LaunchPad

LaunchPad for *Introducing Psychology*, Fifth Edition

Available December 2020 at launchpadworks.com

Each chapter in LaunchPad for *Introducing Psychology*, Fifth Edition, features a collection of activities carefully chosen to help master the major concepts. The site serves students as a comprehensive online study guide, available any time, with opportunities for self-quizzing with instant feedback, exam preparation, and further explorations of topics from the textbook. For instructors, all units and activities can be instantly assigned and students' results and analytics are collected in the Gradebook.

For Students

- Full e-book of *Introducing Psychology,* Fifth Edition
- LearningCurve Quizzing
- Student Video Activities
- Data Visualization Activities
- Concept Practice Activities
- PsychSim 6.0 by Thomas Ludwig and John Krantz

For Instructors

- Gradebook
- Presentation Slides
- iClicker Questions
- Chapter Figures and Photos
- Correlation of *Introducing Psychology,* Fifth Edition, to APA Learning Goals
- Correlation of *Introducing Psychology*, Fifth Edition, to MCAT Topics

Introducing
Psychology

Introducing Psychology

Fifth Edition

Daniel L. Schacter
Harvard University

Daniel T. Gilbert
Harvard University

Matthew K. Nock
Harvard University

Daniel M. Wegner
Harvard University

worth publishers
Macmillan Learning
New York

Senior Vice President, Content Strategy: Charles Linsmeier
Program Director: Shani Fisher
Executive Program Manager: Daniel DeBonis
Senior Development Editor: Valerie Raymond
Assistant Editor: Nicholas Rizzuti
Executive Marketing Manager: Kate Nurre
Marketing Assistant: Steven Huang
Director of Media Editorial and Assessment, Social Sciences:
    Noel Hohnstine
Media Editor: Stefani Wallace
Lead Media Project Manager: Joseph Tomasso
Director, Content Management Enhancement: Tracey Kuehn
Senior Managing Editor: Lisa Kinne
Senior Content Project Manager: Vivien Weiss
Project Manager: Vanavan Jayaraman, Lumina Datamatics, Inc.
Senior Workflow Project Manager: Paul Rohloff
Direction of Design, Content Management: Diana Blume
Design Services Manager: Natasha Wolfe
Cover Designer: John Callahan
Interior Designer: Tamara Newnam
Executive Permissions Editor: Robin Fadool
Photo Researcher and Lumina Project Manager: Krystyna Borgen
Art Manager: Matthew McAdams
Illustrations: Eli Ensor, Matthew McAdams
Composition: Lumina Datamatics, Inc.
Printing and Binding: LSC Communications
Cover Photographs: Henrik Sorensen/DigitalVision/Getty Images

Library of Congress Control Number: 2020939887

ISBN-13: 978-1-319-19077-4
ISBN-10: 1-319-19077-4

1 2 3 4 5 6   25 24 23 22 21 20

Worth Publishers
One New York Plaza
Suite 4600
New York, NY 10004-1562
www.macmillanlearning.com

Dedication

*We dedicate this edition to **Dan Wegner**—coauthor, colleague, and departed friend. His brilliant ideas and beautiful words remain in our pages, and in our hearts. Ad perpetuam rei memoriam.*

About the Authors

Daniel Schacter is William R. Kenan, Jr. Professor of Psychology at Harvard University. Dan received his BA degree from the University of North Carolina at Chapel Hill. He subsequently developed a keen interest in amnesic disorders associated with various kinds of brain damage. He continued his research and education at the University of Toronto, where he received his PhD in 1981. He taught on the faculty at Toronto for the next 6 years before joining the psychology department at the University of Arizona in 1987. In 1991, he joined the faculty at Harvard University. His research explores the relationship between conscious and unconscious forms of memory, the nature of distortions and errors in remembering, and the ways in which we use memory to imagine future events. Many of his studies are summarized in his 1996 book, *Searching for Memory: The Brain, The Mind, and The Past*, and his 2001 book, *The Seven Sins of Memory: How the Mind Forgets and Remembers*, both winners of the American Psychological Association's William James Book Award. He has also received awards for his teaching and research, including the Harvard-Radcliffe Phi Beta Kappa Teaching Prize, the Distinguished Scientific Contributions Award from the American Psychological Association, and the William James Fellow Award from the Association for Psychological Science for "a lifetime of significant intellectual contributions to the basic science of psychology." In 2013, he was elected to the National Academy of Sciences.

Daniel Gilbert is the Edgar Pierce Professor of Psychology at Harvard University. Dan received his BA from the University of Colorado at Denver in 1981 and his PhD from Princeton University in 1985. He taught at the University of Texas at Austin, and in 1996 joined the faculty of Harvard University. He has received the Distinguished Scientific Award for an Early Career Contribution to Psychology from the American Psychological Association; the Diener Award for "outstanding contributions to social psychology" from the Foundation for Personality and Social Psychology; the Campbell Award for "distinguished scholarly achievement and sustained excellence in research in social psychology" from the Society for Personality and Social Psychology; and the William James Fellow Award for "a lifetime of significant intellectual contributions to the basic science of psychology" from the Association for Psychological Science. He teaches Introductory Psychology and has won teaching awards that include the Phi Beta Kappa Teaching Prize and the Harvard College Professorship. His research focuses on how and how well people predict their emotional reactions to future events. He is the author of the best seller *Stumbling on Happiness*, which won the Royal Society's General Prize for best popular science book of the year, and the cowriter and host of the PBS television series *This Emotional Life*.

Matthew Nock is the Edgar Pierce Professor of Psychology at Harvard University. Matt received his BA from Boston University in 1995 and his PhD from Yale University in 2003. He completed his clinical internship at Bellevue Hospital and the New York University Child Study Center, and then joined the faculty of Harvard University in 2003. While an undergraduate, he became interested in understanding why people do things to intentionally harm themselves, and he has been conducting research to answer that question ever since. His research is multidisciplinary and uses a wide range of methodological approaches (e.g., epidemiologic surveys, laboratory-based experiments, and clinic-based studies) to understand how these behaviors develop, how to predict them, and how to prevent their occurrence. He has received many teaching awards at Harvard, as well as four Early Career awards recognizing his research. In 2011 he was named a MacArthur Fellow.

Daniel Wegner was the John Lindsley Professor of Psychology in Memory of William James at Harvard University. He received his BS in 1970 and his PhD in 1974, both from Michigan State University. He began his teaching career at Trinity University in San Antonio, Texas, before joining the faculties at the University of Virginia in 1990 and then Harvard University in 2000. He received the Distinguished Scientific Contributions Award from the American Psychological Association, the William James Fellow Award for "a lifetime of significant intellectual contributions to the basic science of psychology" from the Association for Psychological Science, and the Distinguished Scientist Award from the Society of Experimental Social Psychology. His research focused on thought suppression and mental control, transactive memory in relationships and groups, and the experience of conscious will. His work on thought suppression and consciousness served as the basis of two popular books, *White Bears and Other Unwanted Thoughts* and *The Illusion of Conscious Will*, both of which were named *Choice* Outstanding Academic Books. He was a dedicated mentor, a popular teacher, and a cherished colleague and friend. Dan was diagnosed with ALS and died in 2013.

Brief Contents

1 The Evolution of Psychological Science   1

2 Methods in Psychology   27

3 Neuroscience and Behavior   53

4 Sensation and Perception   89

5 Consciousness   127

6 Memory   159

7 Learning   193

8 Emotion and Motivation   229

9 Language, Thought, and Intelligence   257

10 Development   295

11 Personality   327

12 Social Psychology   353

13 Stress and Health   385

14 Psychological Disorders   413

15 Treatment of Psychological Disorders   449

Appendix: Essentials of Statistics for
    Psychological Science   A-1

Glossary   G-1

References   R-1

Name Index   NI-1

Subject Index   SI-1

Contents

STORIEDEYE/ALAMY

1 The Evolution of Psychological Science 1

Psychology's Philosophical Roots 2
Dualism and Materialism 2
Realism and Idealism 3
Empiricism and Nativism 4

The Late 1800s: Toward a Science of the Mind 4
Structuralism: What Is the Mind Like? 5
Functionalism: What Is the Mind For? 6

OTHER VOICES: Is Psychology a Science? 7

The Early 1900s: Psychoanalysis and Behaviorism 8
Psychoanalysis: The Mind Does Not Know Itself 8
Behaviorism: The Mind Does Not Matter 9

The Early 1900s: Resistance to Behaviorism 12
Gestalt Psychology and Developmental Psychology 12

THE REAL WORLD: Beneath the Ocean of Memory 14
Social Psychology 14

The Late 1900s: The Cognitive Revolution 15
Cognitive Psychology 16
Evolutionary Psychology 16
After the Revolution 17

The Early 2000s: New Frontiers 18
Neuroscience 18
Cultural Psychology 19

A WORLD OF DIFFERENCE: To Have or Have Not 20

Becoming a Psychologist 20
Who Becomes a Psychologist? 20
How Do People Become Psychologists? 21

BRUCE ROLFF/ALAMY

2 Methods in Psychology 27

Empiricism: How to Know Stuff 28
The Scientific Method 28
The Art of Looking 29

A WORLD OF DIFFERENCE: Are Heroes and Sheroes Divided by Zeroes? 30

Methods of Observation: Finding Out What People Do 30
Measurement 30
Demand Characteristics: Doing What Is Expected 31
Observer Bias: Seeing What Is Expected 33

Methods of Explanation: Figuring Out Why People Do What They Do 34

Correlation 34

Causation 34

Drawing Conclusions 38

HOT SCIENCE: Hate Posts and Hate Crimes: Not Just a Correlation 40

Thinking Critically About Evidence 42

We See What We Expect and Want to See 43

We Don't Consider What We Don't See 43

The Skeptical Stance 44

THE REAL WORLD: The Surprisingly High Likelihood of Unlikely Coincidences 45

The Ethics of Science: Doing What's Right 45

Respecting People 45

Respecting Animals 47

Respecting Truth 47

OTHER VOICES: Can We Afford Science? 48

© SPL/SCIENCE SOURCE

3 Neuroscience and Behavior 53

Neurons: The Origin of Behavior 54

Components of the Neuron 54

Major Types of Neurons 56

The Action of Neurons: Information Processing 56

Electric Signaling: Conducting Information Inside a Neuron 56

Chemical Signaling: Transmitting Information Between Neurons 59

The Organization of the Nervous System 62

The Peripheral Nervous System 62

The Central Nervous System 63

Structure of the Brain 65

The Hindbrain 65

The Midbrain 66

The Forebrain 66

A WORLD OF DIFFERENCE: Alzheimer's Disease and the Hippocampus: Sex Differences 69

Brain Plasticity 72

The Adaptive Brain: Understanding Its Evolution 74

Genes, Epigenetics, and the Environment 75

What Are Genes? 75

A Role for Epigenetics 77

Investigating the Brain 78

Studying the Damaged Brain 78

Studying the Brain's Electrical Activity 80

Using Brain Imaging to Study Structure and to Watch the Brain in Action 81

HOT SCIENCE: Big Brain, Smart Brain? 82

OTHER VOICES: Neuromyths 84

PURESTOCK/GETTY IMAGES

4 Sensation and Perception   89

Sensation and Perception Are Distinct Activities   90

Sensory Transduction and Sensory Adaptation   90

Psychophysics   91

Signal Detection   92

THE REAL WORLD: Multitasking   93

Visual Pathways: Connections Between the Eye and the Brain   94

Sensing Light   94

Perceiving Color   98

The Visual Brain   99

Visual Perception: Recognizing What We See   101

Binding Individual Features Into a Whole   101

Recognizing Objects by Sight   102

Perceptual Constancy and Contrast   102

A WORLD OF DIFFERENCE: The Dress   104

Perceiving Depth and Size   105

Perceiving Motion and Change   107

Hearing: More Than Meets the Ear   109

Sensing Sound   109

Perceiving Sound Sources   112

Hearing Loss   113

HOT SCIENCE: Big Technology in Little Ears   114

The Body Senses: More Than Skin Deep   115

Sensing Touch   115

Pain   116

Body Position, Movement, and Balance   117

The Chemical Senses: Adding Flavor   118

Sense of Smell   118

Perceiving Smell   119

Sense of Taste   120

Perceiving Flavor   121

WESTEND61/GETTY IMAGES

5 Consciousness   127

The Mysteries of Consciousness   128

The Problem of Other Minds   128

The Mind–Body Problem   129

The Nature of Consciousness   130

Four Basic Properties   130

Levels of Consciousness   131

Conscious Contents   132

The Unconscious Mind   135

Freudian Unconscious   135

A Modern View of the Cognitive Unconscious   136

Sleep and Dreaming: Good Night, Mind   136

   Sleep   137

   Dreams   141

A WORLD OF DIFFERENCE: Dreaming Blind   144

Drugs and Consciousness: Artificial Inspiration   145

   Drug Use and Addiction   145

   Types of Psychoactive Drugs   148

HOT SCIENCE: Why Is There an Opioid Epidemic and What Can We Do About It?   151

OTHER VOICES: A Judge's Plea for Pot   153

Hypnosis: Open to Suggestion   153

   Induction and Susceptibility   154

   Hypnotic Effects   154

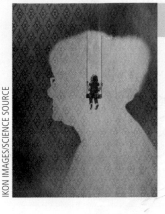

IKON IMAGES/SCIENCE SOURCE

6 Memory   159

What Is Memory?   159

Encoding: Transforming Perceptions Into Memories   160

   Semantic Encoding   160

   Visual Imagery Encoding   160

   Organizational Encoding   162

   Encoding of Survival-Related Information   162

Storage: Maintaining Memories Over Time   163

   Sensory Storage   163

   Short-Term Storage and Working Memory   164

   Long-Term Storage   166

HOT SCIENCE: Can Sleep Enhance Learning? Yes!   168

   Memories, Neurons, and Synapses   169

Retrieval: Bringing Memories to Mind   170

   Retrieval Cues: Reinstating the Past   170

   Consequences of Retrieval   171

Forms of Long-Term Memory: More Than One Kind   173

   Implicit Memory   173

   Explicit Memory: Semantic and Episodic   174

A WORLD OF DIFFERENCE: Do We All Reexperience Our Personal Pasts?   176

THE REAL WORLD: Is Google Hurting Our Memories?   178

Memory Failures: The Seven "Sins" of Memory   179

   1. Transience   179

   2. Absentmindedness   180

   3. Blocking   181

   4. Memory Misattribution   182

HOT SCIENCE: Déjà Vu: Can We Predict the Future?   183

   5. Suggestibility   184

OTHER VOICES: Memories Inside Out   185

6. Bias   186
7. Persistence   187
Are the Seven "Sins" Vices or Virtues?   188

7 Learning   193

What Is Learning?   194

Classical Conditioning: One Thing Leads to Another   194

The Basic Principles of Classical Conditioning   195

THE REAL WORLD: Understanding Drug Overdoses   198

Conditioned Emotional Responses: The Case of Little Albert   199
A Deeper Understanding of Classical Conditioning   199

Operant Conditioning: Reinforcements From the Environment   202

The Development of Operant Conditioning: The Law of Effect   202
B. F. Skinner: The Role of Reinforcement and Punishment   203
The Basic Principles of Operant Conditioning   205
A Deeper Understanding of Operant Conditioning   210

HOT SCIENCE: Dopamine and Reward Learning: From Parkinson's Disease to Gambling   213

Observational Learning: Look at Me   214

Observational Learning in Humans   215
Observational Learning in Animals   216
Neural Elements of Observational Learning   217

Implicit Learning: Under the Radar   217

Cognitive Approaches to Implicit Learning   218
Implicit and Explicit Learning Use Distinct Neural Pathways   219

Learning in the Classroom   220

Techniques for Learning   220

OTHER VOICES: Learning at Jiffy Lube University   221

Testing Aids Attention   223
Control of Learning   223

8 Emotion and Motivation   229

The Nature of Emotion   230

The Emotional Mind   230

OTHER VOICES: Glad to Be Mad?   233

The Emotional Body   233
The Emotional Brain   235

Emotional Communication   236

Communicative Expression   238
Deceptive Expression   239
Lying   240

MARILYN NIEVES/GETTY IMAGES

ECHO/GETTY IMAGES

A WORLD OF DIFFERENCE: Say Cheese 240

The Nature of Motivation 241

Instincts 241

Drives 242

The Hedonic Principle 242

The Motivated Body 244

Hunger 244

Eating Disorders 244

Obesity 245

HOT SCIENCE: This Is Your Brain on Goldfish 248

Sexual Desire 248

The Motivated Mind 250

Intrinsic Versus Extrinsic 250

Conscious Versus Unconscious 251

Approach Versus Avoidance 252

MURIEL DE SEZE/GETTY IMAGES

9 Language, Thought, and Intelligence 257

Language and Communication: From Rules to Meaning 258

The Structure of Human Language 258

Language Development 259

Theories of Language Development 263

Language Development and the Brain 265

Concepts and Categories: How We Think 266

Psychological Theories of Concepts and Categories 266

Concepts, Categories, and the Brain 268

Decision Making: Rational and Otherwise 269

The Rational Ideal 269

The Irrational Reality 269

HOT SCIENCE: Can Framing Effects Make You Rich? 271

Why Do We Make Decision-Making Errors? 272

Decision Making and the Brain 272

Intelligence 274

How Can Intelligence Be Measured? 274

The Intelligence Test 275

What Is Intelligence? 276

Where Does Intelligence Come From? 280

Genetic Influences on Intelligence 280

Environmental Influences on Intelligence 281

Gene–Environment Interactions 283

HOT SCIENCE: Brains Wide Open 284

Who Is Most Intelligent? 284

Individual Differences in Intelligence 284

Group Differences in Intelligence 285

THE REAL WORLD: Racism and Intelligence Testing 287

Improving Intelligence 288

OTHER VOICES: Not by Intelligence Alone 289

JOHN LUND/GETTY IMAGES

10 Development 295

Prenatality: A Womb With a View 296

Prenatal Development 296

Prenatal Environment 298

Infancy and Childhood: Perceiving, Doing, and Thinking 299

Perceptual Development 299

Motor Development 299

Cognitive Development 300

A WORLD OF DIFFERENCE: That's the Dumbest Thing I Never Heard! 304

OTHER VOICES: Shut the Lights Off, Say No More 306

Infancy and Childhood: Bonding and Helping 306

Social Development 307

Moral Development 309

Adolescence: Minding the Gap 311

The Protraction of Adolescence 311

Emerging Sexuality 313

THE REAL WORLD: Coming to Terms With Ourselves 315

From Parents to Peers 316

Adulthood: Change We Can't Believe In 318

Changing Abilities 318

Changing Goals 320

Changing Roles 321

PEOPLEIMAGES/E+/GETTY IMAGES

11 Personality 327

Personality: What It Is and How It Is Measured 328

Describing and Explaining Personality 328

Measuring Personality 328

The Trait Approach: Identifying Patterns of Behavior 331

Traits as Behavioral Dispositions and Motives 331

The Search for Core Traits 331

HOT SCIENCE: Personality on the Surface 333

Traits as Biological Building Blocks 334

A WORLD OF DIFFERENCE: Do Males and Females Have Different Personality Traits? 335

The Psychodynamic Approach: Forces That Lie Beneath Awareness 337

The Structure of the Mind: Id, Ego, and Superego 337

The Humanistic–Existential Approach: Personality as Choice 339

Human Needs and Self-Actualization 339

Personality as Existence 340

The Social–Cognitive Approach: Personalities in Situations 341

Consistency of Personality Across Situations 341

Personal Constructs: The Key to the Perceiver's Personality 341

THE REAL WORLD: Does Your Personality Change Depending on Who You're With? 342

Personal Goals and Expectancies Lead to a Characteristic Style of Behavior 342

The Self: Personality in the Mirror 344

Self-Concept 344

Self-Esteem 346

DAVID GILLIVER/BARCROFT MEDIA

12 Social Psychology 353

Interpersonal Behavior 354

Aggression 354

Cooperation 357

Altruism 359

A WORLD OF DIFFERENCE: Do Me a Favor? 361

Interpersonal Attraction 361

Selectivity 361

Attraction 362

Relationships 364

Interpersonal Perception 365

Stereotyping: Drawing Inferences From Categories 365

THE REAL WORLD: Does Perspective-Taking Work? 370

Attribution: Drawing Inferences From Behavior 370

Interpersonal Influence 372

The Hedonic Motive 373

The Approval Motive 374

OTHER VOICES: 91% of Students Love This Box 376

The Accuracy Motive 378

FOTOSEARCH/AGE FOTOSTOCK

13 Stress and Health   385

Sources of Stress: What Gets to You   386

Stressful Events   386

Chronic Stressors   387

A WORLD OF DIFFERENCE: Can Discrimination Cause Stress and Illness?   387

Perceived Control Over Stressful Events   388

Stress Reactions: All Shook Up   388

Physical Reactions   389

Psychological Reactions   392

Stress Management: Dealing With It   394

Mind Management   394

Body Management   395

Situation Management   397

The Psychology of Illness: Mind Over Matter   399

Psychological Effects of Illness   400

Recognizing Illness and Seeking Treatment   400

THE REAL WORLD: This Is Your Brain on Placebos   401

Somatic Symptom Disorders   402

On Being a Patient   402

Patient–Practitioner Interaction   403

The Psychology of Health: Feeling Good   404

Personality and Health   404

Health-Promoting Behaviors and Self-Regulation   405

OTHER VOICES: The Dangers of Overparenting   408

TREVOR WILLIAMS/GETTY IMAGES

14 Psychological Disorders   413

Defining Mental Disorders: What Is Abnormal?   414

Conceptualizing Mental Disorders   414

Classifying Disorders: The *DSM*   415

A WORLD OF DIFFERENCE: The Impact of Culture on Mental Disorders   417

Causation of Disorders   418

A New Approach to Understanding Mental Disorders: RDoC   419

Dangers of Labeling   419

Anxiety Disorders: Excessive Fear, Anxiety, and Avoidance   420

Phobic Disorders   420

Panic Disorder and Agoraphobia   422

Generalized Anxiety Disorder   423

Obsessive-Compulsive Disorder: Persistent Thoughts and Repetitive Behaviors   424

Posttraumatic Stress Disorder: Distress and Avoidance After a Trauma   425

Depressive and Bipolar Disorders: Extreme Highs and Lows 427

Depressive Disorders 427

Bipolar Disorder 429

Schizophrenia and Other Psychotic Disorders: Losing the Grasp on Reality 431

Symptoms of Schizophrenia 431

OTHER VOICES: Successful and Schizophrenic 434

Disorders of Childhood and Adolescence 436

Autism Spectrum Disorder 436

HOT SCIENCE: Optimal Outcome in Autism Spectrum Disorder 437

Attention-Deficit/Hyperactivity Disorder 437

Conduct Disorder 438

Personality Disorders: Extreme Traits and Characteristics 439

Types of Personality Disorder 439

Antisocial Personality Disorder 439

Self-Harm Behaviors: Intentionally Injuring Oneself 441

Suicidal Behavior 441

Nonsuicidal Self-Injury 443

LÍVIA FERNANDES-BRAZIL/MOMENT SELECT/
GETTY IMAGES

15 Treatment of Psychological Disorders 449

Treatment: Getting Help to Those Who Need It 450

Why Many People Fail to Seek Treatment 450

Approaches to Treatment 451

THE REAL WORLD: Types of Psychotherapists 451

Psychological Treatments: Healing the Mind Through Interaction 452

Psychodynamic Therapy 452

Humanistic and Existential Therapies 454

Behavioral and Cognitive Therapies 455

Group Treatments: Healing Multiple Minds at the Same Time 458

HOT SCIENCE: "Rebooting" Psychological Treatment 459

Biological Treatments: Healing the Mind by Physically Altering the Brain 461

Antipsychotic Medications 461

Antianxiety Medications 462

Antidepressants and Mood Stabilizers 463

Herbal and Natural Products 464

Combining Medication and Psychotherapy 465

OTHER VOICES: Diagnosis: Human 466

Biological Treatments Beyond Medication 466

Treatment Effectiveness: For Better or for Worse   469

Treatment Illusions   469

Treatment Studies: Seeking Evidence   470

Which Treatments Work According to the Evidence?   471

Appendix: Essentials of Statistics for Psychological Science   **A-1**

Glossary   G-1

References   R-1

Name Index   NI-1

Subject Index   SI-1

A Note to Students

Dear Student,

The world is full of mysteries—from stars to fossils, from quarks to cells. But for us, the greatest mystery has always been other people, and that's what drew each of us into our first psychology course in college. What we remember about those courses is that we were blown away by the ideas we encountered and by the lectures we heard, and what we don't remember are the textbooks. That's probably because they were little more than jargon-filled encyclopedias of names and dates that we eagerly sold to some other unsuspecting sucker the moment we finished our final exams.

After we became psychology professors, we started to wonder why textbooks had to be like that. We decided they didn't, and so in 2008 we wrote the textbook that we wished we'd been given when we were students. The reaction to it was nothing short of astounding. We'd never written a textbook before so we had no idea what to expect, but never in our wildest dreams did we imagine that we would end up winning *the Pulitzer Prize*!

Which was good, because we didn't. But what actually happened was even better: We started getting e-mails from students all over the country who told us (with seeming surprise) that they actually *liked* reading our textbook. They liked the content, of course, because psychology is an inherently fascinating subject, but they liked some other things too. First, they liked the fact that our textbook didn't *sound* like a textbook. It wasn't written in the stodgy dad-voice of that guy who always seems to narrate the high school biology films ("Behold the sea otter, nature's furry little scavenger"). Rather, it was written in *our* voices—the same voices we use when we talk to our students, our friends, and our pets (which is why Chapter 12 was originally titled "Stop Chewing My Shoes"). Students also liked the fact that we told the *story* of psychology—that we integrated topics rather than just listing them, that we illustrated ideas rather than just describing them, and that we made fun of ourselves and anyone else who didn't run away fast enough. That kind of feedback is what's kept us going for five editions.

Of course, a textbook has to do more than just tell an interesting and entertaining story. It also has to *help you learn*. That's why in addition to all the stuff that novels, cookbooks, and owner's manuals have—words and sentences, graphs and diagrams—textbooks also have "features" that are meant to help you understand and remember the material you're reading. Designing these features requires a keen understanding of how human beings learn, and as luck would have it, that's one of the subjects on which psychologists happen to be expert. The features in our textbook all make use of basic principles of psychology. To introduce you to those features, we'll start by giving you six tips for reading our textbook, and then, after you've read those tips, we'll explain how the various features will help you implement them.

Six Tips for Reading This Textbook

Reading just happens. You look at a printed page and your eyes instantly start to glide across it, turning black squiggles into words and sentences without any help from you. Unlike reading, understanding and remembering don't just happen, which is why you can read a sentence, look up, and 10 seconds later have no freaking idea what you just read. (If that's happening now, please start this section over.) Research shows that the best way to turn *reading* into *understanding and remembering* is to not just let reading happen, but rather, to take an active role in reading. Here are six ways to do that.

- **Rehearse.** No, we don't mean dress up and recite Shakespeare. In psychology, rehearsal simply means repeating information to yourself, and if you do it right, it turns out to be a remarkably useful way to memorize facts. For example, suppose you wanted to remember the name of the person who built the first psychology laboratory (which you will probably want to do when you read Chapter 1). First you might say something like "Wilhelm Wundt built the first psychology laboratory" a few times to yourself, then wait a few seconds, then say it a few times again, then wait even longer, then say it again, then . . . well, you get the idea. By increasing the interval between rehearsals you will be making it a little bit harder to remember the fact each time—kind of like doing bench presses and adding increasing amounts of weight with each set of repetitions—and research shows that this is an effective way to commit information to memory.

- **Interpret.** Rehearsal is good for memorizing facts, but if you want to learn psychology, you're going to need to understand *ideas*. Research shows that one of the best ways to understand and remember ideas is to stop reading for a moment and *interpret* them—that is, to think about what they mean and how they relate to you. For example, suppose you wanted to learn the basic ideas behind behaviorism (which you will indeed want to do when you read Chapter 7). You will be tempted to read what we've written about behaviorism and move on, but you'd be better off pausing and asking yourself a question such as "How would a behaviorist explain my choice of college majors?" To answer this question, you will not only need to recall what you read about behaviorism, but you will also need to relate it to other things that you already know (e.g., that you struggled to decide whether you should major in psychology or in something your parents incorrectly told you was more important). It turns out that it is much easier to remember new information when you relate it to something with which you are already familiar.

- **Organize.** If someone asked you to memorize the words *greet, ask, beg, sign, fold, insert, lick*, in that order, you might find it difficult—unless you noticed that these are the steps involved in composing a letter that asks for money and then mailing it to your parents. Organizing information in a meaningful way is one of the best ways to learn and remember it, which is why after reading each chapter, you should try telling yourself its story. This doesn't just mean rehearsing the facts or interpreting the various ideas, but rather, it means linking them together and asking how one leads to the other.

- **Test.** You may be tempted to use a yellow highlighter as you read, and then to study by re-reading the material you highlighted. This is a mistake (especially if you have an electronic copy of the textbook) because as you re-read the highlighted material it will start to seem more and more familiar to you, and you will mistakenly assume that because the material is familiar, you know it pretty well. But the fact is that you only "know it" when you're reading it! A much better way to learn is to *test yourself* on the material while you are *not* looking at the textbook. Better yet, study with someone else and test each other.

- **Space.** *When* should you do all this stuff? The wrong answer is "The night before the exam." Research shows that you are much more likely to remember what you learn if you read a bit of the textbook every day and do these exercises while you're reading. Cramming the night before an exam is not only a painful experience (as you might have guessed from the word *cramming*), it is also one of the very worst things you can do if you want to learn, remember what you've learned, and do well on an exam. Reading the textbook the night before is only slightly better than not reading it at all.

- **Sleep.** You already know that it's a good idea to get plenty of sleep the night before an exam. But as you will discover in Chapter 6, it is equally important to get plenty of sleep on the days that you do the study exercises we've just described. When you sleep, your brain rehearses information you encountered during the day, sifting through it, finding patterns in it, and storing it efficiently. Letting your brain "sleep on it" is nearly as important as having your brain "read it" in the first place.

Features That Help You Implement These Tips

So yes, those are six excellent pieces of advice. But how in the world are you supposed to remember them—or remember to use them? Don't worry. We're here to help. Our textbook contains a variety of features that we specifically designed to help you implement these and other research-based learning strategies. In fact, we even wrote one really boring chapter just to help you sleep! (Kidding.)

For example, you'll notice that every chapter is divided into a few major sections, and at the beginning of each major section are a set of **Learning Outcomes** that allow you to "be on the lookout" for key concepts as you are reading. This will help you organize the material in your mind—kind of like how knowing beforehand that Romeo and Juliet are star-crossed lovers can help you make sense of the play when you are watching it. Just as the Learning Outcomes tell you what to look for before you read, the **Build to the Outcomes** questions (which you'll find at the end of each major section) help you decide whether you found what you were looking for. These questions will help you determine whether your reading has produced the level of understanding you should desire—and that your instructor will require! If not, then you can re-read the section, or find the information you missed in the **Chapter Review** that appears at the end of each chapter.

We've also built features to help you interpret the material you're reading. For instance, at the end of each chapter, you will find a series of **Changing Minds** scenarios that describe everyday situations in which misconceptions about human behavior arise, and that then ask you to use the chapter's material to correct them. The **Data Visualization Activities** that are available in LaunchPad invite you to engage with the material by answering questions the way psychologists do—namely, by looking at data! Each activity presents an interactive graph that displays real data from a published study, followed by questions that allow you to test your understanding of the study as well as your ability to reason about the data. The **LearningCurve** adaptive quizzing system will also allow you to test yourself—and it will design quizzes just for you!

A Box of Words

You may have noticed that when people tell stories ("I was in Rome this summer and saw the Trevi Fountain, the Sistine Chapel, the Colosseum . . ."), they occasionally pause to tell you about some related thing they found especially interesting ("Did you know that in the 16th century, the Pope tried to turn the Colosseum into a wool factory?"). Then when they're done, they pick up their story again. Well, every chapter in our textbook also tells a story, and once in a while we pause that story to tell you some related thing that we found especially interesting—not about wool factories, but about psychology. The way you'll know we're pausing is that you will bump into a box of words. These boxes come in four flavors, and we've given each a name.

- One box is called **A World of Difference.** People differ in countless ways—by culture, gender, race, religion, age, wealth, sexual orientation, and a whole host of other differences. These sources of diversity influence just about everything people think, feel, and do, and so in just about every chapter we pause our story to highlight one or more of them.

- A second box is called **Other Voices.** Long before psychologists appeared on earth, poets, pundits, playwrights, and philosophers were having insights into human nature. So we decided to invite some of them to share their insights with you. In most chapters, you will find a short essay by someone who thinks deeply, writes beautifully, and—most importantly—isn't us.

- A third box is called **The Real World.** From rats in mazes to humans in brain scanners, a textbook can sometimes seem like a report from places that aren't much like the place you live. That's why we have included a box that shows how the material you are reading can be applied to the stuff of everyday life.

- Finally, in every chapter you will bump into a box called **Hot Science.** When we wrote the last edition, Donald Trump was a real estate developer and no one had ever heard the phrase "me too," which is to say that things change fast. That's why in every chapter we take a moment to share with you a brand new scientific finding that has changed the way we think, and that might change the way you think as well.

Those are the features and those are the boxes and that's probably enough for one preface. We could drone on because, after all, we *are* professors, but we trust you get the point: We love the science of psychology and we've written a book that we hope will make you fall in love with it as well. Whether or not that happens, we're eager to hear what you think about our new edition. Feel free to reach out to us at MattAnd3Dans@gmail.com. Please don't mention Viagra or your e-mail will end up in our spam filter.

A Note to Instructors

Dear Instructor,

Why do we do this to ourselves? You've spent days and days browsing textbooks when you could have been baking cookies, reading poetry, or binge-watching *The Walking Dead*. We've spent years and years reading papers, writing chapters, and finding photographs when we could have been playing piano, visiting museums, or binge-watching *The Walking Dead.* Why have we all chosen to get lost in Textbookland when there are so many zombies to stream?

For the love of science. You and we may be different ages, genders, races, and religions; we may come from different places or speak different first languages; but much greater than our differences is our common bond, and that is our shared and unshakeable belief that science provides the best tools for understanding the mysteries of human behavior. Somewhere along the way, we all stumbled upon a field called psychology and got stuck there because we fell in love with a simple idea—the idea that the methods scientists use to figure out what causes cancer or to understand how butterflies migrate can also be used to answer age-old questions about the hearts and minds of our kind. Honestly, anyone who stumbles upon that idea and isn't excited by it has to be a zombie.

Is our textbook right for you? We don't know. But we do know that when you choose a textbook, you are entrusting part of your students' education to someone else, and that trust needs to be earned. We've tried to do that by writing a textbook that has a single overarching goal: to make your students fall in love with this amazing young science for just the reasons you and we did. Whatever they do with that passion—whether they become psychologists or just become better parents, smarter consumers, and more dedicated citizens—our job is to ignite it by spreading the good news about our science. That's what we try to do on every one of the pages that follow, and we hope you will tell us if you think we've succeeded.

Okay, give us a minute to dry our eyes. There, that's better. Now let's get into some of the nutsy-boltsy stuff you'll want to know about our textbook, and about our fifth edition in particular.

Ch-ch-ch-changes!

The words *new* and *improved* sell a lot of mobile phones and coffee makers, and they probably sell a lot of textbooks too. But we won't use them here. After all, this is the fifth edition of our textbook, and if everything in it were new and improved, then everything in the previous editions would have to be obsolete or in desperate need of repair. That's simply not the case. We've spent more than a decade working on this textbook, and we've learned a lot—not just from writing and rewriting it, but also from the many instructors and students across the country who have taken the time to tell us what they liked, what they didn't like, and how we could turn the latter into the former.

We've listened, and the reason our fifth edition is the best one ever is that rather than *changing* everything just so we could point to some new bells and whistles, we put most of our energies into *perfecting* the things that were already working well. Instructors told us that our pedagogical tools were strong, so we sharpened them rather than replacing them. They told us that our coverage was right on target, so we steadied our aim rather than aiming elsewhere. And they told us that their students enjoyed our casual and sometimes irreverent narrative voice, so we updated our jokes rather than admitting to ourselves that they were really, really bad. If the fifth edition looks familiar to you, that's because with each edition we've learned to make more babies and less bathwater.

With that said, the fifth edition is by no means the fourth with a new cover. You will see several significant changes right off the bat. For instance, we pretty much burned down Chapter 1 (The Evolution of Psychological Science) for the insurance money and rebuilt it from scratch. We think the new version provides a clearer and more engaging exploration of psychology's rich history. We've also done major renovations of Chapter 4 (Sensation and Perception), Chapter 8 (Emotion and Motivation), and Chapter 9 (Language, Thought, and Intelligence), and added extended coverage to other chapters—for instance, the new section on action potentials that you'll find in Chapter 3 (Neuroscience and Behavior) and the new section on replication that you'll find in Chapter 2 (Methods in Pscyhology). Most importantly, we sneaked a photo of Pete Townshend onto page 321 so that the young people in your class will know who The Who were. Some things are just too important to leave to chance. You'll find a complete list of changes at macmillanlearning.com.

But Wait ... There's More!

Our primary job as textbook authors is to give your students a solid overview of the vast literature in psychological science so that you can spend your class time focusing on the things you really want to tell them, or ask them, or do with them, rather than trying to cover all that territory yourself. Maybe that's all you wanted us to do, in which case . . . um, you're welcome.

But if you think textbook authors can do more than that, well then, we happen to agree with you. That's why we (and *we* of course means "a team of dedicated people whose hard work we will now try to take credit for") have developed a variety of resources to make your job easier and your teaching more effective. Here are just a few of them:

- **LaunchPad** is the name of Macmillan Learning's online platform which combines the full e-book version of our textbook with a whole bunch of interesting activities, award-winning media, and state-of-the-art assessment tools. For students, Launch-Pad is the ultimate online study guide, and for you, it is a place where class documents can be posted, assignments given, quizzes graded, and progress measured. Best of all, LaunchPad integrates seamlessly with all the major learning management systems used by colleges and universities these days, including Blackboard, Brightspace by D2L, Canvas, and Moodle.

- One of the features of LaunchPad that we personally like best is the **LearningCurve** adaptive quizzing system. This system measures a student's performance and then chooses quiz questions based on how well they are doing, which means that every student in your class can take a quiz that has been custom-designed for them. What's more, LearningCurve gives students instant feedback about their performance, while providing you with a report on the progress of individual students and on your class as a whole. You really have to see how beautiful the platform is and how easily it works. Go to launchpadworks.com for a test drive.

- Students hate taking exams. What they don't realize is that we hate making them even more! That's why our book comes with a **Test Bank** that includes more than 300 multiple-choice, true/false, and essay questions for every chapter. You may have designed your class around the APA's "learning goals" for introductory psychology students, and if so, you'll be happy to know that we link the test bank questions to these learning goals, making it easy for you to see which goals are being achieved.

- Can we help you make some **lecture slides**? We hope so, because our book comes with a fully updated set. Can we suggest some **lecture topics and class activities**? We hope so, because our book also comes with a downloadable toolkit that contains plenty of them. Can we get you a cup of coffee? Just checking to see if you were still with us.

- Our textbook gives you access to a large number of **supplements** that your students may find useful, depending on how you've chosen to focus your teaching. For instance, if you focus a lot on critical thinking skills, you might want to supplement our coverage of that topic in Chapter 2 by having your students read "The Critical Thinking Companion for Introductory Psychology" or "The Worth Expert Guide to Scientific Literacy." Or maybe you and your students care a lot about the application of psychology in the real world, in which case you might want to supplement our textbook by having them read "Psychology and the Real World" or "The Psychology Major's Companion." And if none of these or our many other titles quite does the trick, you can use **Macmillan's custom publishing program** to produce a supplement that is specifically tailored to the material you want to emphasize. Pretty much the only supplement we can't provide is CBD oil. But maybe soon.

- Is there a doctor in the house? Some of your students may be preparing to take the **MCAT,** and if so, we've got them covered. We prepared a special resource that links the contents of our textbook to the specific topics that are covered on the MCAT exam. Furthermore, our test bank includes a special set of questions for each chapter that test quantitative reasoning ability in the style of the MCAT.

- In 2020, the American Psychological Association (APA) released the results of its Introductory Psychology Initiative (IPI) in hopes of improving "the quality of the introductory psychology experience" (APA.org/Ed/Precollege/Undergrad/Introductory-Psychology-Initiative). The APA IPI encourages instructors to use *five Integrative Themes* to help students (1) adapt their thinking in response to empirical evidence; (2) recognize general principles but individual differences; (3) acknowledge biological, psychological, and social/cultural influences; (4) be aware of perceptual and thinking errors; and (5) apply psychology's principles to improve their own lives. Additionally, *six Learning Outcomes* charge students to (1) fully understand the five themes; (2) apply psychology in their daily lives; (3) use empirical evidence in judgments and decision making; (4) evaluate claims using psychological science; (5) design, carry out, and evaluate research studies; and (6) know ethical principles for research and therapy. How our text aligns with these goals is detailed at the website, listed just below.

- Macmillan Community is an online forum where teachers can find and share favorite teaching ideas and materials, including videos, animations, images, PowerPoint slides, news stories, articles, Web links, and lecture activities. It is also the home of Worth's abundant social media content, including tweets, blog posts, webinars (featuring Daniel Schacter, Daniel Gilbert, Matthew Nock, and others), and more! Browse the site and share your favorite materials for teaching psychology at https://community.macmillan.com.

These are just a few of the resources that help make our textbook more than the sum of its chapters. Rather than chopping down trees to tell you about the rest of them, we've hired a few photons. You can go online to learn more at macmillanlearning.com.

Acknowledgments

Despite what you might guess by looking at our pictures, we all found women who were willing to marry us after some special pleading. We are grateful to Susan McGlynn, Marilynn Oliphant, and Keesha Nock, who have never complained about those long nights and weekends when we were writing this textbook rather than hanging out with them. You did miss us, didn't you?

Although ours are the only names on the cover, writing a textbook is a team sport, and we've been lucky to have a terrific group of professionals in our dugout. First we want to thank our friend and colleague, Catherine Myers, whose perfect ear and savage blue pencil are essential ingredients in the recipe for a brief edition. We thank the colleagues who reviewed our chapters to make sure we were getting everything right and not missing anything important. We weren't and we were, respectively, so their help was as necessary as it is appreciated. They include Keith Holyoak, Ingrid Johnsrude, Wendy Mendes, Marjorie Rhodes, and Michelle Shiota. These and the dedicated colleagues listed below have helped us more than we can say, and probably more than they realize:

Rebecca Addington
University of Wisconsin–Madison

Christine Bartholomew
Kent State University

Dave Baskind
Delta College

Elizabeth A. Becker
St. Joseph's University

Joan Bihun
University of Colorado Denver

Dawn Brinkley
University of Texas–Dallas

Jennifer L. Butler
Case Western Reserve University

Marci Campbell
Salt Lake Community College

Diana L. Ciesko
Valencia College

Emily Cohen-Shikora
Washington University–St. Louis

Chris De La Ronde
Austin Community College

Rebecca DesRoches
Regis College

Michael Disch
St. Edwards University

Kimberly Duff
Cerritos College

April K. Dye
Carson-Newman University

John E. Edlund
Rochester Institute of Technology

Kim Ernst
Loyola University New Orleans

Lauren Ethridge
University of Oklahoma

Celeste Favela
El Paso Community College

Mark Ferguson
University of Wisconsin-Stevens Point

Sara Finley
Pacific Lutheran University

Jocelyn R. Folk
Kent State University

Jim Fryer
SUNY Potsdam

Sophie A. George
Dixie State University

Afshin Gharib
Dominican University of California

Jerry Green
Tarrant County College

Maria E. Guarneri-White
Pacific Lutheran University

Jane S. Halonen
University of West Florida

Edward Hansen
Florida State University

Shani N. Harris
Spelman College

Erin Henshaw
Denison University

L. E. Holliman
Georgia State University at Perimeter-Clarkston Campus

Keith Holyoak
University of California Los Angeles

George-Harold Jennings
Drew University

Janna Kline
Rutgers University

Michael M. Knepp
University of Mount Union

Karen Kwan
Salt Lake Community College

Christopher B. Mayhorn
North Carolina State University

Michael Jason McCoy
Cape Fear Community College

Wendy Mendes
University of California San Francisco

Dennis K. Miller
University of Missouri–Columbia

Rikki L. A. Miller
University of Southern Maine

Erin M. Myers
Western Carolina University

Khu Nguyen
Washington University in St. Louis

Bradley M. Okdie
Ohio State University–Newark

Caroline Olko
Nassau Community College

Natasha Otto
Morgan State University

Doug A. Peterson
University of South Dakota

Jessica Petok
St. Olaf College

Catherine Phillips
Northwest Vista College

Gary Popoli
Stevenson University

Mixalis Poulakis
University of Indianapolis

G. A. Radvansky
University of Notre Dame

Marjorie Rhodes
New York University

Kiefer Rich
San Diego City College

Blake Riek
Calvin College

Gwendolyn Scott-Jones
Delaware State University

Keith M. Shafritz
Hofstra University

Shubam Sharma
University of Florida

Michelle Shiota
Arizona State University

Hiroko Sotozaki
Western Illinois University

Jonathan N. Sparks
Vance-Granville Community College

Peter Sparks
Oregon State University–Cascades

Helen T. Sullivan
Rider University

Donald Tellinghuisen
Calvin College

David G. Thomas
Oklahoma State University

Travis Tubré
University of Wisconsin–River Falls

Lora Vasiliauskas
Virginia Western Community College

Constance Walsh
Fullerton College

Megan Kozak Williams
Linfield College

James Thomas Wright
Forsyth Technical Community College

Dasa Zeithamova
University of Oregon

We'd also like to thank Chad Galuska, Jeff Henriques, Jennifer Perry, Chelsea Ekstrand, and Russ Frohardt, who wrote the supplemental materials that support our textbook's educational mission. The insight and experience they brought to this task was extraordinary.

As always, we are deeply grateful to our good friends at Worth Publishers, with whom we have happily worked for so many years. They include:

- Senior vice president Chuck Linsmeier, who has been providing much-needed wisdom, encouragement, and gin since our very first day

- Our executive program manager, Dan DeBonis, who has managed our project with panache while keeping the trains, planes, automobiles, submarines, and pachyderms all running on time

- Our brilliant, talented, and preternaturally cheerful senior development editor, Valerie Raymond, without whom we would all jump off a tall building (just behind Dan DeBonis, who might need a push)

- Our director of content management enhancement, Tracey Kuehn; our senior content project manager, Vivien Weiss; our senior project manager, Vanavan Jayaraman; and our assistant editor, Nick Rizzuti, all of whom have mastered the magic that turns a bunch of badly typed pages into a perfect textbook

- Our design services manager, Natasha Wolfe; our cover designer, John Callahan; our art manager, Matt McAdams; our executive permissions editor Robin Fadool; and our photo researcher and Lumina project manager, Krystyna Borgen—all of whom worked together to make our textbook as delightful to behold as it is to read

- Our media editor Stefani Wallace, who along with lead media project manager Joseph Tomasso expertly guided the development and creation of our superb supplements package

- Our executive marketing manager Kate Nurre, who has always been and continues to be a tireless public advocate for our vision

- Our editorial assistants, Molly Evans and Franchesca Ramirez, who provided capable assistance even when we didn't know we needed it

What would we have done without all of you? Gracias, arigato, danke, merci, xie xie, and major thanks!

Daniel L. Schacter
Cambridge, 2020

Daniel T. Gilbert
Cambridge, 2020

Matthew K. Nock
Cambridge, 2020

The Evolution of Psychological Science

1

I n 1860, Abraham Lincoln became the president of the United States, the Pony Express began delivering mail between Missouri and California, and an 18-year-old named William James (1842–1910) started worrying about what to do with the rest of his life. He had hoped to become an artist, but after studying for several months with a famous painter in Rhode Island, he was forced to admit that he wasn't all that talented. At his father's urging, he went to college to study chemistry, then switched to physiology, only to find that neither subject interested him much. After graduation, William went to medical school, but soon took a leave of absence and sailed to Germany, where he began learning about a new science called psychology (from a combination of the Greek *psyche*, which means "soul," and *logos*, which means "to study"). Two years later he returned to America, finished his medical degree, and took a job teaching at Harvard University. There, in the classroom, amidst the blackboards and the chalk, surrounded by bright students who were eager to learn about the new European science of psychology, William finally found what he had been searching for all along. "So far," he wrote to his brother after his first year as a teacher, "I seem to have succeeded in interesting them . . . and I hear expressions of satisfaction on their part."[1] Then, with characteristic understatement, he added, "I should think it not unpleasant as a permanent thing."

[1] All William James quotes are from *The Letters of William James*, edited by his nephew Henry James, first published by Atlantic Monthly Press, Boston, 1920, and now found in a variety of formats and editions.

Psychology's Philosophical Roots

The Late 1800s: Toward a Science of the Mind

The Early 1900s: Psychoanalysis and Behaviorism

The Early 1900s: Resistance to Behaviorism

The Late 1900s: The Cognitive Revolution

The Early 2000s: New Frontiers

Becoming a Psychologist

William James (left) started out as a restless student who didn't know what he wanted to do with his life. Forty years later (middle), he had become the father of American psychology. Throughout his illustrious career, James remained a devoted and beloved teacher who was "so vivacious and humorous that one day a student interrupted and asked him to be serious for a moment" (Hunt, 2007, p. 169). When he gave his final lecture on January 22, 1907, his classroom was packed with students, former students, colleagues, and administrators. James suffered from poor health his entire life and died in 1910, at the age of 68. Today, Harvard's psychology department is housed in William James Hall (right). (MS AM 1092). Houghton Library, Harvard University; Stock Montage/Getty Images; The Harvard Crimson

And a permanent thing it became: William remained at Harvard for the next 35 years, where he taught one of the first psychology courses and created one of the first psychology laboratories in America. He also wrote the first American psychology textbook, *The Principles of Psychology*. As the historian E. G. Boring (1929, p. 624) later wrote, "No other psychological treatise in the English language has in the modern period had such a wide and persistent influence." Today, William James is considered the father of American psychology and his brilliant textbook is still widely read.

"This is no science," James said of psychology in 1892, "it is only the hope of a science." And at that time, he was right. But now, more than a century later, psychology's hope has been realized, and the book you hold in your hand is that realization (see Other Voices: Is Psychology a Science?). How did it happen? How did we get here from there? This chapter tells that story.

Psychology's Philosophical Roots

Psychology is the *scientific study of mind and behavior*. The word *mind* refers to a set of private events that happen inside a person — the thoughts and feelings that we experience at every moment but that no one else can see — and the word *behavior* refers to a set of public events — the things we say and do that can potentially be observed by others. Both human minds and human behaviors have been around for quite a while, and psychologists were not the first to try to make sense of them. That distinction belongs to philosophers, who have been thinking deeply about these topics for several thousand years.

Dualism and Materialism

Our bodies are physical objects that can be seen, smelled, and touched. Our minds are not. You can't hear an emotion or taste a belief. The philosopher René Descartes (1596–1650) thought that the body is made of a material substance, the mind is made of an immaterial substance, and every person is therefore a physical container of a nonphysical thing — what later philosophers called the "ghost in the machine" (Ryle, 1949). Descartes's position is known as **philosophical dualism**, which is *the view that mind and body are fundamentally different things*.

But if the mind and the body are fundamentally different things, then how do they interact? How does the immaterial mind tell the material body to put its best foot forward? And when the material body steps on a rusty nail, why does the immaterial mind say "Ouch"? Philosophers such as Thomas Hobbes (1588–1679) argued that Descartes was wrong and that the mind and body aren't fundamentally different things at all. Rather, the mind is what the brain does. From Hobbes's perspective, looking for a place in the brain where the mind meets the body is like looking for the place on your phone where the picture meets the screen. The picture is what the screen does, and they don't "meet" in some third place. The brain is a physical object whose activity is known as "the mind," and therefore all mental phenomena — every thought and feeling, every sight and sound — is the result of some physical activity in the physical brain. **Philosophical materialism** is *the view that all mental phenomena are reducible to physical phenomena*.

So which philosopher was right? The debate between dualism and materialism cannot be settled by facts. This is an issue about which people pretty much just have to make up their own minds and choose their own sides. Most of the world's religions — from Christianity and Judaism to Hinduism and Islam — have chosen to side with the dualists and embrace the notion of a nonphysical soul. But most psychologists have chosen to embrace materialism (Ecklund et al., 2007), and believe that all mental phenomena — from attention and memory to belief and emotion — are ultimately explainable in terms of the physical processes that produce them. The mind is what

Learning Outcomes

- Explain the distinction between dualism and materialism.
- Explain the distinction between realism and idealism.
- Explain the distinction between empiricism and nativism.

psychology The scientific study of mind and behavior.

philosophical dualism The view that mind and body are fundamentally different things.

philosophical materialism The view that all mental phenomena are reducible to physical phenomena.

René Descartes (left) was a dualist who believed that the mind was a substance that was distinct from the body. "It is certain that this I — that is to say, my soul by which I am what I am — is entirely and absolutely distinct from my body, and can exist without it," he wrote. But Thomas Hobbes (right) was a materialist who thought the idea of a "substance" that was distinct from the body was a contradiction in terms because "substance and body signify the same thing." Album Archivo/Science Source; Fine Art Images/Heritage Images/Getty Images

the brain does — nothing less and nothing more. We are remarkably complex machines whose operations somehow give rise to consciousness, and one of psychology's jobs is to figure out what that "somehow" is.

Realism and Idealism

You probably have the sense that this thing called "you" is somewhere inside your skull, and that right now it is looking out through your eyes and reading the words on this page. It feels as though our eyes are some sort of camera, and that "you" are "in here" seeing pictures of the things "out there." The philosopher John Locke (1632–1704) referred to this theory as **philosophical realism**, which is *the view that perceptions of the physical world are produced entirely by information from the sensory organs.* According to the realist account, light is right now bouncing off the page and hitting your eye, and your brain is using that information and only that information to produce your perception of the book in front of you. And because your eye is like a camera, the pictures it produces are generally accurate depictions of the world.

But philosophers such as Immanuel Kant (1724–1804) suggested that our perceptions of the world are less like photographs and more like paintings. **Philosophical idealism** is *the view that perceptions of the physical world are the brain's interpretation of information from the sensory organs.* According to the idealist account, light is bouncing off the page and hitting your eye, and your brain is using that information — plus all the other information it has about the world — to produce your perception of the book. Before you ever looked at this book, you already knew many things about books in general — what they are made of, how large they are, that the cover is heavier than the pages — and your brain is right now using everything it knows about books to interpret the information it is receiving from your eyes. It is painting a picture of what it believes is out there, and although you think you are "seeing" a book, you are really just seeing that picture.

So which philosopher was right? Modern psychology has come down strongly on the side of idealism. As you will see in many of the upcoming chapters, our perception of the world is an inference — our brain's best guess about what's likely to be out there. Because our brains are such good guessers and such fast guessers, we typically don't realize they are guessing at all. We feel like our eyes are cameras taking photos, but that's only because the artist between our ears can produce realistic paintings at lightning speed.

In his 1781 masterpiece *The Critique of Pure Reason,* Immanuel Kant argued that the mind comes hardwired with certain kinds of knowledge and that it uses this knowledge to create our perceptions of the world. "Perceptions without conceptions are blind," he wrote, meaning that without prior knowledge or "conceptions" of the world, we could not see or "have perceptions" of it. GL Archive/Alamy

philosophical realism The view that perceptions of the physical world are produced entirely by information from the sensory organs.

philosophical idealism The view that perceptions of the physical world are the brain's interpretation of information from the sensory organs.

John Locke was a British philosopher, physician, and political theorist whose writings about the separation of church and state, religious freedom, and liberty strongly influenced America's founding fathers, such as Thomas Jefferson, who incorporated Locke's phrase "the pursuit of happiness" into the Declaration of Independence. John Locke, Kneller, Godfrey (1646–1723), National Trust Images/Lodge Park and Sherborne Estate, UK/Bridgeman Images

Empiricism and Nativism

Here are some other things you know about books: You know that four books are more than two, that pushing a book off the table will cause it to fall, and that when it falls it will go down and not up. How do you know all this stuff? **Philosophical empiricism** is *the view that all knowledge is acquired through experience*. Philosophers such as Locke believed that a newborn baby is a *tabula rasa*, or "blank slate," upon which experience writes its story. As Locke wrote in his 1690 *Essay on Human Understanding*:

> If we will attentively consider new-born children, we shall have little reason to think that they bring many ideas into the world with them. . . . One may perceive how, by degrees, afterwards, ideas come into their minds; and that they get no more, nor other, than what experience, and the observation of things that come in their way, furnish them with; which might be enough to satisfy us that they are not original characters stamped on the mind.

In other words, you know about books — and about teacups and tea kettles and T-shirts and a huge number of other objects — because you've seen them, or interacted with them, or seen someone else interact with them.

Kant thought Locke was wrong about this, too. **Philosophical nativism** is *the view that some knowledge is innate rather than acquired*. Kant argued that human beings must be born with some basic knowledge of the world that allows them to acquire additional knowledge of the world. After all, how could you learn that pushing a book off a table causes it to fall if you didn't already know what causation was? The fact that you can acquire knowledge about what books do when pushed suggests that your mind came with at least a few bits of knowledge already programmed into it. For Kant, those few preprogrammed bits of knowledge were concepts such as space, time, causality, and number. You can't learn these concepts, he argued, and yet you have to have them in order to learn anything else. So they must come factory-installed.

So which philosopher was right? Most modern psychologists embrace some version of nativism. It is all too obvious that much of what we know is acquired through experience. But research suggests that at least some of what we know is indeed hardwired into our brains, just as Kant thought. As you'll see in the Development chapter, even newborn infants seem to have some basic knowledge of the laws of physics and mathematics. The tabula is not rasa, the slate is not blank, which leads to some interesting questions: What exactly is written on the slate at birth? How and when in our evolutionary history did it get there? Can experience erase the slate as well as write on it? Psychologists refer to these types of questions as "nature-versus-nurture" questions, and as you will see in some of the upcoming chapters, they have devised clever techniques for answering them.

philosophical empiricism The view that all knowledge is acquired through experience.

philosophical nativism The view that some knowledge is innate rather than acquired.

Build to the Outcomes

1. How does materialism differ from dualism, and which do modern psychologists favor?

2. How does realism differ from idealism, and which do modern psychologists favor?

3. How does empiricism differ from nativism, and which do modern psychologists favor?

Learning Outcomes

- Define introspection and explain how it was used in structuralism.

- Define natural selection and explain how it influenced functionalism.

The Late 1800s: Toward a Science of the Mind

The psychologist Hermann Ebbinghaus (1908) once remarked that "psychology has a long past but a short history." Indeed, psychology's philosophical roots go back thousands of years, but its history as an independent science began a mere 150 or so years ago, when a few German scientists began to wonder whether the methods of the physical and natural sciences might be used to study the human mind.

Structuralism: What Is the Mind Like?

During his visit to Berlin in 1867, William James sent a letter to a friend:

> It seems to me that perhaps the time has come for psychology to begin to be a science. . . . I am going on to study what is already known and perhaps may be able to do some work at it. Helmholtz and a man called Wundt at Heidelberg are working at it, and I hope I live through this winter to go to them in the summer.

Hermann von Helmholtz (1821–1894) was a German physician and physicist who mainly studied the mathematics of vision, but who had taken to asking people to close their eyes and respond as quickly as possible when he touched different parts of their legs. That's not as creepy as it sounds. Helmholtz recorded each person's **reaction time**, or *the amount of time between the onset of a stimulus and a person's response to that stimulus*. He discovered that people generally took longer to respond when he touched their toes than when he touched their thighs. Why? When something touches your body, your nerves transmit a signal from the point of contact to your brain, and when that signal arrives at your brain, you "feel" the touch. Because your thighs are closer to your brain than your toes are, the signal from your thigh has a shorter distance to travel. By carefully measuring how long it took people to feel a thigh touch and a toe touch and then comparing the two measurements, Helmholtz was able to do something remarkable: He calculated the speed at which nerves transmit information!

Helmholtz's research assistant, Wilhelm Wundt (1832–1920), went on to teach the first course in scientific or "experimental" psychology at the University of Heidelberg in Germany in 1867, published the first psychology textbook in 1874, and opened the world's first psychology laboratory at the University of Leipzig in 1879. Wundt believed that the primary goal of psychology should be to understand "the facts of consciousness, its combinations and relations, so that it may ultimately discover the laws which govern these relations and combinations" (Wundt, 1912/1973, p. 1). Natural scientists had had great success in understanding the physical world by breaking it down into its basic elements, such as cells and molecules and atoms, and Wundt decided to take the same approach to understanding the mind. His approach later came to be known as **structuralism**, which was *an approach to psychology that attempted to isolate and analyze the mind's basic elements*.

reaction time The amount of time between the onset of a stimulus and a person's response to that stimulus.

structuralism An approach to psychology that attempted to isolate and analyze the mind's basic elements.

Wilhelm Wundt (standing in the middle) taught the world's first psychology course and published the world's first psychology textbook, *Principles of Physiological Psychology*. (The word *physiological* simply meant "experimental" back then.) He also opened the world's first psychology laboratory at the University of Leipzig. He was the advisor to a remarkable 184 PhD students, many of whom went on to become well-known psychologists. It is fair to say that modern psychology just Wundt be the same without him. Wontorra, H. M., Meischner-Metge, A. & Schröger, E (Eds.). (2004). Wilhelm Wundt (1832–1920) and the advent of Experimental Psychology. (CD [ISBN 3-00-013477-8.] ed.

introspection The analysis of subjective experience by trained observers.

functionalism An approach to psychology that emphasized the adaptive significance of mental processes.

natural selection The process by which the specific attributes that promote an organism's survival and reproduction become more prevalent in the population over time.

Structuralists often used a technique called **introspection**, which is *the analysis of subjective experience by trained observers*. Volunteers were presented with a wide variety of stimuli, from patches of color to musical tones, and trained to report on the contents of their moment-to-moment "raw experience," such as the hue and luminance of the color, their feelings when they heard the tone, and so on. Structuralists believed that by carefully analyzing the reports from many trained observers who had been exposed to many stimuli, they would eventually discover the basic building blocks of subjective experience.

But structuralism didn't last. Natural scientists had indeed been successful in understanding the natural world by breaking it into small parts, but that approach was successful only because everyone could agree on what those parts were. When two biologists looked at blood under a microscope, they saw the same blood cells. This wasn't true of everyone who looked at the color green or heard C# played on a piano. There was simply no way to tell if a person's description of her experience was accurate, and no way to tell if her experience was the same as or different from someone else's. In fact, William James wrote that introspection was "like seizing a spinning top to catch its motion." So, while the German structuralists were busy introspecting, James began taking a very different approach to the study of the mind — an approach that would forever consign structuralism to the history chapter of psychology textbooks.

Functionalism: What Is the Mind For?

William James felt that subjective experience was less like a molecule made of atoms and more like a river — a "stream of consciousness" as he called it — and that trying to isolate its basic elements was a losing proposition. James thought psychologists should worry less about what mental life was like, and more about what it was for. So James and other psychologists developed a new approach to psychology called **functionalism**, which was *an approach to psychology that emphasized the adaptive significance of mental processes*. What does "adaptive significance" mean?

The answer came from James's contemporary, Charles Darwin (1809–1882), a naturalist who had recently published a book entitled *On the Origin of Species by Means of Natural Selection* (1859). In it, Darwin had proposed the principle of **natural selection**, which refers to *the process by which the specific attributes that promote an organism's survival and reproduction become more prevalent in the population over time*. How does natural selection work? Animals pass their physical attributes to their offspring, and those attributes that are most "adaptive" — that is, those that promote the offspring's survival and reproduction — are more likely to be passed along from one generation to the next. Over time, these adaptive attributes become increasingly prevalent in the population simply because "the population" refers to those animals that have managed to survive and reproduce.

On the Origin of Species (1859) by Charles Darwin (left) is one of the most important scientific books ever written, and it had a big impact on William James and the birth of functionalism. Darwin developed his theory in the 1830s but did not write about it. A naturalist named Alfred Russel Wallace (1823–1913, right) developed the same theory at the same time and in 1855 sent Darwin a paper describing it. The two men decided to announce the theory jointly at a meeting of the Linnean Society in 1858. The next year, Darwin published a book describing the theory, and the world pretty much forgot about good old Wallace. Print Collector/Getty Images; London Stereoscopic & Photographic Company

OTHER VOICES

Is Psychology a Science?

Nobody can deny that you are taking a course in psychology, but are you taking a course in science? We think so, but not everyone agrees. Some critics say that psychology isn't really a science, but we think those critics should have a little chat with Timothy Wilson, a psychology professor at the University of Virginia. Here's what he has to say on the subject:

Once, during a meeting at my university, a biologist mentioned that he was the only faculty member present from a science department. When I corrected him, noting that I was from the Department of Psychology, he waved his hand dismissively, as if I were a Little Leaguer telling a member of the New York Yankees that I too played baseball.

There has long been snobbery in the sciences, with the "hard" ones (physics, chemistry, biology) considering themselves to be more legitimate than the "soft" ones (psychology, sociology). It is thus no surprise that many members of the general public feel the same way. But of late, skepticism about the rigors of social science has reached absurd heights.

The U.S. House of Representatives recently voted to eliminate funding for political science research through the National Science Foundation. In the wake of that action, an opinion writer for the *Washington Post* suggested that the House didn't go far enough. The NSF should not fund any research in the social sciences, wrote Charles Lane, because "unlike hypotheses in the hard sciences, hypotheses about society usually can't be proven or disproven by experimentation."

Lane's comments echoed ones by Gary Gutting in the Opinionator blog of the *New York Times*. "While the physical sciences produce many detailed and precise predictions," wrote Gutting, "the social sciences do not. The reason is that such predictions almost always require randomized controlled experiments, which are seldom possible when people are involved."

This is news to me and the many other social scientists who have spent their careers doing carefully controlled experiments on human behavior, inside and outside the laboratory. What makes the criticism so galling is that those who voice it, or members of their families, have undoubtedly benefited from research in the disciplines they dismiss.

Most of us know someone who has suffered from depression and sought psychotherapy. He or she probably benefited from therapies, such as cognitive behavioral therapy, that have been shown to work in randomized clinical trials.

Problems such as child abuse and teenage pregnancy take a huge toll on society. Interventions developed by research psychologists, tested with the experimental method, have been found to lower the incidence of child abuse and reduce the rate of teenage pregnancies.

Ever hear of stereotype threat? It is the double jeopardy that people face when they are at risk of confirming a negative stereotype of their group. When African American students take a difficult test, for example, they are concerned not only about how well they will do but also about the possibility that performing poorly will reflect badly on their entire group. This added worry has been shown time and again, in carefully controlled experiments, to lower academic performance. But fortunately, experiments have also showed promising ways to reduce this threat. One intervention, for example, conducted in a middle school, reduced the achievement gap by 40%.

If you know someone who was unlucky enough to be arrested for a crime he didn't commit, he may have benefited from social psychological experiments that have resulted in fairer lineups and interrogations, making it less likely that innocent people are convicted.

An often-overlooked advantage of the experimental method is that it can demonstrate what doesn't work. Consider three popular programs that research psychologists have debunked: Critical Incident Stress Debriefing, used to prevent post-traumatic stress disorders in first responders and others who have witnessed horrific events; the D.A.R.E. anti-drug program, used in many schools throughout America; and Scared Straight programs designed to prevent at-risk teens from engaging in criminal behavior.

All three of these programs have been shown, with well-designed experimental studies, to be ineffective or, in some cases, to make matters worse. And as a result, the programs have become less popular or have changed their methods. By discovering what doesn't work, social scientists have saved the public billions of dollars.

To be fair to the critics, social scientists have not always taken advantage of the experimental method as much as they could. Too often, for example, educational programs have been implemented widely without being adequately tested. But increasingly, educational researchers are employing better methodologies. For example, in a recent study, researchers randomly assigned teachers to a program called My Teaching Partner, which is designed to improve teaching skills, or to a control group. Students taught by the teachers who participated in the program did significantly better on achievement tests than did students taught by teachers in the control group.

Are the social sciences perfect? Of course not. Human behavior is complex, and it is not possible to conduct experiments to test all aspects of what people do or why. There are entire disciplines devoted to the experimental study of human behavior, however, in tightly controlled, ethically acceptable ways. Many people benefit from the results, including those who, in their ignorance, believe that science is limited to the study of molecules.

Timothy D. Wilson is a professor of psychology at the University of Virginia and the author of several popular books, including *Redirect: The Surprising New Science of Psychological Change* (2011). Photo by Jen Fariello, Courtesy Timothy D. Wilson.

Wilson says that psychology is a science and we agree. But it isn't the same kind of science that, say, physics is, and that's okay. A penguin isn't the same kind of bird that an ostrich is, and yet, it *is* a bird. What makes psychology unique is that it is an especially young science that has taken upon itself the extraordinarily difficult task of understanding the most complex object in the known universe: the human mind. As you'll see in this chapter, it hasn't always been clear how best to do that; and as a result, psychology has had more than its share of revolutions and counter-revolutions, lurching from one approach to another as it has tried to find the right questions to ask and the best ways to answer them. But so what? Trial and error is how rats learn, so why not psychologists? We hope to convince you in this chapter and all the others that psychology has learned a whole lot since the days of William James. Let's see how we do.

For example, humans have fingers instead of flippers because at some point in the distant past, those of our ancestors who developed fingers were better able to survive and reproduce than those who did not, and they passed their flipperless fingeredness on to us. That's the principle of natural selection at work, shaping the human body. James reasoned that if our physical characteristics had evolved because they were adaptive, then natural selection should also have shaped the mind. "Consciousness," James wrote in 1892, "has in all probability been evolved, like all other functions, for a use." According to James, the task for psychologists was to figure out what that use was.

Build to the Outcomes

1. How did Helmholtz calculate the speed at which nerves transmit impulses?

2. What is introspection and how did Wundt use it?

3. What is structuralism, and what led to its decline?

4. What is natural selection and how did it influence the rise of functionalism?

The Early 1900s: Psychoanalysis and Behaviorism

Learning Outcomes

- Outline the basic ideas behind Freud's psychoanalytic theory.
- Define the basic idea behind behaviorism.
- Give an example of the principle of reinforcement.

Structuralism and functionalism were important ideas — to the hundred or so people who knew anything about them. While 19th-century academics debated the best way to study the mind, the rest of the world paid approximately no attention. But all that would change in the next century, when a restless neurologist from Vienna and a failed writer from Pennsylvania would pull psychology in opposite directions and, in the process, become two of the most influential thinkers of all time.

Psychoanalysis: The Mind Does Not Know Itself

While experimental psychologists were trying to understand the mind, physicians were trying to heal it. The French physicians Jean-Martin Charcot (1825–1893) and Pierre Janet (1859–1947) became interested in patients who had an odd collection of symptoms — some were blind, some were paralyzed, and some were unable to remember their identities — but who had no obvious physical illness or injury. Charcot and Janet referred to their patients' condition as **hysteria**, which is *a loss of function that has no obvious physical origin*. What could possibly explain it?

Enter Sigmund Freud (1856–1939), a handsome young Viennese physician who had begun his career studying the effects of cocaine and the sexual anatomy of eels (though not at the same time). Freud suspected that many patients with hysteria and other "nervous disorders" had suffered a childhood experience so painful that they couldn't allow themselves to remember it. These memories, he reasoned, had been hidden from consciousness and relegated to a place Freud called the **unconscious**, which is *the part of the mind that contains information of which people are not aware*. Freud believed that these exiled or "repressed" memories were the source of his patients' hysterical symptoms, and he spent the next several years developing an elaborate theory of the mind known as **psychoanalytic theory**, which is *a general theory that emphasizes the influence of the unconscious on feelings, thoughts, and behaviors*.

Freud's theory was complex, and you'll learn much more about it in the Consciousness, Personality, Disorders, and Treatment chapters. But, in brief, Freud saw the mind as a set of processes that were largely hidden from our view, and he regarded the conscious thoughts and feelings that the structuralists had worked so hard to identify as little more than flotsam and jetsam, bobbing on the surface of a vast and mysterious ocean. To understand the ocean, Freud suggested, you can't just skim the surface. You have to learn to dive — and when you do, you should expect to encounter some frightening things.

hysteria A loss of function that has no obvious physical origin.

unconscious The part of the mind that contains information of which people are not aware.

psychoanalytic theory A general theory that emphasizes the influence of the unconscious on feelings, thoughts, and behaviors.

Sigmund Freud's first major book, *The Interpretation of Dreams*, sold only 600 copies in the first 8 years. In a letter to a friend, Freud wrote, "Do you suppose that someday a marble tablet will be placed on the house, inscribed with these words: 'In this house on July 24, 1895, the secret of dreams was revealed to Dr. Sigm. Freud'? At the moment I see little prospect of it." But Freud was wrong, and today the site of that house bears a memorial plaque with precisely that inscription.   Photo by Sigmund Freud Copyrights/ullstein bild via Getty Images; volkerpreusser/Alamy

For Freud, those frightening things were the person's anxieties and impulses — the fear of death, the desire to kill, forbidden sexual urges, and so on — all of which were lurking beneath the waves.

Freud believed that the only way to confront these denizens of the deep was through **psychoanalysis**, which is *a therapy that aims to give people insight into the contents of their unconscious minds*. A therapeutic session with Sigmund Freud began with the patient lying on a couch and Freud sitting just behind her (probably smoking a cigar). He might ask the patient to describe her dreams or to "free associate" by talking about anything she wished or by responding quickly to a word ("What pops into your head when I say *mother*?"). Freud believed that his patients' dreams and free associations offered a glimpse into the contents of their unconscious minds, and that if he could see what was there, he could heal them.

William James thought most of Freud's theorizing was nonsense. "I strongly suspect Freud, with his dream theory, of being a regular hallucine," he wrote in a letter to a friend in 1909. *Hallucine* is an old-fashioned word for "lunatic," so this was not meant as a compliment. Most experimental psychologists shared James's assessment and paid scant attention to Freud's ideas. On the other hand, clinicians paid a lot of attention, and Freud's psychoanalytic movement attracted a virtual army of disciples. Indeed, Freud's thinking influenced just about everything in the 20th century — from history and philosophy to literature and art — which is why Freud is ranked as the 44th most influential person in human history (Skiena & Ward, 2013), which puts him a bit behind Albert Einstein but well ahead of Buddha.

Behaviorism: The Mind Does Not Matter

James had a somewhat dim view of Freud, but as the 20th century got rolling, another, much younger psychologist took an even dimmer view of Freud — and of James, Wundt, and everyone else who had ever talked about the "science of the mind." That young psychologist had been born in the tiny town of Traveler's Rest, South Carolina, and went on to the University of Chicago to study the behavior of rats. When his interest changed to the behavior of people, his changing interest changed the world.

Pavlov and Watson

To John Broadus Watson (1878–1958), everything worth knowing about a rat — how it feeds and mates, how it builds its nest and rears its young — could be known just by watching it, and he wondered why human beings couldn't be known the same way.

psychoanalysis A therapy that aims to give people insight into the contents of their unconscious minds.

John B. Watson was the founder of behaviorism, which revolutionized American psychology in the early 20th century. Watson was married, and his academic career was cut short when a scandalous love affair led Johns Hopkins University to dismiss him in 1920. He took a job in advertising, where he spent the remainder of his life working on campaigns for products such as Maxwell House coffee, Johnson & Johnson baby powder, and Pebeco toothpaste. Ferdinand Hamburger Archives, Sheridan Libraries, Johns Hopkins University; The Advertising Archives/Alamy

These historic photos show Ivan Pavlov and one of his dogs, Baika. Both became quite famous: Pavlov won the Nobel Prize in 1904 for his research on digestion, and Baika was immortalized in the 1971 song "Bitch," by the Rolling Stones ("Yeah when you call my name, I salivate like a Pavlov dog"). There is some debate about who earned the higher honor. Everett Collection Historical / Alamy; Courtesy R.K. Lawton

behaviorism An approach to psychology that restricts scientific inquiry to observable behavior.

Why should the study of human behavior require a bunch of idle speculation about the human mind? Mental life was idiosyncratic, undefinable, and unmeasurable, and Watson felt that if psychology wanted to become a real science, it should limit itself to studying the things people do rather than the things they claim to think and feel. Watson called this idea **behaviorism**, which is *an approach to psychology that restricts scientific inquiry to observable behavior.*

Watson was impressed by the work of the Russian physiologist Ivan Pavlov (1849–1936), who studied digestion in dogs. Pavlov knew that dogs naturally start salivating when they are presented with food. But one day he noticed that the dogs in his laboratory started salivating when they heard the footsteps of the research assistant who was coming down the hall to feed them! Pavlov suspected that his dogs had come to associate the feeder's footsteps with the arrival of food and that the dogs were responding to the footsteps as though they were food. He devised an experiment to test this hypothesis. First, he sounded a tone every time he fed his dogs. Then, after a few days, he sounded the tone without feeding the dogs. What happened? The dogs salivated when they heard the tone. Pavlov called the tone a stimulus and the salivation a response.

When Watson read about this research, he quickly realized that these two concepts — stimulus and response — could be the building blocks of a new behaviorist approach. Psychology, Watson argued, should be the scientific study of the relationship between stimuli and responses — nothing less, and certainly nothing more. In his 1919 book *Psychology from the Standpoint of a Behaviorist*, he wrote: "The goal of psychological study is the ascertaining of such data and laws that, given the stimulus, psychology can predict what the response will be." He proudly noted that in his book "the reader will find no discussion of consciousness and no reference to such terms as sensation, perception, attention, will, image and the like" because "I frankly do not know what they mean, nor do I believe that anyone else can use them consistently."

Watson's arguments were wildly persuasive. Before Watson, some psychologists were structuralists, some were functionalists, and some were undecided. "Then," as one historian wrote, "Watson touched a match to the mass, there was an explosion, and only behaviorism was left" (Boring, 1929). But if Watson had convinced psychologists that behaviorism was the one and only proper way to study human behavior, it would take a skinny kid from Pennsylvania to convince the rest of the world of the same thing.

Skinner

Burrhus Frederick Skinner (1904–1990) grew up in Pennsylvania and graduated from Hamilton College in 1926 with the intention of becoming a writer. Like many young people with that aspiration, he took a job at a bookstore in New York City. After a year or so, the writing wasn't going so well, and one day while browsing the shelves he came across books by Pavlov and by Watson. He was captivated. He abandoned his writing career and enrolled as a graduate student in the psychology department at Harvard University — the same department from which William James had retired 20 years earlier.

Skinner greatly admired the work of Pavlov and Watson, but as he studied them, he started to suspect that their simple stimulus–response psychology was missing something important. Pavlov's dogs lived in a laboratory where they sat around and waited to be fed; but in the real world, animals had to act on their environments to find food. How did they learn to do that? To investigate, Skinner built a cage for laboratory animals that the world would soon come to call a Skinner box. The cage had a lever which, when pressed by a hungry rat, delivered food through a tube. Then Skinner rigged up a "cumulative recorder," a device that recorded the frequency of each rat's lever-presses in real time. These inventions don't sound like much today, but in 1930 they were serious technology. Moreover, they allowed Skinner to discover something remarkable.

When Skinner put a rat in one of his special cages, it would typically wander around for a while, sniffing and exploring, until it accidentally bumped the lever, causing a food pellet to appear as if by magic. After this happy accident had happened a few times, the rat would suddenly start pressing the lever — tentatively at first, then more quickly and more often, until it basically looked like the conga player in a hot Latin jazz band. Unlike Pavlov's dogs, which had learned to monitor their environments and anticipate food, Skinner's rats had learned to operate on their environments to produce food. When a rat's behavior produced food (which Skinner called a reinforcement), it would repeat the behavior; and when it didn't, the rat wouldn't. Animals do what they are rewarded for doing, Skinner concluded, and he called this the **principle of reinforcement**, which is *a principle stating that any behavior that is rewarded will be repeated and any behavior that isn't won't.*

Skinner argued that this simple principle could explain how rats learn to find food, but that it could also explain the most complex human behaviors. In a relatively short time, Skinner's theories came to dominate psychology. Structuralism and functionalism had quietly disappeared, and "behaviorism was viewed as the one right way to do psychological science" (Baars, 1986, p. 32).

Like Freud, Skinner's influence went far beyond the ivy-covered walls of the academy. His theories spread across the globe and became the foundation of classroom education, government programs, psychological therapies, and even child-rearing practices. In two controversial best sellers — *Walden II* (1948) and *Beyond Freedom and Dignity*

principle of reinforcement A principle stating that any behavior that is rewarded will be repeated and any behavior that isn't rewarded won't be repeated.

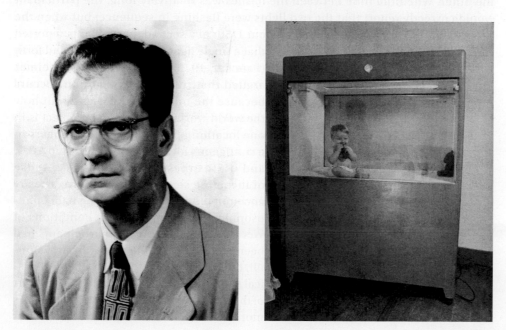

B. F. Skinner's books and ideas were influential but often mischaracterized. For instance, when his second child was born, Skinner designed a device called an "air crib" (right), which was simply a climate-controlled chamber meant to help infants sleep. But when the *Ladies' Home Journal* ran a story entitled "Baby in a Box," outraged readers assumed that Skinner was experimenting on his children at home the way he experimented on rats in his lab and called him "a monster." Skinner died in 1990 at the age of 86, and though psychology had long since renounced its allegiance to behaviorism, he remained a staunch defender. "The appeal to cognitive states and processes is a diversion which could well be responsible for much of our failure to solve our problems. We need to change our behavior and we can do so only by changing our physical and social environments. We choose the wrong path at the very start when we suppose that our goal is to change the 'minds and hearts of men and women' rather than the world in which they live" (Skinner, 1977). B.F. Skinner Foundation; Bernard Hoffman/The LIFE Picture Collection/Getty Images

(1971) — he laid out his vision for a utopian society in which all human behavior was controlled by the judicious application of the principle of reinforcement. In these books, Skinner claimed that free will was an illusion, and that the world could solve its most pressing social problems if only it would realize that people do what they are reinforced for doing, and that their sense of "choosing" and "deciding" is a dangerous fiction.

As you might expect, Skinner's critics were many and fierce. *Time* magazine featured him on its cover beneath the words "B. F. Skinner Says: We Can't Afford Freedom." One reviewer called his book "fascism without tears," and another called it "a corpse patched with nuts, bolts and screws from the junkyard of philosophy." Even the normally nonpartisan *TV Guide* got into the act, warning that Skinner was advocating "the taming of mankind through a system of dog obedience schools for all." These attacks were predictable but mistaken. Skinner did not want to turn classrooms into obedience schools or strip citizens of their civil rights. Rather, he simply believed that a scientific understanding of the principles that govern behavior could be used to improve social welfare and that behaviorists knew what those principles were.

Build to the Outcomes

1. Why did Freud have so little influence on experimental psychology? Where *did* he have influence?

2. What was the key idea behind Watson's behaviorism?

3. How did Skinner's contributions differ from Pavlov's?

The Early 1900s: Resistance to Behaviorism

Learning Outcomes

• Explain why several European psychologists resisted behaviorism.

• Explain why American social psychologists resisted behaviorism.

In the early 1900s, behaviorism was king; but not all its subjects were loyal. In fact, several pockets of resistance could be found throughout the kingdom — groups of psychologists whose work would soon foment a counter-revolution.

Gestalt Psychology and Developmental Psychology

Many of the dissidents were in Europe. For example, the German psychologist Max Wertheimer (1880–1943) studied how people perceive motion. In one of his experiments, participants were shown two lights that flashed quickly on a screen, one after the other. When the time between the flashes was relatively long, the participant would correctly report that the two lights were flashing in sequence; but when the time between flashes was reduced to about 1/5th of a second, participants reported

that a single light was moving back and forth (Fancher, 1979; Sarris, 1989). Wertheimer argued that this "illusory motion" occurs because the mind has theories about how the world works (e.g., "when an object is in one location and then instantly appears in a contiguous location, it probably moved"), and it uses these theories to make sense of incoming sensory data. (You've already encountered this idea under the name philosophical idealism.) In both conditions of Wertheimer's experiment, participants had been shown exactly the same physical stimuli, but they had seen different things. Physical stimuli, Wertheimer concluded, are part of the perceptual experience, but the whole is more than the sum of its parts. The German

Have you ever seen a "news ticker" in which words seem to be scrolling by? The words aren't really moving, of course. Rather, contiguous lights are going on and off in rapid succession. So why do we see motion that isn't really there? This is the question that Gestalt psychologist Max Wertheimer was studying when the rise of Nazism forced him to flee Germany in 1933. He came to New York and taught at the New School for Social Research until his death in 1943. Ramin Talaie/ Bloomberg via Getty Images; AKG Images

word for "whole" is *gestalt*, and Wertheimer and his colleagues called their approach **Gestalt psychology**, which was *an approach to psychology that emphasized the way in which the mind creates perceptual experience.*

While German psychologists were studying why people sometimes see things that aren't really there, the British psychologist Sir Frederic Bartlett (1886–1969) was studying why people sometimes remember things that didn't really happen. Bartlett asked participants to read stories and then try to remember the material — from 15 minutes to several years later. When Bartlett analyzed their errors, he found that participants often remembered what they had expected to read rather than what they actually read, and that this tendency became more pronounced with the passage of time. Bartlett argued that memory is not a simple recording device; rather, our minds use their theories of how the world usually works to construct our memories of past experience (see The Real World: Beneath the Ocean of Memory).

While German and British psychologists were trying to understand the minds of adults, Swiss psychologist Jean Piaget (1896–1980) was trying to understand the minds of children, often by examining the mistakes they made. For example, in one study, Piaget showed 3-year-olds two equally large mounds of clay and then broke one mound into little pieces. When the children were asked which mound now had "more clay," they typically said that the unbroken one did. By the age of 6 or 7, children no longer made this mistake. Piaget concluded that the mind has theories about how the world works ("Breaking a material object into pieces doesn't change the amount of material in it") and that, because small children have not yet learned these theories, they see the world in a fundamentally different way than adults do. Piaget and his contemporaries helped create an area of experimental psychology called **developmental psychology**, which is *the study of the ways in which psychological phenomena change over the life span.*

In short, while the majority of early 20th-century American psychologists were flying the behaviorist flag, a small number of European psychologists were quietly doing the very thing that behaviorism forbade: studying people's perceptions, memories, and judgments in order to understand the nature of an unobservable entity called the mind.

Frederic Bartlett was one of the early-20th-century European psychologists who defied the edicts of behaviorism to study "mentalistic" phenomena such as memory.
Walter Stoneman, ©Godfrey Argent Studio/The Royal Society

Jean Piaget (left) published his first scientific paper at the age of 10. It was about mollusks. A few years later, his interests shifted to people, especially to how they learn to think. Piaget believed the best way to understand children's minds was to ask them questions — a technique that behaviorists considered worse than useless. In 1933, Piaget met a 20-year-old student named Bärbel Inhelder (right) and suggested that she drop a sugar cube into a glass of water and ask children to describe what happened. She did, and the experiment led to her first scientific publication. Inhelder went on to earn a PhD and collaborated with Piaget for nearly 50 years. Although the world rightfully remembers the brilliance of Piaget's work, it often forgets that the work — as well as the brilliance — was also Inhelder's. Ben Martin/Getty Images; Alvaro Donado/Macmillan Learning; © Archives Jean Piaget

Gestalt psychology An approach to psychology that emphasized the way in which the mind creates perceptual experience.

developmental psychology The study of the ways in which psychological phenomena change over the life span.

THE REAL WORLD

Beneath the Ocean of Memory

Sir Frederic Bartlett was interested in how memory worked in "the real world," and despite the ascendance of behaviorism, he spent his life studying it. During World War II, he established the Applied Psychology Unit at the Cambridge Laboratory of Industrial Research to help the British military in its efforts to defeat Hitler. So it was more than fitting that nearly a half century after his death, Bartlett's pioneering studies of human memory helped solve a naval mystery.

During World War II, the Australian warship *Sydney* (shown in the photo) battled the German warship *Kormoran*, and both ships sank in the Indian Ocean. There were just a few survivors, and when they were interrogated months later, each had a different memory of the precise spot where the two ships went down. Despite numerous attempts to locate the ships, the wreckage remained lost at the bottom of the sea.

Then, in 1998, psychologists John Dunn and Kim Kirsner decided to see if they could use Bartlett's research to estimate how the survivors' memories might have become distorted over time (Dunn & Kirsner, 2011). "What we found was that there was a correspondence—that our

Courtesy Sea Power Centre - Australia

data looked like the kind of data that Bartlett had generated in his study," said Dunn (Spiegel, 2011). By combining the survivors' testimony with Bartlett's ideas about memory distortion, the psychologists were able to make a prediction about where the ships might actually be.

"I never really thought that I would ever find out whether it would be right or wrong," said

Dunn. But he did find out, because in 2008, a team of shipwreck-hunters found the ships on the ocean floor—right about where the two psychologists had predicted they would be. Despite what his behaviorist colleagues had claimed, Sir Frederic Bartlett's mentalistic research was "real science" after all.

---

social psychology The study of the causes and consequences of sociality.

Kurt Lewin (left) fled Germany the year that Hitler came to power, and he became deeply interested in the psychological differences between autocracy (in which one person has power over all others) and democracy (in which all people share power). In a series of studies, he and his colleagues (Lewin et al., 1939) assigned 10-year-old boys to work together in autocratic groups on some days and in democratic groups on other days. He observed that "the change from autocracy to democracy seemed to take somewhat more time than from democracy to autocracy" and concluded that this was because "Autocracy is imposed upon the individual. Democracy he has to learn" (Lewin, 1948). Album/Alamy; MBI/Alamy

Social Psychology

Not all the dissidents were in Europe. Some had already come to America. Like many Jews, Kurt Lewin (1890–1947) had fled Europe in the early 1930s when Hitler came to power. After taking a job as a professor at the Massachusetts Institute of Technology, Lewin began studying topics such as leadership, communication, attitude change, and racial prejudice. At the heart of his many different research projects was a single, simple idea: Behavior is not a function of the environment, but of the person's subjective construal of the environment. Responses do not depend on stimuli, as the behaviorists claimed; rather, they depend on how people think about those stimuli.

Lewin's research and theorizing gave birth to a new area of experimental psychology called **social psychology**, which is *the study of the causes and consequences of sociality*. Social psychologists sought to understand how people see the social world. For example, Solomon Asch (1907–1996) told a group of participants about a man who was envious, stubborn, critical, impulsive, industrious, and intelligent — a

Solomon Asch was one of many social psychologists who were influenced by Gestalt psychology and who resisted the edicts of behaviorism by studying how people think about each other. His early studies of the "primacy effect" showed that early information about a person changes the interpretation of later information, which is why first impressions matter so much. If you saw the photo in the middle before the photo on the right, you'd form one impression of the man ("He's a fairly straight-ahead guy who likes to party on weekends"); but if you saw the photos in the opposite order, you'd probably form a very different impression ("He's a total hipster who covers his ink for his day job"). Solomon Asch Center for Study of Ethnopolitical Conflict.; Alvarez/Getty Images

string of adjectives that went from bad to good. He told another group about a man who was intelligent, industrious, impulsive, critical, stubborn, and envious — exactly the same list of adjectives but in the opposite order. Asch discovered that the participants who heard the man's good traits first liked him more. Asch argued that this "primacy effect" occurred because the early words in each list created a theory ("Intelligent and industrious — wow, this is a really great guy") that the mind then used to interpret the later words in that list ("Stubborn probably means that he sticks to his principles"). Asch's studies led to an avalanche of research on how people draw inferences about others.

Other social psychologists studied how people persuade each other to change their beliefs, how people form stereotypes, and how people create identities based on their social groups. Beliefs, stereotypes, identities — concepts like these had been banished from behaviorism but were the heart and soul of social psychology. "The power, the honors, the authority, the textbooks, the money, everything in psychology was owned by the behavioristic school," psychologist George Miller later remembered (Baars, 1986, p. 203). "Those who didn't give a damn, in clinical or social psychology, went off and did their own thing." What the social psychologists didn't know at the time was that their thing would soon be everybody's thing because the behaviorist kingdom was about to be attacked, invaded, and conquered.

Build to the Outcomes

1. What was similar about Wertheimer's and Bartlett's findings?
2. In what way was Piaget's work incompatible with behaviorism?
3. What basic idea underlay Kurt Lewin's work, and why did social psychologists reject behaviorism?

The Late 1900s: The Cognitive Revolution

In 1957, Skinner published a book called *Verbal Behavior*, in which he offered a behaviorist account of how children learn language. The linguist Noam Chomsky decided that there had been enough passive resistance to behaviorism over the past 40 years and that it was time to mount a full-scale attack. In 1959, Chomsky published a devastating critique of Skinner's book, arguing that behaviorist principles could never explain some of the most obvious features of language-learning.

Learning Outcomes

- Summarize Chomsky's critique of Skinner.
- Explain what cognitive psychology is and how it emerged.
- Explain what evolutionary psychology is and why it emerged.

In 1959, the linguist Noam Chomsky (b. 1928) published a critique of Skinner's theory of verbal behavior that heralded the decline of behaviorism in American psychology. Chomsky went on to become an outspoken political activist and social critic. Tom Landers/ The Boston Globe via Getty Images; Cory S. Sheffield

In this 1946 photo, Marlyn Wescoff (left) and Ruth Lichterman (right) are programming ENIAC, the world's first digital computer. This revolutionary device did many things, but one of the most important is that it gave psychologists a scientifically respectable way to talk about mental processes. U.S. Army Photo

cognitive psychology The study of human information processing.

For example, children create novel sentences that they have never heard before. How do they produce them? The obvious answer is that they use grammar — a complex set of rules that tells them which of an infinitely large number of possible sentences are permissible ("The girl ran after the ball") and which are not ("The girl after the ball ran"). So how do they learn these rules? Chomsky argued that a purely behaviorist account of learning could never explain how children learn grammar. Chomsky (1959) suggested that it was time to toss behaviorism into the dustbin of history: "If the study of language is limited in these ways," he wrote, "it seems inevitable that major aspects of verbal behavior will remain a mystery."

The world was listening. But "Out with the old!" is a successful rallying cry only when followed by "In with the new!" and there was indeed something new happening in the 1960s that would push behaviorism to psychology's back burner. It wasn't a new philosophy, scientific discovery, or social movement. It was a mindless, soulless machine.

Cognitive Psychology

ENIAC, the first general-purpose electronic digital computer, was built in 1945. It weighed 30 tons, was the size of a small house, cost the equivalent of $7 million, and performed complicated mathematical calculations that were of interest mainly to a handful of engineers, the U.S. Army, and a few random geeks. But ENIAC and all the other computers that followed did something more important than number-crunching: They gave psychologists permission once again to talk about the mind. How?

A computer's observable behavior is as simple as a rat's. Present the computer with a stimulus ("2 + 2 = ?") and it will produce a response ("4"). But unlike a rat, the way the computer produces its response is neither hidden nor mysterious. It produces its response by processing information — that is, by encoding information, storing it in memory, retrieving it on demand, and combining it in lawful ways. These operations allow computers to do things that from the outside look a whole lot like learning, reasoning, remembering — and maybe even thinking. If those words could legitimately be used to describe the physical information-processing operations that happen inside a machine, why couldn't they also be used to describe the physical information-processing operations that happen inside a brain? If the brain is hardware, then the mind is software — and there is nothing spooky or unmeasurable about the way a software program works.

With the digital computer as their guiding metaphor, psychologists of the 1950s and 1960s suddenly felt emboldened to study topics that everyone but the dissidents had ignored for decades: how people shift their attention from one stimulus to another; how people expand their capacity to process information by combining it into chunks; how a person's desires can shape their perceptions of physical objects; and so on. This dramatic shift in psychology's orientation came to be known — for better or for worse — as the cognitive revolution. **Cognitive psychology** is *the study of human information processing*, and for more than 50 years it has been producing deep insights into the nature of the human mind — many of which you will learn about in the chapters to come.

Evolutionary Psychology

Behaviorism set the mind aside, and cognitive psychology brought it back. But behaviorism also set something else aside: the past. Behaviorists viewed individuals as blank slates who came into the world with nothing but a readiness to be shaped by their environments. As John Watson (1930, p. 89) wrote:

Give me a dozen healthy infants, well-formed, and my own specified world to bring them up in and I'll guarantee to take any one at random and train him to become any type of specialist I might select — doctor, lawyer, artist, merchant-chief and, yes, even beggar-man and thief, regardless of his talents, penchants, tendencies, abilities, vocations, and race of his ancestors.

Watson's view was egalitarian, optimistic, and quintessentially American. But it was also wrong. In the 1960s, the psychologist John Garcia (1917–2012) was studying how rats react to radiation sickness. He noticed that his rats instantly learned to associate their nausea with the taste of the food they ate just before getting sick, and they instantly developed an aversion to that food. On the other hand, no matter how much training they received, his rats could not learn to associate their nausea with a flashing light or the sound of a buzzer. That just didn't make sense. Pavlov had shown that when two stimuli are paired (e.g., a researcher's footsteps and the appearance of food), animals will learn to associate one with the other — and it wasn't supposed to matter whether those stimuli were food, footsteps, lights, or buzzers. It wasn't supposed to matter, but it did. What could that mean?

Garcia thought it meant that every organism is evolved to respond to particular stimuli in particular ways — that animals come into the world "biologically prepared" to learn some associations more easily than others. In the real world of forests and sewers, a rat's nausea is usually caused by eating spoiled food. Although Garcia's rats had been born in a laboratory and had never eaten spoiled food, their ancestors had. Millions of years of evolution had designed the rat brain so that it would quickly learn to associate an episode of nausea with the taste of food, and that's why rats learned this association so quickly and easily. Rats, it turned out, were not blank slates — so why should psychologists think of people that way?

Findings such as these led to **evolutionary psychology**, which is *the study of the ways in which the human mind has been shaped by natural selection*. Evolutionary psychologists began studying topics such as gender differences in sexual promiscuity, how people detect cheaters in a social exchange, and how people select their ideal mate. Evolutionary psychology "is not a specific subfield of psychology, such as the study of vision, reasoning, or social behavior. It is a way of thinking about psychology that can be applied to any topic within it" (Cosmides & Tooby, 2000, p. 115). As you will see in upcoming chapters, modern psychologists now apply evolutionary thinking to a wide array of topics.

evolutionary psychology The study of the ways in which the human mind has been shaped by natural selection.

John Garcia's experiments showed that the ease with which associations are learned can be influenced by an organism's evolutionary history. Later work by other evolutionary psychologists suggested that a great deal of human behavior might be similarly influenced. UCLA Media

After the Revolution

Behaviorism was a valuable approach that led to many important discoveries about human behavior, but it ignored the mind and it ignored the past. Although many modern psychologists still study how rats learn and how reinforcement shapes behavior, few are behaviorists who regard humans as blank slates or who believe that mental processes are unmeasurable fictions. Ironically, the emergence of cognitive and evolutionary psychology has in some ways brought psychology full circle. Like the structuralists, cognitive psychologists now ask what the mind is like; and like the functionalists, evolutionary psychologists now ask what the mind is for. Apparently, some questions are just too interesting to go gently into that good night.

Build to the Outcomes

1. What was wrong with Skinner's explanation of how children learn language?

2. How did the advent of the computer allow psychologists to talk about the mind?

3. What kind of evidence suggested that behaviorism was wrong to ignore the organism's evolutionary history?

Learning Outcomes

- Define neuroscience and explain how modern psychologists study the brain.

- Define cultural psychology and explain why it matters.

The Early 2000s: New Frontiers

The cognitive revolution fundamentally changed psychology at the close of the 20th century. But science never stands still. In the present century, psychology continues to evolve, and several new and exciting areas have emerged. We'll discuss two of them — one that has psychologists looking "down a level" to biology as they search for the neural substrates of mental life, and another that has psychologists looking "up a level" to sociology and anthropology as they seek to understand its cultural origins.

Neuroscience

The mind is what the brain does. But until recently, knowledge of the brain was based primarily on studies of brains that had been damaged. For instance, in 1861, the French physician Paul Broca (1824–1880) performed an autopsy on a man who had been able to understand words but not produce them; he found damage in a small region on the left side of that man's brain. Broca concluded that the ability to speak somehow depended on this particular region — and the fact that this region is today called Broca's area tells you that he was right.

In addition to learning from brains that were damaged by nature, psychologists also learned from brains that they damaged themselves. In the 1930s, for instance, the psychologist Karl Lashley (1890–1958) taught rats to run a maze and then surgically damaged different parts of the rats' cerebral cortices and measured changes in their performance. To his surprise, he found that while brain damage impaired performance, it didn't really matter where on the cortex the damage was inflicted, which led Lashley to conclude that learning was not "localized" or tied to a specific brain area in the same way that language seemed to be.

Of course, damaged brains can teach us only so much. Imagine how hard it would be to figure out how an engine works if all you could do was smash different parts with a hammer and then measure how well the car drove. Fortunately, newer technologies allow psychologists to observe the undamaged brain in action. For example, functional magnetic resonance imaging (fMRI) is a technology that produces the "brain scans" you often hear about in the news. Despite their name, these scans are not photos of the brain; rather, they are maps showing the amount of blood flowing in different parts of a person's brain at a particular moment in time. Because neural activity requires oxygen, and because blood supplies it, these scans can tell us which areas of a brain were processing the most information at any particular time, and this has taught us things we could never have learned by merely examining damaged brains.

For instance, Broca would not have been surprised to learn that people using their hands to speak American Sign Language (ASL) show increased neural

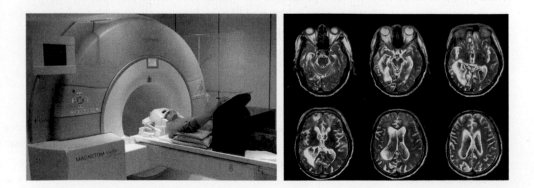

Technologies such as fMRI allow cognitive neuroscientists to determine which areas of the brain are most and least active when people perform various mental tasks, such as reading, writing, thinking, or remembering. The machine (left) produces what are commonly called brain scans (right). Martin Lotze/University of Greifswald; MriMan/Shutterstock

activity in the same region of the left hemisphere that he identified in 1861. But he might have been surprised by research that has used fMRI to show that this left-hemisphere activity occurs only in the brains of speakers who became deaf in adulthood. Speakers who were born deaf show increased neural activity in both the left and right hemispheres, suggesting that they are speaking ASL in a very different way (Newman et al., 2002). The advent of fMRI and other technologies that you'll learn about in the Neuroscience and Behavior chapter has given birth to two new areas of psychology: **cognitive neuroscience**, which is *the study of the relationship between the brain and the mind (especially in humans)*, and **behavioral neuroscience**, which is *the study of the relationship between the brain and behavior (especially in nonhuman animals)*.

cognitive neuroscience The study of the relationship between the brain and the mind (especially in humans).

behavioral neuroscience The study of the relationship between the brain and behavior (especially in nonhuman animals).

cultural psychology The study of how culture influences mental life.

Cultural Psychology

The human beings who inhabit the mountains of India, the plains of China, the cities of Africa, the jungles of Brazil, and the classrooms of America are more alike than they are different, but the differences are important to understanding how they think, feel, and act. Culture refers to the values, traditions, and beliefs that are shared by a particular group of people. Although we usually think of culture in terms of nationality and ethnicity, it can also be defined by age (e.g., youth culture), sexual orientation (e.g., gay culture), religion (e.g., Jewish culture), occupation (e.g., academic culture), and many of the other dimensions on which people differ (see A World of Difference: To Have or Have Not).

Scholars have been interested in cultural differences since at least the days of the ancient Greeks, but most 19th-century psychologists were content to ignore them and to assume that what they were studying was universal, or that exceptions to the rule didn't really matter. In the 20th century, culture became a topic of great interest to the social psychologists, but the behaviorists ignored it. After all, how important could culture be if rats didn't have any?

All of that has now changed. America has become more diverse, and its diversity has become more apparent, which means that the importance of culture is looming larger than ever before. **Cultural psychology** is *the study of how culture influences mental life*, and those influences can be quite profound. For example, in one study, American and Japanese participants were shown two drawings that differed in a few small details and were then asked to spot the differences. The Americans detected more differences in the foreground objects, whereas the Japanese detected more differences in the background objects (Masuda & Nisbett, 2001). Why? Because while Americans live in an independent and individualistic society, Japanese people live in an interdependent society with many role prescriptions that require them to attend to relationships and context, and this cultural difference appears to influence the kinds of visual information to which they naturally attend. Whereas Westerners tend to process visual information "analytically" by attending to objects in the foreground, Easterners tend to process visual information "holistically" by attending to the background. Because culture can influence just about everything psychologists study, you'll learn about work in cultural psychology in every one of the upcoming chapters.

Culture can influence how and what we see. Participants in a study were shown this scene and then another version of this scene in which something was changed. American participants were more likely to spot changes to the red car, but Japanese participants were more likely to spot changes to the buildings. Culture and point of view, Richard E. Nisbett, Takahiko Masuda, Proceedings of the National Academy of Sciences Sep 2003, 100 (19) 11163-11170. © 2003 National Academy of Sciences, U.S.A

Build to the Outcomes

1. What kinds of things can be learned from brain scans?
2. What is the difference between behavioral neuroscience and cognitive neuroscience?
3. Give an example of a way in which culture shapes perception.

A WORLD OF DIFFERENCE

To Have or Have Not

When we think about "other cultures," most of us imagine faraway lands filled with people eating exotic foods, wearing unfamiliar clothes, and speaking languages we can't understand. But you don't have to board an airplane to visit a culture much different from your own because in just about every place on earth, there are two distinctly different cultures living side by side: those who have more — more money, more education, more prestige — and those who have less (Kraus et al., 2011). In even the most egalitarian societies, people can be divided into higher and lower social classes, and as it turns out, social class is a powerful determinant of human behavior.

Consider an example. Because upper-class people have ample material resources, they don't need to depend much on others. When problems arise, upper-class people rely on their bank accounts, whereas lower-class people rely on family, friends, and neighbors with whom they must maintain good relationships. In a way, one of the luxuries that upper-class people enjoy is the luxury of not worrying too much about what others feel or think. Does having that luxury influence their behavior?

Indeed it does. In laboratory studies, upper-class people often prove to be less generous, less charitable, less trusting, and less helpful toward others (Piff et al., 2010), as well as more likely to lie and cheat for personal gain (Gino & Pierce, 2009; Piff et al., 2012). This "me first" orientation is easy to see outside of the laboratory, too. For example, in one study, researchers stood near the intersection of two busy streets and recorded the make, model, and year of the cars that approached. They then watched to see

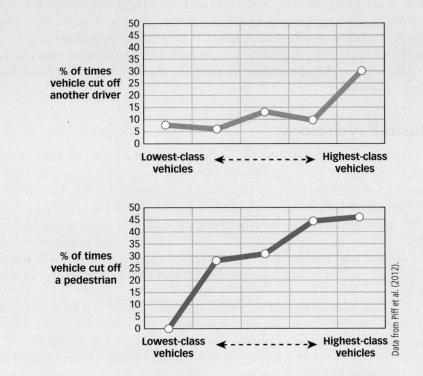

Data from Piff et al. (2012).

whether the drivers cut off other cars and pedestrians in the intersection. As the two graphs show, the drivers of new expensive cars were considerably more likely to zip through intersections without regard for others. Is this because being upper-class makes people selfish? Or is it because being selfish makes people upper-class? Some studies suggest that the first explanation is the right one. For instance, when participants in experiments are randomly assigned to *think* of themselves as upper-class — for instance, when they are asked to compare their incomes to those who have less — they also behave more selfishly (Piff et al., 2012).

Social class matters. So do gender, race, religion, age, and most of the other dimensions on which human beings differ. Psychological science often produces conclusions about "people on average," but it is important to keep in mind that while averages are useful for understanding and predicting behavior, people actually come in nearly infinite varieties, and the things that distinguish them are often as interesting as the things that make them one.

Learning Outcomes

- Describe the diversity of psychology.
- Outline the different kinds of training psychologists may receive.
- Identify some of the careers available to psychologists.

Becoming a Psychologist

Although most ordinary people don't know exactly what psychology is, they have a sneaking suspicion that psychologists can look directly into their minds and read their thoughts, especially the sexual ones. In fact, psychologists can't do this, but they can do other things that are much more useful, such as helping people, doing research, and making lists with three examples. Now that you know where psychology came from, and how it got from there to here, we'll close this chapter by looking at modern psychology as a profession.

Who Becomes a Psychologist?

In July of 1892, William James and six other psychologists decided to form an organization that represented psychology as a profession, so the American Psychological Association (APA) was born. Today their little club boasts more than 75,000 members — and a

In 1890, Harvard was an all-male school, but Mary Whiton Calkins (left) was given special permission to study there with William James. Despite completing all the requirements for a PhD, however, the president of Harvard refused to award her a degree because she was a woman. James was outraged, describing her performance as "the most brilliant examination for the PhD that we have had at Harvard." Calkins went on to become a professor at Wellesley College and the first female president of the APA. In 1894, Margaret Floy Washburn (right) became the first woman to actually receive a PhD in psychology (from Cornell University). She became a professor at Vassar College, and she too went on to serve as the APA's president. Today, women earn the majority of PhDs in psychology from American universities. Macmillan Learning; The Drs. Nicholas and Dorothy Cummings Center for the History of Psychology, The University of Akron

second professional organization, the Association for Psychological Science, formed in 1988 that now has 30,000 members. James and his friends would never have guessed how massive their profession would soon become, or that by 2017, women would make up a majority of the membership of the APA and hold a majority of its governance positions (National Science Foundation, 2018).

Or maybe they would have. After all, just a few years after the APA was founded, Mary Whiton Calkins (1863–1930) became its president, at a time when most American women were presiding over a household rather than a board of directors. Calkins studied at Harvard with James and over the course of her career wrote four books and published more than 100 scientific papers. Today, women play leading roles in all areas of psychology. In fact, women earn about 70% of PhDs in psychology from American universities (National Science Foundation, 2018).

There were no women at the APA's founding meeting in 1892, and neither were there any people of color. But that changed quickly. In 1920, Francis Cecil Sumner (1895–1954) became the first African American to receive a PhD in psychology, and in 1970, his student Kenneth Clark (1914–2005) was the first African American to serve as the APA's president. He and his wife Mamie Phipps Clark studied the ways in which African American children were psychologically harmed by segregation, and in 1954 their groundbreaking research was cited in the U.S. Supreme Court's ruling in *Brown v. Board of Education*, which held that racial segregation of public schools was unconstitutional (Guthrie, 2000). Today, non-White students earn about 30% of PhDs in psychology awarded by American universities. America has changed and so has psychology — in ways that would surely have made the seven founders proud.

How Do People Become Psychologists?

College students who major in psychology usually come away with a bachelor's degree. They can call themselves educated, they can call themselves graduated, and if they really

Mamie Phipps Clark (1917–1983) and Kenneth Clark (1914–2005) studied the psychological effects of prejudice, discrimination, and segregation on children. Based in part on their research, the U.S. Supreme Court declared segregation unconstitutional. Chief Justice Earl Warren concluded that "to separate them [African American children] from others of similar age and qualifications solely because of their race generates a feeling of inferiority as to their status in the community that may affect their hearts and minds in a way unlikely to ever be undone." Without the work of these two pioneering psychologists, the integration of America's schools might not have happened when it did. University Archives, Rare Book & Manuscript Library, Columbia University Libraries; The Topeka Capital-Journal

want to, they can call themselves bachelors. But they can't call themselves psychologists. To be called a psychologist requires earning an additional advanced degree. One of the most common of these is the PhD in psychology. The abbreviation stands for doctor of philosophy (which actually has nothing to do with philosophy and a lot to do with the history of 19th-century German universities — don't ask).

To earn a PhD, students must attend graduate school, where they take classes and learn to do original research by collaborating with professors. Although William James was able to master the entire field of psychology in just a few years because the body of knowledge was so small, graduate students today typically concentrate their training in a specific area of psychology (e.g., social, cognitive, developmental, or clinical). They spend an average of 6 years in graduate school before attaining their PhDs (National Science Foundation, 2018), and afterward many go on for more training in a laboratory or a hospital. (See Data Visualization: Understanding How to Use [or Misuse!] Data at www.launchpadworks.com.)

Some people who receive a PhD in psychology become professors, usually at a college or university where they may do some combination of teaching and scientific research. You are probably taking a class from one of those people right now, and may we take just a moment to say that he or she has excellent taste in textbooks? But many people who receive a PhD in psychology instead take jobs that involve assessing and treating people with psychological problems. These psychologists are informally referred to as therapists, and they typically have private practices, just like your doctor and dentist do.

A practice often includes a variety of mental health professionals, such as psychiatrists (who have earned an MD, or a medical doctor, degree) and counselors (who may have earned one of many master's-level degrees). Other advanced degrees that allow people to call themselves psychologists and provide therapy include the PsyD (doctor of psychology) and the MEd (master of education). Why does a practice need so many different kinds of people? First, different degrees come with different privileges: People with an MD can prescribe medications, but in most states, people with a PhD cannot. Second, most therapists specialize in treating specific problems such as depression, anxiety, eating disorders, and so on, and they may even specialize in treating specific populations, such as children, older adults, or particular ethnic groups (see **FIGURE 1.1**). It takes a village to look after people's mental health.

Psychologists are also employed in a wide variety of other settings. For example, school psychologists offer guidance to students, parents, and teachers; industrial/organizational psychologists help businesses and organizations hire employees and maximize the

Figure 1.1 The Subfields of Psychology
Percentage of PhDs awarded by American universities in various subfields of psychology in 2017. Data from National Science Foundation, 2018.

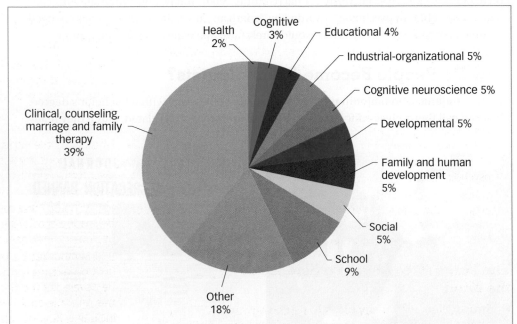

A person earning a PhD in psychology can go on to a wide range of fields, such as these three individuals did (from left to right): Lynne Madden (left) is a clinical psychologist who works with both individuals and groups. Gloria Balague (middle) applies her training as a clinical psychologist to her work with athletes. Lynne Owens Mock (right) directs a community mental health center in Chicago. © Macmillan Learning

employees' performances; sports psychologists help athletes train and compete; forensic psychologists assist attorneys and courts in dealing with crime; consumer psychologists help companies develop and market new products; and the list goes on. Modern psychologists are a diverse set of women and men who teach, do research, help people in distress, and aid the missions of public and private institutions. If you like what you learn in the upcoming chapters, you might even to decide to become one of them.

Build to the Outcomes

1. How has the makeup of psychology changed over the past 150 years?

2. What do most people who earn a PhD in psychology do with that degree?

3. What are some of the careers that psychologists might pursue?

CHAPTER REVIEW

Psychology's Philosophical Roots

- Psychology is the scientific study of mind and behavior, and it has deep philosophical roots.

- Philosophical dualism is the view that mind and body are fundamentally different things; philosophical materialism is the view that all mental phenomena are reducible to physical phenomena. Most modern psychologists are philosophical materialists.

- Philosophical realism is the view that perceptions of the physical world are produced entirely by information from the sensory organs; philosophical idealism is the view that perceptions of the physical world are the brain's interpretation of information from the sensory organs. Most modern psychologists are philosophical idealists.

- Philosophical empiricism is the view that all knowledge is acquired through experience; philosophical nativism is the view that some knowledge is innate rather than acquired. Most modern psychologists are philosophical nativists.

The Late 1800s: Toward a Science of the Mind

- Structuralism was an approach to psychology that attempted to isolate and analyze the mind's basic elements.

- Functionalism was an approach to psychology that was influenced by Darwin's theory of natural selection, emphasizing the adaptive significance of mental processes.

The Early 1900s: Psychoanalysis and Behaviorism

- Sigmund Freud developed psychoanalytic theory, which emphasized the influence of the unconscious on feelings, thoughts, and behaviors. He devised a therapy called psychoanalysis to help people gain insight into the contents of their unconscious minds.

- Freud had little impact on experimental psychology, but a tremendous impact on the treatment of psychological disorders and on the intellectual climate of the Western world.

- John Watson developed behaviorism, which was an approach to psychology that restricted scientific inquiry to observable behavior. Behaviorism soon came to dominate experimental psychology in America.

- B. F. Skinner took a behaviorist approach to understanding how organisms learn to operate on their environments, and he developed the principle of reinforcement. He believed this principle could explain complex human behavior, including how people learn language.

The Early 1900s: Resistance to Behaviorism

- In the first half of the 20th century, behaviorism reigned in America, but some European psychologists continued to do research on mentalistic phenomena such as perception, memory, and judgment.
- At the same time, American social psychologists also resisted behaviorism and continued to do research on mentalistic phenomena such as beliefs, attitudes, stereotypes, identity, and intention.

The Late 1900s: The Cognitive Revolution

- Noam Chomsky's critique of Skinner's theory of language, as well as the advent of the digital computer, helped ignite the "cognitive revolution."
- The emergence of cognitive psychology allowed psychologists to use the language of information processing to once again study mentalistic phenomena.
- In the 1970s and 1980s, psychologists began to incorporate theories from evolutionary biology into their work, which led to the emergence of evolutionary psychology.

The Early 2000s: New Frontiers

- Cognitive neuroscientists study the relationship between psychological processes and neural activity.
- Behavioral neuroscientists study the relationship between behavior and neural activity.
- Cultural psychologists study the ways in which culture influences mental life.

Becoming a Psychologist

- Psychology is a diverse science. In the United States, women earn more than half of all PhDs in psychology, and about a third of all PhDs in psychology are earned by people of color.
- To become a psychologist, one must attain an advanced degree. Many psychologists become therapists or clinicians, but some become professors; and many are employed in a variety of settings including schools, government, and industry.

Key Concept Quiz

1. The philosophical idea that all mental processes in the mind are reducible to physical processes in the brain is known as
   a. philosophical materialism.
   b. philosophical nativism.
   c. philosophical empiricism.
   d. philosophical realism.

2. Introspection is one of the primary methods of
   a. idealism.
   b. structuralism.
   c. behaviorism.
   d. Gestalt psychology.

3. Which of these people most influenced functionalism?
   a. Skinner
   b. Freud
   c. Darwin
   d. Pavlov

4. Psychoanalysis is meant to help people
   a. isolate the basic elements of conscious experience.
   b. respond to stimuli.
   c. obtain reinforcements.
   d. attain insight into their unconscious minds.

5. John Watson thought behaviorism
   a. was the right way to study animals but the wrong way to study people.
   b. should consider the evolutionary history of the organism.
   c. would make psychology an objective science.
   d. could provide glimpses into a person's unconscious mind.

6. B. F. Skinner's principle of reinforcement explains
   a. the emergence of cultural psychology.
   b. why lights can appear to be moving even when they really aren't.

   c. why structuralism failed.
   d. how behavior is shaped by its consequences.

7. The American psychologists who resisted behaviorism in the early 1900s were
   a. social psychologists.
   b. neuroscientists.
   c. evolutionary psychologists.
   d. philosophical dualists.

8. The cognitive revolution was made possible by
   a. Chomsky's critique of Pavlov.
   b. the advent of the digital computer.
   c. the invention of fMRI.
   d. the invention of the Skinner box.

9. John Garcia's experiments showing that rats quickly learn to associate nausea with the taste of food
   a. were important to establishing behaviorism in America.
   b. led to his dismissal from his university.
   c. helped bring about evolutionary psychology.
   d. helped bring about cultural psychology.

10. Two new areas of psychology that have emerged in the 21st century are
    a. behavioral neuroscience and cultural psychology.
    b. cognitive neuroscience and evolutionary psychology.
    c. Gestalt psychology and developmental psychology.
    d. social psychology and cultural psychology.

11. In the 1800s, the French surgeon Paul Broca conducted research that demonstrated a connection between
    a. animals and humans.
    b. the mind and the brain.
    c. brain size and mental ability.
    d. skull indentations and psychological attributes.

12. What was the subject of the famous experiment conducted by Hermann von Helmholtz?
    a. reaction time
    b. childhood learning
    c. phrenology
    d. functions of specific brain areas

13. William James espoused _____, the study of the purpose mental processes serve in enabling people to adapt to their environment.
    a. empiricism
    b. nativism
    c. structuralism
    d. functionalism

14. Mary Calkins
    a. studied with Wilhelm Wundt in the first psychology laboratory.
    b. did research on the self-image of African American children.
    c. was present at the first meeting of the APA.
    d. became the first woman president of the APA.

15. Kenneth Clark
    a. did research that influenced the Supreme Court decision to ban segregation in public schools.
    b. was one of the founders of the APA.
    c. was a student of William James.
    d. did research that focused on the education of African American youth.

LearningCurve Don't stop now! Quizzing yourself is a powerful study tool. Go to LaunchPad to access the LearningCurve adaptive quizzing system and your own personalized learning plan. Visit launchpadworks.com.

Key Terms

psychology (p. 2)
philosophical dualism (p. 2)
philosophical materialism (p. 2)
philosophical realism (p. 3)
philosophical idealism (p. 3)
philosophical empiricism (p. 4)
philosophical nativism (p. 4)

reaction time (p. 5)
structuralism (p. 5)
introspection (p. 6)
functionalism (p. 6)
natural selection (p. 6)
hysteria (p. 8)
unconscious (p. 8)

psychoanalytic theory (p. 8)
psychoanalysis (p. 9)
behaviorism (p. 10)
principle of reinforcement (p. 11)
Gestalt psychology (p. 13)
developmental psychology (p. 13)
social psychology (p. 14)

cognitive psychology (p. 16)
evolutionary psychology (p. 17)
cognitive neuroscience (p. 19)
behavioral neuroscience (p. 19)
cultural psychology (p. 19)

Changing Minds

1. While scrolling through your newsfeed, you come across a story describing some research that shows that when people feel love, particular regions of their brains "light up." You scroll down and see that someone has commented: "This is crazy. Love is more than brain chemistry. It's about the heart!" Given what you know about materialism, dualism, and fMRI, how would you respond?

2. May 6 is Sigmund Freud's birthday. Every year some journalist notices this and describes him as "the father of modern psychology." How accurate is that title? Who else might deserve it more?

3. One of your friends is a chemistry major. She sees your psychology textbook on your desk and starts flipping

through it. "Psychology is just so stupid," she says. "I mean, how can it claim to be a science when it studies things no one can see, like thoughts and memories and emotions? Why don't they just stick to studying what they can actually measure?" Given what you know about the history of psychology, what would you tell your friend?

4. High school students are touring your campus today—and you get to meet them. Yippee! One of them tells you he's considering a major in psychology. "I figure I can get my degree in four years and then start doing therapy." Given what you've learned about careers in psychology, what should you tell him?

Answers to Key Concept Quiz

1. a; 2. b; 3. c; 4. d; 5. c; 6. d; 7. a; 8. b; 9. c; 10. a; 11. b; 12. a; 13. d; 14. d; 15. a

 **LaunchPad** macmillan learning

LaunchPad features the full e-book of *Introducing Psychology*, the LearningCurve adaptive quizzing system, videos, and a variety of activities to boost your learning. Visit LaunchPad at launchpadworks.com.

Methods in Psychology

2

When Louise Hay died in 2017, her net worth was estimated at around $50 million. Her most popular book, *You Can Heal Your Life*, had sold over 35 million copies. In it, she explained that everything that happens to people — including diseases, accidents, and other misfortunes — is a result of the thoughts they choose to think. She claimed that she had cured herself of "incurable" cancer by changing the way she thought, and promised that others could learn to do the same thing if only they attended one of her seminars or bought her videos or books. In a 2010 television interview with one of the authors of this textbook, Hay was asked why she believed her techniques were actually effective.

Gilbert: How do you know what you're saying is right?

Hay: Oh, my inner ding.

Gilbert: Ding?

Hay: My inner ding. It speaks to me. It feels right or it doesn't feel right. Happiness is choosing thoughts that make you feel good. It's really very simple.

Gilbert: But I hear you saying that even if there were no proof for what you believed, or even if there were scientific evidence against it, it wouldn't change?

Hay: Well, I don't believe in scientific evidence, I really don't. Science is fairly new. It hasn't been around that long. We think it's such a big deal, but it's, you know, it's just a way of looking at life.

Louise Hay said that she didn't "believe in scientific evidence" — but what could that possibly mean? After all, if her techniques really did cure cancer, then people with cancer who practice her techniques should on average live longer than those who don't. That isn't "a way of looking at life." It's just plain old common sense — exactly the kind of common sense that lies at the heart of science. Science tells us that there is one and only one way to know for sure whether claims like Louise Hay's are true, and that's to gather evidence. Sorry, but inner dings don't count.

But how exactly should we gather such evidence? Should we show up at a "Hay House" seminar and ask people in the audience whether they think they've been healed by her techniques? Should we examine the medical records of people who have and haven't bought one of her books? Should we invite people to sign up for a class that teaches her techniques and then wait to see how many of them get cancer over the next few years? All of these may strike you as fairly reasonable ways to test Louise Hay's claim, but in fact, every one of them is utterly useless. It turns out that there are a few very good ways to test claims about the world and a whole lot of bad ways, and the main point of this chapter is to teach you the difference between them. Scientists have developed powerful tools for determining when a claim is right and when it is wrong.

Empiricism: How to Know Stuff

Methods of Observation: Finding Out What People Do

Methods of Explanation: Figuring Out Why People Do What They Do

Thinking Critically About Evidence

The Ethics of Science: Doing What's Right

Louise Hay claimed that people can cure cancer with their minds. How can we tell whether her claim is right or wrong? Michele Asselin/Contour by Getty Images

We'll start by examining the general principles that guide scientific research and distinguish it from other human enterprises. Next, we'll see how the methods of psychology allow us to answer two basic questions: What do people do, and why? Psychologists answer the first question by measuring stuff, and they answer the second question by looking for relationships between the stuff they measure. We'll see how scientific evidence allows us to draw certain kinds of conclusions, and that thinking critically about scientific evidence doesn't come naturally to most people. Finally, we'll consider some of the ethical questions that confront scientists who study human beings and other animals.

Empiricism: How to Know Stuff

When ancient Greeks sprained their ankles, caught the flu, or accidentally set their beards on fire, they had to choose between two kinds of doctors. The dogmatists (from *dogmatikos*, meaning "belief") thought the best way to understand illness was to develop theories of the body's functions, and the empiricists (from *empeirikos*, meaning "experience") thought the best way was to observe sick people. The rivalry between these two schools of medicine didn't last long because the people who went to see dogmatists tended to die a lot, which was bad for business. Today we use the word *dogmatism* to describe people's tendency to cling to their beliefs and assumptions, and we use the word **empiricism** to describe *the belief that accurate knowledge can be acquired through observation*. The fact that we can answer questions about the natural world by observing probably seems obvious to you, but this obvious fact has only recently gained wide acceptance. For most of human history, people trusted authority to provide answers to life's important questions, and it is only in the last millennium (and especially in the past three centuries) that people have begun to trust their eyes and ears more than their elders.

Learning Outcomes

- Compare dogmatism and empiricism.
- Outline the process of the scientific method.
- Identify three challenges to studying human behavior.

The astronomer Galileo Galilei (1564–1642) was excommunicated and sentenced to prison for sticking to his empirical observations of the solar system rather than accepting the teachings of the Church. In 1597 he wrote to his friend and fellow astronomer Johannes Kepler (1571–1630), "What would you say of the learned here, who, replete with the pertinacity of the asp, have steadfastly refused to cast a glance through the telescope? What shall we make of this? Shall we laugh, or shall we cry?" As he later learned, the answer was cry.   The Picture Art Collection/Alamy Stock Photo

empiricism The belief that accurate knowledge can be acquired through observation.

scientific method A procedure for using empirical evidence to establish facts.

theory A hypothetical explanation of a natural phenomenon.

hypothesis A falsifiable prediction made by a theory.

The Scientific Method

Empiricism is the backbone of the **scientific method,** which is *a procedure for using empirical evidence to establish facts*. Essentially, the scientific method suggests that when we have an idea about how something in the world works — about how bats navigate, or where the moon came from, or why people can't forget traumatic events — we must go out into the world, make observations, and then use those observations to determine whether our idea is true. Scientists generally refer to these "ideas about how something works" as **theories,** which are *hypothetical explanations of natural phenomena*. So, for instance, we might theorize that bats navigate by making sounds and then listening for the echo, or that the moon was formed when a small planet collided with the earth, or that the brain responds to traumatic events by producing chemicals that facilitate memory. Each of these theories is an explanation of how something in the natural world works and why it works that way.

How do we decide if a theory is right? A good theory makes specific predictions about what we should observe in the world if the theory is true. For example, if bats really do navigate by making sounds and then listening for echoes, then deaf bats should not be able to navigate very well. That "should" statement is technically known as a **hypothesis,** which is *a falsifiable prediction made by a theory*. The word *falsifiable* is a critical part of that definition. Some theories, such as "Things happen the way they do because that's how God wants it," do not tell us what we should observe if the theory is true; therefore, no amount of observation can ever falsify them. That doesn't mean the theory is wrong. It just means that we can't use the scientific method to evaluate its veracity.

So good theories give rise to hypotheses that can be falsified, and when that happens the theory is proved wrong. But how can we prove it *right*? Alas, although a theory can be proved wrong, it can *never* be proved right. For example, imagine that you decided to test the theory that bats navigate by using sound. The theory gives rise to a hypothesis: Deaf bats should not be able to navigate. Now, if you observed a deaf bat navigating perfectly well, your observation would be clearly inconsistent with the predictions of your theory, which must therefore be wrong. On the other hand, if you observed deaf bats navigating badly, that would not prove your theory right. Why? Because even if you didn't see a deaf bat navigating perfectly well today, it is always possible that you will see one tomorrow, or the day after that, or maybe 30 years from now. Observations that are consistent with a theory can increase our confidence that the theory is right, but they can never make us absolutely sure.

The scientific method tells us that the only way to learn the truth about the world is to develop a theory, derive a falsifiable hypothesis from it, and then test that hypothesis by observing the world — or, in fancier language, gathering empirical evidence.

The Art of Looking

Gathering evidence properly requires an **empirical method**, which is *a set of rules and techniques for observation*. In many sciences, the word *method* refers to technologies that enhance the powers of the senses. Biologists use microscopes and astronomers use telescopes because the things they want to observe are invisible to the naked eye. Human behavior, on the other hand, is easy to see, so you might expect psychology's methods to be relatively simple. But human beings have three qualities that make them more difficult to study than either cells or stars.

1. People are highly *complex*. Scientists can describe the birth of a star or the death of a cell in exquisite detail, but they can barely begin to say how the 100 billion interconnected neurons that constitute the human brain give rise to thoughts, feelings, and actions.

2. People are highly *variable*. One ribosome may be a lot like another, but no two people ever do, say, think, or feel exactly the same thing under exactly the same circumstances.

3. People are highly *reactive*. A cesium atom oscillates at the same rate regardless of who might be watching, but people tend to think, feel, and act differently when they are or are not being observed.

The fact that human beings are highly complex, variable, and reactive presents a challenge to the scientific study of their behavior. Psychologists have met this challenge by developing two kinds of methods: *methods of observation*, which allow them to determine what people do, and *methods of explanation*, which allow them to determine why people do it. We'll examine each of these methods in the sections that follow.

Classical thinkers such as Euclid and Ptolemy believed that our eyes work by emitting rays that go out and "touch" the objects we see. But the Persian genius Ibn al-Haytham (965–1039) argued that if this theory was right, then when we open our eyes it should take longer to see something far away than something nearby. And guess what? It doesn't. The classical theory of vision gave rise to a hypothesis, that hypothesis was disconfirmed by observation, and an ancient theory vanished in the blink of an eye. Science Source/Colorization by: Mary Martin

People are highly reactive — that is, they behave differently when they know they are being observed. For example, if actress Mila Kunis had realized that a photographer was lurking nearby, she might have found a more discreet way to express her opinion of passion fruit tea. James Devaney/Wireimage/Getty Images

empirical method A set of rules and techniques for observation.

Build to the Outcomes

1. What is the scientific method?

2. What is the difference between a theory and a hypothesis?

3. Why can theories be proven wrong but not right?

4. What are three reasons that human behavior is especially difficult to study scientifically?

A WORLD OF DIFFERENCE

Are Heroes and Sheroes Divided by Zeroes?

Galileo, Newton, Mendel, Darwin, Faraday, Einstein, Turing, and Skinner were all brilliant scientists. And they were all men. The history of science is pretty much the history of smart men having big ideas and making big discoveries. So where are all the women? One answer is that, until quite recently, educational and employment opportunities for women were limited. For most of history, women were either subtly discouraged or actively prohibited from studying science — and you really can't win the Nobel Prize in Physics if they won't let you take algebra.

A second answer is that men and women may have different interests and talents, and the interests and talents that men have may be the ones needed to become great scientists. Some time ago, a group of male and female scientists surveyed all the scientific evidence on this topic, and concluded: Yes, the evidence does show that men are often more interested in the topics that scientists study (Halpern et al., 2007).

The experts also concluded that men are more *variable* than women on several specific abilities (such as the ability to use numbers) that are important to success in many sciences. Being more variable means that

although men and women have the same average amount of talent on these dimensions, there are more men at both the very lowest and very highest ends of the spectrum. If great scientists tend to come from the highest end of the spectrum, then there will be more men among them. In fact, recent data show that while men are overrepresented in scientific fields that are "math intensive" — such as geoscience, engineering, economics, mathematics, computer science, and the physical sciences — women earn the majority of degrees in other scientific fields, such as the life and social sciences (Ceci et al., 2014). The largest gender gaps in the "hard sciences" emerge in the nations with the *highest* gender equality, suggesting that when women have a choice, they tend not to choose those fields (Stoet & Geary, 2018).

So, why do these sex differences occur? Is it because there is some innate difference in the structure or function of the male and female brains, or is it because men are encouraged to develop their interests and hone their quantitative skills by parents who buy them video games instead of dolls, and by teachers who encourage them to join the math team rather than the debate team? An expert review of the evidence concludes that

In 1834, William Whewell coined the word *scientist* to describe a remarkable astronomer, physicist, and chemist named Mary Somerville. Few people remember that the world's first scientist was a woman. Historia/Shutterstock

men may be more interested in certain scientific topics and may be more likely to be unusually talented (or untalented!) when it comes to math, but there is *no compelling evidence to suggest that these differences are innate* (Ceci et al., 2014).

We agree with the experts who concluded that "there are no single or simple answers to the complex questions about sex differences in science and mathematics" (Halpern et al., 2007, p. 75). But we feel confident that someday a brilliant young psychological scientist will discover the true answers to these complex questions. We hope to be here when she does.

Learning Outcomes

- Name the properties of a good operational definition.
- Identify some of the methods psychologists use to avoid demand characteristics.
- Identify some of the methods psychologists use to avoid observer bias.

Methods of Observation: Finding Out What People Do

When you observe an apple, your brain uses the pattern of light that enters your eyes to make inferences about the apple's color, shape, and size. That kind of observation is good enough for buying fruit, but not for doing science. Why? First, everyday observations are often *inconsistent*: The same apple can appear red in the daylight and crimson at night. Second, everyday observations are often *incomplete:* No matter how long and hard you stared at an apple, you would never be able to determine its pectin content. Luckily, scientists have devised techniques that allow them to overcome these limitations.

Measurement

Whether we want to measure the intensity of an earthquake, the size of an elephant, or the attitude of a registered voter, we must always do two things. First, we must *define* the property we want to measure, and second, we must find a way to *detect* it

(**FIGURE 2.1**). For example, to measure a person's level of happiness, we would start by generating an **operational definition,** which is *a description of a property in measurable terms.* For example, we might operationally define happiness as "a person's self-assessment" or "the number of times a person smiles in an hour." Once we had this definition in hand, we would need to find a detector — that is, some sort of instrument or device that can detect the property as we just defined it — such as a rating scale (to detect a person's self-assessment), or an electromyograph (to detect movement of muscles in the face when a person smiles).

What makes a good operational definition? **Construct validity** is *the extent to which the thing being measured adequately characterizes the property.* For example, most of us would consider the frequency with which a person smiles to be a reasonable way to operationally define the property called "happiness" because we all know from our own experience that happy people tend to smile more than unhappy people do. Do they also eat more or talk more? Well, maybe. But then again, maybe not. And that's why most psychologists would consider "smiles per hour" to be a reasonable way to operationally define happiness, but they would not feel the same way about "number of chocolates eaten" or "number of words spoken." An operational definition is said to have construct validity when most people agree that it adequately characterizes a property.

What makes a good detector? The two key features of a good detector are **power,** which refers to *a detector's ability to detect the presence of differences or changes in the magnitude of a property,* and **reliability,** which refers to *a detector's ability to detect the absence of differences or changes in the magnitude of a property.* If a person smiles a bit more often on Tuesday than on Wednesday, a powerful smile-detector will detect different amounts of smiling on those two days. If a person smiles exactly as much on Wednesday as she did on Tuesday, then a reliable smile-detector will detect no difference in the amounts of smiling on those two days. A good detector detects differences or changes in the magnitude of a property when they do exist (power), but not when they don't (reliability).

Demand Characteristics: Doing What Is Expected

Once we have an operational definition that has construct validity, and a detector that is both powerful and reliable, there is still one problem to solve, which is that when human beings know they are being observed, they will often try to behave as they think the observer wants or expects them to. **Demand characteristics** are *those aspects of an observational setting that cause people to behave as they think someone else wants or expects.* If a friend asked, "Do you think I'm smart?" you would probably say yes whether you meant it or not. You know what your friend is hoping to hear and so you dutifully supply it. Similarly, if a researcher asked, "Do you think it is wrong to cheat on exams?" then you would probably say yes, if only because you know that's the response

operational definition A description of a property in measurable terms.

construct validity The extent to which the thing being measured adequately characterizes the property.

power A detector's ability to detect the presence of differences or changes in the magnitude of a property.

reliability A detector's ability to detect the absence of differences or changes in the magnitude of a property.

demand characteristics Those aspects of an observational setting that cause people to behave as they think someone else wants or expects them to.

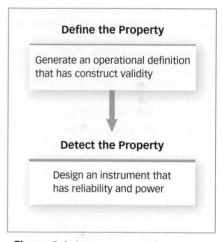

Define the Property

Generate an operational definition that has construct validity

Detect the Property

Design an instrument that has reliability and power

Figure 2.1 Measurement There are two steps in the measurement of a property.

Usain Bolt ran the 100-meter race in 9.58 seconds, and Yohan Blake ran it in 9.75 seconds. If judges did not have powerful speed-detectors, they might have mistakenly concluded that the two men had tied. Carmelita Jeter and Tori Bowie both ran the race in 10.83 seconds. If judges did not have reliable speed-detectors, they might have mistakenly concluded that one of them ran faster than the other. Kyodo News/Getty Images; David J. Phillip/AP Images; Dylan Martinez/Reuters/Newscom

Countries that have a faster pace of life tend to have higher rates of heart disease. How do researchers measure the "pace of life"? They make naturalistic observations — in this case, by measuring the average walking speed of pedestrians in different cities. By the way, the fastest pedestrians are the Irish (left) and the slowest are the Romanians (right) (Levine & Norenzayan, 1999). Izzet Keribar/Getty Images; Mladensky/iStock Editorial/Getty Images

the researcher expects of you. A study that asked such a question would be said to have demand characteristics because the question "demands" or requires participants to give a response that may or may not reflect his or her true feelings. How can we avoid demand characteristics?

One way to avoid demand characteristics is through **naturalistic observation,** which is *a technique for gathering scientific information by unobtrusively observing people in their natural environments.* Naturalistic observation has shown that the biggest groups leave the smallest tips in restaurants (Freeman et al., 1975), that men usually don't approach the most beautiful woman at a club (Glenwick et al., 1978), and that Olympic athletes smile more when they win the bronze medal than the silver medal (Medvec et al., 1995). Each of these conclusions is the result of measurements made by psychologists who observed people who didn't know they were being observed by psychologists. It seems unlikely that the psychologists could have made the same observations if the diners, clubbers, and athletes had realized that they were being observed.

Unfortunately, naturalistic observation isn't always practical. First, some events just don't occur naturally. If we wanted to know whether people who have undergone sensory deprivation perform poorly on fine-motor tasks, we would have to stand on the street corner for a very long time before we just so happened to spot a bunch of blindfolded people with earplugs trying to text with one hand. Second, some events can only be observed through direct interaction, such as by conducting an interview or by hooking someone up to a heart rate monitor. If we wanted to know how often people worried about dying, how accurately they remember their high school graduations, or how much electrical activity their brains produce when they feel jealous, then hiding in the bushes and watching them with binoculars just won't do.

When naturalistic observation isn't possible, there are other ways to reduce demand characteristics.

1. *Privacy.* People are less likely to be influenced by demand characteristics when they are allowed to respond privately (e.g., completing questionnaires when they are alone) and/or anonymously (e.g., their names are not recorded).

2. *Involuntary behaviors.* A person's behavior can't be influenced by demand characteristics if that behavior is not under their voluntary control. If a psychologist asked whether you were interested in stupid celebrity gossip, you might lie and say no. But since our pupils contract when we are bored and dilate when we are interested, the psychologist could record your pupillary dilation as you page through the latest issue of *Us Weekly* to gauge whether you were interested or bored.

naturalistic observation A technique for gathering scientific information by unobtrusively observing people in their natural environments.

3. *Unawareness*. People can't try to behave how they should behave if they don't *know* how they should behave. For example, if you didn't know that a psychologist was studying the effects of classical music on mood, you wouldn't feel obligated to smile when you heard Bach. That's why psychologists typically don't reveal the true purpose of an observation to the people being observed until the study is over.

Observer Bias: Seeing What Is Expected

More than half a century ago, students in a psychology class were asked to measure the speed with which a rat learned to navigate a maze (Rosenthal & Fode, 1963). Some students were told that their rat had been specially bred to be a slow learner, while others were told that their rat had been specially bred to be a fast learner. The truth was that the rats were all exactly the same breed. Nonetheless, students who *thought* they were measuring the speed of a slow learner reported that their rats took longer to navigate the maze, compared to students who *thought* they were measuring the speed of a fast learner. In other words, the measurements revealed precisely what the experimenters had expected them to reveal, even though those expectations had no basis in reality.

There are two reasons this happened. First, *expectations can influence observations.* Just think about all the decisions the students had to make when they were measuring the speed of their rat. Does putting one paw over the finish line count as finishing, or does it have to have all four legs over the line? If a rat runs the maze in 18.5 seconds, should that number be rounded up to 19 or down to 18 before it is recorded? How students answered questions like these may have depended on whether they thought their rats were fast or slow learners. Second, *expectations can influence reality.* Students who expected their rats to be fast learners unwittingly did things that might have helped that learning along — such as handling their rats more often and more gently. The students probably tried their best to be fair and objective, but their expectations nonetheless seem to have influenced both their rat's behavior and their observations of it.

This problem is so significant that psychologists have given it a name: **Observer bias** is *the tendency for observers' expectations to influence both what they believe they observed and what they actually observed.* A common technique to avoid observer bias is called the **double-blind study,** which is *a study in which neither the researcher nor the participant knows how the participants are expected to behave.* For example, if we wanted to know whether people smile more when listening to classical music than hip-hop, we might give participants a task to do while one of these two kinds of music played in the background, and have a research assistant watch them and record how often they smiled. We would take steps to ensure that our participants did not know what we were studying so that they would not feel obliged to behave as we expected them to; we would also ensure that the research assistants did not know how the participants were expected to behave (perhaps by giving them noise-cancelling headphones so that they wouldn't know which kind of music was playing as they recorded the participants' rate of smiling). If the research assistants don't *have* expectations, then their expectations cannot influence either their observations or their participants' behavior.

observer bias The tendency for observers' expectations to influence both what they believe they observed and what they actually observed.

double-blind study A study in which neither the researcher nor the participant knows how the participants are expected to behave.

Robert Parker is one of the world's foremost wine critics. His ratings indicate how good a wine tastes — but can they also *influence* how good a wine tastes? Researchers gave participants a glass of wine and told some of them that Parker had awarded that wine 92 out of 100 points; others were told that he had awarded it only 72 points (Siegrist & Cousin, 2009). Sure enough, participants who thought the wine was highly rated thought the wine tasted much better and were willing to pay about 50% more for a bottle. Abel Alonso/Epa/Shutterstock

Build to the Outcomes

1. What are the essential features of an operational definition?
2. What two properties must a good detector have?
3. What techniques do psychologists use to avoid demand characteristics?
4. What is a technique that psychologists use to avoid observer bias?

Learning Outcomes

- Explain what you can and cannot conclude from correlational research.
- Outline the essential steps of an experiment.
- Explain how experiments solve the third-variable problem.
- Distinguish the kinds of conclusions that can and cannot be drawn from experimental evidence.

	TABLE 2.1 Hypothetical Data Showing the Relationship Between Sleep and Memory	
Participant	Hours of Sleep	No. of Presidents Named
A	0	11
B	0	17
C	2.7	16
D	3.1	21
E	4.4	17
F	5.5	16
G	7.6	31
H	7.9	41
I	8	40
J	8.1	35
K	8.6	38
L	9	43

variable A property that can take on different values.

correlation The relationship that results when variations in the value of one variable are synchronized with variations in the value of the other.

natural correlation A correlation observed in the world around us.

Methods of Explanation: Figuring Out Why People Do What They Do

In 1639, a pastor named John Clarke suggested that "Early to bed and early to rise, makes a man healthy, wealthy, and wise." People have been repeating this little rhyme ever since, but is there any truth to it? The methods you've learned about so far would allow you to measure the health, wealth, and wisdom of a sample of people. That's nice, but is all that health and happiness and wisdom *caused* by getting in and out of bed early? Is there any way to use your new measurement skills to answer questions like this one? Indeed there is, and that's what this part of the chapter is all about.

Correlation

So how do we determine if people who get more sleep are smarter? Suppose you ask a dozen college students how many hours of sleep they got on the prior night, and how many U.S. presidents they can name. You'll keep careful track of their answers in a spread-sheet like the one shown in **TABLE 2.1**. Congratulations! You are now the proud owner of some *data*. If you inspect your data, you might see a pattern: students who report the fewest hours of sleep also tend to name fewer presidents. In collecting these data, you were doing three important things:

1. You measured a pair of **variables,** which are *properties that can take on different values.* When you asked about sleep, you were measuring a variable whose value could vary from *0* to *24,* and when you asked about presidents, you were measuring a second variable whose value could vary from *0* to *44.* (Save this for trivia night: Even though Donald Trump is the 45th president, Grover Cleveland was both the 22nd and the 24th president, which means that someone who recalls the name of every president will recall just 44 names.)

2. You made a *series* of measurements, by asking multiple students rather than just one.

3. You looked at the measurements you made and tried to discern a *pattern of variation.* The values in the second column of Table 2.1 increase from top to bottom, and the numbers in the third column have a similar (though not identical) pattern of variation. In other words, the patterns of variation in these two columns are somewhat synchronized, and this synchrony is known as a **correlation,** which occurs when *variations in the value of one variable are synchronized with variations in the value of the other.* When patterns of variation are synchronized, two variables are said to be correlated — or "co-related."

The direction of a correlation is either positive or negative. A positive correlation exists when two variables have a "more-is-more" relationship. When we say that *more sleep* is associated with *more presidents recalled,* we are describing a positive correlation. A negative correlation exists when two variables have a "less-is-more" relationship; if we said that *less sleep* is associated with *more colds caught,* we would be describing a negative correlation. (See Appendix: Essentials of Statistics for Psychology for more details on how correlations are measured.)

Causation

Natural correlations are *the correlations we observe in the world around us;* and although such observations can tell us that two variables are related, they cannot tell us why. For example, many studies (Anderson & Bushman, 2002; C. A. Anderson et al., 2003, 2017; Huesmann et al., 2003) have observed a positive correlation between the aggressiveness of a child's behavior and the amount of violence to which that child is exposed through media such as television, movies, and video games. The more violence children see, the more aggressively they tend to behave. These two variables clearly have a relationship — they are positively correlated — but *why* are they correlated?

The Third-Variable Problem: Correlation Is Not Causation

One possibility is that exposure to media violence causes aggressiveness. For instance, media violence may teach children that aggression is an acceptable way to vent anger or solve problems. A second possibility is that aggressiveness causes exposure to media violence. For example, children who are naturally aggressive may be especially inclined to play violent video games and watch violent movies. A third possibility is that there is some other factor — a heretofore unnamed "third variable" — which causes children to behave aggressively *and also* causes children to be exposed to media violence (see **FIGURE 2.2**). For instance, it might be that a lack of adult supervision allows children to get away with playing violent video games that adults would normally prohibit, and it may also be that a lack of adult supervision allows children to get away with bullying others simply because no adult is around to stop them. If so, then exposure to media violence and aggressiveness may be correlated only because they are both caused by the same third variable, lack of adult supervision.

How can we tell if two variables are being caused by a third variable? We can't. The **third-variable problem** refers to the fact that *the natural correlation between two variables cannot be taken as evidence of a causal relationship between them because a third variable might be causing them both.* What this means is that if we want to know about the causal relationship between two variables, then observing a natural correlation between them can never tell us what we want to know.

Luckily, another technique can. **Experimentation** is *a technique for determining whether there is a causal relationship between variables.* Experiments do this by using a pair of techniques called *manipulation* and *random assignment.* Let's explore each of them in turn.

Manipulation: Making Different Conditions

Imagine that one evening you are working on your laptop, when your Internet connection suddenly slows to a crawl. Your roommate is upstairs playing with his new Xbox, which you suspect could be sucking up bandwidth, making your laptop run slow. How would you test your suspicion? You now know that simply observing a natural correlation won't be of much help because even if your laptop ran slowly every time your roommate used his Xbox and ran fast every time he didn't, because of the third-variable problem, you still couldn't conclude that the Xbox was *causing* the slowdown. For instance, it is possible that your roommate only uses his Xbox in the evenings, which happens to be

third-variable problem The fact that the natural correlation between two variables cannot be taken as evidence of a causal relationship between them because a third variable might be causing them both.

experimentation A technique for determining whether there is a causal relationship between variables.

In 1949, Dr. Benjamin Sandler noticed a correlation between the incidence of polio and the consumption of ice cream. He concluded that sugar made children susceptible to the disease. Public health officials were so convinced by his findings that they issued public warnings. But as it turned out, the correlation was caused by a third variable: Warm weather had caused an increase in the incidence of polio (because viruses become more active in the summer) and an increase in the consumption of ice cream. George Marks/Getty Images

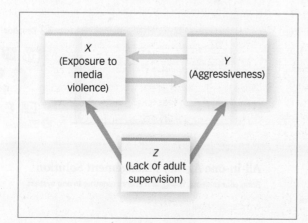

Figure 2.2 Causes of Correlation
Three possible reasons media violence and aggressiveness are correlated: Exposure to media violence (*X*) causes aggressiveness (*Y*), aggressiveness (*Y*) causes increased exposure to media violence (*X*), or a third variable (such as lack of adult supervision, *Z*) causes them both.

manipulation A technique for determining the causal power of a variable by actively changing its value.

independent variable The variable that is manipulated in an experiment.

the time when a whole lot of other people in your neighborhood are home watching Netflix, playing video games, downloading music, and otherwise sucking up bandwidth. "Evening" may be a third variable that causes your roommate to fire up the Xbox and that also causes your laptop to slow down.

So how can you tell whether your slowdown is actually being caused by the Xbox? Well, you could go upstairs when your roommate isn't home and turn his Xbox on and off while observing the speed of your laptop. If your laptop slowed down every time you turned the Xbox on and then sped up again every time you turned the Xbox off, you would know that the Xbox was in fact the cause of the slowdown. What you just did is called **manipulation,** which is *a technique for determining the causal power of a variable by actively changing its value.* Rather than measuring two variables, as we do when we observe correlations, experiments require that we *manipulate* one variable — that is, actively change its value — and then measure the other. Changing the value of the Xbox from on to off is an example of manipulation.

The same technique could be used to determine whether exposure to media violence causes aggressiveness. For instance, we could invite some children to our laboratory and give them one of two experiences: Half could be given a violent video game to play, and the other half could be given a nonviolent video game to play. These two experiences are called the *conditions* of our study, and we could refer to them as "the violent exposure condition" and "the nonviolent exposure condition." At the end of an hour of game playing, we could measure the children's aggressiveness, perhaps by observing whether they push to get to the front of a line. Then we could compare the measurements of aggressiveness in one condition with the measurements of aggressiveness in the other condition.

When we compare these measurements across conditions, we are essentially asking whether the value of aggressiveness went from low to high when we increased the level of exposure to media violence from low to high. Now here is the cool part: Because we *manipulated* exposure rather than just *measuring* it, we'd know for sure that aggressiveness did not cause exposure to media violence, and we'd know that lack of adult supervision did not cause exposure to media violence — and we'd know these two things because we know what *did* cause exposure to media violence: We did! And that would leave just one possibility: Exposure to media violence must have caused aggressiveness.

Can you see the difference between these two ads? Don't worry. It's subtle. The ad on the left has a "Learn More" button and the ad on the right has a "Sign Up" button. By manipulating the label on the button, the advertiser was able to determine whether a label can cause people to click. And it can! The "Learn More" label led 15% more Facebook users to click (Karlson, 2016).
AdExpresso/Scoro

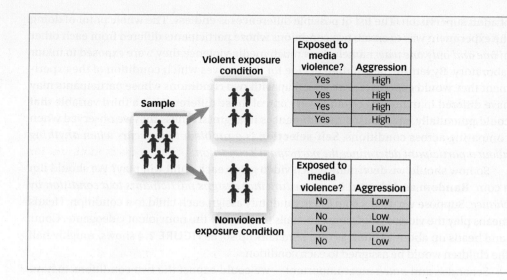

Figure 2.3 The Three Steps of Experimentation Manipulate the independent variable, measure the dependent variable, then compare the values across conditions.

Experimentation involves three simple steps, as illustrated in **FIGURE 2.3**:

1. *Manipulate*: The first step in an experiment is to manipulate a variable. *The variable that is manipulated in an experiment* is called the **independent variable** because its value is determined entirely by the experimenter and therefore does not depend on — or is "independent of" — the participants. A manipulation creates at least two conditions: in our example, a violent exposure condition and a nonviolent exposure condition.

2. *Measure*: The second step in an experiment is to measure a variable. *The variable that is measured in an experiment* is called the **dependent variable** because its value does "depend on" the participants. In our example, the dependent variable is aggression.

3. *Compare*: The third step in an experiment is to compare the value of the variable in one condition with the value of the variable in the other. If the values differ on average, then we know that changes to the value of the independent variable *caused* changes to the value of the dependent variable. In our example, we compare the levels of aggression in each of our two exposure conditions.

Random Assignment: Making Sure Conditions Differ in Just One Way

Manipulation is one essential ingredient in experimentation, but there is another. Let's return to the experiment we just designed in which children were given violent or nonviolent video games to play and then their aggressiveness was measured an hour later. When the children show up at our laboratory to participate in our study, how should we decide which child will play which game?

Suppose we simply ask each child which kind of game he or she would prefer to play, and that half the children choose to play a violent game and the other half choose to play a nonviolent game. We let them play their preferred game for an hour, then measure their aggressiveness and discover that the children who played the violent game were in fact more aggressive than those who played the nonviolent game. Could we now conclude that playing violent video games caused aggressiveness? No! But why not? After all, we manipulated exposure to media violence, switching it on and off as though it were an Xbox, and then we measured aggressiveness and found that it went on and off too. We manipulated, we measured, and we compared. So where did we go wrong?

We went wrong by letting the children *select* which video game to play — because children who *select* violent video games probably differ in many ways from children who don't. They may be older or meaner. They may be younger or sweeter. They may have different brain chemistry, different talents, different numbers of siblings, or different levels

dependent variable The variable that is measured in an experiment.

self-selection A problem that occurs when anything about a participant determines the participant's condition.

random assignment A procedure that assigns participants to a condition by chance.

internal validity An attribute of an experiment that allows it to establish causal relationships.

of adult supervision. The list of possible differences is endless. The whole point of doing the experiment was to create two conditions whose participants differed from each other in *one and only one way,* namely, how much media violence they were exposed to in our laboratory. By letting the children decide for themselves which condition of the experiment they would experience, we ended up with two conditions whose participants may have differed in many ways — and every one of those differences is a third variable that could potentially have caused the differences in aggressiveness that we observed when comparing across conditions. **Self-selection** is *a problem that occurs when anything about a participant determines the participant's condition.*

So how should we determine which video game each child will play? We should flip a coin. **Random assignment** is a *procedure that assigns participants to a condition by chance.* Suppose we used a coin flip to randomly assign each child to a condition: Heads means play the violent videogame, and tails means play the nonviolent videogame. Coins land heads up about as often as they land tails up so, as **FIGURE 2.4** shows, roughly half the children would be assigned to each condition.

Second — and *much* more important — we could expect the two conditions to have roughly equal numbers of mean children and sweet children, of older children and younger children, of children who have a lot of adult supervision at home and children who have little, and so on. In other words, we could expect the two conditions to have roughly equal numbers of children who are anything-you-can-ever-name-and-everything-you-can't! Because the children in the two conditions will be the same *on average* in terms of meanness, age, adult supervision, and every other variable in the known universe *except the variable we manipulated,* we could be sure that the variable we manipulated was the cause of the differences in the variable we measured. Because exposure to media violence would be the *only* difference between the two conditions when we started the experiment, it *must* be the cause of any differences in aggressiveness we observed at the end of the experiment.

There is no evidence that Louise Hay's techniques can cure cancer. Even if cancer victims who bought her books did show a higher rate of remission than those who didn't, there would still be no evidence because buyers are self-selected and thus may differ from nonbuyers in countless ways. Nicosan/Alamy

Drawing Conclusions

If we applied all the techniques discussed so far, we could design an experiment that had a very good chance of establishing the causal relationship between two variables. That experiment would be said to have **internal validity,** which is *an attribute of an experiment that allows it to establish causal relationships.* When we say that an experiment is internally valid, we mean that everything *inside* the experiment is working exactly as it should in order for us to use its results to draw conclusions about the causal relationship between the independent and dependent variables. But exactly *what* conclusions are we entitled to draw? If our imaginary experiment revealed a difference between the

Figure 2.4 Random Assignment
Random assignment ensures that participants in the two conditions are, on average, equal in terms of all possible third variables.

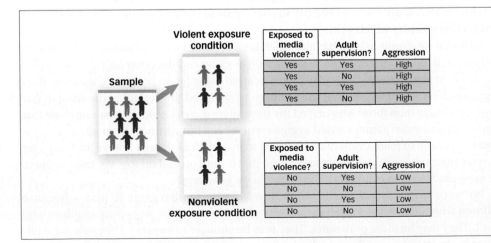

Violent exposure condition	Exposed to media violence?	Adult supervision?	Aggression
	Yes	Yes	High
	Yes	No	High
	Yes	Yes	High
	Yes	No	High

Nonviolent exposure condition	Exposed to media violence?	Adult supervision?	Aggression
	No	Yes	Low
	No	No	Low
	No	Yes	Low
	No	No	Low

aggressiveness of children who were exposed to high or low levels of media violence, could we conclude that media violence causes aggressiveness?

Actually, no. The conclusion we'd be entitled to draw would have to be much more restricted. What we *could* conclude is this: "It is likely that media violence as we defined that variable caused aggressiveness as we defined that variable in the people we studied." That sentence is obnoxiously long and sounds like a legal disclaimer because it contains these phrases: *as we defined that variable,* and *in the people we studied,* and *it is likely that.* Each phrase describes an important restriction on the conclusions we can draw from this or any other experimental result. Let's consider each in turn.

The Representativeness Restriction: "As We Defined That Variable . . ."

The results of an experiment naturally depend on how the independent and dependent variables are operationally defined. For instance, we are more likely to find that exposure to media violence causes aggressiveness if we operationally define exposure as "watching 2 hours of gory axe murders" rather than "watching 10 minutes of football," or if we define aggressiveness as "interrupting another person who is talking" rather than "beating someone with a tire iron." The way we operationally define variables can have a profound influence on what we find, so which is the *right* way?

One common answer is that we should operationally define variables in an experiment as they are defined in the real world. **External validity** is *an attribute of an experiment in which variables have been operationally defined in a normal, typical, or realistic way.* It seems pretty clear that the kind of aggressive behavior that concerns teachers and parents lies somewhere between an interruption and an assault, and that the kind of media violence to which children are typically exposed lies somewhere between sports and torture. If the goal of an experiment is to determine whether the kinds of media violence to which children are typically exposed causes the kinds of aggressiveness with which societies are typically concerned, then external validity is important. When variables are defined in an experiment as they typically are in the real world, we say that the variables are *representative* of the real world.

External validity sounds like such a good idea that you may be surprised to learn that most psychology experiments are externally *in*valid (Mook, 1983). A well-thought-out theory allows us to generate hypotheses about what should happen under particular circumstances; and experiments are usually meant to create some of those circumstances, test the hypotheses, and thereby provide evidence for or against the theory (see also Hot Science: Hate Posts and Hate Crimes: Not Just a Correlation). Experiments are not usually meant to be miniature versions of everyday life, and as such, external invalidity is not usually considered a problem.

The Generalizability Restriction: "In the People We Studied . . ."

Psychologists rarely measure the properties of an entire **population,** which is *a complete collection of people* — such as the population of human beings (about 7 billion), the population of Californians (about 38 million), or the population of people with Down syndrome (about 1 million). Rather, they tend to measure the properties of a **sample,** which is *a partial collection of people drawn from a population.* In some cases, the sample is as small as one. We can learn a lot about, say, memory by studying someone such as Rajveer Meena, who memorized the first 70,000 digits of pi, or about intelligence and creativity by studying someone such as Tanishq Abraham, who graduated from college at the age of 11 and began consulting in the aerospace industry. When psychologists study individuals, they are using the **case method,** which is *a procedure for gathering scientific information by studying a single individual.*

Does piercing make a person more or less attractive? The answer depends on your operational definition of attractiveness.
AP Photo/Keystone, TIPress/Samuel Golay; Dinodia Photos/ Alamy Stock Photo

external validity An attribute of an experiment in which variables have been defined in a normal, typical, or realistic way.

population A complete collection of people.

sample A partial collection of people drawn from a population.

case method A procedure for gathering scientific information by studying a single individual.

Hate Posts and Hate Crimes: Not Just a Correlation

Facebook lets us post videos of our pets, share stories of our vacations, and find out what people we barely know had for lunch. But has it also become a platform in which people's worst impulses are brought together, amplified, and then unleashed upon the world? Do Facebook posts lead people to do terrible things in the real world, such as commit arson, or assault, or even murder?

To investigate, researchers conducted a study in Germany, where a right-wing anti-immigrant party (the Alternative für Deutschland, or AfD) had recently developed a significant presence on Facebook (Müller & Schwarz, 2018). The study involved measuring the number of antirefugee Facebook posts that appeared on the AfD Web site each week and the number of violent crimes against refugees that occurred that same week. The accompanying figure shows what they found. As you can see, the two variables were indeed positively correlated: The more "hate posts" that appeared on AfD's Facebook page in a given week, the more "hate crimes" happened on German streets.

But wait a minute. What about the third-variable problem? Hate posts and hate crimes may well be correlated, but that doesn't mean the former *caused* the latter. Maybe the hate crimes caused the hate posts, or maybe some third variable — such as a change in the weather or the stock market — caused them both. Drawing conclusions about the causal relationship between two variables requires that one of those variables be *manipulated*, right?

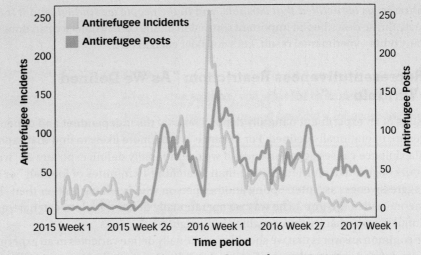

The number of hate crimes and hate posts in Germany from 2015–2017.

Yes, it does, but luckily for the researchers, Internet service in Germany is not as reliable as it is in the United States. German Facebook users experience frequent interruptions that can knock everyone offline for hours or even days at a time. Because service interruptions are basically random events, they serve as a manipulation of one variable (the number of hate posts) whose impact on the other variable (the number of hate crimes) can then be measured. When the researchers did that, the impact was clear: When Facebook went down, hate crimes went down too; and when Facebook came back up again, so did hate crimes. As the researchers themselves concluded, "Social media has

not only become a fertile soil for the spread of hateful ideas but also motivates real-life action" (Müller & Schwarz, 2018, p. 40).

Psychologists are often faced with a tough choice: They can either (a) observe a correlation in the real world but be unsure about causation, or (b) firmly establish causation in the laboratory but be unsure about whether it generalizes to the real world. But every once in a while, nature resolves this dilemma by randomly manipulating a variable in the real world. When that happens, clever researchers may take advantage of the situation and use it to answer pressing social questions — and to produce some very hot science.

Tanishq Abraham graduated from college at the age of 11. He told reporters, "I want to become a doctor, but I also want to become a medical researcher, and also the president of the United States." Is there any reason he can't do all three? Renee C. Byer/Zumapress/Newscom

With that said, the vast majority of studies you will read about in this textbook use samples of 10, 100, 1,000, or even many thousands of people. So how do psychologists determine which people they will include in their sample? One method is by **random sampling,** which is *a technique for selecting participants that ensures that every member of a population has an equal chance of being included in the sample.* (Note to self: Do not confuse random sampling with random assignment. The only thing they have in common is the word *random.*) When we randomly sample participants from a population, the sample is said to be *representative* of the population. This allows us to *generalize* from the sample to the population — that is, to conclude that what we observed in our sample would also have been observed if we had measured the entire population.

Random sampling sounds like an obviously good idea, so you may be surprised once again to find that most psychological studies involve *non*random samples. Indeed, virtually every participant in every psychology experiment you will ever read about was a volunteer, and a large share were college students who were significantly younger, smarter, healthier, wealthier, and Whiter than the average Earthling. About 96% of the people

It can be a mistake to generalize from a nonrandom sample. In 1948, pollsters mistakenly predicted that Thomas Dewey would beat Harry Truman. Why? Because polling was done by telephone, and Dewey Republicans were more likely to have telephones than were Truman Democrats. In 2004, pollsters mistakenly predicted that John Kerry would beat George Bush. Why? Because pollsters solicited voters as they left the polls, and Kerry supporters were more optimistic and therefore more willing to stop and talk to pollsters. In 2016, pollsters mistakenly predicted that Hillary Clinton would beat Donald Trump. Why? Because pollsters solicited too many of the highly educated voters who were likely to support Clinton and not enough of the less educated voters who were likely to support Trump. Ullstein Bild / The Granger Collection, NYC—All Rights Reserved; Pete Marovich/Zumapress/Newscom; Jewel Samad/AFP/ Getty Images

whom psychologists study come from countries that have just 12% of the world's population, and 70% come from the United States alone (Henrich et al., 2010). This is because most psychology experiments are conducted by professors and graduate students at colleges and universities in the Western Hemisphere, and as much as they might *like* to randomly sample the population of our planet, the fact is that they are pretty much stuck studying the local folks who volunteer for their studies.

Is this a fatal flaw in psychological science? No, and there are two reasons why. First, *sometimes the representativeness of a sample doesn't matter*. If one pig flew over the Statue of Liberty just one time, it would instantly disprove the Standard Theory of Porcine Locomotion, and it really wouldn't matter if other pigs could do the same trick. Similarly, if playing *Left 4 Dead* for an hour caused a group of 5th graders from a public school in Ann Arbor, Michigan, to start shoving other kids in the laboratory, then even if the game did not have a similar effect on 9th graders from a private school in Austin, Texas, we would still know that media violence *can* influence aggressiveness — which means that any theory that says it can't is just plain wrong. Sometimes psychologists aren't concerned with whether *everyone* does something; they just want to know if *anyone* does it.

The second reason nonrandom sampling is not a fatal flaw is that *sometimes the representativeness of the sample is a reasonable starting assumption*. Instead of asking, "Do I have a compelling reason to believe that my sample is representative of the population?" we could just as well ask, "Do I have a compelling reason to believe that my sample is *not* representative of the population?" For example, few of us would be willing to take a new medicine if a nonrandom sample of participants took it and died. Indeed, we would probably refuse to take the medicine even if those participants were mice! Although these nonrandomly sampled participants would be different from us in many ways (e.g., tails and whiskers), most of us would assume that anything that kills them has some reasonable chance of killing us. Similarly, if a psychology experiment demonstrated that a sample of American children behaved aggressively after playing violent video games, we might ask whether there is a compelling reason to suspect that Ecuadorian college students or middle-aged Australians would respond any differently. If the answer is yes, then we can conduct experiments to test that possibility.

The bottom line is that learning about *some people* does not necessarily tell us about *all people*, but it can still tell us a lot — and it certainly tells us more than learning about *no people* at all, which is often the only other choice.

The Reliability Restriction: "It Is Likely That . . ."

A **replication** is *an experiment that uses the same procedures as a previous experiment but with a new sample from the same population*. In the past few years, many major media outlets have reported that when psychologists replicate the experiments of other psychologists, they *usually* fail to replicate the earlier results, which suggests that the

random sampling A technique for choosing participants that ensures that every member of a population has an equal chance of being included in the sample.

replication An experiment that uses the same procedures as a previous experiment but with a new sample from the same population.

Headlines suggest that the results of most psychology studies can't be replicated. Should you believe those headlines? Photo Researchers/ Science Source

initial result was some sort of fluke. Could that be right? Are the headlines true, and is psychology experiencing a "replication crisis"?

Recently, teams of psychologists have tried to estimate the proportion of flukes in the scientific literature by selecting a sample of published studies and then attempting to replicate them. (See Appendix: Essentials of Statistics for Psychology for more information about how psychologists try to calculate the likelihood of flukes.) Some teams have found the replication rate in their samples to be frighteningly low (Open Science Collaboration et al., 2015), while others have found it to be reasonably high (Klein et al., 2014). But do any of these findings tell us the actual replication rate of studies in psychology? Probably not (Gilbert et al., 2016). First, the teams who did these replications did not randomly choose which studies to examine. Rather, they chose studies of particular kinds (e.g., those that are easy for anyone to do and do not require a lot of time, money, or expertise) from particular areas of psychology (e.g., almost always from social, and almost never from neuroscience, developmental, or clinical). Because the studies they chose are not representative of psychology as a whole, their results may tell us something about the replicability of those specific studies, but they are unlikely to tell us much about the replication rate of the entire discipline.

Second, the teams did not always use the same methods that were used in the original studies — sometimes because details of the original methods were not known, and sometimes because the teams made mistakes. This means that some of their studies were not really replications at all. Indeed, when the National Academies of Sciences, Engineering, and Medicine recently considered all the evidence, they concluded that contrary to what you may read in the news, "it is not helpful, or justified, to refer to psychology as in a state of 'crisis' " (National Academies of Sciences, Engineering, and Medicine, 2019, p. 124). The bottom line is that no one knows the actual replication rate of experiments in psychology.

Replication serves an important function in psychology, as it does in every science. And it reminds us that even the best experimental evidence does not allow us to conclude that two variables *are* causally related; rather, it allows us to conclude that two variables *are likely to be* causally related. The more easily and more often that evidence is reproduced, the more confident we can be in the causal relationship between the variables. We can never be completely confident in any result, of course, but replications can move us ever closer to certainty.

Build to the Outcomes

1. What is a natural correlation and how can it be measured?

2. What is the third-variable problem?

3. How do manipulation and random assignment solve the third-variable problem?

4. Why is self-selection a problem?

5. What is the difference between a dependent variable and an independent variable?

6. What is the difference between internal validity and external validity?

Learning Outcomes

- Identify two psychological tendencies that make critical thinking so difficult.
- Explain what people can do to help them think critically.

DATA Visualization

Thinking Critically About Evidence

Experiments generate evidence. But interpreting that evidence requires *critical thinking*, which involves asking ourselves tough questions about whether we have interpreted the evidence in an unbiased way, and about whether the evidence tells not just the truth, but the *whole* truth. (See Data Visualization: Does SAT performance correlate with income and education level? at www.launchpadworks.com.) Research suggests that most of us have trouble doing these two things and that educational programs designed to improve our critical thinking skills are not particularly effective (Willingham, 2007). Why do we have so much trouble thinking critically?

We See What We Expect and Want to See

One problem is that our preexisting beliefs color our view of new evidence, causing us to see what we expect to see. As such, evidence often seems to confirm what we believed all along. For instance, participants in one study (Darley & Gross, 1983) learned about a little girl named Hannah. One group of participants was told that Hannah came from an affluent family, while the other group was told that Hannah came from a poor family. All participants were shown a video of Hannah taking a reading test, and they were then asked to rate Hannah. Although the video was exactly the same for all participants, those who believed that Hannah's family was affluent rated her performance more positively than did those who believed that her family was poor. What's more, both groups of participants defended their conclusions by citing evidence from the video! Experiments like this one suggest that when we consider evidence, what we see depends on what we *expected* to see.

Our beliefs and desires can even influence *which* evidence we consider in the first place. Most people surround themselves with others who believe the same things they believe, which means that our friends and families are much more likely to validate our beliefs and desires than to challenge them. Studies also show that, when given the opportunity to search for evidence, people preferentially search for evidence that confirms their beliefs and fulfills their desires (Hart et al., 2009). What's more, when people find evidence that confirms their beliefs and fulfills their desires, they tend to stop looking; yet when they find evidence that does the opposite, they keep searching for more evidence (Kunda, 1990).

Because it is so easy to see what we expect to see, the first rule of critical thinking is this: *Doubt your own conclusions.* One of the best ways to find the truth about the world is to seek out people who don't see the world your way and then listen carefully to what they have to say. Scientists go out of their way to expose themselves to criticism by sending their papers to the colleagues who are most likely to disagree with them or by presenting their findings to audiences full of critics. They do this largely so that they can achieve a more balanced view of their own conclusions.

The first rule of critical thinking is to doubt your own conclusions — but that's hard to do when everyone tells you you're right! Recent research shows that Facebook users create "echo chambers" by sharing stories and links mainly with friends who already share their points of view (Del Vicario et al., 2016).
FluxFactory/E+/Getty Images

We Don't Consider What We Don't See

People rarely pay attention to what they don't see (Kardes & Sanbonmatsu, 2003). For example, participants in one study (Newman et al., 1980) played a game in which they were shown sets of trigrams, which are three-letter combinations such as *SXY, GTR,* and *EVX.* On each trial, the experimenter pointed to one of the trigrams in the set and told the participants that *this* trigram was the special one. The participants' job was to figure out what made the special trigram so special. For half the participants, the special trigram always contained the letter *T,* and participants in this condition needed to see about 34 sets of trigrams before they figured out that the presence of *T* was what made the trigram special. But for the other half of the participants, the special trigram was always the one that *lacked* the letter *T.* These participants *never* figured it out. It is much easier to think about what *is* there than what *isn't.*

The tendency to ignore missing evidence can lead to erroneous conclusions (Wainer & Zwerling, 2006). For instance, consider the red map in **FIGURE 2.5**, which shows the U.S. counties with the lowest rates of kidney cancer. As you can see, they are predominantly rural counties in the South, West, and Midwest. It isn't hard to imagine why the places with the lowest populations might also have the lowest rates of kidney cancer: People who live in these counties probably eat more farm-grown foods, breathe less polluted air, engage in more outdoor activities, and so on. Given the obvious health benefits of "country living," it is no wonder that the most rural counties in America have the lowest kidney cancer rates.

That's a reasonable hypothesis based on the evidence you saw. But it is utterly wrong, and you would have known it was utterly wrong if only you had stopped to think about the

Counties with Lowest Rates (shown in yellow)   Counties with Highest Rates (shown in yellow)

Figure 2.5 Rates of Kidney Cancer in the United States. These maps show (in yellow) the U.S. counties with the lowest rates of kidney cancer (on the left) and the highest rates of kidney cancer (on the right).

evidence you were *not* shown. That evidence is shown in the green map in FIGURE 2.5, which shows the U.S. counties with the *highest* rates of kidney cancer. As you can see, they too are predominantly rural and predominantly in the South, West, and Midwest. Indeed, except for their colors, the two maps in Figure 2.5 look pretty much the same. Why? Because as it turns out, rural counties tend to have *extreme* rates of kidney cancer — that is, they have some of the lowest rates, but they also have some of the highest rates — and that's because rural counties have fewer people in them. Someone who is shown the evidence in the red map and who forgets to ask about the missing evidence in the green map would draw the wrong conclusion about the relationship between kidney cancer and population density. If the first rule of critical thinking is to doubt what you *do* see, then the second rule is to consider what you *don't* see.

The Skeptical Stance

The second rule of critical thinking is to consider what you don't see. Businesses often provide testimonials from satisfied customers — but where are all the dissatisfied customers, and what might they have to say? Daniel Gilbert

Science is a human enterprise and humans make mistakes: They see what they expect to see, they see what they want to see, and they often fail to consider what they can't see at all. What makes science different from most other human enterprises is that scientists actively seek to discover and remedy their mistakes. Scientists are constantly striving to make their observations more accurate and their reasoning more rigorous, and they invite anyone and everyone to examine their evidence and challenge their conclusions. As a result, science is the ultimate democracy in which the lowliest nobody can triumph over the most celebrated somebody. When an unknown Swiss patent clerk with a vivid imagination challenged the greatest physicists of his day, he didn't have a famous father, a fancy degree, powerful friends, or a fat wallet. Albert Einstein won the scientific debate for one reason and one reason alone: He was right.

So think of the remaining chapters in this textbook as a report from the field — a description of the work that psychological scientists have done so far as they stumble toward knowledge. These chapters tell the story of the men and women who have used the scientific method to pry loose small pieces of the truth about who we are; how we think, feel, and behave; and what we are all doing here together on the third rock from the sun. Some of their reports will turn out to be flukes, but every one of them is somebody's best guess about the way people work. Read these reports with interest but think critically about their claims — and for that matter, about everything else. (See The Real World: The Surprisingly High Likelihood of Unlikely Coincidences.)

Build to the Outcomes

1. What two human tendencies are enemies of critical thinking?

2. What does it mean to say, "If you want to be happy, take your friend to lunch; if you want to be right, take your enemy?"

3. What makes science different from most other human enterprises?

The Surprisingly High Likelihood of Unlikely Coincidences

A recent survey found that more than half of college graduates believe in extrasensory perception, or ESP, and it is easy to understand why. Just consider the case of the Truly Amazing Coincidence. One night you dream that a panda is piloting an airplane over the Indian Ocean, and the next day you tell a friend, who says, "Wow, I had exactly the same dream!" Another evening, you and your roommate are sitting around watching television when suddenly you turn to each other and say in perfect unison, "Wanna pizza?" Coincidences like these might make anyone believe in strange and spooky supernatural weirdness.

Well, not anyone. While the Nobel laureate Luis Alvarez was reading the newspaper one day, a particular story got him thinking about an old college friend whom he hadn't seen in years. A few minutes later, he turned the page and was shocked to see the very same friend's obituary. But before concluding that he had suddenly developed an acute case of ESP, Alvarez decided to determine just how amazing this coincidence really was. He estimated the number of friends an average person has, estimated how often an average person thinks about each of those friends, did a few simple calculations, and determined the probability that someone would think about a friend 5 minutes before learning about that friend's death. The odds were astonishing. In a country the size of the United States, Alvarez calculated that this coincidence should happen to 10 people every day (Alvarez, 1965). A fellow Nobel laureate put the number closer to 80 people a day (Charpak & Broch, 2004)!

"In ten years there are five million minutes," says the statistics professor Irving Jack. "That means each person has plenty of opportunity to have some remarkable coincidences in his life" (Neimark, 2004). If 250 million Americans dream for about 2 hours every night, that's a half billion hours of dreaming, so it isn't really surprising that two people might have the same dream, or that someone would dream about something that actually happened the next day. As the mathematics professor John Paulos noted, "In reality, the most astonishingly incredible coincidence imaginable would be the complete absence of all coincidence" (Neimark, 2004).

If all of this seems surprising to you, then you are not alone. Research shows that people routinely underestimate the likelihood of coincidences happening by chance (Diaconis & Mosteller, 1989; Falk & McGregor, 1983; Hintzman et al., 1978). If you want to profit

"Idaho! What a coincidence—I'm from Idaho."

from this fact, just assemble a group of 35 or more people and offer to bet anyone $1 that at least two of the people in the group share a birthday. The odds are in your favor: a remarkable 85%. When everyone starts handing you their dollars and asking how in the world you knew that two of the people in the group shared a birthday, you can honestly tell them it was ESP — also known as Especially Sneaky Psychology.

The Ethics of Science: Doing What's Right

Somewhere along the way, someone probably told you that it isn't nice to treat people like objects. And yet, psychologists may appear to be doing just that when they create experimental situations that cause people to feel fearful or sad, to do things that are embarrassing or immoral, and to learn things about themselves and others that they might not really want to know. Don't be fooled by appearances. The fact is that psychologists go to great lengths to protect the well-being of their research participants, and they are bound by a code of ethics that is as detailed and demanding as the professional codes that bind physicians, lawyers, and accountants. That code requires psychologists to show respect for people, for animals, and for the truth. Let's examine each of these obligations in turn.

Learning Outcomes

- Identify the three basic principles that ethical research must follow.
- Summarize the ways in which psychologists ensure that their research respects people.
- Explain the ways in which psychologists ensure that their research respects truth.

Respecting People

During World War II, Nazi doctors performed barbaric experiments on human subjects, such as removing organs without anesthesia and submerging people in ice water just to

informed consent A verbal agreement to participate in a study made by an adult who has been informed of all the risks that participation may entail.

see how long it would take them to die. After the war ended, the international community developed the Nuremberg Code of 1947 and then the Declaration of Helsinki in 1964, which spelled out rules for the ethical treatment of the people who participate in experiments. Unfortunately, not everyone obeyed the rules. For example, from 1932 until 1972, the U.S. Public Health Service conducted the infamous Tuskegee experiment, in which 399 African American men with syphilis were denied treatment so that researchers could observe the progression of the disease. As one journalist noted, the government "used human beings as laboratory animals in a long and inefficient study of how long it takes syphilis to kill someone" (Jones, 1993, p. 10).

In 1979, the U.S. Department of Health, Education and Welfare released what came to be known as the Belmont Report, which described three basic principles that all research involving human participants must follow:

1. Research should show *respect for persons* and their right to make decisions for and about themselves without undue influence or coercion.

2. Research should be *beneficent,* which means that it should attempt to maximize benefits and reduce risks to the participant.

3. Research should be *just,* which means that it should distribute benefits and risks equally to participants without prejudice toward particular individuals or groups.

The ethical code that psychologists follow incorporates these basic principles and expands them. (You can find the American Psychological Association's *Ethical Principles of Psychologists and Code of Conduct* [2017] at http://www.apa.org/ethics/code.) Here are a few of the most important rules that govern the conduct of psychological research:

- *Informed consent:* Participants may not take part in a psychological study unless they have given **informed consent,** which is *a verbal agreement to participate in a study made by an adult who has been informed of all the risks that participation may entail.* This doesn't mean that the person must know everything about the study (e.g., the hypothesis), but it does mean that the person must know about anything that might potentially be harmful or painful. If people cannot give informed consent (e.g., because they are minors or are mentally incapable), then informed consent must be obtained from their legal guardians. And even after people give informed consent, they always have the right to withdraw from the study at any time without penalty.

- *Freedom from coercion:* Psychologists may not coerce participation. Coercion not only means physical and psychological coercion but monetary coercion as well. It is unethical to offer people large amounts of money to do something that they might otherwise decline to do.

- *Protection from harm:* Psychologists must take every possible precaution to protect their research participants from physical or psychological harm. If there are two equally effective ways to study something, the psychologist must use the safer method.

- *Risk–benefit analysis:* Although participants may be asked to accept small risks, such as a minor shock or a small embarrassment, they may not even be *asked* to accept a large risk, such as severe pain or psychological trauma, that is greater than the risks they would ordinarily take in their everyday lives. Furthermore, even when participants are asked to take small risks, the psychologist must demonstrate that these risks are outweighed by the social benefits of the new knowledge that might be gained from the study.

- *Deception:* Psychologists may use deception only when it is justified by the study's scientific, educational, or applied value and when alternative procedures are not feasible. They may never deceive participants about any aspect of a study that could cause physical or psychological harm or pain.

Why is the man at this bar so upset? He just saw some guy slip a drug into a woman's drink, and he is alerting the bartender. What he doesn't know is that all the people at the bar are actors and that he is being filmed for the television show *What Would You Do?* The man behaved ethically, but what about the producers of the show? Was it ethical for them to put the man in such a stressful situation without his consent?

- *Debriefing:* If a participant is deceived in any way before or during a study, the psychologist must provide a **debriefing,** which is *a verbal description of the true nature and purpose of a study.*

- *Confidentiality:* Psychologists are obligated to keep confidential any private or personal information obtained during a study.

These are just some of the rules that psychologists must follow. But how are those rules enforced? Almost all psychology studies are performed by psychologists who work at colleges and universities. These institutions have institutional review boards (IRBs) that are composed of instructors and researchers, university staff, and laypeople from the community (e.g., business leaders or members of the clergy). If the research is federally funded, the law requires that the IRB include at least one nonscientist and one person who is not affiliated with the institution. (See Other Voices: Can We Afford Science? for more about the federal funding of psychological science.) A psychologist may conduct a study only after the IRB has reviewed and approved it. The code of ethics and the procedure for approval are so strict that many studies simply cannot be performed anywhere, by anyone, at any time, because doing so would require unethical experiments that violate basic human rights.

Respecting Animals

Not all research participants have human rights because not all research participants are human. Some are chimpanzees, rats, pigeons, or other nonhuman animals. The American Psychological Association's code specifically describes the special rights of these nonhuman participants, and some of the more important ones are as follows:

- All procedures involving animals must be supervised by psychologists who are trained in research methods and experienced in the care of laboratory animals and who are responsible for ensuring appropriate consideration of the animals' comfort, health, and humane treatment.

- Psychologists must make reasonable efforts to minimize the discomfort, infection, illness, and pain of animals.

- Psychologists may use a procedure that subjects an animal to pain, stress, or privation only when an alternative procedure is unavailable and when the procedure is justified by the scientific, educational, or applied value of the study.

- Psychologists must perform all surgical procedures under appropriate anesthesia and must minimize an animal's pain during and after surgery.

That's good — but is it good enough? Some people don't think so (e.g., Singer, 1975). They believe that all creatures capable of feeling pain have the same fundamental rights as humans. Some groups, such as People for the Ethical Treatment of Animals, call for an end to all research involving nonhuman animals. But most Americans consider it morally acceptable to use nonhuman animals in research (Gallup, 2018). Indeed, most Americans eat meat, wear leather, and support the rights of hunters, which is to say that most Americans see a sharp distinction between animal and human rights. Science is not in the business of resolving moral controversies, and every individual must draw his or her own conclusions about this issue. But whatever position you take, it is important to note that only a small percentage of psychological studies involve animals, and that only a small percentage of those studies cause animals pain or harm. Psychologists mainly study people, and when they do study animals, they mainly study their behavior.

Respecting Truth

Institutional review boards ensure that data are collected ethically. But once the data are collected, who ensures that they are ethically analyzed and reported? No one. Psychology, like all sciences, works on the honor system. You may find that a bit odd. After all, we don't

debriefing A verbal description of the true nature and purpose of a study.

Some people consider it unethical to use animals for clothing or research. Others see an important distinction between these two purposes.   Paul McErlane/Reuters/Newscom

OTHER VOICES

Can We Afford Science?

Cass R. Sunstein is a law professor at Harvard University and was the administrator of the White House Office of Information and Regulatory Affairs under President Barack Obama. Andrew Toth/ Getty Images

Who pays for all the research described in textbooks like this one? The answer is you. By and large, scientific research is funded by government agencies, such as the National Science Foundation, which give scientists grants (also known as money) to do particular research projects that the scientists have proposed. Of course, this money could be spent on other things, such as feeding the poor, housing the homeless, caring for the ill and elderly, and so on. Does it make sense to spend taxpayer dollars on psychological science when some of our fellow citizens are cold and hungry?

The legal scholar Cass Sunstein argues that research in the behavioral sciences is not an expenditure — it is an investment that pays for itself, and more. Here's some of what he has to say:

When government programs fail, it is often because public officials are clueless about how human beings think and act. Federal, state and local governments make it far too hard for small businesses, developers, farmers, veterans and poor people to get permits, licenses, training and economic assistance. It's one thing to make financial aid available to students, so they can attend college. It's another thing to design forms that students can actually fill out.

Building on impressive new findings from the White House's Social and Behavioral Sciences Team, Mr. Obama ordered his government to use behavioral insights to simplify forms, cut wait times, eliminate administrative hurdles and reduce regulatory burdens. A new report from the team, which has been up and running for more than a year, shows that small reforms can make a big difference.

For example, the team helped to design a new email campaign to increase savings by service members, which nearly doubled enrollment in federal savings plans. It found that simple text messages to lower-income students, reminding them to complete required pre-matriculation tasks, increased college enrollment among those students by 5.7 percentage points. An outreach letter to farmers, designed to promote awareness of a loan program, produced a 22 percent increase in the proportion of farmers who ultimately obtained loans. A new signature box on an online form, requiring vendors to confirm the accuracy of self-reported sales, produced an additional $1.59 million in fees collected by the government in just one quarter, apparently because the box increased honest reporting.

Notwithstanding the success stories, official use of behavioral science raises two legitimate concerns. The first is practical: How much good can it do?

Improvements might be a matter of just a few percentage points — and perhaps a distraction from ambitious fiscal or regulatory reforms that could make a much bigger difference. It's a fair point, but incremental improvements should not be disparaged, especially if they help hundreds of thousands of people. And if the goal is to produce large-scale change, behaviorally informed approaches might accomplish more than we expect. For example, behavioral scientists have found that the default rule, establishing what happens if people do nothing, has surprisingly big effects. If employers automatically enroll new employees in savings programs, they can produce significant increases in participation — in one study, an increase of more than 30 percentage points. And more controversially, if utility companies automatically enrolled people in green energy, there would inevitably be reductions in greenhouse gas emissions, even with the right to opt out.

These examples raise a second concern, about ethics: What about the risk of manipulation? Should the national government really be conducting psychological experiments on the American people? It is true that behavioral science can be misused. A graphic warning, designed to produce fear, might discourage people from purchasing products that create little harm. People might be automatically enrolled in programs that do them no good. The best safeguard against manipulation is accountability. Official uses of behavioral science should never be hidden, and they should always be undertaken within the limits of law and for legitimate ends, such as promoting retirement security, lowering barriers to college, increasing employment and saving taxpayers money. If the law requires people to obtain licenses or permits, to pay taxes, or to apply for benefits or training, the government must select some method of communication. Public officials need to experiment if they want to know the effects of different methods.

Behavioral research shows that efforts at simplification, or slight variations in wording, can make all the difference. Since 2010, Britain has had its own Behavioral Insights Team, which experimented with a brief addition to a letter to late-paying taxpayers: "The great majority of people in your local area pay their tax on time." The change, which is being introduced nationally, produced a 15 percent increase in on-time payments and is projected to bring in millions of dollars worth of revenue. When government programs aren't working, those on the left tend to support more funding, while those on the right want to scrap them altogether. It is better to ask whether the problem is complexity and poor design. We can solve those problems — sometimes without spending a penny.

What do you think? Is Sunstein right? Is psychological science a wise use of public funds? Or is it a luxury that we simply can't afford?

Sunstein, S. (2015, September 19). Making Government Logical, *New York Times*. https://www.nytimes.com/2015/09/20/opinion/sunday/cass-sunstein-making-government-logicalhtml.html

use the honor system in stores ("Take the microwave home and pay us next time you're in the neighborhood"), banks ("I don't need to look up your account, just tell me how much money you want to withdraw"), or courtrooms ("If you say you're innocent, well then, that's good enough for me"), so why would we expect it to work in science? Are scientists more honest than everyone else?

Definitely! Okay, we just lied. But the honor system doesn't depend on scientists being especially honest; it depends on the fact that science is a community enterprise. When scientists claim to have discovered something important, other scientists don't just applaud: They start studying it too. When the physicist Jan Hendrik Schön announced in 2001 that he had produced a molecular-scale transistor, other physicists were deeply impressed — that is, until they tried to replicate his work and discovered that Schön had fabricated his data (Agin, 2007). Schön lost his job and his PhD, but the important point is that such frauds can't last long because one scientist's conclusion is the next scientist's research question.

What exactly are psychologists on their honor to do? At least three things. First, when writing reports of their studies and publishing them in scientific journals, psychologists are obligated to report truthfully on what they did and what they found. They can't fabricate results (e.g., by claiming to have performed studies that they never really performed) or fudge results (e.g., by changing records of data that were actually collected), and they can't mislead by omission (e.g., by reporting only the results that confirm their hypothesis and saying nothing about the results that don't). Second, psychologists are obligated to share credit fairly by including as co-authors of their reports the other people who contributed to the work, as well as by mentioning in their reports the other scientists who have done related work. And third, psychologists are obligated to share their data with other scientists who seek to verify their findings through reanalysis of the data. Most scientific frauds have been uncovered by fellow scientists who became suspicious when they looked closely at the fraudster's data. The fact that anyone can check up on anyone else is part of why the honor system works as well as it does.

Build to the Outcomes

1. What is an institutional review board (IRB)?
2. What is informed consent?
3. What is debriefing?
4. What steps must psychologists take to protect nonhuman subjects?

5. What three things must psychologists do when they report the results of their research?
6. How does science uncover fraud?

CHAPTER REVIEW

Empiricism: How to Know Stuff

- Empiricism is the belief that the best way to understand the world is to observe it firsthand. It is only in the past few centuries that people have begun to systematically collect and evaluate evidence to test the accuracy of their beliefs about the world.
- The scientific method involves (a) developing a theory that gives rise to a falsifiable hypothesis; and then (b) making observations that serve to test that hypothesis. Although these tests may prove that a theory is false, they can never prove that it is true.
- The methods of psychology are special because human beings are more complex, variable, and reactive than almost anything else that scientists study.

Methods of Observation: Finding Out What People Do

- Measurement involves (a) defining a property in measurable terms and then (b) using a device that can detect that property.
- A good definition has construct validity (the condition being measured adequately characterizes the property).

- A good detector has both power (it can tell when properties are different) and reliability (it can tell when properties are the same).
- Demand characteristics are aspects of an observational setting that cause people to behave as they think someone else wants or expects them to. Psychologists try to reduce or eliminate demand characteristics by observing participants in their natural habitats or by hiding their expectations from the participant.
- Observer bias is the tendency for observers' expectations to influence both what they believe they observed and what actually happened. Psychologists try to avoid observer bias by conducting double-blind studies.

Methods of Explanation: Figuring Out Why People Do What They Do

- To determine whether two variables are related, we measure each variable many times and then compare the patterns of variation. If the patterns are synchronized, then the variables are correlated. Correlations allow us to predict the value of one variable from knowledge of the value of the other.
- Even when we observe a correlation between two variables, we can't conclude that they are causally related because a "third variable" could be causing them both.

Experiments solve this third-variable problem by manipulating an independent variable, randomly assigning participants to the conditions that this manipulation creates, and then measuring a dependent variable. These measurements are then compared across conditions.

- An internally valid experiment establishes the likelihood of a causal relationship between variables as they were defined and among the participants who were studied.

- When an experiment mimics the real world, it is externally valid. But most psychology experiments are not attempts to mimic the real world; rather, they test hypotheses derived from theories.

- Random sampling allows researchers to generalize from their samples to the populations from which the samples were drawn. Most psychology studies cannot use random sampling, and therefore there are restrictions on the conclusions that can be drawn from them.

- Replication is an attempt to reproduce a result by using the same procedures and sampling from the same population as the original study.

Thinking Critically About Evidence

- Thinking critically about evidence is difficult because people have a natural tendency to see what they expect and want to see, and to consider what they see but not what they don't see.

- Critical thinkers consider evidence that disconfirms their own opinions. They also consider the evidence that is absent, not just the evidence that is present.

- What makes science different from most other human enterprises is that science actively seeks to discover and remedy its own errors.

The Ethics of Science: Doing What's Right

- Institutional review boards ensure that the rights of human beings who participate in scientific research are based on the principles of respect for persons, beneficence, and justice.

- Psychologists are obligated to uphold these principles by getting informed consent from participants, not coercing their participation, protecting participants from harm, weighing benefits against risks, avoiding deception, and keeping information confidential.

- Psychologists are obligated to respect the rights of animals and to treat them humanely. Most people are in favor of using animals in scientific research.

- Psychologists are obligated to tell the truth about their studies, to share credit appropriately, and to grant others access to their data.

Key Concept Quiz

1. The belief that accurate knowledge can be acquired through observation is the definition of
   a. critical thinking.
   b. dogmatism.
   c. empiricism.
   d. correlation.

2. Which of the following is the best definition of a hypothesis?
   a. empirical evidence
   b. a scientific investigation
   c. a falsifiable prediction
   d. a theoretical idea

3. If a detector is used to measure the same property twice but produces different measurements, then it lacks
   a. validity.
   b. reliability.
   c. power.
   d. concreteness.

4. Aspects of an observational setting that cause people to behave as they think someone wants or expects them to are called
   a. observer biases.
   b. replications.
   c. correlations.
   d. demand characteristics.

5. In a double-blind observation
   a. the participants know what is being measured.
   b. people are observed in their natural environments.

   c. the purpose is hidden from both the observer and the person being observed.
   d. only objective, statistical measures are recorded.

6. The attribute of an experiment that allows conclusions about causal relationships to be drawn is called
   a. external validity.
   b. internal validity.
   c. random assignment.
   d. self-selection.

7. When two variables are correlated, what keeps us from concluding that one is the cause and the other is the effect?
   a. the third-variable problem
   b. observer bias
   c. the strength of the manipulation
   d. the failure of random assignment

8. A researcher administers a questionnaire concerning attitudes toward tax increases to people of all genders and ages who live all across the United States. The dependent variable in the study is the _____ of the participants.
   a. age
   b. gender
   c. attitude
   d. geographic location

9. An experiment that defines variables as they are defined in the real world is
   a. externally valid.
   b. internally valid.
   c. operationally defined.
   d. statistically significant.

10. When people find evidence that confirms their beliefs, they often
   a. stop looking.
   b. seek more evidence.
   c. refuse to believe it.
   d. take their enemies to lunch.

11. What are psychologists ethically required to do when reporting research results?
   a. report findings truthfully
   b. share credit for research
   c. make data available for further research
   d. all of the above

LearningCurve   Don't stop now! Quizzing yourself is a powerful study tool. Go to LaunchPad to access the LearningCurve adaptive quizzing system and your own personalized learning plan. Visit launchpadworks.com.

Key Terms

empiricism (p. 28)
scientific method (p. 28)
theory (p. 28)
hypothesis (p. 28)
empirical method (p. 29)
operational definition (p. 31)
construct validity (p. 31)
power (p. 31)

reliability (p. 31)
demand characteristics (p. 31)
naturalistic observation (p. 32)
observer bias (p. 33)
double-blind study (p. 33)
variable (p. 34)
correlation (p. 34)
natural correlation (p. 34)

third-variable problem (p. 35)
experimentation (p. 35)
manipulation (p. 36)
independent variable (p. 37)
dependent variable (p. 37)
self-selection (p. 38)
random assignment (p. 38)
internal validity (p. 38)

external validity (p. 39)
population (p. 39)
sample (p. 39)
case method (p. 39)
random sampling (p. 40)
replication (p. 41)
informed consent (p. 46)
debriefing (p. 47)

Changing Minds

1. A research study shows that getting a good night's sleep increases people's performance on almost any kind of task. You tell a classmate about this study and she shrugs. "Who didn't already know that? If you ask me, psychology is just common sense. Why conduct experiments to show what everyone already knows?" How would you explain the value of studying something that seems like "common sense"?

2. Your friend texts you a link to a study showing that Europeans who work longer hours are less happy than those who work shorter hours, but that in the United States it's the other way around. The text reads "Cool experiment!" so you reply "Study—not experiment," either because you are very wise or because you don't know much about friendship. Why aren't all research studies experiments? What can't you learn from this study that you *could* learn from an experiment?

3. After the first exam, your professor says she's noticed a positive correlation between the location of students' seats and their exam scores: "The closer students sit to the front of the room, the higher their scores on the exam," she announces. After class, your friend suggests that the two

of you should sit up front for the rest of the semester to improve your grades. Having read about correlation and causation, should you be skeptical? What are some possible reasons for the correlation between seating position and good grades? Could you design an experiment to test whether sitting up front actually causes good grades?

4. A classmate in your criminal justice course suggests that mental illness is a major cause of violent crimes in the United States. As evidence, he mentions a highly publicized murder trial in which the convicted suspect was diagnosed with schizophrenia. What scientific evidence would he need to support this claim?

5. You ask your friend if she wants to go to the gym with you. "No," she says, "I never exercise." You tell her that regular exercise has all kinds of health benefits, including greatly reducing the risk of heart disease. "I don't believe that," she replies. "I had an uncle who got up at 6 a.m. every day of his life to go jogging, and he still died of a heart attack at age 53." What would you tell your friend? Does her uncle's case prove that exercise really doesn't protect against heart disease after all?

Answers to Key Concept Quiz

1. c 2. c 3. b 4. d 5. c 6. b 7. a 8. c 9. a 10. a 11. d

LaunchPad
macmillan learning   LaunchPad features the full e-book of *Introducing Psychology*, the LearningCurve adaptive quizzing system, videos, and a variety of activities to boost your learning. Visit LaunchPad at launchpadworks.com.

© SPL/Science Source

Neuroscience and Behavior

3

Junior Seau was a formidable football player who terrorized opponents in the National Football League (NFL) during a 19-year career. He was widely beloved by fellow players for his leadership qualities and devotion to serving the communities in which he played. Seau struggled after retiring from the NFL in 2009, but it was nonetheless surprising news to many when on May 2, 2012, the 43-year-old Seau ended his own life by gunshot.

Postmortem analyses of Seau's brain revealed the presence of chronic traumatic encephalopathy (CTE), a form of progressive brain damage that has been linked to repeated concussions (Montenigro et al., 2015). Seau is just one of many former NFL players who have been diagnosed with CTE (Mez et al., 2017), including the Hall of Famer and former Monday Night Football broadcaster Frank Gifford, whose death in August 2015 and subsequent CTE diagnosis focused national attention on the problem. CTE has also been observed after repeated head injuries in boxing, wrestling, hockey, and rugby (Costanza et al., 2011; Daneshvar et al., 2011; Lakhan & Kirchgessner, 2012; McKee et al., 2009).

In December 2015, attention to CTE was further heightened by the release of the movie *Concussion,* which focuses on the story of Bennet Omalu (played by Will Smith), the pathologist who first uncovered evidence for CTE in the brain of an NFL player. At present, we don't know for sure whether playing football causes CTE, or whether CTE causes such extreme outcomes as suicide, and scientists are actively debating the nature and consequences of CTE (Castellani et al., 2015). However, we do know that CTE is associated with inability to concentrate, memory loss, irritability, and depression, usually beginning within a decade after repeated concussions and worsening with time (McKee et al., 2009; Montenigro et al., 2015). Fortunately, growing awareness of CTE and its associated symptoms is leading professional sports organizations, as well as colleges, high schools, and others involved in youth sports, to take steps to address the problem. (See Data Visualization: Which Sports Have the Highest Rates of Concussion? at www.launchpadworks.com.)

The symptoms of CTE are reminders that our psychological, emotional, and social well-being depend critically on the health and integrity of the brain. They also highlight that understanding neuroscience isn't just an academic exercise confined to scientific laboratories: The more we know about the brain, the better our chances of finding solutions to problems such as CTE.

Neurons: The Origin of Behavior

The Actions of Neurons: Information Processing

The Organization of the Nervous System

Structure of the Brain

Genes, Epigenetics, and the Environment

Investigating the Brain

DATA Visualization

Junior Seau was both beloved and feared during his NFL career. His suicide devastated his family. Boston Globe/Getty Images; Donald Miralle/Getty Images

neurons Cells in the nervous system that communicate with one another to perform information-processing tasks.

cell body (soma) The part of a neuron that coordinates information-processing tasks and keeps the cell alive.

dendrite The part of a neuron that receives information from other neurons and relays it to the cell body.

In this chapter, we'll consider how the brain works, and what happens when it doesn't. First, we'll introduce the basic unit of information processing in the brain, the neuron. Neurons are the starting point of all behavior, thought, and emotion. Next, we'll consider the anatomy of the central nervous system, focusing especially on the structure and function of the brain. We'll then examine the interplay between genetics and the environment, and the role they each play in directing behavior. Finally, we'll discuss methods that allow us to study both damaged and healthy brains.

Learning Outcomes

- Explain the function of neurons.
- Outline the components of neurons.
- Describe the functions of three major types of neurons.

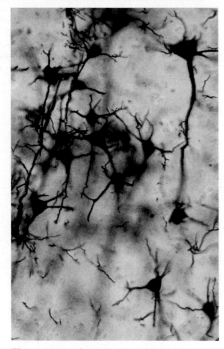

Figure 3.1 Golgi-Stained Neurons
Santiago Ramón y Cajal used a Golgi stain (like the one shown here) to highlight the appearance of neurons. He was the first to see that each neuron is composed of a body with many threads extending outward toward other neurons. In a surprising finding, he also saw that the threads of each neuron do not actually touch other neurons. Oxford Scientific/Getty Images

axon The part of a neuron that carries information to other neurons, muscles, or glands.

myelin sheath An insulating layer of fatty material around the axon of a neuron.

glial cells Support cells found in the nervous system.

Neurons: The Origin of Behavior

An estimated 1 billion people watch the final game of World Cup soccer every 4 years. That's a whole lot of people, but to put it in perspective, it's only a little over 14% of the estimated 7 billion people currently living on earth. But a really, really big number is inside your skull right now: Scientists estimate that there are about *86 billion* nerve cells in your brain (von Bartheld et al., 2016). All of your thoughts, feelings, and behaviors spring from cells in the brain that take in information and produce some kind of output trillions of times a day. These cells are **neurons,** *cells in the nervous system that communicate with each other to perform information-processing tasks.*

Components of the Neuron

In the late 1880s, Santiago Ramón y Cajal used a new technique for staining neurons (**FIGURE 3.1**), discovering that neurons are complex structures composed of three basic parts: the cell body, the dendrites, and the axon (see **FIGURE 3.2**). Like cells in all organs of the body, neurons have a **cell body** (also called the *soma*), the *part of the neuron that coordinates the information-processing tasks and keeps the cell alive.* The cell body contains a *nucleus,* which houses chromosomes that contain your DNA, or the genetic blueprint of who you are. The cell body is enclosed by a porous layer, called a *cell membrane,* that allows some molecules to flow into and out of the cell.

Unlike other cells in the body, neurons have two types of specialized extensions of the cell membrane that allow them to communicate: dendrites and axons. **Dendrites** are the *parts of the neuron that receive information from other neurons and relay it to the cell body.* The term *dendrite* comes from the Greek word for "tree"; indeed, most neurons have many dendrites that look like tree branches. The **axon** is the *part of the neuron that carries information to other neurons, muscles, or glands.* Axons can be very long; in humans, the longest ones stretch about a meter from the base of the spinal cord down to the big toe. While all neurons have the same basic components (cell bodies, dendrites, axons), neurons can vary widely in shape and function; for example, some types of neuron have elaborate dendrites that resemble a dense bush; some have a long major dendrite surrounded by many smaller dendrites; and still others have only a single dendrite.

In many neurons, the axon is covered by a **myelin sheath,** *an insulating layer of fatty material.* The myelin sheath is composed of **glial cells** (named for the Greek word for "glue"), which are *support cells found in the nervous system.* Glial cells serve a variety of roles critical to the function of the nervous system (von Bartheld et al., 2016). Some glial cells digest parts of dead neurons, others provide physical and nutritional support for neurons, and others form the myelin that insulates the axons of nearby neurons and allows those axons to carry information more efficiently. In fact, *demyelinating diseases,* such as multiple sclerosis, cause the myelin sheath to deteriorate, slowing communication from one neuron to another (Schwartz & Westbrook, 2000). This slowdown leads to a variety of problems, including loss of feeling in the limbs, partial blindness, and difficulties in coordinated movement and cognition (Butler et al., 2009).

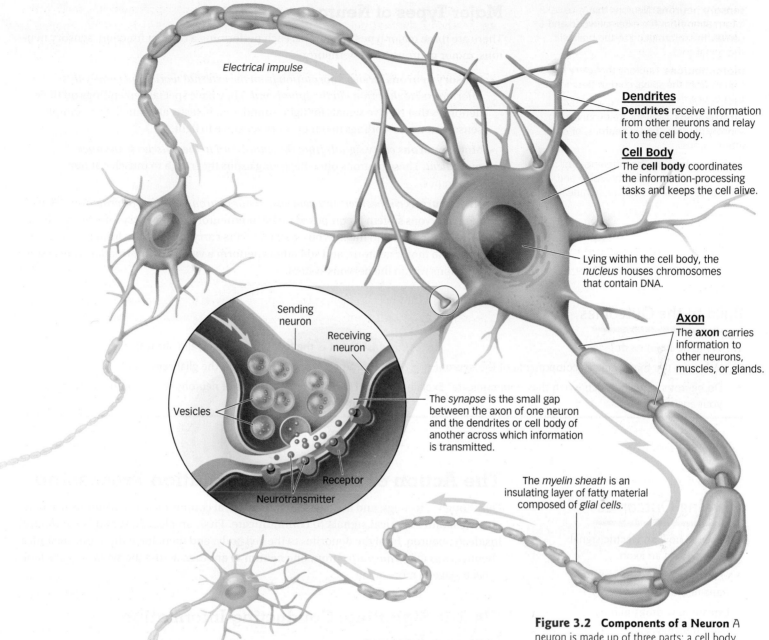

Electrical impulse

Dendrites
Dendrites receive information from other neurons and relay it to the cell body.

Cell Body
The **cell body** coordinates the information-processing tasks and keeps the cell alive.

Lying within the cell body, the *nucleus* houses chromosomes that contain DNA.

Axon
The **axon** carries information to other neurons, muscles, or glands.

Sending neuron

Receiving neuron

Vesicles

The *synapse* is the small gap between the axon of one neuron and the dendrites or cell body of another across which information is transmitted.

Receptor

Neurotransmitter

The *myelin sheath* is an insulating layer of fatty material composed of *glial cells.*

Figure 3.2 **Components of a Neuron** A neuron is made up of three parts: a cell body, dendrites, and an axon. Notice that neurons do not actually touch one another. There is a small synaptic space between them across which information is transmitted.

The dendrites and axons of neurons do not actually touch each other. There's a small gap between the axon of one neuron and the dendrites or cell body of another. This gap is part of the **synapse,** *the junction or region between the axon of one neuron and the dendrites or cell body of another* (see Figure 3.2). Many of the billions of neurons in your brain have a few thousand synaptic junctions, meaning that the adult human brain has trillions of synapses. As you'll read shortly, the transmission of information across the synapse is fundamental to communication between neurons, a process that allows us to think, feel, and behave.

synapse The junction or region between the axon of one neuron and the dendrites or cell body of another.

sensory neurons Neurons that receive information from the external world and convey this information to the brain via the spinal cord.

motor neurons Neurons that carry signals from the spinal cord to the muscles to produce movement.

interneurons Neurons that connect sensory neurons, motor neurons, or other interneurons.

resting potential The difference in electric charge between the inside and outside of a neuron's cell membrane.

Major Types of Neurons

There are three major types of neurons, each performing a distinct function: sensory neurons, motor neurons, and interneurons.

- **Sensory neurons** *receive information from the external world and convey this information to the brain via the spinal cord.* They have specialized endings on their dendrites that receive signals for light, sound, touch, taste, and smell. For example, sensory neurons' endings in our eyes are sensitive to light.
- **Motor neurons** *carry signals from the spinal cord to the muscles to produce movement.* These neurons often have long axons that reach to muscles at our extremities.
- **Interneurons** *connect sensory neurons, motor neurons, or other interneurons.* Most of the nervous system is composed of the interneurons. Some carry information from sensory neurons into the nervous system, others carry information from the nervous system to motor neurons, and still others perform a variety of information-processing functions within the nervous system.

Build to the Outcomes

1. What do neurons do?
2. What are the three primary components of the neuron?
3. Do neurons actually touch when they communicate? Explain your answer.

4. What is the function of the myelin sheath?
5. What critical functions do the glial cells play?
6. How do the three types of neurons work together to transmit information?

Learning Outcomes

- Describe how an electric signal moves down an axon.
- Outline the steps in synaptic transmission.
- Explain how drugs mimic neurotransmitters.

The Action of Neurons: Information Processing

Our thoughts, feelings, and actions depend on neural communication. Neurons use both electrical and chemical signals to communicate. First, an electric signal is *conducted* inside the neuron, from the dendrites to the cell body, and then down the axon. Second, a chemical signal is *transmitted* from one neuron to another, across the synapse. Let's look at each stage in more detail.

Electric Signaling: Conducting Information Inside a Neuron

The neuron's *cell membrane* has small pores that act as channels to allow *ions* to flow in and out of the cell. Ions are atoms or molecules that carry a small positive (+) or negative (–) electric charge. The flow of ions across the neuron's cell membrane creates an electric signal within the neuron.

The Resting Potential: The Origin of the Neuron's Electrical Properties

Normally (when a neuron is "at rest"), some ions such as positively charged potassium ions (K^+) and negatively charged protein ions (A^-) are more abundant *inside* the neuron than outside in the fluid-filled space between neurons (see **FIGURE 3.3a**). Other ions, such as positively charged sodium ions (Na^+) are more abundant *outside* the neuron. The net result is that the inside of the neuron has a slight negative electric charge, relative to the outside. This small imbalance is known as the **resting potential,** *the difference in electric charge between the inside and outside of a neuron's cell membrane* (Kandel, 2000).

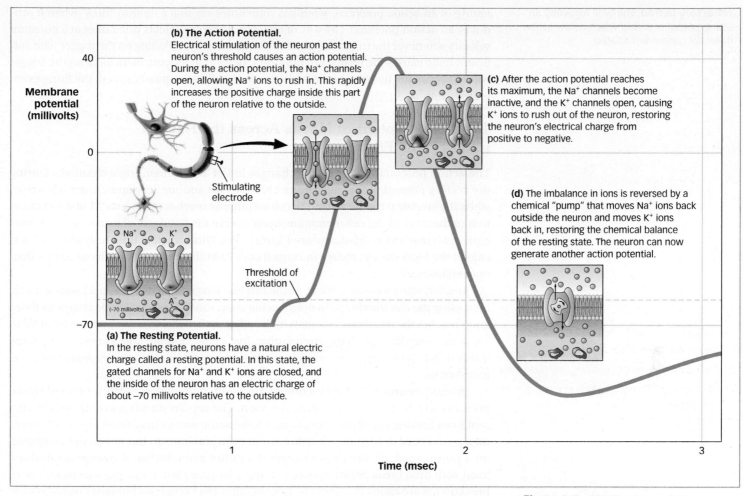

Membrane potential (millivolts)

40

0

−70

(b) The Action Potential.
Electrical stimulation of the neuron past the neuron's threshold causes an action potential. During the action potential, the Na⁺ channels open, allowing Na⁺ ions to rush in. This rapidly increases the positive charge inside this part of the neuron relative to the outside.

Stimulating electrode

(c) After the action potential reaches its maximum, the Na⁺ channels become inactive, and the K⁺ channels open, causing K⁺ ions to rush out of the neuron, restoring the neuron's electrical charge from positive to negative.

(d) The imbalance in ions is reversed by a chemical "pump" that moves Na⁺ ions back outside the neuron and moves K⁺ ions back in, restoring the chemical balance of the resting state. The neuron can now generate another action potential.

Threshold of excitation

Na⁺   K⁺

A⁻
(−70 millivolts)

(a) The Resting Potential.
In the resting state, neurons have a natural electric charge called a resting potential. In this state, the gated channels for Na⁺ and K⁺ ions are closed, and the inside of the neuron has an electric charge of about −70 millivolts relative to the outside.

1   2   3

Time (msec)

Figure 3.3   The Resting and Action Potentials Neurons have a natural electric charge called a resting potential. Electric stimulation causes an action potential.

The resting potential is usually about −70 millivolts. By comparison, a typical AA battery may have about 1.5 volts (1,500 millivolts).

One reason for the difference in concentrations of ions inside and outside the neuron's cell membrane is that special channels in the cell membrane restrict the movement of ions in and out of the cell. During the resting potential, these channels are closed. But, like the floodgates of Hoover Dam, which hold back the Colorado River until they are released, these channels in the cell membrane can be opened, allowing ions to rush across the membrane in a fraction of a second.

The Action Potential: Sending Signals Inside the Neuron

The neuron maintains its resting potential most of the time. But, in a series of classic experiments, biologists Alan Hodgkin and Andrew Huxley noticed that they could produce a signal by stimulating the axon with an electric shock, which set off a much larger electrical impulse that traveled all the way down the axon in a rapid wave (Häusser, 2000; Hodgkin & Huxley, 1939). This electric impulse is called an **action potential,** *an electric signal that is conducted along the length of a neuron's axon to a synapse.*

Hodgkin and Huxley also noticed that the action potential occurred only when the electric shock reached a certain level, or *threshold*. Above that threshold, further increases in the electric shock did *not* increase the strength of the action potential. The action potential is *all or none*: Electric stimulation below the threshold fails to produce an action potential, whereas electric stimulation at or above the threshold always produces the action potential and always at the same strength. Because of the rapid, all-or-nothing

action potential An electric signal that is conducted along a neuron's axon to a synapse.

refractory period The time following an action potential during which a new action potential cannot be initiated.

nature of an action potential, scientists sometimes say that a neuron "fires" when it produces an action potential. (By way of analogy, a revolver ejects one bullet at a constant velocity whenever the trigger is pulled with sufficient force. Pulling on the trigger with sufficient force causes the revolver to fire — but, beyond that point, extra force on the trigger will not cause the bullet to be ejected more forcefully or at greater speed; the firing event is all or nothing.)

The Action Potential Moves Across the Neuron in a Domino Effect

The action potential occurs due to changes in the axon's membrane channels. During the resting potential, the membrane channels for sodium ions are closed. However, when the electrical charge across the cell membrane reaches the threshold, sodium channels in that area of the cell membrane open up like the floodgate of a dam, and Na^+ ions rush in almost instantaneously (see Figure 3.3b). This inrush of positively charged ions causes the local electric charge to surge from −70 millivolts to +40 millivolts in less than one millisecond.

And this starts a domino effect. As the first Na^+ ions rush in, they spread inside the cell, increasing the electric charge in neighboring areas too. When the electric charge in those areas reaches the threshold, channels in the adjacent cell membrane open and let in more Na^+ ions, spreading the charge even farther. Just as one domino knocks over another, the influx of Na^+ ions triggers nearby channels to open, and the process repeats down the entire axon.

In many neurons, the conduction of the action potential is greatly increased by the presence of a myelin sheath around the axon. The myelin sheath prevents electric current from leaking out of the axon, in much the same way as insulation covers the wires on a power cord to keep the electric current from leaking out. But unlike the insulation on a power cord, myelin doesn't cover the entire axon; rather, it clumps around the axon with little break points between clumps, looking kind of like sausage links. These breakpoints are called the *nodes of Ranvier,* after the French pathologist Louis-Antoine Ranvier, who discovered them (see **FIGURE 3.4**). The current seems to "jump" quickly from node to node (Poliak & Peles, 2003). This process is called *saltatory conduction* (*saltare* is Latin for "hop" or "leap"), and it helps speed the flow of information down the axon.

The action potential always spreads onward, never backward, because the Na^+ channels in each region of the axon are temporarily inactivated after the action potential passes over them, just as a domino that has already been knocked over cannot be knocked over twice. This brief period of inactivation is called a **refractory period,** *the time following an action potential during which a new action potential cannot be initiated.* During the refractory period, the electrical and chemical balance of the neuron is restored. To restore the electrical balance, Na^+ channels inactivate themselves for several milliseconds, stopping the inrush of Na^+ ions, and K^+ channels open, allowing excess K^+ ions in the cell to escape (see Figure 3.3c). The rapid exit of positively charged K^+ ions

Figure 3.4 Myelin and Nodes of Ranvier Myelin is formed by a type of glial cell. It wraps around a neuron's axon to speed the movement of the action potential along the length of the axon. Breaks in the myelin sheath are called the nodes of Ranvier. The electric impulse jumps from node to node, speeding the conduction of information down the axon.

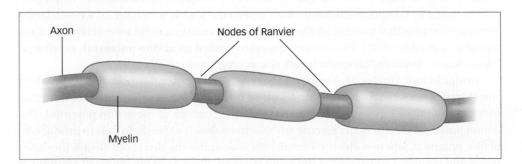

returns the electrical charge of the membrane to a negative state. Then, to restore the chemical balance, a series of special channels, called ion pumps, work to redistribute the ions (e.g., pushing all that excess Na^+ back out of the cell and pulling some K^+ back in), until the concentrations are rebalanced and the resting potential is restored (see Figure 3.3d). At this point, the dominoes are set back up — and ready to be knocked over again if triggered. The entire process is so fast that some neurons fire more than 100 times in a single second.

Chemical Signaling: Transmitting Information Between Neurons

When the action potential reaches the end of an axon, you might think that it stops there. After all, the synapse between neurons means that the axon of one neuron and the neighboring neuron's dendrites do not actually touch one another. However, the information crosses the synaptic gap by relying on a bit of chemistry.

Axons usually end in **terminal buttons,** *knoblike structures at the end of an axon.* Each terminal button is filled with tiny *vesicles* or bags that contain molecules known as **neurotransmitters,** *chemicals that transmit information across the synapse to a receiving neuron's dendrites.* The dendrites of the receiving neuron contain **receptors,** *parts of the cell membrane that receive neurotransmitters and either initiate or prevent a new electric signal.*

Inside the sending neuron, or *presynaptic neuron,* the action potential travels down the length of the axon to the terminal buttons, where it stimulates the release of neurotransmitters from vesicles into the synapses. The neurotransmitters quickly float across the synapse and bind to receptor sites on the nearby dendrite of the receiving neuron, or *postsynaptic neuron.* These receptors may cause membrane channels to open, changing the electric charge in that area of the dendrite. Depending on the strength and timing of these changes, the postsynaptic neuron may reach a threshold and generate an action potential in turn — passing the information along. The sending and receiving of chemical neurotransmitters is called *synaptic transmission* (see **FIGURE 3.5a**), and it ultimately underlies your thoughts, emotions, and behavior.

Neurotransmitters and receptor sites act like a lock-and-key system. Just as a particular key will fit only in a particular lock, so too will only some neurotransmitters bind to specific receptor sites on a dendrite. The molecular structure of the neurotransmitter must fit the molecular structure of the receptor site.

After the chemical message is relayed to the postsynaptic neuron, neurotransmitters must stop acting on neurons; otherwise, there would be no end to the signals that they send. Neurotransmitters leave the synapse through three processes (see Figure 3.5b):

- Neurotransmitters can be absorbed by the terminal buttons of the presynaptic neuron's axon or by neighboring glial cells, a process called *reuptake*.

- Neurotransmitters can be broken down by enzymes in the synapse.

- Neurotransmitters can drift out of the synapse, away from receptors, a process called *diffusion*.

Neurotransmitters can also bind to receptor sites on the presynaptic (sending) neuron called *autoreceptors*. Autoreceptors detect how much of a neurotransmitter has been released into a synapse and may stop the release of more.

Types and Functions of Neurotransmitters

You might wonder how many types of neurotransmitters are floating across synapses in your brain right now. Today, we know of more than 100, each of which help transmit information throughout the brain and body. A few major classes of neurotransmitters play key

terminal buttons Knoblike structures that branch out from an axon.

neurotransmitters Chemicals that transmit information across the synapse to a receiving neuron's dendrites.

receptors Parts of the cell membrane that receive neurotransmitters and either initiate or prevent a new electric signal.

Figure 3.5 Synaptic Transmission
(*a*) The action potential travels down the axon and stimulates the release of neurotransmitters from vesicles (1). The neurotransmitter molecules are released into the synapse (2), where they may float across to bind with receptors on a dendrite of a postsynaptic neuron (3), initiating electrical changes inside that neuron that may reach threshold and trigger a new action potential. (*b*) The neurotransmitter molecules are then cleared out of the synapse by (1) reuptake into the sending neuron, (2) being broken down by enzymes in the synapse, or (3) diffusion away from the synapse. (4) Neurotransmitter molecules can also bind to autoreceptors on the sending neuron, signaling the neuron to stop the release of more neurotransmitters.

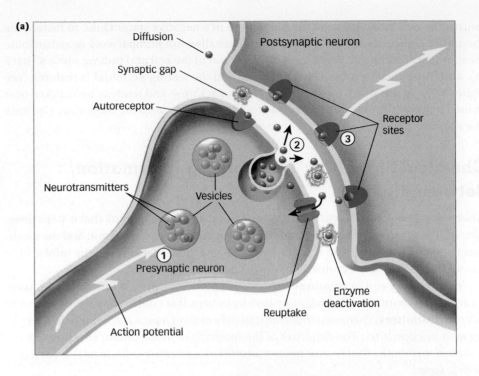

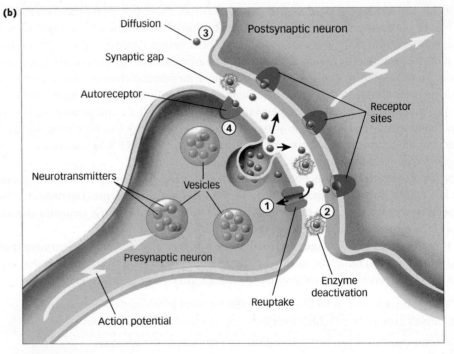

roles in fundamental behaviors. We'll summarize those here, and you'll encounter some of them again in later chapters.

- *Acetylcholine (ACh)* is a neurotransmitter involved in voluntary motor control, as well as attention, learning, sleeping, dreaming, and memory (Gais & Born, 2004; Hasselmo, 2006; Wrenn et al., 2006). Alzheimer's disease, a medical condition involving severe memory impairments (Salmon & Bondi, 2009), is associated with the deterioration of ACh-producing neurons.

- *Dopamine* is a neurotransmitter involved in regulating motor behavior, motivation, and emotional arousal. Because of its role in seeking pleasure and associating actions with rewards, dopamine plays a role in drug addiction (Baler & Volkow, 2006). High levels of dopamine in some brain pathways are linked to schizophrenia (Winterer & Weinberger, 2004), whereas low levels in other brain areas are linked to Parkinson's disease.

- *Glutamate* is the major excitatory neurotransmitter in the brain, meaning that it enhances the transmission of information between neurons. *GABA (gamma-aminobutyric acid),* in contrast, is the primary inhibitory neurotransmitter in the brain, meaning that it tends to prevent the firing of neurons. Too much glutamate, or too little GABA, can cause neurons to become overactive, causing seizures.

- Two related neurotransmitters, *norepinephrine* and *serotonin*, influence mood and arousal. *Norepinephrine* is involved in states of vigilance, or heightened awareness of danger (Ressler & Nemeroff, 1999). *Serotonin* is involved in the regulation of sleep and wakefulness, eating, and aggressive behavior (Dayan & Huys, 2009; Kroeze & Roth, 1998). Low levels of these neurotransmitters have been implicated in mood disorders (Tamminga et al., 2002).

- *Endorphins* are chemicals that help dull the experience of pain and elevate moods (Keefe et al., 2001). The "runner's high" experienced by many athletes as they push their bodies to painful limits of endurance can be explained by the release of endorphins in the brain (Boecker et al., 2008).

Each of these neurotransmitters affects thought, feeling, and behavior in different ways, so normal functioning involves a delicate balance of each. Even a slight imbalance — too much of one neurotransmitter or not enough of another — can dramatically affect behavior. People who smoke, drink alcohol, or take drugs (legal or not) are altering the balance of neurotransmitters in their brains.

How Drugs Mimic Neurotransmitters

Many drugs that affect the nervous system operate by increasing, interfering with, or mimicking the manufacture or function of neurotransmitters (Cooper et al., 2003; Sarter, 2006). **Agonists** are *drugs that increase the action of a neurotransmitter.* **Antagonists** are *drugs that diminish the function of a neurotransmitter.* Some drugs work by altering a step in the production or release of the neurotransmitter. Other drugs have a chemical structure so similar to a neurotransmitter that the drug is able to bind to that neuron's receptor, either mimicking the neurotransmitter (agonists) or blocking the ability of the neurotransmitter to activate that receptor (antagonists).

For example, the drug L-dopa is used to treat Parkinson's disease, a movement disorder characterized by tremors and difficulty initiating movement. Parkinson's disease is caused by the loss of neurons that make the neurotransmitter dopamine. Ingesting L-dopa as a drug spurs the surviving neurons to produce more dopamine. In other words, L-dopa acts as an agonist for dopamine by increasing its production. The use of L-dopa has been reasonably successful in the alleviation of Parkinson's disease symptoms (Muenter & Tyce, 1971; Schapira et al., 2009).

Another agonist, *amphetamine,* is a drug that stimulates the release of norepinephrine and dopamine and also blocks their reuptake. Norepinephrine and dopamine both play a critical role in mood control, such that an increase in either neurotransmitter results in euphoria, wakefulness, and a burst of energy. However, norepinephrine also increases heart rate. An overdose of amphetamine can cause the heart to contract so rapidly that heartbeats do not last long enough to pump blood effectively, leading to fainting and sometimes death.

Opioids are a class of drugs either derived naturally from the opium poppy (such as morphine and heroin) or made synthetically (such as oxycodone and fentanyl). Most opioids work in part by acting as agonists for endorphins, which creates powerful feelings of calm and euphoria. Opioids have been widely prescribed for pain relief because

agonists Drugs that increase the action of a neurotransmitter.

antagonists Drugs that diminish the function of a neurotransmitter.

When long-distance runners complete a marathon, they may experience the subjective highs that result from the release of endorphins — chemical messengers acting in emotion and pain centers that elevate mood and dull the experience of pain.
Sam Barnes/Getty Images

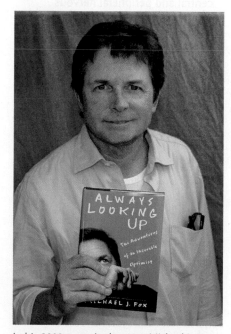

In his 2009 memoir, the actor Michael J. Fox vividly described his struggles with Parkinson's disease, which made it difficult even to control the hand and arm movements needed to brush his own teeth. Fox's visibility has increased public awareness of the disease and spurred greater efforts toward finding a cure. David Livingston/Getty Images Entertainment/Getty Images

they are highly effective at decreasing the perception of pain. At the same time, opioids also diminish the brainstem's sensitivity to rising levels of carbon dioxide in the blood, which depresses breathing. Opioid overdose can therefore lead to asphyxiation and death. Opioids are also highly addictive. In 2017, the Centers for Disease Control and Prevention estimated that 115 people in the United States die from an opioid overdose every day.

These are just a few examples of the many drugs, natural and synthetic, legally prescribed and illegally used, that mimic neurotransmitters. You'll meet more of these later, in the Treatment of Psychological Disorders chapter.

Build to the Outcomes

1. What difference between the inside and outside of the neuron's cell membrane creates the resting potential?

2. How does the neuron's membrane change over the course of an action potential?

3. What is the role of neurotransmitters in neural communication?

4. Choose two neurotransmitters and compare and contrast their functions.

5. Is L-dopa an agonist or an antagonist for dopamine? Explain your answer.

The Organization of the Nervous System

Learning Outcomes

- Differentiate the functions of the central and peripheral nervous systems.
- Understand the nature of the spinal reflex.

We've seen how individual neurons communicate with each other. What's the bigger picture? Neurons are the building blocks that form *nerves,* or bundles of axons and the glial cells that support them. The **nervous system** is *an interacting network of neurons that conveys information throughout the body.*

There are two major divisions of the nervous system: the central nervous system and the peripheral nervous system (see **FIGURE 3.6**). The **central nervous system (CNS)** is *composed of the brain and spinal cord.* It receives sensory information from the external world, processes and coordinates this information, and sends commands to the skeletal and muscular systems for action. The **peripheral nervous system (PNS)** *connects the central nervous system to the body's organs and muscles.* Let's examine each more closely.

The Peripheral Nervous System

nervous system An interacting network of neurons that conveys information throughout the body.

central nervous system (CNS) The part of the nervous system that is composed of the brain and spinal cord.

peripheral nervous system (PNS) The part of the nervous system that connects the central nervous system to the body's organs and muscles.

somatic nervous system A set of nerves that conveys information between voluntary muscles and the central nervous system.

autonomic nervous system (ANS) A set of nerves that carries involuntary and automatic commands that control blood vessels, body organs, and glands.

The peripheral nervous system is composed of two major subdivisions, the somatic nervous system and the autonomic nervous system. The **somatic nervous system** is *a set of nerves that conveys information between voluntary muscles and the central nervous system.* Humans have conscious control over this system and use it to perceive, think, and coordinate their behaviors. For example, reaching for your morning cup of coffee involves the elegantly orchestrated activities of the somatic nervous system: Information from the receptors in your eyes travels to your brain, registering that a cup is on the table; signals from your brain travel to the muscles in your arm and hand; feedback from those muscles tells your brain that the cup has been grasped; and so on.

In contrast, the **autonomic nervous system (ANS)** is *a set of nerves that carries involuntary and automatic commands that control blood vessels, body organs, and glands.* As suggested by its name, this system works on its own ("autonomously") to regulate bodily systems, largely outside of conscious control. The ANS has two major subdivisions, the sympathetic nervous system and the parasympathetic nervous system. Each exerts a different type of control on the body.

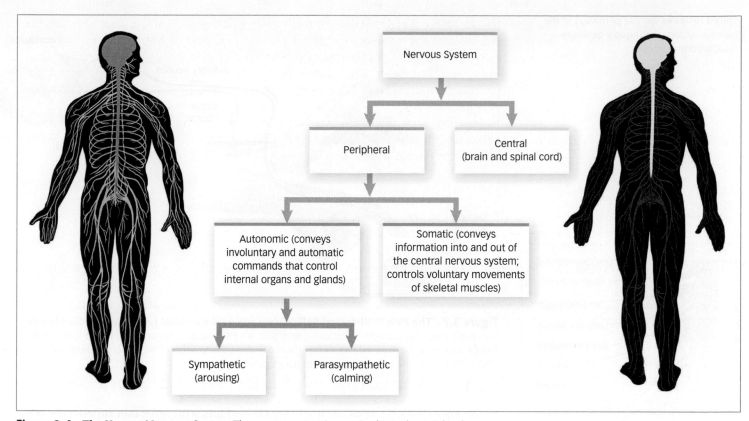

Figure 3.6   The Human Nervous System The nervous system is organized into the peripheral and central nervous systems. The peripheral nervous system is divided into the autonomic and somatic nervous systems. The autonomic nervous system can be divided still further into the sympathetic and parasympathetic nervous systems.

The **sympathetic nervous system** is *a set of nerves that prepares the body for action in challenging or threatening situations*. For example, imagine that you are walking alone late at night and are frightened by footsteps behind you in a dark alley. Your sympathetic nervous system kicks into action at this point: It dilates your pupils to let in more light, increases your heart rate and respiration to pump more oxygen to your muscles, diverts blood flow to your brain and muscles, and activates sweat glands to cool your body. To conserve energy, the sympathetic nervous system inhibits salivation and bowel movements, suppresses the body's immune responses, and suppresses responses to pain and injury. The sum total of these fast, automatic responses is that they increase the likelihood that you can escape.

The **parasympathetic nervous system** *helps the body return to a normal resting state*. When you're far away from your would-be attacker, your body doesn't need to remain on red alert. Now the parasympathetic nervous system kicks in to reverse the effects of the sympathetic nervous system and return your body to its normal state. The parasympathetic nervous system generally mirrors the connections of the sympathetic nervous system. For instance, the parasympathetic nervous system constricts your pupils, slows your heart rate and respiration, diverts blood flow to your digestive system, and decreases activity in your sweat glands.

The Central Nervous System

Compared with the many divisions of the peripheral nervous system, the central nervous system may seem simple. After all, it has only two elements: the brain and the spinal cord. But those two elements are ultimately responsible for most of what we do as humans.

sympathetic nervous system A set of nerves that prepares the body for action in challenging or threatening situations.

parasympathetic nervous system A set of nerves that helps the body return to a normal resting state.

spinal reflexes Simple pathways in the nervous system that rapidly generate muscle contractions.

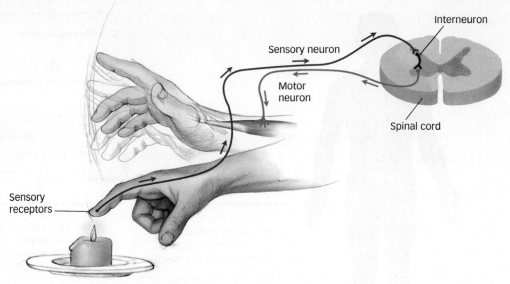

Figure 3.7 **The Pain Withdrawal Reflex** Many actions of the central nervous system don't require the brain's input. For example, withdrawing from pain is a reflexive activity controlled by the spinal cord. Painful sensations (such as the heat of fire) travel directly to the spinal cord via sensory neurons, which then issue a command to motor neurons to retract the hand.

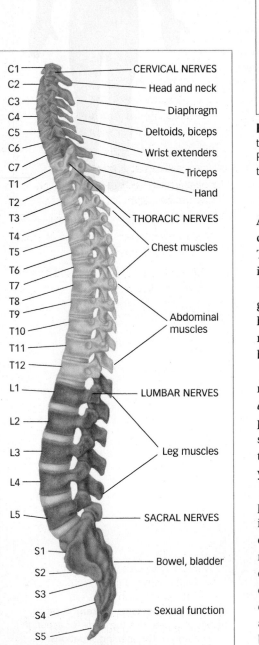

Figure 3.8 **Regions of the Spinal Cord** The spinal cord is divided into four main sections; each controls different parts of the body. Damage higher on the spinal cord usually means greater impairment.

At the top of the CNS rests the brain, which contains structures that support the most complex perceptual, motor, emotional, and cognitive functions of the nervous system. The spinal cord branches down from the brain, and contains nerves that process sensory information and relay commands to the body.

The spinal cord often seems like the brain's poor relation: The brain gets all the glory, and the spinal cord just hangs around, doing relatively simple tasks. Those tasks, however, are pretty important: They keep you breathing, respond to pain, and move your muscles, allowing you to walk. What's more, without the spinal cord, the brain would not be able to put any of its higher processing into action.

Connections between the sensory neurons and motor neurons in the spinal cord mediate **spinal reflexes,** *simple pathways in the nervous system that rapidly generate muscle contractions*. If you touch a hot stove, the sensory neurons that register pain send inputs directly into the spinal cord (see **FIGURE 3.7**). Through just a few synaptic connections within the spinal cord, interneurons relay these sensory inputs to motor neurons that connect to your arm muscles and direct you to quickly retract your hand.

More elaborate tasks require the collaboration of the spinal cord and the brain. The peripheral nervous system sends messages from sensory neurons through the spinal cord into the brain. The brain sends commands for voluntary movement through the spinal cord to motor neurons, whose axons project out to skeletal muscles. Damage to the spinal cord severs the connection from the brain to the sensory and motor neurons that are essential to sensory perception and movement. The location of the spinal injury often determines the extent of the abilities that are lost. As you can see in **FIGURE 3.8,** different regions of the spinal cord control different systems of the body. Individuals with damage at a particular level of the spinal cord lose sensations of touch and pain in body parts below the level of the injury, as well as motor control of the muscles in the same areas. A spinal injury higher up the cord can produce quadriplegia (loss of sensation and motor control over all limbs), resulting in lifelong immobility and the necessity of breathing through a respirator.

On a brighter note, researchers are making progress in understanding the nature of spinal cord injuries and how to treat them by focusing on how the brain changes in response to injury (Blesch & Tuszynski, 2009; Dunlop, 2008), a process that is closely related to the concept of brain plasticity that we will examine later in this chapter. Progress in constructing brain–machine interfaces could also improve the lives of people who have suffered paralysis from spinal cord injuries.

Build to the Outcomes

1. What is the neuron's role in the body's nervous system?
2. What are the two divisions of the peripheral nervous system?
3. What are the two components of the central nervous system?
4. What triggers the increase in your heart rate when you feel threatened?
5. What important functions does the spinal cord perform on its own?

Structure of the Brain

Right now, your neurons and glial cells are busy humming away, giving you potentially brilliant ideas, consciousness, and feelings. But which neurons in which parts of the brain control which functions? To answer that question, it can be helpful to talk about areas of the brain from "bottom to top," noting how the different regions are specialized for different kinds of tasks. In general, simpler functions are performed at the "lower" levels of the brain, whereas more complex functions are performed at successively "higher" levels (see **FIGURE 3.9a**). The brain can also be approached in a "side-by-side" fashion: Although each side (or "hemisphere") of the brain is roughly analogous, one hemisphere specializes in some tasks that the other hemisphere doesn't. Although these divisions make it easier to understand areas of the brain and their functions, keep in mind that none of these divisions of the brain act alone. They are all part of one big, interacting and interdependent whole (Avena-Koenigsberger et al., 2018; Sporns & Betzel, 2016).

Let's look first at the divisions of the brain, moving from the bottom to the top. Using this view, we can divide the brain into three parts: the hindbrain, the midbrain, and the forebrain (see Figure 3.9a).

Learning Outcomes

- Differentiate the functions of the major divisions of the brain.
- Explain the functions of the cerebral cortex according to organization across hemispheres, within hemispheres, and within specific lobes.
- Identify the causes and consequences of brain plasticity.
- Explain the progression of the human brain's evolution.

The Hindbrain

If you follow the spinal cord from your tailbone to where it enters your skull, you'll find it difficult to determine where your spinal cord ends and your brain begins. That's because the spinal cord is continuous with the **hindbrain**, *an area of the brain that coordinates information coming into and out of the spinal cord.* The hindbrain looks like a stalk on which the rest of the brain sits, and it controls the most basic functions of life: respiration, alertness, and motor skills. The structures that make up the hindbrain include the medulla, the reticular formation, the cerebellum, and the pons (see Figure 3.9b).

The **medulla** is *an extension of the spinal cord into the skull that coordinates heart rate, circulation, and respiration.* Beginning inside the medulla and extending upward is a small cluster of neurons called the **reticular formation,** which *regulates sleep, wakefulness, and levels of arousal.* Many general anesthetics work by reducing activity in the reticular formation, rendering the patient unconscious.

Behind the medulla is the **cerebellum,** *a large structure of the hindbrain that controls fine motor skills.* (*Cerebellum* is Latin for "little brain," and this structure does look like a small replica of the brain.) The cerebellum orchestrates the proper sequence of movements when we ride a bike, play the piano, or maintain balance while walking and running. It contributes to the fine-tuning of behavior: smoothing our actions to allow their graceful execution rather than initiating the actions (Smetacek, 2002). The initiation of behavior involves other areas of the brain; as you'll recall, different brain systems interact and are interdependent with each other.

hindbrain The area of the brain that coordinates information coming into and out of the spinal cord.

medulla An extension of the spinal cord into the skull that coordinates heart rate, circulation, and respiration.

reticular formation A brain structure that regulates sleep, wakefulness, and levels of arousal.

cerebellum A large structure of the hindbrain that controls fine motor skills.

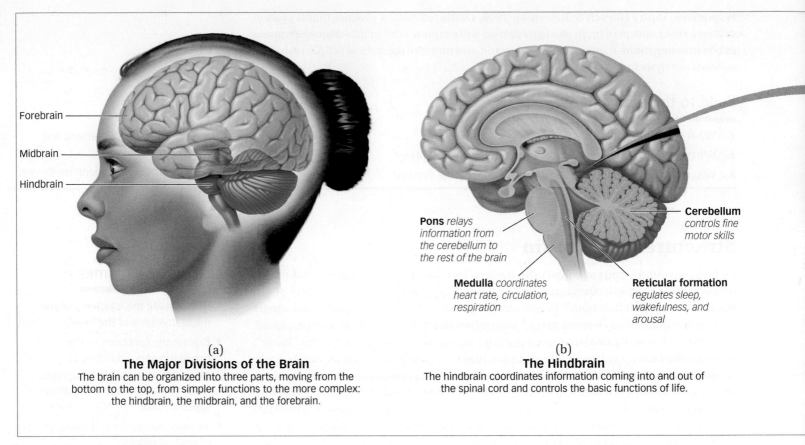

(a)
The Major Divisions of the Brain
The brain can be organized into three parts, moving from the bottom to the top, from simpler functions to the more complex: the hindbrain, the midbrain, and the forebrain.

(b)
The Hindbrain
The hindbrain coordinates information coming into and out of the spinal cord and controls the basic functions of life.

Figure 3.9   Structure of the Brain

The last major area of the hindbrain is the **pons**, *a structure that relays information from the cerebellum to the rest of the brain.* (*Pons* means "bridge" in Latin.) Although the detailed functions of the pons remain poorly understood, it essentially acts as a relay station or bridge between the cerebellum and other structures in the brain.

The Midbrain

Sitting on top of the hindbrain is the *midbrain,* which is relatively small in humans. As you can see in Figure 3.9c, the midbrain contains two main structures: the tectum and the tegmentum. The *tectum* orients an organism in the environment. The tectum receives stimulus input from the eyes, ears, and skin and moves the organism in a coordinated way toward the stimulus. For example, when you're studying in a quiet room and you hear a *click* behind and to the right of you, your body will swivel and orient to the direction of the sound; this is your tectum in action. The *tegmentum* is involved in movement and arousal; it also helps to orient an organism toward sensory stimuli.

The midbrain may be relatively small, but it is critical. You could survive if you had only a hindbrain and a midbrain. The structures in the hindbrain would take care of all the bodily functions necessary to sustain life, and the structures in the midbrain would orient you toward or away from pleasurable or threatening stimuli in the environment. But this wouldn't be much of a life. To understand where the abilities that make us fully human come from, we need to consider the last division of the brain.

The Forebrain

When you appreciate the beauty of a poem, plan to go skiing next winter, or notice the faint glimmer of sadness on a loved one's face, you are enlisting the forebrain. The *forebrain* is the highest level of the brain — literally and figuratively — and controls complex

The high-wire artist Freddy Nock relied on his cerebellum to coordinate the movements necessary to walk on the rope of the Corvatsch cable car from more than 10,000 feet over sea level down to the base station in Silvaplana, Switzerland. Arno Balzarini/Keystone/AP Images

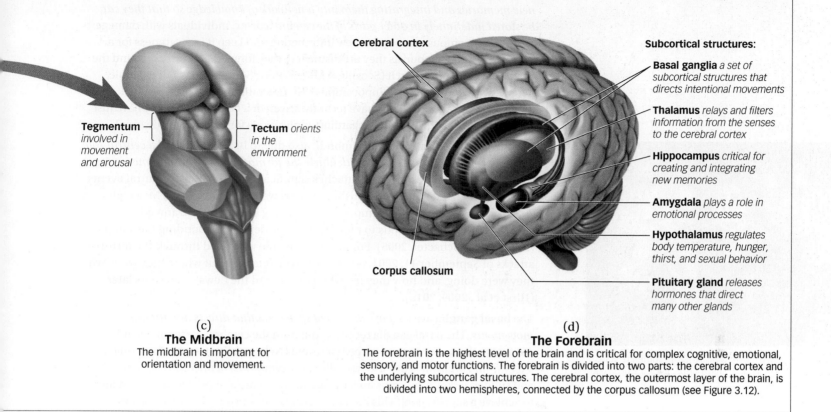

Tegmentum *involved in movement and arousal*   **Tectum** *orients in the environment*

Cerebral cortex

Corpus callosum

Subcortical structures:

Basal ganglia *a set of subcortical structures that directs intentional movements*

Thalamus *relays and filters information from the senses to the cerebral cortex*

Hippocampus *critical for creating and integrating new memories*

Amygdala *plays a role in emotional processes*

Hypothalamus *regulates body temperature, hunger, thirst, and sexual behavior*

Pituitary gland *releases hormones that direct many other glands*

(c)
The Midbrain
The midbrain is important for orientation and movement.

(d)
The Forebrain
The forebrain is the highest level of the brain and is critical for complex cognitive, emotional, sensory, and motor functions. The forebrain is divided into two parts: the cerebral cortex and the underlying subcortical structures. The cerebral cortex, the outermost layer of the brain, is divided into two hemispheres, connected by the corpus callosum (see Figure 3.12).

cognitive, emotional, sensory, and motor functions. The forebrain itself is divided into two main sections: the cerebral cortex and the subcortical structures. The **cerebral cortex** is *the outermost layer of the brain, visible to the naked eye, and divided into two hemispheres.* The **subcortical structures** are *areas of the forebrain housed under the cerebral cortex near the center of the brain* (see Figure 3.9d). Let's examine the subcortical structures first.

Subcortical Structures

The subcortical structures are nestled deep inside the brain (under the cortex), where they are quite protected. They play an important role in relaying information throughout the brain, as well as in performing specific tasks that allow us to think, feel, and behave as humans. Here we'll give you a brief introduction to each, and you'll read more about many of these structures in later chapters.

- The **thalamus** *relays and filters information from the senses and transmits the information to the cerebral cortex.* The thalamus receives inputs from all the major senses except smell, filters the information, giving more weight to some inputs and less weight to others, and then relays the information to a variety of locations in the brain. The thalamus also closes the pathways of incoming sensations during sleep, providing a valuable function in *not* allowing information to pass to the rest of the brain.

- The **hypothalamus,** located below the thalamus (*hypo-* is Greek for "under"), *regulates body temperature, hunger, thirst, and sexual behavior.* Clusters of neurons in the hypothalamus keep body temperature, blood sugar levels, and metabolism within an optimal range for normal human functioning. Lesions to some areas of the hypothalamus result in overeating, whereas lesions to other areas leave an animal with no desire for food at all (Berthoud & Morrison, 2008).

pons A brain structure that relays information from the cerebellum to the rest of the brain.

cerebral cortex The outermost layer of the brain, visible to the naked eye and divided into two hemispheres.

subcortical structures Areas of the forebrain housed under the cerebral cortex near the center of the brain.

thalamus A subcortical structure that relays and filters information from the senses and transmits the information to the cerebral cortex.

hypothalamus A subcortical structure that regulates body temperature, hunger, thirst, and sexual behavior.

- The **hippocampus** (from Latin for "seahorse," due to its shape) is *critical for creating new memories and integrating them into a network of knowledge so that they can be stored indefinitely in other parts of the cerebral cortex.* Individuals with damage to the hippocampus can acquire new information and keep it in awareness for a few seconds, but as soon as they are distracted, they forget the information and the experience that produced it (Scoville & Milner, 1957; Squire, 2009). For example, people with damage to the hippocampus can remember how to drive and talk, but they cannot recall where they have recently driven or a conversation they have just had (see A World of Difference regarding implications for Alzheimer's disease).

- The **amygdala** (from Latin for "almond," also due to its shape), *plays a central role in many emotional processes, particularly the formation of emotional memories* (Aggleton, 1992). The amygdala attaches significance to previously neutral events that are associated with fear, punishment, or reward (LeDoux, 1992; Mcgaugh, 2006, 2015). When we are in emotionally arousing situations, the amygdala stimulates the hippocampus to remember many details surrounding the situation (Kensinger & Schacter, 2005). For instance, people who lived through the terrorist attacks of September 11, 2001, remember vivid details about where they were, what they were doing, and how they felt when they heard the news, even years later (Hirst et al., 2009, 2015).

- The **basal ganglia** are *a set of subcortical structures that directs intentional movements.* The basal ganglia receive input from the cerebral cortex and send outputs to the motor centers in the brainstem (Nelson & Kreitzer, 2015). People who suffer from Parkinson's disease typically show symptoms of uncontrollable shaking and sudden jerks of the limbs and are unable to initiate a sequence of movements to achieve a specific goal. This happens because Parkinson's disease damages parts of the midbrain that normally supply the basal ganglia with dopamine (Dauer & Przedborski, 2003).

The Endocrine System

One way in which the subcortical structures affect behavior is by interacting with the **endocrine system,** *a network of glands that produce and secrete into the bloodstream chemical messages known as hormones, which influence a wide variety of basic functions, including metabolism, growth, and sexual development.* Some of the main glands in the endocrine system include the thyroid gland, which regulates bodily functions such as body temperature and heart rate; the adrenal glands, which regulate stress responses; the pancreas, which controls digestion; the sexual reproductive glands (ovaries in women and testes in men); and the pineal gland, which secretes melatonin, influencing the sleep–wake cycle. The overall functioning of the endocrine system is orchestrated by the **pituitary gland,** *the "master gland" of the body's hormone-producing system, which releases hormones that direct the functions of many other glands in the body* (see **FIGURE 3.10**).

The hypothalamus sends hormonal signals to the pituitary gland, which in turn sends hormonal signals to other glands to control stress, digestive activities, and reproductive processes. For example, when we sense a threat, sensory neurons send signals to the hypothalamus, which stimulates the release of adrenocorticotropic hormone (ACTH) from the pituitary gland. ACTH, in turn, stimulates the adrenal glands to release hormones that activate the sympathetic nervous system (Selye & Fortier, 1950). As you read earlier in this chapter, the sympathetic nervous system prepares the body either to meet the threat head on or to flee from the situation.

The Cerebral Cortex

Our tour of the brain has taken us from the very small (neurons) to the very large: the cerebral cortex. The cortex is the highest level of the brain, and it is responsible for the most complex aspects of perception, emotion, movement, and thought (Fuster, 2003).

A scary movie is designed to stimulate your amygdala, but only a little.   Piola666/Getty Images

hippocampus A brain structure critical for creating new memories and integrating them into a network of knowledge so that they can be stored indefinitely in other parts of the cerebral cortex.

amygdala A brain structure that plays a central role in many emotional processes, particularly the formation of emotional memories.

basal ganglia A set of subcortical structures that directs intentional movements.

endocrine system A network of glands that produce and secrete into the bloodstream chemical messages known as hormones, which influence a wide variety of basic functions, including metabolism, growth, and sexual development.

Alzheimer's Disease and the Hippocampus: Sex Differences

Alzheimer's disease (AD) is a devastating progressive brain disorder that gradually impairs and ultimately wipes out memory and other cognitive functions. AD is estimated to affect more than 5 million Americans (National Institute on Aging, https://www.nia.nih.gov/health/alzheimers-disease-fact-sheet), with 90 million cases expected worldwide by 2050 (Prince et al., 2015).

But AD does not affect men and women equally. Recently, a large group of experts concluded that AD is more prevalent among women than men in many regions of the world (Mazure & Swendsen, 2016; Winblad et al., 2016). Although scientists are just beginning to unravel the reasons this is so, recent evidence indicates that the hippocampus, a brain region critical for learning and memory, shows potentially important sex differences.

One study analyzed the volume of the hippocampus in 43 patients who had been diagnosed with probable AD and in 23 cognitively normal older adults (Ardekani et al., 2016); measurements were made several times in each individual during the course of a year, allowing researchers to assess changes over time. Overall, hippocampal volume was reduced in the AD group compared to the controls, and also declined more over the year in the patients with AD. However, the volume decline among the patients with AD progressed about 1.5 times faster in women than in men. Another study found that changes in hippocampal volume over time are more predictive of an eventual diagnosis of probable AD in women than in men (Burke et al., 2019).

These findings are potentially important clinically because they suggest that measurements of hippocampal volume might be a particularly reliable early indication of the onset of AD in women. Changes in hippocampal volume are not the only sex difference seen in AD. Compared with men, women with AD exhibit more volume decline in several other brain regions (Hua et al., 2010) and also show faster cognitive decline (Ferretti et al., 2018). Researchers and clinicians are increasingly coming to realize that these sex differences likely have important implications for diagnosis and treatment, which should ultimately help scientists craft sex-specific approaches to both diagnosis and treatment of AD (Ferretti et al., 2018; Fisher et al., 2018). Given the worldwide impact of AD, it is difficult to imagine a more important arena for the investigation of sex differences.

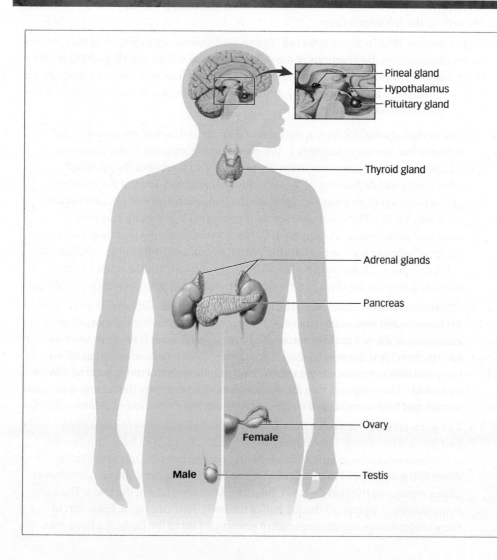

Figure 3.10   Major Glands of the Endocrine System The endocrine system is a network of glands that works with the nervous system and impacts many basic functions by releasing hormones into the bloodstream.

- Pineal gland
- Hypothalamus
- Pituitary gland
- Thyroid gland
- Adrenal glands
- Pancreas
- Ovary
- **Female**
- **Male**
- Testis

pituitary gland The "master gland" of the body's hormone-producing system, which releases hormones that direct the functions of many other glands in the body.

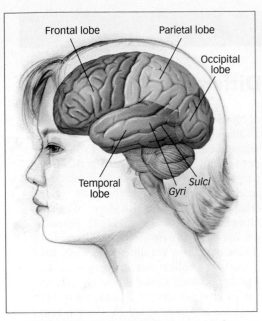

Figure 3.11 **Cerebral Cortex and Lobes**
The four major lobes of the cerebral cortex
are the occipital lobe, the parietal lobe, the
temporal lobe, and the frontal lobe.

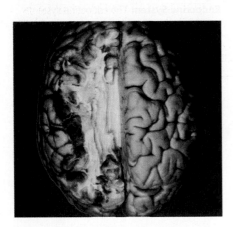

Figure 3.12 **Cerebral Hemispheres** The
corpus callosum connects the two hemispheres
of the brain and supports communication
between them. Parts of the cerebral cortex
(on the left) have been cut away to reveal the
corpus callosum below. The corpus callosum
is composed of myelin-sheathed axons, which
make it appear smooth and whitish. VideoSurgery/
Science Source

corpus callosum A thick band of
nerve fibers that connects large areas of
the cerebral cortex on each side of the
brain and supports communication of
information across the hemispheres.

It sits over the rest of the brain, like a mushroom cap shielding the underside and stem,
and it is the wrinkled surface you see when looking at the brain with the naked eye.

The cerebral cortex occupies roughly the area of a newspaper page, so fitting that
much cortex into a human skull is a tough task. But if you crumple a sheet of newspaper, you'll see that the same surface area now fits compactly into a much smaller space.
The cortex, with its wrinkles and folds, holds a lot of brainpower in a relatively small
package that fits comfortably inside the human skull (see **FIGURE 3.11**). The functions
of the cerebral cortex can be understood at three levels: the separation of the cortex
into two hemispheres, the organization of each hemisphere, and the role of specific
cortical areas.

1. **Organization Across Hemispheres** The two halves of the cortex, called the left
   and right hemispheres, are more or less symmetrical in their appearance and, to
   some extent, in their functions. However, each hemisphere controls the functions of
   the opposite side of the body. This means that your right cerebral hemisphere perceives stimuli from and controls movements on the left side of your body, whereas
   your left cerebral hemisphere perceives stimuli from and controls movement on
   the right side of your body. The two hemispheres are connected to each other by
   commissures, bundles of axons that make possible communication between parallel
   areas of the cortex in each half. The largest of these bundles is the **corpus callosum,**
   *a thick band of nerve fibers that connects large areas of the cerebral cortex on each
   side of the brain and supports communication of information across the hemispheres*
   (see **FIGURE 3.12**). This means, for example, that information received in the right
   hemisphere can pass across the corpus callosum and be registered, virtually instantaneously, in the left hemisphere.

2. **Organization Within Hemispheres** The second level of organization in the cerebral
   cortex distinguishes the functions of the different regions within each hemisphere of the
   brain. Each hemisphere of the cerebral cortex is divided into four areas, or *lobes:* From
   back to front, these are the occipital lobe, the parietal lobe, the temporal lobe, and the
   frontal lobe, as shown in Figure 3.11.

   - The **occipital lobe,** located at the back of the cerebral cortex, *processes visual
     information.* Sensory receptors in the eyes send information to the thalamus,
     which in turn sends information to the primary visual areas of the occipital
     lobe, where simple features of the stimulus are extracted, such as the location
     and orientation of an object's edges (see the Sensation and Perception chapter
     for more details). These features are then combined into a more complex
     representation of what's being seen. Damage to the primary visual areas of the
     occipital lobe can leave a person with partial or complete blindness. Information
     still enters the eyes, but without the ability to process and make sense of the
     information in the cerebral cortex, the information is as good as lost (Zeki, 2001).

   - The **temporal lobe,** located on the lower side of each hemisphere, is *responsible
     for hearing and language.* The *primary auditory cortex* in the temporal lobe is
     analogous to the primary visual areas of the occipital lobe: It receives sensory
     information from the ears (Recanzone & Sutter, 2008). Secondary areas of the
     temporal lobe then process the information into meaningful units, such as speech
     and words. The temporal lobe also houses areas that interpret the meaning of visual
     stimuli and help us recognize common objects in the environment (Martin, 2007).

   - The **parietal lobe,** located in front of the occipital lobe, carries out functions
     that include *processing information about touch.* The parietal lobe contains the
     somatosensory cortex, a strip of brain tissue running from the top of the brain
     down to the sides (see **FIGURE 3.13**). Within each hemisphere, the somatosensory
     cortex represents the skin areas on the *contralateral* surface of the body: The right
     somatosensory represents the left half of the body, and vice versa. Each part of
     the somatosensory cortex maps onto a particular part of the body. If a body area

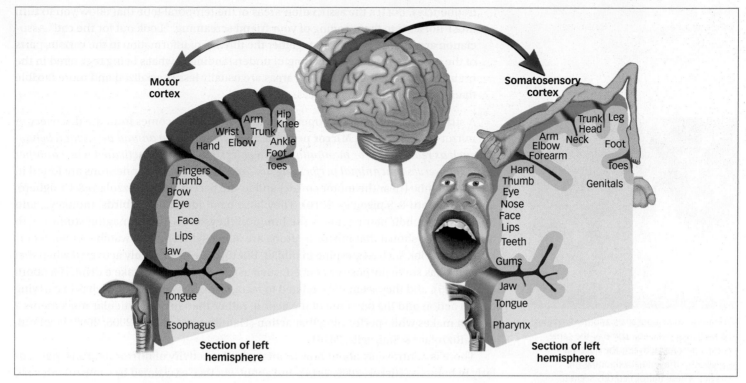

Figure 3.13 Somatosensory and Motor Cortices The motor cortex, a strip of brain tissue in the frontal lobe, represents and controls different skin and body areas on the contralateral side of the body. Directly behind the motor cortex, in the parietal lobe, lies the somatosensory cortex. Like the motor cortex, the somatosensory cortex represents skin areas of particular parts on the contralateral side of the body.

is more sensitive, a larger part of the somatosensory cortex is devoted to it. For example, the part of the somatosensory cortex that corresponds to the lips and tongue is larger than the area corresponding to the feet. The somatosensory cortex can be illustrated as a distorted figure, called a *homunculus* ("little man"), in which the body parts are rendered according to how much of the somatosensory cortex is devoted to them (Penfield & Rasmussen, 1950).

- The **frontal lobe,** which sits behind the forehead, has *specialized areas for movement, abstract thinking, planning, memory, and judgment.* In the frontal lobe, directly in front of the somatosensory cortex, is a parallel strip of brain tissue called the *motor cortex* (see Figure 3.13. Like the somatosensory cortex, different parts of the motor cortex correspond to different body parts. The motor cortex initiates voluntary movements and sends messages to the basal ganglia, cerebellum, and spinal cord, coordinating movements of muscle groups throughout the body. Other areas in the frontal lobe coordinate thought processes that help us manipulate information to plan our behaviors and interact socially with others. In short, the frontal cortex allows us to do the kind of thinking, imagining, planning, and anticipating that sets humans apart from most other species (Schoenemann et al., 2005; Stuss & Benson, 1986; Suddendorf & Corballis, 2007).

3. **Organization Within Specific Lobes** The third level of organization in the cerebral cortex involves the representation of information within specific lobes in the cortex. A hierarchy of processing stages from primary areas handles fine details of information all the way up to **association areas,** which are *composed of neurons that help provide sense and meaning to information registered in the cortex.* For example, neurons in the primary visual cortex are highly specialized: Some detect features of the environment that are in a horizontal orientation, others detect movement, and still others process information about human versus nonhuman forms. Association areas interpret the information extracted by these primary areas (shape, motion, etc.) to make sense of what's being perceived; in this case, perhaps a large cat leaping toward your face (Martin, 2007). Similarly, neurons in the primary auditory cortex register sound

occipital lobe A region of the cerebral cortex that processes visual information.

temporal lobe A region of the cerebral cortex responsible for hearing and language.

parietal lobe A region of the cerebral cortex whose functions include processing information about touch.

frontal lobe The region of the cerebral cortex that has specialized areas for movement, abstract thinking, planning, memory, and judgment.

association areas Areas in the cerebral cortex composed of neurons that help provide sense and meaning to information registered in the cortex.

frequencies, but it's the association areas of the temporal lobe that allow you to turn those noises into the meaning of your friend screaming, "Look out for the cat!" Association areas, then, help stitch together the threads of information in the various parts of the cortex to produce a meaningful understanding of what's being registered in the brain. Neurons in the association areas are usually less specialized and more flexible than neurons in the primary areas.

A striking example of this property of association areas comes from the discovery of the mirror-neuron system. **Mirror neurons** are *active when an animal performs a behavior, such as reaching for or manipulating an object, and are also activated when another animal observes that animal performing the same behavior.* Mirror neurons are found in the frontal lobe (near the motor cortex) and in the parietal lobe (Rizzolatti & Craighero, 2004; Rizzolatti & Sinigaglia, 2010). They have been identified in birds, monkeys, and humans, and their name reflects the function they serve. Neuroimaging studies with humans have shown that mirror neurons are active when people watch someone perform a behavior, such as grasping in midair. But they are more highly activated when that behavior has some purpose or context, such as grasping a cup to take a drink (Iacoboni et al., 2005), and they seem to be related to recognizing the goal someone has in carrying out an action and the outcome of the action, rather than to the particular movements a person makes while performing that action (Hamilton & Grafton, 2006, 2008; Iacoboni, 2009; Rizzolatti & Sinigaglia, 2010).

There is controversy about how to interpret the activity of mirror neurons, particularly in humans (Hickok, 2009, 2014), and about whether, as claimed by some researchers, impairments to the mirror neuron system contribute to difficulties with understanding the minds of other people, as occurs in autism spectrum disorder (Hamilton, 2013; see the chapter on Psychological Disorders). Nonetheless, the existence of mirror neurons is supported by experimental evidence (Rizzolatti & Rozzi, 2018).

Brain Plasticity

The cerebral cortex may seem to be a fixed structure, one big sheet of neurons designed to help us make sense of our external world. Remarkably, however, sensory cortices are not fixed. They can adapt to changes in sensory inputs, a quality that researchers call *plasticity* (i.e., the ability to be molded). As an example, if you lose your left middle finger in an accident, the part of the somatosensory area that represents that finger is initially unresponsive (Kaas, 1991). After all, there's no longer any sensory input going from that finger to that part of the brain. You might expect the neurons in the left-middle-finger-representing part of the somatosensory cortex to wither away. However, over time, that area in the somatosensory cortex becomes responsive to stimulation of the fingers *adjacent* to the missing finger. The brain is plastic: Functions that were assigned to certain areas of the brain may be capable of being reassigned to other areas of the brain to accommodate changing input from the environment (Feldman, 2009).

New Mapping

A striking example comes from amputees who continue to experience sensations where the missing limb would be, a phenomenon called *phantom limb syndrome*. Patients can feel their missing limbs moving, even in coordinated gestures such as shaking hands. Some even report feeling pain in their phantom limbs (Kuffler, 2018; Ramachandran & Brang, 2015). Why does this happen?

To find out, researchers stimulated the skin surface in various regions around the face, torso, and arms while monitoring brain activity in amputee and nonamputee volunteers (Ramachandran & Blakeslee, 1998; Ramachandran et al., 2010; Ramachandran et al.,

When one animal observes another engaging in a particular behavior, some of the same neurons become active in the observer as well as in the animal exhibiting the behavior. These mirror neurons seem to play an important role in social behavior.
David Longstreath/AP Images

mirror neurons Neurons that are active when an animal performs a behavior, such as reaching for or manipulating an object, and are also activated when another animal observes that animal perform the same behavior.

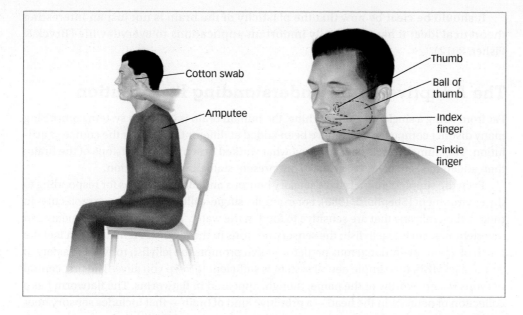

Figure 3.14 Mapping Sensations in Phantom Limbs Researchers lightly touch an amputee's face with a cotton swab, eliciting sensations in the "missing" hand. Touching different parts of the cheek can even result in sensations in particular fingers or the thumb of the missing hand.

1992). Brain-imaging techniques displayed the somatosensory cortical areas that were activated when each area of the skin was stimulated. Stimulating areas of the face and upper arm in amputees activated an area in the somatosensory cortex that previously would have been activated by a now-missing hand (**FIGURE 3.14**). Stimulating the face or arm also produced phantom limb sensations in the amputees; they reported "feeling" a sensation in their missing limbs.

Brain plasticity can explain these results (Pascual-Leone et al., 2005). The cortical representations for the face and the upper arm normally lie on either side of the representation for the hand. The somatosensory areas for the face and upper arm were larger in amputees and had taken over the part of the cortex normally representing the hand!

The Influence of Practice

Plasticity doesn't occur only to compensate for missing digits or limbs, however. An extraordinary amount of stimulation of one finger can result in that finger's "taking over" the representation of the part of the cortex that usually represents other, adjacent fingers (Merzenich et al., 1990). For instance, concert pianists have highly developed cortical areas for finger control: The continued input from the fingers commands a larger area of representation in the somatosensory cortices in the brain. Similar findings have been obtained with quilters (who have highly developed areas for the thumb and forefinger, which are critical to their profession) and taxi drivers (who have overdeveloped brain areas in the hippocampus that are used during spatial navigation) (Maguire et al., 2006).

You might be surprised to learn that plasticity is also related to physical exercise. Physical exercise can increase the number of synapses and even promote the development of new neurons in the hippocampus (Hillman et al., 2008; van Praag, 2009), and may improve brain function and cognitive performance (Colcombe et al., 2004, 2006; Prakash et al., 2015). Although these effects tend to be seen most clearly in older adults (okay, so it's time for your textbook authors to get on a treadmill), benefits have also been documented throughout the life span (Hertig & Nagel, 2012; Hillman et al., 2008). Some evidence indicates that even a single session of moderate-to-intensive exercise can boost aspects of memory and motor skills (Roig et al., 2012; Statton et al., 2015).

Keith Jarrett is a virtuoso who has been playing piano for more than 60 years. Compared with those of a novice, the brain regions that control Jarrett's fingers are likely to have expanded due to brain plasticity in the motor cortex. Jacques Munch/AFP/Getty Images

Flatworms don't have much of a brain, but then again, they don't need much of a brain. The rudimentary brain areas found in simple invertebrates eventually evolved into the complex brain structures found in humans. Blickwinkel/Hecker/Alamy

It should be clear by now that the plasticity of the brain is not just an interesting theoretical idea; it has potentially important applications to everyday life (Bryck & Fisher, 2012).

The Adaptive Brain: Understanding Its Evolution

Far from being a single, elegant machine, the human brain is instead a system comprising many distinct components that have been added at different times over the course of evolution. The human species has retained what worked best in earlier versions of the brain, then added bits and pieces to get us to our present state through evolution.

Even the simplest animals have sensory neurons and motor neurons for responding to the environment (Shepherd, 1988). For example, single-celled protozoa have molecules in their cell membrane that are sensitive to food in the water. The first neurons appeared in invertebrates, such as jellyfish; the sensory neurons in the jellyfish's tentacles can feel the touch of a potentially dangerous predator, which prompts the jellyfish to swim to safety. If you're a jellyfish, this simple neural system is sufficient to keep you alive. The first central nervous system worthy of the name, though, appeared in flatworms. The flatworm has a collection of neurons in the head — a primitive kind of brain — that includes sensory neurons for vision and taste, as well as motor neurons that control feeding behavior. Emerging from the brain is a pair of tracts that form a spinal cord.

During the course of evolution, a major split in the organization of the nervous system occurred between invertebrate animals (those without a spinal column) and vertebrate animals (those with a spinal column). In all vertebrates, the central nervous system is organized into a hierarchy: The lower levels of the brain and spinal cord execute simpler functions, while the higher levels, including the forebrain, perform more complex functions.

In lower vertebrate species such as amphibians (e.g., frogs and newts), the forebrain consists of small clusters of neurons. Reptiles and birds have a larger forebrain that includes subcortical structures, but almost no cerebral cortex. By contrast, mammals have a highly developed cerebral cortex consisting of multiple areas that serve a broad range of higher mental functions. This forebrain development has reached its peak — so far — in humans (**FIGURE 3.15**).

The human brain, then, is not so much one remarkable thing; rather, it is a succession of extensions from a quite serviceable foundation. The forebrain of a bullfrog is about as differentiated as it needs to be to survive in a frog's world. The human forebrain, however,

Figure 3.15 Development of the Forebrain Reptiles and birds have almost no cerebral cortex. Mammals such as rats and cats do have a cerebral cortex, but their frontal lobes are proportionally much smaller than the frontal lobes of humans and other primates. How might this explain the fact that only humans have developed complex language, computer technology, and calculus?

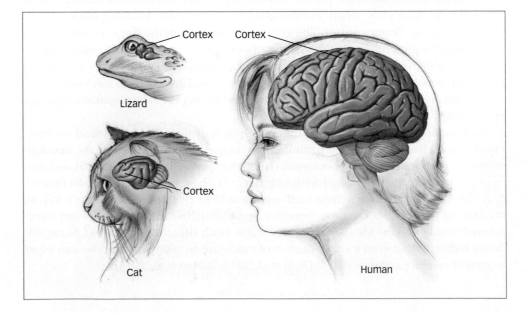

shows substantial refinement, which allows for some remarkable, uniquely human abilities: self-awareness, sophisticated language use, abstract reasoning, and imagining, among others.

Build to the Outcomes

1. Which part of the brain controls the basic functions of life, such as respiration?

2. Which part of the brain helps with orientation to the environment?

3. Which area of the brain is associated with emotional memories?

4. What is the main function of the pituitary gland?

5. Why is the part of the somatosensory cortex relating to the lips bigger than the area corresponding to the feet?

6. What types of thinking occur in the frontal lobe?

7. Give examples of research that proves that the brain is able to change because of a person's life experience.

8. What is a key structural difference between the brain of a reptile or bird, and the brain of a mammal?

Genes, Epigenetics, and the Environment

Is it genetics (nature) or the environment (nurture) that reigns supreme in directing a person's behavior? The emerging picture from current research is that both nature *and* nurture play a role in directing behavior, and the focus has shifted to examining the interaction of the two rather than the absolute contributions of either alone (Gottesman & Hanson, 2005; Rutter & Silberg, 2002; Zhang & Meaney, 2010).

What Are Genes?

A **gene** is *the major unit of hereditary transmission*. Genes are sections on a strand of DNA (deoxyribonucleic acid) that code for the protein molecules that affect traits, such as eye color. Genes are organized into large threads called **chromosomes,** *strands of DNA wound around each other in a double-helix configuration* (see **FIGURE 3.16**). Chromosomes come in pairs, and humans have 23 pairs each. These pairs of chromosomes are similar but not identical: You inherit one of each pair from your father and one from your mother. There's a twist, however: The selection of *which* of each pair is given to you is random.

All humans share about 99% of the same DNA (and almost as much with other apes), which is why we share fundamental characteristics such as breathing oxygen, developing

Learning Outcomes

- Outline the structure of a gene.
- Differentiate between monozygotic and dizygotic twins.
- Give examples of the influence of genetics and the environment to human behavior.

"The title of my science project is 'My Little Brother: Nature or Nurture.'"

Michael Shaw/The New Yorker Collection/Cartoonbank.com

gene The major unit of hereditary transmission.

chromosomes Strands of DNA wound around each other in a double-helix configuration.

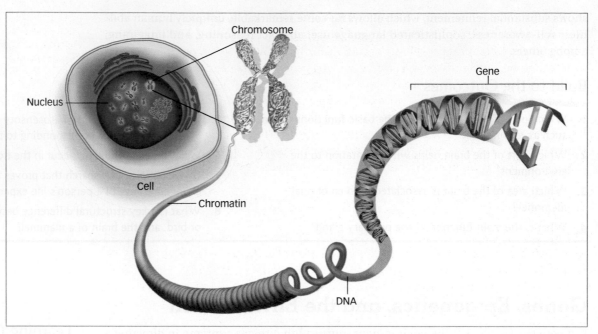

Figure 3.16 **Genes, Chromosomes, and Their Recombination** The cell nucleus houses chromosomes, which are made up of double-helix strands of DNA. Most cells in our bodies have 23 pairs of chromosomes. Genes are segments on the strand of DNA.

a central nervous system, and generating energy from mitochondria. But a portion of DNA varies across individuals, which is why different humans have different biological sexes, eye colors, earlobe shapes, and vulnerability to some diseases. These variations reflect the differences in our genes. Children share half their genes with each parent, a quarter of their genes with their grandparents, an eighth of their genes with cousins, and so on. The most genetically related people are *monozygotic twins* (also called *identical twins*), who develop from the splitting of a single fertilized egg and therefore share 100% of their genes. *Dizygotic twins* (*fraternal twins*) develop from two separate fertilized eggs and therefore share (on average) 50% of their genes, the same as any siblings who share the same parents.

Many researchers have tried to determine the relative influence of genetics on behavior. One way to do this is to compare a trait shown by monozygotic twins with that same trait among dizygotic twins. This type of research usually enlists twins who were raised in the same household so that the impact of environment (socioeconomic status, access to education, parental child-rearing practices, environmental stressors) remains relatively constant. Finding that monozygotic twins have a higher likelihood to share some trait than dizygotic twins do suggests a strong genetic influence (Boomsma et al., 2002).

Monozygotic twins (left) share 100% of their genes in common, whereas dizygotic twins (right) share 50% of their genes, the same as other siblings. Studies of monozygotic and dizygotic twins help researchers estimate the relative contributions of genes and environmental influences on behavior.
Paul Avis/Stockbyte/Getty Images; JBphoto1/Alamy

For example, if one dizygotic twin develops schizophrenia (a mental disorder we'll discuss in greater detail in the Psychological Disorders chapter), there is a 27% likelihood that the other dizygotic twin will *also* develop schizophrenia. However, this statistic rises to 50% for monozygotic twins, suggesting a strong genetic influence on the likelihood of developing schizophrenia. That sounds scarily high — but it's not 100%. That means that genetics are not the only thing determining who develops schizophrenia; environmental influences must also play a role. In short, genetics can contribute to the development, likelihood, or onset of a variety of traits. But a more complete picture of genetic influences on behavior must always take the environmental context into consideration. Genes express themselves within an environment, not in isolation.

A Role for Epigenetics

The idea that genes are expressed within an environment is central to an important and rapidly growing area of research known as **epigenetics:** *the study of environmental influences that determine how and if genes are expressed, without altering the basic DNA sequences that constitute the genes themselves.* To understand how epigenetic influences work, it is useful to think about DNA as analogous to a script for a play or a movie. The biologist Nessa Carey (2012) offers the example of Shakespeare's *Romeo and Juliet,* which has been made into several movies — but each director used Shakespeare's material in different ways, and the actors all gave different performances. Thus, the final products were considerably different from one another, even though Shakespeare's original play still exists. Something similar happens with epigenetics: depending on the environment, a gene can be expressed or not expressed without altering the underlying DNA code.

In the past decade or so, epigenetic influences have turned out to play important roles in learning and memory (Bredy et al., 2007; Day & Sweatt, 2011; Levenson & Sweatt, 2005) and in responses to stress (Zhang & Meaney, 2010). For example, among rats, some mothers spend a lot of time licking and grooming their young pups ("high-grooming" mothers), which rat pups greatly enjoy, whereas others spend little time doing so ("low-grooming" mothers). The researchers found that pups of high-grooming mothers are much less fearful as adults when placed in stressful situations, compared to the adult pups of low-grooming mothers (Francis et al., 1999; Liu et al., 1997). This doesn't simply reflect a genetic profile shared by the mother and her pups, since the same effects are obtained when the offspring of high-grooming mothers are raised by low-grooming mothers, and vice versa. Rather, nurturing behavior by high-grooming mothers triggers release of serotonin in the pups; as you learned earlier in this chapter, increased levels of serotonin are associated with elevated mood. This in turn triggers epigenetic changes which reduce the expression of genes mediating stress hormones, which in turn leads to a corresponding ability to respond more calmly to stress (Weaver et al., 2004).

The early life effects of stress have long-lasting epigenetic effects in humans too. Studies show a role for epigenetics in the persisting effects of childhood abuse in adult men (McGowan et al., 2009). These results have led both clinicians and researchers to increasingly recognize the importance of epigenetics for various psychological disorders in which early life stress is a risk factor, including depression, schizophrenia, and posttraumatic stress disorder (Kundakovic et al., 2015; Provencal & Binder, 2015). Although we are far from fully understanding the complex relationship between epigenetic changes and psychological phenomena, scientists are increasingly recognizing the relevance of epigenetics for psychology (Jones, Moore, & Kobor, 2018; Sweatt, 2019; Zhang & Meaney, 2010).

epigenetics The study of environmental influences that determine how and if genes are expressed, without altering the basic DNA sequences that constitute the genes themselves.

Rodent pups raised by mothers who spend a lot of time licking and grooming them are less fearful as adults in stressful situations. Juniors Bildarchiv GMBH/R211/Alamy

Build to the Outcomes

1. What is a gene?

2. Why do dizygotic twins share 50% of their genes, just as do siblings born separately?

3. What do epigenetic studies suggest about how early life experiences may influence whether genes are expressed?

Learning Outcomes

- Identify the three main ways that researchers study the human brain.
- Compare and contrast advantages and disadvantages of techniques used to study the brain in action.

Investigating the Brain

So far, you've read a great deal about the nervous system: how it's organized, how it works, what its components are, and what those components do. But *how* do we know all of this? Anatomists can dissect a human brain and identify its structures, but they cannot determine which structures play a role in producing which behaviors by dissecting a nonliving brain.

Scientists use a variety of methods to understand how the brain affects behavior. Let's consider three of the main ones: studying people with brain damage; studying the brain's electrical activity; and using brain imaging to study brain structure and watch the brain in action. Let's examine each of these ways of investigating the brain.

Studying the Damaged Brain

To better understand the normal operation of a process, it is instructive to identify what happens when that process fails. Much research in neuroscience correlates the loss of specific perceptual, motor, emotional, or cognitive functions with specific areas of brain damage (Andrewes, 2001; Kolb & Whishaw, 2015). By studying these instances, neuroscientists can theorize about the functions those brain areas normally perform.

The Emotional Functions of the Frontal Lobes

As you've already seen, the human frontal lobes are a remarkable evolutionary achievement. However, psychology's first glimpse at some functions of the frontal lobes came from a 25-year-old railroad worker named Phineas Gage (Macmillan, 2000). In 1848, Gage was packing an explosive charge into a crevice in a rock when the powder exploded, driving a 3-foot, 13-pound iron rod through his head at high speed (Harlow, 1868). As **FIGURE 3.17** shows, the rod entered through his lower left jaw and exited through the middle top of his head. Incredibly, Gage lived to tell the tale. But his personality underwent a significant change.

Figure 3.17 **Phineas Gage** (*a*) Phineas Gage's traumatic accident allowed researchers to investigate the functions of the frontal lobe and its connections with emotion centers in the subcortical structures. (*b*) The likely path of the metal rod through Gage's skull is reconstructed here. Warren Anatomical Museum in the Francis A. Countway Library of Medicine. Gift of Jack and Beverly Wilgus

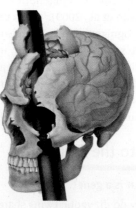

(a)   (b)

Before the accident, Gage had been mild-mannered, quiet, conscientious, and a hard worker. After the accident, he became irritable, irresponsible, indecisive, and given to profanity. The sad change in Gage's personality and emotional life nonetheless provided an unexpected benefit to psychology. His case study was the first to allow researchers to investigate the hypothesis that the frontal lobe is involved in emotion regulation, planning, and decision making.

The Distinct Roles of the Left and Right Hemispheres

You'll recall that the cerebral cortex is divided into two hemispheres, although typically the two hemispheres act as one integrated unit. Sometimes, however, disorders can threaten the ability of the brain to function, and the only way to stop them is with radical methods. This is sometimes the case for people who suffer from severe, intractable epilepsy. Seizures that begin in one hemisphere cross the corpus callosum to the opposite hemisphere and start a feedback loop that results in a kind of firestorm in the brain. To alleviate the severity of the seizures, surgeons can sever the corpus callosum in an operation called a *split-brain procedure.* The result is that a seizure that starts in one hemisphere is isolated in that hemisphere because there is no longer a connection to the other side. This procedure helps people with epilepsy but also produces some unusual, if not unpredictable, behaviors.

Normally, any information that initially enters the left hemisphere is also registered in the right hemisphere and vice versa: The information comes in and travels across the corpus callosum, and both hemispheres understand what's going on (see **FIGURE 3.18**). But in a person with a split brain, information entering one hemisphere stays there. Nobel laureate Roger Sperry (1913–1994) and his colleagues studied split-brain patients, showing that the two brain hemispheres are specialized for different kinds of tasks. For example, language processing is largely a left-hemisphere activity. So, imagine that some information came into the left hemisphere of a person with a split brain, and she was asked to describe verbally what it was. No problem: The left hemisphere has the information, it's the "speaking" hemisphere, and so she should have no difficulty verbally describing what she saw. But her right hemisphere has no

Roger Wolcott Sperry (1913–1994) received the Nobel Prize in Physiology in 1981 for his pioneering work investigating the independent functions of the cerebral hemispheres. Keystone/Getty Images

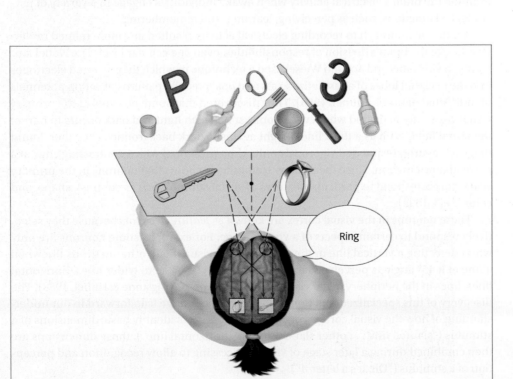

Figure 3.18 Split-Brain Experiment
When a person with a split brain is presented with the picture of a ring on the right and a picture of a key on the left side of a screen, she can verbalize "ring" but not "key" because the left hemisphere "sees" the ring and language is usually located in the left hemisphere. She would be able to choose a key with her left hand from a set of objects behind a screen. She would not, however, be able to pick out a ring with her left hand because what the left hemisphere "sees" is not communicated to the left side of her body.

Ring

electroencephalograph (EEG) A device used to record electrical activity in the brain.

Figure 3.19 **Does the EEG Read Minds?** The electroencephalograph (EEG) records electrical activity in the brain but cannot discern the content of your thoughts. Many states of consciousness, such as wakefulness and stages of sleep, are characterized by particular types of brain waves. This allows researchers to measure variables like a person's level of attention over time. Medically, the EEG can reveal abnormal patterns of activity associated with brain injuries and disorders. AJPhoto/Science Source

David Hubel (left, b. 1926) and Torsten Wiesel (right, b. 1924) received the Nobel Prize in Physiology in 1981 for their work on mapping the visual cortex. AP Photo

clue what the object was because that information was received in the left hemisphere and was unable to travel to the right hemisphere! So even though she saw the object and could verbally describe it, she would be unable to use the right hemisphere to perform other tasks regarding that object, such as using her left hand to select it from a group of objects (see Figure 3.18).

These split-brain studies reveal that the two hemispheres perform different functions and can work together seamlessly as long as the corpus callosum is intact. Without a way to transmit information from one hemisphere to the other, information remains in the hemisphere it initially entered, and we become acutely aware of the different functions of each hemisphere. Of course, a person with a split brain can adapt to this by simply moving her eyes a little so that the same information independently enters both hemispheres. Split-brain studies have continued over the past few decades and continue to play an important role in shaping our understanding of how the brain works (Gazzaniga, 2006).

Studying the Brain's Electrical Activity

A second approach to studying the link between brain structures and behavior involves recording the pattern of electrical activity of neurons. An **electroencephalograph (EEG)** is *a device used to record electrical activity in the brain.* Typically, electrodes are placed on the outside of the head, and even though the source of electrical activity in synapses and action potentials is far removed from these wires, the EEG can amplify the electric signals several thousand times. This provides a visual record of the underlying electrical activity, as shown in **FIGURE 3.19.**

Using this technique, researchers can determine the amount of brain activity during different experiences and states of consciousness. For example, as you'll read in the Consciousness chapter, the brain shows distinctive patterns of electrical activity when awake versus asleep; in fact, different brain-wave patterns are even associated with different stages of sleep. EEG recordings allow researchers to make these fundamental discoveries about the nature of sleep and wakefulness (Dement, 1978). The EEG can also be used to examine the brain's electrical activity when awake individuals engage in a variety of psychological functions, such as perceiving, learning, and remembering.

A different approach to recording electrical activity resulted in a more refined understanding of the brain's division of responsibilities, even at a cellular level. The Nobel laureates David Hubel and Torsten Wiesel used a technique in which they inserted electrodes into the occipital lobes of anesthetized cats and observed the patterns of action potentials of individual neurons (Hubel, 1988). They discovered that some neurons in the primary visual cortex are activated whenever a contrast between light and dark occurs in part of the visual field, such as a thick line of light against a dark background. They then found that each neuron responded vigorously only when presented with a contrasting edge at a particular orientation. Since then, many studies have shown that neurons in the primary visual cortex respond to particular features of visual stimuli, such as contrast, shape, and color (Zeki, 1993).

These neurons in the visual cortex are known as *feature detectors* because they selectively respond to certain aspects of a visual image. For example, some neurons fire only when detecting a vertical line in the middle of the visual field, other neurons fire when a line at a 45° angle is perceived, and still others in response to wider lines, horizontal lines, lines in the periphery of the visual field, and so on (Livingstone & Hubel, 1988). The discovery of this specialized function for neurons was a huge leap forward in our understanding of how the visual cortex works. Feature detectors identify basic dimensions of a stimulus ("slanted line . . . other slanted line . . . horizontal line"); those dimensions are then combined during a later stage of visual processing to allow recognition and perception of a stimulus ("Oh, it's a letter *A*").

Using Brain Imaging to Study Structure and to Watch the Brain in Action

The third major way that neuroscientists can peer into the workings of the human brain involves *neuroimaging techniques* that use advanced technology to create images of the living, healthy brain (Posner & Raichle, 1994; Raichle & Mintun, 2006). *Structural brain imaging* provides information about the basic structure of the brain and allows clinicians or researchers to see abnormalities in brain structure. *Functional brain imaging,* in contrast, provides information about the activity of the brain while people perform various kinds of cognitive or motor tasks.

Structural Brain Imaging

One of the first neuroimaging techniques developed was the *computerized axial tomography* (*CT*) *scan,* in which a scanner rotates a device around a person's head and takes a series of X-ray photographs from different angles. Computer programs then combine these images to provide views of the interior of the brain from any angle. CT scans show different densities of tissue in the brain. For example, the higher-density skull looks white on a CT scan, the cortex shows up as gray, and the least-dense fissures and ventricles in the brain look dark (see **FIGURE 3.20**). CT scans are often used to locate lesions or tumors, which typically appear darker because they are less dense than the cortex.

Magnetic resonance imaging (MRI) uses a strong magnetic field to line up the nuclei of specific molecules in the brain tissue. Brief but powerful pulses of radio waves cause the nuclei to rotate out of alignment. When a pulse ends, the nuclei snap back in line with the magnetic field and give off a small amount of energy in the process. Different molecules have unique energy signatures when they snap back in line with the magnetic field, so these signatures can be used to reveal brain structures with different molecular compositions. MRI produces pictures of soft tissue at a better resolution than a CT scan, as you can see in Figure 3.20. These techniques give psychologists a clearer picture of the structure and volume of the brain (see Hot Science: Big Brain, Smart Brain?) and can help localize brain damage.

Diffusion tensor imaging (DTI) is a type of MRI, developed relatively recently, that is used to visualize white matter pathways, which are fiber bundles that connect both nearby and distant brain regions to each other. DTI measures the rate and direction of diffusion or movement of water molecules along the fibers, revealing where a white matter pathway goes. DTI is a critical tool in mapping the connectivity of the human brain and it plays a central role in an ambitious undertaking known as the Human Connectome Project. This is a collaborative effort funded by the National Institutes of Health that began in 2009 and aims to provide a complete map of the connectivity of neural pathways in the brain (Toga et al., 2012).

DTI allows researchers to visualize white matter pathways in the brain, the fiber bundles that play an important role by connecting brain regions to one another. Laboratory of Neuroimaging at UCLA and Martinos Center for Biomedical Imaging at Massachusetts General Hospital, Human Connectome Project Funded by National Institutes of Health © 2013 Loni. All Rights Reserved

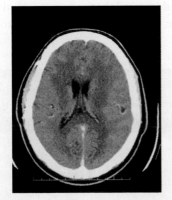
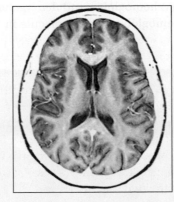

Figure 3.20 Structural Imaging Techniques (CT and MRI) CT (*left*) and MRI (*right*) scans are used to provide information about the structure of the brain and can help to spot tumors and other kinds of damage. Each scan shown here provides a snapshot as if we were viewing a single horizontal "slice" through the brain. Southern Illinois University/Science Source/Getty Images; Neil Borden/Medical Body Scans/Science Source

HOT SCIENCE

Big Brain, Smart Brain?

Is a bigger brain a smarter brain? This seemingly straightforward question has fascinated psychologists, neuroscientists, and philosophers for centuries. For example, the British psychologist Sir Francis Galton noted that study of university students who obtained high honors revealed that these students had considerably larger heads than same-aged peers (Galton, 1869, p. 156). Does that mean you should grab a tape measure to try to predict how you and your friends will do on an upcoming exam? Not so fast. Unfortunately, Galton's conclusions were based on faulty methods, such as attempting to estimate brain volume by measuring head circumference.

Modern brain-imaging techniques such as MRI have made it possible to obtain direct and precise measurements of brain volume. These studies typically report a positive correlation between brain volume and various measures of intelligence (Gignac & Bates, 2017; Pietschnig et al., 2015). But there is still debate about the strength of that correlation, and what it might mean.

A recent large-scale study by Nave and colleagues (2019) used the UK Biobank (UKB), a massive database of health-related information from volunteer participants in the United Kingdom (Miller et al., 2016). UKB has already acquired genetic data from nearly 500,000 adults and, as of April 2018, had acquired structural MRI scans from about 15,000 adults. Nave et al. (2019) used the MRI scans to calculate brain volume and compare it to several cognitive measures from those same participants.

One cognitive measure analyzed by Nave and colleagues focused on the ability to solve novel problems that demand logic and reasoning ability, which is known as *fluid intelligence* (discussed in more detail in the Intelligence chapter). They found a positive correlation between brain volume and fluid intelligence, and showed that this correlation could not be explained by age, socioeconomic status, height, or sex. However, the correlation was not strong, which suggests that brain volume accounts for only a small portion of the variation in fluid intelligence across the sample. Also, because the data are correlational, we still don't know whether larger overall brain volume causes increases in intelligence or vice versa — it is conceivable that people with higher levels of intelligence use their brain in a way that produces increased volume.

Although these results provide a solid basis for evaluating the extent to which a bigger brain is a smarter brain, you should still leave your tape measure in the drawer the next time you try to predict your or anyone else's likelihood of academic success.

Functional Brain Imaging

Functional brain-imaging techniques show researchers much more than just the structure of the brain — they allow us to watch the brain in action. These techniques rely on the fact that activated brain areas demand more energy, which is supplied by increased blood flow; and functional-imaging techniques can detect such changes in blood flow. For instance, in *positron emission tomography* (*PET*), a harmless radioactive substance is injected into a person's bloodstream. The brain is then scanned by radiation detectors as the person performs perceptual or cognitive tasks, such as reading or speaking. Areas of the brain that are activated during these tasks demand more energy and greater blood flow, resulting in a higher amount of radioactivity in that region. The radiation detectors record the level of radioactivity in each region, producing a computerized image of the activated areas (see **FIGURE 3.21**).

For psychologists today, the most widely used functional brain-imaging technique is *functional magnetic resonance imaging* (*fMRI*), which detects the difference between oxygenated hemoglobin and deoxygenated hemoglobin when exposed to magnetic pulses. Hemoglobin is the molecule in the blood that carries oxygen to our tissues,

Figure 3.21 Functional Imaging Techniques (PET and fMRI) PET and fMRI scans provide information about the function of the brain by revealing which brain areas become more or less active in different conditions. The PET scan (directly below) shows areas in the left hemisphere (Broca's area on the left; lower parietal–upper temporal area on the right) that become active when people hold in mind a string of letters for a few seconds. The yellow areas in the fMRI scans (all views to the right, each picturing a different horizontal "slice" through the brain) indicate activity in the auditory cortex of a person listening to music. © WDCN/Univ. College London/Science Source; PR. Michel Zanca/ISM/Phototake

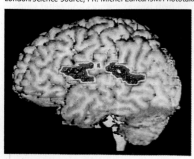

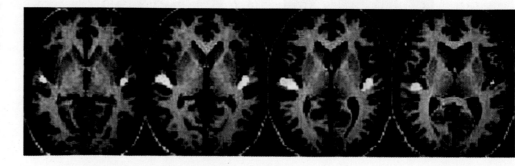

including the brain. When active neurons demand more energy and blood flow, oxygenated hemoglobin concentrates in the active areas; fMRI detects the oxygenated hemoglobin and provides a picture of the level of activation in each brain area (see Figure 3.21).

Both fMRI and PET enable researchers to localize changes in the brain very accurately. However, fMRI has a couple of advantages over PET. First, fMRI does not require any exposure to a radioactive substance. Second, fMRI can localize changes in brain activity across briefer periods than PET, which makes it more useful for analyzing psychological processes that occur extremely quickly, such as reading a word or recognizing a face.

Although the insights being obtained from fMRI are exciting, it is important that we don't get too carried away with them, as sometimes happens in media depictions of fMRI results (Marcus, 2012; Poldrack, 2018). Consider as an example the topic of memory accuracy and distortion. Some fMRI studies have shown that activity in some parts of the brain is greater during the retrieval of accurate rather than inaccurate memories (Schacter & Loftus, 2013). But that doesn't mean that we are ready to use fMRI in the courtroom to determine whether a witness is recounting an accurate memory or an inaccurate memory. For instance, we don't yet know whether the results of laboratory fMRI studies of memory, which typically use simple materials like words or pictures, generalize to the kinds of complex everyday events that are relevant in the courtroom (Schacter & Loftus, 2013). Furthermore, evidence that fMRI can distinguish accurate from inaccurate memories comes from studies in which brain activity is averaged across a *group* of participants. But in the courtroom, we need to determine whether an *individual* is remembering accurately or not, and there is little evidence yet that fMRI can do this. More generally, it is important to think carefully about how fMRI evidence is obtained before we leap to conclusions about how that evidence can be used in everyday life (Poldrack, 2018).

Transcranial Magnetic Stimulation

We noted earlier that researchers have learned a lot about the brain by studying the behavior of people with brain injuries. Scientists have discovered a way to temporarily mimic brain damage with a benign technique called *transcranial magnetic stimulation* (*TMS*) (Barker et al., 1985; Hallett, 2000). TMS delivers a magnetic pulse that passes through the skull and deactivates neurons in the cerebral cortex for a short period. Researchers can direct TMS pulses to particular brain regions (essentially turning those brain regions off) and then measure temporary changes in the way a person moves, sees, thinks, remembers, speaks, or feels.

By manipulating the state of the brain, scientists can perform experiments that establish causal relationships. For example, researchers used TMS to interfere with a region of the parietal lobe, just before people performed memory and imagination tasks (Bonnici et al., 2018; Thakral et al., 2017). TMS reduced the number of details that people remembered from past experiences and imagined in future experiences, thereby establishing that this part of the brain does play a causal role in remembering and imagining.

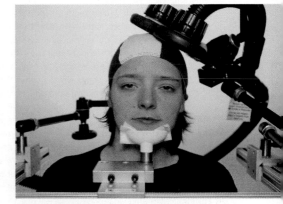

Transcranial magnetic stimulation (TMS) activates and deactivates regions of the brain with a magnetic pulse, temporarily mimicking brain damage. ASTIER/BSIP SA/Alamy

Studies suggest that TMS has no harmful or lasting side effects (Anand & Hotson, 2002; Pascual-Leone et al., 1993), and this new tool has changed the study of how our brains create our thoughts, feelings, and actions. Hopefully, the picture of human brain activity that emerges from these new methods can help to dispel common myths about the brain that remain popular even today (see Other Voices: Neuromyths).

Perhaps the most important takeaway from our review of methods for studying the brain is that each method provides psychologists with a specific type of tool for exploring how various aspects of brain structure or function are related to psychological constructs. Each method has strengths and weaknesses, so an important task for researchers is to decide which of the available tools is the most appropriate for their particular scientific question. Making that decision requires both an understanding of the possibilities and limitations of each tool, as well as framing a scientific question clearly enough to make an informed choice among the available tools.

Neuromyths

You've no doubt heard the phrase "We only use 10% of our brains," and perhaps you've wondered whether there is anything to it. Chabris and Simons (2012) discussed this and other statements about the brain that they believe to be merely myths, based in part on a study by Dekker et al. (2012):

Pop quiz: Which of these statement is false?

1. We use only 10% of our brain.

2. Environments rich in stimuli improve the brains of preschool children.

3. Individuals learn better when they receive information in their preferred learning style, whether auditory, visual, or kinesthetic.

If you picked the first one, congratulations. The idea that we use only 10% of our brain is patently false. Yet it so permeates popular culture that, among psychologists and neuroscientists, it is known as the "10% myth." Contrary to popular belief, the entire brain is put to use—unused neurons die and unused circuits atrophy. Reports of neuroimaging research might perpetuate the myth by showing only a small number of areas "lighting up" in a brain scan, but those are just areas that have more than a base line level of activity; the dark regions aren't dormant or unused.

Did you agree with the other two statements? If so, you fell into our trap. All three statements are false—or at least not substantiated by scientific evidence. Unfortunately, if you got any of them wrong, you're hardly alone.

These "neuromyths," along with others, were presented to 242 primary and secondary school teachers in the Netherlands and the United Kingdom as part of a study by Sanne Dekker and colleagues at VU University Amsterdam and Bristol University, and just published in the journal *Frontiers in Psychology*. They found that 47% of the teachers believed the 10% myth. Even more, 76%, believed that enriching children's environments will strengthen their brains.

This belief might have emerged from evidence that rats raised in cages with amenities like exercise wheels, tunnels, and other rats showed better cognitive abilities and improvements in brain structure compared with rats that grew up isolated in bare cages. But such experiments show only that a truly impoverished and unnatural environment leads to poorer developmental outcomes than a more natural environment with opportunities to play and interact. It follows that growing up locked in a closet or otherwise cut off from human contact will impair a child's brain development. It does not follow that "enriching" a child's environment beyond what is already typical (e.g., by constant exposure to "Baby Einstein"-type videos) will boost cognitive development.

The myth about learning styles was the most popular: 94% of the teachers believed that students perform better when lessons are delivered in their preferred learning style. Indeed, students do have preferences about how they learn; the problem is that these preferences have little to do with how effectively they learn. . . .

Our own surveys of the U.S. population have found even more widespread belief in myths about the brain. About two-thirds of the public agreed with

Christopher Chabris (left) is an associate professor of psychology at Union College. **Daniel Simons** (right) is a professor of psychology at the University of Illinois. Chabris and Simons coauthored *The Invisible Gorilla: And Other Ways Our Intuitions Deceive Us* (2010). Photo by Matt Milless; Courtesy Daniel J. Simons

the 10% myth. Many also believed that memory works like a video recording or that they can tell when someone is staring at the back of their head.

Ironically, in the Dekker group's study, the teachers who knew the most about neuroscience also believed in the most myths. Apparently, teachers who are (admirably) enthusiastic about expanding their knowledge of the mind and brain have trouble separating fact from fiction as they learn. Neuromyths have so much intuitive appeal, and they spread so rapidly in fields like business and self-help, that eradicating them from popular consciousness might be a Sisyphean task. But reducing their influence in the classroom would be a good start.

If for some perverse reason you want to annoy the instructor of your psychology course, you probably could do no better than to claim that "we use only 10% of our brains." Even though, as pointed out by Chabris and Simons (2012), a surprisingly high proportion of elementary and secondary school teachers subscribe to this myth, we don't know any psychologists teaching courses like the one you are taking who would endorse it, and we hope that there aren't any. How did the myth get started? Nobody really knows. Some think it may have arisen from a quotation by the great psychologist William James ("We are making use of only a small part of our possible mental and physical resources") or that it possibly owes to Albert Einstein's attempt to make sense of his own massive intellect (Boyd, 2008).

The key point for our purposes is that when you hear such bold claims from, say, a friend who heard it from somebody else: It's time for you to put into action the kinds of critical thinking skills that we focus on in this text and start asking questions: What's the evidence for the claim? Is there a specific study or studies that your friend can name to provide evidence in support of the claim? Are any such studies published in peer-reviewed scientific journals? Has the finding been replicated? Tall tales such as the 10% myth don't stand much chance of surviving for long if claims for their existence are met head on with critical thinking.

Build to the Outcomes

1. How have brain disorders been central to the study of specific areas of the brain?

2. What role does the corpus callosum play in behavior?

3. How does the EEG record electrical activity in the brain?

4. Compare what can be learned from structural brain imaging with results from functional brain imaging.

5. What does an fMRI track in an active brain?

6. Why should we avoid jumping to conclusions based on fMRI results?

CHAPTER REVIEW

Neurons: The Origin of Behavior

- Neurons process information received from the outside world, communicate with each other, and send messages to the body's muscles and organs.

- Neurons are composed of three major parts: the cell body, dendrites, and the axon. The cell body contains the nucleus, which houses the organism's genetic material. Dendrites receive sensory signals from other neurons and transmit this information to the cell body. Axons carry signals from the cell body to other neurons or to muscles and organs in the body.

- Neurons are separated by a small gap, which is part of the synapse across which signals are transmitted from one neuron to another.

- Glial cells provide support for neurons, usually in the form of the myelin sheath, which coats the axon to facilitate the transmission of information.

- The three major types of neurons include sensory neurons, motor neurons, and interneurons.

The Actions of Neurons: Information Processing

- The neuron's resting potential is due to differences in concentrations of ions inside and outside the cell membrane.

- If electric signals inside the neuron reach a threshold, this initiates an action potential, an all-or-none signal that moves down the entire length of the axon.

- Communication between neurons takes place through synaptic transmission, when an action potential triggers release of neurotransmitters that travel across the synapse to bind with receptors in the receiving neuron's dendrite.

- Some of the major neurotransmitters are acetylcholine (ACh), dopamine, glutamate, GABA, norepinephrine, serotonin, and endorphins.

- Drugs can affect behavior by acting as agonists that facilitate the actions of neurotransmitters, or as antagonists that block or diminish the action of neurotransmitters.

The Organization of the Nervous System

- The nervous system is divided into the peripheral and the central nervous systems. The central nervous system is composed of the spinal cord and the brain.

- The peripheral nervous system connects the central nervous system with the rest of the body. It is itself divided into the somatic nervous system, which controls voluntary muscles, and the autonomic nervous system, which automatically controls the body's organs.

- The autonomic nervous system is further divided into the sympathetic nervous system, which prepares the body for action in threatening situations, and the parasympathetic nervous system, which returns the body to its normal state.

- The spinal cord can control some basic behaviors, such as spinal reflexes, without input from the brain.

Structure of the Brain

- The brain can be divided into the hindbrain, midbrain, and forebrain.

- The hindbrain generally coordinates information coming into and out of the spinal cord with structures such as the medulla (which coordinates breathing and heart rate), the reticular formation (which regulates sleep and arousal), the cerebellum (which coordinates fine motor skills), and the pons (which communicates information from the cerebellum to the cortex).

- The structures of the midbrain coordinate functions such as orientation to the environment and movement toward sensory stimuli.

- The forebrain houses subcortical structures, such as the thalamus, hypothalamus, limbic system (including the hippocampus and amygdala), and basal ganglia; all these structures perform a variety of functions related to motivation and emotion.

- The endocrine system works closely with the nervous system to regulate thoughts, emotions, and behaviors through the release of hormones.

- The cerebral cortex is part of the forebrain and is composed of two hemispheres with four lobes each (occipital, parietal, temporal, and frontal). The cerebral cortex performs tasks that help make us fully human: thinking, planning, judging, perceiving, and behaving purposefully and voluntarily.

- Neurons in the brain can be shaped by experience and by the environment, making the human brain amazingly plastic.

- Nervous systems evolved from simple collections of sensory and motor neurons in simple animals (e.g., flatworms) to the elaborate centralized nervous systems found in mammals. Compared to other animals, mammals have a highly developed cerebral cortex.

Genes, Epigenetics, and the Environment

- The gene, or the unit of hereditary transmission, is built from strands of DNA in a double-helix formation that is organized into chromosomes.

- Monozygotic twins share 100% of their genes, whereas dizygotic twins share 50%, the same as any other siblings.

- Epigenetics refers to the study of environmental influences that determine whether genes are expressed, without altering the basic DNA sequences that constitute the genes themselves. Epigenetic influences play a critical role in the persisting effects of early experiences in rats and humans.

- Both genes and the environment work together to influence behavior.

Investigating the Brain

- The brain can be investigated by observing how perceptual, motor, intellectual, and emotional capacities are affected after brain damage in particular areas of the brain.

- Patterns of electrical activity in large brain areas can be examined from outside the skull, using the electroencephalograph (EEG). Single-cell recordings can indicate which neurons represent particular kinds of stimuli or control particular aspects of behavior.

- Functional brain imaging, such as PET and fMRI, can be used to scan the brain as people perform different perceptual or intellectual tasks, helping to identify which brain areas are involved in specific types of perceptual, motor, cognitive, or emotional processing.

Key Concept Quiz

1. Signals are transmitted from one neuron to another
   a. across a synapse.
   b. through a glial cell.
   c. by the myelin sheath.
   d. in the cell body.

2. Which type of neuron receives information from the external world and conveys this information to the brain via the spinal cord?
   a. sensory neuron
   b. motor neuron
   c. interneuron
   d. axon

3. An electric signal that is conducted along the length of a neuron's axon to the synapse is called a(n)
   a. resting potential.
   b. action potential.
   c. myelin sheath.
   d. ion.

4. The chemicals that transmit information across the synapse to a receiving neuron's dendrites are called
   a. vesicles.
   b. terminal buttons.
   c. postsynaptic neurons.
   d. neurotransmitters.

5. The _____ nervous system automatically controls the organs of the body.
   a. autonomic
   b. parasympathetic
   c. sympathetic
   d. somatic

6. Which part of the hindbrain coordinates fine motor skills?
   a. the medulla
   b. the cerebellum
   c. the pons
   d. the tegmentum

7. What part of the brain is involved in movement and arousal?
   a. the hindbrain
   b. the midbrain
   c. the forebrain
   d. the reticular formation

8. The _____ regulates body temperature, hunger, thirst, and sexual behavior.
   a. cerebral cortex
   b. pituitary gland
   c. hypothalamus
   d. hippocampus

9. What explains the apparent beneficial effects of cardiovascular exercise on aspects of brain function and cognitive performance?
   a. the different sizes of the somatosensory cortices
   b. the position of the cerebral cortex
   c. specialization of association areas
   d. neuron plasticity

10. Genes can be expressed or not expressed depending on the
   a. individual characteristics.
   b. range of variation.
   c. environment.
   d. behavioral standards.

11. Which of these is NOT a function of a neuron?
   a. processing information
   b. communicating with other neurons
   c. nutritional provision
   d. sending messages to organs and muscles

12. Signals from other neurons are received and related to the cell body by
   a. the nucleus.
   b. dendrites.
   c. axons.
   d. glands.

13. When you feel threatened, your _____ nervous system prepares you to either fight or run away.
   a. central
   b. somatic
   c. sympathetic
   d. parasympathetic

14. In the history of evolution, the first true central nervous system appeared in
   a. flatworms.
   b. jellyfish.
   c. reptiles.
   d. early primates.

15. Using _____, researchers can observe relationships between energy consumption in certain brain areas and specific cognitive and behavioral events.
   a. functional brain imaging
   b. electroencephalography
   c. inserting electrodes into individual cells
   d. CT scans

LearningCurve Don't stop now! Quizzing yourself is a powerful study tool. Go to LaunchPad to access the LearningCurve adaptive quizzing system and your own personalized learning plan. Visit launchpadworks.com.

Key Terms

neurons (p. 54)

cell body (soma) (p. 54)

dendrite (p. 54)

axon (p. 54)

myelin sheath (p. 54)

glial cells (p. 54)

synapse (p. 55)

sensory neurons (p. 56)

motor neurons (p. 56)

interneurons (p. 56)

resting potential (p. 56)

action potential (p. 57)

refractory period (p. 58)

terminal buttons (p. 59)

neurotransmitters (p. 59)

receptors (p. 59)

agonists (p. 61)

antagonists (p. 61)

nervous system (p. 62)

central nervous system (CNS) (p. 62)

peripheral nervous system (PNS) (p. 62)

somatic nervous system (p. 62)

autonomic nervous system (ANS) (p. 62)

sympathetic nervous system (p. 63)

parasympathetic nervous system (p. 63)

spinal reflexes (p. 64)

hindbrain (p. 65)

medulla (p. 65)

reticular formation (p. 65)

cerebellum (p. 65)

pons (p. 66)

cerebral cortex (p. 67)

subcortical structures (p. 67)

thalamus (p. 67)

hypothalamus (p. 67)

hippocampus (p. 68)

amygdala (p. 68)

basal ganglia (p. 68)

endocrine system (p. 68)

pituitary gland (p. 68)

corpus callosum (p. 70)

occipital lobe (p. 70)

temporal lobe (p. 70)

parietal lobe (p. 70)

frontal lobe (p. 71)

association areas (p. 71)

mirror neurons (p. 72)

gene (p. 75)

chromosomes (p. 75)

epigenetics (p. 77)

electroencephalograph (EEG) (p. 80)

Changing Minds

1. While watching late-night TV, you come across an infomercial for all-natural BrainGro. "It's a well-known fact that most people use only 10% of their brain," the spokesman promises, "but with BrainGro you can increase that number from 10 to 99%!" Why should you be skeptical of the claim that we use only 10% of our brains? What would happen if a drug actually increased neuronal activity 10-fold?

2. Your friend has been feeling depressed and has gone to a psychiatrist for help. "He prescribed a medication that's supposed to increase serotonin in my brain. But my feelings depend on me, not on a bunch of chemicals in my head," she tells you. What examples could you give your friend to convince her that hormones and neurotransmitters really do influence our cognition, mood, and behavior?

3. A classmate has read the section in this chapter about the evolution of the central nervous system. "Evolution is just a theory," he says. "Not everyone believes in it. And even if it's true that we're all descended from monkeys, that doesn't have anything to do with the psychology of humans alive today." What is your friend misunderstanding about evolution? How would you explain to him the relevance of evolution to modern psychology?

4. A news program reports on a study (Hölzel et al., 2011) in which people who practiced meditation for about 30 minutes a day for 8 weeks showed changes in their brains, including increases in the size of the hippocampus and the amygdala. You tell a friend, who's skeptical, about these results. "The brain doesn't change like that. Basically, the brain you're born with is the brain you're stuck with for the rest of your life," your friend says. Why is her statement wrong? What are several specific ways in which experience can change the brain?

5. A friend of yours announces that he's figured out why he's bad at math. "I read it in a book," he says. "Left-brained people are analytical and logical, but right-brained people are creative and artistic. I'm an art major, so I must be right-brained, and that's why I'm not good at math." Why is your friend's view too simplistic?

Answers to Key Concept Quiz

1. a; 2. a; 3. b; 4. d; 5. a; 6. b; 7. b; 8. c; 9. d; 10. c; 11. c; 12. b; 13. c; 14. a; 15. a

LaunchPad macmillan learning — LaunchPad features the full e-book of *Introducing Psychology*, the LearningCurve adaptive quizzing system, videos, and a variety of activities to boost your learning. Visit LaunchPad at launchpadworks.com.

Sensation and Perception

Sensation and Perception
Are Distinct Activities

Visual Pathways:
Connections Between the
Eye and the Brain

Visual Perception:
Recognizing What We See

Hearing: More Than Meets
the Ear

The Body Senses: More
Than Skin Deep

The Chemical Senses:
Adding Flavor

Daniel Kish is a middle-aged Californian with master's degrees in psychology and education. Growing up, he wanted to be a either a pilot or Batman. He enjoys making music, solo hiking, and mountain biking. He founded and now leads a nonprofit organization and spends much of his time teaching children. Daniel is also totally blind.

When Daniel was a year old, he had to have both eyes removed because of cancer. He "sees" using a form of echolocation, or sonar, rather like that used by bats and dolphins. He clicks his tongue quietly against the roof of his mouth (once every few seconds) as he moves around the world. The clicks are reflected off physical surfaces — trees, walls, fences, lampposts — and Daniel uses the echoes of these clicks to create a mental image of his environment. The echoes inform Daniel about the location of objects, their size and shape, and even what they are made of. The images that are created using this "flash sonar" technique are not as precise as vision would be, but they are informative about the space around him. Daniel says, "You do get a continuous sort of vision, the way you might if you used flashes to light up a darkened scene. It comes into clarity and focus with every flash. . . . You have a depth of structure, and you have position and dimension. You also have a pretty strong sense of density and texture that are sort of like the color, if you will, of flash sonar" (Hurst, 2017). The visual analogies are apt: Recent brain-imaging studies demonstrate that blind users of flash sonar, including Daniel, activate the "visual" parts of their brain, in the occipital lobe, when they are actively echolocating (Thaler et al., 2011).

Daniel taught himself flash sonar as a child so that he could be active and independent. He now teaches blind people of all ages to use echolocation through his nonprofit World Access for the Blind. Daniel, and other blind people who use echolocation, teach us all that, with enough practice, we can all change our brains to do amazing things, even "see" like bats, even if we can't all be Batman.

In this chapter, we'll explore the nature of sensation and perception. We'll look at how physical energy in the world around us is encoded by our senses, is sent to the brain, and then enters our conscious awareness. We'll devote a fair amount of space to understanding how the visual system works. Then we'll discuss how we perceive sounds such as words or music or noise, followed by the body senses, emphasizing touch, pain, and balance. We'll end with the chemical senses of smell and taste, which together allow you to savor the foods you eat. But before doing any of that, we will first distinguish between sensation and perception, to illustrate how perception depends on knowledge and experience as well as on sensory information.

Daniel Kish, who has been totally blind since birth, enjoys solo trips in the mountains of his native California. Volker Corell Photography

Learning Outcomes

- Distinguish between sensation and perception.
- Explain what transduction is.
- Give examples of how sensation and perception are measured.

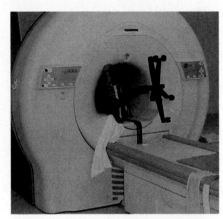

When someone accidentally rolled an office chair into a room containing an MRI system, it flew across the room to the magnet and got stuck as soon as it entered the strong field of the magnet. Some animals can sense magnetic fields, but people can't, which is why accidents like this happen. Provided courtesy of Simply Physics at simplyphysics.com

sensation Simple stimulation of a sense organ.

perception The organization, identification, and interpretation of a sensation in order to form a mental representation.

transduction The process whereby sense receptors convert physical signals from the environment into neural signals that are sent to the central nervous system.

sensory adaptation The process whereby sensitivity to prolonged stimulation tends to decline over time as an organism adapts to current (unchanging) conditions.

Sensation and Perception Are Distinct Activities

Sensation is *simple stimulation of a sense organ*. It is the basic registration of light, sound, pressure, odor, or taste as parts of your body interact with the physical world. As a sensation is registered in your brain, **perception** is the *organization, identification, and interpretation of a sensation in order to form a mental representation.*

For example, your eyes are coursing across these sentences right now. The sensory receptors in your eyeballs are registering different patterns of light reflecting off the page. Your brain is integrating and processing that light information into the meaningful perception of words. Your eyes — the sensory organs — aren't really seeing words; they're simply encoding different lines and curves on a page. Your brain — the perceptual organ — is transforming those lines and curves into a coherent mental representation of words and concepts. Damage to the brain can sometimes interfere with the interpretation of information coming from the senses. For example, particular kinds of damage to visual processing centers of the brain can interfere with the interpretation of information coming from the eyes. In this case, the senses are intact, but perceptual ability is compromised, and the person may be unable to make sense of what she sees.

Sensory Transduction and Sensory Adaptation

How do sensory receptors communicate with the brain? **Transduction** is *the process whereby sense receptors convert physical signals from the environment into neural signals that are sent to the central nervous system*. In vision, light reflected from surfaces provides the eyes with information about the shape, color, and position of objects. In hearing, vibrations (e.g., from vocal cords or a guitar string) cause changes in air pressure that propagate through space to a listener's ears. In touch, the pressure of a surface against the skin signals its shape, texture, and temperature. In taste and smell, molecules dispersed in the air or dissolved in saliva reveal the identity of substances that we may or may not want to eat. In each case, physical energy from the world is converted to electrical signals, which are interpreted by your brain to construct what you perceive as the world "out there."

Our senses act like gates. They allow a limited amount of information in and do not admit other information. For example, bats, rats, and mice communicate with each other using high sound frequencies that humans cannot hear; bees and butterflies find food by seeing "colors" we cannot see. Some animals navigate by sensing magnetic fields that we cannot sense. The illusion of perception is that we perceive a rich, detailed, and complete world around us, despite the sensory signals that we detect being a small subset of what is "out there."

Our sensory systems act like gates in another way too: They are more sensitive to change than to constant stimulation. When you walk into a bakery, the aroma of freshly baked bread overwhelms you, but after a few minutes the smell fades. If you dive into cold water, the temperature is shocking at first, but after a few minutes you get used to it. When you wake up in the middle of the night for a drink of water, the bathroom light blinds you, but after a few minutes you no longer squint. These are all examples of **sensory adaptation,** *the process whereby sensitivity to prolonged stimulation tends to decline over time as an organism adapts to current (unchanging) conditions.*

Sensory adaptation is a useful process. Imagine what your sensory and perceptual world would be like without it. (If you had to be constantly aware of how your tongue feels while it is resting in your mouth, or how your jeans feel brushing against your legs, you'd be driven to distraction.) A sensory signal that doesn't change usually doesn't require any action, and your body discards such signals. This is another way that our bodies perceive only a subset of what is "out there."

Psychophysics

How sensitive are your sensory systems? How fast can information be registered? How quickly does adaptation happen? These are all questions that can be answered using **psychophysics,** *methods that systematically relate the physical characteristics of a stimulus to an observer's perception.* In a simple psychophysics experiment, researchers might ask people to decide whether they see a faint spot of light, for example. The intensity of the light is changed systematically, and the responses of the observer (yes or no) are recorded as a function of intensity.

The simplest measurement in psychophysics is the **absolute threshold,** *the minimal intensity needed to just barely detect a stimulus in 50% of the trials.* **TABLE 4.1** lists the approximate absolute thresholds for each of the five senses. To measure the absolute threshold for detecting a sound, for example, an observer wears headphones linked to a computer. The experimenter repeatedly presents a tone, using the computer to vary its intensity, and records how often the observer reports hearing the tone at each intensity level. The outcome of such an experiment is graphed in **FIGURE 4.1**. Notice from the shape of the curve that the transition from not hearing to hearing is gradual rather than abrupt. (Want to know more about reading data distribution results? See Data Visualization: Finding the Best Way to Describe Experimental Data at www.launchpadworks.com.)

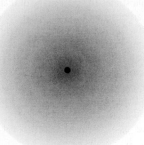

Stare at the central black dot in the image. After several seconds, the grey cloud around the dot will disappear—this phenomenon, called Troxler fading (see Simons et al., 2006), is an example of sensory adaptation.

DATA Visualization

TABLE 4.1	Approximate Sensory Thresholds
Sense	**Absolute Threshold**
Vision	A candle flame 30 miles away on a clear, dark night
Hearing	A clock's tick 20 feet away when all is quiet
Touch	A fly's wing falling on the cheek from 1 centimeter away
Smell	A single drop of perfume diffused through an area equivalent to the volume of six rooms
Taste	A teaspoon of sugar dissolved in two gallons of water

Research from Galanter (1962).

psychophysics Methods that systematically relate the physical characteristics of a stimulus to an observer's perception.

absolute threshold The minimal intensity needed to just barely detect a stimulus in 50% of trials.

Figure 4.1 Absolute Threshold This graph illustrates the percentage of trials on which an observer detected a tone at various intensity. At low intensity, the sound is very quiet, and the observer almost never detected it; at high physical intensities, the sound is very loud, and the observer almost always detected it. The absolute threshold for this tone is the intensity at which the observer detected it on 50% of the trials.

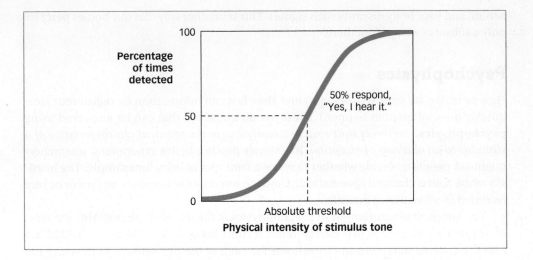

If we repeat this experiment for many different tones, we can record the thresholds for tones ranging from very low to very high pitch. People tend to be most sensitive to the range of tones corresponding to the human voice. If the tone is low enough, such as the lowest note on a pipe organ, most humans cannot hear it at all; we can only feel it. If the tone is high enough, we also cannot hear it, but dogs and many other animals can.

The absolute threshold is useful for assessing **sensitivity,** *how responsive we are to faint stimuli*; but sometimes we also want to know about **acuity,** *how well we can distinguish two very similar stimuli*, such as two tones that differ slightly in loudness or two lights that differ slightly in brightness. The **just noticeable difference (JND)** is *the minimal change in a stimulus (e.g., in its loudness or brightness) that can just barely be detected*.

The JND is not a fixed quantity; rather, it depends on the intensity of the stimulus. This relationship was first noticed by the German physiologist Ernst Weber (Watson, 1978), and is now known as **Weber's law:** *For every sense domain, the change in a stimulus that is just noticeable is a constant proportion of the standard stimulus, over a broad range of intensities.* As an example, if you picked up a 1-ounce envelope, then a 2-ounce envelope, you'd probably notice the difference between them, because the 1-ounce increase represents a doubling in weight. But if you picked up a 20-pound package, then a 20-pound, 1-ounce package, you'd probably detect no difference at all between them, because the 1-ounce increase represents only a small fraction of the original weight.

Signal Detection

The transition from not sensing to sensing is gradual (see Figure 4.1). This is because our nervous systems are noisy. Other sights, sounds, and smells in the world at large compete for attention; you rarely have the luxury of attending to just one stimulus apart from everything else. Furthermore, your expectations, motivations, and goals can all interact with what you are seeing, hearing, and smelling at any given time to influence perception. You might not perceive everything that you sense, and you might even perceive things that you haven't sensed. Have you ever been expecting a text (from a crush, or a notification of a job interview) and thought that your phone had just buzzed, but when you checked your phone, there was nothing?

Signal detection theory (SDT) is *a way of analyzing data from psychophysics experiments that measures an individual's perceptual sensitivity while also taking noise, expectations, motivations, and goals into account.* When sensory stimuli are very intense (e.g., a car alarm, or a flash of light), the sensory evidence is very strong, and background noise, which is at a much lower intensity, doesn't matter. But when sensory stimuli are faint, noise and other factors such as your expectations and motivations can strongly

sensitivity How responsive we are to faint stimuli.

acuity How well we can distinguish two very similar stimuli.

just noticeable difference (JND) The minimal change in a stimulus (e.g., its loudness or brightness) that can just barely be detected.

Weber's law For every sense domain, the change in a stimulus that is just noticeable is a constant proportion of the standard stimulus, over a broad range of intensities.

signal detection theory A way of analyzing data from psychophysics experiments that measures an individual's perceptual sensitivity while also taking noise, expectations, motivations, and goals into account.

THE REAL WORLD

Multitasking

By one estimate, using a cell phone while driving makes having an accident four times more likely (McEvoy et al., 2005). In response to highway safety experts' concerns, and statistics such as this, state legislatures are passing laws that restrict, and sometimes ban, using mobile phones while driving. You might think that's a fine idea . . . for everyone else on the road. But surely *you* can manage to punch in a number on a phone, carry on a conversation, or maybe even text-message while simultaneously driving in a safe and courteous manner. Right? In a word, *wrong*.

Talking on a cell phone while driving demands that you juggle two independent sources of sensory input—vision and hearing—at the same time. This is problematic, because research has found that when attention is directed to hearing, activity in visual areas decreases (Shomstein & Yantis, 2004). This kind of *multitasking* creates problems when you need to react suddenly while driving. Researchers have tested experienced drivers in a highly realistic driving simulator, measuring their response times to brake lights and stop signs while they listened to the radio or carried on phone conversations, among other tasks (Strayer et al., 2003). Drivers reacted significantly more slowly during phone

conversations than during the other tasks. This is because a phone conversation requires memory retrieval, deliberation, and planning what to say and often carries an emotional stake in the conversation topic. Tasks such as listening to the radio require far less attention.

Whether the phone was handheld or hands free made little difference, and similar results have been obtained in field studies of actual driving (Horrey & Wickens, 2006). This suggests that laws requiring drivers to use hands-free phones may have little effect on reducing accidents. The situation is even worse when text messaging is involved: Compared with a no-texting control condition, when either sending or receiving a text message in the simulator, drivers spent dramatically less time looking at the road, had a much harder time staying in their lane, missed numerous lane changes, and had greater difficulty maintaining an appropriate distance behind the car ahead of them (Hosking et al., 2009). Another review concluded that the impairing effect of texting while driving is comparable with that of alcohol consumption and greater than that of smoking marijuana (Pascual-Ferrá et al., 2012).

So how well do we multitask in several thousand pounds of metal hurtling down the

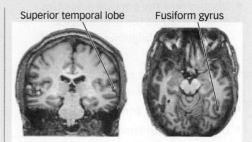

Superior temporal lobe   Fusiform gyrus

Participants received fMRI scans as they performed tasks that required them to shift their attention between visual and auditory information. When participants focused on auditory information, a region in the temporal lobe involved in auditory processing showed increased activity (yellow/orange) but a visual region, the fusiform gyrus, showed decreased activity (blue). Shomstein and Yantis, 2004, Control of Attention Shifts Between Vision and Audition in Human Cortex, The Journal of Neuroscience, 24 November 2004, 24(47): 10702–10706; Doi:10.1523/Jneurosci.2939-04.2004.

highway? Unless you have two heads with one brain each—one to talk and one to concentrate on driving—you would do well to keep your eyes on the road and not on the phone.

affect whether you perceive those stimuli. According to signal detection theory, whether you perceive a stimulus depends on two independent factors: the *strength of the sensory evidence for that stimulus*, and the *amount of evidence necessary for your perceptual system to "decide" that the stimulus is present*, known as the *decision criterion* (Green & Swets, 1966; Macmillan & Creelman, 2005). If the sensory evidence exceeds the decision criterion, the observer perceives the stimulus; if it falls short, the observer does not perceive the stimulus. The decision criterion depends on many factors, such as your expectations (are you waiting for an important call?) and the relative "badness" of different kinds of error; sometimes missing a call is better than checking your phone by mistake (when you're in the shower and it's cold out there!), but sometimes missing a call is worse. For an example of a common everyday task that can interfere with signal detection, see The Real World: Multitasking.

Build to the Outcomes

1. Differentiate between sensation and perception using, as an example, a person with healthy eyes who, after brain damage, can no longer make sense of what she reads.

2. What are the benefits of sensory adaptation?

3. By what process do sensory inputs, such as light and sound waves, become messages sent to the brain?

4. What is an absolute threshold?

5. What is a just noticeable difference?

Visual Pathways: Connections Between the Eye and the Brain

Learning Outcomes

- Discuss how the physical properties of light relate to the psychological dimensions of brightness, color, and saturation.
- Describe how the eye converts light waves into neural impulses.
- Discuss how we perceive color.
- Describe the functions of the dorsal and ventral visual streams.

Your sophisticated visual system has evolved to transduce energy in the world into neural signals in the brain. Humans have sensory receptors in their eyes that respond to wavelengths of light energy. When we look at people, places, and things, patterns of light and color give us information about where one surface stops and another begins. The array of light reflected from those surfaces preserves their shapes and enables us to form a mental representation of a scene (Rodieck, 1998; Snowdon et al., 2012). Understanding vision, then, starts with understanding light.

Sensing Light

Visible light is simply that portion of the electromagnetic spectrum that we can see, and it is an extremely small slice (see **FIGURE 4.2**). You can think of light as waves of energy. Like ocean waves, light waves vary in height and in the distance between their peaks, or *wavelengths*. Light waves vary on three physical dimensions: length, amplitude, and purity (see **TABLE 4.2**). The *length* of a light wave determines its hue, or what humans perceive as color. The intensity, or *amplitude*, of a light wave — how high the peaks

Figure 4.2 Electromagnetic Spectrum The sliver of light waves visible to humans as a rainbow of colors from violet-blue to red is bounded on the short end by ultraviolet rays, which honeybees can see, and on the long end by infrared waves, on which night-vision equipment operates. Someone wearing night-vision goggles, for example, can detect another person's body heat in complete darkness. Light waves are tiny, but the scale along the bottom of this chart offers a glimpse of their varying lengths, measured in nanometers (nm), where I nm = I billionth of a meter.

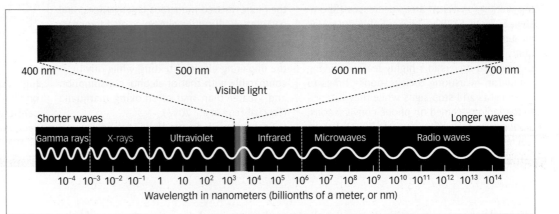

TABLE 4.2	Properties of Light Waves	
Physical Dimension		**Psychological Dimension**
Length		Hue or what we perceive as color
Amplitude		Brightness
Purity		Saturation or richness of color

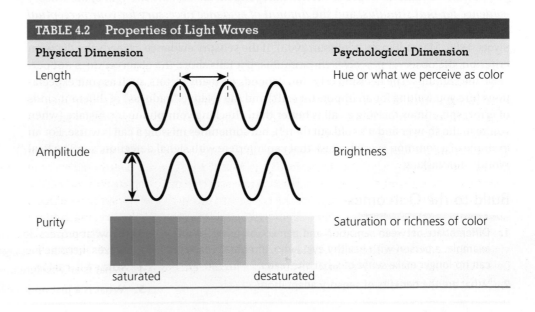

are — determines what we perceive as the brightness of light. The *purity* of a light wave refers to the degree to which a light source is emitting just one wavelength, or a mixture of wavelengths. Very pure light, consisting of just one wavelength, is perceived by humans as having high saturation, or richness of colors. Most light sources (such as the sun, fire, and incandescent lightbulbs) are composed of many different wavelengths of light: The color that is perceived depends on the relative amounts of different wavelengths in the (impure) mixture.

The Eye Detects and Focuses Light

Eyes have evolved as specialized organs to detect light. **FIGURE 4.3a** shows the human eye in cross-section. Light that reaches the eyes passes first through a clear, smooth outer tissue called the *cornea,* which bends the light wave and sends it through the *pupil,* a hole in the colored part of the eye. This colored part is the *iris,* which is a translucent, doughnut-shaped muscle that controls the size of the pupil and hence the amount of light that can enter the eye.

Immediately behind the iris, muscles inside the eye control the shape of the *lens* to bend the light again and focus it onto the **retina,** *a layer of light-sensitive tissue lining the back of the eyeball.* The muscles change the shape of the lens to focus objects at different distances, making the lens flatter for objects that are far away or rounder for nearby objects. This change is called **accommodation,** *the process by which the eye maintains a clear image on the retina.* Figure 4.3b shows how accommodation works. If your eyeballs are a little too long, images are focused in front of the retina, leading to nearsightedness (myopia). If the eyeball is too short, images are focused behind the retina, and the result is farsightedness (hyperopia). Eyeglasses and contact lenses both provide an additional lens to help focus light more appropriately, and procedures such as LASIK physically reshape the eye's existing cornea.

Light Is Converted Into Neural Impulses in the Retina

How does light become a meaningful image? The retina is the interface between the world of light outside the body and the world of vision inside the central nervous system. Two types of *photoreceptor cells* in the retina contain light-sensitive proteins that absorb light and transduce it into electrical signals. **Cones** are photoreceptors that detect color, operate under normal daylight conditions, and allow us to focus on fine detail. **Rods** are photoreceptors that become active only under low-light conditions, for night vision (see Figure 4.3c).

Rods are much more sensitive photoreceptors than cones, but they provide no information about color and sense only shades of gray. Think about this the next time you wake up in the middle of the night and make your way to the bathroom for a drink of water. Using only the moonlight from the window to light your way, do you see the room in color or in shades of gray? About 120 million rods are distributed more or less evenly around each retina except at the very center, known as the **fovea,** *an area of the retina where vision is clearest and there are no rods at all.* The absence of rods in the fovea decreases the sharpness of vision in reduced light.

Cones are far less numerous than rods. Each retina contains only about 6 million cones, which are densely packed in the fovea and much more sparsely distributed over the rest of the retina, as you can see in Figure 4.3c. Light reflected off of objects that you look at directly falls on your fovea. The high density of cones in the fovea means that these objects are seen in great detail, rather like images produced by a state-of-the-art smartphone camera. Objects outside of your direct focus — in other words, objects in your peripheral vision — aren't so clear. The light reflecting from those peripheral objects falls outside the fovea where the cell density is lower, resulting in a fuzzier, grainier image, more like a low-end smartphone camera.

The full-color image on the top is what you'd see if your rods and cones are fully at work. The grayscale image on the bottom is what you'd see if only your rods are functioning. Mike Sonnenberg/iStockphoto/Getty Images

retina A layer of light-sensitive tissue lining the back of the eyeball.

accommodation The process whereby the eye maintains a clear image on the retina.

cones Photoreceptors that detect color, operate under normal daylight conditions, and allow us to focus on fine detail.

rods Photoreceptors that become active under low-light conditions for night vision.

fovea An area of the retina where vision is clearest and there are no rods at all.

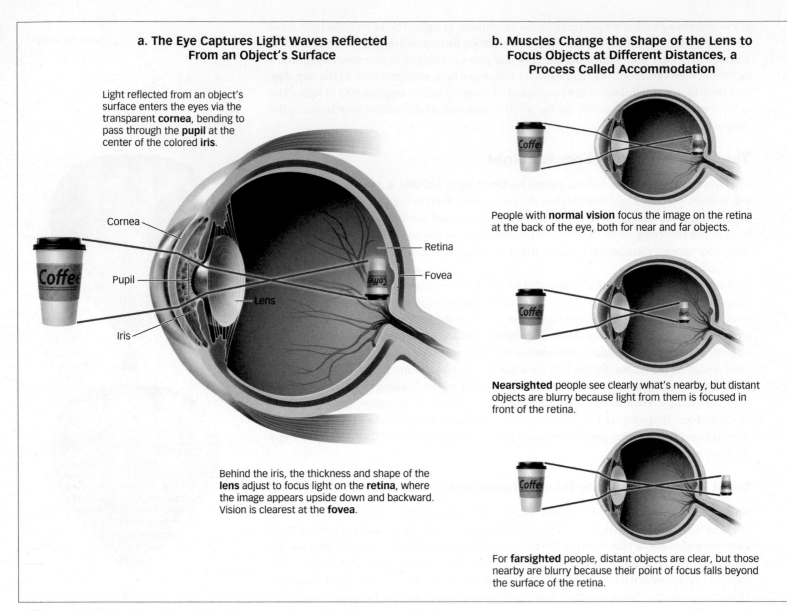

a. The Eye Captures Light Waves Reflected From an Object's Surface

Light reflected from an object's surface enters the eyes via the transparent **cornea**, bending to pass through the **pupil** at the center of the colored **iris**.

Cornea

Pupil

Iris

Lens

Retina

Fovea

Behind the iris, the thickness and shape of the **lens** adjust to focus light on the **retina**, where the image appears upside down and backward. Vision is clearest at the **fovea**.

b. Muscles Change the Shape of the Lens to Focus Objects at Different Distances, a Process Called Accommodation

People with **normal vision** focus the image on the retina at the back of the eye, both for near and far objects.

Nearsighted people see clearly what's nearby, but distant objects are blurry because light from them is focused in front of the retina.

For **farsighted** people, distant objects are clear, but those nearby are blurry because their point of focus falls beyond the surface of the retina.

Figure 4.3 The Eye Transduces Light Waves Into Neural Activity Omikron/Science Source

As seen in Figure 4.3c, the photoreceptor cells (rods and cones) form the innermost layer of the retina. Above them lies a layer of transparent neurons called the bipolar and retinal ganglion cells. The *bipolar cells* collect electrical signals from the rods and cones and transmit them to the *retinal ganglion cells (RGCs),* which organize the signals and send them to the brain. The axons of the RGCs form the optic nerve, which leaves the

The image on the left was taken at a higher resolution than the image on the right. The difference in quality is analogous to light falling on the fovea, rather than on the periphery of the retina. BackyardProduction/Thinkstock/iStock/Getty Images

c. The Retina Is the Interface Between the Eye and the Brain

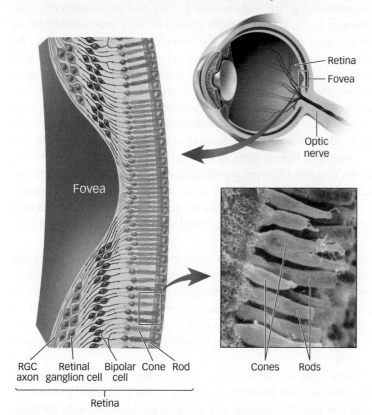

RGC axon | **Retinal ganglion cell** | **Bipolar cell** | **Cone** | **Rod**

Retina

Cones | Rods

The surface of the retina is composed of photoreceptor cells, the rods and cones, beneath a layer of transparent neurons, the bipolar and retinal ganglion cells (RGCs), connected in sequence. The axon of a retinal ganglion cell joins with all other RGC axons to form the **optic nerve**. The optic nerve creates the blind spot on the retina.

The **fovea**, the area of greatest visual acuity, is where most color-sensitive cones are concentrated, allowing us to see fine detail as well as color. Rods, the predominant photoreceptors activated in low-light conditions, are distributed everywhere else on the retina.

d. The Optic Nerve Carries the Neural Energy Into the Brain

Left Visual Field

Right Visual Field

Optic chiasm

Optic nerve

Optic tract

Lateral geniculate nucleus (LGN) in thalamus

Superior colliculus

Area V1

Objects in the right visual field stimulate the left half of each retina, and objects in the left visual field stimulate the right half of each retina. Just before the optic nerves enter the brain about half the nerve fibers from each eye cross. The left half of each optic nerve (representing the right visual field) runs through the brain's left hemisphere via the thalamus, and the right half of each optic nerve (representing the left visual field) travels this route through the right hemisphere. So, information from the right visual field ends up in the left hemisphere and information from the left visual field ends up in the right hemisphere.

eye through a hole in the retina. Because it contains neither rods nor cones and therefore has no mechanism for sensing light, this hole in the retina creates a **blind spot,** *a location in the visual field that produces no sensation on the retina.* Try the demonstration in **FIGURE 4.4** to find the blind spot in your own eyes.

The Optic Nerve Carries Neural Impulses to the Brain

Half of the axons in the optic nerve that leave each eye come from retinal ganglion cells (RGCs) that code information in the right visual field, whereas the other half code information in the left visual field. The right visual field information is relayed to the left hemisphere of the brain, while the left visual field information is relayed to the right hemisphere (see Figure 4.3d). Information first goes to the lateral geniculate nucleus (LGN), located in the thalamus of each hemisphere. As you will recall from the Neuroscience and Behavior chapter, the thalamus receives inputs from all of the senses except smell. From the LGN, the visual signals travel to the back of the brain, to a location called **area V1** (pronounced "vee-one"), *the part of the occipital lobe that contains the primary visual cortex.*

blind spot A location in the visual field that produces no sensation on the retina.

area V1 The part of the occipital lobe that contains the primary visual cortex.

Figure 4.4 Blind Spot Demonstration
To find the blind spot in your right eye, close your left eye and stare at the cross with your right eye. Hold this book 6 to 12 inches (15 to 30 centimeters) away from your eyes and move it slowly toward and away from you until the dot disappears. When that happens, the dot is in your blind spot and so is not visible. At this point the vertical lines may appear as one continuous line, because your visual perceptual system fills in the area occupied by the missing dot! To test your left eye's blind spot, turn the book upside down and repeat the experiment with your right eye closed.

Perceiving Color

Color is not something "in" light waves. In fact, the perception of color is created by our brain. If we see pure light (i.e., only one wavelength at a time), we perceive the shortest visible wavelengths as deep purple. As wavelengths become longer, the colors we perceive change gradually and continuously to blue, then green, yellow, orange, and, with the longest visible wavelengths, red. This rainbow of hues and accompanying wavelengths is called the visible spectrum, illustrated in Figure 4.2. The perception of color from mixtures of wavelengths (as emitted by most light sources) depends on the relative amounts of different wavelengths in the mixture. For example, light is seen as white in color if it contains about the same amounts of many different wavelengths across the visible spectrum, as shown in **FIGURE 4.5**. Notice that in the center of the figure, where the red, green, and blue lights overlap, the surface looks white. This is because the surface is reflecting a broad range of visible wavelengths of light, from long (red) through medium (green) to short (blue).

Rods can signal only the brightness, not the color, of the dim light to which they are sensitive. Cones, by contrast, come in three types; one type is especially sensitive to long wavelengths (L-cones), one to medium wavelengths (M-cones), and one to short wavelengths (S-cones). When light (direct from a source, or reflected off an object) hits a region of the retina, the L-, M-, and S-cones in that region are each excited to the degree that the light contains the wavelengths to which they are sensitive, as shown in **FIGURE 4.6**.

You can think of the three types of cones in the retina (L-, M-, and S-cones) as three channels of information. The relative amount of activity in each channel provides a unique code for each color you see. For example, as illustrated in Figure 4.6, light containing a wavelength of about 570 nanometers would stimulate the L-cones maximally, the M-cones somewhat less strongly, and the S-cones hardly at all, a combination we would perceive as yellowish-green.

Genetic disorders in which one of the cone types is missing — and, in some very rare cases, two or all three cone types — cause a color vision deficiency. Such disorders affect men much more often than women. Color vision deficiency is often referred to as color blindness, but in fact, people who lack only one type of cone can still distinguish many colors, just not as many as someone who has the full complement of three cone types. You can create a kind of temporary color deficiency by exploiting the idea of sensory adaptation. Just like the rest of your body, cones need an occasional break, too. Staring too long at one color fatigues the cones that respond to that color, producing a form of sensory adaptation that results in a color afterimage. To demonstrate this effect for yourself, stare

Figure 4.5 Color Mixing The millions of shades of color that humans can perceive are products of the mixture of wavelengths that sources emit or that objects reflect. Colored spotlights work by causing the surface to reflect light of a particular wavelength, which stimulates the red-, blue-, or green-sensing cones. When all visible wavelengths are present, we see white. Fritz Goro/Getty Images

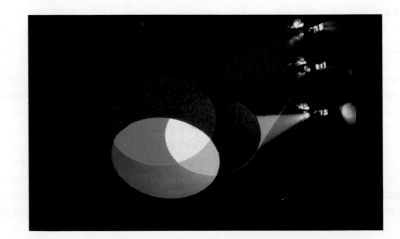

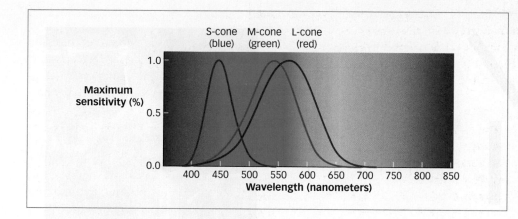

Figure 4.6 Seeing in Color We perceive a spectrum of color because objects selectively absorb some wavelengths of light and reflect others. Color perception corresponds to the relative activity of the three types of cones. The sensitivity of the three types of cones is shown by the three colored lines. Each type is most sensitive to a range of wavelengths — short (bluish light), medium (greenish light), or long (reddish light). (Data from Stockman & Sharpe, 2000.)

at the upper cross in **FIGURE 4.7** for about a minute, trying to keep your eyes as still as possible; then look at the lower cross. You should see a vivid color aftereffect that lasts for a few seconds.

Did you notice that the pinky red patch produces a greenish afterimage and the yellow patch produces a blue afterimage? When you stared at the red patch, the cones that were firing most strongly (the L-cones) became fatigued over time (recall sensory adaptation). Then when you stared at a white or gray patch, which reflects all the wavelengths equally and should make L-, M-, and S-cones equally active, the fatigued L-cones responded relatively weakly compared to the M-cones. Since the M-cones were more active than the L-cones, you perceived the patch as tinted green.

The Visual Brain

The optic nerve carries the neural impulses to area V1 in the brain (Figure 4.3d). Here, the information is systematically mapped into a representation of the visual scene.

Neural Systems for Perceiving Shape

One of the most important functions of vision involves perceiving the shapes of objects; our day-to-day lives would be a mess if we couldn't reliably distinguish between a doughnut and a stalk of celery. Perceiving shape depends on the location and orientation of an object's edges. As you read in the Neuroscience and Behavior chapter, neurons in the primary visual cortex (V1) selectively respond to bars and edges in specific orientations in space (Hubel & Wiesel, 1962, 1998). This means that some neurons fire when we perceive a vertical edge (like the side of a door or window), other neurons fire when we perceive a horizontal edge (like the top of a door or window), still other neurons fire when we perceive edges at a diagonal orientation of 45°, and so on (see **FIGURE 4.8**). All of these edge detectors work together to allow you to distinguish between a doughnut and a celery stalk.

Pathways for What, Where, and How

From area V1, visual information spreads out and is processed through 32 or more (!) distinct brain areas (Felleman & van Essen, 1991). The information spreads through two functionally distinct pathways, called *visual streams* (see **FIGURE 4.9**).

- The *ventral* (lower) *stream* travels across the occipital lobe into the lower levels of the temporal lobes and includes brain areas that represent an object's shape and identity.

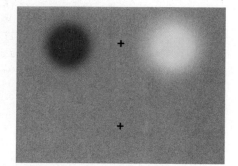

Figure 4.7 Color Afterimage Demonstration Follow the accompanying instructions in the text, and sensory adaptation will do the rest. When the afterimage fades, you can get back to reading the chapter.

Figure 4.8 Single-Neuron Feature Detectors Area V1 contains neurons that respond to specific orientations of edges. Here, a single neuron's responses (action potentials shown as pink lines) are recorded (left) as a monkey views bars at different orientations (right). This neuron fires action potentials at a high rate when the bar is pointing to the right at 45°, less often when the bar is vertical, and hardly at all when the bar is pointing to the left at 45°. Fritz Goro/The Life Picture Collection/Getty Images

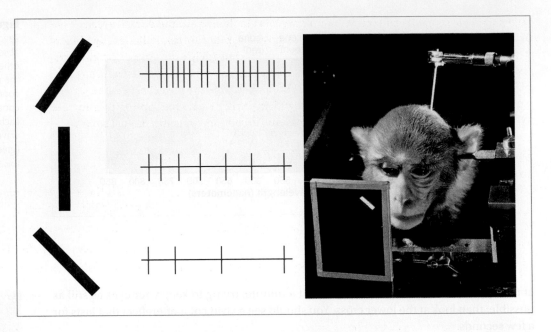

Figure 4.9 Visual Streams One pathway, the ventral stream, courses from the occipital visual regions into the lower temporal lobe, and enables us to identify what we see. Another pathway, the dorsal stream, travels from the occipital lobe through the upper regions of the temporal lobe into the parietal regions, and allows us to locate objects, to track their movements, and to act on them.

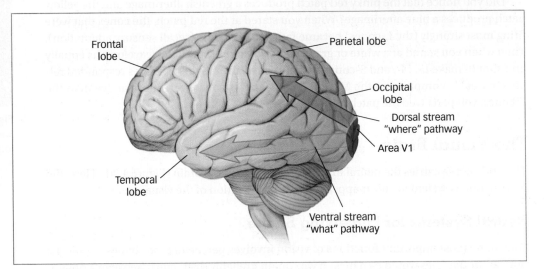

Because this stream represents what an object is, it is often called the "what" pathway (Kravitz et al., 2013; Ungerleider & Mishkin, 1982).

- The *dorsal* (upper) *stream* travels up from the occipital lobe to the parietal lobes (including some of the middle and upper levels of the temporal lobes) and includes brain areas that identify where an object is and how it is moving (Kravitz et al., 2011). Because the dorsal stream allows us to perceive spatial relations, researchers originally dubbed it the "where" pathway (Ungerleider & Mishkin, 1982). Neuroscientists later argued that because the dorsal stream is crucial for guiding actions, such as aiming, reaching, or tracking with the eyes, the "where" pathway is more appropriately called a "perception for action" pathway (Milner & Goodale, 1995).

Some of the most dramatic evidence for the existence of these two pathways comes from studying people with brain injuries. For example, a woman known as DF suffered damage to a large region in the ventral stream (Goodale et al., 1991). Her ability to identify objects by sight was greatly impaired, although her ability to identify them by touch was normal. This suggests that her *visual representation* of objects, but not her *memory* for objects, was damaged. Conversely, people with brain damage to the dorsal stream have difficulty using vision to guide reaching and grasping, but they can still identify objects they see because their ventral streams are intact (Perenin & Vighetto, 1988). We can conclude from these two patterns of impairment that the ventral and dorsal visual streams are functionally distinct. One stream may be damaged, whereas the other remains intact. Normally, though, the two streams work together during visual perception to integrate perception for identification (ventral stream) and perception for action (dorsal stream).

binding problem How the brain links features together so that we see unified objects in our visual world rather than free-floating or miscombined features.

illusory conjunction A perceptual mistake whereby the brain incorrectly combines features from multiple objects.

Build to the Outcomes

1. What are the physical and psychological properties of light waves?

2. What is the importance of the process of accommodation in the eye?

3. What is the function of the photoreceptor cells (rods and cones)?

4. What is the relationship between the right and left eyes, and the right and left visual fields?

5. How does color perception depend on the three types of cone?

6. What happens when the cones in your eyes become fatigued?

7. What are the main jobs of the ventral and dorsal streams?

Visual Perception: Recognizing What We See

Our journey into the visual system has already revealed how it accomplishes some pretty astonishing feats. But the system needs to do much more for us to be able to interact effectively with our visual world. Let's now consider in more detail how the system links together individual visual features into whole objects, allows us to recognize what those objects are, organizes objects into visual scenes, and detects motion and change in those scenes.

Binding Individual Features Into a Whole

Specialized feature detectors in different parts of the visual system analyze each of the multiple features of a visible object: orientation, color, size, shape, and so forth. Ultimately, though, these different features must somehow be integrated into a single, unified perception of an object (Nassi & Callaway, 2009). What allows us to perceive so easily and correctly that the young man in the photo is wearing a gray shirt and the young woman is wearing a red shirt? Why don't we see free-floating patches of gray and red? This is an aspect of the **binding problem**, which is *how the brain links features together so that we see unified objects in our visual world rather than free-floating or miscombined features* (Treisman, 1998, 2006).

In everyday life, we correctly combine features into unified objects so automatically and effortlessly that it may be difficult to appreciate that binding is ever a problem at all. However, occasional errors in binding can reveal important clues about how the process works. One such error is known as an **illusory conjunction,** *a perceptual mistake whereby the brain incorrectly combines features from multiple objects.* In one study, researchers briefly showed study participants visual displays in which black digits flanked colored letters, such as a red *A* and a blue *X*, and instructed the participants first to report the black digits and then the colored letters (Treisman & Schmidt, 1982). Participants frequently reported illusory conjunctions, claiming to have seen, for example, a blue *A* or a red *X* instead of the red *A* and the blue *X* that had actually been shown (see **FIGURE 4.10**). These illusory conjunctions were not just the result of guessing; they occurred more frequently than other kinds of errors, such as reporting a letter or color that was not present in the display (see Figure 4.10c).

Learning Outcomes

- List the principles of perceptual organization that allow us to recognize objects by sight.
- Describe the visual cues essential for depth perception.
- Discuss how we perceive motion and change.

We correctly combine features into unified objects. Thus, we see that the young man is wearing a gray shirt and the young woman is wearing a red shirt. Thomas Barwick/Iconica/Getty Images

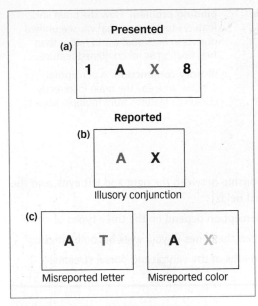

Figure 4.10 Illusory Conjunctions
Illusory conjunctions occur when features such as color and shape are combined incorrectly. For example, when participants are shown a red *A* and a blue *X*, they sometimes report seeing a blue *A* and a red *X*. Other kinds of errors, such as a misreported letter (e.g., reporting *T* when no *T* was presented) or misreported color (reporting green when no green was presented) occur rarely, indicating that illusory conjunctions are not the result of guessing (based on Robertson, 2003).

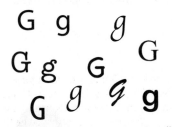

With only a quick glance, you recognize all these letters as *G*, but their varying sizes, shapes, angles, and orientations ought to make this recognition task difficult. What is it about the process of object recognition that allows us to perform this task effortlessly?

attention The active and conscious processing of particular information.

perceptual constancy The principle that even as aspects of sensory signals change, perception remains consistent.

Why do illusory conjunctions occur? Psychologist Anne Treisman and her colleagues have suggested that **attention,** which is *the active and conscious processing of particular information,* provides the "glue" necessary to bind features together. Illusory conjunctions occur when it is difficult for participants to pay full attention to the features that need to be glued together. For example, in the experiments we just considered, participants were required to process the digits that flanked the colored letters, thereby reducing attention to the letters and allowing illusory conjunctions to occur. When experimental conditions are changed so that participants can pay full attention to the colored letters, and they are able to correctly bind those features together, illusory conjunctions disappear (Treisman, 1998; Treisman & Schmidt, 1982).

Recognizing Objects by Sight

Take a quick look at the letters in the accompanying illustration. Even though they're quite different from each other, you probably effortlessly recognized all of them as examples of the letter *G*. Now consider the same kind of demonstration but using your best friend's face. Suppose one day your friend gets a dramatic new haircut — or adds glasses, hair dye, or a nose ring. Even though your friend now looks strikingly different, you still recognize that person with ease. Just like the variability in *G*'s, you somehow are able to extract the underlying features of the face that allow you to accurately identify your friend.

This may seem trivial, but it's no small perceptual feat. Machines still have difficulty recognizing objects from different points of view, or recognizing different instances of a thing, like your friend with different haircuts (Goodfellow et al., 2016). How do we humans recognize patterns, extracting the essential information that makes a *G* a *G* so accurately and effortlessly?

Some researchers argue for a *modular view,* in which specialized brain areas, or modules, detect and represent faces or houses, body parts, and even other objects (Kanwisher, 2010). For example, a classic study using fMRI to examine visual processing in healthy young adults identified a subregion in the temporal lobe that responds more strongly to faces than to just about any other object category, whereas a nearby area responds most strongly to buildings and landscapes (Kanwisher et al., 1997). Much research since is compatible with the idea that different regions of the ventral visual stream respond preferentially to different kinds of objects, such as faces, bodies, scenes, and tools (Kanwisher, 2010; Hutchison et al., 2014).

Recently, researchers have also been exploring the importance of *conceptual knowledge* in recognizing objects — the rich store of facts and other meaningful knowledge we have about a familiar object (Clarke & Tyler, 2015; Schwartz & Yovel, 2016). According to this view, when we perceive an object, we don't merely recognize what it looks like, but we understand what it is — its characteristics and significance to our behavior. There wouldn't be much use in recognizing that the thing approaching you as you cross the street is a car, not a canary, if you don't also know that cars are made of unyielding metal, travel fast, and probably cause some damage if they hit you — so you should get out of the way! An object's visual properties lead to activation of conceptual knowledge at higher levels of the ventral stream, closer to the front of the brain.

Perceptual Constancy and Contrast

The previous section provided examples of **perceptual constancy,** *the principle that even as aspects of sensory signals change, perception remains constant.* When I pick up my coffee cup, then put it down with the handle pointing in a slightly different direction, and later go to pick it up again, I don't notice that it looks slightly different than it did the last time I reached for it. Similarly, if I see my friend outside in bright sunlight, and then illuminated under blacklight in a dark club, she looks pretty much the same to me despite the light reflecting off my friend's face (and thus the signals from my retinas to my brain) being very different in the two situations. Perceptual constancy is the result of your perceptual system organizing the sensory information into meaningful objects, then stripping away potentially distracting, unnecessary sensory data entirely.

In other situations, our perceptual system exhibits **perceptual contrast,** *the principle that although the sensory information from two things may be very similar, we perceive the objects as different.* As with perceptual constancy, perceptual contrast is the result of your perceptual system organizing sensory information into meaningful objects, then stripping away potentially distracting, or even misleading, sensory data so that you can more accurately perceive what the real object is. (See A World of Difference: The Dress for an example of perceptual contrast.)

Principles of Perceptual Organization

Researchers in the Gestalt psychology movement, whom you read about in the Evolution of Psychological Science chapter, were the first to recognize that we tend to perceive not just collections of separate features but whole objects, organized in meaningful ways. We perceptually group features that belong together into one object, while we segregate features that belong to different objects. **Perceptual organization** is *the process of grouping and segregating features to create whole objects organized in meaningful ways.*

The Gestalt perceptual grouping rules govern how humans are likely to perceptually organize things. Here's a sampling:

- *Simplicity:* When confronted with two or more possible interpretations of an object's shape, the visual system tends to select the simplest or most likely interpretation. In **FIGURE 4.11a**, we perceive the complex shape as an arrow, rather than two separate shapes: a triangle sitting atop a rectangle.

- *Closure:* We tend to fill in missing elements of a visual scene, allowing us to perceive edges that are separated by an interruption (e.g., a gap) as belonging to complete objects. In Figure 4.11b, we see an arrow despite the gaps.

- *Continuity:* We tend to group together edges or contours that have the same orientation. In Figure 4.11c, we perceive two crossing lines instead of two V shapes.

- *Similarity:* Regions that are similar in color, lightness, shape, or texture are perceived as belonging to the same object. In Figure 4.11d, we perceive three columns — a column of circles flanked by two columns of triangles.

Our visual systems allow us to identify people as the same individuals even when they change such features as hairstyle and skin color. Despite the extreme changes in these two photos, you can probably tell that they both portray Emma Stone. Sundholm Magnus/action press/Shutterstock; Moviestore/Shutterstock

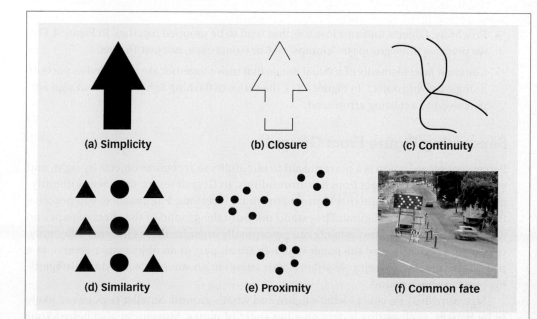

(a) Simplicity   (b) Closure   (c) Continuity

(d) Similarity   (e) Proximity   (f) Common fate

Figure 4.11 Perceptual Grouping Rules Principles first identified by Gestalt psychologists and now supported by a wealth of experimental evidence demonstrate that the brain is predisposed to impose order on incoming sensations in particular ways. This is probably largely due to experience gathered while moving around and interacting with the world, although some principles may be hard-wired from birth. Tony Freeman/Photo Edit

perceptual contrast The principle that although the sensory information from two things may be very similar, we perceive the objects as different.

perceptual organization The process of grouping and segregating features to create whole objects organized in meaningful ways.

A WORLD OF DIFFERENCE

The Dress

On February 25, 2015, a Tumblr user posted a picture of a dress — and triggered a firestorm on social media. The user explained that her friends were divided on the color of the dress — some saw it as white and gold, others as blue and black. Who was right? Over the next 2 days, the post attracted over 400,000 notes on Tumblr. Friends and families across the globe nearly came to blows over the color of the dress, as people insisted that their perception was the correct one and failed to believe that others could see it so differently. In photos of the dress under different lighting conditions posted by the online retailer that sold it, the dress was unambiguously blue and black.

Vision scientists have begun to grapple with the mystery of the dress, and though we don't yet fully understand why people see its color so differently, we do have some clues. Researchers suggest that perception of the dress's color is heavily influenced by how people perceive the lighting of the room where the photo was taken (Lafer-Sousa & Conway, 2017; Gegenfurtner et al., 2015; Uchikawa et al., 2017; Winkler et al., 2015); the lighting is highly ambiguous and thus subject to different interpretations. Daylight consists of both "cool" (perceived as blue) short-wavelength components and

What colors do you see in the dress? Our perceptions of background lighting influence how we perceive the colors.

"warm" (perceived as yellowish) medium wavelengths. If you perceive the lighting in the room as "cool" and "bluish," then your visual system assigns the medium wavelengths to the dress, which you then see as white/gold. But if you perceive the room lighting as "warm" and "yellowish," your visual system attributes the short wavelengths to the dress and you see it as blue/black (Uchikawa et al., 2017).

Still, this hypothesis just raises the question of why some people see the lighting of the room as "cool," while others see it as "warm." Though still not fully understood, "the dress" highlights an important lesson in perceptual contrast. The same stimulus can be seen as very different colors, depending on how we interpret the light hitting it. The colors we perceive are not simply inherent properties of an object; they instead represent our visual system's best guess about color on the basis of complex patterns of incoming sensory data as well as our past experiences.

- *Proximity:* Objects that are close together tend to be grouped together. In Figure 4.11e, we perceive three groups or "clumps" of 5 or 6 dots each, not just 16 dots.
- *Common fate:* Elements of a visual image that move together are perceived as parts of a single moving object. In Figure 4.11f, the series of flashing lights in the road sign are perceived as a moving arrowhead.

Separating Figure From Ground

Perceptual organization is a powerful aid to our ability to recognize objects by sight, and visually separate an object from its surroundings. In Gestalt terms, this means identifying a *figure* apart from the (back)*ground* in which it resides. For instance, you perceive the words on a page as figural: They stand out from the ground of the sheet of paper on which they're printed. You certainly can perceptually organize these elements differently, of course: The words and the paper together are all part of an object you perceive as a page. Typically, our perceptual systems focus attention on some objects, while disregarding others as background.

Size provides one clue to what's figure and what's ground: Smaller regions are likely to be figures, such as tiny letters on a big sheet of paper. Movement also helps: Your instructor is (we hope) a dynamic lecturer, moving around in a static environment, so you perceive your instructor as figure against the background of the classroom.

Figure and ground can also swap roles. A famous illusion called the Rubin vase illustrates this. You can view this "face–vase" illusion in **FIGURE 4.12** in two ways: either as a vase on a black background or as a pair of silhouettes facing each other. Your visual system settles on one or the other interpretation and fluctuates between them every few seconds. This happens because the edge that separates figure and ground equally defines the contours of the vase and the contours of the faces. Evidence from fMRI brain-imaging studies shows that when people are seeing the Rubin image as faces, there is greater activity in the face-selective region of the temporal lobe than when they are seeing it as a vase (Hasson et al., 2001).

Perceiving Depth and Size

Objects in the world (e.g., tables) generally have three dimensions — length, width, and depth — but the retinal image contains only two dimensions, length and width. How does the brain process a flat, 2-D retinal image so that we perceive the depth of an object and how far away it is? The answer is that we have to make an educated guess: educated because our long experience moving around in a 3-D world has taught us that various visual cues indicate depth and distance.

Monocular Depth Cues

Monocular depth cues are *aspects of a scene that yield information about depth when viewed with only one eye.* For instance, even when you have one eye closed, the retinal image of an object grows smaller as that object moves farther away and larger as it moves closer. Our brains routinely use these differences in retinal image size, or *relative size,* to perceive distance. Most adults, for example, fall within a narrow range of heights (perhaps 5–6 feet tall), so retinal image size alone is usually a reliable cue to how far away they are. Our perceptual system automatically corrects for size differences and attributes them to differences in distance. **FIGURE 4.13** demonstrates how strong this effect is.

In addition to relative size, there are several more monocular depth cues, such as:

- *Linear perspective:* Parallel lines seem to converge as they recede into the distance (see **FIGURE 4.14a**).

Figure 4.12 Ambiguous Edges Here's how Rubin's classic illusion works: Fix your eyes on the center of the image. Your perception will alternate between a vase and facing silhouettes, even as the sensory stimulation remains constant.

Figure 4.13 Relative Size When you view images of things that have a familiar size, such as the people in the left-hand photo, your perceptual system automatically interprets the smaller object as the same size as the nearer one, but farther away. With a little image manipulation, you can see in the right-hand photo that the relative size is far greater than you perceive. The image of the person in the blue vest is exactly the same size in both photos. The Photo Works

monocular depth cues Aspects of a scene that yield information about depth when viewed with only one eye.

Figure 4.14 Monocular Depth Cues You can rely on cues such as linear perspective (a), texture gradient (b), interposition (c), and relative height (d) to infer distance, depth, and position, even with only one eye.
(a) DC Productions/Exactostock-1598/Superstock; (b) Age fotostock/Superstock; (c) NP-E07/iStock/Getty Images Plus; (d) Rob Blakers/Lonely Planet Images/Getty Images

(a)

(b)

(c)

(d)

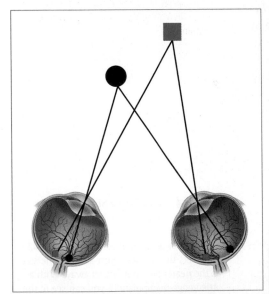

Figure 4.15 Binocular Disparity We see the world in three dimensions because our eyes are a distance apart, so the image of an object falls on a slightly different place on the retina of each eye. In this scene, the images of the square and the circle fall on different points of the retina in each eye. The disparity in positions of the retinal images provides a compelling cue to depth.

binocular disparity The difference in the retinal images of the two eyes that provides information about depth.

- *Texture gradient:* Textures such as parched ground look more detailed close up but more uniform and smoother when farther away (see Figure 4.14b).
- *Interposition:* When one object partly blocks another, the blocking object is closer than the blocked object (e.g., the cherries are closer than the apples in Figure 4.14c).
- *Relative height:* Objects that are closer to you tend to be lower in a visual scene (or in your visual field of view), whereas faraway objects are higher up in your field of view (see Figure 4.14d).

Binocular Depth Cues

We can also obtain information through **binocular disparity,** *the difference in the retinal images of the two eyes.* Because our eyes are slightly separated, each registers a slightly different view of the world. Your brain computes the difference (disparity) between the two retinal images to perceive how far away objects are, as shown in **FIGURE 4.15**. If the images fall in very similar places on the two retinas, demonstrating little disparity, the object is perceived as farther away; if the images are more disparate in their retinal location, the object is perceived as closer. 3-D movies work by showing a slightly different image to each eye to evoke a vivid sense of depth.

Illusions of Depth and Size

The ambiguous relation between size and distance has been used to create elaborate illusions that depend on fooling the visual system about how far away objects are. These illusions depend on the same principle: When you view two objects that project the same retinal image size, the object you perceive as farther away will be perceived as larger. A famous example is the Ames room, a room that is trapezoidal in shape rather than square (see **FIGURE 4.16a**). A person standing in one corner of an Ames room is

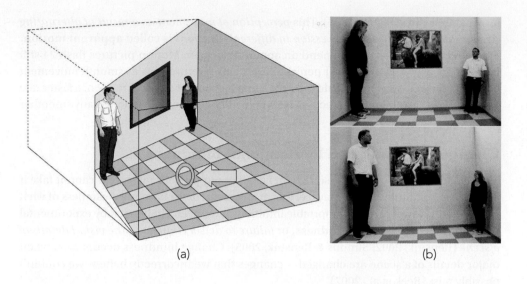

(a)   (b)

Figure 4.16 The Amazing Ames Room
(a) A diagram showing the actual proportions of the Ames room reveals its secrets. The sides of the room form a trapezoid with parallel sides but a back wall that's way off square. The uneven floor makes the room's height shorter in the nearer back corner than in the far corner. (b) Looking into the Ames room through the viewing port (see yellow arrow in part a) with only one eye, the observer infers a normal size–distance relationship — that both people are the same distance away. So the image sizes they project on the retina lead the viewer to conclude that one person is very small and the other is very large. Stephanie Pilick/AFP/Getty Images

Can you see that, by constructing the wagon as a trapezoid similar to an Ames room, Frodo the hobbit (left) appears to be much smaller than Gandalf the wizard (right) in this scene from *The Fellowship of the Ring* (Warner Brothers)?

physically twice as far away from the viewer as a person standing in the other corner. But when viewed with one eye through the small peephole placed in one wall, the Ames room looks square because the shapes of the windows and the flooring tiles are carefully crafted to look square from the viewing port (Ittelson, 1952). As a result, the person standing in the left corner appears to be much larger than a person standing in the right corner (see Figure 4.16b). Similar techniques are commonly used in filmmaking, to make objects or people in the same frame appear to be of different sizes. For example, the actors in the *Lord of the Rings* movies are not very different in size in real life, but you perceive the hobbits as much smaller than the humans, wizards, and elves.

Perceiving Motion and Change

You should now have a good sense of how we see what and where objects are, a process made substantially easier when the objects stay in one place. But in real life, of course, objects change position over time. Understanding how we perceive motion can bring us closer to appreciating how visual perception works in everyday life.

Motion Perception

To sense motion, the visual system must encode information about both space and time. The simplest case to consider is an observer who is not moving, looking at an object that is.

As an object moves across a stationary observer's visual field, it first stimulates one location on the retina, then soon after stimulates another location on the retina. Neural circuits in the brain can detect this change in position over time and respond to specific speeds and directions of motion (Emerson et al., 1992). A region near the back of the temporal lobe (part of the dorsal stream we discussed earlier), is specialized for the perception of visual motion (Born & Bradley, 2005; Newsome & Paré, 1988), and brain damage in this area causes a deficit in normal motion perception (Zihl et al., 1983).

Of course, in the real world, rarely are you a stationary observer: As you move around, your head and eyes move all the time. The motion-perception system must take into account the position and movement of your eyes, head, and body, in order to perceive the motions of objects correctly and allow you to approach or avoid them. The brain accomplishes this by monitoring your eye and head movements and "subtracting" them from the motion in the retinal image.

The movement of objects in the world is not the only event that can evoke the perception of motion. The successively flashing lights of a Las Vegas casino sign can evoke a strong sense of motion because people perceive a series of flashing lights as a whole,

apparent motion The perception of movement as a result of signals appearing in rapid succession in different locations.

change blindness Failure to detect changes to the visual details of a scene.

inattentional blindness A failure to perceive objects that are not the focus of attention.

moving object (see Figure 4.11f). This *perception of movement as a result of alternating signals appearing in rapid succession in different locations* is called **apparent motion.** Filmmaking and animation depend on apparent motion. Motion pictures flash 24 still frames per second (fps), but our perceptual systems interpret this as smooth movement on the screen. A slower rate would produce a much choppier sense of motion; a faster rate would be a waste of resources because we would not perceive the motion as any smoother than it appears at 24 fps.

Change Blindness and Inattentional Blindness

The visual world is very rich — so rich, in fact, that our perceptual system cannot take it all in, although intuitively we may feel that at any moment we have full awareness of what is around us. However, our comfortable intuitions have been challenged by experimental demonstrations of **change blindness,** or *failure to detect changes to the visual details of a scene* (Rensink, 2002; Simons & Rensink, 2005). Change blindness occurs even when major details of a scene are changed — changes that we incorrectly believe we couldn't possibly miss (Beek et al., 2007).

One study dramatically illustrated this idea, by having an experimenter ask a person on a college campus for directions (Simons & Levin, 1998). While they were talking, two men walked between them, holding a door that hid a second experimenter (see **FIGURE 4.17**). Behind the door, the two experimenters traded places so that when the men carrying the door moved on, a different person was asking for directions than the one who had been there just a second or two earlier. Remarkably, only 7 of 15 participants noticed this change.

Although surprising, these findings once again illustrate the importance of focused attention for visual perception. Just as focused attention is critical for binding together the features of objects, it is also necessary for detecting changes to objects and scenes (Rensink, 2002; Simons & Rensink, 2005). Change blindness is most likely to occur when people fail to focus attention on the object that undergoes a change (Rensink et al., 1997).

The role of focused attention in conscious visual experience is also dramatically illustrated by the closely related phenomenon of **inattentional blindness,** *a failure to perceive objects that are not the focus of attention* (Simons & Chabris, 1999). We've already seen that the use of cell phones is a bad idea when driving (see The Real World: Multitasking). In another study, researchers asked whether cell-phone use results in inattentional blindness in other situations (Hyman et al., 2010). They recruited a clown to ride a unicycle in the middle of a college campus. The researchers asked 151 students who had just walked through the area whether they had seen the clown. Seventy-five percent of the students who were using cell phones failed to notice the clown, compared

College students who were using their cell phones while walking through campus failed to notice the unicycling clown more frequently than did students who were not using their cell phones. Republished with permission of John Wiley & Sons, Inc., from Did You See the Unicycling Clown? Inattentional Blindness While Walking and Talking on a Cell Phone, Hyman et al., Applied Cognitive Psychology, 24(5), 2009; permission conveyed through Copyright Clearance Center.

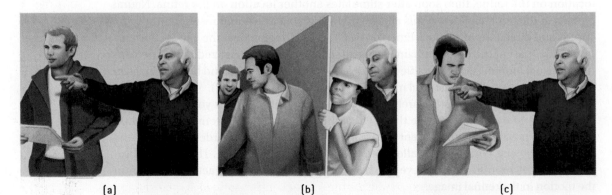

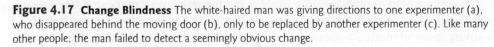

Figure 4.17 Change Blindness The white-haired man was giving directions to one experimenter (a), who disappeared behind the moving door (b), only to be replaced by another experimenter (c). Like many other people, the man failed to detect a seemingly obvious change.

with less than 50% who were not using cell phones. Using cell phones draws on focused attention, resulting in inattentional blindness and emphasizing again that our conscious experience of our visual environment is restricted to those features or objects selected by focused attention.

Build to the Outcomes

1. How does the study of illusory conjunctions help us understand the role of attention in feature binding?

2. How do we recognize our friends, even when they're hidden behind sunglasses?

3. What are the Gestalt rules of perceptual organization?

4. What does the face–vase illusion tell us about perceptual organization?

5. What are perceptual constancy and perceptual contrast?

6. How do monocular depth cues help us with depth perception?

7. What role does binocular disparity have in perceiving depth?

8. How can flashing lights on a casino sign give the impression of movement?

9. How can a failure of focused attention explain inattentional blindness?

Hearing: More Than Meets the Ear

Close your eyes for a few minutes and notice what sounds you hear. Unlike vision, hearing works in the dark, through walls, and around corners.

The sense of hearing depends on sound waves, changes in air pressure unfolding over time. Plenty of things produce sound waves: the impact of two hands clapping, the vibration of vocal cords during a stirring speech, the resonance of a bass guitar string during a thrash metal concert. Just as vision is about the perception of meaningful visual objects, hearing involves transforming changes in air pressure into meaningful sound objects (or *sources*).

Sensing Sound

Striking a tuning fork produces a *pure tone,* a simple sound wave that consists of regularly alternating regions of higher and lower air pressure, radiating outward in all directions from the source. If your ear is in the path of this spreading sound, the alternating pressure wave causes your eardrum to vibrate in time with the wave, hundreds or even thousands of times per second. Just as there are three physical dimensions of light waves that influence visual perception, so, too, are there three physical dimensions of a sound wave that correspond to dimensions of auditory perception: frequency, amplitude, and complexity (see **TABLE 4.3**).

- The *frequency* (or repetition rate) of the sound wave depends on how often the peak in air pressure passes the ear or a microphone, measured in cycles per second, or hertz (Hz). The repetition rate of a sound wave is perceived as the **pitch**, *how high or low a sound is, as ordered on a musical scale.*

- The *amplitude* of a sound wave refers to its intensity, relative to the threshold for human hearing (which is set at zero decibels, or dB). The amplitude is perceived as **loudness,** *a sound's intensity.* The rustling of leaves in a soft breeze is about 20 dB, normal conversation is about 60 dB, and a Slayer concert is about 130 dB — loud enough to cause permanent damage to the auditory system, depending on the length of exposure.

- The *complexity* of sound waves, or the mixture of frequencies, influences perception of **timbre,** *the quality of sound that allows you to distinguish two sources with the same pitch and loudness.* Timbre (pronounced "TAM-ber") allows you to tell the difference between a piano and a guitar both playing the same melody in the same

Learning Outcomes

- Describe the physical properties of sound waves.

- Describe how the ear converts sound waves into neural impulses.

- Explain how the physical properties of a sound relate to pitch, timbre, and loudness.

- Compare the main causes of hearing loss.

pitch How high or low a sound is.

loudness A sound's intensity.

timbre The quality of sound that allows you to distinguish two sources with the same pitch and loudness.

TABLE 4.3	Properties of Sound Waves

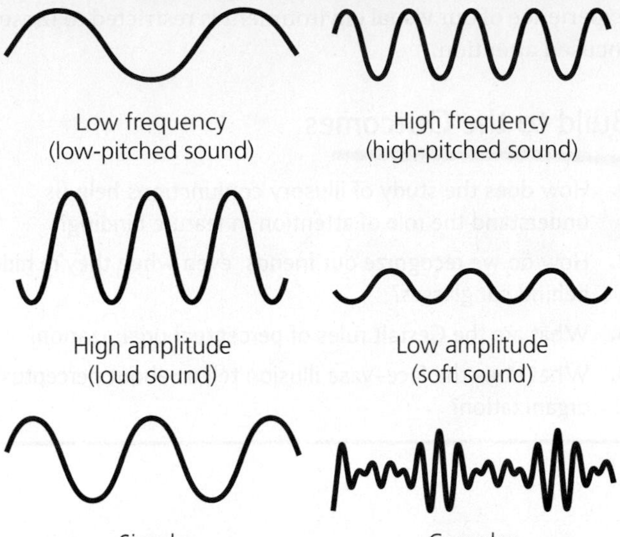

Frequency (repetition rate) corresponds to our perception of pitch.

Low frequency
(low-pitched sound)

High frequency
(high-pitched sound)

Amplitude corresponds to our perception of loudness.

High amplitude
(loud sound)

Low amplitude
(soft sound)

Complexity corresponds to our perception of timbre.

Simple
(pure tone)

Complex
(mix of frequencies)

key, at the same loudness. Timbre (whether it's a piano, guitar, or human voice) is determined, in part, by the relative amounts of the different frequencies in the sound mixture, rather like how color depends on the relative amounts of different wavelengths in an impure light.

Most sound sources that you encounter in real life are a mixture of many different frequencies, and different sources may have frequencies in common. Somehow, we perceive auditory scenes not as incoherent jumbles, but as discrete, recognizable sound sources — such as voices, espresso machines, and traffic — in different auditory locations. How does your brain reconstruct the original sounds such that you can hear and understand your friend over all the other sounds? This is the central problem of auditory perception; to answer it, we need to understand how the auditory system converts sound waves into neural signals.

The Outer Ear Funnels Sound Waves to the Middle Ear

The human ear is divided into three distinct parts, as shown in **FIGURE 4.18**. The *outer ear* collects sound waves and funnels them toward the *middle ear,* which transmits the vibrations to the *inner ear,* embedded in the skull, where they are transduced into neural impulses.

The outer ear consists of the visible part on the outside of the head (called the *pinna*); the auditory canal; and the eardrum, an airtight flap of skin that vibrates in response to sound waves gathered by the pinna and channeled into the canal. The middle ear, a tiny, air-filled chamber behind the eardrum, contains the three smallest bones in the body, called *ossicles.* Named for their appearance as hammer, anvil, and stirrup, the ossicles fit together into a lever that mechanically transmits and amplifies vibrations from the eardrum to the inner ear. Amplification is required because the ossicles push against the oval window, which is a membrane that separates the middle ear from the cochlea of the inner ear. The ossicles take the airborne pressure wave at the eardrum and transfer it into a pressure wave in fluid. Fluid requires more energy to vibrate; if you've ever been poolside, trying to talk to someone who is underwater, you know you have to really shout for the pressure wave of your voice to carry under the water.

cochlea A fluid-filled tube that contains cells that transduce sound vibrations into neural impulses.

basilar membrane A structure in the inner ear that moves up and down in time with vibrations relayed from the ossicles, transmitted through the oval window.

inner hair cells Specialized auditory receptor neurons embedded in the basilar membrane.

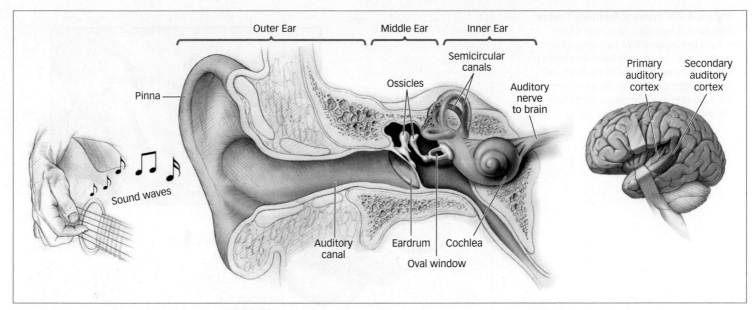

Figure 4.18 Anatomy of the Human Ear The pinna funnels sound waves into the auditory canal, causing the eardrum to vibrate in time with the sound wave. In the middle ear, the ossicles pick up the eardrum vibrations, amplify them, and pass them along, causing vibration of the oval window, and therefore of the fluid-filled cochlea in the inner ear. Here, fluid carries the wave energy to the auditory receptors (inner hair cells) that transduce it into electrical activity, exciting the neurons that form the auditory nerve, leading to the brain.

Sound Is Converted Into Neural Impulses in the Inner Ear

The inner ear contains the spiral-shaped **cochlea** (Latin for "snail"), *a fluid-filled tube containing cells that transduce sound vibrations into neural impulses.* The cochlea is divided along its length by the **basilar membrane,** *a structure in the inner ear that moves up and down in time with vibrations relayed from the ossicles, transmitted through the oval window* (see **FIGURE 4.19**). Sound causes the basilar membrane to move up and down (Békésy, 1960). The frequency of the stimulating sound determines where on the basilar membrane the up-and-down motion is highest. When the frequency is low, the wide, floppy tip (*apex*) of the basilar membrane moves the most; when the frequency is high, the narrow, stiff end closest to the oval window (*base*) moves the most.

When the basilar membrane moves up and down, this stimulates thousands of **inner hair cells,** which are *specialized auditory receptor neurons embedded in the basilar membrane.* The hair cells have long hairs sticking out of their tops that bend back and forth in the cochlear fluid, like seaweed in a current. This back-and-forth bending generates rhythmic action potentials in the auditory nerve axons that travel to the brain.

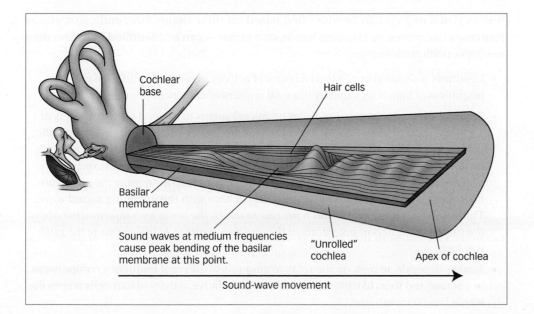

Figure 4.19 Auditory Transduction Inside the cochlea (shown here as though the coiled part had been sliced open and uncoiled), the basilar membrane undulates in response to wave energy in the cochlear fluid. Different locations along the membrane are sensitive to different frequencies, and the movement of the basilar membrane causes the hairs of the hair cells at those locations to bend. This bending generates action potentials in the attached auditory nerve axons, which together form the auditory nerve that emerges from the cochlea.

Figure 4.20 Primary Auditory Cortex
Area A1 is folded into the temporal lobe in each hemisphere. It has a topographic organization (inset), with lower frequencies mapping toward the front of the brain and higher frequencies toward the back, mirroring the organization of the basilar membrane along the cochlea (see Figure 4.19).

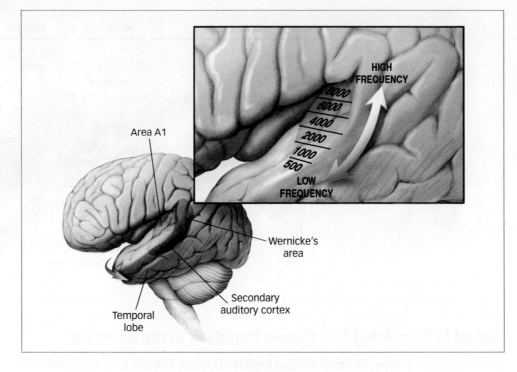

The Auditory Nerve Carries the Neural Impulses to the Brain

From the inner ear, action potentials in the auditory nerve travel to several regions of the brainstem, and then to the thalamus and ultimately to an area of the cerebral cortex called **area A1,** *the primary auditory cortex, located in the temporal lobe* (see **FIGURE 4.20**). There is some evidence that the auditory cortex is composed of two distinct streams, roughly analogous to the dorsal and ventral streams of the visual system. Spatial ("where") auditory features, which allow you to locate the source of a sound in space, are handled by areas toward the back of the temporal lobe that may overlap with the visual dorsal stream. Features that allow you to identify the sound (what it is) are handled by areas in the lower (ventral) part of the temporal lobe that may overlap with the ventral visual pathway.

Perceiving Sound Sources

Just as visual objects can be identified based on their shape, size, and color, sound sources — like voices, or clapping hands, or a guitar — can be identified based on their loudness, pitch, and timbre.

- Loudness is signaled by the total amount of activity in hair cells, rather like how brightness of light is signaled by the total amount of activity in photoreceptors.

- Pitch (of, for example, musical notes or voices) seems to depend on two aspects of auditory nerve activity (Plack, 2018a). First, different frequencies stimulate specific places along the basilar membrane. This provides a **place code,** *a process in which the brain uses information about hair cells (which cells are more active and which are less active) across the whole basilar membrane to help determine the pitch you hear.* Second, hair cell hairs move (and fire) in time with the incoming sound wave. This provides a **temporal code,** *a process in which the brain uses information about the timing of the action potentials in the auditory nerve to help determine the pitch you hear.*

- Timbre depends, in part, on the relative amounts of different frequency components in a sound and thus, like pitch, depends on the relative activity of hair cells across the whole basilar membrane.

area A1 The primary auditory cortex, located in the temporal lobe.

place code The process by which the brain uses information about the relative activity of hair cells (e.g., which ones are more active and which are less active) across the whole basilar membrane to help determine the pitch you hear.

temporal code The process whereby the brain uses the timing of the action potentials on the auditory nerve to help determine the pitch you hear.

We also need to determine the location of a sound source. As in vision, there are monaural (one ear) and binaural (two ear) cues to location (Plack, 2018b). First, your pinnas have intricate folds that alter sound, emphasizing some frequency components over others, depending on where the sound is coming from. You have learned to interpret these changes as indicating a sound's location. Second, the speed of sound is much slower than the speed of light. Sounds arrive a little sooner at the ear nearer to the source than at the far ear. This time difference is effective for indicating the location of a sound even when a sound is only a little off to one side. Third, the higher-frequency components of a sound are more intense in the ear closer to the sound than in the farther ear, because the listener's head blocks higher frequencies. The further a sound is off to the side, the greater the between-ear difference in the level of these high-frequency components. Sometimes you may find yourself turning your head from side to side to localize a sound. By doing this, you are changing the relative intensity and timing of sound waves arriving in your ears and collecting better information about the likely source of the sound. Turning your head also allows you to use your eyes to help locate the source of the sound.

Of course, given all this information about loudness, pitch, timbre, and location, the brain still has to figure out which sound components belong together in a single source (perceptual grouping) and which belong to different sources (allowing you to distinguish the conversation of your dinner companion from that of all the other noises in the restaurant). Just as in vision, our perceptual system organizes and automatically delivers to us the interpretation that is the simplest and most meaningful, consistent with expectations based on experience.

The Gestalt rules you learned about earlier in this chapter also apply to sound. For example, sounds that are similar in the physical properties of frequency or intensity — or that are similar in the perceptual attributes of loudness, pitch, timbre, or location — are grouped together into one source, as are sounds that occur close together in time (proximity). Furthermore, sounds that start together and stop together (like the different frequencies emitted simultaneously by a musical instrument, or a voice) are perceived as coming from the same source.

Hearing Loss

Hearing loss has two main causes. *Conductive hearing loss* arises because the eardrum is or ossicles are damaged to the point that they cannot conduct sound waves effectively to the cochlea. In many cases, medication or surgery can correct the problem. Sound amplification from a hearing aid also can improve hearing through conduction via the bones around the ear directly to the cochlea.

Sensorineural hearing loss is caused by damage to the cochlea, the hair cells, or the auditory nerve. It has two main effects: Sensitivity decreases so sounds have to be more intense to be heard and acuity decreases so sounds smear together on the basilar membrane, making voices harder to understand, especially if other sounds are present. Sensorineural hearing loss has many causes, including genetic disorders, infections, accumulated damage from sound exposure (particularly intense sounds), and aging (these last two causes are hard to tease apart since older people have been exposed to sound for longer). Hearing aids can amplify sounds, but cannot fix the acuity problem.

When hearing loss is severe, a *cochlear implant* may restore some hearing. A cochlear implant is an electronic device that replaces the function of the hair cells (Waltzman, 2006). The external parts of the device include a microphone and a processor (about the size of a USB key), worn behind the ear, and a small flat external transmitter that sits on the scalp behind the ear. The implanted parts include a receiver just inside the skull and a thin wire containing electrodes inserted into the cochlea to stimulate the auditory nerve. Sound picked up by the microphone is transformed into electric signals by the processor,

HOT SCIENCE

Big Technology in Little Ears

More than 90% of infants who are born deaf are born to hearing parents, who communicate using spoken language, which their babies can't hear. Such children are vulnerable to language disorders, because communication with parents and other caregivers in the first few years is crucial if language is to develop normally, as you'll learn in the Development chapter. Some of these parents compensate by learning a signed language, such as American Sign Language, so they can teach it to, and use it with, their baby. If you have ever attempted to learn a second language, you know how difficult it can be — now imagine trying to learn a second language while also caring for a new baby! This requires an extraordinary commitment of time and resources that is sometimes not practical or even possible. Furthermore, even if parents and child successfully learn to use a sign language together, what about that child's relationships with grandparents, family friends, and others in their hearing community?

Giving a baby cochlear implants allows parents and others to interact with the child using their native spoken language, enabling language development. Newborn hearing screening programs now mean that deafness can be identified at birth, and babies are routinely implanted around their first birthday, and sometimes even earlier. This is a serious decision for parents to make; although it enables hearing, cochlear

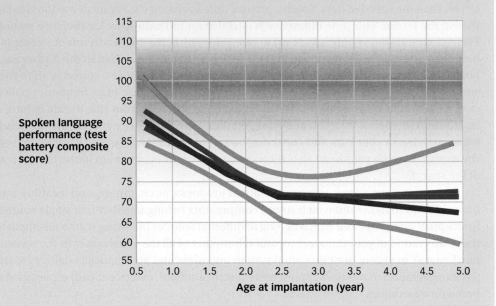

implantation does have risks, such as a higher chance of the child contracting a serious infection such as meningitis. So, is it worth the risks?

Researchers tested 160 children implanted between the ages of 6 months and 5 years of age, to examine the link between spoken language ability and age at which the implant was received (Tobey et al., 2013). The results are shown in the figure. The range of typical scores for normally hearing children, adjusted for age, is given by the gray-shaded rectangle, and ranges between about 85 and 115. The blue

line shows the performance of kids who were tested at 4 years old, maroon at 5 years old, and green at 6 years old. Those lines are all pretty similar, indicating that age at testing didn't affect the results much. What did matter was the age at which the implantation was received: Those who had been implanted at the youngest ages (1 year old or less) showed performance that was in the normal range, while those who were implanted at age 2 or older did not. This suggests that there are disadvantages to waiting to have a child implanted at an older age.

which is essentially a small computer. The signal is transmitted to the implanted receiver, which activates the electrodes in the cochlea. Cochlear implants are now in routine use and can improve hearing to the point that the wearer can understand speech, although background sound still poses a real challenge. (See Hot Science: Big Technology in Little Ears for how cochlear implants are allowing babies to learn the language of their parents and caregivers.)

Build to the Outcomes

1. What are the three properties of sound waves?

2. Why does one note sound so different on a piano and on a guitar?

3. What are the roles of the outer, middle, and inner parts of the ear in hearing?

4. How do hair cells in the ear enable us to hear?

5. How does the frequency of a sound wave relate to what we hear?

6. How do we determine the location of a sound?

7. In which types of hearing loss does sound amplification help?

8. What are some causes of sensorineural hearing loss?

The Body Senses: More Than Skin Deep

Vision and hearing provide information about the world at a distance. By responding to light and sound energy in the environment, these "distance" senses allow us to identify and locate the objects and people around us. In comparison, the body senses, also called somatosenses (*soma* from the Greek for "body"), are up close and personal. **Haptic perception** is *the active exploration of the environment by touching and grasping objects with our hands.* We use sensory receptors in our muscles, tendons, and joints as well as a variety of receptors in our skin to get a feel for the world around us (see **FIGURE 4.21**).

Sensing Touch

Touch begins with the transduction of skin sensations into neural signals. Receptors located under the skin's surface enable us to sense pain, pressure, texture, pattern, or vibration against the skin (see Figure 4.21). Each receptor is sensitive to a small patch of skin. These specialized cells work together to provide a rich tactile (from Latin, "to touch") experience when you explore an object by feeling it or attempting to grasp it. In addition, thermoreceptors, nerve fibers that sense cold and warmth, respond when your skin temperature changes. All these sensations blend seamlessly together in perception, of course, but detailed physiological studies have successfully isolated the parts of the touch system (Hollins, 2010; Johnson, 2002).

The left half of the body is represented in the right half of the brain and vice versa. As you saw in Figure 3.13 in the Neuroscience and Behavior chapter, different locations on the body send sensory signals to different locations in the somatosensory cortex in the parietal lobe. Just as more of the visual brain is devoted to foveal vision, where acuity is greatest, more of the tactile brain is devoted to parts of the skin surface where sensitivity to fine spatial detail (acuity) is greatest. Regions representing the fingertips and lips have high acuity, whereas regions representing body areas such as the calf have lower acuity. You can test this yourself: If you put two chopsticks together so that their tips are about a

Learning Outcomes

- Describe how touch receptors transmit messages to the brain.

- Discuss why pain is a psychological perception.

- Explain how we use various senses to keep our balance.

The Tactile Dome in the Exploratorium in San Francisco was created to be an environment in which only haptic perception could be used. The inside of the dome is pitch black; visitors must crawl, wiggle, slide, and otherwise navigate the unfamiliar terrain using only their sense of touch. How would you feel after being in that environment for an hour or so? © Exploratorium, www.exploratorium.edu

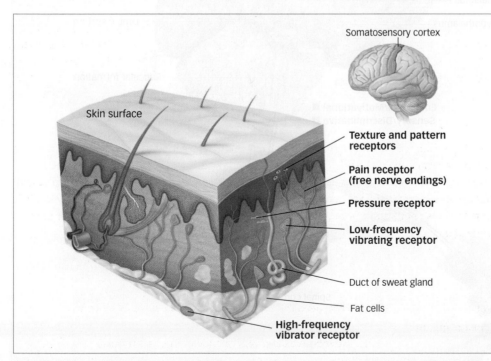

Figure 4.21 Touch Receptors Specialized sensory neurons function as haptic receptors that detect pressure, temperature, or vibrations against the skin. Their axons send signals via the spinal or cranial nerves to the brain's somatosensory cortex. Pain receptors populate all body tissues that feel pain; they are distributed around bones and within muscles and internal organs, as well as under the skin's surface.

haptic perception The active exploration of the environment by touching and grasping objects with our hands.

centimeter apart, and gently press them into the skin of your fingertip, you should be able to tell that there are two tips, not one. If you do the same on your calf, how far apart do the tips have to be before you can tell them apart?

There is mounting evidence for a distinction between "what" and "where" pathways in touch, analogous to similar distinctions we've already considered for vision and hearing. The "what" system for touch provides information about the properties of surfaces and objects; the "where" system provides information about the location in external space that is being touched or a location on the body that is being stimulated (Lederman & Klatzky, 2009).

Pain

Although pain is arguably the least pleasant of sensations, this aspect of touch is among the most important for survival: Pain indicates damage or potential damage to the body. Children born with congenital insensitivity to pain, a rare inherited disorder that specifically impairs pain perception, often accidentally harm themselves (e.g., biting into their tongues or gouging their skin while scratching) and are at increased risk of dying in childhood (Nagasako et al., 2003).

Tissue damage is transduced by the free nerve endings shown in Figure 4.21 that sense painful stimuli. In addition, fast-acting A-delta fibers transmit initial sharp pain,

Figure 4.22 Pain Travels Along Two Pathways Neural signals for pain travel along two pathways: One (shown in red) travels to the thalamus and from there to somatosensory cortex, where the location and type of pain are determined; the other (shown in blue) travels to the motivational and emotional centers of the brain.

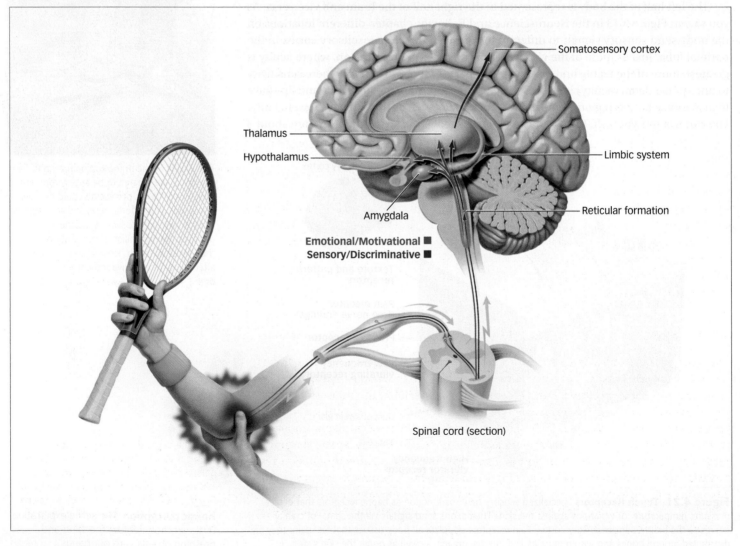

Somatosensory cortex

Thalamus

Hypothalamus

Limbic system

Amygdala

Reticular formation

Emotional/Motivational ■
Sensory/Discriminative ■

Spinal cord (section)

and slower C fibers transmit longer-lasting, duller persistent pain. If you were running barefoot outside and stubbed your toe against a rock, you would first feel a sudden stinging pain transmitted by A-delta fibers that would die down quickly, only to be replaced by the throbbing but longer-lasting pain carried by C fibers.

Neural signals for pain travel to two distinct areas in the brain and evoke two distinct psychological experiences (see **FIGURE 4.22**) (Treede et al., 1999). One pain pathway sends signals to the somatosensory cortex, identifying where the pain is occurring and what sort of pain it is (sharp, burning, or dull). The second pain pathway sends signals to the motivational and emotional centers of the brain, such as the hypothalamus and amygdala, as well as to the frontal lobe. This is the aspect of pain that is unpleasant and motivates us to escape from, or relieve, the pain.

Pain typically feels as though it comes from the site of the tissue damage that caused it. If you burn your finger, you will perceive the pain as originating there. But we have pain receptors in many areas besides the skin, such as around bones and within muscles and internal organs. When pain originates internally, we can feel it on the surface of the body. This kind of **referred pain,** *feelings of pain on the surface of the body, but due to internal damage, occurs when sensory information from internal and external areas converges on the same nerve cells in the spinal cord.* One common example is a heart attack: Victims often feel pain radiating from the left arm rather than from inside the chest.

One influential account of pain perception, known as the **gate-control theory,** *holds that signals arriving from pain receptors in the body can be stopped, or gated, by interneurons in the spinal cord via feedback from the skin or from the brain* (Melzack & Wall, 1965). Pain can be gated by the skin receptors; for example, rubbing your stubbed toe can activate neurons that "close the gate" and stop pain signals from traveling to the brain. Pain can also be gated from the brain; for example, under extreme conditions such as high stress, naturally occurring endorphins can activate brain regions that send inhibitory signals to the spinal cord, suppressing the transmission of pain signals to the brain.

A different kind of feedback signal from the brain can increase the sensation of pain. This system is activated by events such as infection and learned danger signals. When we are quite ill, what we otherwise might experience as mild discomfort can feel quite painful. This pain facilitation signal presumably evolved to motivate people who are ill to rest and avoid strenuous activity, allowing their energy to be devoted to healing. The gate-control theory of pain acknowledges that perception is a two-way street. The senses feed information such as pain sensations to the brain, which processes these sensory data into perceptions. But — just as in vision and hearing — your perceptions of pain are also affected by your knowledge, by your expectations, and by other factors such as your mood and motivational state.

Body Position, Movement, and Balance

Shut your eyes and notice the position of your legs and feet, and arms and hands. Can you feel where they are in space? This is a sense that isn't often talked about — **proprioception** is your *sense of body position*. Your perception of the position (and movement) of your torso, limbs, hands, and feet in space depends on stimulation of receptors in the muscles, tendons, and joints of your body; information about which way is up and about head movement (to serve your balance) originates in the inner ear. These receptors also provide feedback about whether we are performing a desired movement correctly and how resistance from held objects may be influencing the movement. For example, when you swing a baseball bat, the weight of the bat affects how your muscles move your arm. You can use muscle, joint, and tendon feedback about how your arms actually moved to improve performance through learning.

referred pain Feeling of pain on the surface of the body, but due to internal damage, that occurs when sensory information from internal and external areas converges on the same nerve cells in the spinal cord.

gate-control theory A theory of pain perception based on the idea that signals arriving from pain receptors in the body can be stopped, or *gated,* by interneurons in the spinal cord via feedback from the skin or from the brain.

proprioception The sense of body position.

Hitting a ball with a bat or racquet provides feedback about where your arms and body are in space, as well as how the resistance of these objects affects your movement and balance. Successful athletes, such as Serena Williams, have particularly well-developed body senses. Rick Rycroft/AP Images

vestibular system The three fluid-filled semicircular canals and adjacent organs located next to the cochlea in the inner ear.

Maintaining balance depends primarily on the **vestibular system,** *the three fluid-filled semicircular canals and adjacent organs located next to the cochlea in each inner ear* (see Figure 4.18). The semicircular canals are arranged in three perpendicular orientations and studded with hair cells that detect movement of the fluid when the head moves or accelerates. The bending of the hairs of these cells generates activity in the vestibular nerve that is then conveyed to the brain. This detected motion enables us to maintain our balance (Lackner & DiZio, 2005).

Vision also helps us keep our balance. If you see that you are swaying relative to a vertical orientation, such as the walls of a room, you adjust your posture to keep from falling over. Psychologists have experimented with this visual aspect of balance by placing people in rooms where the floor is stationary but the walls sway forward and backward (Bertenthal et al., 1997; Lee & Aronson, 1974). If the room sways enough, people—particularly small children—will topple over as they try to compensate for what their visual system is telling them. When a mismatch between the information provided by visual cues and vestibular feedback occurs, motion sickness can result. Remember this the next time you try reading in the back seat of a moving car!

Build to the Outcomes

1. What is the difference between vision and hearing, and the somatosenses?

2. What types of physical energy stimulate touch receptors?

3. Why might discriminating fine detail be important for fingertips and lips?

4. What is the role of the various parts of the skin in touch and pain?

5. Why does rubbing an injured area sometimes help alleviate pain?

6. What is the vestibular system?

7. Why is it so hard to stand on one foot with your eyes closed?

The Chemical Senses: Adding Flavor

Learning Outcomes

- Describe how odorant molecules are converted into neural impulses.

- Explain the importance of smell in personal and social experiences.

- Describe how taste sensations are converted into neural impulses by the tongue.

- Explain what senses contribute to the perception of flavor.

Vision and hearing begin with physical energy in the world—light and sound waves—and touch is activated by physical energy in or on the body surface. The last two senses we'll consider rely on chemicals that enter our mouths (the sense of taste, or gustation) or float into our noses (the sense of smell, or olfaction). Taste and smell have a common evolutionary basis that allowed our distant ancestors, single-celled organisms swimming in the primordial sea, to sense beneficial and dangerous chemicals in the seawater around them. Smell and taste combine to produce the perceptual experience we call *flavor*.

Sense of Smell

Olfaction is the least understood sense, and one of the most fascinating. Recall from the Neuroscience and Behavior chapter that whereas the other senses connect first to the thalamus, olfactory information enters the frontal lobe, amygdala, hippocampus, and other forebrain structures almost directly. This anatomy indicates that smell has a close relationship with areas involved in emotional and social behavior, as well as memory. Smell can signal whether a creature is unfriendly or friendly (or is a potential mate) or whether a substance is probably delicious or is more likely to be toxic and dangerous; and it has an uncanny ability to remind us of long-ago places and people.

Countless substances release odors into the air. Like natural lights and sounds are mixtures of wavelengths and frequencies, most natural odors (such as baking bread, coffee, and farts) are actually mixtures of different odorant molecules. Odorants are chemicals such as hydrogen sulfide (which on its own smells like rotten eggs), benzaldehyde (which smells like almonds), and vanillin (which gives vanilla its distinctive smell). Odorant molecules make their way into our noses, drifting in on the air we breathe.

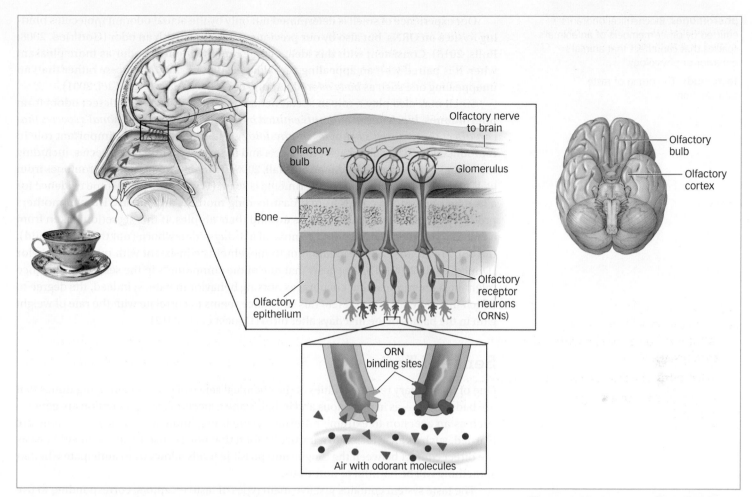

Figure 4.23 Anatomy of Smell Along the roof of the nasal cavity, odorant molecules dissolve in the mucous membrane that forms the olfactory epithelium, then bind to olfactory receptor neurons (ORNs) in the epithelium. Different ORNs have receptors for different odorant molecules. Once activated, ORNs send information to the olfactory bulb. Neurons of the olfactory bulb have axons that form the olfactory nerve, which projects directly into the brain.

Situated along the top of the nasal cavity, shown in **FIGURE 4.23** is a mucous membrane called the *olfactory epithelium*, which contains about 10 million **olfactory receptor neurons (ORNs),** *receptor cells that transduce odorant molecules into neural impulses* (Dalton, 2003). Each ORN has receptors that bind to some odorants but not to others, as if the receptor is a lock and the odorant is the key (see Figure 4.23). Bundles of ORN axons travel from the olfactory epithelium into the **olfactory bulb,** *a brain structure located above the nasal cavity beneath the frontal lobes.* Humans possess about 350 different ORN types that permit us to discriminate up to one trillion (!) odors through the unique combinations of neural activity each odor evokes (Bushdid et al., 2014). This setup is similar to our ability to see a vast range of colors through only a small number of retinal receptor cell types or to feel a range of skin sensations through only a handful of touch-receptor cell types.

Perceiving Smell

The olfactory bulb sends outputs to various centers in the brain, including the parts that are responsible for controlling basic drives, emotions, and memories. The relationship between smell and emotion explains why smells can have immediate strongly positive or negative effects on us. Fortunately, sensory adaptation is at work when it comes to smell, just as it is with the other senses. Whether the associations are good or bad, after just a few minutes the smell fades. Smell adaptation makes sense: It allows us to detect new odors that may require us to act, but after that initial evaluation has occurred, it may be best to reduce our sensitivity to allow us to detect other smells.

olfactory receptor neurons (ORNs) Receptor cells that transduce odorant molecules into neural impulses.

olfactory bulb A brain structure located above the nasal cavity beneath the frontal lobes.

pheromones Biochemical odorants emitted by other members of an animal's species that can affect that animal's behavior or physiology.

taste buds The organ of taste transduction.

Our experience of smell is determined not only by the actual odorant molecules binding to sites on ORNs, but also by our previous experiences with an odor (Gottfried, 2008; Rolls, 2015). Consistent with this idea, people rate the identical odor as more pleasant when it is paired with an appealing verbal label such as *cheddar cheese* rather than an unappealing one such as *body odor* (de Araujo et al., 2005; Herz & von Clef, 2001).

Smell may also play a role in social behavior. Other animals can detect odors from **pheromones,** *biochemical odorants emitted by other members of an animal's species that can affect that animal's behavior or physiology.* Pheromones play an important role in reproductive and social behavior in insects and in several mammalian species, including mice, dogs, and primates (Brennan & Zufall, 2006). Evidence for human pheromones from well-conducted and replicable experiments is scant (Wyatt, 2015), but some evidence for a human pheromone comes from breast-feeding mothers and babies. Human mothers produce a substance from the glands around their nipples. If this secretion, taken from a lactating mother, is put under the nose of a 3-day-old newborn (not their own child), the baby responds with head and mouth movements consistent with nursing behavior (Doucet et al., 2009). This suggests that one of the compounds in the secreted substance might be a pheromone that encourages nursing behavior in babies; indeed, the degree to which first-time mothers secrete this substance seems to correlate with the rate of weight gain in the babies in the first days after birth (Doucet et al., 2012).

Sense of Taste

One of the primary responsibilities of the chemical sense of taste is identifying things that are bad for you — as in poisonous and lethal. Some aspects of taste perception are genetic, such as an aversion to extreme bitterness (which may indicate poison), and some are learned, such as an aversion to a particular food that once caused nausea. In either case, the direct contact between the tongue and possible foods allows us to anticipate whether something will be harmful or nutritious.

The taste system contains just five main types of taste receptors, corresponding to five primary taste sensations: salt, sour, bitter, sweet, and umami (savory). The first four are probably familiar to you, but umami may not be. The umami receptor was discovered by Japanese scientists who attributed its stimulation to the rich savory tastes evoked by foods containing a high concentration of protein, such as miso, meats, and cheeses like blue cheese and old cheddar (Yamaguchi, 1998). Recent research suggests that there may be a sixth basic taste, called oleogustus, that is elicited by fatty acids and is distinct from the five primary taste sensations (Running et al., 2015). (*Oleosus* is Latin for "fatty" or "oily," and *gustus* signifies "taste.")

The tongue is covered with thousands of small bumps, called *papillae*, which are easily visible to the naked eye. Within most of the papilla are hundreds of **taste buds,** *the organs of taste transduction* (see **FIGURE 4.24**). Each taste bud contains several types of taste receptor cells whose tips, called *microvilli,* react with chemical molecules in food (called *tastants*). The mouth contains 5,000 to 10,000 taste buds fairly evenly distributed over the tongue, the roof of the mouth, and the upper throat (Bartoshuk & Beauchamp, 1994; Halpern, 2002). Each taste bud contains 50 to 100 taste receptor cells, and receptors for the different tastes are pretty evenly distributed — any taste can be detected by any part of the tongue.

Taste experiences vary widely across individuals. About 50% of people report a mildly bitter taste in caffeine, saccharine, certain green vegetables, and other substances, whereas roughly 25% report no bitter taste. Members of the first group are called tasters; members of the second group are called nontasters. The remaining 25% of people are supertasters, who report that such substances, especially dark green vegetables, are extremely bitter, to the point of being inedible (Bartoshuk, 2000). There is evidence that genetic factors contribute to individual differences in taste perception (Kim et al., 2003), but much remains to be learned about the specific genes that are

Fussy eater? Or just too sensitive? Our taste perception declines with age. That can make childhood a time of either savory delight or sensory overload of taste. Leslie Banks/iStockPhoto

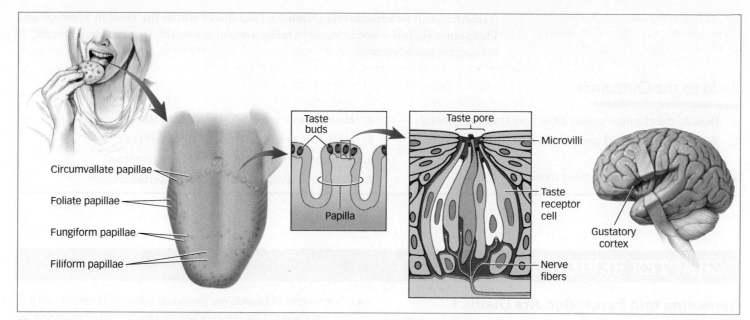

Figure 4.24 A Taste Bud Taste buds stud the bumps (papillae) on the tongue, shown here, as well as the back, sides, and roof of the mouth. Each taste bud contains receptor cells that respond to varying chemical components of foods, called tastants. Tastant molecules dissolve in saliva and stimulate the microvilli at the tips of the taste receptor cells. Each taste bud connects to a cranial nerve that carries taste information to the brainstem, then to the thalamus, and then to the primary gustatory cortex in the brain's frontal lobe.

involved (Hayes et al., 2008; Reed, 2008). Taste perception also fades with age (Methven et al., 2012; Barragán et al., 2018). This may help explain why young children seem to be "fussy eaters," since they may have greater sensitivity to taste sensations.

Perceiving Flavor

Of course, the variety of taste experiences greatly exceeds the five basic taste receptors discussed here. Any food molecules dissolved in saliva evoke specific, combined patterns of activity in the five taste receptor types. Just as odors are typically composed of a mixture of odorants, foods usually contain a mixture of tastants. Furthermore, taste isn't quite the same thing as flavor. Taste is the contribution made by receptors in your mouth alone. Taste and smell collaborate to produce the complex perception of flavor. Have you ever eaten a meal while suffering through a severe head cold that blocks your sense of smell? In that case, food tastes bland, right?

Food perception is multisensory, involving taste, smell, and texture. Neuroimaging studies have suggested that brain areas sensitive to odors from food include not only the primary olfactory cortex (near the amygdala) but also the primary gustatory (taste) cortex (in the frontal lobe) and the mouth region of the primary somatosensory cortex (in the parietal lobe) (Cerf-Ducastel & Murphy, 2001; Small et al., 2005). Indeed, the primary olfactory and gustatory cortices are interconnected, and the gustatory cortex passes "taste" information directly to the olfactory cortex.

One last point about flavor: It is a very easy thing to learn about! In the Learning chapter, we discuss how a strong lifelong aversion to a food (e.g., hummus) can develop after only one nasty experience. This makes sense — if something is bad for you once, it probably will be again, and you learn quickly to stay well away. Learned preferences in food are also important in determining flavor, and they depend dramatically on culture and experience. "It's an acquired taste" is something you may have heard about a food you find disgusting: Acquired tastes include toasted grasshoppers in Mexico (chapulines),

"We would like to be genetically modified to taste like Brussels sprouts."

Sam Gross/The New Yorker Collection/Cartoonbank.com

The full experience of a wine's flavor cannot be appreciated without a finely trained sense of smell. When this wine aficionada raises a glass of wine to her mouth, odorants from the wine enter her nasal cavity via the nostrils, as well as through the back of the throat. The same happens with other foods and beverages. Alain Robert/SIPA via AP

fermented fish in Scandinavia (lutefisk), fetal ducks still in the shell in Vietnam and Philippines (balut) — even cheese in many parts of the world. One person's "yecch!" is another person's "yummy!"

Build to the Outcomes

1. How do the chemical senses differ from the other senses?

2. What roles do various parts of the nose play in the sense of smell?

3. How many odors can humans smell?

4. How do taste and smell contribute to flavor?

5. How does smell contribute to social behavior?

6. What are the five main types of taste receptors?

7. What are tasters, nontasters, and supertasters?

CHAPTER REVIEW

Sensation and Perception Are Distinct Activities

- Sensation is the simple stimulation of a sense organ, whereas perception organizes, identifies, and interprets sensation at the level of the brain.

- The process of transduction converts physical signals from the environment into neural signals carried by sensory neurons into the central nervous system.

- Sensory adaptation occurs when sensitivity to unchanging stimulation declines over time.

- Psychophysics is an approach to studying perception that measures the strength of a stimulus and an observer's sensitivity to that stimulus. An observer's absolute threshold is the smallest intensity needed to just barely detect a stimulus; the just noticeable difference (JND) is the smallest change in a stimulus that can just barely be detected.

- Signal detection theory allows researchers to study an observer's perceptual sensitivity while also considering the effects of noise and the observer's expectations, motivations, and goals.

Visual Pathways: Connections Between the Eye and the Brain

- Light travels in waves that pass through several layers in the eye to reach the retina.

- Two types of photoreceptor cells in the retina transduce light into neural impulses: Cones operate under normal daylight conditions and sense color; rods are active under low-light conditions for night vision.

- Three cone types are critical to color perception: short-wavelength (bluish) light, medium-wavelength (greenish) light, and long-wavelength (reddish) light. The overall pattern of response across the three cone types results in a unique code for each color.

- Information encoded by the retina travels along the optic nerve through the thalamus to the primary visual cortex (area V1) in the occipital lobe.

- The shapes of objects are perceived when different neurons in the visual cortex fire in response to different orientations of the object's edges.

- Two functionally distinct pathways project from the occipital lobe to visual areas in other parts of the brain. The ventral stream travels into the temporal lobes and includes brain areas that represent an object's shape and identity. The dorsal stream travels to the parietal lobes, connecting with brain areas that identify the location and motion of an object.

Visual Perception: Recognizing What We See

- Illusory conjunctions occur when features from separate objects are mistakenly combined. The parietal lobe is important for attention and contributes to feature binding.

- The principle of perceptual constancy holds that even as sensory signals change, perception remains consistent.

- Gestalt principles of perceptual grouping, such as simplicity, closure, and continuity, govern how features are perceptually organized into meaningful objects.

- Depth perception depends on monocular cues, such as familiar size and linear perspective; binocular cues, such as retinal disparity; and motion-based cues, which are based on the movement of the head over time.

- We experience a sense of motion through the differences in the strengths of output from neurons sensitive to motion in different directions.

- Change blindness and inattentional blindness occur when we fail to notice features of our environment, emphasizing that our conscious visual experience depends on focused attention.

Hearing: More Than Meets the Ear

- Perceiving sound depends on three physical dimensions of a sound wave: frequency, which determines the pitch; amplitude, which determines the loudness; and differences in the complexity, or mix, of frequencies, which determines the sound quality, or timbre.

- Auditory pitch perception begins in the ear, which consists of the outer ear which funnels sound waves toward the middle ear, which in turn sends the vibrations to the inner ear, which contains the cochlea.
- Action potentials from the inner ear travel along an auditory pathway through the thalamus to the primary auditory cortex (area A1) in the temporal lobe.
- Auditory perception depends on both a place code and a temporal code. Our ability to localize sound sources depends critically on the placement of our ears on opposite sides of the head.
- Some hearing loss can be overcome with hearing aids that amplify sound. When hair cells are damaged, a cochlear implant is a possible solution.

The Body Senses: More Than Skin Deep

- Sensory receptors on the body send neural signals to locations in the somatosensory cortex, a part of the parietal lobe, which the brain translates as the sensation of touch.

- The experience of pain depends on signals that travel to the somatosensory cortex to indicate the location and type of pain, and to the emotional centers of the brain, which results in unpleasant feelings.
- Balance and acceleration depend primarily on the vestibular system but are also influenced by vision.

The Chemical Senses: Adding Flavor

- Our experience of smell, or olfaction, is associated with odorant molecules that bind to sites on specialized olfactory receptors. The olfactory bulb sends signals to parts of the brain that control drives, emotions, and memories.
- Smell is also involved in social behavior, as illustrated by pheromones, which are related to reproductive behavior and sexual responses in several species.
- Sensations of taste depend on taste buds, which are distributed across the tongue, the roof of the mouth, and the upper throat. Taste buds contain taste receptors corresponding to the five primary taste sensations of salt, sour, bitter, sweet, and umami.

Key Concept Quiz

1. Sensation involves _____, whereas perception involves _____.
   a. organization; coordination
   b. stimulation; interpretation
   c. identification; translation
   d. comprehension; information

2. What process converts physical signals from the environment into neural signals carried by sensory neurons into the central nervous system?
   a. representation
   b. identification
   c. propagation
   d. transduction

3. The smallest intensity needed to just barely detect a stimulus is called
   a. proportional magnitude.
   b. the absolute threshold.
   c. the just noticeable difference.
   d. Weber's law.

4. Light striking the retina, causing a specific pattern of response in the three cone types, leads to our ability to see
   a. motion.
   b. colors.
   c. depth.
   d. shadows.

5. Which part of the brain is the location of the primary visual cortex, where encoded information is systematically mapped into a representation of the visual scene?
   a. the thalamus
   b. the lateral geniculate nucleus
   c. the fovea
   d. area V1

6. The _____ travels from the occipital lobe across brain regions in the temporal lobes that identify what an object is.
   a. optic nerve
   b. dorsal stream
   c. ventral stream
   d. gate-control pathway

7. What kind of cues are relative size and linear perspective?
   a. motion-based
   b. binocular
   c. monocular
   d. template

8. What does the frequency of a sound wave determine?
   a. pitch
   b. loudness
   c. sound quality
   d. timbre

9. The placement of our ears on opposite sides of the head is crucial to our ability to
   a. localize sound sources.
   b. determine pitch.
   c. judge intensity.
   d. recognize complexity.

10. Conductive hearing loss is caused by damage to the
    a. eardrum or ossicles.
    b. cochlea or hair cells.
    c. auditory nerve.
    d. primary auditory cortex (area A1).

11. Which part of the body occupies the greatest area in the somatosensory cortex?

a. calves
b. lips
c. lower back
d. hips

12. The location and type of pain we experience is indicated by signals sent to

a. the amygdala.
b. the spinal cord.
c. pain receptors.
d. the somatosensory cortex.

13. What part of the ear is critically involved in the sense of balance?

a. the pinna
b. the ossicles
c. the semicircular canals
d. the basilar membrane

14. What best explains why smells can have immediate and powerful effects?

a. the involvement in smell of brain centers for emotions and memories
b. the vast number of olfactory receptor neurons we have
c. our ability to detect odors from pheromones
d. the fact that different odorant molecules produce varied patterns of activity

15. About how many taste buds does the mouth contain?

a. 50 to 100
b. 5,000 to 10,000
c. 50,000 to 100,000
d. more than one million

 **LearningCurve** Don't stop now! Quizzing yourself is a powerful study tool. Go to LaunchPad to access the LearningCurve adaptive quizzing system and your own personalized learning plan. Visit launchpadworks.com.

Key Terms

sensation (p. 90)
perception (p. 90)
transduction (p. 90)
sensory adaptation (p. 90)
psychophysics (p. 91)
absolute threshold (p. 91)
sensitivity (p. 92)
acuity (p. 92)
just noticeable difference (JND) (p. 92)
Weber's law (p. 92)
signal detection theory (p. 92)
retina (p. 95)

accommodation (p. 95)
cones (p. 95)
rods (p. 95)
fovea (p. 95)
blind spot (p. 97)
area V1 (p. 97)
binding problem (p. 101)
illusory conjunction (p. 101)
attention (p. 102)
perceptual constancy (p. 102)
perceptual contrast (p. 103)
perceptual organization (p. 103)

monocular depth cues (p. 105)
binocular disparity (p. 106)
apparent motion (p. 108)
change blindness (p. 108)
inattentional blindness (p. 108)
pitch (p. 109)
loudness (p. 109)
timbre (p. 109)
cochlea (p. 111)
basilar membrane (p. 111)
inner hair cells (p. 111)
area A1 (p. 112)

place code (p. 112)
temporal code (p. 112)
haptic perception (p. 115)
referred pain (p. 117)
gate-control theory (p. 117)
proprioception (p. 117)
vestibular system (p. 118)
olfactory receptor neurons (ORNs) (p. 119)
olfactory bulb (p. 119)
pheromones (p. 120)
taste buds (p. 120)

Changing Minds

1. A friend of yours is taking a class in medical ethics. "We discussed a tough case today," she says. "It has to do with a patient who's been in a vegetative state for several years, and the family has to decide whether to take him off life support. The doctors say he has no awareness of himself or his environment, and he is never expected to recover. But when doctors shine a light in his eyes, his pupils contract. That shows he can sense light, so he has to have some ability to perceive his surroundings, doesn't he?" Without knowing any of the details of this particular case, how would you explain to your friend that a patient might be able to sense light but not perceive

it? What other examples from the chapter could you use to illustrate the difference between sensation and perception?

2. In your philosophy class, the professor discusses the proposition that "perception is reality." From the point of view of philosophy, reality is the state of things as they actually exist, whereas perception is how they appear to the observer. What does psychophysics have to say about this issue? What are three ways in which sensory transduction can alter perception, causing perceptions that may differ from absolute reality?

3. A friend comes across the story of an American soldier, Sergeant Leroy Petry, who received the Medal of Honor for saving the lives of two of his men. The soldiers were in a firefight in Afghanistan when a live grenade landed at their feet; Petry picked up the grenade and tried to toss it away from the others, but it exploded, destroying his right hand. According to the news report, Petry didn't initially feel any pain; instead, he set about applying a tourniquet to his own arm while continuing to shout orders to his men as the firefight continued. "That's amazingly heroic," your friend says, "but that bit about not feeling the pain—that's crazy. He must just be so tough that he kept going despite the pain." What would you tell your friend? How can the perception of pain be altered?

Answers to Key Concept Quiz

1. b; 2. d; 3. b; 4. b; 5. d; 6. c; 7. c; 8. a; 9. a; 10. a; 11. b; 12. d; 13. c; 14. a; 15. b

LaunchPad
macmillan learning

LaunchPad features the full e-book of *Introducing Psychology*, the LearningCurve adaptive quizzing system, videos, and a variety of activities to boost your learning. Visit LaunchPad at launchpadworks.com.

Consciousness

5

Unconsciousness is something you don't really appreciate until you need it. Belle Riskin needed it one day on an operating table, when she awoke just as doctors were pushing a breathing tube down her throat. She felt she was choking, but she couldn't see, breathe, scream, or move. Unable even to blink an eye, she couldn't signal to the surgeons that she was conscious. "I was terrified," she explained later. "I knew I was conscious, that something was going on during the surgery. I had just enough awareness to know I was being intubated" (Groves, 2004).

How could this happen? Anesthesia for surgery is supposed to leave the patient unconscious, "feeling no pain," yet in this case — and in about 1 in every 20,000 surgical procedures (Pandit et al., 2014) — the patient regains consciousness at some point. The problem arises because muscle-relaxing drugs are used to keep the patient from moving involuntarily and making unhelpful contributions to the operation. Yet when the drugs that are given to induce unconsciousness fail to do their job, the patient with extremely relaxed muscles is unable to show or tell doctors that there is a problem.

Fortunately, new methods can monitor wakefulness by measuring the electrical activity of the brain. One system uses sensors attached to the patient's head and gives readings on a scale from 0 (no electrical activity in the brain) to 100 (fully alert), providing a kind of "consciousness meter." Anesthesiologists using this index deliver anesthetics to keep the patient in the recommended range of 40 to 60 for general anesthesia during surgery. This system reduces postsurgical reports of consciousness and memory of the surgical experience (Myles et al., 2004). One of these devices in the operating room might have helped Belle Riskin settle into the unconsciousness she so sorely needed.

Most of the time, of course, consciousness is something we cherish. **Consciousness** is *a person's subjective experience of the world and the mind.* Although you might think of consciousness as simply "being awake," the defining feature of consciousness is experience, which you have when you're awake or when you're having a vivid dream. Conscious experience is essential to what it means to be human. The anesthesiologist's dilemma in trying to monitor Belle Riskin's consciousness is a stark reminder, though, that it is impossible for one person to experience another's consciousness.

How can this private world be studied? We'll begin by examining consciousness directly, trying to understand what it is like and how it compares with the mind's *unconscious* processes. Then we'll examine altered states of consciousness: sleep and dreams, intoxication with alcohol and other drugs, and hypnosis. Like the traveler who learns the meaning of *home* by roaming far away, we can learn the meaning of *consciousness* by exploring its exotic variations.

The Mysteries of Consciousness

The Nature of Consciousness

The Unconscious Mind

Sleep and Dreaming: Good Night, Mind

Drugs and Consciousness: Artificial Inspiration

Hypnosis: Open to Suggestion

consciousness A person's subjective experience of the world and the mind.

When it's time for surgery, it's great to be unconscious. Masterfile

Learning Outcomes

- Explain the two dimensions of mind perception.
- Outline the relationship between brain activity, thinking, and acting.

phenomenology The study of how things seem to the conscious person.

problem of other minds The fundamental difficulty we have in perceiving the consciousness of others.

Figure 5.1 Dimensions of Mind Perception When participants judged the mental capacities of 13 entities, such as a baby, a chimp, and an adult woman or man, they tended to perceive minds as varying in both the capacity for experience (such as abilities to feel pain or pleasure) and in the capacity for agency (such as abilities to plan or exert self-control) (Gray et al., 2007). For example, normal adult humans (man, woman, or "you," the respondent) were judged to have both experience and agency; in contrast, the man in a persistent vegetative state ("PVS man") was judged to have some experience but very little capacity for agency, while the robot was judged to have agency but little capacity for experience. Macmillan Learning

The Mysteries of Consciousness

What does it feel like to be you right now? It probably feels as though you are somewhere inside your head, looking out at the world through your eyes. If you shut your eyes, you may be able to imagine things in your mind, even though all the while thoughts and feelings come and go, passing through your imagination. But where are "you," really? Psychologists hope to include an understanding of **phenomenology,** *how things seem to the conscious person,* in their understanding of mind and behavior. But the theater in your mind doesn't have seating for more than one, making it difficult to share what's on your mental screen. Let's look at two of the more vexing mysteries of consciousness: the problem of other minds and the mind–body problem.

The Problem of Other Minds

One great mystery in psychology is called the **problem of other minds,** *the fundamental difficulty we have in perceiving the consciousness of others.* How do you know that anyone else is conscious? They tell you that they are conscious, of course, and are often willing to describe in depth how they feel, how they think, and what they are experiencing. But perhaps they are just *saying* these things. There is no clear way to distinguish a conscious person from someone who might do and say all the same things as a conscious person but who is *not* conscious.

Even the consciousness meter used by anesthesiologists falls short. It certainly doesn't give the anesthesiologist any special insight into what it is like to be the patient on the operating table; it only predicts whether patients will *say* they were conscious. We simply lack the ability to directly perceive the consciousness of others. In short, *you* are the only thing in the universe that you will ever truly know what it is like to be.

The problem of other minds also means there is no way you can tell if another person's experience of anything is at all like yours. Although you know what the color red looks like to you, for instance, you cannot know whether it looks the same to other people. Maybe they're seeing what you see as blue and just calling it red in a consistent way. Of course, most people have come to trust each other in describing their inner lives, reaching the general assumption that other human minds are pretty much like their own. But they don't know this for a fact.

How do people perceive other minds? Researchers asked people to compare the minds of 13 different entities—such as a baby, chimp, or robot (Gray et al., 2007). They found that people judge minds according to two dimensions (see **FIGURE 5.1**): the capacity

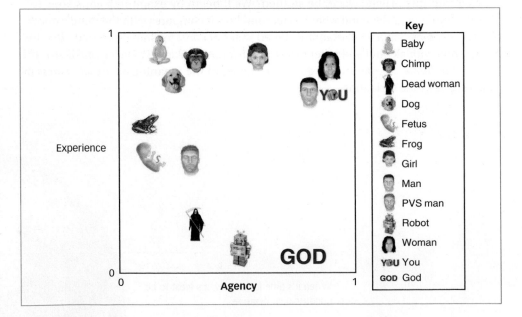

for *experience* (such as the ability to feel pain, pleasure, hunger, consciousness, anger, or fear) and the capacity for *agency* (such as the ability for self-control, planning, memory, or thought).

As shown in Figure 5.1, respondents rated some entities as having little experience or agency (the dead woman), others as having experiences but little agency (the baby), and yet others as having both experience and agency (adult humans). Still others were perceived as having agency without experiences (the robot). People appreciate that minds both have experiences and lead us to perform actions.

As you'll remember from the Methods chapter, the scientific method requires that any observation made by one scientist should, in principle, be available for observation by any other scientist. But if other minds aren't observable, how can consciousness be a topic of scientific study? One radical solution is to eliminate consciousness from psychology entirely and renounce the study of *anything* mental. This was the solution offered by behaviorism, and it turned out to have its own shortcomings, as you saw in the Evolution of Psychological Science chapter. Despite the problem of other minds, modern psychology has embraced the study of consciousness. The astonishing richness of mental life simply cannot be ignored.

The Mind–Body Problem

Another mystery of consciousness is the **mind–body problem**, *the issue of how the mind is related to the brain and body.* The French philosopher and mathematician René Descartes (1596–1650) is famous for proposing, among other things, that the human body is made of physical matter but that the human mind or soul is a separate entity made of a "thinking substance." We now know that the mind and brain are connected everywhere to each other. In other words, "the mind is what the brain does" (Minsky, 1986, p. 287).

But Descartes was right in pointing out the difficulty of reconciling the physical body with the mind. Most psychologists assume that mental events are intimately tied to brain events, such that every thought, perception, or feeling is associated with a particular pattern of activation of neurons in the brain (see the Neuroscience and Behavior chapter). Thinking about a particular person, for instance, occurs with a unique array of neural connections and activations. If the neurons repeat that pattern, then you must be thinking of the same person; conversely, if you think of the person, brain activity occurs in that pattern.

One telling set of studies, however, suggests that the brain's activities *precede* the activities of the conscious mind. Researchers measured the electrical activity in the brains of volunteers by placing sensors on their scalps as they repeatedly decided when to move a hand (Libet, 1985). Participants were also asked to indicate exactly when they consciously chose to move by reporting the position of a dot moving rapidly around the face of a clock just at the point of the decision (**FIGURE 5.2a**). As a rule, the brain begins to

mind–body problem The issue of how the mind is related to the brain and body.

Figure 5.2   The Timing of Conscious Will (a) Participants were asked to move fingers at will while watching a dot move around the face of a clock to mark the moment at which the action was consciously willed. Meanwhile, EEG sensors timed the onset of brain activation. (b) Brain activity (EEG) preceded the willed movement of the finger, but it also preceded the reported time of consciously willing the finger to move.

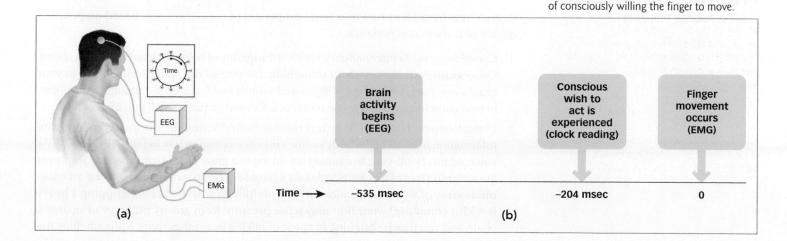

Time →

| Brain activity begins (EEG) | Conscious wish to act is experienced (clock reading) | Finger movement occurs (EMG) |

−535 msec   −204 msec   0

(a)   (b)

Do Alexa or Siri have human consciousness? How could you find out? Frank Duenzl/Picture-Alliance/DPA/AP Images

show electrical activity about half a second before a voluntary action (535 milliseconds, to be exact) but also about one third of a second (331 milliseconds) before the person's conscious decision to move (as shown in Figure 5.2b). Although your personal intuition is that you *think* of an action and *then* do it, these experiments suggest that your brain is getting started before *either* the thinking or the doing, paving the way for both thought and action (Haggard & Tsakiris, 2009; Wegner, 2002).

Over the past several decades, psychologists and computer scientists have attempted to create machines that can mimic human consciousness and intelligence. This work has led to the creation of the field of "artificial intelligence" (AI), which refers to the study and use of machines (including computers) that can independently operate in ways that mimic human intelligence and interactions. AI is used increasingly in our daily lives in ways that attempt to mimic the behavior of human agents — such as through Apple's Siri and Amazon's Alexa. Over the past several decades, psychological scientists have continued to work toward the development of increasingly sophisticated AI methods in an effort to better understand, and mimic, various aspects of human consciousness, such as the abilities for learning, decision making, attention, memory, and planning for the future (Hassabis et al., 2017). Although there is still much progress to be made, since researchers cannot yet see the consciousness of others or know exactly how consciousness arises from the brain, this has not prevented them from collecting people's reports of conscious experiences and learning how these reports reveal the nature of consciousness.

Build to the Outcomes

1. Why is it difficult to study consciousness?

2. How does the capacity for experience differ from the capacity for agency?

3. Which comes first: brain activity or conscious thinking?

The Nature of Consciousness

Learning Outcomes

- Describe the four basic properties of consciousness.

- Compare the three levels of consciousness.

- Explain why we can't always control our conscious thoughts.

How would you describe your own consciousness? Researchers examining people's descriptions suggest that consciousness has four basic properties, that it occurs on three different levels, and that it includes a range of different contents. Let's examine each of these points in turn.

Four Basic Properties

Researchers have identified four basic properties of consciousness, based on people's reports of conscious experience.

1. Consciousness has *intentionality,* which is the quality of being directed toward an object. Consciousness is always *about* something. Despite all the lush detail you see in your mind's eye, the kaleidoscope of sights and sounds and feelings and thoughts, the object of your consciousness at any one moment is focused on just a small part of all of this.

2. Consciousness has *unity,* which is resistance to division, or the ability to integrate information from all of the body's senses into one coherent whole (see **FIGURE 5.3**). As you read this book, your five senses are taking in a great deal of information. Your eyes are scanning lots of black squiggles on a page (or screen) while also sensing an enormous array of shapes and colors in your periphery; your hands are gripping a heavy book (or computer); your butt may sense pressure from gravity pulling you against a chair; and you may be listening to music or talking in another room while smelling the

Figure 5.3 Bellotto's *Dresden* and Closeup (*left*) The people on the bridge in the distance look very finely detailed in *View of Dresden with the Frauenkirche* by Bernardo Bellotto (1721–1780). However, when you examine the detail closely (*right*), you discover that the people are made of brushstrokes merely *suggesting* people—an arm here, a torso there. Consciousness produces a similar impression of "filling in," as it seems to consist of extreme detail even in areas that are peripheral (Dennett, 1991). Dresden from right bank of Elbe upstream from bridge of Augustus, circa 1750, by Bernardo Bellotto, known as Canaletto (1721–1780), oil on canvas, 50×84 cm, Detail/De Agostini Picture Library/A. Dagli Orti/Bridgeman Images

odor of your roommate's dirty laundry. Your brain—amazingly—integrates all of this information into the experience of one unified consciousness.

3. Consciousness has *selectivity,* the capacity to include some objects but not others. While binding the many sensations around you into a coherent whole, your mind must make decisions about which pieces of information to include and which to exclude. The conscious system is most inclined to select information of special interest to the listener. For example, in what has come to be known as the **cocktail-party phenomenon,** *people tune in one message even while they filter out others nearby.* Perhaps you, too, have noticed how abruptly your attention is diverted from whatever conversation you are having when someone else within earshot mentions your name.

4. Consciousness has *transience,* or the tendency to change. William James, whom you met way back in the Evolution of Psychological Science chapter, famously described consciousness as a "stream"—whirling, chaotic, and constantly changing (James, 1890). The stream of consciousness may flow in this way partly because of the limited capacity of the conscious mind. We humans can hold only so much information in mind, so when we select more information, some of what is currently there must disappear. As a result, our focus of attention keeps changing.

The contents of our conscious thoughts are constantly changing, like water in a stream. Black Thought of the musical group The Roots provided an example of a "stream of consciousness" presentation in a 10-minute freestyle performance so impressive that it was recommended listening by the *New York Times.*

Levels of Consciousness

Consciousness can also be understood as having three levels, which involve different qualities of awareness of the world and of the self. These levels of consciousness would probably all register as "conscious" on that wakefulness meter for surgery patients you read about at the beginning of this chapter.

1. **Minimal consciousness** is *a low-level kind of sensory awareness and responsiveness that occurs when the mind inputs sensations and may output behavior* (Armstrong, 1980). This kind of sensory awareness and responsiveness could even happen when someone pokes you while you're asleep and you turn over. Something seems to register in your mind, at least in the sense that you experience it, but you may not think at

cocktail-party phenomenon A phenomenon in which people tune in one message even while they filter out others nearby.

minimal consciousness A low-level kind of sensory awareness and responsiveness that occurs when the mind inputs sensations and may output behavior.

full consciousness A level of consciousness in which you know and are able to report your mental state.

self-consciousness A distinct level of consciousness in which the person's attention is drawn to the self as an object.

Full consciousness involves a consciousness of oneself, such as thinking about the act of driving while driving a car. How is this different from self-consciousness? Photomondo/Photodisc/Getty Images

all about having had the experience. It could be that animals or, for that matter, even plants can have this minimal level of consciousness. But because of the problem of other minds and the notorious reluctance of animals and plants to talk to us, we can't know for sure that they *experience* the things that make them respond.

2. **Full consciousness** occurs when you *know and are able to report your mental state.* That's a subtle distinction: Being fully conscious means that you are aware of having a mental state while you are experiencing the mental state itself. Have you ever been driving a car and suddenly realized that you don't remember the past 15 minutes of driving? Chances are that you were not unconscious, but instead minimally conscious. When you are completely aware and thinking about your driving, you have moved into the realm of full consciousness. Full consciousness involves not only thinking about things but also thinking about the fact that you are thinking about things (Jaynes, 1976).

3. **Self-consciousness** is yet another *distinct level of consciousness in which the person's attention is drawn to the self as an object* (Morin, 2006). Most people report experiencing such self-consciousness when they are embarrassed; when they find themselves the focus of attention in a group; when someone focuses a camera on them; or when they are deeply introspective about their thoughts, feelings, or personal qualities. Looking in a mirror, for example, is all it takes to make people evaluate themselves — thinking not just about their looks but also about whether they are good or bad in other ways. People go out of their way to avoid mirrors when they've done something they are ashamed of (Duval & Wicklund, 1972). However, because it makes them self-critical, the self-consciousness that results when people see their own mirror images can make them briefly more helpful, more cooperative, and less aggressive (Gibbons, 1990).

Most animals don't appear to have self-consciousness. However, chimpanzees sometimes behave in ways that suggest they recognize themselves in a mirror. To examine this, researchers painted an odorless red dye over the eyebrow of an anesthetized chimp and then watched when the chimp was presented with a mirror (Gallup, 1977). If the chimp interpreted the mirror image as a representation of some other chimp with an unusual approach to cosmetics, we would expect it just to look at the mirror or perhaps to reach toward it. But the chimp reached toward its *own eye* as it looked into the mirror — not the mirror image — suggesting that it recognized the image as a reflection of itself. A few other animals, such as chimpanzees and orangutans (Gallup, 1997), possibly dolphins (Reiss & Marino, 2001), and maybe even elephants (Plotnik et al., 2006) and magpies (Prior et al., 2008), recognize their own mirror images. Dogs, cats, crows, monkeys, and gorillas have been tested, too, but don't seem to know they are looking at themselves. Even humans don't have self-recognition right away. Infants don't recognize themselves in mirrors until they've reached about 18 months of age (Lewis & Brooks-Gunn, 1979). The experience of self-consciousness, as measured by self-recognition in mirrors, is limited to a few animals and to humans only after a certain stage of development.

A chimpanzee tries to wipe off the red dye on its eyebrow, suggesting that it recognizes itself in the mirror. The Povinelli Group LLC

Conscious Contents

What's on your mind? For that matter, what's on everybody's mind? One way to learn what is on people's minds is to ask them, and much research has called on people simply to *think aloud* while in a psychological laboratory. A more modern approach is the use of *experience-sampling* or *ecological momentary assessment (EMA)* techniques, in which people are asked to report their conscious experiences at particular times. Equipped with survey apps loaded onto their smartphone, for example, participants record their current thoughts when prompted (e.g., via a push notification) at random times throughout the day (Stone, 2018).

Experience-sampling studies show that consciousness is dominated by the immediate environment — what we see, feel, hear, taste, and smell. What do you experience while

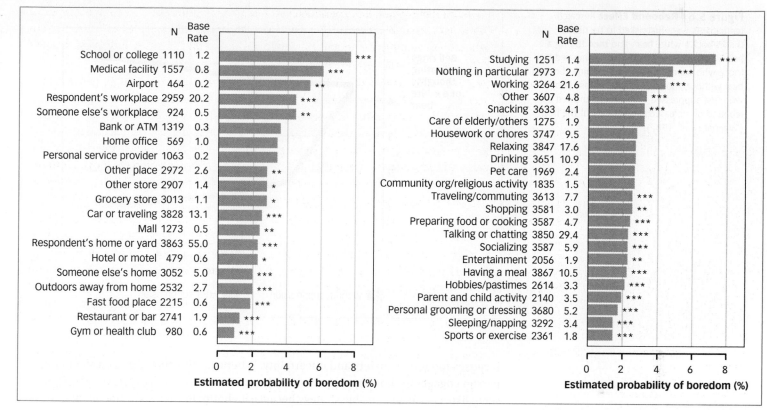

	N	Base Rate	
School or college	1110	1.2	***
Medical facility	1557	0.8	***
Airport	464	0.2	**
Respondent's workplace	2959	20.2	***
Someone else's workplace	924	0.5	**
Bank or ATM	1319	0.3	
Home office	569	1.0	
Personal service provider	1063	0.2	
Other place	2972	2.6	**
Other store	2907	1.4	*
Grocery store	3013	1.1	*
Car or traveling	3828	13.1	***
Mall	1273	0.5	**
Respondent's home or yard	3863	55.0	***
Hotel or motel	479	0.6	*
Someone else's home	3052	5.0	***
Outdoors away from home	2532	2.7	***
Fast food place	2215	0.6	***
Restaurant or bar	2741	1.9	***
Gym or health club	980	0.6	***

Estimated probability of boredom (%)

	N	Base Rate	
Studying	1251	1.4	***
Nothing in particular	2973	2.7	***
Working	3264	21.6	***
Other	3607	4.8	***
Snacking	3633	4.1	***
Care of elderly/others	1275	1.9	
Housework or chores	3747	9.5	
Relaxing	3847	17.6	
Drinking	3651	10.9	
Pet care	1969	2.4	
Community org/religious activity	1835	1.5	
Traveling/commuting	3613	7.7	***
Shopping	3581	3.0	**
Preparing food or cooking	3587	4.7	***
Talking or chatting	3850	29.4	***
Socializing	3587	5.9	***
Entertainment	2056	1.9	**
Having a meal	3867	10.5	***
Hobbies/pastimes	2614	3.3	***
Parent and child activity	2140	3.5	***
Personal grooming or dressing	3680	5.2	***
Sleeping/napping	3292	3.4	***
Sports or exercise	2361	1.8	***

Estimated probability of boredom (%)

Figure 5.4   Locations and Activities Associated with Boredom An experience-sampling study of more than 1 million people revealed the locations and activities associated with the highest (and lowest) probability of being bored. Data from Chin et al. (2016).

actually carrying out the events of your daily life? One recent study used experience sampling to follow 1.1 million people over a 10-day period to better understand what locations and activities are most associated with the experience of boredom (Chin et al., 2016). As shown in **FIGURE 5.4,** people reported the highest likelihood of boredom while at school or college — even more so than while in an airport or a doctor's office. In terms of activities, people reported the highest likelihood of boredom while studying — an activity that was rated as even more boring than doing nothing at all. (Fortunately, you have this very stimulating book to keep you from getting bored!)

Daydreams: The Brain Is Always Active

One reason that we often avoid boredom when doing nothing at all is that our mind shifts into a period of *daydreaming,* a state of consciousness in which a seemingly purposeless flow of thoughts comes to mind. The brain, however, is active even when it has no specific task at hand. Daydreaming was examined in an fMRI study of people resting in the scanner (Mason et al., 2007). Usually, people in brain-scanning studies don't have time to daydream much because they are kept busy with mental tasks — scans cost money and researchers want to get as much data as possible for their bucks. But when people are *not* busy, they still show a widespread pattern of activation in many areas of the brain — now known as the *default network* (Gusnard & Raichle, 2001) (see **FIGURE 5.5**). The areas of the default network are known to be involved in thinking about social life, about the self, and about the past and future — all the usual haunts of the daydreaming mind (Mitchell, 2006).

Efforts to Suppress Current Concerns Can Backfire

The current concerns that populate consciousness can sometimes get the upper hand, transforming daydreams or everyday thoughts into rumination and worry. When this happens, people may exert **mental control,** *the attempt to change conscious states of mind.* For example, someone troubled by a recurring worry about the future ("What if I can't get a decent job when I graduate?") might choose to try *not* to think about this because

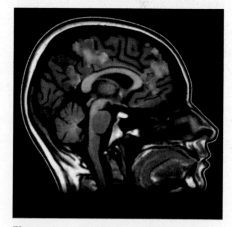

Figure 5.5   The Default Network Activated During Daydreaming An fMRI scan shows that many brain areas, known as the default network, are active when the person is not given a specific mental task to perform during the scan. Data from Science from Wondering Minds, Mason, et al., Vol. 315. January 19, 2007, pp. 393–305

mental control The attempt to change conscious states of mind.

Figure 5.6 Rebound Effect Research participants were first asked to try not to think about a white bear, and then to ring a bell whenever it came to mind. Compared to those who were simply asked to think about a bear without prior suppression, those people who first suppressed the thought showed a rebound of increased thinking about the bear (Wegner et al., 1987).

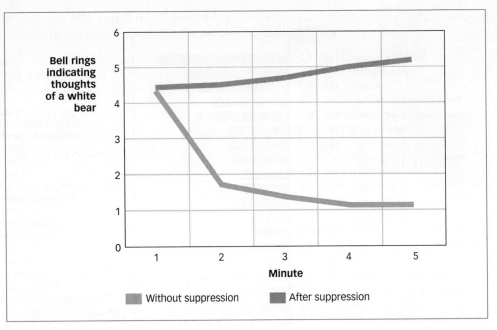

Go ahead, look away from this book for a minute and try not to think about a white bear. Larry Williams/Getty Images

thought suppression The conscious avoidance of a thought.

rebound effect of thought suppression The tendency of a thought to return to consciousness with greater frequency following suppression.

ironic processes of mental control A mental process that can produce ironic errors because monitoring for errors can itself produce them.

it causes too much anxiety and uncertainty. Whenever this thought comes to mind, the person engages in **thought suppression,** the *conscious avoidance of a thought.* This may seem like a perfectly sensible strategy because it eliminates the worry and allows the person to move on to think about something else.

Or does it? Daniel Wegner and his colleagues (1987) asked research participants to try *not* to think about a white bear for 5 minutes while they recorded all their thoughts aloud into a tape recorder. The participants were asked to ring a bell if the thought of a white bear did come to mind. On average, they mentioned the white bear or rang the bell (indicating the thought) more than once per minute. Thought suppression simply didn't work and instead produced a flurry of returns of the unwanted thought.

What's more, when some research participants later were specifically asked to change tasks and deliberately *think* about a white bear, they became oddly preoccupied with it. A graph of their bell rings in **FIGURE 5.6** shows that for these participants, the white bear came to mind far more often than it did for people who had only been asked to think about the bear from the outset, with no prior suppression. This **rebound effect of thought suppression,** *the tendency of a thought to return to consciousness with greater frequency following suppression,* suggests that attempts at mental control may be difficult indeed. The act of trying to suppress a thought may itself cause that thought to return to consciousness in a robust way.

Processes Outside of Consciousness Can Stymie Attempts at Conscious Control

As with thought suppression, other attempts to steer consciousness in any direction can result in mental states that are precisely the opposite of those desired. How ironic: Trying to consciously achieve one task may produce precisely the opposite outcome! These ironic effects seem most likely to occur when the person is distracted or under stress. People who are distracted while they are trying to get into a good mood, for example, tend to become sad (Wegner et al., 1993), and those who are distracted while trying to relax actually become more anxious than those who are not trying to relax (Wegner et al., 1997). Likewise, an attempt not to overshoot a golf putt, undertaken during distraction, often yields the unwanted overshoot (Wegner et al., 1998). The theory of **ironic processes of mental control** proposes that such *ironic errors occur because the mental process* *that monitors errors can itself produce them* (Wegner, 1994, 2009). The irony about the attempt not to think of a white bear, for instance, is that a small part of the mind is *searching* for the white bear.

Build to the Outcomes

1. How does your mind know which information to allow into consciousness and which to filter out?
2. Which characteristic of full consciousness distinguishes it from minimal consciousness?
3. When do people go out of their way to avoid mirrors?
4. Which animals are aware of their own reflection in a mirror?
5. What part of the brain is active during daydreaming?
6. Is consciously avoiding a worrisome thought a sensible strategy?

The Unconscious Mind

Many mental processes are unconscious, in the sense that they occur without our experience of them. For example, think for a moment about the mental processes involved in simple addition. What happens in consciousness between hearing a problem (what's 4 + 5?) and thinking of the answer (9)? At a very young age you may have had to solve such problems by counting on your fingers. Now that you don't have to do that anymore (please tell me you don't have to do that anymore), the answer seems to pop into your head automatically, by virtue of a process that doesn't require you to be aware of any underlying steps and, for that matter, doesn't even *allow* you to be aware of the steps. Nothing conscious seems to bridge this gap, but the answer comes from somewhere, and this emptiness points to the unconscious mind.

Freudian Unconscious

As you read in the Evolution of Psychological Science chapter, Freud's psychoanalytic theory viewed conscious thought as the surface of a much deeper mind made up of unconscious processes — but far more than just a collection of hidden processes. Freud described a **dynamic unconscious** — *an active system encompassing a lifetime of hidden memories, the person's deepest instincts and desires, and the person's inner struggle to control these forces.* The dynamic unconscious might contain hidden sexual thoughts about one's parents, for example, or destructive urges aimed at a helpless infant — the kinds of thoughts people keep secret from others and may not even acknowledge to themselves. According to Freud's theory, the unconscious is a force to be held in check by **repression,** *a mental process that removes unacceptable thoughts and memories from consciousness and keeps them in the unconscious.* Freud believed that without repression, a person might think, do, or say every unconscious impulse or animal urge, no matter how selfish or immoral. With repression, these desires are held in the recesses of the dynamic unconscious.

Freud looked for evidence of the unconscious mind in speech errors and lapses of consciousness, which are commonly called *Freudian slips.* Forgetting the name of someone you dislike, for example, is a slip that seems to have special meaning. Freud believed that errors are not random and instead have meaning that may have been created by an intelligent unconscious mind, even though the person consciously disavows them. Of course, suggesting that there is special meaning to any one thing a person says, or that there is a pattern to a series of random events is not the same as scientifically predicting and explaining when and why an event should happen. Anyone can offer a reasonable, compelling explanation for an event after it has already happened ("That must have been a Freudian slip!"), but the true work of science is to offer testable hypotheses that can be evaluated based on reliable evidence. Unfortunately, Freud's theories about the unconscious have not been supported by scientific research over the past 100 years.

Learning Outcomes

- Compare Freud's conception of the unconscious with the modern view.
- Explain the dual process perspective.

There are no conscious steps between hearing an easy problem (what's 4 + 5?) and thinking of the answer — unless you have to count on your fingers. Fuse/Corbis/Getty Images

dynamic unconscious An active system encompassing a lifetime of hidden memories, the person's deepest instincts and desires, and the person's inner struggle to control these forces.

repression A mental process that removes unacceptable thoughts and memories from consciousness and keeps them in the unconscious.

cognitive unconscious All the mental processes that give rise to a person's thoughts, choices, emotions, and behavior even though they are not experienced by the person.

dual process theories Theories that suggest that we have two different systems in our brains for processing information: one dedicated to fast, automatic, and unconscious processing, and the other dedicated to slow, effortful, and conscious processing.

altered state of consciousness A form of experience that departs significantly from the normal subjective experience of the world and the mind.

A Modern View of the Cognitive Unconscious

Modern psychologists share Freud's interest in the impact of unconscious mental processes on consciousness and on behavior. However, rather than seeing Freud's vision of the unconscious as a teeming menagerie of animal urges and repressed thoughts, the current study of the unconscious mind views it as a rapid, automatic information processor that influences our thoughts, feelings, and behaviors. The **cognitive unconscious** includes *all the mental processes that give rise to a person's thoughts, choices, emotions, and behavior even though they are not experienced by the person.*

Modern views of cognition propose that we have two different types of minds wired into our one little brain. **Dual process theories** suggest that we have *two different systems in our brains for processing information: one dedicated to fast, automatic, and unconscious processing; and the other dedicated to slow, effortful, and conscious processing* (Kahneman, 2011). The fast, automatic system (called System 1) is at work when you effortlessly engage in activities such as reading these words; solving problems such as $2 + 2 =$ _____; and walking down the street avoiding people, cars, and other obstacles. You use the slow, effortful system (called System 2) when you rationally and intentionally work to complete a task, such as answering this chapter's quiz questions, solving problems such as $245 \times 32 =$ _____, and placing an order at a restaurant.

In his book *Thinking Fast and Slow,* Nobel laureate Daniel Kahneman (2011) suggests that Systems 1 and 2 are both continuously active whenever we are awake: System 1 helps you efficiently navigate your daily life, and System 2 becomes engaged when more serious mental effort is involved. For instance, if you are walking around campus from one class to another — a walk that you have taken dozens of times — System 1 will guide you. However, if you happen upon a clown holding a fist full of rubber chickens, System 2 may come online to help you resolve this apparent conflict between what System 1 expected and what it observed. In this way, System 2 uses information and inputs from System 1 to help guide your future behavior.

This dual process perspective is similar in some ways to Freud's idea of the split between the unconscious mind and the conscious mind. However, dual process theories do not incorporate all of Freud's beliefs about hidden urges, defense mechanisms, Freudian slips, and the like. Instead, they simply propose that we have these two different ways of processing information that draw on different neural pathways. Dual process theories have been used to understand the workings of different cognitive processes, such as attention, learning, and memory (e.g., see the discussions of implicit and explicit learning and memory in later chapters on these topics), and continue to guide thinking and research in many different areas of psychology.

Build to the Outcomes

1. According to Freud, what is the source of unconscious errors in speech?

2. What is the difference between System 1 and System 2 ways of processing information?

Sleep and Dreaming: Good Night, Mind

Learning Outcomes

- Describe the stages of sleep.
- Identify the types of sleep disorders.
- Compare the two leading theories of why we dream.

Sleep can produce a state of unconsciousness in which the mind and brain apparently turn off the functions that create experience: The theater in your mind is closed. But this is an oversimplification because the theater seems to reopen during the night for special shows of bizarre cult films: dreams. Dream consciousness involves a transformation of experience that is so radical it is commonly considered an **altered state of consciousness:** *a form of experience that departs significantly from the normal subjective experience of the world and the mind.* Such altered states can be accompanied by changes in thinking, disturbances in the sense of time, feelings of loss of control, changes in emotional expression, alterations in body image and sense of self, perceptual distortions, and changes in meaning or significance (Ludwig, 1966). Sleep and dreams provide two unique perspectives on consciousness: a view of the mind without consciousness and a view of consciousness in an altered state.

Sleep

Consider a typical night. As you begin to fall asleep, the busy, task-oriented thoughts of the waking mind are replaced by wandering thoughts and images, as well as odd juxtapositions, some of them almost dreamlike. This presleep consciousness is called the *hypnagogic state*. On some rare nights you might experience a *hypnic jerk,* a sudden quiver or sensation of dropping, as though missing a step on a staircase. No one is quite sure why these happen. Eventually, your presence of mind goes away entirely. Time and experience stop, you are unconscious, and in fact there seems to be no "you" there to have experiences. But then come dreams, whole vistas of a vivid and surrealistic consciousness you just don't get during the day, a set of experiences that occur with the odd prerequisite that there is nothing "out there" that you are actually experiencing. More patches of unconsciousness may occur, with more dreams here and there. And finally, the glimmerings of waking consciousness return again in a foggy and imprecise form as you enter postsleep consciousness (the *hypnopompic state*) and then awake, often with bad hair.

***Dreamers*, by Albert Joseph Moore (1879/1882)** Although their bodies are in the same room, their minds are probably worlds apart—just as it is for you and those who may be sleeping nearby. Moore, Albert Joseph/Birmingham Museums and Art Gallery/The Bridgeman Art Library

Sleep Cycle

The sequence of events that occurs during a night of sleep is part of one of the major rhythms of human life, the cycle of sleep and waking. This **circadian rhythm** is *a naturally occurring 24-hour cycle*, from the Latin *circa* ("about") and *dies* ("day"). Even people sequestered in underground buildings without clocks, who are allowed to sleep when they want, tend to have a rest–activity cycle of about 25.1 hours (Aschoff, 1965). This slight deviation from 24 hours is not easily explained (Lavie, 2001), but it seems to underlie the tendency many people have to want to stay up a little later each night and wake up a little later each day. We're 25.1-hour people living in a 24-hour world.

The sleep cycle is far more than a simple on–off routine, however, since many bodily and psychological processes ebb and flow in this rhythm. EEG (electroencephalograph) recordings of the human brain reveal a regular pattern of changes in electrical activity in the brain accompanying the circadian cycle. During waking, these changes involve alternating between high-frequency activity (*beta waves*) during alertness and lower-frequency activity (*alpha waves*) during relaxation.

The largest changes in EEG occur during sleep. These changes show a regular pattern over the course of the night that corresponds to five sleep stages (see **FIGURE 5.7**). In the first stage of sleep, the EEG moves to frequency patterns even lower than alpha waves (*theta waves*). In the second stage of sleep, these patterns are interrupted by short bursts of activity called *sleep spindles* and *K complexes,* and the sleeper becomes somewhat more difficult to awaken. The deepest stages of sleep are stages 3 and 4, known as slow-wave sleep, in which the EEG patterns show activity called *delta waves*.

During fifth sleep stage, **REM sleep,** *a stage of sleep characterized by rapid eye movements and a high level of brain activity,* EEG patterns become high-frequency sawtooth waves, similar to beta waves. This suggests that at this time, the mind is as active as it is during waking (see Figure 5.7). Sleepers wakened during REM periods report having dreams much more often than those wakened during non-REM periods (Aserinsky & Kleitman, 1953). During REM sleep, the pulse quickens, blood pressure rises, and there are telltale signs of sexual arousal. At the same time, measurements of muscle movements indicate that the sleeper is very still, except for a rapid side-to-side movement of the eyes. (Watch someone sleeping and you may be able to see the REMs through their closed eyelids. But be careful doing this with strangers down at the bus station.)

circadian rhythm A naturally occurring 24-hour cycle.

REM sleep A stage of sleep characterized by rapid eye movements and a high level of brain activity.

Figure 5.7 EEG Patterns During the Stages of Sleep
The waking brain shows high-frequency beta wave activity, which changes during drowsiness and relaxation to lower-frequency alpha waves. Stage 1 sleep shows lower-frequency theta waves, which are accompanied in stage 2 by irregular patterns called sleep spindles and K complexes. Stages 3 and 4 are marked by the lowest frequencies, delta waves. During REM sleep, EEG patterns return to higher-frequency sawtooth waves that resemble the beta waves of waking.

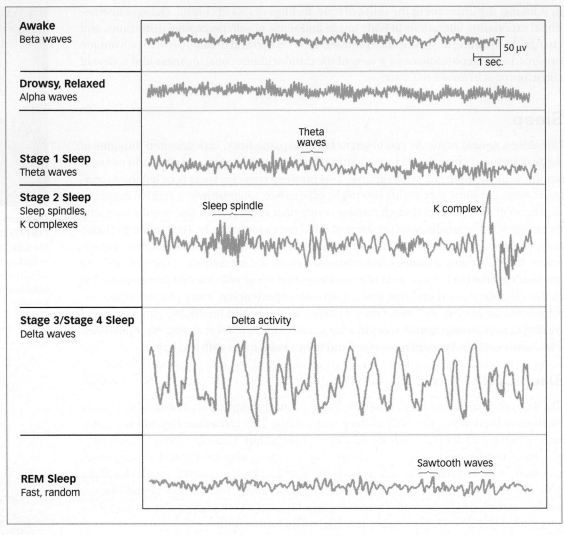

Psychologists learn about what happens when we sleep by collecting EEG and other measurements from research volunteers while they sleep in sleep laboratories such as this one. Ronald Frommann/Laif/Redux

Although many people believe that they don't dream much (if at all), some 80% of people awakened during REM sleep report dreams. If you've ever wondered whether dreams actually take place in an instant or whether they take as long to happen as the events they portray might take, the analysis of REM sleep offers an answer. Researchers woke volunteers either 5 minutes or 15 minutes after the onset of REM sleep and asked them to judge, on the basis of the events in the remembered dream, how long they had been dreaming (Dement & Kleitman, 1957). Sleepers in 92 of 111 cases were correct, suggesting that dreaming occurs in "real time." The discovery of REM sleep has offered many insights into dreaming, but not all dreams occur in REM periods. Some dreams are also reported in other sleep stages, and the dreams that occur at those times are described as less wild than REM dreams and more like normal thinking.

Putting EEG and REM data together produces a picture of how a typical night's sleep progresses through cycles of sleep stages (see **FIGURE 5.8**). In the first hour of the night, you fall all the way from waking to the fourth and deepest stage of sleep, the stage marked by delta waves. You then return to lighter sleep stages, eventually reaching REM and dreamland. You then continue to cycle between REM and slow-wave sleep stages every 90 minutes or so throughout the night. Periods of REM last longer as the night goes on, and lighter sleep stages predominate between these periods, with the deeper slow-wave stages 3 and 4 disappearing halfway through the night. Although you're either unconscious or dream-conscious at the time, your brain and mind cycle through a remarkable array of different states each time you have a night's sleep.

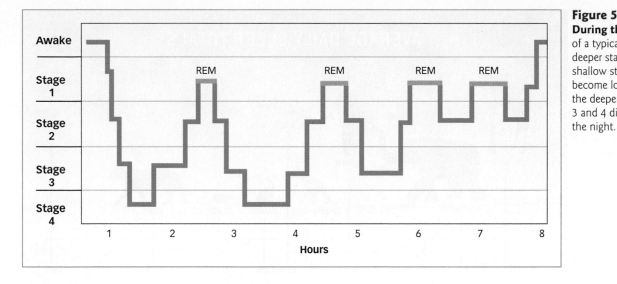

Figure 5.8 Stages of Sleep During the Night Over the course of a typical night, sleep cycles into deeper stages early on and then more shallow stages later. REM periods become longer in later cycles, and the deeper slow-wave sleep of stages 3 and 4 disappears halfway through the night.

Sleep Needs and Sleep Deprivation

How much do people sleep? The answer depends on the age of the sleeper (Dement, 1999). Newborns will sleep 6 to 8 times in 24 hours, often totaling more than 16 hours. Their napping cycle gets consolidated into "sleeping through the night," usually sometime between 9 and 18 months. The typical 6-year-old child might need 11 or 12 hours of sleep, and the progression to less sleep then continues into adulthood, when the average is about 7 to 7.5 hours per night. With aging, people can get along with even a bit less sleep than that. Over a whole lifetime, we get about 1 hour of sleep for every 2 hours we are awake.

This is a lot of sleeping. Could we tolerate less? For a 1965 science project, 17-year-old Randy Gardner stayed up for 264 hours and 12 minutes (just over 11 days). When he finally did go to sleep, he slept only 14 hours and 40 minutes and awakened essentially recovered (Dement, 1978).

Feats such as this one suggest that sleep might be expendable. This is the thinking behind the classic all-nighter that you may have tried just before a big exam. But, as it turns out, this is not the case. When people practice a difficult learning task and are then kept up all night, their learning of the task is wiped out (Stickgold et al., 2000). It is as though memories normally deteriorate unless sleep occurs to help keep them in place (see Hot Science: Can Sleep Enhance Learning? Yes! in the Memory chapter). Studying all night may help you cram for the exam, but it won't make the material stick, which pretty much defeats the whole purpose.

Sleep turns out to be a necessity rather than a luxury in other ways as well. At the extreme, sleep loss can be fatal. When rats are forced to break Randy Gardner's human waking record and stay awake even longer, they have trouble regulating their body temperature and lose weight, although they eat much more than normal. Their bodily systems break down and they die, on average, in 21 days (Rechtschaffen et al., 1983). Even for healthy young humans, a few hours of sleep deprivation each night can have a cumulative detrimental effect: It reduces mental acuity and reaction time, increases irritability and depression, and increases the risk of accidents and injury (Coren, 1997). (See Data Visualization How Does Sleep Affect You? at launchpadworks.com.)

Some researchers have deprived people of different sleep stages selectively by waking them whenever certain stages are detected. Memory problems and excessive aggression are observed in both humans and rats after only a few days of being awakened whenever REM activity starts (Ellman et al., 1991). Such REM deprivation causes a rebound of more REM sleep the next night (Brunner et al., 1990). Deprivation from slow-wave sleep (in stages 3 and 4), in turn, has more physical effects, with just a few nights of deprivation leaving people feeling tired and hypersensitive to pain (Lentz et al., 1999).

Sleep following learning is essential for memory consolidation. Sleep during class, on the other hand, not so much. Sonda Dawes/The Image Works

DATA Visualization

Figure 5.9 Average Daily Sleep Totals All animals seem to require sleep, although in differing amounts. Next time you oversleep and someone accuses you of "sleeping like a baby," you might tell them instead that you were sleeping like a tiger, or a brown bat. Ljerka ILIC/Hermera/Thinkstock

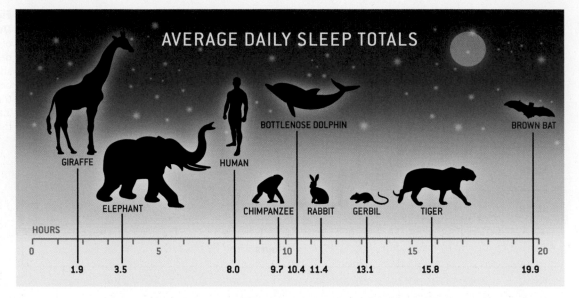

It's clearly dangerous to neglect the need for sleep. But why would we have such a need in the first place? All animals appear to sleep, although the amount of sleep required varies quite a bit (see **FIGURE 5.9**). Giraffes sleep less than 2 hours daily, whereas brown bats snooze for almost 20 hours. These variations in sleep needs, and the very existence of a need, are hard to explain. Sleep is, after all, potentially costly in the course of evolution. The sleeping animal is easy prey, so the habit of sleep would not seem to have developed unless it had significant benefits that made up for this vulnerability. Theories of sleep have not yet determined why the brain and body have evolved to need these recurring episodes of unconsciousness.

Sleep Disorders

In answer to the question "Did you sleep well?" the comedian Stephen Wright said, "No, I made a couple of mistakes." Sleeping well is something everyone would love to do, but for many people, sleep disorders are deeply troubling. The most common disorders that plague sleep include insomnia, sleep apnea, and somnambulism.

Insomnia, *difficulty in falling asleep or staying asleep,* is perhaps the most common sleep disorder. About 30 to 48% of people report symptoms of insomnia, and 6% of people meet criteria for a diagnosis of insomnia, which involves persistent and impairing sleep problems (Bootzin & Epstein, 2011; Ohayon, 2002). Insomnia has many potential causes. In some instances, it results from lifestyle choices such as working night shifts (self-induced insomnia), whereas in other cases it occurs in response to depression, anxiety, or some other condition (secondary insomnia). Regardless of type, insomnia can be exacerbated by worrying about insomnia (Blake, Trinder, & Allen, 2018). No doubt you've experienced some nights when sleeping was a high priority, such as before a class presentation or an important interview, and you've found that you were unable to fall asleep. The desire to sleep initiates an ironic process of mental control — a heightened sensitivity to signs of sleeplessness — and this sensitivity interferes with sleep. Although sedatives can be useful for brief sleep problems associated with emotional events, their long-term use is not effective. Most sleeping pills are addictive and, even in short-term use, can reduce the proportion of time spent in REM and slow-wave sleep (Qureshi & Lee-Chiong, 2004), robbing people of dreams and their deepest sleep stages. As a result, the quality of sleep achieved with pills may not be as high as without them, and people may experience side effects such as grogginess and irritability during the day.

Roz Chast/The New Yorker Collection/www.cartoonbank.com

insomnia Difficulty in falling asleep or staying asleep.

Sleep apnea is *a disorder in which the person stops breathing for brief periods while asleep.* A person with apnea usually snores because apnea involves an involuntary obstruction of the breathing passage. When episodes of apnea occur for over 10 seconds at a time and recur many times during the night, they may cause many awakenings and sleep loss or insomnia. Apnea occurs most often in middle-aged, overweight men (Punjabi, 2008) and may go undiagnosed because it is not easy for the sleeper to notice. Bed partners may be the ones who finally get tired of the snoring and noisy gasping for air when the sleeper's breathing restarts, or the sleeper may eventually seek treatment because of excessive sleepiness during the day. Therapies involving weight loss, drugs, sleep masks that push air into the nasal passage, or surgery may solve the problem.

Somnambulism (or **sleepwalking**) occurs when *a person arises and walks around while asleep.* Sleepwalking is more common in children, peaking between the ages of 4 and 8 years, with 15 to 40% of children experiencing at least one episode (Bhargava, 2011). Sleepwalking tends to happen early in the night, usually during slow-wave sleep. Sleepwalkers may awaken during their walk or return to bed without waking, in which case they will probably not remember the episode in the morning. The sleepwalker's eyes are usually open in a glassy stare. Walking with hands outstretched is uncommon except in cartoons. Sleepwalking is not usually linked to any additional problems and is problematic only in that sleepwalkers sometimes engage in unwise behaviors such leaving the house while still sleeping, and they can trip over furniture or fall down stairs. Contrary to popular belief, it is safe to wake sleepwalkers or lead them back to bed.

Other sleep disorders are less common. **Narcolepsy** is *a disorder in which sudden sleep attacks occur in the middle of waking activities.* Narcolepsy is often accompanied by unrelenting excessive sleepiness and uncontrollable sleep attacks lasting from 30 seconds to 30 minutes. This disorder appears to have a genetic basis because it runs in families, and it can be treated effectively with medication. **Sleep paralysis** is *the experience of waking up unable to move.* This eerie experience usually happens as you are awakening from REM sleep but before you have regained motor control. This period typically lasts only a few seconds or minutes and can be accompanied by hallucinations in which dream content may appear to occur in the waking world. **Night terrors** (or **sleep terrors**) are *abrupt awakenings with panic and intense emotional arousal.* These terrors, which occur most often in children and in only about 2% of adults (Ohayon et al., 1999), happen most often in non-REM sleep early in the sleep cycle and do not usually have dream content the sleeper can report.

To sum up, a lot happens when we close our eyes for the night. Humans follow a pretty regular sleep cycle, going through the five stages of sleep during the night. Disruptions to that cycle, either from sleep deprivation or sleep disorders, can produce consequences for waking consciousness. But something else happens during a night's sleep that affects our consciousness, both while asleep and when we wake up.

Dreams

The pioneering sleep researcher William C. Dement (1959) said, "Dreaming permits each and every one of us to be quietly and safely insane every night of our lives." Indeed, dreams do seem to have a touch of insanity about them. Even more bizarre is the fact that we are the writers, producers, and directors of the crazy things we experience. Just what are these experiences, and how can they be explained?

Dream Consciousness

Dreams depart dramatically from reality. You may dream of being naked in public, of falling from a great height, of your teeth falling out, or of being chased. These things don't happen much in reality unless you're having a terrible, horrible, no good, very bad day.

Sleepwalkers in cartoons often have their arms outstretched and eyes closed, but that's just for cartoons. A real-life sleepwalker usually walks normally with eyes open, sometimes with a glassy look. Matthew Nock

sleep apnea A disorder in which the person stops breathing for brief periods while asleep.

somnambulism (sleepwalking) Occurs when a person arises and walks around while asleep.

narcolepsy A disorder in which sudden sleep attacks occur in the middle of waking activities.

sleep paralysis The experience of waking up unable to move.

night terrors (sleep terrors) Abrupt awakenings with panic and intense emotional arousal.

The quality of consciousness in dreaming is also altered significantly from waking consciousness. Five major characteristics of dream consciousness distinguish it from the waking state (Hobson, 1988).

1. We intensely feel *emotion,* whether it is bliss or terror or love or awe.

2. Dream *thought* is illogical: The continuities of time, place, and person don't apply. You may find you are in one place and then another without any travel in between — or people may change identity from one dream scene to the next.

3. *Sensation* is fully formed and meaningful; visual sensation is predominant, and you may also deeply experience sound, touch, and movement (although pain is uncommon).

4. Dreaming occurs with *uncritical acceptance,* as though the images and events are perfectly normal rather than bizarre.

5. We have *difficulty remembering* the dream after it is over. People often remember dreams only if they are awakened during the dream and even then may lose recall for the dream within just a few minutes of waking. If your waking memory were this bad, you'd be standing around half-naked in the street much of the time, having forgotten your intended destination, clothes, and lunch money.

Not all of our dreams are fantastic and surreal, however. We often dream about mundane topics that reflect prior waking experiences or "day residue." Current concerns pop up (Nikles et al., 1998), along with images from the recent past. For instance, after a fun day at the beach, your dream that night might include cameo appearances by bouncing beach balls or a flock of seagulls. The content of dreams takes snapshots from the day rather than retelling the stories of what you have done or seen. This means that dreams often come without clear plots or story lines, so they may not make a lot of sense.

Some of the most memorable dreams are nightmares, and these frightening dreams can wake up the dreamer (Levin & Nielsen, 2009). One set of daily dream logs from college undergraduates suggested that the average student has about 24 nightmares per year (Wood & Bootzin, 1990), although some people may have them as often as every night. Children have more nightmares than adults, and people who have experienced traumatic events often have nightmares that relive those events.

Dream Theories

Dreams are puzzles that cry out to be solved. The search for dream meaning goes all the way back to biblical figures, who interpreted dreams and looked for prophecies in them. In the Old Testament, the prophet Daniel (a favorite of three of the authors of this book) curried favor with King Nebuchadnezzar of Babylon by interpreting the king's dreams. Unfortunately, the meaning of dreams is usually far from obvious.

In the first psychological theory of dreams, Freud (1900/1965) proposed that dreams are confusing and obscure because the dynamic unconscious creates them precisely *to be* confusing and obscure. According to Freud, dreams represent wishes, and some of these wishes are so unacceptable, taboo, and anxiety-inducing that the mind can express them only in disguised form. Freud believed that many of the most unacceptable wishes are sexual. For instance, he would interpret a dream of a train going into a tunnel as symbolic of sexual intercourse. The problem with Freud's approach is that any dream has infinite potential interpretations. Finding the "correct" one is a matter of guesswork — and of convincing the dreamer that one interpretation is superior to the others.

Although dreams may not represent elaborately hidden wishes, there is evidence that they do feature the return of suppressed thoughts. Researchers asked volunteers to think of a personal acquaintance and then to spend 5 minutes before going to bed writing down whatever came to mind (Wegner et al., 2004). Some participants were

***The Nightmare,* by Henry Fuseli (1790)**
Fuseli depicts not only a mare in this painting but also an incubus — an imp perched on the dreamer's chest that is traditionally associated with especially horrifying nightmares. Goethe House and Museum/Snark/Art Resource, NY

asked to suppress thoughts of this person as they wrote, others were asked to focus on thoughts of the person, and still others were asked to just write freely about anything. The next morning, participants wrote dream reports. All participants mentioned dreaming more about the person they had named than about other people. But they most often dreamed of the person they named if they were in the group that had been assigned to suppress thoughts of the person the night before. This finding suggests that dreams may indeed harbor unwanted thoughts. Perhaps this is why travelers often dream of getting lost, students often dream of missing tests, and professors often dream of forgetting their lectures.

Another key theory of dreaming is the **activation–synthesis model** (Hobson & McCarley, 1977), which proposes that dreams are produced when the brain attempts to make sense of random neural activity that occurs during sleep. During waking consciousness, the mind is devoted to making sense of the wide range of information that arrives through the senses. You figure out that the odd noise you're hearing during class is your cell phone vibrating, for example, or you realize that the strange smell in the hall outside your room must be from burned popcorn. In the dream state, the mind doesn't have access to external sensations, but it keeps on doing what it usually does: interpreting information. Because that information now comes from neural activations that occur in the now-closed system of the brain, without the continuity provided by the perception of reality, the brain's interpretive mechanisms can run free.

The Freudian theory and the activation–synthesis theory differ in the significance they place on the meaning of dreams. In Freud's theory, dreams begin with meaning, whereas in the activation–synthesis theory, dreams begin randomly — but meaning can be added as the mind lends interpretations in the process of dreaming. Dream research has not yet sorted out whether one of these theories or yet another might be the best account of the meaning of dreams.

The Dreaming Brain

What happens in the brain when we dream? Several fMRI studies show that the brain changes during REM sleep correspond with certain alterations of consciousness that occur in dreaming. **FIGURE 5.10** shows some of the patterns of activation and deactivation found in the dreaming brain (Nir & Tononi, 2010; Schwartz & Maquet, 2002).

Many dreams have emotional content: dangerous people lurking about, the occasional monster, some minor worries, and at least once in a while that major exam you've forgotten about until you walk into class. And it turns out that the amygdala,

activation–synthesis model The theory that dreams are produced when the brain attempts to make sense of random neural activity that occurs during sleep.

Freud theorized that dreams represent unacceptable wishes that the mind can express only in disguised form. The activation–synthesis model proposes that dreams are produced when the mind attempts to make sense of random neural activity that occurs during sleep. Suppose you are expecting a visit from an overbearing relative or acquaintance; the night before that person's arrival, you dream that a bus is driven through the living room window of your house. How might Freud have interpreted such a dream? How might the activation–synthesis model interpret such a dream?
© John Davenport/SanAntonio Express-News via ZUMA

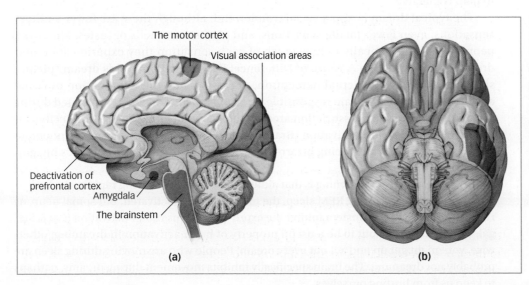

The motor cortex
Visual association areas
Deactivation of prefrontal cortex
Amygdala
The brainstem
(a)   (b)

Figure 5.10   Brain Activation and Deactivation During REM Sleep Brain areas shaded red are activated during REM sleep; those shaded blue are deactivated. (a) The medial view shows activation of the amygdala, the visual association areas, the motor cortex, and the brainstem, and deactivation of the prefrontal cortex. (b) The ventral view shows activation of other visual association areas and deactivation of the prefrontal cortex (Schwartz & Maquet, 2002).

Dreaming Blind

What are your dreams like? Are they mostly visual? Do you hear sounds? Do you experience the sense of touch? taste? smell? We all differ in our experience of dreaming, just as we do in our waking life. Most people have the ability to experience all of their senses during dreaming. But what is the experience of dreaming like for those who are blind? Researchers examined this question by asking people who are blind to keep dream journals each day for several weeks, and comparing their reports of their dreams with those of people with sight (Meaidi et al., 2014). Results revealed that 100% of dreams among sighted people contain visual impressions, compared with only about 75% of dreams among those who had sight and then lost it ("late blind") and 20% of dreams among those who were born blind ("congenitally blind"). It is perhaps not surprising that people who could never see are less likely to "see" during their dreams, but interesting that in 20% of their dreams they can see (although these visual impressions occur only in blind individuals who have at least some amount of light perception).

The lack of visual content in the dreams of people who are blind is made up for by a higher percentage of dreams containing auditory and tactile impressions, as shown in the figure.

Unfortunately, those who are congenitally blind also have a much higher frequency of nightmares, which occur in nearly 25% of their dreams. These nightmares often have the theme that the blind person is doing something wrong (as a result of their lack of sight), which leads to aggressive responses from others (Meaidi et al., 2014). Virtually all of psychology is focused on understanding the waking mind; however, there appear to be a wide range of important individual differences in the experience of the dreaming mind that are just beginning to be understood.

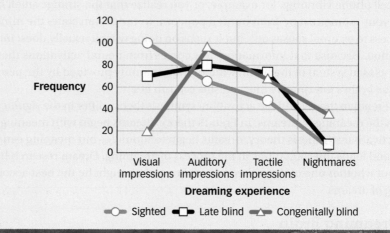

a brain area involved in responses to threatening or stressful events, is quite active during REM sleep. However, the prefrontal cortex shows relatively less arousal than it usually does during waking consciousness. What does this mean for the dreamer? As a rule, the prefrontal cortex is associated with planning and executing actions, and often dreams seem to be unplanned and rambling. Perhaps this is why dreams often don't have very sensible story lines — they've been scripted by an author whose ability to plan is inactive.

The typical dream is also a visual wonderland, although there are fewer auditory sensations, even fewer tactile sensations, and almost no smells or tastes. Moreover, people differ dramatically in how much of each sensation they experience in their dreams, as described in A World of Difference: Dreaming Blind. This dream "picture show" doesn't involve actual perception, of course, just the imagination of visual events. The areas of the brain responsible for visual perception are *not* activated during dreaming, but the visual association areas in the occipital lobe that are responsible for visual imagery *do* show activation (Braun et al., 1998). Your brain is smart enough to realize that it's not really seeing bizarre images but acts instead as though it's imagining bizarre images.

Another odd fact of dreaming is that although the eyes are moving rapidly, the body is otherwise very still. During REM sleep, the motor cortex is activated, but spinal neurons running through the brainstem inhibit the expression of this motor activation (Lai & Siegal, 1999). This turns out to be a useful property of brain activation in dreaming; otherwise, you might get up and act out every dream! People who are moving during sleep are probably not dreaming. The brain specifically inhibits movement during dreams, perhaps to keep us from hurting ourselves.

Build to the Outcomes

1. What do EEG recordings tell us about sleep?

2. What are the stages in a typical night's sleep?

3. What is the relationship between sleep and learning?

4. What are some problems caused by sleeping pills?

5. Is it safe to wake a sleepwalker?

6. What distinguishes dream consciousness from the waking state?

7. According to Freud, what do dreams represent?

8. What does the activation–synthesis model propose about the link between the brain and dreams?

9. What do fMRI studies tell us about why dreams don't have coherent story lines?

Drugs and Consciousness: Artificial Inspiration

The author of the dystopian novel *Brave New World,* Aldous Huxley (1932), once wrote of his experiences with the drug mescaline. His book *The Doors of Perception* described "a world where everything shone with the Inner Light, and was infinite in its significance. The legs, for example, of a chair — how miraculous their tubularity, how supernatural their polished smoothness! I spent several minutes — or was it several centuries? — not merely gazing at those bamboo legs, but actually *being* them" (Huxley, 1954, p. 22).

Being the legs of a chair? This probably is better than being the seat of a chair, but it still sounds like an odd experience. Nevertheless, many people seek out such experiences, often through the use of drugs. **Psychoactive drugs** are *chemicals that influence consciousness or behavior by altering the brain's chemical message system.* You read about several such drugs in the Neuroscience and Behavior chapter when we explored the brain's system of neurotransmitters. And you will read about them in a different light when we turn to their role in the treatment of psychological disorders in the Treatment chapter. Whether these drugs are used for entertainment, for treatment, or for other reasons, they each exert their influence by increasing the activity of a neurotransmitter (the agonists) or decreasing its activity (the antagonists). Like Huxley, who perceived himself becoming the legs of a chair, people using drugs can have experiences unlike any they might find in normal waking consciousness or even in dreams. To understand these altered states, let's explore how people use and abuse drugs, and examine the major categories of psychoactive drugs.

Drug Use and Addiction

Why do children sometimes spin around until they get dizzy and fall down? There is something strangely attractive about states of consciousness that depart from the norm, and people throughout history have sought out these altered states by dancing, fasting, chanting, meditating, and ingesting a bizarre assortment of chemicals to intoxicate themselves (Crocq, 2007). People pursue altered consciousness even when there are costs, from the nausea that accompanies dizziness to the life-wrecking obsession with a drug that can come with addiction. In this regard, the pursuit of altered consciousness can be a fatal attraction.

In one study researchers allowed rats to administer cocaine to themselves intravenously by pressing a lever (Bozarth & Wise, 1985). Over the course of the 30-day study, the rats not only continued to self-administer at a high rate but also occasionally binged to the point of giving themselves convulsions. They stopped grooming themselves and eating until they lost on average almost a third of their body weight. About 90% of the rats died by the end of the study.

Rats are not tiny humans, of course, so such research is not a complete basis for understanding human responses to cocaine. But these results do make it clear that cocaine is addictive and that the consequences of such addiction can be dire. Other laboratory studies show that animals will work to obtain not only cocaine but also alcohol, amphetamines, barbiturates, caffeine, opiates (such as morphine and heroin), nicotine, phencyclidine (PCP), MDMA (Ecstasy), and THC (tetrahydrocannabinol, the active ingredient in marijuana).

Learning Outcomes

- Explain the dangers of addiction.
- Identify categories of psychoactive drugs and their effects on the body.

Why do kids enjoy spinning around until they get so dizzy that they fall down? Even when we are young, there seems to be something enjoyable about altering states of consciousness. Matthew Nock

psychoactive drugs Chemicals that influence consciousness or behavior by altering the brain's chemical message system.

Figure 5.11 Drug Addiction Often Occurs as the Motivation to Use Drugs Shifts from Positive to Negative Reinforcement Recent research suggests that people often start out using drugs because of the positive experiences they have as a result. But over time, addiction can result if people continue to use drugs to avoid the unpleasant effects of drug withdrawal (George & Koob, 2017).

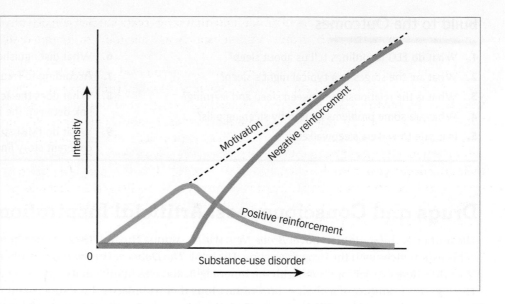

Dangers of Addiction

People usually do not become addicted to a psychoactive drug the first time they use it. They may experiment a few times, then try again, and eventually find that their tendency to use the drug increases over time. Research suggests that drug use is initially motivated by *positive reinforcement,* which refers to an increase in the likelihood of a behavior following the presentation of a reward. In other words, people often try and then repeat the use of psychoactive drugs because those drugs induce a positive psychological state. Over time, however, some drugs become less rewarding and the motivation to continue to take them is driven by *negative reinforcement,* which refers to an increase in the likelihood of a behavior following the removal of an aversive state (see **FIGURE 5.11**). That is, people often continue to use psychoactive drugs to reduce or eliminate withdrawal symptoms that arise after the drug leaves their system (George & Koob, 2017). Three primary factors are influential in this process:

1. **Drug tolerance** refers to *the tendency for larger drug doses to be required over time to achieve the same effect.* Physicians who prescribe morphine to control pain in their patients are faced with tolerance problems because steadily greater amounts of the drug may be needed to dampen the same pain. With increased tolerance comes the danger of drug overdose; recreational users find they need to use more and more of a drug to produce the same high. But then, if a new batch of heroin or cocaine is more concentrated than usual, the "normal" amount the user takes to achieve the same high can be fatal.

2. *Physical dependence* refers to the pain, convulsions, hallucinations, or other unpleasant symptoms that accompany withdrawal from drug use. People who suffer from physical dependence may seek to continue drug use to avoid becoming physically ill. A common example is the "caffeine headache" some people complain of when they haven't had their daily jolt of java.

3. *Psychological dependence* refers to a strong desire to return to the drug even when physical withdrawal symptoms are gone. Drugs can create an emotional need over time that continues to prey on the mind, particularly in circumstances that are reminders of the drug. Some ex-smokers report longing wistfully for an after-dinner smoke, for example, even years after they've successfully quit the habit.

There Are Individual Differences in Risk for Addiction

There continues to be a great deal of debate about the extent to which we should think of addiction as a choice (i.e., a person can simply decide to use drugs or not), or as a disease over which a person has little or no control. Those who suggest that

drug tolerance The tendency for larger doses of a drug to be required over time to achieve the same effect.

choice plays a prominent role in addiction note that large-scale studies consistently show that approximately 75% of those with substance use disorders overcome their addiction (Heyman, 2009).

For instance, one classic study of soldiers who became addicted to heroin in Vietnam found that years after their return, only 12% remained addicted (Robins et al., 1980). Resuming the activities, attractions, and obligations of normal life, as well as leaving behind the places and faces associated with their old drug habit, made it possible for returning soldiers to quit successfully — or so the argument goes. More recent, carefully controlled laboratory studies, in which participants were asked to select between a hit of their drug of choice or a small monetary reward (e.g., $5), show that people addicted to drugs such as crack cocaine and methamphetamine very often choose a small monetary reward over taking the drug. This suggests that the decision to use addictive drugs often can be under a person's control (Hart, 2013).

On the other hand, those who argue that addiction is a disease note research over the past several decades suggesting that some people have clear genetic, neurobiological, and social predispositions to have deficits in their ability to resist the urge to engage in drug use, even when doing so has extremely negative consequences such as losing one's home or family (Volkow & Boyle, 2018; Volkow et al., 2016). Not everyone has these predisposing factors; in fact, studies suggest that even among those who are exposed to drugs of addiction, only about 10% will go on to develop an addiction (Warner et al., 1995). Like the nature-versus-nurture debate more generally, the reality about drug addiction seems not to be an either–or situation. Rather, it seems that most people do not have a genetic, neurobiological, or social predisposition to drug addiction; therefore, even if exposed to addictive drugs, they will be able to resist their short- or long-term use. However, some people are more strongly predisposed to have difficulties resisting the urge to use drugs — difficulties that, at the extreme end of the spectrum, can take the form of a disease that appears beyond a person's behavioral control.

What's Considered "Addictive" Can Change

Although "addiction" as a concept is familiar to most of us, there is no standard clinical definition of what an addiction actually is. The concept of addiction has been extended to many human pursuits beyond drugs and alcohol, giving rise to such terms as *sex addict, gambling addict, workaholic,* and, of course, *chocoholic.* Societies react differently at different times. For instance, in the early 17th century, tobacco use was punishable by death

Many soldiers serving in Vietnam became addicted to heroin while there. Robins and colleagues (1980) found that after returning home to the United States, however, the vast majority left their drug habit behind and were no longer addicted.   Bettmann/Getty Images

The production, sale, and transportation of alcohol was made illegal in the United States in 1920. This period of "prohibition" ended in 1933 due to social and economic pressures. Although most U.S. counties now allow the sale of alcohol (shown on the map in green), there are still many counties with laws that restrict alcohol sales (shown in yellow) and even some "dry" counties where selling alcohol is illegal (shown in red). Why might the prohibition of alcohol have failed nationally?   SZ Photo/Scherl/Sueddeutsche Zeitung Photo/Alamy

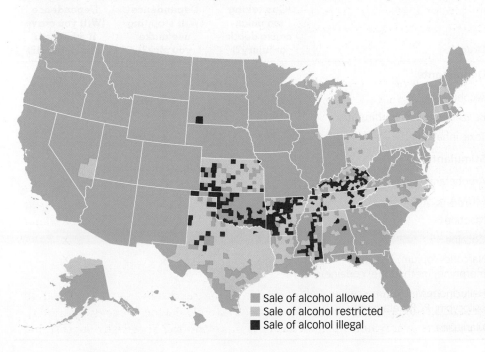

- Sale of alcohol allowed
- Sale of alcohol restricted
- Sale of alcohol illegal

in Germany, by castration in Russia, and by decapitation in China (Corti, 1931). Not a good time or place to be a smoker. By contrast, at several points throughout history, marijuana, cocaine, and heroin have all been popular and even recommended as medicines, each without any stigma of addiction attached (Inciardi, 2001).

In Western society today, the use of some drugs is accepted (e.g., caffeine), others are regulated (alcohol), others are simply taxed (tobacco), and still others are subjected to intense prohibition (marijuana, cocaine, and heroin) (see Hot Science: Why Is There an Opioid Epidemic and What Can We Do About It? for further discussion of drug use in our society). Rather than viewing *all* drug use as a problem, we need to consider the costs and benefits of such use, as well as establish ways to help people choose behaviors that are informed by this knowledge (Parrott et al., 2005).

Types of Psychoactive Drugs

Four in five North Americans use caffeine in some form every day, but not all psychoactive drugs are this familiar. To learn how both the well-known and lesser-known drugs influence the mind, let's consider several broad categories of drugs: depressants, stimulants, narcotics, hallucinogens, and marijuana. **TABLE 5.1** summarizes what is known about the potential dangers of these different types of drugs.

Depressants

Depressants are *substances that reduce the activity of the central nervous system*. Depressants have a sedative or calming effect, tend to induce sleep in high doses, and can arrest breathing in extremely high doses. Depressants can produce both physical and psychological dependence.

The most commonly used depressant is *alcohol,* the "king of the depressants," with its worldwide use beginning in prehistory, its easy availability in most cultures, and its widespread acceptance as a socially approved substance. Fifty-two percent of Americans

depressants Substances that reduce the activity of the central nervous system.

TABLE 5.1 Dangers of Drugs			
	Dangers		
Drug	**Overdose (Can taking too much cause death or injury?)**	**Physical Dependence (Will stopping use make you sick?)**	**Psychological Dependence (Will you crave it when you stop using it?)**
Depressants			
Alcohol	X	X	X
Benzodiazepines/barbiturates	X	X	X
Toxic inhalants	X	X	X
Stimulants			
Amphetamines	X	X	X
MDMA (Ecstasy)	X		?
Nicotine	X	X	X
Cocaine	X	X	X
Narcotics (opium, heroin, morphine, methadone, codeine)	X	X	X
Hallucinogens (LSD, mescaline, psilocybin, PCP, ketamine)	X		?
Marijuana		?	?

over 12 years of age report having had a drink in the past month, and 24% have binged on alcohol (over five drinks in succession) in that time. Young adults (ages 18–25) have even higher rates, with 62% reporting a drink the previous month and 42% reporting a binge (National Center for Health Statistics, 2012).

Alcohol's initial effects, euphoria and reduced anxiety, feel pretty positive. As alcohol is consumed in greater quantities, however, drunkenness results, bringing with it slowed reactions, slurred speech, poor judgment, and other reductions in the effectiveness of thought and action. The exact way in which alcohol influences neural mechanisms is still not understood, but, like other depressants, alcohol increases activity of the neurotransmitter GABA (Koob & Volkow, 2016). As you read in the Neuroscience and Behavior chapter, GABA normally inhibits the transmission of neural impulses; thus one effect of alcohol is to stop the firing of other neurons. Yet people react very differently to alcohol. Some become loud and aggressive, others become emotional and weepy, others become sullen, and still others turn giddy — and the same person can experience each of these effects in different circumstances. How can one drug do all this? Two theories have been offered to account for these variable effects: *expectancy theory* and *alcohol myopia*.

1. **Expectancy theory** suggests that *alcohol's effects can be produced by people's expectations of how alcohol will influence them in particular situations* (Marlatt & Rohsenow, 1980). So, for instance, if you've watched friends or family drink at weddings and notice that this often produces hilarity and gregariousness, you could well experience these effects yourself should you drink alcohol on a similarly festive occasion. Seeing people get drunk and fight in bars, on the other hand, might lead to aggression after drinking. Evidence for expectancy theory comes from studies where participants are given drinks containing alcohol or a substitute nonalcoholic liquid (adjusted for scent and color); some people in each group are led to believe they drank alcohol while others are led to believe they did not. These experiments often show that the mere *belief* that one has had alcohol can influence behavior as strongly as the ingestion of alcohol itself (Goldman et al., 1987).

2. The theory of **alcohol myopia** proposes that *alcohol hampers attention, leading people to respond in simple ways to complex situations* (Steele & Josephs, 1990). This theory recognizes that life is filled with complicated pushes and pulls, and our behavior is often a balancing act. Imagine that you are really attracted to someone who is dating your friend. Do you make your feelings known or focus on your friendship? The myopia theory holds that when you drink alcohol, your fine judgment is impaired. It becomes hard to appreciate the subtlety of these different options, and the inappropriate response is to veer full tilt one way or the other.

Both the expectancy and myopia theories suggest that people using alcohol will often go to extremes (Cooper, 2006). In fact, it seems that drinking is a major contributing factor to social problems that result from extreme behavior. Drinking while driving is a major cause of auto accidents (National Highway Traffic Safety Administration, 2018). Alcohol also has been linked to increased aggression toward others in dozens of studies, including increased likelihood of aggression in general, as well as sexual violence and intimate partner violence (Crane et al., 2015).

Compared to alcohol, the other depressants are much less popular but are still widely used and abused. *Barbiturates* such as Seconal and Nembutal are prescribed as sleep aids and as anesthetics before surgery. *Benzodiazepines* such as Valium and Xanax are tranquilizers and are prescribed as antianxiety drugs. These drugs are prescribed by physicians to treat anxiety or sleep problems, but physical dependence is possible, and psychological dependence is common as well.

Finally, *toxic inhalants* are easily accessible, even to children, in the vapors of household products such as glue, hair spray, nail polish remover, and gasoline. Sniffing or "huffing" vapors from these products can promote temporary effects that resemble drunkenness, but overdoses can be lethal, and continued use holds the potential for permanent neurological damage (Howard et al., 2011).

expectancy theory The idea that alcohol effects can be produced by people's expectations of how alcohol will influence them in particular situations.

alcohol myopia A condition that results when alcohol hampers attention, leading people to respond in simple ways to complex situations.

Which theory, expectancy theory or alcohol myopia, views a person's response to alcohol as being (at least partially) learned, by observing how others respond to alcohol?
Lise Gagne/E+/Getty Images

stimulants Substances that excite the central nervous system, heightening arousal and activity levels.

narcotics (opiates) Highly addictive drugs derived from opium that relieve pain.

Stimulants

Stimulants are *substances that excite the central nervous system, heightening arousal and activity levels.* They include caffeine, amphetamines, nicotine, cocaine, and Ecstasy, some of which sometimes have a legitimate pharmaceutical purpose. *Amphetamines* (also called *speed*), for example, were originally prepared for medicinal uses and as diet drugs; however, amphetamines such as Methedrine and Dexedrine are widely abused, causing insomnia, aggression, and paranoia with long-term use. Stimulants increase the levels of dopamine and norepinephrine in the brain, thereby increasing alertness and energy in the user, often producing a euphoric sense of confidence and a kind of agitated motivation to get things done. Stimulants produce physical and psychological dependence, and their withdrawal symptoms involve depressive effects such as fatigue and negative emotions.

Ecstasy (also known as MDMA, X, or E) is an amphetamine derivative. Ecstasy can make users feel empathic and close to those around them. It is used often as a party drug to enhance the group feeling at dance clubs or raves, but it has unpleasant side effects, such as interfering with the regulation of body temperature, making users highly susceptible to heat stroke and exhaustion. Although Ecstasy is not as likely as some other drugs to cause physical or psychological dependence, it nonetheless can lead to some dependence. What's more, the impurities sometimes found in street pills can be dangerous (Parrott, 2001). Mounting evidence from animal and human studies suggests that sustained use of Ecstasy is associated with damage to serotonergic neurons and may cause problems with mood, attention and memory, and impulse control (Kish et al., 2010; Urban et al., 2012).

Cocaine is derived from leaves of the coca plant, which has been cultivated by indigenous peoples of the Andes for millennia and chewed as a medication. And yes, the urban legend is true: Coca-Cola did contain cocaine until 1903 and may still use coca leaves to this day (with cocaine removed) as a flavoring — although the company's not telling. (Pepsi-Cola never contained cocaine and is probably made from something brown.) Sigmund Freud tried cocaine and wrote effusively about it for a while. Cocaine (usually snorted) and crack cocaine (smoked) produce exhilaration and euphoria and are seriously addictive, both for humans and the rats you read about earlier in this chapter. Dangerous side effects of cocaine use include psychological problems (e.g., insomnia, depression, aggression, and paranoia) as well as physical problems (e.g., death from a heart attack or hyperthermia) (Marzuk et al., 1998). Although cocaine has been used for many years as a party drug, its extraordinary potential to create dependence and its potentially lethal side effects should be taken very seriously.

The popularity of *nicotine* is something of a puzzle, however. This is a drug with almost nothing to recommend it to the newcomer. It usually involves inhaling smoke that doesn't smell that great, and there's not much in the way of a high, either — at best, some dizziness or a queasy feeling. So why do people use it? Tobacco use is motivated far more by the unpleasantness of quitting than by the pleasantness of using. The positive effects people report from smoking — relaxation and improved concentration, for example — come chiefly from relief from withdrawal symptoms (Baker et al., 2004). The best approach to nicotine is to never get started.

Narcotics

Opium, which comes from poppy seeds, and its derivatives heroin, morphine, methadone, and codeine (as well as prescription drugs such as Demerol and Oxycontin) are known as **narcotics** (or **opiates**), *highly addictive drugs derived from opium that relieve pain.* Narcotics induce a feeling of well-being and relaxation that is enjoyable, but they can also induce stupor and lethargy. The addictive properties of narcotics are powerful, and long-term use produces both tolerance and dependence. Because these drugs are often administered with hypodermic syringes, they also introduce the danger of diseases such as HIV when users share syringes. Unfortunately, these drugs are especially alluring because they mimic the brain's own internal relaxation and well-being system.

The brain produces endogenous opioids, or endorphins, which are neuropeptides closely related to opiates. As you learned in the Neuroscience and Behavior chapter, endorphins

Because of the known dangers of smoking cigarettes, many individuals are turning to electronic cigarettes (e-cigarettes) under the assumption that they are a safe alternative. However, an investigation of the chemicals contained in flavored e-cigarettes revealed that 92% of them contain the dangerous chemical diacetyl, which has been linked to severe and irreversible medical problems such as "popcorn lung" (Allen et al., 2016). Dai Sugano/San Jose Mercury News/Zuma Press

Why Is There an Opioid Epidemic and What Can We Do About It?

Opioids have been around in one form or another for thousands of years. For instance, an early medicine called theriac was used for more than 1,500 years to treat a range of illnesses, including anxiety and depression. Its more than 100 ingredients often included things like viper's flesh, roses, and carrots, but the only active ingredient turned out to be opium. Although opium and its derivatives have been consumed in some fashion for some time, our society has seen a startling rise in the use of opioids in the past few years. The rate of opioid overdoses has increased by more than 400% since the year 2000 (see the accompanying figure), leading scientists to declare an opioid epidemic and the U.S. president to call it a "public health emergency" (Blendon & Benson, 2018).

What's the reason for this drastic increase in opioid overdoses? Tragically, most people struggling with opioid dependence first received opioids not from a corner drug dealer, but from a licensed physician. Indeed, the increase in opiate-related overdoses over the past 20 years is mirrored by a similar increase in the number of prescriptions for opioids written by doctors over this same time period (Paulozzi et al., 2014). What seems to be happening is that doctors are (1) increasingly likely to prescribe opiates to patients who report experiencing pain and (2) many doctors are prescribing many more pills than are actually needed (some scientists have argued

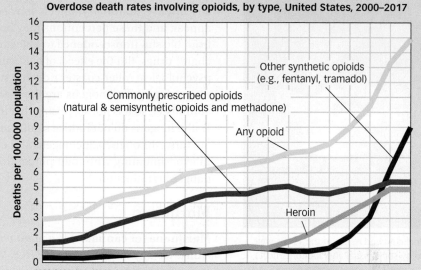

Overdose death rates involving opioids, by type, United States, 2000–2017

this is to avoid getting negative evaluations from patients, as nothing gets you low marks like a patient in pain). And the more pills a person is prescribed, the greater that person's likelihood of developing an opiate addiction over the next year (Shah et al., 2017). When those pills run out, people often turn to illegal sources of opiates (e.g., heroin) to escape their withdrawal symptoms, or they resort to more powerful (and toxic) synthetic opioids (e.g., fentanyl), which are often cheaper and easier to get than prescription opiates (Cicero et al., 2014).

So, what can be done to turn the tide on this epidemic? Scientists and policy makers are arguing for obvious fixes, such as implementing physician training and policy changes to decrease inappropriately high prescription of these drugs, developing less addictive pain medications, and initiating public education campaigns that alert communities and individuals to the dangers of potential opioid addiction (Volkow et al., 2019). It is too early to know if these strategies will be successful, or if other, more effective strategies will be required. What are some other approaches that might be tried?

play a role in how the brain copes internally with pain and stress. These substances reduce the experience of pain naturally. When you exercise for a while and start to feel your muscles burning, for example, you may also find that a time comes when the pain eases—sometimes even *during* exercise. Endorphins are secreted in the pituitary gland and other brain sites as a response to injury or exertion, creating a kind of natural remedy, sometimes referred to as "runner's high," that subsequently reduces pain and increases feelings of well-being.

When people use narcotics, the brain's endorphin receptors are artificially flooded, however, reducing receptor effectiveness and possibly also depressing the production of endorphins. When external administration of narcotics stops, withdrawal symptoms are likely to occur, which might partially explain the current opioid epidemic sweeping the United States (see Hot Science: Why Is There an Opioid Epidemic and What Can We Do About It? for more on this important topic).

Hallucinogens

The drugs that produce the most extreme alterations of consciousness are the **hallucinogens,** *which alter sensation and perception and often cause visual and auditory hallucinations.* These include LSD (lysergic acid diethylamide, or acid), mescaline,

hallucinogens Drugs that alter sensation and perception and often cause visual and auditory hallucinations.

Psychedelic art and music of the 1960s were inspired by some visual and auditory effects of drugs such as LSD. Andrew Herygers/Hurrah

psilocybin, PCP (phencyclidine), and ketamine (an animal anesthetic). Some of these drugs are derived from plants (mescaline from peyote cactus, psilocybin or shrooms from mushrooms) and have been used by people since ancient times. For example, the ingestion of peyote plays a prominent role in some Native American religious practices. The other hallucinogens, including LSD, are largely synthetic.

These drugs produce profound changes in perception. Sensations may seem unusually intense, stationary objects may seem to move or change, patterns or colors may appear, and these perceptions may be accompanied by exaggerated emotions ranging from blissful transcendence to abject terror. These are the "I've-become-the-legs-of-a-chair!" drugs. But the effects of hallucinogens are dramatic and unpredictable, creating a psychological roller-coaster ride that some people find intriguing and others find deeply disturbing. Hallucinogens are the main class of drugs that animals won't work to self-administer, so it is not surprising that in humans these drugs are unlikely to be addictive. Hallucinogens do not induce significant tolerance or dependence, and overdose deaths are rare. Although hallucinogens still enjoy a marginal popularity with people interested in experimenting with their perceptions, they have been more a cultural trend than a dangerous attraction.

Marijuana

Marijuana (or cannabis) is *a plant whose leaves and buds contain a psychoactive drug called tetrahydrocannabinol (THC).* When smoked or eaten, either as is or in concentrated form as *hashish,* this drug produces an intoxication that is mildly hallucinogenic. Users describe the experience as euphoric, with heightened senses of sight and sound and the perception of a rush of ideas. Marijuana affects judgment and short-term memory, and it impairs motor skills and coordination — making driving a car or operating heavy equipment a poor choice during its use. ("Dude, where's my bulldozer?")

Receptors in the brain that respond to THC (Stephens, 1999) are normally activated by a neurotransmitter called *anandamide* that is naturally produced in the brain (Wiley, 1999). Anandamide is involved in the regulation of mood, memory, appetite, and pain perception and has been found to temporarily stimulate overeating in laboratory animals, much as marijuana does in humans (Williams & Kirkham, 1999). Some chemicals found in dark chocolate also mimic anandamide, although very weakly, perhaps accounting for the well-being some people claim they enjoy after a "dose" of chocolate.

The addiction potential of marijuana is not strong because tolerance does not seem to develop, and physical withdrawal symptoms are minimal. Psychological dependence is possible, however, and some people do become chronic users. Marijuana use has been widespread throughout the world throughout recorded history, both as a medicine for pain and/or nausea and as a recreational drug, but its use remains controversial. Marijuana abuse and dependence have been linked with increased risk of depression, anxiety, and other forms of psychopathology. Many people also are concerned that marijuana (along with alcohol and tobacco) is a **gateway drug,** *a drug whose use increases the risk of the subsequent use of more harmful drugs.* Recent studies have challenged the gateway theory, and suggest that early-onset drug use in general, regardless of type of drug, increases the risk of later drug problems (Degenhardt et al., 2008).

Despite the federal laws against the use of marijuana, approximately 42% of adults in the United States have reported using it at some point in their lives — a rate much higher than that observed in most other countries (Degenhardt et al., 2008). Perhaps due to the perceived acceptability of marijuana among the general public, several states recently have taken steps to permit the sale of marijuana for medical purposes, to decriminalize possession of marijuana (so violators pay a fine rather than going to jail), or to legalize its sale and possession outright. The debate about the legal status of marijuana will likely take years to resolve. In the meantime, depending on where you live, the greatest risk of marijuana use may be incarceration (see Other Voices: A Judge's Plea for Pot).

marijuana (cannabis) The leaves and buds of the hemp plant, which contain a psychoactive drug called tetrahydrocannabinol (THC).

gateway drug A drug whose use increases the risk of the subsequent use of more harmful drugs.

A Judge's Plea for Pot

The Honorable Gustin L. Reichbach served as a New York State Supreme Court Justice from 1999 until 2012. He died of pancreatic cancer in July 2012. Rick Kopstein

Should all drugs be illegal? Where should we draw the line between acceptable chemical alteration of one's own consciousness and criminal or pathological behavior? Let's take a specific example — think for a minute about where you stand on the legalization of marijuana. The Honorable Gustin L. Reichbach (2012, p. A27), a New York State Supreme Court justice, wrote a strongly worded piece (slightly condensed here) on this issue, and his position surprised many people.

Three and a half years ago, on my 62nd birthday, doctors discovered a mass on my pancreas. It turned out to be Stage 3 pancreatic cancer. I was told I would be dead in four to six months. Today I am in that rare coterie of people who have survived this long with the disease. But I did not foresee that after having dedicated myself for 40 years to a life of the law, including more than two decades as a New York State judge, my quest for ameliorative and palliative care would lead me to marijuana.

My survival has demanded an enormous price, including months of chemotherapy, radiation hell and brutal surgery. For about a year, my cancer disappeared, only to return. About a month ago, I started a new and even more debilitating course of treatment. Every other week, after receiving an IV booster of chemotherapy drugs that takes three hours, I wear a pump that slowly injects more of the drugs over the next 48 hours.

Nausea and pain are constant companions. One struggles to eat enough to stave off the dramatic weight loss that is part of this disease. Eating, one of the great pleasures of life, has now become a daily battle, with each forkful a small victory. Every drug prescribed to treat one problem leads to one or two more drugs to offset its side effects. Pain medication leads to loss of appetite and constipation. Anti-nausea medication raises glucose levels, a serious problem for me with my pancreas so compromised. Sleep, which might bring respite from the miseries of the day, becomes increasingly elusive.

Inhaled marijuana is the only medicine that gives me some relief from nausea, stimulates my appetite, and makes it easier to fall asleep. The oral synthetic substitute, Marinol, prescribed by my doctors, was useless. Rather than watch the agony of my suffering, friends have chosen, at some personal risk, to provide the substance. I find a few puffs of marijuana before dinner gives me ammunition in the battle to eat. A few more puffs at bedtime permits desperately needed sleep.

This is not a law-and-order issue; it is a medical and a human rights issue. Being treated at Memorial Sloan Kettering Cancer Center, I am receiving the absolute gold standard of medical care. But doctors cannot be expected to do what the law prohibits, even when they know it is in the best interests of their patients. When palliative care is understood as a fundamental human and medical right, marijuana for medical use should be beyond controversy. . . .

Cancer is a nonpartisan disease, so ubiquitous that it's impossible to imagine that there are legislators whose families have not also been touched by this scourge. It is to help all who have been affected by cancer, and those who will come after, that I now speak. Given my position as a sitting judge still hearing cases, well-meaning friends question the wisdom of my coming out on this issue. But I recognize that fellow cancer sufferers may be unable, for a host of reasons, to give voice to our plight. It is another heartbreaking aporia in the world of cancer that the one drug that gives relief without deleterious side effects remains classified as a narcotic with no medicinal value.

Because criminalizing an effective medical technique affects the fair administration of justice, I feel obliged to speak out as both a judge and a cancer patient suffering with a fatal disease. . . . Medical science has not yet found a cure, but it is barbaric to deny us access to one substance that has proved to ameliorate our suffering.

How should we decide which consciousness-altering substances are okay for members of our society to use, and which should be made illegal? What criteria would you propose? Should this decision be based on negative health consequences associated with use of the substance? What weight should be given to positive consequences, such as those described by Justice Reichbach? Research described in this chapter tested, and failed to support, the gateway theory of drug use. If you had the opportunity to design and conduct a study to answer a key question in this area, what would you do?

Build to the Outcomes

1. What is the risk associated with increased tolerance to a drug?
2. Identify both physical and psychological drug withdrawal problems.
3. Why do people experience being drunk differently?
4. Do stimulants create dependency?

5. What are some of the dangerous side effects of cocaine use?
6. Why are narcotics especially alluring?
7. What are the effects of hallucinogens?
8. What are the risks of marijuana use?

Hypnosis: Open to Suggestion

When you think of hypnosis, you may envision people completely under the power of a hypnotist, who is ordering them to dance like a chicken or perhaps "regress" to early childhood and talk in childlike voices. But many common beliefs about hypnosis are false. **Hypnosis** refers to *a social interaction in which one person (the hypnotist) makes suggestions that lead to a change in another person's (the participant's) subjective experience of*

Learning Outcome

• Outline the evidence that hypnosis can lead to mental and behavioral changes.

the world (Kirsch et al., 2011). The essence of hypnosis is in leading people to expect that certain things will happen to them that are outside their conscious will (Wegner, 2002).

Induction and Susceptibility

To induce hypnosis, a hypnotist may ask the person being hypnotized to sit quietly and focus on some item, such as a spot on the wall (or a swinging pocket watch), and may then make suggestions to the person about what effects hypnosis will have (e.g., "your eyelids are slowly closing" or "your arms are getting heavy"). Even without hypnosis, some suggested behaviors might commonly happen just because a person is concentrating on them — just thinking about their eyelids slowly closing, for instance, may make many people shut their eyes briefly or at least blink. In hypnosis, however, suggestions may be made — and followed by people in a susceptible state of mind — for very unusual behavior that most people would not normally do, such as flapping their arms and making loud clucking sounds.

Not everyone is equally hypnotizable. Susceptibility varies greatly. Some highly suggestible people are very easily hypnotized, most people are only moderately influenced, and some people are entirely unaffected by attempts at hypnosis. One of the best indicators of a person's susceptibility is the person's own judgment. So if you think you might be hypnotizable, you may well be (Hilgard, 1965). People respond most strongly to hypnotic suggestions not only when they are highly susceptible but also when hypnotic suggestions are made very specifically and in the context of hypnotic induction rituals (Landry et al., 2017).

Hypnotic Effects

Some impressive demonstrations suggest that real changes occur in those under hypnosis. At the 1849 festivities for Prince Albert of England's birthday, for example, a hypnotized guest was asked to ignore any loud noises and then didn't even flinch when a pistol was fired near his face. These days, hypnotists are discouraged from using firearms during stage shows, but they often have volunteers perform other impressive feats. One common claim for superhuman strength under hypnosis involves asking a hypnotized person to become "stiff as a board" and lie unsupported with shoulders on one chair and feet on another while the hypnotist stands on the hypnotized person's body.

Studies have demonstrated that hypnosis can undermine memory, but with important limitations. People susceptible to hypnosis can be led to experience **posthypnotic amnesia,** *the failure to retrieve memories following hypnotic suggestions to forget.* In one study, a researcher taught a hypnotized person the populations of some remote cities and then suggested that the participant forget the study session; after the session, the person was quite surprised at being able to give the census figures correctly (Hilgard, 1986). Asked how he knew the answers, the individual decided he might have learned them from a TV program. Such amnesia can then be reversed in subsequent hypnosis.

Some important research has found that only memories that were lost while under hypnosis can be retrieved through hypnosis. The false claim that hypnosis helps people unearth memories they are not able to retrieve in normal consciousness seems to have surfaced because hypnotized people often make up memories to satisfy the hypnotist's suggestions. For example, Paul Ingram, a sheriff's deputy accused of sexual abuse by his daughters in the 1980s, was asked by interrogators in session after session to relax and imagine having committed the crimes. He emerged from these sessions having confessed to dozens of horrendous acts of "satanic ritual abuse." These confessions were called into question, however, when the independent investigator used the same technique to ask Ingram about an imaginary crime, something of which Ingram had never been accused. Ingram produced a three-page handwritten confession, complete with dialogue (Ofshe, 1992). Still, prosecutors in the case accepted Ingram's guilty plea; he was released only in 2003 after a public outcry and years of work on his defense. After a person claims to remember something, even under hypnosis, it is difficult to convince others that the memory was false (Loftus & Ketchum, 1994).

Stage hypnotists often perform an induction on the whole audience and then bring some of the more susceptible members on stage for further demonstrations. Photographer: Menelaos Prokos (www.athousandclicks.com) Hypnotist: Eric Walden (https://www.facebook.com/hypnotisteric)

hypnosis A social interaction in which one person (the hypnotist) makes suggestions that lead to a change in another person's (the participant's) subjective experience of the world.

posthypnotic amnesia The failure to retrieve memories following hypnotic suggestions to forget.

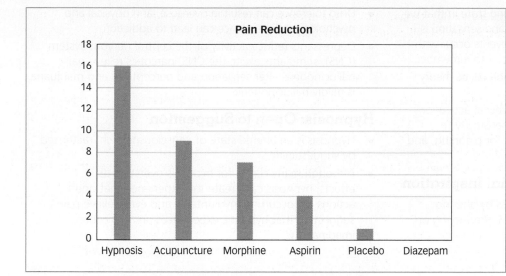

Figure 5.12 Hypnotic Analgesia The degree of pain reduction (values represent differences between experimental and control conditions on a self-reported pain scale) reported by people using different techniques for the treatment of laboratory-induced pain. Hypnosis wins (Stern et al., 1977).

Hypnosis can lead to measurable physical and behavioral changes in the body. One well-established effect is **hypnotic analgesia,** *the reduction of pain through hypnosis in people who are susceptible to hypnosis.* For example, one classic study (see **FIGURE 5.12**) found that for pain induced in volunteers in the laboratory, hypnosis was more effective than morphine, diazepam (Valium), aspirin, acupuncture, or placebos (Stern et al., 1977). The pain-reducing properties of hypnosis have been demonstrated repeatedly over the years, with recent research from controlled trials suggesting that it can even reduce the experience of pain in brain surgery during which the patient is awake (Frati et al., 2019).

It therefore appears that people under hypnotic suggestion are not merely telling the hypnotist what he or she wants to hear. Rather, they seem to be experiencing what they have been asked to experience.

hypnotic analgesia The reduction of pain through hypnosis in people who are susceptible to hypnosis.

Build to the Outcomes

1. What factors make someone more easily hypnotizable?
2. What type of memory can be retrieved through hypnosis?
3. Can hypnosis be as effective for pain relief as anesthesia?

CHAPTER REVIEW

The Mysteries of Consciousness

- People judge mind perception according to the capacities for experience and agency.
- Research suggests that mental activity happens first, paving the way for both conscious thought and action.

The Nature of Consciousness

- Consciousness has four basic properties: intentionality, unity, selectivity, and transience.
- Consciousness can also be understood in terms of three levels: minimal consciousness, full consciousness, and self-consciousness.
- Conscious contents can include current concerns, daydreams, and unwanted thoughts.
- Efforts to suppress a thought—such as of a white bear—may backfire as the mind searches for thoughts of that white bear to suppress.

The Unconscious Mind

- Unconscious processes are sometimes understood as expressions of the Freudian dynamic unconscious, but they are more commonly viewed as processes of the cognitive unconscious that create our conscious thought and behavior.
- The cognitive unconscious is at work when subliminal perception and unconscious decision processes influence thought or behavior without the person's awareness.

Sleep and Dreaming: Good Night, Mind

- During a night's sleep, the brain passes in and out of five stages of sleep; most dreaming occurs in the REM sleep stage.
- Being deprived of sleep and dreams has psychological and physical costs. Sleep can be disrupted through disorders that include insomnia, sleep apnea, somnambulism, narcolepsy, sleep paralysis, and night terrors.

- Dream consciousness differs from the waking state in that we feel emotion intensely, thought is illogical, and sensation is fully formed and meaningful; images and events occur with uncritical acceptance; and dreams are difficult to remember.
- Theories of dreaming include Freud's psychoanalytic theory and the activation–synthesis model.
- fMRI studies of the brain while dreaming reveal activations associated with visual imagery, increased sensitivity to emotions such as fear, lessened capacities for planning, and the prevention of motor movement.

Drugs and Consciousness: Artificial Inspiration

- Psychoactive drugs influence consciousness by altering the brain's chemical messaging system and intensifying or dulling the effects of neurotransmitters.

- Drug tolerance can result in overdose, and physical and psychological dependence can lead to addiction.
- Depressants reduce activity of the central nervous system (CNS); stimulants excite the CNS; narcotics relieve pain; hallucinogens alter sensation and perception; and marijuana is mildly hallucinogenic.

Hypnosis: Open to Suggestion

- Hypnosis is an altered state of consciousness characterized by suggestibility.
- Although many claims for hypnosis overstate its effects, hypnosis can create the experience that one's actions are occurring involuntarily and even relieve pain, suggesting that hypnotic experiences are more than imagination.

Key Concept Quiz

1. Which of the following is NOT a basic property of consciousness?
   a. intentionality
   b. disunity
   c. selectivity
   d. transience

2. Currently, unconscious processes are understood as
   a. a concentrated pattern of thought suppression.
   b. a hidden system of memories, instincts, and desires.
   c. a blank slate.
   d. unexperienced mental processes that give rise to thoughts and behavior.

3. The _____ unconscious is at work when subliminal and unconscious processes influence thought and behavior.
   a. minimal
   b. repressive
   c. dynamic
   d. cognitive

4. The cycle of sleeping and waking is one of the major patterns of human life called
   a. the circadian rhythm.
   b. the sleep stages.
   c. the altered state of consciousness.
   d. subliminal perception.

5. Sleep needs _____ over the life span.
   a. decrease
   b. increase
   c. fluctuate
   d. remain the same

6. During dreaming, the dreamer _____ changes in emotion, thought, and sensation.
   a. is skeptical of
   b. is completely unconscious of
   c. uncritically accepts
   d. views objectively

7. Which explanation of dreams proposes that they are produced when the mind attempts to make

sense of random neural activity that occurs in the brain during sleep?
   a. Freud's psychoanalytic theory
   b. the activation–synthesis model
   c. the cognitive unconscious model
   d. the manifest content framework

8. fMRI studies of the dreaming brain reveal all of these EXCEPT
   a. increased sensitivity to emotions.
   b. activations associated with visual activity.
   c. increased capacity for planning.
   d. prevention of movement.

9. Psychoactive drugs influence consciousness by altering the effects of
   a. agonists.
   b. neurotransmitters.
   c. amphetamines.
   d. spinal neurons.

10. Tolerance for drugs involves
    a. larger doses being required over time to achieve the same effect.
    b. openness to new experiences.
    c. the initial attraction of drug use.
    d. the decrease of the painful symptoms that accompany withdrawal.

11. Drugs that heighten arousal and activity levels by affecting the central nervous system are
    a. depressants.
    b. stimulants.
    c. narcotics.
    d. hallucinogens.

12. Alcohol expectancy refers to
    a. alcohol's initial effects of euphoria and reduced anxiety.
    b. the widespread acceptance of alcohol as a socially approved substance.
    c. alcohol leading people to respond in simple ways to complex situations.
    d. people's beliefs about how alcohol will influence them in particular situations.

13. Hypnosis has been proven to have
    a. an effect on physical strength.
    b. a positive effect on memory retrieval.
    c. an analgesic effect.
    d. an age-regression effect.

14. Which individual is LEAST likely to be a good candidate for hypnosis?
    a. Jake, who spends a lot of time watching movies
    b. Ava, who is convinced she is easily hypnotizable
    c. Evan, who has an active, vivid imagination
    d. Isabel, who loves to play sports

LearningCurve   Don't stop now! Quizzing yourself is a powerful study tool. Go to LaunchPad to access the LearningCurve adaptive quizzing system and your own personalized learning plan. Visit launchpadworks.com.

Key Terms

consciousness (p. 127)
phenomenology (p. 128)
problem of other minds (p. 128)
mind–body problem (p. 129)
cocktail-party phenomenon (p. 131)
minimal consciousness (p. 131)
full consciousness (p. 132)
self-consciousness (p. 132)
mental control (p. 133)
thought suppression (p. 134)

rebound effect of thought suppression (p. 134)
ironic processes of mental control (p. 134)
dynamic unconscious (p. 135)
repression (p. 135)
cognitive unconscious (p. 136)
dual process theories (p. 136)
altered state of consciousness (p. 136)
circadian rhythm (p. 137)

REM sleep (p. 137)
insomnia (p. 140)
sleep apnea (p. 141)
somnambulism (sleepwalking) (p. 141)
narcolepsy (p. 141)
sleep paralysis (p. 141)
night terrors (sleep terrors) (p. 141)
activation–synthesis model (p. 143)
psychoactive drugs (p. 145)
drug tolerance (p. 146)

depressants (p. 148)
expectancy theory (p. 149)
alcohol myopia (p. 149)
stimulants (p. 150)
narcotics (opiates) (p. 150)
hallucinogens (p. 151)
marijuana (cannabis) (p. 152)
gateway drug (p. 152)
hypnosis (p. 153)
posthypnotic amnesia (p. 154)
hypnotic analgesia (p. 155)

Changing Minds

1. "I had a really weird dream last night," your friend tells you. "I dreamed that I was trying to fly like a bird but I kept flying into clotheslines. I looked it up online, and dreams where you're struggling to fly mean that there is someone in your life who's standing in your way and preventing you from moving forward. I suppose that has to be my boyfriend, so maybe I'd better break up with him." Applying what you've read in this chapter, what would you tell your friend about the reliability of dream interpretation?

2. During an early-morning class, you notice your friend yawning, and you ask if he slept well the night before. "On weekdays, I'm in class all day, and I work the night shift," he says. "So I don't sleep much during the week. But I figure it's okay because I make up for it by sleeping late on Saturday mornings." Is it realistic for your friend to assume that he can balance regular sleep deprivation with rebound sleep on the weekends?

3. You and a friend are watching the 2010 movie *Inception,* starring Leonardo DiCaprio as a corporate spy. DiCaprio's character is hired by a businessman named Saito to plant an idea in the unconscious mind of a competitor while he sleeps. According to the plan, when the competitor awakens, he'll be compelled to act on the idea, to the secret benefit of Saito's company. "It's a cool idea," your friend says, "but it's pure science fiction. There's no such thing as an unconscious mind, and no way that unconscious ideas could influence the way you act when you're conscious." What would you tell your friend? What evidence do we have that the unconscious mind does exist and can influence conscious behavior?

Answers to Key Concept Quiz

1. b; 2. d; 3. c; 4. a; 5. a; 6. c; 7. b; 8. c; 9. b; 10. a; 11. b; 12. d; 13. c; 14. d

LaunchPad   LaunchPad features the full e-book of *Introducing Psychology*, the LearningCurve adaptive quizzing system, videos, and a variety of activities to boost your learning. Visit LaunchPad at launchpadworks.com.
macmillan learning

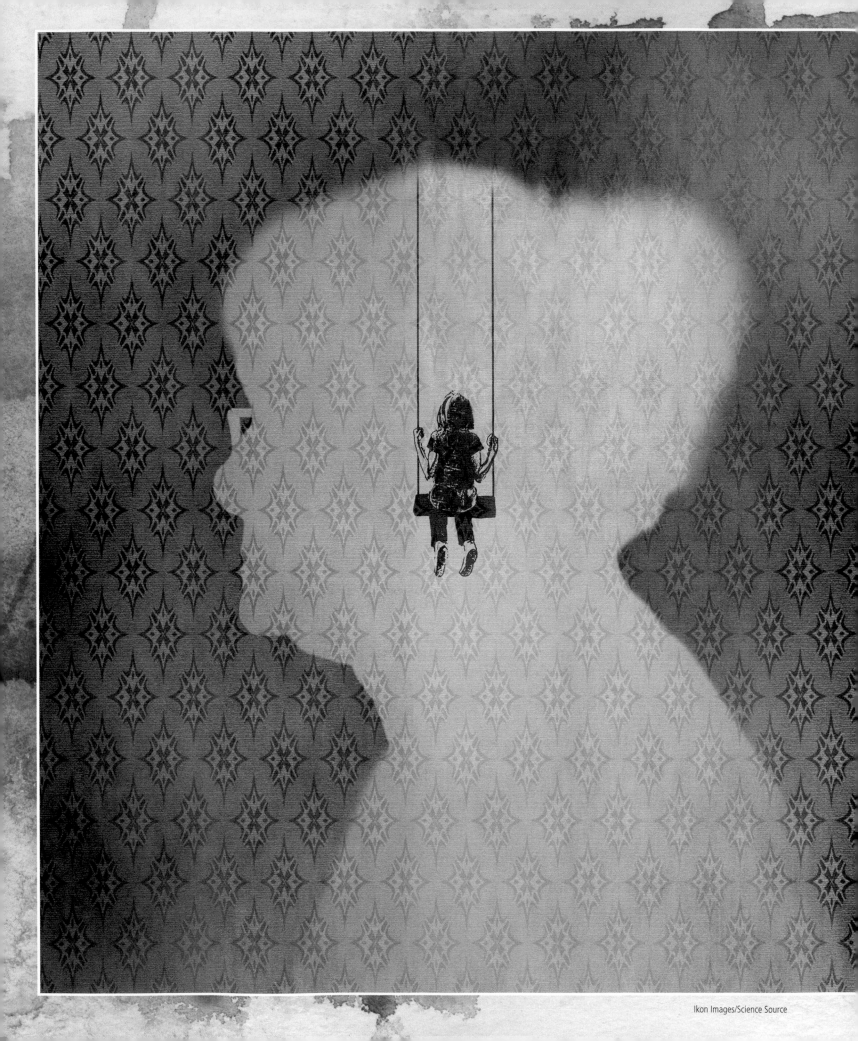

Ikon Images/Science Source

Memory

6

Jill Price was 12 years old when she began to suspect that she possessed an unusually good memory. While she was studying for a 7th-grade science final on May 30, her mind drifted and she became aware that she could recall vividly everything she had been doing on May 30 of the previous year. Remembering specifics of events that occurred a year ago may not seem so extraordinary — you can probably recall what you did for your last birthday or where you spent last Thanksgiving. But can you recall the details of what you did exactly a year ago today? Probably not, but Jill Price can.

Jill can recall clearly and in great detail what has happened to her *every single day since early 1980* (Price & Davis, 2008). This is not just Jill's subjective impression. Memory researchers asked Jill what she had been doing on various randomly chosen dates, and they checked Jill's recall against her personal diary. Each time, Jill answered quickly and accurately: *July 1, 1986?* — "I see it all, that day, that month, that summer. Tuesday. Went with (friend's name) to (restaurant name)." *October 3, 1987?* — "That was a Saturday. Hung out at the apartment all weekend, wearing a sling — hurt my elbow." (Parker et al., 2006, pp. 39–40).

The ease with which someone such as Jill can instantly remember her past shouldn't blind us to appreciating how complex that act of remembering really is. Because memory is so remarkably complex, it is also remarkably fragile (Schacter, 1996). We all have had the experience of forgetting something we desperately wanted to remember or of remembering something that never really happened. Why does memory serve us so well in some situations and play such cruel tricks on us in other cases? Is there just one kind of memory, or are there many? These are among the questions that psychologists have asked and answered, and that we'll discuss in this chapter. We'll start by answering the fundamental question: What is memory?

What Is Memory?

Encoding: Transforming Perceptions Into Memories

Storage: Maintaining Memories Over Time

Retrieval: Bringing Memories to Mind

Forms of Long-Term Memory: More Than One Kind

Memory Failures: The Seven "Sins" of Memory

What Is Memory?

Memory *is the ability to store and retrieve information over time.* Even though few of us possess the extraordinary memory abilities of Jill Price, each of us has a unique identity that is intricately tied to the things we have thought, felt, done, and experienced. Memories are the residue of those events, the enduring changes that experience makes in our brains and leaves behind when it passes. If an experience passes without leaving a trace, it might just as well not have happened.

As you've seen in other chapters, the mind's mistakes provide key insights into its fundamental operation, and there is no better illustration of this than in the realm of memory. In this chapter, we'll explore the three key functions of memory: **encoding,** *the process of transforming what we perceive, think, or feel into an enduring memory;* **storage,** *the process of maintaining information in memory over time;* and **retrieval,** *the process of bringing to mind information that has been previously encoded and stored.*

Jill Price can accurately remember just about everything that has happened to her during the past 30 years, as confirmed by her diary. Dan Tuffs/Getty Images

Learning Outcomes

- Explain how memory is a construction and not a recording of new information.

- Describe the three main ways that information is encoded into the brain.

- Give reasons we remember survival-related information so well.

```
        2 8
       6 9 1
      0 4 7 3
     8 7 4 5 4
    9 0 2 4 8 1
   5 7 4 2 2 9 6
  6 4 7 1 9 3 0 4
 3 5 6 7 1 8 4 8 5
1 0 2 8 8 3 4 7 2 9
4 7 2 0 8 2 7 4 2 6 4
7 3 1 0 9 3 4 3 5 1 3 8
```

Figure 6.1   Digit Memory Test How many digits can you remember? Start on the first row and cover the rows below it with a piece of paper. Study the numbers in the row for a second and then cover that row back up again. After a couple of seconds, try to repeat the numbers. Then uncover the row to see if you were correct. If so, continue down to the next row, using the same instructions, until you can't recall all the numbers in a row. The number of digits in the last row you can remember correctly is your digit span. Bubbles P. could remember 20 random numbers. How did you do?

memory The ability to store and retrieve information over time.

encoding The process of transforming what we perceive, think, or feel into an enduring memory.

storage The process of maintaining information in memory over time.

retrieval The process of bringing to mind information that has been previously encoded and stored.

semantic encoding The process of relating new information in a meaningful way to knowledge that is already stored in memory.

Encoding: Transforming Perceptions Into Memories

Bubbles P., a professional gambler with no formal education who spent most of his time shooting craps at local clubs or playing high-stakes poker, had no difficulty rattling off 20 numbers, in either forward or backward order, after just a single glance (Ceci et al., 1992). Most people can listen to a list of numbers and then repeat them from memory—as long as the list is no more than about seven items long. (Try it for yourself using **FIGURE 6.1**.)

How did Bubbles accomplish his astounding feats of memory? For at least 2,000 years, people have thought of memory as a recording device that makes exact copies of the information that comes in through our senses, and then stores those copies for later use. This idea is simple and intuitive. It is also completely incorrect. We make memories by combining information we *already* have in our brains with new information that comes in through our senses. Memories are *constructed,* not recorded, and encoding is the process by which we transform what we perceive, think, or feel into an enduring memory. Let's look at three types of encoding processes—semantic encoding, visual imagery encoding, and organizational encoding—and then consider how encoding had possible survival value for our ancestors.

Semantic Encoding

Because memories are a combination of old and new information, the nature of any particular memory depends as much on the old information already in our memories as it does on the new information coming in through our senses. In other words, how we remember something depends on how we think about it at the time. For example, as a professional gambler, Bubbles found numbers unusually meaningful, so when he saw a string of digits, he tended to think about their meanings. However, when Bubbles was tested with materials other than numbers—faces, words, objects, or locations—his memory performance was no better than average. Most of us, unlike Bubbles, can't remember 20 digits, but we can remember 20 experiences (a favorite camping trip, a 16th birthday party, a first day at college, and so on). One reason is that we often think about the meaning behind our experiences, so we semantically encode them without even trying (Craik & Tulving, 1975). **Semantic encoding** *is the process of relating new information in a meaningful way to knowledge that is already stored in memory* (Brown & Craik, 2000).

So what's going on in the brain when semantic encoding occurs? Studies reveal that semantic encoding is uniquely associated with increased activity in the lower left part of the frontal lobe and the inner part of the left temporal lobe (**FIGURE 6.2a**) (Demb et al., 1995; Kapur et al., 1994; Wagner et al., 1998). In fact, the amount of activity in each of these two regions during encoding is directly related to whether people later remember an item. The more activity there is in these areas, the more likely the person will remember the information.

Visual Imagery Encoding

In ancient Athens, the Greek poet Simonides had just left a banquet when the ceiling collapsed and killed all the people inside. Simonides was able to name every one of the dead simply by visualizing each chair around the banquet table and recalling the person who had been sitting there. Simonides used **visual imagery encoding,** *the process of storing new information by converting it into mental pictures.* Modern-day "memory athletes," who compete in memory championships, typically rely on visual imagery encoding to accomplish astounding feats of memorization (Dresler et al., 2017). Alex Mullen,

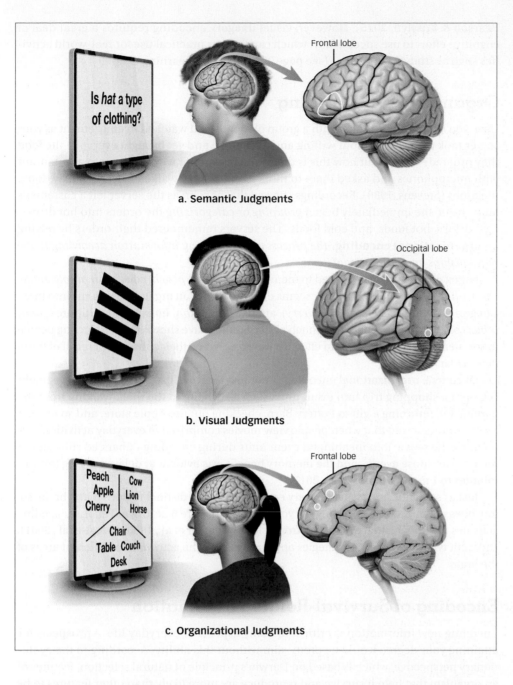

a. Semantic Judgments

b. Visual Judgments

c. Organizational Judgments

Figure 6.2 Brain Activity During Different Types of Judgments fMRI studies reveal that different parts of the brain are active during different types of judgments: (a) During semantic encoding, the lower left frontal lobe is active, along with the inner part of the left temporal lobe (not shown); (b) during visual imagery encoding, the occipital lobe is active; and (c) during organizational encoding, the upper left frontal lobe is active.

a medical student at the University of Mississippi, used visual imagery encoding to memorize the order of a deck of playing cards in under 16 seconds! This helped Alex to win the World Memory Championship in 2017.

Why does visual imagery encoding work so well? First, visual imagery encoding does some of the same things that semantic encoding does: When you create a visual image, you relate incoming information to knowledge already in memory. For example, a visual image of a parked car might help you create a link to your memory of your first kiss.

Second, when you use visual imagery to encode words and other verbal information, you end up with two different mental *placeholders* for the items — a visual one and a verbal one — which gives you more ways to remember them than just a verbal placeholder alone (Paivio, 1971, 1986). Visual imagery encoding activates visual processing regions in the occipital lobe (see Figure 6.2b), which suggests that people actually enlist the visual system when forming memories based on mental images (Kosslyn et al., 1993;

Alex Mullen, world memory champion, can quickly remember a deck of playing cards, and much more. Alex Mullen, Courtesy UMMC Public Affairs

visual imagery encoding The process of storing new information by converting it into mental pictures.

Pearson & Kosslyn, 2015). However, visual imagery encoding requires a great deal of cognitive effort to use successfully, which can limit its practical use for real-world activities such as studying for exams (see page 220–224 in the Learning chapter).

Organizational Encoding

Have you ever ordered dinner with a group of friends and watched in amazement as your server took the order without writing anything down and yet brought everyone the food they ordered? To find out how this is done, one researcher wired servers in a restaurant with microphones and asked them to think aloud as they walked around all day doing their jobs (Stevens, 1988). Recordings showed that as soon as the server left a customer's table, he or she immediately began *grouping* or *categorizing* the orders into hot drinks, cold drinks, hot foods, and cold foods. The servers remembered their orders by relying on **organizational encoding,** *the process of categorizing information according to the relationships among a series of items.*

For example, suppose you had to memorize the words *peach, cow, chair, apple, table, cherry, lion, couch, horse.* The task seems difficult, but if you organize the items into three categories — fruit (*peach, apple, cherry*), animals (*cow, lion, horse*), and furniture (*chair, table, couch*) — the task becomes much easier. Studies have shown that instructing people to sort items into categories is an effective way to enhance their subsequent recall of those items (Mandler, 1967).

Of course, organizational encoding is not just for word lists. For example, we might segment a shopping trip into event units such as driving to the mall, walking from the parking lot, returning a gift to Pottery Barn, checking out the Apple store, and so forth. A recent study showed that when people view movies comprised of everyday activities, segmenting the movie into meaningful event units during encoding enhanced subsequent memory for those events, and the memory benefit was evident at delays ranging from 10 minutes to 1 month (Flores et al., 2017).

Just as semantic and visual imagery encoding activate distinct regions of the brain, so, too, does organizational encoding. As you can see in Figure 6.2c, organizational encoding activates the upper surface of the left frontal lobe (Fletcher et al., 1998; Savage et al., 2001). Different types of encoding strategies appear to rely on the activation of different areas of the brain.

Encoding of Survival-Related Information

Encoding new information is critical to many aspects of everyday life — prospects for attaining your degree would be pretty slim without this ability. According to the evolutionary perspective, which is based on Darwin's principle of natural selection, features of an organism that help it survive and reproduce are more likely than other features to be passed on to subsequent generations (see The Evolution of Psychological Science chapter). Therefore, memory mechanisms that help us survive and reproduce should be preserved by natural selection. Our memory systems should be built in a way that allows us to remember especially well the encoded information that is relevant to our survival, such as sources of food and water and the location of predators. (See Data Visualization: Do Men and Women Differ in the Way They Remember Location Information? Go to launchpadworks.com.)

To test this idea, researchers gave participants three different encoding tasks (Nairne et al., 2007). In the first task, a survival-encoding condition, participants were asked to imagine they were stranded in the grasslands of a foreign land without any survival materials. They were told that over the next few months, they would need supplies of food and water and also need to protect themselves from predators. The researchers then showed participants randomly chosen words (e.g., *stone, meadow, chair*) and asked them to rate

Pen and paper are optional for some servers who have figured out how to use organizational encoding. Efrain Padro/Alamy Stock Photo

DATA Visualization

organizational encoding The process of categorizing information according to the relationships among a series of items.

on a 1–5 scale how relevant each item would be to survival in the hypothetical situation. In a second task, a moving-encoding condition, a second group of participants was asked to imagine that they were planning to move to a new home in a foreign land, and to rate on a 1–5 scale how useful each item might be in helping them set up a new home. In the third task, the pleasantness-encoding condition, a third group was shown the same words and asked to rate on a 1–5 scale the pleasantness of each word.

The findings, displayed in **FIGURE 6.3**, show that participants recalled more words after the survival-encoding task than after either the moving or pleasantness tasks. Exactly what about survival encoding produces such high levels of memory?

Encoding survival-related information requires elements of semantic, visual imagery, and organizational encoding (Burns et al., 2011), which together produce high levels of subsequent memory. Also, survival encoding encourages participants to think in detail about the goals they want to achieve and thus engage in extensive planning, which in turn benefits memory and may account for much of the benefit of survival encoding (Bell, Roer, & Buchner, 2015). Superior recall is also observed for scenarios that *involve planning but not survival,* such as planning a dinner party (Klein et al., 2011). Of course, planning for the future is itself critical for our long-term survival, so these findings are still broadly consistent with the evolutionary perspective that memory is built to enhance our chances of survival (Klein et al., 2011; Schacter, 2012; Suddendorf & Corballis, 2007).

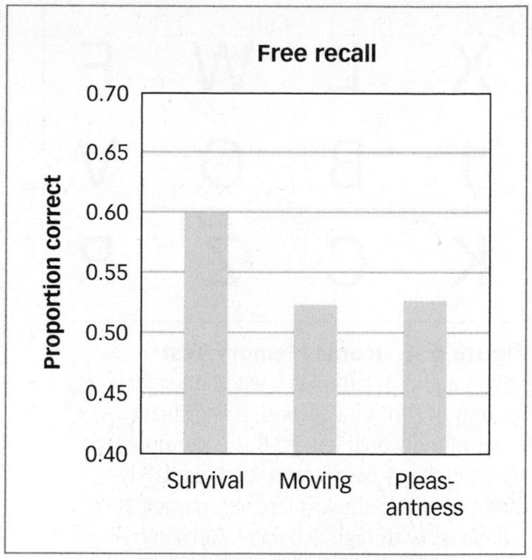

Figure 6.3   Encoding of Survival-Related Information Enhances Later Recall People recall more words after "survival-encoding" tasks than after moving or pleasantness-encoding tasks (Nairne et al., 2007).

Build to the Outcomes

1. Why is memory a "construction," not a recording?

2. What do we consider when making a semantic judgment?

3. What two factors make visual imagery effective?

4. How might you use organizational encoding to remember material before an exam?

5. What is the evolutionary perspective on encoding survival-related information?

Storage: Maintaining Memories Over Time

Encoding is the process of turning perceptions into memories; *storage is the process of maintaining information in memory over time.* There are three major kinds of memory storage: sensory, short-term, and long-term. As these names suggest, the three kinds of storage are distinguished primarily by the amount of time over which a memory is retained.

Sensory Storage

Sensory memory is *a type of storage that holds sensory information for a few seconds or less.* In a classic experiment, participants viewed three rows of four letters each, as shown in **FIGURE 6.4** (Sperling, 1960). The researcher flashed the letters on a screen for just 1/20th of a second. When asked to remember all 12 of the letters they had just seen, participants recalled fewer than half. There were two possible explanations for this: Either people simply couldn't encode all the letters in such a brief period of time, or else they had encoded the letters but forgot them while trying to recall everything they had seen.

To test the two ideas, the researcher relied on a clever trick. Just after the letters disappeared from the screen, a tone sounded that cued the participants to report the letters in a particular row. A *high* tone cued participants to report the contents

Learning Outcomes

- Distinguish sensory memory from short-term memory.

- Describe the elements of the model of working memory.

- Explain the interrelationship between memory and the hippocampus.

- Summarize the role of the neural synapse in long-term memory storage.

sensory memory A type of storage that holds sensory information for a few seconds or less.

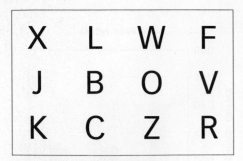

Figure 6.4 Iconic Memory Test
When a grid of letters is flashed on screen for only 1/20th of a second, it is difficult to recall individual letters. But if prompted to remember a particular row immediately after the grid is shown, research participants will do so with high accuracy. Although iconic memory stores the whole grid, the information fades away too quickly for a person to recall everything (Sperling, 1960).

of the top row, a *medium* tone cued participants to report the contents of the middle row, and a *low* tone cued participants to report the contents of the bottom row. When asked to report only a single row, people recalled almost all of the letters in that row! Because the tone sounded after the letters disappeared from the screen and the participants had no way of knowing which of the three rows would be cued, the researcher inferred that virtually all the letters had been encoded. In fact, if the tone was substantially delayed, participants couldn't perform the task because the information had slipped away from their sensory memories. Like the afterimage of a flashlight, the 12 letters flashed on a screen are visual icons, a lingering trace stored in memory for a very short period.

Because we have more than one sense, we have more than one kind of sensory memory. **Iconic memory** is *a fast-decaying store of visual information*. **Echoic memory** is *a fast-decaying store of auditory information*. When you have difficulty understanding what someone has just said, you probably find yourself replaying the last few words — listening to them echo in your "mind's ear," so to speak. What you are actually doing is accessing information that is being held in your echoic memory store. The hallmark of both the iconic and echoic memory stores is that they hold information for a very short time. Iconic memories usually decay in about 1 second or less, and echoic memories usually decay in about 5 seconds (Darwin et al., 1972).

These two sensory memory stores are a bit like doughnut shops: The products come in, they sit briefly on the shelf, and then they are discarded. If you want one, you have to grab it fast. But how to grab it? If information from sensory memory is quickly lost, how do we recall it at all? The key is attention, which brings us to short-term memory (see **FIGURE 6.5**).

Short-Term Storage and Working Memory

Short-term memory is *a type of storage that holds nonsensory information for more than a few seconds but less than a minute*. For example, if someone tells you a telephone number and you pay attention to what they say, you can usually repeat it back with ease — but you will quickly lose the information as soon as your attention focuses on anything else. In one study, research participants were given consonant strings to remember, such as *DBX* and *HLM*. After seeing each string, participants were asked to count backward from 100 by 3s for varying amounts of time and were then asked to recall the consonant strings (Peterson & Peterson, 1959). As shown in **FIGURE 6.6**, memory for the consonant strings declined rapidly, from approximately 80% after a 3-second delay to virtually nothing after a 20-second delay. These results suggest that information can be held in the short-term memory store for about 15 to 20 seconds.

iconic memory A fast-decaying store of visual information.

echoic memory A fast-decaying store of auditory information.

short-term memory A type of storage that holds nonsensory information for more than a few seconds but less than a minute.

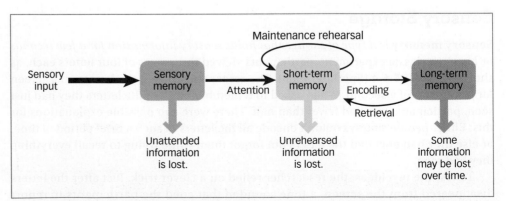

Figure 6.5   The Flow of Information Through the Memory System Information moves through several stages of memory as it gets encoded, stored, and made available for later retrieval.

Rehearsal and "Chunking" Strengthen Memory

What if 15 to 20 seconds isn't enough time? What if we need the information for a while longer? We can use a trick that allows us to get around the natural limitations of our short-term memories. **Rehearsal** is *the process of keeping information in short-term memory by mentally repeating it.* If someone gives you a telephone number and you can't immediately enter it into your cell phone or write it down, you say it over and over to yourself until you can. Each time you repeat the number, you are reentering it into short-term memory, giving it another 15 to 20 seconds of shelf life.

Rehearsal can play a role in the *serial position effect,* which refers to the observation that the first few and last few items in a series are more likely to be recalled than the items in the middle. Enhanced recall of the first few items in, say, a list of words is called the *primacy effect.* It occurs because these items receive more rehearsals than subsequent items in the middle of the list and thus are more likely to be encoded into long-term storage. Enhanced recall of the last few items is called the *recency effect* and can result from rehearsing items that are still in short-term storage (Atkinson & Shiffrin, 1968). Consistent with this interpretation, the recency effect — but not the primacy effect — is eliminated when participants count backward by 3s after the final list item is presented, which prevents them from relying on short-term storage to rehearse the last few items (Glanzer & Cunitz, 1966). However, both primacy and recency effects can be observed in situations that involve only long-term storage, such as recalling the order of the seven Harry Potter books (Kelley et al., 2013).

Short-term memory is limited in *how long* it can hold information, as well as in *how much* information it can hold. Most people keep approximately seven items in short-term memory, but if they put more new ones in, then old ones begin to fall out (Miller, 1956). Those seven items can be numbers or letters or even words or ideas. One way to increase storage is **chunking,** which involves *combining small pieces of information into larger clusters or chunks that are more easily held in short-term memory.* Those restaurant servers who use organizational encoding to organize customer orders into groups are essentially chunking the information, giving themselves less to remember.

Working Memory Stores and Manipulates Information

Short-term memory was originally conceived as a kind of "place" where information is kept for a limited amount of time. More recently, researchers have developed and refined a more dynamic model of a limited-capacity memory system, called **working memory,** which refers to *active maintenance of information in short-term storage* (Baddeley & Hitch, 1974). As illustrated in **FIGURE 6.7**, working memory includes four subsystems.

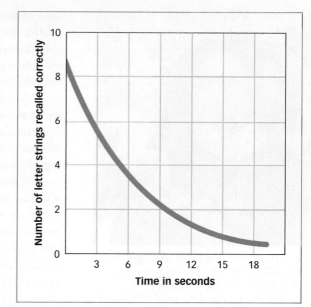

Figure 6.6 The Decline of Short-Term Memory Short-term memory fades quickly without rehearsal. On a test for memory of three-letter strings, participants were highly accurate when tested a few seconds after exposure to each string, but if the test was delayed another 15 seconds, people barely recalled the strings at all (Peterson & Peterson, 1959).

Which of the books in the Harry Potter series are you likely to most easily recall, according to the serial position effect? AP Photo/Bizuayehu Tesfaye

rehearsal The process of keeping information in short-term memory by mentally repeating it.

chunking Combining small pieces of information into larger clusters or chunks that are more easily held in short-term memory.

working memory Active maintenance of information in short-term storage.

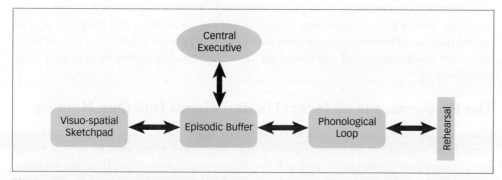

Figure 6.7 A Model of Working Memory The working memory system consists of a central executive that controls the flow of information through the system; a visuo-spatial sketchpad and phonological loop that temporarily hold visual/spatial images and verbal/auditory information, respectively; and an episodic buffer that integrates the various kinds of information.

In everyday life, we draw on working memory when using our phones to navigate novel environments. Andresr/Getty Images

Two of these subsystems store and manipulate information: the *visuo-spatial sketchpad* for visual images and the *phonological loop* for verbal information. There is also an *episodic buffer* that integrates visual and verbal information from the subsystems into a multidimensional code, and a *central executive* that coordinates the subsystems and the episodic buffer (Baddeley, 2001; Baddeley et al., 2011).

In practical terms, say you were using Google Maps on your phone to walk to a new destination and wanted to keep the arrangement of locations on the map in mind as you contemplated your next move. You'd be relying on your visuo-spatial sketchpad to hold the visual representation of the locations on the map. You might also enlist the phonological loop to hold onto the upcoming street names and rely on your central executive to control mental manipulation of the directions and awareness of the flow of information into and out of memory, all stored for a limited amount of time.

Brain-imaging studies indicate that the central executive component of working memory depends on regions within the frontal lobe that are important for controlling and manipulating information on a wide range of cognitive tasks (Baddeley, 2001; D'Esposito & Postle, 2015). Recently, some researchers have suggested that the episodic buffer also integrates other kinds of sensory information, such as smell and taste, as shown in Figure 6.7 (Baddeley et al., 2011), but more research is needed to understand this component of working memory.

Research Is Examining the Link Between Working Memory Training and Cognitive Functioning

Can working memory skills be improved through training, and can such training enhance cognitive functioning? Some studies suggest yes. In one study, elementary school students who were intensively trained on several working memory tasks over several weeks showed improvement on other working memory tasks (Holmes et al., 2009). However, many recent studies have found that working memory training improves performance on the working memory task that was "trained" but not on other cognitive tasks (Redick et al., 2013), including other working memory tasks (De Simoni & von Bastian, 2018). More research will be needed to determine whether working memory training produces any general improvements in cognitive performance and, if so, whether the improvements are large enough to affect performance on everyday cognitive tasks (Au et al., 2015; Redick, 2015; Shipstead et al., 2012).

Long-Term Storage

In contrast to the time-limited sensory and short-term storage stores, **long-term memory** is *a type of storage that holds information for hours, days, weeks, or years*. In contrast to both sensory and short-term storage, long-term memory has no known capacity limits (see Figure 6.5). For example, most people can recall 10,000 to 15,000 words in their native language, tens of thousands of facts (the capital of France is Paris, and $3 \times 3 = 9$), and an untold number of personal experiences. Just think of all the song lyrics you can recite by heart, and you'll understand that you've got a lot of information tucked away in your long-term memory!

The Hippocampus as Index: Linking Pieces Into One Memory

Where is long-term memory located in the brain? The clues to answering this question come from individuals who are unable to store long-term memories. In 1953, a young man, known then by the initials HM, suffered from intractable epilepsy (Scoville & Milner, 1957). In a desperate attempt to stop the seizures, HM's doctors removed parts of his temporal lobes, including the hippocampus and some surrounding regions (**FIGURE 6.8**). After the operation, HM could converse easily, use and understand language, and perform well on intelligence tests, but he could not remember anything that happened to

long-term memory A type of storage that holds information for hours, days, weeks, or years.

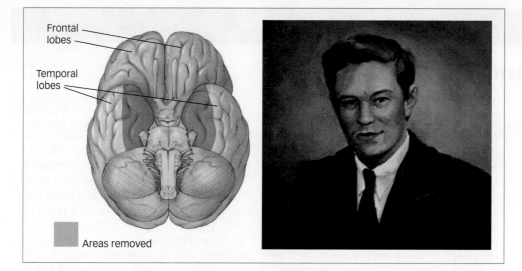

Areas removed

Figure 6.8   The Hippocampus Patient
HM had his hippocampus and adjacent structures of the medial temporal lobe (indicated by the shaded areas) surgically removed to stop his epileptic seizures (*left*). As a result, he could not remember things that happened after the surgery. Henry Molaison (*right*), better known to the world as patient HM, passed away on December 2, 2008, at the age of 82. Molaison participated in countless memory experiments after he became amnesic in 1953, and in so doing made fundamental contributions to our understanding of memory and the brain (Corkin, 2013).   2016 MACMILLAN LEARNING

him after the operation. HM could repeat a telephone number with no difficulty, suggesting that his short-term memory store was just fine (Corkin, 2002, 2013; Hilts, 1995; Squire, 2009). But after information left the short-term store, it was gone forever. For example, he would often forget that he had just eaten a meal or fail to recognize the hospital staff who helped him on a daily basis. Studies of HM and others have shown that the hippocampal region of the brain is critical for putting new information into the long-term store (Clark & Maguire, 2016; Smith et al., 2013). Individuals who have sustained damage to this region suffer from a condition known as **anterograde amnesia**, which is *the inability to transfer new information from the short-term store into the long-term store.*

Some individuals with amnesia also suffer from **retrograde amnesia**, which is *the inability to retrieve information that was acquired before a particular date, usually the date of an injury or surgery.* The fact that HM had much worse anterograde than retrograde amnesia suggests that the hippocampal region is not the site of long-term memory. Indeed, research has shown that different aspects of a single memory — its sights, sounds, smells, emotional content — are stored in different places in the cortex (Damasio, 1989; Schacter, 1996; Squire & Kandel, 1999). Some psychologists have argued that the hippocampal region acts as a kind of "index" that links all these otherwise separate bits and pieces so that we remember them as one memory (Schacter, 1996; Squire, 1992; Teyler & DiScenna, 1986). Recent neuroscience studies support this "index view" (Horner et al., 2015; Tanaka et al., 2018).

Over time, however, the hippocampal index may become less necessary. You can think of the hippocampal region index as a printed recipe. The first time you make a pie, you need the recipe to help you retrieve all the ingredients and then mix them together in the right amounts. As you bake more and more pies, though, you don't need to rely on the printed recipe anymore. Similarly, although the hippocampal region index is critical when a new memory is first formed, it may become less important as the memory ages. Scientists are still debating the extent to which the hippocampal region helps us remember details of our old memories (Bayley et al., 2005; Kirwan et al., 2008; Moscovitch et al., 2016; Squire & Wixted, 2011; Winocur et al., 2010). However, the notion of the hippocampus as an index explains why people such as HM cannot make new memories and why they can remember many old ones.

Consolidation Stabilizes Memories

The idea that the hippocampus becomes less important over time for maintaining memories is closely related to the concept of **consolidation,** *the process by which memories become stable in the brain* (McGaugh, 2000, 2015). Shortly after encoding, memories exist in a fragile state that can be disrupted easily; once consolidation has occurred, they are

anterograde amnesia The inability to transfer new information from the short-term store into the long-term store.

retrograde amnesia The inability to retrieve information that was acquired before a particular date, usually the date of an injury or surgery.

consolidation The process by which memories become stable in the brain.

Can Sleep Enhance Learning? Yes!

Thinking about pulling an all-nighter before your next big test? Here's a reason to reconsider: Our minds don't simply shut off when we sleep (see the Consciousness chapter). In fact, sleep may be as important to our memories as wakefulness.

Nearly a century ago, researchers reported that recall of recently learned information is greater immediately after sleeping than after the same amount of time spent awake (Jenkins & Dallenbach, 1924). Since then, evidence has accumulated that sleep selectively enhances the consolidation of memories that reflect the meaning or gist of an experience (Payne et al., 2009), as well as emotionally important memories (Payne et al., 2008, 2015; Payne & Kensinger, 2018), suggesting that sleep helps us remember what's important and discard what's trivial.

Another recent line of evidence shows that memory consolidation during sleep can be enhanced by presenting sounds during sleep that reactivate specific memories, a procedure known as *targeted memory reactivation* (TMR) (Cellini & Capuozzo, 2018; Oudiette & Paller, 2013). Before sleep, participants viewed objects (such as a kettle) located at particular locations on the screen, and also heard those objects' sounds (such as the kettle's characteristic whistling sound). During a subsequent period of sleep, researchers played for participants the sounds of some of the studied objects in an attempt to reactivate their memories of the object–location associations. In a remarkable result, when tested after awakening, participants showed more accurate memory for the location of the objects whose characteristic sounds had been presented during sleep — even though participants were not aware that any sounds had been presented while they slept. Such targeted memory reactivation effects are strongest for those associations that are not well learned initially (Creery et al., 2015).

These findings suggest that it may be possible to use TMR during sleep to boost learning. One study used TMR to help people acquire new foreign vocabulary (Schreiner & Rasch, 2015). Participants were young adult native German speakers who did not know any items of Dutch vocabulary. While awake in the late evening, all participants learned a series of Dutch words, each paired with their German translation. Participants then slept for 3 hours; one group received TMR, including a recording of some of the previously studied Dutch words. Participants who had received exposure to the Dutch words while sleeping had better recall of the German translation, compared to participants who didn't receive TMR. A later study (Batterink et al., 2017) found similar TMR effects on the learning of novel words by English speakers.

So when you find yourself nodding off after hours of studying for your exam, the science is on the side of a good night's sleep.

more resistant to disruption. One type of consolidation operates over seconds or minutes. For example, when someone experiences a head injury in a car crash and later cannot recall what happened during the few seconds or minutes before the crash — but can recall other events normally — the head injury probably prevented consolidation of short-term memory into long-term memory. Another type of consolidation occurs over much longer periods of time — days, weeks, months, and years — and likely involves transfer of information from the hippocampus to more permanent storage sites in the cortex. The operation of this longer-term consolidation process is why patients such as HM can recall memories from childhood relatively normally but are impaired when recalling experiences that occurred just a few years prior to the time they became amnesic (Kirwan et al., 2008; Squire & Wixted, 2011).

How does a memory become consolidated? The act of recalling a memory, thinking about it, and talking about it with others probably contributes to consolidation (Moscovitch et al., 2006). And consolidation gets a boost from something that you do effortlessly every night: sleep (see Hot Science: Can Sleep Enhance Learning? Yes!).

Recalled Memories May Be Disrupted During Reconsolidation

Many researchers have long believed that a fully consolidated memory becomes a permanent fixture in the brain, more difficult to get rid of than a computer virus. But a fairly recent line of research suggests that things are not so simple. Experiments have shown that even seemingly consolidated *memories can become vulnerable to disruption when they are recalled, thus requiring them to be consolidated again*. This process is called **reconsolidation** (Dudai, 2012; Nader & Hardt, 2009).

Early evidence for reconsolidation came from experiments with rats showing that when animals are cued to retrieve a new memory that was acquired a day earlier, giving the animal a treatment (such as a drug or an electrical shock) can cause forgetting of that memory (Nader et al., 2000; Sara, 2000). But if the animal is not actively retrieving the

reconsolidation The process whereby memories can become vulnerable to disruption when they are recalled, thus requiring them to be consolidated again.

memory, the same treatment has no effect. Researchers have produced similar effects in studies with people (Elsey et al., 2018; Schiller et al., 2010). These findings indicate that each time memories are retrieved, they become vulnerable to disruption and must be reconsolidated.

Might it be possible one day to eliminate or modify painful memories by disrupting reconsolidation? Recent research suggests it could be. When a traumatic event was reactivated in traumatized individuals who had been given a drug to reduce anxiety, there was a subsequent reduction in traumatic symptoms (Brunet et al., 2008, 2018). Related work using fMRI indicates that disrupting reconsolidation can seemingly eliminate a fear memory in a part of the brain called the *amygdala*, which, as we will learn later in this chapter, plays a key role in emotional memory (Agren et al., 2012). Reconsolidation thus appears to be a key memory process with many important implications.

Memories, Neurons, and Synapses

We've already discussed parts of the brain that are related to memory storage, but we haven't said much about how or where memories are stored. Much of what we know about the biological basis of long-term memory comes from the sea slug *Aplysia*, which has an extremely simple nervous system consisting of only 20,000 neurons (compared with roughly 100 billion in the human brain). When an experimenter stimulates *Aplysia*'s tail with a mild electric shock, the slug immediately withdraws its gill; if the experimenter does it again a moment later, *Aplysia* withdraws its gill even more quickly. If the experimenter comes back an hour later and shocks *Aplysia,* the withdrawal of the gill happens as slowly as it did the first time, as if *Aplysia* can't "remember" what happened an hour earlier (Abel et al., 1995). But if the experimenter shocks *Aplysia* over and over, it does develop an enduring "memory" that can last for days or even weeks. Research suggests that this long-term storage involves the growth of new synaptic connections between neurons (Abel et al., 1995; Kandel, 2006; Squire & Kandel, 1999). You'll recall from the Neuroscience and Behavior chapter that neurons communicate by sending neurotransmitter molecules across the synapse, the small space between the axon of a sending neuron and the dendrite of a receiving neuron. Learning in *Aplysia* is based on changes involving the synapses for both short-term storage (enhanced neurotransmitter release) and long-term storage (growth of new synapses).

If you're something more complex than a slug — say, a chimpanzee or your roommate — a similar process of synaptic strengthening happens in the hippocampus, which we've seen is an area crucial for storing new long-term memories. In the early 1970s, researchers applied a brief electrical stimulus to a neural pathway in a rat's hippocampus (Bliss & Lømo, 1973). They found that the electrical current produced a stronger connection between synapses that lay along the pathway and that the strengthening lasted for hours or even weeks. They called this effect **long-term potentiation** (more commonly known as **LTP**), *a process whereby communication across the synapse between neurons strengthens the connection, making further communication easier.* Drugs that block LTP can turn rats into rodent versions of patient HM: The animals have great difficulty remembering where they've been recently and become easily lost in a maze (Bliss, 1999; Morris et al., 1986).

The Boston marathon bombings produced detailed and disturbing memories in people at or near the site of the bombings. However, research shows that the amount of detail in those memories can be reduced by interfering with their reconsolidation. AP Photo/Metrowest Daily News, Ken McGagh

By studying the sea slug *Aplysia californica*'s extremely simple nervous system, researchers were able to determine that long-term memory storage depends on the growth of new synaptic connections between neurons.
Donna Ikenberry/Art Directors/Alamy Stock Photo

long-term potentiation (LTP) A process whereby repeated communication across the synapse between neurons strengthens the connection, making further communication easier.

Build to the Outcomes

1. Define iconic memory and echoic memory.

2. Why is it helpful to repeat a telephone number you're trying to remember?

3. How does working memory expand on the idea of short-term memory?

4. What did researchers learn about the role of the hippocampus and memory from HM?

5. Define anterograde amnesia and retrograde amnesia.

6. How does the process of recalling a memory affect its stability?

7. How does building a memory produce a physical change in the nervous system?

Learning Outcomes

- Explain the encoding specificity principle.
- Explain how memories can be changed by the act of retrieval.
- Describe the difference in brain activity when trying to recall versus successfully recalling information.

Retrieval cues are hints that help bring stored information to mind. How does this explain the fact that most students prefer multiple-choice exams to fill-in-the-blank exams?

AP Photo/*Pocono Record*, Adam Richins

retrieval cue External information that is associated with stored information and helps bring it to mind.

encoding specificity principle The idea that a retrieval cue can be an effective reminder when it helps re-create the specific way in which information was initially encoded.

state-dependent retrieval The process whereby information tends to be better recalled when the person is in the same state during encoding *and* retrieval.

Retrieval: Bringing Memories to Mind

There is something fiendishly frustrating about piggy banks. You can put money in them, you can shake them around to assure yourself that the money is there, but you can't easily get the money out. If memories were like pennies in a piggy bank, stored but inaccessible, what would be the point of saving them in the first place? Retrieval is the process of bringing to mind information that has been previously encoded and stored, and it is perhaps the most important of all memory processes (Roediger, 2000; Schacter, 2001a).

Retrieval Cues: Reinstating the Past

One of the best ways to retrieve information from *inside* your head is to encounter information *outside* your head that is somehow connected to it. The information outside your head is called a **retrieval cue,** *external information that is associated with stored information and helps bring it to mind.* Retrieval cues can be incredibly effective. How many times have you said something such as, "I *know* who played the white cop who stood in for the black cop to infiltrate the Ku Klux Klan in *BlacKkKlansman,* but I just can't remember his name," only to have a friend give you a hint ("He was in *The Last Jedi*"), which instantly brings the answer to mind ("Adam Driver!")? Such incidents suggest that information is sometimes *available* in memory even when it is momentarily *inaccessible* and that retrieval cues help us bring inaccessible information to mind.

In everyday life, retrieval cues can even spontaneously elicit involuntary memories of past experiences (Berntsen, 2010). Encountering a friend may automatically remind you of the movie you recently saw with her, or hearing a song on the radio may remind you of a concert you attended by that band. Involuntary memories occur even more often in everyday life than memories that we voluntarily try to retrieve (Rasmussen & Bernsten, 2011), underscoring the power of retrieval cues to unlock our personal pasts.

External Context Provides Cues

Hints are one kind of retrieval cue, but they are not the only kind. The **encoding specificity principle** states that *a retrieval cue can serve as an effective reminder when it helps re-create the specific way in which information was initially encoded* (Tulving & Thomson, 1973). External contexts often make powerful retrieval cues (Hockley, 2008). For example, in one study divers learned some words on land and some other words underwater; they recalled the words best when they were tested in the same dry or wet environment in which they had initially learned them, because the environment itself was a retrieval cue (Godden & Baddeley, 1975). Recovering alcoholics often experience a renewed urge to drink when visiting places in which they once drank because those places are retrieval cues. There may even be some wisdom to finding a seat in a classroom, sitting in it every day, and then sitting in it again when you take the test. The feel of the chair and the sights you see may help you remember the information you learned while you sat there.

Inner States Also Provide Cues

Retrieval cues need not be external contexts—they can also be inner states. **State-dependent retrieval** is *the process whereby information tends to be better recalled when the person is in the same state during encoding and retrieval.* For example, retrieving information when you are in a sad or happy mood increases the likelihood that you will retrieve sad or happy episodes (Eich, 1995). A person's physiological or psychological state at the time of encoding is part of the information that gets encoded in that memory. So, if the person's state at the time of retrieval matches the person's state at the time of encoding, the state itself is a retrieval cue. Retrieval cues can even be thoughts themselves, as when one thought calls to mind another, related thought (Anderson et al., 1976).

Matching Encoding and Retrieval Contexts Improves Recall

The encoding specificity principle makes some unusual predictions. For example, making semantic judgments about a word usually produces a more durable memory for the word than does making rhyme judgments. Suppose you were shown a cue card of the word *brain* and were then asked to think of a word that rhymes, while your friend was shown the same card and asked to think about what *brain* means. The next day, if we simply asked you both, "Hey, what was that word you saw yesterday?" we would expect your friend to remember it better. However, if instead we asked both of you, "What was that word that rhymed with *train*?" the retrieval cue would match your encoding context better than your friend's, and we would expect you to remember it better than your friend did (Fisher & Craik, 1977). The principle of **transfer-appropriate processing** is *the idea that memory is likely to transfer from one situation to another when the encoding and retrieval contexts of the situations match* (Morris et al., 1977; Roediger et al., 1989).

Consequences of Retrieval

Human memory differs substantially from computer memory. Simply retrieving a file from my computer doesn't have any effect on the likelihood that the file will open again in the future. Not so with human memory. Retrieval doesn't merely provide a readout of what is in memory; it also changes the state of the memory system in important ways.

Retrieval Can Improve Subsequent Memory

The simple act of retrieval can strengthen a retrieved memory, making it easier to remember that information at a later time (Bjork, 1975). For example, in one experiment participants studied brief stories and then either studied them again or were given a test that required retrieving the stories (Roediger & Karpicke, 2006). Participants were then given a final recall test for the stories either 5 minutes, 2 days, or 1 week later. As shown in **FIGURE 6.9**, at the 5-minute delay, studying the stories twice resulted in slightly higher recall than did studying followed by retrieval (testing). But the opposite occurred at the 2-day and 1-week delays: Retrieval (testing) produced much higher levels of recall than did an extra study exposure.

The benefits of retrieval on subsequent retention even occur in grade school children (Jaeger et al., 2015). Furthermore, students are able to learn to use this kind of retrieval practice spontaneously and on their own (Ariel & Karpicke, 2018). These findings have potentially important implications for learning in educational contexts (Karpicke, 2012), which we will explore further in the Learning chapter.

Retrieval Can Also Impair Subsequent Memory

As much as retrieval can help memory, that's not always the case. **Retrieval-induced forgetting** is *a process by which retrieving an item from long-term memory impairs subsequent recall of related items* (Anderson, 2003; Anderson et al., 1994; Murayama et al., 2014). For example, when a speaker selectively talks about some aspects of memories shared with a listener and doesn't mention related information, both the speaker and the listener later have a harder time remembering the omitted events (Cuc et al., 2007; Hirst & Echterhoff, 2012). Retrieval-induced forgetting can affect eyewitness memory. When witnesses to a staged crime are questioned about some details of the crime scene, their ability to later recall related details that they were not asked about is impaired, compared with that of witnesses who were not previously questioned (MacLeod, 2002; Shaw et al., 1995). These findings suggest that initial interviews with eyewitnesses should be as complete as possible to avoid potential retrieval-induced forgetting of significant details that are not probed during an interview (MacLeod & Saunders, 2008).

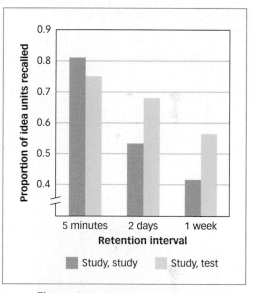

Figure 6.9 Memory Testing Benefits Long-Term Retention With a 5-minute retention interval, the study–study condition results in slightly higher recall. But the results change dramatically with retention intervals of 2 days and 1 week: With these longer delays, the study–test condition yields much higher levels of recall than does the study–study condition (Roediger & Karpicke, 2006).

transfer-appropriate processing The idea that memory is likely to transfer from one situation to another when the encoding and retrieval contexts of the situations match.

retrieval-induced forgetting A process by which retrieving an item from long-term memory impairs subsequent recall of related items.

As part of an experiment, participants wore cameras that took pictures every 15 seconds as the participants toured a museum. Daniel Schacter

Retrieval Can Change Subsequent Memory

In addition to improving and impairing subsequent memory, the act of retrieval also can change what we remember from an experience. In one experiment, participants toured a museum, where they viewed exhibits that each contained several different stops (St. Jacques & Schacter, 2013). The participants wore cameras that, every 15 seconds, automatically took pictures of what was in front of them. Two days later, the participants were given a "reactivation session," during which memories of some of the stops were reactivated by showing photos and asking participants to rate how vividly they reexperienced what had happened at each stop. The participants were also shown novel photos of *unvisited* stops within the exhibit and were asked to judge how closely these novel photos were related to the photos of the stops they had actually seen in that exhibit. Two days after the reactivation session, the participants were given a memory test.

Participants sometimes incorrectly remembered that the stop shown in the novel photo had been part of the original tour. Most important, participants who tended to make this mistake also tended to have more vivid recollections during the reactivation session. In other words, retrieving and vividly reexperiencing memories of what participants actually did see at the museum led them to incorporate into their memory information that was *not* part of their original experience. This finding may be related to the phenomenon of reconsolidation that we discussed earlier, where reactivating a memory temporarily makes it vulnerable to disruption and change. At the very least, this finding reinforces the idea that retrieving a memory involves far more than a simple readout of information.

Separating the Components of Retrieval

Before leaving the topic of retrieval, let's look at how the process actually works. There is reason to believe that *trying* to recall an incident and *successfully* recalling one are fundamentally different processes that occur in different parts of the brain (Moscovitch, 1994; Schacter, 1996). For example, regions in the left frontal lobe show heightened activity when people *try* to retrieve information that was presented to them earlier (Oztekin et al., 2009; Tulving et al., 1994). This activity may reflect the mental effort of struggling to dredge up the past event (Lepage et al., 2000). However, *successfully* remembering a past experience tends to be accompanied by activity in the hippocampal region (see **FIGURE 6.10**) (Eldridge et al., 2000; Giovanello et al., 2004; Schacter et al., 1996). Successful recall also activates parts of the brain that play a role in processing the sensory features of an experience. For instance, recall of previously heard sounds is accompanied by activity in the auditory cortex (in the temporal lobe), whereas recall of previously seen pictures is accompanied by activity in the visual cortex

Figure 6.10 PET Scans of Successful and Unsuccessful Recall (a) When people successfully remembered words they had seen earlier in an experiment (achieving high levels of recall on a test), the hippocampus showed increased activity. (b) When people tried but failed to recall words they had seen earlier (achieving low levels of recall on a test), the left frontal lobe showed increased activity. Schacter DL, Alpert NM, Savage CR, Rauch SL, Albert MS. Conscious recollection and the human hippocampal formation: evidence from positron emission tomography. Proc Natl Acad Sci USA 1996; 93: 321–5.

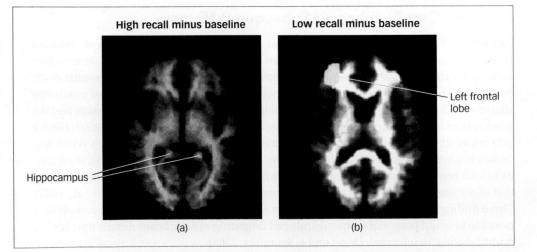

(in the occipital lobe) (Wheeler et al., 2000). Although retrieval may seem like a single process, brain studies suggest that separately identifiable processes are at work.

Build to the Outcomes

1. Why are external contexts powerful retrieval cues?

2. How does mood affect memory?

3. Should students spend more time testing themselves on material (retrieval), or re-reading it over and over?

4. How can retrieval-induced forgetting occur during conversations?

5. How is it possible to remember something you've never seen?

6. How does brain activity differ when you are *trying* to recall an event versus *successfully* recalling it?

Forms of Long-Term Memory: More Than One Kind

In 1977, the neurologist Oliver Sacks interviewed a young man named Greg who had a tumor in his brain that wiped out his ability to remember day-to-day events. One thing Greg could remember, however, was his life during the 1960s, especially attending rock concerts by his favorite band, the Grateful Dead. Greg's memories of those concerts stuck with him over the ensuing years, when he was living in a long-term care hospital. In 1991, Dr. Sacks took Greg to a Grateful Dead concert at New York's Madison Square Garden, wondering whether such a momentous event might jolt his memory into action. "That was fantastic," Greg told Dr. Sacks as they left the concert. "I will always remember it. I had the time of my life." But when Dr. Sacks saw Greg the next morning and asked him whether he recalled the previous night's concert at the Garden, Greg drew a blank: "No, I've never been to the Garden" (Sacks, 1995, pp. 76–77).

Although Greg was unable to make new memories, some of the new things that happened to him did seem to leave a mark. For example, Greg did not recall learning that his father had died, but he did seem sad and withdrawn for years after hearing the news. Similarly, HM could not make new memories after his surgery, but if he played a game in which he had to track a moving target, his performance gradually improved with each round (Milner, 1962). Greg could not consciously remember hearing about his father's death, and HM could not consciously remember playing the game, but both showed clear signs of having been permanently changed by experiences that they so rapidly forgot. In other words, they *behaved* as though they were remembering things while claiming to remember nothing at all. This suggests that there must be several kinds of memory — some that are accessible to conscious recall and some that we cannot consciously access (Eichenbaum & Cohen, 2001; Schacter & Tulving, 1994; Schacter et al., 2000; Squire & Kandel, 1999).

Memories can be broken down into two types. **Explicit memory** occurs *when people consciously or intentionally retrieve past experiences.* Recalling last summer's vacation, incidents from a novel you just read, or facts you studied for a test all involve explicit memory. Indeed, anytime you start a sentence with "I remember . . . ," you are talking about an explicit memory. **Implicit memory** occurs when *past experiences influence later behavior and performance, even without an effort to remember them or an awareness of the recollection* (Graf & Schacter, 1985; Schacter, 1987). Let's look next at both of these.

Implicit Memory

Implicit memories are not consciously recalled, but their presence is "implied" by our actions. Greg's persistent sadness after his father's death, even though he had no

Learning Outcomes

- Distinguish between explicit memory and implicit memory.
- Give examples of semantic memories and episodic memories.
- Describe the pros and cons of collaborative memory.

explicit memory Memory that occurs when people consciously or intentionally retrieve past experiences.

implicit memory Memory that occurs when past experiences influence later behavior and performance, even without an effort to remember them or an awareness of the recollection.

Guitarists such as Janelle Monae rely heavily on procedural memory to acquire and use the skills they need to play their music at a high level. Erika Goldring/Getty Images

conscious knowledge of the event, is an example of implicit memory. So is HM's improved performance on a tracking task that he didn't consciously remember having done before.

The ability to ride a bike or tie your shoelaces or play the guitar are other examples of implicit memory. You may know how to do these things, but you probably can't describe *how* to do them. Such knowledge reflects a particular kind of implicit memory called **procedural memory,** which refers to *the gradual acquisition of skills as a result of practice, or "knowing how" to do things.*

Priming Makes Some Information More Accessible

Not all implicit memories are procedural or "how to" memories. For example, **priming** refers to *an enhanced ability to think of a stimulus, such as a word or object, as a result of a recent exposure to the stimulus during an earlier study task* (Tulving & Schacter, 1990). In one experiment, college students were asked to study a long list of words, including *avocado, mystery, climate, octopus,* and *assassin* (Tulving et al., 1982). Later, implicit memory was tested by showing participants word fragments, and asking them to come up with a word that fitted the fragment. Try the test yourself:

c h - - - - n k   o - t - p - -   - o g - y - - -   - l - m - t e

You probably had difficulty coming up with the answers for the first and third fragments (*chipmunk, bogeyman*) but had little trouble coming up with answers for the second and fourth (*octopus, climate*). Seeing *octopus* and *climate* on the original list made those words more accessible later, during the fill-in-the-blanks test. Just as priming a pump makes water flow more easily, priming the memory system makes some information more accessible. In the fill-in-the-blanks experiment, people showed priming for studied words even when they failed to remember consciously that they had seen them earlier. This suggests that priming is an example of implicit, not explicit, memory. Even more striking evidence on this point comes from a study by Mitchell (2006) in which people who were tested *17 years* after initially participating in a priming experiment still showed significant priming effects, even though some of them had no recollection that they had ever participated in the experiment!

Procedural Memory and Priming Do Not Rely on the Hippocampus

People who have amnesia, such as HM and Greg, can acquire new procedural memories, and they can also show substantial priming effects, even though they have no explicit memory for the items they studied. This indicates that implicit memory does not require the hippocampal structures that are damaged in cases of amnesia (Schacter & Curran, 2000).

So which parts of the brain *are* involved? When research participants are shown the word stem *mot* or *tab* and are asked to provide the first word that comes to mind, parts of the occipital lobe involved in visual processing and parts of the frontal lobe involved in word retrieval become active. But if people perform the same task after being primed by seeing *motel* and *table,* there's less activity in these same regions (Buckner et al., 1995; Schott et al., 2005). Priming seems to make it easier for parts of the cortex that are involved in perceiving a word or object to identify the item after a recent exposure to it (Schacter et al., 2004; Wiggs & Martin, 1998). This suggests that the brain saves a bit of processing time after priming (see **FIGURE 6.11**).

Explicit Memory: Semantic and Episodic

Consider these two questions: (1) What U.S. holiday falls on July 4? (2) What is the most spectacular Fourth of July celebration you've ever seen? Every American knows the answer to the first question (we celebrate the signing of the Declaration of Independence

procedural memory The gradual acquisition of skills as a result of practice, or "knowing how" to do things.

priming An enhanced ability to think of a stimulus, such as a word or an object, as a result of a recent exposure to that stimulus during an earlier study task.

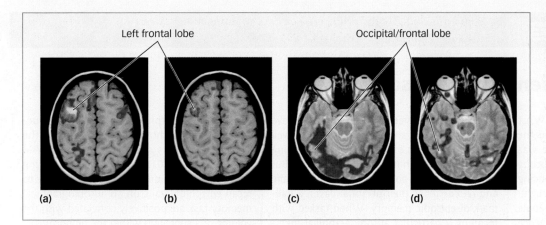

Left frontal lobe

Occipital/frontal lobe

(a)   (b)   (c)   (d)

Figure 6.11   Primed and Unprimed Processing of Stimuli Priming is associated with reduced levels of activation in the cortex on a number of different tasks. These fMRI images show brain regions in the frontal lobe (a) and occipital/temporal lobe (c) that are active during an unprimed task (in this case, providing a word response to a visual word cue). The images in (b) and (d) show reduced activity in the same regions during the primed version of the same task.

on July 4, 1776), but we all have our own answers to the second. Both of these are explicit memories, consciously or intentionally retrieved from past experiences. But the first one requires you to dredge up a fact that every American schoolchild knows and that is not part of your personal autobiography. This is an example of **semantic memory,** *a network of associated facts and concepts that make up our general knowledge of the world*. In contrast, remembering a specific celebration requires you to revisit a particular time and place — or episode — from your personal past. This is an example of **episodic memory,** which is *the collection of past personal experiences that occurred at a particular time and place* (**FIGURE 6.12**).

Episodic memory is special because it is the only form of memory that allows us to engage in mental time travel, projecting ourselves into the past and revisiting events that have happened to us. This ability allows us to connect our pasts and our presents to construct a cohesive story of our lives (see A World of Difference: Do We All Reexperience

semantic memory A network of associated facts and concepts that make up our general knowledge of the world.

episodic memory The collection of past personal experiences that occurred at a particular time and place.

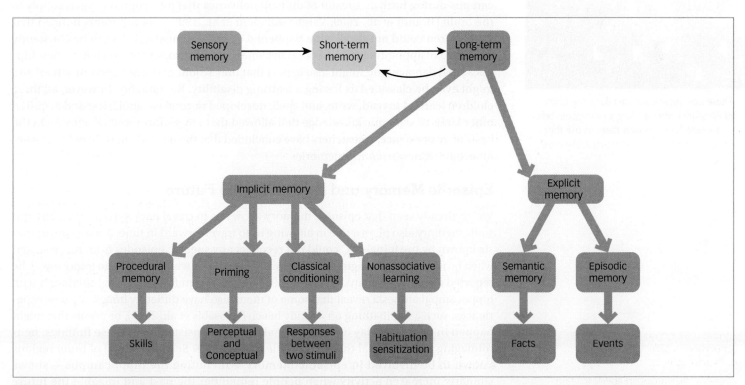

Figure 6.12   Forms of Long-Term Memory Long-term memory consists of explicit and implicit forms, which can be further divided into specific subtypes (see the chapter on Learning for discussion of conditioning, habituation, and sensitization).

A WORLD OF DIFFERENCE

Do We All Reexperience Our Personal Pasts?

Think back to your dinner last night. What did you eat and where? What did the dining room look like? Who else was there? You probably didn't have much difficulty answering these questions and reexperiencing at least a few happenings from dinner last night. But some otherwise high-functioning people seem to lack the ability to vividly reexperience past events, even though they know those events happened. Researchers who recently discovered this condition named it *severely deficient autobiographical memory* (SDAM).

One study examined three middle-aged adults (one woman, two men) with SDAM (Palombo et al., 2015). Each is employed at a full-time job; one has a PhD degree. All three appear to have normal intellectual abilities and all perform well on laboratory tests of verbal memory, showing that they can retain information over time. But they each lack the ability to travel back in time and *reexperience* their personal pasts, a hallmark of episodic memory. When tasked with recalling a particular autobiographical memory from everyday life, they recall few episodic details about what happened and are particularly unable to retrieve visual details, which for most people is an integral part of successful episodic recollection.

Given the established link between the hippocampus and successful recollection, you might not be surprised to learn that structural MRI scans show reduced volume in the right hippocampus of individuals with SDAM (Palombo et al., 2015). Even in healthy young adults, individual differences in the ability to recall episodic details on an autobiographical memory task are positively correlated with the volume of a subregion within the hippocampus known as the *dentate gyrus/$CA_{2/3}$* (Palombo et al., 2018). Previous neuroimaging research had suggested that this same part of the hippocampus may be particularly important for episodic memory, and this new research on individual differences provides additional support for that hypothesis.

These new Americans are taking the Oath of Allegiance after passing a citizenship test that would have required them to use their semantic memories. EPA/Jim Lo Scalzo/Newscom

Our Personal Pasts?). People who have amnesia can usually travel back in time and revisit episodes that occurred before they became amnesic, but they are unable to revisit episodes that happened later. For example, Greg couldn't travel back to any time after 1969, because that's when he stopped being able to create new episodic memories. But can people with amnesia create new semantic memories?

Researchers have studied three young adults who suffered damage to the hippocampus during birth as a result of difficult deliveries that interrupted oxygen supply to the brain (Brandt et al., 2009; Vargha-Khadem et al., 1997). Their parents noticed that the children could not recall what happened during a typical day, had to be constantly reminded of appointments, and often became lost and disoriented. In view of their hippocampal damage, you might also expect that they would perform poorly in school and might even be classified as having a learning disability. Remarkably, however, all three children learned to read, write, and spell; developed normal vocabularies; and acquired other kinds of semantic knowledge that allowed them to perform well in school. On the basis of this evidence, researchers have concluded that the hippocampus is not necessary for acquiring new *semantic* memories.

Episodic Memory and Imagining the Future

We've already seen that episodic memory allows us to travel backward in time, but episodic memory also plays a role in allowing us to travel forward in time. A man with amnesia known by the initials KC could not recollect any specific episodes from his past, and when he was asked to imagine a future episode — such as what he might do tomorrow — he reported a complete "blank" (Tulving, 1985). More recent findings from individuals with hippocampal amnesia reveal that some of them also have difficulty imagining new experiences, such as sunbathing on a sandy beach (Hassabis et al., 2007), or events that might happen in their everyday lives (Race et al., 2011). Consistent with these findings, neuroimaging studies reveal that a *core network* (Benoit & Schacter, 2015) of brain regions known to be involved in episodic memory — including the hippocampus — shows similarly increased activity when people remember the past and imagine the future (Addis et al., 2007; Okuda et al., 2003; Schacter et al., 2012; Szpunar et al., 2007) (see **FIGURE 6.13**).

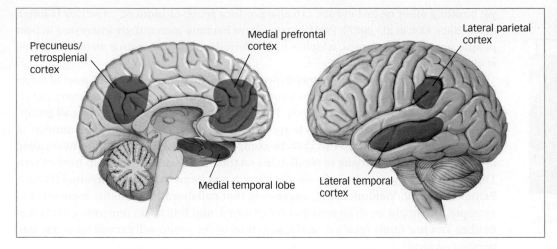

Figure 6.13 Remembering the Past and Imagining the Future Depend on a Common Core Network of Brain Regions A common brain network is activated when people remember episodes that actually occurred in their personal pasts and when they imagine episodes that might occur in their personal futures. This network includes the hippocampus, a part of the medial temporal lobe that plays an important role in episodic memory (Schacter et al., 2007).

Taken together, these observations strongly suggest that we rely heavily on episodic memory to envision our personal futures (Schacter et al., 2008; Szpunar, 2010). Episodic memory allows us to recombine elements of past experience in new ways, so that we can mentally try out different versions of what might happen (Schacter, 2012; Schacter & Addis, 2007; Suddendorf & Corballis, 2007). For example, when you imagine having a difficult conversation with a friend that will take place in a couple of days, you can draw on past experiences to envision different ways in which the conversation might unfold — and hopefully avoid saying things that, based on past experience, are likely to make the situation worse. As we'll discuss later, however, this flexibility of episodic memory might also be responsible for some kinds of memory errors.

Imagining the future by recombining elements of past experiences sounds a lot like what psychologists refer to as *divergent creative thinking:* generating creative ideas by combining different types of information in new ways (Guilford, 1967). One common test of divergent creative thinking, the Alternate Uses Task (AUT) (Guilford, 1967), requires participants to generate unusual uses of common objects, such as a brick.

When people perform the AUT during an fMRI scan, parts of the core brain network that supports episodic memory and future imagining, including the hippocampus, show increased activity (Beaty et al., 2016, 2018; Benedek et al., 2014), suggesting that episodic memory may contribute to divergent creative thinking. A recent study of healthy young adults revealed that brief training in retrieving details from episodic memory enhances divergent creative thinking on the AUT (Madore et al., 2015). Training in how to recall episodic details led participants to rely more on their episodic memories during the AUT, helping them recombine information in novel ways and come up with more unusual uses for objects. fMRI evidence revealed that this episodic training effect is accompanied by increased activity in the hippocampus, as well as increased coupling between the core brain network that supports episodic processing and an executive network that supports working memory and related control functions (Madore et al., 2019). This finding fits well with other evidence indicating that coupling between core and executive networks is a signature feature of divergent creative thinking (Beaty et al., 2016, 2018).

How many unusual uses of a brick can you think of? On the AUT, you would receive credit for coming up with such novel uses as a doorstop, a paperweight, or even a weapon.
Alis Photo/Shutterstock

Collaborative Memory: Social Influences on Remembering

So far, we've focused mainly on memory in individuals functioning on their own. But remembering also serves important social functions, which is why we get together with family to talk about old times, or share our memories with friends by posting our vacation photos on Instagram. Sharing memories with others can strengthen them (Hirst & Echterhoff, 2012), but we've already seen that talking about some aspects of a memory,

Remembering as a collaborative group leads to greater recall than any single member of the group would achieve alone, but less than that produced by a nominal group of individuals remembering on their own. Blend Images/Hill Street Studios/Alamy

yet omitting other related events, can also produce retrieval-induced *forgetting* (Coman et al., 2009; Cuc et al., 2007). Psychologists have become increasingly interested in how people remember in groups, which is now referred to as *collaborative memory* (Meade et al., 2018; Rajaram, 2011).

In a typical collaborative memory experiment, participants first encode a set of target materials, such as a list of words, on their own (just as in the traditional memory experiments that we've already considered). Then participants work together in small groups (usually two or three participants) to try to remember the target items. The number of items recalled by this group can then be compared with the number of items recalled by individuals who are trying to recall items on their own, without any help from others. The collaborative group typically recalls more target items than any individual (Hirst & Echterhoff, 2012; Weldon, 2001), suggesting that collaboration benefits memory. For example, Tim might recall an item that Emily forgot, and Eric might remember items that neither Tim nor Emily recalled, so the sum total of the group will exceed what any one person can recall.

But things get really interesting when we compare the performance of the collaborative group with the performance of several individuals recalling target items on their own. For example, let's assume that after studying a list of eight words, Tim recalls items 1, 2, and 8; Emily recalls items 1, 4, and 7; and Eric recalls items 1, 5, 6, and 8 — in total, seven of the eight items that were presented. (Nobody recalled item 3.) The surprising finding is that Tim, Emily, and Eric together will come up with fewer total items as a group than when they remember on their own (Basden et al., 1997; Hirst & Echterhoff, 2012; Rajaram, 2011; Rajaram & Pereira-Pasarin, 2010; Weldon, 2001). This negative effect of group recall on memory is known as *collaborative inhibition:* The same number of individuals working together recall fewer items than they would on their own.

What's going on here? One possibility is that when recalling items together, the retrieval strategies used by individual members of the group disrupt those used by others (Basden et al., 1997; Hirst & Echterhoff, 2012; Rajaram, 2011). For instance, suppose that

THE REAL WORLD

Is Google Hurting Our Memories?

Take some time to try to answer a simple question before returning to reading this box: What country has a national flag that is not rectangular? Now let's discuss what went through your mind as you searched for an answer. (The correct answer is Nepal.) There probably was a time not too long ago when most people would have tried to conjure up images of national flags or take a mental world tour, but research conducted in the lab of one of your textbook authors indicates that nowadays, most of us think about computers and Google searches when confronted with questions of this kind (Sparrow et al., 2011).

Sparrow and colleagues found that after people were given difficult general-knowledge questions, they were slower to name the color in which a computer-related word (e.g., *Google, Internet, Yahoo*) was printed than the color in which a noncomputer-related word (e.g., *Nike, table, Yoplait*) was printed. This suggests that after being given difficult questions, these people were thinking about things related to computers, which interfered with their ability to name the color in which the word was printed. The researchers concluded that we are now so used to searching for information on Google when we don't immediately know the answer to a question that we immediately think of computers, rather than searching our memories.

This result raises troubling questions: Is reliance on computers and the Internet having an adverse effect on human memory? If we rely on Google for answers, are we unknowingly making our memories obsolete?

In fact, participants had a harder time remembering bits of trivia that they typed into a computer when they were told that the computer would save their answers than when they were told that the answers would be erased; but the same people often remembered where they saved the answers even when they did not remember the information itself (Sparrow et al., 2011). This suggests that people may be adapting their memories to the demands of new technology, relying on computers in a way that is similar to how we sometimes rely on other people (friends, family members, or colleagues) to remember things that we may not remember ourselves. This is similar to what we discussed as *collaborative memory*, and just as collaborative remembering with other people has both helpful and harmful effects, so does collaborative remembering with our computers.

Tim goes first and recalls items in the order that they were presented. This retrieval strategy may be disruptive to Emily, who prefers to recall the last item first and then work backward through the list.

Despite the effects of collaborative inhibition, when individuals recall information together in a group, they are exposed to items recalled by others that they may not recall themselves. This exposure improves their memory when they are retested at a later time (Blumen & Rajaram, 2008). And when group members discuss what they have recalled, they can help each other to correct and reduce memory errors (Ross, Blatz, & Schryer, 2008). (Can you rely on your computer for collaborative remembering? See The Real World: Is Google Hurting Our Memories?)

Build to the Outcomes

1. What is the type of memory in which you just "know how" to do something?

2. How does priming make memory more efficient?

3. What parts of the brain are involved in procedural memory and priming?

4. What form of memory is like a time machine to our past?

5. How does episodic memory help us imagine our futures?

6. Why does a collaborative group typically recall fewer items than the same individuals working independently?

Memory Failures: The Seven "Sins" of Memory

You probably haven't given much thought to breathing today, and the reason is that from the moment you woke up, you've been doing it effortlessly and well. But the moment breathing fails, you are reminded of just how important it is. Memory is like that. Every time we see, think, notice, imagine, or wonder, we are drawing on our ability to use information stored in our brains, but it isn't until this ability fails that we become acutely aware of just how much we should treasure it. Such memory errors — the seven "sins" of memory — cast similar illumination on how memory normally operates and how often it operates well (Schacter, 1999, 2001b). We'll discuss each of the seven "sins" in detail below.

1. Transience

Memories degrade with time. The culprit here is **transience:** *forgetting what occurs with the passage of time.* Transience occurs during the storage phase of memory, after an experience has been encoded and before it is retrieved. This was first illustrated in the late 1870s by Hermann Ebbinghaus, a German philosopher who, after studying lists of nonsense syllables, measured his own memory for those syllables at different delays (Ebbinghaus, 1885/1964). Ebbinghaus charted his recall of the syllables over time, creating the forgetting curve shown in **FIGURE 6.14**. He noted a rapid drop-off in retention during the first few tests, followed by a slower rate of forgetting on later tests — a general pattern confirmed by many subsequent memory researchers (Wixted & Ebbensen, 1991). So, for example, when English-speakers were tested for memory of Spanish vocabulary acquired during high school or college courses taken 1 to 50 years earlier, there was a rapid drop-off in memory during the first 3 years after the students' last class, followed by tiny losses in later years (Bahrick, 1984, 2000). In all these studies, memories didn't fade at a constant rate as time passed; most forgetting happened soon after an event occurred, with increasingly less forgetting as more time passed.

Another way that memories can be forgotten is by interference from other memories. For example, if you carry out the same activities at work each day, by the time Friday rolls around, it may be difficult to remember what you did on Monday because later activities blend in with earlier ones. This is an example of **retroactive interference,**

Learning Outcomes

- Identify each of the memory "sins."
- Describe possible benefits of each memory "sin."

transience Forgetting what occurs with the passage of time.

retroactive interference Situations in which later learning impairs memory for information acquired earlier.

Figure 6.14 The Curve of Forgetting Hermann Ebbinghaus measured his retention at various delay intervals after he studied lists of nonsense syllables. He measured retention in percent savings, that is, the percentage of time he needed to relearn the list compared with the time he needed to learn it initially.

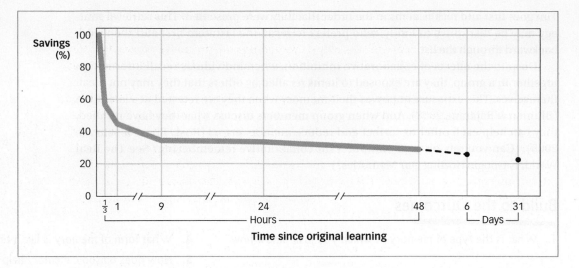

proactive interference Situations in which earlier learning impairs memory for information acquired later.

situations in which later learning impairs memory for information acquired earlier (Postman & Underwood, 1973). **Proactive interference,** in contrast, refers to *situations in which earlier learning impairs memory for information acquired later.* For instance, if you use the same parking lot each day at work or at school, you've probably gone out to find your car and then stood there confused by the memories of having parked it on previous days.

One of the most common types of forgetting over time is that most of us have few or no memories from the first few years of life, due to *childhood amnesia,* or *infantile amnesia.* On average, an individual's first memory dates to about 3 to 3.5 years of age (Dudycha & Dudycha, 1933; Waldfogel, 1948), with women reporting slightly earlier first memories (3.07 years of age) than men (3.4 years) (Howes et al., 1993). These estimates are based on individuals from Western (i.e., North American and European) cultures, which emphasize talking about the past. First memories are seen at even later ages in Asian cultures that place less emphasis on talking about the past, such as Korea and China (MacDonald et al., 2000; Mullen, 1994; Peterson et al., 2009). Culture may thus impact how long our memories last.

2. Absentmindedness

The great cellist Yo-Yo Ma put his treasured $2.5 million instrument in the trunk of a taxicab in Manhattan. He rode to his destination, paid the driver, and left the cab, forgetting his cello. Minutes later, Ma realized what he had done and called the police, who tracked down the taxi and recovered the instrument within hours (Finkelstein, 1999). But how had he forgotten about something so important that had occurred only

First memories are seen later in cultures that place less emphasis on talking about the past. Zhang Bo/Getty Images; Hero Images/Getty Images

10 minutes earlier? Transience is not a likely culprit. As soon as Ma realized what he'd done with his instrument, he recalled where he had put it. This information had not disappeared from his memory (which is why he was able to tell the police where the cello was). Instead, Yo-Yo Ma was a victim of **absentmindedness,** *a lapse in attention that results in memory failure.*

What makes people absentminded? One common cause is lack of attention. Attention plays a vital role in encoding information into long-term memory. Without proper attention, material is much less likely to be stored properly and recalled later. For example, participants in one study listened to lists of 15 words for a later memory test (Craik et al., 1996). They were allowed to pay full attention to certain lists, but while hearing other lists, they simultaneously performed a different task (pressing keys to indicate where asterisks appeared on a screen). On a later test, participants recalled far fewer words from the list they had heard while their attention was divided.

What happens in the brain when attention is divided? As we saw earlier, greater activity in the lower left frontal region during encoding is associated with better memory. But participants show less activity in the lower left frontal lobe when their attention is divided (Shallice et al., 1994). Dividing attention, then, prevents the lower left frontal lobe from playing its normal role in semantic encoding, and the result is absentminded forgetting. Divided attention also leads to less hippocampal involvement in encoding (Kensinger et al., 2003; Uncapher & Rugg, 2008). Given the importance of the hippocampus to episodic memory, this finding may help to explain why absentminded forgetting is sometimes so extreme, as when we forget where we put our keys or glasses only moments earlier.

Another common cause of absentmindedness is forgetting to carry out actions that we plan to do in the future. On any given day, you need to remember the times and places that your classes meet, you need to remember with whom and where you are having lunch, and you need to remember which grocery items to pick up for dinner. In other words, you have to remember to remember, which is called **prospective memory,** *remembering to do things in the future* (Einstein & McDaniel,1990, 2005). Failures of prospective memory are a major source of absentmindedness (Dismukes, 2012).

It is perhaps not surprising in this era of smartphones and Google Calendar that we are increasingly relying on external devices to remind us to carry out future tasks in everyday life, a process referred to as *intention offloading* (Risko & Gilbert, 2016). Studies of patients with memory problems resulting from traumatic brain injury (Baldwin & Powell, 2015) and Alzheimer's disease (El Haj et al., 2017) have shown positive effects on everyday prospective memory from training the patients to use Google Calendar synched to their smartphones. These advantages of technology for improving prospective memory failures are balanced by the costs discussed in The Real World: Is Google Hurting Our Memories?

3. Blocking

Have you ever tried to recall the name of a famous movie actor or a book you've read — and felt that the answer was on the tip of your tongue, rolling around in your head *somewhere* but just out of reach at that moment? This tip-of-the-tongue experience is a classic example of **blocking,** *a failure to retrieve information that is available in memory even though you are trying to produce it.* The sought-after information has been encoded and stored; it has not faded from memory, and you aren't forgetting to retrieve it. Rather, you are experiencing a full-blown retrieval failure, which makes this memory breakdown especially frustrating. Researchers have described the tip-of-the-tongue state, in particular, as "a mild torment, something like [being] on the brink of a sneeze" (Brown & McNeill, 1966, p. 326).

Blocking occurs especially often for the names of people and places (Cohen, 1990; Semenza, 2009; Valentine et al., 1996). Why? Because their links to related concepts and

Talking on a cell phone while driving is an example of divided attention in everyday life; texting is even worse. Texting while driving can be dangerous, and an increasing number of states have banned the practice.
AndreyPopov/Getty Images

absentmindedness A lapse in attention that results in memory failure.

prospective memory Remembering to do things in the future.

blocking A failure to retrieve information that is available in memory even though you are trying to produce it.

Most people watching the Macy's Thanksgiving Day Parade will easily recall this character's name, closely associated with a grumpy attitude: The Grinch! AP Photo/Craig Ruttle

knowledge are weaker than for common names. That somebody's last name is Baker doesn't tell us much about the person, but saying that he *is* a baker does. To illustrate this point, researchers showed people pictures of cartoon and comic strip characters, some with descriptive names that highlight key features of the character (e.g., Grumpy, Snow White, Scrooge) and others with arbitrary names (e.g., Aladdin, Mary Poppins, Pinocchio) (Brédart & Valentine, 1998). Even though the two types of names were equally familiar to participants in the experiment, they blocked less often on the descriptive names than on the arbitrary names.

Although it's frustrating, blocking is a relatively infrequent event for most of us. However, it occurs more often as we grow older, and it is a very common complaint among people in their 60s and 70s (Burke et al., 1991; Schwartz, 2002). Even more striking, some individuals with brain damage live in a nearly perpetual tip-of-the-tongue state (Semenza, 2009). One such individual could recall the names of only 2 of 40 famous people when she saw their photographs, compared with 25 of 40 for healthy volunteers in the control group (Semenza & Zettin, 1989). Yet she could still recall correctly the occupations of 32 of these people — the same number as healthy people could recall. This case and similar ones have given researchers important clues about what parts of the brain are involved in retrieving proper names. Name blocking usually results from damage to parts of the left temporal lobe on the surface of the cortex, most often as a result of a stroke. This idea is supported by studies that show strong activation of regions within the temporal lobe when people recall proper names (Damasio et al., 1996; Gorno-Tempini et al., 1998).

4. Memory Misattribution

Shortly after the devastating 1995 bombing of the federal building in Oklahoma City, police set about searching for two suspects they called John Doe 1 and John Doe 2. John Doe 1 turned out to be Timothy McVeigh, who was quickly apprehended and later convicted of the crime. John Doe 2, who had supposedly accompanied McVeigh when he rented a van before the bombing, was never found. In fact, John Doe 2 had never existed; he was a product of the memory of Tom Kessinger, a mechanic who was present when McVeigh rented the van. The day after, two other men had also rented a van in Kessinger's presence. The first man, like McVeigh, was tall and fair. The second man was shorter and stockier, was dark-haired, wore a blue and white cap, and had a tattoo beneath his left sleeve — a match to the description of John Doe 2. Tom Kessinger had confused his recollections of men he had seen on separate days in the same place. He was a victim of **memory misattribution,** *assigning a recollection or an idea to the wrong source* (see **FIGURE 6.15**).

Part of memory is knowing where our memories came from. This is known as **source memory,** *recall of when, where, and how information was acquired* (Johnson et al., 1993; Mitchell & Johnson, 2009; Schacter et al., 1984). People sometimes correctly recall a fact they learned earlier or accurately recognize a person or object they have seen before but misattribute the source of this knowledge — just as happened to Tom Kessinger. Such

memory misattribution Assigning a recollection or an idea to the wrong source.

source memory Recall of when, where, and how information was acquired.

Figure 6.15 **Memory Misattribution** (a) In 1995, the Murrah Federal Building in Oklahoma City was bombed in an act of terrorism. (b) The police sketch shows John Doe 2, who originally was thought to have been culprit Timothy McVeigh's partner in the bombing. It was later determined that the witness had confused his memories of different men whom he had encountered on different days. Albert Overbeek/ AP Photo; FBI/ *The Oklahoman*/AP Photo

Déjà Vu: Can We Predict the Future?

Pat Long began to experience intense feelings of having previously lived through a current experience despite realizing that he almost certainly had not. These feelings of déjà vu occurred as many as 10 times per day and were associated with the onset of epileptic seizures caused by a tumor in his brain (Long, 2017). Previous reports had linked frequent sensations of déjà vu with epileptic seizures, but many people without epilepsy have similar if less frequent experiences: Surveys indicate that roughly two-thirds of people have experienced déjà vu at least once (Brown, 2004). Yet déjà vu is not only about the past: Déjà vu is often accompanied by a feeling that one knows exactly what is going to happen next (Brown, 2004). Indeed, Pat Long referred to his own déjà vu experience as "a feeling of precognition." But do we actually know what is going to happen next when we experience déjà vu?

To find out, researchers used an innovative virtual reality procedure to induce déjà vu in the lab (Cleary et al., 2012). Participants navigated through a virtual reality video sequence of places, among them scene (*a*). After this encoding phase, participants were shown novel scenes, half of which were similar to a previously viewed scene (as scene (*b*) is to scene (*a*)), and half of which were not similar to any previously presented scenes. Participants were more likely to report an experience of déjà vu when viewing a similar scene than when viewing a completely novel scene—even if they did not remember the original scene. This shows that the experience of déjà vu can be driven by overlap between a novel scene and a previously viewed scene that participants do not recall.

To investigate the feeling of what happens next, Cleary and Claxton (2018) added an important new twist to the earlier procedure. Because in the encoding phase, participants had viewed the images as a video, they had seen many turns that could prime a sense of what might happen next. When participants saw the novel scenes during the test phase, they were told that "Without knowing why, you may also feel a sense of which way to turn next. Indicate which way to turn. Press *L* for left and *R* for right." Would participants claim to have a feeling of which way to turn next more frequently when they reported an experience of déjà vu? The answer was a resounding *yes*. But did participants *actually* know the correct way to turn? The answer was a resounding *no*: Participants could not accurately predict what the next turn would be when shown a novel, configurally similar scene, despite feeling that they knew it.

These findings led Cleary and Claxton to characterize déjà vu as "an illusion of prediction." It may also help Pat Long understand that while the "feeling of precognition" that characterizes his déjà vu experiences is shared by others, that feeling does not contain reliable information about what the future has in store for him.

(a)   (b)

Republished with Permission of SAGE, from Déjà Vu: An Illusion of Prediction, Cleary, A. M., & Claxton, A. B., Psychological Science, 29(4), 2018; permission conveyed through Copyright Clearance Center, Inc.

misattribution could be the cause of déjà vu experiences, when you suddenly feel that you have been in a situation before even though you can't recall any details. A present situation that is similar to a past experience may trigger a general sense of familiarity that is mistakenly attributed to having been in the exact situation previously (Brown, 2004; Reed, 1988) (see Hot Science: Déjà Vu: Can We Predict the Future?).

Individuals with damage to the frontal lobes are especially prone to memory misattribution errors (Schacter et al., 1984; Shimamura & Squire, 1987). This is probably because

TABLE 6.1 False Recognition	
sour	thread
candy	pin
sugar	eye
bitter	sewing
good	sharp
taste	point
tooth	prick
nice	thimble
honey	haystack
soda	pain
chocolate	hurt
heart	injection
cake	syringe
tart	cloth
pie	knitting

the frontal lobes play a significant role in effortful retrieval processes, which are required to dredge up the correct source of a memory. But we are all vulnerable to memory misattribution. Take the following test and there is a good chance that you will experience this for yourself. First, study the two lists of words in **TABLE 6.1** by reading each word for about 1 second. When you are done, return to this paragraph for more instructions, but don't look back at the table! Now try to recognize which of the following words appeared in the lists you just studied: *taste, bread, needle, king, sweet, thread.* If you think that *taste* and *thread* were on the lists you studied, you're right. And if you think that *bread* and *king* weren't on those lists, you're also right. But if you think that *needle* or *sweet* appeared in the lists, you're dead wrong.

Most people make exactly the same mistake, claiming with confidence that they saw *needle* and *sweet* on the lists. This mistaken feeling of familiarity, called *false recognition,* occurs because all the words in the lists are associated with *needle* or *sweet.* Seeing each word in the study lists activates related words. Because *needle* and *sweet* are related to all of the list words, they become so highly activated that, only minutes later, people swear that they actually studied the words (Deese, 1959; Gallo, 2006, 2010; Roediger & McDermott, 1995, 2000). In fact, brain-scanning studies using PET and fMRI show that many of the same brain regions are active during false recognition and true recognition, including the hippocampus (Cabeza et al., 2001; Schacter et al., 1996).

When people experience a strong sense of familiarity about a person, object, or event but lack recollection of specific details, a potentially dangerous recipe for memory misattribution is in place — both in the laboratory and in real-world situations involving eyewitness memory. Understanding this point may be a key to reducing the dangerous consequences of misattribution in eyewitness testimony. However, false recognition can be reduced (Schacter et al., 1999). For example, when participants are given a choice between an object that they actually saw (e.g., a car) and a visually similar new object (a different car that looks like the one they saw), they almost always choose the car that they actually saw and thus avoid making a false recognition error (Guerin et al., 2012a, 2012b). Understanding this point may be a key to reducing the dangerous consequences of misattribution in eyewitness testimony (see Other Voices: Memories Inside Out).

5. Suggestibility

On October 4, 1992, an El Al cargo plane crashed into an apartment building in a southern suburb of Amsterdam, killing 39 residents and all 4 members of the airline crew. The disaster dominated news in the Netherlands for days as people viewed footage of the crash scene and read about the catastrophe. Ten months later, Dutch psychologists asked a simple question of university students: "Did you see the television film of the moment the plane hit the apartment building?" Fifty-five percent answered yes (Crombag et al., 1996). All of this might seem perfectly normal except for one key fact: There was no television film of the moment when the plane actually crashed. The researchers had asked a suggestive question, one that implied that television film of the crash had been shown. Respondents may have viewed television film of the *postcrash* scene, and they may have read, imagined, or talked about what might have happened when the plane hit the building, but they most definitely did not see it. The suggestive question led participants to misattribute information from these or other sources to a film that did not exist. **Suggestibility** is the *tendency to incorporate misleading information from external sources into personal recollections.*

If misleading details can be implanted in people's memories, is it also possible to suggest entire episodes that never occurred? The answer seems to be yes (Loftus, 1993, 2003). In one study, the research participant, a teenager named Chris, was asked by his older brother, Jim, to try to remember the time Chris had been lost in a shopping mall at age 5. He initially recalled nothing, but after several days, Chris produced a detailed recollection of the event. He recalled that he "felt so scared I would never see my family again" and

In 1992, an El Al cargo plane crashed into an apartment building in a suburb of Amsterdam. When Dutch psychologists asked students if they had seen the television film of the plane crashing, a majority said they had. In fact, no such footage exists (Crombag et al., 1996). Albert Overbeek/AP Photo

suggestibility The tendency to incorporate misleading information from external sources into personal recollections.

Memories Inside Out

Karen L. Daniel is the director of the Center on Wrongful Convictions at Northwestern University School of Law. Jasmin Shah Photography

There's a good chance that sometime during the summer of 2015 you saw and enjoyed the hit Pixar movie *Inside Out*, which portrays the emotional struggles of the 11-year-old Riley after her family moves to a new home by drawing on psychological research that distinguishes among basic emotions (see the chapter on Emotion and Motivation). The movie also delved into Riley's memories and provided some realistic insights into how memories can be used to regulate emotions. But as Karen Daniel points out in an opinion piece published when the movie opened, the film's depiction of memory ignored some key findings and ideas from psychological research on memory, with potentially serious consequences:

Let me begin by saying that I love, love, love Pixar movies. Like many adults, I began watching them as part of my parental duties. There was a time when I could recite all the dialogue from *Monsters Inc.* and the first two *Toy Story* films.

It was thus with great anticipation that I tuned in to a radio interview of Pete Docter, the director of the latest Pixar release, *Inside Out*. What a fabulous idea: animating the emotions inside the mind of an 11-year-old child named Riley who is undergoing a major life transition. Docter explained that he researched many aspects of psychology to make the film accurate. When it came to human memory, however, Docter departed from science for the sake of the story line.

As shown in a trailer for *Inside Out*, Riley's memories are portrayed as mini-animations safely preserved inside little globes, which can be pulled out and replayed exactly the way they happened. The character Joy explains that certain of these globes contain "core memories" that form the basis of Riley's personality. This representation of memory is essential to the plot but is not true, as Docter candidly admitted.

I couldn't help but cringe. Given the wide appeal of Pixar movies, a new generation may grow up internalizing the profoundly false notion that memory works like a video recording and that perfect memories of events can be recalled at will. In reality, memory is fallible, malleable, and subject to suggestion and distortion. Docter noted that learning this was a revelation to him, even though he chose not to depict memory that way in *Inside Out*.

One may ask, "Who cares? It's just a movie." In the world of criminal justice, it matters a great deal. One of the most critical moments in a criminal trial is when a victim or witness points at the defendant and declares, "I will never forget that face." The witness usually professes complete certainty, and the prosecutor highlights this as proof of the defendant's guilt — even though experts tell us courtroom certainty does not necessarily correlate to accuracy.

In fact, mistaken identification is a leading cause of conviction of the innocent. Myriad factors that are not necessarily obvious to the average person can affect the reliability of an eyewitness identification, such as distractions at the time of the event, lapse of time, post-event discussions with police, and limitations inherent in cross-racial identifications. Expert witnesses can help explain these factors, but most judges exclude expert testimony on the ground [*sic*] that eyewitness identifications are a matter of "common sense" and expert assistance is not necessary. (The Illinois Supreme Court is now reviewing a case that challenges this approach.)

Which brings us back to *Inside Out*. Absent the input of an expert, jurors are left to draw on personal experiences in evaluating testimony. Today's children (and their parents) may become tomorrow's jurors who believe, incorrectly, that memories are stored intact, and that witnesses can simply compare the pictures within their little memory globes to the person sitting at the defendant's table. Docter explained that this comports with most people's sense of how memory works — which is why relying on "common sense" in criminal trials falls short.

We can never entirely eliminate human error from the justice system, but overconfidence in witnesses and misunderstanding by factfinders leads to many wrongful convictions. Let's enjoy Pixar's new film, but when we return from the movie theater, let's ensure that those charged with deciding guilt or innocence in the courtroom are armed with scientific information about eyewitness identifications rather than with the snow globe concept of memory.

As Daniel and the text point out, faulty eyewitness memories are frequently at work in wrongful convictions. It would be unfortunate if the naive view of memory communicated by *Inside Out* has a lasting influence on any prospective jurors. On a more encouraging note, there are signs that some of the important findings regarding memory's fallibility, such as the seven sins of memory that you learned about in this chapter, are being communicated to participants in the legal system. For example, in 2014 the National Academy of Sciences published a report written by a distinguished committee composed of experts in both psychology and law titled *Identifying the Culprit: Assessing Eyewitness Identification*, which is intended to convey the findings of psychological research on eyewitness memory to participants in the legal system. Though no doubt many more people saw *Inside Out* than will read this important report, it seems likely that accurate characterizations of memory research such as those contained in the National Academy of Sciences' report will ultimately be more influential in the courtroom than the entertaining though misleading depictions of Riley's memory globes.

remembered that a kindly old man wearing a flannel shirt found him crying (Loftus, 1993, p. 532). But according to Jim and other family members, Chris was never lost in a shopping mall. Of 24 participants in a larger study on implanted memories, approximately 25% falsely remembered being lost as a child in a shopping mall or in a similar public place (Loftus & Pickrell, 1995).

People develop false memories for some of the same reasons memory misattribution occurs. We do not store all the details of our experiences in memory, making us vulnerable to accepting suggestions about what might have happened or should have happened. In addition, visual imagery plays an important role in constructing false memories

(Goff & Roediger, 1998). Asking people to imagine an event like spilling punch all over the bride's parents at a wedding increases the likelihood that they will develop a false memory of it (Hyman & Pentland, 1996). Social pressure can also enhance suggestibility, as in cases in which people falsely confess to crimes they did not commit after repeated interrogations by authority figures such as police who are convinced of their guilt and press for a confession (Kassin, 2015). In some instances, these wrongly accused individuals develop false memories of the crime (Kassin, 2007).

All of these factors were operating in a recent study that provides dramatic evidence for the misleading effects of suggestion. Researchers asked college students about a crime that they had supposedly committed between ages 11 and 14 (theft, assault, or assault with a weapon). Although none of the students had actually committed the crime, during three separate interviews, the experimenters required them repeatedly to imagine that they did. The researchers also applied social pressure techniques, such as telling students that their parents or caregivers said they had committed the crime and stating that most people can retrieve seemingly lost memories if they try hard enough. By the end of the third interview, 70% of the students came to believe that they had committed the crime, and some of them even developed detailed false memories of having done so (Shaw & Porter, 2015; Wade et al., 2018).

Suggestibility played a key role in a controversy that arose during the 1980s and 1990s, concerning the accuracy of childhood memories that people recalled during psychotherapy. One highly publicized example involved a woman named Diana Halbrooks (Schacter, 1996). After a few months in psychotherapy, she began recalling disturbing incidents from her childhood — for example, that her mother had tried to kill her and that her father had abused her sexually. Although her parents denied these events had ever occurred, her therapist encouraged her to believe in the reality of her memories. Eventually, Diana Halbrooks stopped therapy and came to realize that the "memories" she had recovered were inaccurate.

How could this have happened? A number of the techniques used by psychotherapists to try to pull up forgotten childhood memories are clearly suggestive (Poole et al., 1995). Importantly, memories that people remember spontaneously on their own are corroborated by other people at about the same rate as the memories of individuals who never forgot their abuse, whereas memories recovered in response to suggestive therapeutic techniques are virtually never corroborated by others (McNally & Geraerts, 2009).

6. Bias

In 2000, the outcome of a very close presidential race between George W. Bush and Al Gore was decided by the Supreme Court 5 weeks after the election had taken place. The day Gore conceded, supporters of each candidate were asked how happy they felt with the outcome (Wilson et al., 2003). Understandably, Bush supporters were happy and Gore supporters were displeased. Four months later, the same participants were asked to recall how happy they had been right after the election was decided. Bush supporters *over*estimated how happy they had felt at the time, and Gore supporters *under*estimated how happy they actually were. In both groups, recollections of happiness were at odds with existing reports of their actual happiness at the time (Wilson et al., 2003).

These results illustrate the problem of **bias,** *the distorting influences of present knowledge, beliefs, and feelings on recollection of previous experiences.* Sometimes what people remember from their pasts says less about what actually happened than about what they think, feel, or believe now about themselves or others (Levine et al., 2018). Researchers have also found that our current moods can bias our recall of past experiences (Bower, 1981; Buchanan, 2007; Eich, 1995). So, in addition to helping you recall actual sad memories (as you saw earlier in this chapter), a sad mood can also bias your recollections of experiences that may not have been so sad.

bias The distorting influences of present knowledge, beliefs, and feelings on recollection of previous experiences.

Sometimes, we exaggerate differences between what we feel or believe now and what we felt or believed in the past. This is called *change bias*. For instance, most of us would like to believe that our romantic attachments grow stronger over time. In one study, dating couples were asked once a year for 4 years to assess the present quality of their relationships and to recall how they felt in past years (Sprecher, 1999). Couples who stayed together for the 4 years recalled that the strength of their love had increased since they last reported on it. Yet their actual ratings at the time did not show any increases in love and attachment. Similarly, when college students tried to remember high school grades and their memories were checked against their actual transcripts, they were highly accurate for grades of A (89% correct) and extremely inaccurate for grades of D (29% correct) (Bahrick et al., 1996). People remember the past as they want it to be rather than the way it actually was.

7. Persistence

The artist Melinda Stickney-Gibson awoke in her apartment to the smell of smoke. She jumped out of bed and saw black plumes rising through cracks in the floor. Raging flames had engulfed the entire building, and she had no chance to escape except by jumping from her third-floor window. Shortly after she crashed to the ground, the building exploded into a brilliant fireball. Although she survived the fire and the fall, Melinda became overwhelmed by memories of the fire. When she sat down in front of a blank canvas to start a new painting, her memories of that awful night intruded. Her paintings, which were previously bright, colorful abstractions, became dark meditations in black, orange, and ochre — the colors of the fire (Schacter, 1996).

Melinda Stickney-Gibson's experiences illustrate memory's seventh and most deadly sin, **persistence:** *the intrusive recollection of events that we wish we could forget*. Melinda's experience is far from unique; persistence frequently occurs after disturbing or traumatic incidents, such as the fire that destroyed her home. Although being able to recall memories quickly is usually considered a good thing, in the case of persistence, that ability mutates into an unwelcome burden.

Intrusive memories are undesirable consequences of emotional experiences because emotional experiences generally lead to more vivid and enduring recollections than nonemotional experiences do. One line of evidence comes from the study of **flashbulb memories,** which are *detailed recollections of when and where we heard about shocking events* (Brown & Kulick, 1977). For example, most Americans can recall exactly where they were and how they heard about the September 11, 2001, terrorist attacks on the World Trade Center and the Pentagon — almost as if a mental flashbulb had gone off automatically and recorded the event in long-lasting and vivid detail (Kvavilashvili et al., 2009). Several studies have shown that flashbulb memories are not always entirely accurate, but they are generally better remembered than mundane news events from the same time (Larsen, 1992; Neisser & Harsch, 1992). Enhanced retention of flashbulb memories is partly attributable to emotional arousal, and partly attributable to the fact that we tend to talk and think a lot about these experiences. Recall that semantic encoding enhances memory: When we talk about flashbulb experiences, we elaborate on them and thus further increase the memorability of those aspects of the experience that we discuss (Hirst et al., 2009, 2015).

Why do our brains succumb to persistence? A key player in the brain's response to emotional events is a small, almond-shaped structure called the *amygdala*, shown in **FIGURE 6.16**. The amygdala influences hormonal systems that kick into high gear when we experience an arousing event; these stress-related hormones, such as adrenaline and cortisol, mobilize the body in the face of threat — and they also enhance memory for the experience. When there is heightened activity in the amygdala as people watch emotional events, there's a better chance that they will recall those events on a later test (Cahill et al., 1996; Kensinger & Schacter, 2005, 2006). Damage to the amygdala does not result

The way each member of this happy couple recalls earlier feelings toward the other depends on how each currently views their relationship. Andersen Ross/Blend Images/Getty Images

Some events are so emotionally charged — such as the terrorist attack on the World Trade Center — that we form unusually detailed memories of when and where we heard about them. These flashbulb memories generally persist much longer than memories for more ordinary events. Kathy Willens/AP Images

persistence The intrusive recollection of events that we wish we could forget.

flashbulb memories Detailed recollections of when and where we heard about shocking events.

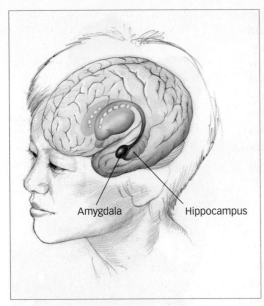

Figure 6.16 The Amygdala's Influence on Memory The amygdala, located next to the hippocampus, responds strongly to emotional events. Individuals with amygdala damage are unable to remember emotional events any better than they can remember nonemotional ones (Cahill & McGaugh, 1998).   Republished by permission of Macmillan Publishers Ltd. from Nature Neuroscience, A Sensory Signature that Distinguishes True from False Memories, Slotnick & Schacter, 7(61), 2004. Permissions conveyed through Copyright Clearance Center, Inc.

in a general memory deficit. Individuals with amygdala damage, however, do not remember emotional events any better than they remember nonemotional events (Cahill & McGaugh, 1998).

In many cases, there are clear benefits to forming strong memories for highly emotional events, particularly those that are life-threatening. In the case of persistence, though, such memories may be too strong — strong enough to interfere with other aspects of daily life.

Are the Seven "Sins" Vices or Virtues?

You may have concluded that evolution has burdened us with an extremely inefficient memory system so prone to error that it often jeopardizes our well-being. Not so. The seven sins are the price we pay for the many benefits that memory provides, the occasional result of the normally efficient operation of the human memory system (Schacter, 2001b).

Consider transience, for example. Wouldn't it be great to remember all the details of every incident in your life, no matter how much time had passed? Not necessarily: If we didn't gradually forget information over time, our minds would be cluttered with details that we no longer need, such as an old phone number (Bjork, 2011; Bjork & Bjork, 1988; Norby, 2015). Memory, in essence, makes a bet that when we haven't used information recently, we probably won't need it in the future. We win this bet more often than we lose it, making transience an adaptive property of memory.

Similarly, absentmindedness and blocking can be frustrating, but they are side effects of our memory's usually successful attempt to sort through incoming information, preserving details that are worthy of attention and recall while discarding those that are less worthy.

Memory misattribution and suggestibility both occur because we often fail to recall the details of exactly when and where we saw a face or learned a fact. Our memories carefully record such details only when we think we may need them later, and most of the time we are better off for it. Furthermore, we often use memories to anticipate possible future events. As discussed earlier, memory is flexible, allowing us to recombine elements of past experience in new ways, so that we can mentally try out different versions of what might happen — even if this sometimes produces misattribution errors in which elements of past experience are miscombined (Carpenter & Schacter, 2017; Dewhurst et al., 2016; Schacter & Addis, 2007; Schacter et al., 2011).

Bias skews our memories so that we depict ourselves in an overly favorable light, but it can also produce the benefit of contributing to our overall sense of contentment, leading to greater psychological well-being (Taylor, 1989). Although persistence can cause us to be haunted by traumas that we'd be better off forgetting, overall, it is probably adaptive to remember threatening or traumatic events that could pose a threat to survival.

Although each of the seven sins can cause trouble in our lives, each has an adaptive side as well. You can think of the seven sins as costs we pay for benefits that allow memory to work as well as it does most of the time.

Build to the Outcomes

1. How might general memories come to distort specific memories?

2. How is memory affected for someone whose attention is divided?

3. Why is Snow White's name easier to remember than Mary Poppins's?

4. What can explain a déjà vu experience?

5. How can eyewitnesses be misled?

6. How does your current outlook color your memory of a past event?

7. How does emotional trauma affect memory?

8. How are we better off with imperfect memories?

CHAPTER REVIEW

Encoding: Transforming Perceptions Into Memories

- Encoding is the process of transforming the information received through our senses into a lasting memory.
- Semantic encoding is characterized by relating new information to previous knowledge in a meaningful way.
- Visual imagery encoding also relates new information to previous knowledge, but features both a visual and a verbal placeholder.
- Organizational encoding is a process of finding relationships between items to make them easier to retrieve.
- Encoding information with respect to its survival value is a particularly effective method for increasing subsequent recall, perhaps because our memory systems have evolved in a way that allows us to remember especially well information that is relevant to our survival, and perhaps because survival scenarios require extensive planning.

Storage: Maintaining Memories Over Time

- Sensory memory holds information for a second or two. "Rehearsal" helps keep memories in short-term storage, and "chunking" combines information into a single, meaningful item.
- Working memory is the active maintenance of information in short-term storage, where information is retained for about 15 to 20 seconds.
- A model of working memory includes the subsystems that store and manipulate visual and verbal information, as well as the episodic buffer that integrates information, and the central executive that coordinates them.
- The hippocampus functions as an index to put information into long-term memory, but it is not the site of long-term memory storage.
- The act of recalling, thinking, and talking about a memory leads to consolidation. Sleep also is an important factor. However, when memories are retrieved, they may also become vulnerable to disruption.
- Memory storage depends on changes in synapses, and long-term potentiation (LTP) increases synaptic connections.

Retrieval: Bringing Memories to Mind

- Whether we remember a past experience depends on whether retrieval cues are available to trigger recall. Retrieval cues are effective when they are given in the same context as when we encoded an experience. Moods and inner states can become retrieval cues.
- Retrieving information from memory can improve subsequent memory of the retrieved information, but it can also suppress memory for related information that is not retrieved.
- Retrieving and vividly reexperiencing memories of objects that were seen makes memory vulnerable to disruption, such that unseen objects may be wrongly incorporated into the memory.

- Neuroimaging studies suggest that trying to remember activates the left frontal lobe, whereas successful recovery of stored information activates the hippocampus and regions in the brain related to the sensory aspects of an experience.

Forms of Long-Term Memory: More Than One Kind

- Long-term memory consists of implicit memory, the unconscious influence of past experiences on later behavior and performance, and explicit memory, the act of consciously or intentionally retrieving past experiences.
- Implicit memory in turn includes procedural memory, the acquisition of skills as a result of practice, and priming, a change in the ability to recognize or identify an object or a word as the result of past exposure to it.
- Explicit memory can be divided into episodic memory, the collection of personal experiences from a particular time and place, and semantic memory, a networked, general, impersonal knowledge of facts, associations, and concepts.
- Collaborative memory refers to remembering in groups. Collaborative remembering can both impair memory (collaborative inhibition) and enhance it by exposing people to new information and helping to correct errors.

Memory Failures: The Seven "Sins" of Memory

- Memory's mistakes can be classified into seven "sins," which are costs we pay for benefits that allow memory to work as well as it does most of the time.
- Some of these "sins" reflect inability to store or retrieve information when we want. *Transience* is reflected by a rapid decline in memory, followed by more gradual forgetting; both decay and interference contribute to transience. *Absentmindedness* results from failures of attention, shallow encoding, and the influence of automatic behaviors; it is often associated with forgetting to do things in the future. *Blocking* occurs when stored information is temporarily inaccessible, as when information is on the "tip of the tongue."
- Conversely, *persistence* reflects the fact that emotional arousal generally leads to enhanced memory, whether we want to remember an experience or not.
- Other "sins" reflect errors in memory content. *Memory misattribution* happens when we experience a sense of familiarity but don't recall the specifics of when and where an experience occurred. *Suggestibility* gives rise to implanted memories of small details or entire episodes. *Bias* can lead us to make the past consistent with the present, to exaggerate changes between past and present, or to remember the past in a way that makes us look good.

Key Concept Quiz

1. Encoding is the process
   a. by which we transform what we perceive, think, or feel into an enduring memory.
   b. of maintaining information in memory over time.
   c. of bringing to mind information that has been previously stored.
   d. through which we recall information we previously learned but have forgotten.

2. What is the process of relating new information in a meaningful way to knowledge that is already in memory?
   a. spontaneous encoding
   b. organization encoding
   c. semantic encoding
   d. visual imagery encoding

3. What kind of memory storage holds information for a second or two?
   a. retrograde memory
   b. working memory
   c. short-term memory
   d. sensory memory

4. The process by which memories become stable in the brain is called
   a. consolidation.
   b. long-term memory.
   c. iconic memory.
   d. hippocampal indexing.

5. Long-term potentiation occurs through
   a. the interruption of communication between neurons.
   b. the strengthening of synaptic connections.
   c. the reconsolidation of disrupted memories.
   d. sleep.

6. The increased likelihood of recalling a sad memory when you are in a sad mood is an illustration of
   a. the encoding specificity principle.
   b. state-dependent retrieval.
   c. transfer-appropriate processing.
   d. memory accessibility.

7. Neuroimaging studies suggest that *trying* to remember activates the
   a. left frontal lobe.
   b. hippocampal region.
   c. occipital lobe.
   d. upper temporal lobe.

8. The act of consciously or intentionally retrieving past experiences is
   a. priming.
   b. procedural memory.
   c. implicit memory.
   d. explicit memory.

9. People who have amnesia are able to retain all of these EXCEPT
   a. explicit memory.
   b. implicit memory.
   c. procedural memory.
   d. priming.

10. Remembering a family reunion that you attended as a child illustrates
    a. semantic memory.
    b. procedural memory.
    c. episodic memory.
    d. perceptual priming.

11. A rapid decline in memory, followed by more gradual forgetting, is reflected by
    a. chunking.
    b. blocking.
    c. absentmindedness.
    d. transience.

12. Eyewitness misidentification or false recognition is most likely a result of
    a. memory misattribution.
    b. suggestibility.
    c. bias.
    d. retroactive interference.

13. The fact that emotional arousal generally leads to enhanced memory is supported by
    a. bias.
    b. persistence.
    c. proactive interference.
    d. source memory.

 **LearningCurve** Don't stop now! Quizzing yourself is a powerful study tool. Go to LaunchPad to access the LearningCurve adaptive quizzing system and your own personalized learning plan. Visit launchpadworks.com.

Key Terms

memory (p. 159)
encoding (p. 159)
storage (p. 159)
retrieval (p. 159)
semantic encoding (p. 160)
visual imagery encoding (p. 160)
organizational encoding (p. 162)
sensory memory (p. 163)
iconic memory (p. 164)
echoic memory (p. 164)
short-term memory (p. 164)
rehearsal (p. 165)

chunking (p. 165)
working memory (p. 165)
long-term memory (p. 166)
anterograde amnesia (p. 167)
retrograde amnesia (p. 167)
consolidation (p. 167)
reconsolidation (p. 168)
long-term potentiation (LTP) (p. 169)
retrieval cue (p. 170)
encoding specificity principle (p. 170)

state-dependent retrieval (p. 170)
transfer-appropriate processing (p. 171)
retrieval-induced forgetting (p. 171)
explicit memory (p. 173)
implicit memory (p. 173)
procedural memory (p. 174)
priming (p. 174)
semantic memory (p. 175)
episodic memory (p. 175)

transience (p. 179)
retroactive interference (p. 179)
proactive interference (p. 180)
absentmindedness (p. 181)
prospective memory (p. 181)
blocking (p. 181)
memory misattribution (p. 182)
source memory (p. 182)
suggestibility (p. 184)
bias (p. 186)
persistence (p. 187)
flashbulb memories (p. 187)

Changing Minds

1. A friend of yours lost her father to cancer when she was a very young child. "I really wish I remembered him better," she says. "I know all the memories are locked in my head. I'm thinking of trying hypnotism to unlock some of those memories." You explain that we don't, in fact, have stored memories of everything that ever happened to us locked in our heads. What examples could you give of ways in which memories can be lost over time?

2. Another friend of yours has a very vivid memory of sitting with his parents in the living room on September 11, 2001, watching live TV as the Twin Towers fell during the terrorist attacks. "I remember my mother was crying," he says, "and that scared me more than the pictures on the TV." Recently, he went home for a visit and discussed the events of 9/11 with his mother—and was stunned when she assured him that he was actually in school on the morning of the attacks and was only sent home at lunchtime, after the towers had fallen. "I don't understand," he tells you afterward. "I think she must be confused, because I have a perfect memory of that morning." Assuming your friend's mother is recalling events correctly, how would you explain to your friend the ways in which his snapshot memory could be wrong? What memory sin might be at work?

3. You ask one of your psychology classmates if she wants to form a study group to prepare for an upcoming exam.

"No offense," she says, "but I can study the material best by just reading the chapter eight or nine times, and I can do that without a study group." What's wrong with your classmate's study plan? In what ways might the members of a study group help each other learn more effectively?

4. You and a friend go to a party on campus where you meet a lot of new people. After the party, your friend says, "I liked a lot of the people we met, but I'll never remember all their names. Some people just have a good memory, and some don't, and there's nothing I can do about it." What advice could you give your friend to help him remember the names of people he meets at the next party?

5. A friend of yours who is taking a criminal justice class reads about a case in which the conviction of an accused murderer was later overturned on the basis of DNA evidence. "It's a travesty of justice," she says. "An eyewitness clearly identified the man by picking him out of a lineup and then identified him again in court during the trial. No results from a chemistry lab should count more than eyewitness testimony." What is your friend failing to appreciate about eyewitness testimony? What sin of memory could lead an eyewitness to honestly believe she is identifying the correct man when she is actually making a false identification?

Answers to Key Concept Quiz

1. a; 2. c; 3. d; 4. a; 5. b; 6. b; 7. a; 8. d; 9. a; 10. c; 11. d; 12. a; 13. b

LaunchPad features the full e-book of *Introducing Psychology*, the LearningCurve adaptive quizzing system, videos, and a variety of activities to boost your learning. Visit LaunchPad at launchpadworks.com.

Marilyn Nieves/Getty Images

Learning

7

Jennifer, a 45-year-old career military nurse, served 19 months abroad during the Iraq war, including 4 months in a prison hospital near Baghdad, where she witnessed many horrifying events, including numerous deaths and serious casualties. Jennifer worked 12- to 14-hour shifts, trying to avoid incoming fire while tending to some of the most egregiously wounded cases.

This repetitive trauma took a toll on Jennifer. Even after she returned home, she thought about her war experiences repeatedly, and they profoundly influenced her reactions to many aspects of everyday life. The sight of blood or the smell of cooking meat made her sick to her stomach, and the previously innocent sound of a helicopter approaching, which in Iraq signaled that new wounded bodies were about to arrive, now triggered heightened feelings of fear and anxiety. She regularly awoke from nightmares concerning the most troubling aspects of her Iraq experiences. Jennifer was "forever changed" by her Iraq experiences (Feczer & Bjorklund, 2009). That is one reason Jennifer's story is a compelling, though disturbing, introduction to the topic of learning.

Much of what happened to Jennifer after she returned home reflects the operation of a kind of learning based on association. Sights, sounds, and smells in Iraq had become associated with negative emotions in a way that created an enduring bond, such that encountering similar sights, sounds, and smells at home elicited similarly intense negative feelings.

Learning is a collection of different techniques, procedures, and outcomes that produce changes in an organism's behavior. In this chapter, we'll discuss the development and basic psychological principles behind two major approaches to learning: classical conditioning and operant conditioning, observational learning that occurs when we watch others and implicit learning that can occur entirely outside of awareness. We'll conclude with a discussion of learning in a context that should matter a lot to you: the classroom.

What Is Learning?

Classical Conditioning:
One Thing Leads to Another

Operant Conditioning:
Reinforcements From the
Environment

Observational Learning:
Look at Me

Implicit Learning:
Under the Radar

Learning in the Classroom

During the 4 months that she served at a prison hospital near Baghdad during the Iraq war, Jennifer learned to associate the sound of an arriving helicopter with wounded soldiers. That learned association had a long-lasting influence on her. AP Photo/John Moore

Learning Outcomes

- Define learning.
- Identify how even the simplest organisms appear to learn.

How might psychologists use the concept of habituation to explain the fact that today's action movies, like *Venom*, tend to show much more graphic violence than movies of the 1980s, which in turn tended to show more graphic violence than movies of the 1950s? Marvel/Sony/Kobal/Rex/Shutterstock

What Is Learning?

Despite the many different kinds of learning that psychologists have discovered, there is a basic principle at the core of all of them. **Learning** involves *the acquisition, from experience, of new knowledge, skills, or responses that result in a relatively permanent change in the state of the learner*. This definition emphasizes three key ideas:

- Learning is based on experience.
- Learning produces changes in the organism.
- These changes are relatively permanent.

Think about Jennifer's time in Iraq and you'll see all of these elements: Experiences that led to associating the sound of an approaching helicopter with the arrival of wounded soldiers changed the way Jennifer responded to certain situations in a way that lasted for years.

Learning can also occur in much simpler, nonassociative forms. You are probably familiar with the phenomenon of **habituation,** *a general process in which repeated or prolonged exposure to a stimulus results in a gradual reduction in responding*. If you've ever lived near a busy highway, you probably noticed the sound of traffic when you first moved in, but eventually you were able to ignore the noise. This welcome reduction in responding reflects the operation of habituation.

Habituation occurs even in the simplest organisms. For example, in the Memory chapter you learned about the sea slug *Aplysia*. *Aplysia* exhibits habituation: When lightly touched, the sea slug initially withdraws its gill, but the response gradually weakens after repeated light touches. In addition, *Aplysia* also exhibits **sensitization,** *a simple form of learning that occurs when presentation of a stimulus leads to an increased response to a later stimulus*. For example, after receiving a strong shock, *Aplysia* shows an increased gill-withdrawal response to a light touch. In a similar manner, people whose houses have been broken into may later become hypersensitive to late-night sounds that wouldn't have bothered them previously.

Although these simple kinds of learning are important, in this chapter we'll focus on more complex kinds of learning. As you'll recall from the Evolution of Psychological Science chapter, the behaviorists insisted on measuring only observable, quantifiable behavior, and dismissed mental activity as irrelevant and unknowable. Behaviorists argued that learning's "permanent change in experience" could be demonstrated equally well in almost any organism: rats, dogs, pigeons, mice, pigs, or humans. But we now know that cognitive considerations (i.e., elements of mental activity) are also fundamental to the learning process.

Build to the Outcomes

1. What are three key ideas that support the definition of learning?

2. How do habituation and sensitization occur?

Learning Outcomes

- Describe the process of classical conditioning.
- Explain how cognitive, neural, and evolutionary aspects influence our understanding of classical conditioning.

Classical Conditioning: One Thing Leads to Another

The American psychologist John B. Watson kick-started the behaviorist movement in the early 20th century, arguing that psychologists should "never use the terms *consciousness, mental states, mind, content, introspectively verifiable, imagery*, and the like" (Watson, 1913, p. 166). Watson's firebrand stance was fueled in large part by the work of a Russian physiologist, Ivan Pavlov (1849–1936).

Pavlov studied the digestive processes of laboratory animals by surgically implanting test tubes into the cheeks of dogs to measure their salivary responses to different kinds of foods. Serendipitously, his explorations into spit and drool revealed the mechanics of one form of learning, which came to be called classical conditioning. **Classical conditioning** is *a type of learning that occurs when a neutral stimulus produces a response after being paired with a stimulus that naturally produces a response.* In his classic experiments, Pavlov showed that dogs learned to salivate to neutral stimuli such as a buzzer or a metronome after the dogs had associated that stimulus with another stimulus that naturally evokes salivation, such as food. Pavlov appreciated the significance of his discovery, and he embarked on a systematic investigation of the mechanisms of classical conditioning. Let's take a closer look at some of these principles.

The Basic Principles of Classical Conditioning

Pavlov's basic experimental setup involved cradling dogs in a harness to administer the foods and to measure the salivary response, as shown in **FIGURE 7.1**. He noticed that dogs that had previously been in the experiment began to produce a kind of "anticipatory" salivary response as soon as they were put in the harness, even before any food was presented. Pavlov and his colleagues regarded these responses as annoyances at first because they interfered with collecting naturally occurring salivary secretions.

In reality, the dogs were behaving in line with the basic elements of classical conditioning. When the dogs were initially presented with a plate of food, they began to salivate. No surprise here. Pavlov called the presentation of food an **unconditioned stimulus (US)**, *something that reliably produces a naturally occurring reaction in an organism* (see **FIGURE 7.2a**). He called the dogs' salivation an **unconditioned response (UR)**, *a reflexive reaction that is reliably produced by an unconditioned stimulus.*

Then Pavlov paired the presentation of food with a stimulus, such as the sound of the ticking of a metronome or the flash of a light (see Figure 7.2b). After repeated pairings of the stimulus with the US, the animal learned to associate the food with the sound.

Eventually, the stimulus alone was able to produce a response: salivation (see Figure 7.2c). At this point, the stimulus has become a **conditioned stimulus (CS)**, *a previously neutral stimulus that produces a reliable response in an organism after being paired with a US*, and the response it evokes is the **conditioned response (CR)**, *a reaction that resembles an unconditioned response but is produced by a conditioned stimulus.* In this example, the dogs' salivation (CR) was eventually prompted by the sound of the metronome (CS) alone because the sound of the metronome and the food (US) had been associated so often in the past.

Now consider your own dog (or cat). Does she always know when dinner's coming? For her the presentation of food (the US) has become associated with a complex CS — your

learning The acquisition, from experience, of new knowledge, skills, or responses that results in a relatively permanent change in the state of the learner.

habituation A general process in which repeated or prolonged exposure to a stimulus results in a gradual reduction in responding.

sensitization A simple form of learning that occurs when presentation of a stimulus leads to an increased response to a later stimulus.

classical conditioning A type of learning that occurs when a neutral stimulus produces a response after being paired with a stimulus that naturally produces a response.

unconditioned stimulus (US) Something that reliably produces a naturally occurring reaction in an organism.

unconditioned response (UR) A reflexive reaction that is reliably produced by an unconditioned stimulus.

conditioned stimulus (CS) A previously neutral stimulus that produces a reliable response in an organism after being paired with a US.

conditioned response (CR) A reaction that resembles an unconditioned response but is produced by a conditioned stimulus.

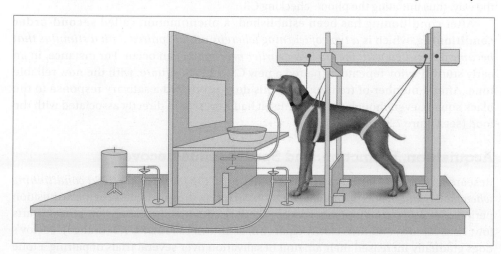

Figure 7.1   Pavlov's Apparatus for Studying Classical Conditioning Using a metronome or a buzzer, Pavlov presented auditory stimuli to the dogs. Visual stimuli could be presented on the screen.

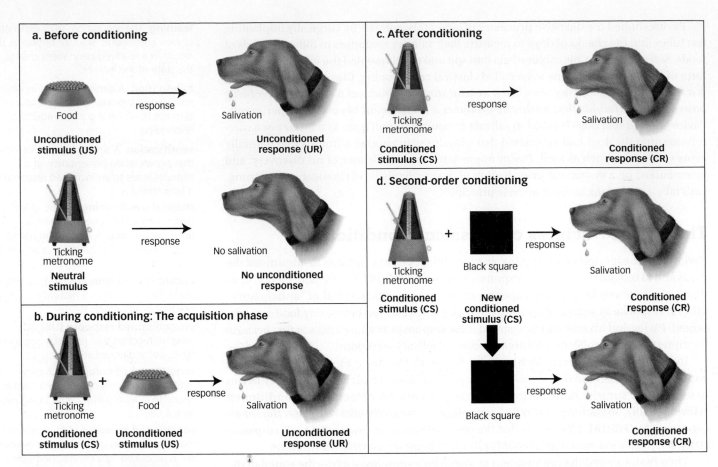

a. Before conditioning

Food
Unconditioned stimulus (US)

→ response →

Salivation
Unconditioned response (UR)

Ticking metronome
Neutral stimulus

→ response →

No salivation
No unconditioned response

b. During conditioning: The acquisition phase

Ticking metronome
Conditioned stimulus (CS)

+ Food
Unconditioned stimulus (US)

→ response →

Salivation
Unconditioned response (UR)

c. After conditioning

Ticking metronome
Conditioned stimulus (CS)

→ response →

Salivation
Conditioned response (CR)

d. Second-order conditioning

Ticking metronome
Conditioned stimulus (CS)

+ Black square
New conditioned stimulus (CS)

→ response →

Salivation
Conditioned response (CR)

Black square

→ response →

Salivation
Conditioned response (CR)

Figure 7.2   The Elements of Classical Conditioning (a) Before conditioning, the dog salivates in response to food, the unconditioned stimulus (US), but not to the ticking of a metronome. (b) During conditioning, the food is paired with the ticking metronome, which becomes a conditioned stimulus (CS). (c) After conditioning, the ticking metronome, now a conditioned stimulus (CS), can produce salivation. (d) In second-order conditioning, the ticking metronome can be used to condition a new stimulus, such as a black square.

Second-order conditioning helps explain why some people desire money to the point that they hoard it and value it even more than the objects it purchases. Money is used to purchase objects that produce gratifying outcomes, such as an expensive car. Although money is not directly associated with the thrill of driving a new sports car, through second-order conditioning, money can become linked with this type of desirable reward. Steven Puetzer/Getty Images

getting up, moving into the kitchen, opening the cabinet, working the can opener — such that the CS alone signals that food is on the way, therefore initiating the CR of her getting ready to eat. And classical conditioning isn't just for dogs. When you hear your smartphone ring announcing the arrival of a new text, you may not salivate but you probably feel an urge to check it right away. Socially important information from friends and others contained in prior texts (the US) has become associated with the text message sound on your phone (the CS), so that the CS alone signals that important information may be on the way, thus initiating the phone-checking CR.

After conditioning has been established, a phenomenon called **second-order conditioning,** which is *a type of learning whereby a CS is paired with a stimulus that became associated with the US in an earlier procedure,* can occur. For instance, in an early study, Pavlov repeatedly paired a new CS, a black square, with the now reliable tone. After a number of training trials, his dogs produced a salivary response to the black square, even though the square itself had never been directly associated with the food (see Figure 7.2d).

Acquisition, Extinction, and Spontaneous Recovery

Researchers use the term **acquisition** to describe *the phase of classical conditioning when the CS and the US are presented together.* During the initial phase of the acquisition period of classical conditioning, typically there is a gradual increase in learning: It starts low, rises rapidly, and then slowly tapers off, as shown in **FIGURE 7.3** (orange). Pavlov's dogs gradually increased their amount of salivation over several trials of pairing a tone

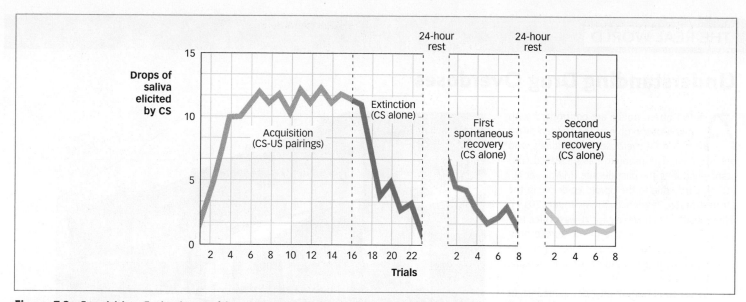

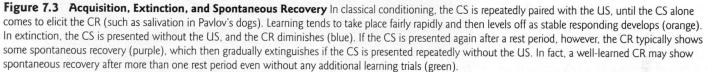

Figure 7.3   Acquisition, Extinction, and Spontaneous Recovery In classical conditioning, the CS is repeatedly paired with the US, until the CS alone comes to elicit the CR (such as salivation in Pavlov's dogs). Learning tends to take place fairly rapidly and then levels off as stable responding develops (orange). In extinction, the CS is presented without the US, and the CR diminishes (blue). If the CS is presented again after a rest period, however, the CR typically shows some spontaneous recovery (purple), which then gradually extinguishes if the CS is presented repeatedly without the US. In fact, a well-learned CR may show spontaneous recovery after more than one rest period even without any additional learning trials (green).

with the presentation of food; similarly, your dog eventually learned to associate your kitchen preparations with the subsequent appearance of food. After learning has been established, in the second-order phase, the CS by itself will reliably elicit the CR.

After Pavlov had explored the process of acquisition extensively, he wondered: What would happen if he continued to present the CS (metronome ticking) but stopped presenting the US (food)? The answer is shown in Figure 7.3 (blue): the CR declines abruptly and continues to drop until eventually the dog ceases to salivate to the sound of the tone. This process is called **extinction,** *the gradual elimination of a learned response that occurs when the CS is repeatedly presented without the US.*

Next, Pavlov wondered whether extinction was permanent. Is a single session of extinction sufficient to knock out the CR completely? Or might the CR reappear? To explore this question, Pavlov extinguished the classically conditioned salivation response and then allowed the dogs to have a short rest period. When they were brought back to the lab and presented with the CS again, they displayed **spontaneous recovery,** *the tendency of a learned behavior to recover from extinction after a rest period.* This phenomenon is shown in Figure 7.3 (purple). Notice that this recovery takes place even though the CS has never again been explicitly paired with the US. With repeated presentations of the CS alone (no US), the CR gradually extinguishes again — only to weakly reappear if the CS is presented again after another period of rest (Figure 7.3, green). Clearly, extinction does not completely erase the learning.

Generalization and Discrimination

Do you think your dog will be stumped, unable to anticipate the presentation of her food, if you get a new can opener? Will you need to establish a whole new round of conditioning with this modified CS?

Probably not. It wouldn't be very adaptive for an organism if each little change in the CS–US pairing required an extensive regimen of new learning. Rather, there tends to be **generalization,** in which *the CR is observed even though the CS is slightly different from the CS used during acquisition.* In other words, the conditioning generalizes to stimuli that are similar to the CS used during the original training. As you might expect, the more the new stimulus changes, the less conditioned responding is observed — which means

second-order conditioning A type of learning in which a CS is paired with a stimulus that became associated with the US in an earlier procedure.

acquisition The phase of classical conditioning when the CS and the US are presented together.

extinction The gradual elimination of a learned response that occurs when the CS is repeatedly presented without the US.

spontaneous recovery The tendency of a learned behavior to recover from extinction after a rest period.

generalization The CR is observed even though the CS is slightly different from the CS used during acquisition.

THE REAL WORLD

Understanding Drug Overdoses

All too often, police are confronted with a perplexing problem: the sudden death from a drug overdose of individuals who are addicted. The problem has increased substantially during the past decade (Martins et al., 2015), partly due to the opioid epidemic in the United States (Lyden & Binswanger, 2019). These deaths are puzzling for at least three reasons: The victims are often experienced drug users; the dose taken is usually not larger than usual; and the deaths tend to occur in unusual settings.

Classical conditioning provides some insight into how these deaths occur (Siegel, 2016). First, when classical conditioning takes place, the conditioned stimulus (CS) is more than a simple buzzer or tone: It also includes the overall *context* within which the conditioning takes place. Second, many conditioned responses (CRs) are compensatory reactions to the unconditioned stimulus (US). Heroin, for example, slows down a person's breathing rate, so the body responds with a compensatory reaction that speeds up breathing to maintain a state of balance, or homeostasis, a critically important CR.

These two finer points of classical conditioning help explain the seeming paradox of fatal heroin overdoses in experienced drug users (Siegel, 1984, 2016). When the drug is injected, the entire setting (the drug paraphernalia, the room, the lighting, the addicted individual's usual companions) functions as the CS, and the brain reacts to the heroin with a compensatory reaction: secreting neurotransmitters that counteract the heroin's effects. Over time, this compensatory physiological response becomes part of the body's reaction to the CS.

Although drug dens and crack houses may be considered blights, it is often safer for individuals who are addicted to use drugs there. The environment becomes part of the CS, so it is ironic that busting crack houses may contribute to deaths from drug overdoses, if individuals who are addicted instead use drugs in new contexts. AP Photo/Chris Gardner

This is why taking drugs in a new environment can be fatal for a longtime drug user. If the usual dose is taken in a new setting, the CS is now altered, and the physiological compensatory CR is not triggered (Siegel et al., 2000). As a result, the usual dose becomes an overdose, possibly fatal.

Understanding these principles has led to treatments for drug addiction. For instance, the brain's compensatory response to a drug—when elicited by the familiar contextual cues ordinarily associated with drug taking—can be experienced by the individual who is addicted as withdrawal symptoms. In *cue exposure therapies*, an individual who is addicted is exposed to drug-related cues without being given the usual dose of the drug itself, eventually resulting in extinction of the association between the contextual cues and the effects of the drug. After such treatment, encountering familiar drug-related cues will no longer result in the compensatory response linked to withdrawal symptoms, thereby making it easier for a person recovering from addiction to remain abstinent (Siegel, 2005).

that if you replaced a manual can opener with an electric can opener, your dog would probably show a much weaker conditioned response (Pearce, 1987; Rescorla, 2006).

When an organism generalizes to a new stimulus, two things are happening. First, by responding to the new stimulus used during generalization testing, the organism demonstrates that it recognizes the similarity between the original CS and the new stimulus. Second, by displaying a *diminished* response to that new stimulus, it also tells us that it notices a difference between the two stimuli. In the second case, the organism shows **discrimination,** *the capacity to distinguish between similar but distinct stimuli.* Generalization and discrimination are two sides of the same coin. The more organisms show one, the less they show the other, and training can modify the balance between the two. (As The Real World: Understanding Drug Overdoses shows, the generalization of classical conditioning can help explain how drug overdoses occur.)

discrimination The capacity to distinguish between similar but distinct stimuli.

Conditioned Emotional Responses: The Case of Little Albert

Behaviorist John Watson and his followers thought that it was possible to develop general explanations of pretty much *any* behavior of *any* organism, based on classical conditioning principles. As a step in that direction, Watson embarked on a controversial study with his research assistant Rosalie Rayner (Watson & Rayner, 1920). Watson and Rayner enlisted the assistance of a healthy 9-month-old boy, known as "Little Albert." They wanted to see if such a child could be classically conditioned to experience a strong emotional reaction—namely, fear.

First, Watson presented Little Albert with a variety of stimuli: a white rat, a dog, a rabbit, various masks, and a burning newspaper. Albert reacted in most cases with curiosity or indifference, and he showed no fear of any of the items. Watson also established that something *could* make Albert afraid: When Watson struck a steel bar with a hammer, the sudden noise caused Albert to cry and tremble.

Watson and Rayner then led Little Albert through the acquisition phase of classical conditioning. Albert was presented with a white rat. As soon as he reached out to touch it, Watson struck the steel bar. This pairing occurred again and again over several trials. Eventually, the sight of the rat alone caused Albert to recoil in terror. In this situation, a US (the loud sound) was paired with a CS (the presence of the rat) such that the CS all by itself was sufficient to produce the CR (a fearful reaction). Little Albert's conditioned response generalized to other stimuli, such as the sight of a white rabbit, a seal-fur coat, and a Santa Claus mask.

This study was controversial in its cavalier treatment of a young child (Harris, 1979). Modern ethical guidelines that govern the treatment of research participants ensure that this kind of study could not be conducted today. So what was Watson's goal in all this? First, he wanted to show that a relatively complex reaction could be conditioned using Pavlovian techniques. Second, he wanted to show that emotional responses such as fear and anxiety could be learned through classical conditioning and therefore need not be the product of deeper unconscious processes or early life experiences as Freud and his followers had argued (see the Evolution of Psychological Science chapter). Third, Watson wanted to confirm that conditioning could be applied to humans as well as to other animals.

The kind of conditioned fear responses that were at work in Little Albert's case were also important in the chapter-opening case of Jennifer, who—as a result of her experiences in Iraq—experienced fear and anxiety when hearing the previously innocent sound of an approaching helicopter. Indeed, a therapy that has proven effective in dealing with such trauma-induced fears is based directly on principles of classical conditioning: Individuals are repeatedly exposed to conditioned stimuli associated with their trauma in a safe setting, in an attempt to extinguish the conditioned fear response (Bouton, 1988; Rothbaum & Schwartz, 2002). However, conditioned emotional responses include much more than just fear and anxiety responses. The warm and fuzzy feelings that envelop you when hearing a song that you used to listen to with a former boyfriend or girlfriend are a type of conditioned emotional response.

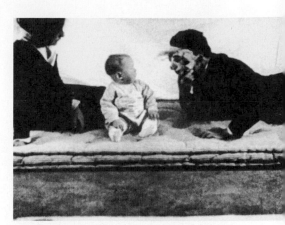

John Watson and Rosalie Rayner show Little Albert an unusual bunny mask. Why isn't the mere presence of these experimenters a conditioned stimulus in itself? (Watson & Rayner, 1920)

What response do you think the advertisers of Pepsi are looking for when they feature Sofia Vergara in an ad? Tim Clayton - Corbis/Getty Images

A Deeper Understanding of Classical Conditioning

As a form of learning, classical conditioning has a simple set of principles and applications to real-life situations. It offers a good deal of utility for psychologists who seek to understand the mechanisms that underlie learning. Since Pavlov's day, classical conditioning has been subjected to deeper scrutiny to understand exactly how, when, and why it works. Let's examine three areas that zero in on the mechanisms of classical conditioning: the cognitive, neural, and evolutionary elements.

The Cognitive Elements of Classical Conditioning

Curiously, although Pavlov's dogs salivated when they heard a metronome that predicted food, they did not salivate when Pavlov approached. Why not? After all, Pavlov delivered the food to the dogs, so why didn't *he* become a CS? Indeed, if Watson was present whenever the unpleasant US was sounded, why didn't Little Albert come to fear *him*?

Somehow, Pavlov's dogs were sensitive to the fact that Pavlov was not a *reliable* indicator of the arrival of food. Pavlov was linked with the arrival of food, but he was also linked with other activities that had nothing to do with food, including checking on the apparatus, bringing the dog from the kennel to the laboratory, and standing around talking with his assistants.

Robert Rescorla and Allan Wagner (1972) were the first to theorize that classical conditioning occurs when an animal has learned to set up an *expectation*. The sound of a metronome, because of its systematic pairing with food, set up this cognitive state for the laboratory dogs; Pavlov, because of the lack of any reliable link with food, did not. The Rescorla–Wagner model introduced a cognitive component that accounted for several features of classical conditioning that were difficult to understand from a simple behaviorist point of view. For example, the model correctly predicted that conditioning would be easier if the CS was an *unfamiliar* event than if it was familiar. The reason is that familiar events, being familiar, already have expectations associated with them, making new conditioning difficult. In short, classical conditioning might appear to be a primitive process, but it is actually quite sophisticated and incorporates a significant cognitive element.

The Neural Elements of Classical Conditioning

Pavlov saw his research as providing insights into how the brain works. Recent research has clarified some of what Pavlov hoped to understand about conditioning and the brain.

For example, Richard Thompson and his colleagues focused on classical conditioning of eyeblink responses in rabbits, using a tone (the CS) immediately followed by a puff of air to the eye. This airpuff (the US) causes a reflexive eyeblink response (the UR), just like you would blink following a puff of air near your eye. After many CS–US pairings, the eyeblink response occurs in response to the CS alone, so that the eye is partially closed and therefore protected when the expected airpuff arrives. Thompson and colleagues showed that the cerebellum is critical for the occurrence of eyeblink conditioning (Thompson, 2005). People with lesions to the cerebellum show impaired eyeblink conditioning: They are able to give a UR (blinking to the airpuff), but cannot learn the protective CR in response to the CS (Daum et al., 1993). Rounding out the picture, more recent neuroimaging findings in healthy young adults show activation in the cerebellum during eyeblink conditioning (Cheng et al., 2008). As you learned in the Neuroscience and Behavior chapter, the cerebellum is part of the hindbrain and plays an important role in motor skills and learning.

Also in the Neuroscience and Behavior chapter you read about the amygdala, which plays an important role in the experience of emotion, including fear and anxiety. So it should come as no surprise that the amygdala is also critical for emotional conditioning. When normal rats are given a sudden painful stimulus, such as a mild electric shock, they show a defensive reaction, known as *freezing*, in which they crouch down and sit motionless. In addition, their autonomic nervous systems go to work: Heart rate and blood pressure increase, and various hormones associated with stress are released. If the rats are trained that a tone (CS) predicts the shock US, these behavioral and autonomic responses occur, except that now they are CRs elicited by the CS. In effect, the rats show fear conditioning, not unlike that shown by

Little Albert. Damage or disruption to the amygdala disrupts fear conditioning in rats (LeDoux et al., 1988) as well as in people and other animals (Olsson & Phelps, 2007; Phelps & LeDoux, 2005).

The Evolutionary Elements of Classical Conditioning

Evolutionary mechanisms also play an important role in classical conditioning. As you learned in the Evolution of Psychological Science chapter, evolution and natural selection go hand in hand with adaptiveness: Behaviors that are adaptive allow an organism to survive and thrive in its environment.

Consider this example: A psychology professor visited southern California, and his hosts took him to lunch at a Middle Eastern restaurant, where he tried the hummus. That night, he got violently ill and developed a lifelong aversion to hummus. In this example, the hummus was the CS, a bacterium or some other source of toxicity was the US, and the resulting nausea was the UR. The UR (the nausea) became linked to the once-neutral CS (the hummus) and became a CR (an aversion to hummus). This aversion was cemented with a single acquisition trial. It usually takes several pairings of a CS and US to establish learning.

Under certain conditions, people may develop taste aversions. This serving of hummus looks inviting and probably tastes delicious, but at least one psychologist avoids all hummus like the plague. Paul Cowan/Shutterstock

The speed of food aversion learning is not so peculiar from an evolutionary perspective. Any species that forages or consumes a variety of foods needs to develop a mechanism by which it can learn to avoid any food that once made it ill. To have adaptive value, this learning should be very rapid — occurring in perhaps one or two trials. If learning takes more trials than this, the animal could die from eating a toxic substance. Also, learned aversions should occur more often with novel foods than with familiar ones. It is not adaptive for an animal to develop an aversion to everything it has eaten on the particular day it got sick. Our psychologist friend didn't develop an aversion to the Coke he drank with lunch or the scrambled eggs he had for breakfast that day; however, the sight and smell of hummus do make him uneasy.

Classical conditioning of food aversion has been intensively studied in rats, using a variety of CSs (visual, auditory, tactile, taste, and smell) and several different USs (injection of a toxic substance, radiation) that caused nausea and vomiting hours later (Garcia & Koelling, 1966). There is typically weak or no conditioning when the CS is a visual, auditory, or tactile stimulus, but a strong food aversion develops with stimuli that have a distinct taste and smell. On the other hand, taste and smell stimuli that produce food aversions in rats do not work with most species of birds. Birds depend primarily on visual cues for finding food and are relatively insensitive to taste and smell. However, it is relatively easy to produce a food aversion in birds using an unfamiliar visual stimulus as the CS, such as a brightly colored food (Wilcoxon et al., 1971). Studies such as these suggest that evolution has provided each species with a kind of **biological preparedness,** *a propensity for learning particular kinds of associations over others,* such that some behaviors are relatively easy to condition in some species but not others (Domjan, 2005).

Research on taste aversion has an interesting application: the development of a technique for dealing with a side effect of radiation and chemotherapy. Patients with cancer who experience nausea from their treatments often develop aversions to foods they ate before the therapy. Broberg and Bernstein (1987) reasoned that if the findings with rats generalized to humans, a simple technique should minimize the negative consequences of this effect. They gave their patients an unusual food (coconut- or root-beer-flavored candy) at the end of the last meal before undergoing treatment. Sure enough, the conditioned food aversions that the patients developed were overwhelmingly for one of the unusual flavors and not for any of the other foods in the meal. Other than any root beer or coconut fanatics among the sample, patients were spared from developing aversions to common foods that they were more likely to eat.

biological preparedness A propensity for learning particular kinds of associations over other kinds.

Build to the Outcomes

1. Why do some dogs seem to know when it's dinnertime?

2. If both an unconditioned and a conditioned stimulus can produce the same effect, what is the difference?

3. What is second-order conditioning?

4. How does a conditioned behavior change when the unconditioned stimulus is removed?

5. Why are generalization and discrimination "two sides of the same coin"?

6. Why did Little Albert fear the rat?

7. How does the role of expectation in conditioning challenge behaviorist ideas?

8. What is the role of the amygdala in fear conditioning?

9. How has the discomfort of patients with cancer been eased by our understanding of food aversions?

Operant Conditioning: Reinforcements From the Environment

Learning Outcomes

- Describe the process of operant conditioning.

- Explain how cognitive, neural, and evolutionary aspects influence our understanding of operant conditioning.

The study of classical conditioning is the study of behaviors that are *reactive*. Most animals don't voluntarily salivate or feel spasms of anxiety; rather, they exhibit these responses involuntarily during the conditioning process. But we also engage in voluntary behaviors to obtain rewards and avoid punishment. **Operant conditioning** is *a type of learning in which the consequences of an organism's behavior determine whether it will repeat that behavior in the future.* The study of operant conditioning is the exploration of behaviors that are *active*.

The Development of Operant Conditioning: The Law of Effect

The study of how active behavior affects the environment began at about the same time as classical conditioning. In the 1890s, Edward L. Thorndike (1874–1949) examined *instrumental behaviors,* that is, behavior that required an organism to *do* something, such as solve a problem or otherwise manipulate elements of its environment (Thorndike, 1898). Some of Thorndike's experiments involved a puzzle box, which was a wooden crate with a door that would open when a concealed lever was moved in the right way (see **FIGURE 7.4**). A hungry cat placed in a puzzle box would try various

Figure 7.4 Thorndike's Puzzle Box In Thorndike's original experiments, food was placed just outside the door of the puzzle box, where the cat could see it. If the cat triggered the appropriate lever, the door would open and the cat could get out.

operant conditioning A type of learning in which the consequences of an organism's behavior determine whether it will repeat that behavior in the future.

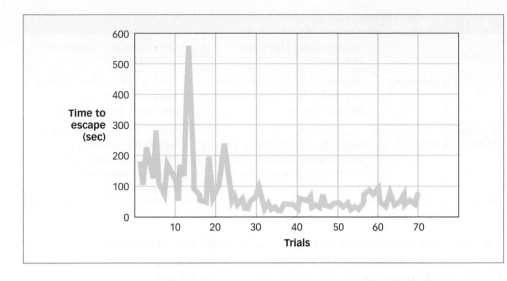

Figure 7.5   The Law of Effect
Thorndike's cats displayed trial-and-error behavior when trying to escape from the puzzle box. For example, they made lots of irrelevant movements and actions until, over time, they discovered the solution. Once they figured out which behavior was instrumental in opening the latch, they stopped all other ineffective behaviors and escaped from the box faster and faster.

behaviors to get out — scratching at the door, meowing loudly, putting its paw through the openings — but only one behavior opened the door and led to food: tripping the lever in just the right way. After the cat earned its reward, Thorndike placed it back in the puzzle box for another round.

Over time, the ineffective behaviors became less and less frequent, and the one instrumental behavior (going right for the latch) became more frequent (see **FIGURE 7.5**). From these observations, Thorndike developed the **law of effect,** the principle that *behaviors that are followed by a "satisfying state of affairs" tend to be repeated, whereas those that produce an "unpleasant state of affairs" are less likely to be repeated.*

Such learning is very different from classical conditioning. Remember that in classical conditioning, the US occurs on every training trial, no matter what the animal does. Pavlov delivered food to the dog whether it salivated or not. But in Thorndike's work, the behavior of the animal determined what happened next. If the behavior was "correct" (i.e., the animal triggered the latch), the animal was rewarded with food. Incorrect behaviors produced no results, and the animal was stuck in the box until it performed the correct behavior. Although different from classical conditioning, Thorndike's work resonated with most behaviorists at the time: It was still observable, quantifiable, and free from explanations involving the mind (Galef, 1998).

law of effect The principle that behaviors that are followed by a "satisfying state of affairs" tend to be repeated, and those that produce an "unpleasant state of affairs" are less likely to be repeated.

operant behavior Behavior that an organism performs that has some impact on the environment.

B. F. Skinner: The Role of Reinforcement and Punishment

Several decades after Thorndike's work, B. F. Skinner (1904–1990) coined the term **operant behavior** to refer to *behavior that an organism performs that has some impact on the environment.* In Skinner's system, all of these emitted behaviors "operated" on the environment in some manner, and the environment responded by providing events that either strengthened those behaviors (i.e., they *reinforced* them) or made them less likely to occur (i.e., they *punished* them). Skinner's elegantly simple observation was that most organisms do *not* behave like a dog in a harness, passively waiting to receive food no matter what the circumstances. Rather, most organisms are like cats in a box, actively engaging the environment in which they find themselves to reap rewards (Skinner, 1938, 1953).

To study operant behavior scientifically, Skinner developed a variation on Thorndike's puzzle box: the *operant conditioning chamber,* or *Skinner box,* as it is commonly called (shown in **FIGURE 7.6**), which allows a researcher to study the behavior of small organisms in a controlled environment.

Skinner's approach to the study of learning focused on *reinforcement* and *punishment.* These terms, which have commonsense connotations, have particular meanings in

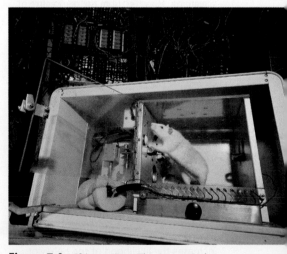

Figure 7.6   Skinner Box This is a typical Skinner box, or operant conditioning chamber. A rat, pigeon, or other suitably sized animal is placed in this environment and observed during learning trials that apply operant conditioning principles.   Walter Dawn/Science Source

TABLE 7.1 Reinforcement and Punishment

	Increases the Likelihood of Behavior	Decreases the Likelihood of Behavior
Stimulus is presented	Positive reinforcement: Parents buy teen a new car as a reward for safe driving.	Positive punishment: Parents assign difficult new chores after teen is stopped for speeding.
Stimulus is removed	Negative reinforcement: Parents reduce restrictions on where teen can drive as a reward for safe driving.	Negative punishment: Parents suspend driving privileges after teen is stopped for speeding.

Negative reinforcement involves the removal of something unpleasant from the environment. When Daddy stops the car, he gets a reward: His little monster stops screaming. However, from the perspective of the child, this is positive reinforcement. The child's tantrum results in something positive added to the environment — stopping for a snack. Michelle Selesnick/Moment/Getty Images

reinforcer Any stimulus or event that increases the likelihood of the behavior that led to it.

punisher Any stimulus or event that decreases the likelihood of the behavior that led to it.

psychology, in terms of their effect on behavior. A **reinforcer** is *any stimulus or event that increases the likelihood of the behavior that led to it,* whereas a **punisher** is *any stimulus or event that decreases the likelihood of the behavior that led to it.*

Whether a particular stimulus acts as a reinforcer or a punisher depends in part on whether it increases or decreases the likelihood of a behavior. Presenting food is usually reinforcing and it produces an increase in the behavior that led to it; removing food is often punishing and leads to a decrease in the behavior. Turning on an electric shock is typically punishing (and decreases the behavior that led to it); turning it off is rewarding (and increases the behavior that led to it).

To keep these possibilities distinct, Skinner used the term *positive* for situations in which a stimulus was presented and *negative* for situations in which it was removed. Consequently, as shown in **TABLE 7.1**, there is *positive reinforcement* (a stimulus is presented that increases the likelihood of a behavior) and a *negative reinforcement* (a stimulus is removed that increases the likelihood of a behavior), as well as *positive punishment* (a stimulus is administered that reduces the likelihood of a behavior) and a *negative punishment* (a stimulus is removed that decreases the likelihood of a behavior). Here the words *positive* and *negative* mean, respectively, something that is *added* or something that is *taken away*; they do not mean "good" or "bad" as they do in everyday speech.

These distinctions can be confusing at first; after all, *negative reinforcement* and *punishment* both sound like they should be "bad" and produce the same type of behavior. However, negative reinforcement, for example, does not involve administering something that decreases the likelihood of a behavior; it's the *removal* of something, such as a shock, that increases the likelihood of a behavior.

Reinforcement is generally more effective than punishment in promoting learning, for many reasons (Gershoff, 2002). One reason is that punishment signals that an unacceptable behavior has occurred, but it doesn't specify what should be done instead. Scolding a young child for starting to run into a busy street certainly stops the behavior, but it doesn't promote any kind of learning about the *desired* behavior.

Primary and Secondary Reinforcement and Punishment

Reinforcers and punishers often gain their functions from basic biological mechanisms. A pigeon that pecks at a target in a Skinner box is usually reinforced with food pellets, just as an animal that learns to escape a mild electric shock has avoided the punishment of tingly paws. Food, comfort, shelter, and warmth are examples of *primary reinforcers* because they help satisfy biological needs or desires. However, the vast majority of reinforcers or punishers in our daily lives have little to do with biology: Verbal approval, a bronze trophy, or money all serve powerful reinforcing functions, yet none of them taste very good or help keep you warm at night.

These *secondary reinforcers* derive their effectiveness from their associations with primary reinforcers through classical conditioning. For example, money starts out as a neutral CS that, through its association with primary USs such as acquiring food or shelter, takes on a conditioned emotional element. Flashing lights, originally a neutral CS, acquire powerful negative elements through association with a speeding ticket and a fine.

Immediate Versus Delayed Reinforcement and Punishment

A key determinant of the effectiveness of a reinforcer is the amount of time between the occurrence of a behavior and the reinforcer: The more time elapses, the less effective the reinforcer (Lattal, 2010; Renner, 1964). This was dramatically illustrated in experiments where food reinforcers were given at varying times after a rat pressed a lever (Dickinson et al., 1992). Delaying reinforcement by even a few seconds led to a reduction in the number of times the rat subsequently pressed the lever, and extending the delay to a minute rendered the food reinforcer completely ineffective (see **FIGURE 7.7**). The most likely explanation for this effect is that delaying the reinforcer made it difficult for the rats to figure out exactly what behavior they needed to perform in order to obtain it. In the same way, parents who wish to use a piece of candy to reinforce their children for playing quietly should provide the candy while the child is still playing quietly; waiting until later, when the child may be engaging in other behaviors — perhaps making a racket with pots and pans — will make it more difficult for the child to link the reinforcer with the behavior of playing quietly (Powell et al., 2009). Similar considerations apply to punishment: As a general rule, the longer the delay between a behavior and the administration of punishment, the less effective the punishment will be in suppressing that behavior (Kamin, 1959; Lerman & Vorndran, 2002).

The greater potency of immediate versus delayed reinforcers and punishers may help us appreciate why it can be difficult to engage in behaviors that have long-term benefits. The smoker who desperately wants to quit smoking will be reinforced immediately by the feeling of relaxation that results from lighting up, but she may have to wait years to be reinforced with the better health that results from quitting; the dieter who sincerely wants to lose weight may easily succumb to the temptation of a chocolate sundae that provides reinforcement now, rather than waiting weeks or months for the reinforcement (looking and feeling better) that would be associated with losing weight. On the other hand, a parent whose child misbehaves at a shopping mall may be unable to punish the child immediately with a time-out because it is impractical in the mall setting; this delay can reduce the effectiveness of the punishment when it does arrive.

The Basic Principles of Operant Conditioning

After establishing how reinforcement and punishment produced learned behavior, Skinner and other scientists began to explore the basic principles of operant conditioning. Let's look at some.

Discrimination and Generalization

Operant conditioning shows both discrimination and generalization effects similar to those we saw with classical conditioning. To demonstrate this, researchers used either an impressionist painting by Claude Monet or a cubist painting by Pablo Picasso (Watanabe et al., 1995). Participants in the experiment were reinforced only if they responded when the appropriate painting was presented. After training, the participants discriminated appropriately: Those trained with the Monet painting responded when other paintings by Monet were presented, but not when cubist paintings by Picasso were shown; those

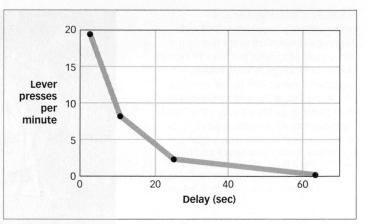

Figure 7.7 Delay of Reinforcement Rats pressed a lever in order to obtain a food reward. Researchers varied the amount of time between the lever press and the delivery of food reinforcement. The frequency of responding (number of lever presses per minute) declined substantially with longer delays.

Suppose you are the mayor of a suburban town, and you want to institute some new policies to decrease the number of drivers who speed on residential streets. How might you use punishment to decrease the undesirable behavior (speeding)? How might you use reinforcement to increase the desirable behavior (safe driving)? Based on the principles of operant conditioning you read about in this section, which approach do you think might be most fruitful? Eden Breitz/Alamy

In a study of discrimination and generalization, participants trained with Picasso paintings, such as the one on the left, responded to other paintings by Picasso or even to paintings by other cubists. Participants trained with Monet paintings, such as the one at the right, responded to other paintings by Monet or by other French impressionists. An interesting detail: The participants in this study were pigeons.
© 2016 Estate of Pablo Picasso/Artists Rights Picasso, Pablo (1881-1973) © ARS, NY *The Weeping Woman* (*Femme En Pleurs*). 1937. Oil on Canvas, 60.8x 50.0 cm. Tate Gallery, London/Art Resource, NY; Tate Gallery, London/Art Resource, NY

trained with a Picasso painting showed the opposite behavior. What's more, the participants could generalize *across* painters from the same artistic tradition: Those trained with Monet responded appropriately to paintings by other impressionist artists, and the Picasso-trained participants responded to paintings by other cubists, despite never having seen those paintings before. These results are particularly striking because the research participants were pigeons that were trained to key-peck to these various works of art.

Extinction

As in classical conditioning, operant behavior undergoes extinction when the reinforcements stop. Pigeons cease pecking at a key if food is no longer presented following that behavior. You wouldn't put more money into a vending machine if it failed to give you its promised candy bar or soda. On the surface, extinction of operant behavior looks like that of classical conditioning.

However, there is an important difference. During acquisition in classical conditioning, the US occurs on *every* trial, no matter what the organism does. In operant conditioning, the reinforcements occur *only* when the proper response has been made, and they don't always occur even then. Not every trip into the forest produces nuts for a squirrel, auto salespeople don't sell to everyone who takes a test drive, and researchers run many experiments that do not work out and thus never get published. Yet these behaviors don't weaken and gradually extinguish. In fact, they typically become stronger and more resilient. Curiously, then, extinction is a bit more complicated in operant conditioning than in classical conditioning because it depends, in part, on how often reinforcement is received. In fact, this principle is an important cornerstone of operant conditioning that we'll examine next.

Schedules of Reinforcement

One day, Skinner was laboriously rolling ground rat meal and water to make food pellets to reinforce the rats in his early experiments. It occurred to him that perhaps he could save time and effort by not giving his rats a pellet for every bar press but instead delivering food on some intermittent schedule. The results of this hunch were dramatic. Not only did the rats continue bar pressing, but they also shifted the rate and pattern of bar pressing depending on the timing and frequency of the presentation of the reinforcers (Skinner, 1979). Unlike in classical conditioning, where the sheer *number* of learning trials was important, the *pattern* with which reinforcements appeared was crucial in operant conditioning.

fixed-interval (FI) schedule An operant conditioning principle whereby reinforcers are presented at fixed time periods, provided that the appropriate response is made.

variable-interval (VI) schedule An operant conditioning principle whereby behavior is reinforced on the basis of an average time that has expired since the last reinforcement.

fixed-ratio (FR) schedule An operant conditioning principle whereby reinforcement is delivered after a specific number of responses have been made.

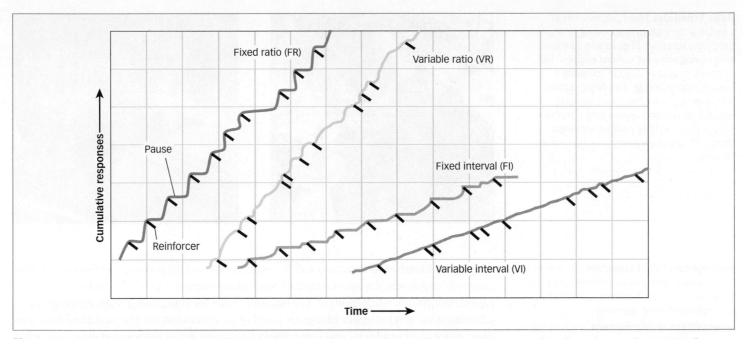

Figure 7.8 **Reinforcement Schedules** Different schedules of reinforcement produce different rates of response. These lines represent the number of responses that occur under each type of reinforcement. The black slash marks indicate when reinforcement was administered. Notice that ratio schedules tend to produce higher rates of responding than do interval schedules, as shown by the steeper lines for fixed-ratio and variable-ratio reinforcement.

Skinner explored dozens of what came to be known as *schedules of reinforcement* (Ferster & Skinner, 1957) (see **FIGURE 7.8**). The two most important are *interval schedules,* based on the time intervals between reinforcements, and *ratio schedules,* based on the ratio of responses to reinforcements.

Interval Schedules Under a **fixed-interval (FI) schedule,** *reinforcers are presented at fixed time periods, provided that the appropriate response is made.* For example, on a 2-minute fixed-interval schedule, a response will be reinforced, but only after 2 minutes have expired since the last reinforcement. Rats and pigeons in Skinner boxes produce predictable patterns of behavior under these schedules. They show little responding right after the presentation of the reinforcement, but as the next time interval draws to a close, they show a burst of responding. Many undergraduates behave exactly like this. They do relatively little work until just before the upcoming exam, then engage in a burst of reading and studying.

Under a **variable-interval (VI) schedule,** *a behavior is reinforced on the basis of an average time that has expired since the last reinforcement.* For instance, on a 2-minute variable-interval schedule, responses will be reinforced every 2 minutes, *on average.* Variable-interval schedules typically produce steady, consistent responding because the time until the next reinforcement is less predictable. One example in real life might be radio promotional giveaways. The reinforcement—say, concert tickets—might occur *on average* once an hour across the span of the broadcasting day, but it might come early in the 10:00 o'clock hour, later in the 11:00 o'clock hour, immediately into the 12:00 o'clock hour, and so on.

Both fixed-interval schedules and variable-interval schedules tend to produce slow, methodical responding because the reinforcements follow a time scale that is independent of how many responses occur. It doesn't matter if a rat on a fixed-interval schedule presses a bar 1 time during a 2-minute period or 100 times: The reinforcing food pellet won't drop out of the chute until 2 minutes have elapsed, regardless of the number of responses.

Ratio Schedules Under a **fixed-ratio (FR) schedule,** *reinforcement is delivered after a specific number of responses have been made.* One schedule might present reinforcement

Interval Schedules Students cramming at the last minute for an exam often show the same kind of behavior as pigeons being reinforced under a fixed-interval schedule. Radio stations offer tickets to hopeful concert goers on a less predictable, variable-interval schedule of reinforcement. Jupiterimages, Brand X Pictures/Stockbyte/Getty Images; © Richard Hutchings/Photoedit

Ratio Schedules These pieceworkers in a textile factory get paid according to a fixed-ratio schedule: They receive payment after sewing some set number of shirts. Slot machines in casinos pay out following a variable-ratio schedule. This helps explain why some gamblers feel incredibly lucky, whereas others can't believe they can play a machine for so long without winning a thing. Jeff Holt/Bloomberg via Getty Images; Stockbroker/MBI/Alamy

variable-ratio (VR) schedule An operant conditioning principle whereby the delivery of reinforcement is based on a particular average number of responses.

intermittent reinforcement An operant conditioning principle whereby only some of the responses made are followed by reinforcement.

intermittent reinforcement effect The fact that operant behaviors that are maintained under intermittent reinforcement schedules resist extinction better than those maintained under continuous reinforcement.

Imagine you own an insurance company, and you want to encourage your salespeople to sell as many policies as possible. You decide to give them bonuses according to the number of policies they sell. How might you set up a system of bonuses using a fixed-ratio schedule? Using a variable-ratio schedule? Which system do you think would encourage your salespeople to work harder, in terms of making more sales? Elenathewise/iStock/Getty Images

after every fourth response, and a different schedule might present reinforcement after every 20 responses; the special case of presenting reinforcement after each response is called *continuous reinforcement.* For example, your local sandwich shop might give you a freebie after a set number of regular purchases; pieceworkers get paid after making a fixed number of products; and some credit card companies return to their customers a percentage of the amount charged. When a fixed-ratio schedule is operating, it is possible, in principle, to know exactly when the next reinforcer is due.

Under a **variable-ratio (VR) schedule,** *the delivery of reinforcement is based on a particular average number of responses.* Slot machines in a modern casino pay off on variable-ratio schedules that are determined by the random number generator controlling the play of the machines. A casino might advertise that its machines pay off on "every 100 pulls, on average," but one player might hit a jackpot after 3 pulls on a slot machine, whereas another player might not hit a jackpot until after 80 pulls. The ratio of responses to reinforcements is variable, which probably helps casinos stay in business.

It should come as no surprise that variable-ratio schedules produce higher rates of responding than fixed-ratio schedules, primarily because the organism never knows when the next reinforcement is going to appear. What's more, the higher the ratio, the higher the response rate tends to be: A 20-response variable-ratio schedule will produce considerably more responding than a 2-response variable-ratio schedule will. When schedules of reinforcement provide **intermittent reinforcement,** *whereby only some of the responses made are followed by reinforcement,* they produce behavior that is much more resistant to extinction than does a continuous reinforcement schedule. One way to think about this effect is to recognize that the more irregular and intermittent a schedule is, the more difficult it becomes for an organism to detect when it has actually been placed on extinction.

For instance, if you've just put a dollar into a soda machine that, unknown to you, is broken, no soda comes out. Because you're used to getting your sodas on a continuous reinforcement schedule — one dollar produces one soda — this abrupt change in the environment is easy to notice, and you are unlikely to put additional money into the machine: You'd quickly show extinction. However, if you've put your dollar into a slot machine that, unknown to you, is broken, do you stop after one or two plays? Almost certainly not. If you're a regular slot player, you're used to going for many plays in a row without winning anything, so it's difficult to tell that anything is out of the ordinary. The **intermittent reinforcement effect** refers to *the fact that operant behaviors that are maintained under intermittent reinforcement schedules resist extinction better than those maintained under continuous reinforcement.* In one extreme case, Skinner gradually extended a variable-ratio schedule until he managed to get a pigeon to make an astonishing 10,000 pecks at an illuminated key for one food reinforcer! Behavior maintained under a schedule like this is virtually immune to extinction.

Shaping Through Successive Approximations

Have you ever been to SeaWorld and wondered how the dolphins learn to jump up in the air, twist around, splash back down, do a somersault, and then jump through a hoop, all in one smooth motion? Well, they don't. At least not all at once. Rather, elements of their behavior are shaped over time until the final product looks like one smooth motion.

Behavior rarely occurs in fixed frameworks where a stimulus is presented and then an organism has to engage in some activity or another. Most of our behaviors are the result of **shaping,** *learning that results from the reinforcement of successive steps to a final desired behavior.* The outcomes of one set of behaviors shape the next set of behaviors, whose outcomes shape the next set of behaviors, and so on.

Skinner noted that if you put a rat in a Skinner box and wait for it to press the bar, you could end up waiting a very long time: Bar pressing just isn't something most rats normally spend a lot of time doing. However, it is relatively easy to shape bar pressing. Wait until the rat turns in the direction of the bar, then deliver a food reward. This will reinforce turning toward the bar, making such a movement more likely. Now wait for the rat to take a step toward the bar before delivering food; this will reinforce moving toward the bar. After the rat walks closer to the bar, wait until it touches the bar before presenting the food. Notice that none of these behaviors is the final desired behavior (reliably pressing the bar). Rather, each behavior is a *successive approximation* to the final desired behavior. In the dolphin example — and indeed, in many instances of animal training in which relatively simple animals seem to perform astoundingly complex behaviors — you can think through how each smaller behavior is reinforced until the overall sequence of behavior is performed reliably.

Superstitious Behavior

Everything we've discussed so far suggests that one of the keys to establishing reliable operant behavior is the correlation between an organism's response and the occurrence of reinforcement. In the case of continuous reinforcement, when every response is followed

shaping Learning that results from the reinforcement of successive steps to a final desired behavior.

B. F. Skinner shaping a dog named Agnes. By reinforcing Agnes for touching successively higher lines on the wall, Skinner taught Agnes a pretty neat trick: after 20 minutes of shaping, Agnes wandered in, stood on her hind legs, and jumped straight to the top line. Look Magazine Photograph Collection, Library of Congress, Prints & Photographs Division, [Reproduction Number E.g., LC-L9-60-8812, Frame 8]

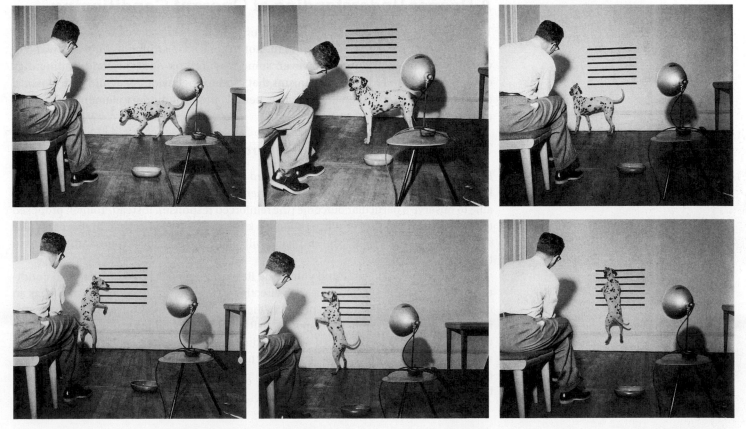

Baseball players who play well on days they happened not to have showered may continue that tradition, mistaking the accidental correlation between poor personal hygiene and a good day as evidence that "stench causes home runs" — just one of many examples of human superstitious behavior (Gilbert et al., 2000; Radford & Radford, 1949).   J. Meric/Getty Images

by the presentation of a reinforcer, there is a one-to-one, or perfect, correlation. In the case of intermittent reinforcement, the correlation is weaker (i.e., not every response is met with the delivery of reinforcement), but it's not zero. As you read in the Methods in Psychology chapter, however, correlation doesn't necessarily mean causation (i.e., just because two things tend to occur together in time and space, we can't conclude that the presence of one actually causes the other to occur).

Skinner (1948) designed an experiment that illustrates this distinction. He put several pigeons in Skinner boxes, set the food dispenser to deliver food every 15 seconds, and left the birds to their own devices. Later he returned and found the birds engaging in odd, idiosyncratic behaviors, such as pecking aimlessly in a corner or turning in circles. He referred to these behaviors as "superstitious" and offered a behaviorist analysis of their occurrence. The pigeons, he argued, were simply repeating behaviors that had been accidentally reinforced. That is, a pigeon might just happened to have pecked randomly in the corner when the food showed up. Because this pecking behavior was reinforced by the delivery of food, the pigeon was likely to repeat it. Now pecking in the corner was more likely to occur, and it was more likely to be reinforced 15 seconds later when the food appeared again. For each pigeon, the behavior that is reinforced would most likely be whatever the pigeon happened to be doing when the food was first delivered. Skinner's pigeons acted as though there was a causal relationship between their behaviors and the appearance of food when it was merely an accidental correlation.

Although some researchers questioned Skinner's characterization of these behaviors as superstitious (Staddon & Simmelhag, 1971), later studies have shown that reinforcing adults or children using schedules in which reinforcement is not contingent on their responses can produce seemingly superstitious behavior. It seems that people, like pigeons, behave as though there's a correlation between their responses and reward when in fact the connection is merely accidental (Bloom et al., 2007; Mellon, 2009; Ono, 1987; Wagner & Morris, 1987).

A Deeper Understanding of Operant Conditioning

To behaviorists such as Watson and Skinner, an organism behaved in a certain way in response to stimuli in the environment, not because the animal in question wanted, wished, or willed anything. However, some research on operant conditioning digs deeper into the underlying mechanisms that produce behavior. As we did with classical conditioning, let's examine the cognitive, neural, and evolutionary elements of operant conditioning.

The Cognitive Elements of Operant Conditioning

Edward Chace Tolman (1886–1959) argued that there was more to learning than just knowing the circumstances in the environment (the properties of the stimulus) and being able to observe a particular outcome (the reinforced response). Instead, Tolman proposed that the conditioning experience produced knowledge or a belief that, in this particular situation, a specific reward (the end state) will appear if a specific response (the means to that end) is made.

Tolman's ideas may remind you of the Rescorla–Wagner model of classical conditioning. In both, the stimulus does not directly evoke a response; rather, it establishes an internal cognitive state that then produces the behavior. These cognitive theories of learning focus less on the stimulus–response (S–R) connection and more on what happens in the organism's mind when faced with the stimulus. During the 1930s and 1940s, Tolman and his students conducted studies that focused on *latent learning* and *cognitive maps,* two phenomena that strongly suggest that simple S–R interpretations of operant learning behavior are inadequate.

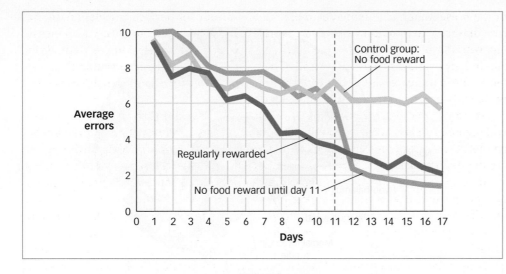

Figure 7.9　Latent Learning Rats in a control group that never received any reinforcement (green curve) improved at finding their way through the maze over 17 days, but not by much. Rats that received regular reinforcements (blue curve) showed fairly clear learning; their error rate decreased steadily over time. Rats in the latent learning group (orange curve) were treated exactly like the control group rats for the first 10 days and then like the regularly rewarded group for the last 7 days. Their dramatic improvement on day 12 shows that these rats had learned a lot about the maze and the location of the goal box even though they had never received reinforcements.

Latent learning is *a process in which something is learned, but it is not manifested as a behavioral change until sometime in the future.* For example, Tolman gave three groups of rats access to a complex maze every day over a span of 17 days. The control group never received any reinforcement — they were simply allowed to run around the maze freely until they happened to reach the goal box at the end of the maze. In **FIGURE 7.9**, you can see that over the 17 days of the study, the control group (in green) got a little better at finding their way through the maze, but not by much. A second group of rats received regular reinforcements; when they reached the goal box, they found a small food reward there. Not surprisingly, these rats showed clear learning, as can be seen in blue in Figure 7.9. A third group was treated exactly like the control group for the first 10 days and then rewarded for the last 7 days. This group's behavior (in orange) was quite striking. For the first 10 days, they behaved like the rats in the control group. However, during the final 7 days, they behaved a lot like the rats in the second group, which had been reinforced every day. Clearly, the rats in this third group had learned a lot about the maze and the location of the goal box during those first 10 days even though they had not received any reinforcements for their behavior. In other words, they showed evidence of latent learning.

These results suggested to Tolman that beyond simply learning "start here, end here," his rats had developed a sophisticated mental picture of the maze. Tolman called this a **cognitive map,** *a mental representation of the physical features of the environment.* Tolman thought that the rats had developed a mental picture of the maze, along the lines of "make two lefts, then a right, then a quick left at the corner," and he devised several experiments to test that idea (Tolman & Honzik, 1930; Tolman et al., 1946). In fact, even if the maze was changed, so that familiar pathways were blocked off, Tolman's rats could quickly find a new route to the goal. These results suggested that the rats had formed a sophisticated cognitive map of their environment and behaved in a way that suggested they were successfully following that map after the conditions changed.

The Neural Elements of Operant Conditioning

The first hint of how specific brain structures might contribute to the process of reinforcement came from James Olds and his associates, who inserted tiny electrodes into different parts of a rat's brain and allowed the animal to control electric stimulation of its own brain by pressing a bar. They discovered that some brain areas, particularly those in the limbic system (see the Neuroscience and Behavior chapter), produced what appeared to be intensely positive experiences: The rats would press the bar repeatedly to stimulate these structures, sometimes ignoring food, water, and other life-sustaining necessities for hours on end. Olds and colleagues called these parts of the brain *pleasure centers* (Olds, 1956) (see **FIGURE 7.10**).

latent learning A process in which something is learned, but it is not manifested as a behavioral change until sometime in the future.

cognitive map A mental representation of the physical features of the environment.

Figure 7.10 Pleasure Centers in the Brain The nucleus accumbens, medial forebrain bundle, and hypothalamus are all major pleasure centers in the brain.

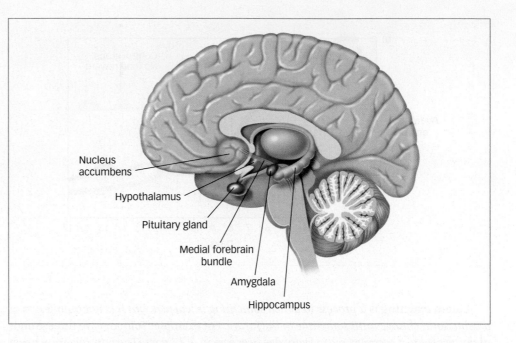

In the years since these early studies, researchers have identified a number of structures and pathways in the brain that deliver rewards through stimulation (Wise, 1989, 2005). The neurons in the *medial forebrain bundle,* a pathway that meanders its way from the midbrain through the *hypothalamus* into the *nucleus accumbens,* are the most susceptible to stimulation that produces pleasure. This is not surprising because psychologists have identified this bundle of cells as crucial to behaviors that clearly involve pleasure, such as eating, drinking, and engaging in sexual activity. Second, the neurons all along this pathway and especially those in the nucleus accumbens itself are all *dopaminergic* (i.e., they secrete the neurotransmitter *dopamine*). Remember from the Neuroscience and Behavior chapter that higher levels of dopamine in the brain are usually associated with positive emotions. During recent years, several competing hypotheses about the precise role of dopamine have emerged, including the idea that dopamine is more closely linked with the expectation of reward than with reward itself (Fiorillo et al., 2008; Schultz, 2016) or that dopamine is more closely associated with wanting or even *craving* something rather than simply liking it (Berridge, 2007). Whichever view turns out to be correct, researchers have found good support for a reward center in which dopamine plays a key role. (For more on the relationship between dopamine and reward, see Hot Science: Dopamine and Reward Learning: From Parkinson's Disease to Gambling.)

The Evolutionary Elements of Operant Conditioning

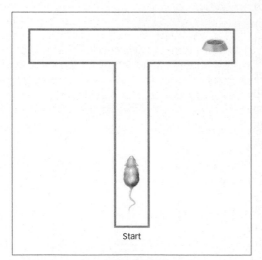

Figure 7.11   A Simple T Maze When rats find food in the right arm of a typical T maze, on the next trial, they will often run to the left arm of the maze. This contradicts basic principles of operant conditioning: If running to the right arm is reinforced, it should be more likely to occur again in the future. However, the rat's actual behavior is perfectly consistent with a rat's evolutionary preparedness. Like most foraging animals, rats explore their environments in search of food and seldom return to where food has already been found. If the rat already has found food in the right arm of the T maze, it quite sensibly will search the left arm next to see if more food is there.

As you'll recall, classical conditioning has an adaptive value that has been fine-tuned by evolution. Not surprisingly, operant conditioning does too. Several behaviorists who were using simple T mazes, such as the one shown in **FIGURE 7.11**, discovered that if a rat found food in one arm of the maze on the first trial of the day, it typically ran down the *other* arm on the very next trial. A staunch behaviorist wouldn't expect the rats to behave this way. According to operant conditioning, prior reinforcement in one arm should *increase* the likelihood of the rats turning in that same direction, not reduce it.

What is puzzling from a behaviorist perspective makes sense when viewed from an evolutionary perspective. Rats are foragers, and like all foraging species, they have evolved a highly adaptive strategy for survival. They move around in their environment, looking for food. If they find it somewhere, they eat it (or store it) and then go look somewhere else for more. If they do not find food, they forage in another part of the environment.

Dopamine and Reward Learning: From Parkinson's Disease to Gambling

The neurotransmitter dopamine plays an important role in reward-based learning, especially *reward prediction error*, the difference between the actual reward received and the amount of predicted or expected reward. For example, when an animal presses a lever and receives an unexpected food reward, a *positive* prediction error occurs (a better-than-expected outcome), and the animal learns to press the lever again. By contrast, when an animal expects to receive a reward from pressing a lever but does not receive it, a *negative* prediction error occurs (a worse-than-expected outcome), and the animal subsequently will be less likely to press the lever again. Reward prediction error can thus be a kind of "teaching signal" that helps the animal learn to behave in a way that maximizes reward.

In pioneering studies, Wolfram Schultz and his colleagues found that dopamine neurons located in the reward centers of a monkey's brain showed increased activity when the monkey received unexpected juice rewards but showed decreased activity when the monkey did not receive expected juice rewards. This suggests that dopamine neurons play an important role in generating the reward prediction error (Schultz, 2016; Schultz et al., 1997). Neuroimaging studies have shown that dopamine is

likewise involved in signaling reward prediction errors in the human brain (Howard & Kahnt, 2018; Pessiglione et al., 2006).

These findings have important implications for people with Parkinson's disease, a movement disorder that involves loss of neurons that produce dopamine. When individuals with Parkinson's perform reward-related learning tasks, the reward prediction error signal is disrupted (Meder et al., 2018; Schonberg et al., 2009). These results may relate to an intriguing feature of Parkinson's disease: Some individuals with the disease develop serious problems with compulsive gambling, shopping, and related impulsive behaviors. Such problems seem to be largely the consequence of Parkinson's drugs that stimulate dopamine receptors (Ahlskog, 2011; Weintraub et al., 2013). Indeed, neuroimaging studies have shown increased dopamine responses to reward cues in Parkinson's patients who develop problems with compulsive gambling as a consequence of drugs that stimulate dopamine receptors (Clark & Dagher, 2014).

These findings linking dopamine and risk-taking behaviors such as gambling may have more general implications. In a study by Rigoli and colleagues (2016), healthy adults performed a task in which they could either choose a guaranteed monetary reward or take a gamble

Recent findings suggest that boosting dopamine levels increases the propensity to gamble. iStock/Getty Images

in which they would receive double or nothing. Participants given a drug that increases brain dopamine levels tended to opt for the risky gamble more often.

Although much remains to be learned about how dopamine impacts reward learning and cognition more generally (Martins et al., 2017; Westbrook & Frank, 2018), future studies that combine drug manipulations, neuroimaging, and controlled learning paradigms should have important scientific and practical implications.

So if the rat just found food in the *right* arm of a T maze, the obvious place to look next time is the *left* arm. The rat knows that there isn't any more food in the right arm because it just ate the food it found there! Indeed, foraging animals such as rats have well-developed spatial representations that allow them to search their environment efficiently. If given the opportunity to explore a complex environment such as a maze with many arms, rats will systematically go from arm to arm collecting food, rarely returning to arms they have previously visited (Olton & Samuelson, 1976).

Two of Skinner's former students, Keller Breland and Marian Breland, were among the first researchers to discover that it wasn't just rats in T mazes that presented a problem for behaviorists (Breland & Breland, 1961). The Brelands, who made a career out of training animals for commercials and movies, often used pigs because pigs are surprisingly good at learning all sorts of tricks. However, they discovered that it was extremely difficult to teach a pig the simple task of dropping coins in a box. Instead of depositing the coins, the pigs persisted in rooting with them as if they were digging them up in soil, tossing them in the air with their snouts and pushing them around. The Brelands tried to train raccoons at the same task, with different but equally dismal results. The raccoons spent their time rubbing the coins between their paws instead of dropping them in the box. Having learned the association between the coins and food, the animals began to treat

The misbehavior of organisms: Pigs are biologically predisposed to root out their food, just as raccoons are predisposed to wash their food. Trying to train either species to behave differently can prove to be an exercise in futility. Gerard Lacz/Science Source; Millard H. Sharp/ Science Source

the coins as stand-ins for food. Pigs are biologically predisposed to root out their food, and raccoons have evolved to clean their food by rubbing it with their paws. That is exactly what each species of animal did with the coins. The Brelands' work shows that all species, including humans, are biologically predisposed to learn some things more readily than others and to respond to stimuli in ways that are consistent with their evolutionary history (Gallistel, 2000).

Build to the Outcomes

1. What is the law of effect?

2. What do *positive* and *negative* mean in operant conditioning?

3. Why is reinforcement often more effective than punishment?

4. What are primary and secondary reinforcers?

5. How does the concept of delayed reinforcement relate to difficulties with quitting smoking?

6. How is the concept of extinction different in operant conditioning than in classical conditioning?

7. How does a radio station use scheduled reinforcements to keep you listening?

8. How do ratio schedules work to keep you spending your money?

9. How can operant conditioning produce complex behaviors?

10. What are cognitive maps? Why are they a challenge to behaviorism?

11. How do specific brain structures contribute to the process of reinforcement?

12. What explains a rat's behavior in a T maze?

Observational Learning: Look at Me

Learning Outcomes

- Describe the process of observational learning.

- Compare evidence of observational learning in animals raised among humans with that in animals raised in the wild.

- Explain the neural elements of observational learning.

observational learning A process in which an organism learns by watching the actions of others.

Four-year-old Rodney and his 2-year-old sister Margie had always been told to keep away from the stove. Being a mischievous imp, however, Rodney one day placed his hand over a burner until the singeing of his flesh led him to recoil, shrieking in pain. Rodney was more scared than hurt, really — and no doubt he learned something important that day. But little Margie, who stood by watching these events unfold, *also* learned the same lesson. Rodney's story is a behaviorist's textbook example: The administration of punishment led to a learned change in his behavior. But how can we explain Margie's learning? She received neither punishment nor reinforcement — indeed, she didn't even have direct experience with the wicked appliance — yet it's arguable that she's just as likely to keep her hands away from stoves in the future as Rodney is.

Margie's is a case of **observational learning**, *a process in which an organism learns by watching the actions of others.* In all societies, appropriate social behavior is passed on from generation to generation, not only through deliberate training of the young but also through young people observing the patterns of behaviors of their elders and each other (Flynn & Whiten, 2008).

Tasks such as using chopsticks or operating a TV's remote control are more easily acquired if we watch these activities being carried out before we try them ourselves. Even complex motor tasks, such as performing surgery, are learned in part through extensive observation and imitation of models. And anyone who is about to undergo surgery is grateful for observational learning. Just the thought of a generation of surgeons acquiring their surgical techniques through the trial-and-error methods that Thorndike studied, or the shaping of successive approximations that captivated Skinner, would make any of us very nervous.

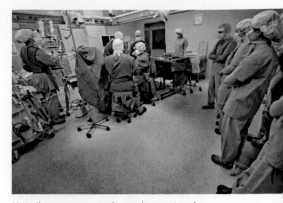

Happily, recent research on observational learning in surgeons and other medical professionals is providing useful new information about how to optimize learning from watching others (Cordovani & Cordovani, 2016; Harris et al., 2018). Carsten Koall/Getty Images

Observational Learning in Humans

In a series of landmark studies, Albert Bandura and his colleagues investigated the parameters of observational learning (Bandura et al., 1961). The researchers escorted individual preschoolers into a play area containing a number of toys that 4-year-olds typically like. An adult then entered the room and started playing with a Bobo doll, which is a large, inflatable plastic toy with a weighted bottom that allows it to bounce back upright when knocked down. The adult played quietly for a bit but then started aggressing toward the Bobo doll, knocking it down, jumping on it, hitting it with a toy mallet, kicking it around the room, and yelling "Pow!" and "Kick him!" When the children who observed these actions were later allowed to play with a child-size Bobo doll, they were more than twice as likely to interact with it in an aggressive manner as a group of children who hadn't observed the aggressive adult (**FIGURE 7.12**).

The children in these studies also showed that they were sensitive to the consequences of the actions they observed. When they saw the adult being punished for behaving aggressively, the children showed considerably less aggression. When the children observed the adult being rewarded and praised for aggressive behavior, they displayed an

Figure 7.12   Beating Up Bobo Children exposed to an adult who behaved aggressively toward a Bobo doll were likely to behave aggressively toward the doll themselves. This behavior occurred in the absence of any direct reinforcement. Observational learning was responsible for producing the children's behaviors. © Albert Bandura, Dept. of Psychology, Stanford University

Coaches rely on observational learning when they demonstrate techniques to athletes.
AP Photo/Robert F. Bukaty

increase in aggression (Bandura et al., 1963). The observational learning seen in Bandura's studies has implications for social learning and cultural transmission of behaviors, norms, and values (Bandura, 1977, 1994).

Observational learning is important in many domains of everyday life. Sports provide a good example. Coaches in just about all sports rely on observational learning when demonstrating critical techniques and skills for their players, and athletes also have numerous opportunities to observe other athletes perform. Studies of athletes in both team and individual sports indicate that they all rely heavily on observational learning to improve their performance (Wesch, Law, & Hall, 2007). In fact, observational learning sometimes results in just as much learning as practicing the task itself (Heyes & Foster, 2002; Mattar & Gribble, 2005; Vinter & Perruchet, 2002).

Observational Learning in Animals

Humans aren't the only creatures capable of learning through observing. A wide variety of species learn by observing. In one study, for example, pigeons watched other pigeons get reinforced for either pecking at the feeder or stepping on a bar. When placed in the box later, the pigeons tended to use whatever technique they had observed the other pigeons use earlier (Zentall et al., 1996).

One of the most important questions about observational learning in animals concerns whether monkeys and chimpanzees can learn to use tools by observing tool use in others, the way young children can. In one study (Nagell, Olguin, & Tomasello, 1993), some chimpanzees saw the experimenter using a rake in its normal position (with the teeth pointed toward the ground) to drag a food reward into reach; this method was rather inefficient because the teeth were widely spaced, and the food sometimes slipped between them. Other chimpanzees saw the experimenter using the rake more efficiently, with the teeth pointed up and the flat edge of the rake touching the ground. Both groups of chimpanzees later used the rake when trying to obtain the food themselves, indicating observational learning. But those chimpanzees who observed the more efficient "teeth up" procedure did not use it any more often than did those who observed the less efficient "teeth down" procedure. By contrast, 2-year-old children exposed to the same conditions used the rake in the exact same way that they had seen the experimenter use it. The chimpanzees seemed only to be learning that the tool could be used to obtain food, whereas the children learned something specific about how to use the tool.

The chimpanzees in these studies had been raised by their mothers in the wild. However, the researchers showed that chimpanzees who had been raised in environments that also included human contact could learn to imitate the exact actions performed by the experimenter, and performed similarly to human children on the task (Tomasello et al., 1993). This finding led Tomasello and colleagues (1993) to suggest that being raised in a human culture has a profound effect on the cognitive abilities of chimpanzees, especially their ability to understand the intentions of others when performing tasks such as using tools, which in turn increases their observational learning capacities.

Figure 7.13 Observational Learning
Monkeys who had been reared in the wild by their mothers or reared by human families watched a model either (*top*) poke a screwdriver through a hole in the center of a box to obtain a food reward or (*bottom*) pry open the lid to obtain the reward. Both groups showed some evidence of observational learning, but the human-reared monkeys were more likely to carry out the exact action they had watched.

More recent research has found something similar in capuchin monkeys, who are known for their tool use in the wild, such as employing branches or stone hammers to crack open nuts (Boinski et al., 2000; Fragaszy et al., 2004) or using stones to dig up buried roots (Moura & Lee, 2004). In one study, the experimenter demonstrated two ways of using a screwdriver to gain access to a food reward hidden in a box (Fredman & Whiten, 2008). Some monkeys observed the experimenter poke through a hole in the center of the box, whereas others watched him pry open the lid at the rim of the box (see **FIGURE 7.13**). Both mother-reared and human-reared monkeys showed evidence of observational learning, but the human-reared monkeys carried out the exact action they had observed more often than did the mother-reared monkeys.

Although this evidence implies that there is a cultural influence on the cognitive processes that support observational learning, more work is needed to understand the exact nature of those processes (Damerius et al., 2017; Mesoudi et al., 2015; Tomasello & Call, 2004).

Neural Elements of Observational Learning

Observational learning involves a neural component as well. *Mirror neurons* are a type of cell found in the frontal and parietal lobes of primates, including humans (see **FIGURE 7.14**). They fire when an animal performs an action, as when a monkey reaches for a food item. But they also fire when an animal watches someone *else* perform the same specific task (Rizzolatti & Craighero, 2004). Although this "someone else" is usually a fellow member of the same species, some research suggests that mirror neurons in monkeys also fire when they observe humans performing an action (Fogassi et al., 2005). For example, monkeys' mirror neurons fire when they observe humans grasping for a piece of food, either to eat it or to place it in a container. Although the exact functions of mirror neurons continue to be debated (Hickok, 2009, 2014; Rizzolatti & Rozzi, 2018), it is thought that they contribute to observational learning.

Studies of observational learning in healthy adults have likewise shown that watching someone else perform a task engages some of the same brain regions that are activated when people actually perform the task themselves. In one study, participants practiced some dance sequence for several days and watched music videos of other dance sequences (Cross et al., 2009). The participants were then given fMRI scans while viewing videos of sequences that they had previously danced or watched, as well as videos of sequences they had not danced or watched (untrained sequences). Viewing the previously danced or watched sequences caused activity in brain regions considered part of the mirror neuron system. A surprise dancing test given to participants after the conclusion of scanning showed that performance was better on sequences previously watched than on the untrained sequences, demonstrating significant observational learning; but performance was best of all on the previously danced sequences (Cross et al., 2009). So although watching *Dancing with the Stars* might indeed improve your dancing skills, practicing on the dance floor should help even more.

Figure 7.14 Mirror Neuron System
Regions in the frontal lobe (area 44) and parietal lobe (area 40) are thought to be part of the mirror neuron system in humans.

Observing skilled dancers, such as this energetic pair on *So You Think You Can Dance*, engages many of the same brain regions as does actual dance practice, and can produce significant learning. Photo by Fox via Getty Images

Build to the Outcomes

1. What is observational learning?
2. Why might a younger sibling appear to learn faster than a firstborn?
3. What did the Bobo doll experiment show about children and aggressive behavior?
4. What are the cognitive differences between chimpanzees raised among humans and those raised in the wild?
5. What do mirror neurons do?

Implicit Learning: Under the Radar

Most people are attuned to linguistic, social, emotional, and sensorimotor events in the world around them—so much so that they gradually build up internal representations of those patterns that they acquired without explicit awareness. This process is often called **implicit learning,** or *learning that takes place largely independent of awareness of both*

Learning Outcomes

- Explain why language studies led to studies of implicit learning.
- Outline the number of ways that implicit and explicit learning differ.

implicit learning Learning that takes place largely independent of awareness of both the process and the products of information acquisition.

Ten years ago, no one knew how to type using their thumbs; now just about all teenagers do it automatically. Mary Altaffer/AP Images

the process and the products of information acquisition. Because it occurs without our awareness, implicit learning is knowledge that sneaks in "under the radar."

Some forms of learning start out explicitly but become more implicit over time. When you first learned to drive a car, for example, you probably devoted a lot of attention to the many movements and sequences that you needed to carry out simultaneously. ("Step lightly on the accelerator while you push the turn indicator, and look in the rearview mirror while you turn the steering wheel.") That complex interplay of motions is now probably quite effortless and automatic for you. Explicit learning has become implicit over time.

These distinctions in learning might remind you of similar distinctions in memory, and for good reason. In the Memory chapter, you read about the differences between *implicit* and *explicit* memories. Do implicit and explicit learning mirror implicit and explicit memory? It's not that simple, but it is true that learning and memory are inextricably linked. Learning produces memories, and, conversely, the existence of memories implies that knowledge was acquired, that experience was registered and recorded in the brain, or that learning has taken place.

Cognitive Approaches to Implicit Learning

Most children, by the time they are 6 or 7 years old, are fairly sophisticated in terms of linguistics and social behavior, but have very little explicit awareness that they have learned something—and they may not even be able to state the general principle underlying their behavior. Yet most kids learn not to eat with their feet, to listen when they are spoken to, and not to kick the dog.

To investigate implicit learning in the laboratory, researchers asked participants to memorize strings of 15 or 20 letters. The letter strings, which at first glance look like nonsense syllables, were actually formed using a complex set of rules called an *artificial grammar.* (For example, one rule might state that "two *J*'s can follow an *X*, but only at the end of a string.") Participants were not told anything about the rules, but, with experience, they gradually developed a vague, intuitive sense of the "correctness" of particular letter groupings (Reber, 1967, 1996). Asked to classify new letter strings according to whether they follow the rules of the grammar, people could usually get 60–70% correct, but they were unable to provide much in the way of explicit awareness of the rules and regularities that they are using.

Other studies of implicit learning have used a *serial reaction time* task (Nissen & Bullemer, 1987). Here, research participants are presented with five small boxes on a computer screen. Each box lights up briefly, and the participant is asked to press the button just beneath that box as quickly as possible. Like the artificial grammar task, the sequence of lights appears to be random but in fact follows a pattern. Research participants eventually get faster with practice as they learn to anticipate which box is most likely to light up next. But if asked, they are generally unaware that there is a pattern to the lights.

Implicit learning is remarkably resistant to various disorders that are known to affect explicit learning (Reber, 2013). For example, patients with profound amnesia not only show normal implicit memories but also display virtually normal implicit learning of artificial grammar (Knowlton et al., 1992), despite having essentially no explicit memory of having been in the learning phase of the experiment! Researchers have also discovered implicit learning of complex, rule-governed auditory patterns in 8-month-old infants (Saffran et al., 1996). Perhaps even more striking, recent evidence indicates that at least one form of implicit learning is *enhanced* in adults with autism (Roser et al., 2015).

In contrast, several studies have shown that children with dyslexia, who fail to acquire reading skills to the same extent as their peers despite normal intelligence and good educational opportunities, exhibit deficits in implicit learning (Bennett et al., 2008; Orban, Lungu, & Doyon, 2008; Pavlidou et al., 2009; Stoodley et al., 2008). These findings suggest that problems with implicit learning play an important role in developmental dyslexia and need to be taken into account in the development of remedial programs (Stoodley et al., 2008).

Implicit and Explicit Learning Use Distinct Neural Pathways

The fact that individuals suffering from amnesia show intact implicit learning strongly suggests that the brain structures that underlie implicit learning are distinct from those that underlie explicit learning. As we learned in the Memory chapter, people with amnesia have damage to the hippocampus and nearby structures in the medial temporal lobe, indicating that these regions are not necessary for implicit learning (Bayley et al., 2005). What's more, it appears that distinct regions of the brain may be activated depending on how people approach a task (Reber, 2013).

For example, in one study, participants saw a series of dot patterns, each of which looked like an array of stars in the night sky (Reber et al., 2003). Actually, all the stimuli were constructed to conform to an underlying prototypical dot pattern. The dots, however, varied so much that it was virtually impossible for a viewer to guess that they all had this common structure. Before the experiment began, half of the participants were told about the existence of the prototype; in other words, they were given instructions that encouraged explicit processing. The others were given standard implicit learning instructions: They were told nothing other than to attend to the dot patterns.

The participants were then asked to categorize new dot patterns according to whether they conformed to the prototype. Interestingly, both groups performed equally well on this task, correctly classifying about 65% of the new dot patterns. However, brain scans revealed that the two groups made these decisions using very different parts of their brains (see **FIGURE 7.15**). Participants who were given the explicit instructions showed *increased* activity in the prefrontal cortex, parietal cortex, hippocampus, and other brain areas known to be associated with explicit memories. Those given the implicit instructions showed *decreased* brain activation primarily in the occipital region, which is involved in visual processing. This finding suggests that participants recruited distinct brain structures in different ways, depending on whether they were approaching the task using explicit or implicit learning.

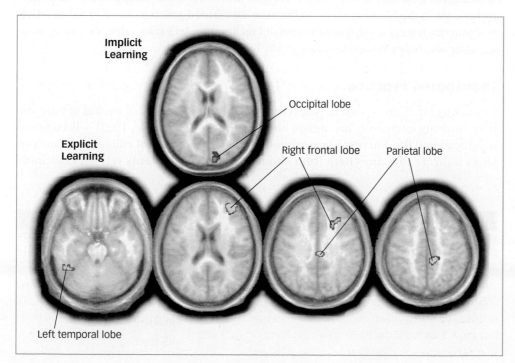

Figure 7.15 Implicit and Explicit Learning Activate Different Brain Areas Research participants were scanned with fMRI while engaged in either implicit learning or explicit learning about the categorization of dot patterns. Some brain regions (in blue), such as the occipital region, showed decreased brain activity after implicit learning. Other brain areas (in yellow), including the left temporal lobe, the right frontal lobe, and the parietal lobe, showed increased brain activity during explicit learning (Reber et al., 2003). Reber, P. J., Gitelman, D. R., Parrish, T. B., & Mesulam, M. M. (2003). Dissociating Explicit and Implicit Category Knowledge with FMRI. *Journal of Cognitive Neuroscience, 15,* 574–583. Permission Conveyed Through Copyright Clearance Center, Inc.

Build to the Outcomes

1. What is the difference between implicit learning and explicit learning?

2. How are learning and memory linked?

3. How can you learn something without being aware of it?

4. Why are tasks learned implicitly difficult to explain to others?

5. What structures of the brain are associated with implicit learning and explicit learning?

Learning Outcomes

- Explain why distributed practice and practice testing are effective study techniques.

- Describe how judgments of learning (JOLs) impact learning.

Learning in the Classroom

In this chapter, we've considered several different types of learning. Yet it may seem strange to you that we haven't discussed the kind of learning to which you are currently devoting much of your life: learning in educational settings such as the classroom. During the past several years, psychologists have published a great deal of work specifically focused on enhancing learning in educational settings. Let's consider what some of this research says about learning techniques and then turn to the equally important topic of exerting control over learning processes.

Techniques for Learning

Students use a wide variety of study techniques in attempts to improve their learning, such as highlighting and underlining, re-reading, summarizing, and visual imagery mnemonics (Annis & Annis, 1982; Wade et al., 1990). How effective are these and other techniques? A comprehensive analysis (Dunlosky et al., 2013) considered the usefulness of each technique and classified it as high, moderate, or low utility (**TABLE 7.2**).

Despite their popularity, highlighting, re-reading, summarizing, and visual imagery mnemonics all received a low utility assessment. That doesn't mean these techniques have no value whatsoever for improving learning, but it does indicate that each one has significant limitations and that students could better spend their time using other approaches—a reason that none of these techniques appeared in the Six Tips for Reading This Textbook section of the Preface. We also discussed some material related to these techniques in the Memory chapter. Because distributed practice, interleaved practice, and practice testing are the most successful techniques, let's take a deeper look at them now (see also Other Voices: Learning at Jiffy Lube University).

Distributed Practice

Cramming for exams—that is, neglecting to study for an extended period of time and then studying intensively just before an exam (Vacha & McBride, 1993)—is common in educational life. Surveys of undergraduates across a range of colleges and universities indicate that anywhere from about 25 to 50% of students rely on cramming

TABLE 7.2	Effectiveness of Study Techniques	
High Effectiveness	**Moderate Effectiveness**	**Low Effectiveness**
Practice testing	Elaborative interrogation	Summarization
Distributed practice	Self-explanation	Highlighting/underlining
	Interleaved practice	Keyword mnemonic
		Imagery for text
		Re-reading

Learning at Jiffy Lube University

Peter C. Brown is a writer in St. Paul, Minnesota. **Henry L. Roediger III** and **Mark A. McDaniel** are both professors of psychology at Washington University in St. Louis, Missouri.

Peter C. Brown

The study techniques we reviewed in this chapter on learning in the classroom can help improve academic performance. But these techniques also have broader applications outside the classroom, in situations where people need to acquire new knowledge and skills. One of the most important everyday applications of learning techniques involves training to perform a job. In an excellent 2014 book called *Make It Stick: The Science of Successful Learning*, which elaborates on several of the key techniques and ideas we have discussed in this section, the writer Peter C. Brown and the cognitive psychologists Henry L. Roediger III and Mark A. McDaniel tell the story of Jiffy Lube University. This is an educational program in which the well-known service-garage business has incorporated practice testing, distributed practice, and other learning techniques to aid in training employees:

If you don't expect innovations in training to spring from your local service garage, Jiffy Lube may surprise you. An integrated suite of educational courses under the felicitous name Jiffy Lube University is helping the company's franchises win customers, reduce employee turnover, broaden their service offerings, and boost sales.

Jiffy Lube is a network of more than two thousand service centers in the United States and Canada that provide oil changes, tire rotation, and other automotive services. Although the company is a subsidiary of Shell Oil Company, every outlet is owned and operated by an independent franchisee, who hires employees to serve customers.

The rapid-oil-change business, like most others, has had to adjust to changes in the marketplace and advances in technology. Synthetic lubricants have made oil changes less frequent, and because cars have become more complicated, garage employees need higher levels of training to understand diagnostic codes and provide appropriate services.

No employee may work on a customer's car until he or she has been certified as proficient. For this, they enter Jiffy Lube University, a Web-based learning platform. Certification starts with interactive e-learning, with frequent quizzing and feedback to learn what a particular job entails and how it's to be performed. When employees score 80 percent or better on an exam, they are eligible to begin training on the job, practicing new skills by following a written guide that breaks each service activity into its component steps. The steps may number as many as thirty and are performed as part of a team, often involving call and response (for example, between a technician working from the top side of an engine and another underneath). A supervisor coaches the employee and rates his or her performance on each step. When the technician demonstrates mastery, certification is recorded in his or her permanent file, signed by the supervisor. Technicians must recertify every two years to keep their mastery up to snuff and adapt to operational and technical changes. Higher-level jobs for advanced services like brake repair or running engine diagnostics are trained in the same manner.

The e-learning and on-the-job training are active learning strategies that incorporate various forms of quizzing, feedback, and spaced and interleaved practice. All progress is displayed by computer on a virtual "dashboard" that provides an individualized learning plan, enabling an employee to track his or her performance, focus on skills that need to be raised, and monitor his or her progress against the company's completion schedule. Jiffy Lube employees are typically eighteen to twenty-five years old and filing for their first jobs. As a technician is certified in one job, he or she begins training in another, until he or she has trained in all store positions, including management.

Ken Barber, Jiffy Lube International's manager of learning and development, says training has to be engaging in order to hold employees' attention. At the time we spoke, Barber was putting the finishing touches on a computer-based simulation game for company managers called "A Day in the Life of a Store Manager." The service center manager is confronted with various challenges and is required to select among a range of possible strategies for resolving them. The manager's choices determine how the game unfolds, providing feedback and the opportunity to strive for better outcomes, sharpening decision-making skill.

In the six years since Jiffy Lube University was launched, it has received many accolades from the training profession and earned accreditation by the American Council on Education. Employees who progress through training in all job certifications can enroll at a postsecondary institution with seven hours of college credit under their belts. Since the program's beginning, employee turnover has dropped and customer satisfaction has increased.

"For most employees of a Jiffy Lube franchisee, this is a way into the workforce, and the training curriculum helps them to grow and expand their knowledge," Barber says. "It helps them find a path to success."

From the results thus far, Jiffy Lube University appears to be a big success. It is notable that, in addition to incorporating the learning techniques described in this chapter, Jiffy Lube University combines e-learning based on a Web platform with actual on-the-job training. The use of e-learning, also referred to as online learning, has expanded rapidly in recent years, and debates about its effectiveness have been spirited (Brooks, 2012; Koller, 2011). Jiffy Lube's successful combination of e-learning and live learning fits with earlier evidence indicating that combining these two formats may be especially effective (Means et al., 2010).

And Jiffy Lube isn't the only company to make use of effective learning techniques. Brown, Roediger, and McDaniel also summarize successful training programs developed by Farmers Insurance, Andersen Windows and Doors, and other companies. So after you complete your studies and enter the workforce, don't be surprised if you find yourself applying practice testing, distributed practice, and related study techniques and principles that promote effective learning.

(McIntyre & Munson, 2008). Although cramming is better than not studying at all, crammers repeatedly study the information to be learned with little or no time between repetitions, a procedure known as *massed practice.* Such students are thus denying themselves the benefits of *distributed practice,* which involves spreading out study activities so that more time intervenes between repetitions of the information to be learned.

(Furthermore, students who rely on cramming are also inviting some of the health and performance problems associated with procrastination that we will address in the Stress and Health chapter).

The benefits of distributed practice relative to massed practice have been demonstrated not only in undergraduates but also in children, older adults, and individuals with memory problems due to brain damage (Dunlosky et al., 2013). A review of 254 separate studies involving more than 14,000 participants concluded that, on average, participants retained 47% of studied information after distributed practice, compared with 37% after massed practice (Cepeda et al., 2006). Distributed practice can also improve long-term retention of actual classroom learning in student populations, including 8th graders and college students (Rohrer, 2015).

Despite all the evidence indicating that distributed practice is an effective learning strategy, we still don't fully understand why that is so. One promising idea is that when we engage in massed practice, retrieving recently studied information is relatively easy, whereas during distributed practice, it is more difficult to retrieve information that we studied less recently. More difficult retrievals benefit subsequent learning more than easy retrievals, what psychologists call "desirable difficulties" (Bjork & Bjork, 2011). Whatever the explanation for the effects of distributed practice, there is no denying its benefits for students.

Interleaved Practice

Researchers have also discovered some novel benefits of the closely related technique of *interleaved practice,* which mixes different kinds of problems or materials within a single study session. Interleaved practice may be particularly effective for learning mathematics. Researchers gave one group of 7th-grade students practice math problems in the traditional blocked form: a set of similar problems that all required the same solution methods. A second group of students received problems in interleaved form: a mixture of different kinds of problems that each required distinct strategies.

The interleaved practice group scored higher than the blocked practice group on surprise tests given 1 day or 30 days after the conclusion of practice (Rohrer et al., 2015). The researchers suggested that interleaved practice was more effective because it requires students to choose a strategy according to the nature of individual problems (as students must do on a test), whereas during blocked practice, students could repeatedly apply the same strategy without having to select among possible strategies.

Practice Testing

Practice testing, like distributed practice, has proven useful across a wide range of materials, including learning of stories, facts, vocabulary, and lectures (Karpicke & Aue, 2015; Roediger & Karpicke, 2018; see also the LearningCurve system associated with this text, which uses practice testing). As you learned in the Memory chapter, practice testing is effective, in part, because actively retrieving an item from memory during a test improves subsequent retention of that item more efficiently than simply studying it again (Roediger & Karpicke, 2006). Yet when asked about their preferred study strategies, students indicated by a wide margin that they prefer re-reading materials to testing themselves (Karpicke, 2012).

The benefits of testing tend to be greatest when the test is difficult and requires considerable retrieval effort (Pyc & Rawson, 2009), also consistent with the desirable difficulties hypothesis (Bjork & Bjork, 2011). Not only does testing increase verbatim learning of the exact material that is tested, but it can also enhance the *transfer* of learning from one situation to another (Carpenter, 2012; Pan & Rickard, 2018). For example, if you are given practice tests with short-answer questions, such testing improves later performance on both short-answer and multiple-choice questions more than restudying does

Studying well in advance of an exam, allowing for breaks and distribution of study time, will generally produce a better outcome than cramming at the last minute. Age Fotostock/ Superstock

(Kang et al., 2007). Testing also improves the ability to draw conclusions from the studied material, which is an important part of learning and often critical to performing well in the classroom (Karpicke & Blunt, 2011). Also important, studies of students' performance in actual classrooms reveal benefits of practice testing that are similar to those observed in the laboratory (McDaniel et al., 2013; McDermott et al., 2014) (see **FIGURE 7.16**).

Testing Aids Attention

Recent research conducted in the laboratory of one of your textbook authors highlights yet another benefit of testing: Including brief tests during a lecture can improve learning by reducing the mind's tendency to wander (Szpunar et al., 2013). How often have you found your mind wandering in the midst of a lecture? It's probably happened more than once. Research indicates that students' minds wander frequently during classroom lectures (Bunce et al., 2011; Lindquist & McLean, 2011; Wilson & Korn, 2007). Such mind wandering critically impairs learning of the lecture material (Risko et al., 2012; Wammes et al., 2016). In a study by Szpunar and colleagues (2013), participants watched a videotaped statistics lecture that was divided into four segments. All of the participants were told they might or might not be tested after each segment; they were also encouraged to take notes during the lectures. However, some participants ("tested group") received brief tests on each segment, while the "nontested group" did not receive a test until after the final segment. A third group ("restudy group") were shown, but not tested on, the same material as the tested group.

At random times during the lectures, participants in all groups were asked about whether they were paying attention to the lecture or whether their minds were wandering off to other topics. Participants in the nontested and restudy groups indicated that their minds wandered in response to about 40% of the inquiries; but in the tested group, the incidence of mind wandering was cut in half, to about 20%. Participants in the tested group took significantly more notes during the lectures and retained significantly more information from the lecture on a final test than did participants in the other two groups, who performed similarly on this test to one another. Participants in the tested group were also less anxious about the final test than those in the other groups.

These results indicate that part of the value of testing comes from encouraging people to sustain attention to a lecture in a way that discourages task-irrelevant activities such as mind wandering, and encourages task-relevant activities such as note taking. A subsequent study (Jing et al., 2016) showed that even when participants in the tested group did mind-wander, they tended to think about other parts of the lecture. The tested group not only showed enhanced verbatim recall of lecture material but also showed an increased ability to integrate information from different parts of the lecture.

Because these benefits of testing were observed in response to a videotaped lecture, they apply most directly to online learning, where taped lectures are the norm (Breslow et al., 2013; Schacter & Szpunar, 2015), but there is every reason to believe that the results would apply to live classroom lectures as well, especially in light of the evidence we just discussed that practice testing enhances classroom performance.

Control of Learning

It's the night before the final exam in your psychology course. You've put in a lot of time reviewing your course notes and the material in this textbook, and you feel that you have learned most of it pretty well. Now you've got to decide whether to devote those precious remaining minutes to studying psychological disorders or social psychology. How do you make that decision? An important part of learning involves assessing how well we know something and how much more time we need to devote to studying it.

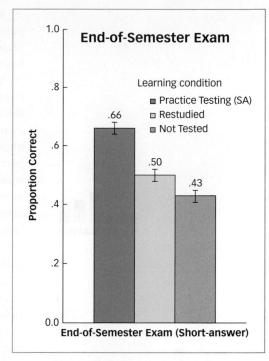

Figure 7.16 In a classroom study, 7th-grade science students received short-answer practice tests for some learning units, restudied other learning units, and received neither practice tests nor restudy for other units. On a short-answer exam at the end of the semester, practice testing produced significantly higher scores than either of the other two conditions (McDermott et al., 2014).

Experimental evidence shows that people's judgments about what they have learned play a critical role in guiding further study and learning (Dunlosky & Thiede, 2013; Metcalfe, 2009). People typically devote more time to studying items that they judge they have not learned well (Metcalfe & Finn, 2008; Son & Metcalfe, 2000).

Unfortunately, judgments of learning (JOLs) are often inaccurate (Castel et al., 2007). For example, after you read and re-read a chapter or article in preparation for a test, the material will likely feel quite familiar, and that feeling may convince you that you've learned the material well enough that you don't need to study it further. However, the feeling of familiarity can be misleading: It may be the result of a low-level process such as perceptual priming (see the Memory chapter), not the kind of learning that will be necessary to perform well on an exam (Bjork & Bjork, 2011). One way to avoid being fooled by misleading JOLs when studying for an exam is to test yourself from time to time, and compare your answers to the actual answers. (See Data Visualization: Do People Differ in How They Learn? at www.launchpadworks.com.)

DATA Visualization

So if you are preparing for the final exam in this course and need to decide whether to devote more time to studying psychological disorders or social psychology, try to exert control over your learning by testing yourself on material from those two chapters; you can use the results of those tests to help you decide which chapter requires further work. Heed the conclusion from researchers (Bjork et al., 2013) that becoming a more sophisticated and effective learner requires understanding: (1) key features of learning and memory; (2) effective learning techniques; (3) how to monitor and control one's own learning; and (4) biases that can undermine judgments of learning.

Build to the Outcomes

1. What are the most and least effective study techniques?

2. What are the benefits of distributed practice?

3. Why does a difficult practice test have the greatest benefit?

4. How does taking practice tests help focus a wandering mind?

5. In what ways can JOLs be misleading?

CHAPTER REVIEW

What Is Learning?

- Learning involves the acquisition of new knowledge, skills, and responses. It is based on experience, it produces a change in the organism, and that change is relatively permanent.

- Even the simplest organisms exhibit simple forms of learning such as habituation and sensitization.

Classical Conditioning: One Thing Leads to Another

- Classical conditioning pairs a neutral stimulus (the conditioned stimulus, CS) with a meaningful event or stimulus (the unconditioned stimulus, US); eventually the CS, all by itself, can elicit a response (the conditioned response, CR).

- Behaviorists viewed classical conditioning as a form of learning in which higher-level functions, such as thinking or awareness, did not need to be invoked to understand behavior.

- Later researchers showed, however, that classical conditioning involves setting up expectations, is sensitive to the degree to which the CS is a genuine predictor of the US, and can involve some degree of cognition.

- The cerebellum plays an important role in eyeblink conditioning, whereas the amygdala is important for fear conditioning.

- Each species is biologically predisposed to acquire particular CS–US associations on the basis of its evolutionary history, showing that classical conditioning is a sophisticated mechanism that evolved because it has adaptive value.

Operant Conditioning: Reinforcements From the Environment

- Operant conditioning is a process by which reinforcements increase the likelihood of behavior and punishments decrease the likelihood of behavior.

- Behaviorists tried to explain behavior without considering cognitive, neural, or evolutionary mechanisms. However, as with classical conditioning, this approach turned out to be incomplete.

- Operant conditioning has clear cognitive components: Organisms behave as though they have expectations about the outcomes of their actions and adjust their actions accordingly.

- The associative mechanisms that underlie operant conditioning have their roots in evolutionary biology, and different species are biologically predisposed to learn some types of association more easily than others.

Observational Learning: Look at Me

- Observational learning is an important process by which species gather information about the world around them and transmit novel behaviors across individuals.
- Chimpanzees and monkeys can benefit from observational learning.
- The mirror neuron system becomes active during observational learning, and many of the same brain regions are active during both observation and performance of a skill.

Implicit Learning: Under the Radar

- Implicit learning is a process that detects, learns, and stores patterns without the application of explicit awareness by the learner.

- Implicit learning can produce simple behaviors such as habituation, but also complex behaviors, such as language use or socialization.
- Neuroimaging studies indicate that implicit and explicit learning recruit different brain structures, sometimes in different ways.

Learning in the Classroom

- Research indicates that some popular study methods, such as highlighting, underlining, and re-reading, have low utility, whereas other techniques, such as practice testing and distributed practice, have high utility.
- Practice testing improves retention and transfer of learning and can also enhance learning and reduce mind-wandering during lectures.
- Judgments of learning play a causal role in determining what material to study, but they can be misleading.

Key Concept Quiz

1. In classical conditioning, a conditioned stimulus is paired with an unconditioned stimulus to produce
   a. a neutral stimulus.
   b. a conditioned response.
   c. an unconditioned response.
   d. another conditioned stimulus.

2. What occurs when a conditioned stimulus is no longer paired with an unconditioned stimulus?
   a. generalization
   b. spontaneous recovery
   c. extinction
   d. acquisition

3. What did Watson and Rayner seek to demonstrate about behaviorism through the Little Albert experiments?
   a. Conditioning involves a degree of cognition.
   b. Classical conditioning has an evolutionary component.
   c. Behaviorism alone cannot explain human behavior.
   d. Even sophisticated behaviors such as emotion are subject to classical conditioning.

4. Which part of the brain is involved in the classical conditioning of fear?
   a. the amygdala
   b. the cerebellum
   c. the hippocampus
   d. the hypothalamus

5. After having a bad experience with a particular type of food, people can develop a lifelong aversion to that food. This suggests that conditioning has a(n) _____ aspect.
   a. cognitive
   b. evolutionary
   c. neural
   d. behavioral

6. Which of the following is NOT an accurate statement concerning operant conditioning?
   a. Actions and outcomes are critical to operant conditioning.
   b. Operant conditioning involves the reinforcement of behavior.
   c. Complex behaviors cannot be accounted for by operant conditioning.
   d. Operant conditioning has its roots in evolutionary behavior.

7. Which of the following mechanisms have no role in Skinner's approach to behavior?
   a. cognitive
   b. neural
   c. evolutionary
   d. all of the above

8. Latent learning provides evidence for a cognitive element in operant conditioning because it
   a. occurs without any obvious reinforcement.
   b. requires both positive and negative reinforcement.
   c. points toward the operation of a neural reward center.
   d. depends on a stimulus–response relationship.

9. Which statement is true of observational learning?
   a. Although humans learn by observing others, nonhuman animals seem to lack this capacity.
   b. If a child sees an adult engaging in a certain behavior, the child is more likely to imitate the behavior.
   c. Humans learn complex behaviors more readily by trial and error than by observation.
   d. Observational learning is limited to transmission of information between individuals of the same species.

10. What kind of learning takes place largely independent of awareness of both the process and the products of information acquisition?
    a. latent
    b. implicit
    c. observational
    d. conscious

11. Which of the following statements about implicit learning is inaccurate?
    a. Some forms of learning start out explicitly but become more implicit over time.
    b. Implicit learning occurs even in the simplest organisms.
    c. People with amnesia tend to be severely impaired at implicit learning tasks.
    d. Children learn language and social conduct largely through implicit learning.

12. Responding to implicit instructions results in decreased brain activation in which part of the brain?
    a. the hippocampus
    b. the parietal cortex
    c. the prefrontal cortex
    d. the occipital cortex

13. Which study strategy has been shown to be the most effective?
    a. highlighting text
    b. re-reading
    c. summarizing
    d. taking practice tests

14. Which of the following statements is true about judgments of learning (JOLs)?
    a. People are generally good judges of how well they have learned new material.
    b. The feeling of familiarity with material is usually an indicator of whether the material is learned.
    c. Based on JOLs, people generally spend more time studying material they feel they know well.
    d. JOLs have a causal influence on learning.

15. Part of the value of self-testing as a study aid comes from:
    a. increasing the feeling of familiarity with the material.
    b. helping to sustain attention during initial learning.
    c. passive re-exposure to the material.
    d. decreasing the need to take careful notes during the lecture.

LearningCurve Don't stop now! Quizzing yourself is a powerful study tool. Go to LaunchPad to access the LearningCurve adaptive quizzing system and your own personalized learning plan. Visit launchpadworks.com.

Key Terms

learning (p. 194)

habituation (p. 194)

sensitization (p. 194)

classical conditioning (p. 195)

unconditioned stimulus (US) (p. 195)

unconditioned response (UR) (p. 195)

conditioned stimulus (CS) (p. 195)

conditioned response (CR) (p. 195)

second-order conditioning (p. 196)

acquisition (p. 196)

extinction (p. 197)

spontaneous recovery (p. 197)

generalization (p. 197)

discrimination (p. 198)

biological preparedness (p. 201)

operant conditioning (p. 202)

law of effect (p. 203)

operant behavior (p. 203)

reinforcer (p. 204)

punisher (p. 204)

fixed-interval (FI) schedule (p. 207)

variable-interval (VI) schedule (p. 207)

fixed-ratio (FR) schedule (p. 207)

variable-ratio (VR) schedule (p. 208)

intermittent reinforcement (p. 208)

intermittent reinforcement effect (p. 208)

shaping (p. 209)

latent learning (p. 211)

cognitive map (p. 211)

observational learning (p. 214)

implicit learning (p. 217)

Changing Minds

1. A friend is taking a class in childhood education. "Back in the old days," she says, "teachers used physical punishment, but of course that's not allowed anymore. Now, a good teacher should only use reinforcement. When children behave, teachers should provide positive reinforcement, like praise. When children misbehave, teachers should provide negative reinforcement, like scolding or withholding privileges." What is your friend misunderstanding about reinforcement? Can you give better examples of how negative reinforcement could be applied productively in an elementary school classroom?

2. A friend of your family is trying to train her daughter to make her bed every morning. You suggest trying positive reinforcement. A month later, the woman reports back to you. "It's not working very well," she says. "Every time Vicky makes her bed, I put a gold star on the calendar, and at the end of the week, if there are seven gold stars, I give her a reward—a piece of licorice. But so far, she's earned the licorice only twice." How could you explain why the desired behavior—bed making—might not increase as a result of this reinforcement procedure?

3. While studying for the psych exam, you ask your study partner to provide a definition of classical conditioning. "In classical conditioning," he says, "there's a stimulus, the CS, that predicts an upcoming event, the US. Usually it's something bad, like an electric shock; nausea; or a loud, frightening noise. The learner makes a response, the CR, to prevent the US. Sometimes, the US is good, like food for Pavlov's dogs, and then the learner makes the response to earn the US." What's wrong with this definition?

4. One of your classmates announces that he liked the last chapter (on memory) better than the current chapter on learning. "I want to be a psychiatrist," he says, "so I mostly care about human learning. Conditioning might be a really powerful way to train animals to push levers or perform tricks, but it really doesn't have much relevance to how humans learn things." How similar is learning in humans and other animals? What real-world examples can you provide to show that conditioning does occur in humans?

Answers to Key Concept Quiz

1. b; 2. c; 3. d; 4. a; 5. b; 6. c; 7. d; 8. a; 9. b; 10. b; 11. c; 12. d; 13. d; 14. d; 15. b

 LaunchPad
macmillan learning

LaunchPad features the full e-book of *Introducing Psychology*, the LearningCurve adaptive quizzing system, videos, and a variety of activities to boost your learning. Visit LaunchPad at launchpadworks.com.

Emotion and Motivation

The Nature of Emotion

Emotional Communication

The Nature of Motivation

The Motivated Body

The Motivated Mind

Leonardo does what you'd expect a 5-year-old child to do. He builds towers of blocks, does puzzles, and plays guessing games. But unlike most children, Leonardo isn't proud when he solves a puzzle or angry when he loses a game. That's because Leonardo has an unusual condition that has made him incapable of experiencing normal human emotions. He does not feel joy or sorrow, delight or despair, shame, envy, annoyance, excitement, gratitude, or regret. Never once has he laughed or cried.

Leonardo's condition has had profound consequences. For instance, interacting with people is quite challenging, and to do it, Leonardo has had to learn how to make just the right facial expression at just the right time — to pull his mouth into a smile when his interaction partner says something nice to him, or to raise his eyebrow once in a while to signal his interest in what they are saying. When his mother comes into the room, Leonardo knows that he is supposed to smile at her, and so he does. She's proud that he has mastered this trick, but she is also keenly aware of the fact that when Leonardo smiles he is simply "making faces" and that he is not actually feeling happy to see her. Most mothers would be bothered by this, but not Cynthia Breazeal. In fact, she's delighted. Because despite Leonardo's limitations, she still thinks he is the cutest robot she ever designed.

Most children experience happiness, fear, surprise, and anger. But Leonardo cannot experience these or any other emotions.
Alex Cao/Photodisc/Getty Images

Leonardo and his "mom," robot designer and MIT professor Cynthia Breazeal. Sam Ogden/Science Source

Learning Outcomes

- Understand how and why psychologists "map" emotional experiences.
- Explain the difference between appraisals and action tendencies.
- Explain the roles that the body and brain play in producing emotions.

It is almost impossible not to feel something when you look at this photograph, but it is almost impossible to say exactly what you are feeling. AP Photo/Stephen Morton

emotion A temporary state that includes unique subjective experiences and physiological activity, and that prepares people for action.

That's right. Leonardo is a robot. He can see and hear, he can remember and reason. But despite his loveable smile and knowing wink, he can't feel a thing — and that makes him infinitely different from us. Our ability to love and to hate, to be amused and annoyed, to feel elated and devastated, is a defining feature of our humanity. But what exactly are emotions? And why are they so essential? In this chapter, we'll explore these questions. We'll start by discussing the nature of emotions and seeing how they relate to the states of our bodies and our brains. Next, we'll see how people express their emotions and how they use those expressions to communicate with each other. We'll then examine the essential role that emotions play in motivation — how they inform us and how they compel us to do everything from making war to making love. Finally, we'll discuss a few of our most powerful motivations — those we share with other animals and those that make us uniquely human.

The Nature of Emotion

Are you alive? You probably answered that question quickly and in the affirmative. But what exactly does the word *alive* mean? Alive is not a thing you can point to. Rather, it is a state that is defined by many features, such as the capacity for reproduction, growth, metabolic activity, and so on. Some entities (such as you) have all these features and so are clearly alive; other entities (such as rocks) have none of these features and so are clearly not alive; and some entities (such as viruses) have a few of these features but not others, which makes it a bit more difficult to say whether they are alive.

Similarly, an emotion is not a thing. There is no place in the brain where it resides and no single way to measure it (Mauss & Robinson, 2009). Rather, an **emotion** is *a temporary state that includes unique subjective experiences and physiological activity, and that prepares people for action*. An emotion has many distinct features (Mauss et al., 2005). Its mental features include what a person thinks, feels, and is prepared to do; and its physical features include the activity of both the body and the brain. When a person's state at a particular moment in time has most or all of these features, we say that person is "experiencing an emotion." What are these features? Let's start by examining the mental ones.

The Emotional Mind

People all over the planet experience an emotion that has no name in English, but that in Sanskrit is called *kama muta* (Zickfeld et al., 2019). When people experience this emotion, they say they are feeling "moved to tears" or "touched." They describe the experience as "stirring" or "heart-warming." You've probably felt this emotion yourself, but how would you describe it to someone who hasn't felt it? You might try telling them about the circumstances that trigger this emotion (e.g., seeing someone making a sacrifice or giving a gift), or you might try telling them about what happens to your body when you experience it (your eyes get moist, your chest gets warm, and your throat gets tight). But in the end, both descriptions would fall a bit flat because one of the essential features of *kama muta* is the feeling of it — and trying to explain a feeling to someone who hasn't had it is a bit like trying to explain green to a person who was born blind. It feels like something to be moved to tears, and what it feels like is one of the emotion's defining features (Heavey et al., 2012).

Emotional Experience

If we can't easily describe our emotional experiences, then how can we study them scientifically? One way is by capitalizing on the fact that even though we can't always say what we are feeling, we usually can say how close one feeling is to another ("*Kama muta* is more like happiness than anger"). That's good news, because knowing how close a bunch of things are allows scientists to map them! Consider the table in **FIGURE 8.1** that lists the distance between — or "closeness" of — six U.S. cities. If you tried to draw a map using the numbers in the table, you would be forced to draw a map of the United States,

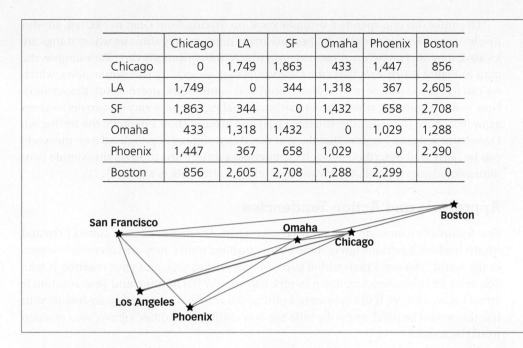

	Chicago	LA	SF	Omaha	Phoenix	Boston
Chicago	0	1,749	1,863	433	1,447	856
LA	1,749	0	344	1,318	367	2,605
SF	1,863	344	0	1,432	658	2,708
Omaha	433	1,318	1,432	0	1,029	1,288
Phoenix	1,447	367	658	1,029	0	2,290
Boston	856	2,605	2,708	1,288	2,299	0

Figure 8.1   From Distances to Maps Knowing the distances between things — like cities, for example — allows us to draw a map that reveals the dimensions on which they vary.

just like the one beneath the table. If you don't believe it, just try moving Chicago. You can't. If you move Chicago even a hair to the right, it will suddenly be too close to Boston and too far from Omaha. Chicago is in the one and only spot that allows it to be exactly 856 miles from Boston and 433 miles from Omaha, while still being 1,749 miles from Los Angeles — and the same is true of every other city on the map. So what does this have to do with emotional experiences? When people say how close two emotional experiences are, they are essentially estimating the "distance" between them, which allows psychologists to draw a map of the feeling-scape. The map of emotional experiences shown in **FIGURE 8.2** is the one that human beings most commonly produce.

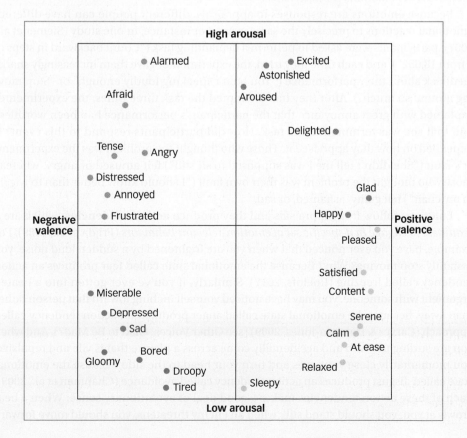

Figure 8.2   The Map of Emotional Experience Just as the locations of cities vary on two dimensions called longitude and latitude, emotional experiences vary on two dimensions called valence and arousal.

Of course, no one spends a summer vacation driving from Glad to Excited, so who needs a map like this one? We do, because maps don't merely show us where things are located; they also reveal the dimensions on which those locations vary. For example, the map in Figure 8.1 reveals that cities' locations vary on exactly two dimensions, which we call longitude (the east–west dimension) and latitude (the north–south dimension). Now look at Figure 8.2, which shows that emotional experiences vary on two dimensions as well: valence (how positive the feeling is) and arousal (how energetic the feeling is). Decades of research suggests that the emotional experiences of people all over the world can be fairly well described by each experiences's unique location on this simple two-dimensional map (Russell, 1980; Watson & Tellegen, 1985; Yik et al., 2011).

Appraisals and Action Tendencies

One feature of an emotion, then, is what it feels like. Another is where it comes from and what it leads to. Emotions rarely come out of nowhere; rather, they are reactions to events in the world. You see a man with a gun running toward you, and your reaction is fear. You see a little boy bending down to pick a flower for his mother, and your reaction is *kama muta*. And yet, if the man were a policeman who was coming to your rescue, your reaction would be relief, and if the little boy was visiting his mother's grave, your reaction would be sorrow.

Our emotions are responses, but they are not responses to events so much as to our interpretation of those events. Psychologists use the word **appraisal** to refer to *conscious or unconscious evaluations and interpretations of the emotion-relevant aspects of a stimulus or event* (Arnold, 1960; Blascovich & Mendes, 2000; Ellsworth & Scherer, 2003; Lazarus, 1984; Roseman, 1984; Roseman & Smith, 2001; Scherer, 1999, 2001). Research suggests that we naturally appraise events on a number of dimensions, such as the event's self-relevance ("Does this affect me?") and importance ("Does this matter?"), our ability to cope with the event ("Can I handle this?") and to control it ("Can I change this?"), and others. How we answer these questions — that is, how we appraise the events — influences the emotions we experience.

Because emotions are responses to appraisals, different people can have different emotional reactions to precisely the same event. For instance, in one study (Siemer et al., 2007), participants were asked to perform a demanding task ("Count backward in steps of 7 from 18,652"), and each time they tried, the experimenter gave them increasingly snarky feedback about their performance ("You aren't speaking loudly enough" or "Stop moving around so much"). After they had attempted the task three times, the experimenter explained with great annoyance that the participant's performance had been worthless and that she was terminating the task. How did participants respond to this event? It depended on how they appraised it. Those who thought the problem was the experimenter's fault ("She didn't tell me I was supposed to sit still") felt amused or angry, whereas those who thought the problem was their own fault ("I should know better than to wiggle in my chair") felt guilty, ashamed, or sad.

Emotions follow from appraisals and they produce **action tendencies,** which are *a readiness to engage in a specific set of emotion-relevant behaviors* (Frijda et al., 1989). For example, have you ever noticed that when you are frightened by a sudden loud noise, you instantly stop moving? Why? Because the emotional state called fear produces an action tendency called freezing (Roelofs, 2017). Similarly, if you've ever gotten into a heated argument with someone, you may have noticed yourself inching toward that person rather than away, because the emotional state called anger produces an action tendency called approach (Carver & Harmon-Jones, 2009) (see Other Voices: Glad to Be Mad?). And when you are surfing the Web and accidentally come across a picture that is vile and repulsive, you momentarily close your eyes and turn your head to the side because the emotional state called disgust produces an action tendency called avoidance (Chapman et al., 2009). Each of these action tendencies makes a good deal of evolutionary sense: When a bear growls at you, you should stand still; when an enemy threatens, you should move forward

appraisal Conscious or unconscious evaluations and interpretations of the emotion-relevant aspects of a stimulus or event.

action tendencies A readiness to engage in a specific set of emotion-related behaviors.

OTHER VOICES

Glad to Be Mad?

Tim Kreider is an essayist and cartoonist. His books include *We Learn Nothing* (2013) and *I Wrote This Book Because I Love You* (2018). Photo by Hayley Young, Courtesy Tim Kreider

Some emotions are positive and some are negative. Happiness is in the first category, sadness is in the second. But what about anger? You're probably tempted to say that it is a negative emotion because it often has such negative effects. But as it turns out, anger has many of the hallmarks of a *positive* emotion: It causes people to approach rather than to avoid, it lowers rather than raises the stress hormone levels in their bodies, and angry people often want to stay angry. Maybe that explains why so many Americans now use social media to stoke their own outrage: It feels *good* to get mad! The essayist Tim Kreider agrees, but thinks there is a dark side to joining the finger-pointing Twitter-mob. Let's listen.

America is generally supposed to have degenerated into a fat indulgent Babylon from its Puritanic origins, and yet the quaint old institution of the public pillory, and the lust for judgment and punishment, is alive and thriving on the internet. See the outing of patrons of the illicit-affair website Ashley Madison, or the campaign of hate against the dentist who mistakenly shot a lion that had a name. Even those who denounced on principle the invasion of privacy in the former case admitted they'd had a hard time repressing a throb of punitive pleasure. And pretty much everyone could feel good about joining the moral pile-on in the latter case, of a man who shot a big charismatic mammal.

. . .

I can understand this impulse; it's universal, one of the oldest and most popular of human pastimes. It's incredibly fun to hate someone's guts who deserves it, to press again and again, like a compulsive masturbator or a rat in a lab, the pleasure-center button of your own self-righteous loathing. A lot of people obviously adore being offended and outraged, casting blame and demanding apologies, at least as much as the less spiritually advanced love doing drugs or having sex. (There's more than a touch of that same pleasure in writing this essay about all the priggish little schoolmarms of the internet.) The insidious difference between moral judgment and those more ordinary vices — what makes it so much more dangerous — is that addictions at least present themselves to the afflicted as problems, whereas being judgmental feels, to those indulging in it, like a virtue.

Maybe this is just a difference of aesthetic taste. In the same way that some people are viscerally offended by hunting or adultery, there's something deeply repugnant to me about moral scolds. They're just ugly: shrill, nasty, humorless, their faces squinched up with prim, complacent hate.

. . .

About 94 percent of the discourse on the internet now consists of this gleeful jeering at someone else's disgrace. I may not condone the transgressor's misdeeds — they may even disgust me as much as they do everyone else — but as soon as this loathsome noise starts up, I find myself always instinctively on the side of the supposed offender. Seeing your own reactions mirrored by other people is instructively repulsive. (When you're flirting with a girl, you always feel you're being genuine and charming, but when you overhear some other guy hitting on someone, it's so transparent and sleazy it makes you cringe.)

I'm not a moral philosopher; I'm just some guy. But when I look at the shrine of hate erected at that dentist's office, or listen to the witch-trial hisses and spitting over the Ashley Madison scandal — or read those commenters who explain, with prim sanctimony, that the latest victim of a police shooting got what he deserved because he was, after all, breaking the law — all I know is, I'd rather be an adulterer than a stone-thrower.

to stop him; and when you see something totally gross, you should move away before you catch something. Action tendencies remind us that emotions are adaptive states that nature designed to ensure our survival.

The Emotional Body

Speaking of bears, what do you think would happen if you walked into your kitchen right now and saw one nosing through the trash? You'd feel afraid, of course. Your heart would start pounding, you'd begin to breathe heavily, and the muscles in your legs would tense as they prepared you to run away. In short, you would feel fear and that feeling would cause your body to respond.

But in the late 19th century, William James suggested that the feeling of fear does not cause these bodily responses; rather, these bodily responses cause the feeling of fear. According to James, first you see the bear, which causes your heart to start pounding, and then you have the feeling called fear, which is your perception of your body's response. The psychologist Carl Lange suggested something similar at about the same time, so this idea became known as the **James–Lange theory** of emotion, which states that *feelings are simply the perception of one's own physiological responses to a stimulus.* According to this theory, our feelings are the consequence — and not the cause — of our body's reactions to events in the world, such as the sudden appearance of bears in our kitchens.

James–Lange theory The theory that feelings are simply the perception of one's own physiological responses to a stimulus.

two-factor theory of emotion The theory that stimuli trigger a general state of physiological arousal which is then interpreted as a specific emotion.

This theory was original, elegant, and provocative — but as the physiologists Walter Cannon and Philip Bard noted, it can't possibly be right. They argued that the James–Lange theory was at odds with three basic facts.

1. Some emotional experiences happen before our bodily responses do. People feel embarrassed at precisely the moment their pants fall off in public, but the bodily response called blushing takes a full 15 to 30 seconds to occur. How could embarrassment simply be "the perception of blushing" if the feeling happens first?

2. Stimuli can cause bodily responses without also causing emotions. When your bedroom gets hot, your heart naturally starts to beat a bit faster, yet you don't feel afraid. If fear were merely "the perception of a rapid heartbeat," then why wouldn't you be scared every time your roommate cranked the thermostat?

3. For the James–Lange theory to work, every human emotion would have to be associated with a unique set of bodily responses — that is, every emotion would have to have a unique "physiological fingerprint," so to speak (Clark-Polner, Johnson, & Barrett, 2017; Siegel et al., 2018). And they don't! Different emotional experiences are sometimes associated with the same set of bodily responses, and different bodily responses are sometimes associated with the same emotional experience.

The James–Lange theory was broken from the start, and nearly a century later, psychologists Stanley Schachter and Jerome Singer (1962) tried to repair it. Like James and Lange, Schachter and Singer believed that our emotional experiences are based on our perceptions of our body's reactions. But instead of suggesting that a specific set of bodily responses correspond to each and every unique emotional experience, they proposed that there is just one bodily response (which they called "undifferentiated physiological arousal") and that how people interpret this response determines which emotion they experience (**FIGURE 8.3**). Their **two-factor theory of emotion** stated that *stimuli trigger a general state of physiological arousal, which is then interpreted as a specific emotion.*

According to this theory, when you see a bear in your kitchen, your body instantly goes on red alert — your heart pounds, your muscles tense, and you start breathing like

Figure 8.3 Classic Theories of Emotion The James–Lange theory suggests that different stimuli (e.g., your favorite singer and a growling bear) trigger different physiological responses that are then experienced as different emotions. The two-factor theory suggests that different stimuli trigger the same general physiological response, which is interpreted or "labeled" differently under different circumstances. Research suggests that neither of these classic theories is quite right.

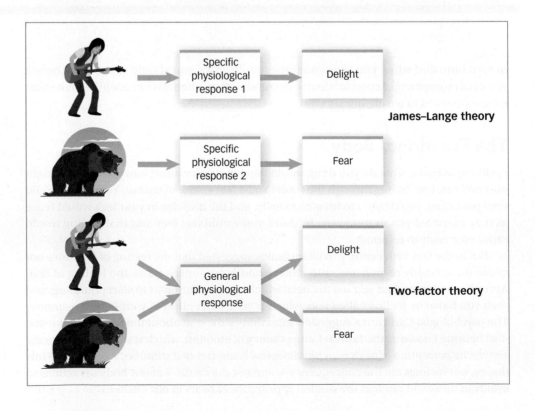

a marathon runner. Your mind notices this heightened physiological arousal and seeks to interpret it. It looks around the room; sees a bear; and, knowing something about how much bears like to eat people, it concludes the bear is causing you to feel fear. But, according to the two-factor theory, if you had seen a pair of cute kittens instead of a bear, your mind would have drawn a completely different conclusion—for instance, that you were feeling delight. The two-factor theory suggests that we have just one bodily response to all emotionally relevant stimuli, but that we interpret that response differently on different occasions. Different emotions are simply different interpretations of the same physiological reaction.

How has the two-factor theory fared? Modern research confirms that a single bodily response can indeed sometimes give rise to different emotional experiences, just as Schacter and Singer suggested. But modern research has not been so kind to the two-factor theory's claim that different emotional experiences are nothing but different interpretations of a single bodily response. For example, anger, fear, and sadness all produce a higher heart rate than disgust does; fear and disgust produce higher galvanic skin response (sweating) than sadness or anger do; and anger produces a larger increase in finger temperature than fear does (Christie & Friedman, 2004; Ekman et al., 1983; Kreibig, 2010; Levenson et al., 1990; Levenson et al., 1991, 1992; Shiota et al., 2011; Stemmler et al., 2007). It seems rather unlikely (as James and Lange maintained) that every human emotion has its own unique "physiological fingerprint," but it seems even more unlikely (as Schachter and Singer maintained) that every human emotion has precisely the same physiological fingerprint. The truth is probably somewhere in the middle, and modern researchers are working to determine exactly where in the middle it lies.

The Emotional Brain

In the late 1930s, two researchers made an accidental discovery (Klüver & Bucy, 1937, 1939). A few days after performing brain surgery on a monkey named Aurora, they noticed that she was acting strangely. First, she would eat just about anything and have sex with just about anyone—as though she could no longer distinguish between good and bad food, or between good and bad mates. Second, she was absolutely fearless and unflappable, remaining perfectly calm when she was handled by researchers or even when confronted by snakes, both of which monkeys generally don't much like. What had happened to Aurora?

As it turned out, during the surgery, the researchers had accidentally damaged a structure in Aurora's brain called the *amygdala,* and subsequent studies confirmed that the amygdala often plays an important role in producing emotions (Cunningham & Brosch, 2012). For instance, most people have better memory for emotionally evocative words such as *death* or *vomit* than for ordinary words such as *box* or *chair,* but this is not true of people whose amygdalae have been damaged (LaBar & Phelps, 1998) or who have been given drugs that temporarily impair neurotransmission in the amygdala (van Stegeren et al., 1998). Although people with amygdala damage do not feel fear when they see a threat, they do feel fear when they experience a threat—for example, when they suddenly find they can't breathe (Feinstein et al., 2013).

Together, these findings provide clues about what the amygdala does. Before an animal feels fear, it must know that there is something to be afraid of—in other words, it must generate an appraisal. The amygdala seems to play a part in that, helping to determine whether stimuli are emotionally relevant. The psychologist Joseph LeDoux discovered that information about a stimulus enters the eye and is then simultaneously transmitted along two different routes: a "fast pathway" that goes from the eye to the thalamus and then directly to the amygdala (shown in green in **FIGURE 8.4**), and a "slow pathway" that goes from the eye to the thalamus and then to the cortex and then to the amygdala

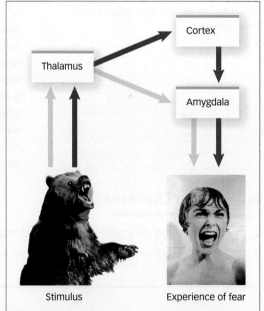

Stimulus   Experience of fear

Figure 8.4 The Fast and Slow Pathways of Fear Information about a stimulus takes two routes simultaneously through the brain: the "fast pathway" (shown in green), which runs from the thalamus directly to the amygdala, and the "slow pathway" (shown in red), which runs from the thalamus to the cortex and then to the amygdala. Because the amygdala receives information from the thalamus before it receives information from the cortex, a person can be afraid of something before he or she knows what it is. Bear: Jim Zuckerman/Getty Images; Woman: Snap/Shutterstock

(shown in red in Figure 8.4). As such, when you see a bear in your kitchen, information about the bear arrives at your amygdala and at your cortex at about the same time. While your cortex conducts a relatively slow, full-scale investigation of the information ("This seems to be an animal, probably a mammal, maybe a member of the genus *Ursus . . .*"), your amygdala uses the information quickly to answer a simple question: "Is this stimulus relevant to my survival?" If your amygdala's answer to that question is yes, it helps produce the bodily responses that, when your cortex is finally done with its investigation, you will come to call fear.

LeDoux's research shows how we get scared. So how do we stop? As Figure 8.4 shows, your amygdala receives information directly from your thalamus via the fast pathway (shown in green), but it also receives information from your cortex via the slow pathway (shown in red). This latter connection allows your cortex to "talk" to your amygdala — and one of the things it sometimes says is, "Chill out!" In a sense, the amygdala's job is to hit the emotional gas pedal, and the cortex's job is to hit the brakes. That's why adults who have cortical damage, and children (whose cortices are not yet well developed), often have trouble inhibiting their emotional responses (Cohen et al., 2016; Stuss & Benson, 1986). When people are asked to make themselves feel sad, afraid, or angry, they show increased activity in the amygdala and decreased activity in the cortex (Damasio et al., 2000); but when they are asked to make themselves not feel these emotions, they show increased cortical activity and decreased amygdala activity (Ochsner et al., 2002).

Does all of this mean that the amygdala is the brain's "fear center"? If only the brain were that simple! Although specific areas of the brain do seem to play special roles in the production of specific emotions — the anterior insula in disgust, the orbitofrontal cortex in anger, the anterior cingulate cortex in sadness — the fact is that the brain simply does not have different "centers" for different emotions (Lindquist et al., 2012). The amygdala's precise role in producing fear is complicated and still not very well understood (Phelps & LeDoux, 2005). There are times when the amygdala is highly active but people do not report feeling afraid, just as there are times when it is not highly active but people do report feeling afraid (Feinstein et al., 2013). What's more, the amygdala appears to play a role in emotions other than fear (Phelps, 2006). The bottom line is that we don't know exactly what the amygdala does, but we do know that the cortex and the amygdala — as well as other limbic and nonlimbic structures — work together in complex ways to produce the reactions of the body and the experiences of the mind that together constitute an emotion.

The tourist and the tiger have something in common: Each has an amygdala that is working at lightning speed to decide whether the other is a threat. Let's hope the tourist's amygdala is working a little faster. AP Photo/ David Longstreath

Build to the Outcomes

1. What are the two dimensions on which emotional experiences vary?

2. What is the difference between an appraisal and an action tendency?

3. What are some problems with the James–Lange theory?

4. How did the two-factor theory build on earlier theories?

5. How do the amygdala and cortex interact to produce fear?

Learning Outcomes

- Describe evidence for and against the universality hypothesis.
- Explain the facial feedback hypothesis.
- Describe how people deceive and detect deception.

Emotional Communication

Leonardo is a robot, so he can't experience emotions. But he can smile and frown, and wink and nod. Indeed, humans who interact with Leonardo quickly forget that he is a machine precisely because he is so good at *expressing* emotions that he isn't actually experiencing. An **emotional expression** is *an observable sign of an emotional state,* and although robots can be taught to exhibit them, human beings do so naturally. Our emotions influence the way we talk — from our intonation and inflection to the volume and duration of our speech — which is why observers can often guess our emotional state from our voice alone (Banse & Scherer, 1996; Cordaro et al., 2016; Frick, 1985;

Sauter et al., 2010). They can also often guess our emotional state from the direction of our gaze, the rhythm of our gait, or the way we touch them on the arm (Dael et al., 2012; Dittrich et al., 1996; Hertenstein et al., 2009; Parkinson et al., 2017; Wallbott, 1998). In some sense, we are all walking, talking advertisements for what's going on inside us.

Of course, no part of our bodies is more exquisitely designed for communicating our emotional state than is our face (Jack & Schyns, 2017). Beneath the skin of your face lie muscles that are capable of creating more than 10,000 unique configurations that enable you to convey information about your emotional state with an astonishing degree of subtlety and specificity (Campos et al., 2013; Ekman, 1965) (see **FIGURE 8.5**). Some of these configurations are reliably associated with specific emotional states (Davidson et al., 1990; Mehu & Scherer, 2015). For example, when you feel happy, your *zygomaticus major* (a muscle that pulls your lip corners up) and your *orbicularis oculi* (a muscle that crinkles the outside edges of your eyes) produce a unique facial expression that we call smiling (Ekman & Friesen, 1982; Martin et al., 2017).

emotional expression An observable sign of an emotional state.

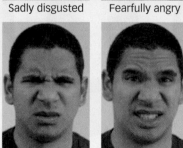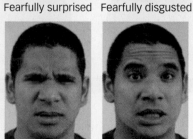

Happy	Sad	Fearful	Angry	Surprised
Disgusted	Happily surprised	Happily disgusted	Sadly fearful	Sadly angry
Sadly surprised	Sadly disgusted	Fearfully angry	Fearfully surprised	Fearfully disgusted
Angrily surprised	Angrily disgusted	Disgustedly surprised	Hatred	Awed

Figure 8.5 Human observers can identify at least 20 distinct facial expressions of emotion, such as those indicated here (Du et al., 2014). Image Courtesy of Aleix M. Martinez

universality hypothesis The theory that all emotional expressions mean the same thing to all people in all places at all times.

Communicative Expression

Why are our emotions written all over our faces? In 1872, Charles Darwin published *The Expression of the Emotions in Man and Animals,* in which he speculated about the evolutionary significance of emotional expression. Darwin noticed that human and nonhuman animals share certain postures and facial expressions, and he suggested that these "displays" were meant to communicate information about internal states. It isn't hard to see how such communications might be useful (Shariff & Tracy, 2011; Tracy et al., 2015). If a dominant animal can bare its teeth and communicate the message "I am angry," and if a subordinate animal can lower its head and communicate the message "I am afraid," then the two can establish a pecking order without any actual pecking. In this sense, emotional expressions are a bit like the words of a nonverbal language.

The Universality of Expression

Of course, a language doesn't work unless everybody speaks the same one, and that's what led Darwin to advance the **universality hypothesis**, which suggests that *all emotional expressions mean the same thing to all people in all places at all times.* For example, every human being naturally expresses happiness with a smile, and every human being naturally understands that a smile signifies happiness.

Evidence suggests that Darwin was partly right. Some facial expressions do seem to be universal. For instance, people who are congenitally blind and have never seen a human face smile when they are happy (Galati et al., 1997; Matsumoto & Willingham, 2009), and 2-day-old infants make a disgust face when bitter chemicals are put in their mouths (Steiner, 1973, 1979). People are also pretty good at identifying the meaning of the emotional expressions made by others, even members of other cultures (Ekman & Friesen, 1971; Elfenbein & Ambady, 2002; Frank & Stennet, 2001; Haidt & Keltner, 1999). In the 1950s, researchers took photographs of Westerners expressing anger, disgust, fear, happiness, sadness, and surprise and showed them to members of the South Fore, a people who lived a Stone Age existence in the highlands of Papua New Guinea and who at that point had had little contact with the modern world. When the researchers asked these participants to match each photograph to a word (such as *happy* or *afraid*), they found that the South Fore made matches that were very similar to those made by Americans.

But research also suggests that some emotional expressions—such as shame, happiness, and sadness—have distinct cultural "accents" (Elfenbein, Beaupré et al., 2007) (see **FIGURE 8.6**). Studies such as these suggest that the universality hypothesis has been overstated. It seems safe to say that human beings show considerable agreement about the emotional meaning of many facial expressions, but this agreement is short of being universal (Cordaro et al., 2018).

Nobuyuki Tsujii is a classical pianist who won the prestigious Van Cliburn International Piano Competition. Although he was born blind and has never seen a facial expression, winning a million-dollar prize immediately gave rise to a million-dollar smile. Kyodo/Newscom

Figure 8.6 The Faces of Pain and Pleasure Westerners and East Asians agree about how the face expresses the experience of intense physical pain, but they disagree about how it expresses the experience of intense physical pleasure. For instance, East Asians expect the physical pleasure of orgasm to produce an expression that is a lot like the expression of happiness, but Westerners expect it to produce an expression that is a lot like the expression of surprise. Distinct Facial Expressions Represent Pain and Pleasure Across Cultures. Chaona Chen, et al. PNAS Oct 2018, 115 (43). Copyright 2018, National Academy of Sciences.

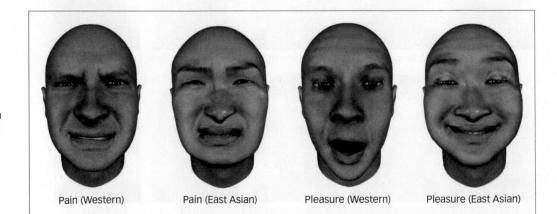

Pain (Western)   Pain (East Asian)   Pleasure (Western)   Pleasure (East Asian)

The Cause and Effect of Expression

You already know that emotions can cause emotional expressions — that happiness can cause smiling and sadness can cause frowning. But you might not know that it can also work the other way around. The **facial feedback hypothesis** (Adelmann & Zajonc, 1989; Izard, 1971; Tomkins, 1981) suggests that *emotional expressions can cause the emotional experiences they typically signify*. For instance, under the right circumstances, people feel happier when they are asked to hold a pencil in their teeth (which causes contraction of the zygomaticus major) than when they are asked to hold a pencil in their lips (Strack et al., 1988; see also Marsh et al., 2018; Noah et al., 2018; Strack, 2016). Similarly, when people are instructed to arch their brows (an expression of surprise), they find facts more surprising, and when they are instructed to wrinkle their noses (an expression of disgust), they find odors less pleasant (Lewis, 2012). These things happen because facial expressions and emotional states become strongly associated with each other over time (Ding! Remember Pavlov?), and eventually each has the power to bring about the other. These effects are not limited to the face: People feel more assertive when instructed to make a fist (Schubert & Koole, 2009) and more confident when instructed to stand with their legs spread and their hands on their hips (Carney et al., 2010).

The fact that emotional expressions can cause emotional experiences may help explain why people are so good at recognizing the emotional expressions of others. When people interact, they unconsciously mimic their interaction partner's body postures and facial expressions (Chartrand & Bargh, 1999; Dimberg, 1982). When our interaction partners smile, we smile, too (Foroni & Semin, 2009). Because facial expressions can cause us to experience the emotions they signify, mimicking our interaction partner's expressions can cause us to *feel* what our partner is feeling, which makes it easy for us to identify our partner's emotions. If your friend's frown makes you frown, and your frown makes you feel sad, then you don't have to think very hard to know what your friend is feeling.

That's why people find it difficult to identify other people's emotions when they are unable to make facial expressions of their own — for instance, if their facial muscles have been paralyzed with Botox (Niedenthal et al., 2005). People also find it difficult to identify other people's emotions when they are unable to experience emotions of their own (Hussey & Safford, 2009; Pitcher et al., 2008). For example, some people with amygdala damage don't feel fear and anger, and as a result, they are typically poor at recognizing the expressions of those emotions in others (Adolphs et al., 1999). On the flip side, the people who are naturally talented at figuring out what others are feeling also tend to be natural mimics (Sonnby-Borgstrom et al., 2003).

Deceptive Expression

Our emotional expressions can communicate our true feelings — or not. When a friend makes a sarcastic remark about your hairstyle, you may express your contempt with an arched brow or an exaggerated eye roll; but when your grandmother makes the same remark, you swallow hard and fake a smile. You know that it is okay to show a bit of contempt for a friend but not for a grandparent, and this knowledge is called a **display rule,** which is *a norm for the appropriate expression of emotion* (Ekman, 1972; Ekman & Friesen, 1968).

People in different cultures use different display rules. In one study, Japanese and American college students watched an unpleasant video of car accidents and amputations (Ekman, 1972; Friesen, 1972). When the students didn't know that the experimenters were observing them, Japanese and American students showed similar facial expressions of disgust; but when they knew the experimenters were observing them, the Japanese students masked their disgust with pleasant expressions and the American students did not. Why? Because in Japan it is considered rude to display negative emotions in the presence of a respected person, so Japanese people tend to mask or neutralize their expressions when being observed. The fact that different cultures have different display rules may be one of

facial feedback hypothesis The theory that emotional expressions can cause the emotional experiences they typically signify.

display rule A norm for the appropriate expression of emotion.

Jonathan Kalb is a theater professor at Hunter College who contracted Bell's palsy and lost the ability to make a smile. "For the past thirteen years, my smile has been an incoherent tug-of-war between a grin on one side and a frown on the other: an expression of joy spliced to an expression of horror. . . . The worst effect of my damaged smile is that it can dampen my experience of joy. . . . my brain doesn't receive the same feedback messages that normal people receive from their smiles, which reinforce their happy feelings as well as relaying them. I've been devastated by the loss" (Kalb, 2015). Jonathan Kalb

Figure 8.7 How Reliable Are the Reliable Muscles? Real smiles (left) are often accompanied by a crinkling of the eye corners, and fake smiles (right) are not. Eye crinkles are reliable signs of happiness. But not perfectly reliable signs! Happy people don't always crinkle their eyes (Crivelli et al., 2015), and although most people can't fake the crinkle, some can (Gunnery et al., 2013).

Courtesy Magda Rychlowska and Paula Niedenthal

the reasons that people are generally better at recognizing the facial expressions of members of their own cultures (Elfenbein & Ambady, 2002) (see A World of Difference: Say Cheese).

Of course, our attempts to obey our culture's display rules don't always work out. Anyone who has ever watched the runner-up in a beauty pageant congratulate the winner knows that voices, bodies, and faces often betray a person's true emotional state. For instance, most people can easily control the zygomaticus major muscles that raise the corners of the mouth but not the orbicularis oculi muscles that crinkle the corners of the eyes, which is why eye crinkles are a good clue to the sincerity of a smile (see **FIGURE 8.7**).

Lying

Sometimes people lie with their smiles, but just as often they lie with their words. Research shows that telling lies affects both our verbal and nonverbal behavior (DePaulo et al., 2003). Liars tend to speak more slowly, take longer to respond to questions, and often respond with less detail than do people who are telling the truth. Oddly enough, one of the signs that a person is lying is that their performance tends to be just a little too good. People who are telling the truth include superfluous details ("I noticed that the robber was wearing the same shoes that I saw on sale last week at Bloomingdale's and I found myself wondering what he paid for them"), they correct themselves ("He was six feet tall . . . well,

A WORLD OF DIFFERENCE

Say Cheese

African Americans, Asian Americans, European Americans, and every other kind of Americans live and work side by side, making the United States one of the most culturally diverse nations on earth. But diversity creates challenges, one of which is communication. Different cultures have different display rules — different ways of nonverbally expressing emotions — which suggests that Americans with different backgrounds should have trouble "reading" their neighbors. And yet, they don't seem to. How come?

To find out, researchers analyzed the accuracy with which people from 82 different cultures could recognize the emotional expressions of people from other cultures (Wood et al., 2016). First, the researchers used historical, genetic, and sociological data to compute the cultural diversity of each of the 82 cultures. Nations such as Brazil and the United States scored high in diversity, whereas nations such as Japan and Ethiopia scored low (see the accompanying map). Second, they computed how easily the facial expressions of people from each of these cultures could be recognized by people from other cultures. When they compared these two measures, they found a positive correlation. The more diverse a culture is, the more easily the facial expressions of its members can be understood

The diversity of cultures: Darker colors indicate greater cultural diversity.

by members of other cultures. Why might that be the case?

The researchers suggest that in nations with little cultural diversity, people can communicate with subtle expressions — a slightly raised eyebrow or the fleeting flare of a nostril — because everyone knows and follows the same display rules. But in diverse nations, people of different backgrounds follow different sets of rules, so to communicate with each other, they have learned to use expressions

that are so perfectly clear that they can be accurately recognized by any human on the planet.

Americans smile a lot (Talhelm et al., 2018), and non-Americans often take this as a sign of our optimism, our phoniness, or our naiveté. But that big, toothy American grin may actually be a clever solution to a knotty communication problem that results from our diversity. When faces speak many languages, they naturally learn to shout.

no, actually more like six-two"), and they express self-doubt ("I think he had blue eyes, but I'm really not sure"). Liars are less likely to do any of these things.

Given the observable differences between truth-tellers and liars, you might think that people would be pretty good at distinguishing one from another. But in most cases, participants in lie-detection experiments don't perform much better than chance (Bond & DePaulo, 2006; cf. ten Brinke, Vohs, & Carney, 2016). One reason is that people have a tendency to believe that others are telling truth, which explains why they tend to mistake liars for truth-tellers much more often than they mistake truth-tellers for liars (Gilbert, 1991). A second reason is that people don't know what to look for when trying to detect lies (Vrij et al., 2011). For instance, people believe that fast talking is a sign of lying when in fact it isn't, and they don't realize that slow talking is a sign of lying when often it is. Not only are people fairly bad lie detectors, but they also don't seem to know they are fairly bad lie detectors: The correlation between a person's ability to detect lies and the person's confidence in that ability is essentially zero (DePaulo et al., 1997).

When we humans can't do something very easily — such as adding huge numbers or lifting huge rocks — we often turn the job over to a machine. Can machines detect lies better than we can? Although several companies claim that they can use brain scans to detect lies, the scientific evidence suggests that they may not . . . um, be telling the truth. At present, at least, brain scans cannot tell us with much accuracy whether a person is lying (Farah et al., 2014). But what about the traditional lie-detecting machine — the polygraph? As you probably know, a polygraph measures a variety of physiological responses that are associated with stress, which people often feel when they are afraid of being caught in a lie. A polygraph can detect lies with better-than-chance accuracy, but its error rate is still far too high to make it reliable or useful. In short, neither people nor machines are particularly good at lie detection, which is probably why lying remains such a popular human sport.

The polygraph machine measures a person's blood pressure, pulse, respiration rate, and skin conductivity during questioning. Does it work? Aldrich Ames (shown above), a former CIA agent who is currently serving a life sentence in prison for selling state secrets to the Russian government, passed several polygraph exams before he was caught, and claims that fooling the machine is easy. Mark Wilson/Getty Images

Build to the Outcomes

1. What evidence suggests that facial expressions of emotion are or are not universal?

2. What are display rules?

3. What features distinguish between sincere and insincere facial expressions?

4. What is the problem with using a polygraph to detect liars in the real world?

The Nature of Motivation

Leonardo is a robot, so he does what he is commanded to do, but nothing more. Because he doesn't have wants and urges — doesn't crave friendship or desire chocolate or hate homework — he doesn't initiate his own behavior. He is reactive rather than proactive, a responder rather than an originator. The spark that you have but that Leonardo lacks is called **motivation,** which refers to *the internal causes of purposeful behavior.* You eat because you feel hungry and you sleep because you feel tired. You find friends because you feel lonely, you ditch friends because you feel bored. Everything you do, you do for a reason — but what are those reasons? Where do they come from? And how do they get you to act on them?

Instincts

When a newborn baby is given a drop of sugar water, she smiles, and when given a check for $10,000, she acts like she couldn't care less. By the time that baby goes to college, these responses pretty much reverse. It seems clear that nature endows us with certain motivations and that experience endows us with others. William James (1890) called the natural tendency to seek a particular goal an *instinct,* and he argued that nature hard-wired people, penguins, parrots, and puppies to want certain things without being taught to want them, and to execute the behaviors that produce these things without ever thinking about it.

Learning Outcomes

- Explain the concept of instinct, and why behaviorists rejected it.
- Describe the concept of drive.
- Explain the hedonic principle and how it influences emotion regulation.

motivation The internal causes of purposeful behavior.

All animals are born with instincts. In the annual running of the bulls in Pamplona, Spain, no one has to teach the bulls to chase the runners, and no one has to teach the runners to flee. AP Photo/Lalo R. Villar

But by 1930, the term *instinct* had fallen out of fashion, in part because it flew in the face of American psychology's hot new trend — behaviorism — which you learned about in the Evolution of Psychological Science and Learning chapters. Behaviorists rejected the concept of instinct on two grounds. First, they believed that behaviors were fully explained by the external stimuli that elicited them and that there was no need to hypothesize about internal states; and second, behaviorists believed that complex behaviors were learned, not hard-wired. Instincts violated these maxims. They were inborn and internal, and therefore of little theoretical value to behaviorists.

Drives

Behaviorists didn't have much use for internal states, but that made it difficult for them to explain certain phenomena. For example, if all behavior is simply a response to an external stimulus, then why does a rat that is sitting quietly in its cage suddenly get up and start wandering around, looking for food? Nothing in the environment has changed, so why has the rat's behavior changed? What visible, measurable, external stimulus is the wandering rat responding to? The obvious answer is that the rat is not responding to an external stimulus but to an internal stimulus, which meant that psychologists were going to have to talk about what happens inside a rat if they were going to explain its behavior. But how could they do that without talking about a rat's "beliefs" and "desires"?

By talking about thermostats. When a thermostat senses that the room is too cold, it sends a signal to the furnace to fire itself up and start blowing heat into the room. Later, when the thermostat senses that the room has reached the optimal temperature, it sends a signal to the furnace to turn itself off and stop blowing heat. When a room is at the optimal temperature, a thermostat is said to be in equilibrium (from the Latin words for "equal" and "balance"). It isn't telling the furnace to turn itself on or to shut itself off. It's just hanging out there on the wall, happily doing nothing.

The brain and body work the same way. The brain monitors the body — its hydration, its glucose levels, its temperature, and so on. When it senses that the body is in disequilibrium, it sends a signal to initiate a corrective action such as drinking, eating, shivering, and so on. When later it senses that equilibrium has been restored, it sends a signal to terminate those actions. The language of equilibrium provided a convenient way for behaviorists to talk about the inside of a rat without talking about its beliefs and desires. According to Clark Hull, one of the most important behaviorists of his day, disequilibrium produces a "need," which Hull called a drive, and his **drive-reduction theory** suggested that *the primary motivation of all organisms is to reduce their drives*. According to this theory, animals are not actually motivated to eat and don't actually find food rewarding. Rather, they are motivated to reduce their drive for food, and it is the reduction of this drive that they find rewarding.

Although the words *instinct* and *drive* are no longer widely used in psychology, both concepts still have something to teach us. The concept of instinct reminds us that nature endows us with certain desires, and the concept of drive reminds us that our actions are often attempts to fulfill them. So what kinds of desires do we have?

The Hedonic Principle

Of all the many things that people are motivated to do, experiencing positive emotion and avoiding negative emotion is chief among them. The **hedonic principle** is *the claim that people are primarily motivated to experience pleasure and avoid pain*. Although we want many things, from peace and prosperity to health and security, we want them for just one reason: They make us happy. Even when we purposefully do things that feel bad, such as paying the dentist to drill our teeth or waking up early for a boring class, we are doing these things because we believe they will make us feel even better later (Michaela et al., 2009; Miyamoto et al., 2014; Tamir & Ford, 2012; Tamir et al., 2015).

drive-reduction theory A theory suggesting that the primary motivation of all organisms is to reduce their drives.

hedonic principle The claim that people are motivated to experience pleasure and avoid pain.

So how do we accomplish that goal? **Emotion regulation** refers to *the strategies people use to influence their own emotional experience*. Nine out of 10 people report that they attempt to regulate their emotional experience at least once a day (Gross, 1998), and they report more than a thousand different strategies for doing so (Parkinson & Totterdell, 1999). Some of these strategies are behavioral (e.g., avoiding situations that trigger unwanted emotions) and some are cognitive (e.g., recruiting memories that trigger the desired emotion); (Webb et al., 2012), but regardless of how they work, people seem to have a poor understanding of which are most effective (Heiy & Cheavens, 2014; Troy et al., 2018).

For example, most people think that *suppression*, which involves inhibiting the outward signs of an emotion, is an effective way to regulate their emotional state. If you're glum, just stand up straight, keep a stiff upper lip, and you'll jolly well feel better in no time! Except that it isn't true (Gross, 2002; Kalokerinos et al., 2015). Not only is suppression a relatively ineffective way to regulate emotions, but it also requires a lot of effort and therefore makes it harder for people to function successfully in their everyday lives (Franchow & Suchy, 2015). On the other hand, most people think that *affect labeling*, which involves putting one's feelings into words, has little or no impact on their emotions. But in fact, affect labeling turns out to be quite an effective way to reduce the intensity of emotional states (Lieberman et al., 2011; Torre & Lieberman, 2018); (see **FIGURE 8.8**).

One of the best strategies for emotion regulation is **reappraisal,** which involves *changing one's emotional experience by changing the way one thinks about the emotion-eliciting stimulus* (Gross, 1998). In one study, participants' brains were scanned as they saw photos that induced negative emotions, such as a photo of a woman crying during a funeral. Some participants were then asked to reappraise the picture, for example, by imagining that the woman in the photo was at a wedding rather than a funeral. The results showed that when participants initially saw the photo, their amygdala was activated; but when they reappraised the picture, their cortex was activated and moments later their amygdala was deactivated (Ochsner et al., 2002). In other words, participants were able to reduce the activity of their own amygdala simply by thinking about the photo in a different way.

Reappraisal is a skill. Like most skills, it can be learned (Denny & Ochsner, 2014; Smith et al., 2018), and like most skills, some people are naturally better at it than others (Malooly et al., 2013). People who are especially good at reappraisal tend to be both mentally and physically healthier (Davidson et al., 2000; Gross & Muñoz, 1995), and to have better relationships (Cooke et al., 2018; Bloch et al., 2014). This should not be surprising, given that reappraisal is one of the skills that therapists commonly try to teach people who are dealing with emotional problems (Jamieson et al., 2013). On the other hand, this skill has a dark side: People who are good at changing how they see things in order to feel better about the things they see can be less compassionate toward those who are suffering (Cameron & Payne, 2011). Given how effective reappraisal is, you might expect people to do it all the time, but you'd be wrong (Heiy & Cheavens, 2014). People tend to underutilize reappraisal in part because it is a strategy that requires some effort to implement (Milyavsky et al., 2018).

emotion regulation The strategies people use to influence their own emotional experiences.

reappraisal The process of changing one's emotional experience by changing the way one thinks about the emotion-eliciting stimulus.

Hours before and after the "I feel" tweet

> **Daniel Gilbert** ✔ @ DanTGilbert . Feb 20 ⌄
>
> I feel sad because the Patriots always win, which makes my friends jealous so they hate me.

Figure 8.8 Labeling Affect with 140 Characters Researchers analyzed the emotional content of the tweets of nearly 75,000 Twitter users over time and discovered that when a user's tweet includes the phrase "I feel" followed by a negative emotion word, within an hour that user's tweets begin to contain much more positive emotion words (Fan et al., 2019). One interpretation of this finding is that labeling their negative emotions helped users overcome them.

Build to the Outcomes

1. How are emotions and motivations related?
2. Why did psychologists abandon the concept of instinct?
3. What is drive-reduction theory?
4. What is the hedonic principle?
5. What are two effective strategies for emotion regulation?

Learning Outcomes

- Describe Maslow's hierarchy of needs.
- Explain how hunger signals get turned on and off.
- Identify the common eating disorders.
- Understand what causes obesity and how it can be prevented.
- Describe the role that hormones play in sexual interest.

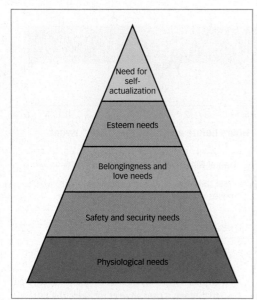

Figure 8.9 Maslow's Hierarchy of Needs The psychologist Abraham Maslow believed that needs form a hierarchy, with physiological needs at the bottom and self-actualization needs at the top.

binge eating disorder (BED) An eating disorder characterized by recurrent and uncontrolled episodes of eating a large number of calories in a short time.

The Motivated Body

People like to feel good. How do they do it? The psychologist Abraham Maslow (1954) believed that people feel good when their needs are met, and he suggested that the list of human needs can be organized by how "pressing" each of those needs is. Maslow designed a hierarchy (see **FIGURE 8.9**) with the most pressing human needs at the bottom and the least pressing needs at the top, and suggested that as a rule, people do not experience a need until the needs below it are met. According to Maslow, people are motivated to experience intellectual fulfillment and moral clarity, but they do not experience this need until their more basic needs for food, water, and sleep are met. In Maslow's hierarchy, the most pressing needs are those we share with other animals, such as the need to eat and the need to mate (Kenrick et al., 2010). Let's start by examining one of the most basic of all needs — a need you had recently had and will have again soon.

Hunger

Animals convert matter into energy by eating, and the drive to eat is called *hunger*. But what exactly is hunger and how is it produced? At every moment, your body is sending reports to your brain about its current energy state. If your body has insufficient energy (i.e., if it is in disequilibrium), it sends a signal to your brain telling it to switch hunger on, and if your body has sufficient energy, it sends a signal to your brain telling it to switch hunger off (Gropp et al., 2005). No one knows precisely what these signals are or how they are sent and received, but research has identified a few candidates.

For example, *ghrelin* is a hormone that is produced in the stomach and appears to be one of the signals that tells the brain to switch hunger *on* (Inui, 2001; Nakazato et al., 2001). When people are injected with ghrelin, they become intensely hungry and eat about 30% more than usual (Wren et al., 2001). In contrast, *leptin* is a chemical secreted by fat cells, and it is a signal that tells the brain to switch hunger *off*. People who are born with a leptin deficiency have trouble controlling their appetites (Montague et al., 1997). Some researchers think the idea that chemicals turn hunger on and off is far too simple. In fact, they argue, there is no general drive called hunger, but rather, there are many different hungers, each of which is a response to a unique nutritional deficit and each of which is switched on by a unique chemical messenger (Rozin & Kalat, 1971). For example, rats that are deprived of protein will seek proteins while turning down fats and carbohydrates, suggesting that they are experiencing a specific "protein hunger" and not a general hunger (Rozin, 1968).

We do not know whether hunger is one signal or many, but we do know that the primary receiver of these signals is the hypothalamus. Different parts of the hypothalamus receive different signals (see **FIGURE 8.10**). The *lateral hypothalamus* receives "hunger-on" signals, and when it is destroyed, animals sitting in a cage full of food will starve themselves to death. The *ventromedial hypothalamus* receives "hunger-off" signals, and when it is destroyed, animals will gorge themselves to the point of illness and obesity (Miller, 1960; Steinbaum & Miller, 1965). These two structures were once thought to be the "hunger center" and the "satiety center" of the brain, respectively, but this view turned out to be far too simple (Woods et al., 1998). Hypothalamic structures clearly play an important role in turning hunger on and off, but the precise way in which they execute these functions remains poorly understood (Stellar & Stellar, 1985).

Eating Disorders

Feelings of hunger tell most of us when to start and stop eating. But for the 10 to 30 million Americans who have eating disorders, eating is a much more complicated affair (Hoek & van Hoeken, 2003; Hudson et al., 2006). Let's take a quick look at three of the better-known eating disorders.

- **Binge eating disorder** (or BED) is *an eating disorder characterized by recurrent and uncontrolled episodes of consuming a large number of calories in a short time.*

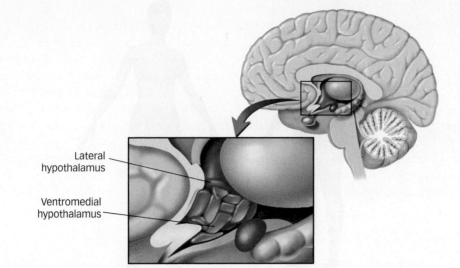

Figure 8.10 Hunger, Satiety, and the Hypothalamus In general, the lateral hypothalamus receives signals that turn hunger on and the ventromedial hypothalamus receives signals that turn hunger off.

People with BED quickly consume large quantities of food over a period of just a few hours, often at night. They frequently report feeling a lack of control over their own behavior — a sense that they "just can't stop eating."

- **Bulimia nervosa** is *an eating disorder characterized by binge eating followed by compensatory behavior.* People with bulimia also binge, but then they take actions to compensate for their eating, such as fasting, excessive exercising, taking diuretics or laxatives, or even inducing vomiting to purge the food from their body. People with BED or bulimia are caught in a cycle: They eat to ease negative emotions such as sadness and anxiety, but then concern about weight gain leads them to experience negative emotions such as guilt and self-loathing (Sherry & Hall, 2009; cf. Haedt-Matt & Keel, 2011).

- **Anorexia nervosa** is *an eating disorder characterized by an intense fear of being overweight and a severe restriction of food intake.* People with anorexia tend to have a distorted body image that leads them to believe they are overweight when they may actually be emaciated. They tend to be high-achieving perfectionists who see their severe control of eating as a triumph of will over impulse. Anorexia is often fatal: It literally leads people to starve themselves to death.

The origins of these eating disorders appear to include genetic (Zerwas & Bulik, 2011), experiential (Innis et al., 2011), and psychological (Klump et al., 2004) factors, but culture may play a role as well (Hogan & Strasburger, 2008). For example, women with anorexia typically believe that thinness equals beauty, and it isn't hard to understand where that idea comes from. The average American woman is 5′ 4″ and weighs 169 pounds (Fryar et al., 2016), but the average fashion model is 5′ 10″ and weighs 119 pounds (Rosenbaum, 2016) (see **FIGURE 8.11**). Although American women's satisfaction with their bodies has increased in the past 30 years (Karazsia et al., 2017), the pressure to be thin remains strong. Anorexia primarily affects women, but men have a sharply increased risk of becoming anorexic if they have a female twin who has the disorder (Procopio & Marriott, 2007), suggesting that anorexia may have something to do with prenatal exposure to female hormones.

Obesity

Bulimia and anorexia are serious problems, but they affect a small fraction of the world's population. The most pervasive eating-related problem today is *obesity,* which is defined as having a body mass index (BMI) of 30 or greater. You can compute your BMI simply by typing "BMI Calculator" into Google, but the odds are that you won't like what you learn. The proportion of U.S. children and teens who are obese has more than tripled since the 1970s

The model Yityish Aynaw was crowned Miss Israel in 2013, the same year that Israel became the first nation to ban advertisements showing models whose body mass index is below 18.5. In the years since, Italy, Spain, and France have all passed similar laws. Noam Galai/Getty Images

bulimia nervosa An eating disorder characterized by binge eating followed by compensatory behavior.

anorexia nervosa An eating disorder characterized by an intense fear of being overweight and a severe restriction of food intake.

Figure 8.11   The Real and the Ideal
These body simulations were made using the BMI Visualizer (http://www.bmivisualizer.com/), and, as you can see, the average American woman (left) and the average fashion model (right) don't look very much alike. Simulations © 2013 Copyright Max Planck Gesellschaft

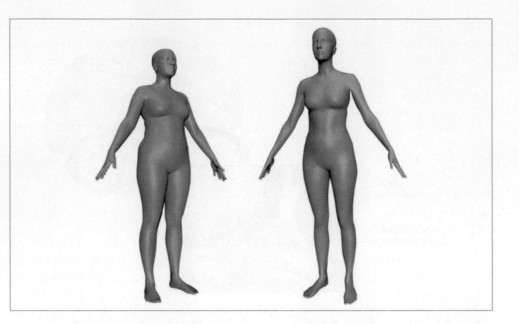

(Fryar et al., 2018), and in 2017, no U.S. state had an obesity rate lower than 20% (see **FIGURE 8.12**; also see Data Visualization: Have BMI and Food Consumption Changed Over Time? at www.launchpadworks.com). The best mathematical models suggest that the *majority* of today's American children will be obese by the time they are 35 years old (Ward et al., 2017). The problem is not unique to America: Nearly 30% of the world's population is overweight or obese, and no country has reduced its obesity rate in the past three decades (Ng et al., 2014).

Most researchers agree that an extremely high BMI is unhealthy. Every year, obesity-related illnesses take upward of 300,000 lives (Mokdad et al., 2003). In addition to the health risks, people who are obese tend to have lower psychological well-being, lower self-esteem, and lower quality of life, and they are viewed more negatively by others (Gallup, 2014; Hebl & Heatherton, 1997; Kolotkin et al., 2001; Sutin et al., 2015). The stigma of obesity is so powerful that average-weight people are viewed negatively if they have a relationship with someone who is obese (Hebl & Mannix, 2003). All of this is true, but sad. As one scientist noted, we need "a war on obesity, not the obese" (Friedman, 2003).

Obesity's Causes

Figure 8.12   The Geography of Obesity
These maps show the U.S. obesity rate in each state in 1990 (left) and in 2017 (right). Obesity is now a serious problem in every state, but especially in the nation's um… midsection.

The primary cause of obesity isn't much of a mystery: We eat too much. But why? After all, we don't breathe ourselves sick or sleep ourselves sick, so why do we eat ourselves sick?

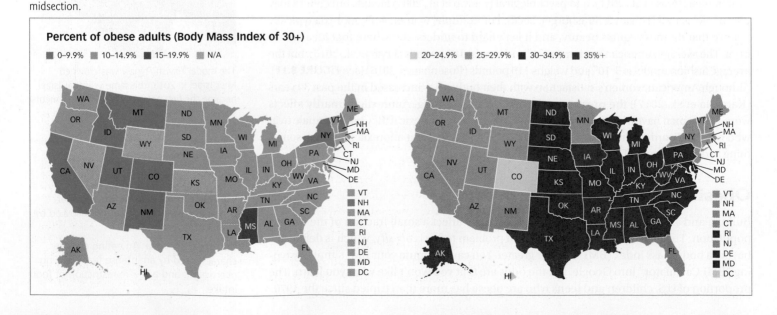

Percent of obese adults (Body Mass Index of 30+)

■ 0–9.9%   ■ 10–14.9%   ■ 15–19.9%   ■ N/A   □ 20–24.9%   ■ 25–29.9%   ■ 30–34.9%   ■ 35%+

Evolutionary mismatch refers to the idea that *traits that were adaptive in an ancestral environment may be maladaptive in a modern environment* (Mayr, 1942; Riggs, 1993). Hundreds of thousands of years ago, the main food-related problem facing our ancestors was starvation, and humans evolved two strategies to avoid it. First, we developed a strong attraction to foods that provide large amounts of energy per bite, which is why most of us prefer cheeseburgers and milkshakes to spinach and tea (see Hot Science: This Is Your Brain on Goldfish). Second, we developed an ability to store excess food energy in the form of fat, which enabled us to eat more than we needed when food was plentiful and then live off our reserves when food was scarce. These two adaptations allowed our species to survive in a world in which calorie-rich food was available only rarely, and the problem is that we don't live in that world anymore (Li et al., 2018). Instead, we live in a world in which the calorie bombs of modern technology—from chocolate cupcakes to sausage pizzas—are inexpensive and readily available (Simpson & Raubenheimer, 2014).

There are other reasons we eat too much. For example, people often eat when they are sad or anxious, or when it is convenient, or when everyone else is doing it (Herman et al., 2003). Sometimes we eat simply because the clock tells us we should, which is why people with amnesia will happily eat a second lunch shortly after finishing an unremembered first one (Rozin et al., 1998). Obesity is also highly heritable (Allison et al., 1996), which suggests that it may have a biological or genetic component. In addition, some studies suggest that toxins in the environment can disrupt the functioning of the endocrine system and predispose people to obesity (Grün & Blumberg, 2006; Newbold et al., 2005), some suggest that obesity can be caused by a dearth of "good bacteria" in the gut (Liou et al., 2013), some suggest that obesity can result from everyday wear-and-tear on the hippocampus (Stevenson & Francis, 2017), and some suggest that the brains of people who are obese are simply more sensitive to rewards (Stice & Yokum, 2016). Whatever the causes, people who are obese are often leptin-resistant (i.e., their brains do not respond to the chemical signal that tells the brain to shut hunger off), and even leptin injections don't seem to help (Friedman & Halaas, 1998; Heymsfield et al., 1999).

Conquering Obesity

Our brains and bodies were engineered for a very different world than this one, which is why it is so easy for us to bulk up and so hard for us to slim down. Just as our bodies seek weight gain, they resist weight loss, and they do this in two ways.

- When we gain weight, we experience an increase in both the size and the number of fat cells in our bodies (usually in our abdomens if we are male and in our thighs and buttocks if we are female). When we lose weight, the size of our fat cells decreases, but the number does not. Once our bodies have added a fat cell, that cell is with us pretty much forever. It may become smaller when we lose weight, but it is unlikely to die. It's always there, just waiting to be re-enlarged.

- Our bodies respond to dieting by decreasing our **metabolism,** which is *the rate at which the body uses energy*. When our bodies sense that there is a famine (which is what they conclude when we refuse to feed them), they find more efficient ways to turn food into fat. This was a great trick for our ancestors, but it is a real problem for us.

All of this explains why avoiding obesity is easier than overcoming it (Casazza et al., 2013). And avoiding it is exactly what some psychologists are trying to help people do by using small interventions that have a big impact (Thaler & Sunstein, 2008). For instance, one study showed that placing hard-boiled eggs just a few inches away from the more healthful ingredients in a salad bar led people to eat 10% fewer eggs (Rozin et al., 2011). Ten percent of an egg may not sound like much to you, but if you are a person who eats two eggs every day, cutting that amount by just 10% would allow you to lose about 1.5 pounds every year, which would make you the slimmest person at your 25th high school reunion. People are less likely to order a sugary soft drink when it appears in the middle of a menu than at the top or bottom (Dayan & Bar-Hillel, 2011); they eat less when they are given a large fork rather than a small one (Mishra et al., 2012); and they

evolutionary mismatch The idea that traits that were adaptive in an ancestral environment may be maladaptive in a modern environment.

metabolism The rate at which the body uses energy.

Sea turtles suffer from evolutionary mismatch. When their eggs hatch on the beach at night, the hatchlings move toward the light. This tendency was adaptive in the turtle's ancestral environment because the ocean, which reflects moonlight, was the brightest thing around. But now the trait is maladaptive because hatchlings are lured away from the ocean by the lights of human habitats, where they inevitably perish. Rene Van Bakel/ASAblanca via Getty Images

One reason that obesity rates are rising is that "normal portions" keep getting larger. When researchers analyzed 52 depictions of the Last Supper that were painted between the years 1000 and 1800, they found that the average plate size had increased by 66% (Wansink & Wansink, 2010). Scala/Art Resource, NY

This Is Your Brain on Goldfish

Are there more calories in an avocado or a Snickers bar? If you are like most people, you'd guess that the candy has more calories than the fruit. And you'd be wrong. An avocado has about 50% more calories than a Snickers bar. Holy guacamole!

Don't feel bad. When it comes to estimating the caloric content of foods, most people haven't got a clue. But research suggests that people's brains may know things that the people who own them don't.

Researchers showed participants photos of 50 food items and then asked the participants to estimate how many calories each of the food items contained (Tang et al., 2014). Panel A of the accompanying figure shows the correlation between the actual caloric density (the number of calories per gram) of each food item and the participants' estimates of caloric density. The utterly flat line indicates that the correlation between these two measures was zero. In other words, the participants were completely unable to say which foods were calorie-rich and which were calorie-poor.

Next, the researchers asked the participants how much they would pay to eat each of the food items. Panel B shows the correlation between the actual caloric density of the food item and how much participants would pay to get a bite. That line has a positive slope, which means that participants were willing to pay more for the opportunity to eat foods that were calorie-rich than calorie-poor. Neural activity in the ventromedial prefrontal cortex (an area of the brain that is involved in computing the value of a stimulus) was also positively correlated with actual caloric content. In other words, the participants *wanted* to eat calorie-rich food, and *their brains responded positively* to calorie-rich food — yet the participants themselves could not say which foods were rich in calories!

People have been counting the calories in food for just a few decades, but their brains have been wanting and valuing food for hundreds of thousands of years. It appears that evolution has wired our brains to detect and delight in the calorie-rich foods that can best fuel them, even if we don't consciously know which foods those are. If you want to know how many calories are in that bagel or banana, just ask yourself how much you'd like to have a bite.

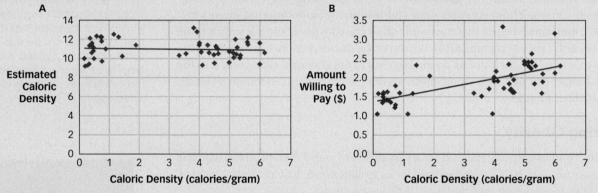

Panel A shows the correlation between participants' estimates of the caloric density and the actual caloric density of the food items. Panel B shows the correlation between the amount participants were willing to pay to eat the food items and the actual caloric density of the food items.

take less cake when they have to cut it themselves (Hagen et al., 2016). These and many other studies show that small changes to the environment can make big differences to our waistlines (Cadario & Chandon, 2019).

Sexual Desire

Food motivates us because without it we die. Although sex is not essential to our personal survival, it is essential to the survival of our DNA, and that's why evolution has wired sexual desire into almost everybody's brain. The general wiring scheme is simple: Glands secrete hormones that travel through the blood to the brain and stimulate our sexual interest. But the details of the wiring scheme are complicated.

Three hormones appear to play key roles. The hormone *dihydroepiandosterone* (DHEA) seems to be involved in the initial onset of sexual desire. Both boys and girls begin producing this slow-acting hormone at about the age of 6, which may explain why boys and girls both experience their initial sexual interest at about the age of 10. Two other hormones have more gender-specific effects. Both males and females produce *testosterone* and *estrogen,* but males produce more of the former and females produce more of

TABLE 8.1 Top 10 Reasons Women and Men Report Having Sex	
Women	**Men**
1 I was attracted to the person.	I was attracted to the person.
2 I wanted to experience the physical pleasure.	It feels good.
3 It feels good.	I wanted to experience the physical pleasure.
4 I wanted to show my affection to the person.	It's fun.
5 I wanted to express my love for the person.	I wanted to show my affection to the person.
6 I was sexually aroused and wanted the release.	I was sexually aroused and wanted the release.
7 I was "horny."	I was "horny."
8 It's fun.	I wanted to express my love for the person.
9 I realized I was in love.	I wanted to achieve an orgasm.
10 I was "in the heat of the moment."	I wanted to please my partner.

Information from Meston & Buss, 2007.

the latter. As you will learn in the Development chapter, these two hormones are largely responsible for the physical and psychological changes that characterize puberty. But are they also responsible for sexual desire in adults?

The answer is yes — as long as those adults are mice. Testosterone regulates sexual desire in male mice and estrogen regulates both sexual desire and fertility in female mice, and the same is true for most mammals. That's why most female mammals have little or no interest in sex except when their estrogen levels are high, which happens when they are ovulating or "in estrus." But humans are different. The level of estrogen in a woman's body changes dramatically over the course of her monthly menstrual cycle, yet her sexual desire changes little.

If estrogen is not the hormonal basis of a woman's sex drive, then what is? Two pieces of evidence suggest that the answer is testosterone — the same hormone that drives male sexuality. First, men naturally have more testosterone than women do, and they generally have stronger sex drives. Men are more likely than women to think about sex, have sexual fantasies, masturbate, want sex at an early point in a relationship, and complain about low sex drive in their partners (Baumeister et al., 2001). Second, when women are given testosterone, their sex drives increase. These facts suggest that testosterone may be the hormonal basis of sexual motivation in both men and women.

Men and women may have different levels of sexual drive on average, but they report similar reasons for having sex. For example, college students report having sex because they are physically attracted to a partner ("Alex has beautiful eyes"), to increase emotional connection ("I wanted to communicate at a deeper level"), to alleviate insecurity ("It was the only way Alex would spend time with me"), as a means to an end ("I wanted to be popular"), or for more than one of these reasons (Meston & Buss, 2007). Although men are more likely than women to report having sex for purely physical reasons, **TABLE 8.1** shows that men and women don't differ dramatically in their most frequent reasons. It is worth noting that not all sex is motivated by any of these reasons: About 1 in 15 U.S. adults reports having been forced to have sex at some time in their lives (Basile et al., 2007). We will have much more to say about sexual attraction and relationships in the Social Psychology chapter.

The red coloration on the female gelada's chest (top photo) indicates that she is ovulating and amenable to sex. Her mate therefore knows exactly when to guard her (to make sure that other males do not inseminate her) and when to go off in search of other mating opportunities. In contrast, the sexual interest of a female human (bottom) is not limited to a particular time in her ovulatory cycle, and her body displays no obvious signs of her fertility.   Michael Nichols/National Geographic/Getty Images; Jupiterimages/Stockbyte/Getty Images

Build to the Outcomes

1. Why do some motivations take precedence over others?
2. What purpose does hunger serve?
3. What causes BED, bulimia, and anorexia?
4. What causes obesity?
5. Why is dieting so difficult and ineffective?
6. Which hormones regulate sexual interest in men and in women?
7. Why do people have sex?

Learning Outcomes

- Explain the advantages of intrinsic and extrinsic motivations.
- Explain how rewards and threats can backfire.
- Explain when people become conscious of their motivations.
- Explain how we know that avoidance motivation is more powerful than approach motivation.

Mohammed Bouazizi was a fruit seller. In 2010, he set himself on fire to protest his treatment by the Tunisian government, and his dramatic suicide ignited the revolution that came to be known as the Arab Spring. Clearly, psychological needs — such as the need for justice — can be even more powerful than biological needs. Fethi Belaid/AFP/Getty Images

intrinsic motivation A motivation to take actions that are themselves rewarding.

extrinsic motivation A motivation to take actions that lead to reward.

The Motivated Mind

Survival and reproduction are every animal's first order of business, so it is no surprise that we are strongly motivated by food and sex. But humans are motivated by other things, too. Yes, we crave kisses of both the chocolate and romantic variety, but we also crave friendship and respect, security and certainty, wisdom and meaning, and a whole lot more. Our psychological motivations can be every bit as powerful as our biological motivations, but they differ in two important ways.

First, although we share our biological motivations with most other animals, our psychological motivations appear to be unique. Chimps and rabbits and robins and turtles are all motivated to have sex, but only human beings seem motivated to imbue the act with deeper meaning. Second, although our biological motivations are of a few basic kinds — food, sex, oxygen, sleep, and a handful of other things — our psychological motivations are so numerous and varied that no psychologist has ever been able to make a complete list of them (Hofmann et al., 2012). Nonetheless, even if you looked at an incomplete list, you'd quickly notice that psychological motivations vary on three key dimensions: extrinsic versus intrinsic, conscious versus unconscious, and approach versus avoidance. Let's examine each of these dimensions in turn.

Intrinsic Versus Extrinsic

Eating a potato chip and taking a psychology exam are different in many ways. One makes you chubby while the other makes you crabby, one requires that you move your lips while the other requires that you don't, and one is so pleasant that you'd pay to have it while the other is so unpleasant that you'd pay not to. But the most significant difference between these activities is that the exam is a means to an end and the potato chip is an end in itself. An **intrinsic motivation** is *a motivation to take actions that are themselves rewarding.* When we eat a potato chip because it tastes good, ride a bicycle because it feels good, or listen to music because it sounds good, we are intrinsically motivated. These activities don't *have* a payoff because they *are* a payoff.

Conversely, an **extrinsic motivation** is *a motivation to take actions that lead to reward.* When we floss our teeth so we can avoid gum disease, when we work hard for money so we can pay our rent, and when we take a psychology exam so we can get a college degree that will allow us to earn enough money to buy dental floss and pay rent, we are extrinsically motivated. None of these things is a source of pleasure in and of itself, but all can increase pleasure in the long run.

Extrinsic Motivation

Extrinsic motivation gets a bad rap. Americans tend to believe that people should "follow their hearts" and "do what they love," and we feel sorry for students who choose courses just to please their parents and for parents who choose jobs just to earn money. But our ability to engage in behaviors that are unrewarding in the present because we believe they will bring greater rewards in the future is one of our species' most significant talents, and no other species can do it quite as well as we can (Gilbert, 2006). In research studies of how well people can put off pleasure, or "delay gratification" (Ayduk et al., 2007; Mischel et al., 2004), participants typically have a choice between getting something they want right now (e.g., a scoop of ice cream today) or getting more of what they want later (e.g., two scoops of ice cream tomorrow). Studies show that 4-year-old children who can delay gratification are more intelligent and socially competent 10 years later and have higher SAT scores when they enter college (Mischel et al., 1989). In fact, the ability to delay gratification is a better predictor of a child's grades in school than is the child's IQ (Duckworth & Seligman, 2005). Apparently, there is something to be said for extrinsic motivation.

Intrinsic Motivation

There is a lot to be said for intrinsic motivation, too (Patall et al., 2008). People work harder when they are intrinsically motivated, they enjoy what they do more, and they do it more creatively. Both kinds of motivation have advantages, which is why many of us try to build lives in which we are both intrinsically and extrinsically motivated by the same activity — lives in which we are paid the big bucks for doing exactly what we like to do best. Who hasn't fantasized about becoming an artist or an athlete or Nicki Minaj's personal party planner?

Alas, research suggests that it is difficult to get paid for doing what you love and still end up loving what you do because rewards can undermine intrinsic motivation (Deci et al., 1999; Henderlong & Lepper, 2002). For example, in one study, college students who were intrinsically motivated to complete a puzzle either were paid to complete it or completed it for free. Those who received money were less likely to play with the puzzle later on (Deci, 1971; see also Lepper Greene & Nisbet, 1973). It appears that under some circumstances, people interpret rewards as information about the intrinsic goodness of an activity ("If they had to pay me to do that puzzle, it couldn't have been a very fun one"), which means that rewards can sometimes undermine intrinsic motivation.

Threats can have the same effect. For example, when a group of day care centers got fed up with parents who picked up their children late, some instituted a small financial penalty for tardiness. As **FIGURE 8.13** shows, the financial penalty did not decrease tardiness — it *increased* it (Gneezy & Rustichini, 2000). Why? Because most parents were already intrinsically motivated to pick up their kids on time. But when the day care centers started punishing them for their tardiness, the parents became extrinsically motivated to pick up their children on time — and because the price of tardiness wasn't particularly high, they decided to pay a small financial penalty to leave their children in day care for an extra hour. When threats and rewards change intrinsic motivation into extrinsic motivation, unexpected consequences can follow.

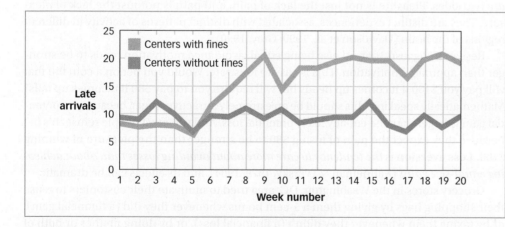

Figure 8.13 When Threats Backfire Threats can cause behaviors that were once intrinsically motivated to become extrinsically motivated. Day care centers that instituted fines for late-arriving parents saw an increase in the number of parents who arrived late.

Conscious Versus Unconscious

When prizewinning artists and scientists are asked to explain how they achieved greatness, they typically say things like "I wanted to liberate color from form" or "I wanted to rid the world of smallpox." They almost never say things like "I wanted to exceed my father's accomplishments, thereby proving to my mother that I was worthy of her love." Prizewinners can articulate their **conscious motivations,** which are *motivations of which people are aware,* but by definition they have trouble articulating their **unconscious motivations,** which are *motivations of which people are not aware* (Aarts et al., 2008; Bargh et al., 2001; Hassin et al., 2009).

Everyone has unconscious motivations. For instance, people vary in their **need for achievement,** which is *the motivation to solve worthwhile problems* (McClelland et al., 1953).

conscious motivations Motivations of which people are aware.

unconscious motivations Motivations of which people are not aware.

need for achievement The motivation to solve worthwhile problems.

Elon Musk is probably high in the need for achievement. The 49-year-old billionaire has built numerous companies, from PayPal and Tesla to SpaceX and Hyperloop, and he intends to build more. "I think it is possible for ordinary people to choose to be extraordinary," he said. "You should not give up unless you are forced to give up." Ray Tamarra/Getty Images

This basic motivation is typically unconscious, but research suggests it can be primed in much the same way that thoughts and feelings can be primed. For example, when words such as *achievement* are presented on a computer screen so rapidly that people cannot consciously perceive them, people will work especially hard to solve a puzzle (Bargh et al., 2001) and will feel especially unhappy if they fail (Chartrand & Kay, 2006).

What determines whether we are conscious of our motivations? Most actions have more than one motivation, and the ease or difficulty of performing the action sometimes determines which of these motivations we will be aware of (Vallacher & Wegner, 1985, 1987). When actions are easy (e.g., screwing in a lightbulb), we are aware of our most general motivations (e.g., to be helpful), but when actions are difficult (e.g., wrestling with a lightbulb that is stuck in its socket), we are aware of our more specific motivations (e.g., to get the threads aligned). For example, participants in one study drank coffee from a normal mug or from a mug that had a heavy weight attached to the bottom, which made the mug difficult to manipulate. When asked what they were doing, those who were drinking from the normal mug explained that they were "satisfying needs," whereas those who were drinking from the weighted mug explained that they were "swallowing" (Wegner et al., 1984). The ease with which we can execute an action is one of many factors that determine which of our motivations we are conscious of.

Approach Versus Avoidance

The poet James Thurber (1956) wrote: "All men should strive to learn before they die/ What they are running from, and to, and why." As these lines remind us, the hedonic principle actually describes two distinct motivations: one that makes us "run to" pleasure and another that makes us "run from" pain. Psychologists — being a lot less poetic and a bit more precise — call these **approach motivation,** which is *the motivation to experience positive outcomes,* and **avoidance motivation,** which is *the motivation to avoid experiencing negative outcomes*. Pleasure and pain may be two sides of the same coin, but they *are* two sides. Pleasure is not just the lack of pain, and pain is not just the lack of pleasure. They are distinct experiences, associated with distinct patterns of activity in different regions of the brain (Davidson et al., 1990; Gray, 1990).

Research suggests that, all else being equal, avoidance motivation tends to be stronger than approach motivation. This is easy to illustrate: Would you bet on a coin flip that will pay you $100 if it comes up heads but will require you to pay $80 if it comes up tails? Mathematically speaking, this should be an extremely attractive wager, because the potential gain is larger than the equally likely potential loss. And yet, most people refuse this bet because they expect the pain of losing $80 to be stronger than the pleasure of winning $100. **Loss aversion** is *the tendency to care more about avoiding losses than about achieving equal-size gains* (Kahneman & Tversky, 1979, 1984), and its effects can be dramatic.

Grocery stores in the Washington, DC, area tried to motivate their customers to reuse their shopping bags by giving them a 5-cent bonus whenever they did (a financial gain), or by taxing them whenever they didn't (a financial loss), or by doing neither or both of these things. As **FIGURE 8.14** shows, the prospect of losing money had a large impact on shoppers' behavior, but the prospect of gaining the same amount of money had no impact at all (Homonoff, 2013).

So what is the one thing that virtually every human being wants to avoid? Death, of course. All animals strive to stay alive, but only human beings know that all that striving is ultimately in vain, because no matter what you do, eventually you will die. Some psychologists have suggested that this knowledge creates a uniquely human "existential terror" that much of human behavior is an attempt to manage. **Terror management theory** is *a theory that suggests that people respond to knowledge of their own mortality by developing a cultural worldview*. A cultural worldview is a shared set of beliefs about what is good and right and true (Greenberg et al., 2008; Solomon et al., 2004). These beliefs allow people to see themselves as more than mortal animals because they inhabit

approach motivation The motivation to experience positive outcomes.

avoidance motivation The motivation to avoid experiencing negative outcomes.

loss aversion The tendency to care more about avoiding losses than about achieving equal-size gains.

terror management theory The theory that people respond to the knowledge of their own mortality by developing a cultural worldview.

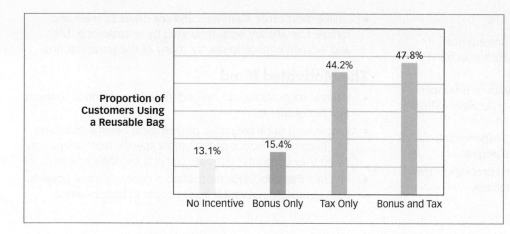

Figure 8.14 The Power of Loss
Avoidance motivation is typically more powerful than approach motivation. Shoppers in the Washington, DC, area were highly motivated to reuse their bags to avoid a 5-cent tax, but they were entirely unmotivated to reuse their bags to get a 5-cent bonus (Homonoff, 2013).

a world of meaning in which they can achieve symbolic immortality (e.g., by leaving a great legacy or having children) and perhaps even literal immortality (e.g., by being pious and earning a spot in the afterlife). According to this theory, a cultural worldview is a kind of shield that buffers people against the overwhelming anxiety that certain knowledge of their own mortality elicits.

Build to the Outcomes

1. What are intrinsic and extrinsic motivations?
2. Why should people delay gratification?
3. Why do rewards sometimes backfire?
4. What makes people conscious of their motivations?
5. What is loss aversion?

CHAPTER REVIEW

The Nature of Emotion

- Emotions have two underlying dimensions: arousal and valence.
- Emotions are reactions to an interpretation or appraisal of an event. Emotions give rise to action tendencies, which prepare people to act in particular ways that make evolutionary sense.
- The James–Lange theory suggests that a stimulus triggers a specific bodily reaction that produces an emotional experience. The two-factor theory suggests that a stimulus triggers general physiological arousal which is then interpreted as a specific emotion.
- Information about a stimulus is sent simultaneously to the amygdala (which plays a role in the rapid appraisal of the stimulus) and the cortex (which conducts a slower and more comprehensive analysis of the stimulus).

Emotional Communication

- The voice, the body, and the face all communicate information about a person's emotional state. Research suggests that some emotional expressions may be universal.
- Emotions cause expressions, but expressions can also cause emotions.

- People follow display rules that tell them when and how to express emotion. Different cultures have different display rules.
- There are reliable differences between sincere and insincere expressions, both verbal and nonverbal, but people are generally poor at telling them apart. The polygraph detects lies at a better-than-chance rate, but its error rate is far too high to make it useful.

The Nature of Motivation

- All organisms are born with some motivations and acquire others through experience.
- Drive-reduction theory suggests that disequilibrium of the body produces drives that organisms are motivated to reduce.
- The hedonic principle suggests that people are motivated to experience pleasure and avoid pain and that this basic motivation underlies all others.
- Research shows that people don't always use the most effective strategies to regulate their emotions. For example, affect labeling (which involves naming and describing one's emotions) and reappraisal (which involves changing the way one thinks about the emotion-eliciting event) are both effective but underutilized.

The Motivated Body

- Physiological motivations generally take precedence over psychological motivations in Maslow's hierarchy of needs.
- One of the most basic physiological motivations is hunger, which is the result of the complex interplay between different kinds of chemical messengers.
- Eating disorders and obesity have genetic, experiential, environmental, psychological, and cultural origins.
- Obesity is the most common eating-related problem in the world, and it is easier to prevent than to remedy.

- Unlike most other mammals, the sex drives of male and female humans are both regulated by testosterone. Men and women engage in sex for many of the same reasons.

The Motivated Mind

- Intrinsic motivations can be undermined by extrinsic rewards and punishments.
- People tend to be conscious of their most general motivations and become conscious of their more specific motivations only when they encounter difficulty carrying out their actions.
- The fact that avoidance motivation is generally more powerful than approach motivation leads people to be loss-averse.

Key Concept Quiz

1. Emotions can be described by their location on the two dimensions of
   a. appraisal and action.
   b. arousal and valence.
   c. instinct and drive.
   d. pain and pleasure.

2. Which theory suggests that emotions are people's interpretations of their own general physiological arousal?
   a. terror management theory
   b. the James–Lange theory
   c. the two-factor theory
   d. drive-reduction theory

3. Which brain structure is most directly involved in the rapid appraisal of whether a stimulus is good or bad?
   a. the cortex
   b. the lateral hypothalamus
   c. the amygdala
   d. the ventromedial hypothalamus

4. _____ is an emotion-regulation strategy that involves thinking about events in new ways.
   a. Affect labeling
   b. Intensification
   c. Suppression
   d. Reappraisal

5. _____ is the idea that emotional expressions can cause emotional experiences.
   a. Display rule
   b. Evolutionary mismatch
   c. The universality hypothesis
   d. The facial feedback hypothesis

6. The hedonic principle states that
   a. smiles mean the same thing in every culture.
   b. people are primarily motivated to experience pleasure and avoid pain.
   c. organisms are motivated to reduce their drives.
   d. some motivations are hard-wired by nature.

7. A natural tendency to seek a particular goal has been called an

   a. instinct.
   b. action tendency.
   c. unconscious motivation.
   d. appraisal.

8. According to Maslow, our most basic needs are
   a. self-actualization and self-esteem.
   b. shared with other animals.
   c. not experienced until higher needs are met.
   d. belongingness and love.

9. Which statement is true?
   a. Men and women engage in sex for many of the same reasons.
   b. Boys and girls experience initial sexual interest at very different ages.
   c. The hormone dihydroepiandosterone (DHEA) plays a role in the onset of sexual interest in males but not females.
   d. The human male sex drive is regulated by testosterone, whereas the human female sex drive is regulated by estrogen.

10. Which of the following does NOT provide any support for the universality hypothesis?
    a. People who are congenitally blind make the facial expressions associated with the basic emotions.
    b. Infants only days old react to bitter tastes with expressions of disgust.
    c. Robots have been engineered to exhibit emotional expressions.
    d. Researchers have discovered that isolated people living a Stone Age existence with little contact with the outside world recognize the emotional expressions of Westerners.

11. Which of the following statements is inaccurate?
    a. Certain facial muscles are reliably engaged by sincere facial expressions.
    b. Fast talking is not a reliable clue that someone is lying.
    c. Studies show that human lie detection ability is extremely good.
    d. Polygraph machines detect lies at a rate better than chance, but their error rate is still quite high.

12. Which of the following is NOT a dimension on which psychological motivations vary?

a. intrinsic–extrinsic
b. conscious–unconscious
c. approach–avoidance
d. appraisal–reappraisal

13. Which of the following activities is most likely the result of extrinsic motivation?

a. completing a crossword puzzle
b. pursuing a career as a musician
c. having ice cream for dessert
d. flossing one's teeth

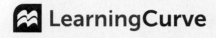 **LearningCurve** Don't stop now! Quizzing yourself is a powerful study tool. Go to LaunchPad to access the LearningCurve adaptive quizzing system and your own personalized learning plan. Visit launchpadworks.com.

Key Terms

emotion (p. 230)

appraisal (p. 232)

action tendencies (p. 232)

James–Lange theory (p. 233)

two-factor theory of emotion (p. 234)

emotional expression (p. 236)

universality hypothesis (p. 238)

facial feedback hypothesis (p. 239)

display rule (p. 239)

motivation (p. 241)

drive-reduction theory (p. 242)

hedonic principle (p. 242)

emotion regulation (p. 243)

reappraisal (p. 243)

binge eating disorder (BED) (p. 244)

bulimia nervosa (p. 245)

anorexia nervosa (p. 245)

evolutionary mismatch (p. 247)

metabolism (p. 247)

intrinsic motivation (p. 250)

extrinsic motivation (p. 250)

conscious motivations (p. 251)

unconscious motivations (p. 251)

need for achievement (p. 251)

approach motivation (p. 252)

avoidance motivation (p. 252)

loss aversion (p. 252)

terror management theory (p. 252)

Changing Minds

1. While watching the news, you and a friend hear about a celebrity who punched a fan in a restaurant. "I just lost it," the celebrity said. "I saw what I was doing, but I just couldn't control myself." According to the news, the celebrity was sentenced to anger management classes. "I'm not excusing the violence," your friend says, "but I'm not sure anger management classes are very useful. I mean, you can't *control* your emotions. They just *happen*." What evidence would you use to explain to your friend why they are wrong?

2. One of your friends has just been dumped by his boyfriend, and he's devastated. He's spent days in his room, refusing to go out. You and your roommate decide to keep a close eye on him during this tough time. "Negative emotions are so destructive," your roommate says. "We'd all be better off without them." How would you convince your roommate that negative emotions are actually critical for our survival?

3. A friend is majoring in education. "We learned today about several cities that tried giving cash rewards to students who passed their classes or did well on achievement tests. That's bribing kids to get good grades, and as soon as you stop paying them, they'll stop studying." Your friend is assuming that extrinsic motivation undermines intrinsic motivation. In what ways is the picture more complicated?

4. One of your friends is a gym rat who spends all his free time working out and is very proud of his ripped abs. His roommate is obese. "I keep telling him to diet and exercise," your friend says, "but he never loses any weight. If he just had a little more willpower, he could slim down." What would you tell your friend? What makes it so hard for people to lose weight?

Answers to Key Concept Quiz

1. b; 2. c; 3. c; 4. d; 5. d; 6. b; 7. a; 8. b; 9. a; 10. c; 11. c; 12. d; 13. d

 **LaunchPad** LaunchPad features the full e-book of *Introducing Psychology*, the LearningCurve
macmillan learning adaptive quizzing system, videos, and a variety of activities to boost your learning. Visit LaunchPad at launchpadworks.com.

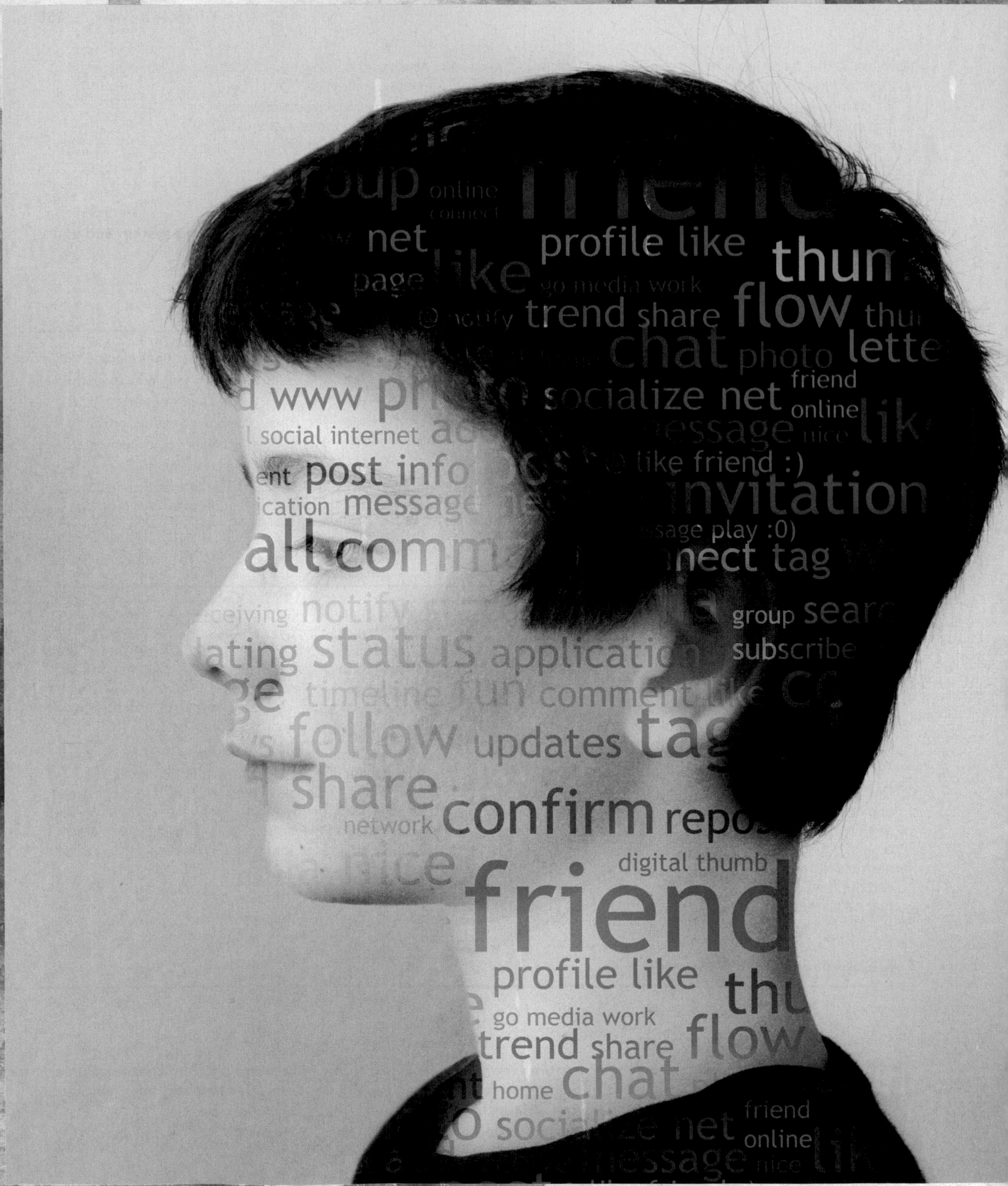

Muriel de Seze/Getty Images

Language, Thought, and Intelligence

9

An English boy named Christopher showed an amazing talent for languages. By the age of 6, he had learned French from his sister's schoolbooks; he acquired Greek from a textbook in only 3 months. His talent was so prodigious that grown-up Christopher could converse fluently in 16 languages. When tested on English–French translations, he scored as well as a native French speaker. Presented with a made-up language, he figured out the complex rules easily, even though advanced language students found them virtually impossible to decipher (Smith & Tsimpli, 1995).

If you've concluded that Christopher is extremely smart, perhaps even a genius, you're wrong. His scores on standard intelligence tests are far below normal. He fails simple cognitive tests that 4-year-old children pass with ease, and he cannot even learn the rules for simple games like tic-tac-toe. Despite his dazzling talent, Christopher lives in a halfway house because he does not have the cognitive capacity to make decisions, reason, or solve problems in a way that would allow him to live independently.

Christopher's strengths and weaknesses offer compelling evidence that cognition is composed of distinct abilities. People who learn languages with lightning speed are not necessarily gifted at decision making or problem solving. People who excel at reasoning may have no special ability to master languages. In this chapter, you will learn about several key higher cognitive functions: acquiring and using language, forming concepts and categories, and making decisions — the components of intelligence itself. You'll also learn about where intelligence comes from, how it's measured, and whether it can be improved.

Language and Communication: From Rules to Meaning

Concepts and Categories: How We Think

Decision Making: Rational and Otherwise

Intelligence

Where Does Intelligence Come From?

Who Is Most Intelligent?

Christopher absorbed languages quickly from textbooks, yet he completely failed simple tests of other cognitive abilities. zoom-zoom /iStock/Getty Images

Language and Communication: From Rules to Meaning

Learning Outcomes

- Describe the basic characteristics of language.
- Explain the milestones of language development.
- Compare the behaviorist, nativist, and interactionist theories of language development.
- Describe the language centers of the brain.

Most social species have systems of communication that allow them to transmit messages to each other. Honeybees communicate the location of food sources by means of a "waggle dance" that indicates both the direction and distance of the food source from the hive (Kirchner & Towne, 1994; Von Frisch, 1974). Vervet monkeys have three different warning calls that uniquely signal the presence of their main predators: a leopard, an eagle, and a snake (Cheney & Seyfarth, 1990). A leopard call provokes monkeys to climb higher into a tree; an eagle call makes them look up into the sky; and a snake signal makes them look down. Each different warning call conveys a particular meaning and functions like a word in a simple language.

Language is *a system for communicating with others using signals that are combined according to rules of grammar and that convey meaning.* **Grammar** is *a set of rules that specify how the units of language can be combined to produce meaningful messages.* Language allows individuals to exchange information about the world, coordinate group action, and form strong social bonds. The complex structure of human language distinguishes it from simpler signaling systems used by other species; it allows us to express a wide range of ideas and concepts, including intangible concepts such as *unicorn* or *democracy*.

The Structure of Human Language

There are approximately 4,000 human languages, which linguists have grouped into about 50 language families (Nadasdy, 1995). Despite their differences, all of these languages share a basic structure involving a set of sounds and rules for combining those sounds to produce meanings.

The smallest units of sound that are recognizable as speech rather than as random noise are called **phonemes**. These building blocks of spoken language differ in how they are produced. For example, when you say *ba*, your vocal cords start to vibrate as soon as you begin the sound, but when you say *pa*, there is a 60-millisecond lag between the time you start the *p* sound and the time your vocal cords start to vibrate.

language A system for communicating with others using signals that are combined according to rules of grammar and that convey meaning.

grammar A set of rules that specify how the units of language can be combined to produce meaningful messages.

phonemes The smallest units of sound that are recognizable as speech rather than as random noise.

Honeybees communicate with each other about the location of food by doing a waggle dance that indicates the direction and distance of food from the hive. DigitalVision/Getty Images; Media Bakery

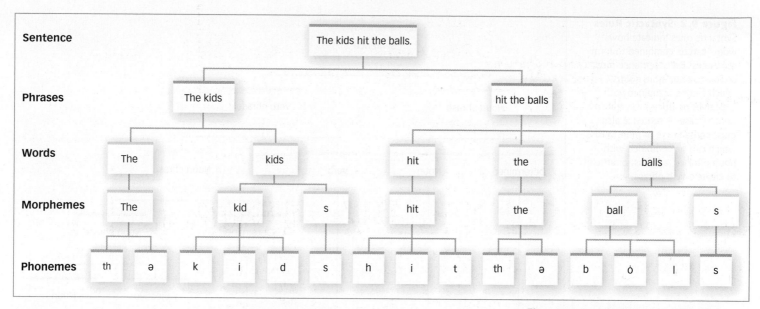

Figure 9.1 Units of Language A sentence can be broken down into progressively smaller units: phrases, morphemes, and phonemes. In all languages, phonemes and morphemes form words, which can be combined into phrases and ultimately into sentences.

Every language has **phonological rules** that *indicate how phonemes can be combined to produce speech sounds.* For example, the initial sound *ts* is acceptable in German but not in English. Typically, people learn these phonological rules without instruction, and if the rules are violated, the resulting speech sounds odd.

Phonemes are combined to make **morphemes**, *the smallest meaningful units of language* (see **FIGURE 9.1**). For example, your brain recognizes the *d* sound you make at the beginning of *dog* as a speech *sound,* but it carries no particular meaning. The morpheme *dog,* on the other hand, is recognized as an element of speech that carries meaning. Adding *s* to *dog (dogs)* changes the meaning of the word, so here *s* functions as a morpheme.

All languages have **morphological rules** that *indicate how morphemes can be combined to form words.* Some morphemes — content morphemes and function morphemes — can stand alone as words. *Content morphemes* refer to things and events (e.g., "cat," "dog," "take"). *Function morphemes* serve grammatical functions, such as tying sentences together ("and," "or," "but") or indicating time ("when"). About half of the morphemes in human languages are function morphemes, and it is the function morphemes that make human language grammatically complex enough to permit us to express abstract ideas rather than simply to point verbally to real objects in the here and now.

Words can be combined to form an infinite number of new sentences, which are governed by **syntactic rules** that *indicate how words can be combined to form phrases and sentences.* A simple syntactic rule in English is that every sentence must contain one or more nouns, which may be combined with adjectives or articles to create noun phrases (see **FIGURE 9.2**), and one or more verbs, which may be combined with adverbs or articles to create verb phrases. So, the utterance "dogs bark" is a full sentence, but "the big gray dog over by the building" is not.

Language Development

Language is a complex cognitive skill, yet we can carry on complex conversations with playmates and family even before we begin school. Three characteristics of language development are worth bearing in mind. First, children learn language at an astonishingly rapid rate. The average 1-year-old has a vocabulary of 10 words, which expands to over *10,000* words in the next 4 years, requiring the child to learn, on average, about 6 or 7 new words *every day.* Second, children make few errors while learning to speak, and as we'll see shortly, the errors they do make usually result from applying, but *overregularizing,* grammatical rules they've learned. This is an extraordinary feat. There are more

phonological rules A set of rules that indicate how phonemes can be combined to produce speech sounds.

morphemes The smallest meaningful units of language.

morphological rules A set of rules that indicate how morphemes can be combined to form words.

syntactic rules A set of rules that indicate how words can be combined to form phrases and sentences.

Figure 9.2 Syntactic Rules
Syntactic rules indicate how words can be combined to form sentences. Every sentence must contain one or more nouns, which can be combined with adjectives or articles to create a noun phrase. A sentence also must contain one or more verbs, which can be combined with noun phrases, adverbs, or articles to create a verb phrase.

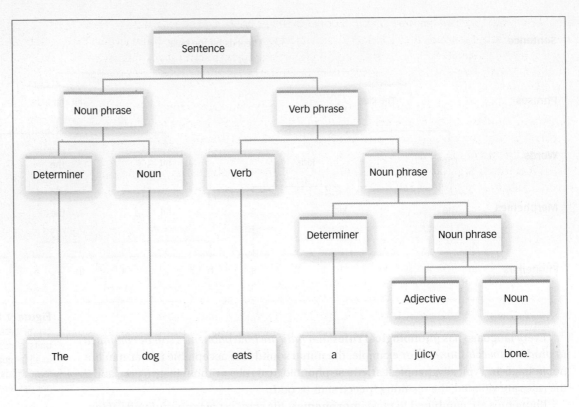

than *3 million* ways to rearrange the words in any 10-word sentence, but only a few of these arrangements will be both grammatically correct and meaningful (Bickerton, 1990). Third, at every stage of language development, children understand language better than they speak it.

Distinguishing Speech Sounds

At birth, infants can distinguish among all of the contrasting sounds that occur in all human languages. Within the first 6 months of life, they lose this ability and, like their parents, can distinguish among the contrasting sounds only in the language they hear being spoken around them. For example, two distinct sounds in English are the *l* sound and the *r* sound, as in *lead* and *read*. These sounds are not distinguished in Japanese; instead, the *l* and *r* sounds fall within the same phoneme. Japanese adults cannot hear the difference between these two phonemes, but American adults can distinguish between them easily — and so can Japanese infants. By the same token, American speakers do not hear many of the contrasts that are common in Japanese.

In one study, researchers played computer synthesized speech of a voice saying "la-la-la" or "ra-ra-ra" repeatedly (Kuhl et al., 2006). They used what is known as a "Head Turn" technique in which infants, seated on a parent's lap as in the accompanying photo, were trained to turn their head toward a lively visual display whenever a background speech sound (e.g., 'ra') was changed to a target speech sound (e.g., 'la'). Both American and Japanese infants aged 6- to 8-months turned their head toward the display when 'ra' changed to 'la' or vice versa, showing that they noticed the difference between the two sounds. At 10-12 months, American infants showed this effect even more strongly, but the Japanese infants showed decreased ability to discriminate the two sounds.

Infants can distinguish among speech sounds, but they cannot produce them dependably and so must rely mainly on cries, laughs, and other vocalizations to communicate. Between the ages of about 4 and 6 months, they begin to babble speech sounds. Babbling involves combinations of vowels and consonants that sound like real syllables but are meaningless. Regardless of the language they hear spoken, all infants go through the same

In this videotaped test, the infant watches an animated toy animal while a single speech sound is repeated. After a few repetitions, the sound changes, the display changes, then they both change again. If the infant switches her attention when the sound changes, she is anticipating the new display, which demonstrates that she can discriminate between the sounds. Courtesy Dr. Patricia K Kuhl, UW Institute For Learning and Brain Sciences

babbling sequence. For example, *d* and *t* appear in infant babbling before *m* and *n*. Even deaf infants babble sounds they've never heard, and they do so in the same order as hearing infants do (Ollers & Eilers, 1988). This is evidence that infants aren't simply imitating the sounds they hear; rather, it suggests that babbling is a natural part of the language development process.

For vocal babbling to continue, though, infants must be able to hear themselves. In fact, delayed babbling or the cessation of babbling merits testing for possible hearing difficulties. Babbling problems can lead to speech impairments, but they do not necessarily prevent language acquisition. Deaf infants whose parents communicate using American Sign Language (ASL) begin to babble with their hands at the same age that hearing children begin to babble vocally — between 4 and 6 months (Petitto & Marentette, 1991).

Deaf infants who learn sign language from their parents start babbling with their hands around the same time that hearing infants babble vocally. Robin Trimarchi/KRT/Newscom

Language Milestones

At about 10 to 12 months of age, infants begin to utter (or sign) their first words. By 18 months, they can say about 50 words and can understand several times more than that. Toddlers generally learn nouns before verbs, and the nouns they learn first are names for everyday concrete objects (e.g., chair, table, milk) (see **TABLE 9.1**). At about this time, their vocabularies undergo explosive growth. By the time the average child begins school, a vocabulary of 10,000 words is not unusual. By 5th grade, the average child knows the meanings of 40,000 words. By college, the average student's vocabulary is about 200,000 words. **Fast mapping**, *the process whereby children map a word onto an underlying concept after only a single exposure,* enables them to learn at this rapid pace (Kan & Kohnert, 2008; Mervis & Bertrand, 1994). This astonishingly easy process contrasts dramatically with the effort required later to learn other concepts and skills, such as arithmetic or writing.

Around 24 months, children begin to form two-word sentences, such as "More milk" or "Throw ball." Such sentences are referred to as **telegraphic speech** because they are *devoid of function morphemes and consist mostly of content words*. Yet despite the absence of function words, such as prepositions or articles, these two-word sentences tend to be grammatical; the words are ordered in a manner consistent with the syntactic rules of the language the children are learning to speak. So, for example, toddlers will say "Throw ball" rather than "Ball throw" when they want you to throw the ball to them, and

TABLE 9.1	Language Milestones
Average Age	**Language Milestones**
0–4 months	Can tell the difference between speech sounds (phonemes); coos, especially in response to speech
4–6 months	Babbles consonants
6–10 months	Understands some words and simple requests
10–12 months	Begins to use single words.
12–18 months	Has vocabulary of 30–50 words (simple nouns, adjectives, and action words)
18–24 months	Two-word phrases ordered according to syntactic rules; vocabulary consists of 50–200 words; understands rules
24–36 months	Has vocabulary of about 1,000 words; produces phrases and incomplete sentences.
36–60 months	Vocabulary grows to more than 10,000 words; produces full sentences; shows mastery of grammatical morphemes (such as *-ed* for past tense) and function words (such as *the, and, but*); can form questions and negations

fast mapping The process whereby children can map a word onto an underlying concept after only a single exposure.

telegraphic speech Speech that is devoid of function morphemes and consists mostly of content words.

they will say "More milk" rather than "Milk more" when they want you to give them more milk. With these seemingly primitive expressions, 2-year-olds show that they have already acquired an appreciation of the syntactic rules of the language they are learning.

The Emergence of Grammatical Rules

If you listen to average 2- or 3-year-old children speaking, you may notice that they use the correct past-tense versions of common verbs, as in the expressions "I ran" and "You ate." By the age of 4 or 5, the same children will be using incorrect forms of these verbs, saying such things as "I runned" and "You eated," forms most children are unlikely ever to have heard (Prasada & Pinker, 1993). The reason is that very young children memorize the particular sounds (i.e., words) that express what they want to communicate. But as children acquire the grammatical rules of their language, they tend to *overregularize*. For example, if a child *overregularizes* the rule that past tense is indicated by *-ed*, then *run* becomes *runned* or even *ranned* instead of *ran*.

These errors show that language acquisition is not simply a matter of imitating adult speech. Instead, children acquire grammatical rules by listening to the speech around them and using those rules to create verbal forms they've never heard. They manage this without explicit awareness of the grammatical rules they've learned. In fact, few children or adults can articulate the grammatical rules of their native language, yet the speech they produce obeys these rules.

By about 3 years of age, children begin to generate complete simple sentences that include function words (e.g., "Give me *the* ball" and "That belongs *to* me"). The sentences increase in complexity over the next 2 years. By the time children are 4 to 5 years of age, many aspects of the language acquisition process are complete. As children continue to mature, their language skills become more refined, with added appreciation of subtler communicative uses of language, such as humor, sarcasm, or irony.

Language Development and Cognitive Development

Language development typically unfolds as a sequence of steps in which children achieve one milestone before moving on to the next. Nearly all infants begin with one-word utterances before progressing to telegraphic speech and then to simple sentences that include function morphemes. This orderly progression could result from general cognitive development that is unrelated to experience with a specific language (Shore, 1986; Wexler, 1999). For example, perhaps infants begin with one- and then two-word utterances because their short-term memories are so limited that initially they can hold in mind only a word or two; additional cognitive development might be necessary before they have the capacity to put together a simple sentence. Alternatively, the orderly progression might depend on experience with a specific language, reflecting a child's emerging knowledge of that language (Bates & Goodman, 1997; Gillette et al., 1999).

To tease apart these possibilities, researchers examined the acquisition of English by internationally adopted children who did not know any English prior to adoption (Snedeker et al., 2007, 2012). If the orderly sequence of milestones that characterizes the acquisition of English by nonadopted infants is a by-product of general cognitive development, then different patterns should be observed in older internationally adopted children, who are more advanced cognitively than infants. However, if the milestones of language development are critically dependent on experience with a specific language — English — then language learning in older adopted children should show the same orderly progression as seen in infants. The main result was clear-cut: Language acquisition in preschool-age adopted children showed the same orderly progression of milestones that characterizes infants' language learning. These children began with one-word utterances before moving on to simple word combinations. Furthermore, their vocabulary, just like that of infants, was initially dominated by nouns, and they produced few function morphemes. These results indicate that some of the key milestones

Chinese preschoolers who are adopted by English-speaking parents progress through the same sequence of linguistic milestones as do infants born into English-speaking families, suggesting that these milestones reflect experience with English in particular rather than general cognitive development. Marvin Joseph/Washington Post/Getty Images

of language development depend on experience with the specific language — in this case, English.

Other aspects of a child's experience also influence language development. A study of the language development of 1- to 2-year-old children in families at different levels of socioeconomic status (SES) — ranging from families on welfare (low SES) to working class (middle SES) and professional (high SES) — highlights that SES has a strong impact: By the time they reached age 3, children in high-SES families were exposed to millions more words than were children in lower-SES families (Hart & Risley, 1995). This came to be widely known as the "30-million-word gap." The researchers also found that these early language differences were highly predictive of how these children performed as 3rd graders on various language and cognitive tests. What exactly produces these troubling lags in low-SES children? A study using video records of mother–child interactions (Hirsh-Pasek et al., 2015) found that both the quantity and the quality of words used by the mother during these interactions mattered: More words from the mother predicted higher performance by the child, highlighting again the importance of linguistic experience for language development.

Theories of Language Development

We know a good deal about how language develops, but what underlies the process? The language acquisition process has been the subject of considerable controversy and (at times) angry exchanges among scientists coming from three different approaches: behaviorist, nativist, and interactionist.

Behaviorist Explanations

According to B. F. Skinner's behaviorist explanation of language learning, we learn to talk in the same way we learn any other skill: through reinforcement, shaping, extinction, and the other basic principles of operant conditioning that you read about in the Learning chapter (Skinner, 1957). As infants mature, they begin to vocalize. Those vocalizations that are not reinforced gradually diminish, and those that are reinforced remain in the developing child's repertoire. So, for example, when the child of English-speaking parents gurgles "prah," the parents are likely to be indifferent. However, a sound that even remotely resembles "da-da" is likely to be reinforced with smiles, whoops, and cackles of "Goooood baaaaaby!" Maturing children also imitate the speech patterns they hear. Then parents or other adults shape the children's speech patterns by reinforcing those that are grammatical and ignoring or punishing those that are ungrammatical. "I no want milk" is likely to be squelched by parental clucks and titters, whereas "No milk for me, thanks" will probably be reinforced.

The behavioral explanation is attractive because it offers a simple account of language development, but this theory cannot account for many fundamental characteristics of language development (Chomsky, 1986; Pinker, 1994; Pinker & Bloom, 1990).

Nativist Explanations

In a blistering rebuttal of Skinner's behaviorist approach, linguist Noam Chomsky (1957, 1959) argued that language-learning capacities are built into the brain, which is specialized to acquire language rapidly through simple exposure to speech. This **nativist theory** holds that *language development is best explained as an innate, biological capacity.* According to Chomsky, the human brain is equipped with a **universal grammar**, *a collection of processes that facilitate language learning.* Language processes naturally emerge as the infant matures, provided the infant receives adequate input to maintain the acquisition process.

The story of Christopher, whom you met earlier in the chapter, is consistent with the nativist view of language development: His genius for language acquisition, despite his

Though behaviorist explanations are widely discredited, parents do indeed reinforce the sounds "da-da" and "ma-ma." UntitledImages /Getty Images

nativist theory The view that language development is best explained as an innate, biological capacity.

universal grammar A collection of processes that facilitate language learning.

"GOT IDEA. TALK BETTER. COMBINE WORDS. MAKE SENTENCES."
© Sidney Harris/Sciencecartoonsplus.com

Immigrants who learn English as a second language are more proficient if they start to learn English before puberty rather than after. Paul Irish/Toronto Star via Getty Images

How does the evolution of the Nicaraguan deaf children's sign language support the interactionist explanation of language development? Susan Meiselas/Magnum

genetic dysphasia A syndrome characterized by an inability to learn the grammatical structure of language despite having otherwise normal intelligence.

low overall intelligence, indicates that language capacity can be somewhat distinct from other mental capacities. Other individuals show the opposite pattern: Some people with normal or nearly normal intelligence can find certain aspects of human language difficult or impossible to learn. This condition is known as **genetic dysphasia**, *a syndrome characterized by an inability to learn the grammatical structure of language despite having otherwise normal intelligence.* For example, when asked to describe what she did over the weekend, one child with genetic dysphasia wrote, "On Saturday I watch TV." Her teacher corrected the sentence to "On Saturday, I watch*ed* TV," drawing attention to the *-ed* rule for describing past events. The following week, the child was asked to write another account of what she did over the weekend. She wrote, "On Saturday I wash myself and I watched TV and I went to bed." Notice that although she had memorized the past-tense forms *watched* and *went,* she could not generalize the rule to form the past tense of another word (*washed*).

Also consistent with the nativist view is evidence that language can be acquired only during a restricted period of development. This was dramatically illustrated by the tragic case of Genie (Curtiss, 1977). At the age of 20 months, Genie was tied to a chair by her parents and kept in virtual isolation. Her father forbade Genie's mother and brother to speak to her, and he himself only growled and barked at her. She remained in this brutal state until the age of 13, when her mother finally sought help for Genie. Genie's life improved substantially, and she received years of language instruction, but it was too late. Her language skills remained extremely primitive. She developed a basic vocabulary and could communicate her ideas, but she could not grasp the grammatical rules of English.

Other studies support the idea that once puberty is reached, acquiring language becomes extremely difficult (Brown, 1958). For example, in one study, researchers found that the proficiency with which immigrants spoke English depended not on how long they'd lived in the United States but on their age at immigration (Johnson & Newport, 1989): Those who had arrived as children were more proficient than those who had immigrated after puberty. More recent work using fMRI shows that acquiring a second language early in childhood (between 1 and 5 years of age) results in very different representation of that language in the brain than does acquiring that language much later (after 9 years of age; Bloch et al., 2009).

Interactionist Explanations

Nativist theories are often criticized because they do not explain *how* language develops; they merely explain why. An interactionist approach holds that although infants are born with an innate ability to acquire language, social interactions play a crucial role. Interactionists point out that parents tailor their verbal interactions with children in ways that simplify the language acquisition process: They speak slowly, enunciate clearly, and use simpler sentences than they do when speaking with adults (Bruner, 1983; Farrar, 1990).

Further evidence of the interaction of biology and experience comes from a fascinating study of the creation of a new language by deaf children (Senghas et al., 2004). Prior to about 1980, deaf children in Nicaragua stayed at home and usually had little contact with other deaf individuals. In 1981, some deaf children began to attend a new vocational school. At first, the school did not teach a formal sign language, and none of the children had learned to sign at home, but the children gradually began to communicate using hand signals they themselves invented. Initially, the gestures were simple, but over the next 30 years, their sign language developed considerably, to the point that it contains many of the same features as mature languages, including signs to describe complex concepts (Pyers et al., 2010). These acts of creation nicely illustrate the interplay of nativism (the predisposition to use language) and experience (growing up in an insulated deaf culture).

Language Development and the Brain

In early infancy, language processing is distributed across many areas of the brain. But language processing gradually becomes more and more concentrated in two areas: Broca's area and Wernicke's area. *Broca's area* is located in the left frontal cortex and is involved in the production of the sequential patterns in vocal and sign languages (see **FIGURE 9.3**). *Wernicke's area,* located in the left temporal cortex, is involved in language comprehension (whether spoken or signed). Together, Broca's area and Wernicke's area are sometimes referred to as the language centers of the brain.

Damage to Broca's area or Wernicke's area results in a condition called **aphasia**, *difficulty in producing or comprehending language.* Individuals with damage to Broca's area understand language relatively well, but they struggle with speech production. Typically, they speak in short, staccato phrases that consist mostly of content morphemes: "Ah, Monday, uh, Casey park. Two, uh, friends, and, uh, 30 minutes." On the other hand, individuals with damage to Wernicke's area can produce grammatical-sounding speech, but it tends to be meaningless: "Feel very well. In other words, I used to be able to work cigarettes. I don't know how. Things I couldn't hear from are here."

As important as Broca's and Wernicke's areas are for language, many other brain areas are also involved. For example, the right cerebral hemisphere contributes to language processing (Jung-Beeman, 2005). A number of neuroimaging studies have revealed evidence of right-hemisphere activation during language tasks, and some children who have had their entire left hemispheres removed during adolescence as a treatment for epilepsy can recover many of their language abilities.

Some studies suggest that learning a second language produces lasting changes in the brain (Mechelli et al., 2004; Stein et al., 2009). For example, the gray matter in a part of the left parietal lobe that is involved in language is denser in bilingual than in monolingual individuals, and the increased density is most pronounced in those who are most proficient in using their second language (Mechelli et al., 2004; see **FIGURE 9.4**). These brain changes may have benefits. For example, bilingual individuals tend to have a later onset of Alzheimer's disease than monolingual individuals do (Schweizer et al., 2012; Woumans et al., 2015), and some (though not all) studies suggest that middle-class children who are fluent in two languages score higher than monolingual children on several measures of cognitive functioning (e.g., Bialystock, 1999, 2009, 2017).

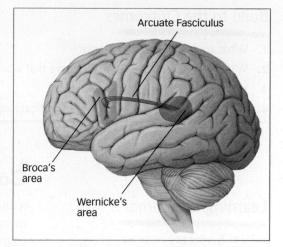

Figure 9.3 Broca's and Wernicke's Areas When Broca's area is damaged, people have a hard time producing sentences, but when speech is produced, it is meaningful. When Wernicke's area is damaged, people can produce sentences, but the sentences tend to be meaningless.

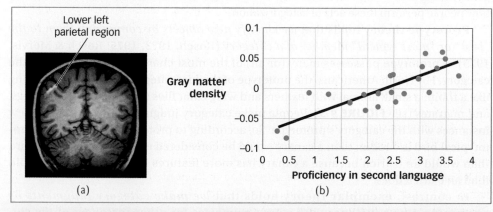
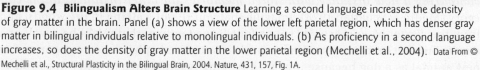

Figure 9.4 Bilingualism Alters Brain Structure Learning a second language increases the density of gray matter in the brain. Panel (a) shows a view of the lower left parietal region, which has denser gray matter in bilingual individuals relative to monolingual individuals. (b) As proficiency in a second language increases, so does the density of gray matter in the lower parietal region (Mechelli et al., 2004). Data From © Mechelli et al., Structural Plasticity in the Bilingual Brain, 2004. Nature, 431, 157, Fig. 1A.

aphasia Difficulty in producing or comprehending language.

Build to the Outcomes

1. What are language and grammar?

2. What language ability do infants have that adults do not?

3. What are the language milestones?

4. How do children learn and use grammatical rules?

5. How do behaviorists, nativists, and interactionists explain language development?

6. What are Broca and Wernicke's areas?

7. How does bilingualism influence brain structure?

Learning Outcomes

- Identify why concepts are fundamental to our ability to think.

- Compare the family prototype and exemplar theories of concepts.

- Describe the involvement of the brain in organizing and processing concepts.

There is family resemblance between family members despite the fact that there is no defining feature that they all have in common. Instead, there are shared common features. Someone who also shares some of those features may be categorized as belonging to the family. Blend Images/Superstock

concept A mental representation that groups or categorizes shared features of related objects, events, or other stimuli.

prototype theory The concept that we classify new objects by comparing them to the "best" or "most typical" member (the *prototype*) of a category.

exemplar theory The concept that we make category judgments by comparing a new instance with stored memories of other instances of the category.

Concepts and Categories: How We Think

A 69-year-old man known by the initials JB began having difficulty understanding the meaning of words, even though he still performed well on many other perceptual and cognitive tasks. Over the next few years, his color language deteriorated dramatically; he had great difficulty naming colors and could not even match objects with their typical colors (e.g., strawberry and red, banana and yellow). Yet he could still classify colors normally, sorting color patches into groups of green, yellow, red, and blue in the exact same manner that healthy participants did. JB retained an intact *concept* of colors despite the decline of his language ability — a finding that suggests we need to look at factors in addition to language in order to understand concepts (Haslam et al., 2007).

A **concept** is a *mental representation that groups or categorizes shared features of related objects, events, or other stimuli.* The brain organizes our concepts about the world, classifying them into categories based on shared similarities. Our category for *dog* may be something like "small, four-footed animal with fur that wags its tail and barks." Our category for *bird* may be something like "small winged, beaked creature that flies." We form these categories in large part by noticing similarities among objects and events that we experience in everyday life. Concepts are fundamental to our ability to think and make sense of the world.

Psychological Theories of Concepts and Categories

What is your definition of *dog*? Can you come up with a rule of "dogship" that includes all dogs and excludes all non-dogs? Most people can't, but they still use the term *dog* intelligently, easily classifying objects as dogs or non-dogs. Two major theories seek to explain how people perform these acts of categorization.

Prototype theory holds that *we classify new objects by comparing them to the "best" or "most typical" member of a category* (Rosch, 1973, 1975; Rosch & Mervis, 1975). A prototype possesses many (or all) of the most characteristic features of the category. For North Americans, the prototype of the *bird* category would be something like a robin: a small animal with feathers and wings that flies through the air, lays eggs, and migrates (see **FIGURE 9.5**). People make category judgments by comparing new instances with the category's prototype. So, according to prototype theory, if your prototypical bird is a robin, then a canary would be considered a better example of a bird than would an ostrich because a canary has more features in common with a robin than an ostrich does.

In contrast, **exemplar theory** holds that *we make category judgments by comparing a new instance with stored memories for other instances of the category* (Medin & Schaffer, 1978). Imagine that you're out walking in the woods, and from the corner of your eye you spot a four-legged animal that might be a wolf or a coyote but that reminds you of your cousin's German shepherd. You categorize this new animal as a dog because it bears a striking resemblance to other dogs you've

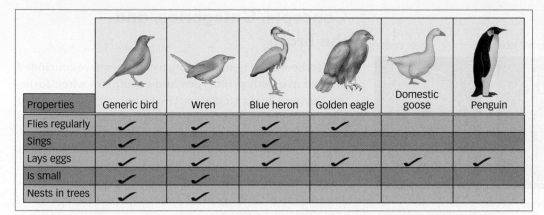

Figure 9.5 Critical Features of a Category We tend to think of a generic bird as possessing a number of critical features, but not every bird possesses all of those features. In North America, a wren is a better example of a bird than is a penguin or an ostrich.

Properties	Generic bird	Wren	Blue heron	Golden eagle	Domestic goose	Penguin
Flies regularly	✔	✔	✔	✔		
Sings	✔	✔	✔			
Lays eggs	✔	✔	✔	✔	✔	✔
Is small	✔	✔				
Nests in trees	✔	✔				

encountered; in other words, it was a good example (or an *exemplar*) of the category *dog*. Exemplar theory does a better job than prototype theory of accounting for certain aspects of categorization (Ashby & Rosedahl, 2017; Nosofsky et al., 2018), especially in that we recall not only what a *prototypical* dog looks like but also what *specific* dogs look like. **FIGURE 9.6** illustrates the difference between prototype theory and exemplar theory.

Exemplars

Prototype

Exemplar Theory

Prototype Theory

New stimulus

Figure 9.6 Prototype Theory and Exemplar Theory According to prototype theory, we classify new objects by comparing them to the "prototype" (or most typical) member of a category. According to exemplar theory, we classify new objects by comparing them with other instances of the category. Juniors Bildarchiv/F237alamy; GK Hart/Vikki Hart/Stone/Getty Images; Age Fotostock/Superstock; Pixtal/Pixtal/Superstock; Imagebroker/Alamy; Otsphoto/Shutterstock

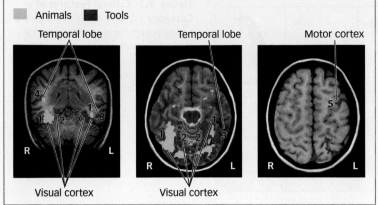

Figure 9.7 Brain Areas Involved in Category-Specific Processing Participants were asked to silently name pictures of animals and tools while they underwent fMRI scanning. The fMRIs revealed greater activity in several brain areas (yellow) when participants named animals, while other areas (purple) showed greater activity when participants named tools. Note that the images are left/right reversed.

Touch is one way that blind individuals could develop category-preferential brain responses.   Rizwan Tabassum/Getty Images

category-specific deficit A neurological syndrome characterized by an inability to recognize objects that belong to a particular category, even when the ability to recognize objects outside the category is undisturbed.

Concepts, Categories, and the Brain

Researchers using neuroimaging techniques have concluded that we use both prototypes and exemplars when forming concepts and categories. The visual cortex is involved in forming prototypes, whereas the prefrontal cortex and basal ganglia are involved in learning exemplars (Ashby & Ell, 2001; Ashby & O'Brien, 2005). This evidence suggests that exemplar-based learning involves analysis and decision making (prefrontal cortex), whereas prototype formation is a more holistic activity involving image processing (visual cortex).

Some of the most striking evidence linking concepts and categories with the brain comes from patients with brain damage. For example, one patient could not recognize a variety of human-made objects or retrieve any information about them, but his knowledge of living things and foods was perfectly normal (Warrington & McCarthy, 1983). Other patients exhibit the reverse pattern: They can recognize information about human-made objects, but not living things or foods (Martin & Caramazza, 2003; Warrington & Shallice, 1984). Such cases are examples of a syndrome called **category-specific deficit**, *an inability to recognize objects that belong to a particular category, although the ability to recognize objects outside the category is undisturbed.*

The type of category-specific deficit suffered depends on where the brain is damaged. Deficits usually result when an individual suffers a stroke or other trauma to areas in the left hemisphere of the cerebral cortex (Mahon & Caramazza, 2009). Damage to the front part of the left temporal lobe results in difficulty identifying humans; damage to the lower left temporal lobe results in difficulty identifying animals; damage to the region where the temporal lobe meets the occipital and parietal lobes impairs the ability to retrieve names of tools (Damasio et al., 1996). Similarly, imaging studies in healthy participants have demonstrated that the same regions of the brain are more active during naming of tools than during naming of animals and vice versa, as shown in **FIGURE 9.7** (Martin, 2007; Martin & Chao, 2001).

How do particular brain regions develop category preferences for objects such as tools or animals? In one neuroimaging study, blind and sighted individuals each heard a series of words referring to animals and tools (Mahon et al., 2009). In both groups, regions in the visual cortex and temporal lobe responded to animals and tools in much the same manner as shown in Figure 9.7. These results provide compelling evidence that category-specific organization of visual regions does not depend on an individual's visual experience. One possibility is that category-specific organization in blind individuals could arise from interactions with other senses, such as touch, but others argue that category-specific brain organization may be innately determined (Bedny & Saxe, 2012; Mahon et al., 2009).

Build to the Outcomes

1. What are concepts?

2. Why are concepts useful to us?

3. How do the prototype and exemplar theories differ?

4. What evidence suggests that the brain is "prewired" to organize perceptual and sensory inputs?

Decision Making: Rational and Otherwise

We use categories and concepts to guide the hundreds of decisions and judgments we make during the course of an average day. Some decisions are easy (what to wear; what to eat for breakfast; whether to walk, ride a bicycle, or drive to class) and some are more difficult (which car to buy, which apartment to rent, who to hang out with on Friday night, and even which job to take after graduation). Some decisions are based on sound judgments. Others are not.

The Rational Ideal

Economists contend that if we are rational thinkers, free to make our own decisions, we will behave as predicted by **rational choice theory**: *We make decisions by determining how likely something is to happen, judging the value of the outcome, and then multiplying the two* (Edwards, 1955). This means that our judgments will vary depending on the value we assign to the possible outcomes. Suppose, for example, you were asked to choose between a 10% chance of gaining $500 and a 20% chance of gaining $2,000. The rational person would choose the second alternative because the expected payoff is $400 ($2,000 × 20%), whereas the first offers an expected gain of only $50 ($500 × 10%). Selecting the option with the highest expected value seems very straightforward. But how well does this theory describe decision making in our everyday lives? In many cases, the answer is: not very well.

The Irrational Reality

Is the ability to classify new events and objects into categories always a useful skill? Alas, no. The same principles that allow cognition to occur easily and accurately can pop up to bedevil our decision making.

Judging Frequencies and Probabilities

Consider the following list of words:

> *block table block pen telephone block disk glass table block telephone block watch table candy*

You probably noticed that the words *block* and *table* occur more frequently than the other words do. In fact, studies have shown that people are quite good at estimating *frequency,* or the number of times something will happen. In contrast, we perform poorly on tasks that require us to think in terms of *probabilities,* or the likelihood that something will happen.

In one experiment, 100 physicians were asked to predict the incidence of breast cancer among women whose mammogram screening tests showed possible evidence of breast cancer. The physicians were told to take into consideration the rarity of breast cancer (1% of the population at the time the study was done) and radiologists' record in diagnosing the condition (correctly recognized only 79% of the time and falsely diagnosed almost 10% of the time). Of the 100 physicians, 95 estimated the probability that cancer was present to be about *75%!* The correct answer was 8% (Eddy, 1982). But dramatically different results were obtained when the study was repeated using *frequency* information instead of *probability* information. Stating the problem as "10 out of every 1,000 women actually have breast cancer" instead of "1% of women actually have breast cancer" led 46% of the physicians to derive the right answer (Hoffrage & Gigerenzer, 1998). This finding suggests, at a minimum, that when seeking advice (even from a highly skilled decision maker), make sure your problem is described using frequencies rather than probabilities.

Learning Outcomes

- Explain why people sometimes fail to make rational decisions.
- Summarize the ideas underlying prospect theory.
- Describe the role of the brain in decision making.

People don't always make rational choices. When a lottery jackpot is larger than usual, more people will buy lottery tickets, thinking that they might well win big. However, more people buying lottery tickets reduces the likelihood of any one person winning the lottery. Ironically, people have a better chance at winning a lottery with a relatively small jackpot. Santa Rosa Press Democrat/Zumapress.com /Alamy

rational choice theory The classical view that we make decisions by determining how likely something is to happen, judging the value of the outcome, and then multiplying the two.

Jennifer Aniston	Robert Kingston
Judy Smith	Gilbert Chapman
Frank Carson	Gwyneth Paltrow
Elizabeth Taylor	Martin Mitchell
Daniel Hunt	Thomas Hughes
Henry Vaughan	Michael Drayton
Agatha Christie	Julia Roberts
Arthur Hutchinson	Hillary Clinton
Jennifer Lopez	Jack Lindsay
Allen Nevins	Richard Gilder
Jane Austen	George Nathan
Joseph Litton	Britney Spears

Figure 9.8 Availability Bias Read this list of names, then look away and estimate the number of women's and men's names.

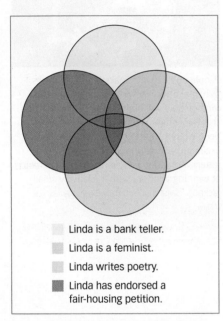

- Linda is a bank teller.
- Linda is a feminist.
- Linda writes poetry.
- Linda has endorsed a fair-housing petition.

Figure 9.9 The Conjunction Fallacy People often think that with each additional bit of information, the probability that all the facts are simultaneously true increases. In fact, the probability decreases dramatically. Notice how the intersection of *all* these possibilities is much smaller than the area of any one possibility alone.

availability bias The concept that items that are more readily available in memory are judged as having occurred more frequently.

conjunction fallacy Thinking that two events are more likely to occur together than is either individual event alone.

Availability Bias

Take a look at the list of names in **FIGURE 9.8**. Now look away from the book and estimate the number of male names and female names in the figure. Did you notice that some of the women on the list are famous and none of the men are? Was your estimate off because you thought the list contained more women's names than men's names (Tversky & Kahneman, 1973, 1974)? The reverse would have been true if you had looked at a list with the names of famous men and unknown women because people typically fall prey to **availability bias:** *Items that are more readily available in memory are judged as having occurred more frequently.*

The availability bias affects our estimates because memory strength and frequency of occurrence are directly related. Frequently occurring items are remembered more easily than *in*frequently occurring items, so you naturally conclude that items for which you have better memory must also have been more frequent. Unfortunately, better memory in this case was due not to greater *frequency* but to greater *familiarity.*

The Conjunction Fallacy

Consider the following description:

> Linda is 31 years old, single, outspoken, and very bright. In college, she majored in philosophy. As a student, she was deeply concerned with issues of discrimination and social justice and also participated in antinuclear demonstrations.

Which state of affairs is more probable?

a. Linda is a bank teller.

b. Linda is a bank teller and is active in the feminist movement.

In one study, 89% of participants rated option b as more probable than option a (Tversky & Kahneman, 1983).

This situation is called the **conjunction fallacy** because *people think that two events are more likely to occur together than either individual event.* Actually, the reverse is true: As you can see in **FIGURE 9.9**, the probability of two or more events both occurring (in conjunction) is always *less* than the probability of either event occurring alone. However unlikely it may seem that Linda is a bank teller, it is even *less* likely that she is a bank teller who is *also* an activist.

Representativeness Heuristic

A panel of psychologists wrote descriptions of 100 people, including 70 engineers and 30 lawyers. A random selection of these descriptions is shown below. Read each one and then pause and decide if it is more likely that the person is an engineer or a lawyer. Note your decision and read on.

1. Jack enjoys reading books on social and political issues. During the interview, he displayed particular skill at argument.

2. Tom is a loner who enjoys working on mathematical puzzles during his spare time. During the interview, his speech remained fairly abstract and his emotions were well controlled.

3. Harry is a bright man and an avid racquetball player. During the interview, he asked many insightful questions and was very well spoken.

When research participants read a series of descriptions like these, most thought that Jack was more likely to be a lawyer, and Tom was more likely to be an engineer. Harry's description doesn't sound like a lawyer's or an engineer's, so most people said he was *equally likely* to hold either occupation (Kahneman & Tversky, 1973). But, remember, the pool of descriptions included more than twice as many engineers as lawyers, so it is far *more* likely that Harry is an engineer. People seem to ignore information about *base rate,* or the existing probability of an event, basing their judgments on similarities to categories.

Researchers call this the **representativeness heuristic**: *a mental shortcut (or "heuristic") that involves making a probability judgment by comparing an object or event with a prototype of the object or event* (Kahneman & Tversky, 1973).

Framing Effects

If people are told that a particular drug has a 70% effectiveness rate, they're usually pretty impressed. Tell them instead that a drug has a 30% failure rate, and they typically perceive it as risky and potentially harmful. Notice that the information is the same: A 70% effectiveness rate means that 30% of the time, it's ineffective. The way the information is presented, or framed, leads to substantially different conclusions (Tversky & Kahneman, 1981). This is an example of how **framing effects**, *a bias whereby people give different answers to the same problem depending on how the problem is phrased (or framed)*, can influence the assignment of value.

One of the most striking framing effects is the **sunk-cost fallacy**, which occurs when *people make decisions about a current situation on the basis of what they have previously invested in the situation.* Imagine waiting in line for 3 hours, paying $100 for a ticket to see your favorite bands, and waking on the day of the outdoor concert to find that it's bitterly cold and rainy. If you go, you'll feel miserable. But you go anyway, reasoning that the $100 you paid for the ticket and the time you spent in line will have been wasted if you stay home.

Notice that you have two choices: (1) stay comfortably at home or (2) endure many uncomfortable hours in the rain. The $100 is gone in either case: It's a sunk cost, irretrievable at the moment of your decision. But because you invested time and money, you feel obligated to follow through, even though it's something you no longer want.

Even the National Basketball Association (NBA) is guilty of sunk-cost fallacies. Coaches should play their most productive players and keep them on the team longer, but they don't. The most *expensive* players are given more time on court and are kept on the team longer than are cheaper players, even if the costly players are not performing up to par (Staw & Hoang, 1995). Coaches act to justify their team's investment in an expensive player rather than recognize the loss. Framing effects can be costly, but they can also be exploited to increase wealth (see Hot Science: Can Framing Effects Make You Rich?).

representativeness heuristic A mental shortcut that involves making a probability judgment by comparing an object or event with a prototype of the object or event.

framing effects A bias whereby people give different answers to the same problem depending on how the problem is phrased (or framed).

sunk-cost fallacy A framing effect in which people make decisions about a current situation on the basis of what they have previously invested in the situation.

HOT SCIENCE

Can Framing Effects Make You Rich?

Financial experts agree that it is critically important to save money for future needs, yet nearly 40% of American adults report having no retirement savings (Martin, 2018). From 2016 to 2018, American adults reported that their biggest financial regret was not saving for retirement, yet only about half of those with a financial regret said they had a plan to address it (Tepper, 2018). Finding ways to help people save more could thus contribute to their financial health and likely relieve some psychological distress. One possible avenue is to use framing effects.

In one study, researchers questioned nearly 1,000 adults on how adequate various amounts of wealth would be in retirement (Goldstein et al., 2016). They framed the amounts either as a lump sum (e.g., $100,000) or as an equivalent amount of monthly payments for life (e.g., $500/

per month). For relatively small amounts, people value the lump sum more. The researchers surmised that when framed as a monthly payment, the amount is small enough that people can see how little it would actually purchase, but the lump sum seems substantial.

Flipping this around, Hershfield, Shu, and Benartzi (2019) reasoned that it may be more psychologically painful to *part* with a lump sum than an equivalent amount of money meted out in smaller amounts. They conducted a study in collaboration with the financial company Acorns, which allows people to invest spare change or larger amounts of money in an online account through a smartphone app (for details, go to www.acorns.com). In this study, new users who had just established an account at Acorns were asked if they wanted to sign up to deposit $150 each month. For some users, this

was framed as depositing $5/day, for others it was framed as depositing $35/week, while for a third group it was framed as one $150 deposit.

If people find it psychologically more painful to part with the larger sum than equivalent smaller amounts, then more users should sign up for the small daily deposits than for the larger weekly or monthly deposits. This is exactly what happened: when given the daily framing, 29% of users signed up, compared with 10% for the weekly framing and only 7% for the monthly framing. People in the daily framing also remained in the program longer than people in the other two conditions.

These results suggest that there is a way to avoid financial regrets later in life: Put away a small amount of money — small enough that parting with it doesn't cause psychological pain — as frequently as possible.

Optimism Bias

In addition, human decision making often reflects the effects of **optimism bias:** *People believe that compared with other individuals, they are more likely to experience positive events and less likely to experience negative events in the future* (Sharot, 2011). For example, people believe they are more likely than others to own their own homes and live a long life and that they are less likely to have a heart attack or a drinking problem (Weinstein, 1980). Although optimism about the future is often a good thing for our mental and physical health — optimistic individuals are usually well adjusted psychologically and are able to handle stress well (Nes & Sergerstrom, 2006) — too much optimism can be detrimental because it may prevent us from taking the necessary steps to achieve our goals.

Why Do We Make Decision-Making Errors?

As you have seen, everyday decision making seems riddled with errors and shortcomings. Our decisions vary wildly, depending on how a problem is presented (e.g., framed in terms of frequencies versus probabilities or in terms of losses rather than savings). We are also prone to fallacies, such as the sunk-cost fallacy, the conjunction fallacy, or optimism bias. Psychologists have developed several theories to explain why everyday decision making suffers from these failings. The most influential theory, **prospect theory**, proposes that *people choose to take on risks when evaluating potential losses and to avoid risks when evaluating potential gains* (Tversky & Kahneman, 1992).

For instance, imagine you are tasked with deciding which of two apartments to rent: both cost $400 a month, but apartment A offers you a $300 rebate on your first month's rent, while apartment B will let you spin a wheel that offers an 80% chance of getting a $400 rebate. You'll most likely choose the sure $300 over the risky $400. However, given a choice between a sure fine of $300 for damaging an apartment or spinning a wheel that has an 80% chance of a $400 fine, most people take the gamble of spinning the wheel, hoping to avoid the fine, even though the odds are they'll wind up paying more than the original $300. This asymmetry in risk preferences shows that we are willing to take on risk if we think it will ward off a loss, but we're risk averse if we expect to lose some benefits.

Decision Making and the Brain

A man identified as Elliot was a successful businessman, husband, and father prior to developing a brain tumor. After surgery, his intellectual abilities seemed intact, but he was unable to differentiate between important and unimportant activities and would spend hours doing mundane tasks. He lost his job and got involved in several risky financial ventures that bankrupted him. He had no difficulty discussing what had happened, but his descriptions were so detached and dispassionate that it seemed as though his abstract intellectual functions had become dissociated from his social and emotional abilities.

Research confirms that this interpretation of Elliot's downfall is right on track. In one study, researchers looked at how healthy volunteers differed from people with prefrontal lobe damage on a gambling task that involves risky decision making (Bechara et al., 1994, 1997). Participants chose cards one at a time from any of four decks; each card specified an amount of play money won or lost. Unbeknownst to the participants, two of the decks usually provided large payoffs or large losses ("risky decks"), whereas the other two provided smaller payoffs and losses ("safe decks").

Early on, participants selected cards equally from the risky and the safe decks, but healthy participants gradually shifted to choosing primarily from the safe decks. In contrast, patients with prefrontal damage continued to select equally from the risky and safe decks, leading most to go bankrupt in the game. This performance mirrors Elliot's real-life problems. In both groups, participants' galvanic skin response (GSR) showed strong emotional reactions to big gains and losses. But as the game progressed, the healthy

optimism bias A bias whereby people believe that compared with other individuals, they are more likely to experience positive events and less likely to experience negative events in the future.

prospect theory The theory that people choose to take on risk when evaluating potential losses and avoid risks when evaluating potential gains.

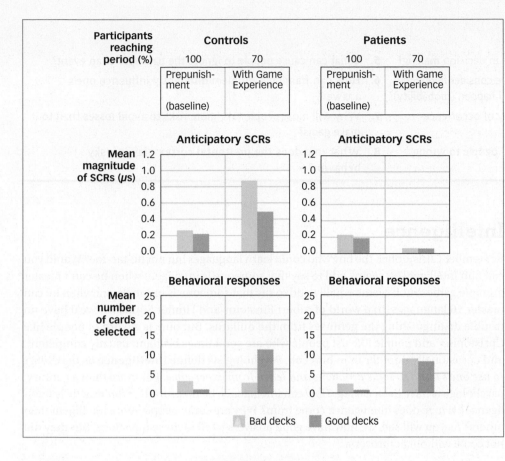

Figure 9.10 The Neuroscience of Risky Decision Making In a study of risky decision making, participants played a game in which they selected cards from one of four decks. Two of the decks were made up of riskier cards, that is, cards that provided large payoffs or large losses. The other two decks contained safer cards with much smaller payoffs and losses. At the beginning of the game, both groups chose cards from all four decks with equal frequency. Over the course of the game, however, healthy participants avoided the risky decks and showed large emotional responses (SCRs, or skin conductance responses) when they even considered choosing a card from a risky deck. Participants with prefrontal brain damage, on the other hand, continued to choose cards from all four decks with equal frequency; they showed no evidence of emotional learning and eventually went bankrupt in the game (data from Bechara et al., 1997).

participants began to show anticipatory emotional reactions when they even *considered* choosing a card from the risky deck (Bechara et al., 1997). The participants with prefrontal damage didn't show these anticipatory feelings when they were thinking about selecting a card from the risky deck. Apparently, their emotional reactions did not guide their thinking, so they continued to make risky decisions, as shown in **FIGURE 9.10**.

The risky decision making by participants with prefrontal damage suggests that the patients are insensitive to the future consequences of their behavior (Naqvi, Shiv, & Bechara, 2006). Unable to think beyond immediate consequences, they cannot shift their choices in response to a rising rate of losses or a declining rate of rewards (Bechara, Tranel, & Damasio, 2000). Interestingly, substance-dependent individuals, such as alcoholics and cocaine addicts, act the same way. Most perform as poorly on the gambling task as do individuals with prefrontal damage (Bechara et al., 2001).

These findings have potentially important implications for such everyday issues as road safety. In one study, people who had been convicted of driving while impaired with alcohol (DWI) were tested on the gambling task; offenders who performed poorly were much more likely to commit repeated DWI offenses than those who performed well (Bouchard et al., 2012). Related recent work has documented gambling-task impairments in binge eaters, another group who demonstrate an insensitivity to the future consequences of behavior (Danner et al., 2012).

Neuroimaging studies of healthy individuals show that during the gambling task, an area in the prefrontal cortex is activated when participants make risky decisions as compared to safe decisions. Indeed, the activated region is in the part of the prefrontal cortex that is typically damaged in participants who perform poorly on the gambling task; greater activation in this region is correlated with better task performance in healthy individuals (Fukui et al., 2005; Lawrence et al., 2009). Taken together, the neuroimaging and lesion studies show clearly that aspects of risky decision making depend critically on the contributions of the prefrontal cortex.

Build to the Outcomes

1. What is the importance of rational choices in decision making?

2. Why is a better decision more likely when we consider frequency, rather than the likelihood that something will happen (probability)?

3. How are strength of memory and frequency of occurrence related?

4. How can more information sometimes lead people to wrong conclusions?

5. What can cause people to ignore the base rate of an event?

6. How can framing a problem differently influence one's answer?

7. Why will most people take more risks to avoid losses than to make gains?

8. What role does the prefrontal cortex play in risky behavior?

Learning Outcomes

- Define intelligence.
- Explain how and why intelligence tests were developed.
- Explain why intelligence matters.
- Explain the three-level hierarchy of intelligence.

intelligence The ability to use one's mind to solve novel problems and learn from experience.

Intelligence

Remember Christopher, the boy who could learn languages but not tic-tac-toe? Would you call him intelligent? It seems odd to say that someone is intelligent when he can't master a simple game, but it seems equally odd to say that someone is unintelligent when he can master 16 languages. In a world of Albert Einsteins and Homer Simpsons we'd have no trouble distinguishing the geniuses from the dullards. But ours is a word of people like Christopher and people like us: people who are sometimes brilliant, usually competent, and occasionally dimmer than broccoli. Psychologists define **intelligence** as *the ability to use one's mind to solve problems and learn from experience.* For more than a century, psychologists have been asking: *How* can intelligence be measured? *What* exactly is intelligence? *Where* does intelligence come from? *Why* are some people more intelligent than others? As you will see, we now have good answers to all of these questions, but they did not come without controversy.

How Can Intelligence Be Measured?

Few things are more dangerous than a man with a mission. In the 1920s, the psychologist Henry Goddard administered intelligence tests to immigrants arriving at Ellis Island and concluded that the overwhelming majority of Jews, Hungarians, Italians, and Russians

During the early 20th century, laws required the involuntary sterilization of people with low intelligence. These laws were widely supported, and the U.S. Supreme Court upheld their constitutionality. The Harry H. Laughlin Papers, Truman State University

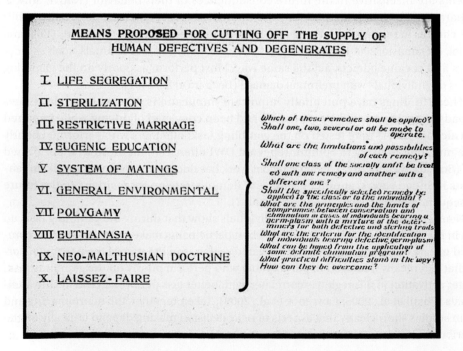

MEANS PROPOSED FOR CUTTING OFF THE SUPPLY OF HUMAN DEFECTIVES AND DEGENERATES

I. LIFE SEGREGATION

II. STERILIZATION

III. RESTRICTIVE MARRIAGE

IV. EUGENIC EDUCATION

V. SYSTEM OF MATINGS

VI. GENERAL ENVIRONMENTAL

VII. POLYGAMY

VIII. EUTHANASIA

IX. NEO-MALTHUSIAN DOCTRINE

X. LAISSEZ-FAIRE

Which of these remedies shall be applied?
Shall one, two, several or all be made to operate.

What are the limitations and possibilities of each remedy?

Shall one class of the socially unfit be treated with one remedy and another with a different one?

Shall the specifically selected remedy be applied to the class or to the individual?

What are the principles and the limits of compromise between conservation and elimination in cases of individuals bearing a germ-plasm with a mixture of the determiners for both defective and sterling traits?

What are the criteria for the identification of individuals bearing defective germ-plasm?

What can be hoped from the application of some definite elimination program?

What practical difficulties stand in the way? How can they be overcome?

were "feebleminded." Goddard also used his tests to identify feebleminded American families (who, he claimed, were largely responsible for the nation's social problems) and suggested that the government should segregate them in isolated colonies and "take away from these people the power of procreation" (Goddard, 1913, p. 107). The United States subsequently passed laws restricting the immigration of people from southern and eastern Europe, and the majority of U.S. states passed laws requiring the sterilization of "mental defectives."

From Goddard's day to our own, intelligence tests have been used to rationalize prejudice and discrimination on the basis of race, religion, and nationality. This is especially ironic because those tests were originally developed for the noblest of purposes: to help underprivileged children succeed in school. Toward the end of the 19th century, France instituted a sweeping set of social reforms that for the first time required all boys and girls between the ages of 6 and 13 to attend school. The problem was that not all children of the same age were equally prepared to learn. The psychologist Alfred Binet argued that the schools should use an objective method to determine the learning capabilities of each child. He and his student Théodore Simon created a series of tasks that included solving logic problems, remembering words, copying pictures, distinguishing edible and inedible foods, making rhymes, and answering questions such as "Before deciding something important, what should you do?"

Binet and Simon designed their test to measure a child's *aptitude* for learning, independent of the child's prior educational *achievement*. Moreover, they designed it to allow psychologists to estimate a student's "mental level" simply by computing the average test score of many students in different age groups, then finding the age group whose average test score best matched the test score of the particular student. For example, a 10-year-old child whose test score was about the same as the average test score of all 8-year-olds was said to have the mental level of an 8-year-old and thus to need remedial education.

However, psychologists quickly realized that comparing mental age to chronological age works fairly well for kids but not for adults because adults of different ages don't have remarkably different intellectual capacities (Ackerman, 2017). To solve this problem, psychologists began to measure intelligence by computing what is now known as the **intelligence quotient (IQ)**, which is *a statistic obtained by dividing an adult's test score by the average adult's test score and then multiplying the quotient by 100.* An adult who scores the same as the average adult has an IQ of 100.

At 4 years old, Heidi Hankins became one of the youngest people ever admitted to Mensa, an organization for people with unusually high IQs. Heidi's IQ is 159—about the same as Albert Einstein's. Solent News/Shutterstock

The Intelligence Test

Most modern intelligence tests have their roots in the test that Binet and Simon developed more than a century ago. The most widely used modern intelligence tests are the *Wechsler Adult Intelligence Scale* (WAIS) and the *Wechsler Intelligence Scale for Children* (WISC), which are named after their originator, psychologist David Wechsler. Like Binet and Simon's original test, the WAIS and the WISC measure intelligence by asking people to answer questions and solve problems, to see similarities and differences between ideas and objects, to articulate the meaning of words, and so forth. Some sample problems from the WAIS are shown in **TABLE 9.2**.

Decades of research show that a person's performance on tests like the WAIS predict an astonishing number of important life outcomes (Borghans et al., 2016; Deary et al., 2008a; Deary et al., 2008b; Der et al., 2009; Leon et al., 2009; Richards et al., 2009; Rushton & Templer, 2009). For example, intelligence test scores are excellent predictors of income. One study comparing siblings who had significantly different IQs found that the less intelligent sibling earned roughly half of what the more intelligent sibling earned over the course of their lifetimes (Murray, 2002;

intelligence quotient (IQ) A statistic obtained by dividing an adult's test score by the average adult's test score and then multiplying the quotient by 100.

TABLE 9.2   The Tests and Core Subtests of the Wechsler Adult Intelligence Scale IV

WAIS-IV Test	Core Subtest	Questions and Tasks
Verbal comprehension test	Vocabulary	The test taker is asked to tell the examiner what certain words mean. For example: *chair* (easy), *hesitant* (medium), and *presumptuous* (hard).
	Similarities	The test taker is asked what 19 pairs of words have in common. For example: In what way are an apple and a pear alike? In what way are a painting and a symphony alike?
	Information	The test taker is asked several general knowledge questions. These cover people, places, and events. For example: How many days are in a week? What is the capital of France? Name three oceans. Who wrote *The Inferno?*
Perceptual reasoning test	Block design	The test taker is shown 2-D patterns made up of red and white squares and triangles and is asked to reproduce these patterns using cubes with red and white faces.
	Matrix reasoning	The test taker is asked to add a missing element to a pattern so that it progresses logically. For example: Which of the four symbols at the bottom goes in the empty cell of the table?
	Visual puzzles	The test taker is asked to complete visual puzzles like this one: Which three of these pictures go together to make this puzzle?
Working memory test	Digit span	The test taker is asked to repeat a sequence of numbers. Sequences run from two to nine numbers in length. In the second part of this test, the sequences must be repeated in reversed order. An easy example is to repeat 3-7-4. A harder one is 3-9-1-7-4-5-3-9.
	Arithmetic	The test taker is asked to solve arithmetic problems, progressing from easy to difficult ones.
Processing speed test	Symbol search	The test taker is asked to indicate whether one of a pair of abstract symbols is contained in a list of abstract symbols. There are many of these lists, and the test taker does as many as he or she can in 2 minutes.
	Coding	The test taker is asked to write down the number that corresponds to a code for a given symbol (e.g., a cross, a circle, and an upside-down *T*) and does as many as he or she can in 90 seconds.

Figure 9.11   Income and Intelligence Among Siblings This graph shows the average annual salary of a person who has an IQ of 90–109 (shown in pink) and of their siblings who have higher or lower IQs (shown in blue).

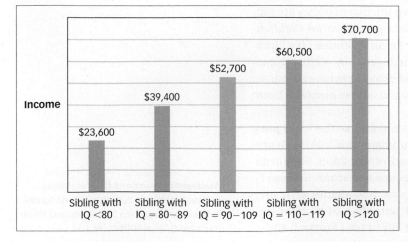

see **FIGURE 9.11**). In part, this is because intelligent people are more patient, better at calculating risk, and better at predicting how other people will act and how they should respond (Burks et al., 2009). But the main reason that intelligent people earn much more money than their less intelligent counterparts (or siblings!) is that they get more education (Deary et al., 2005; Nyborg & Jensen, 2001) and perform better in school (Roth et al., 2015).

Intelligent people aren't just wealthier, they are healthier as well (Calvin et al., 2011; Wraw et al., 2015). They are less likely to smoke and drink alcohol and are more likely to exercise and eat well (Batty et al., 2007; Ciarrochi et al., 2012; Weiser et al., 2010). Not surprisingly, they also live longer. The bottom line is clear: Intelligence matters for almost everything people value.

What Is Intelligence?

Sean Penn is one of the most critically acclaimed actors of his generation, having won two Academy Awards for best actor, two Golden Globes for best actor, and more. So when he released his first novel in 2018, he may have been surprised by the reviews. For example, the *New York Times* called it "conspicuously un-fun." The *Washington Post* wrote that "Sean Penn is not up to it as a novelist" and hoped that he "never quit his day job." The *Guardian*

Intelligence is a good predictor of success. Thomas Jefferson is considered the most intelligent of all U.S presidents, and Calvin Coolidge is considered the least intelligent (Simonton, 2006). Jefferson gave us the Declaration of Independence and Coolidge gave us the Great Depression. John Parrot /Stocktrek Images/Getty Images; Stock Montage/Getty Images

said that "Penn's prose is more reminiscent of bot than man." Other critics were less kind.

Penn's brilliance as an actor and mediocrity as a writer suggest that these two artistic endeavors require different abilities that are not necessarily possessed by the same individual. But if acting and writing require different abilities, then what does it mean to say that someone has "artistic talent"? Is that just a meaningless phrase, or does it refer to a single ability that some people have and others don't? The science of intelligence has grappled with a similar question for more than a century. Intelligence test scores predict important outcomes, from academic success to longevity, but is that because they measure a single ability called intelligence?

A Hierarchy of Abilities

If there really is a single ability called intelligence that enables people to perform a variety of intelligent behaviors, then those who have this ability should do well at just about everything, and those who lack it should do well at just about nothing. In other words, if intelligence is a single ability, then there should be a very strong positive correlation between people's performances on many different kinds of tests. Psychologist Charles Spearman (1904) set out to examine this hypothesis. He began by measuring how well school-age children could discriminate small differences in color, auditory pitch, and weight. He discovered that performances on these different tests were positively correlated, which is to say that children who performed well on one test (e.g., distinguishing two musical notes) tended to perform well on other tests (e.g., solving algebraic equations). But although performances on different tests were positively correlated, they were not *perfectly* correlated. In other words, the child who had the very highest score on one test didn't necessarily have the very highest score on every test. Spearman combined these two facts into his **two-factor theory of intelligence**, which suggests that *a person's performance on a test is due to a combination of general ability and skills that are specific to the test*. Spearman referred to general ability as *g* and to specific ability as *s*.

As sensible as Spearman's theory was, not everyone agreed with it. Louis Thurstone (1938) noticed that although the correlations between performances on different tests were all correlated, the correlations were much *stronger* when the tests had something in common. For example, performances on a verbal test were more strongly correlated with scores on another verbal test than with scores on a perceptual test. Thurstone took this to mean that there was actually no such thing as general ability; rather, there were a few stable and independent mental abilities — such as perceptual ability, verbal ability, and numerical ability. Thurstone called these the *primary mental abilities* and argued that they were neither general like *g* (e.g., a person might have strong verbal abilities and weak numerical abilities) nor specific like *s* (e.g., a person who has strong verbal abilities might tend both to speak and read well). In essence, Thurstone argued that we have abilities such as verbal ability and perceptual ability but no general ability called intelligence.

Social psychologist Jennifer Richeson received a so-called "Genius Award" from the MacArthur Foundation for her research on the dynamics of interracial interaction. Spearman's notion of *g* suggests that because she's really good at psychology, she's probably pretty good at most other things too. John D. & Catherine T. Macarthur Foundation

two-factor theory of intelligence Spearman's theory suggesting that a person's performance on a test is due to a combination of general ability and skills that are specific to the test.

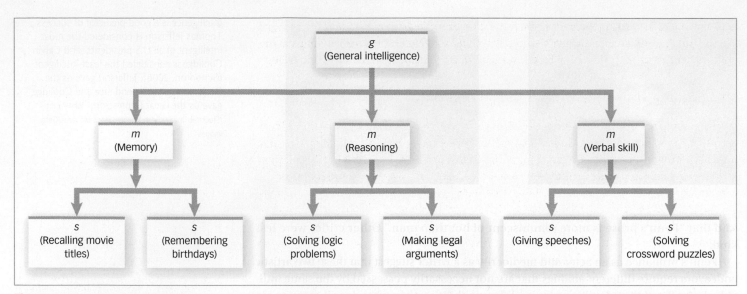

Figure 9.12 A Three-Level Hierarchy
Most intelligence test data are best described by a three-level hierarchy with general intelligence (*g*) at the top, specific abilities (*s*) at the bottom, and a small number of middle-level abilities (*m*) in the middle.

We now know that Spearman and Thurstone were both partly right. A massive reanalysis of data collected over 60 years from more than 130,000 people suggests a three-level hierarchy (see **FIGURE 9.12**) with a *general factor* (much like Spearman's *g*) at the top, *specific factors* (much like Spearman's *s*) at the bottom, and a set of factors called *group factors* (much like Thurstone's *primary mental abilities*) in the middle (Carroll, 1993; Gustafsson, 1984). This hierarchy suggests that people do indeed have a very general ability called intelligence, which is made up of a small set of middle-level abilities, which are made up of a large set of specific abilities that are unique to particular tasks. Research suggests that there are eight of these mid-level abilities: *memory and learning, visual perception, auditory perception, retrieval ability, cognitive speediness, processing speed, crystallized intelligence,* and *fluid intelligence* (Carroll, 1993).

Most of these mid-level abilities are self-explanatory, but the last two are not (Horn & Cattell, 1966). **Crystallized intelligence** refers to the *ability to apply knowledge that was acquired through experience,* and it is generally measured with tests of vocabulary and factual information. **Fluid intelligence** refers to the *ability to solve and reason about novel problems,* and it is generally measured with tests that present people with abstract problems in new domains that must be solved under time pressure (see **FIGURE 9.13**). Problems that require crystallized or fluid intelligence appear to activate different networks in the brain (Barbey, 2018), which may explain why impairment of one kind of intelligence

crystallized intelligence The ability to apply knowledge that was acquired through experience.

fluid intelligence The ability to solve and reason about novel problems.

Figure 9.13 Measuring Fluid Intelligence
Problems like this one from Raven's Progressive Matrices Test (Rave et al., 2004) measure fluid intelligence rather than crystallized intelligence. Raven's Progressive Matrices (Standard, Sets A-E) (SPM). Copyright © 1998, 1976, 1958, 1938 NCS Pearson, Inc. Reproduced with permission. All rights reserved.

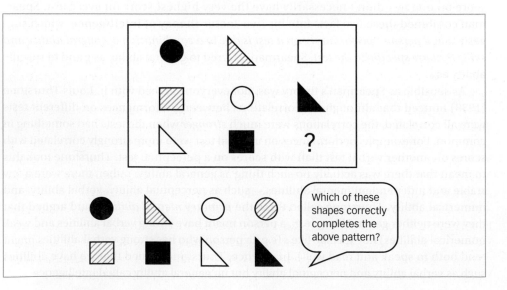

does not always lead to impairment of the other. For example, both autism and Alzheimer's disease impair crystallized intelligence more than fluid intelligence, whereas damage to the prefrontal cortex impairs fluid intelligence more than crystallized intelligence (Blair, 2006).

What Standard Intelligence Tests Don't Measure

Although the data from standard intelligence tests are best described by the three-level hierarchy, some psychologists have argued that there are other kinds of intelligence that these tests do not measure. For example, psychologist Robert Sternberg (1999, 2006) has distinguished between *analytic intelligence,* which is the ability to identify and define problems and to find strategies for solving them; *creative intelligence,* which is the ability to generate solutions that other people do not; and *practical intelligence,* which is the ability to implement these solutions in everyday settings. In one study, workers at milk-processing plants developed complex strategies for efficiently combining partially filled cases of milk. Not only did they outperform highly educated white-collar workers, but their performance was unrelated to their scores on intelligence tests, suggesting that practical and analytic intelligence are not the same thing (Scribner, 1984). Sternberg has argued that tests of practical intelligence are actually better than tests of analytic intelligence at predicting a person's job performance (cf. Brody, 2003; Gottfredson, 2003).

Another kind of intelligence that standard IQ tests don't measure is **emotional intelligence**, *the ability to reason about emotions and to use emotions to enhance reasoning* (Mayeret et al., 2008; Salovey & Grewal, 2005). Emotionally intelligent people know what kinds of emotions a particular event will trigger; they can identify, describe, and manage their emotions; they know how to use their emotions to improve their decisions; and they can identify other people's emotions from facial expressions and tones of voice. Emotionally intelligent people have better social skills and more friends (Eisenberg et al., 2000; Mestre et al., 2006; Schultz et al., 2004), they are judged to be more competent in their interactions (Brackett et al., 2006), and they have better romantic relationships (Brackett et al., 2005) and workplace relationships (Elfenbein et al., 2007; Lopes et al., 2006). Given all this, it isn't surprising that emotionally intelligent people tend to be happier (Brackett & Mayer, 2003; Brackett et al., 2006), healthier (Mikolajczak et al., 2015), and more satisfied with their lives (Ciarrochi et al., 2000; Mayer et al., 1999).

Standard IQ tests may also fail to measure middle-level abilities that are valued in non-Western cultures. For instance, Westerners regard people as intelligent when they speak quickly and often, but Africans regard people as intelligent when they are deliberate and quiet (Irvine, 1978). The Confucian tradition's conception of intelligence emphasizes flexibility in thinking and the ability to identify wisdom in others (Pang, Esping, & Plucker, 2017), the Taoist tradition emphasizes humility and self-knowledge, and the Buddhist tradition emphasizes determination and mental effort (Yang & Sternberg, 1997). Unlike Western societies, many African and Asian societies conceive of intelligence as including social responsibility and cooperativeness (Azuma & Kashiwagi, 1987; Serpell, 1974; White & Kirkpatrick, 1985). In Zimbabwe, the word for "intelligence" is *ngware,* which means to be wise and cautious in social relationships (Sternberg & Grigorenko, 2004).

Some researchers take all this to mean that different cultures have radically different conceptualizations of intelligence, but others are convinced that what appear to be differences in the conceptualization of intelligence are really just differences in language. They argue that every culture values the ability to solve important problems and that what really distinguishes cultures is the *kinds* of problems that are considered important.

ITEM 1	

Photo Courtesy Daniel Gilbert

Emotion	Select one:
a. Happy	O
b. Angry	O
c. Fearful	O
d. Sad	O

ITEM 2

Scott felt worried when he thought about all the work he needed to do. He believed he could handle it—if only he had the time. When his supervisor brought him an additional project, he felt _____. (Select the best choice.)

Emotion	Select one:
a. Frustrated and anxious	O
b. Content and calm	O
c. Ashamed and accepting	O
d. Sad and guilty	O

Two items from a test of emotional intelligence (Mayer et al., 2008). Item I measures the accuracy with which a person can read emotional expressions (left). Item 2 measures the ability to predict emotional responses to events (right). The correct answer on both items is a.

emotional intelligence The ability to reason about emotions and to use emotions to enhance reasoning.

The Hungarian chess grandmaster Judit Polgar (left) and the Korean actress Ryu Si-Hyeon (right) both have genius-level IQs. But their cultures construe intelligence differently. Westerners tend to think of intelligence as an individual's ability to engage in rational thinking, but Easterners tend to think of it as the ability to recognize contradictions and complexities. AP Photo/Keystone/Peter Schneider; Park Sea-Yeon/Epa/Alamy

Build to the Outcomes

1. Why were intelligence tests originally developed?
2. What is an intelligence quotient (IQ)?
3. What important life outcomes do intelligence test scores predict?
4. What was the debate between Spearman and Thurstone, and how was it resolved?
5. How does fluid intelligence differ from crystallized intelligence?
6. What are some of the skills of emotionally intelligent people?

Learning Outcomes

- Describe the influence of genes on intelligence.
- Explain how environmental factors influence intelligence.

DATA Visualization

Where Does Intelligence Come From?

No one is born knowing calculus, and no one has to be taught how to blink. Some things are learned, others are not. But almost all of the really *interesting* things about people are a joint product of the experiences they have and the characteristics with which they were born. Intelligence is one of those really interesting things, and it is influenced both by nature and by nurture. (See Data Visualization: How Do Nature and Nurture Influence Intelligence? Go to Launchpadworks.com.) Let's examine these in turn.

Genetic Influences on Intelligence

Although intelligence does appear to "run in families," that isn't very good evidence of genetic influence because family members share experiences as well as genes. Parents and children typically live in the same house and eat the same foods; siblings often go to the same schools, watch the same TV shows and movies; and so on. Family members may have similar levels of intelligence because they share genes, because they share environments, or both. If we want to know how much influence each of these factors has on intelligence, we need to measure and compare the intelligence scores of people who share one, both, or neither. For example, siblings who are raised together share both genes and environments; siblings who are separated at birth and raised by different families share genes but not environments; and adopted children who are raised together share environments but not genes.

Furthermore, different kinds of siblings share different amounts of their genes. Siblings who were born on different dates share, on average, about 50% of their genes. And so do **fraternal** (or **dizygotic**) **twins**, who are *siblings who develop from two different eggs that were fertilized by two different sperm*. On the other hand, **identical** (or **monozygotic**) **twins** are *siblings who develop from the splitting of a single egg that was fertilized by a single sperm,* and they share 100% of their genes. By comparing people who have different amounts and combinations of shared genes and environments, psychologists have been able to assess the influence of on intelligence.

The conclusion is clear: The IQs of biologically unrelated children raised in the same household are more weakly correlated than the IQs of identical twins raised in different households (Bouchard & McGue, 2003). This suggest that genes play an unusually important role in determining intelligence — and that shouldn't surprise you. After all, intelligence is influenced by the structure and function of the brain, and the structure and function of the brain are influenced by the genes that provide the blueprint for it. Indeed, given that genes influence just about every other human trait (Polderman et al., 2015), it would be rather remarkable if they *didn't* influence intelligence.

Tamara Rabi and Adriana Scott were 20 years old when they met for the first time in a McDonald's parking lot in New York. "I'm just standing there looking at her," Adriana recalled. "It was a shock. I saw me" (Gootman, 2003). It turned out that the two women were identical twins who had been separated at birth and adopted by different families. ©Angel Franco/The New York Times/Redux

Environmental Influences on Intelligence

Intelligence is influenced by genes, but it is also affected by the environment and changes over time. As **FIGURE 9.14** shows, intelligence changes over the life span (Owens, 1966; Schaie, 1996, 2005; Schwartzman et al., 1987). For most people, the direction of this change is upward between adolescence and middle age and downward thereafter (cf. Ackerman, 2014). The sharpest decline occurs in old age (Kaufman, 2001; Salthouse, 1996a, 2000; Schaie, 2005) and may be due to a general decrease in the brain's processing speed (Salthouse, 1996b; Zimprich & Martin, 2002).

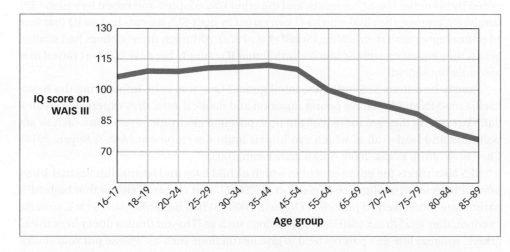

Figure 9.14 Intelligence Changes Over Time Intelligence changes over the life span, rising early, peaking in middle age, and declining thereafter.

Intelligence also changes over generations (see **FIGURE 9.15**). The *Flynn effect* refers to the fact that the average IQ score today is roughly 30 points higher than it was a century ago (Dickens & Flynn, 2001; Flynn, 2012; cf. Lynn, 2013). This is a striking number. It means that the average person today is smarter than 95% of the people who were alive in 1900! Why is each generation outscoring the one before it? Some researchers give the credit to improved nutrition, schooling, and parenting (Baker et al., 2015; Lynn, 2009; Neisser, 1998). But most scientists believe that the industrial and technological revolutions have changed the nature of daily living such that people now spend more and more time solving precisely the kinds of abstract problems that intelligence tests include — and as we all know, practice makes perfect (Bordone et al., 2015; Bratsberg & Rogeberg, 2018; Flynn, 2012).

How do genes and environments work together to influence intelligence? Our genes determine the range in which our IQ is *likely* to fall, but our environments determine

fraternal (dizygotic) twins Twins who develop from two different eggs that were fertilized by two different sperm.

identical (monozygotic) twins Twins who develop from the splitting of a single egg that was fertilized by a single sperm.

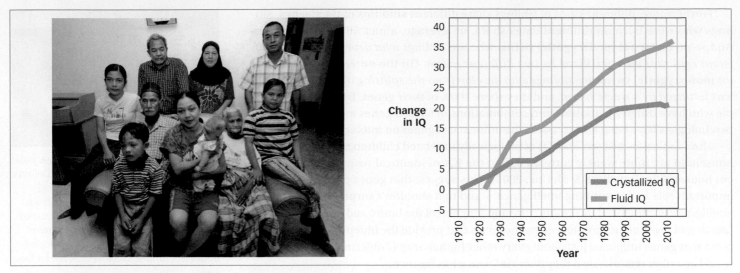

Figure 9.15 The Flynn Effect Khatijah, who is 105 years old (front row, second from right), sits with five generations of her family. As the graph shows, human intelligence has been increasing across generations for at least the past century, though some recent studies suggest that this increase may recently have ended (information from Pietschnig & Voracek, 2015). Binsar Bakkara/AP Images

To encourage low-SES parents to talk more to their children, the city of Providence, Rhode Island, created a program called Providence Talks. Once a month, a child wears a small recording device for the day, which allows a computer to calculate how many words she spoke, how many were spoken by adults in her vicinity, and how many conversational exchanges she experienced. A caseworker then visits her parent and provides a progress report. Katherine Taylor/The New York Times/Redux Pictures

the exact point in that range where it actually *does* fall (Hunt, 2011). Two of the most powerful such environmental influences involve economics and education.

Economics: Poverty Is Intelligence's Enemy

Maybe money can't buy love, but it can buy intelligence. One of the best predictors of a person's intelligence is the material wealth of the family in which he or she was raised — what psychologists call *socioeconomic status* (SES). Studies suggest that being raised in a high-SES family rather than a low-SES family is worth between 12 and 18 IQ points (Nisbett, 2009; van IJzendoorn et al., 2005). For instance, one study compared pairs of siblings who were born to low-SES parents. In each case, one of the siblings was raised by his or her low-SES parents, and the other was adopted and raised by a high-SES family. On average, the child who had been raised by high-SES parents had an IQ that was 14 points higher than their sibling (Schiff et al., 1978). Although these siblings had similar genes, they ended up with dramatically different IQs simply because one was raised in a wealthier household.

Exactly how does SES influence intelligence? One way is by influencing the brain itself. Low-SES children have poorer nutrition and medical care, they experience greater daily stress, and they are more likely to be exposed to environmental toxins such as air pollution and lead — all of which can impair brain development (Ash & Boyce, 2018; Chen et al., 2010; Evans, 2006; Hackman & Farah, 2008).

SES also affects the environment in which a child lives and learns. Intellectual stimulation increases intelligence (Nelson et al., 2007), and research shows that high-SES parents are more likely to provide it (Nisbett, 2009). When high-SES parents talk to their children, they tend to ask stimulating questions such as "Do you think a ducky likes to eat grass?", whereas low-SES parents tend to give instructions such as "Please put your ducky away" (Hart & Risley, 1995). By the age of 3, the average high-SES child has heard 30 million different words, whereas the average low-SES child has heard only 10 million different words. As a result, the high-SES child knows 50% more words than his or her low-SES counterpart. Clearly, poverty is the enemy of intelligence (Evans & Kim, 2012).

Education: School Is Intelligence's Friend

If poverty is intelligence's enemy, then education is its BFF. There is a strong positive correlation between the amount of formal education a person receives and his or her intelligence (Ceci, 1991; Neisser et al., 1996). One reason is that smart people tend to stay in school, but the other reason is that school makes people smarter (Ceci & Williams, 1997). When schooling is delayed because of war, pandemic, or the simple lack of qualified teachers, children show a measurable decline in intelligence (Nisbett, 2009).

Does this mean that anyone can become a lifelong genius just by showing up for class? Unfortunately not. Although education does increase intelligence, its effects tend to vanish when education ends (Protzko, 2015, 2016). For example, prekindergarten programs for low-SES children tend to raise their IQs, but the effects fade once these children leave their intellectually enriched environments and go to elementary school.

Although education does not always produce long-lasting increases in intelligence, it does seem to produce long-lasting increases in other important skills such as reading. In terms of just about every important outcome — from health to wealth to happiness — the difference between an illiterate person with an IQ of 100 and a literate person with an IQ of 101 is much larger than a single IQ point would suggest.

Gene–Environment Interactions

Although genes and environments have independent effects on the brain, they can also interact in fascinating ways. As you read in the Neuroscience and Behavior chapter, epigenetics refers to the fact that environmental factors can determine whether or not a gene will actually *do* anything. You can think of a gene as a little switch that the environment can turn to the *on* or *off* position. If the environment turns it on, then the gene plays a role in the development and function of the brain; if the environment turns it off, then the gene is silent and does nothing. Scientists have discovered more than 50 genes that can influence intelligence (Sniekers et al., 2017), and whether a person has these genes depends on their parents, of course, but whether these genes actually influence the person's intelligence may depend on whether the person's environment turns them.

There is another way in which genes and environments can interact to influence intelligence: Genes can also cause people to be drawn toward or away from particular environments (Dickens & Flynn, 2001; Nisbett, 2009; Plomin et al., 2001; Tucker-Drob et al., 2013). For example, if a particular set of genes makes people more outgoing and more sociable, then those genes may cause some people to enjoy the company of their peers more than others, which may cause them to stay in school longer, which may cause them to become smarter. Those genes would not be playing a direct role in promoting intelligence — say, by altering the structure of the person's brain — but would instead, be playing an indirect role by "pushing" people into the environments that promote their intelligence and "pulling" them away from environments that don't.

The fact that genes and environments can interact challenges the way most of us think about them. For instance, if a gene that lowers intelligence by impairing brain function is normally switched off, but in a particular child's case it was switched on by the stress of their impoverished environment, should we attribute that child's low intelligence to their "low intelligence gene" or to their "stressful environment"? If another child has a gene that causes them to be extraverted, which in turn causes them to join all the clubs at school, which in turn causes them to read more books and attend more lectures, should we attribute that child's high intelligence to their "extraversion gene" or to their extra education? These difficult questions highlight the fact that genes and environments work together in complex ways that scientists are just beginning to understand, which is why the obvious distinction between nature and nurture is becoming less obvious every day (see Hot Science: Brains Wide Open).

Build to the Outcomes

1. What do twin studies teach us about the influence of genes and environments on intelligence?

2. What are the most important environmental influences on intelligence?

3. How do genes and environments interact to influence intelligence?

Brains Wide Open

One of the things that makes our species so smart is that our brains are designed to be programmed by our environments. Turtles, lizards, and houseflies are all prewired by evolution to react in specific ways to specific stimuli. But mammalian brains — and especially human brains — are built to be *environmentally sensitive,* which means that humans are born with minimal hard-wiring and are instead wired by experiences. This is one of the things that allows human beings to function so effectively in a wide variety of physical and cultural environments.

But the brain's remarkable openness to experience doesn't last forever. By the age of 18 or so, the cerebral cortex has thickened, and the brain is never again as environmentally sensitive as it was in childhood. If the brain's environmental sensitivity is one of the things that makes our species so smart, it stands to reason that the smartest people among us might have brains that remain environmentally sensitive for longer than usual. Is that true?

To find out, researchers examined data from nearly 11,000 sets of monozygotic (MZ) and dizygotic (DZ) twins who had taken IQ tests sometime between infancy and adulthood (Brant et al., 2013). They computed the extent to which differences in IQ scores at each age

had been influenced by genes or by the environment. What they found was fascinating. Children's brains were relatively open to environmental influence, while adult's brains were relatively closed — but whereas the brains of low-IQ people closed by early adolescence, the brains of high-IQ people remained open to influence well into adolescence.

The accompanying graph shows the magnitude of both environmental and genetic influences at different ages. Whether you look at the effect of genes (in orange) or the effect of environment (in purple), you'll notice that the high- and low-IQ people end in the same place, but they get there at different speeds — specifically, low-IQ people get there faster.

No one knows why the brains of high-IQ people remain sensitive to the environment for longer, and no one knows if this is a cause or a consequence of their intelligence. All we know is that the longer the brain retains its childlike openness to experience, the more effectively it functions for the rest of its life.

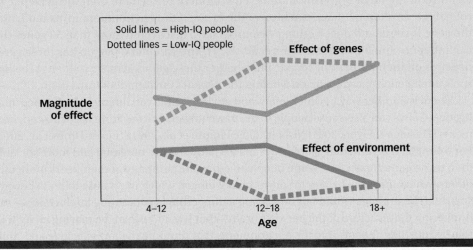

Who Is Most Intelligent?
Individual Differences in Intelligence

Learning Outcomes

The average IQ is 100, and 68% of us have IQs between 85 and 115 (see **FIGURE 9.16**). The people who score well above this middle range are said to be *intellectually gifted,* and the people who score well below it are said to be *intellectually disabled.* Although these

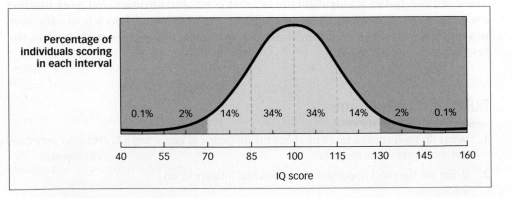

Figure 9.16 The Curve of Intelligence
This graph shows the percentage of people who score in each range of IQ.

people live at opposite ends of the intelligence continuum, they do have one thing in common: They are more likely to be male than female. Males and females have the same average IQ, but the distribution of males' IQ scores is wider and more variable than the distribution of females' IQ scores, which means that there are more males than females at both the very top and the very bottom of the IQ range (Hedges & Nowell, 1995; Lakin, 2013; Wai et al., 2012). Some of this difference is certainly due to the different ways in which boys and girls are socialized. Whether any of this difference is due to innate biological differences between males and females remains a hotly debated issue in psychology (Ceci et al., 2009; Nisbett et al., 2012; Spelke, 2005).

Those of us who occupy the large middle of the intelligence distribution tend to have a number of misconceptions about those who live at the extremes. For example, movies often portray the "tortured genius" as a person who is brilliant, creative, misunderstood, despondent, and more than a little bit weird. But, in fact, people with very high intelligence are *less* susceptible to mental illness than are people with very low intelligence (Dekker & Koot, 2003; Didden et al., 2012; Walker et al., 2002). Just as intelligence seems to buffer people against physical illness, so it seems to buffer people against mental illness as well.

Gifted children are rarely gifted in all departments, but instead have gifts in particular domains such as math, language, or music (Achter et al., 1996; Makel et al., 2016). Because gifted children tend to be single-gifted, they also tend to be single-minded, displaying a "rage to master" the domain in which they excel. Some research suggests that what most clearly distinguishes gifted children from their less gifted peers is the sheer amount of time they spend engaged in their domain of excellence (Ericsson & Charness, 1999). Their ability to devote themselves passionately to a single activity may help explain why gifted children so often become high-achieving adults (Lubinski, 2016).

On the other end of the intelligence spectrum are people with intellectual disabilities, about 70% of whom are male. Two of the most common causes of intellectual disability are Down syndrome (caused by the presence of a third copy of chromosome 21) and fetal alcohol syndrome (caused by a mother's excessive alcohol use during pregnancy). The intellectual disabilities associated with these two causes tend to be quite general, and people who have them typically show impaired performance on most or all cognitive tasks. Perhaps the greatest myth about the intellectually disabled is that they are unhappy. The fact is that nearly all people with Down syndrome are happy with their lives, like who they are, and like how they look (Skotko et al., 2011b). People with intellectual disabilities face many challenges, but being misunderstood by those who don't know them is among the most difficult.

Group Differences in Intelligence

In the early 1900s, Stanford University professor Lewis Terman improved on Binet and Simon's work and produced the intelligence test now known as the Stanford–Binet Intelligence Scale. Among the things this test revealed was that Whites performed better than non-Whites. "Are the inferior races really inferior, or are they merely unfortunate in their lack of opportunity to learn?" Terman asked, and then answered unequivocally: "Their dullness seems to be racial, or at least inherent in the family stocks from which they come" (Terman, 1916, pp. 91–92).

A century later, Terman's words make most of us cringe. But which words are the cringe-worthy ones? Terman claimed that (1) intelligence is influenced by genes, (2) members of some racial groups score better than others on intelligence tests, and (3) members of some racial groups score better than others on intelligence tests *because* of differences in their genes. Virtually all modern scientists who study intelligence consider Terman's

The artist Vincent van Gogh was the iconic "tortured genius." But data suggest that low intelligence, not high intelligence, is most strongly associated with mental illness. Lee Foster/Alamy

Isabella Springmuhl Tejada is a fashion designer who has Down syndrome. Her work has been showcased during London Fashion Week, and the BBC voted her one of the 100 most inspiring and innovative women of 2016. Leonardo Alvarez Hernandez/Getty Images

first two claims to be well-established facts: Intelligence *is* influenced by genes, and some groups *do* perform better than others on intelligence tests. But Terman's third claim — that differences in genes are the *reason* some groups outperform others — is a controversial conjecture that has been the subject of acrimonious debate. What does science have to tell us about it?

Before answering that question, let's be clear about one thing: Group differences in intelligence are not inherently problematic. No one is troubled by the possibility that this year's winners of the Nobel Prize are on average more intelligent than this year's winners of the Super Bowl, or that people who graduate from college are on average more intelligent than people who never attended school. On the other hand, most of us *are* troubled by the possibility that people of one gender, race, or nationality may be more intelligent than people of another. Intelligence is a valuable trait, and it doesn't seem fair for some people to have more of it than others simply because of an accident of birth or geography.

But fair or not, some people do. Women routinely outscore men on tests that require rapid access to and use of semantic information, production and comprehension of complex prose, fine motor skills, and perceptual speed or verbal intelligence. Men routinely outscore women on tests that require transformations in visual or spatial memory, certain motor skills, spatiotemporal responding, and fluid reasoning in abstract mathematical and scientific domains (Halpern et al., 2007; Nisbett et al., 2012). Asians routinely outscore Whites, who routinely outscore Blacks, on standard intelligence tests (Neisser et al., 1996; Nisbett et al., 2012). Indeed, group differences on intelligence tests are "among the most thoroughly documented findings in psychology" (Suzuki & Valencia, 1997, p. 1104). Although the average difference between groups is considerably less than the average difference within groups, there is no doubt that some groups outperform others — and the only important question is why?

Tests and Test Takers

One possibility is that there is something wrong with the tests. In fact, the earliest intelligence tests did ask questions whose answers were more likely to be known by members of one group (usually White Europeans) than by members of another. For example, one of Binet and Simon's questions was this: "When anyone has offended you and asks you to excuse him, what ought you to do?" Binet and Simon were looking for answers such as "accept the apology like a gentleman or explain why it is insufficient." Answers such as "challenge him to a fight" or "demand three goats" would have been counted as wrong despite the fact that in some cultures those answers would have been right. Early intelligence tests were clearly culturally biased. But testing has come a long way in a century, and one would have to look hard to find such blatantly biased questions on a modern intelligence test (Suzuki & Valencia, 1997).

Of course, even when test *questions* are unbiased, testing *situations* may not be. For example, studies show that African American students (but not European American students) perform more poorly on tests if they are asked to report their race at the top of the answer sheet, presumably because doing so leads them to feel anxious about confirming racial stereotypes (Steele & Aronson, 1995), and anxiety naturally interferes with test performance (Reeve et al., 2009). **Stereotype threat** is *the fear of confirming the negative beliefs that others may hold* (Aronson & Steele, 2004; Schmader et al., 2008; Walton & Spencer, 2009), and it can influence people's test performances. When Asian American women are reminded of their gender, they perform poorly on tests of mathematical skill if they are aware of stereotypes suggesting that women can't do math; but when the same women are instead reminded of their ethnicity, they perform well on such tests if they are aware of stereotypes suggesting that Asians are especially good

stereotype threat The fear of confirming the negative beliefs that others may hold.

THE REAL WORLD

Racism and Intelligence Testing

In the 19th century, Binet and Simon argued that children would be much better served if schools used an objective test to measure students' intelligence rather than allowing teachers, who might harbor a variety of preconceptions and prejudices, to make subjective evaluations of the children. In the early 20th century, however, intelligence tests acquired a bad reputation because they were used to justify some of the most heinous forms of discrimination, including the forced sterilization of poor and uneducated people who tended not to score well. Today, many people still consider *intelligence testing* and *racism* to be synonymous.

But history is irony. For decades, the state of Florida eschewed intelligence tests and instead used the subjective evaluations of teachers and parents to decide which children would be admitted to the "gifted and talented" programs in public schools. Minority children were severely underrepresented in these programs,

so, in 2005, Florida decided to try something new — or, more correctly, something old: It began to require that all 2nd graders take a screening test and that those who scored well take an actual intelligence test. The schools then used the results of the intelligence tests (rather than subjective evaluations) to determine which children would be placed in gifted and talented programs. What happened? The intelligence test did precisely what Binet and Simon had designed it to do: It eliminated the all-too-human prejudices that naturally bedevil subjective evaluations. In just a few years, the number of Black students admitted to gifted and talented programs had increased by a remarkable 74%, and the number of Hispanic students admitted had increased by an even more remarkable 118% (Card & Giuliano, 2016).

Unfortunately, this story does not have a happy ending. In 2010, the state of Florida instituted a series of budget cuts that forced

schools to discontinue the use of intelligence tests and to rely once again on subjective evaluations. As you might expect, the number of minority children admitted to gifted and talented programs plummeted. Intelligence tests, it seems, are neither good nor bad. They are tools — and like all tools, they can be used to make the real world a worse place or a better one.

at math (Gibson et al., 2014; Shih et al., 1999). Findings such as these remind us that the situations in which intelligence tests are administered can affect members of different groups differently and may cause group differences in *performance* that do not reflect group differences in actual *intelligence*. (See The Real World: Racism and Intelligence Testing).

Environments and Genes

Biases in the testing situation may explain some of the between-group differences in intelligence test scores, but there is broad agreement among scientists that environment also plays a major role. For example, African American children have lower birth weights, poorer diets, higher rates of chronic illness, and poorer medical care; attend worse schools; and are three times more likely than European American children to live in single-parent households (Acevedo-Garcia et al., 2007; National Center for Health Statistics, 2016a). Given the vast differences between the SES of European Americans and African Americans, it isn't very surprising that African Americans score, on average, 10 points lower on IQ tests than do European Americans.

What explains group differences like this one? So far, scientists have not found any evidence to suggest that genes explain these differences, but they have found evidence that makes such an explanation unlikely. For example, the average African American has about 20% European genes; yet individuals who have more of these genes are no smarter than those who have fewer, which is not what we'd expect if European genes made people smart (Loehlin, 1973; Nisbett et al., 2012; Scarr et al., 1977). Similarly, African American children and multi-racial children have different amounts of European genes; yet when they are adopted into middle-class families, their IQs don't differ (Moore, 1986), which is once again not what we'd expect if European genes made people smart. These facts do not prove that there is no genetic basis of the between-group differences in intelligence, but they do make that possibility less plausible. Unless researchers can isolate genes that are clearly connected to intelligence and then show that they are more prevalent in one group than another, most scientists are unlikely to embrace a genetic explanation of between-group differences in intelligence.

Improving Intelligence

Intelligence can be improved — by money, for example, and by education. But most people can't just snap their fingers and become wealthier, and education takes time. Is there anything that average parents can do to raise their child's IQ? Researchers analyzed the data from all the high-quality scientific studies on this question that have been performed over the past few decades (Protzko et al., 2013), and they found four things that seem to reliably raise a child's intelligence:

- Supplementing the diets of pregnant women and neonates with long-chain polyunsaturated fatty acids (substances found in breast milk) appears to raise children's IQ by up to 4 points (Boutwell et al., 2018).

- Enrolling low-SES infants in so-called early educational interventions tends to raise their IQ by about 6 points.

- Reading to children in an interactive manner raises their IQ by about 6 points.

- Sending children to preschool raises their IQ by about 6 points.

Parents are constantly looking for things they can do to make their kids smarter. Some studies suggest that learning to play a musical instrument can increase a child's intelligence (Protzko, 2017), while others suggest that musical training and intelligence are not causally related (Sala & Gobet, 2018). Jose Luis Pelaez Inc/Getty Images

There are also things parents can do to make themselves smarter as well. Some studies suggest that training for long periods of time with complex "mental exercises" can increase fluid intelligence (Jaeggi et al., 2008; cf. Mackey et al., 2011; Redick et al., 2013; Tranter & Koutstaal, 2007), and perhaps even slow cognitive decline in older adults (Salthouse, 2015). The jury is still out on whether these techniques produce significant and lasting increases in intelligence (Katz et al., 2018), but at least some of them appear promising.

Of course, improving intelligence does not have to take so much work. **Cognitive enhancers** are *drugs that improve the psychological processes that underlie intelligent performance.* Stimulants such as Ritalin and Adderall can enhance cognitive performance (Elliott et al., 1997; Halliday et al., 1994; McKetin et al., 1999) by temporarily improving people's ability to focus attention, manipulate information in working memory, and flexibly control their responses, which is why there has been an alarming increase in their use by healthy students over the past few decades (Sahakian & Morein-Zamir, 2007). These drugs enhance cognitive performance, but they can also have damaging side effects and lead to abuse.

In the near future, cognitive enhancement may be achieved not with chemicals that alter the brain's function but with techniques that alter its structure. By manipulating the genes that guide hippocampal development, for instance, scientists have created a strain of "smart mice" that have extraordinary memory and learning abilities (Tang et al., 1999, p. 64), and new "gene-editing" techniques may allow these animals to pass their genetic modifications on to their young. Although no one has yet developed a safe and powerful "smart pill" or a gene-editing technique that enhances intelligence in mammals, many experts believe that both of these things will happen in the very near future (Farah et al., 2004; Rose, 2002; Turner & Sahakian, 2006).

There is no bright line between technological enhancements and the more traditional kinds. If Adderall and "mental exercise" both enhance cognition by altering brain function, then what's the difference between them? Some think the answer is more ethical

cognitive enhancers Drugs that improve the psychological processes that underlie intelligent performance.

than biological: Both drugs and memory training enhance fluid intelligence, but one requires hard work and commitment while the other requires just a prescription. Do we want to live in a world in which a highly prized human attribute such as intelligence can be purchased, rather than being earned or endowed by nature? That's a question we will all soon be asking, and we will need a whole lot of intelligence to answer it (see Other Voices: Not by Intelligence Alone).

Not by Intelligence Alone

Barry Schwartz is the Dorwin Cartwright Professor of Social Theory and Social Action at Swarthmore College. He is the author of numerous books, including *The Paradox of Choice* (2004) and *Practical Wisdom: The Right Way to Do the Right Thing* (2010).
©Toby Madden/eyevine/Redux

Intelligence matters. But is it all that matters? Professor Barry Schwartz thinks not. He believes that intelligence alone cannot make us happy, productive, and successful citizens unless it is combined with a list of "intellectual virtues" that enable us to *use* our intelligence properly. In his view, colleges and universities should focus less on teaching students *what* to think and focus more on teaching students *how* to think by demonstrating and instilling nine key intellectual virtues. What are they?

Knowing how to think demands a set of cognitive skills—quantitative ability, conceptual flexibility, analytical acumen, expressive clarity. But beyond those skills, learning how to think requires the development of a set of intellectual virtues that make good students, good professionals, and good citizens . . . .

Love of truth. Students need to love the truth to be good students. . . . It has become intellectually fashionable to attack the very notion of truth. You have your truth, and I have mine. You have one truth today, but you may have a different one tomorrow. Everything is relative, a matter of perspective. People who claim to know the "truth," it is argued, are in reality just using their positions of power and privilege to shove their truth down other people's throats.

This turn to relativism is in part a reflection of something good and important that has happened to intellectual inquiry. People have caught on to the fact that much of what the intellectual elite thought was the truth *was* distorted by limitations of perspective. Slowly the voices of the excluded have been welcomed into the conversation. And their perspectives have enriched our understanding. But the reason they have enriched our understanding is that they have given the rest of us an important piece of the truth that was previously invisible to us. Not *their* truth, but *the* truth. It is troubling to see how quickly an appreciation that each of us can attain only a partial grasp of the truth degrades into a view that there really isn't any truth out there to be grasped. . . .

Honesty. Honesty enables students to face the limits of what they themselves know; it encourages them to own up to their mistakes. And it allows them to acknowledge uncongenial truths about the world. . . .

Fair-mindedness. Students need to be fair-minded in evaluating the arguments of others. . . .

Humility. Humility allows students to face up to their own limitations and mistakes and to seek help from others. . . .

Perseverance. Students need perseverance, since little that is worth knowing or doing comes easily. . . .

Courage. Students need intellectual courage to stand up for what they believe is true, sometimes in the face of disagreement from others, including people in authority, like their professors. And they need courage to take risks, to pursue intellectual paths that might not pan out.

Good listening. Students can't learn from others, or from their professors, without listening. It takes courage to be a good listener, because good listeners know that their own views of the world, along with their plans for how to live in it, may be at stake whenever they have a serious conversation.

Perspective-taking and empathy. It may seem odd to list perspective-taking and empathy as intellectual virtues, but it takes a great deal of intellectual sophistication to get perspective-taking right. Young children "feel" for a peer who is upset but are clueless about how to comfort her. They try to make a crying child feel better by doing what would make them feel better. And teachers, at all levels, must overcome "the curse of knowledge." If they can't remind themselves of what they were like before they understood something well, they will be at a loss to explain it to their students. Everything is obvious once you know it. . . .

Wisdom. Finally, students need what Aristotle called practical wisdom. Any of the intellectual virtues I've mentioned can be carried to an extreme. Wisdom is what enables us to find the balance (Aristotle called it the "mean") between timidity and recklessness, carelessness and obsessiveness, flightiness and stubbornness, speaking up and listening up, trust and skepticism, empathy and detachment. Wisdom is also what enables us to make difficult decisions when intellectual virtues conflict. Being empathetic, fair, and open-minded often rubs up against fidelity to the truth. Practical wisdom is the master virtue. . . .

Cultivation of intellectual virtues is not in conflict with training in specific occupations. On the contrary, intellectual virtues will help to create a work force that is flexible, able to admit to and learn from mistakes, and open to change. People with intellectual virtues will be persistent, ask for help when they need it, provide help when others need it, and not settle for expedient but inaccurate solutions to tough problems. . . . Workplaces need people who have intellectual virtues, but workplaces are not in a good position to instill them. Colleges and universities should be doing this training for them.

Schwartz believes that without a love of truth, honesty, fair-mindedness, and the rest, intelligence itself just can't get us very far. Is he right? And if so, can these virtues be taught? How? Is his list complete, and if not, what's missing? These are difficult but important questions, which, if you believe Schwartz, will never be answered by intelligence alone.

Build to the Outcomes

1. What are the most common misconceptions about the intellectually gifted and the intellectually disabled?

2. What one thing most clearly distinguishes gifted children from other children?

3. How can the testing situation affect a person's performance on an IQ test?

4. What evidence suggests that genes are unlikely to be the cause of between-group differences in intelligence?

5. In what ways can intelligence be enhanced? What ethical questions are raised?

CHAPTER REVIEW

Language and Communication: From Rules to Meaning

- Human language is characterized by a complex organization—from phonemes to morphemes to phrases and finally to sentences.

- Children can distinguish between all contrasting sounds of human language, but they lose that ability within the first 6 months. Vocal babbling occurs at about 4 to 6 months, and first words are uttered or signed by 10 to 12 months. Sentences emerge around 24 months.

- Children acquire grammatical rules in development, even without being taught explicitly.

- The behaviorist explanation for language learning is based on operant conditioning, whereas nativists hold that humans are biologically predisposed to process language. Interactionists explain it as both a biological and a social process.

- Our abilities to produce and comprehend language depend on distinct but interacting regions of the brain, with Broca's area critical for language production and Wernicke's area critical for comprehension.

Concepts and Categories: How We Think

- We organize knowledge about objects, events, or other stimuli by creating concepts, prototypes, and exemplars.

- We acquire concepts using processes suggested by two theories: Prototype theory states that we use the most typical member of a category to assess new items; exemplar theory states that we compare new items with stored memories of other members of the category.

- Prototypes and exemplars are processed in different parts of the brain.

- The brain organizes concepts into distinct categories, such as living things and human-made things; visual experience is not necessary for the development of such categories.

Decision Making: Rational and Otherwise

- Human decision making often departs from a completely rational process. The mistakes that accompany this departure tell us a lot about how the human mind works.

- When people are asked to make probability judgments, they will turn the problem into something they know how to solve, such as judging memory strength, judging similarity to prototypes, or estimating frequencies. This can lead to errors of judgment.

- Because we feel that avoiding losses is more important than achieving gains, framing effects can affect our choices. Emotional information also strongly influences our decision making, even when we are not aware of it.

- The prefrontal cortex plays an important role in decision making, and patients with prefrontal damage make more risky decisions than healthy individuals do.

Intelligence

- *Intelligence* is the ability to use one's mind to solve problems and learn from experience. Binet and Simon developed a test that was meant to measure a child's natural aptitude for learning, independent of previous experience.

- Intelligence tests produce a score known as an *intelligence quotient,* or IQ, which is the deviation of an adult's test score from the average adult's test score.

- People who score well on one test of mental ability *tend to* score well on others, which suggests that each person has a particular level of general intelligence *(g),* but they don't *always* score well on every other test, which suggests that different people have different specific abilities *(s).* Research reveals several *middle-level abilities* between *g* and *s.*

- Practical intelligence, creative intelligence, and emotional intelligence are middle-level abilities that standard intelligence tests don't measure.

Where Does Intelligence Come From?

- Both genes and environment have a powerful influence on intelligence.

- SES and education can both have powerful influences on IQ, though the effects of education are sometimes short-lived.

- Whether or not a person has a specific gene depends on that person's parents, but environmental factors can determine whether that gene is expressed.

Who Is Most Intelligent?

- Intelligence is correlated with mental health, and gifted children are as well-adjusted as their peers. Despite conventional wisdom, people with intellectual disabilities are typically happy with themselves and their lives.

- Some groups outscore others on intelligence tests, in part because testing situations can impair the performance of some groups more than others, and in part because low-SES environments have an adverse impact on intelligence.

- There is no compelling evidence to suggest that group differences on intelligence tests are due to the genetic differences between the groups.

- Human intelligence can be increased by a variety of means, from preschool to mental exercise to pharmaceuticals. Some of these methods carry greater risks, and raise more difficult ethical questions, than others.

Key Concept Quiz

1. The combining of words to form phrases and sentences is governed by
   a. phonological rules.
   b. morphological rules.
   c. structural rules.
   d. syntactic rules.

2. Language development as an innate, biological capacity is explained by
   a. fast mapping.
   b. behaviorism.
   c. nativist theory.
   d. interactionist explanations.

3. Damage to the brain region called Broca's area results in
   a. failure to comprehend language.
   b. difficulty in producing grammatical speech.
   c. the reintroduction of infant babbling.
   d. difficulties in writing.

4. The "most typical" member of a category is a(n)
   a. prototype.
   b. exemplar.
   c. concept.
   d. definition.

5. Evidence suggests that exemplar-based learning involves analysis and decision making, involving which area of the brain:
   a. visual cortex
   b. prefrontal cortex
   c. primary auditory cortex
   d. somatosensory cortex

6. People give different answers to the same problem, depending on how the problem is phrased, because of
   a. the availability bias.
   b. the conjunction fallacy.
   c. the representativeness heuristic.
   d. framing effects.

7. Intelligence tests were originally developed
   a. to help place children in the most appropriate classroom.
   b. to measure educational achievement rather than aptitude.
   c. by governments that wanted to halt immigration.
   d. in Russia.

8. Intelligence tests have been shown to be predictors of
   a. academic performance.
   b. mental health.
   c. physical health.
   d. all of the above.

9. People who score well on one test of mental ability usually score well on others, suggesting that
   a. tests of mental ability are perfectly correlated.
   b. intelligence cannot be measured meaningfully.
   c. there is a general ability called intelligence.
   d. intelligence is genetic.

10. Most scientists now believe that intelligence is best described
    a. as a set of group factors.
    b. by a two-factor framework.
    c. as a single, general ability.
    d. by a three-level hierarchy.

11. Standard intelligence tests typically measure
    a. analytic intelligence.
    b. practical intelligence.
    c. creative intelligence.
    d. all of the above.

12. Intelligence is influenced by
    a. genes alone.
    b. genes and environment.
    c. environment alone.
    d. neither genes nor environment.

13. Intelligence changes
    a. over the life span and across generations.
    b. over the life span but not across generations.
    c. across generations but not over the life span.
    d. neither across generations nor over the life span.

14. A person's socioeconomic status has a(n) _____ effect on intelligence.
    a. powerful
    b. negligible
    c. unsubstantiated
    d. unknown

15. About which of these statements is there a broad agreement among scientists?

  a. Differences in the intelligence test scores of different ethnic groups are clearly due to genetic differences between those groups.

  b. Differences in the intelligence test scores of different ethnic groups are caused in part by factors such as low birth weight and poor diet, which are more prevalent in some groups than in others.

  c. Differences in the intelligence test scores of different ethnic groups always reflect real differences in intelligence.

  d. Genes that are strongly associated with intelligence have been found to be more prevalent in some ethnic groups than in others.

LearningCurve   Don't stop now! Quizzing yourself is a powerful study tool. Go to LaunchPad to access the LearningCurve adaptive quizzing system and your own personalized learning plan. Visit launchpadworks.com.

Key Terms

language (p. 258)

grammar (p. 258)

phonemes (p. 258)

phonological rules (p. 259)

morphemes (p. 259)

morphological rules (p. 259)

syntactic rules (p. 259)

fast mapping (p. 261)

telegraphic speech (p. 261)

nativist theory (p. 263)

universal grammar (p. 263)

genetic dysphasia (p. 264)

aphasia (p. 265)

concept (p. 266)

prototype theory (p. 266)

exemplar theory (p. 266)

category-specific deficit (p. 268)

rational choice theory (p. 269)

availability bias (p. 270)

conjunction fallacy (p. 270)

representativeness heuristic (p. 271)

framing effects (p. 271)

sunk-cost fallacy (p. 271)

optimism bias (p. 272)

prospect theory (p. 272)

intelligence (p. 274)

intelligence quotient (IQ) (p. 275)

two-factor theory of intelligence (p. 277)

crystallized intelligence (p. 278)

fluid intelligence (p. 278)

emotional intelligence (p. 279)

fraternal (dizygotic) twins (p. 281)

identical (monozygotic) twins (p. 281)

stereotype threat (p. 286)

cognitive enhancers (p. 288)

Changing Minds

1. You mention to a friend that you've just learned that the primary language we learn can shape the way that we think. Your friend says that people are people everywhere and that this can't be true. What evidence could you describe to support your point?

2. In September 2011, *Wired* magazine ran an article discussing the fourth-down decisions of NFL coaches. On fourth down, a coach can choose to play aggressively and go for a first down (or even a touchdown), or the coach can settle for a punt or a field goal, which are safer options but result in fewer points than a touchdown. Statistically, the riskier play results in greater point gain, on average, than playing it safe. But in reality, coaches choose the safer plays over 90% of the time. Reading this article, one of your friends is incredulous. "Coaches aren't stupid, and they want to win," he says. "Why would they always make the wrong decision?" Your friend is assuming that humans are rational decision makers. In what ways is your friend wrong? What might be causing the football coaches to make irrational decisions?

3. In biology class, the topic turns to genetics. The professor describes how scientists used gene editing to make a smarter mouse. Your classmate turns to you. "I knew it," she said. "There's a 'smart gene' after all. Some people have it, and some people don't, and that's why some people are intelligent, and some people aren't." What would you tell her about the ways in which genes and environment affect intelligence?

4. One of your friends tells you about his sister. "We're very competitive," he says. "But she's smarter. We both took IQ tests when we were kids, and she scored 104, but I only scored 102." What would you tell your friend about the relationship between IQ scores and intelligence? What kinds of intelligence do traditional IQ tests measure? What other abilities contribute to an individual's overall intelligence?

5. A survey shows that in mathematics departments all over the country, tenured male professors outnumber tenured female professors by about 9 to 1. One of your friends says, "But it's a fact—girls just don't do as well as boys at math, so it's not surprising that fewer girls choose math-related careers." Considering what you've read in this chapter about group differences in intelligence, how might you explain this fact to your friend?

Answers to Key Concept Quiz

1. d; 2. c; 3. b; 4. a; 5. b; 6. d; 7. a; 8. d; 9. c; 10. d; 11. a; 12. b; 13. a; 14. a; 15. b

 **LaunchPad**
macmillan learning

LaunchPad features the full e-book of *Introducing Psychology*, the LearningCurve adaptive quizzing system, videos, and a variety of activities to boost your learning. Visit LaunchPad at launchpadworks.com.

John Lund/Getty Images

Development

10

His mother called him Adi and showered him with affection, but his father was not so kind. As his sister later recalled, Adi "got his sound thrashing every day." Although his father wanted him to become a civil servant, Adi's true love was art, and his mother quietly encouraged that gentle interest. Adi was just 18 years old when his mother was diagnosed with terminal cancer. His sister noted that Adi "spoiled my mother during this time of her life with overflowing tenderness. He was indefatigable in his care for her, wanted to comply with any desire she could possibly have and did all to demonstrate his great love for her." He was heartbroken when she died but had little time for grieving. As he later wrote, "Poverty and hard reality compelled me to make a quick decision. I was faced with the problem of somehow making my own living." Adi decided to defy his father's wishes and become an artist. He applied to art school but was flatly rejected, and so—motherless, homeless, and penniless—Adi wandered the streets for years, sleeping on park benches, living in shelters, and eating in soup kitchens, all the while trying desperately to sell his sketches and watercolors.

But this is not the story of a forgotten artist. Indeed, Adi ultimately achieved great fame, and today, collectors from all across the world compete to buy his paintings. The largest collection of his work is not, however, in private hands or even in a museum. Rather, it is owned by the U.S. government and kept locked away in a windowless room in Washington, DC. "I often looked at them and wondered, 'What if?'" said Marylou Gjernes, the longtime curator of this collection. "What if he had been accepted into art school? Would World War II have happened?'"

Prenatality: A Womb With a View

Infancy and Childhood: Perceiving, Doing, and Thinking

Infancy and Childhood: Bonding and Helping

Adolescence: Minding the Gap

Adulthood: Change We Can't Believe In

Adi painted in many styles, including the precise and well-structured watercolor shown here. In 2013, one of his paintings sold at auction for $40,000. Interfoto/Alamy

Why did the curator of Adi's artwork ask herself that question? Because although his mother called him Adi, the rest of us know him as Adolf Hitler.

Why is it so difficult to imagine the worst mass murderer of the 20th century as a gentle child who loved to draw, as a compassionate adolescent who cared for his ailing mother, or as a dedicated young adult who suffered for the sake of his art? After all, *you* didn't start out as the person you are today. You are utterly different from the baby you once were, and utterly different from the elderly person you will someday become. From birth to infancy, from childhood to adolescence, from young adulthood to old age, human beings are transformed by time. They experience dramatic changes in the way they look, think, feel, and act, but they also display some surprising consistencies. **Developmental psychology** is *the study of continuity and change across the life span,* and in the past century, developmental psychologists have discovered some truly amazing things about this metamorphosis.

The story of human development starts where humans do: at conception. First, we'll examine the 9-month period between conception and birth and see how prenatal events set the stage for so much of what's to come. Then we'll examine infancy and childhood, the periods during which children learn how to think about the world and about their relationships with others. Next, we'll examine a relatively new invention called adolescence, the stage at which children become both independent and sexual creatures. Finally, we'll examine adulthood, the stage at which people typically leave their parents, find mates, and have children of their own.

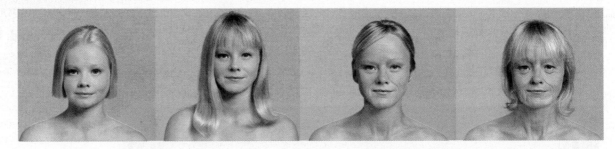

Throughout the life span, human beings show both continuity and change in how they look, think, feel, and behave. Peter Dazeley/ Getty Images

Learning Outcomes

- Describe the three prenatal stages of development.
- Give reasons it is advantageous for humans to be born with underdeveloped brains.
- Explain how the prenatal environment influences fetal development.

developmental psychology The study of continuity and change across the life span.

germinal stage The 2-week period of prenatal development that begins at conception.

Prenatality: A Womb With a View

Most of us calculate our age by counting our birthdays, but on the day we are born we are already 9 months old. The *prenatal stage* of development ends with birth, but it begins 9 months earlier when about 200 million sperm set out on a journey from a woman's vagina, through her uterus, and to her fallopian tubes. Many are called, but few are chosen. Some of the sperm don't swim vigorously enough to make any progress; others take a wrong turn and end up in the fallopian tube that does not contain an egg. When all is said and done, only one out of every million sperm manages to get close to an egg and then release digestive enzymes that erode the egg's protective outer coating. The moment the first sperm does this, the egg releases a chemical that reseals its coating and keeps all the other sperm from entering. After triumphing over 199,999,999 of its fellow travelers, this single successful sperm sheds its tail and fertilizes the egg. About 12 hours later, the egg merges with the nuclei of the sperm, and the prenatal development of a unique human being begins.

Prenatal Development

That unique human being has a name. A *zygote* is a fertilized egg that contains genetic material from both the egg and the sperm, and its brief lifetime is called the **germinal stage**, which is *the 2-week period that begins at conception.* During this stage, the

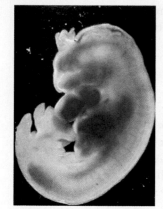
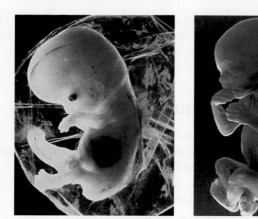

Figure 10.1 Prenatal Development
Humans undergo dramatic changes during the 9 months of prenatal development. These images show an embryo at 30 days (about the size of a poppyseed), an embryo at 8 weeks (about the size of a raspberry), and a fetus at 5 months (about the size of a banana). Claude Edelmann/Science Source; Biophoto Associates/Science Source; James Stevenson/Science Source

one-celled zygote divides into two cells that then divide into four cells that then divide into eight cells, and so on. By the time an infant is born, its body contains trillions of cells, each of which came from the original zygote. During the germinal stage, the zygote migrates down the fallopian tube and implants itself in the wall of the uterus. This is a difficult journey, and about half of all zygotes don't complete it, either because they are defective or because they implant themselves in an inhospitable part of the uterus. Male zygotes are especially unlikely to complete this journey and no one understands why, though several comedians have suggested it's because male zygotes are especially unwilling to stop and ask for directions.

The moment the zygote successfully implants itself in the uterine wall, it loses its old name and earns a new one: *embryo*. The **embryonic stage** is *a period that starts at about the 2nd week after conception and lasts until about the 8th week* (see **FIGURE 10.1**). During this stage, the implanted embryo continues to divide, and its cells begin to differentiate. Although it is only an inch long, the embryo already has arms, legs, and a beating heart. It also has the beginnings of female reproductive organs, and if it is a male embryo, it begins to produce a hormone called testosterone that will masculinize those organs.

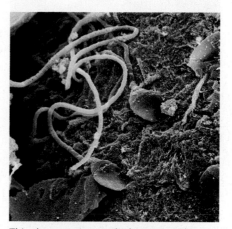

This electron micrograph shows several human sperm, one of which is fertilizing an egg. Contrary to what many people think, fertilization does not happen right away. It typically happens 1 to 2 days after intercourse, but can happen as many as 5 days later. Eye of Science/Science Source

The embryo doesn't have a lot of time to get used to its new name, however, because at about 9 weeks it becomes a *fetus*. The **fetal stage** is *a period that lasts from about the 9th week after conception until birth*. The fetus has a skeleton and muscles that make it capable of movement. During the fetal stage, brain cells begin to generate axons and dendrites that allow them to communicate with other brain cells. They also begin to undergo a process (described in the Neuroscience and Behavior chapter) known as **myelination**, which is *the formation of a fatty sheath around the axons of a neuron*. Just as plastic sheathing insulates the wires in a kitchen appliance, myelin insulates the neurons in the brain, preventing the leakage of the signals that travel along the axon. Myelination starts during the fetal stage, but it doesn't end until adulthood.

The human brain grows rapidly during the fetal period, but unlike the brains of other primates, it does not come close to achieving its adult size. A newborn chimpanzee's brain is nearly 60% of its adult size, but a newborn human's brain is only 25% of its adult size, which is to say that 75% of a human's brain development occurs after birth. Why are humans born with such underdeveloped brains? First, humans have really big heads, and if a newborn baby's head were anywhere close to its adult size, the baby could never pass through its mother's birth canal. Second, one of our species' greatest talents is its ability to adapt to a wide range of novel environments that differ in climate, social structure, and so on. So rather than arriving in the world with a highly developed brain that may or may not meet the requirements of its environment, human beings arrive with underdeveloped

embryonic stage The period of prenatal development that lasts from the 2nd week until about the 8th week.

fetal stage The period of prenatal development that lasts from the 9th week until birth.

myelination The formation of a fatty sheath around the axons of a neuron.

brains that do much of their developing *within* the very environments in which they ultimately must function, thereby gaining the unique capacities that each environment requires.

Prenatal Environment

The word *environment* probably makes you think of green fields and blue skies. But the womb is also an environment, and it has a powerful impact on development (Coe & Lubach, 2008; Glynn & Sandman, 2011; Wadhwa et al., 2001). Although a woman's bloodstream is separated from the bloodstream of her unborn child by the placenta, many substances can pass through the placenta. A **teratogen** is *any substance that passes from mother to unborn child and impairs development.*

Teratogens include the mercury in fish, the lead in water, and the paint dust in air, but the most common teratogens are alcohol and tobacco. **Fetal alcohol syndrome (FAS)** is *a developmental disorder that stems from heavy alcohol use by the mother during pregnancy,* and children born with FAS have a variety of brain abnormalities and cognitive deficits (Carmichael Olson et al., 1997; Streissguth et al., 1999). Some studies suggest that light drinking does not harm the fetus, but there is little consensus about how much drinking is "light" (Warren & Hewitt, 2009). On the other hand, everyone agrees that "none" is a perfectly safe amount.

There is no such debate about tobacco. Mothers who smoke during pregnancy have children who are smaller, more likely to be born prematurely, and more likely to have perceptual and attentional problems in both infancy (Wiebe et al., 2014) and childhood (Espy et al., 2011; Fried & Watkinson, 2000). Even secondhand smoke can lead to reduced birth weight and deficits in attention and learning (Makin et al., 1991; Windham et al., 1999). Exactly how dangerous is smoking during pregnancy? Very! Research suggests that smoking during pregnancy increases a woman's odds of having a stillborn child by a whopping 47% (Marufu et al., 2015).

The things a pregnant woman ingests can harm her unborn child, but so too can the things she *fails* to ingest. Women who don't get enough nutrition during pregnancy have children who are at increased risk for a variety of physical and mental illnesses (Neugebauer et al., 1999; Susser et al., 1999).

The prenatal environment is rich with chemicals that affect the unborn child, but it is also rich with information. The fetus can hear its mother's heartbeat, the gastrointestinal sounds associated with her digestion, and her voice. Newborns will suck a nipple more vigorously when they hear the sound of their mother's voice than when they hear the voice of a female stranger (Querleu et al., 1984), indicating that even at birth they are already more familiar with the former. Newborns who listen to strangers speaking two languages will suck more vigorously when they hear words from their mother's native language, indicating that they are already familiar with the tempo and rhythm of their mother's speech (Byers-Heinlein et al., 2010). What fetuses hear in the womb even influences the sounds they will ultimately make themselves. French newborns cry with a rising pitch, and German newborns cry with a falling pitch, both mimicking the cadence of their mother's native tongue (Mampe et al., 2009). Clearly, the fetus is listening.

This child has some of the telltale facial features associated with fetal alcohol syndrome (FAS): short eye openings, a flat midface, a flat ridge under the nose, a thin upper lip, and an underdeveloped jaw.
Rick's Photography/Shutterstock

teratogen Any substance that passes from mother to unborn child and impairs development.

fetal alcohol syndrome (FAS) A developmental disorder that stems from heavy alcohol use by the mother during pregnancy.

Build to the Outcomes

1. What are the three stages of prenatal development?

2. What is the adaptive benefit of being born with an underdeveloped brain?

3. How does the uterine environment affect the unborn child?

4. What evidence suggests that "the fetus is listening"?

Infancy and Childhood: Perceiving, Doing, and Thinking

Newborn babies don't look like they can do much more than poop, burp, sleep, and cry. But looks can be deceiving. **Infancy** is *the stage of development that begins at birth and lasts between 18 and 24 months,* and in the past few decades, researchers have discovered that much more is going on inside the infant than meets the untrained eye.

Perceptual Development

Grandparents, aunts, uncles, and other assorted relatives might not stand around the crib and make goofy faces if they realized that the baby can't see them. Newborns have a limited range of vision, and the amount of detail they can see from 20 feet away is roughly equivalent to the amount of detail that you can see from 600 feet away (Banks & Salapatek, 1983). On the other hand, newborns can see things that are 8 to 12 inches away, which just so happens to be the distance between a mother's face and her nursing infant's eyes.

How do psychologists know what a newborn can and can't see? Recall from the Learning chapter that *habituation* is the tendency for organisms to respond less intensely to a stimulus each time it is presented. So if a newborn habituates to a stimulus after several presentations, that means he or she must have been able to see it. If newborns are shown an object over and over again, they will stare a lot at first and then less and less each time the object is presented. If the object is then rotated 90°, the newborns will begin staring at it again (Slater et al., 1988), indicating that they noticed the change. Newborns are especially attentive to objects that look like faces (Biro et al., 2014). For example, when newborns in one study were shown moving shapes (see **FIGURE 10.2**) they tracked the movement with their eyes longer if those shapes had facial features (Johnson et al., 1991; cf. Kwon et al., 2016). Clearly, babies are watching—and what they are watching most closely is us!

Motor Development

Infants can use their eyes and ears right away, but they have to spend some time learning to use their other parts. **Motor development** is *the emergence of the ability to execute physical actions* such as reaching, grasping, crawling, and walking. Infants are born with a small set of **motor reflexes**, which are *motor responses that are triggered by specific patterns of sensory stimulation.* For example, the *rooting reflex* causes infants to move their mouths toward any object that touches their cheek, and the *sucking reflex* causes them to suck any object that enters their mouth. Together, these two reflexes allow newborn infants to find their mother's nipple and begin feeding—a behavior so vitally important that nature took no chances and hard-wired it into every one of us.

The development of more sophisticated motor behaviors tends to obey two general rules. The first is the **cephalocaudal rule** (or the "top-to-bottom" rule), which describes *the tendency for motor skills to emerge in sequence from the head to the feet.* Infants tend to gain control over their heads first, their arms and trunks next, and their legs last. A young infant who is placed on her stomach may lift her head and her chest by using her arms for support, but she typically has little control over her legs. The second rule is the **proximodistal rule** (or the "inside-to-outside" rule), which describes *the tendency for motor skills to emerge in sequence from the center to the periphery.* Infants learn to control their trunks before their elbows and knees, which they learn to control before their hands and feet (see **FIGURE 10.3**). Although motor skills develop in an orderly sequence, they do not develop on a strict timetable. Rather, the timing of these skills is influenced by many factors, such as the infant's body weight, muscular development, and general level of activity.

Learning Outcomes

- Describe the evidence suggesting that newborns can see.
- Explain the two rules of motor development.
- Describe the stages of Piaget's theory of cognitive development.
- Differentiate between egocentrism and theory of mind.
- Describe the key skills that allow infants to learn from others.

Figure 10.2 Infants Track Social Stimuli Newborns will track the shapes with facial features (left) longer than shapes with scrambled facial features (middle) or no facial features (right). Adapted from Johnson et al., 1991

infancy The stage of development that begins at birth and lasts between 18 and 24 months.

motor development The emergence of the ability to execute physical actions.

motor reflexes Motor responses that are triggered by specific patterns of sensory stimulation.

cephalocaudal rule The "top-to-bottom" rule that describes the tendency for motor skills to emerge in sequence from the head to the feet.

proximodistal rule The "inside-to-outside" rule that describes the tendency for motor skills to emerge in sequence from the center to the periphery.

Figure 10.3 Motor Development Infants learn to control their bodies from head to feet and from center to periphery. These skills do not emerge on a strict timetable, but they do emerge in a strict sequence.

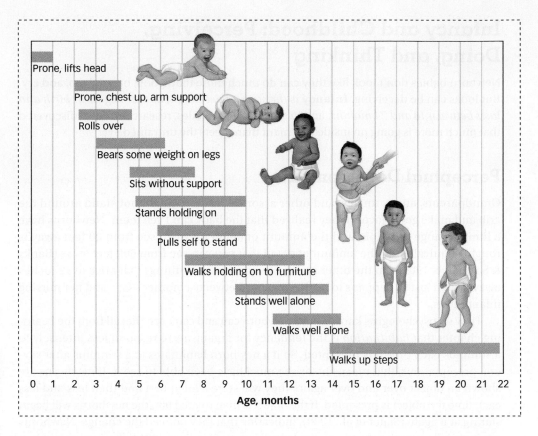

Age, months

Prone, lifts head
Prone, chest up, arm support
Rolls over
Bears some weight on legs
Sits without support
Stands holding on
Pulls self to stand
Walks holding on to furniture
Stands well alone
Walks well alone
Walks up steps

0 1 2 3 4 5 6 7 8 9 10 11 12 13 14 15 16 17 18 19 20 21 22

Jean Piaget (1896–1980) was the father of modern developmental psychology, as well as the last man who actually looked cool wearing a beret. Patrick Grehan/Getty Images

cognitive development The process by which infants and children gain the ability to think and understand.

sensorimotor stage A stage of cognitive development that begins at birth and lasts through infancy, during which infants acquire information about the world by sensing it and moving around within it.

schemas Theories about the way the world works.

assimilation The process by which infants apply their schemas in novel situations.

Cognitive Development

Infants can see and hear and move their bodies. But can they think? In the first half of the 20th century, Swiss biologist Jean Piaget began to study **cognitive development**, which is *the process by which infants and children gain the ability to think and understand.* Piaget suggested that during this process, infants and children learn how the physical world works, how their own minds work, and how other people's minds work. Let's see how they achieve all three of these understandings.

Discovering the World

Piaget (1954) suggested that cognitive development occurs in four discrete stages: the sensorimotor stage, the preoperational stage, the concrete operational stage, and the formal operational stage (see **TABLE 10.1**).

The **sensorimotor stage** is *a stage of cognitive development that begins at birth and lasts through infancy, during which infants acquire information about the world by sensing it and moving around within it.*

By actively exploring their environments with their eyes, mouths, and fingers, infants begin to construct **schemas**, which are *theories about the way the world works.* If an infant learns that tugging at a stuffed animal brings the toy closer, then that observation is incorporated into the infant's theory about how physical objects behave ("Things come closer if I pull them"), and the infant can later use that theory when she wants a different object to come closer, such as a rattle or a ball. Piaget called this **assimilation**, *the process by which infants apply their schemas in novel situations.* Of course, if the infant applies this theory to the family cat, the cat is likely to sprint in the opposite direction. Infants' theories about the world are sometimes disconfirmed by experience, which causes infants to take special notice (Stahl & Feigenson, 2015) and to adjust their theories ("Inanimate things come closer when I pull them, but animate things just hiss and run"). Piaget called

TABLE 10.1	Piaget's Four Stages of Cognitive Development
Stage	**Characteristic**
Sensorimotor (birth–2 years)	Infant experiences the world by sensing it and moving in it, develops schemas, begins to act intentionally, and shows evidence of understanding object permanence
Preoperational (2–6 years)	Child acquires motor skills but does not understand conservation of physical properties; child begins this stage by thinking egocentrically but ends with a basic understanding of other minds
Concrete operational (6–11 years)	Child can think logically about physical objects and events, and understands conservation of physical properties
Formal operational (11 years and up)	Child can think logically about abstract propositions and hypotheticals

this **accommodation**, *the process by which infants revise their schemas in light of new information.*

Piaget suggested that infants are surprisingly clueless about some of the most basic properties of the physical world and must acquire information about those properties through experience. For example, when you put your shoes in the closet, you know that they are still there even after you close the closet door, and you would be surprised if you opened the door a moment later and found the closet empty. But according to Piaget, this wouldn't surprise an infant because infants do not yet have an understanding of **object permanence**, which refers to *the fact that objects exist even when they are not visible.* Piaget noted that in the first few months of life, infants act as though objects stop existing the moment they are out of sight.

But modern researchers have discovered that infants know more about object permanence than Piaget suspected. For instance, in one study, infants were shown a miniature drawbridge that flipped up and down (see **FIGURE 10.4**). Once the infants got used to this, a solid box was placed behind the drawbridge—in the path of the drawbridge, but out of the infant's sight. Some infants then saw a *possible* event: The drawbridge began to flip and then it suddenly stopped, as if its motion was being impeded by the unseen solid box. Other infants saw an *impossible* event: The drawbridge began to flip—and then it didn't stop, as if its motion was unimpeded by the unseen solid box. Four-month-old

accommodation The process by which infants revise their schemas in light of new information.

object permanence The fact that objects continue to exist even when they are not visible.

Habituation   Possible event   Impossible event

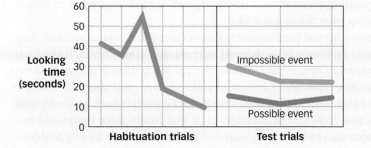

Looking time (seconds)

Habituation trials   Test trials

Impossible event

Possible event

Figure 10.4 The Impossible Event During the habituation trials, infants watch a drawbridge flip back and forth with nothing in its path until they grow bored. During the test trials, a box is placed behind the drawbridge, and the infants are shown either a possible event (in which the motion of the drawbridge is impeded) or an impossible event (in which the motion of the drawbridge is not impeded). The graph shows the infants' looking times during the habituation trials and the test trials. During the test trials, the infants showed more interest in the impossible event than the possible event (Baillargeon et al., 1985).

When preoperational children are shown two equal-size glasses filled with equal amounts of liquid, they correctly say that neither glass "has more." But when the contents of one glass are poured into a taller, thinner glass, they incorrectly say that the taller glass now "has more." Concrete operational children don't make this mistake because they recognize that operations such as pouring change the appearance of the liquid but not its actual volume. Maya Barnes Johansen/The Image Works

childhood The stage of development that begins at about 18 to 24 months and lasts until about 11 to 14 years.

preoperational stage The stage of cognitive development that begins at about 2 years and ends at about 6 years, during which children develop a preliminary understanding of the physical world.

concrete operational stage The stage of cognitive development that begins at about 6 years and ends at about 11 years, during which children learn how various actions, or *operations,* can transform the concrete objects of the physical world.

conservation The understanding that the quantitative properties of an object are invariant despite changes in the object's appearance.

formal operational stage The final stage of cognitive development that begins around the age of 11, during which children learn to reason about abstract concepts.

infants stared longer at the impossible event than at the possible event, suggesting that they were puzzled by it (Baillargeon et al., 1985). The only thing that made the impossible event impossible was the fact that an unseen box should have—but didn't—impede the motion of the drawbridge, which means that the infants must have realized that the box continued to exist even when it could no longer be seen. Studies such as these suggest that infants acquire an understanding of object permanence earlier than Piaget suspected (Shinskey & Munakata, 2005; Wang & Baillargeon, 2008).

Discovering the Mind

The long period following infancy is called **childhood**, which is *the period that begins at about 18 to 24 months and lasts until about 11 to 14 years.* According to Piaget, people enter childhood at the **preoperational stage**, which is *the stage of cognitive development that begins at about 2 years and ends at about 6 years, during which children develop a preliminary understanding of the physical world.* They exit childhood at the **concrete operational stage**, which is *the stage of cognitive development that begins at about 6 years and ends at about 11 years, during which children learn how various actions, or "operations," can transform the concrete objects of the physical world.*

The difference between these stages is nicely illustrated by one of Piaget's clever experiments, in which he showed children a row of cups and asked them to place an egg in each. Preoperational children were able to do this, and afterward they readily agreed that there were just as many eggs as there were cups. Then Piaget took the eggs and spread them out in a long line that extended beyond the row of cups. Preoperational children incorrectly claimed that there were now more eggs than cups, pointing out that the row of eggs was longer than the row of cups and hence there must be more of them. Concrete operational children, on the other hand, correctly reported that the number of eggs did not change when they were merely spread out in a longer line. They understood that *quantity* is a property of a set of concrete objects that does not change when an operation such as *spreading out* alters the set's appearance (Piaget, 1954). Piaget called the child's insight **conservation**, which is *the understanding that the quantitative properties of an object are invariant, despite changes in the object's appearance.*

Why don't preoperational children grasp the notion of conservation? Adults naturally distinguish between the subjective and the objective, between appearances and realities, between the way things look and the way things are. We know that a wagon can *be* red but *look* gray at dusk, and that a highway can *be* dry but *look* wet in the heat. Visual illusions delight us precisely because we know that they look one way but are really another. Preoperational children don't make this distinction. They assume that when something *looks* gray or wet it must *be* gray or wet. As they move from the preoperational to the concrete operational stage, they come to realize that the way the world *appears* and the way the world *is* are sometimes very different things.

Once children have this insight, they can understand that when a ball of clay is rolled, stretched, or flattened, it is still the same amount of clay despite the fact that it looks larger in one form than in another. They can understand that when water is poured from a short, wide beaker into a tall, thin cylinder, it is still the same amount of water despite the fact that the water level in the tall cylinder is higher. In short, they understand that certain operations—such as squishing, pouring, and spreading out—can change what an object *looks* like without changing what the object *is* like.

Children learn to solve physical problems at the concrete operational stage, and they learn to solve nonphysical problems at the **formal operational stage**, which is *the final stage of cognitive development that begins around the age of 11, during which children learn to reason about abstract concepts.* Childhood ends when formal operations begin, and people are able to reason systematically about abstract concepts such as *liberty* and *love,* and about events that have not yet happened or that might have happened but didn't. There are no concrete objects in the world to which the words *liberty* and *love* refer, yet people at the formal operational stage can think and reason about such concepts in the same way that a concrete operational child can think and reason about squishing and spreading out. The ability to generate, consider, reason about, or mentally "operate on" abstract concepts is the hallmark of formal operations.

Discovering Other Minds

As children develop, they discover their own minds. But they also discover the minds of others. Because preoperational children don't fully grasp the fact that they have minds that mentally represent objects, they also don't fully grasp the fact that other people have minds that may mentally represent the same objects in different ways. That's why preoperational children mistakenly expect others to see the world as they do. When 3-year-old children are asked what a person on the opposite side of a table is seeing, they typically claim that the other person sees what they themselves see (see **FIGURE 10.5**). **Egocentrism** is *the failure to understand that the world appears different to different people* and it is a hallmark of the preoperational stage.

Just as 3-year-old children fail to realize that other people don't always see what they see, they also fail to realize that other people don't always know what they know. This fact has been demonstrated using the *false-belief task* (Wimmer & Perner, 1983). In the standard version of this task, children see a puppet named Maxi deposit some chocolate in a cupboard and then leave the room. A second puppet arrives a moment later, finds the chocolate, and moves it to a different cupboard. The children are then asked where Maxi will look for the chocolate when he returns: in the first cupboard where he initially put it, or in the second cupboard, where the children know it currently is?

Most 5-year-olds realize that Maxi will search the first cupboard because Maxi did not see the chocolate being moved. But 3-year-olds typically claim that Maxi will look in the second cupboard. Why? Because that's where *the children* know the chocolate is—and they assume that what they know, everyone knows! Children are able to give the right answer in the false-belief task somewhere between the ages of 4 and 6 (Callaghan et al., 2005), though children in some cultures are able to give it earlier than children in others (Liu et al., 2008). But eventually, the vast majority of children ultimately come to understand that they and others have minds and that these minds represent the world in different ways. Once children understand these things, they are said to have acquired a **theory of mind**, which is *the understanding that the mind produces representations of the world and that these representations guide behavior.*

The age at which most children acquire a theory of mind appears to be influenced by a variety of factors, such as the number of siblings the child has, the frequency with

When small children are told to hide, they sometimes cover their eyes. Because they can't see you, they assume that you can't see them (Russell, Gee, & Bullard, 2012).   Courtesy of Daniel Gilbert

egocentrism The failure to understand that the world appears different to different people.

theory of mind The understanding that the mind produces representations of the world and that these representations guide behavior.

Figure 10.5 Egocentrism Preoperational children mistakenly believe that others share their points of view. The child can see the tree, but when asked what the adult sees, she will say, "A tree." The child doesn't seem to realize that although she can see the tree, the adult cannot.

That's the Dumbest Thing I Never Heard!

Everyone sees the world a bit differently. As children develop, they acquire a theory of mind, and one component of that theory is the realization that different people may hold different beliefs.

Piaget thought children came to this realization in the course of their social interactions, where they inevitably encountered disagreement. A child says, "That dog is mean," and his father replies, "No, he's very nice." A playmate says, "My house is red," and another responds, "You're wrong. It's blue!" All the disagreements that children hear eventually lead them to understand that different people have different beliefs about the world.

Although being disagreeable is a popular pastime in Western societies, not all cultures appreciate a good argument as much as Americans do. For instance, many Eastern cultures encourage respect for one's elders and family harmony, and they encourage people to avoid interpersonal conflict. In such cultures, if a person doesn't have something agreeable to say, they often say nothing at all. Thus, children who grow up in these cultures do not normally hear people challenging each other's beliefs. So how do they come to understand that different people *have* different beliefs?

The answer seems to be: s-l-o-w-l-y! For example, in one study, 77% of Australian preschoolers understood that different people have different beliefs, but only 47% of Iranian preschoolers understood the same (Shahaeian et al., 2011). Were the Iranian children just slow learners? Nope. In fact, they were just as likely as the Australian children to have acquired other components of a theory of mind—for instance, the realization that different people *like* different things—and they were even *more* likely than the Australian children to realize that people know what they see and not what they don't. Iranian preschoolers appear to learn just as fast as Australian preschoolers do, but it takes them a bit longer to understand that people have different beliefs because they are exposed to fewer debates about them. The pattern seen in Australia is also seen in the United States, and the pattern seen in Iran is also seen in China, suggesting that this may be a stable difference between Western and Eastern cultures (Wellman et al., 2006).

In the end, of course, everyone comes to realize that human beings don't always see eye to eye. But people who live in places where they are encouraged to speak their minds and air their differences in public seem to figure that out a bit earlier than most. At least that's what research suggests. Do you agree? Well, why not? What's the matter with you anyway?

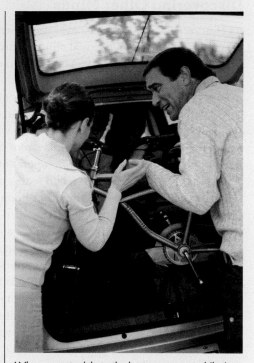

When parents debate the best way to get a bike into a car, their children learn that people have different beliefs. For example, Mom believes that Dad should shut up, and Dad doesn't. But he will. And probably soon. Photoalto/Laurence Mouton/Getty Images

People with autism often have an unusual ability to concentrate on small details, words, and numbers for extended periods of time. Thorkil Sonne (right) started a company called Specialisterne.com, which places people who have autism—such as his son Lars (left)—at jobs that they can do better than more "neurotypical" people can. Joachim Ladefoged/VII/Redux

which the child engages in pretend play, whether the child has an imaginary companion, the socioeconomic status of the child's family, and even culture (see A World of Difference: That's the Dumbest Thing I Never Heard!). But of all the factors researchers have studied, language seems to be the most important (Astington & Baird, 2005). Children's language skills are an excellent predictor of how well they perform on false-belief tasks (Happé, 1995). Deaf children whose parents do not know sign language are slow to acquire a theory of mind (DeVilliers, 2005; Peterson & Siegal, 1999; Peterson et al., 2016; Pyers & Senghas, 2009), as are children with *autism*, a disorder we'll cover in more depth in the Disorders chapter. Children with autism are slow to recognize that other people can believe what they don't believe themselves (Baron-Cohen et al., 1985; Senju et al., 2009), and have trouble understanding belief-based emotions such as embarrassment and shame (Baron-Cohen, 1991; Heerey et al., 2003).

Piaget's ideas about cognitive development were nothing short of groundbreaking. Few psychologists have had such a profound and enduring impact. But while some of his ideas have held up quite well, Piaget got a few things wrong. First, Piaget thought that children graduated from one stage to another in the same way that they graduated from kindergarten to first grade. Modern psychologists see development as more continuous and less step-like. In a sense, cognitive development is more like the gradual change of seasons than it is like graduation day.

Second, transitions between stages generally occur *earlier* than Piaget realized (Gopnik, 2012). Every year, clever researchers find new ways of testing infants and children, and every year, textbook authors must lower the age at which cognitive milestones are achieved. Don't be too surprised if in the coming years, someone discovers that zygotes can do algebra.

Discovering Our Cultures

Piaget saw the child as a lone scientist who goes out into the world and makes observations, develops theories, and revises those theories in light of new evidence. But scientists rarely go it alone. Rather, they receive training from more experienced scientists, inherit the theories and methods of their forebears, and seek each other's opinions. According to the Russian psychologist Lev Vygotsky, children do the same thing. Vygotsky believed that cognitive development was largely the result of the child's interaction with members of their own culture rather than their interaction with concrete objects. For example, most infants cannot open a jar on their own, but they can learn to open a jar if an adult shows them how. Children receive the accumulated wisdom of their species because, unlike most other animals, they have three essential skills that allow them to learn from others (Meltzoff et al., 2009; Striano & Reid, 2006; Whiten, 2017):

As Vygotsky pointed out, children are not lone explorers who discover the world for themselves; rather, they are members of families, communities, and societies that teach them much of what they need to know. Dragon Images/Shutterstock

1. *Joint attention* is the ability to focus on what another person is focused on. If an adult turns their head to the left, 3-month-old infants and 9-month-old infants will look to the left. But if the adult first closes their eyes and then looks to the left, the younger infant will look to the left, but the older infant will not (Brooks & Meltzoff, 2002). This suggests that younger infants are following the adult's head movements but that older infants are following the adult's gaze (see **FIGURE 10.6**). That is, they are trying to see what they think the adult is seeing (Rossano et al., 2012).

2. *Imitation* is the tendency to do what another person does (Jones, 2007). Children imitate adults, but early on they begin to imitate the adult's intentions, rather than their actual actions. When an 18-month-old sees an adult's hand slip as the adult tries to pull the lid off a jar, the child won't copy the slip but will instead perform the *intended* action of removing the lid (Meltzoff, 1995, 2007; Yu & Kushnir, 2014).

3. *Social referencing* is the ability to use another person's reactions as information about how to think (Kim et al., 2010; Walden & Ogan, 1988). An infant who approaches a new toy will often stop and look back to examine their parent's face for cues about whether their parent thinks the toy is or isn't dangerous. This is just one of the many instances in which children rely on adults to tell them what they should and shouldn't fear (see Other Voices: Shut the Lights Off, Say No More).

Joint attention ("I see what you see"), imitation ("I do what you do"), and social referencing ("I think what you think") are three of the basic abilities that allow infants to learn from other members of their species and to discover things about the world that they might never discover alone (Heyes, 2016).

Figure 10.6 Joint Attention Joint attention allows children to learn from others. When a 12-month-old infant interacts with an adult (a) who then looks at an object (b), the infant will typically look at the same object (c)—but only when the adult's eyes are open (Meltzoff et al., 2009). Republished with permission of AAAS, A.N. Meltzoff, et al. Foundations for a New Science of Learning, Science, Vol. 325, 2009; permission conveyed through Copyright Clearance Center

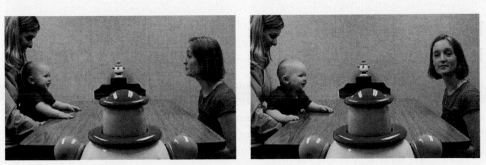

(a)   (b)   (c)

Shut the Lights Off, Say No More

Americans from both the left and right sides of the political spectrum agree that gun violence is one of our nation's most frightening problems. In response to the surge of school shootings in recent years, many public schools are now conducting "active shooter drills" that teach children how to protect themselves during an attack. At first blush, this sounds like a good idea—after all, what's the harm of being prepared?

According to author and educator Erika Christakis, the harm is this: We are scaring our kids to death—and for no good reason! Here's her argument:

Around the country, young children are being taught to run in zigzag patterns so as to evade bullets. I've heard of kindergartens where words like *barricade* are added to the vocabulary list, as 5- and 6-year-olds are instructed to stack chairs and desks "like a fort" should they need to keep a gunman at bay. In one Massachusetts kindergarten classroom hangs a poster with lockdown instructions that can be sung to the tune of "Twinkle, Twinkle, Little Star": *Lockdown, Lockdown, Lock the door/Shut the lights off, Say no more.* . . .

In the 2015–16 school year, 95 percent of public schools ran lockdown drills, according to a report by the National Center for Education Statistics. . . . A recent analysis by *The Washington Post* found that during the 2017–18 school year, more than 4.1 million students experienced at least one lockdown or lockdown drill, including some 220,000 students in kindergarten or preschool. . . .

Deaths from shootings on school grounds remain extremely rare compared with those resulting from accidental injury, which is the leading cause of death for children and teenagers. In 2016, there were 787 accidental deaths (a category that includes fatalities due to drowning, fires, falls, and car crashes) among American children ages 5 to 9—a small number, considering that there are more than 20 million children in this group. Cancer was the next-most-common cause of death, followed by congenital anomalies. Homicide of *all* types came in fourth. To give these numbers yet more context: *The Washington Post* has identified fewer than 150 people (children and adults) who have been shot to death in America's schools since the 1999 shooting at Columbine High School,

in Colorado. Not 150 people a year, but 150 in nearly two decades.

Preparing our children for profoundly unlikely events would be one thing if that preparation had no downside. But in this case, our efforts may exact a high price. . . . A 2018 survey by the Pew Research Foundation determined that, despite the rarity of such events, 57 percent of American teenagers worry about a shooting at their school. This comes at a time when children are already suffering from sharply rising rates of anxiety, self-mutilation, and suicide. According to a landmark study funded by the National Institute of Mental Health, 32 percent of 13-to-18-year-olds have anxiety disorders, and 22 percent suffer from mental disorders that cause severe impairment or distress. Among those suffering from anxiety, the median age of onset is 6.

. . . Our feverish pursuit of disaster preparedness lays bare a particularly sad irony of contemporary life. Among modernity's gifts was supposed to be childhood—a new life stage in which young people had both time and space to grow up, without fear of dying or being sent down a coal mine. To a large extent, this has been achieved. American children are manifestly safer and healthier than in previous eras. The mortality rate of children under 5 in the United States today is less than 1 percent (or 6.6 deaths per 1,000 children), compared with more than 40 percent in 1800. The reduction is miraculous. But as in so many other realms, we seem determined to snatch defeat from the jaws of victory. At just the moment when we should be able to count on childhood, we are in danger of abandoning it. . . . Our children may be relatively safe, but childhood itself is imperiled.

Erika Christakis is an early childhood educator and the author of *The Importance of Being Little: What Young Children Really Need from Grownups* (2017). Photo by Andrea Reese, courtesy Erika Christakis

Build to the Outcomes

1. How does habituation enable researchers to understand what a newborn can or cannot see?

2. What are the cephalocaudal and proximodistal rules?

3. What happens at each of Piaget's stages of cognitive development?

4. What does the false-belief task demonstrate?

5. What is the most important factor determining how early a child will acquire a theory of mind?

6. What three skills allow children to learn from other members of their cultures?

Learning Outcomes

- Describe attachment and its four styles.

- Describe the three shifts that Piaget claimed characterize children's moral development.

- Describe Kohlberg's three stages of the development of moral reasoning.

- Explain why moral reasoning is only part of the picture of moral development.

Infancy and Childhood: Bonding and Helping

Infants and children learn how to think about the world, about their minds, and about other minds. But they also learn to form relationships and establish emotional bonds with these other minds, as well as to reason about right and wrong and behave accordingly. Social development and moral development are among the most important projects of infancy and childhood, so let's explore each in turn.

Social Development

When Konrad Lorenz was a child, his neighbor gave him a day-old duckling that soon began to follow Lorenz wherever he went. A few decades later, Lorenz was awarded the Nobel Prize in Physiology for explaining how and why that had happened (Lorenz, 1952). Everyone who had ever raised a duckling already knew that it would follow its mother and assumed that this behavior was some sort of hard-wired instinct. But Lorenz realized that evolution had not designed ducklings to follow their mothers; rather, it had designed them to follow the first noisy moving object they saw upon hatching. In most cases, that object was indeed their mother, but if it just so happened to be a little boy, then the duckling would ignore its mother and follow the boy instead. Ducklings were not prepared to follow their mothers in particular; they were prepared to form a bond.

Becoming Attached

Like ducklings, human infants need adults to survive, and therefore they too come into the world prepared to form a bond. Because they cannot waddle after an adult, they instead do things to make adults waddle after them: They cry, gurgle, coo, and smile, and these signals cause adults to move toward them, pick them up, comfort them, change them, and feed them. At first, newborns will send these signals to any adult within range, but by about 6 months they begin to direct those signals toward the adult who responds first, best, fastest, and most often.

That person is known as the *primary caregiver,* and they quickly become the emotional center of the infant's universe. Infants feel safe in the primary caregiver's presence and will happily crawl around and explore the environment. If their primary caregiver gets a little too far away, the infant will begin to feel unsafe and will take action to close the gap, either by moving toward the primary caregiver or by crying until the caregiver moves toward them. The *emotional bond with a primary caregiver* is called an **attachment** (Bowlby, 1969, 1973, 1980). This bond is so important that infants who, by unfortunate circumstances, are deprived of the opportunity to form one are at serious risk for a wide range of physical, mental, and emotional impairments (Gillespie & Nemeroff, 2007; Kessler et al., 2008; O'Connor & Rutter, 2000; Rutter et al., 2004).

Attachment Styles

Infants form attachments, but not all attachments are of the same quality (Ainsworth et al., 1978). A common method for measuring the quality of an attachment involves bringing an infant and their primary caregiver (usually the mother) to a laboratory room and then staging a series of episodes in which the primary caregiver briefly leaves the room and then returns. Infants tend to react to these episodes in one of four ways, which

Like hatchlings, human infants need to stay close to their mothers to survive. Unlike hatchlings, human infants know how to get their mothers to come to them rather than the other way around.   John St. Germain/Alamy; Peter Burian/Corbis

attachment The emotional bond with a primary caregiver.

In a series of classic studies, psychologist Harry Harlow (1958) raised baby rhesus monkeys in isolation and then put them in a cage with two "artificial mothers." One was made of wire and dispensed food while the other was made of cloth and did not. The baby monkeys spent most of their time clinging to the cloth mother, leading Harlow to conclude that even monkeys are "born to bond."   PR INC/Science Source

Figure 10.7 Attachment Styles How an infant responds when the primary caregiver leaves and returns allows researchers to identify the infant's attachment style. If the infant does not consistently show one of these three patterns, then the infant's attachment style is said to be disorganized.

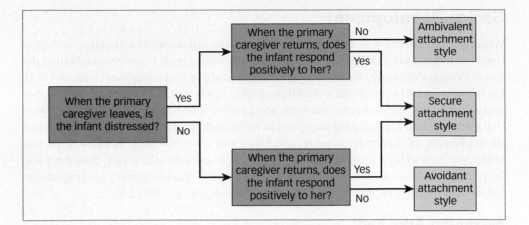

Some parents worry that placing their child in day care may impair the attachment process. But a massive long-term study showed that while attachment style is strongly influenced by maternal sensitivity and responsiveness, the quality, amount, stability, and type of day care have little or no influence (Friedman & Boyle, 2008). David Grossman/Alamy

attachment styles Characteristic patterns of reacting to the absence and presence of one's primary caregiver.

temperament A biologically based pattern of attentional and emotional reactivity.

internal working model A set of beliefs about the way relationships work.

are known as **attachment styles**, or *characteristic patterns of reacting to the presence and absence of one's primary caregiver* (**FIGURE 10.7**).

1. *Secure attachment.* The infant may or may not be distressed when the caregiver leaves the room. When the caregiver returns, the distressed infant goes to them for calming, and the nondistressed infant acknowledges them with a glance or a smile. The majority of infants in all cultures have a secure attachment style.

2. *Ambivalent attachment.* The infant is distressed when the caregiver leaves the room, but when they return the infant responds negatively to them—either by rebuffing them or by refusing the caregiver's attempts at calming.

3. *Avoidant attachment.* The infant is not distressed when the caregiver leaves the room, and ignores the caregiver when they return.

4. *Disorganized attachment.* The infant shows no consistent pattern of response to the caregiver's absence or return.

Infants' attachment styles are determined in part by their **temperament**, which is a *biologically based pattern of attentional and emotional reactivity* (Kagan, 1997; Rothbart & Bates, 2006; Thomas & Chess, 1977). For example, babies who react fearfully to novel stimuli—such as sudden movements, loud sounds, or unfamiliar people—tend to become quiet, cautious, and shy adults who avoid unfamiliar people and novel situations (Schwartz et al., 2003). Nature clearly plays a role in how infants react to situations, including the absence and return of their primary caregiver.

But nurture seems to play an even bigger role. How caregivers think, feel, and act has a strong influence on an infant's attachment style. For instance, mothers of securely attached infants tend to be especially sensitive to signs of their child's emotional state, especially good at detecting their infant's "requests" for reassurance, and especially responsive to those requests (Ainsworth et al., 1978; De Wolff & van IJzendoorn, 1997; van IJzendoorn & Sagi, 1999).

A mother's behavior is correlated with her infant's attachment style—but is it actually a cause of her infant's attachment style? It appears so. Researchers studied a group of young mothers whose 6-month-old infants were particularly irritable or difficult. Half the mothers participated in a training program designed to sensitize them to their infants' emotional signals and to encourage them to be more responsive. A year later, infants whose mothers had received the training were more likely to be securely attached than were infants whose mothers did not (van den Boom, 1994, 1995). Clearly, it takes two to make a bond.

The Effects of Attachment Styles

As a result of interactions with their primary caregivers, infants develop what psychologists call an **internal working model**: *a set of beliefs about the way relationships work*

(Bretherton & Munholland, 1999). For example, infants with a secure attachment style seem to be confident that their primary caregiver will respond when they feel insecure, whereas infants with an avoidant attachment style seem to be confident that they won't (see **FIGURE 10.8**). Infants with an ambivalent attachment style seem to be uncertain about whether their primary caregiver will respond on any particular occasion. Finally, infants with a disorganized attachment style just seem to be confused about their relationships with their primary caregiver, which has led some psychologists to speculate that this style primarily characterizes children who have been abused (Carolson, 1998; Cicchetti & Toth, 1998).

An infant's attachment style, and the internal working model that goes with it, have a long-lasting influence (Waters et al., 2015). For example, adults who were securely attached as infants have greater academic success (Jacobson & Hoffman, 1997), superior cognitive functioning (Bernier et al., 2015), higher psychological well-being (Madigan et al., 2013), and more successful social relationships (McElwain et al., 2011; Schneider et al., 2001; Simpson et al., 2011; Sroufe et al., 1990; Steele et al., 1999; Vondra et al., 2001). The bond we form with that first noisy moving object—the one that most of us call Mom—is a powerful force that impacts our development for years to come.

Moral Development

Infants can make one distinction quickly and well, and that's the distinction between pleasure and pain. Before their bottoms hit their very first diaper, infants can tell when something feels good or bad and can demonstrate to anyone within earshot that they strongly prefer the former. But over the next few years, they begin to notice that their pleasures ("Throwing food is fun") can be someone else's pains ("Throwing food makes Mom mad"), which is a problem because infants need those other people to survive, and making them mad is not a winning strategy. So infants learn to balance their needs with the needs of those around them, and they do this in part by developing a distinction between *right* and *wrong*. How does this happen?

Moral Reasoning

Piaget spent time playing games with children and quizzing them about how they came to know the rules of those games and what they thought should happen to children who broke those rules. By listening carefully to what children said, Piaget concluded that as they develop, children's thinking about right and wrong—that is, their moral reasoning—changes in three ways (Piaget, 1932/1965):

1. A shift *from realism to relativism.* Very young children regard moral rules as real, inviolable truths about the world that do not depend on what people think or say. Young children generally don't believe that a bad action such as hitting someone can ever be good, even if everyone agrees to allow it. But as they mature, children begin to realize that some moral rules are human inventions and that people can agree to change them, or abandon them entirely.

2. A shift *from prescriptions to principles.* Young children think of moral rules as guidelines for specific actions in specific situations ("Each child can play with the iPad for 5 minutes and must then pass it to the child sitting to the left"). As they mature, children come to see that these rules are expressions of more general principles, such as fairness and equity, which means that specific rules can be abandoned or modified when they fail to uphold the general principle ("If Jason missed his turn with the iPad, then he should get two turns now").

3. A shift *from outcomes to intentions.* For the young child, an unintentional action that causes great harm ("Reiko accidentally broke the iPad") seems "more wrong" than an intentional action that causes slight harm ("Reiko got mad and broke the pencil") because young children tend to judge the morality of an action by its outcome rather than by the actor's intentions. As they mature, children begin to see that the morality of an action depends on the actor's state of mind (Cushman et al., 2013; Nobes et al., 2017).

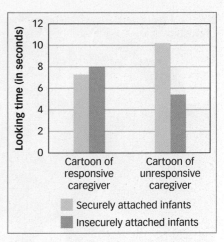

Figure 10.8 Internal Working Models Infants stare longer when they see something they don't expect, and securely attached infants will stare longer at a cartoon of a mother ignoring rather than comforting her child. Infants who are not securely attached do just the opposite (Johnson et al., 2007).

According to Piaget, young children do not realize that moral rules can vary across persons and cultures. For example, Hindus consider it immoral to eat cows, but Americans eat more than a billion pounds of beef each year at McDonald's alone! Noah Seelam/Getty Images; Alex Segre/Alamy

The psychologist Lawrence Kohlberg used Piaget's insights as the basis of a detailed theory of the development of moral reasoning (Kohlberg, 1958, 1963, 1986). Kohlberg asked both children and adults how they would resolve a series of "moral dilemmas" (e.g., should a poor husband steal a drug from a pharmacy to save his dying wife?). On the basis of their responses, he concluded that there are three distinct stages of moral development. According to Kohlberg:

1. Most children are at the **preconventional stage**, which is *a stage of moral development in which the morality of an action is primarily determined by its consequences for the actor.* A person at this stage might reason: "If the husband steals the drug he could end up in jail, so he shouldn't."

2. Most adolescents are at the **conventional stage**, which is *a stage of moral development in which the morality of an action is primarily determined by the extent to which it conforms to social rules.* A person at this stage might reason: "Stealing is against the law, so the husband shouldn't steal the drug."

3. Most adults are at the **postconventional stage**, which is *a stage of moral development in which the morality of an action is determined by a set of general principles that reflect core values.* A person at this stage might reason: "Human life is sacred, so the husband should steal the drug."

Beyond Moral Reasoning

Although the development of moral reasoning does seem to follow the basic trajectory described by Kohlberg's theory, we now know that the three stages are not as discrete as Kohlberg thought. For instance, a person might apply preconventional, conventional, and postconventional thinking in different circumstances, which suggests that the person did not "reach a stage" so much as "acquire a skill" that they may or may not use at a particular time.

Moreover, moral reasoning turns out to be just a piece of the story of moral development. For example, long before children are capable of deliberate reasoning, they display a surprising amount of "moral sense" (Blake et al., 2014; Zahn-Waxler et al., 1992). When 16-month-olds watch a puppet show in which one puppet helps others and another puppet hinders others, they are more likely to reach out and touch the puppet who helped (Hamlin et al., 2007; Margoni & Surian, 2018). One-year-olds will helpfully point toward an object that they can see an adult searching for (Liszkowski et al., 2006), and 2-year-olds smile more after giving someone else a tasty treat than after receiving one themselves (Aknin et al., 2012). In short, infants and young children seem to have many of the moral sensibilities of adults.

preconventional stage A stage of moral development in which the morality of an action is primarily determined by its consequences for the actor.

conventional stage A stage of moral development in which the morality of an action is primarily determined by the extent to which it conforms to social rules.

postconventional stage A stage of moral development in which the morality of an action is determined by a set of general principles that reflect core values.

They also seem to have many of the same moral limitations: They favor people who have been kind to them in the past (Paulus, 2016), they favor familiar people over strangers, they favor members of their own group over members of other groups, and so on (Wynn et al., 2018). Studies such as these suggest that morality is not simply the result of reasoning but also of basic psychological tendencies—such as a sense of fairness or a desire to help and cooperate—whose roots may be part of our evolutionary heritage.

Build to the Outcomes

1. How is attachment assessed?

2. How do caregivers influence an infant's attachment style?

3. According to Piaget, what three shifts characterize moral development?

4. What are Kohlberg's three stages of moral development?

5. What kind of evidence suggests that infants and children have a "moral sense"?

Adolescence: Minding the Gap

Between childhood and adulthood is a developmental stage that may not qualify for a hood of its own, but that is clearly distinct from the stages that come before and after. **Adolescence** is *the period of development that begins with the onset of sexual maturity (about 11 to 14 years of age) and lasts until the beginning of adulthood (about 18 to 21 years of age)*. Unlike the transition from embryo to fetus or from infant to child, this transition is abrupt and well-marked. In just 3 or 4 years, the average adolescent gains about 40 pounds and grows about 10 inches. For girls, all this growing starts at about the age of 10 and ends at about age 16; for boys, it starts and ends about 2 years later.

The beginning of this growth spurt signals the onset of **puberty**, which is *the onset of bodily changes associated with sexual maturity*. These changes involve the **primary sex characteristics**, which are *bodily structures that change at puberty and are directly involved in reproduction* (e.g., girls begin to menstruate and boys begin to ejaculate), as well as the **secondary sex characteristics**, which are *bodily structures that change at puberty but are not directly involved in reproduction* (e.g., girls develop breasts and boys develop facial hair). All of these changes are caused by the increased production of hormones—specifically, estrogen in girls and testosterone in boys.

Just as the body changes during adolescence, so too does the brain. For example, just before puberty there is a marked increase in the growth rate of the tissue that connects different regions of the brain (Thompson et al., 2000). Between the ages of 6 and 13, the connections between the temporal lobe (the region specialized for language) and the parietal lobe (the region specialized for understanding spatial relations) multiply rapidly—and then stop suddenly, just about the time that the critical period for learning a language ends. There is also a massive increase in the number of synapses in the prefrontal cortex before puberty. Then, during puberty, the brain undergoes synaptic "pruning" in which the connections that are not frequently used are eliminated. The adolescent brain seems to be a work in progress (see **FIGURE 10.9**).

The Protraction of Adolescence

The age at which puberty begins varies across individuals (e.g., people tend to reach puberty at about the same age as their same-sexed parent did) and across ethnic groups (e.g., African American girls tend to reach puberty before European American girls do). It also varies across generations (Malina et al., 1988; Sawyer et al., 2018). For example, in the 19th century, girls in Scandinavia, the United Kingdom, and the United States tended to have their first menstrual periods when they were about 17 years old, but by 1960, that age had fallen to about 13 years (Patton & Viner, 2007). In newly industrialized countries

Learning Outcomes

- Explain why the protraction of adolescence matters.

- Describe the determinants of sexual orientation and sexual behavior.

- Explain how adolescents are influenced by their peers.

The famous Leipzig Boy's Choir is in trouble. Boys enter the choir at the age of 9 and sing soprano until their voices change. Back in 1723, when Johann Sebastian Bach was the choirmaster, that change happened at about the age of 17. Today, it happens at about the age of 12. As a result, by the time a boy learns to sing, he isn't a soprano anymore. As a result, the choir is struggling. Wolfgang Kluge/AP Images

adolescence The period of development that begins with the onset of sexual maturity (about 11 to 14 years of age) and lasts until the beginning of adulthood (about 18 to 21 years of age).

puberty The onset of bodily changes associated with sexual maturity.

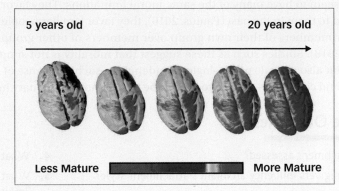

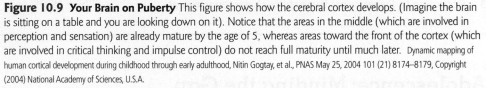

Figure 10.9 Your Brain on Puberty This figure shows how the cerebral cortex develops. (Imagine the brain is sitting on a table and you are looking down on it). Notice that the areas in the middle (which are involved in perception and sensation) are already mature by the age of 5, whereas areas toward the front of the cortex (which are involved in critical thinking and impulse control) do not reach full maturity until much later. Dynamic mapping of human cortical development during childhood through early adulthood, Nitin Gogtay, et al., PNAS May 25, 2004 101 (21) 8174–8179, Copyright (2004) National Academy of Sciences, U.S.A.

About 60% of preindustrial societies don't have a word for adolescence because there is no such stage. When a Krobo girl menstruates for the first time, older women take her into seclusion for 2 weeks and teach her about sex, birth control, and marriage. Afterward, a public ceremony is held, and the young woman who was regarded as a child just days earlier is thereafter regarded as an adult. MyLoupe/Getty Images

primary sex characteristics Bodily structures that change at puberty and are directly involved in reproduction.

secondary sex characteristics Bodily structures that change at puberty but are not directly involved in reproduction.

like China, the age at which girls have their first menstrual period has decreased by almost 5 months every decade for the past 25 years (Song et al., 2014). Similarly, the average age at which American boys show the early signs of puberty has fallen to between 9 and 10 years old (Herman-Giddens et al., 2012).

Why is puberty happening much earlier today than it did just a few decades ago? For girls at least, the main reason appears to be diet (Ellis & Garber, 2000). Young women have more body fat today than ever before, and body fat secretes estrogen, which hastens puberty. Some evidence suggests that exposure to environmental toxins that mimic estrogen may also play a role (Buck Louis et al., 2008). Stress appears to be another cause of early puberty in girls (Belsky, 2012; Belsky et al., 2015). Studies show that girls reach puberty earlier if they grow up in unpredictable households with high levels of conflict, in households without a biological father, or if they are victims of early sexual abuse (Greenspan & Deardorff, 2014).

Whatever its causes, early puberty has important psychological consequences. Just two centuries ago, the gap between childhood and adulthood was relatively brief because people became physically mature at roughly the same time that they were ready to accept adult roles in society—that is, to marry and get a job. But today, people typically spend 3 to 10 more years in school, and they take jobs and get married much later than they once did (Fitch & Ruggles, 2000). So while the age at which people become physically adult has gone down, the age at which they take on adult roles and responsibilities has gone up, resulting in a protracted period of adolescence.

Adolescents may have adult bodies, but society does not treat them like adults. Indeed, American teenagers are subject to twice as many restrictions as active-duty U.S. marines or incarcerated felons (Epstein, 2007a)! Adolescents often do things to protest these restrictions and to demonstrate their adulthood, such as smoking, drinking, using drugs, having sex, and committing crimes. And yet, the problems of adolescence are not nearly as prevalent as Netflix might lead us to believe (Steinberg & Morris, 2001). Research suggests that the "moody adolescent" who is a victim of "raging hormones" is largely a myth. Adolescents are no moodier than children (Buchanan et al., 1992), and fluctuations in their hormone levels have a very small impact on their moods (Brooks-Gunn et al., 1994). Although they can be more impulsive and susceptible to peer influence than adults (see **FIGURE 10.10**), they are just as capable of making wise decisions based on good information (Steinberg, 2007). The fact is that adolescence

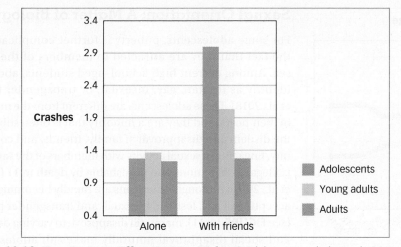

Figure 10.10 How Do Peers Affect Decision Making? Adolescents make better decisions when no one is around! Participants in one study played a video driving game with or without their peers in the room. The presence of peers greatly increased the number of risks taken and crashes experienced by adolescents but had little or no effect on adults (Gardner & Steinberg, 2005).

is not a terribly troubled time for most adolescents, who tend to "age out" of whatever troubles they do manage to get themselves into (Epstein, 2007b; Martin et al., 2014; Sampson & Laub, 1995).

Adolescents who experiment with reckless behavior generally don't become reckless adults—if they live that long. 17-year-old Maria Droesch was sending a text to her mother when she crashed the car she was driving and died. Her mother now hauls the wreckage of Maria's car from town to town to persuade people not to text while driving. In 2017, about 40% of high school age students admitted to texting while driving at least once in the past 30 days (Kann et al., 2018).

Emerging Sexuality

Adolescence is more difficult for some people than others. It is a particularly difficult time for girls who reach puberty before the majority of their peers do. These early bloomers are at elevated risk for depression, delinquency, and disease (Mendle et al., 2018; Mendle et al., 2007). Early bloomers don't have as much time as their peers do to develop the skills necessary to cope with adolescence (Petersen & Grockett, 1985), and yet, because they look so mature, people expect them to act like adults. Furthermore, older men may draw these girls into activities that they are not ready to engage in, from drinking to sex (Ge et al., 1996). Some research suggests that for girls, the *timing* of puberty has a greater influence on emotional and behavioral problems than does the occurrence of puberty itself (Buchanan et al., 1992).

The timing of puberty does not have such a consistent effect on boys. Some studies suggest that early-maturing boys do better than their peers, some suggest they do worse, and some suggest that it makes no difference at all (Ge et al., 2001).

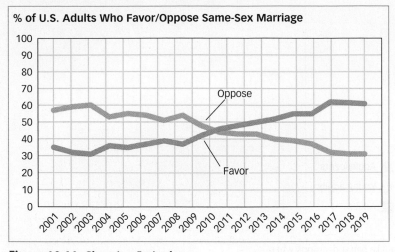

% of U.S. Adults Who Favor/Oppose Same-Sex Marriage

Figure 10.11 Changing Attitudes Toward Same-Sex Marriage In 1965, homosexuality was illegal in America, and most Americans thought it was a mental illness. Things have changed. For example, in fewer than 10 years there has been a complete reversal of Americans' attitudes toward same-sex marriage, which was legalized throughout the United States in 2015.

Sexual Orientation: A Matter of Biology

For some adolescents, puberty is further complicated by the fact that they are attracted to members of the same sex. Among current high school–aged students, about 8% identify as lesbian, gay, bisexual, or transgender (Kann et al., 2018). These adolescents are different from the majority of their peers, and they are a minority that is often subject to the disdain and disapproval of family, friends, and community. Engaging in sexual activity with members of the same sex is illegal in 75 nations and punishable by death in 11 (Bailey et al., 2016). Although Americans are rapidly becoming more accepting of gay, lesbian, bisexual, and transgender people (see **FIGURE 10.11**), many still disapprove to varying degrees, and social disapproval naturally makes an adolescent's life difficult.

What determines whether a person's sexuality is primarily oriented toward the same or the opposite sex? For a long time, psychologists thought the answer was upbringing. But modern research has failed to identify *any* aspect of parenting—including the parents' own sexual orientation—that has a significant impact on a child's ultimate sexual orientation (Patterson, 2013). Similarly, peers have a measurable influence on the decision to engage in sexual activity, but they have no influence on an adolescent's sexual orientation (Brakefield et al., 2014).

So what *does* determine sexual orientation? Considerable evidence suggests that biology and genetics play major roles. For instance, the fraternal twin of a gay man (with whom he shares 50% of his genes) has a 15% chance of being gay, but the identical twin of a gay man (with whom he shares 100% of his genes) has about a 50% chance (Bailey & Pillard, 1991; Gladue, 1994). A similar pattern characterizes women (Bailey et al., 1993). Furthermore, the brains of gay and lesbian people look in some ways like the brains of opposite-gendered straight people (Savic & Lindström, 2008). For example, the cerebral hemispheres of straight men and gay women (both of whom are *gynephilic,* or attracted to women) tend to be of different sizes, whereas the hemispheres of straight women and gay men (both of whom are *androphilic,* or attracted to men) tend to be the same size. Some evidence suggests that high levels of androgens in the womb may predispose a fetus—whether male or female—to become an androphilic adult (Ellis & Ames, 1987; Meyer-Bahlberg et al., 1995), while other studies suggest that a mother's immune system may play a role in determining her male child's sexual orientation (Balthazart, 2018).

The science of sexual orientation is still young and fraught with conflicting findings, but at least two conclusions are noncontroversial. First, whatever the complete story of its determinants turns out to be, sexual orientation clearly has biological and genetic components. It is not just a "lifestyle choice," and there is no evidence to suggest that "conversion" or "reparative" therapies can transform gay, lesbian, or bisexual people into heterosexuals (American Psychological Association, 2009).

Second, human sexual orientation is far more complex and diverse than one-word labels like *straight* and *gay* suggest. Psychological attraction, sexual behavior, biological sex, and gender identity are different things that combine in seemingly endless variations that defy the simple categorization that language imposes (see The Real World: Coming to Terms With Ourselves). Indeed, in a recent survey of U.S. adults, the percentage who identified as gay or lesbian was only slightly larger than the percentage who identified as "something else" or who said they didn't know the answer (Ward et al., 2014). Human beings are sexual creatures who still have a great deal to learn about themselves.

THE REAL WORLD

Coming to Terms With Ourselves

Sexuality involves both the body and the mind. But people's bodies are hidden beneath their clothes, and people's minds are hidden behind their eyes, so the complexity and diversity of sexuality in the real world is all too easy to miss. Understanding it requires understanding three distinct but related concepts.

1. *Sex* refers to the bodies we are born with. Most (though not all) human bodies are either male (i.e., they have XY chromosomes and a penis) or female (i.e., they have XX chromosomes and a vagina).
2. *Gender* refers to our identities—how we see ourselves, and how we want others to see us. Most (though not all) adults identify themselves as men or women.
3. *Sexual orientation* refers to the kinds of people to whom we find ourselves attracted. Most (though not all) adults are attracted to people of the opposite sex and gender.

These three dimensions don't capture every important aspect of human sexuality, but they help us understand and talk to each other. The accompanying table shows the terms that are typically used to refer to people who differ on these dimensions. (For more on this topic, go to http://www.glaad.org/reference/transgender.)

In Latin, the prefix *trans* means "on the other side of," and the prefix *cis* means "on this side of." So the term *transgender* refers to anyone whose gender and sex do not match, and the term *cisgender* refers to anyone whose gender

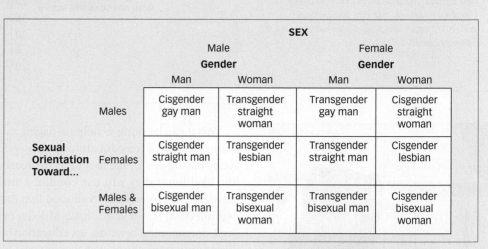

		SEX			
		Male		Female	
		Gender		Gender	
		Man	Woman	Man	Woman
Sexual Orientation Toward...	Males	Cisgender gay man	Transgender straight woman	Transgender gay man	Cisgender straight woman
	Females	Cisgender straight man	Transgender lesbian	Transgender straight man	Cisgender lesbian
	Males & Females	Cisgender bisexual man	Transgender bisexual woman	Transgender bisexual man	Cisgender bisexual woman

and sex do match. Notice also that the terms *male* and *female* refer to a person's sex, whereas the terms *man* and *woman* refer to a person's gender. Most people prefer to be described in terms of their gender rather than their sex, so both transgender and cisgender women typically prefer to be called *she*, and both cisgender and transgender men typically prefer to be called *he*. There are some people who feel that none of these adjectives or pronouns properly describe them. In general, it makes sense to think about other people's sex, gender, and orientation the way they think about it themselves.

It also makes sense to talk about them that way. Over time, descriptors of marginalized groups often take on pejorative connotations. The word *homosexual*, for example, has traditionally been used as a neutral description of people with same-sex orientations, but in some circles it has become an unflattering way to refer to gay and lesbian people. Conversely, terms that were once pejorative are occasionally reclaimed by the people whom they were initially meant to demean. For example, in some circles, *queer* is now a positive description of anyone who is not cisgender and straight. The National Queer Arts Festival has been thriving in San Francisco since 1998, but its name would have been an unthinkable slur just 20 years earlier.

The vast majority of humans are cisgender and straight, and all these other complicated terms and categories make some of them wistful for simpler times. But the truth is that there never were simpler times—just times in which the complexity of human sexuality was a secret, hidden from our view. In America, those times have now passed, and the full range of our diversity is proudly on display.

Sexual Behavior: A Matter of Choice

Sexual orientation may not be a choice, but sexual activity is—and many teenagers choose it. Although the percentage of American high school students who are sexually active has been declining in recent years (see **FIGURE 10.12**), it is still close to a third. Sex is a positive and rewarding experience for many teenagers (Basilenko et al., 2015), but it is a problem for others—especially for those who start having it too early. Teenagers who begin having sex before the age of 15 have a lower sense of self-worth and higher rates of anxiety, depression, aggressiveness, and substance abuse (Golden et al., 2016). Only about half of sexually active high school students report using a condom during their last sexual encounter (Kann et al., 2018), making them more likely to end up with a sexually transmitted infection.

Figure 10.12 Teenagers Are Having Less Sex The number of American high school students who are sexually active (defined as having had intercourse in the past 3 months) has been dropping over the past decade. Adapted from the Centers for Disease Control and Prevention's "Youth Risk Behavior Survey 1991–2017," https://www.cdc.gov/healthyyouth/data/yrbs/pdf/trendsreport.pdf

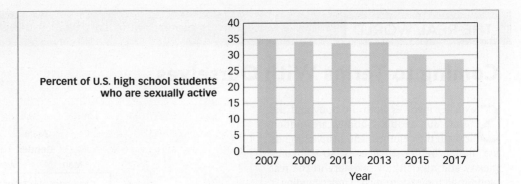

Percent of U.S. high school students who are sexually active

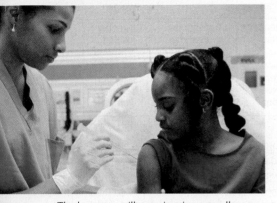

The human papilloma virus is a sexually transmitted infection that can lead to cervical cancer. Luckily, there is a vaccine that can prevent it. Some parents worry that being vaccinated will encourage their daughters to have sex early, but studies show that young women who have been vaccinated do not have sex any earlier than those who have not been vaccinated (Cook et al., 2018). Blend Images/ERproductions Ltd/Getty Images

"You're free-range when I say you're free-range."
© Charles Barsotti/The New Yorker [www.cartoonbank.com]

What can be done to help teenagers make wise choices about their sexual behavior? Comprehensive sex education is a powerful tool. Research shows that it leads teens to delay having sex for the first time, decreases the number of partners they have, increases the likelihood they will use condoms and other forms of birth control when they do have sex, and lowers the likelihood that they will get pregnant or get a sexually transmitted infection (Chin et al., 2012; Mueller et al., 2008; Satcher, 2001). And yet, despite its well-documented benefits, sex education in American schools is often absent, sketchy, or based entirely on the goal of abstinence. This is unfortunate because abstinence-only programs turn out to be largely ineffective (Kohler et al., 2008; Santelli et al., 2017), and some studies even suggest that teens who take abstinence pledges are just as likely to have sex as those who don't but are less likely to use birth control when they do (Rosenbaum, 2009). That's unfortunate too, because teenage mothers fare more poorly than teenage women without children on almost every measure of academic and economic achievement, and their children fare more poorly on most measures of educational success and emotional well-being than do the children of older mothers (Olausson et al., 2001).

From Parents to Peers

Children's views of themselves and their world are tightly tied to the views of their parents, but puberty creates a new set of needs that snip away at those bonds by orienting adolescents toward peers rather than parents. The psychologist Erik Erikson (1959) characterized each stage of life by the major task (or "key event") confronting the individual at that stage. His *stages of psychosocial development* (shown in **TABLE 10.2**) suggest that the major task of adolescence is the development of an adult identity (Becht et al., 2017). Adolescents achieve their identities in different ways: Some explore a variety of identities before finally committing to one of them, while others do little personal exploration and instead adopt the identities prescribed for them by family, religion, or culture (Kroger, 2017; Marcia, 1966, 1993). Regardless of how and when they find them, adolescent identities all have one thing in common: an expanded focus on peers (Roisman et al., 2004).

This shift from parents to peers can be difficult for several reasons. First, children cannot choose their parents, but adolescents can choose their peers and therefore have the power to shape themselves by joining groups that will lead them to develop new values, attitudes, beliefs, and perspectives (Shin & Ryan, 2014). The responsibility this opportunity entails can be overwhelming (Tarantino et al., 2014). Second, as adolescents strive for greater autonomy, their parents naturally rebel. For instance, parents and adolescents tend to disagree about the age at which certain adult behaviors—such as staying out late or having sex—are permissible, and you don't need a psychologist to tell you which position each party in this conflict tends to hold (Deković et al., 1997; Holmbeck & O'Donnell, 1991). Because adolescents and parents often have different ideas about who should control the adolescent's behavior, their relationships become more conflictive and less close, and their interactions become briefer and less frequent (Larson & Richards, 1991).

When adolescents pull away from their parents, they move toward their peers. Across a wide range of cultures, historical epochs, and even species, these peer relations evolve

TABLE 10.2   Erikson's Stages of Psychosocial Development

According to Erikson, at each "stage" of development a "key event" creates a challenge or "crisis" that a person can resolve positively or negatively.

Age	Key Event	Crisis	Positive Resolution
Birth to 12–18 months	Feeding	Trust vs. mistrust	Child develops a belief that the environment can be counted on to meet his or her basic physiological and social needs
18 months to 3 years	Toilet training	Autonomy vs. shame/doubt	Child learns what he or she can control and develops a sense of free will and a corresponding sense of regret and sorrow for inappropriate use of self-control
3–6 years	Independence	Initiative vs. guilt	Child learns to initiate action, to explore, to imagine, and to feel remorse for actions
6–12 years	School	Industry vs. inferiority	Child learns to do things well or correctly in comparison to a standard or to others
12–18 years	Peer relationships	Identity vs. role confusion	Adolescent develops a sense of self in relation to others and to own internal thoughts and desires
19–40 years	Love relationships	Intimacy vs. isolation	Person develops the ability to give and receive love; begins to make long-term commitment to relationships
40–65 years	Parenting	Generativity vs. stagnation	Person develops interest in guiding the development of the next generation
65 to death	Reflection on and acceptance of one's life	Ego integrity vs. despair	Person develops a sense of acceptance of life as it was lived and the importance of the people and relationships that the individual developed over the life span

in a similar way (Dunphy, 1963; Weisfeld, 1999). Most young adolescents initially form groups or "cliques" with same-sex peers, many of whom were friends during childhood (Brown et al., 1994). Next, male cliques and female cliques begin to meet in public places, such as town squares or shopping malls, and they begin to interact—but only in groups and only in public. After a few years, the older members of these same-sex cliques peel off and form smaller, mixed-sex cliques, which may assemble in private as well as in public, but they usually assemble as a group (Molloy et al., 2014). Finally, couples (typically, but not always, a male and a female) peel off from the small, mixed-sex clique and begin romantic relationships.

Although peers exert considerable influence on adolescents' beliefs and behaviors, this influence generally occurs because adolescents like their peers and want to impress

Adolescents form same-sex cliques that meet opposite-sex cliques in public places. Eventually, most of them will form mixed-sex cliques, pair off into romantic relationships, get married, have children, and then worry about those kids when they do all the same things. Adriansherratt/Alamy

them, and not because the peers exert pressure (Smith et al., 2014; Susman et al., 1994). As they age, adolescents show an increasing tendency to resist whatever peer pressure they do experience (Steinberg & Monahan, 2007). Acceptance by peers is of tremendous importance to adolescents, and those who are rejected by their peers tend to be withdrawn, lonely, and depressed (Pope & Bierman, 1999), in part because adolescents take negative feedback from their peers much more seriously than adults do (Rodman et al., 2017). Fortunately for those of us who were 7th-grade nerds, people who are unpopular in early adolescence can become popular in later adolescence as their peers become less rigid and more tolerant (Kinney, 1993).

Build to the Outcomes

1. How does the brain change at puberty?

2. What are the consequences of early puberty?

3. What are some factors that can make adolescence especially difficult?

4. What determines sexual orientation?

5. Why do many adolescents make unwise choices about sex?

6. What are Erikson's stages of psychosocial development?

7. How do family and peer relationships change during adolescence?

Adulthood: Change We Can't Believe In

Learning Outcomes

- Describe the physical and psychological changes that occur in adulthood.

- Describe how marriage and children relate to adults' happiness.

Adulthood is *the stage of development that begins around 18 to 21 years and lasts for the remainder of life.* Many of us think of adulthood as the destination to which the process of development finally delivers us, and that once we've arrived, our journey is pretty much complete, as though middle-aged adults were just young adults with mortgages, and older adults were just middle-aged adults with wrinkles. But this conception of development is wrong. Although they are a bit more difficult to see, a whole host of physical, cognitive, and emotional changes take place between our first legal beer and our last legal breath.

Changing Abilities

The early 20s are the peak years for health, stamina, vigor, and prowess, and because our psychology is so closely tied to our biology, these are also the years during which many of our cognitive abilities are at their sharpest. If you are a typical college student, then at this very moment you see farther, hear better, and remember more easily than you ever will again. Enjoy it while you can. Somewhere between the ages of 26 and 30, your body will start the slow process of breaking down. Your muscles will be replaced by fat, your skin will become less elastic, your sensory abilities will become less acute, and your brain cells will die at an accelerated rate.

These physical changes will have psychological consequences (Hartshorne & Germine, 2015; Salthouse, 2006). For instance, as your brain ages, your prefrontal cortex and its subcortical connections will deteriorate more quickly than the other areas of your brain (Raz, 2000), and you will experience a noticeable decline in cognitive tasks that require effort, initiative, or strategy. Your memory will get worse overall, and some kinds will get worse faster than others. For example, you will experience a greater decline in working memory (the ability to hold information "in mind") than in long-term memory (the ability to retrieve information), and a greater decline in episodic memory (the ability to remember particular past events) than in semantic memory (the ability to remember general information such as the meanings of words). As **FIGURE 10.13** shows, performance on most (but not all) cognitive tasks peaks when people are young.

adulthood The stage of development that begins around 18 to 21 years and lasts for the remainder of life.

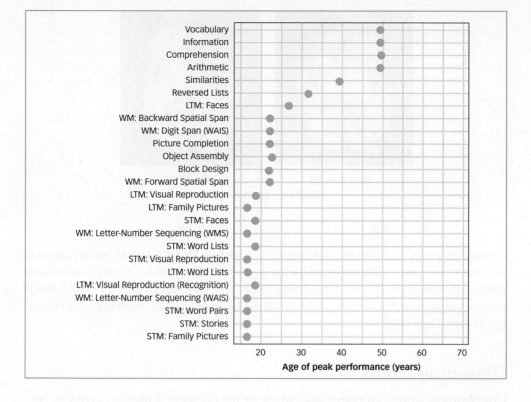

Figure 10.13 Age-Related Changes in Cognitive Performance This chart shows the age of peak performances on a test of working memory (WM), short-term memory (STM), long-term memory (LTM) and other cognitive abilities. Data from Hartshorne & Germine (2015)

So the bad news is that older adults experience declines in memory and attention. The good news is that they often compensate by doing things differently (Bäckman & Dixon, 1992; Park & McDonough, 2013; Salthouse, 1987). For example, older chess players *remember* chess positions more poorly than younger players do, but they *play* just as well because they learn to search the board more efficiently (Charness, 1981). Older typists *react* more slowly than younger typists do, but they *type* just as quickly and accurately because they are better at anticipating the next word (Salthouse, 1984). Older airline pilots are worse than younger pilots when it comes to remembering a list of nonsense words, but they are just as good at remembering the heading commands that they receive from the control tower on every flight (Morrow et al., 1994).

The brain compensates too. As you know from the Neuroscience and Behavior chapter, young brains are highly differentiated—that is, they have different parts that do different things. But as the brain ages, it becomes *de-differentiated* (Lindenberger & Baltes, 1994). For example, when young adults try to keep verbal information in working memory, the left prefrontal cortex is more strongly activated than the right, and when they try to keep spatial information in working memory, the right prefrontal cortex is more strongly activated than the left (Smith & Jonides, 1997). But this *bilateral*

One week before his 58th birthday, US Airways pilot Chesley "Sully" Sullenberger made a perfect emergency landing in the Hudson River and saved the lives of everyone on board. None of the passengers wished they'd had a younger pilot. Noah Berger/AP Images; Steven Day/AP Images

Figure 10.14 Bilaterality in Older and Younger Brains These are brain scans of younger and older adults as they take a memory test. The brains of younger adults show much more activity on one side than on the other, whereas the brains of older adults show about equal activity on both sides. Roberto Cabeza, Center for Cognitive Neuroscience, Duke University. Research from Cabeza et al. (1997) and Madden et al. (1999).

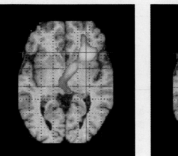
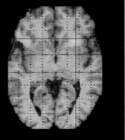

Young Adult   **Old Adult**

Word-Pair Cued Recall

asymmetry pretty much disappears in older adults (see **FIGURE 10.14**), which suggests that the older brain is compensating for the declining abilities of each individual area by calling on other areas to help out (Cabeza, 2002). The physical machinery breaks down as time passes, and one of the ways in which the brain meets that challenge is by changing its division of labor.

Changing Goals

One reason Grandpa can't remember where he left his socks is that his prefrontal cortex doesn't work as well as it used to. But another reason is that the location of socks isn't the sort of thing that grandpas care all that much about remembering (Haase et al., 2013). Whereas younger adults are largely oriented toward the acquisition of information that will be useful to them in the future (e.g., reading restaurant reviews to help them plan an upcoming evening out), older adults are generally oriented toward information that brings emotional satisfaction in the present (e.g., reading detective novels). Because young people have such long futures, they invest their time attending to, thinking about, and remembering potentially useful information that may fill their needs tomorrow. Because older people have much shorter futures, they spend their time attending to, thinking about, and remembering positive information that fills their emotional needs today (Carstensen & Turk-Charles, 1994). (See Data Visualization: Is There a Cognitive Decline With Age Regardless of Cognitive Stimulation? Go to launch-padworks.com.)

DATA Visualization

For example, older people perform *much* more poorly than younger people when they are asked to remember a series of unpleasant faces, but only *slightly* more poorly when they are asked to remember a series of pleasant faces (Mather & Carstensen, 2003). Compared with younger adults, older adults are generally better at sustaining positive emotions and curtailing negative ones (Ford et al., 2018; Isaacowitz, 2012; Isaacowitz & Blanchard-Fields, 2012; Mather & Carstensen, 2005), and they experience fewer negative emotions in their daily lives (Carstensen et al., 2000; Charles et al., 2001; Mroczek & Spiro, 2005; Schilling et al., 2013; Stone et al., 2010). Given all this, you shouldn't be surprised to learn that people find late adulthood to be one of the happiest and most satisfying periods of life.

Because they are not concerned about "saving for tomorrow," older people are also more willing than younger people to forego personal financial gain and instead contribute to the public good (Freund & Blanchard-Fields, 2014). And because they are oriented toward emotionally satisfying rather than profitable experiences, older adults choose to spend time with family and a few close friends rather than with a large circle

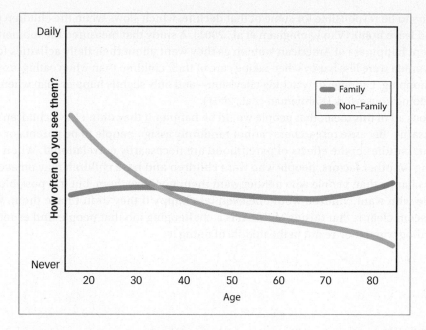

Figure 10.15 Friends but Not Family Become Less Important as We Age
The amount of time people spend with their families doesn't change much over the course of their lives, but the amount of time they spend with friends diminishes dramatically. Adapted from Sander, Schupp, & Richter (2017)

of acquaintances (Chui et al., 2014; David-Barrett et al., 2016; see **FIGURE 10.15**). "Let's go meet some new people" isn't something that most 60-year-olds tend to say, but "Let's go hang out with some old friends" is. It is sad but instructive to note that many of these same cognitive and emotional changes can be observed among younger people who have discovered that their futures will be short because of a terminal illness (Carstensen & Fredrickson, 1998; Sullivan-Singh et al., 2015).

Changing Roles

The psychological separation from parents that begins in adolescence usually becomes a physical separation in adulthood. In virtually all human societies, young adults leave home, get married, and have children of their own. Marriage and parenthood are two of the most significant aspects of adult life. If you are a college-age American, then you are likely to get married at around the age of 27 and have approximately 1.8 children because you believe that marriage and children will make you happy. But do they?

In fact, married people do report being somewhat happier than unmarried people— whether those unmarried people are single, widowed, divorced, or cohabiting (Dion, 2005; Johnson & Wu, 2002; Lucas & Dyrenforth, 2005). But some researchers suggest that married people may be happier simply because happy people are more likely to get married and that marriage may be an effect—not a cause—of happiness (Lucas et al., 2003). The general consensus among scientists seems to be that both of these positions have some merit: Even before marriage, people who will end up married tend to be happier than those who will never marry, but marriage does seem to confer some further happiness benefit (Helliwell & Grover, 2014). It is worth noting that marriage has become less popular over the past few decades in most Western nations and that being single has become an increasingly attractive and satisfying option for many (DePaulo & Morris, 2006; Pepping et al., 2018). If these trends continue, the happiness boost that marriage seems to provide may soon be a thing of the past.

Children are another story. Research shows that on average, children do not increase their parents' happiness—and may even decrease it (Stanca, 2016). Marital satisfaction decreases dramatically over the course of a marriage, and the presence of children

Young adults overestimate the problems of aging. In the 1965 hit song "My Generation," Pete Townshend of The Who sang, "Things they do look awfully cold, I hope I die before I get old." At the age of 75, Townshend is still touring and making records, so apparently he's reconsidered his position. Jeff Kravitz/Getty Images

Research suggests that marriage has a positive impact on happiness. Especially in the first 5 minutes. Courtesy of Daniel Gilbert

appears to be responsible for some of that decline, which slows when the children grow up and leave home (Van Laningham et al., 2001). A study that measured the moment-to-moment happiness of American women as they went about their daily activities found that women were less happy when taking care of their children than when eating, exercising, shopping, napping, or watching television—and only slightly happier than when they were doing housework (Kahneman et al., 2004).

Does all of this mean that people would be happier if they didn't have children? Not necessarily. Because researchers cannot randomly assign people to be parents or nonparents, studies of the effects of parenthood are necessarily correlational. When controlling for other factors, people who want children and have children may on average be less happy than people who neither want them nor have them, but it is possible that people who want children would be even less happy if they didn't have them. What does seem clear is that raising children is a challenging job that people find especially rewarding when they're not in the middle of doing it.

Build to the Outcomes

1. What cognitive changes are associated with adulthood?
2. How do adults compensate for their declining abilities?
3. In what ways do people's goals change in adulthood?
4. Why is late adulthood such a happy time for most people?
5. What does research say about how marriage and children relate to happiness?

CHAPTER REVIEW

Prenatality: A Womb With a View

- Developmental psychology studies continuity and change across the life span.
- The prenatal stage of development begins when a sperm fertilizes an egg, producing a zygote. The zygote develops into an embryo at 2 weeks and then into a fetus at 8 weeks.
- Humans are born with underdeveloped brains, which is essential to the birth process and allows for adaptation to the social and physical environment after birth.
- The fetal environment has important physical and psychological effects. In addition to the food a pregnant woman eats, teratogens—agents that impair fetal development—can affect the fetus. The most common teratogens are tobacco and alcohol.
- The fetus can hear and becomes familiar with its mother's voice.

Infancy and Childhood: Perceiving, Doing, and Thinking

- Infants have a limited range of vision, but they can see and remember objects that appear within it.
- Infants learn to control their bodies from the top down and from the center out.
- Infants slowly develop theories about how the world works. Piaget believed that these theories developed through four stages in which children learn basic facts about the

world, such as the facts that objects continue to exist even when they are out of sight and that objects have enduring properties that are not changed by superficial transformations. Children also learn that their minds represent objects; hence objects may not be as they appear, and others may not see them as the child does.

- Hearing language about thoughts and feelings helps children acquire a theory of mind.
- Cognitive development is also driven by social interactions, and infants have several abilities that allow them to learn from others.

Infancy and Childhood: Bonding and Helping

- At a very early age, human beings develop strong emotional ties to their primary caregivers. The quality of these ties is determined both by the caregiver's behavior and the child's temperament.
- Piaget concluded that children's reasoning about right and wrong is initially based on inviolable truths about the world, but as they mature, children begin to consider the actor's intentions as well as the extent to which the action obeys abstract moral principles.
- Kohlberg outlined a theory of moral development that progresses from evaluation of an action's consequences, to determination of whether it obeys social rules, and finally to how it aligns with core values.

- Infants seem to have some "moral sense," such as an affinity toward kind people and a concern with fairness.

Adolescence: Minding the Gap

- Adolescence begins with puberty, the onset of sexual maturity of the human body.
- Puberty now occurs earlier than ever before, and the entrance of young people into adult society occurs later.
- Adolescents are more likely to do things that are risky or illegal, but they rarely inflict serious or enduring harm on themselves or others.
- Research suggests that biology and genetics play key roles in determining a person's sexual orientation. Sex education has been shown to reduce risky sexual behavior.
- As adolescents seek to develop their adult identities, they seek increasing autonomy from their parents and become

more peer oriented, forming single-sex cliques, followed by mixed-sex cliques. Finally, they pair off as couples.

Adulthood: Change We Can't Believe In

- Performance on most cognitive tasks peaks when people are in their 20s.
- Older people develop a variety of strategies to compensate for their cognitive declines.
- Older adults are more oriented toward emotional satisfaction, which influences the way they attend to and remember information, the size and structure of their social networks, and their happiness.
- For most people, adulthood means leaving home, getting married, and having children. The responsibilities that parenthood entails present a significant challenge to people's happiness.

Key Concept Quiz

1. The sequence of prenatal development is
   a. fetus, embryo, zygote.
   b. zygote, embryo, fetus.
   c. embryo, zygote, fetus.
   d. zygote, fetus, embryo.

2. Learning begins
   a. in the womb.
   b. at birth.
   c. in the newborn stage.
   d. in infancy.

3. The proximodistal rule states that
   a. motor skills emerge in sequence from the center to the periphery.
   b. motor skills emerge in sequence from the top to the bottom.
   c. motor skills such as rooting are hard-wired by nature.
   d. simple motor skills disappear as more sophisticated motor skills emerge.

4. Which statement is true of vulnerability to teratogens?
   a. Heavy alcohol use during the early stages of pregnancy will probably not damage the fetus because critical brain systems have not yet developed.
   b. Exposure of the mother to environmental poisons such as lead in the drinking water can interfere with the development of the fetus.
   c. The babies of women who smoke while pregnant may have impaired development, but exposure to secondhand smoke is okay.
   d. All of the above.

5. According to Piaget, a child's theories about the way the world works are known as
   a. assimilation.
   b. accommodation.

   c. schemas.
   d. habituation.

6. Once children understand that human behavior is guided by mental representations, they are said to have acquired
   a. joint attention.
   b. a theory of mind.
   c. formal operational ability.
   d. egocentrism.

7. When infants in a new situation examine their mother's face for cues about what to do, they are demonstrating an ability known as
   a. joint attention.
   b. social referencing.
   c. imitation.
   d. all of the above.

8. The capacity for attachment may be innate, but the quality of attachment is influenced by
   a. the child's temperament.
   b. the primary caregiver's ability to read the child's emotional state.
   c. the interaction between the child and the primary caregiver.
   d. all of the above.

9. According to Kohlberg, each stage in the development of moral reasoning is characterized by a specific focus. What is the correct sequence of these stages?
   a. focus on consequences, focus on ethical principles, focus on social rules
   b. focus on ethical principles, focus on social rules, focus on consequences
   c. focus on consequences, focus on social rules, focus on ethical principles
   d. focus on social rules, focus on consequences, focus on ethical principles

10. Evidence indicates that American adolescents are
   a. moodier than children.
   b. victims of raging hormones.
   c. likely to develop drinking problems.
   d. living in a protracted gap between childhood and adulthood.

11. Scientific evidence suggests that _____ play(s) a key role in determining a person's sexual orientation.
   a. personal choices
   b. parenting styles
   c. sibling relationships
   d. biology and genetics

12. Adolescents place the greatest emphasis on relationships with
   a. peers.
   b. parents.
   c. siblings.
   d. nonparental authority figures.

13. The peak years for health, stamina, vigor, and prowess are
   a. childhood.
   b. the early teens.
   c. the early 20s.
   d. the early 30s.

14. Data suggest that for most people, the last decades of life are
   a. characterized by an increase in negative emotions.
   b. spent attending to the most useful information.
   c. very satisfying.
   d. a time during which they begin to interact with a much wider circle of people.

15. Data suggest that on average, having children...
   a. increases people's happiness.
   b. decreases people's happiness.
   c. has no effect on people's happiness.
   d. decreases happiness for fathers but increases it for mothers.

LearningCurve Don't stop now! Quizzing yourself is a powerful study tool. Go to LaunchPad to access the LearningCurve adaptive quizzing system and your own personalized learning plan. Visit launchpadworks.com.

Key Terms

developmental psychology (p. 296)

germinal stage (p. 296)

embryonic stage (p. 297)

fetal stage (p. 297)

myelination (p. 297)

teratogen (p. 298)

fetal alcohol syndrome (FAS) (p. 298)

infancy (p. 299)

motor development (p. 299)

motor reflexes (p. 299)

cephalocaudal rule (p. 299)

proximodistal rule (p. 299)

cognitive development (p. 300)

sensorimotor stage (p. 300)

schemas (p. 300)

assimilation (p. 300)

accommodation (p. 301)

object permanence (p. 301)

childhood (p. 302)

preoperational stage (p. 302)

concrete operational stage (p. 302)

conservation (p. 302)

formal operational stage (p. 302)

egocentrism (p. 303)

theory of mind (p. 303)

attachment (p. 307)

attachment styles (p. 308)

temperament (p. 308)

internal working model (p. 308)

preconventional stage (p. 310)

conventional stage (p. 310)

postconventional stage (p. 310)

adolescence (p. 311)

puberty (p. 311)

primary sex characteristics (p. 311)

secondary sex characteristics (p. 311)

adulthood (p. 318)

Changing Minds

1. One of your friends recently got married, and she and her wife are planning to have children. You mention to your friend that once she becomes pregnant, she'll have to stop drinking. She scoffs. "They make it sound as though a pregnant woman who drinks alcohol is murdering her baby. Look, my mom drank wine every weekend when she was pregnant with me, and I'm just fine." What is your friend failing to understand about the effects of alcohol on prenatal development? What other teratogens might you tell her about?

2. You are at the grocery store when a mother with a crying child in a stroller walks by. A grocery clerk is standing next to you, stocking the shelves. He shakes his head, leans over, and says, "I bet that kid spends his whole day in day-care. I mean, being away from their moms all day has to screw a kids up, right?" What do you think? Do scientific studies provide any support for the clerk's hypothesis?

3. You and your roommate are watching a movie in which a young man tells his parents that he's gay. The parents react badly and decide that they should send him to a "camp" where he can learn to change his sexual orientation. Your roommate turns to you and says, "Do you know anything about this? Can people really be changed from gay to straight?" What would you tell your friend about "conversion therapy" and about the factors that determine sexual orientation?

4. One of your cousins has just turned 30 and, to his horror, has discovered a gray hair. "This is the end," he says. "Soon I'll start losing my eyesight, growing new chins, and forgetting how to use a cell phone. Aging is just one long, slow, agonizing decline." What could you tell your cousin to cheer him up? Does everything in life get worse with age?

Answers to Key Concept Quiz

1. b; 2. a; 3. a; 4. b; 5. c; 6. b; 7. b; 8. d; 9. c; 10. d; 11. d; 12. a; 13. c; 14. c; 15. b

 LaunchPad
macmillan learning

LaunchPad features the full e-book of *Introducing Psychology*, the LearningCurve adaptive quizzing system, videos, and a variety of activities to boost your learning. Visit LaunchPad at launchpadworks.com.

Personality

11

Growing up, Stefani Joanne Angelina Germanotta seemed to have personality. As a child, she was said to have shown up at the occasional family gathering naked. As the pop star now known as Lady Gaga, she continues the tradition of being different. Her first albums, *The Fame* and *The Fame Monster*, as well as the fact that she calls her fans Little Monsters and herself the Mother Monster, hinted she might have issues. But she, like most of us, is not one dimensional. Yes, her style is eccentric (sometimes a dress made of meat, sometimes feathers), but she also is a serious supporter of humanitarian and personal causes, including equality for people who are gay, bisexual, lesbian, or transgender (as in her song "Born This Way"). Lady Gaga is one of a kind. She has personality in an important sense—she has qualities that make her psychologically different from other people.

The forces that create any one personality are always something of a mystery. Your personality is different from anyone else's and expresses itself pretty consistently across settings—at home, in the classroom, and elsewhere. But how and why do people differ psychologically? By studying many unique individuals, psychologists seek to gather enough information to answer these central questions of personality psychology scientifically.

Personality is *an individual's characteristic style of behaving, thinking, and feeling.* Whether Lady Gaga's quirks are real or merely for publicity, they certainly are identifiably hers and they show her distinct personality. In this chapter, we will explore personality, first by looking at what it is and how it is measured, and then by focusing on four main approaches to understanding personality. At the end of the chapter, we discuss the psychology of self to see how our views of what we are like can shape and define our personality.

Personality: What It Is and How It Is Measured

The Trait Approach: Identifying Patterns of Behavior

The Psychodynamic Approach: Forces That Lie Beneath Awareness

The Humanistic–Existential Approach: Personality as Choice

The Social–Cognitive Approach: Personalities in Situations

The Self: Personality in the Mirror

The singer Lady Gaga in her meat dress at the MTV Video Music Awards (2010) and her feather dress at the Golden Globes (2019).
PA Wire/AP Images; Vittorio Zunino Celotto/Getty Images

personality An individual's characteristic style of behaving, thinking, and feeling.

Learning Outcomes

- Explain how prior and anticipated events explain personality differences.

- Compare personality inventories and projective techniques.

Donald Trump

Ruth Bader Ginsberg

Dwayne Johnson

Oprah Winfrey

How would you describe each of these personalities? The White House; Chip Somodevilla/ Getty Images; Frazer Harrison/Getty Images; Michael Kovac/ Getty Images

self-report A method in which people provide subjective information about their own thoughts, feelings, or behaviors, typically via questionnaire or interview.

Personality: What It Is and How It Is Measured

If someone said, "You have no personality," how would you feel? Like a boring, grayish lump who should go out and get a personality as soon as possible? As a rule, people don't strive for a personality—one seems to develop naturally as we travel through life. As psychologists have tried to understand the process of personality development, they have pondered questions of description (*how* do people differ?), explanation (*why* do people differ?), and the more quantitative question of measurement (how can personality be *assessed*?).

Describing and Explaining Personality

As the first biologists attempted to classify all plants and animals (whether lichens or ants or fossilized lions), personality psychologists began by labeling and describing different personalities. And just as biology came of age with Darwin's theory of evolution, which *explained* how biological differences among species arose, the maturing study of personality also has developed explanations of the basis for psychological differences among people.

What leads Lady Gaga to all of her entertaining extremes? Many psychologists attempt to study and explain personality differences by thinking about them in terms of *prior events* that may have shaped an individual's personality or *anticipated events* that motivate the person to reveal particular personality characteristics. In a biological prior event, Stefani Germanotta inherited genes from her parents that may have led her to develop into the sort of person who loves putting on a display (not to mention putting on meat and feathers) and stirring up controversy. Researchers interested in events that happen prior to our behavior study our genes, brains, and other aspects of our biological makeup; they also delve into our subconscious, as well as into our circumstances and interpersonal surroundings. The consideration of anticipated events emphasizes the person's own subjective perspective and often seems intimate and personal in its reflection of the person's hopes, fears, and aspirations.

Of course, our understanding of how the baby named Stefani Germanotta grew into the adult Lady Gaga (or of the life of any woman or man) also depends on insights into the interaction between the prior and anticipated events: We need to know how her history may have shaped her motivations.

Measuring Personality

Of all the things psychologists have set out to measure, personality may be one of the toughest. How do you capture the uniqueness of a person? What aspects of people's personalities are important to know about? How should we quantify them? Personality measures can be classified broadly into two types: personality inventories and projective techniques.

Personality Inventories Rely on Self-Reporting

To learn about an individual's personality, you could follow the person around, clipboard in hand, and record every single thing the person does, says, thinks, and feels (including how long this goes on before the person calls the police). Some observations might involve your own impressions (Day 5: seems to be getting irritable); others would involve objectively observable events that anyone could verify (Day 7: grabbed my pencil and broke it in half, then bit my hand).

Psychologists have figured out ways to obtain objective data on personality without driving their subjects to violence. The most popular technique is **self-report**, *a method in* *which people provide subjective information about their own thoughts, feelings, or behaviors, typically via questionnaire or interview.* Scales based on the content of self-reports have been devised to assess a whole range of personality characteristics, all the way from general tendencies such as overall happiness (Lyubomirsky, 2008) to specific ones such as responding rapidly to insults (Swann & Rentfrow, 2001) or complaining about poor service (Lerman, 2006).

One of the most commonly used personality tests is the **Minnesota Multiphasic Personality Inventory (MMPI)**, *a well-researched clinical questionnaire used to assess personality and psychological problems.* The MMPI was developed in 1939 and has been revised several times over the years, leading up to the current version, the MMPI-2-RF (restructured form) (Ben-Porath & Tellegen, 2008). The MMPI-2-RF consists of 338 self-descriptive statements to which the respondent answers "true," "false," or "cannot say." The MMPI-2-RF measures a wide range of psychological constructs: clinical problems (e.g., antisocial behavior, thought dysfunction), somatic problems (e.g., head pain, cognitive complaints), internalizing problems (e.g., anxiety, self-doubt), externalizing problems (e.g., aggression, substance abuse), and interpersonal problems (e.g., family problems, avoidance). The MMPI-2-RF also includes *validity scales* that assess a person's attitudes toward test taking and any tendency to try to distort the results by faking answers.

Personality inventories such as the MMPI-2-RF are easy to administer: All that is needed is the test and a pencil (or a computer-based version). The respondent's scores are then calculated and compared with the average ratings of thousands of other test takers. Because no human interpretation of the responses is needed (i.e., "true" means true, "false" means false, and so on), any potential biases of the person giving the test are minimized. Although self-report test results are easy to obtain, critics of this approach highlight several limitations. One problem is that many people have a tendency to respond in a socially desirable way, such that they underreport things that are unflattering or embarrassing. Perhaps even more problematic is that there are many things we don't know about ourselves and are thus unable to report them!

Projective Techniques Rely on Analysis of Ambiguous Information

A second, somewhat controversial, class of tools for evaluating personality are designed to circumvent the limitations of self-report. These tests, known as **projective techniques**, are *designed to reveal inner aspects of individuals' personalities by analysis of their responses to a standard series of ambiguous stimuli.* The developers of projective tests assume that people will project personality factors that are below awareness—wishes, concerns, impulses, and ways of seeing the world—onto the ambiguous stimuli and will not censor these responses.

Probably the best known of these tests is the **Rorschach Inkblot Test**, *a projective technique in which respondents' inner thoughts and feelings are believed to be revealed by analysis of their responses to a set of unstructured inkblots.* An example inkblot is shown in **FIGURE 11.1**. Responses are scored according to complicated systems (derived in part from research involving people with psychological disorders) that classify what people see (Exner, 1993; Rapaport, 1946). For instance, most people who look at Figure 11.1 report seeing birds or people. Someone who reports seeing something very unusual (e.g., "I see two purple tigers eating a velvet cheeseburger") may be experiencing thoughts and feelings that are very different from those of most other people.

The **Thematic Apperception Test (TAT)** is *a projective technique in which respondents' underlying motives and concerns and the way they see the social world are believed to be revealed through analysis of the stories they make up about ambiguous pictures of people.* To get a sense of the test, look at **FIGURE 11.2**. The test administrator shows the respondent the card and asks him or her to tell a story about the picture, asking

Personality inventories ask people to report what traits they possess. Can we rely on people to accurately report on their personality? Spencer Grant/Photoedit

Figure 11.1 Sample Rorschach Inkblot Test takers are shown a card such as this sample and asked, "What might this be?" What they perceive, where they see it, and why they believe it looks that way are assumed to reflect unconscious aspects of their personality. Science Source

Minnesota Multiphasic Personality Inventory (MMPI) A well-researched clinical questionnaire used to assess personality and psychological problems.

projective techniques Tests designed to reveal inner aspects of individuals' personalities by analysis of their responses to a standard series of ambiguous stimuli.

Rorschach Inkblot Test A projective technique in which respondents' inner thoughts and feelings are believed to be revealed by analysis of their responses to a set of unstructured inkblots.

Thematic Apperception Test (TAT) A projective technique in which respondents' underlying motives, concerns, and the way they see the social world are believed to be revealed through analysis of the stories they make up about ambiguous pictures of people.

Figure 11.2 TAT Test takers are shown cards that display ambiguous scenes and are asked to tell a story about what is happening in the picture. The main themes of the story, the thoughts and feelings of the characters, and how the story develops and resolves are considered useful indices of unconscious aspects of an individual's personality (Murray, 1943). Lewis J. Merrim/Science Source

questions such as: Who are the people shown on the card? What is happening to them? What led them to this moment? What will happen next? Different people tell very different stories about the images. In creating the stories, the respondent is thought to identify with the main characters and to project his or her view of others and the world onto the other details in the drawing. Thus, any details that are not obviously drawn from the picture are believed to be projected onto the story from the respondent's own desires and internal conflicts.

The value of projective tests is debated by psychologists. For example, if the respondent tells a story about an abusive father, the examiner must add an interpretation (was this about the respondent's actual father, or was the respondent merely trying to be funny or provocative?). Thus, despite the rich picture of a personality that these tests may offer, we should understand projective tests primarily as a way in which a psychologist can try to get to better know someone personally and intuitively (McClelland et al., 1953). When measured by rigorous scientific criteria, projective tests such as the TAT and the Rorschach have not been found to be reliable or valid in predicting behavior (Lilienfeld et al., 2003).

Methods Using Technology

Newer personality measurement methods are moving beyond both self-report inventories and projective tests (Robins et al., 2007). High-tech methods such as wireless communication, real-time computer analysis, and automated behavior identification open the door to personality measurements that are leaps beyond following the person around with a clipboard—and can lead to surprising findings. The stereotype that women are more talkative than men, for example, was challenged by research that involved 396 college students in the United States and Mexico who each spent several days wearing an EAR (electronically activated recorder) that captured random snippets of their talk (Mehl et al., 2007). The result? Women and men were *equally* talkative, each averaging about 16,000 words per day. The advanced measurement of how people differ (and how they do not) is a key step in understanding personality.

Psychologists are also using social media to better understand personality traits and how people express themselves. An important advantage of this approach, as with the EAR, is that it allows psychologists to study people as they actually behave out in the world while interacting with others (as opposed to in the lab under experimental conditions). For example, one study analyzed more than 700 million words and phrases that 75,000 people posted on their Facebook pages and compared them to the results from personality tests given to the same people (Schwartz et al., 2013). The results revealed significant differences in how males and females express themselves, as well as differences by age and personality. For instance, females use more words about emotions, whereas males use more words about objects and more swear words. People who posted about going out and partying scored high on extraversion; people who posted about being "sick of" things scored high on neuroticism; and people who posted about computers and Pokémon cards scored high on introversion. As the world creates newer forms of communicating, psychologists benefit by having newer ways of studying personality.

The EAR (electronically activated recorder) sampled conversations of hundreds of participants and found that women and men are equally talkative (Mehl et al., 2007). Thanks to Stephanie Levitt; © Matthias Mehl, University of Arizona

Build to the Outcomes

1. What does it mean to say that personality is in the eye of the beholder?

2. Compare the reliability of personality inventories and projective tests.

3. What is the advantage of measurements taken with the EAR and social media?

The Trait Approach: Identifying Patterns of Behavior

Imagine writing a story about the people you know. To capture their special qualities, you might describe their traits: Keesha is *friendly, aggressive,* and *domineering;* Seth is *flaky, humorous,* and *superficial.* With a thesaurus and a free afternoon, you might even be able to describe William as *perspicacious, flagitious,* and *callipygian.* The trait approach to personality uses such trait terms to characterize differences among individuals. Trait theorists face two significant challenges: narrowing down an almost infinite set of adjectives to a set of traits, and determining whether those traits arise from biological or hereditary foundations.

Learning Outcomes

- Describe how the trait approach to personality has changed over time.
- Describe the traits in the Big Five Factor Model.
- Explain the biological basis for personality traits.

Traits as Behavioral Dispositions and Motives

One way to think about personality is as a combination of traits. This was the approach of Gordon Allport (1937), one of the first trait theorists, who believed people could be described in terms of traits just as an object could be described in terms of its properties. He saw a **trait** as *a relatively stable disposition to behave in a particular and consistent way.* For example, a person who keeps his books organized alphabetically on bookshelves, hangs his clothing neatly in the closet, and keeps a clear agenda in a smartphone or daily planner can be said to have the trait of *orderliness.* This trait consistently manifests itself in a variety of settings.

The orderliness trait *describes* a person but doesn't *explain* his or her behavior. Why does the person behave in this way? The trait may be a preexisting disposition of the person that causes the person's behavior, or it may be a motivation that guides the person's behavior. Allport saw traits as preexisting dispositions, causes of behavior that reliably trigger that behavior. The person's orderliness, for example, is an inner property of the person that will cause the person to straighten things up and be tidy in a wide array of situations. Other personality theorists have suggested instead that traits reflect motives. Just as a hunger motive might explain someone's many trips to the snack bar, a need for orderliness might explain the neat closet, organized calendar, and alphabetically organized bookshelves (Murray & Kluckhohn, 1953).

The Search for Core Traits

Picking a single trait such as orderliness and studying it in depth doesn't get us very far in the search for the core of human character: the basic set of traits that defines how humans differ from each other. Researchers have used several different approaches in an effort to discover the core personality traits.

Early Research Focused on Adjectives That Describe Personality

Generation after generation, people have described people with words, so early psychologists proposed that core traits could be discerned by finding the main themes in all the adjectives used to describe personality. In one such analysis, a painstaking count of relevant words in a dictionary of English resulted in a list of more than 18,000 potential traits (Allport & Odbert, 1936)! Attempts to narrow down the list to a more manageable set depend on the idea that traits might be related in a hierarchical pattern (see **FIGURE 11.3**), with more general or abstract traits at higher levels than more specific or concrete traits. The highest-level traits are sometimes called dimensions or *factors* of personality.

But how many factors are there? Different researchers have proposed different answers. Cattell (1950) proposed a 16-factor theory of personality (way down from 18,000,

trait A relatively stable disposition to behave in a particular and consistent way.

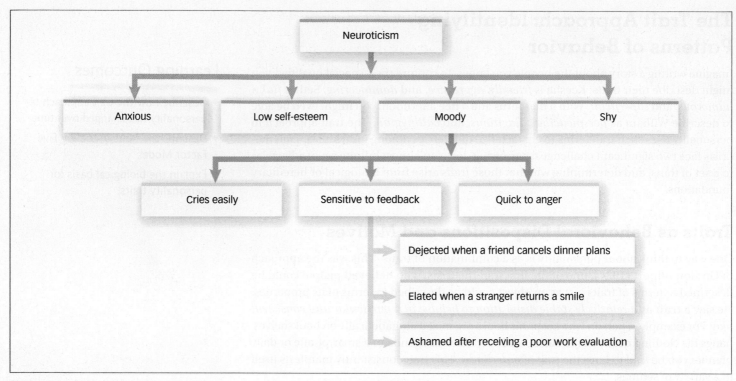

Figure 11.3 Hierarchical Structure of Traits Traits may be organized in a hierarchy in which many specific behavioral tendencies are associated with a higher-order trait, such as neuroticism (Eysenck, 1990).

TABLE 11.1	The Big Five Factor Model	
	High on trait . . . Low on trait	
Openness to experience	imaginative ...... down-to-earth	
	variety .... routine	
	independent .... conforming	
Conscientiousness	organized .... disorganized	
	careful .... careless	
	self-disciplined .. weak-willed	
Extraversion	social .... retiring	
	fun loving .... sober	
	affectionate ..... reserved	
Agreeableness	softhearted ...... ruthless	
	trusting .... suspicious	
	helpful .... uncooperative	
Neuroticism	worried .... calm	
	insecure .... secure	
	self-pitying .... self-satisfied	

Big Five The traits of the five-factor model: openness to experience, conscientiousness, extraversion, agreeableness, and neuroticism.

but still a lot), whereas others have proposed theories with far fewer basic dimensions (John et al., 2008). Hans Eysenck (1967) simplified things nicely with a model of personality with only two major traits (although he later expanded it to three). Eysenck identified one dimension, extroversion, that distinguished people who are sociable and active (extraverts) from those who are quiet and introspective (introverts). He also identified a second dimension, neuroticism, ranging from the tendency to be very neurotic or emotionally unstable to the tendency to be more emotionally stable. He believed that many behavioral tendencies could be understood in terms of their relation to the core traits of extraversion and neuroticism. The third factor he proposed was psychoticism, which refers to the extent to which a person is impulsive or hostile. (Note that nowadays, the term *psychotic* refers to an abnormal mental state marked by detachment from reality. This is discussed further in the Disorders chapter.)

A Consensus Is Reached: The Big Five Dimensions of Personality

Today most researchers agree that personality is best captured by 5 factors rather than 2, 3, 16, or 18,000 (Denissen et al., 2019; John & Srivastava, 1999). The **Big Five**, as they are affectionately called, are *the traits of the five-factor personality model: openness to experience, conscientiousness, extraversion, agreeableness, and neuroticism* (see **TABLE 11.1**) (remember them by the initials OCEAN). The five-factor model, which overlaps with the pioneering work of Cattell and Eysenck, is now widely preferred for several reasons. First, this set of five factors strikes the right balance between accounting for wide variation in personality while avoiding overlapping traits. Second, in a large number of studies using different kinds of data (people's descriptions of their own personalities, other people's descriptions of their personalities, interviewer checklists, and behavioral observation), the same five factors have emerged. Third, and perhaps most important, the basic five-factor structure seems to show up across a wide range of participants, including children, adults in other cultures, and even those who use other languages, suggesting that the Big Five may be universal (Denissen et al., 2019). The Big Five personality traits even predict people's online behavior on social networking sites such as Facebook (see Hot Science: Personality on the Surface).

Research on the Big Five has shown that people's personalities tend to remain fairly stable through their lifetime: Scores at one time in life correlate strongly with scores at later dates, even decades later (Caspi et al., 2005). William James offered the opinion that "in most of us, by the age of thirty, the character has set like plaster, and will never soften again" (James, 1890, p. 121), but this turns out to be too strong a view. Some variability is typical in childhood, and, though there is less in adolescence, some personality change can even occur in adulthood for some people (Srivastava et al., 2003). In general, people become slightly more conscientious in their 20s (got to keep that job!) and a bit more agreeable in their 30s (got to keep those friends!). Neuroticism decreases with age, but only among women (Srivastava et al., 2003). So enjoy the personality you have now, because it may be changing soon. (See Data Visualization: Does Personality Remain Stable Over Time? at www.launchpadworks.com.)

DATA Visualization

Personality on the Surface

When you judge someone as friend or foe, interesting or boring, how do you do it? It's nice to think that your impressions of personality are based on solid foundations. You wouldn't judge personality based on something as shallow as someone's looks, or what's on their Instagram or Twitter feed, would you? These criteria may seem to be flimsy bases for understanding personality, but it turns out that some valid personality judgments can be made from exactly such superficial cues.

It turns out that you *can* get some accurate information about a book by judging its cover. Researchers are increasingly using advances in computer science to study people's *digital footprints*—or the electronic information that they post online about themselves, including their written posts, photos, and videos. It turns out that digital footprints can tell us quite a bit about people's personalities. One recent analysis examined data from 14 different studies showing that the contents of a person's social media posts (e.g., on Instagram, Twitter, Facebook) correlate pretty well with self-reported ratings of Big Five personality traits (Azucar et al., 2018). The signs of personality that appear on the surface may be more than skin deep.

Beyond social media use, studies of personality also have shown that digital and social behavior correlates with personality in expected ways. For instance, analysis of smartphone data reveals that those who score high on extraversion and agreeableness spend more time with others (Wilt & Revelle, 2019). Extraverts also spend more time messaging friends via apps such as WhatsApp, whereas people high on conscientiousness spend much less time messaging (Montag et al., 2015). We can hope that those conscientious people are using the time they save to do other important things, such as their assigned Intro Psych reading.

They say you can't judge a book by its cover, but some new research suggests you can judge people by their Instagram feeds. Courtesy Matthew Nock

Traits as Biological Building Blocks

Can we explain *why* a person has a stable set of personality traits? Many trait theorists have argued that unchangeable brain and biological processes produce the remarkable stability of traits over the life span. Brain damage certainly can produce personality change, as the classic case of Phineas Gage so vividly demonstrates (see the Neuroscience and Behavior chapter). You may recall that after the blasting accident that blew a steel rod through his frontal lobes, Gage showed a dramatic loss of social appropriateness and conscientiousness (Damasio, 1994). In fact, when someone experiences a profound change in personality, testing often reveals the presence of such brain pathologies as Alzheimer's disease, stroke, or brain tumor (Boyle, 2018). Pharmaceutical treatments that change brain chemistry can also trigger personality changes, such as making people somewhat more extraverted and less neurotic (Bagby et al., 1999).

Genes, Traits, and Personality

Some of the most compelling evidence for the importance of biological factors in personality comes from genetics. Simply put, the more genes you have in common with someone, the more similar your personalities are likely to be. A recent study of data from more than 100,000 participants suggested that roughly 40% of the variability in personality among individuals results from genetic factors (Vukasović & Bratko, 2015). Of course, genetic factors do not account for everything; the remaining 60% of the variability in personality remains to be explained by differences in life experiences and other factors.

Our genes influence our personality in various ways, such as affecting how rigidly versus flexibly we think about things. This causes family members to share such traits, but not enough to prevent all political and religious disagreements during Thanksgiving dinner. Simonkr/Getty Images

Is some of this variability explained by differences in parenting? Apparently not. Identical twins, who share 100% of their genes, have highly similar personalities, regardless of whether they grow up together or are reared apart, by different adoptive families (McGue & Bouchard, 1998; Tellegen et al., 1988). Indeed, one provocative related finding is that environmental factors such as parental divorce or parenting style may have little direct impact on personality (Plomin & Caspi, 1999). According to these researchers, simply growing up in the same family does not make people very similar. Rather, when two siblings are similar, this is thought to be due primarily to genetic similarities.

People who share genes often have striking similarities in behavior and attitude. One such study examined the DNA of 13,000 people and measured the extent to which they reported conservative versus liberal attitudes. The researchers found associations between conservatism–liberalism and genetic markers linked to mental flexibility, or the extent to which people change their thinking in response to shifts in their environment, which could be one of the factors influencing our views on social and political issues (Hatemi et al., 2011). Current research by psychological scientists is aimed at better understanding how variations in our genetic code may contribute to the development of personality.

Gender Differences: Biology or Culture?

Do you think there is a typical female personality or a typical male personality? On a variety of personality characteristics, including helpfulness, men and women on average show no reliable differences. Overall, men and women seem to be far more similar in personality than they are different (Hyde, 2005). However, researchers have found some reliable differences between men and women with respect to their traits, attitudes, and behaviors. For example, males report having greater assertiveness, self-esteem, and sensation seeking, whereas women are higher on neuroticism, agreeableness, and conscientiousness (Costa et al., 2001; Schmitt et al., 2008).

Interestingly, many of the gender differences that do exist among adults seem to have developed over time. For instance, a review of more than 150 previous studies that included more than 20,000 participants found gender differences in the expression of emotion (with boys showing more externalizing emotions like anger and girls showing more internalizing emotions such as sadness and anxiety—consistent with the study noted in the preceding paragraph) (Chaplin & Aldao, 2013). However, these differences were much more pronounced as children aged into adolescence, suggesting that cultural factors play a role in how children learn to express their emotions. The finding that gender differences in personality do not begin to emerge until adolescence also has been reported in studies conducted across dozens of different cultures around the world, suggesting that this is a universal phenomenon (De Bolle et al., 2015) (see A World of Difference: Do Males and Females Have Different Personality Traits?).

Another factor that may contribute to the emergence of personality differences in adolescence is the simultaneous emergence of differences in sex hormones during puberty. As you know from the Development chapter, a lot of things change during adolescence (e.g., more hormones, more interactions with friends, less time spent with parents), and it can be difficult to know what changes are causing what other changes. Interestingly, however, the effect of hormones on personality can be studied experimentally. One recent

A WORLD OF DIFFERENCE

Do Males and Females Have Different Personality Traits?

Although the gender differences in personality are quite small, they tend to get a lot of attention—and spur a lot of debate. An evolutionary perspective holds that men and women have evolved different personality characteristics, in part because their reproductive success depends on different behaviors. For instance, aggressiveness in men may have an adaptive value in intimidating sexual rivals, whereas being agreeable and nurturing may have evolved among women to protect and ensure the survival of their offspring (Campbell, 1999). In actuality, science has yet to reveal conclusive and replicable differences between the brains of men and women (Rippon, 2019).

On the other hand, a social–cognitive perspective suggests that personality characteristics and behavioral differences between men and women result from cultural standards and expectations that assign them: socially permissible jobs, activities, and family positions (Eagly & Wood, 1999). Because of their physical size and their freedom from childbearing, men historically have taken roles of greater power—roles that in postindustrial society don't necessarily require physical strength. These differences then snowball, with men generally taking roles that require assertiveness and aggression (e.g., executive, school principal, surgeon) and women pursuing roles that emphasize greater supportiveness and nurturance (e.g., nurse, day care worker, teacher).

Regardless of the source of gender differences in personality, the degree to which

Cultures differ in their appreciation of male and female characteristics, but the Hindu deity Ardhanarishvara represents the value of combining both parts of human nature. Male on one side and female on the other, this god is symbolic of the dual nature of the sacred. The only real problem with such side-by-side androgyny comes in finding clothes that fit. Ardhanarishvara, University of California, Berkeley Art Museum and Pacific Film Archive, gift of Jean and Francis Marshall, 1999.15.10. Photographed by Ben Blackwell

people identify personally with masculine and feminine stereotypes may tell us about important personality differences between individuals. Sandra Bem (1974) designed a scale (the Bem Sex Role Inventory) that assesses the degree of identification with stereotypically masculine traits (such as self-reliance, independence, and assertiveness) and stereotypically feminine traits (such as affection, sympathy, and kindness). Bem suggested that psychologically *androgynous* people (those who adopt the best of both worlds and identify with positive feminine traits such as kindness and positive masculine traits such as assertiveness) might be better adjusted than people who identify strongly with only one sex role or who don't identify much with either one. So far, the data seem to support this idea. For instance, those who endorse an androgynous sex role report fewer symptoms of depression than those with a masculine or feminine role, regardless of their biological sex (Vafaei et al., 2016). This is also good news for the Hindu deity pictured here.

Research has shown that there are small differences in the personalities of men versus women; however, these differences are largely absent during childhood and don't emerge until adolescence, suggesting that they may be learned based on cultural expectations. This brother and sister seem to have the same personality. Their dog looks happy though. Eric Raptosh Photography/Getty Images

study followed a sample of transgender men over a 3-month period during which they were undergoing testosterone treatment (in an effort to make their bodies more masculine). Personality tests administered before and after testosterone treatment revealed that significant changes occurred, with the transgender men viewing themselves as being more masculine and their scores more closely matching those of nontransgender men (Keo-Meier et al., 2015).

Traits Are Wired in the Brain

What neurophysiological mechanisms might influence the development of personality traits? Eysenck (1967) speculated that extraversion and introversion might arise from individual differences in cortical arousal. Eysenck suggested that extraverts pursue stimulation because their *reticular formation* (the part of the brain that regulates arousal or alertness, as described in the Neuroscience and Behavior chapter) is not easily stimulated. To achieve greater cortical arousal and feel fully alert, Eysenck argued, extraverts seek out social interaction, parties, and other activities to achieve mental stimulation. In contrast, introverts may prefer reading or other quiet activities because their cortex is very easily stimulated to a point higher than optimal alertness.

Behavioral and physiological research generally supports Eysenck's view. When introverts and extraverts are presented with a range of intense stimuli, introverts respond more strongly, including salivating more when a drop of lemon juice is placed on their tongues and reacting more negatively to electric shocks or loud noises (Bartol & Costello, 1976; Stelmack, 1990). This reactivity has an impact on the ability to concentrate: Extraverts tend to perform well at tasks that are done in a noisy, arousing context (such as bartending or teaching), whereas introverts are better at tasks that require concentration in tranquil contexts (such as the work of a librarian or nighttime security guard) (Lieberman & Rosenthal, 2001; Matthews & Gilliland, 1999).

In a refined version of Eysenck's ideas, Jeffrey Gray (1970) proposed that the dimensions of extraversion–introversion and neuroticism reflect two basic brain systems. The *behavioral activation system (BAS),* essentially a "go" system, activates approach behavior in response to the anticipation of reward. The extravert has a highly reactive BAS and will actively engage the environment, seeking social reinforcement and being on the go. The *behavioral inhibition system (BIS),* a "stop" system, inhibits behavior in response to stimuli signaling punishment. The anxious or introverted person, in turn, has a highly reactive BIS and will focus on negative outcomes and be on the lookout for stop signs.

Extraverts pursue stimulation in the form of people, loud noise, and bright colors. Introverts tend to prefer softer, quieter settings. Pop quiz: Miley Cyrus—introvert or extravert? Kevin Winter/Getty Images

Brain imaging studies suggest that the core personality traits may arise from individual variations in the volume of the different brain regions associated with each trait. For instance, self-reported neuroticism is correlated with the volume of brain regions involved in sensitivity to threat; agreeableness with areas associated with processing information about the mental states of other people; conscientiousness with regions involved in self-regulation; and extraversion with areas associated with processing information about reward (DeYoung et al., 2010). Research aimed at understanding how the structure and activity of our brains can contribute to the formation of our personality traits is still in its early stages, but it is a growing area of the field that many believe holds great promise for helping us better understand how we each develop into the unique humans that we are.

Build to the Outcomes

1. How might traits explain behavior?
2. What are the strengths of the five-factor model?
3. What do studies of twins tell us about personality?

4. Are there significant personality differences between the genders?
5. What neurological differences explain why extraverts pursue more stimulation than introverts?

The Psychodynamic Approach: Forces That Lie Beneath Awareness

Rather than trying to understand personality in terms of broad theories for describing individual differences, Freud looked for personality in the details: the meanings and insights revealed by careful analysis of the tiniest blemishes in a person's thought and behavior. Working with patients who came to him with disorders that did not seem to have any physical basis, he began by interpreting the origins of their everyday mistakes and memory lapses, errors that have come to be called *Freudian slips*.

The theories of Freud and his followers (discussed in the Treatment chapter) are referred to as the **psychodynamic approach**, which *regards personality as formed by needs, strivings, and desires largely operating outside of awareness—motives that can produce emotional disorders.* The real engines of personality, in this view, are forces of which we are largely unaware.

Learning Outcomes

- Differentiate the id, ego, and superego.
- Explain how defense mechanisms reduce anxiety.

The Structure of the Mind: Id, Ego, and Superego

To explain the emotional difficulties that beset his patients, Freud proposed that the mind consists of three independent, interacting, and often conflicting systems: the id, the superego, and the ego.

The most basic system, the **id**, is *the part of the mind containing the drives present at birth; it is the source of our bodily needs, wants, desires, and impulses, particularly our sexual and aggressive drives.* The id operates according to the tendency to seek immediate gratification of any impulse. If governed by the id alone, you would never be able to tolerate the buildup of hunger while waiting to be served at a restaurant but would simply grab food from tables nearby.

Opposite the id is the **superego**, *the mental system that reflects the internalization of cultural rules, mainly learned as parents exercise their authority.* The superego acts as a kind of conscience, punishing us when it finds we are doing or thinking something wrong (by producing guilt or other painful feelings) and rewarding us (with feelings of pride or self-congratulation) for living up to ideal standards.

psychodynamic approach An approach that regards personality as formed by needs, strivings, and desires largely operating outside of awareness—motives that also can produce emotional disorders.

id The part of the mind containing the drives present at birth; it is the source of our bodily needs, wants, desires, and impulses, particularly our sexual and aggressive drives.

superego The mental system that reflects the internalization of cultural rules, mainly learned as parents exercise their authority.

Sigmund Freud was the first psychology theorist to be honored with his own bobblehead doll. Let's hope he's not the last. The Photo Works

ego The component of personality, developed through contact with the external world, that enables us to deal with life's practical demands.

defense mechanisms Unconscious coping mechanisms that reduce the anxiety generated by threats from unacceptable impulses.

The final system of the mind, according to psychoanalytic theory, is the **ego**, *the component of personality, developed through contact with the external world, that enables us to deal with life's practical demands.* The ego is the regulating mechanism that enables us to delay gratifying immediate needs and function effectively in the real world. It is the mediator between the id and the superego. The ego helps you resist the impulse to snatch others' food and also finds the restaurant and pays the check.

Freud believed that the relative strength of the interactions among the three systems of mind (i.e., which system is usually dominant) determines an individual's basic personality structure. He believed that the dynamics among the id, superego, and ego are largely governed by *anxiety,* an unpleasant feeling that arises when unwanted thoughts or feelings occur, such as when the id seeks a gratification that the ego thinks will lead to real-world dangers or that the superego sees as leading to punishment. When the ego receives an "alert" signal in the form of anxiety, it launches into a defensive position in an attempt to ward off the anxiety. According to Freud, it does so using one of several different **defense mechanisms**, *unconscious coping mechanisms that reduce the anxiety generated by threats from unacceptable impulses* (see **TABLE 11.2**). Psychodynamically oriented psychologists believe that defense mechanisms help us overcome anxiety and engage effectively with the outside world and that our characteristic style of defense becomes our signature in dealing with the world—and an essential aspect of our personality.

Freud also proposed that a person's basic personality is formed before 6 years of age during a series of sensitive periods, or life stages, when experiences influence all that will follow. Freud called these periods *psychosexual stages,* distinct early life stages through which personality is formed as children experience sexual pleasures from specific body areas and as caregivers redirect or interfere with those pleasures (see **TABLE 11.3**). He argued that as a result of adult interference with pleasure-seeking energies, the child experiences conflict. At each stage, a different bodily region dominates the child's subjective experience. Problems and conflicts encountered at any psychosexual stage, Freud believed, will influence personality in adulthood.

TABLE 11.2 Defense Mechanisms		
Defense Mechanism	**Description**	**Example**
Repression	Removing painful experiences and unacceptable impulses from the conscious mind: "motivated forgetting"	Not lashing out physically in anger; putting a bad experience out of your mind
Rationalization	Supplying a reasonable-sounding explanation for unacceptable feelings and behavior to conceal (mostly from oneself) one's underlying motives or feelings	Dropping calculus, allegedly because of poor ventilation in the classroom
Reaction formation	Unconsciously replacing threatening inner wishes and fantasies with an exaggerated version of their opposite	Being rude to someone you're attracted to
Projection	Attributing one's own threatening feelings, motives, or impulses to another person or group	Judging others as being dishonest because you believe that you are dishonest
Regression	Reverting to an immature behavior or earlier stage of development, a time when things felt more secure, to deal with internal conflict and perceived threat	Using baby talk, even though able to use appropriate speech, in response to distress
Displacement	Shifting unacceptable wishes or drives to a neutral or less threatening alternative	Slamming a door; yelling at someone other than the person you're mad at
Identification	Dealing with feelings of threat and anxiety by unconsciously taking on the characteristics of another person who seems more powerful or better able to cope	A bullied child becoming a bully
Sublimation	Channeling unacceptable sexual or aggressive drives into socially acceptable and culturally enhancing activities	Diverting anger to the football or rugby field, or other contact sport

TABLE 11.3	Freud's Psychosexual Stages
Stage	Description
Oral	The stage in which experience centers on the pleasures and frustrations associated with the mouth, sucking, and being fed
Anal	The stage in which experience is dominated by the pleasures and frustrations associated with the anus, retention and expulsion of feces and urine, and toilet training
Phallic	The stage in which experience is dominated by the pleasure, conflict, and frustration associated with the phallic–genital region, as well as coping with powerful incestuous feelings of love, hate, jealousy, and conflict
Latency	The stage in which the primary focus is on the further development of intellectual, creative, interpersonal, and athletic skills
Genital	The time for the coming together of the mature adult personality with a capacity to love, work, and relate to others in a mutually satisfying and reciprocal manner

What should we make of all this? Critics argue that psychodynamic explanations lack any real evidence and tend to focus on provocative after-the-fact interpretation rather than testable prediction. The psychosexual stage theory offers a compelling set of story lines for interpreting lives once they have unfolded, but it has not generated clear-cut predictions supported by research.

Build to the Outcomes

1. According to Freud, how is personality shaped by the interaction of the id, superego, and ego?

2. What are some of the defense mechanisms we use to reduce anxiety?

The Humanistic–Existential Approach: Personality as Choice

During the 1950s and 1960s, psychologists began trying to understand personality from a very different viewpoint: understanding how humans make *healthy choices* that create their personalities. *Humanistic psychologists* emphasized a positive, optimistic view of human nature that highlights people's inherent goodness and their potential for personal growth. *Existentialist psychologists* focused on the individual as a responsible agent who is free to create and live his or her life while negotiating the issue of meaning and the reality of death. The *humanistic–existential approach* integrates these insights with a focus on how a personality can become optimal.

Human Needs and Self-Actualization

Humanists see the **self-actualizing tendency**, *the human motive toward realizing our inner potential,* as a major factor in personality. The pursuit of knowledge, the expression of one's creativity, the quest for spiritual enlightenment, and the desire to give to society are all examples of self-actualization. As you saw in the Emotion and Motivation chapter, the humanistic theorist Abraham Maslow (1943) proposed a *hierarchy of needs,* a model of essential human needs arranged according to their priority, in which basic physiological and safety needs must be satisfied before a person can afford to focus on higher-level psychological needs. Only when these basic needs are met can one pursue higher needs, culminating in *self-actualization,* the need to be good, to be fully alive, and to find meaning in life.

Humanist psychologists explain individual personality differences as arising from the various ways that the environment facilitates—or blocks—attempts to satisfy

Learning Outcomes

- Describe the humanistic–existential approach to personality.
- Explain the role of self-actualization and angst in personality development.

self-actualizing tendency The human motive toward realizing our inner potential.

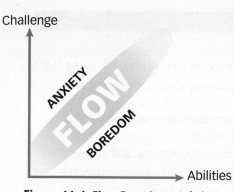

Figure 11.4 Flow Experience It feels good to do things that challenge your abilities but that don't challenge them too much. This feeling between boredom and anxiety is the "flow experience" (Csikszentmihalyi, 1990).

psychological needs. For example, someone with the inherent potential to be a great scientist, artist, parent, or teacher might never realize these talents if his or her energies and resources are instead directed toward meeting basic needs of security, belongingness, and the like. Research indicates that when people shape their lives around goals that do not match their true nature and capabilities, they are less likely to be happy than those whose lives and goals do match (Ryan & Deci, 2000).

It feels great to be doing exactly what you are capable of doing. Engagement in tasks that exactly match one's abilities creates a mental state of energized focus called *flow* (see **FIGURE 11.4**) (Csikszentmihalyi, 1990). Tasks that are below our abilities cause boredom, those that are too challenging cause anxiety, and those that are "just right" lead to the experience of flow. If you know how to play the piano, for example, and are playing a Chopin prelude that you know well enough that it just matches your abilities, you are likely to experience this optimal state. People report being happier at these times than at any other times. Humanists believe that such peak experiences, or states of flow, reflect the realization of one's human potential and represent the height of personality development.

Personality as Existence

Existentialists agree with humanists about many of the features of personality but focus on challenges to the human condition that are more profound than the lack of a nurturing environment. For existentialists, specific aspects of the human condition, such as awareness of our own existence and the ability to make choices about how to behave, have a double-edged quality: They bring an extraordinary richness and dignity to human life, but they also force us to confront realities that are difficult to face, such as the prospect of our own death. The **existential approach** is *a school of thought that regards personality as governed by an individual's ongoing choices and decisions in the context of the realities of life and death.*

According to the existential perspective, the difficulties we face in finding meaning in life and in accepting the responsibility of making free choices provoke a type of anxiety that existentialists call *angst* (the anxiety of fully being). The human ability to consider limitless numbers of goals and actions is exhilarating, but it can also open the door to profound questions such as "Why am I here?" and "What is the meaning of my life?"

Thinking about the meaning of existence also can evoke an awareness of the inevitability of death. What is the purpose of living if life as we know it will end one day? Alternatively, does life have *more* meaning, given that it is so temporary? Existential theorists do not suggest that people consider these profound existential issues on a day-to-day and moment-to-moment basis. Rather than ruminating about death and meaning, people typically pursue superficial answers that help them deal with the angst and dread they experience, and the defenses they construct form the basis of their personalities (May, 1983). Some people organize their lives around obtaining material possessions; others may immerse themselves in drugs or addictive behaviors such as compulsive Web browsing, video gaming, or television watching to numb the mind to existential realities.

For existentialists, a healthier solution is to face the issues head on and learn to accept and tolerate the pain of existence. Indeed, being fully human means confronting existential realities rather than denying them or embracing comforting illusions. This requires the courage to accept the inherent anxiety and the dread of nonbeing that is part of being alive. Such courage may be bolstered by developing supportive relationships with others who can supply unconditional positive regard. Something about being loved helps relieve the angst.

existential approach A school of thought that regards personality as being governed by an individual's ongoing choices and decisions in the context of the realities of life and death.

Build to the Outcomes

1. How does the humanistic–existential approach differ from the trait and psychodynamic approaches?

2. What does it mean to be self-actualized?

3. How is "flow" created?

4. What is the existential approach to personality?

5. What is angst? How is it created?

The Social–Cognitive Approach: Personalities in Situations

What is it like to be a person? The **social–cognitive approach** *views personality in terms of how a person thinks about the situations encountered in daily life and behaves in response to them.* Bringing together insights from social psychology, cognitive psychology, and learning theory, this approach emphasizes how the person experiences and interprets situations (Bandura, 1986; Mischel & Shoda, 1999; Wegner & Gilbert, 2000).

Researchers in social cognition believe that both the current situation and learning history are key determinants of behavior, and focus on how people *perceive* their environments. People think about their goals, the consequences of their behavior, and how they might achieve certain objectives in different situations (Lewin, 1951). The social–cognitive approach looks at how personality and situation interact to cause behavior, how personality contributes to the way people construct situations in their own minds, and how people's goals and expectancies influence their responses to situations.

Learning Outcomes

- Describe the social–cognitive approach to personality.
- Explain how personal constructs are key to personality differences.
- Identify how one's perception of control influences behavior.

Consistency of Personality Across Situations

At the core of the social–cognitive approach is a natural puzzle, the **person–situation controversy**, which focuses on *the question of whether behavior is caused more by personality or by situational factors.* This controversy began in earnest when Walter Mischel (1968) argued that measured personality traits often do a poor job of predicting individuals' behavior. Mischel also noted that knowing how a person will behave in one situation is not particularly helpful in predicting that person's behavior in another situation. For example, in classic studies, Hugh Hartshorne and M. A. May (1928) assessed children's honesty by examining their willingness to cheat on a test and found that such dishonesty was not consistent from one situation to another (Hartshorne & May, 1928). The assessment of a child's trait of honesty in a cheating situation was of almost no use in predicting whether that child would act honestly in a different situation, such as when given the opportunity to steal money. Mischel proposed that measured traits do not predict behaviors very well because behaviors are determined more by situational factors than personality theorists were willing to acknowledge.

Is there no personality, then? Do we all just do what situations require? It turns out that information about both personality and situation are necessary to predict behavior accurately (Fleeson, 2004; Mischel, 2004). Some situations are particularly powerful, leading most everyone to behave similarly regardless of personality (Cooper & Withey, 2009). At a funeral, almost everyone looks somber, and during an earthquake, almost everyone shakes. But in more moderate situations, personality can come to the fore to influence behavior (Funder, 2001). Among the children in Hartshorne and May's (1928) studies, cheating versus not cheating on a test was actually a fairly good predictor of cheating on a test later—as long as the situation was similar. Personality consistency, then, appears to be a matter of when and where a certain kind of behavior tends to be shown (see The Real World: Does Your Personality Change Depending on Who You're With?).

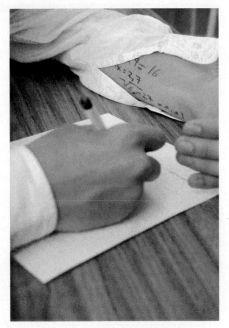

Is a student who cheats on a test more likely than others to steal candy or lie to her grandmother? Social–cognitive research indicates that behavior in one situation does not necessarily predict behavior in a different situation.   Glow Images/Getty Images

Personal Constructs: The Key to the Perceiver's Personality

How can we understand differences in how situations are interpreted? Recall our notion that personality often exists in the eye of the beholder. Situations may exist in the eye of the beholder as well. One person's gold mine may be another person's useless hole in the ground. George Kelly (1955) long ago realized that these differences in perspective could be used to understand the *perceiver's* personality. He suggested that people view the social world from differing perspectives and that these different views arise through

social–cognitive approach An approach that views personality in terms of how the person thinks about the situations encountered in daily life and behaves in response to them.

Does Your Personality Change Depending on Who You're With?

Social–cognitive psychologists suggest that how you behave is influenced by both your personality and the situations you are in. For instance, you act differently when sitting in a classroom than you do when dancing at a club (unless it's a really fun class). But do your personality and behavior also change when you're talking to different people?

For most people, the answer is yes. For example, we speak and act differently when interacting with our parents ("Hello mother, hello father") than with our friends ("Yo! Sup, punk?!"). And the personality traits of bilingual speakers shift slightly when they are speaking in one language versus another (Ramirez-Esparza et al., 2004).

Why would our personality characteristics change when we are interacting with one person versus another? One possibility is that we shift our personality and language to match the people with whom we are interacting to signal closeness or affiliation with them. Another possibility is that we do this to influence what other people think about us. For instance, one recent study found that people in positions of power tend to downplay their competence when interacting with subordinates to appear warmer and more like-able, whereas subordinates tend to conceal their warmth to appear more competent (Swencionis & Fiske, 2016). The authors suggest that in both situations, the participants are attempting to increase the perceived similarity between them and the person with whom they are interacting. The fact that things such as personality, similarity, and perceived competence can influence decisions about hiring and promotions (Rivera, 2012; Tews et al., 2011) means that personality actually has a huge impact on the experiences you have in the real world.

the application of **personal constructs**, *dimensions people use in making sense of their experiences.* Consider, for example, different individuals' personal constructs of a clown: One person may see him as a source of fun, another as a tragic figure, and yet another as so frightening that McDonald's must be avoided at all costs.

Kelly proposed that different personal constructs are the key to personality differences, and lead people to engage in different behaviors. Taking a long break from work for a leisurely lunch might seem lazy to you. To your friend, the break might seem an ideal opportunity for catching up with friends and she might wonder why *you* always choose to eat at your desk. Social–cognitive theory explains different responses to situations with the idea that people experience and interpret the world in different ways.

Personal Goals and Expectancies Lead to a Characteristic Style of Behavior

Social–cognitive theories also recognize that a person's unique perspective on situations is reflected in his or her personal goals, which are often conscious. In fact, people can usually tell you their goals, whether to find a date for this weekend, get a good grade in psych,

Are two of these people taller and one shorter? Are two bareheaded while one wears a hood? Or are two the daughters and one the mom? George Kelly held that the personal constructs we use to distinguish among people in our lives are basic elements of our own personalities. Daniel Wegner

person–situation controversy The question of whether behavior is caused more by personality or by situational factors.

personal constructs Dimensions people use in making sense of their experiences.

establish a fulfilling career, or just get this darn bag of chips open. These goals often reflect the tasks that are appropriate to the person's situation and, in a larger sense, fit the person's role and stage of life (Cantor, 1990; Vallacher & Wegner, 1985). For instance, common goals for adolescents include being popular, achieving greater independence from parents and family, and getting into a good college. Common goals for adults include developing a meaningful career, finding a mate, securing financial stability, and starting a family.

People translate goals into behavior in part through **outcome expectancies**, *a person's assumptions about the likely consequences of a future behavior.* Just as a laboratory rat learns that pressing a bar releases a food pellet, we learn that "if I am friendly toward people, they will be friendly in return" and "if I ask people to pull my finger, they will withdraw from me." So we learn to perform behaviors that we expect will have the outcome of moving us closer to our goals. We learn outcome expectancies through direct experience, both bitter and sweet, and through merely observing other people's actions and the resulting consequences.

People also differ in their expectancy for achieving goals. Some people seem to feel that they are fully in control of what happens to them in life, whereas others feel that the world doles out rewards and punishments to them irrespective of their actions. A person's **locus of control** is that *person's tendency to perceive the control of rewards as internal to the self or external in the environment* (Rotter, 1966). People who believe they control their own destiny are said to have an *internal* locus of control, whereas those who believe that outcomes are random, determined by luck, or controlled by other people are described as having an *external* locus of control. These beliefs translate into individual differences in emotion and behavior. For example, people with an internal locus of control tend to be less anxious, achieve more, and cope better with stress than do people with an external orientation (Lefcourt, 1982). To get a sense of your standing on this trait dimension, choose one of the options for each of the sample items from the locus-of-control scale in **TABLE 11.4.**

Some days you feel like a puppet on a string. If you have an external locus of control and believe you are at the mercy of other people, or of fate, you may feel that way most days. Asia Images/Superstock

---

TABLE 11.4   Rotter's Locus-of-Control Scale

For each pair of items, choose the option that most closely reflects your personal belief. Then check the answer key below to see if you have more of an internal or external locus of control.

1. a. Many of the unhappy things in people's lives are partly due to bad luck.
   b. People's misfortunes result from the mistakes they make.

2. a. I have often found that what is going to happen will happen.
   b. Trusting to fate has never turned out as well for me as making a decision to take a definite course of action.

3. a. Becoming a success is a matter of hard work; luck has little or nothing to do with it.
   b. Getting a good job depends mainly on being in the right place at the right time.

4. a. When I make plans, I am almost certain that I can make them work.
   b. It is not always wise to plan too far ahead because many things turn out to be a matter of good or bad fortune anyhow.

Information from Rotter, 1966.
Answers: A more internal locus of control would be reflected in choosing options 1b, 2b, 3a, and 4a.

---

outcome expectancies A person's assumptions about the likely consequences of a future behavior.

locus of control A person's tendency to perceive the control of rewards as internal to the self or external in the environment.

Build to the Outcomes

1. Do researchers in social cognition think that personality arises from past experiences or from the current environment?

2. How well do measured personality traits predict behavior, according to the social–cognitive approach?

3. Does personality or the current situation predict a person's behavior?

4. What are personal constructs?

5. What is the advantage of an internal, over an external, locus of control?

The Self: Personality in the Mirror

- Describe the features that make up the self-concept.
- Identify three possible reasons we desire self-esteem.

Imagine that you wake up tomorrow morning, drag yourself to the bathroom, look in the mirror, and don't recognize the face looking back at you. This was the plight of a woman, married for 30 years and the mother of two grown children, who one day began to respond to her mirror image as if it were a different person (Feinberg, 2001). She talked to and challenged the person in the mirror. When she got no response, she tried to attack it as if it were an intruder. Her husband, shaken by this bizarre behavior, brought her to a neurologist, who was gradually able to convince her that the image in the mirror was in fact herself.

Most of us are pretty familiar with the face that looks back at us from every mirror. We develop the ability to recognize ourselves in mirrors by 18 months of age (as discussed in the Consciousness chapter), and we share this skill with chimpanzees and other apes that have been raised in the presence of mirrors. Self-recognition in mirrors signals our amazing capacity for reflexive thinking, for directing attention to our own thoughts, feelings, and actions—an ability that enables us to construct ideas about our own personality. Unlike a cow, which will never know that it has a poor sense of humor, or a cat, which will never know that it is awfully friendly, humans have rich and detailed self-knowledge.

Self-Concept

If asked to describe yourself, you might mention your physical characteristics (male or female, tall or short, dark-skinned or light); your activities (listening to hip-hop, alternative rock, jazz, or classical music); your personality traits (extraverted or introverted, agreeable or independent); or your social roles (student, son or daughter, member of a hiking club, krumper). These features make up the **self-concept**, *a person's explicit knowledge of his*

What do these self-portraits of Vincent van Gogh, Pablo Picasso, Frida Kahlo, Wanda Wulz, Jean-Michel Basquiat, and Salvador Dalí reveal about each artist's self-concept?
©DeAgostini/SuperStock; © 2019 Estate of Pablo Picasso/ARS, NY. Photo: Painting/Alamy; © 2019 Banco de México Diego Rivera Frida Kahlo Museum Trust, Mexico, D.F./ARS, NY. Photo: Albright-Knox Art Gallery/Art Resource, NY; Alinari/Art Resource, NY; © The Estate of Jean-Michel Basquiat/ADAGP, Paris/ARS, New York 2019. Photo: Banque D'Images, ADAGP/Art Resource, NY; © 2019 Salvador Dalí, Fundació Gala-Salvador Dalí, ARS, NY. Photo: ©Philippe Halsman/Magnum

self-concept A person's explicit knowledge of his or her own behaviors, traits, and other personal characteristics.

or her own behaviors, traits, and other personal characteristics. A person's self-concept is an organized body of knowledge that develops from social experiences and has a profound effect on a person's behavior throughout life.

Self-Concept Organization

Our knowledge of ourselves seems to be organized naturally in two ways: as narratives about episodes in our lives and in terms of personality traits (as would be suggested by the distinction between episodic memory and semantic memory discussed in the Memory chapter).

The aspect of the self-concept that is a *self-narrative* (a story that we tell about ourselves) can be brief or very lengthy. Your life story could start with your birth and upbringing, describe a series of defining moments, and end where you are today. You could select specific experiences that have influenced you. Self-narrative organizes the highlights (and low blows) of your life into a story in which you are the leading character and binds them together into your self-concept (McAdams, 1993; McLean, 2008).

Self-concept is also organized in terms of more abstract personality traits—whether you judge yourself to be considerate or smart or lazy or active. Each person finds certain unique personality traits particularly important for conceptualizing the self (Markus, 1977). One person might define herself as independent, for example, whereas another might not care much about her level of independence but instead emphasize her sense of style.

Our self-narratives and trait self-concepts don't always match up. You may think of yourself as an honest person, for example, but also recall that time you nabbed a handful of change from your parents' dresser and conveniently forgot to replace it. The traits we use to describe ourselves are generalizations, and not every episode in our life stories may fit them. In fact, research suggests that the stores of knowledge about our behaviors and traits are not very well integrated (Kihlstrom et al., 2002). In people who develop amnesia, for example, memory for behaviors can be lost even though the trait self-concept remains stable (Klein, 2004). People can have a pretty strong sense of who they are even though they may not remember a single example of when they acted that way.

Causes and Effects of Self-Concept

How do self-concepts arise, and how do they affect us? Although we can gain self-knowledge in private moments of insight, we more often arrive at our self-concepts through interacting with others. Young children in particular receive plenty of feedback from their parents, teachers, siblings, and friends about their characteristics, which helps them form an idea of who they are. Even adults would find it difficult to hold a view of the self as "kind" or "smart" if no one else ever shared this impression. The sense of self, then, is largely developed and maintained in relationships with others.

Over the course of a lifetime, however, we become less and less impressed with what others have to say about us. All the things people have said about us accumulate after a while into a general view of ourselves, and we hold onto this view stubbornly. Just as we might argue vehemently with someone who tried to tell us a refrigerator is a pair of underpants, we are likely to defend our self-concept against anyone whose view of us departs from our own.

Because it is so stable, a major effect of the self-concept is to promote consistency in behavior across situations (Lecky, 1945). We tend to engage in **self-verification**, *the tendency to seek evidence to confirm the self-concept,* and we find it disconcerting if someone sees us quite differently from the way we see ourselves (Swann, 1983, 2012). In one study, people who considered themselves submissive were given feedback that they seemed very dominant and forceful (Swann, 1983). Rather than accepting this discrepant information, they went out of their way to act in an extremely submissive manner. As existential theorists emphasize, people derive a comforting sense of familiarity and stability from knowing who they are.

Think about your own self-narrative (what you have done) and self-concept (how you view yourself). Are there areas that don't match up? Are there things that you've done, good or bad, that are not part of your self-concept? How might you explain that? Cavan Images/Getty Images

"I don't want to be defined by who I am."
P.C. Vey/ The New Yorker Collection/Cartoonbank.com

self-verification The tendency to seek evidence to confirm the self-concept.

TABLE 11.5 Rosenberg Self-Esteem Scale				
Consider each statement and circle SA for strongly agree, A for agree, D for disagree, and SD for strongly disagree.				
1. On the whole, I am satisfied with myself.	SA	A	D	SD
2. At times, I think I am no good at all.	SA	A	D	SD
3. I feel that I have a number of good qualities.	SA	A	D	SD
4. I am able to do things as well as most other people.	SA	A	D	SD
5. I feel I do not have much to be proud of.	SA	A	D	SD
6. I certainly feel useless at times.	SA	A	D	SD
7. I feel that I'm a person of worth, at least on an equal plane with others.	SA	A	D	SD
8. I wish I could have more respect for myself.	SA	A	D	SD
9. All in all, I am inclined to feel that I am a failure.	SA	A	D	SD
10. I take a positive attitude toward myself.	SA	A	D	SD

Information from Rosenberg, 1965.

Scoring: For items 1, 3, 4, 7, and 10, SA = 3, A = 2, D = 1, SD = 0; for items 2, 5, 6, 8, and 9, the scoring is reversed, with SA = 0, A = 1, D = 2, SD = 3. The higher the total score, the higher one's self-esteem.

These are the men's snowboarding halfpipe medalists at the 2018 Winter Olympics. From left, Ayumu Hirano of Japan, silver; Shaun White of the United States, gold; and Scotty James of Australia, bronze, pose with their medals. Notice the expression on Hirano's face compared with those of the gold- and bronze-medal winners. Andreas Rentz/Getty Images

Self-Esteem

When you think about yourself, do you feel good and worthy? Do you like yourself? Or do you feel bad and have negative, self-critical thoughts? **Self-esteem** is *the extent to which an individual likes, values, and accepts the self.* Researchers who study self-esteem typically ask participants to fill out a self-esteem questionnaire such as the one shown in **TABLE 11.5** (Rosenberg, 1965). People who strongly agree with the positive statements about themselves and strongly disagree with the negative statements are considered to have high self-esteem.

In general, compared with people with low self-esteem, those with high self-esteem tend to live happier and healthier lives, cope better with stress, and be more likely to persist at difficult tasks (Baumeister et al., 2003). How does this aspect of personality develop? And why does everyone—whether high or low in self-esteem—seem to *want* high self-esteem?

Sources of Self-Esteem

An important factor in determining self-esteem is who people choose for comparison. For example, James (1890) noted that an accomplished athlete who is the second best in the world should feel pretty proud, but this athlete might not feel that way if the standard of comparison involves being best in the world. In fact, athletes in the 1992 Olympics who had won silver medals looked less happy during the medal ceremony than those who had won bronze medals (Medvec et al., 1995). If people see the actual self as falling short of the ideal self (the person that they would like to be), they tend to feel sad or dejected. When they become aware that the actual self is inconsistent with the self they have a duty to be, they are likely to feel anxious or agitated (Higgins, 1987).

The Desire for Self-Esteem

What's so great about self-esteem? Why do people want to see themselves in a positive light and avoid seeing themselves negatively? Three key theories on the benefits of self-esteem focus on social status, belonging, and security.

self-esteem The extent to which an individual likes, values, and accepts the self.

1. *Social status.* People with high self-esteem seem to carry themselves in a way that is similar to how high-status animals of other social species carry themselves. Dominant

male gorillas, for example, appear confident and comfortable, not anxious or withdrawn. Perhaps high self-esteem in humans reflects high social status or suggests that the person is worthy of respect, and this perception triggers natural affective responses (Barkow, 1980; Maslow, 1937).

2. *Belonging.* Evolutionary theory holds that early humans who managed to survive and pass on their genes were those able to maintain good relations with others rather than being cast out to fend for themselves. Thus, self-esteem could be a kind of inner gauge of how much a person feels included by others at any given moment (Leary & Baumeister, 2000). According to evolutionary theory, then, we seek higher self-esteem because we have evolved to seek out belongingness in our families, work groups, and culture, and higher self-esteem indicates that we are being accepted.

3. *Security.* Existential and psychodynamic approaches to personality suggest that the source of distress underlying negative self-esteem is ultimately the fear of death (Solomon et al., 1991). In this view, humans find it terrifying to contemplate their own mortality, so they try to defend against this awareness by immersing themselves in activities (e.g., earning money or dressing up to appear attractive) that their culture defines as meaningful and valuable. The desire for self-esteem may stem from a need to find value in ourselves as a way of escaping the anxiety associated with recognizing our mortality. The higher our self-esteem, the less anxious we feel with the knowledge that someday we will no longer exist.

Survivor, The Bachelor, Big Brother. Why are shows in which everyone is fighting to remain a part of the group so popular today? Is it because these shows exploit the evolutionary desire to belong? (Or do people just like to see other people get kicked out of the club?) CBS Photo Archive/Getty Images

But Can We All Be Above Average?

Whatever the reason that low self-esteem feels so bad and high self-esteem feels so good, people are generally motivated to see themselves positively. In fact, we often process information in a biased manner in order to feel good about the self. Research on the **self-serving bias** shows that *people tend to take credit for their successes but downplay responsibility for their failures.* You may have noticed this tendency in yourself, particularly in terms of the attributions you make about exams when you get a good grade ("I studied really intensely, and I'm good at that subject") or a bad grade ("The test was ridiculously tricky, and the professor is unfair").

On the whole, most people satisfy the desire for high self-esteem and maintain a reasonably positive view of self by engaging in the self-serving bias (Miller & Ross, 1975; Shepperd et al., 2008). For example, 90% of drivers describe their driving skills as better than average, and 86% of workers rate their performance on the job as above average. Even among university professors, 94% feel they are above average in teaching ability compared with other professors (Cross, 1977). These kinds of judgments simply cannot be accurate, statistically speaking, because the average of a group of people has to be the average, not better than average! This particular error may be adaptive, however. People who do not engage in this self-serving bias to boost their self-esteem tend to be more at risk for depression, anxiety, and related health problems (Taylor & Brown, 1988).

On the other hand, a few people take positive self-esteem too far—a trait called **narcissism**, *a grandiose view of the self, combined with a tendency to seek admiration from and exploit others.* At its extreme, narcissism is considered a personality disorder (see the Psychological Disorders chapter). Research has documented disadvantages of an overinflated view of self, most of which arise from the need to defend that grandiose view at all costs. For example, when highly narcissistic adolescents were given reason to be ashamed of their performance on a task, their aggressiveness increased in the form of willingness to deliver loud blasts of noise to punish their opponents in a laboratory game (Thomaes et al., 2008).

The self is the part of personality that the person knows and can report about. Some of the personality measures we have seen in this chapter (such as personality inventories based on self-reports) are really no different from measures of self-concept.

"I suffer from accurate self-esteem."
Ariel Molvig/The New Yorker Collection/www.cartoonbank.com

self-serving bias People's tendency to take credit for their successes but downplay responsibility for their failures.

narcissism A trait that reflects a grandiose view of the self, combined with a tendency to seek admiration from and exploit others.

Both depend on the person's perceptions and memories of the self's behavior and traits. But personality runs deeper than this as well. The unconscious forces identified in psychodynamic approaches provide themes for behavior and sources of mental disorder that are not accessible for self-report. The humanistic and existential approaches remind us of the profound concerns we humans face and the difficulties we may have in understanding all the forces that shape our self-views. Finally, in emphasizing how personality shapes our perceptions of social life, the social–cognitive approach brings the self back to center stage. The self, after all, is the hub of each person's social world.

Build to the Outcomes

1. What makes up our self-concept?
2. How does our self-narrative contribute to our self-concept?
3. Why don't traits always reflect knowledge of behavior?
4. How does self-concept influence behavior?
5. What impact does self-verification have on our behaviors?

6. What is self-esteem? Why do we want to have a high level of it?
7. How do comparisons with others affect self-esteem?
8. How might self-esteem have played a role in evolution?
9. Why is it possible to have too much self-esteem?

CHAPTER REVIEW

Personality: What It Is and How It Is Measured

- In psychology, *personality* refers to a person's characteristic style of behaving, thinking, and feeling.
- Personality differences can be studied from two points of view: *prior events,* such as biological makeup, life circumstances, and culture; and *anticipated events,* as reflected in a person's hopes, dreams, and fears.
- Personality can be measured by personality inventories such as the MMPI–2–RF that rely on self-report, and projective techniques, such as the Rorschach Inkblot Test and the TAT, that rely on responses to ambiguous stimuli.
- Newer high-tech methods are proving to be even more effective in measuring personality.

The Trait Approach: Identifying Patterns of Behavior

- The trait approach tries to identify personality dimensions that can be used to characterize an individual's behavior. Researchers have attempted to boil down the potentially huge array of things people do, think, and feel into some core personality factors.
- Many personality psychologists currently focus on the Big Five personality factors: openness to experience, conscientiousness, extraversion, agreeableness, and neuroticism.
- Twin studies indicate that the more genes you have in common with someone else, the more similar your personalities will be.

- The reticular formation, a part of the brain that regulates arousal and alertness, is more easily stimulated in introverts than in extraverts, who may need to seek out more interaction and activity to achieve mental stimulation.

The Psychodynamic Approach: Forces That Lie Beneath Awareness

- Freud believed that the personality results from forces that are largely unconscious, shaped by the interplay among id, superego, and ego.
- Defense mechanisms are techniques the mind may use to reduce anxiety generated by unacceptable impulses.
- Freud also believed that personality is formed as the developing person passes through a series of psychosexual stages.
- Critics argue that psychodynamic explanations lack real evidence and are after-the-fact interpretations.

The Humanistic–Existential Approach: Personality as Choice

- The humanistic–existential approach to personality focuses on how people make healthy choices that form their personalities.
- Humanists see personality as directed by an inherent striving toward self-actualization and development of our unique human potentials.
- Existentialists focus on angst and the defensive response people often have to questions about the meaning of life and the inevitability of death.

The Social–Cognitive Approach: Personalities in Situations

- The social–cognitive approach focuses on personality as arising from individuals' behavior in situations. According to social–cognitive personality theorists, the same person may behave differently in different situations but should behave consistently in similar situations.

- Personal constructs are dimensions that people use to make sense of their experiences and that reveal the perceiver's personality.

- People translate their goals into behavior through outcome expectancies.

- People who believe they control their own destiny (internal locus of control) tend to be better able to cope with stress and achieve more, compared with people who believe they are at the mercy of fate or of other people (external locus of control).

The Self: Personality in the Mirror

- The self-concept is a person's knowledge of self, including both specific self-narratives and more abstract personality traits.

- People's self-concept develops through social feedback, and people often act to try to confirm these views through a process of self-verification.

- Self-esteem is a person's evaluation of self; it is derived from being accepted by others, as well as by how we evaluate ourselves in comparison to others. We may seek positive self-esteem to achieve perceptions of status, or belonging, or of being symbolically protected against mortality.

- People strive for positive self-views through self-serving biases.

Key Concept Quiz

1. From a psychological perspective, personality refers to
   a. a person's characteristic style of behaving, thinking, and feeling.
   b. physiological predispositions that manifest themselves psychologically.
   c. past events that have shaped a person's current behavior.
   d. choices people make in response to cultural norms.

2. Which statement does NOT present a drawback of self-report measures such as the MMPI–2–RF?
   a. People may respond in ways that put themselves in a flattering light.
   b. Some people tend to always agree or always disagree with the statements on the test.
   c. Interpretation is subject to the biases of the researcher.
   d. People are unaware of some of their personality characteristics and thus cannot answer accurately.

3. Projective techniques to assess personality involve
   a. personal inventories.
   b. self-reporting.
   c. responses to ambiguous stimuli.
   d. actuarial methodology.

4. A relatively stable disposition to behave in a particular and consistent way is a
   a. motive.
   b. goal.
   c. trait.
   d. reflex.

5. Which of the following is NOT one of the Big Five personality factors?
   a. conscientiousness
   b. agreeableness
   c. neuroticism
   d. orderliness

6. Compelling evidence for the importance of biological factors in personality is best seen in studies of
   a. parenting styles.
   b. identical twins reared apart.
   c. brain damage.
   d. factor analysis.

7. Which of Freud's systems of the mind would lead you to, if hungry, start grabbing food off people's plates upon entering a restaurant?
   a. the id
   b. the ego
   c. the superego
   d. repression

8. After performing poorly on an exam, you drop a class, saying that you and the professor are just a poor match. According to Freud, what defense mechanism are you employing?
   a. regression
   b. rationalization
   c. projection
   d. reaction formation

9. Humanists see personality as directed toward the goal of
   a. existentialism.
   b. self-actualization.
   c. ego control.
   d. sublimation.

10. According to the existential perspective, the difficulties we face in finding meaning in life and in accepting responsibility for making free choices provoke a type of anxiety called
   a. angst.
   b. flow.
   c. the self-actualizing tendency.
   d. mortality salience.

11. According to social–cognitive theorists, _____ are the dimensions people use in making sense of their experiences.
    a. personal constructs
    b. outcome expectancies
    c. loci of control
    d. personal goals

12. Tyler has been getting poor evaluations at work. He attributes this to having a mean boss who always assigns him the hardest tasks. This suggests Tyler has
    a. an external locus of control.
    b. an internal locus of control.
    c. high performance anxiety.
    d. poorly developed personal constructs.

13. What we think about ourselves is referred to as our _____, and how we feel about ourselves is referred to as our _____.

a. self-narrative; self-verification
b. self-concept; self-esteem
c. self-concept; self-verification
d. self-esteem; self-concept

14. On what do the key theories on the benefits of self-esteem focus?
    a. status
    b. belonging
    c. security
    d. all of the above

15. When people take credit for their successes but downplay responsibility for their failures, they are exhibiting
    a. narcissism.
    b. implicit egotism.
    c. the self-serving bias.
    d. the name-letter effect.

LearningCurve Don't stop now! Quizzing yourself is a powerful study tool. Go to LaunchPad to access the LearningCurve adaptive quizzing system and your own personalized learning plan. Visit launchpadworks.com.

Key Terms

personality (p. 327)

self-report (p. 328)

Minnesota Multiphasic Personality Inventory (MMPI) (p. 329)

projective techniques (p. 329)

Rorschach Inkblot Test (p. 329)

Thematic Apperception Test (TAT) (p. 329)

trait (p. 331)

Big Five (p. 332)

psychodynamic approach (p. 337)

id (p. 337)

superego (p. 337)

ego (p. 338)

defense mechanisms (p. 338)

self-actualizing tendency (p. 339)

existential approach (p. 340)

social–cognitive approach (p. 341)

person–situation controversy (p. 341)

personal constructs (p. 342)

outcome expectancies (p. 343)

locus of control (p. 343)

self-concept (p. 344)

self-verification (p. 345)

self-esteem (p. 346)

self-serving bias (p. 347)

narcissism (p. 347)

Changing Minds

1. A presidential candidate makes a Freudian slip on live TV, calling his mother "petty"; he corrects himself quickly and says he meant to say "pretty." By the next day, the video has gone viral, and the morning talk shows discuss the possibility that the candidate has an unresolved psychosexual conflict and is stuck in the phallic stage—meaning that he is likely a relatively unstable person preoccupied with coping with incestuous feelings of love for his mother and jealousy of his father. Your roommate knows you're taking a psychology class and asks for your opinion: "Can we really tell that a person is sexually repressed, and maybe in love with his own mother, just because he stumbled over a single word?" How would you reply? How widely are Freud's ideas about personality accepted by modern psychologists?

2. While reading a magazine, you come across an article on the nature–nurture controversy in personality. The magazine describes several studies in which adopted children (who share no genes with each other but grow up in the same household) are no more like each other than complete strangers. This suggests that family environment—and the influence of parental behavior—on personality is very weak. You show the article to a friend, who has trouble believing the results: "I always thought parents who don't show affection produce kids who have trouble forming lasting relationships." How would you explain to your friend the relationship between nature, nurture, and personality?

3. One of your friends has found an online site that offers personality testing. He takes the test and reports that the

results prove he's an "intuitive" rather than a "sensing" personality, who likes to look at the big picture rather than focusing on tangible here-and-now experiences. "This explains a lot," he says, "like why I have trouble remembering details like other people's birthdays, and why it's hard for me to finish projects before the deadline." Aside from warning your friend about the dangers of self-diagnosis via Internet quizzes, what would you tell him about the relationship between personality types and behavior? How well do scores on personality tests predict a person's actual behavior?

4. One of your friends tells you that her boyfriend cheated on her, so she will never date him again or date anyone who has ever been unfaithful because "once a cheat, always a cheat." She goes on to explain that personality and character are stable over time, so people will always make the same decisions and repeat the same mistakes over time. What do we know about the interaction between personality and situations that might confirm or deny her statements?

Answers to Key Concept Quiz

1. a; 2. c; 3. c; 4. c; 5. d; 6. b; 7. a; 8. b; 9. b; 10. a; 11. a; 12. a; 13. b; 14. d; 15. c

 LaunchPad
macmillan learning

Social Psychology

12

Long before he was elected to the U.S. Senate, John McCain was a navy pilot. His plane was shot down by the North Vietnamese and he spent 5 years as a prisoner of war. And long before he was elected President of South Africa, Nelson Mandela was a political activist whose protests against an apartheid regime earned him 27 years in prison. Both men experienced a variety of tortures at the hands of their captors, and both agreed about which was the worst. It had nothing to do with electric shock or waterboarding. It did not involve ropes or razor blades. It was a remarkably simple technique that has been used for millennia to break the body and destroy the mind. That technique is called solitary confinement. "It crushes your spirit and weakens your resistance more effectively than any other form of mistreatment," McCain later said. "Nothing is more dehumanizing," wrote Mandela.

Torture involves depriving people of something they desperately need, such as oxygen, water, food, or sleep, and as torturers have known for ages, the need for social interaction is every bit as vital. "I found solitary confinement the most forbidding aspect of prison life," Mandela wrote. "I have known men who took half a dozen lashes in preference to being locked up alone." Studies of prisoners show that extensive periods of isolation can induce symptoms of psychosis (Grassian, 2006), and even in smaller doses, social isolation takes a toll. Ordinary people who are socially isolated are more likely to become depressed, to become ill, and to die prematurely. Indeed, being socially isolated is as dangerous to your health as is smoking or being obese (Cacioppo & Patrick, 2008; Holt-Lunstad, 2018).

But why? Snails and centipedes don't need each other. Neither do skunks, moose, badgers, or aardvarks. In fact, the majority of the earth's animals are loners that rely on no one but themselves and lead a solitary existence. Why are we so different? **Social psychology** is *the study of the causes and consequences of sociality,* and it provides an answer to this question. Like all other animals, human beings must solve the twin problems of survival and reproduction, and, as you will see in this chapter, sociality is our brilliant solution to both of these problems. You'll also see how people learn to understand and predict each other, so that they know who they can and cannot trust. Finally, you'll see some of the ingenious techniques that human beings have developed to manipulate and control each other—sometimes for the better, and sometimes for the worse.

Interpersonal Behavior
Interpersonal Attraction
Interpersonal Perception
Interpersonal Influence

Both John McCain and Nelson Mandela spent years in solitary confinement, and both described it as the worst form of torture. Brooks Kraft LLC/Corbis via Getty Images; GETTY IMAGES

social psychology The study of the causes and consequences of sociality.

Learning Outcomes

- Identify biological and cultural influences on aggression.
- Explain why cooperation is risky.
- Describe the costs and benefits of groups.
- Distinguish between apparent and genuine altruism.

Interpersonal Behavior

All animals need food and water, some need mates and shelter, and one appears to need the limited-edition iPhone on the day it is released. All these things are resources, and the problem with resources is that there are rarely enough to go around—so if somebody gets them, then somebody else doesn't. We'd all rather be the one who gets them, of course, and human beings have developed two tactics to make sure that happens: hurting and helping. Although these words are antonyms, they turn out to be two solutions to the same problem.

Aggression

Whether the scarce resource is a carrot, a cave, or an iPhone, the simplest way to make sure you get one is simply to take it—and kick the stuffing out of anyone who tries to stop you. **Aggression** is *behavior that is meant to cause harm* (Anderson & Bushman, 2002; Bushman & Huesmann, 2010), and it is a strategy used by virtually all animals to achieve their goals. The **frustration–aggression hypothesis** suggests that *animals aggress when their goals are frustrated* (Berkowitz, 1989; Dollard et al., 1939). The word *frustration* here refers not to a feeling but rather to the obstruction of a goal. A chimp that wants a banana (goal) that is in the hands of another chimp (frustration) may attack to get that banana (aggression), just as a person who wants money (goal) that is in the hands of another person (frustration) may attack (aggression) to get that money.

Strategic behavior of this kind is known as **proactive aggression,** which is *aggression that is planned and purposeful* (Wrangham, 2017). The mafia hit man who executes a rival gangster in cold blood is engaging in proactive aggression. Because this kind of aggression is a means to an end, it tends to be specifically directed toward a relevant target (the hit man's task is to kill the gangster and not just anybody who happens to be eating in the restaurant that day), it tends to occur only when the aggressor believes that the benefits will outweigh the costs (the hit man won't pull the trigger if he thinks there's a good chance he'll be caught), and it is not associated with a heightened state of arousal (hey, it's just a job).

But not all aggression is proactive. **Reactive aggression** is *aggression that occurs spontaneously in response to a negative affective stat*e. The man who gets fired, gets angry, and yells at his wife when he gets home is engaging in reactive aggression. This kind of aggression is strongly associated with the experience of pain or anger and is not always directed toward a relevant target. When rats are given painful electric shocks, they will attack whatever happens to be in their cage, whether that's another rat or a tennis ball (Kruk et al., 2004), and when experimental participants are made to experience physical pain (which can safely be done by having people immerse their hands in ice water), they will hurt others who had nothing to do with their pain (Anderson, 1989; Anderson et al., 1997).

Unlike proactive aggression, reactive aggression occurs even when the costs outweigh the benefits: The angry man who screams at his wife has done nothing to get his job back, and he's probably made his life worse instead of better. Reactive aggression is typically a response to the experience of negative affect (Berkowitz, 1990), which explains why so many acts of violence—from murders to brawls—are more likely to occur on hot days, when people are already feeling uncomfortable, irritated, and easily angered (Rinderu, Bushman, & Van Lange, 2018) (see **FIGURE 12.1**). Indeed, the relationship between temperature and violence is so reliable that scientists can predict precisely how much more violence the United States will experience over the next few decades due to climate change (Burke et al., 2015). *Hint:* It's a lot.

aggression Behavior that is meant to cause harm.

frustration–aggression hypothesis A principle stating that animals aggress when their goals are frustrated.

proactive aggression Aggression that is planned and purposeful.

reactive aggression Aggression that occurs spontaneously in response to a negative affective state.

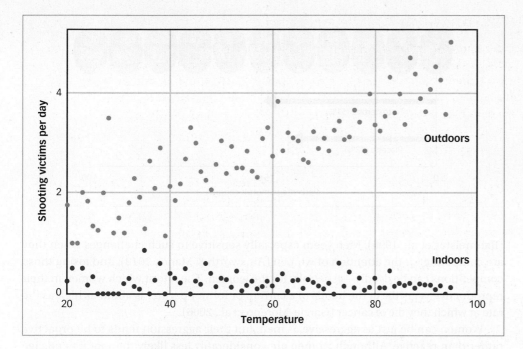

Figure 12.1 Heat and Aggression
This graph shows the relationship between outdoor temperature and the number of shooting victims in Philadelphia from 2015–2017. Notice that as the outdoor temperature goes up, so does the rate of outdoor violence—but the rate of indoor violence stays the same. Data from Asher, 2018

How Biology Influences Aggression

If you want to know whether someone is likely to engage in reactive aggression and you can ask them just one question, it should be this: "Are you a man?" Violence is one of the most gendered of all behaviors. Crimes such as assault, battery, and murder are almost exclusively perpetrated by men (and especially by young men), who are responsible for about 90% of the murders and 80% of the violent crimes in the United States (Strueber et al., 2006). Although socialization practices all over the world encourage males to be more aggressive than females (more on that shortly), male aggressiveness is not merely the product of playing with toy soldiers or watching ice hockey. Studies show that aggression is associated with the presence of a hormone called testosterone, which is typically much higher in men than in women, and much higher in younger men than in older men (Carré & Archer, 2018).

A man's testosterone levels wax and wane, and when those levels wax, men tend to feel more powerful and confident in their ability to prevail in interpersonal conflicts (Eisenegger et al., 2011; Eisenegger et al., 2010). Testosterone also makes men more sensitive to provocations (Ronay & Galinsky, 2011) and less sensitive to signs of retaliation. For example, participants in one experiment watched a face as its expression changed from neutral to threatening and were asked to respond as soon as the expression became threatening (see **FIGURE 12.2**). Participants who were given a small dose of testosterone were slower to recognize the threatening expression (van Honk & Schutter, 2007; see also Olsson et al., 2016). As you can imagine, feeling powerful while simultaneously failing to realize that the guy whose parking space you just stole looks really, really mad is a good way to end up in a fist fight.

One of the most reliable methods for raising a man's testosterone levels and provoking an aggressive response is to challenge his beliefs about his own status or dominance. Indeed, three-quarters of all murders can be classified as "status competitions" or "contests to save face" (Daly & Wilson, 1988). Contrary to popular wisdom, it isn't men with unusually low self-esteem who are most prone to this sort of aggression, but men with unusually high self-esteem, because those men are especially likely to perceive other people's actions as a challenge to their inflated sense of self-worth

Figure 12.2 I Spy Threat Subjects who were given testosterone needed to see a more threatening expression before they were able to recognize it as such. Research from Van Honk, J., & Schutter, D. J. (2007).

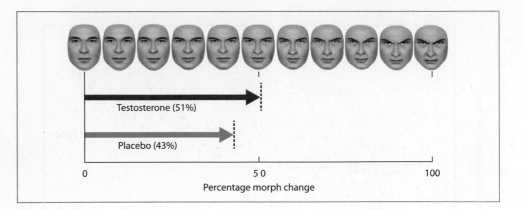

(Baumeister et al., 1996). Men seem especially sensitive to such challenges when they are competing for the attention of women (Ainsworth & Maner, 2012), and losing those competitions can be deadly—especially for the women. The rate at which women in their reproductive years die at the hands of a current or former partner is about as high as the rate at which they die of cancer (Garcia-Moreno et al., 2006).

Women can be just as aggressive as men, but their aggression tends to be proactive rather than reactive. Although women are considerably less likely than men to engage in physical aggression, they are just as likely to engage in verbal aggression (Denson et al., 2018) and cyber-bullying (Barlett & Coyne, 2014). Indeed, women may even be more likely than men to aggress by causing social harm—for example, by ostracizing others (Benenson et al., 2011) or by spreading malicious rumors about them (Bjorkqvist, 2018; Card et al., 2008; Richardson, 2014). Men and women both use aggression as a tool, but they use it in different ways.

How Culture Influences Aggression

Aggression has a biological basis, but it is also strongly influenced by culture. For example, violent crime in the United States is more prevalent in the South, where men are taught to react aggressively when they feel their status has been challenged, than in the North, where men are taught to resolve conflicts by appealing to authority (Brown et al., 2009; Nisbett & Cohen, 1996). In one set of experiments (Cohen et al., 1996), researchers insulted American men from northern and southern states. When a large man walked directly toward them as they were leaving the experiment, the previously insulted southerners got right up in the man's face before letting him pass, whereas the previously insulted northerners simply stepped aside. Are northern men just nicer? Nope. Because in another condition of the study in which the participants were *not* insulted, southern men stepped aside *before* northern men did. Southern men, it seems, are more aggressive when insulted but more polite otherwise.

Aggression is also more prevalent in cultures that make it easy. The U.S. murder rate is three times higher than the murder rate in Canada, and one reason is that while Americans are just 4% of the world's population, they own about half the world's guns. Aggression is also more likely to occur when it is easy to imagine (Labella & Masten, 2017). Research suggests that watching violent movies and playing violent video games makes people (and especially children) behave more aggressively (Anderson et al., 2010; Anderson et al., 2017; Bender et al., 2017; Calvert et al., 2017) and less cooperatively (cf. Ferguson, 2010; Sheese & Graziano, 2005).

The good news is that just as a culture can encourage aggression, so too can it discourage it (Fry, 2012). For example, the Inuit people of the Canadian Arctic do not resolve conflicts with guns or knives, but with song contests in which the person who delivers the most effective musical put-down of his opponent is declared the winner (Briggs, 2000). Replacing war with *American Idol* sounds like a remarkably sane idea.

Major League Baseball pitchers have extremely good aim, so when they hit a batter with a "bean ball" you can assume they meant it. Statistics show that pitchers born in southern states are 40% more likely to throw a bean ball than are pitchers born in northern states (Timmerman, 2007). Matt Brown/Getty Images

Depending on where you live, violence can be ordinary or unthinkable. In Iraq, where children are exposed to the brutality of extremist groups such as ISIS, mock executions can be part of daily play. In contrast, the Jains of India believe that every form of life is sacred, and children wear masks so that they do not accidentally harm insects or microbes by inhaling them. Hadi Mizban/AP Images; Manish Swarup/AP Images

Cooperation

Aggression may be the simplest way to solve the problem of scarce resources, but it is rarely the most effective way, because when individuals work together, they can often each get more than either could get alone. **Cooperation** is *behavior by two or more individuals that leads to mutual benefit* (Rand & Nowak, 2016), and it is one of our species' greatest achievements—right up there with language, fire, and free two-day delivery (Axelrod, 1984; Henrich, 2018; Nowak, 2006; Rand, 2016). Every roadway and supermarket, every toothbrush and smartphone, every ballet and surgery is the result of cooperation, and it is hard to think of any important human accomplishment that could possibly have happened without it. But if the benefits of cooperation are clear, why don't we cooperate all the time?

Why Cooperation Is Risky

Cooperation is potentially beneficial, but it is also risky, as demonstrated by a game called the *prisoner's dilemma*. Imagine that you and your friend Tucker have been arrested for hacking into a bank's mainframe and stealing a few million dollars. The police have found some stolen bank codes on your laptops, but they don't know which of you actually did the hacking. You and Tucker are now being interrogated in separate rooms, and the detectives ask each of you to sign a statement saying that the other was the actual hacker. They explain that if you sign and Tucker doesn't, then you'll go free and Tucker will go to prison for 3 years. On the other hand, if Tucker signs and you don't, then you'll be the one spending 3 years in the pen and Tucker will be the one going home tonight. Okay, but what if you agree to sign and then Tucker decides to sign too? If that happens, then you'll both go to prison for 2 years. And what if you refuse to sign and Tucker refuses as well? Well, you'll still go to prison together, but only for a year. So what should you do (other than math)? As **FIGURE 12.3**

cooperation Behavior by two or more individuals that leads to mutual benefit.

Figure 12.3 The Prisoner's Dilemma Game The prisoner's dilemma game illustrates the risk of cooperation. Mutual cooperation leads to a moderate benefit to both players, but if one player cooperates and the other doesn't, the cooperator gets no benefit and the noncooperator gets a large benefit.

	Tucker refuses to sign (i.e., he cooperates with you)	Tucker signs (i.e., he does not cooperate with you)
You refuse to sign (i.e., you cooperate with Tucker)	You both serve 1 year	You serve 3 years Tucker goes free
You sign (i.e., you do not cooperate with Tucker)	You go free Tucker serves 3 years	You both serve 2 years

At the Dirty Lemon Beverage Store in New York City, customers walk in, select their drinks, and leave. They are expected to text the company later so their accounts can be charged. If a few people cheat, it won't matter much; but if a lot of people cheat, then the store will have to close. "Honor systems" such as these are real-world versions of the prisoner's dilemma.   Richard Levine/Alamy

shows, it would be best if you and Tucker cooperated and refused to implicate each other, because you'd both get off with a very light sentence. But if you agree to cooperate and then Tucker gets sneaky and decides to sign, you'll serve a long sentence while Tucker goes free. As this game cooperation can be beneficial, but it is also risky because others can take advantage of you. You should only cooperate with Tucker if you can trust him to do the same. But can you?

How Groups Minimize the Risks of Cooperation

Maybe Tucker is an old friend and you know you can trust him to cooperate with you. But what if he's just some guy you barely know? Then how will you decide? As it turns out, people all over the world make this decision based on the groups to which the other person belongs. A **group** is *a collection of people who have something in common that distinguishes them from others*. Every one of us is a member of many groups—from families and teams to religions and nations. All these groups have one thing in common: The members can generally trust that other members will be nice to them. **Prejudice** is *an evaluation of another person based solely on their group membership* (Dovidio & Gaertner, 2010), and although most people use this word to denote negative evaluations, psychologists use it to denote both positive and negative evaluations (Allport, 1954). Research suggests that although people are not always negatively prejudiced against members of other groups, they are almost always positively prejudiced toward members of their own groups (Brewer, 1999; DiDonato et al., 2011). Even when people are randomly assigned to be members of meaningless groups such as Group 1 or Group 2, they still favor members of their own group (Hodson & Sorrentino, 2001; Locksley et al., 1980). It appears that simply knowing that "You're one of us and not one of them" is sufficient to create ingroup favoritism (Tajfel et al., 1971). You may not know Tucker, but if he graduated from your high school, lives in your town, and shares your religion, skin tone, and taste in foot-ware, odds are that you will choose to trust him.

Because group members can be trusted to favor each other, group membership makes cooperation less risky. That's one of its benefits. But groups can also have costs. For example, when groups try to make decisions, they rarely do better than the best member would have done alone—and they often do much worse (Baumeister et al., 2016; Minson & Mueller, 2012). There are several reasons for this:

- Groups usually don't capitalize fully on the expertise of their members (Hackman & Katz, 2010). For instance, groups (such as a school board) often give too little weight to the opinions of members who are experts (the financial advisor) and too much weight to the opinions of members who happen to be high in status (the mayor) or especially talkative (the mayor).

- The **common knowledge effect** is *the tendency for group discussions to focus on information that all members share* (Gigone & Hastie, 1993; Kerr & Tindale, 2004). The problem is that the information everyone shares (the cost of running the cafeteria) may be relatively unimportant, whereas the truly important information (how a school in Sweden solved a similar budget crisis) may be known to just a few.

- A group whose members come to the table with moderate opinions ("We probably shouldn't renovate the gym this year") can end up making an extreme decision ("Let's shut down the gym and fire the entire athletic staff") simply because, in the course of discussion, each member was exposed to many different arguments in favor of a single position (Isenberg, 1986). **Group polarization** is *the tendency for groups to make decisions that are more extreme than any member would have made alone* (Myers & Lamm, 1975).

- Group members usually care about how other members feel and are sometimes reluctant to "rock the boat" even when it needs a good rocking. **Groupthink** is *the tendency for groups to reach consensus in order to facilitate interpersonal harmony* (Janis, 1982). Harmony is important (especially if the group is a choir), but studies show that groups often sacrifice the soundness of their decisions to achieve it (Turner & Pratkanis, 1998).

group A collection of people who have something in common that distinguishes them from others.

prejudice A positive or negative evaluation of another person based on their group membership.

common knowledge effect The tendency for group discussions to focus on information that all members share.

group polarization The tendency of groups to make decisions that are more extreme than any member would have made alone.

groupthink The tendency of groups to reach consensus in order to facilitate interpersonal harmony.

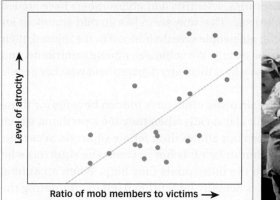

Figure 12.4 Mob Size and Level of Atrocity Mobs often do horrible things. These two men were rescued by police just as residents of their town prepared to lynch them for stealing a car. Because larger mobs provide more opportunity for diffusion of responsibility, their atrocities become more horrible as they become larger (Leader et al., 2007; Ritchey & Ruback, 2018). AP Images

The costs of groups go beyond making suboptimal decisions. People in groups sometimes do truly terrible things that none of their members would do alone (Yzerbyt & Demoulin, 2010). Lynching, rioting, gang-raping—why do human beings sometimes behave so badly when they assemble? One reason is **deindividuation,** *a phenomenon that occurs when immersion in a group causes people to become less concerned with their personal values* (Postmes & Spears, 1998). Deindividuation can lead people in groups to do things that they would not do on their own (Baumeister et al., 2016). You would never smash a store window and grab a Rolex on your own because looting conflicts with your personal values; but if you're pressed tightly into a big crowd and someone suddenly breaks a window, you may be so busy attending to what others are saying and doing (and stealing!) that you don't even stop to consider what you personally believe.

A second reason for the bad behavior of people in groups is **diffusion of responsibility,** which is the *tendency of individuals to feel diminished responsibility for their actions when they are surrounded by others who are acting the same way.* For example, studies of **bystander intervention**—which is *the act of helping strangers in an emergency situation*—show that people are less likely to help an innocent person in distress when there are many other bystanders present, simply because they assume the other bystanders are collectively more responsible than they are (Darley & Latané, 1968; Fischer et al., 2011). If you saw a fellow student fall off her bicycle in the middle of campus, you'd probably feel more responsible for stopping to help if you were the only person watching than if hundreds of other students were standing nearby because, in the former case, you'd own a greater share of the responsibility (see **FIGURE 12.4**).

So groups make bad decisions and foster bad behavior. Might we be better off without them? Not bloody likely. Groups not only minimize the risks of cooperation (which makes human civilization possible), but they also contribute to our general health, happiness, and well-being (which makes human civilization worthwhile). Being excluded from groups is one of the most painful experiences people can have (Eisenberger et al., 2003; Uskul & Over, 2014; Williams, 2007), so it isn't any wonder that people who are routinely excluded are anxious, lonely, depressed, and at increased risk for illness and premature death (Cacioppo & Patrick, 2008; Cohen, 1988; Leary, 1990). Groups sometimes cause us to misjudge and to misbehave, but they are essential to our cooperativeness, our health, and our happiness. Can't live with 'em, but can't live without 'em. (See Data Visualization: Do Humans Have a "Social Brain"? Go to launchpadworks.com.)

Altruism

Cooperation solves the problem of scarce resources: We can do better by cooperating than we can by competing. But is "doing better" the only reason we cooperate with others? Aren't we ever just . . . well, nice? **Altruism** is *intentional behavior that benefits another*

deindividuation A phenomenon in which immersion in a group causes people to become less concerned with their personal values.

diffusion of responsibility The tendency of individuals to feel diminished responsibility for their actions when surrounded by others who are acting the same way.

bystander intervention The act of helping strangers in an emergency situation.

altruism Intentional behavior that benefits another at a potential cost to oneself.

at a potential cost to oneself, and for centuries, scientists and philosophers have argued about whether people are ever truly altruistic. That may seem like an odd argument for a bunch of smart folks to be having. After all, people give their blood to the injured, their food to the homeless, and their time to the elderly. We volunteer, donate, contribute, and tithe. People do nice things all the time—so why is there any debate about whether people are altruistic?

Because behaviors that appear to be altruistic often have hidden benefits for those who do them. For example, squirrels emit alarm calls when they see a predator, which puts them at increased risk of being eaten but allows their fellow squirrels to escape. This behavior appears to be altruistic, but in fact it is not because the squirrels who give the alarm are genetically related to the individuals they help. When an animal promotes the survival of its relatives, it is actually benefiting itself by promoting the survival of its own genes (Hamilton, 1964). **Kin selection** is *the process by which evolution selects for individuals who cooperate with their relatives,* and although cooperating with relatives looks like altruism, many scientists consider it selfishness in disguise.

Cooperating with unrelated individuals isn't necessarily altruistic either. Male baboons will sometimes risk injury to help an unrelated male baboon win a fight, and monkeys will spend time grooming unrelated monkeys when they could be doing something else. But, as it turns out, in most primate societies, the animal that gives favors today tends to get favors tomorrow. **Reciprocal altruism** is *behavior that benefits another with the expectation that those benefits will be returned in the future,* and despite the second word in the term, many scientists think there is nothing altruistic about it (Trivers, 1972). In many ways, reciprocal altruism is merely cooperation over time.

The behavior of nonhuman animals does not provide clear evidence of genuine altruism (cf. Bartal et al., 2011). So what about us? Are we any different? Yes and no. Like other animals, we tend to help our kin more than strangers (Burnstein et al., 1994; Komter, 2010), and we tend to expect those we help to help us in return (Burger et al., 2009). But unlike other animals, humans clearly do provide benefits to complete strangers who have no chance of repaying them (Batson, 2002; Warneken & Tomasello, 2009). We hold the door for people who share precisely none of our genes and tip waiters in restaurants to which we will never return. We give strangers directions, advice, and sometimes even our parking spots (see A World of Difference: Do Me a Favor?). And we do much more than that. When Wesley Autrey saw a student stumble and fall on the subway tracks just as a train was approaching, he didn't ask whether they shared genes or how he would be repaid in the future. He just jumped onto the tracks and lay on top of the student, holding him down while the train passed over them both—with less than an inch to spare. That's altruism.

Humans do help other humans, sometimes at a staggering cost to themselves, and we even may be more altruistic than we realize (Gerbasi & Prentice, 2013; Miller & Ratner, 1998). Indeed, some scientists believe that our altruistic orientation is the single essential characteristic that gave our species dominion over all others (Hare, 2017).

Wesley Autrey jumped onto the subway tracks to save a stranger's life. "I had a split-second decision to make. . . . I don't feel like I did something spectacular; I just saw someone who needed help. I did what I felt was right" (Buckley, 2007). Said no ground squirrel ever. Robert Kalfus/Splash News/Newscom

kin selection The process by which evolution selects for individuals who cooperate with their relatives.

reciprocal altruism Behavior that benefits another with the expectation that those benefits will be returned in the future.

Build to the Outcomes

1. How does the frustration–aggression hypothesis explain aggressive behaviors?
2. How and why does gender influence aggression?
3. What evidence suggests that culture can influence aggression?
4. What are the potential costs and benefits of cooperation?
5. How do groups lower the risks of cooperation?
6. How and why do individuals behave differently when they are in groups?
7. How can we explain selfish behaviors that appear to be altruistic?

A WORLD OF DIFFERENCE

Do Me a Favor?

One of the many things that distinguish human beings from other animals is that we often do favors for strangers. Often, but not always. Some requests are reasonable, and some are outrageous. So which are which?

The answer, it seems, depends on your cultural background. In one study (Jonas et al., 2009), researchers approached college students in a campus parking lot and asked them for one of two favors. Some students were asked to give up their parking privileges for a week ("Could I borrow your parking card this week so I can participate in a research project in a nearby building?") and others were asked to give up *everyone's* parking privileges for a week ("Would you mind if we closed the entire parking lot this week for a tennis tournament?"). Both of these requests required the students to relinquish their parking spots to a stranger, so both were a bit irritating. But which one was more irritating?

As the figure shows, European American students were more irritated when the researchers asked them—but *only* them—to give up their parking privileges. As members of families that came from individualistic cultures, in which every person is expected to look out for his own interests, these students were especially annoyed when the researcher singled them out and asked them to give up something that

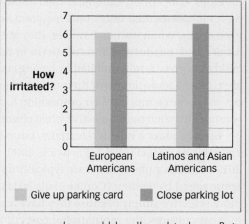

How irritated? (y-axis: 0 to 7)

Groups: European Americans; Latinos and Asian Americans

Legend: Give up parking card; Close parking lot

everyone else would be allowed to keep. But Latino students and Asian American students had precisely the opposite reactions. As members of families that came from collectivist cultures, in which the needs of the many outweigh the needs of the few, these students were especially annoyed when the researcher suggested that many students should give up their parking privileges so that a few students could participate in a tennis tournament. Latino and Asian American students didn't mind suffering as long as everyone didn't have to. Most people will do a reasonable favor for a stranger, but what counts as reasonable may depend on the culture in which one has been marinated.

Social life involves favors—soliciting them, offering them, doing them, and denying them. When is a request too big to grant? It all depends on who you ask. Mint Images/Getty Images

Interpersonal Attraction

Social behavior is useful for survival, but it is essential for reproduction, which generally doesn't happen unless two people get extremely social with each other. The first step on the road to reproduction is finding someone who wants to travel that road with us, and psychologists know a lot about how people do that.

Selectivity

People don't mate randomly, at least not outside of Hollywood. Rather, they carefully select their sexual partners, and, as anyone who has lived on earth for more than a few minutes knows, women tend to be more selective than men (Feingold, 1992a; Fiore et al., 2010). When researchers arranged for a trained actor to approach opposite-sex strangers on a college campus and ask, "Would you go out with me?" they found that roughly half of both the men and the women who were approached agreed to the request. On the other hand, when the actor asked the stranger, "Would you go to bed with me?" precisely

Learning Outcomes

- Explain the biological and cultural factors that influence selectivity in mate choice.

- Describe the situational, physical, and psychological factors that determine feelings of attraction.

- Describe the factors that cause people to get married and divorced.

Among sea horses, it is the male that carries the young, and, not coincidentally, males are more selective than are females. George Grall/ National Geographic Image Collection

none of the women said yes, but *three-quarters* of the men did (Clark & Hatfield, 1989). There are many reasons other than "being selective" that a woman might turn down a sexual offer from a strange man who approaches her in a public place (Conley, 2011), but research suggests that women tend to be choosier than men under most ordinary circumstances as well (Buss & Schmitt, 1993; Schmitt et al., 2012).

But why? One reason is biology. Women produce a small number of eggs in their lifetimes, conception eliminates their ability to conceive for at least 9 months, and pregnancy increases their nutritional requirements and puts them at risk of illness and maybe even death. When women have sex, they are taking a serious long-term risk. Men, on the other hand, produce billions of sperm in their lifetimes, and their ability to conceive a child tomorrow is not inhibited by having conceived one today. When men have sex, they are risking a few minutes of their time and roughly a teaspoon of bodily fluid. Basic biology makes sex a much riskier proposition for women than for men, so it makes sense that women are much more selective when choosing a sexual partner.

Biology plays a role in selectivity, but culture and personal experience play important roles as well (Finkel & Eastwick, 2009; Petersen & Hyde, 2010; Zentner & Mitura, 2012). For example, women are typically approached by men more often than men are approached by women (Conley et al., 2011), which means that women can afford to be more selective simply because they have a larger pool from which to select. In addition, in most cultures, the reputational costs of promiscuity are higher for women than for men (Eagly & Wood, 1999; Kasser & Sharma, 1999). Interestingly, on those occasions when selecting a sexual partner has major consequences for men (e.g., when selecting a wife instead of a date), they suddenly become every bit as choosy as women ordinarily are (Kenrick et al., 1990).

Attraction

Many things go into choosing a date, a lover, or a life partner, but one of the most important is the simple feeling we call attraction (Berscheid & Reis, 1998). Research suggests that this powerfully important feeling is the result of situational, physical, and psychological factors.

How Situational Factors Influence Attraction

One of the most powerful determinants of attraction is proximity, because the closer someone lives to us, the more likely we are to encounter them (Festinger et al., 1950), and research shows that humans and other animals generally prefer familiar to unfamiliar stimuli. For instance, in one experiment, faces were flashed on a computer screen so quickly that participants were unaware of having seen them. Next, participants were shown (at normal speed) some of the faces that had been flashed as well as some new faces. Although participants could not reliably distinguish between faces that had been flashed and faces that hadn't, they liked more the faces that had been flashed previously (Monahan et al., 2000). The **mere exposure effect** is *the tendency for liking of a stimulus to increase with the frequency of exposure to that stimulus* (Bornstein, 1989; Van Dessel et al., 2019; Zajonc, 1968). Familiarity, it seems, does not typically breed contempt. It breeds attraction.

How Physical Factors Influence Attraction

mere exposure effect The tendency for liking of a stimulus to increase with the frequency of exposure to that stimulus.

Once people are in the same place at the same time, they can begin to learn about each other's personal qualities, and the first personal quality they usually learn about is the other person's appearance. The influence of appearance on attraction is remarkably strong.

For instance, one study found that a man's height and a woman's weight are among the best predictors of how many responses a personal ad receives (Lynn & Shurgot, 1984), and another study found that physical attractiveness is the only factor that predicts the online dating choices of both women and men (Green et al., 1984). Physically attractive people have more sex, more friends, and more fun than the rest of us do (Curran & Lippold, 1975). They even earn about 10% more money over the course of their lives (Hamermesh & Biddle, 1994; see **FIGURE 12.5**). Physical appearance is so powerful that it even influences nonromantic relationships: For example, mothers are more affectionate and playful when their children are cute than when they are not (Langlois et al., 1995).

So yes, it pays to be beautiful, but what exactly constitutes beauty? Although different cultures have different standards of beauty, it turns out that those standards have a surprising amount in common (Cunningham et al., 1995).

- *Body shape*. In most cultures, male bodies are considered attractive when they are shaped like a triangle (i.e., broad shoulders with a narrow waist and hips), and female bodies are considered attractive when they are shaped like an hourglass (i.e., broad shoulders and hips with a narrow waist; Deady & Law Smith, 2015; Singh, 1993).

- *Symmetry*. People in all cultures seem to prefer faces and bodies that are bilaterally symmetrical—that is, faces and bodies whose left half is a mirror image of the right half (Perilloux et al., 2010; Perrett et al., 1999).

- *Age*. In every culture, straight women tend to prefer older men, and straight men tend to prefer younger women (Buss, 1989).

Each of these features can be thought of as a signal—either of general health (symmetry), of the ability to bear children (female body shape and youth), or of social dominance and the potential to command resources (male body shape and maturity). The feeling we call attraction may simply be nature's way of telling us that we are in the presence of a fertile person who has healthy genes and the ability to provide for children.

How Psychological Factors Influence Attraction

Physical appearance is assessed easily, early, and from across a crowded room (Lenton & Francesconi, 2010; Rogers & Hammerstein, 1949), and it definitely determines who first draws our attention and quickens our pulse. But once people begin interacting, they move beyond appearances (Cramer et al., 1996; Regan, 1998), which is why physical attractiveness

When actress Tallia Storm looks at herself in the mirror, she probably likes what she sees, as do her many fans. But she and her fans aren't seeing the same thing. Tallia's fans usually see her face on a screen, so they probably prefer the image on the left; but Tallia usually sees her face in a mirror, so she probably prefers the "reversed image" on the right. Research on the mere exposure effect shows that people do indeed prefer mirror-reversed images of themselves, but not of others (Mita et al., 1977). Wenn Rights Ltd/Alamy Stock Photo

Figure 12.5 Yes, Size Matters NFL quarterback Tom Brady is 6′ 4″ tall, and his wife, supermodel Gisele Bundchen, is 5′ 10″ tall. Research shows that tall people earn about $800 more per inch per year. The graph shows the average hourly wage of adult White men in the United States classified by height (Mankiw & Weinzierl, 2010). Kevin Mazur/Getty Images

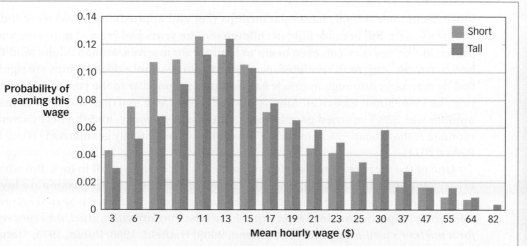

Standards of beauty can vary across cultures. Mauritanian women long to be heavy (left), and Ghanian men are grateful to be short (right). Seyllou/AFP/Getty Images; Michael Dwyer/Alamy

matters less when people have known each other for a long time (Hunt et al., 2015). People's *inner* qualities—their personalities, points of view, attitudes, beliefs, values, ambitions, and abilities—play an important role in determining their sustained interest in each other, and there isn't much mystery about the kinds of inner qualities that most people find attractive. For instance, intelligence, loyalty, trustworthiness, and kindness seem to be high on just about everybody's list (Daniel et al., 1985; Farrelly et al., 2007; Fletcher et al., 1999).

Another quality that is on everybody's list is similarity. (Byrne et al., 1970; Iyengar et al., 2018; Montoya & Horton, 2013). We marry people of a similar age, with similar levels of education, similar religious backgrounds, similar ethnicities, similar socioeconomic statuses, similar personalities, similar political beliefs, and so on (Botwin et al., 1997; Buss, 1985; Caspi & Herbener, 1990).

Why is similarity so attractive? There are at least three reasons. First, it's easy to interact with people who are similar to us because we can easily agree on a wide range of issues, such as what to eat, where to live, how to raise children, and how to spend our money. Second, when someone shares our attitudes and beliefs, we feel validated, and we become more confident that our attitudes and beliefs are right (Byrne & Clore, 1970). Third, because we like people who share our attitudes and beliefs, we expect them to like us for exactly the same reason, and *being liked* is a powerful source of attraction (Aronson & Worchel, 1966; Backman & Secord, 1959; Condon & Crano, 1988).

Relationships

Most nonhuman animals have relationships that end approximately seven seconds after sex is over. But because human children require years and years of nurturing and protection before they can even begin to fend for themselves, human adults tend to have relatively long-term relationships. In most cultures, those relationships are signified by marriage. Although marriage has become less popular in the past few decades (e.g., in 1960, about 22% of all Americans had never been married, but by 2018 that number was 32%), married people are still the large majority, and the best current estimate is that about 75% of today's 20-year-olds will eventually get married (Wang & Parker, 2014).

One of the main reasons people get married is because they fall in love. But what exactly does that mean? Love, it seems, comes in different kinds: **passionate love** is *an experience involving feelings of euphoria, intimacy, and intense sexual attraction,* and **companionate love** is *an experience involving affection, trust, and concern for a partner's well-being* (Acevedo & Aron, 2009; Hatfield, 1988; Rubin, 1973; Sternberg, 1986). The ideal romantic relationship gives rise to both types of love, but the speeds, trajectories, and durations of the two experiences are markedly different (see **FIGURE 12.6**). Passionate love is what brings people together: It has a rapid onset,

passionate love An experience involving feelings of euphoria, intimacy, and intense sexual attraction.

companionate love An experience involving affection, trust, and concern for a partner's well-being.

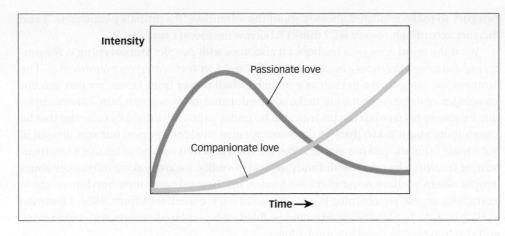

Figure 12.6 Passionate and Companionate Love Passionate and companionate love have different time courses and trajectories. Passionate love begins to cool within just a few months, but companionate love can grow slowly yet steadily over years.

reaches its peak quickly, and begins to diminish within just a few months (Aron et al., 2005). Companionate love is what keeps people together: It takes some time to get started, grows slowly, and need never stop growing (Gonzaga et al., 2001).

Marriage offers benefits (such as love, sex, and financial security), but it also imposes costs (such as additional responsibility, loss of personal freedom, and the potential for interpersonal conflict). More than a third of those Americans who are currently married will eventually decide to terminate that relationship. Why? People tend to remain in relationships only as long as they perceive a favorable ratio of costs to benefits (Homans, 1961; Thibaut & Kelley, 1959). Whether a person considers a particular cost–benefit ratio to be favorable depends on at least two things (Le & Agnew, 2003; Lemay, 2016; Rusbult & Van Lange, 2003). First, it depends on whether the person believes he or she could do better in another relationship. Second, it depends on how much the person has already invested in the relationship. A ratio that seems favorable to people who have been married for many years may seem unfavorable to people who have been married for just a few months, which is one of the reasons new marriages are more likely to end than old ones are (Bramlett & Mosher, 2002; Cherlin, 1992).

Build to the Outcomes

1. Why are women generally more selective in choosing mates than are men?

2. What situational factors play a role in attraction?

3. Why is physical appearance so important?

4. What kind of information does physical appearance convey?

5. Why is similarity such a powerful determinant of attraction?

6. What are the two basic kinds of love?

7. How do people weigh the costs and benefits of their relationships?

Interpersonal Perception

Of the millions of objects you encounter on a daily basis, other human beings are the single most important. **Social cognition** is *the processes by which people come to understand others,* and your brain is doing it all day long. Whether you know it or not, your brain is constantly making inferences about other people's thoughts and feelings, beliefs and desires, abilities and aspirations, intentions, needs, and characters. These inferences are based on two kinds of information: the social categories to which a person belongs and that person's individual behavior.

Stereotyping: Drawing Inferences From Categories

One of the mind's best tricks is that it can put new things into old categories. As soon as you categorize a novel stimulus ("That's a textbook"), you can use your knowledge of the

Learning Outcomes

- Explain how stereotypes cause people to draw inaccurate conclusions about others.

- Explain why stereotypes are so difficult to overcome.

- Define an attribution and describe common attribution errors.

social cognition The processes by which people come to understand others.

category to make educated guesses about the stimulus ("It's probably expensive") and then act accordingly toward it ("I think I'll borrow my friend's copy").

What the mind does with textbooks it also does with people. **Stereotyping** is *the process of drawing inferences about individuals based on their category membership*. The moment we categorize a person as a male baseball player from Japan, we can use our knowledge of those categories to make some educated guesses about him—for example, that he shaves his face but not his legs, that he understands the infield fly rule, and that he knows more about Tokyo than we do. When we give an elderly person our seat instead of our phone number, quiz our server about the fried zucchini instead of Fermat's last theorem, or comfort a lost child with candy instead of vodka, we are making inferences about people whom we have never met based solely on their category membership. As these examples suggest, stereotyping is not just useful—it is essential (Allport, 1954; Liberman et al., 2017). Without it, the world would be filled with perplexed seniors, irritated waiters, and children hoping to get lost more often.

And yet, ever since the journalist Walter Lippmann coined the word *stereotype* in 1936, it has had a distasteful connotation because stereotyping is a helpful process that often produces harmful results. Research suggests that this happens because stereotypes have four properties that make them subject to misuse. Let's examine each of those properties in turn.

1. Stereotypes Can Be Inaccurate

Some of our stereotypes are accurate: Men *are* more likely than women to be sports fanatics (Gough, 2020), and the people who go to Starbucks really *are* younger and hipper than the people who go to Dunks (Moskowitz, 2013). But many of our stereotypes are inaccurate. So where do they come from? Other people! We read tweets, watch TV, listen to song lyrics, overhear our parents talking—and all of these can be sources of inaccurate stereotypes. But inaccurate stereotypes also come from direct observation. For example, participants in one study were shown a long series of positive and negative behaviors and were told that each behavior had been performed by a member of one of two groups: group A or group B (see **FIGURE 12.7**). The behaviors were carefully arranged so that each group behaved negatively exactly one-third of the time. However, there were more positive than negative behaviors, and more members of group A than of group B. Thus, negative behaviors were less common than positive behaviors, and group B members were less common than group A members.

After seeing all the behaviors, participants were given a memory test. They correctly reported that group A had behaved negatively one-third of the time, but they incorrectly reported that group B had behaved negatively more than half the time (Hamilton & Gifford, 1976). Why? Both bad behavior and group B membership were uncommon, and when two uncommon things happen at the same time, people pay special attention ("Look! There's one of those group B'ers doing something terrible"). This is why members of majority groups tend to overestimate the number of violent crimes (which are relatively uncommon events) that are committed by members of minority groups (who are relatively uncommon people). The bottom line is that even when we directly observe people, we can still end up with inaccurate beliefs about the groups to which they belong.

2. Stereotypes Can Be Overused

Because all thumbtacks are pretty much alike, our stereotypes about thumbtacks (small, cheap, and painful when chewed) will rarely be mistaken if we generalize from one thumbtack to another. But human categories are so variable that our stereotypes may offer only the vaguest of clues about the individuals who populate those categories.

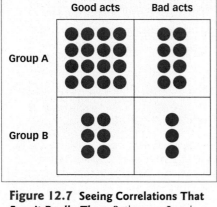

	Good acts	Bad acts
Group A		
Group B		

Figure 12.7 Seeing Correlations That Aren't Really There Both group A and group B engage in bad behavior 1/3 of the time, so there is no difference in the average "badness" of the two groups. However, bad behavior and group B membership are both uncommon, and when two uncommon things happen at the same time, we tend to notice and remember. This tendency can lead us to see a relationship between group membership and bad behavior that isn't really there.

stereotyping The process of drawing inferences about individuals based on their category membership.

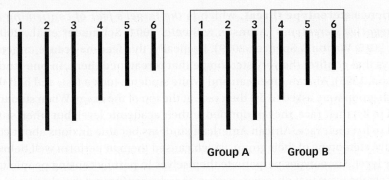

Figure 12.8 Categorization Reduces Perceived Variability People see less variability among lines 1–3 (and also among lines 4–6) if they see them labeled as they are on the right (group A and group B boxes), than if they see them unlabeled (as in the left box).

You probably believe that men have greater upper body strength than women do, and this belief is right—on average. But the upper body strength of the individuals within each of these gender categories is so varied that knowing a person's gender doesn't give you a lot of insight into how much weight that person can lift.

So stereotypes are least useful when variability within groups is high—and in human groups, variability is almost always high. Alas, the mere act of categorizing a stimulus makes people *see* variability as lower than it actually is. Participants in one study were shown a series of lines of different lengths (see **FIGURE 12.8**; McGarty & Turner, 1992; Tajfel & Wilkes, 1963). For some participants, the longest lines were labeled Group A and the shortest lines were labeled Group B, as shown on the right side of Figure 12.8. When participants were later asked to remember the lengths of the lines, participants who had seen the category labels tended to *underestimate* the variability of the lines that shared a label.

What's true of lines is true of people as well. The mere act of categorizing people as Asian or Native American, as Jews or Gentiles, as artists or accountants, can cause us to underestimate the variability within those categories, which leads us to overestimate how useful our stereotypes about those categories will be (Park & Hastie, 1987; Rubin & Badea, 2012).

3. Stereotypes Can Be Self-Perpetuating

When we meet a linebacker who likes ballet more than wrestling, or a Mexican who likes gefilte fish more than tacos, why don't we revise or even abandon our stereotypes of these groups? The answer is that stereotypes tend to be self-perpetuating. Like viruses and parasites, once they take up residence inside us, they resist even our most concerted efforts to eradicate them. This happens for two reasons.

First, **perceptual confirmation** is *the tendency of observers to see what they expect to see*, which can further perpetuate stereotypes. In one study, participants listened to a radio broadcast of a men's college basketball game (Stone, Perry, & Darley, 1997). Some participants were led to believe that a particular player was Black while others were led to believe that he was White. After listening to the game, participants evaluated the player's performance. When participants thought the player was Black, they reported that he had shown more athletic ability and played a better game; when they thought he was White, they reported that he had shown more basketball intelligence and hustle. Keep in mind that the participants who drew these disparate conclusions had all listened to the same game! Stereotypes perpetuate themselves in part by biasing our perception of individuals, leading us to believe that those individuals have confirmed our stereotypes even when they have not (Fiske, 1998).

Second, **behavioral confirmation** (also known as "self-fulfilling prophecy") is *the tendency of targets to behave as observers expect them to behave*. For instance, when people know that observers have a negative stereotype about them, they may

Stereotypes can be inaccurate. Shlomo Koenig does not fit most people's stereotype of a police officer or a rabbi, but he is both.
Gino Domenico/AP Images

perceptual confirmation The tendency of observers to see what they expect to see.

behavioral confirmation The tendency of targets to behave as observers expect them to behave.

The Implicit Association Test measures how easily people can learn to associate two things (Greenwald, McGhee, & Schwartz, 1998). Studies using the test show that 70% of White Americans find it easier to associate White faces with positive concepts, such as "peace," and Black faces with negative concepts, such as "bomb," than the other way around. Surprisingly, 40% of African Americans show this same pattern. You can take the IAT yourself at https://implicit .harvard.edu/implicit/. Colorblind Images/Blend Images/Alamy; Radius Images/Alamy

stereotype threat A target's fear of confirming an observer's negative stereotypes.

Violinist Lorien Benet is auditioning for a job with the Pittsburgh Symphony Orchestra from behind a screen so that the judges will not know her gender (left). Why? Because some data suggest that when judges cannot see the musicians, they may end up hiring more women (Goldin & Rouse, 2000). If that's true, it means that the underrepresentation of women in major symphony orchestras is due at least in part to perceptual confirmation and/ or behavioral confirmation. By the way, Benet (right) got the job, and has been fiddling around with the PSO since 2001. Copyright ©, Pittsburgh Post-Gazette, 2019, All Rights Reserved. Reprinted with permission; Photo by Karissa Shivone, courtesy Lorien Benet Hart

experience **stereotype threat,** which is *the target's fear of confirming the observer's negative stereotypes* (Aronson & Steele, 2004; Schmader et al., 2008; Spencer et al., 2016; Walton & Spencer, 2009). Ironically, this fear may cause targets to behave in ways that confirm the very stereotype that threatened them. In one study (Steele & Aronson, 1995), African American and White students took a test, and half the students in each group were asked to list their race at the top of the exam. When students were not asked to list their race, they performed at their academic level; but when students were asked to list their race, African American students became anxious about confirming a negative stereotype of their group, which caused them to perform well below their academic level. Stereotypes perpetuate themselves in part by causing people to behave in precisely the ways that observers expect, thereby confirming the observers' stereotypes (Klein & Snyder, 2003).

4. Stereotyping Can Be Unconscious and Automatic

Once we recognize that a stereotype is inaccurate and self-perpetuating, why don't we just make a firm resolution to stop using it? Because stereotyping often happens *unconsciously* (which means that we don't always know we are doing it) and *automatically* (which means that we often cannot avoid doing it even when we try) (Banaji & Heiphetz, 2010; Greenwald et al., 1998; Greenwald & Nosek, 2001).

For example, in one study, participants played a video game in which photos of Black or White men holding either guns or cameras were flashed on the screen for less than 1 second each. Participants earned money by shooting men with guns and lost money by shooting men with cameras. The results showed that participants tended to make two kinds of mistakes: They shot Black men holding cameras and didn't shoot White men holding guns (Correll et al., 2002). The photos appeared on the screen so quickly that participants did not have enough time to consciously consider their stereotypes, but that didn't matter because their stereotypes worked unconsciously, causing them to mistake a camera for a gun when it was in the hands of a Black man and to mistake a gun for a camera when it was in the hands of a White man (Correll et al., 2015). Interestingly, Black participants were just as likely to show this pattern as White participants were.

Why? Because stereotypes comprise all the information about human categories that we have encountered and absorbed over the years—information from friends and uncles, books and blogs, jokes and movies and late-night television. When we see Black men holding guns in crime dramas and rap videos, our minds naturally associate these two things, and although we consciously recognize that we are seeing art and not news, our brains make and remember the association anyway because, as you saw in the Memory chapter and the Learning chapter, making associations is one of the things brains do best. Once our brains have made these associations, we can't just decide not to be influenced

by them any more than Pavlov's dogs could decide not to salivate when they heard the tone that they had come to associate with the appearance of food. In fact, some research suggests that consciously trying not to use a stereotype can cause people to use it even more (Macrae et al., 1994).

Are the Undesirable Consequences of Stereotyping Inevitable?

Although stereotyping is unconscious and automatic, that does not mean its undesirable consequences are inevitable (Blair, 2002; Kawakami et al., 2000; Milne & Grafman, 2001; Rudman et al., 2001). For instance, police officers who receive special training before playing the camera-or-gun video game described earlier do not show the same biases that ordinary people do (Correll et al., 2007; Johnson et al., 2018). Like ordinary people, they take a few milliseconds longer to decide not to shoot a Black man than a White man, indicating that their stereotypes are still unconsciously and automatically influencing their perception. But unlike ordinary people, they don't actually shoot Black men more often than White men, indicating that they have learned how to keep those stereotypes from influencing their behavior (Phills et al., 2011; Todd et al., 2011).

So which techniques are most effective? In 2014, a team of psychologists held a contest in which they invited researchers to submit techniques for reducing unconscious stereotyping of Blacks, and then tested each of the techniques against the other. As **FIGURE 12.9** shows, about half the techniques had some effect, and these tended to be techniques that exposed Whites to examples of Blacks who defied their stereotypes. For example, the most effective technique asked participants to imagine in detail that they were being assaulted by a White man and then rescued by a Black man. The least effective techniques were those that simply encouraged people to feel compassion toward or to take the perspective of a Black person (see The Real World: Does Perspective-Taking Work?). And yet, even the best techniques were not very good: They tended to produce small and short-lived changes in unconscious bias, and those changes were not associated with any changes in people's conscious beliefs or actual behavior (Forscher et al., 2019).

These findings are troubling for many reasons, not the least of which is that many of the failed techniques look a lot like the programs that are commonly used in schools, businesses, and other organizations to reduce unconscious stereotyping or "implicit bias." Indeed, a team of psychologists conducted a review of the scientific literature on a host of

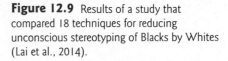

Figure 12.9 Results of a study that compared 18 techniques for reducing unconscious stereotyping of Blacks by Whites (Lai et al., 2014).

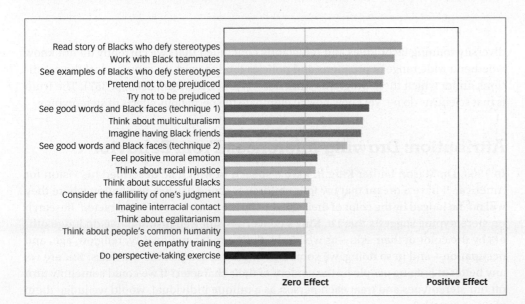

THE REAL WORLD

Does Perspective-Taking Work?

To encourage diversity and inclusion, many organizations ask their members to participate in "perspective-taking exercises" that are meant to help them understand the world from other people's points of view. Maybe it works and maybe it doesn't, but what could be the harm of thinking about what it's like to live inside another person's skin?

To find out, a team of researchers blindfolded participants, then asked them to perform a variety of ordinary tasks, ranging from filling a glass with water to finding the stairwell in a hallway (Silverman et al., 2014). Participants in a control condition merely watched the first group perform these tasks. Later, all participants reported their feelings toward blind people and also estimated how capable blind people are of working and living independently.

Wearing the blindfold did precisely what we might hope it would do: It made participants feel more friendly, open, sympathetic, and warm toward blind people. But compared with observers, participants who wore the blindfold also came to believe that blind people are much less competent and capable—less able to get around a city, to cook, to own their own business, and so on. In other words, taking a blind person's perspective for a few minutes led participants to conclude that blind people were not capable of doing most of the tasks that daily life requires.

And that's not true. Most blind people are perfectly capable of performing ordinary tasks, such as pouring water and finding a stairwell, and perfectly capable of performing jobs from schoolteacher to accountant. Blindness is a disability to which people adapt extraordinarily well over time, and although there are a few things that blind people can't do as well as sighted people can (e.g., driving a car on the street), there are other things they can do even better (e.g., hearing a car on the street). Participants in this study had enough time to experience blindness but not enough time to adapt to it. Being blindfolded for a few minutes made them more compassionate toward blind people, but it also led them to mistakenly believe that they understood what a lifetime of blindness was like. Rather than becoming more accurate about what it is like to be disabled, they became less accurate.

None of us can ever really know what another person's experience of the world is like. Well-meaning exercises that are designed to expand our perspectives can sometimes do the opposite, suggesting that organizations would do well to consult with psychologists before implementing remedies that can make problems worse instead of better.

Paul Scruggs is blind, but that doesn't prevent him from working as a machine operator in a factory that makes military uniforms. You could probably run this machine with your eyes closed—but not in the first hour of trying. Jay Mallin/Bloomberg via Getty Images

diversity training techniques and reluctantly concluded that "we currently do not know whether a wide range of programs and policies tend to work on average, [or] the conditions under which these programs work best" (Paluck & Green, 2009, p. 357). The truth is that scientists do not yet know how to eliminate the pernicious effects of stereotyping.

Attribution: Drawing Inferences From Behavior

In 1963, Dr. Martin Luther King Jr. gave a speech in which he described his vision for America: "I have a dream that my four children will one day live in a nation where they will not be judged by the color of their skin but by the content of their character." Research on stereotyping suggests that Dr. King's concern is still well justified. We do judge others by the color of their skin—as well as by their gender, nationality, religion, age, and occupation—and in so doing, we sometimes make consequential mistakes. But are we any better at judging people by the content of their character? If we could somehow turn off our stereotypes and treat each person as a unique individual, would we judge them more accurately?

Dispositions Versus Situations

Not necessarily. Treating people as individuals means judging them by their own words and deeds. This is more difficult than it sounds because what a person says and does is not always a good indicator of what that person is actually like. Honest people sometimes lie to save a friend from embarrassment, and dishonest people sometimes tell the truth to bolster their credibility. Happy people have weepy moments, polite people can be rude in traffic, and people who despise us can be flattering when they need a favor. In short, people's behavior sometimes tells us about the kinds of people they are, but sometimes it simply tells us about the kinds of situations they happen to be in.

To understand people, we need to know not only *what* they say and do but also *why* they say and do it. Is the politician who gave the pro-life speech really opposed to abortion, or was she just trying to win the conservative vote? Is the batter who hit the home run a talented slugger, or was the wind blowing in just the right direction at just the right time? When we answer questions such as these, we are making **attributions,** which are *inferences about the causes of people's behaviors* (Epley & Waytz, 2010; Gilbert, 1998). We make *situational attributions* when we decide that a person's behavior was caused by some temporary aspect of the situation in which it happened ("He was lucky that the wind carried the ball into the stands"), and we make *dispositional attributions* when we decide that a person's behavior was caused by a relatively enduring tendency (or "disposition") to think, feel, or act in a particular way ("He's got a great eye and a powerful swing").

Attribution Errors

Research suggests that when people try to decide whether to make a dispositional or situational attribution, they often make mistakes. The **correspondence bias** is *the tendency to make a dispositional attribution when we should instead make a situational attribution* (Gilbert & Malone, 1995; Jones & Harris, 1967; Ross, 1977). This bias is so common that it is often called the *fundamental attribution error*.

For example, volunteers in one experiment (Ross et al., 1977) observed a trivia game in which a quizmaster made up a list of unusual questions, while a contestant tried to answer those questions. The quizmasters tended to ask tricky questions based on their own idiosyncratic knowledge ("What store sells the shoes I am wearing?"), and contestants were unable to answer most of them. After the game, the observers were asked to decide how smart the quizmaster and the contestant were. Although the quizmasters had asked good questions and the contestants had given bad answers, it should have been clear to the observers that all this asking and answering was a product of the situation: Quizmasters had been given an easy job and contestants had been given a hard one. If their roles had been reversed, the contestants would have asked equally difficult questions and the quizmasters would have given equally bad answers. Instead, observers attributed the quizmasters' and contestants' performances to their dispositions, concluding that the quizmasters were actually smarter than the contestants. Even when we know that a successful athlete had a home-field advantage or that a successful entrepreneur had family connections, we tend to attribute their success to talent and tenacity.

The correspondence bias is stronger in some cultures than in others (Choi et al., 1999) and among some people than others (D'Agostino et al., 1992; Li et al., 2012). People are also more likely to show this bias when making attributions for other people's behavior than when making attributions for their own. The **actor–observer effect** is *the tendency to make situational attributions for our own behaviors while making dispositional attributions for the identical behavior of others* (Jones & Nisbett, 1972). When college students are asked to explain why they and their friends chose their majors, they tend to make situational attributions for their own choices ("I chose economics because my parents told me I have to support myself as soon as I'm done with college") and dispositional attributions for their friends' choices ("Leah chose economics because she likes money") (Nisbett et al., 1973).

"I think success is all perspiration. You make your own luck," said Robert Herjavec, a successful businessman and a judge on *Shark Tank.* But research on the correspondence bias suggests that it is all too easy to credit success to intelligence and tenacity, and all too easy to blame failure on stupidity and laziness. John Lamparski/WireImage/Getty Images

attribution An inference about the cause of a person's behavior.

correspondence bias The tendency to make a dispositional attribution even when we should instead make a situational attribution.

actor–observer effect The tendency to make situational attributions for our own behaviors while making dispositional attributions for the identical behavior of others.

The actor–observer effect occurs because people typically have more information about the situations that caused their own behavior than about the situations that caused other people's behavior. We remember getting the please-major-in-something-practical lecture from our parents, but we weren't at Leah's house to see her get the same lecture. As observers, our eyes are focused on another person's behavior, but as actors, our eyes are quite literally focused on the situations in which our own behavior occurs. That's why when people see themselves on video (which allows them to see their own behavior as observers see it), they suddenly make dispositional attributions about themselves (Storms, 1973; Taylor & Fiske, 1975).

Build to the Outcomes

1. Where do stereotypes come from? What purpose do they serve?
2. When are stereotypes least likely to be useful?
3. Why do stereotypes sometimes seem more accurate than they really are?
4. Why is it difficult not to use stereotypes?
5. What errors do people make when making attributions?

Learning Outcomes

- Describe the hedonic motive and explain how appeals to it can backfire.
- Describe the approval motive and distinguish normative influence, conformity, and obedience.
- Describe the accuracy motive and distinguish informational influence, persuasion, and consistency.

Interpersonal Influence

If you grew up on X-Men and the Avengers, you've probably thought a bit about which of the standard superpowers you'd most like to have. Super strength and super speed have obvious benefits, invisibility and X-ray vision could be interesting as well as lucrative, and there's a lot to be said for flying. But when it comes down to it, the ability to control other people would probably be the most useful superpower of all. Why get in a death match with an alien overlord or rescue children from a burning building when you can convince someone else to do these dangerous jobs for you? The things we want from life—gourmet food, interesting jobs, big houses, fancy cars—can all be given to us by others, and the things we want most—loving families, loyal friends, admiring children, appreciative employers—cannot be acquired in any other way.

Social influence is *the ability to change or direct another person's behavior* (Cialdini & Goldstein, 2004). People have three basic motivations that underlie almost all attempts at social influence (Bargh et al., 2010; Fiske, 2010). First, people are motivated to experience pleasure and to avoid experiencing pain (the *hedonic motive*). Second, people are motivated to be accepted and to avoid being rejected (the *approval motive*). Third, people

Huda Kattan is a social media influencer with more than 42 million followers on Instagram, which is roughly the population of Spain. Although her posts may change people's choices of skin care products, they probably have less impact on people's choices of careers, political candidates, and investments. Is Huda influential? That depends on whether you think influence should be defined more by its importance or its magnitude.

hudabeauty ✓   Follow   ▼   •••

449 posts   42.8m followers   773 following

HUDA KATTAN
Makeup Artist & Blogger
Turned Business Woman
Love my InstaFam 😊
New SKINCARE @wishfulskin
Personal Page 👉 @huda
hudabeauty.com

social influence The ability to change or direct another person's behavior.

are motivated to believe what is right and to avoid believing what is wrong (the *accuracy motive*). As you are about to see, most attempts at social influence appeal to one or more of these three motives.

The Hedonic Motive

Pleasure seeking is the most basic of all motives, and social influence often involves creating situations in which others can achieve more pleasure by doing what we want them to do than by doing something else. Parents, teachers, governments, and businesses influence our behavior by offering rewards and threatening punishments (see **FIGURE 12.10**). There's nothing mysterious about how these influence attempts work, and they are often quite effective. When the Republic of Singapore warned its citizens that anyone caught chewing gum in public would face a year in prison and a $5,500 fine, most Americans were either outraged or amused; but when the protesting and giggling subsided, it was hard to ignore the fact that gum chewing in Singapore had fallen to an all-time low. A prison term will get your attention every time.

Rewards and punishments can be effective, but they can also backfire. The **overjustification effect** occurs when *a reward decreases a person's intrinsic motivation to perform a behavior* (Deci et al., 1999). For example, children in one study (Lepper et al., 1973) were allowed to play with colored markers, and then some children received a reward. When the children were given markers the next day, those who had received a reward the previous day were least likely to play with the markers. Why? Because children who had received a reward the first day came to think of drawing as something one does to receive rewards, not as something that was intrinsically rewarding—and if no one was going to give them a reward on the second day, then why the heck should they play with the markers?

Rewards and punishments can also backfire simply because people resent being bribed and threatened. **Reactance** is an *unpleasant feeling that arises when people feel they are being coerced,* and when people experience reactance, they often try to alleviate it by doing the very thing they were being coerced not to do. In one study (Pennebaker & Sanders, 1976), researchers placed signs in two restrooms on a college campus. One sign read "Please don't write on these walls" and the other read "Do not write on these walls under any circumstances." Two weeks later, the researchers returned to find that the walls in the second restroom had more graffiti than the walls in the first, presumably because students didn't appreciate the threatening tone of the second sign and wrote on the walls just to show that they could.

overjustification effect An effect that occurs when a reward decreases a person's intrinsic motivation to perform a behavior.

reactance An unpleasant feeling that arises when people feel they are being coerced.

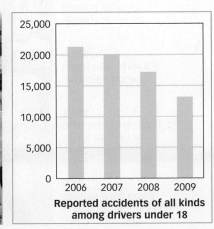

Figure 12.10 The Cost of Speeding
The penalty for speeding in Massachusetts used to be a modest fine. Then the legislature changed the law so that drivers under 18 who are caught speeding lose their licenses for 90 days—and to get them back, they have to pay $500, attend 8 hours of training classes, and retake the state's driving exam. Guess what? Deaths among drivers under 18 fell by 38% in just 3 years. In other words, more than 8,000 young lives were saved by appealing to the hedonic motive. Journal-Courier/Clayton Stalter /The Image Works

The Approval Motive

Other humans are the only thing standing between us and starvation, predation, loneliness, and all the other things that make getting shipwrecked such a bad idea. We depend on others for safety, sustenance, and solidarity, which is why being rejected or excluded by others is one of the most painful of all human experiences (Eisenberger et al., 2003; Uskul & Over, 2014; Williams, 2007). We are powerfully motivated to have others accept us, like us, and approve of us (Baumeister & Leary, 1995; Leary, 2010)—a noble motive to be sure, but one that leaves us vulnerable to several forms of social influence.

Normative Influence: We Do What We Think Is Appropriate

When you get on an elevator you are supposed to face forward and not talk to the person next to you even if you were talking to that person before you got on the elevator—unless you are the only two people on the elevator, in which case it's okay to talk and face sideways but still not backward. Although no one ever taught you this long-winded rule, you probably picked it up somewhere along the way. The unwritten rules that govern social behavior are called **norms,** which are *customary standards for behavior that are widely shared by members of a culture* (Cialdini, 2013; Hawkins et al., 2019; Miller & Prentice, 1996). We learn norms with exceptional ease and obey them with exceptional fidelity because we know that if we don't, others won't approve of us (Centola & Baronchelli, 2015). For example, every human culture has a **norm of reciprocity,** which is *the unwritten rule that people should benefit those who have benefited them* (Gouldner, 1960). When a friend buys you lunch, you return the favor, and if you don't, your friend gets miffed. The norm of reciprocity is so strong that when researchers randomly pulled the names of strangers from a telephone directory and sent them all Christmas cards, they received Christmas cards back from most (Kunz & Woolcott, 1976).

Norms are a powerful weapon in the game of social influence (Miller & Prentice, 2016). **Normative influence** is *a phenomenon in which another person's behavior provides information about what is appropriate* (see **FIGURE 12.11**). For example, restaurant servers often give customers a piece of candy along with the bill because they know about the norm of reciprocity. Studies show that customers who receive a candy feel obligated to do "a little extra" for the server who did "a little extra" for them (Strohmetz et al., 2002).

Have you ever wondered who put the $20 bill in the guitar case? Probably the person who owns it because they know that the presence of a large bill will suggest to you that others are leaving big tips and that it would be socially appropriate for you to do the same. Don Paulson Photography/Purestock/Superstock

Figure 12.11 The Perils of Connection Other people's behavior defines what is normal, so we tend to do the things we see others doing. Overeating is one of those things. Research shows that if someone you know becomes obese, your chances of becoming obese can increase dramatically (Christakis & Fowler, 2007). Francis Dean/Dean Pictures/The Image Works

norms Customary standards for behavior that are widely shared by members of a culture.

norm of reciprocity The unwritten rule that people should benefit those who have benefited them.

normative influence A phenomenon in which another person's behavior provides information about what is appropriate.

On average, your risk of becoming obese increases by . . .

. . . **57%** if someone you consider a friend becomes obese.

. . . **171%** if a very close friend becomes obese.

. . . **100%** if you are a man and your male friend becomes obese.

. . . **38%** if you are a woman and your female friend becomes obese.

. . . **37%** if your spouse becomes obese.

. . . **40%** if one of your siblings becomes obese.

. . . **67%** if you are a woman and your sister becomes obese.

. . . **44%** if you are a man and your brother becomes obese.

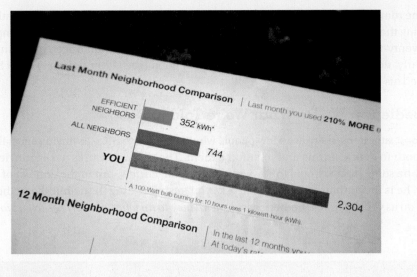

Conformity: We Do What We See Others Do

People can influence us by invoking familiar norms, such as the norm of reciprocity. But if you've ever found yourself at a fancy dinner, sneaking a peek at the person next to you in the hopes of discovering whether the little fork is supposed to be used for the shrimp or the salad, then you know that other people can also influence us by defining new norms in ambiguous, confusing, or novel situations. **Conformity** is *the tendency to do what others do,* and it results in part from normative influence.

In a classic study, the psychologist Solomon Asch (1951, 1956) had participants sit in a room with seven other people who appeared to be ordinary participants but who were actually trained actors. An experimenter explained that the participants would be shown cards with three printed lines, and their job was simply to say which of the three lines matched a "standard line" that was printed on another card (see **FIGURE 12.12**). The experimenter held up a card and then asked each person to answer in turn. The real participant was among the last to be called on. Everything went well on the first two trials, but then on the third trial, something weird happened: The actors all began giving the same wrong answer! What did the real participants do? Although most participants continued to give the right answer on most trials, 75% of them conformed and gave the wrong answer on at least one trial. Subsequent research has shown that these participants didn't actually misperceive the length of the lines but were instead succumbing to normative influence (Asch, 1955; Nemeth & Chiles, 1988). Giving the wrong answer was apparently the "right thing to do" in this confusing, novel, and ambiguous situation, so participants did it.

The behavior of others can tell us what is proper, appropriate, expected, and accepted—in other words, it can define a norm—and once a norm is defined, we feel obliged to honor it. For instance, researchers left a variety of different "message cards"

conformity The tendency to do what others do.

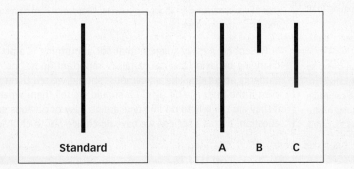

Standard   **A   B   C**

Figure 12.12 Asch's Conformity Study If you were asked which of the lines on the right (A, B, or C) matches the standard line on the left, what would you say? Research on conformity suggests that your answer would depend, in part, on how other people in the room answered the same question.

in the rooms of a hotel in the hopes of convincing guests to reuse their towels rather than having them laundered every day. The most effective message? The one that simply read: "Seventy-five percent of our guests use their towels more than once" (Cialdini, 2005). Clearly, normative influence can be a force for good (see Other Voices: 91% of Students Love This Box).

Obedience: We Do What We're Told to Do

obedience The tendency to do what authorities tell us to do.

In most situations, there are a few people whom we all recognize as having special authority both to define norms and to enforce them. The guy who works at the movie theater may be some high-school fanboy with a 10:00 p.m. curfew, but in the context of the theater, he is the authority. So when he asks you to stop texting in the middle of the movie, you do as you are told. **Obedience** is *the tendency to do what authorities tell us to do.*

OTHER VOICES

91% of Students Love This Box

Binge drinking is a problem on college campuses across America (Wechsler & Nelson, 2001). About half of all students report doing it, and those who do are much more likely to miss classes, fall behind in their school work, drive drunk, and have unprotected sex. So what to do? Writer Tina Rosenberg has a suggestion.

Like most universities, Northern Illinois University in DeKalb has a problem with heavy drinking. In the 1980s, the school was trying to cut down on student use of alcohol with the usual strategies. One campaign warned teenagers of the consequences of heavy drinking. "It was the 'don't run with a sharp stick you'll poke your eye out' theory of behavior change," said Michael Haines, who was the coordinator of the school's Health Enhancement Services. When that didn't work, Haines tried combining the scare approach with information on how to be well: "It's O.K. to drink if you don't drink too much—but if you do, bad things will happen to you."

That one failed, too. In 1989, 45 percent of students surveyed said they drank more than five drinks at parties. This percentage was slightly higher than when the campaigns began. And students thought heavy drinking was even more common; they believed that 69 percent of their peers drank that much at parties.

But by then Haines had something new to try. In 1987 he had attended a conference on alcohol in higher education sponsored by the United States Department of Education. There Wes Perkins, a professor of sociology at Hobart and William Smith Colleges, and Alan Berkowitz, a psychologist in the school's counseling center, presented a paper that they had just published on how student drinking is affected by peers. "There are decades of research on peer influence—that's nothing new," Perkins said at the meeting. What was new was their survey showing that when students were asked how much their peers drank, they grossly overestimated the amount. If the students were responding to peer pressure, the researchers said, it was coming from imaginary peers.

The "aha!" conclusion Perkins and Berkowitz drew was this: maybe students' drinking behavior could be changed by just telling them the truth.

Haines surveyed students at Northern Illinois University and found that they also had a distorted view of how much their peers drink. He decided to try a new campaign, with the theme "most students drink moderately." The centerpiece of the campaign was a series of ads in the Northern Star, the campus newspaper, with pictures of students and the caption "two thirds of Northern Illinois University students (72%) drink 5 or fewer drinks when they 'party.' " . . .

Haines's staff also made posters with campus drinking facts and told students that if they had those posters on the wall when an inspector came around, they would earn $5. (35 percent of the students did have them posted when inspected.) Later they made buttons for students in the fraternity and sorority system—these students drank more heavily—that said "Most of Us," and offered another $5 for being caught wearing one. The buttons were deliberately cryptic, to start a conversation.

After the first year of the social norming campaign, the perception of heavy drinking had fallen from 69 to 61 percent. Actual heavy drinking fell from 45 to 38 percent. The campaign went on for a decade, and at the end of it NIU students believed that 33 percent of their fellow students were episodic heavy drinkers, and only 25 percent really were—a decline in heavy drinking of 44 percent. . . .

Why isn't this idea more widely used? One reason is that it can be controversial. Telling college students "most of you drink moderately" is very different than saying "don't drink." (It's so different, in fact, that the National Social Norms Institute, with headquarters at the University of Virginia, gets its money from Anheuser Busch—a decision that has undercut support for the idea of social norming.) The approach angers people who lobby for a strong, unmuddied message of disapproval—even though, of course, disapproval doesn't reduce bad behavior, and social norming does.

Tina Rosenberg is a writer and winner of the Pulitzer Prize, the National Book Award, and the McArthur "Genius" Award. Her latest book is *Join the Club: How Peer Pressure Can Transform the World.* Noah Greenberg Photography

Rosenberg's essay suggests that social norming is a powerful tool for changing behavior, but its use raises important questions. When we tell students about drinking on campus, should we tell them what's true—even if the truth is a bit ugly? Or should we tell them what's best—even if they are unlikely to do it? There are no easy or obvious answers to this question, but as a society, we have no choice but to choose one.

Why do we obey authorities? Well, okay, yes, sometimes they have guns. But while authorities are often capable of rewarding and punishing us, research shows that much of their influence is *normative* (Tyler, 1990). The psychologist Stanley Milgram (1963) demonstrated this in one of psychology's most infamous experiments. The participants in this experiment reported to a laboratory at Yale University where they met a man who was introduced as another participant but who was actually a trained actor. An experimenter in a lab coat (the authority) explained that the participant would play the role of teacher and the actor would play the role of learner. The teacher and the learner would sit in different rooms, the teacher would read words to the learner over an intercom, and the learner would then repeat the words back to the teacher. If the learner made a mistake, the teacher would press a button on a machine that would deliver increasing amounts of electric shock to the learner (see **FIGURE 12.13**). The shock machine was fake, but its switches appeared to allow teachers to deliver 30 different levels of shock, ranging from 15 volts (labeled *slight shock*) to 450 volts (labeled *Danger: severe shock*).

After the learner was strapped into his chair, the experiment began. When the learner made his first mistake, the participant dutifully delivered a 15-volt shock. As the learner made more mistakes, he received more shocks, each stronger than the one before it. When the teacher delivered the 75-volt shock, the learner cried out in pain. At 150 volts, the learner screamed, "I refuse to go on. Let me out!" With every shock, the learner's screams became more agonized. Then, after receiving the 330-volt shock, the learner stopped responding altogether. Participants were naturally upset by all this and typically asked the experimenter to stop, but the experimenter simply replied, "You have no choice. You must go on." The experimenter never threatened the participant with punishment of any kind. Rather, he just stood there with his clipboard in hand, looking very authoritative, and calmly instructed the participant to continue.

So what did the participants do? Eighty percent of the participants continued to shock the learner even after he screamed, complained, pleaded, and then fell silent. And 62% of them delivered the highest possible voltage. Although Milgram's study was conducted nearly half a century ago, more recent replications reveal about the same rate of obedience (Burger, 2009; Grzyb et al., 2017).

Would normal people electrocute a stranger just because some guy in a lab coat told them to? The answer, it seems, is yes—as long as *normal* means being sensitive to social norms (Zimbardo, 2007). The participants in this experiment knew that hurting others is *often* wrong but not *always* wrong: Doctors give painful injections and teachers give painful exams. In these and many other situations, it is permissible for authorities to cause someone to suffer in the service of a higher goal. In Milgram's experiments, the experimenter's calm demeanor and persistent instruction suggested that he, and not the participants, knew what was appropriate in this particular situation, so the participants typically did as ordered. Obedience, it seems, is not just for soldiers and dogs.

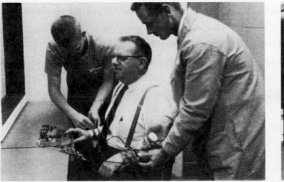

Figure 12.13 Milgram's Obedience Studies In these historic photos from Stanley Milgram's obedience studies, an actor who is playing the role of "the learner" (left) is being hooked up to the fake shock generator (right) From the Film Obedience © 1968 by Stanley Milgram, © Renewed 1993 by Alexandra Milgram; and Distributed by Alexander Street Press; Stanley Milgram, from the Film "Obedience." Rights held by Alexandra Milgram

Why do publishers and booksellers go out of their way to remind people that a book is a "best seller"? Because they know that people are more inclined to buy books when they think that others are buying them, too.
Joey Kotfica/Getty Images

attitude An enduring positive or negative evaluation of a stimulus.

belief An enduring piece of knowledge about a stimulus.

informational influence A phenomenon that occurs when another person's behavior provides information about what is good or true.

persuasion A phenomenon that occurs when a person's attitudes or beliefs are influenced by a communication from another person.

systematic persuasion The process by which attitudes or beliefs are changed by appeals to reason.

heuristic persuasion The process by which attitudes or beliefs are changed by appeals to habit or emotion.

The Accuracy Motive

When you are hungry, you open the refrigerator and grab an apple because you know that apples (a) taste good and (b) are in the refrigerator. This action, like most actions, relies on both an **attitude,** which is *an enduring positive or negative evaluation of a stimulus* ("Apples taste good") and a **belief,** which is *an enduring piece of knowledge about a stimulus* ("Apples are in the fridge"). If our attitudes or beliefs are inaccurate—that is, if we can't tell good from bad or true from false—then our actions are likely to be fruitless. Because we rely so much on our attitudes and beliefs, it isn't surprising that we are motivated to have the right ones, and that motivation leaves us vulnerable to many kinds of social influence.

Informational Influence: We Do What We Think Is Correct

If everyone in the mall suddenly ran screaming for the exit, you'd probably join them—not because you were afraid that they would disapprove of you if you didn't, but because their behavior would suggest to you that there was something worth running from. **Informational influence** occurs *when another person's behavior provides information about what is good or true.* You can observe the power of informational influence yourself just by standing in the middle of the sidewalk, tilting back your head, and staring at the top of a tall building. Research shows that within just a few minutes, other people will stop and stare too (Milgram et al., 1969). Why? Because they will assume that if you are looking up, then there must be something worth looking at.

You are the constant target of informational influence. Advertisements that refer to soft drinks as "popular" or books as "best sellers" remind you that other people are buying them, which suggests that they know something you don't and that you'd be wise to follow their example. Situation comedies use laugh tracks because the producers know that when you hear other people laughing, you will mindlessly assume that something must be funny (Fein et al., 2007; Nosanchuk & Lightstone, 1974). Restaurants and clubs sometimes force people to stand in line outside even when there is room to stand inside, because they know that people walking by will see the line and assume there is something worth waiting for. In short, the world is full of stimuli about which we know little, and we often cure our ignorance by paying attention to other people's behavior. This tendency is useful, but it also leaves us susceptible to social influence.

Persuasion: We Do What We Believe In

People can influence us with their actions, but they can also influence us with their words. **Persuasion** occurs when *a person's attitudes or beliefs are influenced by a communication from another person* (Albarracín & Shavitt, 2018; Berger, 2014; Petty & Wegener, 1998). How does it work? Candidates for political office often try to win votes by making thoughtful arguments about important issues, but they also try to win votes by standing next to popular celebrities and American flags. The first of these is called **systematic persuasion,** which is *the process by which attitudes or beliefs are changed by appeals to reason*, and the second is called **heuristic persuasion,** which is *the process by which attitudes or beliefs are changed by appeals to habit or emotion* (Chaiken, 1980; Petty & Cacioppo, 1986). Sometimes people think carefully about a communication, weighing the evidence and analyzing the arguments. Other times they don't think deeply and just use simple heuristics or "rules of thumb" to help them decide what to believe. Which form of persuasion is more effective? It depends on whether the person is motivated to weigh evidence and analyze arguments.

High-Status Primate   High-Status Primate   Low-Status Primate

Heuristic persuasion can be powerful. Samsung hopes that pairing soccer star David Beckham with their newest phone (left) will cause you to prefer it—and it probably does. In fact, this effect is so basic that it even occurs in other species. When rhesus monkeys were shown various corporate logos paired with pictures of high-status monkeys (middle) and low-status monkeys (right), they came to prefer the former logos to the latter (Acikalin et al., 2018).

For example, in one study, students heard a speech that contained either strong or weak arguments in favor of instituting comprehensive exams at their school (Petty et al., 1981). Some students were told that the speaker was a high-status university professor, and others were told that the speaker was a low-status high school student—a bit of information that the students could use as a heuristic to decide whether to believe the speech (Hanel et al., 2018). In addition, some students were told that their university was considering implementing these exams right away, which made them motivated to analyze the evidence carefully (because the outcome would affect them directly) Others were told that their university was considering implementing these exams 10 years later, which made them unmotivated to analyze the evidence (because they themselves would have graduated by the time the exams were given). As **FIGURE 12.14** shows, when students were motivated to analyze the evidence, they were systematically persuaded—that is, their attitudes and beliefs were influenced by the strength of the arguments but not by the status of the speaker. But when students were not motivated to analyze the evidence, they were heuristically persuaded—that is, their attitudes and beliefs were influenced by the status of the speaker but not by the strength of the arguments.

Consistency: We Believe in What We Do

If a friend told you that rabbits had just staged a coup in Antarctica and were halting all carrot exports, you probably wouldn't bother to check CNN. You'd know right away that your friend was joking, stoned, or extremely gullible, because the statement is logically inconsistent with other things that you know are true—for example, that rabbits do not

Figure 12.14 Two Types of Persuasion When participants were motivated, they were systematically persuaded, agreeing with strong arguments and disagreeing with weak ones, regardless of the speaker's status. But when participants were unmotivated, they were heuristically persuaded, agreeing with high-status speakers and disagreeing with low-status speakers, regardless of the strength of the arguments (Petty et al., 1981).

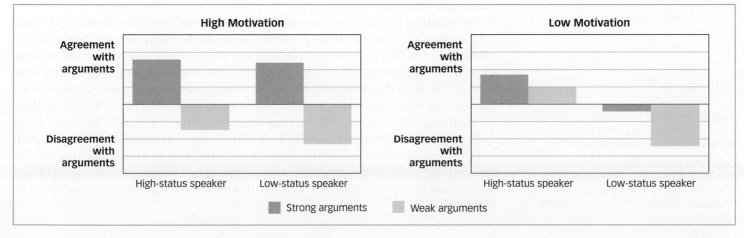

foment revolution and that Antarctica does not export carrots. People evaluate the accuracy of new beliefs by assessing their consistency with old beliefs. Although this is not a foolproof method for determining whether something is true, it provides a pretty good approximation (Kruglanski et al., 2018). Because we are motivated to be accurate, and, because consistency is a rough indicator of accuracy, we are motivated to be consistent as well (Cialdini et al., 1995).

Like other motivations, this one leaves us vulnerable to social influence. For example, the **foot-in-the-door technique** involves *making a small request and then following it with a larger request* (Burger, 1999). In one study (Freedman & Fraser, 1966), experimenters went to a neighborhood and knocked on doors to see if they could convince homeowners to install a big ugly "Drive Carefully" sign in their front yards. One group of homeowners was simply asked to install the sign, and only 17% said yes. A second group of homeowners was first asked to sign a petition urging the state legislature to promote safe driving (which almost all agreed to do) and was *then* asked to install the ugly sign. A full 55% said yes to both requests! Why would homeowners—or anyone else, for that matter—be more likely to grant two requests than one?

Well, just imagine how the homeowners in the second group felt. They had just signed a petition saying that they cared a lot about safe driving, and yet they didn't really want to say yes to installing an ugly sign. As they wrestled with the inconsistency between their actions ("I signed a petition") and their attitudes ("I hate that ugly sign"), they began to experience **cognitive dissonance,** which is *an unpleasant state that arises when a person recognizes the inconsistency of their actions, attitudes, or beliefs* (Festinger, 1957). To eliminate that feeling they had to eliminate the inconsistency that caused it—and so they changed their attitudes and agreed to install the ugly sign (Aronson, 1969; Cooper & Fazio, 1984; Harmon-Jones et al., 2015). The lesson for any would-be social influencer is clear: You can get people to do something by first getting them to express an attitude with which that action is consistent. For instance, hotel guests who were subtly induced at check-in to say they were "Friends of the Earth" were 25% more likely to reuse their towels during their stay (Baca-Motes et al., 2013).

But not all inconsistencies cause cognitive dissonance. For example, participants in one study (Festinger & Carlsmith, 1959) were asked to perform a dull task. After the participants were sufficiently bored, the experimenter explained that he desperately needed a few more people to volunteer for the study, and he asked the participants to go into the hallway, find another person, and untruthfully tell them that the task was fun and they should participate. The experimenter offered some participants $1 to tell this lie, and he offered other participants $20. All participants succumbed to the social pressure to help the experimenter by telling a lie, and after they did so, they were asked to report their true enjoyment of the task.

Think about the situation these participants were in: They did something (i.e., they told a fellow student that the task was fun) that was inconsistent with their true attitudes (i.e., they thought the task was boring). Did this inconsistency cause them to experience cognitive dissonance and therefore change their attitudes? Yes if they were paid $1, but no if they were paid $20. Why? Because earning a measly dollar does not justify lying to a fellow student, and so those participants had to justify their actions by changing their attitudes ("It was okay to tell them the task was fun because I really believe it!"). But earning $20 in 1959 is equal to earning $175 today, so those participants did not need to change their attitudes to justify telling a harmless little lie. The money was justification enough! The bottom line is that people just hate being inconsistent, and under the right circumstances, this fact can be a powerful weapon of social influence.

foot-in-the-door technique A technique that involves making a small request and following it with a larger request.

cognitive dissonance An unpleasant state that arises when a person recognizes the inconsistency of their actions, attitudes, or beliefs.

Build to the Outcomes

1. What are the three basic motives that social influence involves?

2. Why do attempts to influence others with rewards and punishments sometimes backfire?

3. How can the norm of reciprocity be used to influence people?

4. Why do people sometimes do what they see others doing?

5. When and why do people obey authority?

6. What is the difference between normative and informational influence?

7. When is it more effective to engage in systematic persuasion rather than in heuristic persuasion?

8. Why does the accuracy motive lead to a desire for consistency?

9. What is cognitive dissonance? How do people alleviate it?

CHAPTER REVIEW

Interpersonal Behavior

- Survival and reproduction require scarce resources, and aggression and cooperation are two ways to get them.

- Aggressions can be proactive or reactive. Proactive aggression is planned and purposeful. Reactive aggression typically results from negative affect, and the likelihood that people will engage in it is influenced both by biological and cultural factors.

- Cooperation is an excellent strategy for attaining resources, but it entails the risk that others will take advantage of us. One way to reduce that risk is to cooperate with members of one's own groups, who are likely to show ingroup favoritism.

- Groups also have costs. They can promote unethical behavior by causing people to lose sight of their personal values, and they often make decisions that are worse than the decisions their best members would have made on their own.

- Many behaviors that appear to be altruistic have hidden benefits for the person who performs them. But unlike other animals, human beings do appear to exhibit genuine altruism.

Interpersonal Attraction

- Both biology and culture make the costs of sex and reproduction higher for women than for men, which is one reason women tend to be choosier when selecting mates.

- Attraction is determined by situational, physical, and psychological factors.

- Most people have long-term romantic relationships, which are often signified by marriage. People usually remain in these relationships as long as they believe the benefits outweigh the costs.

Interpersonal Perception

- We make inferences about people on the basis of the social categories to which they belong, as well as on the basis of their individual behaviors.

- Inferences based on the category to which others belong can be mistaken, because our stereotypes about categories are often inaccurate, overused, self-perpetuating, and unconscious and automatic.

- Inferences can also be mistaken when people attribute behavior to the actor's dispositions rather than to the situation in which the behavior was performed.

Interpersonal Influence

- People are motivated to experience pleasure and avoid pain (the hedonic motive), and thus can be influenced by rewards and punishments. These influence attempts can sometimes backfire by changing how people think about their own behavior or by making them feel as though they are being manipulated.

- People are motivated to attain the approval of others (the approval motive), and thus can be influenced by social norms, such as the norm of reciprocity. People often look to the behavior of others to determine what kinds of behavior are normative. People tend to obey authorities even when they should not.

- People are motivated to know what is true (the accuracy motive). People often look to the behavior of others to determine what is true.

- People can be persuaded by appeals to reason or emotion. Each is effective under different circumstances.

- People feel bad when they notice inconsistency between their attitudes and actions, and they will sometimes change their attitudes to alleviate this feeling of "cognitive dissonance" and achieve consistency.

Key Concept Quiz

1. What best predicts whether a person will engage in reactive aggression?
   a. the outdoor temperature
   b. the person's gender
   c. the person's culture
   d. the availability of violent video games

2. When women aggress, they usually
   a. engage in reactive rather than proactive aggression.
   b. have high testosterone.
   c. cause social harm rather than physical harm.
   d. experience frustration.

3. The prisoner's dilemma game illustrates
   a. ingroup favoritism.
   b. the diffusion of responsibility.
   c. group polarization.
   d. the benefits and costs of cooperation.

4. Which of the following is NOT a downside of being in a group?
   a. People in groups tend to treat members well.
   b. People in groups tend to treat non-members badly.
   c. Groups sometimes make poor decisions.
   d. Groups may take extreme actions that an individual member would not take alone.

5. The apparently altruistic behavior of nonhuman animals can often be explained by
   a. kin selection.
   b. obedience.
   c. informational influence.
   d. cognitive dissonance.

6. Which of the following best describes reciprocal altruism?
   a. cognitive dissonance
   b. diminished responsibility in groups
   c. cooperation over time
   d. cooperation with relatives

7. Which of the following is an explanation for increased selectivity by women in choosing a mate?
   a. Sex is potentially more costly for women than for men.
   b. The reputational costs of promiscuity are often higher for women than for men.
   c. Pregnancy increases a woman's nutritional requirements and carries risk of illness and death.
   d. all of the above

8. Which of the following is a situational factor that influences attraction?
   a. proximity
   b. similarity
   c. bilateral symmetry
   d. personality

9. People tend to stay in relationships as long as there is
   a. passionate love.
   b. bilateral symmetry.
   c. a favorable cost-benefit ratio.
   d. normative influence.

10. The fact that people prefer to experience pleasure rather than pain is known as
    a. group polarization.
    b. heuristic persuasion.
    c. cognitive dissonance.
    d. the hedonic motive.

11. The tendency to do what authorities tell us to do is known as
    a. persuasion.
    b. obedience.
    c. conformity.
    d. behavioral confirmation.

12. What is the process by which people come to understand others?
    a. social influence
    b. reciprocal altruism
    c. social cognition
    d. cognitive dissonance

13. Which of the following is NOT a problem with stereotypes?
    a. they are often inaccurate.
    b. they are over-used.
    c. they are used automatically and unconsciously.
    d. they are based on the false assumption that social categories can sometimes provide useful information about individuals.

14. The tendency to make a dispositional attribution even when a person's behavior was caused by the situation is referred to as
    a. groupthink.
    b. the mere exposure effect.
    c. normative influence.
    d. correspondence bias.

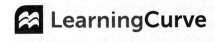 **LearningCurve**   **Don't stop now! Quizzing yourself is a powerful study tool.**
Go to LaunchPad to access the LearningCurve adaptive quizzing system and your own personalized learning plan. Visit launchpadworks.com.

Key Terms

social psychology (p. 353)	groupthink (p. 358)	stereotyping (p. 366)	normative influence (p. 374)
aggression (p. 354)	deindividuation (p. 359)	perceptual confirmation (p. 367)	conformity (p. 375)
frustration–aggression hypothesis (p. 354)	diffusion of responsibility (p. 359)	behavioral confirmation (p. 367)	obedience (p. 376)
proactive aggression (p. 354)	bystander intervention (p. 359)	stereotype threat (p. 368)	attitude (p. 378)
reactive aggression (p. 354)	altruism (p. 359)	attribution (p. 371)	belief (p. 378)
cooperation (p. 357)	kin selection (p. 360)	correspondence bias (p. 371)	informational influence (p. 378)
group (p. 358)	reciprocal altruism (p. 360)	actor–observer effect (p. 371)	persuasion (p. 378)
prejudice (p. 358)	mere exposure effect (p. 362)	social influence (p. 372)	systematic persuasion (p. 378)
common knowledge effect (p. 358)	passionate love (p. 364)	overjustification effect (p. 373)	heuristic persuasion (p. 378)
group polarization (p. 358)	companionate love (p. 364)	reactance (p. 373)	foot-in-the-door technique (p. 380)
	social cognition (p. 365)	norms (p. 374)	cognitive dissonance (p. 380)
		norm of reciprocity (p. 374)	

Changing Minds

1. One of the senators from your state supports a bill that would impose heavy fines on aggressive drivers who run red lights. One of your classmates thinks this is a good idea. "The textbook taught us a lot about punishment and reward. It's simple. If we punish aggressive driving, its frequency will decline." Is your classmate right? Might the new law backfire? Might another policy be more effective in promoting safe driving?

2. One of your friends is outgoing, funny, and a star athlete on the men's basketball team. He has started to date someone who is introverted and prefers playing computer games to attending parties. You tease him about the contrast in their personalities, and he replies, "Well, opposites attract." Is he right?

3. A large law firm is found guilty of discriminatory hiring practices. Your friend reads about the case and scoffs, "People are always so quick to claim racism. Sure, there are still a few racists out there, but surveys that ask Americans what they think about people of other races show that they feel just fine about them." What would you tell your friend?

4. One of your friends wears a neon orange track suit and a battered fedora. Every. Single. Day. "Most people follow the crowd," your friend says. "But not me. I'm an individual, and I'm just not influenced by other people." Could your friend be right? What examples might you provide for or against your friend's claim?

5. A classmate learns about Stanley Milgram's 1963 study in which participants were willing to obey orders to administer painful electric shocks to a learner who begged them to stop. "Some people are such sheep!" she says. "I would never have done that." Is she right? What evidence would you give her to support or oppose her claim?

6. Your family gathers for a holiday dinner, and your cousin Wendy brings her fiancée, Amanda. It's the first time Amanda has met the whole family, and she seems nervous. She talks too much, laughs too loudly, and rubs everyone the wrong way. Later, one of your uncles says to you, "It's hard to imagine Wendy wanting to spend the rest of her life married to someone so annoying." Has your uncle fallen prey to the correspondence bias? How could you know?

Answers to Key Concept Quiz

1. b; 2. c; 3. d; 4. a; 5. a; 6. c; 7. d; 8. a; 9. c; 10. d; 11. b; 12. c; 13. d; 14. d

Fotosearch/Age Fotostock

Stress and Health

13

"I have a knife to your neck. Don't make a sound. Get out of bed and come with me or I will kill you and your family." These are the words that awoke 14-year-old Elizabeth Smart in the middle of the night on June 5, 2002. Fearing for her life, and the lives of her family, she kept quiet and left with her abductor, Brian David Mitchell, a man Elizabeth's parents had hired previously to do some roof work on their home. Mitchell and his wife held Elizabeth in captivity for 9 months, during which time Mitchell repeatedly raped her and threatened to kill her and her entire family. Mitchell, his wife, and Smart were spotted walking down the street by a couple who recognized them from a recent episode of the television show *America's Most Wanted* and called the police. Mitchell and his wife were apprehended and Elizabeth was returned to her family.

Elizabeth suffered under unimaginable circumstances for a prolonged period of time in what can be thought of as one of the most stressful situations possible. Fortunately, she is now safe and sound, happily married, and working as an activist. She endured life-threatening stressors for months, and those experiences undoubtedly affected her in ways that will last her entire lifetime. Yet, despite the very difficult hand she was dealt, she appears to have bounced back and to be leading a happy, productive, and rewarding life. Hers is a story of both stress and health.

Fortunately, few of us will ever have to endure the type of stress that Elizabeth Smart lived through. But life has its **stressors**, *specific events or chronic pressures that place demands on a person or threaten the person's well-being.* Although such stressors rarely involve threats of death, they do have both immediate and cumulative effects that can influence health.

In this chapter, we'll look at what psychologists have learned about the kinds of life events that produce **stress**, *the physical and psychological response to internal or external stressors*; typical responses to such stressors; and ways to manage stress. Stress has such a profound influence on health that we consider stress and health together in this chapter. And because sickness and health are not merely features of the physical body, we then consider the more general topic of **health psychology**, *the subfield of psychology concerned with how psychological factors influence the causes and treatment of physical illness and the maintenance of health.* You will see how perceptions of illness can affect its course and how health-promoting behaviors can improve the quality of people's lives.

Sources of Stress: What Gets to You

Stress Reactions: All Shook Up

Stress Management: Dealing With It

The Psychology of Illness: Mind Over Matter

The Psychology of Health: Feeling Good

stressors Specific events or chronic pressures that place demands on a person or threaten the person's well-being.

stress The physical and psychological response to internal or external stressors.

health psychology The subfield of psychology concerned with how psychological factors influence the causes and treatment of physical illness and the maintenance of health.

This smiling young face is that of Elizabeth Smart, who, between the times of these two photographs, was kidnapped, raped, and tortured for nearly a year. Stressful life events often affect us in ways that cannot be seen from the outside. Fortunately, there are things that we can do in response to even the most stressful of life events that can get us smiling again. SLCPD UPI Photo Service/Newscom; Michael Loccisano/Getty Images

Sources of Stress: What Gets to You

A natural catastrophe, such as a hurricane, earthquake, or volcanic eruption, is an obvious source of stress. But for most of us, stressors are personal events that affect the comfortable pattern of our lives and the little annoyances that bug us day after day. Let's look at the life events that can cause stress, chronic sources of stress, and the relationship between lack of perceived control and the impact of stressors.

Learning Outcomes

- Compare the impact of stressful events and chronic stress.
- Identify the importance of perceived control.

Stressful Events

People often seem to get sick after major life events. In fact, simply adding up the stress ratings of each life change experienced is a significant indicator of a person's likelihood of future illness (Miller, 1996). Someone who gets divorced, loses a job, and has a friend die all in the same year, for example, is more likely to get sick than someone who escapes the year with only a divorce.

A checklist adapted for the life events of college students (and sporting the snappy acronym CUSS, for College Undergraduate Stress Scale) is shown in **TABLE 13.1**. To assess your stressful events, check off any events that have happened to you in the past year and

TABLE 13.1 **College Undergraduate Stress Scale**

Event	Stress Rating	Event	Stress Rating
Being raped	100	Lack of sleep	69
Finding out that you are HIV positive	100	Change in housing situation (hassles, moves)	69
Being accused of rape	98	Competing or performing in public	69
Death of a close friend	97	Getting in a physical fight	66
Death of a close family member	96	Difficulties with a roommate	66
Contracting a sexually transmitted disease (other than AIDS)	94	Job changes (applying, new job, work hassles)	65
Concerns about being pregnant	91	Declaring a major or concerns about future plans	65
Finals week	90	A class you hate	62
Concerns about your partner being pregnant	90	Drinking or use of drugs	61
Oversleeping for an exam	89	Confrontations with professors	60
Flunking a class	89	Starting a new semester	58
Having a boyfriend or girlfriend cheat on you	85	Going on a first date	57
Ending a steady dating relationship	85	Registration	55
Serious illness in a close friend or family member	85	Maintaining a steady dating relationship	55
Financial difficulties	84	Commuting to campus or work or both	54
Writing a major term paper	83	Peer pressures	53
Being caught cheating on a test	83	Being away from home for the first time	53
Drunk driving	82	Getting sick	52
Sense of overload in school or work	82	Concerns about your appearance	52
Two exams in one day	80	Getting straight A's	51
Cheating on your boyfriend or girlfriend	77	A difficult class that you love	48
Getting married	76	Making new friends; getting along with friends	47
Negative consequences of drinking or drug use	75	Fraternity or sorority rush	47
Depression or crisis in your best friend	73	Falling asleep in class	40
Difficulties with parents	73	Attending an athletic event	20
Talking in front of class	72		

Note: To compute your personal life change score, sum the stress ratings for all events that have happened to you in the last year.

Information from Renner & Mackin (1998).

sum your point total. In a large sample of students in an introductory psychology class, the average was 1,247 points, ranging from 182 to 2,571 (Renner & Mackin, 1998).

Looking at the list, you may wonder why positive events, such as getting married, are included. Isn't a wedding supposed to be fun? Indeed, compared with negative events, positive events produce less psychological distress and fewer physical symptoms (McFarlane et al., 1980). However, because positive events often require readjustment and preparedness that many people find extremely stressful (Brown & McGill, 1989), these events are included in computing life-change scores.

Chronic Stressors

Life would be simpler if an occasional stressful event such as a wedding or a lost job were the only pressures we faced. At least each event would be limited in scope, with a beginning, a middle, and, ideally, an end. But unfortunately, life brings with it continued exposure to **chronic stressors**, *sources of stress that occur continuously or repeatedly*. Strained relationships, discrimination, bullying, overwork, money troubles — small stressors that may be easy to ignore if they happen only occasionally — can accumulate to produce distress and illness. People who report being affected by daily hassles also report more psychological symptoms (LaPierre et al., 2012) and physical symptoms (Piazza et al., 2013), and these effects often have a greater and longer-lasting impact than major life events.

Many chronic stressors are linked to social relationships. For instance, as described in the Social Psychology chapter, people often form different social groups based on race, culture, interests, popularity, and so on. Being outside the ingroup can be stressful. Being actively targeted by members of the ingroup can be even more stressful, especially if this happens repeatedly over time (see A World of Difference: Can Discrimination Cause Stress and Illness?). Chronic stressors also can be linked to particular environments. For example, features of city life — noise, traffic, crowding, pollution, and even the threat of violence — provide particularly insistent sources of chronic stress (Evans, 2006). People who live in cities show more amygdala activity in response to stressors than do those who live in towns, and people who live in rural regions show the least of all (Lederbogen et al., 2011).

As the movie *Crazy Rich Asians* showcased perfectly, although weddings are positive events, they also can be stressful due to the often overwhelming amount of planning and decision making involved (and occasionally because of the difficulties in managing the interactions of friends and family). Warner Bros/Kobal/Shutterstock

chronic stressors Sources of stress that occur continuously or repeatedly.

Can Discrimination Cause Stress and Illness?

Have you ever been discriminated against because of your race, gender, sexual orientation, or some other characteristic? If so, then you know that this can be a pretty stressful experience. But what exactly does it *do* to people?

There are a number of ways in which discrimination can lead to elevated stress and negative health outcomes. People from socially disadvantaged groups who experience higher levels of stress as a result of discrimination engage more frequently in maladaptive behaviors (e.g., drinking, smoking, and overeating) in efforts to cope with stress. They also can experience difficulties in their interactions with health care professionals, such as clinician biases or patient suspiciousness about treatment (Major, Mendes, & Dovidio, 2013). This may help explain why

members of socially disadvantaged groups have significantly higher rates of health problems than do members of socially advantaged groups (Penner et al., 2010).

One study exposed Black and White participants to social rejection by a person of the same race or by a person of a different race to test whether there is something particularly harmful about discrimination, compared with social rejection in general (Jamieson et al., 2013). In the study, research participants delivered a speech to two confederates in different rooms via a video chat program, after which the confederates provided negative feedback about the participant's speech. The confederates were not seen by the participant but were represented by computer avatars that either matched the participant's race or did not. The results showed

that whereas being rejected by people of your own race was associated with greater displays of shame and physiological changes associated with an avoidance state (i.e., increased cortisol), being rejected by members of a different race was associated with displays of anger, greater vigilance for danger, physiological changes associated with an approach state (i.e., higher cardiac output and lower vascular resistance), and higher risk taking.

Studies such as this one help explain some of the health disparities that currently exist across different social groups. The results suggest that discrimination can lead to physiological, cognitive, and behavioral changes that in the short term prepare a person for action, but that in the long term could lead to negative health outcomes.

Some stressful life events, such as those associated with drunk driving, are within our power to control. We gain control when we give the car keys to a designated driver.
Kwame Zikomo/Purestock/Alamy

The realization that chronic stressors are linked to environments has spawned the subfield of *environmental psychology,* the scientific study of environmental effects on behavior and health.

Perceived Control Over Stressful Events

What do catastrophes, stressful life changes, and daily hassles have in common? Right off the bat, of course, their threat to the person or the status quo is easy to see. Stressors challenge you to *do something*—to take some action to eliminate or overcome the stressors.

Paradoxically, events are most stressful when there is *nothing to do*—no way to deal with the challenge. In classic studies of *perceived control,* researchers looked at the after-effects of loud noise on people who could or could not control it (Glass & Singer, 1972). Participants were asked to solve puzzles and proofread in a quiet room or in a room filled with loud noise. Bursts of such noise hurt people's performance on the tasks after the noise was over. However, this dramatic decline in performance did not occur among participants who were told during the noise period that they could stop the noise just by pushing a button. They didn't actually take this option, but just having access to the "panic button" shielded them from the detrimental effects of the noise.

Subsequent studies have found that a lack of perceived control underlies other stressors, too. The stressful effects of crowding, for example, appear to stem from the feeling that you can't control getting away from the crowded conditions (Evans & Stecker, 2004). Being jammed into a crowded dormitory room may be easier to handle once you realize you could take a walk and get away from it all.

Build to the Outcomes

1. Which of the events on the stress rating scale relate to you? Do any of the ratings surprise you?

2. How can positive events be stressful?

3. Give examples of chronic stressors.

4. What are some examples of environmental factors that cause chronic stress?

5. What makes events most stressful?

Learning Outcomes

- Explain physical responses to stress.
- Identify possible psychological responses to stress.

Stress Reactions: All Shook Up

It was a regular Tuesday morning in New York City. College students were sitting in their morning classes. People were arriving at work, and the streets were beginning to fill with shoppers and tourists. Then, at 8:46 a.m., American Airlines Flight 11 crashed into the North Tower of the World Trade Center. People watched in horror. How could this have happened? It seemed like a terrible accident. Then at 9:03 a.m., United Airlines Flight 175 crashed into the South Tower of the World Trade Center. There were reports of a plane crashing into the Pentagon. And another somewhere in Pennsylvania. America was under attack, and no one knew what would happen next on this terrifying morning of September 11, 2001.

The 9/11 terrorist attacks were an enormous stressor that had a lasting impact on many people, physically and psychologically. Research done several years after this event revealed that people who lived in close proximity to the World Trade Center (within 1.5 miles) on 9/11 now had less gray matter in the amygdala, hippocampus, insula, anterior cingulate, and medial prefrontal cortex than did those who lived more than 200 miles away during the attacks; this suggested that the stress associated with the attacks may have reduced the size of these parts of the brain that play an important role in emotion, memory, and decision making (Ganzel et al., 2008). Children who watched more television coverage of 9/11 had higher symptoms of posttraumatic stress disorder than did children who watched less coverage (Otto et al., 2007). Stress can produce changes in every system of the body and mind, stimulating both physical reactions and psychological reactions. Let's consider each in turn.

Physical Reactions

The **fight-or-flight response** is *an emotional and physiological reaction to an emergency that increases readiness for action.* The mind asks, "Should I stay and fight? Or should I flee this situation?" And the body prepares to react.

Brain activation in response to threat occurs in the hypothalamus, initiating a cascade of bodily responses that includes stimulation of the nearby pituitary gland, which releases a hormone known as ACTH (short for adrenocorticotropic hormone). ACTH in turn stimulates the adrenal glands atop the kidneys (see **FIGURE 13.1**). This pathway is sometimes called the HPA (hypothalamic–pituitary–adrenocortical) axis.

The adrenal glands release hormones, including *catecholamines* (epinephrine and norepinephrine), which increase sympathetic nervous system activation (and therefore increase heart rate, blood pressure, and respiration rate) and decrease parasympathetic activation (see the Neuroscience and Behavior chapter). The increased respiration and blood pressure make more oxygen available to the muscles to energize attack or to initiate escape. The adrenal glands also release *cortisol,* a hormone that increases the concentration of glucose in the blood to make fuel available to the muscles. Everything is prepared for a full-tilt response to the threat.

General Adaptation Syndrome

What might have happened if the terrorist attacks of 9/11 were spaced out over a period of days or weeks? In the 1930s, Canadian physician Hans Selye subjected rats to heat, cold, infection, trauma, hemorrhage, and other prolonged stressors. His stressed-out rats developed physiological responses that included enlargement of the adrenal cortex, shrinking

The threat of death or injury, such as many in New York City experienced at the time of the 9/11 attacks, can cause significant and lasting physical and psychological stress reactions. Spencer Platt/Getty Images

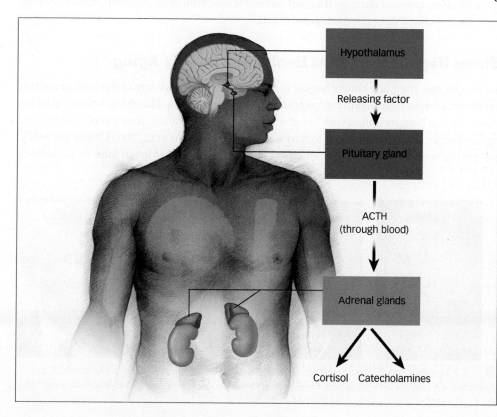

Figure 13.1 HPA Axis Just a few seconds after a fearful stimulus is perceived, the hypothalamus activates the pituitary gland, which in turn activates the adrenal glands to release catecholamines and cortisol, which energize the fight-or-flight response.

fight-or-flight response An emotional and physiological reaction to an emergency that increases readiness for action.

Figure 13.2 Selye's Three Phases of Stress Response In Selye's theory, resistance to stress builds over time, but then can last only so long before exhaustion sets in.

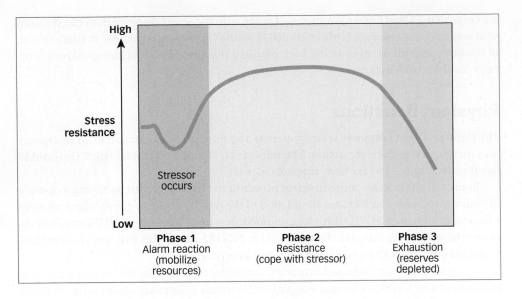

of the lymph glands, and ulceration of the stomach. Noting that many different kinds of stressors caused similar patterns of physiological change, he called the reaction the **general adaptation syndrome (GAS)**, which he defined as *a three-stage physiological stress response that appears regardless of the stressor that is encountered.*

The GAS has three stages (**FIGURE 13.2**):

1. First, in the *alarm phase,* which is equivalent to the fight-or-flight response, the body rapidly mobilizes its resources to respond to the threat.

2. Next, in the *resistance phase,* the body tries to adapt and cope with the stressor by shutting down unnecessary processes such as digestion, growth, and sex drive.

3. If the GAS continues long enough, the *exhaustion phase* sets in: The body's resistance collapses, creating damage that can include susceptibility to infection, tumor growth, aging, irreversible organ damage, or death.

Hans Selye with rat. Given all the stress Selye put rats under, this one looks surprisingly calm. Yousuf Karsh/Julie Grahame

general adaptation syndrome (GAS) A three-stage physiological response that appears regardless of the stressor that is encountered.

Stress Negatively Affects Health and Speeds Aging

As people age, the body slowly begins to break down. (Just ask any of the authors of this textbook.) Stress significantly accelerates this aging process. Elizabeth Smart's parents noted that on being reunited with her after 9 months of separation, they almost did not recognize her because she appeared to have aged so much (Smart et al., 2003). More generally, people exposed to chronic stress, whether due to their relationships or jobs, or something

Chronic stress can actually speed the aging process. Just look at how much each of our last three presidents aged while in office. College can be stressful, too, but hopefully not so much so that you have gray hair by graduation. Jüschke/Ullstein Bild via Getty Images; Tim Sloan/AFP/Getty Images; Stephen Jaffe/AFP/Getty Images; Yuri Gripas-Pool/Getty Images; Alex Wong/Getty Images; Max Mumby/Indigo/Getty Images

Dr. Elizabeth Blackburn was awarded a Nobel Prize in Physiology or Medicine in 2009 for her groundbreaking discoveries on the functions of telomeres (shown here in yellow). Nathan Devery/Science Source; Thor Swift/ *The New York Times*/Redux Pictures

else, experience actual wear and tear on their bodies and accelerated aging. Take a look at the pictures of three presidents before and after their terms as president of the United States (arguably, one of the most stressful jobs in the world). As you can see, they appear to have aged much more than the 8 years that passed between their first and second photographs. How exactly can stressors in the environment speed up the aging process?

Understanding this process requires knowing a little bit about how aging occurs. The cells in our bodies are constantly dividing, and as part of this process, our chromosomes are repeatedly copied so that our genetic information is carried into the new cells. Each time a cell divides, caps (called *telomeres*) at the tips of the chromosomes become slightly shorter (think of telomeres like the tape wrapped around the end of your shoelaces that keep them from fraying). Over time, if they become too short, cells can no longer divide properly. The recent discovery of the function of telomeres and their relation to aging and disease by Elizabeth Blackburn and colleagues has been one of the most exciting advances in science in the past several decades (earning Dr. Blackburn a Nobel Prize in 2009).

Interestingly, social stressors can play an important role in this process. People exposed to chronic stress have shorter telomere length (Epel et al., 2004). Laboratory studies suggest that cortisol can lead to shortened telomeres, which in turn can lead to accelerated aging and increased risk of a wide range of diseases, including cancer, cardiovascular disease, diabetes, and depression (Blackburn et al., 2015). The good news is that activities such as exercise and meditation seem to prevent chronic stress from shortening telomere length, providing a potential explanation of how these activities may convey health benefits such as longer life and lower risk of disease (Epel et al., 2009; Puterman et al., 2010).

Chronic Stress Affects the Immune Response

The **immune system** is *a complex response system that protects the body from bacteria, viruses, and other foreign substances*. The immune system is remarkably responsive to psychological influences, such as the presence of stressors. Stressors can cause hormones known as *glucocorticoids* (e.g., cortisol) to flood the brain (described in the Neuroscience and Behavior chapter), wearing down the immune system and making it less able to fight invaders (Webster Marketon & Glaser, 2008). For example, in one study, medical students volunteered to receive small wounds to the roof of the mouth. These wounds healed more slowly during exam periods than during summer vacation (Marucha et al., 1998).

The effect of stress on immune response may help explain why social status is related to health. The stress of living life at the bottom levels of society increases the risk of infection by weakening the immune system. People who perceive themselves as low in social

immune system A complex response system that protects the body from bacteria, viruses, and other foreign substances.

status and/or support are more likely to suffer from respiratory problems, for example, than those who do not bear this social burden (Lan et al., 2018).

Stress Affects Cardiovascular Health

The heart and circulatory system are also sensitive to stress. For example, people who experience major stressors are at higher odds of developing coronary heart disease (CHD) over the next few years (Crum-Cianflone et al., 2014; Song et al., 2019). Chronic stress, leading to prolonged arousal of the sympathetic nervous system, raises blood pressure, gradually damaging blood vessels. The damaged vessels accumulate plaque, in a process known as *atherosclerosis,* and the more plaque, the greater the likelihood of CHD.

A revolutionary study demonstrated a link between work-related stress and CHD (Friedman & Rosenman, 1974). Researchers interviewed and tested 3,000 healthy middle-aged men and then tracked their subsequent cardiovascular health. Some of the men displayed a **Type A behavior pattern:** *a tendency toward easily aroused hostility, impatience, a sense of time urgency, and competitive achievement strivings.* Other men had a less-driven behavior pattern (sometimes called *Type B*). The Type A men were identified not only by their answers to questions in the interview (agreeing that they walk and talk fast, work late, set goals for themselves, work hard to win, and easily get frustrated and angry at others) but also by the pushy and impatient way in which they answered the questions. In the 9 years following the interview, Type A men were twice as likely to have heart attacks, compared to Type B men.

Hostility, particularly in men, predicts heart disease better than smoking, diet, or even high levels of LDL cholesterol (Niaura et al., 2002). Stress affects the cardiovascular system to some degree in everyone, but it is particularly harmful in those people who respond to stressful events with hostility.

Psychological Reactions

The body's response to stress is intertwined with responses of the mind. Perhaps the first thing the mind does is try to sort things out — to interpret whether an event is threatening — and if it is, whether something can be done about it.

Stress Interpretation Is a Two-Step Process

The interpretation of a stimulus as being stressful or not is called *primary appraisal* (Lazarus & Folkman, 1984). Primary appraisal allows you to realize that a small dark spot on your shirt is a stressor (spider!) or that a 70-mile-per-hour drop from a great height in a small car full of screaming people may not be (roller coaster!).

The next step in interpretation is *secondary appraisal,* determining whether the stressor is something you can handle; that is, whether you have control over the event (Lazarus & Folkman, 1984). Interestingly, the body responds differently depending on whether the stressor is perceived as a *threat* (a stressor you believe you might not be able to overcome) or a *challenge* (a stressor you feel fairly confident you can control) (Blascovich & Tomaka, 1996). The same midterm exam is seen as a challenge if you are well prepared, but a threat if you didn't study.

Although both threats and challenges raise the heart rate, threats increase vascular reactivity (such as constriction of the blood vessels), which can lead to high blood pressure.

Chronic Stress Can Lead to Burnout

Did you ever take a class from an instructor who had lost interest in the job? The syndrome is easy to spot: The teacher looks distant and blank, almost robotic, giving predictable and humdrum lessons each day, as if it doesn't matter whether anyone is listening.

Chris Rock's joke that "rich 50 is like poor 35!" matches up with data suggesting that wealthier people tend to be healthier and younger looking than poorer people.

Andrew Toth/FilmMagic/Getty Images

Type A behavior pattern The tendency toward easily aroused hostility, impatience, a sense of time urgency, and competitive achievement strivings.

Now imagine being this instructor. You decided to teach because you wanted to shape young minds. You worked hard, and for a while things were great. But one day, you looked up to see a room full of students who were bored and didn't care about anything you had to say. They texted while you talked and started shuffling papers and putting things away long before the end of class. You're happy at work only when you're not in class. When people feel this way, especially about their jobs or careers, they are suffering from **burnout**, *a state of physical, emotional, and mental exhaustion resulting from long-term involvement in an emotionally demanding situation and accompanied by lowered performance and motivation.*

Burnout is a particular problem in the helping professions (Fernandez Nievas & Thaver, 2015). Teachers, nurses, clergy, doctors, dentists, psychologists, social workers, police officers, and others who repeatedly encounter emotional turmoil on the job may be able to work productively only for a limited time. Eventually, many succumb to symptoms of burnout: overwhelming exhaustion, a deep cynicism and detachment from the job, and a sense of ineffectiveness and lack of accomplishment (Maslach, 2003). Their unhappiness can even spread to others; people with burnout tend to become disgruntled employees who revel in their coworkers' failures and ignore their coworkers' successes (Brenninkmeijer et al., 2001).

What causes burnout? One theory suggests that the culprit is using your job to give meaning to your life (Pines, 1993). If you define yourself only by your career and gauge your self-worth by success at work, you risk having nothing left when work fails. For example, a teacher in danger of burnout might do well to invest time in family, hobbies, or other forms of self-expression. Others argue that some emotionally stressful jobs lead to burnout no matter how they are approached and that active efforts to overcome the stress before burnout occurs are important. The stress management techniques discussed in the next section may be lifesavers for people in such jobs.

> **burnout** A state of physical, emotional, and mental exhaustion resulting from long-term involvement in an emotionally demanding situation and accompanied by lowered performance and motivation.

Is there anything worse than taking a horribly boring class? How about being the teacher of that class? What techniques would prevent burnout from stress in people in helping professions (teachers, doctors, nurses, and so on)? Stock4B GMBH/Alamy

Build to the Outcomes

1. How does the body react to a fight-or-flight situation?
2. What are the three phases of GAS?
3. What is a telomere? What do telomeres do for us?
4. How does stress affect the immune system?
5. How does chronic stress increase the chance of a heart attack?
6. What is the difference between a threat and a challenge?
7. Why is burnout a problem, especially in the helping professions?

Learning Outcomes

- Explain techniques for coping with psychological stress.
- Identify physical activities that reduce stress.
- Define and give examples of situation management.

The school shooting at Marjory Stoneman Douglas High School in February 2018 in Parkland, Florida, left 17 students and staff members dead and another 17 wounded. People deal with major stressful life events such as this in different ways. Repressive copers use avoidance; rational copers use acceptance, exposure, and understanding; and reframers try to think about the situation in more positive ways. John McCall/Sun Sentinel via Getty Images

repressive coping Avoiding feelings, thoughts, or situations that are reminders of a stressor and maintaining an artificially positive viewpoint.

rational coping Facing a stressor and working to overcome it.

reframing Finding a new or creative way to think about a stressor that reduces its threat.

Stress Management: Dealing With It

More than 90% of college students say they occasionally feel overwhelmed by the tasks they face, and over a third say they have dropped courses or received low grades in response to severe stress (Duenwald, 2002). No doubt you are among the lucky few who are entirely cool and report no stress. But just in case you're not, you may be interested in stress management techniques.

Mind Management

A significant part of stress management is control of the mind. Changing the way you think about potentially stressful events can change how you respond to them. Three ways of changing your thinking about stressors involve the use of repression, rationalization, and reframing.

1. Repressive Coping: Holding an Artificially Positive Viewpoint

Controlling your thoughts is not easy, but some people do seem to be able to banish unpleasant thoughts from the mind. **Repressive coping** is characterized by *avoiding feelings, thoughts, or situations that are reminders of a stressor and maintaining an artificially positive viewpoint*. Like Elizabeth Smart, who for years after her rescue focused in interviews on what was happening in her life now, rather than repeatedly discussing her past in captivity, people often rearrange their lives to avoid stressful situations. It may make sense to try to avoid stressful thoughts and situations if you're the kind of person who is good at putting unpleasant thoughts and emotions out of mind (Coifman et al., 2007). For some people, however, the avoidance of unpleasant thoughts and situations is so difficult that it can turn into a grim preoccupation (Parker & McNally, 2008; Wegner & Zanakos, 1994). For those who can't avoid negative emotions effectively, it may be better to come to grips with them. This is the basic idea of rational coping.

2. Rational Coping: Working to Overcome

Rational coping involves *facing the stressor and working to overcome it*. This strategy is the opposite of repressive coping, so it may seem to be the most unpleasant and unnerving thing you could do when faced with stress. It requires approaching, rather than avoiding, a stressor in order to diminish its longer-term negative impact (Hayes et al., 1999).

Rational coping is a three-step process. The first step is *acceptance,* coming to realize that the stressor exists and cannot be wished away. The second step is *exposure,* attending to the stressor, thinking about it, and even seeking it out. The third step is *understanding,* working to find the meaning of the stressor in your life.

When the trauma is particularly intense, rational coping may be difficult to undertake. In rape trauma, for example, even accepting that the rape happened takes time and effort; the initial impulse is to deny the event and try to live as though it had never occurred. Psychological treatment may help during the exposure step by aiding victims in confronting and thinking about what happened. Using a technique called *prolonged exposure,* rape survivors relive the traumatic event in their imaginations by recording a verbal account of the event and then listening to the recording daily. This sounds like bitter medicine indeed, but it is remarkably effective, producing significant reductions in anxiety and symptoms of posttraumatic stress disorder compared with other therapies that promote more gradual and subtle forms of exposure (Foa & McLean, 2016).

3. Reframing: Changing Your Thinking

Changing the way you think is another way to cope with stressful thoughts. **Reframing** involves *finding a new or creative way to think about a stressor that reduces its threat*. If you experience anxiety at the thought of public speaking, for example, you might reframe

Nervous about a class presentation or performance? Reframing that anxiety as arousal, which can help you perform better, can actually improve your performance. Get out there and reframe! CAIAImage/Martin Barraud/Getty Images

by shifting from thinking of an audience as evaluating you to thinking of yourself as evaluating them, which might make speech giving easier.

Reframing can take place spontaneously if people are given the opportunity to spend time thinking and writing about stressful events. For example, one series of studies found that the physical health of college students improved after they spent a few hours writing about their deepest thoughts and feelings (Pennebaker, 1989). Compared with students who had written about something else, members of the self-disclosure group were less likely in subsequent months to visit the student health center; they also used less aspirin and achieved better grades (Pennebaker & Chung, 2007). In fact, engaging in such expressive writing was found to improve immune function as well (Pennebaker et al., 1988), whereas suppressing emotional topics weakened it (Petrie et al., 1998). The positive effect of self-disclosing writing may reflect its usefulness in reframing trauma and reducing stress.

Body Management

Stress can express itself as tension in your neck, back pain, a knot in your stomach, sweaty hands, or that distressed face you may glimpse in the mirror. Because stress often manifests itself through bodily symptoms, body management can help reduce stress. Here are four techniques.

1. Meditation: Turning Inward

Meditation is *the practice of intentional contemplation*. Techniques of meditation are associated with a variety of religious traditions and are increasingly being practiced outside religious contexts. Some forms of meditation call for attempts to clear the mind of thought; others involve focusing on a single thought (e.g., thinking about a candle flame); still others involve concentration on breathing or on a *mantra* (a repetitive sound, such as *om*). At a minimum, these techniques have in common a period of quiet.

Time spent meditating can be restful and revitalizing. Beyond these immediate benefits, many people also meditate in an effort to experience deeper or transformed consciousness. Whatever the reason, meditation appears to have positive psychological effects (Hölzel et al., 2011). Many believe it does so, in part, by improving control over attention. The focus of many forms of meditation, such as mindfulness meditation, is on teaching ourselves how to remain focused on, and to accept, our immediate experience.

Recent research suggests that those who engage in several weeks of intensive meditation show lengthening of their telomeres, which suggests a slight reversal of the effects of stress and aging as described earlier (Conklin et al., 2015). Taken together, these findings

Prince Harry of England, who has been a prominent advocate for mental health and wellness, recently shared that he engages in daily meditation, which has been shown to reduce stress and improve health.
Adrian Dennis-WPA Pool/Getty Images

meditation The practice of intentional contemplation.

relaxation therapy A technique for reducing tension by consciously relaxing muscles of the body.

relaxation response A condition of reduced muscle tension, cortical activity, heart rate, breathing rate, and blood pressure.

biofeedback The use of an external monitoring device to obtain information about a bodily function and then to possibly gain control over that function.

indicate that meditators may be better able to regulate their thoughts and emotions, which may translate to a better ability to manage interpersonal relations, anxiety, and a range of other activities that require conscious effort (Sedlmeier et al., 2012).

2. Relaxation: Picturing Peace

Imagine for a moment that you are scratching your chin. Don't actually do it; just think about it and notice that your body participates by moving ever so slightly, tensing and relaxing in the sequence of the imagined action. Our bodies respond to all the things we think about doing every day. These thoughts create muscle tension even when we think we're doing nothing at all.

Relaxation therapy is *a technique for reducing tension by consciously relaxing muscles of the body*. A person in relaxation therapy may be asked to relax specific muscle groups one at a time or to imagine warmth flowing through the body or to think about a relaxing situation. This activity draws on a **relaxation response**, *a condition of reduced muscle tension, cortical activity, heart rate, breathing rate, and blood pressure* (Benson, 1990). Basically, as soon as you get in a comfortable position, quiet down, and focus on something repetitive or soothing that holds your attention, you relax.

Setting aside time (e.g., 45 minutes) to relax on a regular basis can reduce symptoms of stress and even reduce blood levels of cortisol, the biochemical marker of the stress response (Cruess et al., 2000). How can you use this in your daily life? Quite simply: Take a break. Go for a walk and take in nature. Experimental studies have shown that going for short walks in the park during workers' lunch breaks decreased their feelings of stress (de Bloom et al., 2017) and that 90-minute walks in nature (versus those in urban settings) decrease rumination and activity in parts of the brain associated with increased risk for mental disorders (Bratman et al., 2015).

3. Biofeedback: Enlisting the Help of an External Monitor

Wouldn't it be nice if, instead of having to learn to relax, you could just flip a switch and relax as fast as possible? **Biofeedback**, *the use of an external monitoring device to obtain information about a bodily function and then to possibly gain control over that function*, was developed with the goal of high-tech relaxation in mind. You might not be aware right now of whether your fingers are warm or cold, for example, but with an electronic thermometer displayed before you, the ability to sense your temperature might allow you (with a bit of practice) to make your hands warmer or cooler at will (e.g., Roberts & McGrady, 1996).

Biofeedback can help people control physiological functions they are not otherwise aware of. For instance, you probably have no idea what brain-wave patterns you are producing right now. But people can change their brain waves from alert beta patterns to relaxed alpha patterns and back again when permitted to monitor their brains using the electroencephalograph or EEG (which you read about in the Neuroscience and Behavior chapter). Often, however, the use of biofeedback to produce relaxation in the brain turns out to be a bit of technological overkill and may not be much more effective than simply having the person stretch out in a hammock and hum a happy tune.

4. Aerobic Exercise: Boosting Mood

Studies indicate that *aerobic exercise* (exercise that increases heart rate and oxygen intake for a sustained period) is associated with psychological well-being (Hassmen et al., 2000). In various studies, researchers have randomly assigned people to aerobic exercise activities and no-exercise comparison groups and have found that exercise actually does promote stress relief and happiness. One review compiled data from 90 studies in which people with chronic illness were randomly assigned either to an exercise or a no-exercise condition, and found that people assigned to the aerobic exercise condition experienced

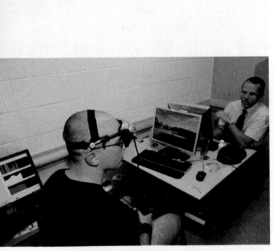

Biofeedback gives people access to visual or audio feedback showing physiological functions — such as heart rate, breathing, brain electrical activity, or skin temperature — that they would otherwise be unable to sense directly. Photo by Charles Baldwin of East Carolina University/Courtesy Dr. Carmen Russoniello

a significant reduction in depressive symptoms (Herring et al., 2012). Other reviews found that exercise is as effective as the strongest psychological interventions for depression (Rimer et al., 2012) and that exercise even shows positive physical and mental health benefits for individuals with schizophrenia (Gorczynski & Faulkner, 2011). Pretty good effects for a simple intervention with no side effects!

The reasons for these positive effects are unclear. Researchers have suggested that the effects result from increases in the body's production of neurotransmitters such as serotonin, which can have a positive effect on mood (as discussed in the Neuroscience and Behavior chapter) or from increases in the production of endorphins (the endogenous opioids discussed in the Neuroscience and Behavior and Consciousness chapters).

Beyond boosting positive mood, exercise also stands to keep you healthy into the future. Recent research has shown that engaging in bouts of aerobic exercise helps you to recover more quickly from future stressors (Bernstein & McNally, 2017). Perhaps the simplest thing you can do to improve your happiness and health, then, is to participate regularly in an aerobic activity. Pick something you find fun: Sign up for a dance class, get into a regular basketball game, or start paddling a canoe — just not all at once.

Situation Management

After you have tried to manage stress by managing your mind and managing your body, what's left to manage? Look around and you'll notice a whole world out there. Situation management involves changing your life situation as a way of reducing the impact of stress on your mind and body.

1. Social Support: "Swimming With a Buddy"

The wisdom of the National Safety Council's first rule — "Always swim with a buddy" — is obvious when you're in water over your head, but people often don't realize that the same principle applies whenever danger threatens. Other people can offer help in times of stress. **Social support** is *aid gained through interacting with others*. Good ongoing relationships with friends and family and participation in social activities and religious groups can be as healthy for you as exercising and not smoking (Umberson et al., 2006).

Many first-year college students experience something of a crisis of social support. No matter how outgoing and popular they were in high school, newcomers typically find the task of developing satisfying new social relationships quite daunting. It's not surprising that students who report the greatest feelings of isolation also show reduced immune responses to flu vaccinations (Pressman et al., 2005). Time spent getting to know people in new social situations can be an investment in your own health.

The value of social support in protecting against stress may be very different for women and men: Whereas women seek support under stress, men are less likely to do so. The fight-or-flight response to stress may be largely a male reaction, according to research on sex differences by Shelley Taylor (2002). Taylor suggested that the female response to stress is to *tend-and-befriend* by taking care of people and bringing them together. After a hard day at work, a

Exercise helps reduce stress — unless, as for John Stibbard, your exercise involves carrying the Olympic torch on a wobbly suspension bridge over a 70-meter gorge. Matt Dunham/ AP Images

social support The aid gained through interacting with others.

Women are more likely than men to seek social support when under stress. Chinaface/ Getty Images; Image Source/Getty Images

man may come home frustrated and worried about his job and end up drinking a beer and fuming alone. A woman under the same type of stress may be more likely to instead play with her kids or talk to friends on the phone. The tend-and-befriend response to stress may help explain why women are healthier and have a longer life span than men. The typical male response amplifies the unhealthy effects of stress, whereas the female response takes less of a toll on a woman's mind and body and provides social support for the people around her as well.

2. Religious Experiences: Reaping Earthly Rewards

National polls indicate that more than 90% of Americans believe in God and that most who do pray at least once per day. Although many who believe in a higher power believe that their faith will be rewarded in an afterlife, it turns out that there may be some benefits here on earth as well. An enormous body of research has suggested that *religiosity* (affiliation with or engagement in the practices of a particular religion) and *spirituality* (having a belief in and engagement with some higher power, not necessarily linked to any particular religion) are associated with positive health outcomes, including lower rates of heart disease, decreases in chronic pain, and improved psychological health (Seybold & Hill, 2001).

Why do people who endorse religiosity or spirituality have better mental and physical health? Is it divine intervention? Engagement in religious or spiritual practices, such as attendance at weekly religious services, may lead to the development of a stronger and more extensive social network, which has well-known health benefits. Those who are religious or spiritual also may fare better psychologically and physically as a result of following the healthy recommendations offered in many religious or spiritual teachings. That is, they may be more likely to observe dietary restrictions, abstain from the use of drugs or alcohol, or endorse a more hopeful and optimistic perspective of daily life events, all of which can lead to more positive health outcomes (Seeman et al., 2003; Seybold & Hill, 2001). However, many claims made by some religious groups have not been supported, such as the beneficial effects of intercessory prayer (see **FIGURE 13.3**). Psychologists are actively testing the effectiveness of various religious and spiritual practices with the goal of better understanding how they might help explain, and improve, the human condition.

3. Humor: Laughing It Off

Wouldn't it be nice to laugh at your troubles and move on? Most of us recognize that humor can defuse unpleasant situations and reduce stress. Is laughter truly the best medicine? Should we close down the hospitals and send in the clowns?

Figure 13.3 Pray for Me? To test whether praying for someone in his or her time of need actually helped, researchers randomly assigned patients about to undergo major surgery to one of three conditions: those who were told they might be prayed for and were; those who were told they might be prayed for and weren't; and those who were told they definitely would be prayed for and were. Unfortunately, there were no differences in the presence of medical complications between those who were or were not prayed for. To make matters worse, those who knew they would be prayed for and who were prayed for experienced significantly more complications than the other two groups (Benson et al., 2006).

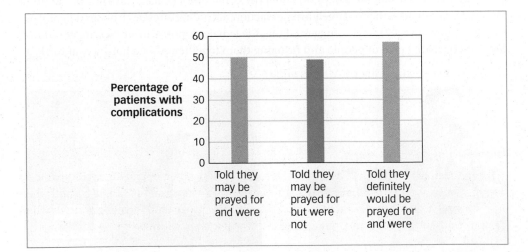

There is a kernel of truth to the theory that humor can help us cope with stress. In one study, volunteers wearing an overinflated blood pressure cuff were more tolerant of the pain during a laughter-inducing comedy audiotape than during a neutral tape or guided relaxation (Cogan et al., 1987).

Humor can also reduce the time needed to calm down after a stressful event. For instance, men viewing a highly stressful film about industrial accidents were asked to narrate the film aloud, either by describing the events seriously or by making their commentary as funny as possible. Although men in both groups reported feeling tense while watching the film and showed increased levels of sympathetic nervous arousal (increased heart rate and skin conductance, decreased skin temperature), those looking for humor in the experience bounced back to normal arousal levels more quickly than did those in the serious story group (Newman & Stone, 1996).

4. Scheduling and Activating: Getting It Done

At one time or another, most of us have avoided carrying out a task or put it off to a later time. College students report procrastinating on academic activities — such as writing a term paper or preparing for a test — between 30 and 60% of the time (Rabin et al., 2011). Some procrastinators defend this practice by claiming that they tend to work best under pressure or by noting that as long as a task gets done, it doesn't matter all that much if it is completed just before the deadline. Is there any merit to such claims? Or are they just feeble excuses for counterproductive behavior?

Among students, higher levels of procrastination are associated with poorer academic performance (Moon & Illingworth, 2005) and higher levels of psychological distress (Rice et al., 2012). In fact, recent evidence indicates that habitual procrastinators show higher levels of self-reported hypertension and cardiovascular disease, even when controlling for other personality traits associated with these health problems (Sirois, 2015). Although there is no proven method of eliminating procrastination, there is some evidence that procrastination in college students can be reduced by interventions that use training in time management or behavioral methods that target the processes that are believed to be responsible for procrastination (Glick & Orsillo, 2015). If you tend toward procrastination, we hope that the research discussed here can alert you to its pitfalls.

When Andrew Mason, CEO of the Internet company Groupon, left his position, his resignation letter read: "After four and a half intense and wonderful years as CEO of Groupon, I've decided that I'd like to spend more time with my family. Just kidding—I was fired today." He went on to add, "I am so lucky to have had the opportunity to take the company this far with all of you. I'll now take some time to decompress (FYI I'm looking for a good fat camp to lose my Groupon 40, if anyone has a suggestion), and then maybe I'll figure out how to channel this experience into something productive." This seems like a textbook case of using humor to mitigate stress, which is why we put it, um, you know where.   Justin Lane/European Pressphoto Agency/Newscom

Build to the Outcomes

1. When is it useful to avoid stressful thoughts? When is avoidance a problem?

2. What are the three steps in rational coping?

3. What is the difference between repressive and rational coping?

4. How has writing about stressful events been shown to be helpful?

5. What are some positive outcomes of meditation?

6. How does biofeedback work?

7. What are the benefits of exercise?

8. What are the benefits of social support?

9. Why are religiosity and spirituality associated with health benefits?

10. How does humor mitigate stress?

11. How do good study habits support good health?

The Psychology of Illness: Mind Over Matter

One of the mind's most important influences on the body's health and illness is the mind's sensitivity to bodily symptoms. Noticing what is wrong with the body can be helpful when it motivates a search for treatment, but sensitivity can also lead to further problems when it snowballs into a preoccupation with illness that itself can cause harm.

Learning Outcome

- Describe the interrelationship between the mind and body relating to illness.

Psychological Effects of Illness

Why does it feel so bad to be sick? You notice scratchiness in your throat or the start of sniffles, and you think you might be coming down with something. And in just a few short hours, you're achy all over, energy gone, no appetite, feverish, feeling dull and listless. You're sick. The question is, why does it have to be like this? As long as you're going to have to stay at home and miss out on things anyway, couldn't sickness be less of a pain?

Sickness makes you miserable for good reason. Misery is part of the *sickness response,* a coordinated, adaptive set of reactions to illness organized by the brain (Hart, 1988; Watkins & Maier, 2005). Feeling sick keeps you home, where you'll spread germs to fewer people. More important, the sickness response makes you withdraw from activity and lie still, conserving the energy for fighting illness that you'd normally expend on other behavior. Appetite loss is similarly helpful: The energy spent on digestion is conserved. Thus, the behavioral changes that accompany illness are not random side effects; they help the body fight disease.

How does the brain know it should do this? The immune response to an infection begins with one of the components of the immune response, the activation of white blood cells that "eat" microbes and also release cytokines, proteins that circulate through the body (Maier & Watkins, 1998). Cytokines do not enter the brain, but they activate the vagus nerve, which runs from the intestines, stomach, and chest to the brain and convey the "I am infected" message (Goehler et al., 2000; Klarer et al., 2014). Perhaps this is why we often feel sickness in the "gut," a gnawing discomfort in the very center of the body.

Interestingly, the sickness response can be prompted without any infection at all, merely by the introduction of stress. The stressful presence of a predator's odor, for instance, can trigger the sickness response of lethargy in an animal, along with symptoms of infection such as fever and increased white blood cell count (Maier & Watkins, 2000). In humans, the connection among sickness response, immune reaction, and stress is illustrated in depression, a condition in which all the sickness machinery runs at full speed. So in addition to fatigue and malaise, depressed people show signs characteristic of infection, including high levels of cytokines circulating in the blood (Maes, 1995). Just as illness can make you feel a bit depressed, severe depression seems to recruit the brain's sickness response and make you feel ill (Watkins & Maier, 2005).

Recognizing Illness and Seeking Treatment

You probably weren't thinking about your breathing a minute ago, but now that you're reading this sentence, you notice it. Sometimes we are very attentive to our bodies. At other times, the body seems to be on "automatic," running along unnoticed until specific symptoms announce themselves or are pointed out by an annoying textbook writer.

People differ substantially in the degree to which they attend to and report bodily symptoms. People who report many physical symptoms tend to be negative in other ways as well, describing themselves as anxious, depressed, and under stress (Watson & Pennebaker, 1989). Do people with many symptom complaints truly have a lot of problems? Or are they just high-volume complainers? In one study, volunteers underwent several applications of a thermal stimulus (110–120°F) to the leg; as you might expect, some of the participants found it more painful than did others. fMRI brain scans during the painful events revealed that the anterior cingulate cortex, somatosensory cortex, and prefrontal cortex (brain areas known to respond to painful body stimulation) were particularly active in those participants who reported higher levels of pain experience (see **FIGURE 13.4**), suggesting that people can report accurately on the extent to which they experience pain (Coghill et al., 2003) (see The Real World: This Is Your Brain on Placebos).

In contrast to complainers, other people underreport symptoms and pain or ignore or deny the possibility that they are sick. Insensitivity to symptoms comes with costs: It

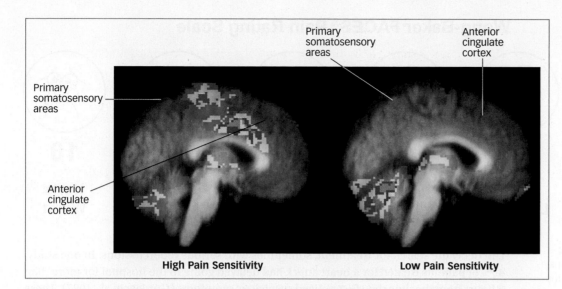

Primary somatosensory areas

Anterior cingulate cortex

Primary somatosensory areas

Anterior cingulate cortex

High Pain Sensitivity   **Low Pain Sensitivity**

Figure 13.4 The Brain in Pain
These fMRI scans show brain activation in high- (*left*) and low-pain-sensitive (*right*) individuals during painful stimulation. The anterior cingulate cortex and primary somatosensory areas show greater activation in high-pain-sensitive individuals. Levels of activation are highest in yellow and red, then light blue and dark blue (Coghill et al., 2003). Neural Correlates of Interindividual Differences in the Subjective Experience of Pain, Coghill, McHaffie, & Yen. Copyright 2003 National Academy of Sciences, USA

THE REAL WORLD

This Is Your Brain on Placebos

There is something miraculous about Band-Aids. Your standard household toddler typically requires one for any injury at all, expecting and often achieving immediate relief. It is not unusual to find a child who reports that aches or pains are "cured" if a Band-Aid has been applied by a helpful adult. Of course, the Band-Aid is not really helping the pain — or is it?

Physicians and psychologists have long puzzled over the *placebo effect*, a clinically significant psychological or physiological response to a therapeutically inert substance or procedure. The classic placebo is the sugar pill, but Band-Aids, injections, heating pads, neck rubs, homeopathic remedies, and kind words can have placebo effects (Diederich & Goetz, 2008).

How do placebos operate? Do people being treated for pain really feel the pain but distort their report of the experience to make it fit their beliefs about treatment? Or does the placebo actually reduce the pain a patient experiences? Howard Fields and Jon Levine (1984) discovered that placebos trigger the release of endorphins (or *endogenous opioids*), painkilling chemicals similar to morphine that are produced by the brain (see the Consciousness chapter).

Placebos can also lower the activation of specific brain areas associated with pain. One study examined brain activation as volunteers were exposed to electric shock or heat (Wager et al., 2004). Beforehand, some participants were given a placebo cream applied to the skin, and told it was an analgesic that would reduce the pain. Other participants merely experienced the pain. As you can see in the accompanying images, patients given placebo showed decreased activation in the *thalamus, anterior cingulate cortex*, and *insula*, pain-sensitive brain regions that were activated during untreated pain. These findings suggest that placebos do not lead people to misreport their pain experience, but, rather, they reduce brain activity in areas that normally are active during pain experiences.

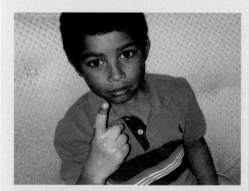

Many children, like this little guy, report immediate pain relief following application of a Band-Aid to whatever spot hurts. Although most adults know that Band-Aids don't treat pain, the placebo effect remains powerful throughout the life span. Courtesy Matthew Nock

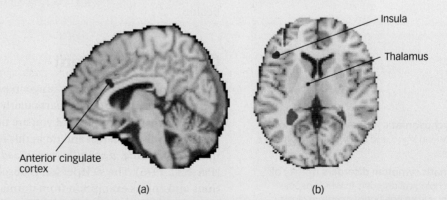

Insula

Thalamus

Anterior cingulate cortex

(a)   (b)

The Brain's Response to Placebo These fMRI scans reveal that some brain regions that are normally activated when individuals report pain in response to shocks are deactivated when those individuals are given a placebo analgesic during the shock. These regions include (a) the anterior cingulate cortex and (b) the insula and thalamus (Wager et al., 2004). Courtesy of Tor Wager

Wong-Baker FACES® Pain Rating Scale

0	2	4	6	8	10
No Hurt	**Hurts Little Bit**	**Hurts Little More**	**Hurts Even More**	**Hurts Whole Lot**	**Hurts Worst**

How much does it hurt? Pain is a psychological state that can be difficult to measure. One way to put a number on a pain is to have people judge with reference to the external expression of the internal state. © 1983 Wong-Baker FACES Foundation. www.Wong BakerFACES.org. Used with permission. Originally published in Whaley & Wong's Nursing Care of Infants and Children. © Elsevier Inc.

can delay the search for treatment, sometimes with serious repercussions. In one study, 40% of patients treated for a heart attack had delayed going to the hospital for more than 6 hours from the time they first noticed suspicious symptoms (Gurwitz et al., 1997). These people often waited around for hours, just hoping the problem would go away. This is not a good idea, because many of the treatments that can reduce the damage of a heart attack are most useful when provided early. When it comes to your own health, protecting your mind from distress through the denial of illness can result in exposing your body to great danger.

Somatic Symptom Disorders

The flip side of denial is excessive sensitivity to illness, and it turns out that sensitivity also has its perils. Indeed, hypersensitivity to symptoms or to the possibility of illness underlies a variety of psychological problems and can also undermine physical health. Psychologists studying **psychosomatic illness**, *an interaction between mind and body that can produce illness,* explore ways in which mind (*psyche*) can influence body (*soma*) and vice versa. The study of mind–body interactions focuses on **somatic symptom disorders**, *the set of psychological disorders in which* a *person with at least one bodily symptom displays significant health-related anxiety, expresses disproportionate concerns about their symptoms, and devotes excessive time and energy to their symptoms or health concerns.* These disorders will be discussed in the Psychological Disorders chapter, but their association with symptoms in the body makes them relevant to this chapter's concern with stress and health.

On Being a Patient

Getting sick is more than a change in physical state; it can involve a transformation of identity. This change can be particularly profound with a serious illness: A kind of cloud settles over you, a feeling that you are now different, and this transformation can influence everything you feel and do in this new world of illness. You even take on a new role in life, a **sick role**, *a socially recognized set of rights and obligations linked with illness* (Parsons, 1975). The sick person is absolved of responsibility for many everyday obligations and enjoys exemption from normal activities. For example, in addition to skipping school and homework and staying on the couch all day, a sick child can watch TV and avoid eating anything unpleasant at dinner. At the extreme, the sick person can get away with being rude, lazy, demanding, and picky. In return for these exemptions, the sick role also incurs obligations. The properly "sick" individual cannot appear to enjoy the illness or reveal signs of wanting to be sick and must also take care to pursue treatment to end this "undesirable" condition.

psychosomatic illness An interaction between mind and body that can produce illness.

somatic symptom disorders The set of psychological disorders in which people with at least one bodily symptom display significant health-related anxiety, express disproportionate concerns about their symptoms, and devote excessive time and energy to their symptoms or health concerns.

sick role A socially recognized set of rights and obligations linked with illness.

Some people feign medical or psychological symptoms to achieve something they want, a type of behavior called *malingering*. Because many symptoms of illness cannot be faked, malingering is possible only with a small number of illnesses. Faking illness is suspected when the secondary gains of illness — such as the ability to rest, to be freed from performing unpleasant tasks, or to be helped by others — outweigh the costs. Such gains can be very subtle, as when a child stays in bed because of the comfort provided by an otherwise distant parent, or they can be obvious, as when insurance benefits turn out to be a cash award for best actor. For this reason, malingering can be difficult to diagnose and treat (Bass & Halligan, 2014).

Patient–Practitioner Interaction

Medical care usually occurs through a strange interaction. On one side is a patient, often miserable, who expects to be questioned and examined and possibly prodded, pained, or given bad news. On the other side is a health care provider, who hopes to quickly obtain information from the patient by asking lots of extremely personal questions (and examining extremely personal parts of the body); to identify the problem and help in some way; and to achieve all of this as efficiently as possible because more patients are waiting. It seems less like a time for healing than an occasion for major awkwardness.

One of the keys to an effective medical care interaction is physician empathy (Kelm et al., 2014). To offer successful treatment, the clinician must simultaneously understand the patient's physical state *and* psychological state. Physicians often err on the side of failing to acknowledge patients' emotions, focusing instead on technical issues of the case (Suchman et al., 1997). This is particularly unfortunate, because a substantial percentage of patients who seek medical care do so for treatment of psychological and emotional problems (Wiegner et al., 2015). The best physician treats the patient's mind as well as the patient's body.

Another important part of the medical care interaction is motivating the patient to follow the prescribed regimen of care (Miller & Rollnick, 2012). When researchers check compliance by counting the pills remaining in a patient's bottle after a prescription has been started, they find that patients often do an astonishingly poor job of following doctors' orders (see **FIGURE 13.5**). Compliance deteriorates when the treatment must be frequent, as when eye drops for glaucoma are required every few hours, or is inconvenient

Is staying home with a cold socially acceptable? Or is it considered malingering? Image Source/ Getty Images

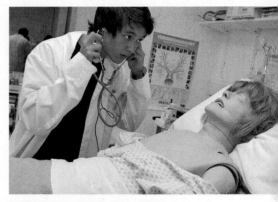

Medical training with robot patients may help doctors learn the technical side of health care, but it is likely to do little to improve the interpersonal side. Dan Atkin/Alamy

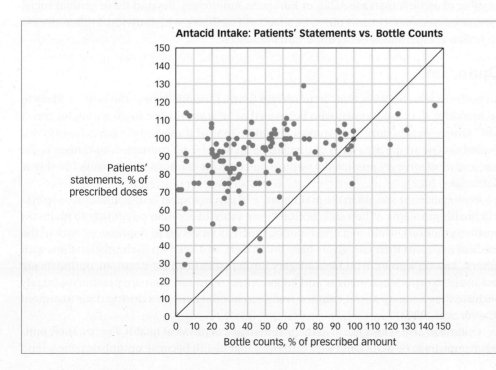

Antacid Intake: Patients' Statements vs. Bottle Counts

Patients' statements, % of prescribed doses (y-axis: 0–150)

Bottle counts, % of prescribed amount (x-axis: 0–150)

Figure 13.5 Antacid Intake A scatterplot of actual antacid intake (measured by counting the number of pills remaining in the bottle) plotted against patient's stated intake for 116 patients. When the actual and stated intakes are the same, the point lies on the diagonal line; when stated intake is greater than actual, the point lies above the line. Most patients exaggerated their intake (Roth & Caron, 1978).

or painful, such as drawing blood or performing injections in managing diabetes. Finally, compliance decreases as the number of treatments increases. This is a worrisome problem, especially for older patients, who may have difficulty remembering when to take which pill. Failures in medical care may stem from the failure of health care providers to recognize the psychological challenges that are involved in self-care. Helping people follow doctors' orders involves psychology, not medicine, and is an essential part of promoting health.

Build to the Outcomes

1. What are the physical benefits of the sickness response?
2. What is the relationship between pain and activity in the brain?
3. How can hypersensitivity to symptoms undermine health?
4. What benefits might come from being ill?
5. Why is it important that a physician express empathy?

The Psychology of Health: Feeling Good

Learning Outcome

- Explain the attitudes and behaviors that lead to good health.

Two kinds of psychological factors influence personal health: health-relevant personality traits and health behavior. Personality can influence health through relatively enduring traits that make some people particularly susceptible to health problems while sparing or protecting others. The Type A behavior pattern is an example. Because personality is not typically something we choose ("I'd like a bit of that sense of humor and extraversion over there, please, but hold the whininess"), this source of health can be beyond personal control. In contrast, engaging in positive health behaviors is something anyone can do, at least in principle.

Personality and Health

Different health problems seem to plague different social groups. For example, men are more susceptible to heart disease than are women, and African Americans are more susceptible to asthma than are Asian or European Americans. Beyond these general social categories, personality turns out to be a factor in wellness, with individual differences in optimism and hardiness being important influences.

Optimism

An optimist who believes that "in uncertain times, I usually expect the best" is likely to be healthier than a pessimist who believes that "if something can go wrong for me, it will." One review of dozens of studies including tens of thousands of participants concluded that of all the measures of psychological well-being examined, optimism is the one that most strongly predicted a positive outcome for cardiovascular health (Boehm & Kubzansky, 2012).

Optimism seems to aid in the maintenance of psychological health in the face of physical health problems. When sick, optimists are more likely than pessimists to maintain positive emotions, avoid negative emotions such as anxiety and depression, stick to the medical regimens their caregivers have prescribed, and keep up their relationships with others. Among women who have surgery for breast cancer, for example, optimists are less likely to experience distress and fatigue after treatment than are pessimists, largely because they keep up social contacts and recreational activities during their treatment (Carver et al., 2003).

Optimism also seems to aid in the maintenance of physical health. For instance, optimism appears to be associated with cardiovascular health because optimistic people tend to engage in healthier behaviors such as eating a balanced diet and exercising, which in turn decreases the risk of heart disease (Boehm et al., 2013).

The benefits of optimism raise an important question: If the traits of optimism and pessimism are stable over time — even resistant to change — can pessimists ever hope to gain any of the advantages of optimism? Research has shown that even die-hard pessimists can be trained to become significantly more optimistic and that this training can improve their psychosocial health outcomes. For example, patients with breast cancer who were pessimistic and who received 10 weeks of training in stress management techniques became more optimistic and were less likely than those who only engaged in relaxation exercises to suffer distress and fatigue during their cancer treatments (Antoni et al., 2001).

Hardiness

Some people seem to be thick-skinned, somehow able to take stress or abuse that could be devastating to others. In one study, a group of stress-resistant business executives reported high levels of stressful life events but relatively few illnesses compared with a similar group who succumbed to stress by getting sick (Kobasa, 1979). The stress-resistant group (labeled *hardy*) shared several traits, all conveniently beginning with the letter *C*. They showed a sense of *commitment*, an ability to become involved in life's tasks and encounters rather than just dabbling. They exhibited a belief in *control*, the expectation that their actions and words have a causal influence over their lives and environment. And they were willing to accept *challenge*, undertaking change and accepting opportunities for growth.

Can anyone develop hardiness? In one study, participants attended 10 weekly hardiness-training sessions, in which they were encouraged to examine their stresses, develop action plans for dealing with them, explore their bodily reactions to stress, and find ways to compensate for unchangeable situations without falling into self-pity. Compared with control groups (who engaged in relaxation and meditation training or in group discussions about stress), the hardiness-training group reported greater reductions in their perceived personal stress, as well as fewer symptoms of illness (Maddi et al., 1998). Hardiness training can have similar positive effects in college students, for some even boosting their GPA (Maddi et al., 2009).

Health-Promoting Behaviors and Self-Regulation

Even without changing our personalities, we can do certain things to be healthy. The importance of healthy eating, safe sex, and giving up smoking are common knowledge. But we don't seem to be acting on the basis of this knowledge. Forty percent of Americans over age 20 are obese (Hales et al., 2017). The prevalence of unsafe sex is difficult to estimate, but 65 million Americans currently suffer from an incurable sexually transmitted infection (STI), and 20 million contract one or more new STIs each year (Satterwhite et al., 2013). And despite endless warnings, 14% of U.S. adults still smoke cigarettes (CDC, 2019b). What's going on?

Self-Regulation

Doing what is good for you is not necessarily easy. Mark Twain once remarked, "The only way to keep your health is to eat what you don't want, drink what you don't like, and do what you'd rather not." Engaging in health-promoting behaviors involves **self-regulation**, *the exercise of voluntary control over the self to bring the self into line with preferred standards.* When you decide on a salad rather than a cheeseburger, for instance, you control your impulse and behave in a way that will help make you the kind of person you would prefer to be — a healthy one. Self-regulation often involves putting off immediate gratification for longer-term gains.

Adrianne Haslet was approximately 4 feet away from one of the bombs that exploded at the Boston Marathon in 2013. Although the explosion caused her to lose her left foot, Adrianne (center) vowed that she would continue her career as a dancer — and she actually ran in the Boston Marathon in 2016. She is an optimist, and optimism can lead to positive health outcomes. Bill Greene/The Boston Globe via Getty Images

Sometimes hardiness tips over the edge into foolhardiness. Members of the Coney Island Polar Bear Club take the plunge every Sunday of winter. Kathy Willens/AP Images

self-regulation The exercise of voluntary control over the self to bring the self into line with preferred standards.

Nobody ever said self-control was easy. Probably the only reason you're able to keep yourself from eating this cookie is that it's just a picture of a cookie. Really. Don't eat it. Jean Sander/FeaturePics

DATA Visualization

One of the reasons that people in France are leaner than people in the United States is that the average French diner spends 22 minutes to consume a fast-food meal, whereas the average American diner spends only 15 minutes. How could the length of the average meal influence an individual's body weight? Jeff Gilbert/Alamy

One theory suggests that self-control is a kind of strength that can be fatigued (Baumeister et al., 2007). In other words, trying to exercise control in one area may exhaust self-control, leaving behavior in other areas unregulated. To test this theory, researchers seated hungry volunteers near a batch of fresh, hot, chocolate chip cookies. They asked some participants to leave the cookies alone but help themselves to a healthy snack of radishes, whereas others were allowed to indulge. When later challenged with an impossibly difficult figure-tracing task, the self-control group was more likely than the self-indulgent group to abandon the difficult task — behavior interpreted as evidence that they had depleted their pool of self-control (Baumeister et al., 1998). The take-home message from this experiment is that to control behavior successfully, we need to choose our battles, exercising self-control mainly on the personal weaknesses that are most harmful to health. Most important, however, the exact nature of this effect is still being debated; several research teams have failed to replicate this earlier work (e.g., Lurquin et al., 2016).

Sometimes self-regulation is less a matter of brute force than of strategy. Martial artists claim that anyone can easily overcome a large attacker with the right moves, and overcoming our own unhealthy impulses may also be a matter of finesse. Let's look carefully at healthy approaches to some key challenges for self-regulation — eating, safe sex, and smoking — to learn which "smart moves" can aid us in our struggles.

Eating Wisely

In many Western cultures, the weight of the average citizen is increasing alarmingly. One explanation is based on our evolutionary history: To ensure survival, our ancestors found it useful to eat well in times of plenty to store calories for leaner times. In 21st-century postindustrial societies, however, most people can't burn all of the calories they consume (Pinel et al., 2000). But why, then, are people in France leaner on average than Americans, even though their foods are high in fat? One reason has to do with the fact that activity level in France is higher. Another reason is that portion sizes in France are significantly smaller than in the United States, but at the same time, people in France take longer to finish their smaller meals (Rozin, Kabnick, et al., 2003). Right now, Americans seem to be involved in some kind of national eating contest, whereas in France people are eating less food more slowly, perhaps leading them to be more conscious of what they are eating. This, ironically, probably leads to lower French fry consumption.

Short of moving to France, what can you do? Studies indicate that dieting doesn't always work because the process of conscious self-regulation can easily be undermined by stress, causing people who are trying to control themselves to lose control by overindulging in the very behavior they had been trying to overcome. This may remind you of a general principle we discussed in the Consciousness chapter: Trying hard not to do something can often directly result in the unwanted behavior (Wegner, 1994a, 1994b, 2009). (See Data Visualization: How Are Stress and Eating Habits Related? at www.launchpadworks.com.)

Rather than dieting, then, heading toward normal weight should involve a new emphasis on exercise and nutrition (Prochaska & Sallis, 2004). In emphasizing what is good to eat, a person can think freely about food rather than trying to suppress thoughts about it. A focus on increasing activity rather than reducing food intake, in turn, gives people another positive and active goal to pursue. Self-regulation is more effective when it focuses on what to do rather than on what not to do (Molden et al., 2009; Wegner & Wenzlaff, 1996).

Avoiding Sexual Risks

People put themselves at risk when they have unprotected vaginal, oral, or anal intercourse. Sexually active adolescents and adults are usually aware of such risks, not to mention the risk of unwanted pregnancy, yet many behave in risky ways nonetheless. Why doesn't awareness translate into avoidance? Risk takers harbor an *illusion of unique invulnerability,* a systematic bias toward believing that they are less likely to fall victim to the problem than are others (Perloff & Fetzer, 1986). For example, a study of sexually active female college students found that they judged their own likelihood of getting pregnant in the next year as less than 10%, but estimated the average for other women at the university to be 27% (Burger & Burns, 1988).

Unprotected sex often is the impulsive result of last-minute emotions. When thought is further blurred by alcohol or recreational drugs, people often fail to use the latex condoms that can reduce their exposure to the risks of pregnancy, HIV, and many other STIs. One approach to reducing sexual risk taking, then, is simply finding ways to help people plan ahead. Sex education programs offer adolescents just such a chance by encouraging them, at a time when they have not had much sexual experience, to think about what they might do when they need to make decisions. Although sex education is sometimes criticized as increasing adolescents' awareness of and interest in sex, the research evidence is clear: Sex education reduces the likelihood that college students will engage in unprotected sexual activity, and it benefits their health (Li et al., 2017).

Not Smoking

One in two smokers dies prematurely from smoking-related diseases such as lung cancer, heart disease, emphysema, and cancer of the mouth and throat. Although the overall rate of smoking in the United States is declining, new smokers abound, and many can't seem to stop. College students are puffing away along with everyone else; according to the Centers for Disease Control and Prevention (CDC), about 13% of college students currently smoke. In the face of all the devastating health consequences, why don't people quit?

Nicotine, the active ingredient in cigarettes, is addictive, so smoking is difficult to stop once the habit is established (as discussed in the Consciousness chapter). As with other forms of self-regulation, the resolve to quit smoking is fragile and seems to break down under stress. In the months following 9/11, for example, cigarette sales jumped 13% in Massachusetts (Phillips, 2002). And for some time after quitting, ex-smokers remain sensitive to cues in the environment: Eating or drinking, a bad mood, anxiety, or just seeing someone else smoking is enough to make them want a cigarette (Shiffman et al., 1996). The good news is that the urge diminishes, and people become less likely to relapse the longer they've been away from nicotine.

Psychological programs and techniques to help people kick the habit include nicotine replacement systems such as gum and skin patches, counseling programs, and hypnosis, but these programs are not always successful. Trying again and again in different ways is apparently the best approach (Schachter, 1982). After all, to quit smoking forever, you need to quit only one more time than you start up. But like the self-regulation of eating and sexuality, the self-regulation of smoking can require effort and thought. Keeping healthy by behaving in healthy ways is one of the great challenges of life (see Other Voices: The Dangers of Overparenting).

Build to the Outcomes

1. Why do optimists tend to have better health?
2. What is hardiness?
3. Why is it difficult to achieve and maintain self-control?
4. Why is exercise a more effective weight-loss choice than dieting?
5. Why does planning ahead reduce sexual risk taking?
6. To quit smoking forever, how many times do you need to quit?

OTHER VOICES

The Dangers of Overparenting

Julie Lythcott-Haims Photo Courtesy of Veronica Weber/Palo Alto Weekly

Many parents want to protect their children from experiencing any stress or hardship. This is only natural; we want to protect the ones we love from being hurt, and we want to ensure that they have the best life possible. But is there a downside to doing so? Julie Lythcott-Haims, who for a decade served as Stanford University's dean of freshman, believes that "overparenting" can cause significant harm by depriving children of opportunities to learn creativity, competence, and confidence, and to develop a true sense of who they really are. In her book *How to Raise an Adult*, Lythcott-Haims describes how overbearing "helicopter parenting" can backfire among college students.

I became a university dean because I'm interested in supporting humans in growing to become who they're meant to become, unfettered by circumstances or other people's expectations. I expected that the kids who would need my help would be first-generation college students or low-income kids, and these populations certainly benefited from the mentorship and support that a dean could provide. But it was my solidly middle- or upper-middle-class students who had the most bewildered looks on their faces, looks that turned to relief when Mom or Dad handled the situation, whatever it was. These parents seemed involved in their college students' lives in ways that held their kids back instead of propelling them forward.

In 2013 the news was filled with worrisome statistics about the mental health crisis on college campuses, particularly the number of students medicated for depression. Charlie Gofen, the retired chairman of the board at the Latin School of Chicago, a private school serving about 1,100 students, emailed the statistics off to a colleague at another school and asked, "Do you think parents at your school would rather their kid be depressed at Yale or happy at University of Arizona?" The colleague quickly replied, "My guess is 75 percent of the parents would rather see their kids depressed at Yale. They figure that the kid can straighten the emotional stuff out in his/her 20's, but no one can go back and get the Yale undergrad degree."

In 2013 the American College Health Association surveyed close to 100,000 college students from 153 different campuses about their health. When asked about their experiences, at some point over the past 12 months:

- 84.3 percent felt overwhelmed by all they had to do
- 60.5 percent felt very sad
- 57.0 percent felt very lonely
- 51.3 percent felt overwhelming anxiety
- 8.0 percent seriously considered suicide

You're right to be thinking *Yes, but do we know whether overparenting causes this rise in mental health problems?* The answer is that we don't have studies proving causation, but a number of recent studies show correlation.

In 2010, psychology professor Neil Montgomery of Keene State College in New Hampshire surveyed 300 college freshmen nationwide and found that students with helicopter parents were less open to new ideas and actions and more vulnerable, anxious, and self-conscious. "[In s]tudents who were given responsibility and not constantly monitored by their parents—so-called 'free rangers'—the effects were reversed," Montgomery's study found. A 2011 study by Terri LeMoyne and Tom Buchanan at the University of Tennessee at Chattanooga looking at more than 300 students found that students with "hovering" or "helicopter" parents are more likely to be medicated for anxiety and/or depression.

When parents have tended to do the stuff of life for kids—the waking up, the transporting, the reminding about deadlines and obligations, the bill-paying, the question-asking, the decision-making, the responsibility-taking, the talking to strangers, and the confronting of authorities, kids may be in for quite a shock when parents turn them loose in the world of college or work. They will experience setbacks, which will feel to them like failure. Lurking beneath the problem of whatever thing needs to be handled is the student's inability to differentiate the self from the parent.

Here's the point—and this is so much more important than I realized until rather recently when the data started coming in: The research shows that figuring out for themselves is a critical element to people's mental health. Your kids have to be there for themselves. That's a harder truth to swallow when your kid is in the midst of a problem or worse, a crisis, but taking the long view, it's the best medicine for them.

Is being exposed to stressful situations necessarily a bad thing? How else will we learn how to cope with difficult situations? If we never learn to do so, we may be more likely to experience some of the bad outcomes that Lythcott-Haims writes about. So get out there, get stressed, and manage it!

CHAPTER REVIEW

Sources of Stress: What Gets to You

- Stressors are events and threats that place specific demands on a person or threaten well-being.
- Sources of stress include major life events (even happy ones), and also chronic stressors that occur repeatedly.
- Events are most stressful when we perceive that there is no way to control or deal with the challenge.

Stress Reactions: All Shook Up

- The body responds to stress with an initial fight-or-flight reaction, which activates the hypothalamic–pituitary–adrenocortical (HPA) axis and prepares the body to face the threat or run away from it.
- The general adaptation syndrome (GAS) outlines three phases of stress response: alarm, resistance, and exhaustion.

- Chronic stress can wear down the immune system, causing susceptibility to infection, aging, tumor growth, organ damage, and death. People who respond to stress with anger are most at risk of heart disease.
- The response to stress will vary depending on whether it's interpreted as something that can be overcome or not.
- If prolonged, the psychological response to stress can lead to burnout.

Stress Management: Dealing With It

- The management of stress involves strategies for influencing the mind, the body, and the situation.
- Mind management strategies include suppressing stressful thoughts or avoiding the situations that produce them, rationally coping with the stressor, and reframing.
- Body management strategies involve attempting to reduce stress symptoms through meditation, relaxation, biofeedback, and aerobic exercise.
- Situation management strategies can involve seeking out social support, engaging in religious experiences, or attempting to find humor in stressful events.

The Psychology of Illness: Mind Over Matter

- The psychology of illness concerns how sensitivity to the body leads people to recognize illness and seek treatment.
- Somatic symptom disorders can stem from excessive sensitivity to physical problems.
- The sick role is a set of rights and obligations linked with illness; some people fake illness to accrue those rights.
- Successful health care providers interact with their patients to understand both the physical state and the psychological state.

The Psychology of Health: Feeling Good

- The connection between mind and body can be revealed through the influences of personality and self-regulation of behavior on health.
- The personality traits of optimism and hardiness are associated with reduced risk for illnesses, perhaps because people with these traits can better fend off stress.
- The self-regulation of behaviors such as eating, sexuality, and smoking is difficult for many people because self-regulation is easily disrupted by stress.

Key Concept Quiz

1. What kinds of stressors are you likely to be exposed to if you live in a dense urban area with considerable traffic, noise, and pollution?
   a. cultural stressors
   b. intermittent stressors
   c. chronic stressors
   d. positive stressors

2. In an experiment, two groups are subjected to distractions while attempting to complete a task. Those in group A are told they can quiet the distractions by pushing a button. This information is withheld from group B. Why will group A's performance at the task likely be better than group B's?
   a. Group B is working in a different environment.
   b. Group A has perceived control over a source of performance-impeding stress.
   c. Group B is less distracted than group A.
   d. The distractions affecting group B are now chronic.

3. The brain activation that occurs in response to a threat begins in the
   a. pituitary gland.
   b. hypothalamus.
   c. adrenal gland.
   d. corpus callosum.

4. According to the general adaptation syndrome, during the _____ phase, the body adapts to its high state of arousal as it tries to cope with a stressor.
   a. exhaustion
   b. alarm

   c. resistance
   d. energy

5. Which statement most accurately describes the physiological response to stress?
   a. Type A behavior patterns have psychological but not physiological ramifications.
   b. The link between work-related stress and coronary heart disease is unfounded.
   c. Stressors can cause hormones to flood the brain, strengthening the immune system.
   d. The immune system is remarkably responsive to psychological influences.

6. Meditation is an altered state of consciousness that occurs
   a. with the aid of drugs.
   b. through hypnosis.
   c. naturally or through special practices.
   d. as a result of dreamlike brain activity.

7. Engaging in aerobic exercise is a way of managing stress by managing the
   a. environment.
   b. body.
   c. situation.
   d. intake of air.

8. Finding a new or creative way to think about a stressor that reduces its threat is called
   a. stress inoculation.
   b. repressive coping.
   c. reframing.
   d. rational coping.

9. The positive health outcomes associated with religiosity and spirituality are believed to be the result of all of the following except
  a. enhanced social support.
  b. engagement in healthier behavior.
  c. endorsement of hope and optimism.
  d. intercessory prayer.

10. A person who is preoccupied with minor symptoms and believes they signify a life-threatening illness is likely to be diagnosed with
  a. cytokines.
  b. repressive coping.
  c. burnout.
  d. a somatic symptom disorder.

11. Faking an illness is a violation of
  a. malingering.
  b. somatoform disorder.
  c. the sick role.
  d. the Type B pattern of behavior.

12. Which statement describes a successful health care provider?
  a. The provider displays empathy.
  b. The provider pays attention to both the physical and psychological states of the patient.

  c. The provider uses psychology to promote patient compliance.
  d. The provider uses all of the above.

13. When sick, optimists are more likely than pessimists to
  a. maintain positive emotions.
  b. become depressed.
  c. ignore their caregiver's advice.
  d. avoid contact with others.

14. Which of the following is NOT a trait associated with hardiness?
  a. a sense of commitment
  b. an aversion to criticism
  c. a belief in control
  d. a willingness to accept challenge

15. Stress _____ the self-regulation of behaviors such as eating and smoking.
  a. strengthens
  b. has no effect on
  c. disrupts
  d. normalizes

LearningCurve Don't stop now! Quizzing yourself is a powerful study tool. Go to LaunchPad to access the LearningCurve adaptive quizzing system and your own personalized learning plan. Visit launchpadworks.com.

Key Terms

stressors (p. 385)
stress (p. 385)
health psychology (p. 385)
chronic stressors (p. 387)
fight-or-flight response (p. 389)

general adaptation syndrome (GAS) (p. 390)
immune system (p. 391)
Type A behavior pattern (p. 392)
burnout (p. 393)
repressive coping (p. 394)

rational coping (p. 394)
reframing (p. 394)
meditation (p. 395)
relaxation therapy (p. 396)
relaxation response (p. 396)
biofeedback (p. 396)

social support (p. 397)
psychosomatic illness (p. 402)
somatic symptom disorders (p. 402)
sick role (p. 402)
self-regulation (p. 405)

Changing Minds

1. In 2002, researchers compared severe acne in college students during a relatively stress-free period with acne during a highly stressful exam period. After adjusting for other variables such as changes in sleep or diet, the researchers concluded that increased acne severity was strongly correlated with increased levels of stress. Learning about the study, your roommate is surprised. "Acne is a skin disease," your roommate says. "I don't see how it could have anything to do with your mental state." How would you weigh in on the role of stress in medical diseases? What

other examples could you give of ways in which stress can affect health?

2. A friend of yours who is taking a heavy course load confides that he's feeling overwhelmed. "I can't take the stress," he says. "Sometimes I daydream of living on an island somewhere, where I can just lie in the sun and have no stress at all." What would you tell your friend about stress? Is all stress bad? What would a life with no stress really be like?

3. One of your classmates spent the summer interning in a neurologist's office. "One of the most fascinating things," she says, "was the patients with psychosomatic illness. Some had seizures or partial paralysis of an arm, and there were no neurological causes. The neurologist tried to refer these patients to psychiatrists, but a lot of the patients thought the doctor was accusing them of faking their symptoms, and were very insulted." What would you tell your friend about psychosomatic illness? Could a disease that's "all in the head" really produce symptoms such as seizures or partial paralysis, or are these patients definitely faking their symptoms?

Answers to Key Concept Quiz

1. c; 2. b; 3. b; 4. c; 5. d; 6. c; 7. b; 8. c; 9. d; 10. d; 11. c; 12. d; 13. a; 14. b; 15. c

LaunchPad
macmillan learning

LaunchPad features the full e-book of *Introducing Psychology*, the LearningCurve adaptive quizzing system, videos, and a variety of activities to boost your learning. Visit LaunchPad at launchpadworks.com.

Psychological Disorders

14

Robin Williams was one of the funniest and most beloved comedians in history, best known for his zany improvisational style. He appeared in more than 100 films and television shows, including four major movies released in 2014. Then, on August 11, 2014, Williams locked himself in his bedroom and hanged himself with his belt. Why would a person who was so successful and beloved purposely end his life?

Many people familiar with Robin Williams's professional career did not know that he had suffered from mental illness for years. Throughout his life, Williams struggled with drug- and alcohol-use disorders. He also suffered from major depressive disorder, a condition characterized by long periods of depressed mood, diminished interest in pleasurable activities, feelings of worthlessness, and problems with eating and sleeping. Shortly before his death, he also was diagnosed with Parkinson's disease and dementia, conditions associated with a progressive decline of physical and mental abilities. Many people who are suicidal say that their motivation is not necessarily to be dead, but rather to escape from some seemingly intolerable situation, such as a long-term struggle with mental illness. That may have been the reason for Williams's suicide, although we will never know for sure.

Williams's case highlights several important facts about mental disorders. They can affect anyone, regardless of the amount of perceived happiness or success. They are characterized by extreme distress and impairment, often limiting a person's ability to carry out daily activities. At the same time, however, many people suffer silently, unknown to those around them. And finally, in extreme cases, mental disorders can be lethal, leading to severe self-injury or death by suicide. Thus, there is a great need for us to better understand what mental disorders are and what causes them.

In this chapter, we first consider how psychologists decide when a person's thoughts, emotions, and behaviors are "abnormal." What key factors must be weighed in making such a decision? We'll then focus on several major forms of *mental disorder*: depressive and bipolar disorders; anxiety, obsessive-compulsive, and trauma-related disorders; schizophrenia; disorders that begin in childhood and adolescence; personality disorders; and self-harm behaviors. As we view each type of disorder, we will examine how they manifest and what is known about their prevalence and causes. In the Treatment chapter, we'll discuss how these disorders are currently treated.

The actor and comedian Robin Williams (1951–2014) in 2009. Williams was a brilliant performer who had audiences laughing for more than 40 years. In his personal life, however, he suffered with bouts of addiction, depression, and dementia, ending with his suicide. CBS Photo Archive/ Getty Images

Defining Mental Disorders: What Is Abnormal?

Anxiety Disorders: Excessive Fear, Anxiety, and Avoidance

Obsessive-Compulsive Disorder: Persistent Thoughts and Repetitive Behaviors

Posttraumatic Stress Disorder: Distress and Avoidance After a Trauma

Depressive and Bipolar Disorders: Extreme Highs and Lows

Schizophrenia and Other Psychotic Disorders: Losing the Grasp on Reality

Disorders of Childhood and Adolescence

Personality Disorders: Extreme Traits and Characteristics

Self-Harm Behaviors: Intentionally Injuring Oneself

Learning Outcomes

- Explain why the *DSM* has become a more credible diagnostic tool over the course of revisions to each edition.
- Identify the fundamental ideas behind the medical model, the biopsychosocial perspective, and the diathesis–stress model.
- Relate how the RDoC expands on the *DSM*.
- Explain the negative consequences of labeling someone with a disorder.

mental disorder A persistent disturbance or dysfunction in behavior, thoughts, or emotions that causes significant distress or impairment.

medical model An approach that conceptualizes abnormal psychological experiences as illnesses that, like physical illnesses, have biological and environmental causes, defined symptoms, and possible cures.

Although mental disorders are deviations from normal behavior, not all deviations from the norm are disordered. Indeed, people thinking differently about the world, and behaving in ways that deviate from the norm, have brought remarkable advances, such as Mickey Mouse, iPhones, and progress toward racial equality. Lawrence Schiller/Polaris Communications/Getty Images; Shaun Curry/AFP/Getty Images; Howard Sochurek/ The Life Picturecollection/Getty Images

Defining Mental Disorders: What Is Abnormal?

The concept of a mental disorder seems simple at first glance, but it turns out to be very complex and quite tricky (similar to clearly defining "consciousness," "stress," or "personality"). Any extreme variation in your thoughts, feelings, or behaviors is not a mental disorder. For instance, severe anxiety before a test, sadness after the loss of a loved one, or a night of excessive alcohol consumption—although unpleasant—is not necessarily pathological. Similarly, a persistent pattern of deviating from the norm does not qualify as a mental disorder. If it did, we would diagnose mental disorders in the most creative and visionary people—anyone whose ideas deviate from those of people around them.

So what *is* a mental disorder? Although there is no universal agreement on a precise definition, a **mental disorder** can be broadly defined as *a persistent disturbance or dysfunction in behavior, thoughts, or emotions that causes significant distress or impairment* (Stein et al., 2010; Wakefield, 2007). One way to think about mental disorders is as dysfunctions or deficits in the normal human psychological processes you have learned about throughout this textbook. People with mental disorders have problems with their perception, memory, learning, emotions, motivation, thinking, and social processes. Of course, this definition leaves many questions unanswered. What kinds of disturbances count as mental disorders? How long must they last to be considered "persistent"? And how much distress or impairment is required? These are all still hotly debated questions in the field.

Conceptualizing Mental Disorders

Since ancient times, there have been reports of people acting strangely or reporting bizarre thoughts or emotions. Until fairly recently, such difficulties were conceptualized as the result of religious or supernatural forces. In some cultures, psychopathology is still interpreted as possession by spirits or demons, as enchantment by a witch or shaman, or as God's punishment for wrongdoing. In many societies, including our own, people with psychological disorders have been feared and ridiculed, and often treated as criminals: punished, imprisoned, or put to death for their "crime" of deviating from what is considered to be normal. However, focusing solely on deviating from the norm is problematic, as deviations from the norm can be extremely helpful to society—such as the case with creativity, athleticism, and entertainment.

Over the past 200 years, these ways of looking at psychological abnormalities have largely been replaced in most parts of the world by a **medical model**, an *approach that conceptualizes abnormal psychological experiences as illnesses that, like physical illnesses, have biological and environmental causes, defined symptoms, and possible cures*. Conceptualizing abnormal thoughts and behaviors as illness suggests that a first step is to determine the nature of the problem through *diagnosis*.

In diagnosis, clinicians seek to determine the nature of a person's mental disorder by assessing *signs* (objectively observed indicators of a disorder) and *symptoms* (subjectively reported behaviors, thoughts, and emotions) that suggest an underlying illness. So, for example, just as self-reported sniffles and a cough are symptoms of a cold, Robin Williams's depressed mood and struggles to control his use of mind-altering substances can be seen as symptoms of his depressive and substance-use disorders. It is important to note the differences among three related general medical and classification terms:

- A *disorder* is a common set of signs and symptoms.
- A *disease* is a known pathological process affecting the body.
- A *diagnosis* is a determination as to whether a disorder or disease is present (Kraemer et al., 2007).

It is important to note that knowing that a disorder is present (i.e., diagnosed) does not necessarily mean that we know the underlying disease process in the body that gives rise to the signs and symptoms of the disorder.

Viewing mental disorders as medical problems reminds us that people who are suffering deserve care and treatment, not condemnation. Nevertheless, there are some criticisms of the medical model. Some psychologists argue that it is inappropriate to use clients' subjective self-reports, rather than physical tests of pathology (as in other areas of medical diagnostics), to determine underlying illness. Others argue that the model often "medicalizes" or "pathologizes" normal human behavior. For instance, extreme sadness can be considered to be an illness called *major depressive disorder,* extreme shyness can be diagnosed as an illness called *social anxiety disorder,* and trouble concentrating in school is called *attention-deficit/hyperactivity disorder.* Although there are some valid concerns about the current method of defining and classifying mental disorders, it is a huge advance over older alternatives, such as viewing mental disorders as the product of witchcraft or as punishment for sin.

Classifying Disorders: The *DSM*

So how is the medical model used to classify the wide range of abnormal behaviors that occur among humans? Most people working in the area of mental disorders use the **Diagnostic and Statistical Manual of Mental Disorders (DSM),** *a classification system that describes the symptoms used to diagnose each recognized mental disorder and indicates how the disorder can be distinguished from other, similar problems.* Each disorder is named and classified as a distinct illness. The initial version of the *DSM*, published in 1952, provided a common language for talking about disorders, although the diagnostic criteria were quite vague. Over the decades, revised editions of the *DSM* moved toward very detailed lists of symptoms (or *diagnostic criteria*) that had to be present for a disorder to be diagnosed. For instance, to be diagnosed with major depressive disorder, a person must report feeling extremely sad or depressed for at least 2 weeks, and must also have at least five of nine agreed-on symptoms of depression, such as diminished interest in normally enjoyable activities, significant weight loss or gain, loss of energy, feelings of worthlessness or guilt, and trouble concentrating. The use of these detailed lists of symptoms led to a dramatic increase in the reliability, or consistency, of diagnoses of mental disorders. Two clinicians interviewing the same individual were now much more likely to agree on what mental disorders were present, greatly increasing the credibility of the diagnostic process (and the fields of psychiatry and clinical psychology).

In May 2013, the American Psychiatric Association released the current version of the manual, the *DSM–5.* The *DSM–5* describes 22 major categories containing more than 200 different mental disorders (see **TABLE 14.1**).

Each of the 22 chapters in the main body of the *DSM–5* lists the specific criteria that must be met for a person to be diagnosed with each disorder. Studies of large,

Professional baseball player Zack Greinke was unable to play baseball in 2006, early in his professional career, due to social phobia. Fortunately, through effective treatment, he was able to return to the game and has gone on to a very successful professional career.
AP Photo/Eric Christian Smith

Diagnostic and Statistical Manual of Mental Disorders (DSM) A classification system that describes the features used to diagnose each recognized mental disorder and indicates how that disorder can be distinguished from other, similar problems.

TABLE 14.1 **Main _DSM–5_ Categories of Mental Disorders**
1. **Neurodevelopmental disorders:** These conditions begin early in development and cause significant impairments in functioning; they include intellectual disability (formerly called mental retardation), autism spectrum disorder (ASD), and attention-deficit/hyperactivity disorder (ADHD).
2. **Schizophrenia spectrum and other psychotic disorders:** This group of disorders is characterized by major disturbances in perception, thought, language, emotion, and behavior.
3. **Bipolar and related disorders:** These disorders include major fluctuations in mood—from mania to depression—and also can include psychotic experiences.
4. **Depressive disorders:** These conditions are characterized by extreme and persistent periods of depressed mood.
5. **Anxiety disorders:** These disorders are characterized by excessive fear and anxiety that are extreme enough to impair a person's functioning; they include panic disorder, generalized anxiety disorder, and specific phobias.
6. **Obsessive-compulsive and related disorders:** These conditions are characterized by the presence of obsessive thinking followed by compulsive behavior in response to that thinking.
7. **Trauma- and stressor-related disorders:** These disorders develop in response to a traumatic event, such as posttraumatic stress disorder.
8. **Dissociative disorders:** These conditions are characterized by disruptions to or discontinuities in consciousness, memory, or identity, such as dissociative identity disorder (formerly called multiple personality disorder).
9. **Somatic symptom and related disorders:** These are conditions in which a person experiences bodily symptoms (e.g., pain, fatigue) associated with significant distress or impairment.
10. **Feeding and eating disorders:** These are problems with eating such as anorexia nervosa and bulimia nervosa that impair health or functioning.
11. **Elimination disorders:** These involve inappropriate elimination of urine or feces (e.g., bedwetting).
12. **Sleep–wake disorders:** These are problems with the sleep–wake cycle, such as insomnia, narcolepsy, and sleep apnea.
13. **Sexual dysfunctions:** These are problems related to unsatisfactory sexual activity, such as erectile disorder and premature ejaculation.
14. **Gender dysphoria:** This is a disorder characterized by incongruence between a person's experienced/expressed gender and assigned gender.
15. **Disruptive, impulse-control, and conduct disorders:** These conditions involve problems controlling emotions and behaviors; they include conduct disorder, intermittent explosive disorder, and kleptomania.
16. **Substance-related and addictive disorders:** This collection of disorders involves persistent use of substances or some other behavior (e.g., gambling) despite the fact that it leads to significant problems.
17. **Neurocognitive disorders:** These are disorders of thinking caused by conditions such as Alzheimer's disease or traumatic brain injury.
18. **Personality disorders:** These are enduring patterns of thinking, feeling, and behaving that lead to significant life problems.
19. **Paraphilic disorders:** These conditions are characterized by inappropriate sexual activity, such as pedophilic disorder.
20. **Other mental disorders:** This is a residual category for conditions that do not fit into one of the aforementioned categories but are associated with significant distress or impairment (such as an unspecified mental disorder due to a medical condition).
21. **Medication-induced movement disorders and other adverse effects of medication:** These are problems with physical movement (e.g., tremors, rigidity) that are caused by medication.
22. **Other conditions that may be the focus of clinical attention:** These include disorders related to abuse, neglect, relationship, and other problems.

Information from _DSM–5_ (American Psychiatric Association, 2013).

DATA
Visualization

comorbidity The co-occurrence of two or more disorders in a single individual.

representative samples of the U.S. population reveal that approximately half of Americans report experiencing at least one mental disorder during the course of their lives (Kessler et al., 2005a). And most of those with a mental disorder (over 80%) report **comorbidity**, _the co-occurrence of two or more disorders in a single individual_ (Gadermann et al., 2012). (See also Data Visualization: Comorbidity: How Often Do Multiple Disorders Occur? at launchpadworks.com.)

The mental disorders that we see in the United States are also experienced by people around the world (see **FIGURE 14.1**). For instance, all over the globe, anxiety and mood disorders are always the most common, followed by impulse-control and substance

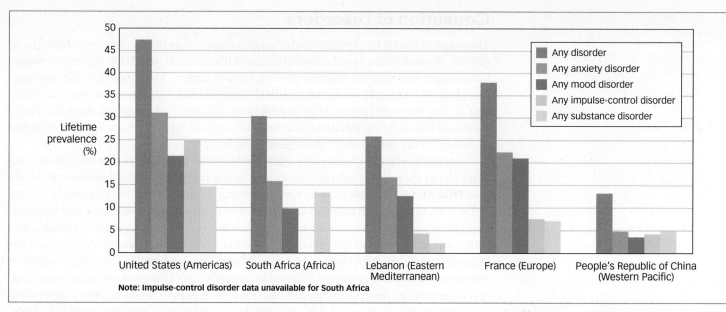

Note: Impulse-control disorder data unavailable for South Africa

Figure 14.1 Lifetime Prevalence of Mental Disorders Around the World
(Data from Kessler et al., 2007)

use disorders (Kessler et al., 2007). But although all countries appear to have common mental disorders, cultural context can influence how mental disorders are experienced, described, assessed, and treated (see A World of Difference: The Impact of Culture on Mental Disorders). To address this issue, the *DSM–5* includes a section devoted to helping the clinician understand how the client's culture might influence the experience, expression, and explanation of his or her mental disorder.

A WORLD OF DIFFERENCE

The Impact of Culture on Mental Disorders

Just as language, traditions, customs, and other factors differ across cultures, so does the manifestation of mental disorders. The disorders you will learn about in this chapter appear in every culture, but cultural factors often influence the way these disorders are experienced, talked about, and explained. The *DSM–5* provides a framework for thinking about differences in cultural concepts of distress. It distinguishes among three important concepts:

- *Cultural syndromes* are groups of symptoms that tend to cluster together in specific cultures. For instance, *taijin kyofusho* is a cultural syndrome seen in Japan that is a combination of two *DSM–5* conditions: social anxiety disorder (in which a person fears negative feedback from others) and body dysmorphic disorder (in which a person is preoccupied with perceived flaws in his or her own physical appearance).

- *Cultural idioms of distress* are ways of talking about or expressing distress that can differ across cultures. For instance, *kufungisisa*, or "thinking too much," is an idiom of distress in Zimbabwe that is associated with a number of depressive and anxiety disorders.

- *Cultural explanations* are culturally recognized descriptions of what causes the symptoms, distress, or disorder. For example, in many South Asian cultures, mental disorder is believed to be caused by the loss of *dhat* or *dhatu*, a white substance believed to be in the body and essential for health that can exit the body in the form of semen or during urination or defecation.

The cultural context in which we are living can have an impact on how we experience, talk about, and explain mental disorders. This is important to keep in mind when trying to understand mental disorders within your own

Taijin kyofusho is a Japanese syndrome in which people fear and avoid social contact due to the belief that they are inadequate or offensive in some way. This syndrome appears to be a combination of two *DSM–5* conditions: social anxiety disorder and body dysmorphic disorder. Arief Juwono/Getty Images

cultures, and also when trying to understand mental disorders among those from cultures other than your own.

Causation of Disorders

The medical model of mental disorder suggests that just as different viruses, bacteria, or genetic abnormalities cause different physical illnesses, a specifiable pattern of causes (or *etiology*) may exist for different psychological disorders. The medical model also suggests that each category of mental disorder is likely to have a common *prognosis,* a typical course over time and susceptibility to treatment and cure. Unfortunately, this basic medical model is usually an oversimplification; it is rarely useful to focus on a *single cause* that is *internal* to the person and that suggests a *single cure.*

Instead, most psychologists take a **biopsychosocial perspective** that *explains mental disorders as the result of interactions among biological, psychological, and social factors* (see **FIGURE 14.2a**). Biological factors promoting mental disorders can include genetic influences, biochemical imbalances, and abnormalities in brain structure and function. Psychological factors can include maladaptive learning and coping, cognitive biases, dysfunctional attitudes, and interpersonal problems. Social factors can include poor socialization, stressful life experiences, and cultural and social inequities. The large number of interacting factors suggests that different individuals can experience a similar psychological disorder (e.g., depression) for different reasons. A person might fall into a depression as a result of biological causes (e.g., genetics, hormones), psychological causes (e.g., faulty beliefs, hopelessness, poor strategies for coping with loss), environmental causes (e.g., stress or loneliness), or a combination of these factors. And, of course, multiple causes mean there may not be a single cure.

The observation that most disorders have both internal (biological/psychological) *and* external (environmental) causes has given rise to a theory known as the **diathesis–stress model**, which suggests that *a person may be predisposed to a psychological disorder that remains unexpressed until triggered by stress* (see **FIGURE 14.2b**). The diathesis is the internal predisposition, and the stress is the external trigger. For example, most people were able to cope with their strong emotional reactions to the terrorist attacks of September 11, 2001. However, for some who had a predisposition to negative emotions, the horror of the events may have overwhelmed their ability to cope, thereby precipitating a psychological disorder. Although diatheses can be inherited, it's important to remember that heritability is not destiny. A person who inherits a diathesis may never encounter the precipitating stress, whereas someone with little genetic propensity to a disorder may come to suffer from it, given the right pattern of stress.

biopsychosocial perspective Explains mental disorders as the result of interactions among biological, psychological, and social factors.

diathesis–stress model Suggests that a person may be predisposed to a psychological disorder that remains unexpressed until triggered by stress.

Figure 14.2 Proposed Models of How Mental Disorders Develop (a) The biopsychosocial model suggests that biological, psychological, and social factors all interact to produce mental health or mental illness. (b) The diathesis–stress model suggests that mental illness develops when a person who has some predisposition or vulnerability to mental illness (the "diathesis") experiences a major life stressor (the "stress").

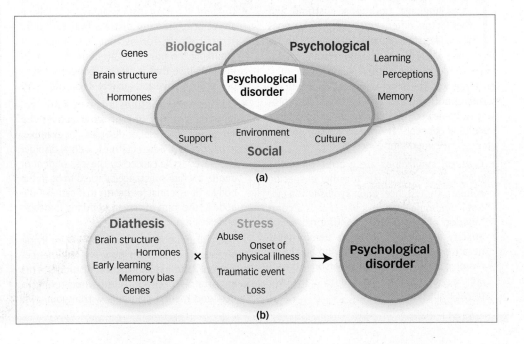

A New Approach to Understanding Mental Disorders: RDoC

Although the *DSM* provides a useful framework for classifying disorders, concern has been growing over the fact that the findings from scientific research on the biopsychosocial factors that appear to cause psychopathology do not map neatly onto individual *DSM* diagnoses. Researchers at the National Institute of Mental Health (NIMH) have proposed a new framework for thinking about mental disorders, focused not on the currently defined *DSM* categories but on the more basic biological, cognitive, and behavioral constructs that are believed to be the building blocks of mental disorders. This new system is called the **Research Domain Criteria Project (RDoC)**, *an initiative that aims to guide the classification and understanding of mental disorders by revealing the basic processes that give rise to them.* The RDoC is not intended to immediately replace the *DSM* but to inform future revisions to it in the coming years.

Using the RDoC, researchers study the causes of mental disorders by focusing on multiple levels of analysis that include biological factors from genes to cells to brain circuits; psychological domains, such as learning, attention, and memory; and social processes and behaviors. The RDoC approach aims to shift researchers' focus away from classifications based on surface symptoms and toward an understanding of the underlying processes that give rise to disordered behavior. For instance, rather than studying cocaine addiction as a distinct disorder, from the RDoC perspective researchers might try to understand what causes abnormalities in "responsiveness to reward" in those with excessive cocaine use as well as in those with other addictive behaviors. The basic idea is that some people seem to have trouble inhibiting their reward-seeking behavior, which in turn could predispose those people to develop addiction. Importantly, understanding what processes cause problems such as addiction will help us to develop more effective treatments, a topic we address in more detail in the Treatment chapter.

The Research Domain Criteria (RDoC) may help us understand why some people seem to have addictive personalities and have trouble limiting their engagement in pleasurable experiences. Fstop/Superstock

Dangers of Labeling

An important complication in the diagnosis and classification of psychological disorders is the effect of labeling. Psychiatric labels can have negative consequences because many carry the baggage of negative stereotypes and stigma, such as the idea that a mental disorder is a sign of personal weakness or the idea that all psychiatric patients are dangerous. The stigma associated with mental disorders may explain why most people with diagnosable psychological disorders (approximately 60%) do not seek treatment (Kessler et al., 2005c; Wang et al., 2005).

Unfortunately, educating people about mental disorders does not dispel the stigma borne by those with such conditions (Phelan et al., 1997). In fact, expectations created by psychiatric labels can sometimes even compromise the judgment of mental health professionals (Garb, 1998). In a classic demonstration of this phenomenon, researchers reported to different mental hospitals complaining of "hearing voices," a symptom sometimes found in people with schizophrenia. Each was admitted to a hospital, and each promptly reported that the symptom had ceased. Even so, hospital staff were reluctant to identify these people as normal: It took an average of 19 days for these "patients" to secure their release, and even then they were released with the diagnosis of "schizophrenia in remission" (Rosenhan, 1973). Apparently, once hospital staff had labeled these patients as having a psychological disease, the label stuck.

These effects of labeling are particularly disturbing in light of evidence that hospitalizing people with mental disorders is seldom necessary. One set of studies in Vermont followed the lives of patients who were thought to be too dangerous to release and therefore had been kept in institutions for years. Their release resulted in no harm to the community (Harding et al., 1987), and further studies have shown that those with a mental disorder are no more likely to be violent than those without a disorder (Elbogen & Johnson, 2009).

Although we label mental disorders, we should not apply those labels to people. For instance, rather than saying someone "is ADHD," we would say that the person currently meets diagnostic criteria for ADHD. Robin Nelson/Photo Edit

Research Domain Criteria Project (RDoC) An initiative that aims to guide the classification and understanding of mental disorders by revealing the basic processes that give rise to them.

Labeling may even affect how labeled individuals view themselves; persons given such a label may come to view themselves not just as mentally disordered but as hopeless or worthless. Such a view may cause them to develop an attitude of defeat and, as a result, to fail to work toward their own recovery. As one small step toward counteracting such consequences, clinicians have adopted the important practice of applying labels to the disorder, not to the person with the disorder. For example, an individual might be described as "a person with schizophrenia," not as "a schizophrenic." You'll notice that we follow this convention in this text.

Build to the Outcomes

1. What is a mental disorder?

2. How does the medical model explain abnormal behavior?

3. What is the first step in helping someone with a mental disorder?

4. What are the differences among disorder, disease, and diagnosis?

5. What is the *DSM*? How has it changed over time?

6. How do the biopsychosocial perspective and the diathesis–stress model explain disorders?

7. Why does assessment require looking at a number of factors?

8. What is the RDoC? How does it differ from the *DSM*?

9. Why might someone avoid seeking help for a disorder?

10. What are the dangers of labeling?

Anxiety Disorders: Excessive Fear, Anxiety, and Avoidance

Learning Outcomes

- Explain the major symptoms of anxiety disorders, including phobias, panic disorder, and GAD.

- Describe factors that contribute to phobias, panic disorder, and GAD.

"Okay, time for a pop quiz that will count for half your grade in this class." If your instructor said that, you would probably experience a wave of anxiety. Your reaction would not be a sign that you have a mental disorder. In fact, situation-related anxiety is normal and adaptive: in this case, perhaps by reminding you to keep up with your textbook assignments so you are prepared for pop quizzes. But when anxiety arises that is out of proportion to real threats and challenges, it is maladaptive: It can take hold of people's lives, stealing their peace of mind and undermining their ability to function normally. **Anxiety disorders** are *the class of mental disorders in which anxiety is the predominant feature.* People commonly experience more than one type of anxiety disorder at a given time, and there is significant comorbidity between anxiety and depression (Brown & Barlow, 2002; Jacobson & Newman, 2017). Among the anxiety disorders recognized in the *DSM-5* are phobic disorders, panic disorder, and generalized anxiety disorder.

Phobic Disorders

anxiety disorders The class of mental disorders in which anxiety is the predominant feature.

phobic disorders Disorders characterized by marked, persistent, and excessive fear and avoidance of specific objects, activities, or situations.

specific phobia A disorder that involves an irrational fear of a particular object or situation that markedly interferes with an individual's ability to function.

Mary, a 47-year-old mother of three, sought treatment for *claustrophobia*—an intense fear of enclosed spaces. She traced her fear to her childhood, when her older siblings would scare her by locking her in closets. She wanted to find a job but could not because of a terror of elevators and other confined places that, she felt, shackled her to her home (Carson et al., 2000). Many people feel a little anxious in enclosed spaces, but Mary's fears were abnormal and dysfunctional because they were disproportionate to any actual risk and impaired her ability to carry out a normal life. The *DSM-5* describes **phobic disorders** as characterized by *marked, persistent, and excessive fear and avoidance of specific objects, activities, or situations.* An individual with a phobic disorder recognizes that the fear is irrational but cannot prevent it from interfering with everyday functioning.

A **specific phobia** is *an irrational fear of a particular object or situation that markedly interferes with an individual's ability to function.* Specific phobias fall into five categories: (1) animals (e.g., dogs, cats, rats, snakes, spiders); (2) natural environments (e.g., heights, darkness, water, storms); (3) situations (e.g., bridges, elevators, tunnels, enclosed places);

(4) blood, injections, and injury; and (5) other phobias, including choking or vomiting, and in children, loud noises or costumed characters. Approximately 12% of people in the United States will develop a specific phobia during their lives (Kessler et al., 2005a), with rates slightly higher among women than men (Kessler et al., 2012).

Social phobia involves *an irrational fear of being publicly humiliated or embarrassed.* Social phobia can be restricted to situations—such as public speaking or eating in public—or can be generalized to a variety of social situations that involve being observed or interacting with unfamiliar people. Individuals with social phobia try to avoid situations where unfamiliar people might evaluate them, and they experience intense anxiety and distress when public exposure is unavoidable. Social phobia typically emerges between early adolescence and early adulthood (Kessler et al., 2005a). About 12% of men and 14% of women qualify for a diagnosis of social phobia at some time in their lives (Kessler et al., 2012).

Who Is at Risk?

Why are phobias so common? The high rates of both specific and social phobias suggest a predisposition to be fearful of certain objects and situations. Indeed, most of the situations and objects of people's phobias could pose a real threat, such as falling from a high place or being attacked by a vicious dog or a poisonous snake. A roomful of strangers could form impressions that affect your prospects for friends, jobs, or marriage. And of course, in some very rare cases, they could attack or bite.

Observations such as these are the basis for the **preparedness theory** of phobias, which maintains that *people are instinctively predisposed toward certain fears* (Seligman, 1971). The preparedness theory is supported by research showing that both humans and monkeys can quickly be conditioned to have a fear response for stimuli such as snakes and spiders, but not for neutral stimuli such as flowers or toy rabbits (Cook & Mineka, 1989). Phobias are particularly likely to form for objects that evolution has predisposed us to avoid.

Biological and Environmental Factors

Neurobiological factors may also play a role. For example, individuals with phobias often show abnormalities in the neurotransmitters serotonin and dopamine (Frick et al., 2015; Plavén-Sigray et al., 2017), and sometimes show abnormally high levels of activity in the amygdala, an area of the brain linked with emotional associations (discussed in the chapter on Emotion and Motivation). Interestingly, although people with social phobia report feeling much more distressed than those without social phobia during tasks involving

social phobia A disorder that involves an irrational fear of being publicly humiliated or embarrassed.

preparedness theory The idea that people are instinctively predisposed toward certain fears.

The preparedness theory explains why most merry-go-rounds carry children on beautiful horses. This mom might have some trouble getting her daughter to ride on a big spider or snake. Courtesy of Daniel Wegner

Some phobias may be learned through classical conditioning, in which a conditioned stimulus (CS) that is paired with an anxiety-evoking unconditioned stimulus (US) itself comes to elicit a conditioned fear response (CR). Suppose your friend has a phobia of dogs that is so intense that he is afraid to go outside in case his neighbors' dog barks at him. Applying the principles of classical conditioning you studied in the Learning chapter, how might you help him overcome his fear? Mathew Nock

panic disorder A disorder characterized by the sudden occurrence of multiple psychological and physiological symptoms that contribute to a feeling of stark terror.

agoraphobia A specific phobia involving a fear of public places.

social evaluation (such as giving a speech), they are actually no more physiologically aroused than others (Jamieson et al., 2013). This suggests that social phobia may be due to a person's subjective experience of the situation, rather than an abnormal physiological stress response to such situations.

This evidence does not rule out the influence of environments and upbringing on the development of phobic overreactions. As the learning theorist John Watson (1924) demonstrated many years ago, phobias can be classically conditioned (see the discussion of Little Albert and the white rat in the Learning chapter). Similarly, the discomfort of a dog bite could create a conditioned association between dogs and pain, resulting in an irrational fear of all dogs. The idea that phobias are learned from emotional experiences with feared objects, however, is not a complete explanation for the occurrence of phobias. Most studies find that people with phobias are no more likely than people without phobias to recall personal experiences with the feared object that could have provided the basis for classical conditioning (Craske, 1999; McNally & Steketee, 1985). Moreover, many people are bitten by dogs, but few develop phobias. Despite its shortcomings, however, the idea that phobias are a matter of learning provides a useful model for therapy (see the Treatment chapter).

Panic Disorder and Agoraphobia

Wesley, a 20-year-old college student, began having panic attacks with increasing frequency, often two or three times a day. The attacks would begin with a sudden wave of intense, terrifying fear that seemed to come out of nowhere, often accompanied by dizziness, a tightening of the chest, and the thought that he was going to pass out or possibly die. Wesley finally decided to seek treatment because he had begun to avoid buses, trains, and public places for fear that he would have an attack like this and not be able to escape.

Wesley's condition, called **panic disorder**, is characterized by *the sudden occurrence of multiple psychological and physiological symptoms that contribute to a feeling of stark terror.* The acute symptoms of a panic attack typically last only a few minutes and include shortness of breath, heart palpitations, sweating, dizziness, depersonalization (a feeling of being detached from one's body) or derealization (a feeling that the external world is strange or unreal), and a fear that one is going crazy or about to die. Not surprisingly, panic attacks often send people rushing to emergency departments or to their physicians' offices for what they believe are heart attacks. Unfortunately, because many of the symptoms mimic various medical disorders, a correct diagnosis may take years (Meuret et al., 2017). According to the *DSM–5* diagnostic criteria, a person has panic disorder only if he or she experiences recurrent unexpected attacks and reports significant anxiety about having another attack.

A disorder that sometimes co-occurs with panic disorder is **agoraphobia**, *a specific phobia involving a fear of public places.* Many people with agoraphobia, including Wesley, are not frightened of public places in themselves; instead, they are afraid that something terrible will happen (e.g., panic symptoms) while they are in a public place and that they will not be able to escape or get help. In severe cases, people who have agoraphobia are unable to leave home, sometimes for years.

Who Is at Risk?

Approximately 22% of the U.S. population reports having had at least one panic attack (Kessler et al., 2005b), typically during a period of intense stress (Telch et al., 1989). An occasional episode is not sufficient for a diagnosis of panic disorder: The individual also has to experience significant dread and anxiety about having another attack. When this criterion is applied, approximately 5% of people will have diagnosable panic disorder sometime in their lives (Kessler et al., 2005b). Panic disorder is more prevalent among women (7%) than men (3%) (Kessler et al., 2012).

Agoraphobia is the fear of being in public because something bad is going to happen and escape will not be possible. It may prevent a person from going outside at all.
Lolostock/Shutterstock

Biological Factors

People who experience panic attacks may be hypersensitive to physiological signs of anxiety, which they interpret as having disastrous consequences for their well-being. Thus, panic attacks may be conceptualized as a "fear of fear" itself. To test this idea, researchers compared the responses of participants with and without panic disorder to *sodium lactate,* a chemical that produces rapid, shallow breathing and heart palpitations—similar to the symptoms of a panic attack. Those with panic disorder were acutely sensitive to the chemical: Within a few minutes, 60 to 90% experienced a panic attack. In contrast, participants without panic disorder rarely responded to the drug with a panic attack.

Generalized Anxiety Disorder

Gina, a 24-year-old woman, began to experience debilitating anxiety during her 1st year of graduate school. At first, she worried about whether she was sufficiently completing all of her assignments. Soon her concerns spread to focus on her own health (Did she have an undiagnosed medical problem?) as well as that of her boyfriend (He smokes cigarettes . . . is he giving himself cancer?). She worried incessantly for a year and ultimately took time off from school to get treatment for her worries, extreme agitation, fatigue, and feelings of sadness and depression.

Gina's symptoms are typical of **generalized anxiety disorder (GAD)**—called *generalized* because the unrelenting worries are not focused on any particular threat; they are, in fact, often exaggerated and irrational. GAD is *chronic excessive worry accompanied by three or more of the following symptoms: restlessness, fatigue, concentration problems, irritability, muscle tension, and sleep disturbance.* In people suffering from GAD, the uncontrollable worrying produces a sense of loss of control that can so erode self-confidence that simple decisions seem fraught with dire consequences. For example, Gina struggled to make everyday decisions as basic as which vegetables to buy at the market and how to prepare her dinner.

Who Is at Risk?

Approximately 6% of people in the United States suffer from GAD at some time in their lives (Kessler et al., 2005a), with women experiencing GAD at higher rates (8%) than men (5%) (Kessler et al., 2012). Research suggests that both biological and psychological factors contribute to the risk of GAD.

generalized anxiety disorder (GAD)
A disorder characterized by chronic excessive worry accompanied by three or more of the following symptoms: restlessness, fatigue, concentration problems, irritability, muscle tension, and sleep disturbance.

Biological and Environmental Factors

Biological explanations of GAD suggest that neurotransmitter imbalances may play a role in the disorder, although the precise nature of this imbalance is not clear. Psychological explanations focus on anxiety-provoking situations in explaining high levels of GAD. The condition is especially prevalent among people who have low incomes, live in large cities, and/or face environments that are rendered unpredictable by political and economic strife. Unpredictable traumatic experiences in childhood increase the risk of developing GAD (Bandoli et al., 2017), as does the experience of a loss or situation associated with future perceived danger (Kendler et al., 2003), such as loss of a home due to foreclosure (McLaughlin et al., 2012). Still, many people who might be expected to develop GAD don't, supporting the diathesis–stress notion that personal vulnerability must also be a key factor in this disorder.

Build to the Outcomes

1. What is an anxiety disorder?
2. When is anxiety helpful? When is it harmful?
3. What is a phobic disorder? What are the different types?
4. Why might we be predisposed to certain phobias?
5. What is a panic disorder?
6. What is it about public places that many people with agoraphobia fear?
7. What is generalized anxiety disorder (GAD)? What factors contribute to it?

Obsessive-Compulsive Disorder: Persistent Thoughts and Repetitive Behaviors

Learning Outcome

• Describe the symptoms and potential causes of OCD.

You may have had an irresistible urge to go back to check whether you actually locked the door or turned off the oven, even when you're pretty sure that you did. Or you may have been unable to resist engaging in some superstitious behavior, such as not walking under a ladder or stepping on a crack. For some people, such thoughts and actions spiral out of control and become a serious problem.

Karen, a 34-year-old with four children, sought treatment after several months of experiencing intrusive, repetitive thoughts in which she imagined that one or more of her children was having a serious accident. In addition, an extensive series of protective counting rituals hampered her daily routine. For example, when grocery shopping, Karen had the feeling that if she selected the first item (say, a box of cereal) on a shelf, something terrible would happen to her oldest child. If she selected the second item, some unknown disaster would befall her second child, and so on for all four children. Her preoccupation with numbers extended to other activities: If she drank one cup of coffee, she felt compelled to drink four more to protect her children from harm. She acknowledged that her counting rituals were irrational, but she became extremely anxious when she tried to stop (Oltmanns et al., 1991).

Karen's symptoms are typical of **obsessive-compulsive disorder (OCD)**, in which *repetitive, intrusive thoughts (obsessions) and ritualistic behaviors (compulsions) designed to fend off those thoughts interfere significantly with an individual's functioning.* Anxiety plays a role in this disorder because the obsessive thoughts typically produce anxiety, and the compulsive behaviors are performed to reduce it. In OCD, these obsessions and compulsions are intense, frequent, and experienced as irrational and excessive. Attempts to cope with the obsessive thoughts by trying to suppress or ignore them are of little or no benefit. In fact (as discussed in the Consciousness chapter), thought suppression can backfire, increasing the frequency and intensity of the obsessive thoughts (Wegner, 1989; Wenzlaff & Wegner, 2000). Despite anxiety's role, *DSM–5* classifies OCD

obsessive-compulsive disorder (OCD) A disorder in which repetitive, intrusive thoughts (obsessions) and ritualistic behaviors (compulsions) designed to fend off those thoughts interfere significantly with an individual's functioning.

separately from anxiety disorders because researchers believe that this disorder has a distinct cause and is maintained via different neural circuitry in the brain than the anxiety disorders.

Who Is At Risk?

Although 28% of adults in the United States report experiencing obsessions or compulsions at some point in their lives (Ruscio et al., 2010), only 2% will develop actual OCD (Kessler et al., 2005a). Similar to anxiety disorders, rates of OCD are higher among women than men (Kessler et al., 2012). Compulsive behavior can vary considerably in intensity and frequency. For example, fear of contamination may lead to 15 minutes of hand washing in some individuals, whereas others may need to spend hours with disinfectants and extremely hot water, scrubbing their hands until they bleed.

Biological and Evolutionary Factors

The obsessions that plague individuals with OCD typically derive from concerns that could pose a real threat (such as contamination or disease), which supports preparedness theory. Thinking repeatedly about whether we've left a stove burner on when we leave the house makes sense, after all, if we want to return to a house that is not "well done." The concept of preparedness places OCD in the same evolutionary context as phobias (Szechtman & Woody, 2006). However, as with phobias, fears that may have served an evolutionary purpose become distorted and maladaptive.

OCD has been recognized by clinicians for more than 200 years, but the precise biological mechanisms driving this behavior have eluded scientific understanding (Stone, 1997). Brain-imaging research over the past few decades suggests that one key component is abnormally high activity or connectedness in a specific brain circuit involved in habitual behavior: the cortico-striato-thalamo-cortical loop (which connects parts of the cortex with the striatum and thalamus) (Dougherty et al., 2018; Milad & Rauch, 2012). Treatments for OCD that decrease the activity of this brain circuit have shown some promise, but they are still being developed and tested (see the Treatment chapter for more on these approaches).

Howie Mandel is a successful comedian, but his struggle with OCD is no laughing matter. Mandel struggles with extreme fears of being contaminated by germs and engages in repeated checking and cleaning behaviors that often interfere with his daily life. He has spoken publicly about his struggles with OCD and about the importance of seeking effective treatment for this condition. Charles Sykes/ AP Images

Build to the Outcomes

1. What is obsessive-compulsive disorder (OCD)?
2. How effective is willful effort in curing OCD?

3. What factors may contribute to OCD?

Posttraumatic Stress Disorder: Distress and Avoidance After a Trauma

Psychological reactions to traumatic or stressful events can lead to stressor-related disorders. For example, a person who lives through a terrifying and uncontrollable experience may develop **posttraumatic stress disorder (PTSD)**, which is characterized by *chronic physiological arousal, recurrent unwanted thoughts or images of the trauma, and avoidance of things that call the traumatic event to mind.*

Who Is At Risk?

Psychological disorders following exposure to traumatic events are perhaps nowhere more apparent than in war. Many soldiers returning from combat experience symptoms of PTSD, including flashbacks of battle, exaggerated anxiety, and startle reactions. Most of these symptoms are normal, appropriate responses to horrifying events, and for most

Learning Outcome

• Describe the symptoms and potential causes of PTSD.

posttraumatic stress disorder (PTSD)
A disorder characterized by chronic physiological arousal, recurrent unwanted thoughts or images of the trauma, and avoidance of things that call the traumatic event to mind.

The traumatic events of war leave many debilitated by PTSD. But PTSD does not leave any visible wounds, so it can be difficult to diagnose with certainty. Because of this, the Pentagon has determined that psychological casualties of war are not eligible for the Purple Heart—the hallowed medal given to those wounded or killed in action (Alvarez & Eckholm, 2009). Jim Barber/Shutterstock

people, the symptoms subside with time. In PTSD, however, the symptoms can last much longer. For example, approximately 12% of U.S. veterans of recent operations in Iraq met the criteria for PTSD after their deployment; and the observed rates of PTSD are even higher in non-Western and developing countries (Keane et al., 2006). The effects of PTSD are now recognized not only among victims, witnesses, and perpetrators of war but also among ordinary people who are traumatized by terrible events in civilian life. At some time over the course of their lives, about 7% of Americans are estimated to suffer from PTSD (Kessler et al., 2005a).

Biological and Environmental Factors

Not everyone who is exposed to a traumatic event develops PTSD, suggesting that people differ in their degree of sensitivity to trauma. Research using brain-imaging techniques has found that those with PTSD show heightened activity in the amygdala (a region associated with the evaluation of threatening information and fear conditioning), decreased activity in the medial prefrontal cortex (a region important in the extinction of fear conditioning), and a smaller-size hippocampus (the part of the brain most linked with memory, as described in the Neuroscience and Behavior and Memory chapters) (Shin et al., 2006).

Of course, an important question is whether people whose brains have these characteristics are at greater risk for PTSD if traumatized, or if these characteristics are the consequences of trauma in some people. For instance, does reduced hippocampal volume reflect a preexisting condition that makes the brain sensitive to stress? Or does the traumatic stress itself somehow kill hippocampal cells? One important study suggests that although a group of combat veterans with PTSD showed reduced hippocampal volume, so did the identical (monozygotic) twins of those men (see **FIGURE 14.3**), even though the twins had never had any combat exposure or developed PTSD (Gilbertson et al., 2002). This suggests that the veterans' reduced hippocampal volumes weren't caused by the combat exposure; instead, both these veterans and their twin brothers might have had a smaller hippocampus to begin with, a preexisting condition that made them susceptible to developing PTSD when they were later exposed to trauma.

Figure 14.3 Hippocampal Volumes of Vietnam Veterans and Their Identical Twins Average hippocampal volumes for (1) combat-exposed veterans who developed PTSD and (2) their combat-unexposed twins with no PTSD were smaller than in (3) combat-exposed veterans who never developed PTSD and (4) their unexposed twins with no PTSD. These findings suggest that an inherited smaller hippocampus may make some people sensitive to conditions that cause PTSD (Gilbertson et al., 2002).

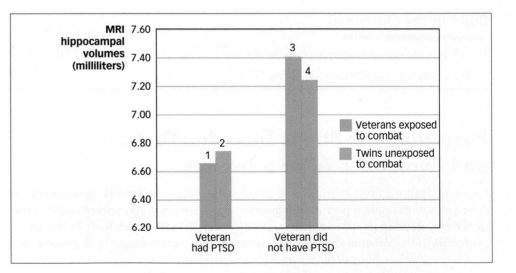

Build to the Outcomes

1. What is posttraumatic stress disorder (PTSD)?

2. How might brain structure and functioning be related to susceptibility to PTSD?

Depressive and Bipolar Disorders: Extreme Highs and Lows

You're probably in a mood right now. Maybe you're happy that it's almost time to get a snack or saddened by something you heard from a friend—or you may feel good or bad without having a clue why. As you learned in the Emotion and Motivation chapter, moods are relatively long-lasting, nonspecific emotional states—and *nonspecific* means we often may have no idea what has caused a mood. Changing moods lend variety to our experiences, like different-colored lights shining on the stage as we play out our lives. However, for people like Robin Williams and others with mood disorders, moods can become so intense that they are pulled or pushed into life-threatening actions. **Mood disorders** are *mental disorders that have mood disturbance as their predominant feature* and take two main forms: *depression* (also called *unipolar depression*) and *bipolar disorder* (so named because people go from one end of the emotional pole [extreme depression] to the other [extreme mania]).

Depressive Disorders

Everyone feels sad, pessimistic, and unmotivated from time to time. For most people, these periods are relatively short lived and mild, but depression is much more than typical sadness. Consider Mark, a 34-year-old man who visited his primary-care physician complaining of difficulties falling asleep and staying asleep that left him chronically tired, so much so that he feared that maybe he had some kind of medical problem. He no longer had the energy to exercise and had gained 10 pounds. He also lost all interest in going out with his friends. Nothing he normally enjoyed, even sexual activity, gave him pleasure anymore; he had trouble concentrating and was forgetful, irritable, impatient, and frustrated. Mark's change in mood and behavior, and the sense of hopelessness and weariness he felt, go far beyond normal sadness. Instead, depressive disorders fall outside the range of socially or culturally expected responses.

Major depressive disorder (or **unipolar depression**), which we refer to here simply as "depression," is characterized by *a severely depressed mood and/or inability to experience pleasure that lasts 2 or more weeks and is accompanied by feelings of worthlessness, lethargy, and sleep and appetite disturbance.* Some people experience **seasonal affective disorder (SAD)**, *recurrent depressive episodes in a seasonal pattern.* In most cases,

mood disorders Mental disorders that have mood disturbance as their predominant feature.

major depressive disorder (unipolar depression) A disorder characterized by a severely depressed mood and/or inability to experience pleasure that lasts 2 or more weeks and is accompanied by feelings of worthlessness, lethargy, and sleep and appetite disturbance.

seasonal affective disorder (SAD) Recurrent depressive episodes in a seasonal pattern.

Seasonal affective disorder is not merely having the blues because of the weather. It appears to be due to reduced exposure to light in the winter months. Ragnar TH Sigurdsson/Arctic Images/Alamy; Andrey Arkusha/Shutterstock

Postpartum depression can strike women out of nowhere, often causing new mothers to feel extreme sadness, guilt, and disconnection, and even to experience serious thoughts of suicide. The actress Brooke Shields wrote about her experience with postpartum depression in a popular book on this condition. Nancy Kaszerman/ZUMA Press/Newscom

SAD episodes begin in fall or winter and remit in spring, in a pattern that is due to reduced levels of light over the colder seasons (Westrin & Lam, 2007). Nevertheless, recurrent summer depressive episodes have been reported. A winter-related pattern of depression appears to be more prevalent in higher latitudes.

Who Is at Risk?

Approximately 18% of people in the United States meet the criteria for depression at some point in their lives (Kessler et al., 2012). On average, major depression lasts about 12 weeks (Eaton et al., 2008). However, without treatment, approximately 80% of individuals will experience at least one recurrence of the disorder (Judd, 1997; Mueller et al., 1999).

Similar to that of anxiety disorders, the rate of depression is much higher in women (22%) than in men (14%) (Kessler et al., 2012). Socioeconomic standing has been invoked as an explanation for women's heightened risk: Their incomes are lower than those of men, and poverty could cause depression. Sex differences in hormones are another possibility: Estrogen, androgen, and progesterone influence depression; some women experience *postpartum depression* (depression following childbirth) due to changing hormone levels. It is also possible that the higher rate of depression in women reflects their greater willingness to face their depression and seek help, leading to higher rates of diagnosis (Nolen-Hoeksema, 2012).

Biological Factors

Beginning in the 1950s, researchers noticed that drugs that increased levels of the neurotransmitters norepinephrine and serotonin could sometimes reduce depression. This observation suggested that depression might be caused by a depletion of these neurotransmitters (Schildkraut, 1965), which led to the development and widespread use of popular prescription drugs such as Prozac and Zoloft, which increase the availability of serotonin in the brain. However, reduced levels of these neurotransmitters cannot be the whole story regarding the causes of depression. For example, some studies have found *increases* in norepinephrine activity among depressed individuals (Thase & Howland, 1995). Moreover, even though these antidepressant medications change neurochemical transmission in less than a day, they typically take at least 2 weeks to relieve depressive symptoms. In many cases, they are not effective in decreasing depressive symptoms. A biochemical model of depression has yet to be developed that accounts for all the evidence.

Nevertheless, research has begun to tell us what parts of the brain show abnormalities in depression. For instance, a recent review of 24 brain-imaging studies concluded that when viewing negative stimuli (words or images), people suffering from depression show both increased activity in regions of the brain associated with processing emotional information and decreased activity in areas associated with cognitive control (see **FIGURE 14.4**) (Hamilton et al., 2012). Given that depression arises from the interactions of many biological systems that each give rise to the different psychological traits seen in depression, it will likely be many years before we fully understand the biological causes of this disorder (Young et al., 2016).

Negative Thoughts Contribute to Depression

If optimists see the world through rose-colored glasses, people who suffer from depression tend to view the world through dark gray lenses. Their negative cognitive style is remarkably consistent and, some argue, begins in childhood with experiences that create a pattern of negative self-thoughts (Blatt & Homann, 1992; Gibb et al., 2001). Aaron T. Beck (1967), one of the first theorists to emphasize the role of thought in depression, noted that his depressed patients distorted perceptions of their experiences and embraced dysfunctional attitudes that promoted and maintained negative mood states.

Figure 14.4 The Brain and Depression
When presented with negative information, people with depression show increased activation in regions of the brain associated with emotional processing, such as the amygdala, insula, and dorsal anterior cingulate cortex (ACC), and decreased activity in regions associated with cognitive control such as the dorsal striatum and dorsolateral prefrontal cortex (DLPFC) (Hamilton et al., 2012).

Structure	Direction of Effect
A) amygdala	increased in MDD
B) dorsal anterior cingulate cortex	increased in MDD
C) insula and superior temporal gyrus	increased in MDD
D) dorsolateral prefrontal cortex	decreased in MDD
E) caudate body	decreased in MDD

His observations led him to develop a *cognitive model of depression,* which states that biases in how information is attended to, processed, and remembered lead to and maintain depression.

Elaborating on this initial idea, researchers proposed a theory of depression that emphasizes the role of people's negative inferences about the causes of their experiences (Abramson et al., 1978). **Helplessness theory** maintains that *individuals who are prone to depression automatically attribute negative experiences to causes that are internal (i.e., their own fault), stable (i.e., unlikely to change), and global (i.e., widespread).* For example, a student at risk for depression might view a bad grade on a math test as a sign of low intelligence (internal) that will never change (stable) and that will lead to failure in all his or her future endeavors (global). In contrast, a student without this tendency might have the opposite response, attributing the grade to something external (poor teaching), unstable (a missed study session), and/or specific (boring subject).

More recent research suggests that people with depression may have biases to interpret neutral information negatively (seeing the world through gray glasses), coupled with better recall of negative information and trouble turning their attention away from negative information (Gotlib & Joormann, 2010). For example, a student at risk for depression who gets a bad grade on a test might interpret a well-intentioned comment from the teacher ("Good job on the test") negatively ("She's being sarcastic!"); might have trouble forgetting about both the test score and the perceived negative comment; and might have better memory about this test in the future ("Sure, I did well on my English exam, but don't forget about that bad math test last month"). These cognitive biases may reflect differences in brain structure and function. For instance, people with depression show abnormalities in parts of the brain that are involved in attention and memory, especially when presented with negative information (Disner et al., 2011). Although we don't fully understand the causes of depression, pieces of the puzzle are being discovered and fit together even as you read this.

Bipolar Disorder

Julie, a 20-year-old college sophomore, had gone 5 days without sleep and was expressing bizarre thoughts and ideas. She proclaimed to friends that she did not menstruate because she was "of a third sex, a gender above the two human sexes." She claimed to be a "superwoman," capable of avoiding human sexuality and yet still able to give birth.

The cognitive model of depression is based on approaches to thinking developed by the Stoic philosophers of ancient Greece and Rome. Epictetus' famous quote "Men are disturbed not by things, but by the principles and notions which they form concerning things" is commonly cited by cognitive theorists as a guiding principle of the cognitive model of depression.   Mary Evans Picture Library/Alamy

helplessness theory The idea that individuals who are prone to depression automatically attribute negative experiences to causes that are internal (i.e., their own fault), stable (i.e., unlikely to change), and global (i.e., widespread).

The psychologist Kay Redfield Jamison has written several best-selling books about her own struggles with bipolar disorder. Leonardo Cendamo/Getty Images

She felt that she could save the world from nuclear destruction, and began to campaign for an elected position in the U.S. government (even though no elections were scheduled at that time). Worried that she would forget some of her thoughts, she had been leaving hundreds of notes about her ideas and activities everywhere, including on the walls and furniture of her dormitory room (Vitkus, 1999).

In addition to her manic episodes, Julie had a history of depression. The diagnostic label for this constellation of symptoms is **bipolar disorder**, *a condition characterized by cycles of abnormal, persistent high mood (mania) and low mood (depression)*. In about two-thirds of people with bipolar disorder, manic episodes immediately precede or immediately follow depressive episodes (Whybrow, 1997). The depressive phase of bipolar disorder is often clinically indistinguishable from major depression (Johnson et al., 2009). In the manic phase, which must last at least 1 week to meet *DSM* requirements, mood can be elevated, expansive, or irritable. Other prominent symptoms include grandiosity, decreased need for sleep, talkativeness, racing thoughts, distractibility, and reckless behavior (such as compulsive gambling, sexual indiscretions, and unrestrained spending sprees). Psychotic features such as hallucinations (erroneous perceptions) and delusions (erroneous beliefs) may be present, so the disorder can be misdiagnosed as schizophrenia (described in a later section of this chapter).

Who Is at Risk?

The lifetime risk for bipolar disorder is about 2.5% and does not differ between men and women (Kessler et al., 2012). Unfortunately, bipolar disorder tends to be persistent. In one study, 24% of the participants had relapsed within 6 months of recovery from an episode, and 77% had at least one new episode within 4 years of recovery (Coryell et al., 1995).

Some researchers have suggested that people with psychotic and mood (especially bipolar) disorders have higher creativity and intellectual ability (Andreasen, 2011). In bipolar disorder, this suggestion goes, before the mania becomes too pronounced, the energy, grandiosity, and ambition that it supplies may help people achieve great things. Notable individuals thought to have had bipolar disorder include Isaac Newton, Vincent van Gogh, Abraham Lincoln, Ernest Hemingway, Winston Churchill, and Theodore Roosevelt.

Biological and Environmental Factors

Like most other mental disorders, bipolar disorder likely arises from the interaction of multiple genes; however, these genes have been difficult to identify. Adding to the complexity, there is evidence that genetic risk factors for bipolar disorder are also associated with vulnerability for schizophrenia, as well as major depression, autism spectrum disorder, and attention-deficit/hyperactivity disorder. These disorders all share overlapping symptoms such as problems with mood regulation, cognitive impairments, and social withdrawal (Cross-Disorder Group of the Psychiatric Genomics Consortium, 2013). Findings like these are exciting because they help us begin to understand why we see similar symptoms in people with what we previously thought were unrelated disorders. Although some genetic links have been made, we currently lack an understanding of how different biological factors work together to cause the symptoms observed in bipolar and other disorders.

There is growing evidence that epigenetic changes (which you learned about in the Neuroscience and Behavior chapter) can help explain how genetic risk factors influence the development of bipolar and related disorders. Remember how rat pups whose moms spent less time licking and grooming them experienced epigenetic changes that led to a poorer stress response? Epigenetic effects also seem to help explain who develops symptoms of mental disorders and who doesn't. For instance, studies examining identical (monozygotic) twin pairs (who share 100% of their DNA), where one twin develops bipolar disorder or schizophrenia and the other twin doesn't, reveal significant epigenetic

bipolar disorder A condition characterized by cycles of abnormal, persistent high mood (mania) and low mood (depression).

differences between the two, particularly at genetic locations known to be important in brain development and the occurrence of bipolar disorders and schizophrenia (Dempster et al., 2011; Labrie et al., 2012).

Stressful life experiences often precede manic and depressive episodes (S. L. Johnson et al., 2008). One study found that severely stressed individuals took an average of three times longer to recover from an episode than did individuals not affected by stress (Johnson & Miller, 1997). Personality characteristics such as neuroticism and conscientiousness also predict increases in bipolar symptoms over time (Lozano & Johnson, 2001). Finally, people living with family members who express hostility and criticism when speaking about the individual with the mental disorder are more likely to relapse, compared to people with supportive families (Miklowitz & Johnson, 2006). This is true not just of those with bipolar disorder, but across a wide range of mental disorders (Hooley, 2007).

Build to the Outcomes

1. What is a mood disorder?
2. What is the difference between depression and sadness?
3. What are the types of depressive disorders?
4. What factors may explain why women experience higher rates of depression than men?
5. What is the helplessness theory of depression?
6. What is bipolar disorder?
7. Why is bipolar disorder sometimes misdiagnosed as schizophrenia?
8. How does stress relate to manic-depressive episodes?

Schizophrenia and Other Psychotic Disorders: Losing the Grasp on Reality

Margaret, a 39-year-old mother, believed that God was punishing her for marrying a man she did not love and bringing two children into the world. As her punishment, God had made her and her children immortal so that they would have to suffer in their unhappy home life forever—a realization that came to her one evening when she was washing dishes and saw a fork lying across a knife in the shape of a cross. A local television station was rerunning old episodes of a sitcom in which the main characters often argue and shout at each other; Margaret saw this as a sign from God that her own marital conflict would go on forever. She believed (falsely) that the pupils of her children's eyes were fixed in size and would neither dilate nor constrict—a sign of their immortality.

Margaret was suffering from the best-known, most widely studied psychotic disorder: **schizophrenia**, *a psychotic disorder* (*psychosis* is a break from reality) *characterized by the profound disruption of basic psychological processes; a distorted perception of reality; altered or blunted emotion; and disturbances in thought, motivation, and behavior.* To be diagnosed with schizophrenia, the *DSM-5* requires that two or more symptoms emerge during a period of at least 1 month, and that signs of the disorder persist for at least 6 months.

Symptoms of Schizophrenia

The symptoms of schizophrenia often are separated into *positive, negative,* and *cognitive symptoms.*

Positive symptoms of schizophrenia include *thoughts and behaviors, such as delusions and hallucinations, not seen in those without the disorder:*

- **Hallucinations** are *false perceptual experiences that have a compelling sense of being real despite the absence of external stimulation.* The perceptual disturbances

Learning Outcomes

- Compare the negative, positive, and cognitive symptoms of schizophrenia.
- Describe the biological factors contributing to schizophrenia.
- Explain the evidence for the influence of environmental factors.

schizophrenia A disorder characterized by the profound disruption of basic psychological processes; a distorted perception of reality; altered or blunted emotion; and disturbances in thought, motivation, and behavior.

positive symptoms Thoughts and behaviors, such as delusions and hallucinations, present in schizophrenia but not seen in those without the disorder.

hallucination A false perceptual experience that has a compelling sense of being real despite the absence of external stimulation.

Those suffering from schizophrenia often experience hallucinations and delusions, and they are unable to determine what is real and what their own minds have created. The experience of John Nash, a Nobel Prize–winning economist with schizophrenia, was depicted in the book and movie *A Beautiful Mind.* Eli Reed/Dreamworks/Universal/Kobal/Shutterstock

delusion A false belief, often bizarre and grandiose, that is maintained in spite of its irrationality.

disorganized speech A severe disruption of verbal communication in which ideas shift rapidly and incoherently among unrelated topics.

grossly disorganized behavior Behavior that is inappropriate for the situation or ineffective in attaining goals, often with specific motor disturbances.

catatonic behavior A marked decrease in all movement or an increase in muscular rigidity and overactivity.

negative symptoms Deficits in or disruptions of normal emotions and behaviors (e.g., emotional and social withdrawal; apathy; poverty of speech; and other indications of the absence or insufficiency of normal behavior, motivation, and emotion) that are present in those with schizophrenia.

cognitive symptoms Deficits in cognitive abilities, specifically executive functioning, attention, and working memory, present in those with schizophrenia.

associated with schizophrenia can include hearing, seeing, smelling, or having a tactile sensation of things that are not there. Some 65% of people with schizophrenia report hearing voices repeatedly (Frith & Fletcher, 1995). The voices typically command, scold, suggest bizarre actions, or offer snide comments.

- **Delusions** are *false beliefs, often bizarre and grandiose, that are maintained in spite of their irrationality.* For example, an individual with schizophrenia may believe that he or she is Jesus Christ, Napoleon, Joan of Arc, or some other well-known person. Delusions of persecution are also common. Some individuals believe that the CIA, demons, extraterrestrials, or other malevolent forces are conspiring to harm them or control their minds, which may represent an attempt to make sense of the tormenting delusions (Roberts, 1991).

- **Disorganized speech** is *a severe disruption of verbal communication in which ideas shift rapidly and incoherently among unrelated topics.* The abnormal speech patterns in schizophrenia reflect difficulties in organizing thoughts and focusing attention. For example, asked by her doctor, "Can you tell me the name of this place?" one patient with schizophrenia responded, "I have not been a drinker for 16 years. I am taking a mental rest after a 'carter' assignment of 'quill.' You know, a 'penwrap.' I had contracts with Warner Brothers Studios and Eugene broke phonograph records but Mike protested" (Carson et al., 2000, p. 474).

- **Grossly disorganized behavior** is *behavior that is inappropriate for the situation or ineffective in attaining goals,* often with specific motor disturbances. An individual might exhibit constant childlike silliness, improper sexual behavior (such as masturbating in public), disheveled appearance, or loud shouting or swearing. Specific motor disturbances might include strange movements, rigid posturing, odd mannerisms, bizarre grimacing, or hyperactivity.

- **Catatonic behavior** is *a marked decrease in all movement or an increase in muscular rigidity and overactivity.* Individuals with catatonia may actively resist movement (when someone is trying to move them) or become completely unresponsive and unaware of their surroundings, in a stupor. In addition, individuals receiving drug therapy may exhibit motor symptoms (such as rigidity or spasm) as a side effect of the medications of the sort commonly used to treat schizophrenia.

Negative symptoms are *deficits in or disruptions of normal emotions and behaviors.* These include emotional and social withdrawal; apathy; poverty of speech; and other indications of the absence or insufficiency of normal behavior, motivation, and emotion. Whereas positive symptoms are "added" in individuals with schizophrenia, negative symptoms refer to things that are missing (or reduced) in people with schizophrenia.

Cognitive symptoms are *deficits in cognitive abilities, specifically in executive functioning, attention, and working memory.* These are the least noticeable symptoms because they are much less bizarre and public than the positive and negative symptoms. However, these cognitive deficits often play a large role in preventing people with schizophrenia from achieving a high level of functioning, such as maintaining friendships and holding down a job (Green et al., 2000).

Who Is at Risk?

Schizophrenia occurs in about 0.5% of the population (Simeone et al., 2015) and is slightly more common in men than in women (McGrath et al., 2008). Schizophrenia rarely develops before early adolescence (Rapoport et al., 2009). Despite its relatively low frequency, people with schizophrenia are overrepresented among psychiatric inpatients and have inpatient hospital stays that are significantly longer than those for other psychiatric patients (Chen et al., 2017). The disproportionate rate and length of hospitalization for schizophrenia is a testament to the devastation it causes in people's lives.

Many people with this disorder experience a lifetime of suffering and impairment, but see Other Voices: Successful and Schizophrenic for a discussion of the fact that many with this disorder have very successful careers and fulfilling lives.

Biological Factors

Genetic factors play a strong role in schizophrenia. Family studies indicate that the closer a person's genetic relatedness to someone with schizophrenia, the greater his or her likelihood of developing the disorder (Gottesman, 1991). For example, as shown in **FIGURE 14.5,** the identical twin of someone with schizophrenia has a higher risk of developing the disorder, compared with someone whose dizygotic twin, or other sibling, has the disorder (Hilker et al., 2018).

A major breakthrough came in the 1950s, when researchers discovered drugs that could reduce the symptoms of schizophrenia by lowering levels of the neurotransmitter dopamine. This finding suggested the **dopamine hypothesis,** *the idea that schizophrenia involves an excess of dopamine activity.* The hypothesis has been invoked to explain why amphetamines, which increase dopamine levels, often exacerbate symptoms of schizophrenia (Harro, 2015).

If only things were so simple. Considerable evidence suggests that this hypothesis is inadequate (Moncrieff, 2009). For example, many individuals with schizophrenia do not respond favorably to dopamine-blocking drugs, and those who do respond seldom show a complete remission of symptoms. Moreover, the drugs block dopamine receptors very rapidly, yet individuals with schizophrenia typically do not show a beneficial response for weeks. Finally, research has implicated other neurotransmitters in schizophrenia, suggesting that the disorder may involve a complex interaction among a host of different biochemicals (Risman et al., 2008; Sawa & Snyder, 2002). In sum, the precise role of neurotransmitters in schizophrenia has yet to be determined.

Finally, neuroimaging studies provide evidence of a variety of brain abnormalities associated with schizophrenia. One study examined the brains of adolescents with schizophrenia (Thompson et al., 2001). By superimposing the adolescents' brain scans onto an image of a standardized brain, the researchers were able to detect progressive tissue loss beginning in the parietal lobe and eventually encompassing much of the

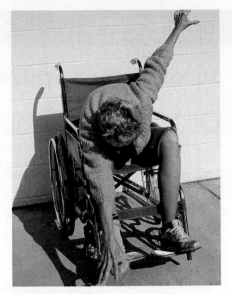

A person suffering from catatonic schizophrenia may assume an unusual posture and fail to move for hours. Grunnitus Studio/Science Source

dopamine hypothesis The idea that schizophrenia involves an excess of dopamine activity.

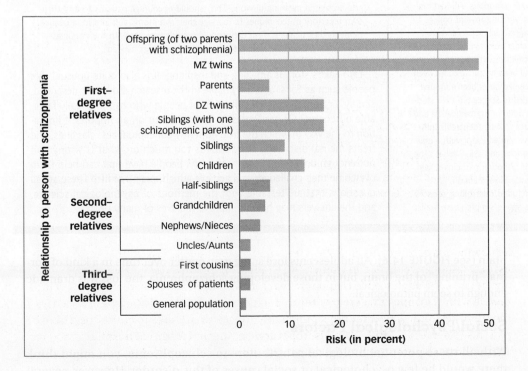

Figure 14.5 Average Risk of Developing Schizophrenia The risk of schizophrenia among biological relatives is greater for those with greater degrees of relatedness. For example, an identical (monozygotic, MZ) twin of a person with schizophrenia has a higher risk of developing schizophrenia, compared with a fraternal (dizygotic, DZ) twin or other sibling. Offspring of two parents with schizophrenia have a higher risk of developing this disorder, compared to those having only one parent, or other more distant relatives such as aunts and uncles, with the disorder (data from Gottesman, 1991).

Successful and Schizophrenic

People diagnosed with schizophrenia often are informed that it is a lifelong condition; and although current treatments show some effectiveness in decreasing the delusional thinking and hallucinations often associated with schizophrenia, people with this disorder often are unable to hold down a full-time job, maintain healthy relationships, or achieve a high quality of life.

Elyn Saks received a diagnosis of schizophrenia and was informed of this prognosis. She described what happened next in a longer version of the following article, which appeared in the *New York Times*.

Thirty years ago, I was given a diagnosis of schizophrenia. My prognosis was "grave": I would never live independently, hold a job, find a loving partner, get married. My home would be a board-and-care facility, my days spent watching TV in a day room with other people debilitated by mental illness. . . .

Then I made a decision. I would write the narrative of my life. Today I am a chaired professor at the University of Southern California Gould School of Law. I have an adjunct appointment in the department of psychiatry at the medical school of the University of California, San Diego. The MacArthur Foundation gave me a genius grant.

Although I fought my diagnosis for many years, I came to accept that I have schizophrenia and will be in treatment the rest of my life. . . . What I refused to accept was my prognosis.

Conventional psychiatric thinking and its diagnostic categories say that people like me don't exist. Either I don't have schizophrenia (please tell that to the delusions crowding my mind), or I couldn't have accomplished what I have (please tell that to U.S.C.'s committee on faculty affairs). But I do, and I have. And I have undertaken research with colleagues at U.S.C. and U.C.L.A. to show that I am not alone. There are others with schizophrenia and such active symptoms as delusions and hallucinations who have significant academic and professional achievements.

Over the last few years, my colleagues . . . and I have gathered 20 research subjects with high-functioning schizophrenia in Los Angeles. They suffered from symptoms like mild delusions or hallucinatory behavior. Their average age was 40. Half were male, half female, and more than half were minorities. All had high school diplomas, and a majority either had or were working toward college or graduate degrees. They were graduate students, managers, technicians and professionals, including a doctor, lawyer, psychologist and chief executive of a nonprofit group. At the same time, most were unmarried and childless, which is consistent with their diagnoses. . . . More than three-quarters had been hospitalized between two and five times because of their illness, while three had never been admitted.

How had these people with schizophrenia managed to succeed in their studies and at such high-level jobs? We learned that, in addition to medication and therapy, all the participants had developed techniques to keep their schizophrenia at bay. For some, these techniques were cognitive. An educator with a master's degree said he had learned to face his hallucinations and ask, "What's the evidence for that? Or is it just a perception problem?" Another participant said, "I hear derogatory voices all the time. . . . You just gotta blow them off." . . .

Other techniques that our participants cited included controlling sensory inputs. For some, this meant keeping their living space simple (bare walls,

no TV, only quiet music), while for others, it meant distracting music. "I'll listen to loud music if I don't want to hear things," said a participant who is a certified nurse's assistant. Still others mentioned exercise, a healthy diet, avoiding alcohol and getting enough sleep. . . .

One of the most frequently mentioned techniques that helped our research participants manage their symptoms was work. "Work has been an important part of who I am," said an educator in our group. "When you become useful to an organization and feel respected in that organization, there's a certain value in belonging there." This person works on the weekends too because of "the distraction factor." In other words, by engaging in work, the crazy stuff often recedes to the sidelines. . . .

That is why it is so distressing when doctors tell their patients not to expect or pursue fulfilling careers. Far too often, the conventional psychiatric approach to mental illness is to see clusters of symptoms that characterize people. Accordingly, many psychiatrists hold the view that treating

Elyn R. Saks is a law professor at the University of Southern California and the author of the memoir *The Center Cannot Hold: My Journey Through Madness.* Photo by Mikel Healey, Courtesy Elyn R. Saks

symptoms with medication is treating mental illness. But this fails to take into account individuals' strengths and capabilities, leading mental health professionals to underestimate what their patients can hope to achieve in the world. . . . A recent *New York Times Magazine* article described a new company that hires high-functioning adults with autism, taking advantage of their unusual memory skills and attention to detail. . . .

An approach that looks for individual strengths, in addition to considering symptoms, could help dispel the pessimism surrounding mental illness. Finding "the wellness within the illness," as one person with schizophrenia said, should be a therapeutic goal. Doctors should urge their patients to develop relationships and engage in meaningful work. They should encourage patients to find their own repertory of techniques to manage their symptoms and aim for a quality of life as they define it. And they should provide patients with the resources—therapy, medication and support—to make these things happen.

Elyn Saks's story is amazing and inspiring. It is also quite unusual. Are people such as Saks, and the people in the research study she described, simply a carefully selected collection of people who had unusually favorable outcomes? Or has Professor Saks touched on an important limitation to the way in which the field currently conceptualizes, classifies, and treats mental disorders? Do we focus too much on what is wrong and not enough on what inherent strengths people have that can help them overcome their challenges and achieve a high quality of life? These are all questions that are testable with the methods of psychological science, and the answers may help to improve the lives of many people.

brain (see **FIGURE 14.6**). All adolescents lose some gray matter over time in a kind of normal "pruning" of the brain, but in those developing schizophrenia, the loss was dramatic enough to seem pathological.

Social/Psychological Factors

With all these potential biological contributors to schizophrenia, you might think there would be few psychological or social causes of this disorder. However, several

Side views   Top view

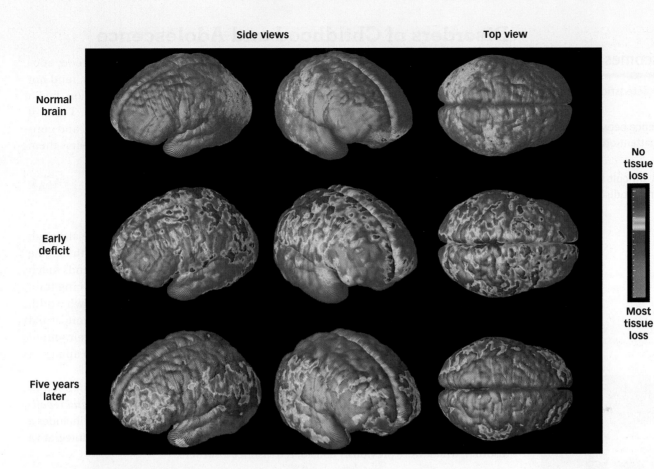

Figure 14.6 Brain Tissue Loss in Adolescent Schizophrenia MRI studies reveal brain tissue loss in adolescents diagnosed with schizophrenia. Normal adolescent brains show some loss due to normal "pruning" (*top*). By contrast, scans of adolescents who recently developed schizophrenia ("early deficit") reveal loss in the parietal areas (*middle*); individuals at this stage may experience symptoms such as hallucinations or bizarre thoughts. Scans taken 5 years later reveal extensive tissue loss over much of the cortex (*bottom*); individuals at this stage are likely to suffer from delusions, disorganized speech and behavior, and negative symptoms such as social withdrawal. Thompson et al., (2001), National Academy of Sciences, USA

studies suggest that family environment plays a role in the development of and recovery from the condition. One large-scale study compared the risk of schizophrenia in children adopted into healthy families to those adopted into severely disturbed families (Tienari et al., 2004). (Disturbed families were defined as those with extreme conflict, lack of communication, or chaotic relationships.) Among children whose biological mothers had schizophrenia, the disturbed environment increased their likelihood of developing schizophrenia—an outcome that was not found among children who were also reared in disturbed families but whose biological mothers did *not* have schizophrenia. This finding provides support for the diathesis–stress model described earlier.

Build to the Outcomes

1. What is schizophrenia?

2. What are the positive, negative, and cognitive symptoms of schizophrenia?

3. What is the role of genetics in schizophrenia?

4. How do biological factors contribute to schizophrenia?

5. What changes appear in the brains of people with schizophrenia?

6. What environmental factors contribute to schizophrenia?

Learning Outcomes

- Describe the characteristic indications of autism.
- Define the difference between normal problems with inattention and ADHD.
- Explain why it is difficult to pin down the causes of conduct disorder.

Disorders of Childhood and Adolescence

Most of the disorders described thus far can have their onset during childhood, adolescence, or adulthood. Some, such as bipolar disorder and schizophrenia, tend not to begin until early adulthood. However, other disorders *always,* by definition, begin in childhood or adolescence—and if they don't, they will never manifest. Three of these—autism spectrum disorder, attention-deficit/hyperactivity disorder, and conduct disorder—are among the most common and best known, so we will review them briefly here.

Autism Spectrum Disorder

Marco is a 4-year-old only child. His parents have become worried because although his mother stays home with him all day and tries to talk with him and play with him, he still has not spoken a single word and he shows little interest in trying. He spends much of his time playing with his toy trains, often sitting for hours staring at spinning train wheels or pushing a single train back and forth, seeming completely in his own world, uninterested in playing with anyone else. Marco's parents have become concerned about his apparent inability to speak, lack of interest in others, and development of some peculiar mannerisms, such as flapping his arms repeatedly for no apparent reason.

Autism spectrum disorder (ASD) is *a condition beginning in early childhood in which a person shows persistent communication deficits, as well as restricted and repetitive patterns of behaviors, interests, or activities.* As defined in the *DSM–5,* ASD includes a range of conditions, including autism, Asperger's syndrome, and childhood disintegrative disorder, which were previously considered distinct disorders.

Who Is at Risk?

The true rate of ASD is difficult to pinpoint, especially given the recent change in diagnostic definition. Estimates from the 1960s indicated that autism was a rare diagnosis, occurring in 4 per 10,000 children. Estimates have been creeping up over time and now stand at approximately 10 to 20 per 10,000 children. If one considers the full range of disorders that now fall under the ASD umbrella in the *DSM–5,* the rate is 60 per 10,000 children (Newschaffer et al., 2007).

It is unclear whether this increased rate is due to increased awareness and recognition of ASD, better screening and diagnostic tools, or some other factor. Boys have higher rates of ASD than girls by a ratio of about 4:1. Although the causes of ASD are not yet fully understood, a great deal of research has provided no evidence that ASD is caused by vaccinations (Mandy & Lai, 2016).

Biological Factors

One model suggests that ASD can be understood as an impaired capacity for *empathizing,* or knowing the mental states of others, combined with a superior ability for *systematizing,* or understanding the rules that organize the structure and function of objects (Baron-Cohen & Belmonte, 2005). Consistent with this model, brain-imaging studies show that people with autism have comparatively decreased activity in regions associated with understanding the minds of others and greater activation in regions related to basic object perception (Sigman et al., 2006).

Although many people with ASD experience impairments throughout their lives that prevent them from having relationships and holding down a job, many go on to very successful careers. The renowned behavioral scientist and author Temple Grandin has

Temple Grandin, a professor of animal sciences at Colorado State University, is living proof that people with autism spectrum disorder can have very successful professional careers. Vera Anderson/WireImage/Getty Images

autism spectrum disorder (ASD)
A condition beginning in early childhood in which a person shows persistent communication deficits as well as restricted and repetitive patterns of behaviors, interests, or activities.

Optimal Outcome in Autism Spectrum Disorder

Many people consider autism spectrum disorder (ASD) a lifelong condition and believe that those affected will forever experience significant difficulties and disabilities in their interpersonal, education, and occupational functioning. However, recent studies are helping to change this outlook.

New research describes people who had been diagnosed with autism as children, but who no longer meet the criteria for ASD (e.g., Shulman et al., 2019). In one study, 17% of children diagnosed with ASD at age 2 no longer met diagnostic criteria at age 4 (Moulton et al., 2016). There are several potential explanations for this change. The most obvious is that some portion of children diagnosed with ASD are misdiagnosed and don't really have this disorder. Perhaps they are overly shy or quiet, or develop speech later than other children, which is misinterpreted as ASD. Another possibility is that children who lose their ASD diagnosis were identified and treated earlier.

The possibility of effectively treating ASD was raised in an important study, in which children with autism were assigned either to an intensive behavioral intervention including over 40 hours per week of one-on-one behavior therapy for 2 years, or to control conditions, in which they received fewer than 10 hours per week of treatment. Amazingly, 47% of the children in the intensive behavior therapy condition obtained a normal level of intellectual and educational functioning—passing through a normal 1st-grade class—compared with only 2% of those in the control conditions. Later studies suggested that toddlers with ASD who received intensive, long-term behavioral treatment show significant improvements in IQ, language, and social functioning (Dawson et al., 2010). Many of these gains persisted for years after the treatment ended (Estes et al., 2015).

Given that early detection and treatment can lead to such positive outcomes for those with ASD, should we be screening all young children for ASD so we can catch it early and intervene? This is an area of intense debate. A recent report concluded that there is insufficient evidence to conclude that the benefits of universal screening outweigh the potential risks of misdiagnosis (Siu & U.S. Preventive Task Force, 2016). However, others argue that because we have methods for accurately detecting and effectively treating ASD in young children, we should screen all children for this disorder to maximize their chances of optimal outcomes (e.g., Dawson & Sapiro, 2019). Researchers and policy makers will be working actively on this issue in the years ahead.

Autism was once viewed as a condition with lifelong impairments. New research suggests that early intervention can help many of those diagnosed with ASD to achieve normal levels of functioning.   Courtesy UC Davis MIND Institute

---

written of her personal experience with autism. She was diagnosed with autism at age 3, started learning to talk late, and then suffered teasing for odd habits and "nerdy" behavior. Fortunately, she developed ways to cope and found a niche through her special talent—the ability to understand animal behavior (Sacks, 1996). She is now a professor, an author, and the central character in an HBO movie based on her life. Temple Grandin's story lets us know that there are happy endings. Overall, those diagnosed with ASD as children have highly variable trajectories, with some achieving normal or better-than-normal functioning and others struggling with profound disorder (see Hot Science: Optimal Outcome in Autism Spectrum Disorder).

Attention-Deficit/Hyperactivity Disorder

Chances are you have had the experience of being distracted during a lecture or while reading one of your *other* textbooks. We all have trouble focusing from time to time. Far beyond normal distraction, however, **attention-deficit/hyperactivity disorder (ADHD)** is *a persistent pattern of severe problems with inattention and/or hyperactivity or impulsiveness that cause significant impairments in functioning.* This is quite different from occasional mind-wandering or bursts of activity. Meeting the criteria for ADHD requires having multiple symptoms of inattention (e.g., persistent problems with sustained attention, organization, memory, following instructions), hyperactivity–impulsiveness (e.g., persistent difficulties with remaining still, waiting for a turn, interrupting others), or both. Most children experience some of these behaviors at some point, but to meet the criteria

attention-deficit/hyperactivity disorder (ADHD) A persistent pattern of severe problems with inattention and/or hyperactivity or impulsiveness that cause significant impairments in functioning.

for ADHD, a child has to have many of these behaviors for at least 6 months in at least two settings (e.g., home and school)—to the point where they impair the child's ability to perform at school or get along at home.

Who Is at Risk?

Approximately 10% of boys and 4% of girls meet criteria for ADHD (Polanczyk et al., 2007). For a long time, ADHD was thought of as a disorder that affects only children and adolescents and that people "age out" of it. However, we now know that in many instances, this disorder persists into adulthood. The same symptoms are used to diagnose both children and adults. (For example, children with ADHD may struggle with attention and concentration in the classroom, whereas adults may experience the same problems in meetings.)

Approximately 4% of adults meet the criteria for ADHD; they are more likely to be male, divorced, and unemployed—and most did not receive any treatment for their ADHD (Kessler et al., 2006). Unfortunately, most people still think of ADHD as a disorder of childhood and don't realize that adults can suffer from it as well. This could be why so few adults with ADHD receive treatment and why the disorder often wreaks havoc on job performance and relationships.

Biological Factors

Because ADHD, like most disorders, is defined by the presence of a wide range of symptoms, it is unlikely that it emerges from one single cause. Some studies suggest a strong genetic influence (Faraone et al., 2005). Brain-imaging studies suggest that those with ADHD have smaller brain volumes (Castellanos et al., 2002) as well as abnormalities in brain networks associated with attention and behavioral inhibition (Makris et al., 2009). The good news is that current drug treatments for ADHD are effective and appear to decrease the risk of later psychological and academic problems (Biederman et al., 2009).

Conduct Disorder

Psychologists are attempting to identify the causes of conduct disorder in the hope of being able to decrease harmful behaviors, such as bullying, that often accompany it.
FatCamera/Getty Images

Michael is an 8-year-old boy whose mother brought him into a local clinic because his behavior had been getting progressively out of control, and his parents and teachers could no longer handle him. At home, he routinely bullied his siblings, threw glasses and dishes at family members, and even punched and kicked his parents. Outside of the house, Michael had been getting into trouble for stealing from the local store and yelling at his teacher. Nothing his parents tried seemed to change Michael's behavior. A psychiatrist diagnosed Michael with **conduct disorder**, a condition in which a child or adolescent engages in a *persistent pattern of deviant behavior involving aggression to people or animals, destruction of property, deceitfulness or theft, or serious rule violations.*

Who Is at Risk?

conduct disorder A persistent pattern of deviant behavior involving aggression toward people or animals, destruction of property, deceitfulness or theft, or serious rule violations.

Approximately 9% of people in the United States report a lifetime history of conduct disorder (12% of boys and 7% of girls; Nock et al., 2006). Meeting the criteria for conduct disorder requires having any 3 of the 15 symptoms of conduct disorder. This means that approximately 32,000 different combinations of symptoms could lead to a diagnosis, which makes those with conduct disorder a pretty diverse group. This diversity makes it difficult to pin down the causes of conduct disorder.

Biological and Environmental Factors

Researchers are currently attempting to better understand the pathways through which inherited genetic factors interact with environmental stressors (e.g., childhood adversities) to create characteristics in brain structure and function (e.g., reduced activity in brain regions associated with planning and decision making) that interact with environmental factors (e.g., affiliation with deviant peers) to lead to the behaviors that are characteristic of conduct disorder.

Build to the Outcomes

1. What is autism spectrum disorder (ASD)?

2. What is the relationship between ASD and empathy?

3. What is attention-deficit/hyperactivity disorder (ADHD)?

4. What are the criteria for an ADHD diagnosis?

5. What is conduct disorder?

6. How is it possible that there are 32,000 different combinations of symptoms that could lead to a diagnosis of conduct disorder? What does this say about the population of people who have been given this diagnosis?

Personality Disorders: Extreme Traits and Characteristics

As discussed in the chapter on Personality, we all have one, and we all differ in our ways of behaving, thinking, and feeling. Sometimes, personality traits can become so extreme that they can be considered mental disorders. **Personality disorders** are *enduring patterns of thinking, feeling, or relating to others or controlling impulses that deviate from cultural expectations and cause distress or impaired functioning.* Personality disorders begin in adolescence or early adulthood and are relatively stable over time.

Let's look at the types of personality disorders and then more closely examine one that sometimes lands people in jail: antisocial personality disorder.

Learning Outcomes

- Define personality disorders.
- Explain the diagnostic signs of antisocial personality disorder.

Types of Personality Disorder

The *DSM-5* lists 10 specific personality disorders (see **TABLE 14.2**). They fall into three clusters: (1) *odd/eccentric,* (2) *dramatic/erratic,* and (3) *anxious/inhibited.*

Personality disorders have been a bit controversial for several reasons. First, critics question whether having a problematic personality is really a disorder. Given that approximately 15% of the U.S. population has a personality disorder according to the *DSM-5,* perhaps it might be better just to admit that a lot of people can be difficult to interact with and leave it at that. Another question is whether personality problems correspond to "disorders" with distinct *types,* or whether such problems might be better understood as extreme values on trait *dimensions* such as the Big Five traits discussed in the Personality chapter (Trull & Durrett, 2005).

Antisocial Personality Disorder

One of the most thoroughly studied of all the personality disorders is **antisocial personality disorder (APD),** *a pervasive pattern of disregard for and violation of the rights of others that begins in childhood or early adolescence and continues into adulthood.* The terms *sociopath* and *psychopath* describe people with APD who are especially coldhearted, manipulative, and ruthless—yet may appear friendly and charming (Cleckley, 1976; Hare, 1998). For example, in 1914 a man named Henri Desiré Landru

personality disorders Enduring patterns of thinking, feeling, or relating to others or controlling impulses that deviate from cultural expectations and cause distress or impaired functioning.

antisocial personality disorder (APD) A pervasive pattern of disregard for and violation of the rights of others that begins in childhood or early adolescence and continues into adulthood.

TABLE 14.2   Clusters of Personality Disorders

Cluster	Personality Disorder	Characteristics
A. Odd/Eccentric	Paranoid	Distrust in others, suspicion that people have sinister motives; apt to challenge the loyalties of friends and read hostile intentions into others' actions; prone to anger and aggressive outbursts but otherwise emotionally cold; often jealous, guarded, secretive, overly serious
	Schizoid	Extreme introversion and withdrawal from relationships; prefers to be alone, little interest in others; humorless, distant, often absorbed with own thoughts and feelings, a day-dreamer; fearful of closeness, with poor social skills, often seen as a "loner"
	Schizotypal	Peculiar or eccentric manners of speaking or dressing; strange beliefs; "magical think-ing," such as belief in ESP or telepathy; difficulty forming relationships; may react oddly in conversation, not respond, or talk to self; speech elaborate or difficult to follow (possi-bly a mild form of schizophrenia)
B. Dramatic/Erratic	Antisocial	Impoverished moral sense or "conscience"; history of deception, crime, legal problems, impulsive and aggressive or violent behavior; little emotional empathy or remorse for hurt-ing others; manipulative, careless, callous; at high risk for substance abuse and alcoholism
	Borderline	Unstable moods and intense, stormy personal relationships; frequent mood changes and anger, unpredictable impulses; self-mutilation or suicidal threats or gestures to get atten-tion or manipulate others; self-image fluctuation and a tendency to see others as "all good" or "all bad"
	Histrionic	Constant attention seeking; grandiose language, provocative dress, exaggerated illnesses, all to gain attention; believes that everyone loves them; emotional, lively, overly dramatic, enthusiastic, and excessively flirtatious; shallow and labile emotions; "onstage"
	Narcissistic	Inflated sense of self-importance, absorbed by fantasies of self and success; exaggerates own achievements, assumes others will recognize they are superior; good first impres-sions but poor longer-term relationships; exploitative of others
C. Anxious/Inhibited	Avoidant	Socially anxious and uncomfortable unless they are confident of being liked; in contrast with schizoid person, yearns for social contact; fears criticism and worries about being embarrassed in front of others; avoids social situations due to fear of rejection
	Dependent	Submissive, dependent, requiring excessive approval, reassurance, and advice; clings to people and fears losing them; lacking self-confidence; uncomfortable when alone; may be devastated by end of close relationship or suicidal if breakup is threatened
	Obsessive-compulsive	Conscientious, orderly, perfectionist; excessive need to do everything "right"; inflexibly high standards and caution can interfere with their productivity; fear of errors can make them strict and controlling; poor expression of emotions (not the same as obsessive-compulsive disorder)

Information from *DSM–5* (American Psychiatric Association, 2013).

Henri Desiré Landru (1869–1922) was a serial killer who met widows through newspaper ads. After obtaining enough information to embezzle money from them, he murdered 10 women and the son of one of the women. He was executed for serial murder in 1922. Three Lions/Hulton Archive/Getty Images

began using personal ads to attract women "interested in matrimony," and he suc-ceeded in seducing 10 of them. He bilked them of their savings, poisoned them, and cremated them in his stove, also disposing of a boy and two dogs along the way. He recorded his murders in a notebook and maintained a marriage and a mistress all the while. The gruesome actions of serial killers such as Landru leave us frightened and wondering; however, bullies, compulsive liars, and even drivers who regularly speed through a school zone share the same shocking blindness to human pain.

Who Is at Risk?

Many people with APD commit crimes, and many are caught because of the frequency and flagrancy of their infractions. Among 22,790 prisoners in one study, 47% of the men and 21% of the women were diagnosed with APD (Fazel & Danesh, 2002). Statistics such as these support the notion of a "criminal personality."

Adults with an APD diagnosis typically have a history of *conduct disorder* before the age of 15. In adulthood, a diagnosis of APD is given to individuals who show three or more of a set of seven diagnostic signs: illegal behavior, deception, impulsivity, physical aggression, recklessness, irresponsibility, and a lack of remorse for wrongdoing. About 3.6% of the general population has APD, and the rate of occurrence in men is three times the rate in women (Grant et al., 2004).

Biological Factors

Evidence of brain abnormalities in people with APD is accumulating (Blair et al., 2005). For example, criminal psychopaths who are shown negative emotional words such as *hate* or *corpse* exhibit less activity in the amygdala and hippocampus (two areas involved in fear conditioning) than do noncriminals (Kiehl et al., 2001). Research like this has suggested that psychopaths experience fear but appear to have decreased abilities for detecting and responding to threats in their environment (Hoppenbrouwers et al., 2016).

Build to the Outcomes

1. What are personality disorders?
2. What are the characteristics of a person with antisocial personality disorder (APD)?
3. Why do prison statistics support the idea of a "criminal personality"?

Self-Harm Behaviors: Intentionally Injuring Oneself

We all have an innate drive to keep ourselves alive. We eat when we are hungry, get out of the way of fast-moving vehicles, and go to school so we can earn a living to keep ourselves, and our families, alive. One of the most extreme manifestations of abnormal human behavior is revealed when a person acts in direct opposition to this drive for self-preservation and engages in intentionally self-destructive behavior. Accounts of people intentionally harming themselves date back to the beginning of recorded history. However, it is only over the past several decades that we have begun to gain an understanding of why people purposely do things to hurt themselves. *DSM–5* includes two self-destructive behaviors in a special section devoted to disorders in need of further study: suicidal behavior disorder and nonsuicidal self-injury disorder.

Suicidal Behavior

Tim, a 35-year-old accountant, had by all appearances been living a pretty happy, successful life. He was married to his high school sweetheart and had two young children. Over the past several years, though, his workload had increased, and he started to experience severe job-related stress. At around the same time, he and his wife began to experience some financial problems, and his alcohol consumption increased, all of which put significant strain on the family and began to affect his work. One evening, after a heated argument with his wife, Tim went into the bathroom and swallowed a bottle full of prescription medicine in an effort to end his life. He was taken to the hospital and kept there to be treated for suicidal behavior.

Suicide, *intentional self-inflicted death,* is the tenth leading cause of death in the United States and the second leading cause of death among people 15 to 24 years old. It

Learning Outcomes

- Explain the factors that increase the risk of suicide.

- Explain what is currently known about the motivation behind nonsuicidal self-injury.

suicide Intentional self-inflicted death.

We all have an innate desire to keep ourselves alive. So why do some people purposely do things to harm themselves? Piotr Powietrzynski/ Getty Images

takes the lives of more than 5 times as many people as HIV/AIDS each year in the United States, and more than twice as many people as homicide (Murphy et al., 2018).

Nonfatal **suicide attempts**, in which people engage in *potentially harmful behavior with some intention of dying,* occur much more frequently than suicide deaths. In the United States, approximately 15% of adults report that they have seriously considered suicide at some point in their lives, and 5% have actually made a suicide attempt.

Suicidal thoughts and behaviors are virtually nonexistent before age 10 but increase dramatically from ages 12 to 18 (see **FIGURE 14.7**) before leveling off during early adulthood (Nock et al., 2013).

Who Is at Risk?

Approximately 80% of suicides around the world occur among men. Although many more men than women die by suicide, women experience suicidal thoughts and (nonfatal) suicide attempts at significantly higher rates than do men (Nock et al., 2008). White people are much more likely to kill themselves than members of other racial and ethnic groups, accounting for 90% of all suicides (Centers for Disease Control and Prevention, 2019). Unfortunately, we currently do not have a good understanding of why these enormous sociodemographic differences exist.

Environmental Factors

So the numbers are staggering, but *why* do people try to kill themselves? The short answer is: We do not yet know, and it's complicated. When interviewed in the hospital following their suicide attempt, most people who have tried to kill themselves report that they did so to escape from an intolerable state of mind or impossible situation (Boergers et al., 1998). Consistent with this explanation, research has documented that the risk of suicidal behavior is significantly increased if a person experiences severely distressing states, such as the presence of multiple mental disorders (more than 90% of people who die by suicide have at least one mental disorder); the experience of significant negative life events during childhood and adulthood (e.g., physical or sexual assault); and the presence of severe medical problems (Nock et al., 2012). The search is ongoing for a more comprehensive understanding of how and why some people respond to negative life events with suicidal

suicide attempt Engagement in potentially harmful behavior with some intention of dying.

Figure 14.7 Age of Onset of Suicidal Behavior During Adolescence A survey of a nationally representative sample of U.S. adolescents shows that although suicidal thoughts ("ideation") and behaviors (e.g., suicide planning, suicide attempt) are quite rare among young children, they increase dramatically starting around age 12 and continue to climb throughout adolescence (data from Nock et al., 2013).

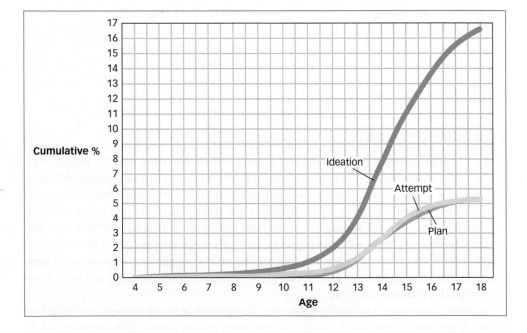

thoughts and behaviors, as well as for methods of how to better predict and prevent these devastating outcomes.

Nonsuicidal Self-Injury

Louisa, an 18-year-old college student, secretly cuts her lower abdomen and upper thighs about once per week, typically when she is feeling intense anger and hatred, either toward herself or someone else. She was 14 when she started to use self-injury as a way to calm herself down. Louisa says that she feels a little ashamed after each episode of cutting, but she doesn't know how else to calm down when she gets really upset, so she has no plans to stop this behavior.

Louisa is engaging in a behavior called **nonsuicidal self-injury (NSSI)**, the *direct, deliberate destruction of body tissue in the absence of any intent to die.*

Who Is at Risk?

NSSI has been reported since the beginning of recorded history; however, it is a behavior that appears to be on the rise over the past few decades. As many as 15 to 20% of adolescents and 3 to 6% of adults report engaging in NSSI at some point in their lifetime (Muehlenkamp et al., 2012). The rates appear to be even between males and females, and for people of different races and ethnicities. Like suicidal behavior, NSSI is virtually absent during childhood, increases dramatically during adolescence, and then appears to decrease across adulthood.

Environmental Factors

In some parts of the world, cutting or scarification of the skin is socially accepted, and in some cases encouraged as a rite of passage (Favazza, 2011). In parts of the world where self-cutting is not socially encouraged, why would a person purposely cause such hurt if not to die? Studies suggest that people who engage in self-injury have very strong emotional and physiological responses to negative events, that they perceive this response as intolerable, and that NSSI serves to diminish the intensity of this response (Nock, 2009). There also is some evidence that in many instances people engage in self-injury as a means to communicate distress or elicit help from others (Nock, 2010).

Unfortunately, like suicidal behavior, our understanding of the genetic and neurobiological influences on NSSI is limited, and there currently are no effective medications for these problems. There also is limited evidence for behavioral interventions or prevention programs (Mann et al., 2005). So, whereas suicidal behavior and NSSI are some of the most disturbing and dangerous mental disorders, they also, unfortunately, are among the most perplexing. The field has made significant strides in our understanding of these behavior problems in recent years, but there is a long way to go before we are able to predict and prevent them accurately and effectively.

Although in Western cultures self-injury is considered pathological, in some parts of the world scarification of the skin is viewed as a rite of passage into adulthood and a symbol of one's tribe, as in the case of this young man from the Republic of Benin in West Africa. Eric Lafforgue/Art in All of US/Getty Images

nonsuicidal self-injury (NSSI) Direct, deliberate destruction of body tissue in the absence of any intent to die.

Build to the Outcomes

1. What factors contribute to the distressing states that can lead to suicide?

2. What reason has been given in hospital interviews for suicide attempts?

3. What is nonsuicidal self-injury (NSSI)?

4. How does culture play a role in the view of self-injury as pathological?

5. Why might people engage in self-injury?

CHAPTER REVIEW

Defining Mental Disorders: What Is Abnormal?

- The *DSM–5* is a classification system that defines a mental disorder as occurring when a person experiences disturbances of thought, emotion, or behavior that produce distress or impairment. The *DSM–5* includes detailed lists of criteria, including cultural considerations, designed to increase the validity of the process.

- The medical model conceptualizes abnormal thought and behaviors as illnesses with defined symptoms and possible cures.

- According to the biopsychosocial model, mental disorders arise from an interaction of biological, psychological, and social factors.

- The diathesis–stress model suggests that a person may be predisposed for a disorder that may manifest if triggered by stress.

- The RDoC is a classification system that focuses on biological, cognitive, and behavioral aspects of mental disorders.

- Psychiatric labels may create negative stereotypes and may be one reason many people do not seek help.

Anxiety Disorders: Excessive Fear, Anxiety, and Avoidance

- People with anxiety disorders have irrational worries and fears that undermine their ability to function normally.

- Phobic disorders involve excessive fear and avoidance of specific objects, activities, or situations. The preparedness theory posits that people are instinctively predisposed toward certain fears.

- People who suffer from panic disorder experience a sudden, terrifying attack of intense anxiety. Agoraphobia can lead people to be housebound for fear of public humiliation.

- Generalized anxiety disorder (GAD) involves a chronic state of anxiety, not tied to a specific object or situation.

Obsessive-Compulsive Disorder: Persistent Thoughts and Repetitive Behaviors

- People with obsessive-compulsive disorder (OCD) experience recurring, anxiety-provoking thoughts that compel them to engage in ritualistic, irrational behavior.

- OCD derives from concerns that could be real, supporting the preparedness theory.

Posttraumatic Stress Disorder: Distress and Avoidance After a Trauma

- In posttraumatic stress disorder (PTSD), a person experiences chronic physiological arousal, unwanted thoughts or images of the event, and avoidance of things or situations that remind the person of the event.

- Research has identified neural correlates of PTSD.

Depressive and Bipolar Disorders: Extreme Highs and Lows

- Mood disorders are mental disorders in which a disturbance in mood is the predominant feature.

- Major depression (or unipolar depression) is characterized by a severely depressed mood and/or inability to experience pleasure lasting at least 2 weeks; symptoms include excessive self-criticism, guilt, difficulty concentrating, suicidal thoughts, sleep and appetite disturbances, and lethargy.

- Bipolar disorder involves extreme mood swings of depression and mania. The manic phase is characterized by periods of abnormally and persistently elevated, expansive, or irritable mood.

- Depression has at its roots socioeconomic, hormonal, genetic, and neural factors. Helplessness theory indicates that biases in how information is processed can lead to depression.

Schizophrenia and Other Psychotic Disorders: Losing the Grasp on Reality

- Schizophrenia is a severe psychological disorder involving hallucinations, disorganized thoughts and behavior, and emotional and social withdrawal.

- Positive symptoms are thoughts and behaviors *not* seen in those without the disorder; negative symptoms indicate an *absence* of normal behavior; cognitive symptoms are impairments in executive functioning, attention, and working memory.

- Schizophrenia affects only 1% of the population, but it accounts for a disproportionate share of psychiatric hospitalizations. The likelihood of getting the disorder increases with biological relatedness.

- Early studies with drugs that reduced the availability of dopamine sometimes reduced the symptoms of schizophrenia, suggesting that the disorder involved an excess of dopamine activity; but recent research suggests that schizophrenia may involve a complex interaction among a variety of neurotransmitters.

Disorders of Childhood and Adolescence

- Autism spectrum disorder (ASD) emerges in early childhood and involves persistent communication deficits, including difficulty empathizing with others, as well as restricted and repetitive patterns of behaviors, interests, or activities.

- Attention-deficit/hyperactivity disorder (ADHD) begins by age 12 and involves persistent severe problems with inattention and/or hyperactivity or impulsiveness that cause significant impairments in functioning.

- Conduct disorder begins in childhood or adolescence and involves deviant behavior involving aggression toward people or animals, destruction of property, deceitfulness or theft, or serious rule violations.

Personality Disorders: Extreme Traits and Characteristics

- Personality disorders are enduring patterns of thinking, feeling, relating to others, or controlling impulses that cause distress or impaired functioning.
- Antisocial personality disorder (APD) is associated with a lack of moral emotions and behavior. People with APD can be manipulative, dangerous, and reckless, often hurting others and sometimes hurting themselves.

Self-Harm Behaviors: Intentionally Injuring Oneself

- Suicide is among the leading causes of death in the United States and the world.
- Most people who die by suicide have a mental disorder.
- Nonsuicidal self-injury (NSSI) is performed without suicidal intent.
- Both suicide and NSSI are most often motivated by an attempt to escape from painful mental states.

Key Concept Quiz

1. The conception of psychological disorders as diseases that have symptoms and possible cures is referred to as
   a. the medical model.
   b. physiognomy.
   c. the root syndrome framework.
   d. a diagnostic system.

2. The *DSM–5* is best described as a
   a. medical model.
   b. classification system.
   c. set of theoretical assumptions.
   d. collection of physiological definitions.

3. *Comorbidity of disorders* refers to
   a. symptoms stemming from internal dysfunction.
   b. the relative risk of death arising from a disorder.
   c. the co-occurrence of two or more disorders in a single individual.
   d. the existence of disorders on a continuum from normal to abnormal.

4. Irrational worries and fears that undermine one's ability to function normally are an indication of
   a. a genetic abnormality.
   b. dysthymia.
   c. diathesis.
   d. an anxiety disorder.

5. The RDoC aims to
   a. replace the *DSM–5*.
   b. shift researchers from focusing on a symptom-based classification of mental disorders to a focus on underlying processes that may lead to mental disorders.
   c. prevent the negative consequences of labeling individuals with mental disorders.
   d. help researchers better classify mental disorders based on psychodynamic symptoms.

6. A(n) _____ disorder involves anxiety tied to a specific object or situation.
   a. generalized anxiety
   b. environmental
   c. panic
   d. phobic

7. Agoraphobia often develops as a result of
   a. preparedness theory.
   b. obsessive-compulsive disorder.
   c. panic disorder.
   d. social phobia.

8. Kelly's fear of germs leads her to wash her hands repeatedly throughout the day, often for 30 minutes or more, under extremely hot water. From which disorder does Kelly most likely suffer?
   a. panic attacks
   b. obsessive-compulsive disorder
   c. phobia
   d. generalized anxiety disorder

9. Which of these is *not* a symptom of PTSD?
   a. chronic physiological arousal
   b. avoidance of things or places that might serve as reminders of the traumatic event
   c. recurrent, intrusive thoughts about the traumatic event
   d. impaired acquisition of conditioned fear responses

10. Extreme mood swings between _____ characterize bipolar disorder.
    a. depression and mania
    b. stress and lethargy
    c. anxiety and arousal
    d. obsessions and compulsions

11. Schizophrenia is characterized by which of the following?
    a. hallucinations
    b. disorganized thoughts and behavior
    c. emotional and social withdrawal
    d. all of the above

12. Autism spectrum disorder is characterized most often by which of the following?
    a. communication deficits and restricted, repetitive behavior
    b. hallucinations and delusions
    c. suicidal thoughts
    d. schizophrenia

13. Attention-deficit/hyperactivity disorder
    a. must begin before the age of 7 years.
    b. never persists into adulthood.

c. sometimes persists into adulthood.

d. affects only boys.

14. Jim was diagnosed as having antisocial personality disorder. This diagnosis was most likely based on the fact that he

a. is emotionally distant, suspicious of others, and has an intense fear of rejection.

b. avoids social interaction, has very poor social skills, and is often seen as a "loner."

c. is very peculiar in his speech and dress and has difficulty forming relationships.

d. is manipulative, impulsive, and shows little emotional empathy.

15. In the United States, those at highest risk for suicide are

a. men.

b. White people.

c. those with a mental disorder.

d. all of the above.

LearningCurve

Don't stop now! Quizzing yourself is a powerful study tool. Go to LaunchPad to access the LearningCurve adaptive quizzing system and your own personalized learning plan. Visit launchpadworks.com.

Key Terms

mental disorder (p. 414)

medical model (p. 414)

Diagnostic and Statistical Manual of Mental Disorders (DSM) (p. 415)

comorbidity (p. 416)

biopsychosocial perspective (p. 418)

diathesis–stress model (p. 418)

Research Domain Criteria Project (RDoC) (p. 419)

anxiety disorders (p. 420)

phobic disorders (p. 420)

specific phobia (p. 420)

social phobia (p. 421)

preparedness theory (p. 421)

panic disorder (p. 422)

agoraphobia (p. 422)

generalized anxiety disorder (GAD) (p. 423)

obsessive-compulsive disorder (OCD) (p. 424)

posttraumatic stress disorder (PTSD) (p. 425)

mood disorders (p. 427)

major depressive disorder (or unipolar depression) (p. 427)

seasonal affective disorder (SAD) (p. 427)

helplessness theory (p. 429)

bipolar disorder (p. 430)

schizophrenia (p. 431)

positive symptoms (p. 431)

hallucination (p. 431)

delusion (p. 432)

disorganized speech (p. 432)

grossly disorganized behavior (p. 432)

catatonic behavior (p. 432)

negative symptoms (p. 432)

cognitive symptoms (p. 432)

dopamine hypothesis (p. 433)

autism spectrum disorder (ASD) (p. 436)

attention-deficit/hyperactivity disorder (ADHD) (p. 437)

conduct disorder (p. 438)

personality disorders (p. 439)

antisocial personality disorder (APD) (p. 439)

suicide (p. 441)

suicide attempt (p. 442)

nonsuicidal self-injury (NSSI) (p. 443)

Changing Minds

1. You catch a TV interview with a celebrity who describes his difficult childhood, living with a mother who suffered from major depression. "Sometimes my mother stayed in her bed for days, not even getting up to eat," he says. "At the time, the family hushed it up. My parents came from a culture where it was considered shameful to have mental problems. You are supposed to have enough strength of will to overcome your problems, without help from anyone else. So my mother never got treatment." How might the idea of a medical model of psychiatric disorders have helped this celebrity's mother and her family in the decision to seek treatment?

2. You're studying for your upcoming psychology exam when your roommate breezes in, saying, "I was just at the gym and I ran into Sue. She's totally schizophrenic: nice one minute, mean the next." You can't resist the opportunity to set the record straight. How does the behavior your roommate is describing differ from that of a person with schizophrenia?

3. A friend of yours has a family member who is experiencing severe mental problems, including delusions and loss of motivation. "We went to one psychiatrist," she says, "and got a diagnosis of schizophrenia. We went for a second opinion, and the other doctor said it was probably bipolar disorder. They're both good doctors, and they're both using the same *DSM*. How can they come up with different diagnoses?"

4. After reading the chapter, one of your classmates turns to you with a sigh of relief. "I finally figured it out. I have a deadbeat brother who always gets himself into trouble and then blames other people for his problems. Even when he gets a ticket for speeding, he never thinks it's his fault—the police were picking on him, or his passengers were urging him to go too fast. I always thought he was just a loser, but now I realize he has a personality disorder!" Do you agree with your classmate's diagnosis of his brother? How would you caution your classmate about the dangers of self-diagnosis, or diagnosis of friends and family?

Answers to Key Concept Quiz

1. a; 2. b; 3. c; 4. d; 5. b; 6. d; 7. c; 8. b; 9. d; 10. a; 11. d; 12. a; 13. c; 14. d; 15. d

LaunchPad
macmillan learning

LaunchPad features the full e-book of *Introducing Psychology*, the LearningCurve adaptive quizzing system, videos, and a variety of activities to boost your learning. Visit LaunchPad at launchpadworks.com.

Treatment of Psychological Disorders

15

Treatment: Getting Help to Those Who Need It

Psychological Treatments: Healing the Mind Through Interaction

Biological Treatments: Healing the Mind by Physically Altering the Brain

Treatment Effectiveness: For Better or for Worse

"Today we're going to be touching a dead mouse I found in the parking lot outside my office building this morning," Dr. Jenkins said. "Okay, let's do it, I'm ready," Christine responded. The pair walked down to the parking lot and spent the next 50 minutes touching, then stroking, the dead mouse. They then went back upstairs to plan out what other disgusting things Christine was going to touch over the next 7 days before coming back for her next therapy session.

This is all part of the psychological treatment of Christine's obsessive-compulsive disorder (OCD). It is an approach called *exposure and response prevention* (ERP), in which people are gradually exposed to the content of their obsessions and prevented from engaging in their compulsions. Christine's obsessions include the fear that she is going to be contaminated by germs and die of cancer; her compulsive behavior involves several hours per day of washing her body and scrubbing everything around her with alcohol wipes to decrease the possibility of her developing cancer. After dozens and dozens of exposures to the focus of their obsessions, without performing the compulsive behaviors that they believe have been keeping them safe, people undergoing ERP eventually learn that their obsessive thoughts are not accurate and that they don't have to act out their compulsions. ERP can be scary, but it has proven amazingly effective at decreasing obsessions and compulsions and helping people with OCD return to a high level of daily functioning. The condition was widely considered untreatable until the development of ERP, which is now considered to be the most effective way to treat it (Foa & McLean, 2016). Exposure and response prevention is just one of many approaches currently being used to help people overcome the mental disorders you learned about in the last chapter.

In this chapter, we will examine why people seek psychological help in the first place. Then we'll explore the most common approaches to psychological treatment, including psychological treatments built on psychoanalytic, humanistic, existential, behavioral, and cognitive theories, as well as biological treatment approaches that directly modify brain structure and function. We'll discuss which treatments are most effective and we'll also look to the future by exploring some exciting new directions in the assessment and treatment of disorders using innovative technologies.

Exposure-based treatments, in which a person learns to face the source of their fear and anxiety, have proven to be an effective way to treat anxiety disorders. Keith Binns/Getty Images

Learning Outcomes

- Describe reasons people with mental disorders may fail to get treatment.
- Outline different approaches to treatment.

Treatment: Getting Help to Those Who Need It

Estimates suggest that 46.4% of people in the United States suffer from a mental disorder at some point in their lifetime (Kessler, Berglund, et al., 2005), and 26.2% suffer from at least one disorder during a given year (Kessler, Chiu, et al., 2005). The personal costs of these disorders include the anguish of the sufferers as well as interference in their ability to carry on the activities of daily life. Think about Christine from the example above. Her OCD was causing major problems in her life. She had to quit her job at the local coffee shop because she was no longer able to touch money or anything else that had been touched by other people without washing her hands immediately afterward. Her relationship with her boyfriend was in trouble because he was growing tired of her constantly seeking reassurance regarding cleanliness (hers and his). All of these problems in turn increased her anxiety and depression, making her obsessions even stronger. She desperately wanted some way to break out of this vicious cycle. She needed an effective treatment.

The personal burdens of mental disorders are enormous, and there are financial costs, too. Depression is the second leading cause of all disability worldwide (Ferrari et al., 2013), and recent estimates suggest that depression-related lost work productivity costs somewhere from $30 to $50 billion per year (Kessler, 2012). If we add in similar figures for all other psychological problems, the overall costs are astronomical. In addition to the personal benefits of treatment, then, society also stands to benefit from the effective treatment of psychological disorders.

Unfortunately, only about 18% of people in the United States with a mental disorder in a given 12-month period receive treatment during the same time frame. Treatment rates are even lower elsewhere around the world, especially in low-income or developing countries (Wang et al., 2007). Even among those who do receive treatment, the average delay from onset until first receiving treatment is more than a decade (Wang et al., 2004)!

Why Many People Fail to Seek Treatment

A physical symptom such as a toothache would send most people to the dentist—a trip that usually results in a successful treatment. The clear source of pain and the obvious solution make for a quick and effective response. In contrast, the path from a mental disorder to a successful treatment is often far less clear. Here are three of the most often reported reasons people fail to get treatment:

1. *People may not realize that they have a mental disorder that can be effectively treated.* Approximately 45% of those with a mental disorder who do not seek treatment report that they did not do so because they didn't think they needed to be treated (Mojtabai et al., 2011). Mental disorders often are not taken nearly as seriously as physical illness, perhaps because the origin of mental illness is "hidden" and usually cannot be diagnosed by a blood test or X-ray.

2. *People's beliefs may keep them from getting help.* Individuals may believe that they should be able to handle things themselves. In fact, this is the primary reason that people with a mental disorder give for not seeking treatment (72.6%) and for dropping out of treatment prematurely (42.2%) (Mojtabai et al., 2011). Other beliefs that can form barriers to treatment include the belief that treatment would be ineffective, and perceived stigma from others.

3. *Structural barriers prevent people from physically getting to treatment.* Like finding a good lawyer or plumber, finding the right psychologist can be difficult. This confusion is understandable given the plethora of different types of treatments available (see The Real World: Types of Psychotherapists). Other structural barriers include not being able to afford treatment, lack of clinician availability, the inconvenience of attending treatment, and trouble finding transportation to the clinic (Mojtabai et al., 2011).

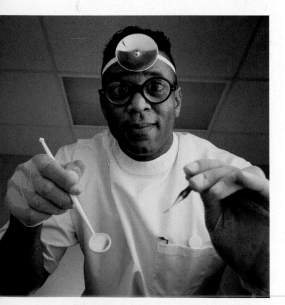

When your tooth hurts, you go to a dentist. But how do you know when to see a psychologist? Allison Leach/The Image Bank/Getty Images

Even when people seek and find help, they sometimes do not receive the most effective treatment, which further complicates things. For starters, most treatment for mental disorders is not provided by mental health specialists, but by general medical practitioners (Wang et al., 2007). And even when people make it to a mental health specialist, they do not always receive the most effective treatment possible. In fact, less than 40% of those with a mental disorder receive minimally adequate treatment. Clearly, before choosing or prescribing a therapy, we need to know what kinds of treatments are available and understand which treatments are best for particular disorders.

Approaches to Treatment

Treatments can be divided broadly into two kinds: (1) psychological treatment, in which people interact with a clinician in order to use the environment to change their brain and behavior and (2) biological treatment, in which drugs, surgery, or some other direct

---

THE REAL WORLD

Types of Psychotherapists

Where should you turn if you're ready to seek the help of a mental health professional? Therapists have widely varying backgrounds and training, which affects the kinds of services they offer. There are several major "flavors" of therapists.

- *Psychologist* A psychologist who practices psychotherapy holds a doctorate (a PhD or PsyD) and has extensive training in therapy, assessment of psychological disorders, and research. The psychologist will sometimes have a specialty, such as working with adolescents or helping people overcome sleep disorders, and will usually conduct therapy that involves talking. Psychologists must be licensed by the state.

- *Psychiatrist* A psychiatrist is a medical doctor who has completed an MD with specialized training in assessing and treating mental disorders. Psychiatrists can prescribe medications, and some also practice psychotherapy. General-practice physicians can also prescribe medications for mental disorders, but they do not typically receive much training in the diagnosis or treatment of mental disorders, and they do not practice psychotherapy.

- *Clinical/psychiatric social worker* Social workers have a master's degree in social work and have training in working with people in dire life situations such as poverty, homelessness, or family conflict. They also receive special training to help people in these situations who have mental disorders.

- *Counselor* In some states, a counselor must have a master's degree and extensive training in therapy; other states require minimal relevant education. Counselors who work in schools usually have a master's degree and specific training in counseling in educational settings.

Some people offer therapy under made-up terms that sound professional—"mind–body healing therapist," for example, or "marital adjustment adviser." Often these are simply terms invented to avoid licensing boards. To be safe, it is important to shop wisely for a therapist whose training and credentials reflect expertise and inspire confidence.

People you know, such as your general-practice physician, a school counselor, or a trusted friend or family member, might know of and be able to recommend a good therapist. Or you can visit your college clinic or the Web site of the American Psychological Association for referrals to licensed mental health care providers. When you do contact someone, he or she will often be able to provide you with further advice about who would be just the right kind of therapist to consult.

Before you agree to see a therapist for treatment, you should ask questions (such as those below) to evaluate whether the therapist's style or background is a good match for your problem:

- What type of treatment do you provide?

- How effective is this type of therapy for the type of problem I'm having?

Maskot/Getty Images

- How will you know if my problem is improving? What kind of measures do you use to test this?

Not only will the therapist's answers to these questions tell you about his or her background and experience, but they will also tell you about his or her approach to treating clients. You can then make an informed decision about the type of service you need.

DATA Visualization

intervention directly treat(s) the brain. In some cases, patients receive both psychological *and* biological treatments. Christine's OCD, for example, might be treated not only with ERP but also with medication that mitigates her obsessive thoughts and compulsive urges. As we learn more about the biology and chemistry of the brain, approaches to mental health that begin with the brain are becoming increasingly widespread. (See also Data Visualization: How Has the Rate of ADHD Diagnosis Changed Over Time? at www.launchpadworks.com.)

Build to the Outcomes

1. What are some of the personal, social, and financial costs of mental illness?

2. What are the obstacles to treatment for people with mental illness?

3. What are the two broad types of treatment?

Learning Outcomes

- Outline each of the major approaches to psychotherapy.
- Describe the pros and cons of group treatment.

psychotherapy An interaction between a socially sanctioned clinician and someone suffering from a psychological problem, with the goal of providing support or relief from the problem.

eclectic psychotherapy A form of psychotherapy that involves drawing on techniques from different forms of therapy, depending on the client and the problem.

Psychological Treatments: Healing the Mind Through Interaction

Psychological treatment, or **psychotherapy**, *is an interaction between a socially sanctioned clinician and someone suffering from a psychological problem, with the goal of providing support or relief from the problem.* More than 500 different forms of psychotherapy exist. A survey asked psychotherapists to describe their main theoretical orientation (Norcross & Rogan, 2013) (see **FIGURE 15.1**). One out of four reported using **eclectic psychotherapy**, *a form of psychotherapy that involves drawing on techniques from different forms of therapy, depending on the client and the problem.* This approach allows therapists to apply an appropriate theoretical perspective suited to the problem at hand, rather than adhering to a single theoretical perspective for all clients and all types of problems. Nevertheless, as Figure 15.1 shows, the majority of psychotherapists use a single approach, such as psychodynamic therapy, humanistic and existential therapies, or behavioral and cognitive therapies. We'll examine each of those major approaches to psychotherapy in turn.

Psychodynamic Therapy

Psychodynamic psychotherapy has its roots in Freud's psychoanalytically oriented theory of personality. **Psychodynamic psychotherapies** *explore childhood events and*

Figure 15.1 Approaches to Psychotherapy in the 21st Century This chart shows the percentage of psychologists who have various primary psychotherapy orientations (data from Norcross & Rogan, 2013).

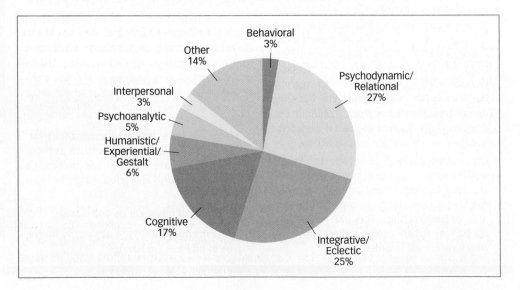

encourage individuals to use the understanding gained from the exploration to develop insight into their psychological problems. Psychoanalysis was the first psychodynamic therapy to be developed, but it has largely been replaced by modern psychodynamic therapies, such as interpersonal psychotherapy.

Psychoanalysis

As we saw in the Personality chapter, *psychoanalysis* assumes that people are born with aggressive and sexual urges that are repressed during childhood development through the use of defense mechanisms. Psychoanalysts encourage their clients to bring these repressed conflicts into consciousness so that the clients can understand them and reduce their unwanted influences.

Traditional psychoanalysis involves four or five sessions per week over an average of 3 to 6 years (Ursano & Silberman, 2003). During a session, the client reclines on a couch, facing away from the analyst, who asks the client to make *free associations,* in which the client expresses whatever thoughts and feelings come to mind. Occasionally, the therapist may comment on some information the client presents, but the therapist does not express his or her values and judgments. The goal of psychoanalysis is for the client to understand the unconscious through a process Freud called *developing insight.*

The stereotypic image you might have of psychological therapy—a person lying on a couch talking to a person sitting in a chair—springs from the psychoanalytic approach.   Antoine Devourard/Patrick Allard/Rea/Redux

Psychodynamic Therapy

Freud's original version of psychoanalysis is practiced by only about 5% of clinicians today (see Figure 15.1). However, many of his insights and techniques remain very influential in a broader range of psychodynamic treatments that are used more frequently today (by about 30% of therapists); the new treatments differ from classic psychoanalysis in both their content and their procedures. One of the most common psychodynamic treatments is **interpersonal psychotherapy (IPT)**, *a form of psychotherapy that focuses on helping clients improve current relationships* (Weissman et al., 2000). Therapists using IPT talk to clients about their interpersonal behaviors and feelings. They pay particular attention to the client's grief (e.g., an exaggerated reaction to the loss of a loved one), role disputes (e.g., conflicts with a significant other), role transitions (e.g., starting a new job, getting married, or retiring), or interpersonal deficits (e.g., lack of the skills needed to start or maintain a relationship). The treatment focuses on interpersonal functioning, with the assumption that as interpersonal relations improve, symptoms will subside.

Modern psychodynamic psychotherapies such as IPT also differ from classical psychoanalysis in what procedures are used. For starters, in modern psychodynamic therapy the therapist and client typically sit face to face. In addition, therapy is less intensive, with meetings often occurring only once a week and therapy lasting months rather than years. In contrast to classical psychoanalysis, modern psychodynamic therapists are more likely to offer support or advice in addition to interpretation (Barber et al., 2013). Therapists are also now less likely to interpret a client's statements as a sign of unconscious sexual or aggressive impulses, as was commonly the case in psychoanalysis. However, other concepts, such as fostering insight into unconscious processes, remain features of most psychodynamic therapies. Freud's couch casts a long shadow.

In the classic movie *Good Will Hunting*, the lead character, played by Matt Damon, forms a strong bond with his therapist, played by Robin Williams. As in psychodynamic therapy, the therapist in the movie uses the doctor–patient relationship to help break down the patient's defense mechanisms and resolve an inner conflict. The amazing bond that was formed between therapist and patient and the life-changing treatment delivered are the stuff of therapists' dreams (and Hollywood scripts).   Miramax/Kobal/Shutterstock

What Is the Evidence?

Although psychodynamic therapy has been around for a long time and continues to be widely practiced, there is limited evidence for its effectiveness. Some researchers suggest that there is evidence that psychodynamic therapies are effective (Shedler, 2010), while other studies conclude that cognitive behavioral therapy (described below) may be more effective than psychodynamic therapies (Tolin, 2010; Watzke et al., 2012).

psychodynamic psychotherapies
Therapies that explore childhood events and encourage individuals to use this understanding to develop insight into their psychological problems.

interpersonal psychotherapy (IPT)
A form of psychotherapy that focuses on helping clients improve current relationships.

Humanistic and Existential Therapies

Humanistic and existential therapies emerged in the middle of the 20th century, in part as a reaction to the negative views that psychoanalysis holds about human nature (for instance, that we are focused primarily on sex and death). Humanistic and existential therapies assume that human nature is generally positive, and they emphasize the natural tendency of each individual to strive for personal improvement. Humanistic and existential therapies share the assumption that psychological problems stem from feelings of alienation and loneliness, and that those feelings can be traced to failure to reach one's potential (in the humanistic approach) or from failure to find meaning in life (in the existential approach). Although interest in these approaches peaked in the 1960s and 1970s, some therapists continue to practice these approaches today. Two well-known types are person-centered therapy (a humanistic approach) and gestalt therapy (an existential approach).

Person-Centered Therapy

Person-centered therapy (or **client-centered therapy**) *assumes that all individuals have a tendency toward growth and that this growth can be facilitated by acceptance by and genuine reactions from the therapist.* This approach assumes that each person is qualified to determine his or her own goals for therapy, such as becoming more confident or making a career decision, and even the frequency and length of therapy. In this type of nondirective treatment, the therapist tends not to provide advice or suggestions about what the client should be doing, but instead paraphrases the client's words, mirroring the client's thoughts and sentiments (e.g., "I think I hear you saying . . ."). Person-centered therapists believe that with adequate support, the client will recognize the right things to do.

Person-centered therapists should demonstrate three basic qualities:

1. *Congruence,* which means openness and honesty in the therapeutic relationship and ensuring that the therapist communicates the same message at all levels. For example, the therapist must communicate the same message in words, in facial expressions, and in body language. Saying "I think your concerns are valid" while smirking simply will not do.

2. *Empathy,* which is the process of trying to understand the client by seeing the world from the client's perspective, in order to better appreciate the client's apprehensions, worries, or fears.

3. *Unconditional positive regard,* which means providing a nonjudgmental, warm, and accepting environment in which the client can feel safe expressing his or her thoughts and feelings.

The goal of person-centered therapy is not to uncover repressed conflicts, as in psychodynamic therapy, but instead to try to understand the client's experience and reflect that experience back to the client in a supportive way, encouraging the client's natural tendency toward growth. This style of therapy, however, is reminiscent of psychoanalysis in the way it encourages the client toward the free expression of thoughts and feelings.

Gestalt Therapy

Gestalt therapy *has the goal of helping the client become aware of his or her thoughts, behaviors, experiences, and feelings and to "own" or take responsibility for them.* Gestalt therapists are encouraged to be enthusiastic and warm toward their clients, an approach they share with person-centered therapists. To help facilitate the client's awareness, gestalt therapists also reflect back to the client their impressions of the client.

Gestalt therapy emphasizes the experiences and behaviors that are occurring at that particular moment in the therapy session. For example, if a client is talking about

person-centered therapy (or client-centered therapy) A form of psychotherapy that assumes that all individuals have a tendency toward growth and that this growth can be facilitated by acceptance and genuine reactions from the therapist.

gestalt therapy A form of psychotherapy whose goal is helping the client become aware of his or her thoughts, behaviors, experiences, and feelings and "own" or take responsibility for them.

something stressful that occurred during the previous week, the therapist might shift the attention to the client's current experience by asking "How do you feel as you describe what happened to you?" This technique is known as focusing. Clients are also encouraged to put their feelings into action. One way to do this is the empty chair technique, in which the client imagines that a person in their life (e.g., a spouse, a parent, a coworker) is in an empty chair sitting directly across from the client. The client then moves from chair to chair, alternating from role-playing what he or she would say to the other person and then role-playing how he or she imagines the other person would respond.

As part of gestalt therapy, clients may be encouraged to imagine a conversation with another person sitting across from them in a chair. Photoalto/Alamy

Behavioral and Cognitive Therapies

Unlike the talk therapies described above, behavioral and cognitive treatments emphasize actively changing a person's current thoughts and behaviors as a way to mitigate or eliminate their psychopathology. In the evolution of psychological treatments, clients started out lying down in psychoanalysis and then sitting in psychodynamic and related approaches, but in behavioral and cognitive therapies, they often stand and engage in behavior-change homework assignments in their everyday life.

Behavior Therapy: Changing Maladaptive Behavior Patterns

Whereas Freud developed psychoanalysis as an offshoot of hypnosis and other clinical techniques that clinicians used before him, behavior therapy was developed based on laboratory findings of behavioral psychologists. As you read in the Evolution of Psychological Science chapter, behaviorists rejected theories based on "invisible" mental properties that were difficult to test and impossible to observe directly. Behaviorists found psychoanalytic ideas particularly hard to test: How do you know whether a person has an unconscious conflict or whether insight has occurred? Behavioral principles, in contrast, focused solely on behaviors that could be observed (e.g., avoidance of a feared object, such as refusing to get on an airplane). **Behavior therapy** assumes that *disordered behavior is learned and that symptom relief is achieved through changing overt, maladaptive behaviors into more constructive behaviors.* A variety of behavior therapy techniques have been developed for many disorders, based on the learning principles you encountered in the Learning chapter, including operant conditioning procedures (which focus on reinforcement and punishment) and classical conditioning procedures (which focus on extinction). Here are three examples of behavior therapy techniques in action:

1. *Eliminating unwanted behaviors* How would you change a 3-year-old's habit of throwing tantrums at the grocery store? A behavior therapist might investigate what happens immediately before and after the tantrum: Did the child get candy to "shut him up"? The study of operant conditioning shows that behavior can be influenced by its *consequences* (the reinforcing or punishing events that follow). Adjusting these might help change the behavior. Making the consequences less reinforcing (no candy!) and more punishing (a period of time-out facing the wall in the grocery store) could eliminate the problem behavior.

2. *Promoting desired behaviors* Candy and time-outs can have a strong influence on child behavior, but they work less well with adults. How might you get an individual with schizophrenia to engage in activities of daily living, or get an individual addicted to cocaine to stop using drugs? A behavior therapy technique that has proven to be quite effective in such cases is the **token economy**, which *involves giving clients "tokens" for desired behaviors that they can later trade for rewards.* In the case of cocaine dependence, for instance, the desired behavior is not using cocaine. Programs that reward non-use with vouchers (that can be exchanged for rewards such as money, bus passes, clothes, and so on), have been shown to significantly reduce cocaine use (Petry et al., 2013).

A behavioral psychologist might treat a temper tantrum using time-out, a method that is based on the behavioral principle of operant conditioning and one that ensures that a child will not be rewarded for her undesired behavior. Matthew Nock

behavior therapy A type of therapy that assumes that disordered behavior is learned and that symptom relief is achieved through changing overt maladaptive behaviors into more constructive behaviors.

token economy A form of behavior therapy in which clients are given "tokens" for desired behaviors, which they can later trade for rewards.

TABLE 15.1 Exposure Hierarchy for Social Phobia	
Item	Fear (0–100)
1. Have a party and invite everyone from work	99
2. Go to a holiday party for 1 hour without drinking	90
3. Invite Cindy to have dinner and see a movie	85
4. Go for a job interview	80
5. Ask boss for a day off work	65
6. Ask questions in a meeting at work	65
7. Eat lunch with coworkers	60
8. Talk to a stranger on the bus	50
9. Talk to cousin on the telephone for 10 minutes	40
10. Ask for directions at the gas station	35

Information from Ellis (1991).

An exposure therapy client with obsessive-compulsive disorder who fears contamination in public restrooms might be given the "homework" of visiting three such restrooms in a week, touching the toilets, and then not washing up. Benkrut/iStock/Getty Images

exposure therapy An approach to treatment that involves confronting an emotion-arousing stimulus directly and repeatedly, ultimately leading to a decrease in the emotional response.

cognitive therapy Focuses on helping a client identify and correct any distorted thinking about self, others, or the world.

cognitive restructuring A therapeutic approach that teaches clients to question the automatic beliefs, assumptions, and predictions that often lead to negative emotions and to replace negative thinking with more realistic and positive beliefs.

Similar systems are used to promote desired behaviors in classrooms, the workplace, and commercial advertising (e.g., airline and credit card rewards programs).

3. *Reducing unwanted emotional responses* One of the most powerful ways to reduce anxious behavior is by gradual exposure to the feared object or situation. **Exposure therapy** is an *approach to treatment of the client that involves confronting an emotion-arousing stimulus directly and repeatedly, ultimately leading to a decrease in the emotional response.* This technique depends on the processes of habituation and response extinction. For example, in Christine's case her clinician gradually exposed her to the content of her obsessions (dirt and germs), which became less and less distressing with repeated exposure (as she learned that she would not actually be harmed by coming into contact with the previously feared stimulus). Similarly, for clients who are afraid of social interaction and unable to function at school or work, a behavioral treatment might involve exposure first to imagined situations in which they talk briefly with one person, then talk a bit longer to a medium-sized group, and finally, give a speech to a large group. Behavioral therapists use an exposure hierarchy to accustom the client gradually to the feared object or situation. Easier situations are practiced first, and as fear decreases, the client progresses to more difficult or frightening situations (see **TABLE 15.1**).

Cognitive Therapy: Changing Distorted Thoughts

Whereas behavior therapy focuses primarily on changing a person's behavior, **cognitive therapy**, as the name suggests, *focuses on helping a client identify and correct any distorted thinking about self, others, or the world* (Beck, 2019). For example, behaviorists might explain a phobia as the outcome of a classical conditioning experience such as being bitten by a dog; the dog bite leads to the development of a dog phobia through the association of the dog with the experience of pain. Cognitive theorists might instead emphasize the *interpretation* of the event, and might focus on a person's new or strengthened belief that dogs are dangerous.

Cognitive therapies use a technique called **cognitive restructuring**, which *teaches clients to question the automatic beliefs, assumptions, and predictions that often lead to negative emotions and to replace negative thinking with more realistic and positive beliefs.* Specifically, clients are taught to examine the evidence for and against a particular belief or to be more accepting of outcomes that may be undesirable yet still manageable. For example, a client who is depressed may believe that she is stupid and will never pass her college courses—all on the basis of one poor grade. In this situation, the therapist would work with the client to examine the validity of this belief. The therapist would consider relevant evidence such as grades on previous exams, performance on other coursework, and examples of her intelligence outside school. In therapy sessions, the cognitive therapist will help the client to identify evidence that either supports or fails to support each negative thought, to help the client generate more balanced thoughts that more accurately reflect the true state of affairs. In other words, the clinician tries to remove the dark lens through which the client views the world, not with the goal of replacing it with rose-colored glasses, but instead with the goal of replacing it with clear glass. Here is a brief sample transcript of what part of a cognitive therapy session might sound like.

Clinician: Last week I asked you to keep a thought record of situations that made you feel very depressed, at least one per day, and the automatic thoughts that popped into your mind. Were you able to do that?

Client: Yes.

Clinician: Wonderful, I'm glad you were able to complete this assignment. Let's take a look at this together. What's the first situation that you recorded?

Client: Well . . . I went out on Friday night with my friends, which I thought would be fun and help me to feel better. But I was feeling kind of down about things and I ended up not really talking to anyone, which led me to just sit in the corner and drink all night, which caused me to get so drunk that I passed out at the party. I woke up the next day feeling embarrassed and more depressed than ever.

Clinician: Okay, and what thoughts automatically popped into your head?

Client: I can't control myself. I'll never be able to control myself. My friends think I'm a loser and will never want to hang out with me again.

Clinician: What evidence can you think of that supports this thought?

Client: Well . . . um . . . I got really drunk and so they *have* to think I'm a loser. I mean, who does that?

Clinician: All right. Now let's take a moment to think about whether there is any evidence that doesn't support those thoughts. Did anything happen that suggests that your friends don't think you are a loser or that they do want to keep hanging out with you?

Client: Well . . . my friends brought me home safely and then called the next day and joked about what happened and my one friend Tommy said something like "we've all been there" and that he wants to hang out again this weekend.

Clinician: This is very interesting. So on one hand, you feel depressed and have thoughts that you are a loser and your friends don't like you. But on the other hand, you have some pretty real-world evidence that even though you drank too much, they were still there for you and they do in fact want to hang out with you again, yes?

Client: Yeah, I guess you're right if you put it that way. I didn't think about it like that.

Clinician: So now if we were going to replace your first thoughts, which don't seem to have a lot of real-world evidence, with a more balanced thought based on the evidence, what would that new thought be?

Client: Probably something like, my friends probably weren't happy about the fact that I got so drunk because then they had to take care of me, but they are my friends and were there for me and want to keep hanging out with me.

Clinician: Excellent job. I think that sounds just right based on the evidence.

In addition to cognitive restructuring techniques, which try to change a person's thoughts to be more balanced or accurate, some forms of cognitive therapy also include techniques for coping with unwanted thoughts and feelings, techniques that resemble meditation (see the Consciousness chapter). One such technique, called **mindfulness meditation**, *teaches an individual to be fully present in each moment; to be aware of his or her thoughts, feelings, and sensations; and to detect symptoms before they become a problem.* In one study, people recovering from depression were about half as likely to

Whereas traditional forms of cognitive therapy focused largely on changing maladaptive thoughts, some newer forms incorporate meditation practices to help people become more aware of such thoughts and to simply let them pass on by—like clouds in the sky. Filadendron/Getty Images

mindfulness meditation Teaches an individual to be fully present in each moment; to be aware of his or her thoughts, feelings, and sensations; and to detect symptoms before they become a problem.

relapse during a 60-week assessment period if they received mindfulness meditation-based cognitive therapy than if they received treatment as usual (Teasdale et al., 2000).

Cognitive Behavioral Therapy: Blending Approaches

Historically, cognitive and behavioral therapies were considered distinct systems of therapy. Today, most therapists working with anxiety and depression use **cognitive behavioral therapy (CBT)**, *a blend of cognitive and behavioral therapeutic strategies.* In contrast to traditional behavior therapy and cognitive therapy, CBT is *problem-focused,* meaning that it is undertaken for specific problems (e.g., reducing the frequency of panic attacks or returning to work after a bout of depression), and *action-oriented,* meaning that the therapist tries to assist the client in selecting specific strategies that could help address those problems. The client is expected to *do* things, such as engage in exposure exercises, practice behavior-change skills, or use a diary to monitor relevant symptoms (e.g., the severity of depressed mood, panic attack symptoms). This is in contrast to psychodynamic or other therapies in which goals may not be explicitly discussed or agreed on and the client's only necessary action is to attend the therapy session.

Cognitive behavioral therapies have been found to be effective for a number of disorders (Butler et al., 2006) (see Hot Science: "Rebooting" Psychological Treatment). Substantial positive effects of CBT have been found for clients with unipolar depression, generalized anxiety disorder, panic disorder, social phobia, posttraumatic stress disorder, and childhood depressive and anxiety disorders.

Group Treatments: Healing Multiple Minds at the Same Time

It is natural to think of psychopathology as an illness that affects only one individual. Yet each person lives in a world of other people, and interactions with others may intensify and even cause disorders. A person who is depressed may be lonely after moving away from friends and loved ones, or a person who is anxious could be worried about pressure from parents. These ideas suggest that people might be able to recover from disorders in the same way they got into them—not just as an individual effort, but through social processes.

Couple and Family Therapy

When a couple is "having problems," it may be that neither individual suffers from any psychopathology. Rather, it may be the relationship itself that is disordered. In *couple therapy*, a married, cohabitating, or dating couple is seen together in therapy to work on problems usually arising within the relationship. For example, a couple might seek help because they are unhappy with their relationship. In this scenario, both members of the couple are expected to attend therapy sessions because the problem is seen as arising from their interaction rather than from the problem(s) of one half of the couple. Treatment strategies would target changes in *both* parties, focusing on ways to break their repetitive dysfunctional pattern.

In some cases, therapy with even larger groups is warranted. An individual may be having a problem—say, an adolescent is abusing alcohol—but the source of the problem is the individual's relationships with family members; perhaps the mother is herself an alcoholic who subtly encourages the adolescent to drink, and the father travels and neglects the family. In this case, it could be useful for the therapist to work with the whole group at once in *family therapy*—psychotherapy involving members of a family. Family therapy can be particularly effective when adolescent children are having problems (Masten, 2004).

Families enter therapy for many reasons, sometimes to help particular members and other times because there are problems in one or more of the relationships in the family. Anna Goldberg/AgeFotostock

cognitive behavioral therapy (CBT)
A blend of cognitive and behavioral therapeutic strategies.

"Rebooting" Psychological Treatment

Modern psychological treatments reflect recent advances in psychological science, and are supported by experimental studies that show they actually do decrease peoples' psychological suffering. However, psychological treatment is still pretty primitive in many ways. It usually involves weekly meetings in which a clinician attempts to talk a patient out of his or her psychological disorder—just as in Freud's day. Psychology researcher Alan Kazdin has called for a "rebooting" of psychotherapy research and practice to take advantage of recent advances in technology (Kazdin, 2018; Kazdin & Blase, 2011).

For instance, using apps that monitor people's symptoms by having them answer daily surveys sent to their smartphones, psychologists have learned that among people experiencing suicidal thoughts, those thoughts tend to come and go repeatedly throughout the week (Kleiman et al., 2018). Since traditional therapists see patients once per week, what should suicidal patients do when their thoughts come and go between sessions? Researchers have begun to create computer- and phone-based apps that can identify people at risk and beam interventions to their computers and phones at any time. For instance, one platform uses artificial intelligence and automated chat-bots to scan the content of people's text messages to identify periods of psychological distress and then encourage them to reach out to others for help (e.g., Jaroszewski et al., 2019).

Another smartphone-based app, called Therapeutic Evaluative Conditioning (TEC), has users repeatedly pair suicidal or self-injury-related images with aversive images such as snakes or spiders. The idea is that, as with classical conditioning, by

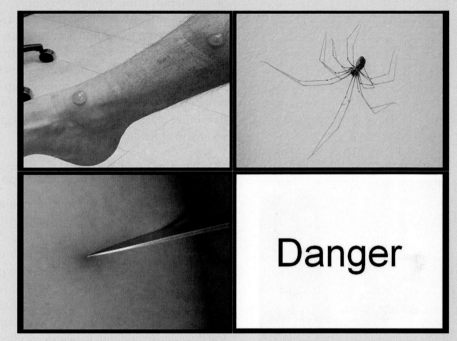

In Therapeutic Evaluative Conditioning (TEC), patients are trained to pair suicidal or self-injury-related images (left) with aversive images (right). Over time, the patients develop an aversion to suicide/self-injury and show a decrease in these self-harm behaviors. Joseph C. Franklin

repeatedly pairing these images, over time people will come to associate the suicidal or self-injury-related images with the aversive feeling evoked by the pictures of snakes and spiders. Researchers found that people who played this matching game for a few minutes each day for a month showed significant reductions in self-injury and suicidal behavior (Franklin et al., 2016).

The development of computer- or smartphone-based interventions has been extremely exciting, although so far few of these apps can show data supporting their effectiveness (Wisniewski et al., 2019). So, although the development of computerized approaches has opened up lots of new opportunities for intervention, it is important that psychologists carefully evaluate which ones can help improve health outcomes and which are simply fancier ways of providing ineffective treatment.

Group Therapy

Taking these ideas one step further, if individuals (or families) can benefit from talking with a psychotherapist, perhaps they can also benefit from talking with other clients who are talking with the therapist. This is **group therapy**, *a type of therapy in which multiple participants (who often do not know one another at the outset) work on their individual problems in a group atmosphere.* The therapist in group therapy serves more as a group facilitator than as a personal therapist, conducting the sessions both by talking with individuals and by encouraging them to talk with each other.

group therapy A type of therapy in which multiple participants (who often do not know each other at the outset) work on their individual problems in a group atmosphere.

Why do people choose group therapy? One advantage is that attending a group with others who have similar problems shows clients that they are not alone in their suffering. In addition, group members model appropriate behaviors for each other and share their insights about how to deal with their problems. Group therapy is often just as effective as individual therapy (e.g., Jonsson & Hougaard, 2008). From a societal perspective, then, group therapy is much more efficient.

Group therapy also has disadvantages. It may be difficult to assemble a group of individuals who have similar needs. This is particularly an issue with CBT, which tends to focus on specific problems such as depression or panic disorder. Group therapy may also become a problem if one or more members undermine the treatment of other group members. This can occur if some group members dominate the discussions, threaten other group members, or make others in the group uncomfortable (e.g., attempting to date other members). Finally, clients in group therapy get less attention than each might receive in individual psychotherapy.

Self-Help and Support Groups

Self-help groups are a cost-effective, time-effective, and treatment-effective solution for dealing with some types of psychological problems. Many people like self-help groups, but are they effective? How could you test this? Sturti/Getty Images

Some important types of group therapy are *self-help groups* and *support groups*, which are discussion groups that focus on a particular disorder or difficult life experience; they are often run by peers (rather than a clinician) who have themselves struggled with the same issues. The most famous self-help and support groups are Alcoholics Anonymous (AA), Gamblers Anonymous, and Al-Anon (a program for families and friends of those with alcohol problems). Other self-help groups offer support to cancer survivors or to parents of children with autism or to people with mood disorders, eating disorders, and substance abuse problems. In fact, self-help and support groups exist for just about every psychological disorder. In addition to being cost effective, self-help and support groups allow people to realize that they are not the only ones with a particular problem, and the groups give them the opportunity to offer guidance and support to each other that have arisen from their own personal experiences of success.

In some cases, though, self-help and support groups can do more harm than good. Some members may be disruptive or aggressive, or they may encourage each other to engage in behaviors that are countertherapeutic (e.g., continuing to avoid feared situations or using alcohol to cope). People with moderate problems who may be exposed to others with severe problems may become over-sensitized to symptoms they might not otherwise have found disturbing. Because self-help and support groups are usually not led by trained therapists, mechanisms to evaluate these groups and to ensure their quality are rarely in place.

AA has more than 1.3 million members in the United States, with 117,000 group meetings that occur around the world (Alcoholics Anonymous, 2016). Members are encouraged to follow *12 steps* to reach the goal of lifelong abstinence from all drinking; the steps include believing in a higher power, practicing prayer and meditation, and making amends for harm to others. Most members attend group meetings several times per week, and between meetings they receive additional support from their "sponsor." A few studies have examined the effectiveness of AA, and it appears that 12-step programs like AA can be as effective as cognitive and behavioral interventions at helping people to stop using addictive substances (Kelly et al., 2017).

Considered together, the many social approaches to psychotherapy reveal how important interpersonal relationships are for each of us. It may not always be clear how psychotherapy works, whether one approach is better than another, or what particular theory best explains how problems have developed. What *is* clear, however, is that social interactions among people—both in individual therapy and in all the different forms of group therapy—can be useful in treating psychological disorders.

Build to the Outcomes

1. What is the basis for psychoanalysis and what are its key techniques?

2. In what common ways do modern psychodynamic theories differ from Freudian analysis?

3. How does a humanistic view of human nature differ from a psychodynamic view?

4. What are the characteristics of person-centered and gestalt therapies?

5. What did the behaviorists see as problems with psychoanalytic ideas?

6. What is the idea behind the concept of cognitive restructuring?

7. How is CBT both *problem-focused* and *action-oriented*?

8. When is group therapy the best option?

9. How do self-help and support groups differ from traditional psychotherapy?

Biological Treatments: Healing the Mind by Physically Altering the Brain

People have ingested foreign substances in an attempt to change or improve their mental state since the beginning of recorded history. Humans have been fermenting fruits and other natural substances to create alcohol since about 7000 BCE (McGovern et al., 2004). Ancient Greek physicians prescribed a substance called *theriac* to treat a wide range of ailments, including anxiety and depression. Although theriac contained many ingredients (including red roses, carrots, and viper's flesh), one ingredient in particular (opium) likely was responsible for its positive effects. In the late 1800s, physicians found that cocaine also worked wonders as a cure for depression, headaches, indigestion, and a range of other problems, although its many negative side effects led to it falling out of favor as a sanctioned medicine (Markel, 2011). Since then, drug treatments have been developed that don't lead users to feel euphoric (as is the case with opium and cocaine). Instead they target specific neurotransmitters in the brain that researchers believe are involved in different mental disorders. These treatments are now the most common medical approach in treating psychological disorders.

Antipsychotic Medications

Antipsychotic drugs *treat schizophrenia and related psychotic disorders.* The first antipsychotic drug was chlorpromazine (brand name Thorazine), which was originally developed back in the 1950s as a sedative. Related medications, such as thioridazine (Mellaril) and haloperidol (Haldol), followed. Before antipsychotic drugs were introduced, people with schizophrenia often exhibited bizarre symptoms and were sometimes so disruptive and difficult to manage that the only way to protect them (and other people) was to keep them in psychiatric hospitals. After the antipsychotic drugs were introduced, the number of people in psychiatric hospitals decreased by more than two-thirds. The drugs led to the deinstitutionalization of hundreds of thousands of people and gave a major boost to the field of **psychopharmacology**, *the study of drug effects on psychological states and symptoms.*

Antipsychotic medications appear to exert their effect by blocking dopamine receptors in certain parts of the brain. The effectiveness of these medications for schizophrenia led to the dopamine hypothesis (described in the Psychological Disorders chapter), which suggests that schizophrenia may be caused by excess dopamine. Research has indeed found that dopamine overactivity in some parts of the brain is related to the more bizarre positive symptoms of schizophrenia, such as hallucinations and delusions (Marangell et al., 2003).

Learning Outcomes

- Explain how antipsychotic medications affect the brain.
- Identify the risks of antianxiety medications.
- Explain how modern antidepressants affect the brain.
- Identify which herbal supplements have been proven to be effective.
- Debate pros and cons of combining psychological therapy with drug therapy.
- Identify the more extreme treatment options when psychotherapy and medications are unsuccessful.

antipsychotic drugs Medications that are used to treat schizophrenia and related psychotic disorders.

psychopharmacology The study of drug effects on psychological states and symptoms.

Although antipsychotic drugs work well for positive symptoms, the negative symptoms of schizophrenia, such as emotional numbing and social withdrawal, may be related to dopamine *under*activity in other parts of the brain, which may help explain why antipsychotic medications do not relieve negative symptoms well. Instead of a drug that blocks dopamine receptors, negative symptoms require one that *increases* the amount of dopamine available. This is a good example of how medical treatments can have broad psychological effects but do not target specific psychological symptoms.

Over the past few decades, a new class of antipsychotic drugs has been introduced that includes clozapine (Clozaril), risperidone (Risperdal), and olanzapine (Zyprexa). These newer drugs are often referred to as *atypical* antipsychotics. (The older drugs are now often referred to as *conventional* or *typical* antipsychotics.) Unlike the older antipsychotic medications, these newer drugs appear to affect both the dopamine and serotonin systems, blocking both types of receptors. Serotonin has been implicated in some of the core difficulties in schizophrenia, such as cognitive and perceptual disruptions, as well as mood disturbances. This may explain why atypical antipsychotics can provide relief for both the positive and negative symptoms of schizophrenia (Galling et al., 2017).

Like most medications, antipsychotic drugs have side effects. The side effects of conventional antipsychotic drugs can include involuntary movements of the face, mouth, and extremities. In fact, people often need to take another medication to treat the unwanted side effects of the conventional antipsychotic drugs. Side effects of the newer medications tend to be different from and are sometimes milder than those of the older ones. For that reason, the atypical antipsychotics are now usually the frontline treatments for schizophrenia (Meltzer, 2013).

Antianxiety Medications

Antianxiety medications are *drugs that help reduce a person's experience of fear or anxiety.* The most commonly used antianxiety medications are the benzodiazepines, a type of tranquilizer that works by facilitating the action of the neurotransmitter gamma-aminobutyric acid (GABA). As you learned in the Neuroscience and Behavior chapter, GABA inhibits certain neurons in the brain. This inhibitory action can produce a calming effect for the person. Commonly prescribed benzodiazepines include diazepam (Valium), lorazepam (Ativan), and alprazolam (Xanax). The benzodiazepines typically take effect in a matter of minutes and are extremely effective for reducing symptoms of anxiety disorders.

Nonetheless, doctors are relatively cautious when prescribing benzodiazepines, since they can be highly addictive (Bandelow et al., 2017). They also have side effects, including drowsiness, and negative effects on coordination and memory. And benzodiazepines combined with alcohol can depress respiration, potentially causing accidental death.

"The drug has, however, proved more effective than traditional psychoanalysis."

Paul Noth/The New Yorker Collection/Cartoonbank.com

If you watch television you have seen advertisements for specific drugs. Does this direct-to-consumer advertising really work? Sure does! One recent study sent people posing as patients to physicians' offices asking for specific drugs and found that patient requests had a huge impact on doctors' behavior: Those asking about specific drugs were much more likely to receive a prescription than those who did not make a request (Kravitz et al., 2005). Monkey Business/ Getty Images

antianxiety medications Drugs that help reduce a person's experience of fear or anxiety.

Antidepressants and Mood Stabilizers

Antidepressants are *a class of drugs that help lift people's moods.* Two types of antidepressants, the *monoamine oxidase inhibitors (MAOIs)* and *tricyclic antidepressants,* were introduced in the 1950s. MAOIs prevent the enzyme monoamine oxidase from breaking down neurotransmitters such as norepinephrine, serotonin, and dopamine. Tricyclic antidepressants block the reuptake of norepinephrine and serotonin, thereby increasing the amount of neurotransmitter in the synaptic space between neurons. These two classes of antidepressants are used sparingly due to their side effects, which include potentially dangerous increases in blood pressure, constipation, difficulty urinating, blurred vision, and a racing heart (Marangell et al., 2003).

Among the most commonly used antidepressants today are the *selective serotonin reuptake inhibitors,* or SSRIs, which include drugs such as fluoxetine (Prozac), citalopram (Celexa), and paroxetine (Paxil). The SSRIs work by blocking the reuptake of serotonin in the brain, which makes more serotonin available in the synaptic space between neurons. The greater availability of serotonin in the synapse gives the neuron a better chance of "recognizing" and using this neurotransmitter in sending the desired signal. The SSRIs were developed on the basis of the hypothesis that low levels of serotonin are a causal factor in depression. Supporting this hypothesis, SSRIs are effective for depression, as well as for a wide range of other problems. SSRIs are called *selective* because, unlike the tricyclic antidepressants, which work on the serotonin and norepinephrine systems, SSRIs work more specifically on the serotonin system (see **FIGURE 15.2**).

Finally, antidepressants such as venlafaxine (Effexor) and bupropion (Wellbutrin) offer other alternatives. Effexor is an example of a serotonin and norepinephrine reuptake inhibitor (SNRI). Whereas SSRIs act only on serotonin, SNRIs act on both serotonin and norepinephrine. Wellbutrin, in contrast, is a norepinephrine and dopamine reuptake inhibitor. These and other newly developed antidepressants appear to have fewer (or at least different) side effects than the tricyclic antidepressants and MAOIs.

Most antidepressants can take up to a month before they start to have an effect on mood. Besides relieving symptoms of depression, almost all of the antidepressants effectively treat anxiety disorders. However, a review based on all published and unpublished data held by the U.S. Food and Drug Administration found that antidepressants are only slightly more effective than a placebo (i.e., a sugar pill containing no active medicine) (Kirsch et al., 2008).

Although antidepressants are commonly used to treat major depression, they are not recommended for treating bipolar disorder because, in the process of lifting the person's mood, they might actually trigger a manic episode (see the Psychological Disorders chapter).

antidepressants A class of drugs that help lift people's moods.

Figure 15.2 Antidepressant Drug Actions Antidepressant drugs, such as MAOIs, SSRIs, and tricyclic antidepressants, act on neurotransmitters such as serotonin, dopamine, and norepinephrine by inhibiting their breakdown and blocking reuptake. These actions make more of the neurotransmitter available for release and leave more of the neurotransmitter in the synaptic gap to activate the receptor sites on the postsynaptic neuron.

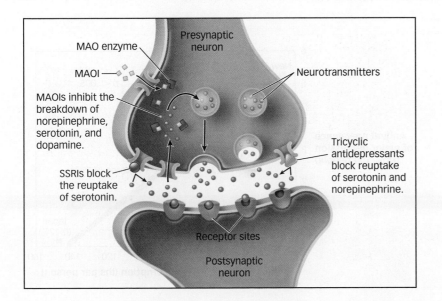

Instead, bipolar disorder is treated with *mood stabilizers,* which are medications used to suppress swings between mania and depression. Lithium and valproate are commonly used mood stabilizers.

Herbal and Natural Products

In a survey of more than 2,000 Americans, 7% of those suffering from anxiety disorders and 9% of those suffering from severe depression reported using alternative "medications" such as herbal medicines, megavitamins, homeopathic remedies, or naturopathic remedies to treat these problems (Kessler et al., 2001). People use these products because they are available over the counter, are less expensive, and are perceived as "natural" alternatives to synthetic or human-made "drugs." Are herbal and natural products effective in treating mental health problems? Or are they just "snake oil"?

The answer to this question isn't simple. Herbal products are not considered medications by regulatory agencies such as the Food and Drug Administration, so they are exempt from rigorous research to establish their safety and effectiveness. There is little scientific information about herbal products, including possible interactions with other medications, side effects, appropriate dosages, how they work, or even *whether* they work—and the purity of the products often varies from brand to brand (Jordan et al., 2010).

There is research support for the effectiveness of some herbal and natural products, but the evidence is not overwhelming (Lake, 2009). For example, some studies have shown that St. John's wort has an advantage over a placebo (Lecrubier et al., 2002) for the treatment of depression, but other studies show no advantage (Hypericum Depression Trial Study Group, 2002). Omega-3 fatty acids have been linked with lower rates of depression and suicide (see **FIGURE 15.3**), and several treatment studies have shown that omega-3s are superior to placebos at decreasing depression (Lewis et al., 2011; Parker et al., 2006). Overall, although herbal medications and treatments are worthy of continued research, these products should be closely monitored and used judiciously until more is known about their safety and effectiveness.

Phototherapy, *a therapy that involves repeated exposure to bright light,* is another natural treatment that may be helpful to people who have a seasonal pattern to their depression. This could include people suffering with seasonal affective disorder (SAD) (see the Psychological Disorders chapter). Typically, people are exposed to bright light in the morning using a lamp designed for this purpose. Some studies suggest that phototherapy is about as effective as antidepressant medication in the treatment of SAD (Thaler et al., 2011) and that it can show positive effects (and no side effects) in the treatment of nonseasonal depression as well (Perera et al., 2018).

phototherapy A therapy that involves repeated exposure to bright light.

Figure 15.3 Omega-3 Fatty Acids and Depression Countries that consume more fish (a main dietary source of omega-3s) have significantly lower rates of depression (Hibbeln, 1998). But remember, correlation does not mean causation! It could be that some other factor explains this association. For instance, it could be that living closer to the ocean or having a greater focus on health predicts both greater omega-3 consumption and lower rates of depression.

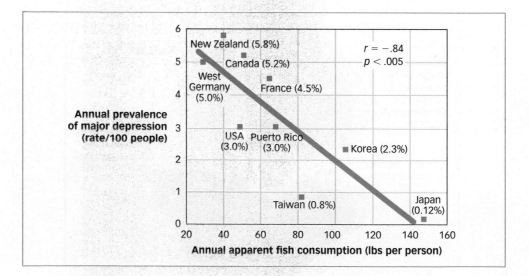

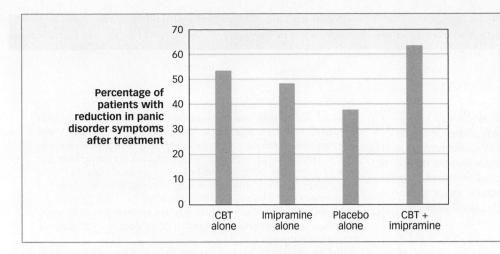

Figure 15.4 The Effectiveness of Medication and Psychotherapy for Panic Disorder One study of CBT and medication (imipramine) for panic disorder found that the effects of CBT, medication, and treatment that combined both CBT and medication were not significantly different, although all three conditions were superior to the placebo condition (Barlow et al., 2000).

Combining Medication and Psychotherapy

Given that psychological treatments and medications both have shown an ability to treat mental disorders effectively, some natural next questions are: Which is more effective? Is the combination of psychological and medicinal treatments better than either by itself?

The answer often depends on the particular problem being considered. For example, in the cases of schizophrenia and bipolar disorder, researchers have found that medication is more effective than psychological treatment and so is considered a necessary part of treatment. But in the case of mood and anxiety disorders, medication and psychological treatments are equally effective. One landmark study compared cognitive behavioral therapy (CBT), imipramine (an antidepressant), the combination of these treatments (CBT plus imipramine), and an inert placebo for the treatment of panic disorder (Barlow et al., 2000). After 12 weeks of treatment, either CBT alone or imipramine alone was found to be superior to a placebo, but the combination of treatments was not significantly better than either treatment alone (see **FIGURE 15.4**). More is not always better (see Other Voices: Diagnosis: Human).

Given that both therapy and medications are effective, another question is whether they work through similar mechanisms. A study of people with social phobia examined patterns of cerebral blood flow following treatment with either citalopram (an SSRI) or CBT (Furmark et al., 2002). Participants in both groups were alerted to the possibility that they would soon have to speak in public. In both groups, those who responded to treatment showed decreased activation in the amygdala, hippocampus, and neighboring cortical areas during the public speaking challenge (see **FIGURE 15.5**); the amygdala, located next to the hippocampus, plays a significant role in memory for emotional information. These findings suggest that both therapy and medication affect the brain in regions associated with a reaction to threat.

One problem in combining medication and psychotherapy is that the two treatments are often provided by different people. Psychiatrists are MDs trained in the administration of medication (although they may also provide psychological treatment), whereas psychologists

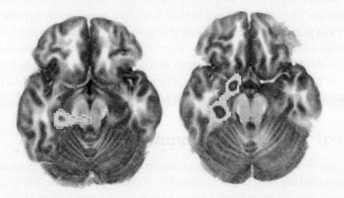

Figure 15.5 The Effects of Medication and Therapy in the Brain Neuroimaging (PET) scans of individuals with social phobia showed similar reductions in activation of the amygdala–hippocampus region after they received treatment with CBT (*left*) or with citalopram (*right*), an SSRI (from Furmark et al., 2002).

OTHER VOICES

Diagnosis: Human

Ted Gup is an author and a Visiting Lecturer in English at Brown University. Courtesy Ted Gup

Should more people receive psychological treatment or medications? Or should fewer? On one hand, data indicate that most people with a mental disorder do not receive treatment and that untreated mental disorders are an enormous source of pain and suffering. On the other hand, some argue that we have become too quick to label normal human behavior as "disordered" and too willing to medicate any behavior, thought, or feeling that makes us uncomfortable. Ted Gup is one of these people. The following is a version of his op-ed piece that appeared in the *New York Times* on April 3, 2013, under the headline "Diagnosis: Human."

The news that 11 percent of school-age children now receive a diagnosis of attention deficit hyperactivity disorder—some 6.4 million—gave me a chill. My son David was one of those who received that diagnosis.

In his case, he was in the first grade. Indeed, there were psychiatrists who prescribed medication for him even before they met him. One psychiatrist said he would not even see him until he was medicated. For a year I refused to fill the prescription at the pharmacy. Finally, I relented. And so David went on Ritalin, then Adderall, and other drugs that were said to be helpful in combating the condition.

In another age, David might have been called "rambunctious." His battery was a little too large for his body. And so he would leap over the couch, spring to reach the ceiling and show an exuberance for life that came in brilliant microbursts.

As a 21-year-old college senior, he was found on the floor of his room, dead from a fatal mix of alcohol and drugs. The date was Oct. 18, 2011. No one made him take the heroin and alcohol, and yet I cannot help but hold myself and others to account. I had unknowingly colluded with a system that devalues talking therapy and rushes to medicate, inadvertently sending a message that self-medication, too, is perfectly acceptable.

My son was no angel (though he was to us) and he was known to trade in Adderall, to create a submarket in the drug among his classmates who were themselves all too eager to get their hands on it. What he did cannot be excused, but it should be understood. What he did was to create a market that perfectly mirrored the society in which he grew up, a culture where Big Pharma itself prospers from the off-label uses of drugs, often not tested in children and not approved for the many uses to which they are put.

And so a generation of students, raised in an environment that encourages medication, are emulating the professionals by using drugs in the classroom as performance enhancers.

And we wonder why it is that they use drugs with such abandon. As all parents learn—at times to their chagrin—our children go to school not only in the classroom but also at home, and the culture they construct for themselves as teenagers and young adults is but a tiny village imitating that to which they were introduced as children. . . .

Ours is an age in which the airwaves and media are one large drug emporium that claims to fix everything from sleep to sex. I fear that being human is itself fast becoming a condition. It's as if we are trying to contain grief, and the absolute pain of a loss like mine. We have become increasingly disassociated and estranged from the patterns of life and death, uncomfortable with the messiness of our own humanity, aging and, ultimately, mortality.

Challenge and hardship have become pathologized and monetized. Instead of enhancing our coping skills, we undermine them and seek shortcuts where there are none, eroding the resilience upon which each of us, at some point in our lives, must rely.

Have we gone too far in the labeling and treatment of mental disorders? Or have we not gone far enough? On one hand, we shouldn't rush to diagnose and medicate normal behavior, but on the other hand, we must provide help to those who are suffering with a true mental disorder. One possible way forward is to ensure that people are diagnosed and treated only after a thorough evaluation by a well-trained professional. This way, we will know that a mental health professional has carefully considered whether the problems a person is having are truly disordered and in need of intervention, or just part of being human.

provide psychological treatment but cannot prescribe medication. Thus, the coordination of treatment often requires cooperation between psychologists and psychiatrists.

The question of whether psychologists should be licensed to prescribe medications has long been a source of debate among psychologists and physicians. To date, only five states have passed legislation allowing psychologists to prescribe medication (Louisiana, New Mexico, Illinois, Iowa, and Idaho), with five more states currently considering it. Opponents of prescription privileges argue that psychologists do not have the medical training to understand how medications interact with other drugs. Proponents argue that patient safety would not be compromised as long as rigorous training procedures were established. At present, the coordination of medication and psychological treatment usually involves a team effort of psychiatry and psychology.

Biological Treatments Beyond Medication

Medication can be an effective biological treatment, but for some people medications do not work, or their side effects are intolerable. If these people don't respond to psychotherapy either, what other options do they have for symptom relief? There are additional avenues of help available, but some are risky or poorly understood.

Electroconvulsive therapy (ECT), sometimes referred to as *shock therapy, is a treatment that involves inducing a brief seizure by delivering an electrical shock to the brain.* The shock is applied to the person's scalp for less than a second. ECT is used primarily to treat severe depression that has not responded to antidepressant medications, although it may also be useful for treating bipolar disorder (Khalidet al., 2008; Poon et al., 2012). Patients are pretreated with muscle relaxants and are under general anesthetic during treatment, so they are not conscious of the procedure. The main side effect of ECT is impaired short-term memory, which usually improves over the first month or two after the end of treatment. In addition, patients sometimes report headaches and muscle aches afterward. Despite these side effects, the treatment can be helpful: It is more effective than simulated ECT, a placebo, and antidepressant drugs such as tricyclics and MAOIs (Pagnin et al., 2008).

Transcranial magnetic stimulation (TMS) is *a treatment that involves placing a powerful pulsed magnet over a person's scalp to alter neuronal activity in the brain.* When TMS is used as a treatment for depression, the magnet is placed just above the right or left eyebrow in an effort to stimulate the right or left prefrontal cortex (areas of the brain implicated in depression). TMS is noninvasive and has fewer side effects than ECT: The side effects of TMS may include mild headache and a small risk of seizure, but no impact on memory or concentration. TMS applied daily to the left prefrontal cortex for 4 to 6 weeks has been found to be effective in treating depression in patients who have not responded to medication (Perera et al., 2016). In fact, a study comparing TMS with ECT found that both procedures were effective, with no significant differences between them (Janicak et al., 2002). Other studies have found that TMS can also be used to treat auditory hallucinations in patients with schizophrenia (Aleman et al., 2007).

In very rare cases, **psychosurgery**, *the surgical destruction of specific brain areas,* may be used to treat severe and unresponsive psychological disorders. Psychosurgery has a controversial history, beginning in the 1930s with the invention of the lobotomy. Lobotomies involved inserting an instrument into the brain through the patient's eye socket or through holes drilled in the side of the head. The objective was to sever connections between the frontal lobes and inner brain structures, such as the thalamus, known to be involved in emotion. Although some lobotomies produced highly successful results, there were often permanent and devastating side effects, such as extreme lethargy or childlike impulsiveness. The development of antipsychotic drugs during the 1950s provided a safer way to treat violent individuals, and the practice of lobotomy was brought to an end (Swayze, 1995).

Today, psychosurgery is reserved for extremely severe cases for which no other interventions have been effective, and when the symptoms of the disorder are intolerable to the patient. Modern psychosurgery involves a very precise destruction of brain tissue to disrupt the brain circuits known to be involved in generating symptoms. For example,

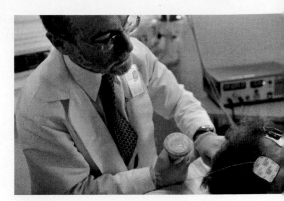

Electroconvulsive therapy (ECT) can be an effective treatment for severe depression. To reduce side effects, it is administered under general anesthesia. Richard Perry/The New York Times/Redux

electroconvulsive therapy (ECT) A treatment that involves inducing a brief seizure by delivering an electrical shock to the brain.

transcranial magnetic stimulation (TMS) A treatment that involves placing a powerful pulsed magnet over a person's scalp to alter neuronal activity in the brain.

psychosurgery Surgical destruction of specific brain areas.

Transcranial magnetic stimulation (TMS) is a technique that allows researchers and clinicians to change brain activity using a magnetic wand—no surgery is required. Orlando Sentinel/Getty Images

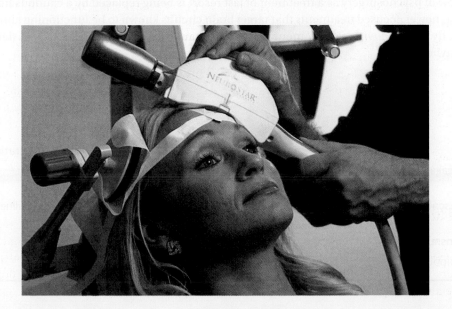

Figure 15.6 DBS Deep brain stimulation involves the insertion of battery-powered electrodes that deliver electrical pulses to specific areas of the brain believed to be causing a person's mental disorder. National Institute of Mental Health, National Institutes of Health, Department of Health and Human Services

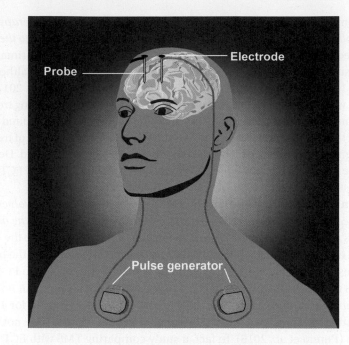

people suffering from OCD who fail to respond to treatment (including several trials of medication and cognitive behavioral treatment) may benefit from specific surgical procedures to destroy part of the corpus callosum (see Figure 3.18) and the cingulate gyrus (the ridge just above the corpus callosum), two brain regions known to be involved in the generation of obsessions and compulsions. Because of the relatively small number of cases of psychosurgery, there are not as many studies of these techniques as there are for other treatments. However, available studies have shown that psychosurgery typically leads to substantial improvements in both the short and long term for people with severe OCD (Csigó et al., 2010; van Vliet et al., 2013).

A final approach, called *deep brain stimulation* (DBS), combines the use of psychosurgery with electrical currents (as in ECT and TMS). In DBS, a small, battery-powered device is implanted in the patient's body to deliver electrical stimulation to specific areas of the brain known to be involved in the disorder (**FIGURE 15.6**). This technique has been successful for OCD treatment (Abelson et al., 2009), for treating the tremor that accompanies Parkinson's disease (Perlmutter & Mink, 2006), and for some cases of severe depression that were otherwise untreatable (Mayberg et al., 2005). The early view of psychosurgery as a treatment of last resort is being replaced by a cautious hope that newer, focused treatments that target brain circuits known to be functioning abnormally in those with certain mental disorders can have beneficial effects (Ressler & Mayberg, 2007).

Build to the Outcomes

1. What do antipsychotic drugs do?

2. What are the advantages of the newer, atypical antipsychotic medications?

3. What are some reasons for caution when prescribing antianxiety medications?

4. How do antidepressant drugs affect neurotransmitters?

5. Why are antidepressants not prescribed for bipolar disorder?

6. Why aren't herbal and natural products given the same scrutiny as pharmacological drugs are given?

7. Which herbal remedies have been proven to be effective?

8. Do therapy and medications work similarly in treating mental illness?

9. What are the benefits of ECT? The risks?

10. What is the procedure for TMS?

11. When would psychosurgery be appropriate?

Treatment Effectiveness: For Better or for Worse

Think back to Christine and the dead mouse at the beginning of this chapter. What if, instead of ERP, Christine had been treated with psychoanalysis or psychosurgery? Would those alternatives have been just as effective for treating her OCD? Throughout this chapter, we have explored various psychological and biological treatments that might help people with psychological disorders. But do these treatments actually work? Which ones work better than the others?

As you learned in the Methods in Psychology chapter, pinning down a specific cause for an effect can be a difficult detective exercise. Detection is made even more difficult because clients and doctors may approach treatment evaluation very unscientifically, often by simply noticing an improvement (or no improvement, or even a worsening of symptoms) and reaching a conclusion based on that sole observation. Determining a treatment's effectiveness can be misdirected by illusions that can only be overcome by careful, scientific evaluation.

Learning Outcomes

- Describe treatment illusions.
- Explain research methods used in treatment studies.

Treatment Illusions

Imagine you're sick and the doctor says, "Take this pill." You follow the doctor's orders and you get better. To what do you attribute your improvement? One possibility is that the pill cured you, but you might have fallen victim to an illusion of treatment. Three types of treatment illusion are produced by natural improvement, by placebo effects, and by reconstructive memory. Let's look more closely at each.

1. Natural Improvement

Natural improvement is the tendency of symptoms to return to their mean or average level. The illusion in this case happens when you conclude, mistakenly, that a treatment has made you better when you would have gotten better anyway. People typically turn to therapy or medication when their symptoms are at their worst. When this is the case, the client's symptoms will often improve regardless of whether there was any treatment at all; when you're at rock bottom, there's nowhere to move but up. In most cases, for example, depression that becomes severe enough to make individuals candidates for treatment will tend to lift in several months *no matter what they do*. A person who enters therapy for depression may develop the illusion that the therapy works because the therapy coincides with the typical course of the illness and the person's natural return to health. How can we know a treatment is effective, or if the change we observe following that treatment is caused by natural improvement? As discussed in the Methods in Psychology chapter, we could do an experiment in which we assign half of the people who are depressed to receive treatment and the other half to receive no treatment, and then monitor them over time to see if the ones who got treatment actually show greater improvement. This is precisely how researchers test out different interventions, as described in more detail below.

2. Placebo Effects

Recovery also could be the result of *nonspecific treatment effects* that are not related to the proposed active ingredient of the treatment. For example, positive influences can be produced by a **placebo**, *an inert substance or procedure that has been applied with the expectation that it will produce a healing response.* For example, if you have a headache and take a sugar pill that does not contain any painkiller, thinking it is Tylenol or aspirin, the pill is a placebo if the headache goes away. Placebos can have profound effects in the case of psychological treatments. Research shows that a large percentage of individuals with anxiety, depression, and other emotional and medical problems experience significant improvement after a placebo treatment.

placebo An inert substance or procedure that has been applied with the expectation that it will produce a healing response.

"If this doesn't help you don't worry, it's a placebo."

Peter C. Vey/The New Yorker Collection/Cartoonbank.com

3. Reconstructive Memory

A third treatment illusion can come about when the client's motivation to get well causes errors in *reconstructive memory* for the original symptoms. You might think that you've improved because of a treatment when in fact you're simply misremembering, mistakenly believing that your symptoms before treatment were worse than they actually were. For example, a client who forms a strong expectation of therapy success might later conclude that even a useless treatment had worked wonders by recalling past symptoms and troubles as worse than they had been, which would make the treatment seem effective.

Treatment Studies: Seeking Evidence

How can we make sure that we use treatments that actually work and not waste time with procedures that may be useless or even harmful? Research psychologists use approaches covered in the Methods in Psychology chapter to run experiments that test which treatments are effective for different mental disorders.

Treatment outcome studies are designed to evaluate whether a particular treatment works to decrease a person's symptoms. For example, to study the outcome of a new treatment for depression, researchers might recruit a sample of people with depression and randomly assign half to receive 6 weeks of the new treatment and the other half to a 6-week no-treatment control condition. Comparing the change in the depressive symptoms of both groups, we can learn how much more of a change in depressive symptoms was caused by the treatment compared to the control condition.

On the other hand, we also know that receiving any treatment can cause a change in symptoms via the placebo effect. To rule out that the observed changes are due to such an effect, we can randomly assign half of our patients to our preferred treatment, and the other half to another condition that *appears* to be an effective treatment. Ideally, a treatment should be assessed in a *double-blind experiment,* a study in which neither the participant nor the researcher/therapist knows which treatment the participant is receiving. In drug studies, this isn't hard to arrange because active drugs and placebos can be made to look the same to both the participants and the researchers during the study. Keeping all involved "in the dark" is much harder in the study of psychological treatments. Nevertheless, by comparing treatments either with no treatment or with other active interventions (such as other psychological treatments or medications), researchers can determine which treatments work and which are most effective for different disorders.

TABLE 15.2	Selected List of Specific Psychological Treatments Compared With Medication or Other Treatments	
Disorder	**Treatment**	**Results**
Depression	CBT	CBT = meds; CBT + meds > either alone
Panic disorder	CBT	CBT > meds at follow-up; CBT = meds at end of treatment; both > placebo
Posttraumatic stress disorder	CBT	CBT > present-centered therapy
Insomnia	CBT	CBT > medication or placebo
Depression and physical health in Alzheimer's patients	Exercise and behavioral management	Treatment > routine medical care
Gulf War veterans' illnesses	CBT and exercise	Treatment > usual care or alternative treatments

Note: CBT = cognitive behavioral therapy; meds = medication.
Information from Barlow et al. (2013).

Which Treatments Work According to the Evidence?

The distinguished psychologist Hans Eysenck (1916–1997) reviewed the relatively few studies of psychotherapy's effectiveness available in 1957 and raised a furor among therapists by concluding that psychotherapy—particularly psychoanalysis—not only was ineffective but seemed to *impede* recovery (Eysenck, 1957). Since then, studies support a more optimistic conclusion: The typical psychotherapy client is better off than three-quarters of untreated individuals (Seligman, 1995; Smith et al., 1980), and strong evidence generally supports the effectiveness of many different treatments (Nathan & Gorman, 2007). The key question then becomes: Which treatments are effective for which problems (Hunsley & Di Giulio, 2002)?

Some psychologists have argued for years that evidence supports the conclusion that most psychotherapies work about equally well, due to common factors such as contact with and empathy from a professional (Luborsky et al., 2002). Others have argued that some treatments are more effective than others, especially for treating particular types of problems. A recent review highlighted several specific psychological treatments that have been shown to work as well as, or even better than, other available treatments, including medication (Barlow et al., 2013). **TABLE 15.2** lists several of these treatments.

Some researchers and clinicians have questioned whether treatments shown to work in well-controlled studies conducted at university clinics will work in the real world.

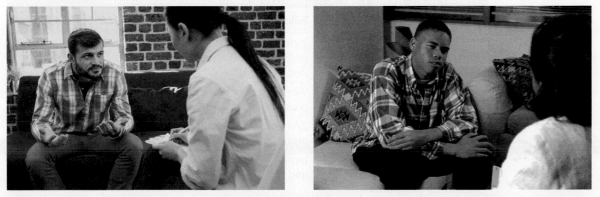

Treatments shown to be effective in research studies (which often include only a small percentage of ethnic minority patients) have been found to work equally well with people of different ethnicities (Miranda et al., 2005). Wavebreak Media Ltd/Alamy; Mary Kate Denny/Photoedit

For instance, some psychologists have noted that most treatment studies reported in the literature do not have large numbers of ethnic minority participants, and so it is unclear if these treatments will work with ethnically and culturally diverse groups. A review of available data suggests that, despite gaps in the literature, many psychological treatments work as well with ethnic minority clients as with White clients (Miranda et al., 2005).

Even trickier than the question of establishing whether a treatment works is whether it might actually do harm. The dangers of drug treatment should be clear to anyone who has read a magazine ad for a drug and studied the fine print, with its list of side effects, potential drug interactions, and complications. Some drugs used in psychological treatment can be addictive, creating long-term dependency and serious withdrawal symptoms. The strongest critics of drug treatment claim that drugs do no more than trade one unwanted symptom for another: trading depression for lack of sexual interest, trading anxiety for intoxication, or trading agitation for lethargy and dulled emotion (Breggin, 2000).

The dangers of psychotherapy are more subtle, but one is clear enough in some cases that there is actually a name for it. **Iatrogenic illness** is *a disorder or symptom that occurs as a result of a medical or psychotherapeutic treatment itself* (Boisvert & Faust, 2002). Such an illness might arise, for instance, when a psychotherapist becomes convinced that a client has a disorder that in fact the client does not have. As a result, the therapist works to help the client accept that diagnosis and participate in psychotherapy to treat the disorder. Being treated for a disorder can, under certain conditions, make a person show signs of that very disorder—and so an iatrogenic illness is born. For example, there are cases of clients who have been influenced through hypnosis and repeated suggestions in therapy to "recover" memories of traumatic childhood events, when an investigation reveals no evidence for these problems prior to therapy (McNally, 2003).

Just as psychologists have created lists of treatments that work, they have also begun to establish lists of treatments that *harm*. The purpose of doing so is to inform other researchers, clinicians, and the public which treatments they should avoid. Did your high school have a D.A.R.E. (Drug Abuse and Resistance Education) program? Have you heard of critical-incident stress debriefing (CISD), Scared Straight, and boot-camp programs? They all sound as if they might work, but careful scientific experiments have determined that people who participate in these interventions are actually worse off afterward (see **TABLE 15.3**) (Lilienfeld, 2007)!

To regulate the potentially powerful influence of different therapies, psychologists hold themselves to a set of ethical standards for the treatment of people with mental disorders (American Psychological Association, 2002). Adherence to these standards is required for membership in the American Psychological Association, and state licensing boards also monitor adherence to ethical principles in therapy. The ethical standards

iatrogenic illness A disorder or symptom that occurs as a result of a medical or psychotherapeutic treatment itself.

TABLE 15.3 Some Psychological Treatments That Cause Harm		
Type of Treatment	**Potential Harm**	**Source of Evidence**
Critical-incident stress debriefing (CISD)	Increased risk of posttraumatic stress disorder (PTSD)	Randomized controlled trials
Scared Straight	Worsening of conduct problems	Randomized controlled trials
Boot-camp interventions for conduct problems	Worsening of conduct problems	Meta-analysis (review of studies)
Drug Abuse and Resistance Education (D.A.R.E.) programs	Increased use of alcohol and drugs	Randomized controlled trials

Information from Lilienfeld (2007).

include (1) striving to benefit clients and taking care to do no harm; (2) establishing relationships of trust with clients; (3) promoting accuracy, honesty, and truthfulness; (4) seeking fairness in treatment and taking precautions to avoid biases; and (5) respecting the dignity and worth of all people. When people suffering from mental disorders come to psychologists for help, adhering to these guidelines is the least that psychologists can do. Ideally, in the hope of relieving suffering, they can do much more.

Build to the Outcomes

1. What are the three kinds of treatment illusions?
2. What is the placebo effect?
3. What methods are used in treatment outcome studies?
4. Why is a double-blind experiment so important in assessing treatment effectiveness?
5. How do psychologists know which treatments work and which might be harmful?
6. How might psychotherapy cause harm?

CHAPTER REVIEW

Treatment: Getting Help to Those Who Need It

- Mental illness is often misunderstood, and because of this, it too often goes untreated.
- Untreated mental illness can be extremely costly, affecting an individual's ability to function and causing social and financial burdens.
- Many people who suffer from mental illness do not get the help they need: They may be unaware that they have a problem, they may have beliefs that keep them from getting help, or they may face structural barriers to getting treatment.
- Treatments include psychotherapy, which focuses on the mind; medical and biological methods, which focus on the brain and body; and a combination of the two approaches.

Psychological Treatments: Healing the Mind Through Interaction

- Psychodynamic therapies, including psychoanalysis, emphasize helping clients gain insight into their unconscious conflicts.
- Humanistic approaches (e.g., person-centered therapy) and existential approaches (e.g., gestalt therapy) focus on helping people develop a sense of personal worth.
- Behavior therapy applies learning principles to specific behavior problems. Cognitive therapy is focused on helping people change the way they think about events in their lives. Cognitive behavioral therapy (CBT) merges cognitive and behavioral approaches.
- Group therapies target couples, families, or groups of clients brought together for the purpose of working together to solve their problems.

Biological Treatments: Healing the Mind by Physically Altering the Brain

- Antipsychotic medications block dopamine receptors in parts of the brain, thus reducing dopamine activity. They are used to treat the positive symptoms of schizophrenia.
- Antianxiety medications are used to treat anxiety disorders but have the potential for abuse.
- Antidepressants affect the level of serotonin in the brain and are used to treat depression and related disorders.
- Herbal and natural products are not considered medications by regulatory agencies and so are not subject to strict scrutiny. Although there is little scientific information on their effectiveness, some do seem to have mild positive effects.
- Medications are often combined with psychotherapy.
- Other biomedical treatments include electroconvulsive therapy (ECT), transcranial magnetic stimulation (TMS), deep brain stimulation (DBS), and psychosurgery—this last used in extreme cases, when other methods of treatment have been exhausted.

Treatment Effectiveness: For Better or for Worse

- Observing improvement during treatment does not necessarily mean that the treatment was effective; it might instead reflect natural improvement, nonspecific treatment effects (e.g., the placebo effect), and reconstructive memory processes.
- Treatment studies apply scientific research methods such as placebo controls and double-blind techniques to determine which treatments work.
- Some treatments are more effective than others for certain disorders; both medication and psychotherapy have dangers that ethical practitioners must consider carefully.

Key Concept Quiz

1. Which statement does NOT present a reason that people fail to get treatment for mental illness?
   a. People may not realize that their disorder needs to be treated.
   b. Levels of impairment for people with mental illness are comparable to or higher than those of people with chronic medical illnesses.
   c. There may be barriers to treatment, such as beliefs and circumstances that keep people from getting help.
   d. Even people who acknowledge they have a problem may not know where to look for services.

2. Which of the following statements is true?
   a. Mental illness is very rare, with only 1 person in 100 suffering from a psychological disorder.
   b. The majority of individuals with psychological disorders seek treatment.
   c. Women and men are equally likely to seek treatment for psychological disorders.
   d. Mental illness is often not taken as seriously as physical illness.

3. The most effective treatment for psychological disorders is often
   a. yoga.
   b. hypnosis.
   c. psychotherapy, medication, or a combination of the two.
   d. doing nothing, since most people improve anyway.

4. Eclectic psychotherapy
   a. concentrates on the interpretation of dreams.
   b. introduces clients to strange situations.
   c. draws on techniques from different forms of therapy.
   d. focuses on the analysis of resistance.

5. The different psychodynamic therapies all share an emphasis on
   a. the influence of the collective unconscious.
   b. the importance of taking responsibility for psychological problems.
   c. combining behavioral and cognitive approaches.
   d. developing insight into the unconscious sources of psychological disorders.

6. Which type of therapy would likely work best for someone with an irrational fear of heights?
   a. psychodynamic therapy
   b. gestalt therapy
   c. behavioral therapy
   d. humanistic therapy

7. Mindfulness meditation is part of which kind of therapy?
   a. interpersonal therapy
   b. humanistic therapy
   c. psychodynamic therapy
   d. cognitive therapy

8. Which type of therapy emphasizes action on the part of the client?
   a. cognitive behavioral therapy
   b. humanistic therapy
   c. existential therapy
   d. group therapy

9. Examining the failure to reach one's potential reflects the _____ approach, whereas examining one's failure to find meaning in life reflects the _____ approach.
   a. cognitive; behavioral
   b. humanistic; existential
   c. psychodynamic; cognitive behavioral
   d. existential; humanistic

10. Antipsychotic drugs were developed to treat
    a. depression.
    b. schizophrenia.
    c. anxiety.
    d. mood disorders.

11. Atypical antipsychotic drugs
    a. act on different neurotransmitters depending on the individual.
    b. affect only the dopamine system.
    c. affect only the serotonin system.
    d. act on both the dopamine and serotonin systems.

12. Antidepressant medications have the strongest effects for people with _____ depression.
    a. no
    b. mild
    c. moderate
    d. severe

13. What do electroconvulsive therapy, transcranial magnetic stimulation, and phototherapy all have in common?
    a. They incorporate herbal remedies in their treatment regimens.
    b. They may result in the surgical destruction of certain brain areas.
    c. They are considered biological treatments beyond medication.
    d. They are typically used in conjunction with psychotherapy.

14. Which treatment illusion occurs when a client or therapist attributes the client's improvement to a feature of treatment, although that feature wasn't really the active element that caused improvement?
    a. nonspecific treatment effects
    b. natural improvement
    c. error in reconstructive memory
    d. regression to the mean

15. Current studies indicate that the typical psychotherapy client is better off than _____ of untreated individuals.
    a. one-half.
    b. the same number.
    c. one-fourth.
    d. three-fourths.

LearningCurve Don't stop now! Quizzing yourself is a powerful study tool.
Go to LaunchPad to access the LearningCurve adaptive quizzing system and your
own personalized learning plan. Visit launchpadworks.com.

Key Terms

psychotherapy (p. 452)

eclectic psychotherapy (p. 452)

psychodynamic psychotherapies (p. 452)

interpersonal psychotherapy (IPT) (p. 453)

person-centered therapy (or client-centered therapy) (p. 454)

gestalt therapy (p. 454)

behavior therapy (p. 455)

token economy (p. 455)

exposure therapy (p. 456)

cognitive therapy (p. 456)

cognitive restructuring (p. 456)

mindfulness meditation (p. 457)

cognitive behavioral therapy (CBT) (p. 458)

group therapy (p. 459)

antipsychotic drugs (p. 461)

psychopharmacology (p. 461)

antianxiety medications (p. 462)

antidepressants (p. 463)

phototherapy (p. 464)

electroconvulsive therapy (ECT) (p. 467)

transcranial magnetic stimulation (TMS) (p. 467)

psychosurgery (p. 467)

placebo (p. 469)

iatrogenic illness (p. 472)

Changing Minds

1. One of your friends recently lost a close family member in a tragic car accident, and he's devastated. He hasn't been attending classes, and when you check up on him you learn that he's not sleeping well or eating regularly. You want to help him but feel out of your depth. You suggest he visit the campus counseling center and talk to a therapist. "Only crazy people go to therapy," he says. What could you tell your friend to dispel this wrong assumption?

2. While you're talking to your bereaved friend, his roommate comes in. The roommate agrees with your suggestion about therapy but takes it further. "I'll give you the name of my therapist. He helped me quit smoking—he'll be able to cure your depression in no time." Why is it dangerous to assume that a good therapist can cure anyone and anything?

3. In the Methods in Psychology chapter you read about Louise Hay, whose best-selling book, *You Can Heal Your Life*, promotes a kind of psychotherapy: teaching readers how to change their thoughts and thereby improve not only their inner lives but also their physical health. The chapter quotes Hay as saying that scientific evidence is unnecessary to validate her claims. Is her view correct? Is

there a scientific basis for the major types of psychotherapy described in this chapter? How is scientific experimentation used to assess their effectiveness?

4. In June 2009, the pop icon Michael Jackson died from a fatal dose of the anesthetic propofol, which is sometimes used off-label as an antianxiety drug. An autopsy confirmed that his body contained a cocktail of prescription drugs, including the benzodiazepines lorazepam and diazepam. (Jackson's cardiologist, Dr. Conrad Murray, was later convicted of involuntary manslaughter for administering the fatal propofol dose.) Other celebrities whose deaths have been attributed to medications commonly prescribed for anxiety and depression include Heath Ledger in 2008, Prince in 2016, musicians Lil Peep and Tom Petty in 2017, and baseball pitcher Tyler Skaggs in 2019. "These drugs are dangerous," your roommate notes. "People who have psychological problems should seek out talk therapy for their problems and stay away from the medications, even if they're prescribed by a responsible doctor." You agree that medications can be dangerous if misused, but how would you justify the use of drug treatment for serious mental disorders?

Answers to Key Concept Quiz

1. b; 2. d; 3. c; 4. c; 5. d; 6. c; 7. d; 8. a; 9. b; 10. b; 11. d; 12. d; 13. c; 14. a; 15. d

LaunchPad macmillan learning   LaunchPad features the full e-book of *Introducing Psychology*, the LearningCurve adaptive quizzing system, videos, and a variety of activities to boost your learning. Visit LaunchPad at launchpadworks.com.

Essentials of Statistics for Psychological Science

Picturing the Measurements

When psychologists collect data, they end up with a big spreadsheet filled with numbers. To help them make sense of those numbers, they often use graphic representations. The most common kind of graphic representation is called a **frequency distribution**, which is *a graphic representation showing the number of times in which the measurement of a property takes on each of its possible values*. For example, the graph at the top of **Figure A.1** shows the results of a city-wide census in which residents of Somerville, Massachusetts, were asked to report their current level of happiness by using a rating scale that ranged from 1 (very unhappy) to 10 (very happy). The property being measured was happiness, the operational definition of happiness was a scale rating, and all the possible values of that rating (1 through 10) are shown on the horizontal axis. The vertical axis shows the number of men and women who responded to the census and used each of these values to rate their happiness. (People who identified as something other than male or female are not shown in this graph.) So, for example, the graph shows that 1,677 women and 646 men rated their happiness as 8 on a 10-point scale. The graph at the bottom left shows exactly the same data, but it uses smooth lines rather than bars, which is an equally common way to display a frequency distribution.

frequency distribution A graphic representation showing the number of times that the measurement of a property takes on each of its possible values.

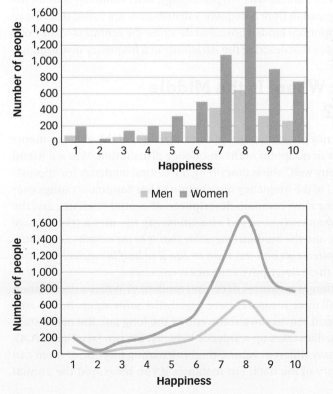

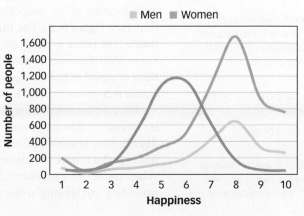

Figure A.1 Frequency Distributions The graph at the top uses bars to show the number of male residents (shown in green) and female residents (shown in orange) of Somerville, Massachusetts, who rated their happiness at each value on a 10-point scale. The graph at the bottom left shows the same data using smoothed lines. The graph at the bottom right adds a hypothetical normal distribution (shown in purple).

In a single glance, these graphs reveal things about the sample that a page full of numbers does not. For instance, when you look at the shape of the distributions, you instantly know that the people in this sample tend to be fairly happy, that far fewer men than women responded to the census, that 8 is the most popular rating for both men and women, and that both genders are about 3 times as likely to rate their happiness as 10 than to rate it as 1. All of that information from a simple drawing!

The distributions in Figure A.1 are *negatively skewed* (which means that they lean to the right) rather than *positively skewed* (which means that they lean to the left) because very few people use numbers that are below the midpoint of the scale to rate their happiness. Although a frequency distribution can have just about any shape, a special shape is shown in purple in the graph at the bottom right of Figure A.1. As you can see, this distribution has a peak exactly in the middle and then trails off in the same way at both ends. This distribution is unskewed or *symmetrical,* which is to say that the left half is a mirror image of the right half. This is called the **normal distribution**, which is *a mathematically defined distribution in which the frequency of measurements is highest in the middle and decreases symmetrically in both directions.* The normal distribution is important because it appears so often in real-world data—as long as you have a lot of it! For example, if you graphed the height, blood pressure, IQ, or shoe size of all Americans, you'd see a normal distribution every time. By the way, the normal distribution is often called a *bell curve,* but if you'd like to be single for the rest of your life you can refer to it in public as a *Gaussian distribution.*

Describing the Measurements

A frequency distribution depicts every measurement in a sample and therefore provides a full and complete picture of that sample. But sometimes a full and complete picture is more than we want to know. When we ask a friend how she's been doing, we don't really want her to show us a frequency distribution of her happiness ratings on each day of the previous 6 months. Rather, we want her to provide a brief summary statement that captures the essential information from that graph—for example, "I've been doing pretty well," or maybe "I've been having a few ups and downs." In psychology, brief summary statements that capture the essential information from a frequency distribution are called *descriptive statistics,* and there are two important kinds: those that describe the *central tendency* of a frequency distribution, and those that describe the *variability* in a frequency distribution.

Central Tendency: Where Is the Middle of the Distribution?

Descriptions of central tendency are statements about the values of the measurements that *tend* to lie near the *center* or midpoint of the frequency distribution. When a friend says that she's been "doing pretty well," she is describing the central tendency (or approximate location of the midpoint) of the frequency distribution of her happiness ratings over time (see **Figure A.2**). The three most common descriptions of central tendency are: the **mode** (*the value of the most frequently observed measurement*); the **mean** (*the average value of all the measurements*); and the **median** (*the value that is in the middle, i.e., greater than or equal to half the measurements and less than or equal to half the measurements*). **Figure A.3** shows how each of these descriptive statistics is calculated.

Why do we need three different measures of central tendency? When a distribution is normal we don't, because all three measures have exactly the same value. But when a distribution is skewed, the mean moves toward the end of the long tail, the mode stays home at the hump, and the median takes up residence between the two (see **Figure A.4**). When these three measures have different values, then calculating just one of them can provide a misleading summary of the data. For instance, if you measured the annual

normal distribution A mathematically defined distribution in which the frequency of measurements is highest in the middle and decreases symmetrically in both directions.

mode The value of the most frequently observed measurement.

mean The average value of all the measurements.

median The value that is greater than or equal to half the measurements and less than or equal to half the measurements.

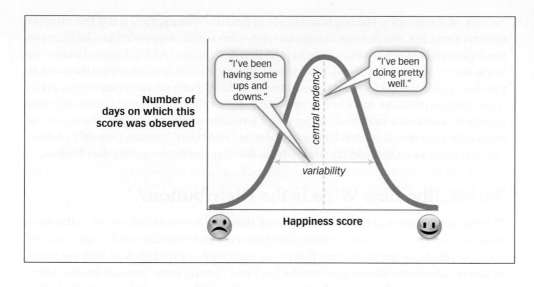

Figure A.2   Two Kinds of Descriptive Statistics The most common descriptive statistics describe a frequency distribution's central tendency (where do most of the measurements lie?) and variability (how much do the measurements differ from one another?).

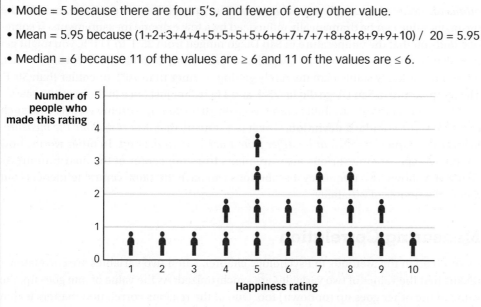

- Mode = 5 because there are four 5's, and fewer of every other value.

- Mean = 5.95 because (1+2+3+4+4+5+5+5+5+6+6+7+7+7+8+8+8+9+9+10) / 20 = 5.95

- Median = 6 because 11 of the values are ≥ 6 and 11 of the values are ≤ 6.

Figure A.3   Calculating Descriptive Statistics This frequency distribution shows the data from 20 individuals who rated their happiness on a 10-point scale. Descriptive statistics include measures of central tendency (such as the mean, median, and mode) and measures of variability (such as the range and the standard deviation).

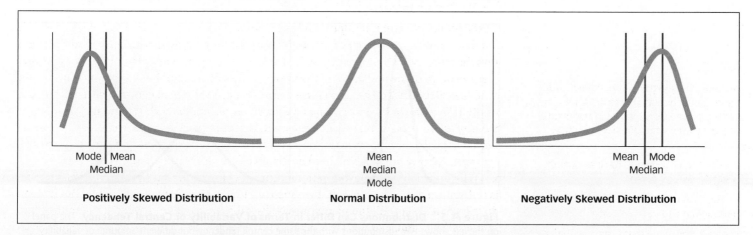

Figure A.4   Differently Shaped Distributions When a frequency distribution is normal, the mean, median, and mode all have the same value, but when it is positively or negatively skewed, these three measures of central tendency have different values.

range The value of the largest measurement in a frequency distribution minus the value of the smallest measurement.

standard deviation A statistic that describes how the measurements in a frequency distribution differ from the mean on average.

income of the roughly 400,000 households in Seattle, Washington, you'd find that the mean is about $84,000. But that sample includes a few unusual households—for example, the households of Bill Gates (whose net worth is $95 billion) and Jeff Bezos (whose net worth is over $150 billion). But if, in addition to the mean, you also calculated the median, you'd find it has the considerably lower value of $62,000. Each measure can potentially be misleading in isolation, but when considered together they paint a much more accurate picture of Seattle as a middle-class city with a few ultra-wealthy residents. You should be very suspicious whenever you hear some new fact about the "average person" but don't hear anything about the median, the mode, or the shape of the frequency distribution.

Variability: How Wide Is the Distribution?

Whereas descriptions of central tendency are statements about the location of the measurements in a frequency distribution, descriptions of variability are statements about the extent to which the measurements differ from each other, or roughly how *wide* the distribution is. When your friend says that she has been "having some ups and downs," she is describing the variability among her happiness ratings. The simplest measure of variability is the **range**, which is *the value of the largest measurement in a frequency distribution minus the value of the smallest measurement.* The range is easy to compute, but like the mean, its value can be dramatically influenced by a few extreme measurements. If someone told you that the temperature in San Diego ranged from 25°F to 111°F, you might get the mistaken impression that San Diego has a remarkably variable climate when, in fact, it has a remarkably stable climate, rarely getting warmer than 76°F or colder than 50°F. The temperature in San Diego did hit 25°F and 111°F, but just once in the past 100 years.

Other measures of variability aren't as easily distorted by extreme values. One such measure is the **standard deviation**, which is a statistic that describes *how the measurements in a frequency distribution differ from the mean on average.* In other words, how far, on average, are the various measurements from the center of the distribution? As **Figure A.5** shows, two frequency distributions can have the same central tendencies but different amounts of variability.

Measuring Correlation

As you read in the Methods in Psychology chapter, when two variables are correlated it means that the values of two variables are synchronized: As the value of one goes up, the value of the other goes up (or down) too. One of the reasons correlation matters is that when two variables are correlated, you can use your knowledge of the value of one to predict the value of the other. For example, most of us have learned from experience that

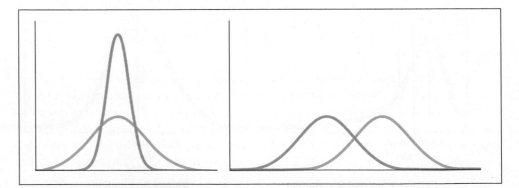

Figure A.5   Distributions Can Differ in Terms of Variability or Central Tendency The panel on the left shows two distributions with the same central tendency but different amounts of variability. The panel on the right shows two distributions with the same amount of variability but different central tendencies.

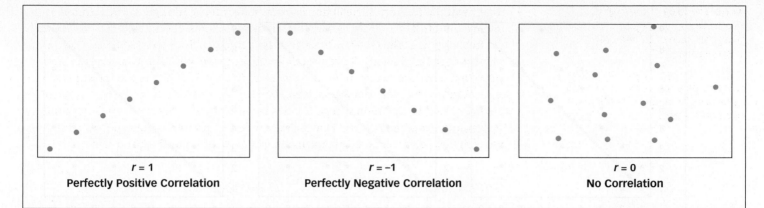

$r = 1$	$r = -1$	$r = 0$
Perfectly Positive Correlation	**Perfectly Negative Correlation**	**No Correlation**

Figure A.6 **Graphing Correlations** This is what three different kinds of correlations look like when graphed.

height and weight are positively correlated. So, if you know that a man is 6′7″ tall, you can make an educated guess that he probably weighs more than 200 pounds. Your guess will be right most of the time—but not every time. For example, professional basketball player Terrance Ferguson is 6′7″ but weighs just 184 pounds. How often your prediction would be right would depend on the *strength* of the correlation between height and weight. If that correlation were strong, then your prediction would be right almost all the time, and if it were weak, your prediction would be right much less often. The **correlation coefficient** is *a mathematical measure of both the direction and strength of a correlation,* and it is symbolized by the letter *r.* The value of *r* can range from −1 to 1.

correlation coefficient (*r*) A mathematical measure of both the direction and strength of a correlation, which is symbolized by the letter *r.*

- When *r* = 1, then the variables have a *perfect positive correlation* (see **Figure A.6**). For example, if every 1-inch increase in height were associated with a fixed amount (say, 2.5 pounds) increase in weight, then the correlation between these two variables would be perfectly positive. In this case, if you knew exactly how tall a person was, you could predict exactly how much they weighed.

- When *r* = −1, then the variables have a *perfect negative correlation* (see Figure A.6). For example, if every 1-inch increase in height were associated with a decrease in weight, then the correlation between these two variables would be perfectly negative. And once again, if you knew exactly how tall a person was, you could predict exactly how much they weighed.

- If *r* = 0, then the variables have *no correlation* (see Figure A.6). For example, if a 1-inch increase in height were sometimes associated with an increase in weight, sometimes associated with a decrease in weight, and sometimes associated with no change in weight at all, then there would be no correlation between the two variables. In this case, knowing how tall a person was would not allow you to predict anything about their weight.

Correlations of 1 and −1 are extremely rare in the real world. Yes, height and weight *do* have a positive correlation—that is, people who have more of one tend to have more of the other—but they have an *imperfect* positive correlation (i.e., an extra unit of weight is not inevitably associated with a corresponding increase in height). We note this by giving *r* intermediate values, somewhere between 0 and 1 (for positive correlations) or between 0 and −1 (for negative correlations). In each case, the more exceptions to the rule, the closer *r* is to 0.

Figure A.7 illustrates three cases in which two variables are positively correlated. In each graph, the diagonal line shows the data you would expect to see if the two variables were perfectly positively correlated (i.e., if *r* = 1). In a sense, the diagonal line represents "the rule" that "when one variable increases by 1 unit, then the other variable increases by

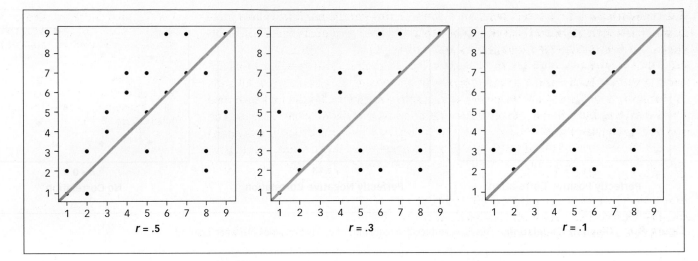

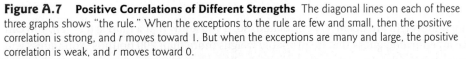

Figure A.7   **Positive Correlations of Different Strengths** The diagonal lines on each of these three graphs shows "the rule." When the exceptions to the rule are few and small, then the positive correlation is strong, and r moves toward 1. But when the exceptions are many and large, the positive correlation is weak, and r moves toward 0.

1 unit." Therefore, every dot that is not on the diagonal line is "an exception to the rule." The farther a dot is from the line, the greater an exception it is. As you can see, the size and number of the "exceptions to the rule" change the value of r quite dramatically. The two variables shown in the left panel of Figure A.7 have a strong correlation of $r = .5$, the two variables shown in the middle panel have a moderate correlation of $r = .3$, and the two variables shown in the right panel have a weak correlation of $r = .1$. The only difference between these graphs is that as you move from left to right you see more data points that are farther from the line. The sign of r (plus or minus) tells you the direction of the relationship (positive or negative), and the absolute value of r (between 0 and 1) tells you about the number and size of the exceptions to the rule—hence, about how accurate you are likely to be when using knowledge of one variable to make predictions about the other.

Statistical Testing: Making Sure Conditions Don't Differ by Chance

If you flip a coin 100 times, you expect it to come up heads *roughly* 50 of those times. But every once in a very, very long while, it will come up heads 60 times, or 70 times, or even 100 times, by sheer chance alone. This will not happen often, of course, but if you execute 100 coin flips enough times, it will happen eventually. So what? Who cares about coin flips?.

Remember in the Methods in Psychology chapter when we did that experiment in which we randomly assigned supervised and unsupervised kids to play violent or nonviolent video games? The random assignment was done by flipping a coin to assign each child to an experimental condition. Normally, this would ensure that approximately equal numbers of supervised and unsupervised kids were assigned to each condition. But because of the nature of coin flips, every once in a long while a coin flip will assign more unsupervised kids to play violent video games and more supervised kids to play nonviolent video games by sheer chance alone. When this happens, scientists say that "random assignment has failed" (though they should actually say that the coin has failed to produce random assignment). When random assignment fails, we can no longer be sure that changes in our dependent variable (in this experiment it was aggression) were caused by the changes we made to our independent variable (in this experiment it was video game violence). They may instead have been caused by the different amounts of parental supervision, which were not equally represented in our two groups.

If random assignment can fail, then how do psychologists know whether this has happened when they do an experiment? Unfortunately, they can never know for sure. But what they *can* do is calculate the *odds* that random assignment has failed each time they conduct an experiment. Psychologists perform this calculation every time they do an experiment, and they generally do not accept the results of their experiments unless the calculation suggests that there is less than a 5% chance that those results would have occurred if random assignment had failed. Such results are said to be *statistically significant,* and psychologists typically indicate this by writing "$p < .05$," which simply means that the probability (p) that the result would have been observed if random assignment had failed is less than 5% ($< .05$).

Psychologists accept their results only when the odds that random assignment failed are less than 5% ($p < .05$), but that means that about 5% of the time, they are making a **Type I error**, which occurs *when researchers conclude that there is a causal relationship between two variables when in fact there is not.* If a psychologist concluded that playing violent video games had increased aggressiveness in a sample of children when in fact it hadn't, that conclusion would be a Type I error, also known as a *false positive.* As you might guess, a **Type II error** occurs *when researchers conclude that there is not a causal relationship between two variables when in fact there is.* If a psychologist concluded that playing violent video games had not increased aggressiveness in a sample of children when in fact it had, that conclusion would be a Type II error, also known as a *false negative.*

When psychologists design experiments and conduct data analyses they do their best to minimize these errors, but some risk of making them always remains. That's why replication (which means doing the same experiment many times to see whether it produces the same results each time) serves an important function in psychology, as it does in every science. Even the best experimental evidence does not allow us to conclude that two variables *are* causally related; it only allows us to conclude that two variables *are likely to be* causally related. The more easily and more often that evidence is reproduced, the more confident we can be in the causal relationship between the variables.

Type I error An error that occurs when researchers conclude that there is a causal relationship between two variables when in fact there is not.

Type II error An error that occurs when researchers conclude that there is not a causal relationship between two variables when in fact there is.

Key Terms

frequency distribution (p. A-1)

normal distribution (p. A-2)

mode (p. A-2)

mean (p. A-2)

median (p. A-2)

range (p. A-4)

standard deviation (p. A-4)

correlation coefficient (r) (p. A-5)

Type I error (p. A-7)

Type II error (p. A-7)

absentmindedness A lapse in attention that results in memory failure.

absolute threshold The minimal intensity needed to just barely detect a stimulus in 50% of trials.

accommodation The process by which infants revise their schemas in light of new information.

accommodation (visual system) The process whereby the eye maintains a clear image on the retina.

acquisition The phase of classical conditioning when the CS and the US are presented together.

action potential An electric signal that is conducted along a neuron's axon to a synapse.

action tendencies A readiness to engage in a specific set of emotion-related behaviors.

activation–synthesis model The theory that dreams are produced when the brain attempts to make sense of random neural activity that occurs during sleep.

actor–observer effect The tendency to make situational attributions for our own behaviors while making dispositional attributions for the identical behavior of others.

acuity How well we can distinguish two very similar stimuli.

adolescence The period of development that begins with the onset of sexual maturity (about 11 to 14 years of age) and lasts until the beginning of adulthood (about 18 to 21 years of age).

adulthood The stage of development that begins around 18 to 21 years and lasts for the remainder of life.

aggression Behavior that is meant to cause harm.

agonists Drugs that increase the action of a neurotransmitter.

agoraphobia A specific phobia involving a fear of public places.

alcohol myopia A condition that results when alcohol hampers attention, leading people to respond in simple ways to complex situations.

altered state of consciousness A form of experience that departs significantly from the normal subjective experience of the world and the mind.

altruism Intentional behavior that benefits another at a potential cost to oneself.

amygdala A brain structure that plays a central role in many emotional processes, particularly the formation of emotional memories.

anorexia nervosa An eating disorder characterized by an intense fear of being overweight and a severe restriction of food intake.

antagonists Drugs that diminish the function of a neurotransmitter.

anterograde amnesia The inability to transfer new information from the short-term store into the long-term store.

antianxiety medications Drugs that help reduce a person's experience of fear or anxiety.

antidepressants A class of drugs that help lift people's moods.

antipsychotic drugs Medications that are used to treat schizophrenia and related psychotic disorders.

antisocial personality disorder (APD) A pervasive pattern of disregard for and violation of the rights of others that begins in childhood or early adolescence and continues into adulthood.

anxiety disorders The class of mental disorders in which anxiety is the predominant feature.

aphasia Difficulty in producing or comprehending language.

apparent motion The perception of movement as a result of signals appearing in rapid succession in different locations.

appraisal Conscious or unconscious evaluations and interpretations of the emotion-relevant aspects of a stimulus or event.

approach motivation The motivation to experience positive outcomes.

area A1 The primary auditory cortex, located in the temporal lobe.

area V1 The part of the occipital lobe that contains the primary visual cortex.

assimilation The process by which infants apply their schemas in novel situations.

association areas Areas in the cerebral cortex composed of neurons that help provide sense and meaning to information registered in the cortex.

attachment The emotional bond with a primary caregiver.

attachment styles Characteristic patterns of reacting to the absence and presence of one's primary caregiver.

attention The active and conscious processing of particular information.

attention-deficit/hyperactivity disorder (ADHD) A persistent pattern of severe problems with inattention and/or hyperactivity or impulsiveness that cause significant impairments in functioning.

attitude An enduring positive or negative evaluation of a stimulus.

attribution An inference about the cause of a person's behavior.

autism spectrum disorder (ASD) A condition beginning in early childhood in which a person shows persistent communication deficits as well as restricted and repetitive patterns of behaviors, interests, or activities.

autonomic nervous system (ANS) A set of nerves that carries involuntary and automatic commands that control blood vessels, body organs, and glands.

availability bias The concept that items that are more readily available in memory are judged as having occurred more frequently.

avoidance motivation The motivation to avoid experiencing negative outcomes.

axon The part of a neuron that carries information to other neurons, muscles, or glands.

basal ganglia A set of subcortical structures that directs intentional movements.

basilar membrane A structure in the inner ear that moves up and down in time with vibrations relayed from the ossicles, transmitted through the oval window.

behavior therapy A type of therapy that assumes that disordered behavior is learned and that symptom relief is achieved through changing overt maladaptive behaviors into more constructive behaviors.

behavioral confirmation The tendency of observers to see what they expect to see.

behavioral neuroscience The study of the relationship between the brain and behavior (especially in nonhuman animals).

behaviorism An approach to psychology that restricts scientific inquiry to observable behavior.

belief An enduring piece of knowledge about a stimulus.

bias The distorting influences of present knowledge, beliefs, and feelings on recollection of previous experiences.

Big Five The traits of the five-factor model: openness to experience, conscientiousness, extraversion, agreeableness, and neuroticism.

binding problem How the brain links features together so that we see unified objects in our visual world rather than free-floating or miscombined features.

binge eating disorder (BED) An eating disorder characterized by recurrent and uncontrolled episodes of eating a large number of calories in a short time.

binocular disparity The difference in the retinal images of the two eyes that provides information about depth.

biofeedback The use of an external monitoring device to obtain information about a bodily function and then to possibly gain control over that function.

biological preparedness A propensity for learning particular kinds of associations over other kinds.

biopsychosocial perspective Explains mental disorders as the result of interactions among biological, psychological, and social factors.

bipolar disorder A condition characterized by cycles of abnormal, persistent high mood (mania) and low mood (depression).

blind spot A location in the visual field that produces no sensation on the retina.

blocking A failure to retrieve information that is available in memory even though you are trying to produce it.

bulimia nervosa An eating disorder characterized by binge eating followed by compensatory behavior.

burnout A state of physical, emotional, and mental exhaustion resulting from long-term involvement in an emotionally demanding situation and accompanied by lowered performance and motivation.

bystander intervention The act of helping strangers in an emergency situation.

case method A procedure for gathering scientific information by studying a single individual.

catatonic behavior A marked decrease in all movement or an increase in muscular rigidity and overactivity.

category-specific deficit A neurological syndrome characterized by an inability to recognize objects that belong to a particular category, even when the ability to recognize objects outside the category is undisturbed.

cell body (soma) The part of a neuron that coordinates information-processing tasks and keeps the cell alive.

central nervous system (CNS) The part of the nervous system that is composed of the brain and spinal cord.

cephalocaudal rule The "top-to-bottom" rule that describes the tendency for motor skills to emerge in sequence from the head to the feet.

cerebellum A large structure of the hindbrain that controls fine motor skills.

cerebral cortex The outermost layer of the brain, visible to the naked eye and divided into two hemispheres.

change blindness Failure to detect changes to the visual details of a scene.

childhood The stage of development that begins at about 18 to 24 months and lasts until about 11 to 14 years.

chromosomes Strands of DNA wound around each other in a double-helix configuration.

chronic stressors Sources of stress that occur continuously or repeatedly.

chunking Combining small pieces of information into larger clusters or chunks that are more easily held in short-term memory.

circadian rhythm A naturally occurring 24-hour cycle.

classical conditioning A type of learning that occurs when a neutral stimulus produces a response after being paired with a stimulus that naturally produces a response.

cochlea A fluid-filled tube that contains cells that transduce sound vibrations into neural impulses.

cocktail-party phenomenon A phenomenon in which people tune in one message even while they filter out others nearby.

cognitive behavioral therapy (CBT) A blend of cognitive and behavioral therapeutic strategies.

cognitive development The process by which infants and children gain the ability to think and understand.

cognitive dissonance An unpleasant state that arises when a person recognizes the inconsistency of their actions, attitudes, or beliefs.

cognitive enhancers Drugs that improve the psychological processes that underlie intelligent performance.

cognitive map A mental representation of the physical features of the environment.

cognitive neuroscience The study of the relationship between the brain and the mind (especially in humans).

cognitive psychology The study of human information processing.

cognitive restructuring A therapeutic approach that teaches clients to question the automatic beliefs, assumptions, and predictions that often lead to negative emotions and to replace negative thinking with more realistic and positive beliefs.

cognitive symptoms Deficits in cognitive abilities, specifically executive functioning, attention, and working memory, present in those with schizophrenia.

cognitive therapy Focuses on helping a client identify and correct any distorted thinking about self, others, or the world.

cognitive unconscious All the mental processes that give rise to a person's thoughts, choices, emotions, and behavior even though they are not experienced by the person.

common knowledge effect The tendency for group discussions to focus on information that all members share.

comorbidity The co-occurrence of two or more disorders in a single individual.

companionate love An experience involving affection, trust, and concern for a partner's well-being.

concept A mental representation that groups or categorizes shared features of related objects, events, or other stimuli.

concrete operational stage The stage of cognitive development that begins at about 6 years and ends at about 11 years, during which children learn how various actions, or *operations,* can transform the concrete objects of the physical world.

conditioned response (CR) A reaction that resembles an unconditioned response but is produced by a conditioned stimulus.

conditioned stimulus (CS) A previously neutral stimulus that produces a reliable response in an organism after being paired with a US.

conduct disorder A persistent pattern of deviant behavior involving aggression toward people or animals, destruction of property, deceitfulness or theft, or serious rule violations.

cones Photoreceptors that detect color, operate under normal daylight conditions, and allow us to focus on fine detail.

conformity The tendency to do what others do.

conjunction fallacy Thinking that two events are more likely to occur together than is either individual event alone.

conscious motivations Motivations of which people are aware.

consciousness A person's subjective experience of the world and the mind.

conservation The understanding that the quantitative properties of an object are invariant despite changes in the object's appearance.

consolidation The process by which memories become stable in the brain.

construct validity The extent to which the thing being measured adequately characterizes the property.

conventional stage A stage of moral development in which the morality of an action is primarily determined by the extent to which it conforms to social rules.

cooperation Behavior by two or more individuals that leads to mutual benefit.

corpus callosum A thick band of nerve fibers that connects large areas of the cerebral cortex on each side of the brain and supports communication of information across the hemispheres.

correlation The relationship that results when variations in the value of one variable are synchronized with variations in the value of the other.

correlation coefficient (*r*) A mathematical measure of both the direction and strength of a correlation, which is symbolized by the letter *r*.

correspondence bias The tendency to make a dispositional attribution even when we should instead make a situational attribution.

crystallized intelligence The ability to apply knowledge that was acquired through experience.

cultural psychology The study of how culture influences mental life.

debriefing A verbal description of the true nature and purpose of a study.

defense mechanisms Unconscious coping mechanisms that reduce the anxiety generated by threats from unacceptable impulses.

deindividuation A phenomenon in which immersion in a group causes people to become less concerned with their personal values.

delusion A false belief, often bizarre and grandiose, that is maintained in spite of its irrationality.

demand characteristics Those aspects of an observational setting that cause people to behave as they think someone else wants or expects them to.

dendrite The part of a neuron that receives information from other neurons and relays it to the cell body.

dependent variable The variable that is measured in an experiment.

depressants Substances that reduce the activity of the central nervous system.

developmental psychology The study of continuity and change across the life span.

Diagnostic and Statistical Manual of Mental Disorders (DSM) A classification system that describes the features used to diagnose each recognized mental disorder and indicates how that disorder can be distinguished from other, similar problems.

diathesis–stress model Suggests that a person may be predisposed to a psychological disorder that remains unexpressed until triggered by stress.

diffusion of responsibility The tendency of individuals to feel diminished responsibility for their actions when surrounded by others who are acting the same way.

discrimination The capacity to distinguish between similar but distinct stimuli.

disorganized speech A severe disruption of verbal communication in which ideas shift rapidly and incoherently among unrelated topics.

display rule A norm for the appropriate expression of emotion.

dopamine hypothesis The idea that schizophrenia involves an excess of dopamine activity.

double-blind study A study in which neither the researcher nor the participant knows how the participants are expected to behave.

drive-reduction theory A theory suggesting that the primary motivation of all organisms is to reduce their drives.

drug tolerance The tendency for larger doses of a drug to be required over time to achieve the same effect.

dual process theories Theories that suggest that we have two different systems in our brains for processing information: one dedicated to fast, automatic, and unconscious processing, and the other dedicated to slow, effortful, and conscious processing.

dynamic unconscious An active system encompassing a lifetime of hidden memories, the person's deepest instincts and desires, and the person's inner struggle to control these forces.

echoic memory A fast-decaying store of auditory information.

eclectic psychotherapy A form of psychotherapy that involves drawing on techniques from different forms of therapy, depending on the client and the problem.

ego The component of personality, developed through contact with the external world, that enables us to deal with life's practical demands.

egocentrism The failure to understand that the world appears different to different people.

electroconvulsive therapy (ECT) A treatment that involves inducing a brief seizure by delivering an electrical shock to the brain.

electroencephalograph (EEG) A device used to record electrical activity in the brain.

embryonic stage The period of prenatal development that lasts from the 2nd week until about the 8th week.

emotion A temporary state that includes unique subjective experiences and physiological activity, and that prepares people for action.

emotion regulation The strategies people use to influence their own emotional experiences.

emotional expression An observable sign of an emotional state.

emotional intelligence The ability to reason about emotions and to use emotions to enhance reasoning.

empirical method A set of rules and techniques for observation.

empiricism The belief that accurate knowledge can be acquired through observation.

encoding The process of transforming what we perceive, think, or feel into an enduring memory.

encoding specificity principle The idea that a retrieval cue can be an effective reminder when it helps re-create the specific way in which information was initially encoded.

endocrine system A network of glands that produce and secrete into the bloodstream chemical messages known as hormones, which influence a wide variety of basic functions, including metabolism, growth, and sexual development.

epigenetics The study of environmental influences that determine how and if genes are expressed, without altering the basic DNA sequences that constitute the genes themselves.

episodic memory The collection of past personal experiences that occurred at a particular time and place.

evolutionary mismatch The idea that traits that were adaptive in an ancestral environment may be maladaptive in a modern environment.

evolutionary psychology The study of the ways in which the human mind has been shaped by natural selection.

exemplar theory The concept that we make category judgments by comparing a new instance with stored memories of other instances of the category.

existential approach A school of thought that regards personality as being governed by an individual's ongoing choices and decisions in the context of the realities of life and death.

expectancy theory The idea that alcohol effects can be produced by people's expectations of how alcohol will influence them in particular situations.

experimentation A technique for determining whether there is a causal relationship between variables.

explicit memory Memory that occurs when people consciously or intentionally retrieve past experiences.

exposure therapy An approach to treatment that involves confronting an emotion-arousing stimulus directly and repeatedly, ultimately leading to a decrease in the emotional response.

external validity An attribute of an experiment in which variables have been defined in a normal, typical, or realistic way.

extinction The gradual elimination of a learned response that occurs when the CS is repeatedly presented without the US.

extrinsic motivation A motivation to take actions that lead to reward.

facial feedback hypothesis The theory that emotional expressions can cause the emotional experiences they typically signify.

fast mapping The process whereby children can map a word onto an underlying concept after only a single exposure.

fetal alcohol syndrome (FAS) A developmental disorder that stems from heavy alcohol use by the mother during pregnancy.

fetal stage The period of prenatal development that lasts from the 9th week until birth.

fight-or-flight response An emotional and physiological reaction to an emergency that increases readiness for action.

fixed-interval (FI) schedule An operant conditioning principle whereby reinforcers are presented at fixed time periods, provided that the appropriate response is made.

fixed-ratio (FR) schedule An operant conditioning principle whereby reinforcement is delivered after a specific number of responses have been made.

flashbulb memories Detailed recollections of when and where we heard about shocking events.

fluid intelligence The ability to solve and reason about novel problems.

foot-in-the-door technique A technique that involves making a small request and following it with a larger request.

formal operational stage The final stage of cognitive development that begins around the age of 11, during which children learn to reason about abstract concepts.

fovea An area of the retina where vision is clearest and there are no rods at all.

framing effects A bias whereby people give different answers to the same problem depending on how the problem is phrased (or framed).

fraternal (dizygotic) twins Twins who develop from two different eggs that were fertilized by two different sperm.

frequency distribution A graphic representation showing the number of times that the measurement of a property takes on each of its possible values.

frontal lobe The region of the cerebral cortex that has specialized areas for movement, abstract thinking, planning, memory, and judgment.

frustration–aggression hypothesis A principle stating that animals aggress when their goals are frustrated.

full consciousness A level of consciousness in which you know and are able to report your mental state.

functionalism An approach to psychology that emphasized the adaptive significance of mental processes.

gate-control theory A theory of pain perception based on the idea that signals arriving from pain receptors in the body can be stopped, or *gated*, by interneurons in the spinal cord via feedback from the skin or from the brain.

gateway drug A drug whose use increases the risk of the subsequent use of more harmful drugs.

gene The major unit of hereditary transmission.

general adaptation syndrome (GAS) A three-stage physiological response that appears regardless of the stressor that is encountered.

generalization The CR is observed even though the CS is slightly different from the CS used during acquisition.

generalized anxiety disorder (GAD) A disorder characterized by chronic excessive worry accompanied by three or more of the following symptoms: restlessness, fatigue, concentration problems, irritability, muscle tension, and sleep disturbance.

genetic dysphasia A syndrome characterized by an inability to learn the grammatical structure of language despite having otherwise normal intelligence.

germinal stage The 2-week period of prenatal development that begins at conception.

Gestalt psychology An approach to psychology that emphasized the way in which the mind creates perceptual experience.

gestalt therapy A form of psychotherapy whose goal is helping the client become aware of his or her thoughts, behaviors, experiences, and feelings and "own" or take responsibility for them.

glial cells Support cells found in the nervous system.

grammar A set of rules that specify how the units of language can be combined to produce meaningful messages.

grossly disorganized behavior Behavior that is inappropriate for the situation or ineffective in attaining goals, often with specific motor disturbances.

group A collection of people who have something in common that distinguishes them from others.

group polarization The tendency of groups to make decisions that are more extreme than any member would have made alone.

group therapy A type of therapy in which multiple participants (who often do not know each other at the outset) work on their individual problems in a group atmosphere.

groupthink The tendency of groups to reach consensus in order to facilitate interpersonal harmony.

habituation A general process in which repeated or prolonged exposure to a stimulus results in a gradual reduction in responding.

hallucination A false perceptual experience that has a compelling sense of being real despite the absence of external stimulation.

hallucinogens Drugs that alter sensation and perception and often cause visual and auditory hallucinations.

haptic perception The active exploration of the environment by touching and grasping objects with our hands.

health psychology The subfield of psychology concerned with how psychological factors influence the causes and treatment of physical illness and the maintenance of health.

hedonic principle The claim that people are motivated to experience pleasure and avoid pain.

helplessness theory The idea that individuals who are prone to depression automatically attribute negative experiences to causes that are internal (i.e., their own fault), stable (i.e., unlikely to change), and global (i.e., widespread).

heuristic persuasion The process by which attitudes or beliefs are changed by appeals to habit or emotion.

hindbrain The area of the brain that coordinates information coming into and out of the spinal cord.

hippocampus A brain structure critical for creating new memories and integrating them into a network of knowledge so that they can be stored indefinitely in other parts of the cerebral cortex.

hypnosis A social interaction in which one person (the hypnotist) makes suggestions that lead to a change in another person's (the participant's) subjective experience of the world.

hypnotic analgesia The reduction of pain through hypnosis in people who are susceptible to hypnosis.

hypothalamus A subcortical structure that regulates body temperature, hunger, thirst, and sexual behavior.

hypothesis A falsifiable prediction made by a theory.

hysteria A loss of function that has no obvious physical origin.

iatrogenic illness A disorder or symptom that occurs as a result of a medical or psychotherapeutic treatment itself.

iconic memory A fast-decaying store of visual information.

id The part of the mind containing the drives present at birth; it is the source of our bodily needs, wants, desires, and impulses, particularly our sexual and aggressive drives.

identical (monozygotic) twins Twins who develop from the splitting of a single egg that was fertilized by a single sperm.

illusory conjunction A perceptual mistake whereby the brain incorrectly combines features from multiple objects.

immune system A complex response system that protects the body from bacteria, viruses, and other foreign substances.

implicit learning Learning that takes place largely independent of awareness of both the process and the products of information acquisition.

implicit memory Memory that occurs when past experiences influence later behavior and performance, even without an effort to remember them or an awareness of the recollection.

inattentional blindness A failure to perceive objects that are not the focus of attention.

independent variable The variable that is manipulated in an experiment.

infancy The stage of development that begins at birth and lasts between 18 and 24 months.

informational influence A phenomenon that occurs when another person's behavior provides information about what is good or true.

informed consent A verbal agreement to participate in a study made by an adult who has been informed of all the risks that participation may entail.

inner hair cells Specialized auditory receptor neurons embedded in the basilar membrane.

insomnia Difficulty in falling asleep or staying asleep.

intelligence The ability to use one's mind to solve novel problems and learn from experience.

intelligence quotient (IQ) A statistic obtained by dividing an adult's test score by the average adult's test score and then multiplying the quotient by 100.

intermittent reinforcement An operant conditioning principle whereby only some of the responses made are followed by reinforcement.

intermittent reinforcement effect The fact that operant behaviors that are maintained under intermittent reinforcement schedules resist extinction better than those maintained under continuous reinforcement.

internal validity An attribute of an experiment that allows it to establish causal relationships.

internal working model A set of beliefs about the way relationships work.

interneurons Neurons that connect sensory neurons, motor neurons, or other interneurons.

interpersonal psychotherapy (IPT) A form of psychotherapy that focuses on helping clients improve current relationships.

intrinsic motivation A motivation to take actions that are themselves rewarding.

introspection The analysis of subjective experience by trained observers.

ironic processes of mental control A mental process that can produce ironic errors because monitoring for errors can itself produce them.

James–Lange theory The theory that feelings are simply the perception of one's own physiological responses to a stimulus.

just noticeable difference (JND) The minimal change in a stimulus (e.g., its loudness or brightness) that can just barely be detected.

kin selection The process by which evolution selects for individuals who cooperate with their relatives.

language A system for communicating with others using signals that are combined according to rules of grammar and that convey meaning.

latent learning A process in which something is learned, but it is not manifested as a behavioral change until sometime in the future.

law of effect The principle that behaviors that are followed by a "satisfying state of affairs" tend to be repeated, and those that produce an "unpleasant state of affairs" are less likely to be repeated.

learning The acquisition, from experience, of new knowledge, skills, or responses that results in a relatively permanent change in the state of the learner.

locus of control A person's tendency to perceive the control of rewards as internal to the self or external in the environment.

long-term memory A type of storage that holds information for hours, days, weeks, or years.

long-term potentiation (LTP) A process whereby repeated communication across the synapse between neurons strengthens the connection, making further communication easier.

loss aversion The tendency to care more about avoiding losses than about achieving equal-size gains.

loudness A sound's intensity.

major depressive disorder (or unipolar depression) A disorder characterized by a severely depressed mood and/or inability to experience pleasure that lasts 2 or more weeks and is accompanied by feelings of worthlessness, lethargy, and sleep and appetite disturbance.

manipulation A technique for determining the causal power of a variable by actively changing its value.

marijuana (cannabis) The leaves and buds of the hemp plant, which contain a psychoactive drug called tetrahydrocannabinol (THC).

mean The average value of all the measurements.

median The value that is greater than or equal to half the measurements and less than or equal to half the measurements.

medical model An approach that conceptualizes abnormal psychological experiences as illnesses that, like physical illnesses, have biological and environmental causes, defined symptoms, and possible cures.

meditation The practice of intentional contemplation.

medulla An extension of the spinal cord into the skull that coordinates heart rate, circulation, and respiration.

memory The ability to store and retrieve information over time.

memory misattribution Assigning a recollection or an idea to the wrong source.

mental control The attempt to change conscious states of mind.

mental disorder A persistent disturbance or dysfunction in behavior, thoughts, or emotions that causes significant distress or impairment.

mere exposure effect The tendency for liking of a stimulus to increase with the frequency of exposure to that stimulus.

metabolism The rate at which the body uses energy.

mind–body problem The issue of how the mind is related to the brain and body.

mindfulness meditation Teaches an individual to be fully present in each moment; to be aware of his or her thoughts, feelings, and sensations; and to detect symptoms before they become a problem.

minimal consciousness A low-level kind of sensory awareness and responsiveness that occurs when the mind inputs sensations and may output behavior.

Minnesota Multiphasic Personality Inventory (MMPI) A well-researched clinical questionnaire used to assess personality and psychological problems.

mirror neurons Neurons that are active when an animal performs a behavior, such as reaching for or manipulating an object, and are also activated when another animal observes that animal perform the same behavior.

mode The value of the most frequently observed measurement.

monocular depth cues Aspects of a scene that yield information about depth when viewed with only one eye.

mood disorders Mental disorders that have mood disturbance as their predominant feature.

morphemes The smallest meaningful units of language.

morphological rules A set of rules that indicate how morphemes can be combined to form words.

motivation The internal causes of purposeful behavior.

motor development The emergence of the ability to execute physical actions.

motor neurons Neurons that carry signals from the spinal cord to the muscles to produce movement.

motor reflexes Motor responses that are triggered by specific patterns of sensory stimulation.

myelin sheath An insulating layer of fatty material around the axon of a neuron.

myelination The formation of a fatty sheath around the axons of a neuron.

narcissism A trait that reflects a grandiose view of the self, combined with a tendency to seek admiration from and exploit others.

narcolepsy A disorder in which sudden sleep attacks occur in the middle of waking activities.

narcotics (opiates) Highly addictive drugs derived from opium that relieve pain.

nativist theory The view that language development is best explained as an innate, biological capacity.

natural correlation A correlation observed in the world around us.

natural selection The process by which the specific attributes that promote an organism's survival and reproduction become more prevalent in the population over time.

naturalistic observation A technique for gathering scientific information by unobtrusively observing people in their natural environments.

need for achievement The motivation to solve worthwhile problems.

negative symptoms Deficits in or disruptions of normal emotions and behaviors (e.g., emotional and social withdrawal; apathy; poverty of speech; and other indications of the absence or insufficiency of normal behavior, motivation, and emotion) that are present in those with schizophrenia.

nervous system An interacting network of neurons that conveys information throughout the body.

neurons Cells in the nervous system that communicate with one another to perform information-processing tasks.

neurotransmitters Chemicals that transmit information across the synapse to a receiving neuron's dendrites.

night terrors (sleep terrors) Abrupt awakenings with panic and intense emotional arousal.

nonsuicidal self-injury (NSSI) Direct, deliberate destruction of body tissue in the absence of any intent to die.

norm of reciprocity The unwritten rule that people should benefit those who have benefited them.

normal distribution A mathematically defined distribution in which the frequency of measurements is highest in the middle and decreases symmetrically in both directions.

normative influence A phenomenon in which another person's behavior provides information about what is appropriate.

norms Customary standards for behavior that are widely shared by members of a culture.

obedience The tendency to do what authorities tell us to do.

object permanence The fact that objects continue to exist even when they are not visible.

observational learning A process in which an organism learns by watching the actions of others.

observer bias The tendency for observers' expectations to influence both what they believe they observed and what they actually observed.

obsessive-compulsive disorder (OCD) A disorder in which repetitive, intrusive thoughts (obsessions) and ritualistic behaviors (compulsions) designed to fend off those thoughts interfere significantly with an individual's functioning.

occipital lobe A region of the cerebral cortex that processes visual information.

olfactory bulb A brain structure located above the nasal cavity beneath the frontal lobes.

olfactory receptor neurons (ORNs) Receptor cells that transduce odorant molecules into neural impulses.

operant behavior Behavior that an organism performs that has some impact on the environment.

operant conditioning A type of learning in which the consequences of an organism's behavior determine whether it will repeat that behavior in the future.

operational definition A description of a property in measurable terms.

optimism bias A bias whereby people believe that compared with other individuals, they are more likely to experience positive events and less likely to experience negative events in the future.

organizational encoding The process of categorizing information according to the relationships among a series of items.

outcome expectancies A person's assumptions about the likely consequences of a future behavior.

overjustification effect An effect that occurs when a reward decreases a person's intrinsic motivation to perform a behavior.

panic disorder A disorder characterized by the sudden occurrence of multiple psychological and physiological symptoms that contribute to a feeling of stark terror.

parasympathetic nervous system A set of nerves that helps the body return to a normal resting state.

parietal lobe A region of the cerebral cortex whose functions include processing information about touch.

passionate love An experience involving feelings of euphoria, intimacy, and intense sexual attraction.

perception The organization, identification, and interpretation of a sensation in order to form a mental representation.

perceptual confirmation The tendency of targets to behave as observers expect them to behave.

perceptual constancy The principle that even as aspects of sensory signals change, perception remains consistent.

perceptual contrast The principle that although the sensory information from two things may be very similar, we perceive the objects as different.

perceptual organization The process of grouping and segregating features to create whole objects organized in meaningful ways.

peripheral nervous system (PNS) The part of the nervous system that connects the central nervous system to the body's organs and muscles.

persistence The intrusive recollection of events that we wish we could forget.

personal constructs Dimensions people use in making sense of their experiences.

personality An individual's characteristic style of behaving, thinking, and feeling.

personality disorders Enduring patterns of thinking, feeling, or relating to others or controlling impulses that deviate from cultural expectations and cause distress or impaired functioning.

person-centered therapy (or client-centered therapy) A form of psychotherapy that assumes that all individuals have a tendency toward growth and that this growth can be facilitated by acceptance and genuine reactions from the therapist.

person–situation controversy The question of whether behavior is caused more by personality or by situational factors.

persuasion A phenomenon that occurs when a person's attitudes or beliefs are influenced by a communication from another person.

phenomenology The study of how things seem to the conscious person.

pheromones Biochemical odorants emitted by other members of an animal's species that can affect that animal's behavior or physiology.

philosophical dualism The view that mind and body are fundamentally different things.

philosophical empiricism The view that all knowledge is acquired through experience.

philosophical idealism The view that perceptions of the physical world are the brain's interpretation of information from the sensory organs.

philosophical materialism The view that all mental phenomena are reducible to physical phenomena.

philosophical nativism The view that some knowledge is innate rather than acquired.

philosophical realism The view that perceptions of the physical world are produced entirely by information from the sensory organs.

phobic disorders Disorders characterized by marked, persistent, and excessive fear and avoidance of specific objects, activities, or situations.

phonemes The smallest units of sound that are recognizable as speech rather than as random noise.

phonological rules A set of rules that indicate how phonemes can be combined to produce speech sounds.

phototherapy A therapy that involves repeated exposure to bright light.

pitch How high or low a sound is.

pituitary gland The "master gland" of the body's hormone-producing system, which releases hormones that direct the functions of many other glands in the body.

place code The process by which the brain uses information about the relative activity of hair cells (e.g., which ones are more active and which are less active) across the whole basilar membrane to help determine the pitch you hear.

placebo An inert substance or procedure that has been applied with the expectation that it will produce a healing response.

pons A brain structure that relays information from the cerebellum to the rest of the brain.

population A complete collection of people.

positive symptoms Thoughts and behaviors, such as delusions and hallucinations, present in schizophrenia but not seen in those without the disorder.

postconventional stage A stage of moral development in which the morality of an action is determined by a set of general principles that reflect core values.

posthypnotic amnesia The failure to retrieve memories following hypnotic suggestions to forget.

posttraumatic stress disorder (PTSD) A disorder characterized by chronic physiological arousal, recurrent unwanted thoughts or images of the trauma, and avoidance of things that call the traumatic event to mind.

power A detector's ability to detect the presence of differences or changes in the magnitude of a property.

preconventional stage A stage of moral development in which the morality of an action is primarily determined by its consequences for the actor.

prejudice A positive or negative evaluation of another person based on their group membership.

preoperational stage The stage of cognitive development that begins at about 2 years and ends at about 6 years, during which children develop a preliminary understanding of the physical world.

preparedness theory The idea that people are instinctively predisposed toward certain fears.

primary sex characteristics Bodily structures that change at puberty and are directly involved in reproduction.

priming An enhanced ability to think of a stimulus, such as a word or an object, as a result of a recent exposure to that stimulus during an earlier study task.

principle of reinforcement A principle stating that any behavior that is rewarded will be repeated and any behavior that isn't rewarded won't be repeated.

proactive aggression Aggression that is planned and purposeful.

proactive interference Situations in which earlier learning impairs memory for information acquired later.

problem of other minds The fundamental difficulty we have in perceiving the consciousness of others.

procedural memory The gradual acquisition of skills as a result of practice, or "knowing how" to do things.

projective techniques Tests designed to reveal inner aspects of individuals' personalities by analysis of their responses to a standard series of ambiguous stimuli.

proprioception The sense of body position.

prospect theory The theory that people choose to take on risk when evaluating potential losses and avoid risks when evaluating potential gains.

prospective memory Remembering to do things in the future.

prototype theory The concept that we classify new objects by comparing them to the "best" or "most typical" member (the *prototype*) of a category.

proximodistal rule The "inside-to-outside" rule that describes the tendency for motor skills to emerge in sequence from the center to the periphery.

psychoactive drugs Chemicals that influence consciousness or behavior by altering the brain's chemical message system.

psychoanalysis A therapy that aims to give people insight into the contents of their unconscious minds.

psychoanalytic theory A general theory that emphasizes the influence of the unconscious on feelings, thoughts, and behaviors.

psychodynamic approach An approach that regards personality as formed by needs, strivings, and desires largely operating outside of awareness — motives that also can produce emotional disorders.

psychodynamic psychotherapies Therapies that explore childhood events and encourage individuals to use this understanding to develop insight into their psychological problems.

psychology The scientific study of mind and behavior.

psychopharmacology The study of drug effects on psychological states and symptoms.

psychophysics Methods that systematically relate the physical characteristics of a stimulus to an observer's perception.

psychosomatic illness An interaction between mind and body that can produce illness.

psychosurgery Surgical destruction of specific brain areas.

psychotherapy An interaction between a socially sanctioned clinician and someone suffering from a psychological problem, with the goal of providing support or relief from the problem.

puberty The onset of bodily changes associated with sexual maturity.

punisher Any stimulus or event that decreases the likelihood of the behavior that led to it.

random assignment A procedure that assigns participants to a condition by chance.

random sampling A technique for choosing participants that ensures that every member of a population has an equal chance of being included in the sample.

range The value of the largest measurement in a frequency distribution minus the value of the smallest measurement.

rational choice theory The classical view that we make decisions by determining how likely something is to happen, judging the value of the outcome, and then multiplying the two.

rational coping Facing a stressor and working to overcome it.

reactance An unpleasant feeling that arises when people feel they are being coerced.

reaction time The amount of time between the onset of a stimulus and a person's response to that stimulus.

reactive aggression Aggression that occurs spontaneously in response to a negative affective state.

reappraisal The process of changing one's emotional experience by changing the way one thinks about the emotion-eliciting stimulus.

rebound effect of thought suppression The tendency of a thought to return to consciousness with greater frequency following suppression.

receptors Parts of the cell membrane that receive neurotransmitters and either initiate or prevent a new electric signal.

reciprocal altruism Behavior that benefits another with the expectation that those benefits will be returned in the future.

reconsolidation The process whereby memories can become vulnerable to disruption when they are recalled, thus requiring them to be consolidated again.

referred pain Feeling of pain on the surface of the body, but due to internal damage, that occurs when sensory information from internal and external areas converges on the same nerve cells in the spinal cord.

refractory period The time following an action potential during which a new action potential cannot be initiated.

reframing Finding a new or creative way to think about a stressor that reduces its threat.

rehearsal The process of keeping information in short-term memory by mentally repeating it.

reinforcer Any stimulus or event that increases the likelihood of the behavior that led to it.

relaxation response A condition of reduced muscle tension, cortical activity, heart rate, breathing rate, and blood pressure.

relaxation therapy A technique for reducing tension by consciously relaxing muscles of the body.

reliability A detector's ability to detect the absence of differences or changes in the magnitude of a property.

REM sleep A stage of sleep characterized by rapid eye movements and a high level of brain activity.

replication An experiment that uses the same procedures as a previous experiment but with a new sample from the same population.

representativeness heuristic A mental shortcut that involves making a probability judgment by comparing an object or event with a prototype of the object or event.

repression A mental process that removes unacceptable thoughts and memories from consciousness and keeps them in the unconscious.

repressive coping Avoiding feelings, thoughts, or situations that are reminders of a stressor and maintaining an artificially positive viewpoint.

Research Domain Criteria Project (RDoC) An initiative that aims to guide the classification and understanding of mental disorders by revealing the basic processes that give rise to them.

resting potential The difference in electric charge between the inside and outside of a neuron's cell membrane.

reticular formation A brain structure that regulates sleep, wakefulness, and levels of arousal.

retina A layer of light-sensitive tissue lining the back of the eyeball.

retrieval The process of bringing to mind information that has been previously encoded and stored.

retrieval cue External information that is associated with stored information and helps bring it to mind.

retrieval-induced forgetting A process by which retrieving an item from long-term memory impairs subsequent recall of related items.

retroactive interference Situations in which later learning impairs memory for information acquired earlier.

retrograde amnesia The inability to retrieve information that was acquired before a particular date, usually the date of an injury or surgery.

rods Photoreceptors that become active under lowlight conditions for night vision.

Rorschach Inkblot Test A projective technique in which respondents' inner thoughts and feelings are believed to be revealed by analysis of their responses to a set of unstructured inkblots.

sample A partial collection of people drawn from a population.

schemas Theories about the way the world works.

schizophrenia A disorder characterized by the profound disruption of basic psychological processes; a distorted perception of reality; altered or blunted emotion; and disturbances in thought, motivation, and behavior.

scientific method A procedure for using empirical evidence to establish facts.

seasonal affective disorder (SAD) Recurrent depressive episodes in a seasonal pattern.

secondary sex characteristics Bodily structures that change at puberty but are not directly involved in reproduction.

second-order conditioning A type of learning in which a CS is paired with a stimulus that became associated with the US in an earlier procedure.

self-actualizing tendency The human motive toward realizing our inner potential.

self-concept A person's explicit knowledge of his or her own behaviors, traits, and other personal characteristics.

self-consciousness A distinct level of consciousness in which the person's attention is drawn to the self as an object.

self-esteem The extent to which an individual likes, values, and accepts the self.

self-regulation The exercise of voluntary control over the self to bring the self into line with preferred standards.

self-report A method in which people provide subjective information about their own thoughts, feelings, or behaviors, typically via questionnaire or interview.

self-selection A problem that occurs when anything about a participant determines the participant's condition.

self-serving bias People's tendency to take credit for their successes but downplay responsibility for their failures.

self-verification The tendency to seek evidence to confirm the self-concept.

semantic encoding The process of relating new information in a meaningful way to knowledge that is already stored in memory.

semantic memory A network of associated facts and concepts that make up our general knowledge of the world.

sensation Simple stimulation of a sense organ.

sensitivity How responsive we are to faint stimuli.

sensitization A simple form of learning that occurs when presentation of a stimulus leads to an increased response to a later stimulus.

sensorimotor stage A stage of cognitive development that begins at birth and lasts through infancy, during which infants acquire information about the world by sensing it and moving around within it.

sensory adaptation The process whereby sensitivity to prolonged stimulation tends to decline over time as an organism adapts to current (unchanging) conditions.

sensory memory A type of storage that holds sensory information for a few seconds or less.

sensory neurons Neurons that receive information from the external world and convey this information to the brain via the spinal cord.

shaping Learning that results from the reinforcement of successive steps to a final desired behavior.

short-term memory A type of storage that holds nonsensory information for more than a few seconds but less than a minute.

sick role A socially recognized set of rights and obligations linked with illness.

signal detection theory A way of analyzing data from psychophysics experiments that measures an individual's perceptual sensitivity while also taking noise, expectations, motivations, and goals into account.

sleep apnea A disorder in which the person stops breathing for brief periods while asleep.

sleep paralysis The experience of waking up unable to move.

social cognition The processes by which people come to understand others.

social influence The ability to change or direct another person's behavior.

social phobia A disorder that involves an irrational fear of being publicly humiliated or embarrassed.

social psychology The study of the causes and consequences of sociality.

social support The aid gained through interacting with others.

social–cognitive approach An approach that views personality in terms of how the person thinks about the situations encountered in daily life and behaves in response to them.

somatic nervous system A set of nerves that conveys information between voluntary muscles and the central nervous system.

somatic symptom disorders The set of psychological disorders in which people with at least one bodily symptom display significant health-related anxiety, express disproportionate concerns about their symptoms, and devote excessive time and energy to their symptoms or health concerns.

somnambulism (sleepwalking) Occurs when a person arises and walks around while asleep.

source memory Recall of when, where, and how information was acquired.

specific phobia A disorder that involves an irrational fear of a particular object or situation that markedly interferes with an individual's ability to function.

spinal reflexes Simple pathways in the nervous system that rapidly generate muscle contractions.

spontaneous recovery The tendency of a learned behavior to recover from extinction after a rest period.

standard deviation A statistic that describes how each of the measurements in a frequency distribution differs from the mean.

state-dependent retrieval The process whereby information tends to be better recalled when the person is in the same state during encoding *and* retrieval.

stereotype threat A target's fear of confirming an observer's negative stereotypes.

stereotyping The process of drawing inferences about individuals based on their category membership.

stimulants Substances that excite the central nervous system, heightening arousal and activity levels.

storage The process of maintaining information in memory over time.

stress The physical and psychological response to internal or external stressors.

stressors Specific events or chronic pressures that place demands on a person or threaten the person's well-being.

structuralism An approach to psychology that attempted to isolate and analyze the mind's basic elements.

subcortical structures Areas of the forebrain housed under the cerebral cortex near the center of the brain.

suggestibility The tendency to incorporate misleading information from external sources into personal recollections.

suicide Intentional self-inflicted death.

suicide attempt Engagement in potentially harmful behavior with some intention of dying.

sunk-cost fallacy A framing effect in which people make decisions about a current situation on the basis of what they have previously invested in the situation.

superego The mental system that reflects the internalization of cultural rules, mainly learned as parents exercise their authority.

sympathetic nervous system A set of nerves that prepares the body for action in challenging or threatening situations.

synapse The junction or region between the axon of one neuron and the dendrites or cell body of another.

syntactic rules A set of rules that indicate how words can be combined to form phrases and sentences.

systematic persuasion The process by which attitudes or beliefs are changed by appeals to reason.

taste buds The organ of taste transduction.

telegraphic speech Speech that is devoid of function morphemes and consists mostly of content words.

temperament A biologically based pattern of attentional and emotional reactivity.

temporal code The process whereby the brain uses the timing of the action potentials on the auditory nerve to help determine the pitch you hear.

temporal lobe A region of the cerebral cortex responsible for hearing and language.

teratogen Any substance that passes from mother to unborn child and impairs development.

terminal buttons Knoblike structures that branch out from an axon.

terror management theory The theory that people respond to the knowledge of their own mortality by developing a cultural worldview.

thalamus A subcortical structure that relays and filters information from the senses and transmits the information to the cerebral cortex.

Thematic Apperception Test (TAT) A projective technique in which respondents' underlying motives, concerns, and the way they see the social world are believed to be revealed through analysis of the stories they make up about ambiguous pictures of people.

theory A hypothetical explanation of a natural phenomenon.

theory of mind The understanding that the mind produces representations of the world and that these representations guide behavior.

third-variable problem The fact that the natural correlation between two variables cannot be taken as evidence of a causal relationship between them because a third variable might be causing them both.

thought suppression The conscious avoidance of a thought.

timbre The quality of sound that allows you to distinguish two sources with the same pitch and loudness.

token economy A form of behavior therapy in which clients are given "tokens" for desired behaviors, which they can later trade for rewards.

trait A relatively stable disposition to behave in a particular and consistent way.

transcranial magnetic stimulation (TMS) A treatment that involves placing a powerful pulsed magnet over a person's scalp to alter neuronal activity in the brain.

transduction The process whereby sense receptors convert physical signals from the environment into neural signals that are sent to the central nervous system.

transfer-appropriate processing The idea that memory is likely to transfer from one situation to another when the encoding and retrieval contexts of the situations match.

transience Forgetting what occurs with the passage of time.

two-factor theory of emotion The theory that stimuli trigger a general state of physiological arousal which is then interpreted as a specific emotion.

two-factor theory of intelligence Spearman's theory suggesting that a person's performance on a test is due to a combination of general ability and skills that are specific to the test.

Type A behavior pattern The tendency toward easily aroused hostility, impatience, a sense of time urgency, and competitive achievement strivings.

Type I error An error that occurs when researchers conclude that there is a causal relationship between two variables when in fact there is not.

Type II error An error that occurs when researchers conclude that there is not a causal relationship between two variables when in fact there is.

unconditioned response (UR) A reflexive reaction that is reliably produced by an unconditioned stimulus.

unconditioned stimulus (US) Something that reliably produces a naturally occurring reaction in an organism.

unconscious The part of the mind that contains information of which people are not aware.

unconscious motivations Motivations of which people are not aware.

universal grammar A collection of processes that facilitate language learning.

universality hypothesis The theory that all emotional expressions mean the same thing to all people in all places at all times.

variable A property that can take on different values.

variable-interval (VI) schedule An operant conditioning principle whereby behavior is reinforced on the basis of an average time that has expired since the last reinforcement.

variable-ratio (VR) schedule An operant conditioning principle whereby the delivery of reinforcement is based on a particular average number of responses.

vestibular system The three fluid-filled semicircular canals and adjacent organs located next to the cochlea in the inner ear.

visual imagery encoding The process of storing new information by converting it into mental pictures.

Weber's law For every sense domain, the change in a stimulus that is just noticeable is a constant proportion of the standard stimulus, over a broad range of intensities.

working memory Active maintenance of information in short-term storage.

Aarts, H., Custers, R., & Marien, H. (2008). Preparing and motivating behavior outside of awareness. *Science, 319,* 1639.

Abel, T., Alberini, C., Ghirardi, M., Huang, Y.-Y., Nguyen, P., & Kandel, E. R. (1995). Steps toward a molecular definition of memory consolidation. In D. L. Schacter (Ed.), *Memory distortion: How minds, brains and societies reconstruct the past* (pp. 298–328). Harvard University Press.

Abelson, J., Curtis, G., Sagher, O., Albucher, R., Harrigan, M., Taylor, S., Martis, B., & Giordani, B. (2009). Deep brain stimulation for refractory obsessive-compulsive disorder. *Biological Psychiatry, 57,* 510–516.

Abramson, L. Y., Seligman, M. E. P., & Teasdale, J. D. (1978). Learned helplessness in humans: Critique and reformulation. *Journal of Abnormal Psychology, 87,* 49–74.

Acevedo, B. P., & Aron, A. (2009). Does a long-term relationship kill romantic love? *Review of General Psychology, 13,* 59–65.

Acevedo-Garcia, D., McArdle, N., Osypuk, T. L., Lefkowitz, B., & Krimgold, B. K. (2007). *Children left behind: How metropolitan areas are failing America's children.* Harvard School of Public Health.

Achter, J. A., Lubinski, D., & Benbow, C. P. (1996). Multipotentiality among the intellectually gifted: "It was never there and already it's vanishing." *Journal of Counseling Psychology, 43,* 65–76.

Acikalin, M. Y., Watson, K. K., Fitzsimons, G. J., & Platt, M. L. (2018). Rhesus macaques form preferences for brand logos through sex and social status based advertising. *PLoS ONE, 13*(3), e0193055. https://doi.org/10.1371/journal.pone.0194055

Ackerman, P. L. (2014). Adolescent and adult intellectual development. *Current Directions in Psychological Science, 23*(4), 246–251. https://doi.org/10.1177/0963721414534960

Ackerman, P. L. (2017). Adult intelligence: The construct and the criterion problem. *Perspectives on Psychological Science, 12*(6), 987–998. https://doi.org/10.1177/1745691617703437

Addis, D. R., Wong, A. T., & Schacter, D. L. (2007). Remembering the past and imagining the future: Common and distinct neural substrates during event construction and elaboration. *Neuropsychologia, 45,* 1363–1377.

Addis, D. R., Wong, A. T., & Schacter, D. L. (2008). Age-related changes in the episodic simulation of future events. *Psychological Science, 19,* 33–41.

Adelmann, P. K., & Zajonc, R. B. (1989). Facial efference and the experience of emotion. *Annual Review of Psychology, 40,* 249–280.

Adolph, K. E., Cole, W. G., Komati, M., Garciaguirre, J. S., Badaly, D., Lingeman, J. M., Chan, G. L. Y., & Sotsky, R. B. (2012). How do you learn to walk? Thousands of steps and dozens of falls per day. *Psychological Science, 23*(11), 1387–1394. https://doi.org/10.1177/0956797612446346

Adolphs, R., Russell, J. A., & Tranel, D. (1999). A role for the human amygdala in recognizing emotional arousal from unpleasant stimuli. *Psychological Science, 10,* 167–171.

Aggleton, J. (Ed.). (1992). *The amygdala: Neurobiological aspects of emotion, memory and mental dysfunction.* Wiley-Liss.

Agin, D. (2007). *Junk science: An overdue indictment of government, industry, and faith groups that twist science for their own gain.* Macmillan.

Agren, T., Engman, J., Frick, A., Björkstrand, J., Larsson, E. M., Furmark, T., & Fredrikson, M. (2012). Disruption of reconsolidation erases a fear memory trace in the human amygdala. *Science, 337,* 1550–1552.

Ahlskog, J. E. (2011). Pathological behaviors provoked by dopamine agonist therapy of Parkinson's disease. *Physiology & Behavior, 104,* 168–172.

Ainsworth, M. D. S., Blehar, M. C., Waters, E., & Wall, S. (1978). *Patterns of attachment: A psychological study of the strange situation.* Erlbaum.

Ainsworth, S. E., & Maner, J. K. (2012). Sex begets violence: Mating motives, social dominance, and physical aggression in men. *Journal of Personality and Social Psychology, 103*(5), 819–829. https://doi.org/10.1037/a0029428

Aknin, L. B., Hamlin, J. K., & Dunn, E. W. (2012). Giving leads to happiness in young children. *PLoS ONE, 7*(6), e39211. https://doi.org/10.1371/journal.pone.0039211

Albarracín, D., & Shavitt, S. (2018). Attitudes and attitude change. *Annual Review of Psychology, 69*(1), 299–327.

Alcoholics Anonymous. (2016). Estimated worldwide A.A. individual and group membership. http://www.aa.org/assets/en_US/smf-132_en.pdf

Aleman, A., Sommer, I. E., & Kahn, R. S. (2007). Efficacy of slow repetitive transcranial magnetic stimulation in the treatment of resistant auditory hallucinations in schizophrenia: A meta-analysis. *Journal of Clinical Psychiatry, 68,* 416–421.

Allen, J. G., Flanigan, S. S., LeBlanc, M., Vallarino, J., MacNaughton, P., Stewart, J. H., & Christiani, D. C. (2016). Flavoring chemicals in e-cigarettes: Diacetyl, 2,3-pentanedione, and acetoin in a sample of 51 products, including fruit-, candy-, and cocktail-flavored e-cigarettes. *Environmental Health Perspectives, 124*(6), 733–739.

Allison, D. B., Kaprio, J., Korkeila, M., Koskenvuo, M., Neale, M. C., & Hayakawa, K. (1996). The heritability of body mass index among an international sample of monozygotic twins reared apart. *International Journal of Obesity, 20*(6), 501–506.

Allport, G. W. (1937). *Personality: A psychological interpretation.* Holt.

Allport, G. W. (1954). *The nature of prejudice.* Addison-Wesley.

Allport, G. W., & Odbert, H. S. (1936). Trait-names: A psycholexical study. *Psychological Monographs, 47,* 592.

Alvarez, L. W. (1965). A pseudo experience in parapsychology. *Science, 148,* 1541.

Alvarez, L., & Eckholm, E. (2009, January 7). Purple heart is ruled out for traumatic stress. *New York Times.* http://www.nytimes.com/2009/01/08/us/08purple.html

American Psychiatric Association. (2013). *Diagnostic and Statistical Manual of Mental Disorders (DSM-5)* (5th ed.). American Psychiatric Publishing.

American Psychological Association. (2002). *Ethical principles of psychologists and code of conduct.* Author. apa.org/code/ethics/index.aspx [includes 2010 amendments].

American Psychological Association. (2009). *Report of the American Psychological Association task force on appropriate therapeutic responses to sexual orientation.* Author.

Anand, S., & Hotson, J. (2002). Transcranial magnetic stimulation: Neurophysiological applications and safety. *Brain and Cognition, 50,* 366–386.

Anderson, C. A. (1989). Temperature and aggression: Ubiquitous effects of heat on occurrence of human violence. *Psychological Bulletin, 106,* 74–96.

Anderson, C. A., Berkowitz, L., Donnerstein, E., Huesmann, L. R., Johnson, J. D., Linz, D., Malamuth, N. M., & Wartella, E. (2003). The influence of media violence on youth. *Psychological Science in the Public Interest, 4,* 81–110.

Anderson, C. A., & Bushman, B. J. (2002). Human aggression. *Annual Review of Psychology, 53,* 27–51.

Anderson, C. A., Bushman, B. J., & Groom, R. W. (1997). Hot years and serious and deadly assault: Empirical tests of the heat hypothesis. *Journal of Personality and Social Psychology, 73,* 1213–1223.

Anderson, C. A., Shibuya, A., Ihori, N., Swing, E. L., Bushman, B. J., Sakamoto, A., Rothstein, H. R., & Saleem, M. (2010). Violent video game effects on aggression, empathy, and prosocial behavior in Eastern and Western countries: A meta-analytic review. *Psychological Bulletin, 136*(2), 151–173. https://doi.org/10.1037/a0018251

Anderson, C. A., Suzuki, K., Swing, E. L., Groves, C. L., Gentile, D. A., Prot, S., Lam, C. P., Sakamoto, A., Horiuchi, Y., Krahé, B., Jelic, M., Liuquing, W., Toma, R., Warburton, W., Zhang, X-M., Tajima, S., Quing, F., & Petrescu, P. (2017). Media violence and other aggression risk factors in seven nations. *Personality and Social Psychology Bulletin, 43*(7), 986–998. https://doi.org/10.1177/0146167217703064

Anderson, M. C. (2003). Rethinking interference theory: Executive control and the mechanisms of forgetting. *Journal of Memory and Language, 49,* 415–445.

Anderson, M. C., Bjork, R. A., & Bjork, E. L. (1994). Remembering can cause forgetting: Retrieval dynamics in long-term memory. *Journal of Experimental Psychology: Learning, Memory, and Cognition, 20,* 1063–1087.

Anderson, R. C., Pichert, J. W., Goetz, E. T., Schallert, D. L., Stevens, K. V., & Trollip, S. R. (1976). Instantiation of general terms. *Journal of Verbal Learning and Verbal Behavior, 15,* 667–679.

Andreasen, N. C. (2011). A journey into chaos: Creativity and the unconscious. *Mens Sana Monographs, 9,* 42–53.

Andrewes, D. (2001). *Neuropsychology: From theory to practice.* Psychology Press.

Annis, L. F., & Annis, D. B. (1982). A normative study of students' reported preferred study techniques. *Literacy Research and Instruction, 21,* 201–207.

Antoni, M. H., Lehman, J. M., Klibourn, K. M., Boyers, A. E., Culver, J. L., Alferi, S. M., Yount, S. E., McGregor, B. A., Arena, P. L., Harris, S. D., Price, A. A., & Carver, C. S. (2001). Cognitive-behavioral stress management intervention decreases the prevalence of depression and enhances benefit finding among women under treatment for early-stage breast cancer. *Health Psychology, 20,* 20–32.

Ardekani, B. A., Convit, A., & Bachman, A. H. (2016). Analysis of the MIRIAD data shows sex differences in hippocampal atrophy progression. *Journal of Alzheimer's Disease, 50,* 847–857.

Ariel, R., & Karpicke, J. D. (2018). Improving self-regulated learning with a retrieval practice intervention. *Journal of Experimental Psychology: Applied, 24,* 43–56

Armstrong, D. M. (1980). *The nature of mind.* Cornell University Press.

Arnold, M. B. (Ed.). (1960). *Emotion and personality: Psychological aspects* (Vol. 1). Columbia University Press.

Aron, A., Fisher, H., Mashek, D., Strong, G., Li, H., & Brown, L. (2005). Reward, motivation, and emotion systems associated with early-stage intense romantic love. *Journal of Neurophysiology, 93,* 327–337.

Aronson, E. (1969). The theory of cognitive dissonance: A current perspective. In L. Berkowitz (Ed.), *Advances in experimental social psychology* (Vol. 4, pp. 1–34). Academic Press.

Aronson, E., & Worchel, P. (1966). Similarity versus liking as determinants of interpersonal attractiveness. *Psychonomic Science, 5,* 157–158.

Aronson, J., & Steele, C. M. (2004). Stereotypes and the fragility of academic competence, motivation, and self-concept. In A. J. Elliot & C. S. Dweck (Eds.), *Handbook of competence and motivation* (pp. 436–456). Guilford Press.

Asch, S. E. (1951). Effects of group pressure on the modification and distortion of judgments. In H. Guetzkow (Ed.), *Groups, leadership, and men* (pp. 177–190). Carnegie Press.

Asch, S. E. (1955). Opinions and social pressure. *Scientific American, 193,* 31–35.

Asch, S. E. (1956). Studies of independence and conformity: 1. A minority of one against a unanimous majority. *Psychological Monographs: General and Applied, 70,* 1–70.

Aschoff, J. (1965). Circadian rhythms in man. *Science, 148,* 1427–1432.

Aserinsky, E., & Kleitman, N. (1953). Regularly occurring periods of eye motility, and concomitant phenomena, during sleep. *Science, 118,* 273–274.

Ash, M., & Boyce, J. K. (2018). Racial disparities in pollution exposure and employment at U.S. industrial facilities. *Proceedings of the National Academy of Sciences, USA, 115,* 10636 LP–10641.

Ashby, F. G., & Ell, S. W. (2001). The neurobiology of human category learning. *Trends in Cognitive Sciences, 5,* 204–210.

Ashby, F. G., & O'Brien, J. B. (2005). Category learning and multiple memory systems. *Trends in Cognitive Sciences, 9,* 83–89.

Ashby, F. G., & Rosedahl, L. (2017). A neural interpretation of exemplar theory. *Psychological Review, 124,* 472–482.

Astington, J. W., & Baird, J. (2005). *Why language matters for theory of mind.* Oxford University Press.

Atkinson, R. C., & Shiffrin, R. M. (1968). Human memory: A proposed system and its control processes. In K. W. Spence & J. T. Spence (Eds.), *The psychology of learning and motivation* (Vol. 2, pp. 89–195). Academic Press.

Au, J., Sheehan, E., Tsai, N., Duncan, G. J., Buschkuehl, M., & Jaeggi, S. (2015). Improving fluid intelligence with training on working memory: A meta-analysis. *Psychonomic Bulletin & Review, 22,* 366–377.

Avena-Koenigsberger, A., Misic, B., & Sporns, O. (2018). Communication dynamics in complex brain networks. *Nature Reviews Neuroscience, 19,* 17–33.

Axelrod, R. (1984). *The evolution of cooperation.* Basic Books.

Axelrod, R., & Hamilton, W. D. (1981). The evolution of cooperation. *Science, 211,* 1390–1396.

Ayduk, O., Shoda, Y., Cervone, D., & Downey, G. (2007). Delay of gratification in children: Contributions to social-personality psychology. In G. Downey, Y. Shoda, & C. Cervone (Eds.), *Persons in context: Building a science of the individual* (pp. 97–109). Guilford Press.

Azucar, D., Marengo, D., & Settanni, M. (2018). Predicting the Big 5 personality traits from digital footprints on social media: A meta-analysis. *Personality and Individual Differences, 124,* 150–159.

Azuma, H., & Kashiwagi, K. (1987). Descriptors for an intelligent person: A Japanese study. *Japanese Psychological Research, 29,* 17–26.

Baars, B. J. (1986). *The cognitive revolution in psychology.* Guilford Press.

Baca-Motes, K., Brown, A., Gneezy, A., Keenan, E. A., & Nelson, L. D. (2013). Commitment and behavior change: Evidence from the field. *Journal of Consumer Research, 39*(5), 1070–1084. https://doi.org/10.1086/667226

Backman, C. W., & Secord, P. F. (1959). The effect of perceived liking on interpersonal attraction. *Human Relations, 12,* 379–384.

Bäckman, L., & Dixon, R. A. (1992). Psychological compensation: A theoretical framework. *Psychological Bulletin, 112,* 259–283.

Baddeley, A. D. (2001). Is working memory still working? *American Psychologist, 56,* 851–864.

Baddeley, A. D., Allen, R. J., & Hitch, G. J. (2011). Binding in visual working memory: The role of the episodic buffer. *Neuropsychologia, 49,* 1393–1400.

Baddeley, A. D., & Hitch, G. J. (1974). Working memory. In S. Dornic (Ed.), *Attention and performance* (Vol. 6, pp. 647–667). Erlbaum.

Bagby, R. M., Levitan, R. D., Kennedy, S. H., Levitt, A. J., & Joffe, R. T. (1999). Selective alteration of personality in response to noradrenergic and serotonergic antidepressant medication in depressed sample: Evidence of non-specificity. *Psychiatry Research, 86,* 211–216.

Bahrick, H. P. (1984). Semantic memory content in permastore: 50 years of memory for Spanish learned in school. *Journal of Experimental Psychology: General, 113,* 1–29.

Bahrick, H. P. (2000). Long-term maintenance of knowledge. In E. Tulving & F. I. M. Craik (Eds.), *The Oxford handbook of memory* (pp. 347–362). Oxford University Press.

Bahrick, H. P., Hall, L. K., & Berger, S. A. (1996). Accuracy and distortion in memory for high school grades. *Psychological Science, 7,* 265–271.

Bailey, J. M., & Pillard, R. C. (1991). A genetic study of male sexual orientation. *Archives of General Psychiatry, 48,* 1089–1096.

Bailey, J. M., Pillard, R. C., Neale, M. C., & Agyes, Y. (1993). Heritable factors influence sexual orientation in women. *Archives of General Psychiatry, 50,* 217–223.

Bailey, J. M., Vasey, P. L., Diamond, L. M., Breedlove, S. M., Vilain, E., & Epprecht, M. (2016). Sexual orientation, controversy, and science. *Psychological Science in the Public Interest, 17*(2), 45–101. https://doi.org/10.1177/1529100616637616

Baillargeon, R., Spelke, E. S., & Wasserman, S. (1985). Object permanence in 5-month-old infants. *Cognition, 20,* 191–208.

Baker, D. P., Eslinger, P. J., Benavides, M., Peters, E., Dieckmann, N. F., & Leon, J. (2015). The cognitive impact of the education revolution: A possible cause of the Flynn Effect on population IQ. *Intelligence, 49,* 144–158. https://doi.org/10.1016/j.intell.2015.01.003

Baker, P. (2015, June 10). Michelle Obama talks about race and success, and makes it personal. *New York Times.* http://www.nytimes.com/2015/06/11/us/michelle-obama-king-college-prep-and-tuskegee-graduation-speeches.html

Baker, T. B., Brandon, T. H., & Chassin, L. (2004). Motivational influences on cigarette smoking. *Annual Review of Psychology, 55,* 463–491.

Baldwin, V. N., & Powell, T. (2015). Google Calendar: A single case experimental design study of a man with severe memory problems. *Neuropsychological Rehabilitation, 25,* 617–636.

Baler, R. D., & Volkow, N. D. (2006). Drug addiction: The neurobiology of disrupted self-control. *Trends in Molecular Medicine, 12,* 559–566.

Balthazart, J. (2018). Fraternal birth order effect on sexual orientation explained. *Proceedings of the National Academy of Sciences, USA, 115,* 234–236.

Banaji, M. R., & Heiphetz, L. (2010). Attitudes. In S. T. Fiske, D. T. Gilbert, & G. Lindzey (Eds.), *The handbook of social psychology* (5th ed., Vol. 1, pp. 348–388). Wiley.

Bandelow, B., Michaelis, S. S., & Wedekind, D. (2017). Treatment of anxiety disorders. *Dialogues in Clinical Neuroscience, 19,* 93–107.

Bandoli, G., Campbell-Sills, L., Kessler, R. C., Heeringa, S. G., Nock, M. K., Rosellini, A. J., Sampson, N. A., Schoenbaum, M., Ursano, R. J., & Stein, M. B. (2017). Childhood adversity, adult stress, and the risk of major depression or generalized anxiety disorder in U.S. soldiers: A test of the stress sensitization hypothesis. *Psychological Medicine, 47,* 2379–2392.

Bandura, A. (1977). *Social learning theory.* Prentice Hall.

Bandura, A. (1986). *Social foundations of thought and action: A social cognitive theory.* Prentice Hall.

Bandura, A. (1994). Social cognitive theory of mass communication. In J. Bryant & D. Zillmann (Eds.), *Media effects: Advances in theory and research* (pp. 61–90). Erlbaum.

Bandura, A., Ross, D., & Ross, S. (1961). Transmission of aggression through imitation of adult models. *Journal of Abnormal and Social Psychology, 63,* 575–582.

Bandura, A., Ross, D., & Ross, S. (1963). Vicarious reinforcement and imitative learning. *Journal of Abnormal and Social Psychology, 67,* 601–607.

Banks, M. S., & Salapatek, P. (1983). Infant visual perception. In M. Haith & J. Campos (Eds.), *Handbook of child psychology: Biology and infancy* (pp. 435–572). Wiley.

Banse, R., & Scherer, K. R. (1996). Acoustic profiles in vocal emotion expression. *Journal of Personality and Social Psychology, 70,* 614–636.

Barber, J. P., Muran, J. C., McCarthy, K. S., & Keefe, J. R. (2013). Research on dynamic therapies. In M. Lambert (Ed.), *Bergin and Garfield's handbook of psychotherapy and behavior change* (6th ed., pp. 443–494). Wiley.

Barbey, A. K. (2018). Network neuroscience theory of human intelligence. *Trends in Cognitive Sciences, 22*(1), 8–20. https://doi.org/10.1016/j.tics.2017.10.001

Bargh, J. A., Gollwitzer, P. M., Lee-Chai, A., Barndollar, K., & Trötschel, R. (2001). The automated will: Nonconscious activation and pursuit of behavioral goals. *Journal of Personality and Social Psychology, 81,* 1014–1027.

Bargh, J. A., Gollwitzer, P. M., & Oettingen, G. (2010). Motivation. In S. T. Fiske, D. T. Gilbert, & G. Lindzey (Eds.), *The handbook of social psychology* (5th ed., Vol. 1, pp. 263–311). Wiley.

Barker, A. T., Jalinous, R., & Freeston, I. L. (1985). Noninvasive magnetic stimulation of the human motor cortex. *Lancet, 2,* 1106–1107.

Barkow, J. (1980). Prestige and self-esteem: A biosocial interpretation. In D. R. Omark, F. F. Stayer, & D. G. Freedman (Eds.), *Dominance relations* (pp. 319–322). Garland.

Barlett, C., & Coyne, S. M. (2014). A meta-analysis of sex differences in cyber-bullying behavior: The moderating role of age. *Aggressive Behavior, 40,* 474–488. https://doi.org/10.1002/ab.21555

Barlow, D. H., Bullis, J. R., Comer, J. S., & Ametaj, A. A. (2013). Evidence-based psychological treatments: An update and a way forward. *Annual Review of Clinical Psychology, 9,* 1–27.

Barlow, D. H., Gorman, J. M., Shear, M. K., & Woods, S. W. (2000). Cognitive-behavioral therapy, imipramine, or their combination for panic disorder: A randomized controlled trial. *Journal of the American Medical Association, 283*(19), 2529–2536.

Baron-Cohen, S. (1991). Do people with autism understand what causes emotion? *Child Development, 62,* 385–395.

Baron-Cohen, S., & Belmonte, M. K. (2005). Autism: A window onto the development of the social and analytic brain. *Annual Review of Neuroscience, 28,* 109–126.

Baron-Cohen, S., Leslie, A., & Frith, U. (1985). Does the autistic child have a "theory of mind"? *Cognition, 21,* 37–46.

Barragán, R., Coltell, O., Portolés, O., Asensio, E. M., Sorlí, J. V., Ortega-Azorin, C., González, J. I., Sáiz, C., Fernández-Carrión, R., Ordovas, J. M., & Corella, D. (2018). Bitter, sweet, salty, sour and umami taste perception decreases with age: Sex-specific analysis, modulation by genetic variants and taste-preference associations in 18- to 80-year-old subjects. *Nutrients, 10*(10), E1539. https://doi.org/10.3390/nu10101539

Bartal, I. B.-A., Decety, J., & Mason, P. (2011). Empathy and pro-social behavior in rats. *Science, 334*(6061), 1427–1430.

Bartol, C. R., & Costello, N. (1976). Extraversion as a function of temporal duration of electric shock: An exploratory study. *Perceptual and Motor Skills, 42,* 1174.

Bartoshuk, L. M. (2000). Comparing sensory experiences across individuals: Recent psychophysical advances illuminate genetic variation in taste perception. *Chemical Senses, 25,* 447–460.

Bartoshuk, L. M., & Beauchamp, G. K. (1994). Chemical senses. *Annual Review of Psychology, 45,* 419–445.

Basden, B. H., Basden, D. R., Bryner, S., & Thomas, R. L. (1997). A comparison of group and individual remembering: Does collaboration disrupt retrieval strategies? *Journal of Experimental Psychology: Learning, Memory, and Cognition, 23,* 1176–1191.

Basile, K. C., Chen, J., Black, M. C., & Saltzman, L. E. (2007). Prevalence and characteristics of sexual violence victimization among U.S. adults, 2001–2003. *Violence and Victims, 22*(4), 437–448.

Bass, C. & Halligan, P. (2014). Factitious disorders and malingering: Challenges for clinical assessment and management. *Lancet, 383,* 1422–1432.

Bates, E., & Goodman, J. C. (1997). On the inseparability of grammar and the lexicon: Evidence from acquisition, aphasia, and real-time processing. *Language and Cognitive Processes, 12,* 507–584.

Batson, C. D. (2002). Addressing the altruism question experimentally. In S. G. Post & L. G. Underwood (Eds.), *Altruism & altruistic love: Science, philosophy, & religion in dialogue* (pp. 89–105). Oxford University Press.

Batterink, L. J., Westerberg, C. E., & Paller, K. A. (2017). Vocabulary learning benefits from REM after slow-wave sleep. *Neurobiology of Learning & Memory, 144,* 102–113.

Batty, G. D., Deary, I. J., Schoon, I., & Gale, C. R. (2007). Mental ability across childhood in relation to risk factors for premature mortality in adult life: The 1970 British Cohort Study. *Journal of Epidemiology & Community Health, 61*(11), 997–1003. https://doi.org/10.1136/jech.2006.054494

Baumeister, R., Ainsworth, S., & Vohs, K. (2016). Are groups more or less than the sum of their members? The moderating role of individual identification. *Behavioral and Brain Sciences, 39,* e137. https://doi.org/10.1017/S0140525X15000618

Baumeister, R. F., Bratslavsky, E., Muraven, M., & Tice, D. M. (1998). Ego depletion: Is the active self a limited resource? *Journal of Personality and Social Psychology, 74,* 1252–1265.

Baumeister, R. F., Campbell, J. D., Krueger, J. I., & Vohs, K. D. (2003). Does high self-esteem cause better performance, interpersonal success, happiness, or healthier lifestyles? *Psychological Science in the Public Interest, 4,* 1–44.

Baumeister, R. F., Cantanese, K. R., & Vohs, K. D. (2001). Is there a gender difference in strength of sex drive? Theoretical views, conceptual distinctions, and a review of relevant evidence. *Personality and Social Psychology Review, 5,* 242–273.

Baumeister, R. F., & Leary, M. R. (1995). The need to belong: Desire for interpersonal attachments as a fundamental human motivation. *Psychological Bulletin, 117,* 497–529.

Baumeister, R. F., Smart, L., & Boden, J. M. (1996). Relation of threatened egotism to violence and aggression: The dark side of high self-esteem. *Psychological Review, 103,* 5–33.

Baumeister, R. F., Vohs, K. D., & Tice, D. M. (2007). The strength model of self-control. *Current Directions in Psychological Science, 16,* 351–355.

Bayley, P. J., Frascino, J. C., & Squire, L. R. (2005). Robust habit learning in the absence of awareness and independent of the medial temporal lobe. *Nature, 436,* 550–553.

Bayley, P. J., Gold, J. J., Hopkins, R. O., & Squire, L. R. (2005). The neuroanatomy of remote memory. *Neuron, 46,* 799–810.

Beaty, R. E., Benedek, M., Silvia, P. J., & Schacter, D. L. (2016). Creative cognition and brain network dynamics. *Trends in Cognitive Sciences, 20,* 87–95.

Beaty, R. E., Thakral, P. P., Madore, K. P., Benedek, M., & Schacter, D. L. (2018). Core network contributions to remembering the past, imagining the future, and thinking creatively. *Journal of Cognitive Neuroscience. 30*(12), 1939–1951.

Bechara, A., Damasio, A. R., Damasio, H., & Anderson, S. W. (1994). Insensitivity to future consequences following damage to human prefrontal cortex. *Cognition, 50,* 7–15.

Bechara, A., Damasio, H., Tranel, D., & Damasio, A. R. (1997). Deciding advantageously before knowing the advantageous strategy. *Science, 275,* 1293–1295.

Bechara, A., Dolan, S., Denburg, N., Hindes, A., & Anderson, S. W. (2001). Decision-making deficits, linked to a dysfunctional ventromedial prefrontal cortex, revealed in alcohol and stimulant abusers. *Neuropsychologia, 39,* 376–389.

Bechara, A., Tranel, D., & Damasio, H. (2000). Characterization of the decision-making deficit of patients with ventromedial prefrontal cortex lesions. *Brain, 123,* 2189–2202.

Becht, A. I., Nelemans, S. A., Branje, S. T., Vollebergh, W. M., Koot, H. M., & Meeus, W. J. (2017). Identity uncertainty and commitment making across adolescence: Five-year within-person associations using daily identity reports. *Developmental Psychology, 53*(11), 2103–2112. https://doi.org/10.1037/dev0000374

Beck, A. T. (1967). *Depression: Causes and treatment.* University of Pennsylvania Press.

Beck, A. T. (2019). A 60-year evolution of cognitive theory and therapy. *Perspectives on Psychological Science, 14*(1), 16–20.

Bedny, M., & Saxe, R. (2012). Insights into the origins of knowledge from the cognitive neuroscience of blindness. *Cognitive Neuropsychology, 29,* 56–84.

Beek, M. R., Levin, D. T., & Angelone, B. (2007). Change blindness: Beliefs about the roles of intention and scene complexity in change detection. *Consciousness and Cognition, 16,* 31–51.

Békésy, G. von. (1960). *Experiments in hearing.* McGraw-Hill.

Bell, R., Roer, J. P., & Buchner, A. (2015). Adaptive memory: Thinking about function. *Journal of Experimental Psychology: Learning, Memory, & Cognition, 41,* 1038–1048.

Belsky, J. (2012). The development of human reproductive strategies: Progress and prospects. *Current Directions in Psychological Science, 21*(5), 310–316. https://doi.org/10.1177/0963721412453588

Belsky, J., Ruttle, P. L., Boyce, W. T., Armstrong, J. M., & Essex, M. J. (2015). Early adversity, elevated stress physiology, accelerated sexual maturation, and poor health in females. *Developmental Psychology, 51*(6), 816–822. https://doi.org/10.1037/dev0000017

Bem, S. L. (1974). The measure of psychological androgyny. *Journal of Consulting and Clinical Psychology, 42,* 155–162.

Bender, P. K., Plante, C., & Gentile, D. A. (2017). The effects of violent media content on aggression. *Current Opinion in Psychology, 19,* 104–108.

Benedek, M., Jauk, E., Fink, A., Koschutnig, K., Reishofer, G., Ebner, F., & Neubauer, A. C. (2014). To create or to recall? Neural mechanisms underlying the generation of creative new ideas. *NeuroImage, 88,* 125–133.

Benenson, J. F., Markovits, H., Thompson, M. E., & Wrangham, R. W. (2011). Under threat of social exclusion, females exclude more than males. *Psychological Science, 22*(4), 538–544. https://doi.org/10.1177/0956797611402511

Bennett, I. J., Romano, J. C., Howard, J. H., & Howard, D. V. (2008). Two forms of implicit learning in young adults with dyslexia. *Annals of the New York Academy of Sciences, 1145,* 184–198.

Benoit, R. G., & Schacter, D. L. (2015). Specifying the core network supporting episodic simulation and episodic memory by activation likelihood estimation. *Neuropsychologia, 75,* 450–457.

Ben-Porath, Y. S., & Tellegen, A. (2008). *Minnesota Multiphasic Personality Inventory–2–Restructured Form: Manual for administration, scoring, and interpretation.* Minneapolis: University of Minnesota Press.

Benson, H. (Ed.). (1990). *The relaxation response.* Harper Torch.

Benson, H., Dusek, J. A., Sherwood, J. B., Lam, P., Bethea, C. F., Carpenter, W., Levitsky, S., Hill, P. C., Clem, D. W., Jr., Jain, M. K., Drumel, D., Kopecky, S. L., Mueller, P. S., Marek, D., Rollins, S., & Hibberd, P. L. (2006). Study of the therapeutic effects of intercessory prayer (STEP) in cardiac bypass patients: A multicenter randomized trial of uncertainty and certainty of receiving intercessory prayer. *American Heart Journal, 151,* 934–942.

Berger, J. (2014). Word of mouth and interpersonal communication: A review and directions for future research. *Journal of Consumer Psychology, 24*(4), 586–607.

Berkowitz, L. (1989). Frustration-aggression hypothesis: Examination and reformulation. *Psychological Bulletin, 106*(1): 59–73. https://doi.org/10.1037/0033-2909.106.1.59

Berkowitz, L. (1990). On the formation and regulation of anger and aggression: A cognitive-neoassociationistic analysis. *American Psychologist, 45,* 494–503.

Bernier, A., Beauchamp, M. H., Carlson, S. M., & Lalonde, G. (2015). A secure base from which to regulate: Attachment security in toddlerhood as a predictor of executive functioning at school entry. *Developmental Psychology, 51*(9), 1177–1189. https://doi.org/10.1037/dev0000032

Bernstein, E. E., & McNally, R. J. (2017). Acute aerobic exercise hastens emotional recovery from a subsequent stressor. *Health Psychology, 36,* 560–567.

Berntsen, D. (2010). The unbidden past: Involuntary autobiographical memories as a basic mode of remembering. *Current Directions in Psychological Science, 19,* 138–142.

Berridge, K. C. (2007). The debate over dopamine's role in reward: The case for incentive salience. *Psychopharmacology, 191,* 391–431.

Berscheid, E., & Reis, H. T. (1998). Interpersonal attraction and close relationships. In D. T. Gilbert, S. T. Fiske, & G. Lindzey (Eds.), *The handbook of social psychology* (4th ed., Vol. 2, pp. 193–281). McGraw-Hill.

Bertenthal, B. I., Rose, J. L., & Bai, D. L. (1997). Perception–action coupling in the development of visual control of posture. *Journal of Experimental Psychology: Human Perception & Performance, 23,* 1631–1643.

Berthoud, H.-R., & Morrison, C. (2008). The brain, appetite, and obesity. *Annual Review of Psychology, 59,* 55–92.

Bhargava, S. (2011). Diagnosis and management of common sleep problems in children. *Pediatrics in Review, 32,* 91.

Bialystok, E. (1999). Cognitive complexity and attentional control in the bilingual mind. *Child Development, 70,* 636–644.

Bialystok, E. (2009). Bilingualism: The good, the bad, and the indifference. *Bilingualism: Language and Cognitive Processes, 12,* 3–11.

Bialystok, E. (2017). The bilingual adaptation: How minds accommodate experience. *Psychological Bulletin, 143,* 233–262.

Bickerton, D. (1990). *Language and species.* University of Chicago Press.

Biederman, J., Monuteaux, M. C., Spencer, T., Wilens, T. E., & Faraone, S. V. (2009). Do stimulants protect against psychiatric disorders in youth with ADHD? A 10-year follow-up study. *Pediatrics, 124,* 71–78.

Bilalić, M., McLeod, P., & Gobet, F. (2008). Why good thoughts block better ones: The mechanisms of the pernicious Einstellung (set) effect. *Cognition, 108*, 652–661.

Biro, S., Alink, L. R., van IJzendoorn, M. H., & Bakermans-Kranenburg, M. J. (2014). Infants' monitoring of social interactions: The effect of emotional cues. *Emotion, 14*(2), 263–271. https://doi.org/10.1037/a0035589

Bjork, E. L., & Bjork, R. A. (2011). Making things hard on yourself, but in a good way: Creating desirable difficulties to enhance learning. In M. A. Gernsbacher, R. W. Pewe, L. M. Hough, & J. R. Pomerantz (Eds.), *Psychology and the real world: Essays illustrating fundamental contributions to society* (pp. 56–64). Worth Publishers.

Bjork, R. A. (1975). Retrieval as a memory modifier. In R. Solso (Ed.), *Information processing and cognition: The Loyola Symposium* (pp. 123–144). Erlbaum.

Bjork, R. A. (2011). On the symbiosis of remembering, forgetting, and learning. In A. S. Benjamin (Ed.), *Successful remembering and successful forgetting: A festschrift in honor of Robert A. Bjork* (pp. 1–22). Psychology Press.

Bjork, R. A., & Bjork, E. L. (1988). On the adaptive aspects of retrieval failure in autobiographical memory. In M. M. Gruneberg, P. E. Morris, & R. N. Sykes (Eds.), *Practical aspects of memory: Current research and issues* (pp. 283–288). Wiley.

Bjork, R. A., Dunlosky, J., & Kornell, N. (2013). Self-regulated learning: Beliefs, techniques, and illusions. *Annual Review of Psychology, 64*, 417–444.

Bjorkqvist, K. (2018). Gender differences in aggression. *Current Opinion in Psychology, 19*, 39–42.

Blackburn, E. H., Epel, E. S., & Lin, J. (2015). Human telomere biology: A contributory and interactive factor in aging, disease risks, and protection. *Science, 350*, 1193–1198.

Blair, C. (2006). How similar are fluid cognition and general intelligence? A developmental neuroscience perspective on fluid cognition as an aspect of human cognitive ability. *Behavioral and Brain Sciences, 29*(2), 109–125 (article),125–160 (discussion). https://doi.org/10.1017/S0140525X06009034

Blair, I. V. (2002). The malleability of automatic stereotypes and prejudice. *Personality and Social Psychology Review, 6*, 242–261.

Blair, J., Peschardt, K., & Mitchell, D. R. (2005). *Psychopath: Emotion and the brain*. Blackwell.

Blake, M. J., Trinder, J. A., & Allen, N. B. (2018). Mechanisms underlying the association between insomnia, anxiety, and depression in adolescence: Implications for behavioral sleep interventions. *Clinical Psychology Review, 63*, 25–40.

Blake, P. R., McAuliffe, K., & Warneken, F. (2014). The developmental origins of fairness: The knowledge-behavior gap. *Trends in Cognitive Sciences, 18*(11), 559–561. https://doi.org/10.1016/j.tics.2014.08.003

Blascovich, J., & Mendes, W. B. (2000). Challenge and threat appraisals: The role of affective cues. In J. P. Forgas (Ed.), *Studies in emotion and social interaction, Second Series. Feeling and thinking: The role of affect in social cognition* (pp. 59–82). Cambridge University Press.

Blascovich, J., & Tomaka, J. (1996). The biopsychosocial model of arousal regulation. In M. P. Zanna (Ed.), *Advances in experimental social psychology* (Vol. 28, pp. 1–51). Academic Press.

Blatt, S. J., & Homann, E. (1992). Parent–child interaction in the etiology of dependent and self-critical depression. *Clinical Psychology Review, 12*, 47–91.

Blendon, R. J., & Benson, J. M. (2018). The public and the opioid abuse epidemic. *New England Journal of Medicine, 378*, 407–411.

Blesch, A., & Tuszynski, M. H. (2009). Spinal cord injury: Plasticity, regeneration and the challenge of translational drug development. *Trends in Neurosciences, 32*, 41–47.

Bliss, T. V. P. (1999). Young receptors make smart mice. *Nature, 401*, 25–27.

Bliss, T. V. P., & Lømo, W. T. (1973). Long-lasting potentiation of synaptic transmission in the dentate area of the anesthetized rabbit following stimulation of the perforant path. *Journal of Physiology, 232*, 331–356.

Bloch, C., Kaiser, A., Kuenzli, E., Zappatore, D., Haller, S., Franceschini, R., Luedi, G., Radue, E.-W., & Nitsch, C. (2009). The age of second language acquisition determines the variability in activation elicited by narration in three languages in Broca's and Wernicke's area. *Neuropsychologia, 47*, 625–633.

Bloch, L., Haase, C. M., & Levenson, R. W. (2014). Emotion regulation predicts marital satisfaction: More than a wives' tale. *Emotion, 14*(1), 130–144. https://doi.org/10.1037/a0034272

Bloom, C. M., Venard, J., Harden, M., & Seetharaman, S. (2007). Non-contingent positive and negative reinforcement schedules of superstitious behaviors. *Behavioural Process, 75*, 8–13.

Blumen, H. M., & Rajaram, S. (2008). Influence of re-exposure and retrieval disruption during group collaboration on later individual recall. *Memory, 16*, 231–244.

Boecker, H., Sprenger, T., Spilker, M. E., Henriksen, G., Koppenhoefer, M., Wagner, K. J., Valet, M., Berthele, A., & Tolle, T. R. (2008). The runner's high: Opioidergic mechanisms in the human brain. *Cerebral Cortex, 18*, 2523–2531.

Boehm, J. K., & Kubzansky, L. D. (2012). The heart's content: The association between positive psychological well-being and cardiovascular health. *Psychological Bulletin, 138*, 655–691.

Boehm, J. K., Williams, D. R., Rimm, E. B., Ryff, C., & Kubzansky, L. D. (2013). Relation between optimism and lipids in midlife. *American Journal of Cardiology, 111*, 1425–1431.

Boergers, J., Spirito, A., & Donaldson, D. (1998). Reasons for adolescent suicide attempts: Associations with psychological functioning. *Journal of the American Academy of Child and Adolescent Psychiatry, 37*, 1287–1293.

Boinski, S., Quatrone, R. P., & Swartz, H. (2000). Substrate and tool use by brown capuchins in Suriname: Ecological contexts and cognitive bases. *American Anthropologist, 102*, 741–761.

Boisvert, C. M., & Faust, D. (2002). Iatrogenic symptoms in psychotherapy: A theoretical exploration of the potential impact of labels, language, and belief systems. *American Journal of Psychotherapy, 56*, 244–259.

Bond, C. F., & DePaulo, B. M. (2006). Accuracy of deception judgments. *Personality and Social Psychology Review, 10*, 214–234.

Bonnici, H. M., Cheke, L. G., Green, D. A. E., FitzGerald, T. H. M. B., & Simons, J. S. (2018). Specifying a causal role for angular gyrus in episodic memory. *Journal of Neuroscience, 38*, 10438–10443.

Boomsma, D., Busjahn, A., & Peltonen, L. (2002). Classical twin studies and beyond. *Nature Reviews Genetics, 3*, 872–882.

Bootzin, R. R., & Epstein, D. R. (2011). Understanding and treating insomnia. *Annual Review of Clinical Psychology, 7*, 435–458.

Bordone, V., Scherbov, S., & Steiber, N. (2015). Smarter every day: The deceleration of population ageing in terms of cognition. *Intelligence, 52*, 90–96. https://doi.org/10.1016/j.intell.2015.07.005

Borghans, L., Golsteyn, B. H. H., Heckman, J. J., & Humphries, J. E. (2016). What grades and achievement tests measure. *Proceedings of the National Academy of Sciences, 113*(47), 13354–13359. https://doi.org/10.1073/pnas.1601135113

Boring, E. G. (1929). *A history of experimental psychology*. The Century Company.

Born, R. T., & Bradley, D. C. (2005). Structure and function of visual area MT. *Annual Review of Neuroscience, 28*, 157–189.

Bornstein, R. F. (1989). Exposure and affect: Overview and metaanalysis of research, 1968–1987. *Psychological Bulletin, 106*, 265–289.

Botwin, M. D., Buss, D. M., & Shackelford, T. K. (1997). Personality and mate preferences: Five factors in mate selection and marital satisfaction. *Journal of Personality, 65*, 107–136.

Bouchard, S. M., Brown, T. G., & Nadeau, L. (2012). Decision making capacities and affective reward anticipation in DWI recidivists compared to non-offenders: A preliminary study. *Accident Analysis and Prevention, 45*, 580–587.

Bouchard, T. J., & McGue, M. (2003). Genetic and environmental influences on human psychological differences. *Journal of Neurobiology, 54*, 4–45.

Bouton, M. E. (1988). Context and ambiguity in the extinction of emotional learning: Implications for exposure therapy. *Behaviour Research and Therapy, 26,* 137–149.

Boutwell, B. B., Young, J. T. N., & Meldrum, R. C. (2018). On the positive relationship between breastfeeding & intelligence. *Developmental Psychology, 54*(8), 1426–1433. https://doi.org/10.1037/dev0000537

Bower, G. H. (1981). Mood and memory. *American Psychologist, 36,* 129–148.

Bowlby, J. (1969). *Attachment and loss: Vol. 1. Attachment.* Basic Books.

Bowlby, J. (1973). *Attachment and loss: Vol. 2. Separation.* Basic Books.

Bowlby, J. (1980). *Attachment and loss: Vol. 3. Loss: Sadness and depression.* Basic Books.

Boyd, R. (2008, February 7). Do people use only 10 percent of their brains? *Scientific American.* http://www.scientificamerican.com/article .cfm?id=people-only-use-10-percent-of-brain&page=2

Boyle, L. L. (2018). Psychological and neuropsychological testing. In R. R. Tampi, D. J. Tampi, & L. L. Boyle (Eds.), *Psychiatric disorders late in life: A comprehensive review* (pp. 81–90). Springer International Publishing.

Bozarth, M. A., & Wise, R. A. (1985). Toxicity associated with long-term intravenous heroin and cocaine self-administration in the rat. *Journal of the American Medical Association, 254,* 81–83.

Brackett, M. A., & Mayer, J. D. (2003). Convergent, discriminant, and incremental validity of competing measures of emotional intelligence. *Personality and Social Psychology Bulletin, 29,* 1147.

Brackett, M. A., Rivers, S. E., Shiffman, S., Lerner, N., & Salovey, P. (2006). Relating emotional abilities to social functioning: A comparison of self-report and performance measures of emotional intelligence. *Journal of Personality and Social Psychology, 91,* 780.

Brackett, M. A., Warner, R. M., & Bosco, J. (2005). Emotional intelligence and relationship quality among couples. *Personal Relationships, 12*(2), 197–212.

Brakefield, T. A., Mednick, S. C., Wilson, H. W., De Neve, J. E., Christakis, N. A., & Fowler, J. H. (2014). Same-sex sexual attraction does not spread in adolescent social networks. *Archives of Sexual Behavior, 43*(2), 335–344. https://doi.org/10.1007/s10508-013-0142-9

Bramlett, M. D., & Mosher, W. D. (2002). *Cohabitation, marriage, divorce, and remarriage in the United States* (Vital and Health Statistics Series 23, No. 22). Hyattsville, MD: National Center for Health Statistics.

Brandt, K. R., Gardiner, J. M., Vargha-Khadem, F., Baddeley, A. D., & Mishkin, M. (2009). Impairment of recollection but not familiarity in a case of developmental amnesia. *Neurocase, 15,* 60–65.

Brant, A. M., Munakata, Y., Boomsma, D. I., Defries, J. C., Haworth, C. M. A., Keller, M. C., Martin, N. G., McGue, M., Petrill, S. A., Plomin, R., Wadsworth, S. J., Wright, M. J., & Hewitt, J. K. (2013). The nature and nurture of high IQ: An extended sensitive period for intellectual development. *Psychological Science, 24*(8), 1487–1495. https://doi.org/10.1177/0956797612473119

Bratman, G. N., Hamilton, J. P., Hahn, K. S., Daily, G. C., & Gross, J. J. (2015). Nature experience reduces rumination and subgenual prefrontal cortex activation. *Proceedings of the National Academy of Science, USA, 112,* 8567–8572.

Bratsberg, B., & Rogeberg, O. (2018). Flynn effect and its reversal are both environmentally caused. *Proceedings of the National Academy of Sciences, USA, 115*(26), 6674–6678. https://doi.org/10.1073/pnas.1718793115

Braun, A. R., Balkin, T. J., Wesensten, N. J., Gwadry, F., Carson, R. E., Varga, M., Baldwin, P., Belenky, G., & Herscovitch, P. (1998). Dissociated pattern of activity in visual cortices and their projections during rapid eye movement sleep. *Science, 279,* 91–95.

Brédart, S., & Valentine, T. (1998). Descriptiveness and proper name retrieval. *Memory, 6,* 199–206.

Bredy, T. W., Wu, H., Crego, C., Zellhoefer, J., Sun, Y. E., & Barad, M. (2007). Histone modifications around individual BDNF gene promoters in prefrontal cortex are associated with extinction of conditioned fear. *Learning and Memory, 14,* 268–276.

Breggin, P. R. (2000). *Reclaiming our children.* Perseus Books.

Breland, K., & Breland, M. (1961). The misbehavior of organisms. *American Psychologist, 16,* 681–684.

Brennan, P. A., & Zufall, F. (2006). Pheromonal communication in vertebrates. *Nature, 444,* 308–315.

Brenninkmeijer, V., Vanyperen, N. W., & Buunk, B. P. (2001). I am not a better teacher, but others are doing worse: Burnout and perceptions of superiority among teachers. *Social Psychology of Education, 4*(3–4), 259–274.

Breslow, L., Pritchard, D. E., DeBoer, J., Stump, G. S., Ho, A. D., & Seaton, D. T. (2013). Studying learning in the worldwide classroom: Research into edX's first MOOC. *Research & Practice in Assessment, 8,* 13–25.

Bretherton, I., & Munholland, K. A. (1999). Internal working models in attachment relationships: A construct revisited. In J. Cassidy & P. R. Shaver (Eds.), *Handbook of attachment: Theory, research and clinical applications* (pp. 89–114). Guilford Press.

Brewer, M. B. (1999). The psychology of prejudice: Ingroup love or outgroup hate? *Journal of Social Issues, 55*(3), 429–444. https://doi.org/10.1111 /0022-4537.00126

Briggs, J. (2000). Conflict management in a modern Inuit community. In P. P. Schweitzer, M. Biesele, & R. K. Hitchcock (Eds.), *Hunters and gatherers in the modern world: Conflict, resistance, and self-determination* (pp. 110–124). Berghahn Books.

Broberg, D. J., & Bernstein, I. L. (1987). Candy as a scapegoat in the prevention of food aversions in children receiving chemotherapy. *Cancer, 60,* 2344–2347.

Brody, N. (2003). Construct validation of the Sternberg Triarchic Abilities Test: Comment and reanalysis. *Intelligence, 31*(4), 319–329.

Brooks, D. (2012, May 3). The campus tsunami. *New York Times.* http://www .nytimes.com/2012/05/04/opinion/brooks-the-campus-tsunami.html

Brooks, R., & Meltzoff, A. N. (2002). The importance of eyes: How infants interpret adult looking behavior. *Developmental Psychology, 38,* 958–966.

Brooks-Gunn, J., Graber, J. A., & Paikoff, R. L. (1994). Studying links between hormones and negative affect: Models and measures. *Journal of Research on Adolescence, 4,* 469–486.

Brown, A. S. (2004). *The déjà vu experience.* Psychology Press.

Brown, B. B., Mory, M., & Kinney, D. (1994). Casting crowds in a relational perspective: Caricature, channel, and context. In G. A. R. Montemayor & T. Gullotta (Eds.), *Advances in adolescent development: Personal relationships during adolescence* (Vol. 5, pp. 123–167). Sage.

Brown, J. D., & McGill, K. L. (1989). The cost of good fortune: When positive life events produce negative health consequences. *Journal of Personality and Social Psychology, 57,* 1103–1110.

Brown, R. (1958). *Words and things.* Free Press.

Brown, R., & Kulik, J. (1977). Flashbulb memories. *Cognition, 5,* 73–99.

Brown, R., & McNeill, D. (1966). The "tip-of-the-tongue" phenomenon. *Journal of Verbal Learning and Verbal Behavior, 5,* 325–337.

Brown, R. P., Osterman, L. L., & Barnes, C. D. (2009). School violence and the culture of honor. *Psychological Science, 20*(11), 1400–1405.

Brown, S. C., & Craik, F. I. M. (2000). Encoding and retrieval of information. In E. Tulving & F. I. M. Craik (Eds.), *The Oxford handbook of memory* (pp. 93–107). Oxford University Press.

Brown, T. A., & Barlow, D. H. (2002). Classification of anxiety and mood disorders. In D. H. Barlow (Ed.), *Anxiety and its disorders: The nature and treatment of anxiety and panic* (2nd ed.). Guilford Press.

Bruner, J. S. (1983). Education as social invention. *Journal of Social Issues, 39,* 129–141.

Brunet, A., Orr, S. P., Tremblay, J., Robertson, K., Nader, K., & Pitman, R. K. (2008). Effects of post-retrieval propranolol on psychophysiologic responding during subsequent script-driven traumatic imagery in posttraumatic stress disorder. *Journal of Psychiatric Research, 42,* 503–506.

Brunet, A., Saumier, D., Liu, A., Streiner, D. L., Tremblay, J., & Pitman, R. K. (2018). Reduction of PTSD symptoms with pre-reactivation propranolol therapy: A randomized controlled trial. *American Journal of Psychiatry 175,* 427–433. https://doi-org.ezp-prod1.hul.harvard.edu/10.1176/appi .ajp.2017.17050481

Brunner, D. P., Dijk, D. J., Tobler, I., & Borbely, A. A. (1990). Effect of partial sleep deprivation on sleep stages and EEG power spectra. *Electroencephalography and Clinical Neurophysiology, 75,* 492–499.

Bryck, R. L., & Fisher, P. A. (2012). Training the brain: Practical applications of neural plasticity from the intersection of cognitive neuroscience, developmental psychology, and prevention science. *American Psychologist, 67,* 87–100.

Buchanan, C. M., Eccles, J. S., & Becker, J. B. (1992). Are adolescents the victims of raging hormones? Evidence for activational effects of hormones on moods and behavior at adolescence. *Psychological Bulletin, 111,* 62–107.

Buchanan, T. W. (2007). Retrieval of emotional memories. *Psychological Bulletin, 133,* 761–779.

Buck Louis, G. M., Gray, L. E., Marcus, M., Ojeda, S. R., Pescovitz, O. H., Witchel, S. F., Sippell, W., Abbott, D. H., Soto, A., Tyl, R. W., Bourguignon, J.-P., Skakkebaek, N. E., Swan, S. H., Golub, M. S., Wabitsch, M., Toppari, J., & Euling, S. Y. (2008). Environmental factors and puberty timing: Expert panel research. *Pediatrics, 121*(Suppl. 3), S192–S207. https://doi.org/10.1542/peds1813E

Buckley, C. (2007, January 3). Man is rescued by stranger on subway tracks. *New York Times.* http://www.nytimes.com/2007/01/03/nyregion/03life.html

Buckner, R. L., Petersen, S. E., Ojemann, J. G., Miezin, F. M., Squire, L. R., & Raichle, M. E. (1995). Functional anatomical studies of explicit and implicit memory retrieval tasks. *Journal of Neuroscience, 15,* 12–29.

Bunce, D. M., Flens, E. A., & Neiles, K. Y. (2011). How long can students pay attention in class? A study of student attention decline using clickers. *Journal of Chemical Education, 87,* 1438–1443.

Burger, J. M. (1999). The foot-in-the-door compliance procedure: A multiple-process analysis and review. *Personality and Social Psychology Review, 3,* 303–325.

Burger, J. M. (2009). Replicating Milgram: Would people still obey today? *American Psychologist, 64,* 1–11.

Burger, J. M., & Burns, L. (1988). The illusion of unique invulnerability and the use of effective contraception. *Personality and Social Psychology Bulletin, 14,* 264–270.

Burger, J. M., Sanchez, J., Imberi, J. E., & Grande, L. R. (2009). The norm of reciprocity as an internalized social norm: Returning favors even when no one finds out. *Social Influence, 4*(1), 11–17.

Burke, D., MacKay, D. G., Worthley, J. S., & Wade, E. (1991). On the tip of the tongue: What causes word failure in young and older adults? *Journal of Memory and Language, 30,* 237–246.

Burke, M., Hsiang, S. M., & Miguel, E. (2015). Climate and conflict. *Annual Review of Economics, 7*(1), 577–617.

Burke, S. L., Hu, T., Fava, N. M, Li, T., Rodriguez, M., Schuldiner, K. L., Burgess, A., & Laird, A. (2019). Sex differences in the development of mild cognitive impairment and probable Alzheimer disease as predicted by hippocampal volume or white matter hyperintensities. *Journal of Women and Aging, 31,* 140–164.

Burks, S. V., Carpenter, J. P., Goette, L., & Rustichini, A. (2009). Cognitive skills affect economic preferences, strategic behavior, and job attachment. *Proceedings of the National Academy of Sciences, 106*(19), 7745–7750. https://doi.org/10.1073/pnas. 0812360106

Burns, D. J., Hwang, A. J., & Burns, S. A. (2011). Adaptive memory: Determining the proximate mechanisms responsible for the memorial advantages of survival processing. *Journal of Experimental Psychology: Learning, Memory, and Cognition, 37,* 206–218.

Burnstein, E., Crandall, C., & Kitayama, S. (1994). Some neo-Darwinian decision rules for altruism: Weighing cues for inclusive fitness as a function of the biological importance of the decision. *Journal of Personality and Social Psychology, 67,* 773–789.

Bushdid, C., Magnasco, M. O., Vosshall, L. B., & Keller, A. (2014). Humans can discriminate more than one trillion olfactory stimuli. *Science, 343*(6177), 1370–1372. https://doi.org/10.1126/science.1249168

Bushman, B. J., & Huesmann, L. R. (2010). Aggression. In S. T. Fiske, D. T. Gilbert, & G. Lindzey (Eds.), *The handbook of social psychology* (5th ed., Vol. 2, pp. 833–863). Wiley.

Buss, D. M. (1985). Human mate selection. *American Scientist, 73,* 47–51.

Buss, D. M. (1989). Sex differences in human mate preferences: Evolutionary hypotheses tested in 37 cultures. *Behavioral and Brain Sciences, 12,* 1–49.

Buss, D. M., & Schmitt, D. P. (1993). Sexual strategies theory: An evolutionary perspective on human mating. *Psychological Review, 100,* 204–232.

Butler, A. C., Chapman, J. E., Forman, E. M., & Beck, A. T. (2006). The empirical status of cognitive-behavioral therapy: A review of meta-analyses. *Clinical Psychology Review, 26,* 17–31.

Butler, M. A., Corboy, J. R., & Filley, C. M. (2009). How the conflict between American psychiatry and neurology delayed the appreciation of cognitive dysfunction in multiple sclerosis. *Neuropsychology Review, 19,* 399–410.

Byers-Heinlein, K., Burns, T. C., & Werker, J. F. (2010). The roots of bilingualism in newborns. *Psychological Science, 21*(3), 343–348. https://doi.org/10.1177/0956797609360758

Byrne, D., & Clore, G. L. (1970). A reinforcement model of evaluative responses. *Personality: An International Journal, 1,* 103–128.

Byrne, D., Ervin, C. R., & Lamberth, J. (1970). Continuity between the experimental study of attraction and real-life computer dating. *Journal of Personality and Social Psychology, 16,* 157–165.

Cabeza, R. (2002). Hemispheric asymmetry reduction in older adults: The HAROLD model. *Psychology and Aging, 17,* 85–100.

Cabeza, R., Rao, S., Wagner, A. D., Mayer, A., & Schacter, D. L. (2001). Can medial temporal lobe regions distinguish true from false? An event-related fMRI study of veridical and illusory recognition memory. *Proceedings of the National Academy of Sciences, USA, 98,* 4805–4810.

Cacioppo, J. T., & Patrick, B. (2008). *Loneliness: Human nature and the need for social connection.* Norton.

Cadario, R., & Chandon, P. (2019). Which healthy eating nudges work best? A meta-analysis of field experiments. *Marketing Science* (forthcoming). Available at SSRN: https://ssrn.com/abstract=3090829 or http://dx.doi.org/10.2139/ssrn.3090829

Cahill, L., Haier, R. J., Fallon, J., Alkire, M. T., Tang, C., Keator, D., Wu, J., & McGaugh, J. L. (1996). Amygdala activity at encoding correlated with long-term, free recall of emotional information. *Proceedings of the National Academy of Sciences, USA, 93,* 8016–8021.

Cahill, L., & McGaugh, J. L. (1998). Mechanisms of emotional arousal and lasting declarative memory. *Trends in Neurosciences, 21,* 294–299.

Callaghan, T., Rochat, P., Lillard, A., Claux, M. L., Odden, H., Itakura, S., Tapanya, S., & Singh, S. (2005). Synchrony in the onset of mental-state reasoning: Evidence from five cultures. *Psychological Science, 16,* 378–384.

Calvert, S. L., Appelbaum, M., Dodge, K. A., Graham, S., Nagayama Hall, G. C., Hamby, S., Fasig-Caldwell, L. G., Citkowicz, M., Galloway, D. P., & Hedges, L. V. (2017, Feb–Mar). The American Psychological Association Task Force assessment of violent video games: Science in the service of public interest. *American Psychologist, 72*(2), 126–143.

Calvin, C. M., Deary, I. J., Fenton, C., Roberts, B. A., Der, G., Leckenby, N., & Batty, G. D. (2011). Intelligence in youth and all-cause-mortality: Systematic review with meta-analysis. *International Journal of Epidemiology, 40*(3), 626–644. https://doi.org/10.1093/ije/dyq190

Cameron, C. D., & Payne, B. K. (2011). Escaping affect: How motivated emotion regulation creates insensitivity to mass suffering. *Journal of Personality and Social Psychology, 100*(1), 1–15.

Campbell, A. (1999). Staying alive: Evolution, culture, and women's intrasexual aggression. *Behavioral & Brain Sciences, 22,* 203–252.

Campbell, C. M., & Edwards, R. R. (2012). Ethnic differences in pain and pain management. *Pain Management, 2,* 219–230.

Campbell, C. M., Edwards, R. R., & Fillingim, R. B. (2005). Ethnic differences in responses to multiple experimental pain stimuli. *Pain, 113,* 20–26.

Campbell, F. A., Ramey, C. T., Pungello, E., Sparling, J., & Miller-Johnson, S. (2002). Early childhood education: Young adult outcomes from the Abecedarian Project. *Applied Developmental Science, 6*(1), 42–57. https://doi.org/10.1207/S1532480XADS0601_05

Campos, B., Shiota, M. N., Keltner, D., Gonzaga, G. C., & Goetz, J. L. (2013). What is shared, what is different? Core relational themes and expressive displays of eight positive emotions. *Cognition & Emotion, 27*(1), 37–52. https://doi.org/10.1080/02699931.2012.683852

Cantor, N. (1990). From thought to behavior: "Having" and "doing" in the study of personality and cognition. *American Psychologist, 45,* 735–750.

Card, D., & Giuliano, L. (2016). Can tracking raise the test scores of high-ability minority students? *American Economic Review, 106*(10), 2783–2816.

Card, N. A., Stucky, B. D., Sawalani, G. M., & Little, T. D. (2008). Direct and indirect aggression during childhood and adolescence: A meta-analytic review of gender differences, intercorrelations, and relations to maladjustment. *Child Development, 79,* 1185–1229. http://dx.doi.org/10.1111/j.1467-8624.2008.01184.x

Carey, N. (2012). *The epigenetics revolution: How modern biology is rewriting our understanding of genetics, disease, and inheritance.* Columbia University Press.

Carmichael Olson, H., Streissguth, A. P., Sampson, P. D., Barr, H. M., Bookstein, F. L., & Thiede, K. (1997). Association of prenatal alcohol exposure with behavioral and learning problems in early adolescence. *Journal of the American Academy of Child & Adolescent Psychiatry, 36*(9), 1187–1194.

Carney, D. R., Cuddy, A. J. C., & Yap, A. J. (2010). Power posing: Brief nonverbal displays affect neuroendocrine levels and risk tolerance. *Psychological Science, 21*(10), 1363–1368. https://doi.org/10.1177/0956797610383437

Carolson, E. A. (1998). A prospective longitudinal study of attachment disorganization/disorientation. *Child Development, 69,* 1107–1128.

Carpenter, A. C., & Schacter, D. L. (2017). Flexible retrieval: When true inferences produce false memories. *Journal of Experimental Psychology: Learning, Memory, and Cognition, 43,* 335–349.

Carpenter, S. K. (2012). Testing enhances the transfer of learning. *Current Directions in Psychological Science, 21,* 279–283.

Carré, J. M., & Archer, J. (2018). Testosterone and human behavior: The role of individual and contextual variables. *Current Opinion in Psychology, 19,* 149–153. https://doi.org/10.1016/j.copsyc.2017.03.021

Carroll, J. B. (1993). *Human cognitive abilities.* Cambridge University Press.

Carson, R. C., Butcher, J. N., & Mineka, S. (2000). *Abnormal psychology and modern life* (11th ed.). Allyn & Bacon.

Carstensen, L. L., & Fredrickson, B. L. (1998). Influence of HIV status and age on cognitive representations of others. *Health Psychology, 17,* 1–10.

Carstensen, L. L., Pasupathi, M., Mayr, U., & Nesselroade, J. R. (2000). Emotional experience in everyday life across the adult life span. *Journal of Personality and Social Psychology, 79,* 644–655.

Carstensen, L. L., & Turk-Charles, S. (1994). The salience of emotion across the adult life span. *Psychology and Aging, 9,* 259–264.

Carver, C. S., & Harmon-Jones, E. (2009). Anger is an approach-related affect: Evidence and implications. *Psychological Bulletin, 135*(2), 183–204.

Carver, C. S., Lehman, J. M., & Antoni, M. H. (2003). Dispositional pessimism predicts illness-related disruption of social and recreational activities among breast cancer patients. *Journal of Personality and Social Psychology, 84,* 813–821.

Casazza, K., Fontaine, K. R., Astrup, A., Birch, L. L., Brown, A. W., Bohan Brown, M. M., Durant, N., Dutton, G., Foster, E. M., Heymsfield, S. B., McIver, K., Mehta, T., Menachemi, N., Newby, P. K., Pate, R., Rolls, B. J., Sen, B., Smith, D. L., Jr., Thomas, D. M., & Allison, D. B. (2013). Myths, presumptions, and facts about obesity. *New England Journal of Medicine, 368*(5), 446–454.

Caspi, A., & Herbener, E. S. (1990). Continuity and change: Assortative marriage and the consistency of personality in adulthood. *Journal of Personality and Social Psychology, 58,* 250–258.

Caspi, A., Roberts, B. W., & Shiner, R. L. (2005). Personality development: Stability and change. *Annual Review of Psychology, 56,* 453–484.

Castel, A. D., McCabe, D. P., & Roediger, H. L., III. (2007). Illusions of competence and overestimation of associate memory for identical items: Evidence from judgments of learning. *Psychonomic Bulletin & Review, 14,* 197–111.

Castellani, R. J., Perry, G., & Iverson, G. L. (2015). Chronic effects of mild neurotrauma: Putting the cart before the horse? *Journal of Neuropathology & Experimental Neurology, 74,* 493–499.

Castellanos, F. X., Patti, P. L., Sharp, W., Jeffries, N. O., Greenstein, D. K., Clasen, L. S., Blumenthal, J. D., James, R. S., Ebens, C. L., Walter, J. M., Zijdenbos, A., Evans, A. C., Giedd, J. N., & Rapoport, J. L. (2002). Developmental trajectories of brain volume abnormalities in children and adolescents with attention-deficit/hyperactivity disorder. *Journal of the American Medical Association, 288,* 1740–1748. https://doi.org/10.1001/jama.288.14.1740

Cattell, R. B. (1950). *Personality: A systematic, theoretical, and factual study.* McGraw-Hill.

Ceci, S. J. (1991). How much does schooling influence general intelligence and its cognitive components? A reassessment of the evidence. *Developmental Psychology, 27,* 703–722.

Ceci, S. J., DeSimone, M., & Johnson, S. (1992). Memory in context: A case study of "Bubbles P.," a gifted but uneven memorizer. In D. J. Herrmann, H. Weingartner, A. Searleman, & C. McEvoy (Eds.), *Memory improvement: Implications for memory theory* (pp. 169–186). Springer-Verlag.

Ceci, S. J., Ginther, D. K., Kahn, S., & Williams, W. M. (2014). Women in academic science: A changing landscape. *Psychological Science in the Public Interest, 15*(3), 75–141. https://doi.org/10.1177/1529100614541236

Ceci, S. J., & Williams, W. M. (1997). Schooling, intelligence, and income. *American Psychologist, 52,* 1051–1058.

Ceci, S. J., Williams, W. M., & Barnett, S. M. (2009). Women's underrepresentation in science: Sociocultural and biological considerations. *Psychological Bulletin, 135*(2), 218–261. https://doi.org/10.1037/a0014412

Cellini, N., & Capuozzo, A. (2018). Shaping memory consolidation via targeted memory reactivation during sleep. *Annals of the New York Academy of Sciences, 1426,* 52–71.

Centers for Disease Control and Prevention (CDC). (2019a). HIV in the United States and dependent areas. https://www.cdc.gov/hiv/pdf/statistics/overview/cdc-hiv-us-ataglance.pdf

Centers for Disease Control and Prevention (CDC). (2019b). Smoking and tobacco use fact sheet. https://www.cdc.gov/tobacco/data_statistics/fact_sheets/index.htm?s_cid=osh-stu-home-spotlight-001

Centers for Disease Control and Prevention (CDC). (2019c). WISQARS. Fatal injury data visualization tool. https://wisqars-viz.cdc.gov:8006/

Centola, D., & Baronchelli, A. (2015). The spontaneous emergence of conventions: An experimental study of cultural evolution. *Proceedings of the National Academy of Sciences, USA, 112*(7), 1989–1994. https://doi.org/10.1073/pnas.1418838112

Cepeda, N. J., Pashler, H., Vul, E., Wixted, J. T., & Rohrer, D. (2006). Distributed practice in verbal recall tests: A review and quantitative synthesis. *Psychological Bulletin, 132,* 354–380.

Cerf-Ducastel, B., & Murphy, C. (2001). fMRI activation in response to odorants orally delivered in aqueous solutions. *Chemical Senses, 26*(6), 625–637.

Chabris, C., & Simons, D. (2010). *The invisible gorilla: And other ways our intuitions deceive us.* Crown.

Chabris, C., & Simons, D. (2012, November 16). Using just 10% of your brains? Think again. *Wall Street Journal Online.* https://www.wsj.com/articles/SB10001424127887324556304578119351875421218

Chaiken, S. (1980). Heuristic versus systematic information processing and the use of source versus message cues in persuasion. *Journal of Personality and Social Psychology, 39,* 752–766.

Chaplin, T. M., & Aldao, A. (2013). Gender differences in emotion expression in children: A meta-analytic review. *Psychological Bulletin, 139,* 735–765.

Chapman, H. A., Kim, D. A., Susskind, J. M., & Anderson, A. K. (2009). In bad taste: Evidence for the oral origins of moral disgust. *Science, 27,* 1222–1226.

Charles, S. T., Reynolds, C. A., & Gatz, M. (2001). Age-related differences and change in positive and negative affect over 23 years. *Journal of Personality and Social Psychology, 80,* 136–151.

Charness, N. (1981). Aging and skilled problem solving. *Journal of Experimental Psychology: General, 110,* 21–38.

Charpak, G., & Broch, H. (2004). *Debunked! ESP, telekinesis, and other pseudoscience* (B. K. Holland, Trans.). Johns Hopkins University Press.

Chartrand, T. L., & Bargh, J. A. (1999). The chameleon effect: The perception-behavior link and social interaction. *Journal of Personality and Social Psychology, 76,* 893–910.

Chartrand, T. L., & Kay, A. (2006). *Mystery moods and perplexing performance: Consequences of succeeding and failing at a nonconscious goal.* Unpublished manuscript.

Chen, E., Cohen, S., & Miller, G. E. (2010). How low socioeconomic status affects 2-year hormonal trajectories in children. *Psychological Science, 21*(1), 31–37.

Chen, S., Collins, A., Anderson, K., McKenzie, K., & Kidd, S. (2017). Patient characteristics, length of stay, and functional improvement for schizophrenia spectrum disorders: A population study of inpatient care in Ontario 2005–2015. *Canadian Journal of Psychiatry, 62,* 854–863.

Cheney, D. L., & Seyfarth, R. M. (1990). *How monkeys see the world.* University of Chicago Press.

Cheng, D. T., Disterhoft, J. F., Power, J. M., Ellis, D. A., & Desmond, J. E. (2008). Neural substrates underlying human delay and trace eyeblink conditioning. *Proceedings of the National Academy of Sciences, USA, 105,* 8108–8113.

Cherlin, A. J. (Ed.). (1992). *Marriage, divorce, remarriage* (2nd ed.). Harvard University Press.

Chin, A., Markey, A., Bhargava, S., Kassam, K. S., & Loewenstein, G. (2016). Bored in the USA: Experience sampling and boredom in everyday life. *Emotion, 17,* 359–368.

Chin, H. B., Sipe, T. A., Elder, R., Mercer, S. L., Chattopadhyay, S. K., Jacob, V., Wethington, H. R., Kirby, D., Elliston, D. B., Griffith, M., Chuke, S. O., Briss, S. C., Ericksen, I., Galbraith, J. S., Herbst, J. H., Johnson, R. L., Kraft, J. M., Noar, S. M., Romero, L. M., & Santelli, J. (2012). The effectiveness of group-based comprehensive risk-reduction and abstinence education interventions to prevent or reduce the risk of adolescent pregnancy, human immunodeficiency virus, and sexually transmitted infections: Two systematic reviews for the Guide to Community Preventive Services. *American Journal of Preventive Medicine, 42,* 272–294.

Choi, I., Nisbett, R. E., & Norenzayan, A. (1999). Causal attribution across cultures: Variation and universality. *Psychological Bulletin, 125,* 47–63.

Chomsky, N. (1957). *Syntactic structures.* The Hague: Mouton.

Chomsky, N. (1959). A review of *Verbal Behavior* by B. F. Skinner. *Language, 35,* 26–58.

Chomsky, N. (1986). *Knowledge of language: Its nature, origin, and use.* Praeger.

Christakis, N. A., & Fowler, J. H. (2007). The spread of obesity in a large social network over 32 years. *New England Journal of Medicine, 357*(4), 370–379.

Christie, I. C., & Friedman, B. H. (2004). Autonomic specificity of discrete emotion and dimensions of affective space: A multivariate approach. *International Journal of Psychophysiology, 51,* 143–153. https://doi.org/10.1016/j.ijpsycho.2003.08.002

Chui, H., Hoppmann, C. A., Gerstorf, D., Walker, R., & Luszcz, M. A. (2014). Social partners and momentary affect in the oldest-old: The presence of others benefits affect depending on who we are and who we are with. *Developmental Psychology, 50*(3), 728–740. https://doi.org/10.1037/a0033896

Cialdini, R. B. (2005). Don't throw in the towel: Use social influence research. *American Psychological Society, 18,* 33–34.

Cialdini, R. B. (2013). The focus theory of normative conduct. In P. A. M. van Lange, A. W. Kruglanski, & E. T. Higgins (Eds.), *Handbook of theories of social psychology* (Vol. 3, pp. 295–312). Sage.

Cialdini, R. B., & Goldstein, N. J. (2004). Social influence: Compliance and conformity. *Annual Review of Psychology, 55*(1), 591–621. https://doi.org/10.1146/annurev.psych.55.090902.142015

Cialdini, R. B., Trost, M. R., & Newsom, J. T. (1995). Preference for consistency: The development of a valid measure and the discovery of surprising behavioral implications. *Journal of Personality and Social Psychology, 69,* 318–328.

Ciarrochi, J. V., Chan, A. Y., & Caputi, P. (2000). A critical evaluation of the emotional intelligence concept. *Personality & Individual Differences, 28,* 539.

Ciarrochi, J., Heaven, P. C. L., & Skinner, T. (2012). Cognitive ability and health-related behaviors during adolescence: A prospective study across five years. *Intelligence, 40*(4), 317–324. https://doi.org/10.1016/j.intell.2012.03.003

Cicchetti, D., & Toth, S. L. (1998). Perspectives on research and practice in developmental psychopathology. In I. E. Sigel & K. A. Renninger (Eds.), *Handbook of child psychology: Vol. 4. Child psychology in practice* (5th ed., pp. 479–583). Wiley.

Cicero, T. J., Ellis, M. S., Surratt, H. L., & Kurtz, S. P. (2014). The changing face of heroin use in the United States: A retrospective analysis of the past 50 years. *Journal of the American Medical Association Psychiatry, 71,* 821–826.

Clark, C. A., & Dagher, A. (2014). The role of dopamine in risk taking: A specific look at Parkinson's disease and gambling. *Frontiers in Behavioral Neuroscience, 8,* 196. https://doi.org/10.3389/fnbeh.2014.00196

Clark, I. A., & Maguire, E. A. (2016). Remembering preservation in hippocampal amnesia. *Annual Review of Psychology, 67,* 51–82.

Clark, R. D., & Hatfield, E. (1989). Gender differences in receptivity to sexual offers. *Journal of Psychology and Human Sexuality, 2,* 39–55.

Clarke, A., & Tyler, L. K. (2015). Understanding what we see: How we derive meaning from vision. *Trends in Cognitive Sciences, 19*(11), 677–687. https://doi.org/10.1016/j.tics.2015.08.008

Clark-Polner, E., Johnson, T., & Barrett, L. F. (2017). Multivoxel pattern analysis does not provide evidence to support the existence of basic emotions. *Cerebral Cortex, 27,* 1944–1948. https://doi.org/10.1093/cercor/bhw028

Cleary, A. M., Brown, A. S., Sawyer, B. D., Nomi, J. S., Ajoku, A. C., & Ryals, A. J. (2012). Familiarity from the configuration of objects in 3-dimensional space and its relation to déjà vu: A virtual reality investigation. *Consciousness and Cognition, 21,* 969–975.

Cleary, A. M., & Claxton, A. B. (2018). Déjà vu: An illusion of prediction. *Psychological Science, 29,* 635–644.

Cleckley, H. M. (1976). *The mask of sanity* (5th ed.). Mosby.

Coates, T. (2015). *Between the world and me.* Spiegel & Grau.

Coe, C. L., & Lubach, G. R. (2008). Fetal programming prenatal origins of health and illness. *Current Directions in Psychological Science, 17,* 36–41.

Cogan, R., Cogan, D., Waltz, W., & McCue, M. (1987). Effects of laughter and relaxation on discomfort thresholds. *Journal of Behavioral Medicine, 10,* 139–144.

Coghill, R. C., McHaffie, J. G., & Yen, Y. (2003). Neural correlates of individual differences in the subjective experience of pain. *Proceedings of the National Academy of Sciences, USA, 100,* 8538–8542.

Cohen, A. O., Breiner, K., Steinberg, L., Bonnie, R. J., Scott, E. S., Taylor-Thompson, K. A., Rudolph, M. D., Chein, J., Richeson, J. A., Heller, A. S., Silverman, M. R., Dellarco, D. V., Fair, D. A., Galván, A., & Casey, B. J. (2016). When is an adolescent an adult? Assessing cognitive control in emotional and nonemotional contexts. *Psychological Science, 27*(4), 549–562.

Cohen, D., Nisbett, R. E., Bowdle, B. F., & Schwarz, N. (1996). Insult, aggression, and the southern culture of honor: An "experimental ethnography." *Journal of Personality and Social Psychology, 70,* 945–960.

Cohen, G. (1990). Why is it difficult to put names to faces? *British Journal of Psychology, 81,* 287–297.

Cohen, S. (1988). Psychosocial models of the role of social support in the etiology of physical disease. *Health Psychology, 7,* 269–297.

Coifman, K. G., Bonanno, G. A., Ray, R. D., & Gross, J. J. (2007). Does repressive coping promote resilience? Affective-autonomic response discrepancy during bereavement. *Journal of Personality and Social Psychology, 92,* 745–758.

Colcombe, S. J., Erickson, K. I., Scalf, P. E., Kim, J. S., Prakash, R., McAuley, E., Elavsky, S., Marquez, D. X., Hu, L., & Kramer, A. F. (2006). Aerobic exercise training increases brain volume in aging humans. *Journals of Gerontology Series A: Biological Sciences and Medical Sciences, 61,* 1166–1170.

Colcombe, S. J., Kramer, A. F., Erickson, K. I., Scalf, P., McAuley, E., Cohen, N. J., Webb, A., Jerome, G. J., Marquez, D. X., & Elavsky, S. (2004). Cardiovascular fitness, cortical plasticity, and aging. *Proceedings of the National Academy of Sciences, USA, 101,* 3316–3321.

Coman, A., Manier, D., & Hirst, W. (2009). Forgetting the unforgettable through conversation: Social shared retrieval-induced forgetting of September 11 memories. *Psychological Science, 20,* 627–633.

Condon, J. W., & Crano, W. D. (1988). Inferred evaluation and the relation between attitude similarity and interpersonal attraction. *Journal of Personality and Social Psychology, 54,* 789–797.

Conklin, Q., King, B., Zanesco, A., Pokorny, J., Hamidi, A., Lin, J., Epel, E., Blackburn, E., & Saron, C. (2015). Telomere lengthening after three weeks of an intensive insight meditation retreat. *Psychoneuroendocrinology, 61*, 26–27.

Conley, T. D. (2011). Perceived proposer personality characteristics and gender differences in acceptance of casual sex offers. *Journal of Personality and Social Psychology, 100*(2), 309–329. https://doi.org/10.1037/a0022152

Conley, T. D., Moors, A. C., Matsick, J. L., Ziegler, A., & Valentine, B. A. (2011). Women, men, and the bedroom: Methodological and conceptual insights that narrow, reframe, and eliminate gender differences in sexuality. *Current Directions in Psychological Science, 20*(5), 296–300. https://doi.org/10.1177/0963721411418467

Cook, E. E., Venkataramani, A. S., Kim, J. J., Tamimi, R. M. & Holmes, M. D. (2018). Legislation to increase uptake of HPV vaccination and adolescent sexual behaviors. *Pediatrics, 142*(3), e20180458. https://doi.org/10.1542/peds.2018-0458

Cook, M., & Mineka, S. (1989). Observational conditioning of fear to fear-relevant versus fear-irrelevant stimuli in rhesus monkeys. *Journal of Abnormal Psychology, 98*(4), 448–459.

Cooke, J. E., Kochendorfer, L. B., Stuart-Parrigon, K. L., Koehn, A. J., & Kerns, K. A. (2018). Parent-child attachment and children's experience and regulation of emotion: A meta-analytic review. *Emotion*. https://doi.org/10.1037/emo0000504

Cooper, J., & Fazio, R. H. (1984). A new look at dissonance theory. In L. Berkowitz (Ed.), *Advances in experimental social psychology* (Vol. 17, pp. 229–266). Academic Press.

Cooper, J. R., Bloom, F. E., & Roth, R. H. (2003). *Biochemical basis of neuropharmacology*. Oxford University Press.

Cooper, M. L. (2006). Does drinking promote risky sexual behavior? A complex answer to a simple question. *Current Directions in Psychological Science, 15*, 19–23.

Cooper, W. H., & Withey, W. J. (2009). The strong situation hypothesis. *Personality and Social Psychology Review, 13*, 62–72.

Cordaro, D. T., Keltner, D., Tshering, S., Wangchuk, D., & Flynn, L. M. (2016). The voice conveys emotion in ten globalized cultures and one remote village in Bhutan. *Emotion, 16*(1), 117–128. https://doi.org/10.1037/emo0000100

Cordaro, D. T., Sun, R., Keltner, D., Kamble, S., Huddar, N., & McNeil, G. (2018). Universals and cultural variations in 22 emotional expressions across five cultures. *Emotion, 18*(1), 75–93. https://doi.org/10.1037/emo0000302

Cordovani, L., & Cordovani, D. (2016). A literature review on observational learning for medical motor skills and anesthesia teaching. *Advances in Health Sciences Education: Theory and Practice, 21*, 1113–1121.

Coren, S. (1997). *Sleep thieves*. Free Press.

Corkin, S. (2002). What's new with the amnesic patient HM? *Nature Reviews Neuroscience, 3*, 153–160.

Corkin, S. (2013). *Permanent present tense: The unforgettable life of the amnesic patient, H.M.* Basic Books.

Correll, J., Park, B., Judd, C. M., & Wittenbrink, B. (2002). The police officer's dilemma: Using ethnicity to disambiguate potentially threatening individuals. *Journal of Personality and Social Psychology, 83*, 1314–1329.

Correll, J., Park, B., Judd, C. M., Wittenbrink, B., Sadler, M. S., & Keesee, T. (2007). Across the thin blue line: Police officers and racial bias in the decision to shoot. *Journal of Personality and Social Psychology, 92*, 1006–1023.

Correll, J., Wittenbrink, B., Crawford, M. T., & Sadler, M. S. (2015). Stereotypic vision: How stereotypes disambiguate visual stimuli. *Journal of Personality and Social Psychology, 108*(2), 219–233. https://doi.org/10.1037/pspa0000015

Corti, E. (1931). *A history of smoking* (P. England, Trans.). Harrap.

Coryell, W., Endicott, J., Maser, J. D., Mueller, T., Lavori, P., & Keller, M. (1995). The likelihood of recurrence in bipolar affective disorder: The importance of episode recency. *Journal of Affective Disorders, 33*, 201–206.

Cosmides, L., & Tooby, J. (2000). The evolutionary psychology of the emotions and their relationship to internal regulatory variables. In M. Lewis, J. M. Haviland-Jones, & L. Feldman Barrett (Eds.), *Handbook of emotions* (3rd ed.). Guilford Press.

Costa, P. T., Terracciano, A., & McCrae, R. R. (2001). Gender differences in personality traits across cultures: Robust and surprising findings. *Journal of Personality and Social Psychology, 81*, 322–331.

Costanza, A., Weber, K., Gandy, S., Bouras, C., Hof, P. R., Giannakopoulos, G., & Canuto, A. (2011). Contact sport–related chronic traumatic encephalopathy in the elderly: Clinical expression and structural substrates. *Neuropathology and Applied Neurobiology, 37*, 570–584.

Craik, F. I. M., Govoni, R., Naveh-Benjamin, M., & Anderson, N. D. (1996). The effects of divided attention on encoding and retrieval processes in human memory. *Journal of Experimental Psychology: General, 125*, 159–180.

Craik, F. I. M., & Tulving, E. (1975). Depth of processing and the retention of words in episodic memory. *Journal of Experimental Psychology: General, 104*, 268–294.

Cramer, R. E., Schaefer, J. T., & Reid, S. (1996). Identifying the ideal mate: More evidence for male-female convergence. *Current Psychology, 15*, 157–166.

Crane, C. A., Godleski, S. A., Przybyla, S. M., Schlauch, R. C., & Testa, M. (2015). The proximal effects of acute alcohol consumption on male-to-female aggression: A meta-analytic review of the experimental literature. *Trauma, Violence, & Abuse*. https://doi.org/10.1177/1524838015584374

Craske, M. G. (1999). *Anxiety disorders: Psychological approaches to theory and treatment*. Westview Press.

Creery, J. D., Oudiette, D., Antony, J. W., & Paller, K. A. (2015). Targeted memory reactivation during sleep depends on prior learning. *Sleep, 38*, 755–763.

Crivelli, C., Carrera, P., & Fernández-Dols, J.-M. (2015). Are smiles a sign of happiness? Spontaneous expressions of judo winners. *Evolution and Human Behavior, 36*(1), 52–58.

Crocq, M.-A. (2007). Historical and cultural aspects of man's relationship with addictive drugs. *Dialogues in Clinical Neuroscience, 9*, 355–361.

Crombag, H. F. M., Wagenaar, W. A., & Van Koppen, P. J. (1996). Crashing memories and the problem of "source monitoring." *Applied Cognitive Psychology, 10*, 95–104.

Cross, E. S., Kraemer, D. J. M., Hamilton, A. F. de C., Kelley, W. M., & Grafton, S. T. (2009). Sensitivity of the action observation network to physical and observational learning. *Cerebral Cortex, 19*, 315–326.

Cross, P. (1977). Not can but will college teachers be improved? *New Directions for Higher Education, 17*, 1–15.

Cross-Disorder Group of the Psychiatric Genomics Consortium. (2013). Identification of risk loci with shared effects on five major psychiatric disorders: A genome-wide analysis. *Lancet, 381*, 1371–1379.

Cruess, D. G., Antoni, M. H., Kumar, M., & Schneiderman, N. (2000). Reductions in salivary cortisol are associated with mood improvement during relaxation training among HIV-seropositive men. *Journal of Behavioral Medicine, 23*, 107–122.

Crum-Cianflone, N. F., Bagnell, M. E., Schaller, E., Boyko, E. J., Smith, B., Maynard, C., Ulmer, C. S., Vernalis, M., & Smith, T. C. (2014). Impact of combat deployment and posttraumatic stress disorder on newly reported coronary heart disease among U.S. active duty and reserve forces. *Circulation, 129*, 1813–1820.

Csigó, K., Harsányi, A., Demeter, G., Rajkai, C., Németh, A., & Racsmány, M. (2010). Long-term follow-up of patients with obsessive-compulsive disorder treated by anterior capsulotomy: A neuropsychological study. *Journal of Affective Disorders, 126*, 198–205.

Csikszentmihalyi, M. (1990). *Flow: The psychology of optimal experience*. Harper & Row.

Cuc, A., Koppel, J., & Hirst, W. (2007). Silence is not golden: A case of socially shared retrieval-induced forgetting. *Psychological Science, 18*, 727–733.

Cunningham, M. R., Roberts, A. R., Barbee, A. P., Druen, P. B., & Wu, C.-H. (1995). "Their ideas of beauty are, on the whole, the same as ours": Consistency and variability in the cross-cultural perception of female physical attractiveness. *Journal of Personality and Social Psychology, 68*, 261–279.

Cunningham, W. A., & Brosch, T. (2012). Motivational salience: Amygdala tuning from traits, needs, values, and goals. *Current Directions in Psychological Science, 21*(1), 54–59.

Curran, J. P., & Lippold, S. (1975). The effects of physical attraction and attitude similarity on attraction in dating dyads. *Journal of Personality, 43,* 528–539.

Curtiss, S. (1977). *Genie: A psycholinguistic study of a modern-day "wild-child."* Academic Press.

Cushman, F., Sheketoff, R., Wharton, S., & Carey, S. (2013). The development of intend-based moral judgment. *Cognition, 127,* 6–21.

Dael, N., Mortillaro, M., & Scherer, K. R. (2012). Emotion expression in body action and posture. *Emotion, 12,* 1085–1101.

D'Agostino, P. R., & Fincher-Kiefer, R. (1992). Need for cognition and correspondence bias. *Social Cognition, 10,* 151–163.

Dalton, P. (2003). Olfaction. In H. Pashler & S. Yantis (Eds.), *Stevens' handbook of experimental psychology: Vol. 1. Sensation and perception* (3rd ed., pp. 691–746). Wiley.

Daly, M., & Wilson, M. (1988). Evolutionary social psychology and family homicide. *Science, 242,* 519–524.

Damasio, A. R. (1989). Time-locked multiregional retroactivation: A systems-level proposal for the neural substrates of recall and recognition. *Cognition, 33,* 25–62.

Damasio, A. R. (1994). *Descartes' error: Emotion, reason, and the human brain.* Putnam.

Damasio, A. R., Grabowski, T. J., Bechara, A., Damasio, H., Ponto, L. L. B., Parvisi, J., & Hichwa, R. D. (2000). Subcortical and cortical brain activity during the feeling of self-generated emotions. *Nature Neuroscience, 3,* 1049–1056.

Damasio, H., Grabowski, T. J., Tranel, D., Hichwa, R. D., & Damasio, A. R. (1996). A neural basis for lexical retrieval. *Nature, 380,* 499–505.

Damerius, L. A., Forss, S. I. F., Kosonen, Z. K., Willems, E. P., Burkart, J. M., Call, J., Galdikas, B. M. F., Liebal, K., Haun, D. B. M., & van Schaik, C. P. (2017). Orientation toward humans predicts cognitive performance in orang-utans. *Scientific Reports, 7,* Art. No.: 40052.

Daneshvar, D. H., Nowinski, C. J., McKee, A. C., & Cantu, R. C. (2011). The epidemiology of sport-related concussion. *Clinical Sports Medicine, 30,* 1–17.

Daniel, H. J., O'Brien, K. F., McCabe, R. B., & Quinter, V. E. (1985). Values in mate selection: A 1984 campus survey. *College Student Journal, 19,* 44–50.

Danner, U. N., Ouwehand, C., van Haastert, N. L., Homsveld, H., & de Ridder, D. T. (2012). Decision-making impairments in women with binge eating disorder in comparison with obese and normal weight women. *European Eating Disorders Review, 20,* e56–e62.

Darley, J. M., & Gross, P. H. (1983). A hypothesis-confirming bias in labeling effects. *Journal of Personality and Social Psychology, 44,* 20–33.

Darley, J. M., & Latané, B. (1968). Bystander intervention in emergencies: Diffusion of responsibility. *Journal of Personality and Social Psychology, 8,* 377–383.

Darwin, C. J., Turvey, M. T., & Crowder, R. G. (1972). An auditory analogue of the Sperling partial report procedure: Evidence for brief auditory storage. *Cognitive Psychology, 3,* 255–267.

Dauer, W., & Przedborski, S. (2003). Parkinson's disease: Mechanisms and models. *Neuron, 39,* 889–909.

Daum, I., Schugens, M. M., Ackermann, H., Lutzenberger, W., Dichgans, J., & Birbaumer, N. (1993). Classical conditioning after cerebellar lesions in humans. *Behavioral Neuroscience, 107,* 748–756.

David-Barrett, T., Kertesz, J., Rotkirch, A., Ghosh, A., Bhattacharya, K., Monsivais, D., & Kaski, K. (2016). Communication with family and friends across the life course. *PLoS ONE, 11*(11), 1–15. https://doi.org/10.1371/journal.pone.0165687

Davidson, R. J., Ekman, P., Saron, C., Senulis, J., & Friesen, W. V. (1990). Emotional expression and brain physiology I: Approach/withdrawal and cerebral asymmetry. *Journal of Personality and Social Psychology, 58,* 330–341.

Davidson, R. J., Putnam, K. M., & Larson, C. L. (2000). Dysfunction in the neural circuitry of emotion regulation—a possible prelude to violence. *Science, 289,* 591–594.

Dawson, G., Rogers, S., Munson, J., Smith, M., Winter, J., Greenson, J., Donaldson, A., & Varley, J. (2010). Randomized, controlled trial of an intervention for toddlers with autism: The Early Start Denver Model. *Pediatrics, 125,* e17–e23.

Dawson, G., & Sapiro, G. (2019). Potential for digital behavioral measurement tools to transform the detection and diagnosis of autism spectrum disorder. *Journal of the American Medical Association Pediatrics, 173,* 305–306.

Day, J. J., & Sweatt, J. D. (2011). Epigenetic mechanisms in cognition. *Neuron, 70,* 813–829.

Dayan, E., & Bar-Hillel, M. (2011). Nudge to obesity. II: Menu positions influence food orders. *Judgment and Decision Making, 6*(4), 333.

Dayan, P., & Huys, Q. J. M. (2009). Serotonin in affective control. *Annual Review of Neuroscience, 32,* 95–126.

de Araujo, I. E., Rolls, E. T., Velazco, M. I., Margot, C., & Cayeux, I. (2005). Cognitive modulation of olfactory processing. *Neuron, 46,* 671–679.

De Bloom, J., Sianoja, M., Korpela, K., Tuomisto, M., Lilja, A., Geurts, S., & Kinnunen, U. (2017). Effects of park walks and relaxation exercises during lunch breaks on recovery from job stress: Two randomized controlled trials. *Journal of Environmental Psychology, 51,* 14–30.

De Bolle, M., De Fryut, F., McCrae, R. R., Löckenhoff, C. E., Costa, P. T., Jr., Aguilar-Valfae, M. E., Ahn, C.-k., Ahn, H.-n., Alcalay, L., Allik, J., Avdeyeva, T. V., Bratko, D., Brunner-Sciarra, M., Cain, T. R., Chan, W., Chittcharat, N., Crawford, J. T., Fehr, R., Ficková, E., . . . Terracciano, A. (2015). The emergence of sex differences in personality traits in early adolescence: A cross-sectional, cross-cultural study. *Journal of Personality and Social Psychology, 108,* 171–185.

De Simoni, C., & von Bastian, C. C. (2018). Working memory updating and binding training: Bayesian evidence supporting the absence of transfer. *Journal of Experimental Psychology: General, 147,* 829–858.

De Wolff, M., & van IJzendoorn, M. H. (1997). Sensitivity and attachment: A meta-analysis on parental antecedents of infant attachment. *Child Development, 68,* 571–591.

Deady, D. K., & Law Smith, M. J. (2015) Changing male preferences for female body type in the U.S.: An adaptive response to a changing socioeconomic climate. *Journal of Behavioral and Brain Science, 5,* 570–577. http://dx.doi.org/10.4236/jbbs.2015.513054

Deary, I. J., Batty, G. D., & Gale, C. R. (2008). Bright children become enlightened adults. *Psychological Science, 19*(1), 1–6.

Deary, I. J., Batty, G. D., Pattie, A., & Gale, C. R. (2008). More intelligent, more dependable children live longer: A 55-year longitudinal study of a representative sample of the Scottish nation. *Psychological Science, 19,* 874.

Deary, I. J., Taylor, M. D., Hart, C. L., Wilson, V., Smith, G. D., Blane, D., & Starr, J. M. (2005). Intergenerational social mobility and mid-life status attainment: Influences of childhood intelligence, childhood social factors, and education. *Intelligence, 33*(5), 455–472. https://doi.org/10.1016/j.intell.2005.06.003

Deci, E. L. (1971). Effects of externally mediated rewards on intrinsic motivation. *Journal of Personality and Social Psychology, 18,* 105–115.

Deci, E. L., Koestner, R., & Ryan, R. M. (1999). A meta-analytic review of experiments examining the effects of extrinsic rewards on intrinsic motivation. *Psychological Bulletin, 125,* 627–668.

Deese, J. (1959). On the prediction of occurrence of particular verbal intrusions in immediate recall. *Journal of Experimental Psychology, 58,* 17–22.

Degenhardt, L., Chiu, W. T., Sampson, N., Kessler, R. C., Anthony, J. C., Angermeyer, M., Bruffaerts, R., de Girolamo, G., Gureje, O., Huang, Y., Karam, A., Kostyuchenko, S., Lepine, J. P., Medina Mora, M. E., Neumark, Y., Ormel, J. H., Pinto-Meza, A., Posada-Villa, J., Stein, D. J., . . . Wells, J. E. (2008). Toward a global view of alcohol, tobacco, cannabis, and cocaine use: Findings from the WHO World Mental Health surveys. *PLoS Medicine, 5,* e141.

Dekker, M. C., & Koot, H. M. (2003). *DSM–IV* disorders in children with borderline to moderate intellectual disability: I. Prevalence and impact. *Journal of the American Academy of Child and Adolescent Psychiatry, 42*(8), 915–922. https://doi.org/10.1097/01.CHI.0000046892.27264.1A

Dekker, S., Lee, N. C., Howard-Jones, P., & Jolles, J. (2012). Neuromyths in education: Prevalence and predictors of misconceptions among teachers. *Frontiers in Psychology, 3,* 429. https://doi.org/10.3389/fpsyg.2012.00429

Deković, M., Noom, M. J., & Meeus, W. (1997). Expectations regarding development during adolescence: Parental and adolescent perceptions. *Journal of Youth and Adolescence, 26,* 253–272. http://dx.doi.org/10.1007/s10964-005-0001-7

Del Vicario, M., Bessi, A., Zollo, F., Petroni, F., Scala, A., Caldarelli, G., Stanley, H. E., & Quattrociocchi, W. (2016). The spreading of misinformation online. *Proceedings of the National Academy of Sciences, PNAS, 113*(3), 554–559. https://doi.org/10.1073/pnas.1517441113

Demb, J. B., Desmond, J. E., Wagner, A. D., Vaidya, C. J., Glover, G. H., & Gabrieli, J. D. E. (1995). Semantic encoding and retrieval in the left inferior prefrontal cortex: A functional MRI study of task difficulty and process specificity. *Journal of Neuroscience, 15,* 5870–5878.

Dement, W. C. (1959, November 30). Dreams. *Newsweek.*

Dement, W. C. (1978). *Some must watch while some must sleep.* W. W. Norton.

Dement, W. C. (1999). *The promise of sleep.* Delacorte Press.

Dement, W. C., & Kleitman, N. (1957). The relation of eye movements during sleep to dream activity: An objective method for the study of dreaming. *Journal of Experimental Psychology, 53,* 339–346.

Dempster, E. L., Pidsley, R., Schalkwyk, L. C., Owens, S., Georgiades, A., Kane, F., Kalidindi, S., Picchioni, M., Kravariti, E., Toulopoulou, T., Murray, R. M., & Mill, J. (2011). Disease-associated epigenetic changes in monozygotic twins discordant for schizophrenia and bipolar disorder. *Human Molecular Genetics, 20,* 4786–4796.

Denissen, J. J., Geenen, R., Soto, C. J., John, O. P., & van Aken, M. A. G. (2019). The Big Five Inventory-2: Replication of psychometric properties in a Dutch adaptation and first evidence for the discriminant predictive validity of the facet scales. *Journal of Personality Assessment.* https://doi.org/10.1080/00233891.2018.1539004

Dennett, D. (1991). *Consciousness explained.* Basic Books.

Denny, B. T., & Ochsner, K. N. (2014). Behavioral effects of longitudinal training in cognitive reappraisal. *Emotion, 14*(2), 425–433. https://doi.org/10.1037/a0035276

Denson, T. F., O'Dean, S. M., Blake, K. R., & Beames, K. R. (2018). Aggression in women: Behavior, brain and hormones. *Frontiers in Behavioral Neuroscience, 12.* https://doi-org.ezp-prod1.hul.harvard.edu/10.3389/fnbeh.2018.00081

DePaulo, B. M., Charlton, K., Cooper, H., Lindsay, J. J., & Muhlenbruck, L. (1997). The accuracy–confidence correlation in the detection of deception. *Personality and Social Psychology Review, 1,* 346–357.

DePaulo, B. M., Lindsay, J. J., Malone, B. E., Muhlenbruck, L., Charlton, K., & Cooper, H. (2003). Cues to deception. *Psychological Bulletin, 129,* 74–118.

DePaulo, B. M., & Morris, W. L. (2006). The unrecognized stereotyping and discrimination against singles. *Current Directions in Psychological Science, 15,* 251–254.

Der, G., Batty, G. D., & Deary, I. J. (2009). The association between IQ in adolescence and a range of health outcomes at 40 in the 1979 U.S. national longitudinal study of youth. *Intelligence, 37*(6), 573–580.

D'Esposito, M., & Postle, B. R. (2015). The cognitive neuroscience of working memory. *Annual Review of Psychology, 66,* 115–142.

DeVilliers, P. (2005). The role of language in theory-of-mind development: What deaf children tell us. In J. W. Astington & J. A. Baird (Eds.), *Why language matters for theory of mind* (pp. 266–297). Oxford University Press.

Dewhurst, S. A., Anderson, R. J., Grace, L., & van Esch, L. (2016). Adaptive false memories: Imagining future scenarios increases false memories in the DRM paradigm. *Memory & Cognition, 44,* 1076–1084.

DeYoung, C. G., Hirsh, J. B., Shane, M. S., Papademetris, X., Rajeevan, N., & Gray, J. R. (2010). Testing predictions from personality neuroscience: Brain structure and the Big Five. *Psychological Science, 21,* 820–828.

Diaconis, P., & Mosteller, F. (1989). Methods for studying coincidences. *Journal of the American Statistical Association, 84,* 853–861.

Dickens, W. T., & Flynn, J. R. (2001). Heritability estimates versus large environmental effects: The IQ paradox resolved. *Psychological Review, 108,* 346–369.

Dickinson, A., Watt, A., & Griffiths, J. H. (1992). Free-operant acquisition with delayed reinforcement. *Quarterly Journal of Experimental Psychology Section B: Comparative and Physiological Psychology, 45,* 241–258.

Didden, R., Sigafoos, J., Lang, R., O'Reilly, M., Drieschner, K., & Lancioni, G. E. (2012). Intellectual disabilities. In P. Sturmey & M. Hersen (Eds.), *Handbook of evidence-based practice in clinical psychology.* Wiley. https://doi.org/10.1002/9781118156391.ebcp001006

DiDonato, T. E., Ullrich, J., & Krueger, J. I. (2011). Social perception as induction and inference: An integrative model of intergroup differentiation, ingroup favoritism, and differential accuracy. *Journal of Personality and Social Psychology, 100*(1), 66–83. https://doi.org/10.1037/a0021051

Diederich, N. J., & Goetz, C. G. (2008). The placebo treatments in neurosciences: New insights from clinical and neuroimaging studies. *Neurology, 71,* 677–684.

Dimberg, U. (1982). Facial reactions to facial expressions. *Psychophysiology, 19,* 643–647.

Dion, K. L. (2005). Marital status as stimulus variable and subject variable. *Psychological Inquiry, 16,* 104–110.

Dismukes, R. K. (2012). Prospective memory in workplace and everyday situations. *Current Directions in Psychological Science, 21,* 215–220.

Disner, S. G., Beevers, C. G., Haigh, E. A., & Beck, A. T. (2011). Neural mechanisms of the cognitive model of depression. *Nature Reviews Neuroscience, 12,* 467–477.

Dittrich, W. H., Troscianko, T., Lea, S., & Morgan, D. (1996). Perception of emotion from dynamic point-light displays represented in dance. *Perception, 25,* 727–738. https://doi.org/10.3389/fpsyg.2011.00337

Dollard, J., Doob, L. W., Miller, N. E., Mowrer, O. H., & Sears, R. R. (1939). *Frustration and aggression.* Yale University Press.

Domjan, M. (2005). Pavlovian conditioning: A functional perspective. *Annual Review of Psychology, 56,* 179–206.

Doucet, S., Soussignan, R., Sagot, P., & Schaal, B. (2009). The secretion of areolar (Montgomery's) glands from lactating women elicits selective, unconditional responses in neonates. *PLoS ONE, 4,* e7579. https://doi.org/10.1371/journal.pone.0007579

Doucet, S., Soussignan, R., Sagot, P., & Schaal, B. (2012). An overlooked aspect of the human breast: Areolar glands in relation with breast-feeding pattern, neonatal weight gain, and the dynamics of lactation. *Early Human Development, 88,* 119–128. https://doi.org/10.1016/j.earlhumdev.2011.07.020

Dougherty, D. D., Brennan, B. P., Stewart, S. E., Wilhelm, S., Widge, A. S., & Rauch, S. L. (2018). Neuroscientifically informed formulation and treatment planning for patients with obsessive-compulsive disorder: A review. *Journal of the American Medical Association Psychiatry, 75,* 1081–1087.

Dovidio, J. F., & Gaertner, S. L. (2010). Intergroup bias. In S. T. Fiske, D. T. Gilbert, & G. Lindzey (Eds.), *The handbook of social psychology* (5th ed., Vol. 2, pp. 1085–1121). Wiley.

Dresler, M., Shirer, W. R., Konrad, B. N., Müller, N. C. J., Wagner, I. C., Fernández, G., Czisch, M., & Greicius, M. D. (2017). Mnemonic training reshapes brain networks to support superior memory. *Neuron, 93*(5), 1227–1235.

Duckworth, A. L., & Seligman, M. E. P. (2005). Self-discipline outdoes IQ in predicting academic performance of adolescents. *Psychological Science, 16,* 939–944.

Dudai, Y. (2012). The restless engram: Consolidations never end. *Annual Review of Neuroscience, 35,* 227–247.

Dudycha, G. J., & Dudycha, M. M. (1933). Some factors and characteristics of childhood memories. *Child Development, 4,* 265–278.

Duenwald, M. (2002, September 12). Students find another staple of campus life: Stress. *New York Times.* http://www.nytimes.com/2002/09/17/health/students-find-another-staple-of-campus-life-stress.html?pagewanted=all&src=pm

Dunlop, S. A. (2008). Activity-dependent plasticity: Implications for recovery after spinal cord injury. *Trends in Neurosciences, 31,* 410–418.

Dunlosky, J., Rawson, K. A., Marsh, E. J., Nathan, M. J., & Willingham, D. T. (2013). Improving students' learning with effective learning techniques: Promising directions from cognitive and educational psychology. *Psychological Science in the Public Interest, 14*(1), 4–58.

Dunlosky, J., & Thiede, K. W. (2013). Four cornerstones of calibration research: Why understanding students' judgments can improve their achievement. *Learning and Instruction, 24,* 58–61.

Dunn, J. C., & Kirsner, K. (2011). The search for HMAS Sydney II: Analysis and integration of survivor reports. *Journal of Applied Cognitive Psychology, 25,* 513–527.

Dunphy, D. C. (1963). The social structure of urban adolescent peer groups. *Sociometry, 26,* 230–246.

Duval, S., & Wicklund, R. A. (1972). *A theory of objective self-awareness.* Academic Press.

Eagly, A. H., & Wood, W. (1999). The origins of sex differences in human behavior: Evolved dispositions versus social roles. *American Psychologist, 54,* 408–423.

Eaton, W. W., Shao, H., Nestadt, G., Lee, B. H., Bienvenu, O. J., & Zandi, P. (2008). Population-based study of first onset and chronicity of major depressive disorder. *Archives of General Psychiatry, 65,* 513–520.

Ebbinghaus, H. (1908). *Psychology: An elementary textbook.* Heath.

Ebbinghaus, H. (1964). *Memory: A contribution to experimental psychology.* Dover. (Original work published 1885.)

Ecklund, E. H., Scheitle, C. P., & Pennsylvania, T. (2007). Religion among academic scientists: Distinctions, disciplines, and demographics. *Social Problems, 54*(2), 289–307. https://doi.org/10.1525/sp.2007.54.2.289.290

Eddy, D. M. (1982). Probabilistic reasoning in clinical medicine: Problems and opportunities. In D. Kahneman, P. Slovic, & A. Tversky (Eds.), *Judgments under uncertainty: Heuristics and biases* (pp. 249– 267). Cambridge University Press.

Edwards, W. (1955). The theory of decision making. *Psychological Bulletin, 51,* 201–214.

Eich, J. E. (1995). Searching for mood dependent memory. *Psychological Science, 6,* 67–75.

Eichenbaum, H., & Cohen, N. J. (2001). *From conditioning to conscious recollection: Memory systems of the brain.* Oxford University Press.

Eimas, P. D., Siqueland, E. R., Jusczyk, P., & Vigorito, J. (1971). Speech perception in infants. *Science, 171,* 303–306.

Einstein, G. O., & McDaniel, M. A. (1990). Normal aging and prospective memory. *Journal of Experimental Psychology: Learning, Memory, and Cognition, 16,* 717–726.

Einstein, G. O., & McDaniel, M. A. (2005). Prospective memory: Multiple retrieval processes. *Current Direction in Psychological Science, 14,* 286–290.

Eisenberg, N., Fabes, R. A., Guthrie, I. K., & Reiser, M. (2000). Dispositional emotionality and regulation: Their role in predicting quality of social functioning. *Journal of Personality and Social Psychology, 78,* 136.

Eisenberger, N. I., Lieberman, M. D., & Williams, K. D. (2003). Does rejection hurt? An fMRI study of social exclusion. *Science, 302,* 290–292. https://doi.org/10.1126/science.1089134

Eisenegger, C., Haushofer, J., & Fehr, E. (2011). The role of testosterone in social interaction. *Trends in Cognitive Sciences, 15*(6), 263–271. https://doi.org/10.1016/j.tics.2011.04.008

Eisenegger, C., Naef, M., Snozzi, R., Heinrichs, M., & Fehr, E. (2010). Prejudice and truth about the effect of testosterone on human bargaining behaviour. *Nature, 463,* 356–359.

Ekman, P. (1965). Differential communication of affect by head and body cues. *Journal of Personality and Social Psychology, 2,* 726–735.

Ekman, P. (1972). Universals and cultural differences in facial expressions of emotion. In J. K. Cole (Ed.), *Nebraska Symposium on Motivation, 1971* (pp. 207–283). Lincoln: University of Nebraska Press.

Ekman, P., & Friesen, W. V. (1968). Nonverbal behavior in psychotherapy research. In J. M. Shlien (Ed.), *Research in psychotherapy* (Vol. 3, pp. 179–216). American Psychological Association.

Ekman, P., & Friesen, W. V. (1971). Constants across cultures in the face and emotion. *Journal of Personality and Social Psychology, 17,* 124–129.

Ekman, P., & Friesen, W. V. (1982). Felt, false, and miserable smiles. *Journal of Nonverbal Behavior, 6,* 238–252.

Ekman, P., Levenson, R. W., & Friesen, W. V. (1983). Autonomic nervous system activity distinguishes among emotions. *Science, 221,* 1208–1210.

El Haj, M., Gallouj, K., & Antoine, P. (2017). Google Calendar enhances prospective memory in Alzheimer's disease: A case report. *Journal of Alzheimer's disease, 57,* 285–291.

Elbogen, E. B., & Johnson, S. C. (2009). The intricate link between violence and mental disorder. *Archives of General Psychiatry, 66*(2), 152–161.

Eldridge, L. L., Knowlton, B. J., Furmanski, C. S., Bookheimer, S. Y., & Engel, S. A. (2000). Remembering episodes: A selective role for the hippocampus during retrieval. *Nature Neuroscience, 3,* 1149–1152.

Elfenbein, H. A., & Ambady, N. (2002). On the universality and cultural specificity of emotion recognition: A meta-analysis. *Psychological Bulletin, 128,* 203–235.

Elfenbein, H. A., Beaupré, M., Lévesque, M., & Hess, U. (2007). Toward a dialect theory: Cultural differences in the expression and recognition of posed facial expressions. *Emotion, 7*(1), 131–146. https://doi.org/10.1037/1528-3542.7.1.131

Elfenbein, H. A., Der Foo, M. D., White, J., & Tan, H. H. (2007). Reading your counterpart: The benefit of emotion recognition accuracy for effectiveness in negotiation. *Journal of Nonverbal Behavior, 31,* 205–223.

Elliott, R., Sahakian, B. J., Matthews, K., Bannerjea, A., Rimmer, J., & Robbins, T. W. (1997). Effects of methylphenidate on spatial working memory and planning in healthy young adults. *Psychopharmacology, 131,* 196–206.

Ellis, A. (1991). *Reason and emotion in psychotherapy.* Carol.

Ellis, B. J., & Garber, J. (2000). Psychosocial antecedents of variation in girls' pubertal timing: Maternal depression, stepfather presence, and marital and family stress. *Child Development, 71,* 485–501.

Ellis, L., & Ames, M. A. (1987). Neurohormonal functioning in sexual orientation: A theory of homosexuality–heterosexuality. *Psychological Bulletin, 101,* 233–258.

Ellman, S. J., Spielman, A. J., Luck, D., Steiner, S. S., & Halperin, R. (1991). REM deprivation: A review. In S. J. Ellman & J. S. Antrobus (Eds.), *The mind in sleep: Psychology and psychophysiology* (2nd ed., pp. 329–376). Wiley.

Ellsworth, P. C., & Scherer, K. R. (2003). Appraisal processes in emotion. In R. J. Davidson, K. R. Scherer, & H. H. Goldsmith (Eds.), *The handbook of affective science* (pp. 572–595). Oxford University Press.

Elsey, J. W. B., Van Ast, V. A., & Kindt, M. (2018). Human memory reconsolidation: A guiding framework and critical review of the evidence. *Psychological Bulletin, 144,* 797–848.

Emerson, R. C., Bergen, J. R., & Adelson, E. H. (1992). Directionally selective complex cells and the computation of motion energy in cat visual cortex. *Vision Research, 32,* 203–218.

Epel, E. S., Blackburn, E. H., Lin, J., Dhabhar, F. S., Adler, N. E., Morrow, J. D., & Cawthorn, R. M. (2004). Accelerated telomere shortening in response to life stress. *Proceedings of the National Academy of Sciences, USA, 101,* 17312–17315.

Epel, E. S., Daubenmier, J., Moskowitz, J. T., Foldman, S., & Blackburn, E. H. (2009). Can meditation slow rate of cellular aging? Cognitive stress, mindfulness, and telomerase. *Annals of the New York Academy of Sciences, 1172,* 34–53.

Epley, N., & Waytz, A. (2010). Mind perception. In S. T. Fiske, D. T. Gilbert, & G. Lindzey (Eds.), *The handbook of social psychology* (5th ed., Vol. 1, pp. 498–541). Wiley.

Epstein, R. (2007a). *The case against adolescence: Rediscovering the adult in every teen.* Quill Driver.

Epstein, R. (2007b). The myth of the teen brain. *Scientific American Mind, 18*, 27–31.

Ericsson, K. A., & Charness, N. (1999). Expert performance: Its structure and acquisition. In S. J. Ceci & W. M. Williams (Eds.), *The nature–nurture debate: The essential readings* (pp. 200–256). Blackwell.

Erikson, E. H. (1959). *Identity and the life cycle*. International Universities Press.

Espy, K. A., Fang, H., Johnson, C., Stopp, C., Wiebe, S. A., & Respass, J. (2011). Prenatal tobacco exposure: Developmental outcomes in the neonatal period. *Developmental Psychology, 47*(1), 153–169. https://doi.org/10.1037/a0020724

Estes, A., Munson, J., Rogers, S. J., Greenson, J., Winter, J., & Dawson, G. (2015). Long-term outcomes of early intervention in 6-year-old children with Autism Spectrum Disorder. *Journal of the American Academy of Child and Adolescent Psychiatry, 54*, 580–587.

Evans, G. W. (2006). Child development and the physical environment. *Annual Review of Psychology, 57*, 423–451.

Evans, G. W., & Stecker, R. (2004). Motivational consequences of environmental stress. *Journal of Environmental Psychology, 24*, 143–165.

Evans, S. W., & Kim, P. (2012). Childhood poverty and young adults' allostatic load: The mediating role of childhood cumulative risk exposure. *Psychological Science, 23*(9), 979–983. https://doi.org/10.1177/0956797612441218

Exner, J. E. (1993). *The Rorschach: A comprehensive system.* Vol. 1. *Basic Foundations.* Wiley.

Eysenck, H. J. (1957). The effects of psychotherapy: An evaluation. *Journal of Consulting Psychology, 16*, 319–324.

Eysenck, H. J. (1967). *The biological basis of personality*. Charles C. Thomas.

Eysenck, H. J. (1990). Biological dimensions of personality. In L. A. Pervin (Ed.), *Handbook of personality: Theory and research* (pp. 244–276). Guilford Press.

Falk, R., & McGregor, D. (1983). The surprisingness of coincidences. In P. Humphreys, O. Svenson, & A. Vari (Eds.), *Analysing and aiding decision processes* (pp. 489–502). North Holland.

Fan, R., Varol, O., Varamesh, A., Barron, A., van de Leemput, I. A., Scheffer, M., & Bollen, J. (2019). The minute-scale dynamics of online emotions reveal the effects of affect labeling. *Nature Human Behaviour, 3*(1), 92–100. https://doi.org/10.1038/s41562-018-0490-5

Fancher, R. E. (1979). *Pioneers in psychology*. W. W. Norton.

Farah, M. J., Hutchinson, J. B., Phelps, E. A., & Wagner, A. D. (2014). Functional MRI-based lie detection: Scientific and societal challenges. *Nature Reviews Neuroscience, 15*(2), 123–131. http://www.ncbi.nlm.nih.gov/pubmed/24588019

Farah, M. J., Illes, J., Cook-Deegan, R., Gardner, H., Kandel, E., King, P., Parens, E., Sahakian, B., & Wolpe, P. R. (2004). Neurocognitive enhancement: What can we do and what should we do? *Nature Reviews Neuroscience, 5*, 421–426.

Faraone, S. V., Perlis, R. H., Doyle, A. E., Smoller, J. W., Goralnick, J. J., Holmgren, M. A., & Sklar, P. (2005). Molecular genetics of attention-deficit/hyperactivity disorder. *Biological Psychiatry, 57*, 1313–1323.

Farrar, M. J. (1990). Discourse and the acquisition of grammatical morphemes. *Journal of Child Language, 17*, 607–624.

Farrelly, D., Lazarus, J., & Roberts, G. (2007). Altruists attract. *Evolutionary Psychology, 5*, 313–329.

Favazza, A. (2011). *Bodies under siege: Self-mutilation, nonsuicidal self-injury, and body modification in culture and psychiatry*. Johns Hopkins University Press.

Fazel, S., & Danesh, J. (2002). Serious mental disorder in 23,000 prisoners: A review of 62 surveys. *Lancet, 359*, 545–550.

Feczer, D., & Bjorklund, P. (2009). Forever changed: Posttraumatic stress disorder in female military veterans, a case report. *Perspectives in Psychiatric Care, 45*, 278–291.

Fein, S., Goethals, G. R., & Kugler, M. B. (2007). Social influence on political judgments: The case of presidential debates. *Political Psychology, 28*, 165–192.

Feinberg, T. E. (2001). *Altered egos: How the brain creates the self*. Oxford University Press.

Feingold, A. (1992). Gender differences in mate selection preferences: A test of the parental investment model. *Psychological Bulletin, 112*, 125–139.

Feinstein, J. S., Buzza, C., Hurlemann, R., Follmer, R. L., Dahdaleh, N. S., Coryell, W. H., Welsh, M. J., Tranel, D., & Wemmie, J. A. (2013). Fear and panic in humans with bilateral amygdala damage. *Nature Neuroscience, 16*(3), 270–272.

Feldman, D. E. (2009). Synaptic mechanisms for plasticity in neocortex. *Annual Review of Neuroscience, 32*, 33–55.

Felleman, D. J., & Van Essen, D. C. (1991). Distributed hierarchical processing in the primate cerebral cortex. *Cerebral Cortex, 1*, 1–47.

Ferguson, C. J. (2010). Blazing angels or resident evil? Can violent video games be a force for good? *Review of General Psychology, 14*(2), 68–81. https://doi.org/10.1037/a0018941

Fernandez Nievas, I. F., & Thaver, D. (2015). Work-life balance: A different scale for doctors. *Frontiers in Pediatrics, 3*, 115.

Ferrari, A. J., Charlson, F. J., Norman, R. E., Patten, S. B., Freedman, G., Murray, C. J. L., Vos, T., & Whiteford, H. A. (2013). Burden of depressive disorders by country, sex, age, and year: Findings from the Global Burden of Disease Study 2010. *PLoS Medicine, 10*, e1001547.

Ferretti, M. T., Iulita, M. F., Cavedo, M., Chiesa, P. A., Dimech, A. S., Chadha, A. S., Baracchi, F., Girouard, H., Misoch, S., Giacobini, E., Depypere, H., Hampel, H., & Women's Brain Project and the Alzheimer Precision Medicine Initiative. (2018). Sex differences in Alzheimer's disease—the gateway to precision medicine. *Nature Reviews Neuroscience, 14*, 457–469.

Ferster, C. B., & Skinner, B. F. (1957). *Schedules of reinforcement*. Appleton-Century-Crofts.

Festinger, L. (1957). *A theory of cognitive dissonance*. Stanford University Press.

Festinger, L., & Carlsmith, J. M. (1959). Cognitive consequences of forced compliance. *Journal of Abnormal and Social Psychology, 58*, 203–210.

Festinger, L., Schachter, S., & Back, K. (1950). *Social pressures in informal groups: A study of human factors in housing*. Harper & Row.

Fields, H. L., & Levine, J. D. (1984). Placebo analgesia: A role for endorphins? *Trends in Neurosciences, 7*, 271–273.

Finkel, E. J. (2017). *The all-or-nothing marriage: How the best marriages work*. Dutton.

Finkel, E. J., & Eastwick, P. W. (2009). Arbitrary social norms influence sex differences in romantic selectivity. *Psychological Science, 20*, 1290–1295.

Finkel, E. J., Eastwick, P. W., Karney, B. R., Reis, H. T., & Sprecher, S. (2012). Online dating: A critical analysis from the perspective of psychological science. *Psychological Science in the Public Interest, 13*(1), 3–66. https://doi.org/10.1177/1529100612436522

Finkelstein, K. E. (1999, October 17). In concert, searchers retrieve Yo-Yo Ma's lost Stradivarius. *New York Times*. http://www.nytimes.com/1999/10/17/nyregion/in-concert-searchers-retrieve-yo-yo-ma-s-lost-stradivarius.html

Fiore, A. T., Taylor, L. S., Zhong, X., Mendelsohn, G. A., & Cheshire, C. (2010). Who's right and who writes: People, profiles, contacts, and replies in online dating. *Proceedings of 43rd Hawaii International Conferences on System Sciences* (pp. 1–10). IEEE Computer Society. https://doi.org/10.1109/HICSS.2010.444.

Fiorillo, C. D., Newsome, W. T., & Schultz, W. (2008). The temporal precision of reward prediction in dopamine neurons. *Nature Neuroscience, 11*, 966–973.

Fischer, P., Krueger, J. I., Greitemeyer, T., Vogrincic, C., Kastenmüller, A., Frey, D., Heene, M., Wicher, M., & Kainbacher, M. (2011). The bystander-effect: A meta-analytic review on bystander intervention in dangerous and non-dangerous emergencies. *Psychological Bulletin, 137*(4), 517–537. https://doi.org/10.1037/a0023304

Fisher, D. W., Bennett, D. A., & Dong, H. (2018). Sexual dimorphism in predisposition to Alzheimer's disease. *Neurobiology of Aging, 70*, 308–324.

Fisher, R. P., & Craik, F. I. M. (1977). The interaction between encoding and retrieval operations in cued recall. *Journal of Experimental Psychology: Human Learning and Perception, 3,* 153–171.

Fiske, S. T. (1998). Stereotyping, prejudice, and discrimination. In D. T. Gilbert, S. T. Fiske, & G. Lindzey (Eds.), *The handbook of social psychology* (4th ed., Vol. 2, pp. 357–411). McGraw-Hill.

Fiske, S. T. (2010). *Social beings: A core motives approach to social psychology.* Wiley.

Fitch, C. A., & Ruggles, S. (2000). Historical trends in marriage formation, United States 1850–1990. In L. J. Waite (Ed.), *The ties that bind: Perspectives on marriage and cohabitation* (pp. 59–88). Transaction Publishers.

Fleeson, W. (2004). Moving personality beyond the person-situation debate: The challenge and opportunity of within-person variability. *Current Directions in Psychological Science, 13,* 83–87.

Fletcher, G. J. O., Simpson, J. A., Thomas, G., & Giles, L. (1999). Ideals in intimate relationships. *Journal of Personality and Social Psychology, 76,* 72–89. https://doi.org/10.1037/0022-3514.76.1.72

Fletcher, P. C., Shallice, T., & Dolan, R. J. (1998). The functional roles of prefrontal cortex in episodic memory. I. Encoding. *Brain, 121,* 1239–1248.

Flores, S., Bailey, H. R., Eisenberg, M. L., & Zacks, J. M. (2017). Event segmentation improves memory up to one month later. *Journal of Experimental Psychology: Learning, Memory, & Cognition, 43,* 1183–1202.

Flynn, E., & Whiten, A. (2008). Cultural transmission of tool-use in young children: A diffusion chain study. *Social Development, 17,* 699–718.

Flynn, J. R. (2012). *Are we getting smarter? Rising IQ in the twenty-first century.* Cambridge University Press.

Foa, E. B., & McLean, C. P. (2016). The efficacy of exposure therapy for anxiety-related disorders and its underlying mechanisms: The case of OCD and PTSD. *Annual Review of Clinical Psychology, 12,* 1–28.

Fogassi, L., Ferrari, P. F., Gesierich, B., Rozzi, S., Chersi, F., & Rizzolatti, G. (2005). Parietal lobe: From action organization to intention understanding. *Science, 308,* 662–667.

Ford, J. H., DiBiase, H. D., Ryu, E., & Kensinger, E. A. (2018). It gets better with time: Enhancement of age-related positivity effect in the six months following a highly negative public event. *Psychology and Aging, 33*(3), 419–424. https://doi.org/10.1037/pag0000250

Foroni, F., & Semin, G. R. (2009). Language that puts you in touch with your bodily feelings: The multimodal responsiveness of affective expressions. *Psychological Science, 20*(8), 974–980.

Forscher, P. S., Lai, C. K., Axt, J., Ebersole, C. R., Herman, M., Devine, P. G., & Nosek, B. A. (in press). A meta-analysis of procedures to change implicit measures. *Journal of Personality and Social Psychology.* https://doi.org/10.31234/osf.io/dv8tu

Fragaszy, D. M., Izar, P., Visalberghi, E., Ottoni, E. B., & de Oliveria, M. G. (2004). Wild capuchin monkeys (*Cebus libidinosus*) use anvils and stone pounding tools. *American Journal of Primatology, 64,* 359–366.

Franchow, E. I., & Suchy, Y. (2015). Naturally-occurring expressive suppression in daily life depletes executive functioning. *Emotion, 15*(1), 78–89. https://doi.org/10.1037/emo0000013

Francis, D., Diorio, J., Liu, D., & Meaney, M. J. (1999). Nongenomic transmission across generations of maternal behavior and stress responses in the rat. *Science, 286,* 1155–1158.

Frank, M. G., & Stennet, J. (2001). The forced-choice paradigm and the perception of facial expressions of emotion. *Journal of Personality and Social Psychology, 80,* 75–85.

Franklin, J. C., Fox, K. R., Franklin, C. R., Kleiman, E. M., Ribeiro, J. D., Jaroszewski, A. C., Hooley, J. M., & Nock, M. K. (2016). A brief mobile app reduces nonsuicidal and suicidal self-injury: Evidence from three randomized controlled trials. *Journal of Consulting and Clinical Psychology, 84,* 544–557.

Frati, A., Pesce, A., Palmieri, M., Iasanzaniro, M., Familiari, P., Angelini, A., Salvati, M., Rocco, M., & Raco, A. (2019). Hypnosis-aided awake surgery for the management of intrinsic brain tumors versus standard awake-asleep-awake protocol: A preliminary, promising experience. *World Neurosurgery, 121,* e882–e891.

Fredman, T., & Whiten, A. (2008). Observational learning from tool using models by human-reared and mother-reared capuchin monkeys (*Cebus apella*). *Animal Cognition, 11,* 295–309.

Freedman, J. L., & Fraser, S. C. (1966). Compliance without pressure: The foot-in-the-door technique. *Journal of Personality and Social Psychology, 4,* 195–202.

Freeman, S., Walker, M. R., Borden, R., & Latané, B. (1975). Diffusion of responsibility and restaurant tipping: Cheaper by the bunch. *Personality and Social Psychology Bulletin, 1,* 584–587.

Freud, S. (1965). *The interpretation of dreams* (J. Strachey, Trans.). Avon. (Original work published 1900.)

Freund, A. M., & Blanchard-Fields, F. (2014). Age-related differences in altruism across adulthood: Making personal financial gain versus contributing to the public good. *Developmental Psychology, 50*(4), 1125–1136. https://doi.org/10.1037/a0034491

Frick, A., Ahs, F., Engman, J., Jonasson, M., Alaie, I., Björkstrand, J., Frans, Ö., Faria, V., Linnman, C., Appel, L., Wahlstedt, K., Lubberink, M., Fredrikson, M., & Furmark, T. (2015). Serotonin synthesis and reuptake in social anxiety disorder: A positron emission tomography study. *Journal of the American Medical Association Psychiatry, 72,* 794–802.

Frick, R. W. (1985). Communicating emotion: The role of prosodic features. *Psychological Bulletin, 97,* 412–429.

Fried, P. A., & Watkinson, B. (2000). Visuoperceptual functioning differs in 9- to 12-year-olds prenatally exposed to cigarettes and marijuana. *Neurotoxicology and Teratology, 22,* 11–20.

Friedman, J. M. (2003). A war on obesity, not the obese. *Science, 299*(5608), 856–858.

Friedman, J. M., & Halaas, J. L. (1998). Leptin and the regulation of body weight in mammals. *Nature, 395*(6704), 763–770.

Friedman, M., & Rosenman, R. H. (1974). *Type A behavior and your heart.* Knopf.

Friedman, S. L., & Boyle, D. E. (2008). Attachment in U.S. children experiencing nonmaternal care in the early 1990s. *Attachment & Human Development, 10*(3), 225–261.

Friesen, W. V. (1972). *Cultural differences in facial expressions in a social situation: An experimental test of the concept of display rules* (Doctoral dissertation, University of California, San Francisco).

Frijda, N., Kuipers, P., & ter Schure, E. (1989). Relations among emotion, appraisal, and emotional action readiness. *Journal of Personality and Social Psychology, 57*(2), 212–228.

Frith, C. D., & Fletcher, P. (1995). Voices from nowhere. *Critical Quarterly, 37,* 71–83.

Fry, D. P. (2012). Life without war. *Science, 336*(6083), 879–884. https://doi.org/10.1126/science.1217987

Fryar, C. D., Gu, Q., Ogden, C. L., & Flegal, K. M. (2016). Anthropometric reference data for children and adults: United States, 2011–2014. *National Center for Health Statistics. Vital Health Stat, 3*(39), 1–46.

Fukui, H., Murai, T., Fukuyama, H., Hayashi, T., & Hanakawa, T. (2005). Functional activity related to risk anticipation during performance of the Iowa gambling task. *NeuroImage, 24,* 253–259.

Funder, D. C. (2001). Personality. *Annual Review of Psychology, 52,* 197–221.

Furmark, T., Tillfors, M., Marteinsdottir, I., Fischer, H., Pissiota, A., Långström, B., & Fredrikson, M. (2002). Common changes in cerebral blood flow in patients with social phobia treated with citalopram or cognitive behavioral therapy. *Archives of General Psychiatry, 59*(5), 425–433.

Fuster, J. M. (2003). *Cortex and mind.* Oxford University Press.

Gadermann, A. M., Alonso, J., Vilagut, G., Zaslavsky, A. M., & Kessler, R. C. (2012). Comorbidity and disease burden in the National Comorbidity Survey Replication (NCS-R). *Depression and Anxiety, 29,* 797–806.

Gais, S., & Born, J. (2004). Low acetylcholine during slow-wave sleep is critical for declarative memory consolidation. *Proceedings of the National Academy of Sciences, USA, 101,* 2140–2144.

Galanter, E. (1962). Contemporary psychophysics. In R. Brown, E. Galanter, E. H. Hess, & G. Mandler (Eds.), *New directions in psychology.* Holt, Rinehart, & Winston.

Galati, D., Scherer, K. R., & Ricci-Bitt, P. E. (1997). Voluntary facial expression of emotion: Comparing congenitally blind with normally sighted encoders. *Journal of Personality and Social Psychology, 73,* 1363–1379.

Galef, B. (1998). Edward Thorndike: Revolutionary psychologist, ambiguous biologist. *American Psychologist, 53,* 1128–1134.

Galling, B., Roldan, A., Hagi, K., Rietschel, L., Walyzada, F., & Correll, C. U. (2017). Antipsychotic augmentation vs. monotherapy in schizophrenia: Systematic review, meta-analysis and meta-regression analysis. *World Psychiatry, 16,* 77–89.

Gallistel, C. R. (2000). The replacement of general-purpose learning models with adaptively specialized learning modules. In M. S. Gazzaniga (Ed.), *The new cognitive neurosciences* (pp. 1179–1191). MIT Press.

Gallo, D. A. (2006). *Associative illusions of memory.* Psychology Press.

Gallo, D. A. (2010). False memories and fantastic beliefs: 15 years of the DRM illusion. *Memory & Cognition, 38,* 833–848.

Gallup. (2014, July 9). Obesity linked to lower social well-being. https://news.gallup.com/poll/172253/obesity-linked-lower-social.aspx

Gallup. (2018, October). Two in three Americans now support legalizing marijuana. https://news.gallup.com/poll/243908/two-three-americans-support-legalizing-marijuana.aspx.

Gallup, G. G. (1977). Self-recognition in primates: A comparative approach to the bidirectional properties of consciousness. *American Psychologist, 32,* 329–338.

Gallup, G. G. (1997). On the rise and fall of self-conception in primates. *Annals of the New York Academy of Sciences, 818,* 73–84.

Galton, F. (1869). *Hereditary genius: An inquiry into its laws and consequences.* Macmillan/Fontana.

Ganzel, B. L., Kim, P., Glover, G. H., & Temple, E. (2008). Resilience after 9/11: Multimodal neuroimaging evidence for stress-related change in the healthy adult brain. *NeuroImage, 40,* 788–795.

Garb, H. N. (1998). *Studying the clinician: Judgment research and psychological assessment.* American Psychological Association.

Garcia, J., & Koelling, R. A. (1966). Relation of cue to consequence in avoidance learning. *Psychonomic Science, 4,* 123–124.

Garcia-Moreno, C., Jansen, H. A. F. M., Ellsberg, M., Heise, L., & Watts, C. H. (2006). Prevalence of intimate partner violence: Findings from the WHO multi-country study on women's health and domestic violence. *Lancet, 368*(9543), 1260–1269. https://doi.org/10.1016/S0140-6736(06)69523-8

Gardner, M., & Steinberg, L. (2005). Peer influence on risk taking, risk preference, and risky decision making in adolescence and adulthood: An experimental study. *Developmental Psychology, 41*(4), 625–635. https://doi.org/10.1037/0012-1649.41.4.625

Gazzaniga, M. S. (2006). Forty-five years of split brain research and still going strong. *Nature Reviews Neuroscience, 6,* 653–659.

Ge, X. J., Conger, R. D., & Elder, G. H. (1996). Coming of age too early: Pubertal influences on girls' vulnerability to psychological distress. *Child Development, 67,* 3386–3400.

Ge, X. J., Conger, R. D., & Elder, G. H., Jr. (2001). Pubertal transition, stressful life events, and the emergence of gender differences in adolescent depressive symptoms. *Developmental Psychology, 37*(3), 404–417. https://doi.org/10.1037/0012-1649.37.3.404

Gegenfurtner, K. R., Bloj, M., & Toscani, M. (2015). The many colours of "the dress." *Current Biology, 25,* R543–R544.

George, O., & Koob, G. F. (2017). Individual differences in the neuropsychopathology of addiction. *Dialogues in Clinical Neuroscience, 19*(3), 217–229.

Gerbasi, M. E., & Prentice, D. A. (2013). The self- and other-interest inventory. *Journal of Personality and Social Psychology, 105*(3), 495–514. https://doi.org/10.1037/a0033483

Gershoff, E. T. (2002). Corporal punishment by parents and associated child behaviors and experiences: A meta-analytic and theoretical review. *Psychological Bulletin, 128,* 539–579.

Gibb, B. E., Alloy, L. B., & Tierney, S. (2001). History of childhood maltreatment, negative cognitive styles, and episodes of depression in adulthood. *Cognitive Therapy and Research, 25,* 425–446.

Gibbons, F. X. (1990). Self-attention and behavior: A review and theoretical update. In M. P. Zanna (Ed.), *Advances in experimental social psychology* (Vol. 23, pp. 249–303). Academic Press.

Gibson, C. E., Losee, J., & Vitiello, C. (2014). A replication attempt of stereotype susceptibility (Shih, Pittinsky, & Ambady, 1999): Identity salience and shifts in quantitative performance. *Social Psychology, 45*(3), 194–198. http://dx.doi.org/10.1027/1864-9335/a000184

Gignac, G. E., & Bates, T. C. (2017). Brain volume and intelligence: The moderating role of intelligence measurement quality. *Intelligence, 64,* 18–29.

Gigone, D., & Hastie, R. (1993). The common knowledge effect: Information sharing and group judgment. *Journal of Personality and Social Psychology, 54,* 959–974.

Gilbert, D. T. (1991). How mental systems believe. *American Psychologist, 46,* 107–119.

Gilbert, D. T. (1998). Ordinary personology. In D. T. Gilbert, S. T. Fiske, & G. Lindzey (Eds.), *The handbook of social psychology* (4th ed., Vol. 2, pp. 89–150). McGraw-Hill.

Gilbert, D. T. (2006). *Stumbling on happiness.* Knopf.

Gilbert, D. T., Brown, R. P., Pinel, E. C., & Wilson, T. D. (2000). The illusion of external agency. *Journal of Personality and Social Psychology, 79,* 690–700.

Gilbert, D. T., King, G., Pettigrew, S., & Wilson, T. D. (2016). Comment on "Estimating the reproducibility of psychological science." *Science, 351* (6277). https://doi.org/10.1126/science.aad7243

Gilbert, D. T., & Malone, P. S. (1995). The correspondence bias. *Psychological Bulletin, 117,* 21–38.

Gilbertson, M. W., Shenton, M. E., Ciszewski, A., Kasai, K., Lasko, N. B., Orr, S. P., & Pitman, R. K. (2002). Smaller hippocampal volume predicts pathological vulnerability to psychological trauma. *Nature Neuroscience, 5,* 1242–1247.

Gillespie, C. F., & Nemeroff, C. B. (2007). Corticotropin-releasing factor and the psychobiology of early-life stress. *Current Directions in Psychological Science, 16,* 85–89.

Gillette, J., Gleitman, H., Gleitman, L., & Lederer, A. (1999). Human simulation of vocabulary learning. *Cognition, 73,* 135–176.

Gino, F., & Pierce, L. (2009). The abundance effect: Unethical behavior in the presence of wealth. *Organizational Behavior and Human Decision Processes, 109*(2), 142–155. https://doi.org/10.1016/j.obhdp.2009.03.003

Giovanello, K. S., Schnyer, D. M., & Verfaellie, M. (2004). A critical role for the anterior hippocampus in relational memory: Evidence from an fMRI study comparing associative and item recognition. *Hippocampus, 14,* 5–8.

Gladue, B. A. (1994). The biopsychology of sexual orientation. *Current Directions in Psychological Science, 3,* 150–154.

Glanzer, M., & Cunitz, A. R. (1966). Two storage mechanisms in free recall. *Journal of Verbal Learning and Verbal Behavior, 5,* 351–360.

Glass, D. C., & Singer, J. E. (1972). *Urban stress.* Academic Press.

Glenwick, D. S., Jason, L. A., & Elman, D. (1978). Physical attractiveness and social contact in the singles bar. *Journal of Social Psychology, 105,* 311–312.

Glick, D. M., & Orsillo, S. M. (2015). An investigation of the efficacy of acceptance-based behavioral therapy for academic procrastination. *Journal of Experimental Psychology: General, 144,* 400–409.

Glynn, L. M., & Sandman, C. A. (2011). Prenatal origins of neurological development: A critical period for fetus and mother. *Current Directions in Psychological Science, 20*(6), 384–389. https://doi.org/10.1177/0963721411422056

Gneezy, U., & Rustichini, A. (2000). A fine is a price. *Journal of Legal Studies, 29,* 1–17.

Goddard, H. H. (1913). *The Kallikak family: A study in the heredity of feeble-mindedness.* Macmillan.

Godden, D. R., & Baddeley, A. D. (1975). Context-dependent memory in two natural environments: On land and underwater. *British Journal of Psychology, 66,* 325–331.

Goehler, L. E., Gaykema, R. P. A., Hansen, M. K., Anderson, K., Maier, S. F., & Watkins, L. R. (2000). Vagal immune-to-brain communication: A visceral chemosensory pathway. *Autonomic Neuroscience: Basic and Clinical, 85,* 49–59.

Goff, L. M., & Roediger, H. L., III. (1998). Imagination inflation for action events—repeated imaginings lead to illusory recollections. *Memory & Cognition, 26,* 20–33.

Gogtay, N., Giedd, J. N., Lusk, L., Hayashi, K. M., Greenstein, D., Vaituzis, A. C., Nugent, T. F. III, Herman, D. H., Clasen, L. S., Toga, A. W., Rapoport, J. L., & Thompson, P. M. (2004). Dynamic mapping of human cortical development during childhood through early adulthood. *PNAS, 101,* 8174–8179. https://doi.org/10.1073/pnas.0402680101

Golden, R. L., Furman, W., & Collibee, C. (2016). The risks and rewards of sexual debut. *Developmental Psychology, 52*(11), 1913–1925. https://doi.org/10.1037/dev0000206

Goldin, C., & Rouse, C. (2000). Orchestrating impartiality: The impact of "blind" auditions on female musicians. *American Economic Review, 90*(4), 715–741.

Goldman, M. S., Brown, S. A., & Christiansen, B. A. (1987). Expectancy theory: Thinking about drinking. In H. T. Blane & K. E. Leonard (Eds.), *Psychological theories of drinking and alcoholism* (pp. 181–266). Guilford Press.

Goldstein, D. G., Hershfield, H. E., & Benartzi, S. (2016). The illusion of wealth and its reversal. *Journal of Marketing Research, 53,* 804–813.

Goldstein, M. H., Schwade, J. A., Briesch, J., & Syal, S. (2010). Learning while babbling: Prelinguistic object-directed vocalizations signal a readiness to learn. *Infancy, 15,* 362–391.

Gonzaga, G. C., Keltner, D., Londahl, E. A., & Smith, M. D. (2001). Love and the commitment problem in romantic relations and friendship. *Journal of Personality and Social Psychology, 81,* 247–262.

Goodale, M. A., Milner, A. D., Jakobson, L. S., & Carey, D. P. (1991). A neurological dissociation between perceiving objects and grasping them. *Nature, 349,* 154–156.

Goodfellow, I., Bengio, Y., & Courville, A. (2016). Introduction. In *Deep learning* (Chap. 1, pp. 1–26). MIT Press.

Gootman, E. (2003, March 3). Separated at birth in Mexico, united at campuses on Long Island. *New York Times.* http://www.nytimes.com/2003/03/03/nyregion/separated-at-birth-in-mexico-reunited-at-campuses-on-li.html?_r=0

Gopnik, A. (2012). Scientific thinking in young children: Theoretical advances, empirical research, and policy implications. *Science, 337*(6102), 1623–1627. https://doi.org/10.1126/science.1223416

Gorczynski, P., & Faulkner, G. (2011). Exercise therapy for schizophrenia. *Cochrane Database of Systematic Reviews, 5,* CD004412.

Gorno-Tempini, M. L., Price, C. J., Josephs, O., Vandenberghe, R., Cappa, S. F., Kapur, N., & Frackowiak, R. S. (1998). The neural systems sustaining face and proper-name processing. *Brain, 121,* 2103–2118.

Gotlib, I. H., & Joormann, J. (2010). Cognition and depression: Current status and future directions. *Annual Review of Clinical Psychology, 6,* 285–312.

Gottesman, I. I. (1991). *Schizophrenia genesis: The origins of madness.* Freeman.

Gottesman, I. I., & Hanson, D. R. (2005). Human development: Biological and genetic processes. *Annual Review of Psychology, 56,* 263–286.

Gottfredson, L. S. (2003). Dissecting practical intelligence theory: Its claims and evidence. *Intelligence, 31*(4), 343–397.

Gottfried, J. A. (2008). Perceptual and neural plasticity of odor quality coding in the human brain. *Chemosensory Perception, 1,* 127–135.

Gough, C. (2020). Share of sports fans in the US as of March 2020, by gender. Retrieved from Statista website: https://www.statista.com/statistics/1018814/sports-fans-usa-gender/

Gouldner, A. W. (1960). The norm of reciprocity. *American Sociological Review, 25,* 161–178.

Graf, P., & Schacter, D. L. (1985). Implicit and explicit memory for new associations in normal subjects and amnesic patients. *Journal of Experimental Psychology: Learning, Memory, and Cognition, 11,* 501–518.

Grant, B. F., Hasin, D. S., Stinson, F. S., Dawson, D. A., Chou, S. P., & Ruan, W. J. (2004). Prevalence, correlates, and disability of personality disorders in the U.S.: Results from the National Epidemiologic Survey on Alcohol and Related Conditions. *Journal of Clinical Psychiatry, 65,* 948–958.

Grassian, S. (2006). Psychiatric effects of solitary confinement. *Washington University Journal of Law and Policy, 22,* 1–24.

Gray, H. M., Gray, K., & Wegner, D. M. (2007). Dimensions of mind perception. *Science, 315,* 619.

Gray, J. A. (1970). The psychophysiological basis of introversion–extraversion. *Behavior Research and Therapy, 8,* 249–266.

Gray, J. A. (1990). Brain systems that mediate both emotion and cognition. *Cognition and Emotion, 4,* 269–288.

Green, D. A., & Swets, J. A. (1966). *Signal detection theory and psychophysics.* Wiley.

Green, M. F., Kern, R. S., Braff, D. L., & Mintz, J. (2000). Neurocognitive deficits and functional outcome in schizophrenia: Are we measuring the "right stuff"? *Schizophrenia Bulletin, 26,* 119–136.

Green, S. K., Buchanan, D. R., & Heuer, S. K. (1984). Winners, losers, and choosers: A field investigation of dating initiation. *Personality and Social Psychology Bulletin, 10,* 502–511.

Greenberg, J., Solomon, S., & Arndt, J. (2008). A basic but uniquely human motivation: Terror management. In J. Y. Shah & W. L. Gardner (Eds.), *Handbook of motivation science* (pp. 114–134). Guilford Press.

Greenspan, L., & Deardorff, J. (2014). *The new puberty: How to navigate early development in today's girls.* Rodale Books.

Greenwald, A. G., McGhee, D. E., & Schwartz, J. L. K. (1998). Measuring individual differences in implicit cognition: The Implicit Association Test. *Journal of Personality and Social Psychology, 74,* 1464–1480.

Greenwald, A. G., & Nosek, B. A. (2001). Health of the Implicit Association Test at age 3. *Zeitschrift für Experimentelle Psychologie, 48,* 85–93.

Gropp, E., Shanabrough, M., Borok, E., Xu, A. W., Janoschek, R., Buch, T., Plum, L., Balthasar, N., Hampel, B., Waisman, A., Barsh, G. S., Horvath, T. L., & Brüning, J. C. (2005). Agouti-related peptide-expressing neurons are mandatory for feeding. *Nature Neuroscience, 8,* 1289–1291.

Gross, J. J. (1998). Antecedent- and response-focused emotion regulation: Divergent consequences for experience, expression, and physiology. *Journal of Personality and Social Psychology, 74*(1), 224–237.

Gross, J. J. (2002). Emotion regulation: Affective, cognitive, and social consequences. *Psychophysiology, 39,* 281–291.

Gross, J. J., & Muñoz, R. F. (1995). Emotion regulation and mental health. *Clinical Psychology: Science and Practice, 2,* 151–164.

Groves, B. (2004, August 2). Unwelcome awareness. *San Diego Union-Tribune,* p. 24.

Grün, F., & Blumberg, B. (2006). Environmental obesogens: Organotins and endocrine disruption via nuclear receptor signaling. *Endocrinology, 147,* s50–s55.

Grzyb, T., Trojanowski, J., Grzybała, P., Dolin´ski, D., Folwarczny, M., Krzyszycha, K., & Martynowska, K. (2017). Would you deliver an electric shock in 2015? Obedience in the experimental paradigm developed by Stanley Milgram in the 50 years following the original studies. *Social Psychological and Personality Science, 8*(8), 927–933. https://doi.org/10.1177/1948550617693060

Guerin, S. A., Robbins, C. A., Gilmore, A. W., & Schacter, D. L. (2012a). Interactions between visual attention and episodic retrieval: Dissociable contributions of parietal regions during gist-based false recognition. *Neuron, 75,* 1122–1134.

Guerin, S. A., Robbins, C. A., Gilmore, A. W., & Schacter, D. L. (2012b). Retrieval failure contributes to gist-based false recognition. *Journal of Memory and Language, 66,* 68–78.

Guilford, J. P. (1967). *The nature of human intelligence.* McGraw-Hill.

Gunnery, S. D., Hall, J. A., & Ruben, M. A. (2013). The deliberate Duchenne smile: Individual differences in expressive control. *Journal of Nonverbal Behavior, 37,* 29–41.

Gup, T. (2013, April 3). Diagnosis: Human. *New York Times.* http://www.nytimes.com/2013/04/03/opinion/diagnosis-human.html

Gurwitz, J. H., McLaughlin, T. J., Willison, D. J., Guadagnoli, E., Hauptman, P. J., Gao, X., & Soumerai, S. B. (1997). Delayed hospital presentation in patients who have had acute myocardial infarction. *Annals of Internal Medicine, 126,* 593–599.

Gusnard, D. A., & Raichle, M. E. (2001). Searching for a baseline: Functional imaging and the resting human brain. *Nature Reviews Neuroscience, 2,* 685–694.

Gustafsson, J.-E. (1984). A unifying model for the structure of intellectual abilities. *Intelligence, 8,* 179–203.

Gutchess, A. H., & Schacter, D. L. (2012). The neural correlates of gist-based true and false recognition. *NeuroImage, 59,* 3418–3426.

Guthrie, R. V. (2000). Kenneth Bancroft Clark (1914–2005). In A. E. Kazdin (Ed.), *Encyclopedia of Psychology* (Vol. 2, p. 91). American Psychological Association.

Haase, C. M., Heckhausen, J., & Wrosch, C. (2013). Developmental regulation across the life span: Toward a new synthesis. *Developmental Psychology, 49*(5), 964–972. https://doi.org/10.1037/a0029231

Hackman, D. A., & Farah, M. J. (2008). Socioeconomic status and the developing brain. *Trends in Cognitive Sciences, 13,* 65–73.

Hackman, J. R., & Katz, N. (2010). Group behavior and performance. In S. T. Fiske, D. T. Gilbert, & G. Lindzey (Eds.), *The handbook of social psychology* (5th ed., Vol. 2, pp. 1208–1251). Wiley.

Haedt-Matt, A. A., & Keel, P. K. (2011). Revisiting the affect regulation model of binge eating: A meta-analysis of studies using ecological momentary assessment. *Psychological Bulletin, 137*(4), 660–681.

Hagen, L., Krishna, A., & McFerran, B. (2016). Rejecting responsibility: Low physical involvement in obtaining food promotes unhealthy eating. *Journal of Marketing Research, 54*(4), 589–604.

Haggard, P., & Tsakiris, M. (2009). The experience of agency: Feelings, judgments, and responsibility. *Current Directions in Psychological Science, 18,* 242–246.

Haidt, J., & Keltner, D. (1999). Culture and facial expression: Open-ended methods find more expressions and a gradient of recognition. *Cognition and Emotion, 13*(3), 225–266.

Hales, C. M., Carroll, M. D., Fryar, C. D., & Ogden, C. L. (2017). Prevalence of obesity among adults and youth: United States, 2015–2016. *NCHS data brief, no. 288.* Hyattsville, MD: National Center for Health Statistics.

Hallett, M. (2000). Transcranial magnetic stimulation and the human brain. *Nature, 406,* 147–150.

Halliday, R., Naylor, H., Brandeis, D., Callaway, E., Yano, L., & Herzig, K. (1994). The effect of D-amphetamine, clonidine, and yohimbine on human information processing. *Psychophysiology, 31,* 331–337.

Halpern, B. (2002). Taste. In H. Pashler & S. Yantis (Eds.), *Stevens' handbook of experimental psychology: Vol. 1. Sensation and perception* (3rd ed., pp. 653–690). Wiley.

Halpern, D. F., Benbow, C. P., Geary, D. C., Gur, R. C., Hyde, J. S., & Gernsbacher, M. A. (2007). The science of sex differences in science and mathematics. *Psychological Science in the Public Interest, 8*(1), 1–51.

Hamermesh, D. S., & Biddle, J. E. (1994). Beauty and the labor market. *American Economic Review, 84,* 1174–1195.

Hamilton, A. F., & Grafton, S. T. (2006). Goal representation in human anterior intraparietal sulcus. *Journal of Neuroscience, 26,* 1133–1137.

Hamilton, A. F., & Grafton, S. T. (2008). Action outcomes are represented in human inferior frontoparietal cortex. *Cerebral Cortex, 18,* 1160–1168.

Hamilton, A. F. C. (2013). Reflecting on the mirror neuron system in autism: A systematic review of current theories. *Developmental Cognitive Neuroscience, 3,* 91–105.

Hamilton, D. L., & Gifford, R. K. (1976). Illusory correlation in interpersonal perception: A cognitive basis of stereotypic judgements. *Journal of Experimental Social Psychology, 12,* 392–407.

Hamilton, J. P., Etkin, A., Furman, D. J., Lemus, M. G., Johnson, R. F., & Gotlib, I. H. (2012). Functional neuroimaging of major depressive disorder: A meta-analysis and new integration of baseline activation and neural response data. *American Journal of Psychiatry, 169,* 693–703.

Hamilton, W. D. (1964). The genetical evolution of social behaviour. *Journal of Theoretical Biology, 7,* 1–16.

Hamlin, J. K., Wynn, K., & Bloom, P. (2007). Social evaluation by preverbal infants. *Nature, 450*(7169), 557–559.

Hanel, P. H. P., Wolfradt, U., Maio, G. R., & Manstead, A. S. R. (2018). The source attribution effect: Demonstrating pernicious disagreement between ideological groups on non-divisive aphorisms. *Journal of Experimental Social Psychology, 79,* 51–63. https://doi.org/10.1016/j.esp.2018.07.002

Happé, F. G. E. (1995). The role of age and verbal ability in the theory of mind performance of subjects with autism. *Child Development, 66,* 843–855.

Harding, C. M., Brooks, G. W., Ashikaga, T., Strauss, J. S., & Brier, A. (1987). The Vermont longitudinal study of persons with severe mental illness, II: Long-term outcome of subjects who retrospectively met DSM–III criteria for schizophrenia. *American Journal of Psychiatry, 144,* 727–735.

Hare, B. (2017). Survival of the friendliest: *Homo sapiens* evolved via selection for prosociality. *Annual Review of Psychology, 68*(1), 155–186.

Hare, R. D. (1998). *Without conscience: The disturbing world of the psychopaths among us.* Guilford Press.

Harlow, H. F. (1958). The nature of love. *American Psychologist, 13,* 573–685.

Harlow, J. M. (1868). Recovery from the passage of an iron bar through the head. *Publications of the Massachusetts Medical Society, 2,* 327–347.

Harmon-Jones, E., Harmon-Jones, C., & Levy, N. (2015). An action-based model of cognitive-dissonance processes. *Current Directions in Psychological Science, 24*(3), 184–189. https://doi.org/10.1177/0963721414566449

Harris, B. (1979). Whatever happened to Little Albert? *American Psychologist, 34,* 151–160.

Harris, D. J., Vine, S. J., Wilson, M. R., McGrath, J. S., LeBel, M.-E., & Buckingham, G. (2018). Action observation for sensorimotor learning in surgery. *British Journal of Surgery, 105,* 1713–1720.

Harro, J. (2015). Neuropsychiatric adverse effects of amphetamine and methamphetamine. *International Review of Neurobiology, 120,* 179–204.

Hart, B., & Risley, T. R. (1995). *Meaningful differences in the everyday experience of young American children.* Brookes.

Hart, B. L. (1988). Biological basis of the behavior of sick animals. *Neuroscience and Biobehavioral Reviews, 12,* 123–137.

Hart, C. L. (2013). *High price: A neuroscientist's journey of self-discovery that challenges everything you know about drugs and society.* Harper Collins.

Hart, W., Albarracin, D., Eagly, A. H., Lindberg, M. J., Merrill, L., & Brechan, I. (2009). Feeling validated versus being correct: A meta-analysis of selective exposure to information. *Psychological Bulletin, 135,* 555–588.

Hartshorne, H., & May, M. (1928). *Studies in deceit.* Macmillan.

Hartshorne, J. K., & Germine, L. T. (2015). When does cognitive functioning peak? The asynchronous rise and fall of different cognitive abilities across the life span. *Psychological Science, 26* (4), 433–443. https://doi.org/10.1177/0956797614567339

Haslam, C., Wills, A. J., Haslam, S. A., Kay, J., Baron, R., & McNab, F. (2007). Does maintenance of colour categories rely on language? Evidence to the contrary from a case of semantic dementia. *Brain and Language, 103,* 251–263.

Hassabis, D., Kumaran, D., Summerfield, C., & Botvinick, M. (2017). Neuroscience-inspired artificial intelligence. *Neuron, 95,* 245–258.

Hassabis, D., Kumaran, D., Vann, S. D., & Maguire, E. A. (2007). Patients with hippocampal amnesia cannot imagine new experiences. *Proceedings of the National Academy of Sciences, USA, 104,* 1726–1731.

Hasselmo, M. E. (2006). The role of acetylcholine in learning and memory. *Current Opinion in Neurobiology, 16,* 710–715.

Hassin, R. R., Bargh, J. A., & Zimerman, S. (2009). Automatic and flexible: The case of non-conscious goal pursuit. *Social Cognition, 27,* 20–36.

Hassmen, P., Koivula, N., & Uutela, A. (2000). Physical exercise and psychological well-being: A population study in Finland. *Preventive Medicine, 30,* 17–25.

Hasson, U., Hendler, T., Bashat, D. B., & Malach, R. (2001). Vase or face? A neural correlate of shape-selective grouping processes in the human brain. *Journal of Cognitive Neuroscience, 13,* 744–753.

Hatemi, P. K., Gillespie, N. A., Eaves, L. J., Maher, B. S., Webb, B. T., Heath, A. C., Medland, S. E., Smyth, D. C., Beeby, H. N., Gordon, S. D., Montgomery, G. W., Zhu, G., Byrne, E. M., & Martin, N. G. (2011). A genome-wide analysis of liberal and conservative political attitudes. *Journal of Politics, 73,* 271–285.

Hatfield, E. (1988). Passionate and companionate love. In R. J. Sternberg & M. L. Barnes (Eds.), *The psychology of love* (pp. 191–217). Yale University Press.

Häusser, M. (2000). The Hodgkin–Huxley theory of the action potential. *Nature Neuroscience, 3,* 1165.

Hawkins, R. X. D., Goodman, N. D., & Goldstone, R. L. (2019). The emergence of social norms and conventions. *Trends in Cognitive Sciences, 23*(2), 158–169.

Hayes, J. E., Bartoshuk, L. M., Kidd, J. R., & Duffy, V. B. (2008). Supertasting and PROP bitterness depends on more than the TAS2R38 gene. *Chemical Senses, 23,* 255–265.

Hayes, S. C., Strosahl, K., & Wilson, K. G. (1999). *Acceptance and commitment therapy: An experiential approach to behavior change.* Guilford Press.

Heavey, C. L., Hurlburt, R. T., & Lefforge, N. L. (2012). Toward a phenomenology of feelings. *Emotion, 12*(4), 763–777.

Hebb, D. O. (1949). *The organization of behavior.* Wiley.

Hebl, M. R., & Heatherton, T. F. (1997). The stigma of obesity in women: The difference is Black and White. *Personality and Social Psychology Bulletin, 24,* 417–426.

Hebl, M. R., & Mannix, L. M. (2003). The weight of obesity in evaluating others: A mere proximity effect. *Personality and Social Psychology Bulletin, 29,* 28–38.

Hedges, L. V., & Nowell, A. (1995). Sex differences in mental test scores, variability, and numbers of high-scoring individuals. *Science, 269*(5220), 41–45.

Heerey, E. A., Keltner, D., & Capps, L. M. (2003). Making sense of self-conscious emotion: Linking theory of mind and emotion in children with autism. *Emotion, 3,* 394–400.

Heiy, J. E., & Cheavens, J. S. (2014). Back to basics: A naturalistic assessment of the experience and regulation of emotion. *Emotion, 14*(5), 878–891. https://doi.org/10.1037/a0037231

Helliwell, J., & Grover, S. (2014, December). How's life at home? New evidence on marriage and the set point for happiness. NBER Working Paper No. 20794.

Henderlong, J., & Lepper, M. R. (2002). The effects of praise on children's intrinsic motivation: A review and synthesis. *Psychological Bulletin, 128,* 774–795.

Henrich, J. (2018). Human cooperation: The hunter-gatherer puzzle. *Current Biology, 28*(19), R1143–R1145. https://doi.org/10.1016/j.cub.2018.08.005

Henrich, J., Heine, S. J., & Norenzayan, A. (2010). Most people are not WEIRD. *Nature, 466,* 29.

Herman, C. P., Roth, D. A., & Polivy, J. (2003). Effects of the presence of others on food intake: A normative interpretation. *Psychological Bulletin, 129,* 873–886.

Herman-Giddens, M. E., Steffes, J., Harris, D., Slora, E., Hussey, M., Dowshen, S. A., & Reiter, E. O. (2012). Secondary sexual characteristics in boys: Data from the pediatric research in office settings network. *Pediatrics, 130*(5), e1058–e1068. https://doi.org/10.1542/peds.2011-3291

Herring, M. P., Puetz, T. W., O'Connor, P. J., & Dishman, R. K. (2012). Effect of exercise training on depressive symptoms among patients with chronic illness: A systematic review and meta-analysis of randomized controlled trials. *Archives of Internal Medicine, 172,* 101–111.

Hershfield, H. E., Shu, S., & Benartzi, S. (2019). Temporal reframing and savings: A field experiment. *Marketing Science.*

Hertenstein, M. J., Holmes, R., McCullough, M., & Keltner, D. (2009). The communication of emotion via touch. *Emotion, 9,* 566–573.

Hertig, M. M., & Nagel, B. J. (2012). Aerobic fitness relates to learning on a virtual Morris water maze task and hippocampal volume in adolescents. *Behavioral Brain Research, 233,* 517–525.

Herz, R. S., & von Clef, J. (2001). The influence of verbal labeling on the perception of odors. *Perception, 30,* 381–391.

Heyes, C. (2016). Born pupils? Natural pedagogy and cultural pedagogy. *Perspectives on Psychological Science, 11*(2), 280–295. https://doi.org/10.1177/1745691615621276

Heyes, C. M., & Foster, C. L. (2002). Motor learning by observation: Evidence from a serial reaction time task. *Quarterly Journal of Experimental Psychology (A), 55,* 593–607.

Heyman, G. M. (2009). *Addiction: A disorder of choice.* Harvard University Press.

Heymsfield, S. B., Greenberg, A. S., Fujioka, K., Dixon, R. M., Kushner, R., Hunt, T., Lubina, J. A., Patane, J., Self, B., Hunt, P., & McCarnish, M. (1999). Recombinant leptin for weight loss in obese and lean adults: A randomized, controlled, dose-escalation trial. *Journal of the American Medical Association, 282*(16), 1568–1575.

Hibbeln, J. R. (1998). Fish consumption and major depression. *Lancet, 351,* 1213.

Hickok, G. (2009). Eight problems for the mirror neuron theory of action understanding in monkeys and humans. *Journal of Cognitive Neuroscience, 21,* 1229–1243.

Hickok, G. (2014). *The myth of mirror neurons: The real neuroscience of communication and cognition.* W. W. Norton

Higgins, E. T. (1987). Self-discrepancy theory: A theory relating self and affect. *Psychological Review, 94,* 319–340.

Hilgard, E. R. (1965). *Hypnotic susceptibility.* Harcourt, Brace and World.

Hilgard, E. R. (1986). *Divided consciousness: Multiple controls in human thought and action.* Wiley-Interscience.

Hilker, R., Helenius, D., Fagerlund, B., Skytthe, A., Christensen, K., Werge, T. M., Nordentoft, M., & Glenthøj, B. (2018). Heritability of schizophrenia and schizophrenia spectrum based on the nationwide Danish twin register. *Biological Psychiatry, 83,* 492–498.

Hillman, C. H., Erickson, K. I., & Kramer, A. F. (2008). Be smart, exercise your heart: Exercise effects on brain and cognition. *Nature Reviews Neuroscience, 9,* 58–65.

Hilts, P. (1995). *Memory's ghost: The strange tale of Mr. M and the nature of memory.* Simon & Schuster.

Hintzman, D. L., Asher, S. J., & Stern, L. D. (1978). Incidental retrieval and memory for coincidences. In M. M. Gruneberg, P. E. Morris, & R. N. Sykes (Eds.), *Practical aspects of memory* (pp. 61–68). Academic Press.

Hirsh-Pasek, K., Adamson, L. B., Bakeman, R., Owen, M. T., Golinkoff., R. M., Pace, A., Yust, P. K. S., & Suma, K. (2015). The contribution of early communication quality to low-income children's language success. *Psychological Science, 26,* 1071–1083.

Hirst, W., & Echterhoff, G. (2012). Remembering in conversations: The social sharing and reshaping of memory. *Annual Review of Psychology, 63,* 55–79.

Hirst, W., Phelps, E. A., Buckner, R. L., Budson, A. E., Cuc, A., Gabrieli, J. D. E., Johnson, M. K., Lustig, C., Lyle, K. B., Mather, M., Meksin, R., Mitchell, K. J., Ochsner, K. N., Schacter, D. L., Simons, J. S., & Vaidya, C. J. (2009). Long-term memory for the terrorist attack of September 11: Flashbulb memories, event memories, and the factors that influence their retention. *Journal of Experimental Psychology: General, 138,* 161–176.

Hirst, W., Phelps, E. A., Meksin, R., Vaidya, C. J., Johnson, M. K., Mitchell, K. J., Buckner, R. L., Budson, A. E., Gabrieli, J. D. E., Lustig, C., Mather, M., Ochsner, K. N., Schacter, D., Simons, J. S., Lyle, K. B., Cuc, A. F., & Olsson, A. (2015). A ten-year follow-up of a study of memory for the attack of September 11, 2001: Flashbulb memories and memories for flashbulb events. *Journal of Experimental Psychology: General, 144,* 604–623.

Hobson, J. A. (1988). *The dreaming brain.* Basic Books.

Hobson, J. A., & McCarley, R. W. (1977). The brain as a dreamstate generator: An activation–synthesis hypothesis of the dream process. *American Journal of Psychiatry, 134,* 1335–1368.

Hockley, W. E. (2008). The effects of environmental context on recognition memory and claims of remembering. *Journal of Experimental Psychology: Learning, Memory, and Cognition, 34,* 1412–1429.

Hodgkin, A. L., & Huxley, A. F. (1939). Action potential recorded from inside a nerve fibre. *Nature, 144,* 710–712.

Hodson, G., & Sorrentino, R. M. (2001). Just who favors the ingroup? Personality differences in reactions to uncertainty in the minimal group paradigm. *Group Dynamics, 5,* 92–101.

Hoek, H. W., & van Hoeken, D. (2003). Review of the prevalence and incidence of eating disorders. *International Journal of Eating Disorders, 34,* 383–396.

Hoffrage, U., & Gigerenzer, G. (1998). Using natural frequencies to improve diagnostic inferences. *Academic Medicine, 73,* 538–540.

Hofmann, W., Vohs, K. D., & Baumeister, R. F. (2012). What people desire, feel conflicted about, and try to resist in everyday life. *Psychological Science, 23,* 582–588.

Hogan, M. J., & Strasburger, V. C. (2008). Body image, eating disorders, and the media. *Adolescent Medicine: State of the Art Reviews, 19*(3), 521–546, x–xi. http://www.ncbi.nlm.nih.gov/pubmed/19227390

Hollins, M. (2010). Somesthetic senses. *Annual Review of Psychology, 61,* 243–271.

Holmbeck, G. N., & O'Donnell, K. (1991). Discrepancies between perceptions of decision making and behavioral autonomy. In R. L. Paikoff (Ed.), *New directions for child development: Shared views in the family during adolescence* (no. 51, pp. 51–69). San Francisco: Jossey-Bass.

Holmes, J., Gathercole, S. E., & Dunning, D. L. (2009). Adaptive training leads to sustained enhancement of poor working memory in children. *Developmental Science, 12,* F9–F15.

Holt-Lunstad, J. (2018). Why social relationships are important for physical health: A systems approach to understanding and modifying risk and protection. *Annual Review of Psychology, 69*(1), 437–458.

Hölzel, B. K., Carmody, J., Vangel, M., Congleton, C., Yerramsetti, S. M., Gard, T., & Lazar, S. W. (2011). Mindfulness practice leads to increases in regained gray matter density. *Psychiatry Research: Neuroimaging, 191*(1), 36–43.

Homans, G. C. (1961). *Social behavior.* Harcourt, Brace and World.

Homonoff, T. (2013, March 27). Can small incentives have large effects? The impact of taxes versus bonuses on disposable bag use. Working Papers (Princeton University. Industrial Relations Section). http://arks.princeton.edu/ark:/88435/dsp014q77fr47j

Hooley, J. M. (2007). Expressed emotion and relapse of psychopathology. *Annual Review of Clinical Psychology, 3,* 329–352.

Hoppenbrouwers, S. S., Bulten, B. H., & Brazil, I. A. (2016). Parsing fear: A reassessment of the evidence for fear deficits in psychopathy. *Psychological Bulletin, 142,* 573–600.

Horn, J. L., & Cattell, R. B. (1966). Refinement and test of the theory of fluid and crystallized general intelligences. *Journal of Educational Psychology, 5,* 253–270.

Horner, A. J., Bisby, J. A., Bush, D., Lin, W.-J., & Burgess, N. (2015). Evidence for holistic episodic recollection via hippocampal pattern completion. *Nature Communications, 6,* 7462. https://doi.org/10.1038/ncomms8462

Horrey, W. J., & Wickens, C. D. (2006). Examining the impact of cell phone conversation on driving using meta-analytic techniques. *Human Factors, 48,* 196–205.

Hosking, S. G., Young, K. L., & Regan, M. A. (2009). The effects of text messaging on young drivers. *Human Factors, 51,* 582–592.

Howard, J. D., & Kahnt, T. (2018). Identity prediction errors in the human midbrain update reward–identity expectations in the orbitofrontal cortex. *Nature Communication, 9,* Art. No.: 1611.

Howard, M. O., Brown, S. E., Garland, E. L., Perron, B. E., & Vaughn, M. G. (2011). Inhalant use and inhalant use disorders in the United States. *Addiction Science & Clinical Practice, 6,* 18–31.

Howes, M., Siegel, M., & Brown, F. (1993). Early childhood memories—accuracy and affect. *Cognition, 47,* 95–119.

Hua, X., Hibar, D. P., Lee, S., Toga, A. W., Jack, C. R., Jr., Weiner, M. W., Thompson, P. M., & Alzheimer's Disease Neuroimaging Initiative.
(2010). Sex and age differences in atrophic rates: An ADNI study with n = 1368 MRI scans. *Neurobiology of Aging, 31,* 1463–1480.

Hubel, D. H. (1988). *Eye, brain, and vision.* W. H. Freeman.

Hubel, D. H., & Wiesel, T. N. (1962). Receptive fields, binocular interaction and functional architecture in the cat's visual cortex. *Journal of Physiology, 160,* 106–154.

Hubel, D. H., & Wiesel, T. N. (1998). Early exploration of the visual cortex. *Neuron, 20,* 401–412.

Hudson, J. I., Hiripi, E., Pope, H. G., & Kessler, R. C. (2006). The prevalence and correlates of eating disorders in the National Comorbidity Survey Replication. *Biological Psychiatry, 61*(3), 348–358.

Huesmann, L. R., Moise-Titus, J., Podolski, C.-L., & Eron, L. D. (2003). Longitudinal relations between children's exposure to TV violence and their aggressive and violent behavior in young adulthood: 1977–1992. *Developmental Psychology, 39,* 201–221.

Hull, C. L. (1943). *Principles of behavior.* Appleton-Century-Crofts.

Hunsley, J., & Di Giulio, G. (2002). Dodo bird, phoenix, or urban legend? The question of psychotherapy equivalence. *Scientific Review of Mental Health Practice, 1,* 13–24.

Hunt, E. B. (2011). *Human intelligence.* Cambridge University Press.

Hunt, L. L., Eastwick, P. W., & Finkel, E. J. (2015). Leveling the playing field: Longer acquaintance predicts reduced assortative mating on attractiveness. *Psychological Science, 26*(7), 1046–1053. https://doi.org/10.1177/0956797615579273

Hunt, M. (2007). *The story of psychology* (exp. & rev. ed.). Anchor Books.

Hurst, N. (2017). How does human echolocation work? Smithsonian.com, https://www.smithsonianmag.com/innovation/how-does-human-echolocation-work-180965063/

Hussey, E., & Safford, A. (2009). Perception of facial expression in somatosensory cortex supports simulationist models. *Journal of Neuroscience, 29*(2), 301–302.

Hutchison, R. M., Culham, J. C., Everling, S., Flanagan, J. R., & Gallivan, J. P. (2014). Distinct and distributed functional connectivity patterns across cortex reflect the domain-specific constraints of object, face, scene, body, and tool category-selective modules in the ventral visual pathway. *Neuroimage, 96,* 216–236. https://doi.org/10.1016/j.neuroimage.2014.03.068

Huxley, A. (1932). *Brave new world.* Chatto and Windus.

Huxley, A. (1954). *The doors of perception.* Harper & Row.

Hyde, J. S. (2005) The gender similarities hypothesis. *American Psychologist, 60,* 581–592.

Hyman, I. E., Jr., Boss, S. M., Wise, B. M., McKenzie, K. E., & Caggiano, J. M. (2010). Did you see the unicycling clown? Inattentional blindness while walking and talking on a cell phone. *Applied Cognitive Psychology, 24*(5), 597–607.

Hyman, I. E., Jr., & Pentland, J. (1996). The role of mental imagery in the creation of false childhood memories. *Journal of Memory and Language, 35,* 101–117.

Hypericum Depression Trial Study Group. (2002). Effect of Hypericum perforatum (St. John's wort) in major depressive disorder: A randomized controlled trial. *Journal of the American Medical Association, 287,* 1807–1814.

Iacoboni, M. (2009). Imitation, empathy, and mirror neurons. *Annual Review of Psychology, 60,* 653–670.

Iacoboni, M., Molnar-Szakacs, I., Gallese, V., Buccino, G., Mazziotta, J. C., & Rizzolatti, G. (2005). Grasping the intentions of others with one's own mirror neuron system. *PLoS Biology, 3,* 529–535.

Inciardi, J. A. (2001). *The war on drugs III.* Allyn & Bacon.

Ingvar, M., Ambros-Ingerson, J., Davis, M., Granger, R., Kessler, M., Rogers, G. A., Schehr, R. S., & Lynch, G. (1997). Enhancement by an ampakine of memory encoding in humans. *Experimental Neurology, 146,* 553–559.

Inniss, D., Steiger, H., & Bruce, K. (2011). Threshold and subthreshold post-traumatic stress disorder in bulimic patients: Prevalences and clinical correlates. *Eating and Weight Disorders, 16*(1), e30–e36. https://doi.org/10.1007/BF03327518

Inui, A. (2001). Ghrelin: An orexigenic and somatotrophic signal from the stomach. *Nature Reviews Neuroscience, 2,* 551–560.

Irvine, J. T. (1978). Wolof magical thinking: Culture and conservation revisited. *Journal of Cross-Cultural Psychology, 9,* 300–310.

Isaacowitz, D. M. (2012). Mood regulation in real time: Age differences in the role of looking. *Current Directions in Psychological Science, 21*(4), 237–242. https://doi.org/10.1177/0963721412448651

Isaacowitz, D. M., & Blanchard-Fields, F. (2012). Linking process and outcome in the study of emotion and aging. *Perspectives on Psychological Science, 7*(1), 3–17. https://doi.org/10.1177/1745691611424750

Isenberg, D. J. (1986). Group polarization: A critical review and meta-analysis. *Journal of Personality and Social Psychology, 50*(6), 1141–1151. https://doi.org/10.1037/0022-3514.50.6.1141

Ittelson, W. H. (1952). *The Ames demonstrations in perception.* Princeton University Press.

Iyengar, S., Konitzer, T., & Tedin, K. (2018). The home as a political fortress: Family agreement in an era of polarization. *Journal of Politics, 80*(4), 1326–1338. https://doi.org/10.1086/698929

Izard, C. E. (1971). *The face of emotion.* Appleton-Century-Crofts.

Jack, R. E., & Schyns, P. G. (2017). Toward a social psychophysics of face communication. *Annual Review of Psychology, 68,* 269–297. https://doi.org/10.1146/annurev-psych-010416-044242

Jacobson, N. C., & Newman, M. G. (2017). Anxiety and depression as bidirectional risk factors for one another: A meta-analysis of longitudinal studies. *Psychological Bulletin, 143,* 1155–1200.

Jacobson, T., & Hoffman, V. (1997). Children's attachment representations: Longitudinal relations to school behavior and academic competency in middle childhood and adolescence. *Developmental Psychology, 33,* 703–710.

Jaeger, A., Eisenkraemer, R. E., & Stein, L. M. (2015). Test-enhanced learning in third-grade children. *Educational Psychology, 35,* 513–521.

Jaeggi, S. M., Buschkuehl, M., Jonides, J., & Perrig, W. J. (2008). Improving fluid intelligence with training on working memory. *Proceedings of the National Academy of Sciences, USA, 105,* 6829–6833. https://doi.org/10.1073/pnas.0801268105

James, W. (1890). *The principles of psychology.* Harvard University Press.

Jamieson, J. P., Koslov, K., Nock, M. K., & Mendes, W. B. (2013). Experiencing discrimination increases risk-taking. *Psychological Science, 24,* 131–139.

Jamieson, J. P., Nock, M. K., & Mendes, W. B. (2013). Changing the conceptualization of stress in social anxiety disorder: Affective and physiological consequences. *Clinical Psychological Science, 1*(4), 363–374. https://doi.org/10.1177/2167702613482119

Janicak, P. G., Dowd, S. M., Martis, B., Alam, D., Beedle, D., Krasuski, J., Strong, M. J., Sharma, R., Rosen, C., & Viana, M. (2002). Repetitive transcranial magnetic stimulation versus electroconvulsive therapy for major depression: Preliminary results of a randomized trial. *Biological Psychiatry, 51,* 659–667.

Janis, I. L. (1982). *Groupthink: Scientific studies of policy decisions and fiascoes.* Houghton-Mifflin.

Jaroszewski, A. C., Morris, R., & Nock, M. K. (2019). Randomized controlled trial of an online machine learning-driven risk assessment and intervention platform for increasing the use of crisis services. *Journal of Consulting and Clinical Psychology, 87*(4), 370–379.

Jaynes, J. (1976). *The origin of consciousness in the breakdown of the bicameral mind.* Allen Lane.

Jenkins, J. G., & Dallenbach, K. M. (1924). Obliviscence during sleep and waking. *American Journal of Psychology, 35,* 605–612.

Jing, H. G., Madore, K. P., & Schacter, D. L. (2017). Preparing for what might happen: An episodic specificity induction impacts the generation of alternative future events. *Cognition, 169,* 118–128.

Jing, H. G., Szpunar, K. K., & Schacter, D. L. (2016). Interpolated testing influences focused attention and improves integration of information during a video-recorded lecture. *Journal of Experimental Psychology: Applied, 22,* 305–318.

John, O. P., Naumann, L. P., & Soto, C. J. (2008). Paradigm shift to the integrative Big-Five trait taxonomy: History, measurement, and conceptual issues. In O. P. John, R. W. Robins, & L. A. Pervin (Eds.), *Handbook of personality: Theory and research* (3rd ed., pp. 114–158). Guilford Press.

John, O. P., & Srivastava, S. (1999). The Big Five trait taxonomy: History, measurement, and theoretical perspectives. In L. A. Pervin & O. P. John (Eds.), *Handbook of personality: Theory and research* (2nd ed., pp. 102–138). Guilford Press.

Johnson, D. J., Cesario, J., & Pleskac, T. J. (2018). How prior information and police experience impact decisions to shoot. *Journal of Personality and Social Psychology, 115*(4), 601–623.

Johnson, D. R., & Wu, J. (2002). An empirical test of crisis, social selection, and role explanations of the relationship between marital disruption and psychological distress: A pooled time-series analysis of four-wave panel data. *Journal of Marriage and the Family, 64,* 211–224.

Johnson, J. S., & Newport, E. L. (1989). Critical period effects in second language learning: The influence of maturational state on the acquisition of English as a second language. *Cognitive Psychology, 21,* 60–99.

Johnson, K. (2002). Neural basis of haptic perception. In H. Pashler & S. Yantis (Eds.), *Stevens' handbook of experimental psychology: Vol. 1. Sensation and perception* (3rd ed., pp. 537–583). Wiley.

Johnson, M. H., Dziurawiec, S., Ellis, H. D., & Morton, J. (1991). Newborns' preferential tracking of face-like stimuli and its subsequent decline. *Cognition, 40,* 1–19.

Johnson, M. K., Hashtroudi, S., & Lindsay, D. S. (1993). Source monitoring. *Psychological Bulletin, 114,* 3–28.

Johnson, S. C., Dweck, C. S., & Chen, F. S. (2007). Evidence for infants' internal working models of attachment. *Psychological Science, 18,* 501–2. https://doi.org/10.1111/j.1467-9280.2007.01929.x

Johnson, S. L., Cuellar, A. K., & Miller, C. (2009). Unipolar and bipolar depression: A comparison of clinical phenomenology, biological vulnerability, and psychosocial predictors. In I. H. Gottlib & C. L. Hammen (Eds.), *Handbook of depression* (2nd ed., pp. 142–162). Guilford Press.

Johnson, S. L., Cuellar, A. K., Ruggiero, C., Winnett-Perman, C., Goodnick, P., White, R., & Miller, I. (2008). Life events as predictors of mania and depression in bipolar 1 disorder. *Journal of Abnormal Psychology, 117,* 268–277.

Johnson, S. L., & Miller, I. (1997). Negative life events and time to recover from episodes of bipolar disorder. *Journal of Abnormal Psychology, 106,* 449–457.

Jonas, E., Graupmann, V., Kayser, D. N., Zanna, M., Traut-Mattausch, E., & Frey, D. (2009). Culture, self, and the emergence of reactance: Is there a "universal" freedom? *Journal of Experimental Social Psychology, 45,* 1068–1080.

Jones, E. E., & Harris, V. A. (1967). The attribution of attitudes. *Journal of Experimental Social Psychology, 3,* 1–24.

Jones, E. E., & Nisbett, R. E. (1972). The actor and the observer: Divergent perceptions of the causes of behavior. In E. E. Jones, D. E. Kanouse, H. H. Kelley, R. E. Nisbett, S. Valins, & B. Weiner (Eds.), *Attribution: Perceiving the causes of behavior* (pp. 79–94). General Learning Press.

Jones, J. H. (1993). *Bad blood: The Tuskegee Syphilis Experiment.* Simon & Schuster.

Jones, M. J., Moore, S. R., & Kobor, M. S. (2018). Principles and challenges of applying epigenetic epidemiology to psychology. *Annual Review of Psychology, 69,* 459–485.

Jones, S. S. (2007). Imitation in infancy. *Psychological Science, 18*(7), 593–599.

Jonsson, H., & Hougaard, E. (2008). Group cognitive behavioural therapy for obsessive-compulsive disorder: A systematic review and meta-analysis. *Acta Psychiatrica Scandinavica, 117,* 1–9.

Jordan, S. A., Cunningham, D. G., & Marles, R. J. (2010). Assessment of herbal medicinal products: Challenges and opportunities to increase the knowledge base for safety assessment. *Toxicology and Applied Pharmacology, 243,* 198–216.

Judd, L. L. (1997). The clinical course of unipolar major depressive disorders. *Archives of General Psychiatry, 54,* 989–991.

Jung-Beeman, M. (2005). Bilateral brain processes for comprehending natural language. *Trends in Cognitive Sciences, 9,* 512–518.

Kaas, J. H. (1991). Plasticity of sensory and motor maps in adult mammals. *Annual Review of Neuroscience, 14,* 137–167.

Kagan, J. (1997). Temperament and the reactions to unfamiliarity. *Child Development, 68,* 139–143.

Kahneman, D. (2011). *Thinking fast and slow.* Farrar, Straus and Giroux.

Kahneman, D., Krueger, A. B., Schkade, D. A., Schwarz, N., & Stone, A. A. (2004). A survey method for characterizing daily life experience: The day reconstruction method. *Science, 306,* 1776–1780.

Kahneman, D., & Tversky, A. (1973). On the psychology of prediction. *Psychological Review, 80,* 237–251.

Kahneman, D., & Tversky, A. (1979). Prospect theory: An analysis of decision under risk. *Econometrica, 47,* 263–291.

Kahneman, D., & Tversky, A. (1984). Choices, values, and frames. *American Psychologist, 39,* 341–350.

Kalb, J. (2015, January 12). Give me a smile. *New Yorker.*

Kalokerinos, E. K., Greenaway, K. H., & Denson, T. F. (2015). Reappraisal but not suppression downregulates the experience of positive and negative emotion. *Emotion, 15*(3), 271–275. https://doi.org/10.1037/emo0000025

Kamin, L. J. (1959). The delay-of-punishment gradient. *Journal of Comparative and Physiological Psychology, 52,* 434–437.

Kan, P. F., & Kohnert, K. (2008). Fast mapping by bilingual preschool children. *Journal of Child Language, 35,* 495–514.

Kandel, E. R. (2000). Nerve cells and behavior. In E. R. Kandel, G. H. Schwartz, & T. M. Jessell (Eds.), *Principles of neural science* (pp. 19–35). McGraw-Hill.

Kandel, E. R. (2006). *In search of memory: The emergence of a new science of mind.* Norton.

Kang, S. H. K., McDermott, K. B., & Roediger, H. L., III. (2007). Test format and corrective feedback modify the effect of testing on long-term retention. *European Journal of Cognitive Psychology, 19,* 528–558.

Kann, L., McManus, T., Harris, W. A., Shanklin, S. L., Flint, K. H., Queen, B., Lowry, R., Chyen, D., Whittle, L., Thornton, J., Lim, C., Bradford, D., Yamakawa, Y., Leon, M., Brener, N., & Ethier, K. A. (2018). Youth Risk Behavior Surveillance—United States, 2017. *MMWR Surveillance Summaries.* https://www.cdc.gov/healthyyouth/data/yrbs/pdf/2017/ss6708.pdf

Kanwisher, N. (2010). Functional specificity in the human brain: A window into the functional architecture of the mind. *Proceedings of the National Academy of Sciences, USA, 107,* 11163–11170.

Kanwisher, N., McDermott, J., & Chun, M. M. (1997). The fusiform face area: A module in human extrastriate cortex specialized for face perception. *Journal of Neuroscience, 17,* 4302–4311.

Kapur, S., Craik, F. I. M., Tulving, E., Wilson, A. A., Houle, S., & Brown, G. M. (1994). Neuroanatomical correlates of encoding in episodic memory: Levels of processing effects. *Proceedings of the National Academy of Sciences, USA, 91,* 2008–2011.

Karazsia, B. T., Murnen, S. K., & Tylka, T. L. (2017). Is body dissatisfaction changing across time? A cross-temporal meta-analysis. *Psychological Bulletin, 143*(3), 293–320. https://doi.org/10.1037/bul0000081

Kardes, F. R., & Sanbonmatsu, D. M. (2003). Omission neglect: The importance of missing information. *Skeptical Inquirer, 27,* 42–16.

Karlson, K. (2016). We tested over 100 different Facebook ads in one month—here's what we learned. https://adespresso.com/blog/test-100-facebook-ads-one-month-what-we-learned/

Karpicke, J. D. (2012). Retrieval-based learning: Active retrieval promotes meaningful learning. *Current Directions in Psychological Science, 21,* 157–163.

Karpicke, J. D., & Aue, W. R. (2015). The testing effect is alive and well with complex materials. *Educational Psychology Review, 27,* 317–326.

Karpicke, J. D., & Blunt, J. R. (2011). Retrieval practice produces more learning than elaborative studying with concept mapping. *Science, 331,* 772–775.

Kasser, T., & Sharma, Y. S. (1999). Reproductive freedom, educational equality, and females' preference for resource-acquisition characteristics in mates. *Psychological Science, 10,* 374–377.

Kassin, S. M. (2007). Internalized false confessions. In M. Toglia, J. Read, D. Ross, & R. Lindsay (Eds.), *Handbook of eyewitness psychology: Vol. 1, Memory for events* (pp. 175–192). Erlbaum.

Kassin, S. M. (2015). The social psychology of false confessions. *Social Issues and Policy Review, 9,* 25–51.

Katz, B., Shah, P., & Meyer, D. E. (2018). How to play 20 questions with nature and lose: Reflections on 100 years of brain-training research. *Proceedings of the National Academy of Sciences, USA, 115*(40), 9897–9904.

Kaufman, A. S. (2001). WAIS-III IQs, Horn's theory, and generational changes from young adulthood to old age. *Intelligence, 29,* 131–167.

Kawakami, K., Dovidio, J. F., Moll, J., Hermsen, S., & Russin, A. (2000). Just say no (to stereotyping): Effects of training in the negation of stereotypic associations on stereotype activation. *Journal of Personality and Social Psychology, 78,* 871–888.

Kazdin, A. E. (2018). *Innovations in psychological interventions and their delivery: Leveraging cutting-edge science to improve the world's mental health.* Oxford University Press.

Kazdin, A. E., & Blaise, S. L. (2011). Rebooting psychotherapy research and practice to reduce the burden of mental illness. *Perspectives on Psychological Science, 6,* 21–37.

Keane, T. M., Marshall, A. D., & Taft, C. T. (2006). Posttraumatic stress disorder: Etiology, epidemiology, and treatment outcome. *Annual Review of Clinical Psychology, 2,* 161–197.

Keefe, F. J., Lumley, M., Anderson, T., Lynch, T., & Carson, K. L. (2001). Pain and emotion: New research directions. *Journal of Clinical Psychology, 57,* 587–607.

Kelley, M. R., Neath, I., & Surprenant, A. M. (2013). Three more semantic serial position functions and a SIMPLE explanation. *Memory & Cognition, 41,* 600–610.

Kelly, G. (1955). *The psychology of personal constructs.* Norton.

Kelly, J. F., Karminer, Y., Kahler, C. W., Hoeppner, B., Yeterian, J., Cristello, J. V., & Timko, C. (2017). A pilot randomized clinical trial testing integrated 12-step facilitation (iTSF) treatment for adolescent substance use disorder. *Addiction, 112,* 2155–2166.

Kelm, Z., Womer, J., Walter, J. K., & Feudtner, C. (2014). Interventions to cultivate physician empathy: A systematic review. *BMC Medical Education, 14,* 219.

Kendler, K. S., Hettema, J. M., Butera, F., Gardner, C. O., & Prescott, C. A. (2003). Life event dimensions of loss, humiliation, entrapment, and danger in the prediction of onsets of major depression and generalized anxiety. *Archives of General Psychiatry, 60,* 789–796.

Kenrick, D. T., Griskevicius, V., Neuberg, S. L., & Schaller, M. (2010). Renovating the pyramid of needs: Contemporary extensions built upon ancient foundations. *Perspectives on Psychological Science, 5*(3), 292–314. https://doi.org/10.1177/1745691610369469

Kenrick, D. T., Sadalla, E. K., Groth, G., & Trost, M. R. (1990). Evolution, traits, and the stages of human courtship: Qualifying the parental investment model. *Journal of Personality, 58,* 97–116.

Kensinger, E. A., Clarke, R. J., & Corkin, S. (2003). What neural correlates underlie successful encoding and retrieval? A functional magnetic resonance imaging study using a divided attention paradigm. *Journal of Neuroscience, 23,* 2407–2415.

Kensinger, E. A., & Schacter, D. L. (2005). Emotional content and reality monitoring ability: fMRI evidence for the influence of encoding processes. *Neuropsychologia, 43,* 1429–1443.

Kensinger, E. A., & Schacter, D. L. (2006). Amygdala activity is associated with the successful encoding of item, but not source, information for positive and negative stimuli. *Journal of Neuroscience, 26,* 2564–2570.

Keo-Meier, C. L., Herman, L. I., Reisner, S. L., Pardo, S. T., Sharp, C., & Babcock, J. C. (2015). Testosterone treatment and MMPI-2 improvement in transgender men: A prospective controlled study. *Journal of Consulting and Clinical Psychology, 83,* 143–156.

Kerr, N. L., & Tindale, R. S. (2004). Group performance and decision making. *Annual Review of Psychology, 55,* 623–655. https://doi.org/10.1146/annurev.psych.55.090902.142009

Kessler, R. C. (2012). The costs of depression. *Psychiatric Clinics of North America, 35,* 1–14.

Kessler, R. C., Adler, L., Barkley, R., Biederman, J., Connors, C. K., Demler, O., Faraone, S. V., Greenhill, L. L., Howes, M. J., Secnik, K., Spencer, T., Ustun, B., Walters, E. E., & Zaslavsky, A. M. (2006). The prevalence and correlates of adult ADHD in the United States: Results from the National Comorbidity Study Replication. *American Journal of Psychiatry, 163,* 716–723.

Kessler, R. C., Angermeyer, M., Anthony, J. C., deGraaf, R., Demyittenaere, K., Gasquet, I., de Girolamo, G., Gluzman, S., Gureje, O., Haro, J. M., Kawakami, N., Karam, A., Levinson, D., Medina Mora, M. E., Oakley Browne, M. A., Posada-Villa, J., Stein, D. J., Tsang, C. H. A., Aguilar-Gaxiola, S., . . . Üstün, T. B. (2007). Lifetime prevalence and age-of-onset distributions of mental disorders in the World Health Organization World Mental Health Survey Initiative. *World Psychiatry, 6,* 168–176.

Kessler, R. C., Berglund, P., Demler, M. A., Jin, R., Merikangas, K. R., & Walters, E. E. (2005a). Lifetime prevalence and age-of-onset distributions of *DSM-IV* disorders in the National Comorbidity Survey replication. *Archives of General Psychiatry, 62,* 593–602.

Kessler, R. C., Chiu, W. T., Dernier, O., & Walters, E. E. (2005b). Prevalence, severity, and comorbidity of 12-month *DSM-IV* disorders in the National Comorbidity Survey replication. *Archives of General Psychiatry, 62,* 617–627.

Kessler, R. C., Demler, O., Frank, R. G., Olfson, M., Pincus, H. A., Walters, E. E., Wang, P., Wells, K. B., & Zaslavsky, A. M. (2005). Prevalence and treatment of mental disorders, 1990 to 2003. *New England Journal of Medicine, 352*(24), 2515–2523.

Kessler, R. C., Pecora, P. J., Williams, J., Hiripi, E., O'Brien, K., English, D., White, J., Zerbe, R., Downs, A. C., Plotnick, R., Hwang, I., & Sampson, N. A. (2008). Effects of enhanced foster care on the long-term physical and mental health of foster care alumni. *Archives of General Psychiatry, 65,* 625–633.

Kessler, R. C., Petukhova, M., Sampson, N. A., Zaslavsky, A. M., & Wittchen, H. U. (2012). Twelve-month and lifetime prevalence and lifetime morbid risk of anxiety and mood disorders in the United States. *International Journal of Methods in Psychiatric Research, 21*(3), 169–184.

Kessler, R. C., Soukup, J., Davis, R. B., Foster, D. F., Wilkey, S. A., Van Rompay, M. I., & Eisenberg, D. M. (2001). The use of complementary and alternative therapies to treat anxiety and depression in the United States. *American Journal of Psychiatry, 158,* 289–294.

Khalid, N., Atkins, M., Tredget, J., Giles, M., Champney-Smith, K., & Kirov, G. (2008). The effectiveness of electroconvulsive therapy in treatment-resistant depression: A naturalistic study. *Journal of ECT, 24,* 141–145.

Kiehl, K. A., Smith, A. M., Hare, R. D., Mendrek, A., Forster, B. B., Brink, J., & Liddle, P. F. (2001). Limbic abnormalities in affective processing by criminal psychopaths as revealed by functional magnetic resonance imaging. *Biological Psychiatry, 50,* 677–684.

Kihlstrom, J. F., Beer, J. S., & Klein, S. B. (2002). Self and identity as memory. In M. R. Leary & J. P. Tangney (Eds.), *Handbook of self and identity* (pp. 68–90). Guilford Press.

Kim, G., Walden, T. A., & Knieps, L. J. (2010). Impact and characteristics of positive and fearful emotional messages during infant social referencing. *Infant Behavior and Development, 33,* 189–195.

Kim, U. K., Jorgenson, E., Coon, H., Leppert, M., Risch, N., & Drayna, D. (2003). Positional cloning of the human quantitative trait locus underlying taste sensitivity to phenylthiocarbamide. *Science, 299,* 1221–1225.

Kinney, D. A. (1993). From nerds to normals—the recovery of identity among adolescents from middle school to high school. *Sociology of Education, 66,* 21–40.

Kirchner, W. H., & Towne, W. F. (1994). The sensory basis of the honeybee's dance language. *Scientific American, 270*(6), 74–80.

Kirsch, I., Cardena, E., Derbyshire, S., Dienes, Z., Heap, M., Kallio, S., Mazzoni, G., Naish, P., Oakley, D., Potter, C., Walters, V., & Whalley, M. (2011). Definitions of hypnosis and hypnotizability and their relation to suggestion and suggestibility: A consensus statement. *Contemporary Hypnosis and Integrative Therapy, 28,* 107–115.

Kirsch, I., Deacon, B. J., Huedo-Medine, T. B., Scoboria, A., Moore, T. J., & Johnson, B. T. (2008). Initial severity and antidepressant benefits: A meta-analysis of data submitted to the Food and Drug Administration. *PLoS Medicine, 5,* e45.

Kirwan, C. B., Bayley, P. J., Galvan, V. V., & Squire, L. R. (2008). Detailed recollection of remote autobiographical memory after damage to the medial temporal lobe. *Proceedings of the National Academy of Sciences, USA, 105,* 2676–2680.

Kish, S. J., Lerch, J., Furukawa, Y., Tong, J., McCluskey, T., Wilkins, D., Houle, S., Meyer, J., Mundo, E., Wilson, A. A., Rusjan, P. M., Saint-Cyr, J. A., Guttman, M., Collins, D. L., Shapiro, C., Warsh, J. J., & Bioleau, I. (2010). Decreased cerebral cortical serotonin transporter binding in ecstasy users: A positron emission tomography [11c] DASB and structural brain imaging study. *Brain, 133,* 1779–1797.

Klarer, M., Arnold, M., Günther, L., Winter, C., Langhans, W., & Meyer, U. (2014). Gut vagal afferents differentially modulate innate anxiety and learned fear. *Journal of Neuroscience, 34,* 7067–7076.

Kleiman, E. M., Turner, B. J., Fedor, S., Beale, E. E., Picard, R. W., Huffman, J. C., & Nock, M. K. (2018). Digital phenotyping of suicidal thoughts. *Depression and Anxiety, 35,* 601–608.

Klein, O., & Snyder, M. (2003). Stereotypes and behavioral confirmation: From interpersonal to intergroup perspectives. In M. P. Zanna (Ed.), *Advances in experimental social psychology* (Vol. 35, pp. 153–234). Elsevier Academic Press. http://dx.doi.org/10.1016/S0065-2601(03)01003-7

Klein, R. A., Ratliff, K. A., Vianello, M., Adams, R. B., Jr., Bahník, Š., Bernstein, M. J., Bocian, K., Brandt, M. J., Brooks, B., Brumbaugh, C. C., Cernalcilar, Z., Chandler, J., Cheong, W., Davis, W. E., Devos, T., Eisner, M., Frankowska, N., Furrow, D., Galliani, E. M., . . . Nosek, B. A. (2014). Investigating variation in replicability: A "many labs" replication project. *Social Psychology, 45*(3), 142–152. http://dx.doi.org/10.1027/1864-9335/a000178

Klein, S. B. (2004). The cognitive neuroscience of knowing one's self. In M. Gazzaniga (Ed.), *The cognitive neurosciences* (3rd ed., pp. 1077–1089). MIT Press.

Klein, S. B., Robertson, T. E., & Delton, A. W. (2011). The future orientation of memory: Planning as a key component mediating the high levels of recall found with survival processing. *Memory, 19,* 121–139.

Klump, K. L., Strober, M., Bulik, C. M., Thornton, L., Johnson, C., Devlin, B., Fichter, M. M., Halmi, K. A., Kaplan, A. S., Woodside, D. B., Crow, S., Mitchell, J., Rotondo, A., Keel, P. K., Berrettini, W. H., Plotnicov, K., Pollice, C., Lilenfeld, L. R., & Kaye, W. H. (2004). Personality characteristics of women before and after recovery from an eating disorder. *Psychological Medicine, 34*(8), 1407–1418. https://doi.org/10.1017/S0033291704002442

Klüver, H., & Bucy, P. C. (1937). "Psychic blindness" and other symptoms following bilateral temporary lobectomy in rhesus monkeys. *American Journal of Physiology, 119,* 352–353.

Klüver, H., & Bucy, P. C. (1939). Preliminary analysis of the temporal lobes in monkeys. *Archives of Neurology and Psychiatry, 42,* 979–1000.

Knowlton, B. J., Ramus, S. J., & Squire, L. R. (1992). Intact artificial grammar learning in amnesia: Dissociation of classification learning and explicit memory for specific instances. *Psychological Science, 3,* 173–179.

Kobasa, S. (1979). Stressful life events, personality, and health: An inquiry into hardiness. *Journal of Personality and Social Psychology, 37,* 1–11.

Kohlberg, L. (1958). *The development of modes of thinking and choices in years 10 to 16* (Unpublished doctoral dissertation, University of Chicago).

Kohlberg, L. (1963). Development of children's orientation towards a moral order: I. Sequencing in the development of moral thought. *Vita Humana, 6,* 11–36.

Kohlberg, L. (1986). A current statement on some theoretical issues. In S. Modgil & C. Modgil (Eds.), *Lawrence Kohlberg: Consensus and controversy* (pp. 485–546). Falmer.

Kohler, P. K., Manhart, L. E., & Lafferty, E. (2008). Abstinence-only and comprehensive sex education and the initiation of sexual activity and teen pregnancy. *Journal of Adolescent Health, 42,* 344–351.

Kolb, B., & Whishaw, I. Q. (2015). *Fundamentals of human neuropsychology* (7th ed.). Worth Publishers.

Koller, D. (2011, December 5). Death knell for the lecture: Technology as a passport to personalized education. http://www.nytimes.com/2011/12/06/science/daphne-koller-technology-as-a-passport-to-personalized-education.html?pagewanted=all

Kolotkin, R. L., Meter, K., & Williams, G. R. (2001). Quality of life and obesity. *Obesity Reviews, 2,* 219–229.

Komter, A. (2010). The evolutionary origins of human generosity. *International Sociology, 25*(3), 443–464.

Koob, G. F., & Volkow, N. D. (2016). Neurobiology of addiction: A neurocircuitry analysis. *Lancet Psychiatry, 3,* 760–773.

Kosslyn, S. M., Alpert, N. M., Thompson, W. L., Chabris, C. F., Rauch, S. L., & Anderson, A. K. (1993). Visual mental imagery activates topographically organized visual cortex: PET investigations. *Journal of Cognitive Neuroscience, 5,* 263–287.

Kraemer, H. C., Shrout, P. E., & Rubio-Stipec, M. (2007). Developing the *Diagnostic and Statistical Manual-V:* What will "statistical" mean in *DSM-V? Social Psychiatry and Psychiatric Epidemiology, 42,* 259–267.

Kraus, M. W., Piff, P. K., & Keltner, D. (2011). Social class as culture: The convergence of resources and rank in the social realm. *Current Directions in Psychological Science, 20*(4), 246–250. https://doi.org/10.1177/0963721411414654

Kravitz, D. J., Saleem, K. S., Baker, C. I., & Mishkin, M. (2011). A new neural framework for visuospatial processing. *Nature Reviews Neuroscience, 12,* 217–230.

Kravitz, D. J., Saleem, K. S., Baker, C. I., Ungerleider, L. G., & Mishkin, M. (2013). The ventral visual pathway: An expanded neural framework for the processing of object quality. *Trends in Cognitive Sciences, 17,* 26–49.

Kravitz, R. L., Epstein, R. M., Feldman, M. D., Franz, C. E., Azari, R., Wilkes, M. S., Hinton, L., & Franks, P. (2005). Influence of patients' requests for direct-to-consumer advertised antidepressants: A randomized controlled trial. *Journal of the American Medical Association, 293,* 1995–2002.

Kreibig, S. D. (2010). Autonomic nervous system activity in emotion: A review. *Biological Psychology, 84*(3), 394–421. https://doi.org/10.1016/j.biopsycho.2010.03.010

Kroeze, W. K., & Roth, B. L. (1998). The molecular biology of serotonin receptors: Therapeutic implications for the interface of mood and psychosis. *Biological Psychiatry, 44,* 1128–1142.

Kroger, J. (2017, February). Identity development in adolescence and adulthood. *Oxford Research Encyclopedia of Psychology.* http://psychology.oxfordre.com/view/10.1093/acrefore/9780190236557.001.0001/acrefore-9780190236557-e-54

Kruglanski, A. W., Jasko, K., Milyavsky, M., Chernikova, M., Webber, D., Pierro, A., & Di Santo, D. (2018). Cognitive consistency theory in social psychology: A paradigm reconsidered. *Psychological Inquiry 29*(2), 45–59. https://doi.org/10.1080/1047840X.2018.1480656

Kruk, M. R., Halasz, J., Meelis, W., & Haller, J. (2004). Fast positive feedback between the adrenocortical stress response and a brain mechanism involved in aggressive behavior. *Behavioral Neuroscience, 118,* 1062–1070.

Kuffler, D. P. (2018). Origins of phantom limb pain. *Molecular Neurobiology, 55,* 60–69.

Kuhl, P. K., Stevens, E., Hayashi, A., Deguchi, T., Kiritani, S., & Iverson, P. (2006). Infants show a facilitation effect for native language phonetic perception between 6 and 12 months. *Developmental Science, 9,* F13–F21.

Kunda, Z. (1990). The case for motivated reasoning. *Psychological Bulletin, 108,* 480–498.

Kundakovic, M., Gudsnuk, K, Herbstman, J. B., Tang, D. L., Perera, F. P., & Champagne, F. A. (2015). DNA methylation of BDNF as a biomarker of early-life adversity. *Proceedings of the National Academy of Sciences, USA, 112,* 6807–6813.

Kunz, P. R., & Woolcott, M. (1976). Season's greetings: From my status to yours. *Social Science Research, 5,* 269–278.

Kvavilashvili, L., Mirani, J., Schlagman, S., Foley, K., & Kornbrot, D. E. (2009). Consistency of flashbulb memories of September 11 over long delays: Implications for consolidation and wrong time slice hypotheses. *Journal of Memory and Language, 61,* 556–572.

Kwon, M.-K., Setoodehnia, M., Baek, J., Luck, S. J., & Oakes, L. M. (2016). The development of visual search in infancy: Attention to faces versus salience. *Developmental Psychology, 52*(4), 537–555. https://doi.org/10.1037/dev0000080

LaBar, K. S., & Phelps, E. A. (1998). Arousal-mediated memory consolidation: Role of the medial temporal lobe in humans. *Psychological Science, 9,* 490–493.

Labella, M. H., & Masten, A. S. (2017). Family influences on the development of aggression and violence. *Current Opinion in Psychology, 19,* 11–13.

Labrie, V., Pai, S., & Petronis, A. (2012). Epigenetics of major psychosis: Progress, problems, and perspectives. *Trends in Genetics, 28,* 427–435.

Lackner, J. R., & DiZio, P. (2005). Vestibular, proprioceptive, and haptic contributions to spatial orientation. *Annual Review of Psychology, 56,* 115–147.

Lafer-Sousa, R., & Conway, B. R. (2017). #TheDress: Categorical perception of an ambiguous color image. *Journal of Vision, 17*(12), 25. https://doi.org/10.1167/17.12.25

Lai, C. K., Marini, M., Lehr, S. A., Cerruti, C., Shin, J.-E. L., Joy-Gaba, J. A., Ho, A. K., Teachman, B. A., Wojcik, S. P., Koleva, S. P., Frazier, R. S., Heiphetz, L., Chen, E. E., Turner, R. N., Haidt, J., Kesebir, S., Hawkins, C. B., Schaefer, H. S., Rubichi, S., . . . Nosek, B. A. (2014). Reducing implicit racial preferences: I. A comparative investigation of 17 interventions. *Journal of Experimental Psychology, General, 143*(4), 1765–1785. https://doi.org/10.1037/a0036260

Lai, Y., & Siegal, J. (1999). Muscle atonia in REM sleep. In B. Mallick & S. Inoue (Eds.), *Rapid eye movement sleep* (pp. 69–90). Narosa Publishing House.

Lake, J. (2009). Natural products used to treat depressed mood as monotherapies and adjuvants to antidepressants: A review of the evidence. *Psychiatric Times, 26,* 1–6.

Lakhan, S. E., & Kirchgessner, A. (2012, March 12). Chronic traumatic encephalopathy: The dangers of getting "dinged." *Springer Plus, 1*:2. https://doi.org/10.1186/2193-1801-1-2

Lakin, J. M. (2013). Sex differences in reasoning abilities: Surprising evidence that male–female ratios in the tails of the quantitative reasoning distribution have increased. *Intelligence, 41*(4), 263–274. https://doi.org/10.1016/j.intell.2013.04.004

Lan, P. H., Miller, G. E., Chiang, J. J., Levine, C. S., Le, V., Shalowitz, M. U., Story, R. E., & Chen, E. (2018). One size does not fit all: Links between shift-and-persist and asthma in youth are moderated by perceived social status and experience of unfair treatment. *Development and Psychopathology, 30,* 1699–1714.

Landry, M., Lifshitz, M., & Raz, A. (2017). Brain correlates of hypnosis: A systematic review and meta-analytic exploration. *Neuroscience & Biobehavioral Reviews, 81,* 75–98.

Langlois, J. H., Ritter, J. M., Casey, R. J., & Sawin, D. B. (1995). Infant attractiveness predicts maternal behaviors and attitudes. *Developmental Psychology, 31,* 464–472.

LaPierre, S., Boyer, R., Desjardins, S., Dubé, M., Lorrain, D., Préville, M., & Brassard, J. (2012). Daily hassles, physical illness, and sleep problems in older adults with wishes to die. *International Psychogeriatrics, 24,* 243–252.

Larsen, S. F. (1992). Potential flashbulbs: Memories of ordinary news as baseline. In E. Winograd & U. Neisser (Eds.), *Affect and accuracy in recall: Studies of "flashbulb memories"* (pp. 32–64). Cambridge University Press.

Larson, R., & Richards, M. H. (1991). Daily companionship in late childhood and early adolescence—changing developmental contexts. *Child Development, 62,* 284–300.

Lattal, K. A. (2010). Delayed reinforcement of operant behavior. *Journal of the Experimental Analysis of Behavior, 93,* 129–139.

Lavie, P. (2001). Sleep–wake as a biological rhythm. *Annual Review of Psychology, 52,* 277–303.

Lawrence, N. S., Jollant, F., O'Daly, O., Zelaya, F., & Phillips, M. L. (2009). Distinct roles of prefrontal cortical subregions in the Iowa Gambling Task. *Cerebral Cortex, 19,* 1134–1143.

Lazarus, R. S. (1984). On the primacy of cognition. *American Psychologist, 39,* 124–129.

Lazarus, R. S., & Folkman, S. (1984). *Stress, appraisal, and coping.* Springer.

Le, B., & Agnew, C. R. (2003). Commitment and its theorized determinants: A meta-analysis of the Investment Model. *Personal Relationships, 10*(1), 37–57. https://doi.org/10.1111/1475-6811.00035

Leader, T., Mullen, B., & Abrams, D. (2007). Without mercy: The immediate impact of group size on lynch mob atrocity. *Personality and Social Psychology Bulletin, 33*(10), 1340–1352.

Leary, M. R. (1990). Responses to social exclusion: Social anxiety, jealousy, loneliness, depression, and low self-esteem. *Journal of Social and Clinical Psychology, 9,* 221–229.

Leary, M. R. (2010). Affiliation, acceptance, and belonging: The pursuit of interpersonal connection. In S. T. Fiske, D. T. Gilbert, & G. Lindzey (Eds.), *The handbook of social psychology* (5th ed., Vol. 2, pp. 864–897). Wiley.

Leary, M. R., & Baumeister, R. F. (2000). The nature and function of self-esteem: Sociometer theory. In M. P. Zanna (Ed.), *Advances in experimental social psychology* (Vol. 32, pp. 1–62). Academic Press.

Lecky, P. (1945). *Self-consistency: A theory of personality.* Island Press.

Lecrubier, Y., Clerc, G., Didi, R., & Kieser, M. (2002). Efficacy of St. John's wort extract WS 5570 in major depression: A double-blind, placebo-controlled trial. *American Journal of Psychiatry, 159,* 1361–1366.

Lederbogen, F., Kirsch, P., Haddad, L., Streit, F., Tost, H., Schuch, P., Wüst, S., Pruessner, J. C., Rietschel, M., Deuschle, M., & Meyer-Lindenberg, A. (2011). City living and urban upbringing affect neural social stress processing in humans. *Nature, 474,* 498–501.

Lederman, S. J., & Klatzky, R. L. (2009). Haptic perception: A tutorial. *Attention, Perception, & Psychophysics, 71,* 1439–1459.

LeDoux, J. E. (1992). Brain mechanisms of emotion and emotional learning. *Current Opinion in Neurobiology, 2,* 191–197.

LeDoux, J. E., Iwata, J., Cicchetti, P., & Reis, D. J. (1988). Different projections of the central amygdaloid nucleus mediate autonomic and behavioral correlates of conditioned fear. *Journal of Neuroscience, 8,* 2517–2529.

Lee, D. N., & Aronson, E. (1974). Visual proprioceptive control of standing in human infants. *Perception & Psychophysics, 15,* 529–532.

Lefcourt, H. M. (1982). *Locus of control: Current trends in theory and research* (2nd ed.). Erlbaum.

Lemay, E. P. (2016). The forecast model of relationship commitment. *Journal of Personality and Social Psychology, 111*(1), 34–52. https://doi.org/10.1037/pspi0000052

Lenton, A. P., & Francesconi, M. (2010). How humans cognitively manage an abundance of mate options. *Psychological Science, 21*(4), 528–533. https://doi.org/10.1177/0956797610364958

Lentz, M. J., Landis, C. A., Rothermel, J., & Shaver, J. L. (1999). Effects of selective slow wave sleep disruption on musculoskeletal pain and fatigue in middle-aged women. *Journal of Rheumatology, 26,* 1586–1592.

Leon, D. A., Lawlor, D. A., Clark, H., Batty, G. D., & Macintyre, S. (2009). The association of childhood intelligence with mortality risk from adolescence to middle age: Findings from the Aberdeen children of the 1950s cohort study. *Intelligence, 37*(6), 520–528.

Lepage, M., Ghaffar, O., Nyberg, L., & Tulving, E. (2000). Prefrontal cortex and episodic memory retrieval mode. *Proceedings of the National Academy of Sciences, USA, 97,* 506–511.

Lepper, M. R., Greene, D., & Nisbett, R. E. (1973). Undermining children's intrinsic interest with extrinsic rewards: A test of the "overjustification" hypothesis. *Journal of Personality and Social Psychology, 28,* 129–137.

Lerman, D. (2006). Consumer politeness and complaining behavior. *Journal of Services Marketing, 20,* 92–100.

Lerman, D. C., & Vorndran, C. M. (2002). On the status of knowledge for using punishment: Implications for treating behavior disorders. *Journal of Applied Behavior Analysis, 35,* 4312–4464.

Levenson, J. M., & Sweatt, J. D. (2005). Epigenetic mechanisms in memory formation. *Nature Reviews Neuroscience, 6,* 108–118.

Levenson, R. W., Cartensen, L. L., Friesen, W. V., & Ekman, P. (1991). Emotion, physiology, and expression in old age. *Psychology and Aging, 6,* 28–35.

Levenson, R. W., Ekman, P., & Friesen, W. V. (1990). Voluntary facial action generates emotion-specific autonomic nervous system activity. *Psychophysiology, 27,* 363–384.

Levenson, R. W., Ekman, P., Heider, K., & Friesen, W. V. (1992). Emotion and automatic nervous system activity in the Minangkabau of West Sumatra. *Journal of Personality and Social Psychology, 62,* 972–988.

Levin, R., & Nielsen, T. (2009). Nightmares, bad dreams, and emotion dysregulation: A review and new neurocognitive model of dreaming. *Current Directions in Psychological Science, 18,* 84–88.

Levine, L. J., Lench, H. C., Karnaze, M. M., & Carlson, S. J. (2018). Bias in predicted and remembered emotion. *Current Opinion in Behavioral Sciences, 19,* 73–77.

Levine, R. V., & Norenzayan, A. (1999). The pace of life in 31 countries. *Journal of Cross-Cultural Psychology, 30*(2), 178–205.

Lewin, K. (1948). *Resolving social conflicts; selected papers on group dynamics.* (G. W. Lewin, Ed.). Harper & Row.

Lewin, K. (1951). Behavior and development as a function of the total situation. In K. Lewin (Ed.), *Field theory in social science: Selected theoretical papers* (pp. 791–843). Harper & Row.

Lewin, K., Lippitt, R., & White, R. K. (1939). Patterns of aggressive behavior in experimentally created social climates. *Journal of Social Psychology, 10,* 271–299.

Lewis, M., & Brooks-Gunn, J. (1979). *Social cognition and the acquisition of self.* Plenum Press.

Lewis, M. B. (2012). Exploring the positive and negative implications of facial feedback. *Emotion, 12*(4), 852–859.

Lewis, M. D., Hibbeln, J. R., Johnson, J. E., Lin, Y. H., Hyun, D. Y., & Loewke, J. D. (2011). Suicide deaths of active-duty U.S. military and omega-3 fatty acid status: A case control comparison. *Journal of Clinical Psychiatry, 72,* 1585–1590.

Li, G., Kung, K. F., & Hines, M. (2017). Childhood gender-typed behavior and adolescent sexual orientation: A longitudinal population-based study. *Developmental Psychology, 53*(4), 764–777. https://doi.org/10.1037/dev0000281

Li, N. P., van Vugt, M., & Colarelli, S. M. (2018). The evolutionary mismatch hypothesis: Implications for psychological science. *Current Directions in Psychological Science, 27*(1). https://doi.org/10.1177/0963721417731378

Li, Y. J., Johnson, K. A., Cohen, A. B., Williams, M. J., Knowles, E. D., & Chen, Z. (2012). Fundamental(ist) attribution error: Protestants are dispositionally focused. *Journal of Personality and Social Psychology, 102*(2), 281–290. https://doi.org/10.1037/a0026294

Liberman, Z., Woodward, A. L., & Kinzler, K. D. (2017). The origins of social categorization. *Trends in Cognitive Sciences, 21*(7), 556–568. https://doi.org/10.1016/j.tics.2017.04.004

Libet, B. (1985). Unconscious cerebral initiative and the role of conscious will in voluntary action. *Behavioral and Brain Sciences, 8,* 529–566.

Lieberman, M. D., Inagaki, T. K., Tabibnia, G., & Crockett, M. J. (2011). Subjective responses to emotional stimuli during labeling, reappraisal, and distraction. *Emotion, 11,* 468–480.

Lieberman, M. D., & Rosenthal, R. (2001). Why introverts can't always tell who likes them: Multitasking and nonverbal decoding. *Journal of Personality and Social Psychology, 80,* 294–310.

Lilienfeld, S. O. (2007). Psychological treatments that cause harm. *Perspectives on Psychological Science, 2,* 53–70.

Lilienfeld, S. O., Lynn, S. J., & Lohr, J. M. (Eds.). (2003). *Science and pseudoscience in clinical psychology.* Guilford Press.

Lindenberger, U., & Baltes, P. B. (1994). Sensory functioning and intelligence in old age: A strong connection. *Psychology and Aging, 9*(3), 339–355. https://doi.org/10.1037/0882-7974.9.3.339

Lindquist, K., Wager, T., Kober, H., Bliss-Moreau, E., & Barrett, L. (2012). The brain basis of emotion: A meta-analytic review. *Behavioral and Brain Sciences, 35*(3), 121–143. https://doi.org/10.1017/S0140525X11000446

Lindquist, S. I., & McLean, J. P. (2011). Daydreaming and its correlates in an educational environment. *Learning and Individual Differences, 21,* 158–167.

Liou, A. P., Paziuk, M., Luevano, J.-M., Machineni, S., Turnbaugh, P. J., & Kaplan, L. M. (2013). Conserved shifts in the gut microbiota due to gastric bypass reduce host weight and adiposity. *Science Translational Medicine, 5*(178), 178ra41.

Liszkowski, U., Carpenter, M., Striano, T., & Tomasello, M. (2006). 12- and 18-month-olds point to provide information for others. *Journal of Cognition and Development, 7*(2), 173–187. https://doi.org/10.1207/s15327647jcd0702_2

Liu, D., Diorio, J., Tannenbaum, B., Caldji, C., Francis, D., Freedman, A., Sharma, S., Pearson, D., Plotsky, P. M., & Meaney, M. J. (1997). Maternal care, hippocampal glucocorticoid receptors, and hypothalamic-pituitary–adrenal responses to stress. *Science, 277,* 1659–1662.

Liu, D., Wellman, H. M., Tardif, T., & Sabbagh, M. A. (2008). Theory of mind development in Chinese children: A meta-analysis of false belief understanding across cultures and languages. *Developmental Psychology, 44,* 523–531.

Livingstone, M., & Hubel, D. (1988). Segregation of form, color, movement, and depth: Anatomy, physiology, and perception. *Science, 240,* 740–749.

Locke, J. (1690). *Essay on human understanding.* Pennsylvania State University, *Electronic Classics Series.* Pennsylvania State University.

Locksley, A., Ortiz, V., & Hepburn, C. (1980). Social categorization and discriminatory behavior: Extinguishing the minimal intergroup discrimination effect. *Journal of Personality and Social Psychology, 39,* 773–783.

Loehlin, J. C. (1973). Blood group genes and Negro–White ability differences. *Behavior Genetics, 3*(3), 263–270.

Loftus, E. F. (1993). The reality of repressed memories. *American Psychologist, 48,* 518–537.

Loftus, E. F. (2003). Make-believe memories. *American Psychologist, 58,* 867–873.

Loftus, E. F., & Ketchum, K. (1994). *The myth of repressed memory.* St. Martin's Press.

Loftus, E. F., & Pickrell, J. E. (1995). The formation of false memories. *Psychiatric Annals, 25,* 720–725.

Long. P. (2017, May 30). My déjà vu is so extreme I can't tell what's real any more. https://mosaicscience.com/story/my-deja-vu-so-extreme-i-cant-tell-whats-real-any-more/

Lopes, P. N., Grewal, D., Kadis, J., Gall, M., & Salovey, P. (2006). Emotional intelligence and positive work outcomes. *Psichothema, 18,* 132.

Lorenz, K. (1952). *King Solomon's ring.* Crowell.

Lozano, B. E., & Johnson, S. L. (2001). Can personality traits predict increases in manic and depressive symptoms? *Journal of Affective Disorders, 63,* 103–111.

Lubinski, D. (2016). From Terman to today: A century of findings on intellectual precocity. *Review of Educational Research, 86*(4), 900–944. https://doi.org/10.3102/0034654316675476

Luborsky, L., Rosenthal, R., Diguer, L., Andrusyna, T. P., Berman, J. S., Levitt, J. T., Seligman, D. A., & Krause, E. D. (2002). The dodo bird verdict is alive and well—mostly. *Clinical Psychology: Science and Practice, 9,* 2–12.

Lucas, R. E., Clark, A. E., Georgellis, Y., & Diener, E. (2003). Reexamining adaptation and the set point model of happiness: Reactions to changes in marital status. *Journal of Personality and Social Psychology, 84,* 527–539.

Lucas, R. E., & Dyrenforth, P. S. (2005). The myth of marital bliss? *Psychological Inquiry, 16*(2/3), 111–115.

Ludwig, A. M. (1966). Altered states of consciousness. *Archives of General Psychiatry, 15,* 225–234.

Lurquin, J. H., Michaelson, L. E., Barker, J. E, Gustavson, D. E., von Bastian, C. C., Carruth, N. P., & Miyake, A. (2016). No evidence of the ego-depletion effect across task characteristics and individual differences: A pre-registered study. *PLoS ONE, 11*(2), e0147770.

Lyden, J., & Binswanger, I. A. (2019). The United States opioid epidemic. *Seminars in Perinatology.* https://doi.org/doi.10.1053/j.semperi.2019.01.001

Lynn, M., & Shurgot, B. A. (1984). Responses to lonely hearts advertisements: Effects of reported physical attractiveness, physique, and coloration. *Personality and Social Psychology Bulletin, 10,* 349–357.

Lynn, R. (2009). What has caused the Flynn effect? Secular increases in the development quotients of infants. *Intelligence, 37*(1), 16–24.

Lynn, R. (2013). Who discovered the Flynn effect? A review of early studies of the secular increase of intelligence. *Intelligence, 41*(6), 765–769. https://doi.org/10.1016/j.intell.2013.03.008

Lyons, D. E., Young, A. G., & Keil, F. C. (2007). The hidden structure of overimitation. *Proceedings of the National Academy of Sciences, 104*(50), 19751–19756. https://doi.org/10.1073/pnas.0704452104.

Lythcott-Haims, J. (2015). *How to raise an adult.* Henry Holt.

Lyubomirsky, S. (2008). *The how of happiness: A scientific approach to getting the life you want.* Penguin.

MacDonald, S., Uesiliana, K., & Hayne, H. (2000). Cross-cultural and gender differences in childhood amnesia. *Memory, 8,* 365–376.

Mackey, A. P., Hill, S. S., Stone, S. I., & Bunge, S. A. (2011). Differential effects of reasoning and speed training in children. *Developmental Science, 14,* 582–590. https://doi.org/10.1111/j.1467-7687.2010.01005x

MacLeod, M. D. (2002). Retrieval-induced forgetting in eyewitness memory: Forgetting as a consequence of remembering. *Applied Cognitive Psychology, 16,* 135–149.

MacLeod, M. D., & Saunders, J. (2008). Retrieval inhibition and memory distortion: Negative consequences of an adaptive process. *Current Directions in Psychological Science, 17,* 26–30.

Macmillan, M. (2000). *An odd kind of fame: Stories of Phineas Gage.* MIT Press.

Macmillan, N. A., & Creelman, C. D. (2005). *Detection theory.* Erlbaum.

Macrae, C. N., Bodenhausen, G. V., Milne, A. B., & Jetten, J. (1994). Out of mind but back in sight: Stereotypes on the rebound. *Journal of Personality and Social Psychology, 67,* 808–817.

Maddi, S. R., Harvey, R. H., Khoshaba, D. M., Fazel, M., & Resurreccion, N. (2009). Hardiness training facilitates performance in college. *Journal of Positive Psychology, 4,* 566–577.

Maddi, S. R., Kahn, S., & Maddi, K. L. (1998). The effectiveness of hardiness training. *Consulting Psychology Journal: Practice and Research, 50,* 78–86.

Madigan, S., Atkinson, L., Laurin, K., & Benoit, D. (2013). Attachment and internalizing behavior in early childhood: A meta-analysis. *Developmental Psychology, 49*(4), 672–689. https://doi.org/10.1037/a0028793

Madore, K. P., Addis, D., & Schacter, D. L. (2015). Creativity and memory: Effects of an episodic specificity induction on divergent thinking. *Psychological Science, 26,* 1461–1468.

Madore, K. P., Thakral, P. P., Beaty, R. E., Addis, D. R., & Schacter, D. L. (2019). Neural mechanisms of episodic retrieval support divergent creative thinking. *Cerebral Cortex, 29,* 150–166.

Maes, M. (1995). Evidence for an immune response in major depression: A review and hypothesis. *Progress in Neuro-Psychopharmacology and Biological Psychiatry, 19,* 11–38.

Maguire, E. A., Woollett, K., & Spiers, H. J. (2006). London taxi drivers and bus drivers: A structural MRI and neuropsychological analysis. *Hippocampus, 16,* 1091–1101.

Mahon, B. Z., Anzellotti, S., Schwarzbach, J., Zampini, M., & Caramazza, A. (2009). Category-specific organization in the human brain does not require visual experience. *Neuron, 63,* 397–405.

Mahon, B. Z., & Caramazza, A. (2009). Concepts and categories: A cognitive neuropsychological perspective. *Cognitive Neuropsychology, 60,* 27–51.

Maier, S. F., & Watkins, L. R. (1998). Cytokines for psychologists: Implications of bidirectional immune-to-brain communication for understanding behavior, mood, and cognition. *Psychological Review, 105,* 83–107.

Maier, S. F., & Watkins, L. R. (2000). The immune system as a sensory system: Implications for psychology. *Current Directions in Psychological Science, 9,* 98–102.

Major, B., Mendes, W. B., & Dovidio, J. F. (2013). Intergroup relations and health disparities: A social psychological perspective. *Health Psychology, 32,* 514–524.

Makel, M. C., Kell, H. J., Lubinski, D., Putallaz, M., & Benbow, C. P. (2016). When lightning strikes twice: Profoundly gifted, profoundly accomplished. *Psychological Science, 27*(7), 1004–1018. https://doi.org /10.1177/0956797616644735

Makin, J. E., Fried, P. A., & Watkinson, B. (1991). A comparison of active and passive smoking during pregnancy: Long-term effects. *Neurotoxicology and Teratology, 16,* 5–12.

Makris, N., Biederman, J., Monuteaux, M. C., & Seidman, L. J. (2009). Towards conceptualizing a neural systems-based anatomy of attention-deficit/hyperactivity disorder. *Developmental Neuroscience, 31,* 36–49.

Malina, R. M., Bouchard, C., & Beunen, G. (1988). Human growth: Selected aspects of current research on well-nourished children. *Annual Review of Anthropology, 17,* 187–219.

Malooly, A. M., Genet, J. J., & Siemer, M. (2013). Individual differences in reappraisal effectiveness: The role of affective flexibility. *Emotion, 13*(2), 302–313. https://doi.org/10.1037/a0029980

Mampe, B., Friederici, A. D., Christophe, A., & Wermke, K. (2009). Newborns' cry melody is shaped by their native language. *Current Biology, 19,* 1–4.

Mandler, G. (1967). Organization and memory. In K. W. Spence & J. T. Spence (Eds.), *The psychology of learning and motivation* (Vol. 1, pp. 327–372). Academic Press.

Mandy, W., & Lai, M. C. (2016). The role of the environment in the developmental psychopathology of autism spectrum condition. *Journal of Child Psychology and Psychiatry, 57,* 271–292.

Mankiw, N. G., & Weinzierl, M. (2010). The optimal taxation of height: A case study of utilitarian income redistribution. *American Economic Journal: Economic Policy, 2,* 155–176.

Mann, J. J. (2005). The medical management of depression. *New England Journal of Medicine, 353,* 1819–1834.

Mann, J. J., Apter, A., Bertolote, J., Beautrais, A., Currier, D., Haas, A., Hegerl, U., Lohnqvist, J., Malone, K., Marusic, A., Mehlum, L., Patton, G., Phillips, M., Rutz, W., Rihmer, Z., Schmidtke, A., Shaffer, D., Silverman, M., Takahashi, Y., . . . Hendin, H. (2005). Suicide prevention strategies: A systematic review. *Journal of the American Medical Association, 294*(16), 2064–2074. https://doi.org/10.1001/jama.294.16.2064

Marangell, L. B., Silver, J. M., Goff, D. M., & Yudofsky, S. C. (2003). Psychopharmacology and electroconvulsive therapy. In R. E. Hales & S. C. Yudofsky (Eds.), *The American Psychiatric Publishing textbook of clinical psychiatry* (4th ed., pp. 1047–1149). American Psychiatric Publishing.

Marcia, J. E. (1966). Development and validation of ego-identity status. *Journal of Personality and Social Psychology, 3,* 551–558. http://dx.doi .org/10.1037/h0023281

Marcia, J. E. (1993). The ego identity status approach to ego identity. In J. E. Marcia, A. S. Waterman, D. R. Matteson, S. L. Archer, & J. L. Orlofsky (Eds.), *Ego identity: A handbook for psychosocial research* (pp. 3–21). Springer.

Marcus, G. (2012, December 3). Neuroscience fiction. *New Yorker.* http: //www.newyorker.com/news/news-desk/neuroscience-fiction

Margoni, F., & Surian, L. (2018). Infants' evaluation of prosocial and antisocial agents: A meta-analysis. *Developmental Psychology, 54,* 1445–1455.

Markel, H. (2011). *An anatomy of addiction: Sigmund Freud, William Halsted, and the miracle drug cocaine.* Pantheon.

Markus, H. (1977). Self-schemata and processing information about the self. *Journal of Personality and Social Psychology, 35,* 63–78.

Marlatt, G. A., & Rohsenow, D. (1980). Cognitive processes in alcohol use: Expectancy and the balanced placebo design. In N. K. Mello (Ed.), *Advances in substance abuse: Behavioral and biological research* (pp. 159–199). Greenwich, CT: JAI Press.

Marsh, A. A., Rhoads, S. A., & Ryan, R. M. (2018). A multi-semester classroom demonstration yields evidence in support of the facial feedback effect. *Emotion.* https://doi.org/10.1037/emo0000532

Martin, A. (2007). The representation of object concepts in the brain. *Annual Review of Psychology, 58,* 25–45.

Martin, A., & Caramazza, A. (2003). Neuropsychological and neuroimaging perspectives on conceptual knowledge: An introduction. *Cognitive Neuropsychology, 20,* 195–212.

Martin, A., & Chao, L. L. (2001). Semantic memory and the brain: Structure and processes. *Current Opinion in Neurobiology, 11,* 194–201.

Martin, D. (2018). Use the behavioral tips to "science" your clients on savings. *Journal of Financial Planning, 31,* 20–21.

Martin, J., Rychlowska, M., Wood, A., & Niedenthal, P. (2017). Smiles as multipurpose social signals. *Trends in Cognitive Sciences, 21*(11), 864–877. https://doi.org/10.1016/j.tics.2017.08.007

Martin, M. J., Blozis, S. A., Boeninger, D. K., Masarik, A. S., & Conger, R. D. (2014). The timing of entry into adult roles and changes in trajectories of problem behaviors during the transition to adulthood. *Developmental Psychology, 50*(11), 2473–2484. https://doi.org/10.1037/a0037950

Martins, D., Mehta, M. A., & Prata, D. (2017). The "highs and lows" of the human brain on dopaminergics: Evidence from neuropharmacology. *Neuroscience and Biobehavioral Reviews, 80,* 351–371.

Martins, S. S., Sampson, L., Cerda, M., & Galea, S. (2015). Worldwide prevalence and trends in unintentional drug overdose: A systematic review of the literature. *American Journal of Public Health, 105,* E29–E49.

Marucha, P. T., Kiecolt-Glaser, J. K., & Favagehi, M. (1998). Mucosal wound healing is impaired by examination stress. *Psychosomatic Medicine, 60,* 362–365.

Marufu, T. C., Ahankari, A., Coleman, T., & Lewis, S. (2015). Maternal smoking and the risk of stillbirth: Systematic review and meta-analysis. *BMC Public Health, 15*(1), 239. https://doi.org/10.1186/s12889-015-1552-5

Marzuk, P. M., Tardiff, K., Leon, A. C., Hirsch, C., Portera, L., Iqbal, M. I., Nock, M. K., & Hartwell, N. (1998). Ambient temperature and mortality from unintentional cocaine overdose. *Journal of the American Medical Association, 279,* 1795–1800.

Maslach, C. (2003). Job burnout: New directions in research and intervention. *Current Directions in Psychological Science, 12,* 189–192.

Maslow, A. (1943). A theory of human motivation. *Psychological Review, 50,* 370–396.

Maslow, A. H. (1937). Dominance-feeling, behavior, and status. In R. J. Lowry (Ed.), *Dominance, self-esteem, self-actualization: Germinal papers by A. H. Maslow* (pp. 49–70). Brooks-Cole.

Maslow, A. H. (1954). *Motivation and personality.* Harper & Row.

Mason, M. F., Norton, M. I., Van Horn, J. D., Wegner, D. M., Grafton, S. T., & Macrae, C. N. (2007). Wandering minds: The default network and stimulus-independent thought. *Science, 3154,* 393–395.

Masten, A. S. (2004). Family therapy as a treatment for children: A critical review of outcome research. *Family Process, 18,* 323–335.

Masuda, T., & Nisbett, R. E. (2001). Attending holistically vs. analytically: Comparing the context sensitivity of Japanese and Americans. *Journal of Personality and Social Psychology, 81,* 922–934.

Mather, M., & Carstensen, L. L. (2003). Aging and attentional biases for emotional faces. *Psychological Science, 14,* 409–415.

Mather, M., & Carstensen, L. L. (2005). Aging and motivated cognition: The positivity effect in attention and memory. *Trends in Cognitive Sciences, 9*(10), 496–502.

Matsumoto, D., & Willingham, B. (2009). Spontaneous facial expressions of emotion of congenitally and noncongenitally blind individuals. *Journal of Personality and Social Psychology, 96,* 1–10.

Mattar, A. A. G., & Gribble, P. L. (2005). Motor learning by observing. *Neuron, 46,* 153–160.

Matthews, G., & Gilliland, K. (1999). The personality theories of H. J. Eysenck and J. A. Gray: A comparative review. *Personality and Individual Differences, 26,* 583–626.

Mauss, I. B., Levenson, R. W., McCarter, L., Wilhelm, F. H., & Gross, J. J. (2005). The tie that binds? Coherence among emotion experience, behavior, and physiology. *Emotion, 5*(2), 175–190. https://doi.org/10.1037/1528-3542.5.2.175

Mauss, I. B., & Robinson, M. D. (2009). Measures of emotion: A review. *Cognition and Emotion, 23,* 209–237.

Max, A. (2006, September 16). Dutch reach new heights. *USA Today.* http://usatoday30.usatoday.com/news/offbeat/2006-09-16-dutch-tall_x.htm

May, R. (1983). *The discovery of being: Writings in existential psychology.* Norton.

Mayberg, H., Lozano, A., Voon, V., McNeely, H., Seminowicz, D., Hamani, C., Schwalb, J. M., & Kennedy, S. H. (2005). Deep brain stimulation for treatment-resistant depression. *Neuron, 45,* 651–660.

Mayer, J. D., Caruso, D. R., & Salovey, P. (1999). Emotional intelligence meets traditional standards for an intelligence. *Intelligence, 27,* 267.

Mayer, J. D., Roberts, R. D., & Barsade, S. G. (2008). Human abilities: Emotional intelligence. *Annual Review of Psychology, 59,* 507–536.

Mayr, E. (1942). *Systematics and the origin of species, from the viewpoint of a zoologist.* Columbia University Press.

Mazure, C. M., & Swendsen, J. (2016). Sex differences in Alzheimer's disease and other dementias. *Lancet Neurology, 15,* 451–452.

McAdams, D. (1993). *The stories we live by: Personal myths and the making of the self.* Morrow.

McClelland, D. C., Atkinson, J. W., Clark, R. A., & Lowell, E. L. (1953). *The achievement motive.* Appleton-Century-Crofts.

McDaniel, M. A., Thomas, R. C., Agarwal, P. K., McDermott, K. B., & Roediger, H. L. (2013). Quizzing in middle-school science: Successful transfer performance on classroom exams. *Applied Cognitive Psychology, 27,* 360–372.

McDermott, K. B., Agarwal, P. K., D'Antonio, L., Roediger, H. L., & McDaniel, M. A. (2014). Both multiple-choice and short-answer quizzes enhance later exam performance in middle and high school classes. *Journal of Experimental Psychology: Applied, 20,* 3–21.

McElwain, N. L., Booth-LaForce, C., & Wu, X. (2011). Infant–mother attachment and children's friendship quality: Maternal mental state talk as an intervening mechanism. *Developmental Psychology, 47*(5), 1295–1311. https://doi.org/10.1037/a0024094

McEvoy, S. P., Stevenson, M. R., McCartt, A. T., Woodward, M., Haworth, C., Palamara, P., & Circarelli, R. (2005). Role of mobile phones in motor vehicle crashes resulting in hospital attendance: A case-crossover study. *British Medical Journal, 331,* 428–430.

McFarlane, A. H., Norman, G. R., Streiner, D. L., Roy, R., & Scott, D. J. (1980). A longitudinal study of the influence of the psychosocial environment on health status: A preliminary report. *Journal of Health and Social Behavior, 21,* 124–133.

McGarty, C., & Turner, J. C. (1992). The effects of categorization on social judgement. *British Journal of Social Psychology, 31,* 253–268.

McGaugh, J. L. (2000). Memory: A century of consolidation. *Science, 287,* 248–251.

McGaugh, J. L. (2006). Make mild moments memorable: Add a little arousal. *Trends in Cognitive Sciences, 10,* 345–347.

McGaugh, J. L. (2015). Consolidating memories. *Annual Review of Psychology, 66,* 1–24.

McGovern, P. E., Zhang, J., Tang, J., Zhang, Z., Hall, G. R., Moreau, R. A., Nuñez, A., Butrym, E. D., Richards, M. P., Wang, C.-s., Cheng, G., Zhao, Z., & Wang, C. (2004). Fermented beverages of pre- and proto-historic China. *Proceedings of the National Academy of Sciences of the United States of America, 101,* 17593–17598.

McGowan, P. O., Sasaki, A., D'Alessio, A. C., Dymov, S., Labonté, B., Szyf, M., Turecki, G., & Meaney, M. J. (2009). Epigenetic regulation of the glucocorticoid receptor in human brain associates with childhood abuse. *Nature Neuroscience, 12,* 342–348.

McGrath, J., Saha, S., Chant, D., & Welham, J. (2008). Schizophrenia: A concise overview of incidence, prevalence, and mortality. *Epidemiologic Reviews, 30,* 67–76.

McGue, M., & Bouchard, T. J. (1998). Genetic and environmental influences on human behavioral differences. *Annual Review of Neuroscience, 21,* 1–24.

McIntyre, S. H., & Munson, J. M. (2008). Exploring cramming: Student behaviors, beliefs, and learning retention in the Principles of Marketing course. *Journal of Marketing Education, 30,* 226–243.

McKee, A. C., Cantu, R. C., Nowinski, C. J., Hedley-Whyte, E. T., Gavett, B. E., Budson, A. E., Santini, V. E., Lee, H.-S., Kubilus, C. A., & Stern, R. A. (2009). Chronic traumatic encephalopathy in athletes: Progressive tauopathy after repetitive head injury. *Journal of Neuropathology and Experimental Neurology, 68,* 709–735.

McKetin, R., Ward, P. B., Catts, S. V., Mattick, R. P., & Bell, J. R. (1999). Changes in auditory selective attention and event-related potentials following oral administration of D-amphetamine in humans. *Neuropsychopharmacology, 21,* 380–390.

McLaughlin, K. A., Nandi, A., Keyes, K. M., Uddin, M., Aiello, A. E., Galea, S., & Koenen, K. C. (2012). Home foreclosure and risk of psychiatric morbidity during the recent financial crisis. *Psychological Medicine, 42,* 1441–1448.

McLean, K. C. (2008). The emergence of narrative identity. *Social and Personality Psychology Compass, 2*(4), 1685–1702.

McNally, R. J. (2003). *Remembering trauma.* Belknap Press of Harvard University Press.

McNally, R. J., & Geraerts, E. (2009). A new solution to the recovered memory debate. *Perspective on Psychological Science, 4,* 126–134.

McNally, R. J., & Steketee, G. S. (1985). Etiology and maintenance of severe animal phobias. *Behavioral Research and Therapy, 23,* 431–435.

Meade, M. L., Harris, C. B., Van Bergen, P., Sutton, J., & Barnier, A. J. (Eds.). (2018). *Collaborative remembering: Theories, research and applications.* Oxford University Press.

Meaidi, A., Jennum, P., Ptito, M., & Kupers, R. (2014). The sensory construction of dreams and nightmare frequency in congenitally blind and late blind individuals. *Sleep Medicine, 15,* 586–595.

Means, B., Toyama, Y., Murphy, R., Bakia, M., & Jones, K. (2010). *Evaluation of evidence based practices in online learning: Meta-analysis and review of online learning studies.* U.S. Department of Education. https://www2.ed.gov/rschstat/eval/tech/evidence-based-practices/finalreport.pdf

Mechelli, A., Crinion, J. T., Noppeney, U., O'Doherty, J., Ashburner, J., Frackowiak, R. S., & Price, C. J. (2004). Neurolinguistics: Structural plasticity in the bilingual brain. *Nature, 431,* 757.

Meder, D., Herz, D. M., Rowe, J. B., Lehéricy, S., & Siebner, H. R. (2018). The role of dopamine in the brain—lessons learned from Parkinson's disease. *NeuroImage.* https://doi.org/10.1016/j.neuroimage.2018.11.021

Medin, D. L., & Schaffer, M. M. (1978). Context theory of classification learning. *Psychological Review, 85,* 207–238.

Medvec, V. H., Madey, S. F., & Gilovich, T. (1995). When less is more: Counterfactual thinking and satisfaction among Olympic medalists. *Journal of Personality and Social Psychology, 69,* 603–610.

Mehl, M. R., Vazire, S., Ramirez-Esparza, N., Slatcher, R. B., & Pennebaker, J. W. (2007). Are women really more talkative than men? *Science, 317,* 82.

Mehu, M., & Scherer, K. R. (2015). Emotion categories and dimensions in the facial communication of affect: An integrated approach. *Emotion, 15*(6), 798–811. https://doi.org/10.1037/a0039416

Mellon, R. C. (2009). Superstitious perception: Response-independent reinforcement and punishment as determinants of recurring eccentric interpretations. *Behaviour Research and Therapy, 47,* 868–875.

Meltzer, H. Y. (2013). Update on typical and atypical antipsychotic drugs. *Annual Review of Medicine, 64,* 393–406.

Meltzoff, A. N. (1995). Understanding the intentions of others: Reenactment of intended acts by 18-month-old children. *Developmental Psychology, 31,* 838–850.

Meltzoff, A. N. (2007). "Like me": A foundation for social cognition. *Developmental Science, 10*(1), 126–134. https://doi.org/10.1111/j.1467-7687 .2007.00574x

Meltzoff, A. N., Kuhl, P. K., Movellan, J., & Sejnowski, T. J. (2009). Foundations for a new science of learning. *Science, 325,* 284–288.

Melzack, R., & Wall, P. D. (1965). Pain mechanisms: A new theory. *Science, 150,* 971–979.

Mendle, J., Ryan, R. M., & McKone, K. M. P. (2018). Age at menarche, depression, and antisocial behavior in adulthood. *Pediatrics, 141*(1), e20171703.

Mendle, J., Turkheimer, E., & Emery, R. E. (2007). Detrimental psychological outcomes associated with early pubertal timing in adolescent girls. *Developmental Review, 27,* 151–171.

Mervis, C. B., & Bertrand, J. (1994). Acquisition of the Novel Name– Nameless Category (N3C) principle. *Child Development, 65,* 1646–1662. https://doi.org/10.2307/1131285

Merzenich, M. M., Recanzone, G. H., Jenkins, W. M., & Grajski, K. A. (1990). Adaptive mechanisms in cortical networks underlying cortical contributions to learning and nondeclarative memory. *Cold Spring Harbor Symposia on Quantitative Biology, 55,* 873–887.

Mesoudi, A., Chang, L., Dall, S. R. X., & Thornton, A. (2015). The evolution of individual and cultural variation in social learning. *Trends in Ecology & Evolution, 31,* 215–225.

Meston, C. M., & Buss, D. M. (2007). Why humans have sex. *Archives of Sexual Behavior, 36,* 477–507.

Mestre, J. M., Guil, R., Lopes, P. N., Salovey, P., & Gil-Olarte, P. (2006). Emotional intelligence and social and academic adaptation to school. *Psicothema, 18,* 112.

Metcalfe, J. (2009). Metacognitive judgments and control of study. *Current Directions in Psychological Science, 18,* 159–163.

Metcalfe, J., & Finn, B. (2008). Evidence that judgments of learning are causally related to study choice. *Psychonomic Bulletin & Review, 15,* 174–179.

Methven, L., Allen, V. J., Withers, G. A., & Gosney, M. A. (2012). Ageing and taste. *Proceedings of the Nutrition Society, 71,* 556–565.

Meuret, A. E., Kroll, J., & Ritz, T. (2017). Panic disorder comorbidity with medical conditions and treatment implications. *Annual Review of Clinical Psychology, 13,* 209–240.

Meyer-Bahlberg, H. F. L., Ehrhardt, A. A., Rosen, L. R., & Gruen, R. S. (1995). Prenatal estrogens and the development of homosexual orientation. *Developmental Psychology, 31,* 12–21.

Mez, J., Daneshvar, D. H., Kiernan, P. T., Abdolmohammadi, B., Alvarez, V. E., Huber, B. R., Alosco, M. L., Solomon, T. M., Nowinski, C. J., McHale, L., Cormier, K. A., Kubilus, C. A., Martin, B. M., Murphy, L., Baugh, C. M., Montenigro, P. H., Chaisson, C. E., Tripodis, Y., Kowall, N. W., . . . McKee, A. C. (2017). Clinicopathological evaluation of chronic traumatic encephalopathy in players of American football. *Journal of the American Medical Association, 318,* 360–370.

Michaela, R., Florian, S., Gert, G. W., & Ulman, L. (2009). Seeking pleasure and seeking pain: Differences in prohedonic and contrahedonic motivation from adolescence to old age. *Psychological Science, 20*(12), 1529–1535.

Miklowitz, D. J., & Johnson, S. L. (2006). The psychopathology and treatment of bipolar disorder. *Annual Review of Clinical Psychology, 2,* 199–235.

Mikolajczak, M., Avalosse, H., Vancorenland, S., Verniest, R., Callens, M., van Broeck, N., Fantini-Hauwel, C., & Mierop, A. (2015). A nationally representative study of emotional competence and health. *Emotion, 15*(5), 653–667. https://doi.org/10.1037/emo0000034

Milad, M. R., & Rauch, S. L. (2012). Obsessive-compulsive disorder: Beyond segregated cortico-striatal pathways. *Trends in Cognitive Sciences, 16,* 43–51.

Milgram, S. (1963). Behavioral study of obedience. *Journal of Abnormal and Social Psychology, 67,* 371–378.

Milgram, S., Bickman, L., & Berkowitz, O. (1969). Note on the drawing power of crowds of different size. *Journal of Personality and Social Psychology, 13,* 79–82.

Miller, D. T., & Prentice, D. A. (1996). The construction of social norms and standards. In E. T. Higgins & A. W. Kruglanski (Ed.), *Social psychology: Handbook of basic principles* (pp. 799–829). Guilford Press.

Miller, D. T., & Prentice, D. A. (2016). Changing norms to change behavior. *Annual Review of Psychology, 67*(1), 339–361.

Miller, D. T., & Ratner, R. K. (1998). The disparity between the actual and assumed power of self-interest. *Journal of Personality and Social Psychology, 74,* 53–62.

Miller, D. T., & Ross, M. (1975). Self-serving biases in the attribution of causality: Fact or fiction? *Psychological Bulletin, 82,* 213–225.

Miller, G. A. (1956). The magical number seven, plus or minus two: Some limits on our capacity for processing information. *Psychological Review, 63,* 81–96.

Miller, M. L. Alfaro-Almagro, F., Bangerter, N. K., Thomas, D. L., Yacoub, E., Xu, J., Bartsch, A. J., Jbabdi, S., Sotiropoulos, S. N., Andersson, J. L. R., Griffanti, L., Douaud, G., Okell, T. W., Weale, P., Dragonu, I., Garratt, S. Hudson, S., Collins, R., Jenkinson, M., . . . Smith, S. M. (2016). Multimodal population brain imaging in the UK Biobank prospective epidemiological study. *Nature Neuroscience, 19,* 1523–1536.

Miller, N. E. (1960). Motivational effects of brain stimulation and drugs. *Federation Proceedings, 19,* 846–854.

Miller, T. W. (Ed.). (1996). *Theory and assessment of stressful life events.* Madison, CT: International Universities Press.

Miller, W. R., & Rollnick, S. (2012). *Motivational interviewing: Helping people change* (3rd ed.). Guilford Press.

Milne, E., & Grafman, J. (2001). Ventromedial prefrontal cortex lesions in humans eliminate implicit gender stereotyping. *Journal of Neuroscience, 21,* 1–6.

Milner, A. D., & Goodale, M. A. (1995). *The visual brain in action.* Oxford University Press.

Milner, B. (1962). Laterality effects in audition. In V. B. Mountcastle (Ed.), *Interhemispheric relations and cerebral dominance* (pp. 177–195). Johns Hopkins University Press.

Milyavsky, M., Webber, D., Fernandez, J. R., Kruglanski, A. W., Goldenberg, A., Suri, G., & Gross, J. J. (2018). To reappraise or not to reappraise? Emotion regulation choice and cognitive energetics. *Emotion.* https://doi .org/10.1037/emo0000498

Minsky, M. (1986). *The society of mind.* Simon & Schuster.

Minson, J. A., & Mueller, J. S. (2012). The cost of collaboration: Why joint decision making exacerbates rejection of outside information. *Psychological Science, 23*(3), 219–224. https://doi.org/10.1177/0956797611429132

Miranda, J., Bernal, G., Lau, A., Kihn, L., Hwang, W. C., & LaFramboise, T. (2005). State of the science on psychological interventions for ethnic minorities. *Annual Review of Clinical Psychology, 1,* 113–142.

Mischel, W. (1968). *Personality and assessment.* Wiley.

Mischel, W. (2004). Toward an integrative science of the person. *Annual Review of Psychology, 55,* 1–22.

Mischel, W., Ayduk, O., Baumeister, R. F., & Vohs, K. D. (2004). Willpower in a cognitive-affective processing system: The dynamics of delay of gratification. In *Handbook of self-regulation: Research, theory, and applications* (pp. 99–129). Guilford Press.

Mischel, W., & Shoda, Y. (1999). Integrating dispositions and processing dynamics within a unified theory of personality: The cognitive-affective personality system. In L. A. Pervin & O. P. John (Eds.), *Handbook of personality: Theory and research* (pp. 197–218). Guilford Press.

Mischel, W., Shoda, Y., & Rodriguez, M. L. (1989). Delay of gratification in children. *Science, 244,* 933–938.

Mishra, A., Mishra, H., & , T. M. (2012). The influence of bite size on quantity of food consumed: A field study. *Journal of Consumer Research, 38*(5), 791–795. http://dx.doi.org/10.1086/660838

Mita, T. H., Dermer, M., & Knight, J. (1977). Reversed facial images and the mere-exposure hypothesis. *Journal of Personality and Social Psychology, 35,* 597–601.

Mitchell, K. J., & Johnson, M. K. (2009). Source monitoring 15 years later: What have we learned from fMRI about the neural mechanisms of source memory? *Psychological Bulletin, 135,* 638–677.

Mitchell, J. P. (2006). Mentalizing and Marr: An information processing approach to the study of social cognition. *Brain Research, 1079,* 66–75.

Miyamoto, Y., Ma, X., & Petermann, A. G. (2014). Cultural differences in hedonic emotion regulation after a negative event. *Emotion, 14*(4), 804–815. https://doi.org/10.1037/a0036257

Mojtabai, R., Olfson, M., Sampson, N. A., Jin, R., Druss, B., Wang, P. S., Wells, K. B., Pincus, H. A., & Kessler, R. C. (2011). Barriers to mental health treatment: Results from the National Comorbidity Survey replication. *Psychological Medicine, 41*(8), 1751–1761.

Mokdad, A. H., Ford, E. S., Bowman, B. A., Dietz, W. H., Vinicor, F., Bales, V. S., & Marks, J. S. (2003). Prevalence of obesity, diabetes, and obesity-related health risk factors, 2001. *Journal of the American Medical Association, 289*(1), 76–79. https://doi.org/10.1001/jama.289.1.76

Molden, D., Lee, A. Y., & Higgins, E. T. (2009). Motivations for promotion and prevention. In J. Shah & W. Gardner (Eds.), *Handbook of motivation science* (pp. 169–187). Guilford Press.

Molloy, L. E., Gest, S. D., Feinberg, M. E., & Osgood, D. W. (2014). Emergence of mixed-sex friendship groups during adolescence: Developmental associations with substance use and delinquency. *Developmental Psychology, 50*(11), 2449–2461. https://doi.org/10.1037/a0037856

Monahan, J. (1992). Mental disorder and violent behavior: Perceptions and evidence. *American Psychologist, 47*, 511–521.

Monahan, J. L., Murphy, S. T., & Zajonc, R. B. (2000). Subliminal mere exposure: Specific, general, and diffuse effects. *Psychological Science, 11*, 462–466.

Moncrieff, J. (2009). A critique of the dopamine hypothesis of schizophrenia and psychosis. *Harvard Review of Psychiatry, 17*, 214–225.

Montag, C., Błaszkiewicz, K., Sariyska, R., Lachman, B., Andone, I., Trendafilov, B., Eibes, M., & Markowetz, A. (2015). Smartphone usage in the 21st century: Who is active on WhatsApp? *BMC Research Notes, 81*(1), 331.

Montague, C. T., Farooqi, I. S., Whitehead, J. P., Soos, M. A., Rau, H., Wareham, N. J., Sewter, C. P., Digby, J. E., Mohammed, S. N., Hurst, J. A., Cheetham, C. H., Earley, A. R., Barnett, A. H., Prins, J. B., & O'Rahilly, S. (1997). Congenital leptin deficiency is associated with severe early-onset obesity in humans. *Nature, 387*(6636), 903–908.

Montenigro, P. H., Corp, D. T., Stein, T. D., Cantu, R. C., & Stern, R. A. (2015). Chronic traumatic encephalopathy: Historical origins and current perspective. *Annual Review of Clinical Psychology, 11*, 309–330.

Montoya, R. M., & Horton, R. S. (2013). A meta-analytic investigation of the processes underlying the similarity-attraction effect. *Journal of Social and Personal Relationships, 30*(1), 64–94. https://doi. org/10.1177/0265407512452989

Mook, D. G. (1983). In defense of external invalidity. *American Psychologist, 38*, 379–387.

Moon, S. M., & Illingworth, A. J. (2005). Exploring the dynamic nature of procrastination: A latent growth curve analysis of academic procrastination. *Personality and Individual Differences, 38*, 297–309.

Moore, E. G. J. (1986). Family socialization and the IQ test performance of traditionally and transracially adopted Black children. *Developmental Psychology, 22*, 317–326.

Morin, A. (2006). Levels of consciousness and self-awareness: A comparison of various neurocognitive views. *Consciousness & Cognition, 15*, 358–371.

Morris, C. D., Bransford, J. D., & Franks, J. J. (1977). Levels of processing versus transfer-appropriate processing. *Journal of Verbal Learning and Verbal Behavior, 16*, 519–533.

Morris, R. G., Anderson, E., Lynch, G. S., & Baudry, M. (1986). Selective impairment of learning and blockade of long-term potentiation by an N-methyl-D-aspartate receptor antagonist, AP5. *Nature, 319*, 774–776.

Morrow, D., Leirer, V., Altiteri, P., & Fitzsimmons, C. (1994). When expertise reduces age differences in performance. *Psychology and Aging, 9*, 134–148.

Moscovitch, M. (1994). Memory and working-with-memory: Evaluation of a component process model and comparisons with other models. In D. L. Schacter & E. Tulving (Eds.), *Memory systems 1994* (pp. 269–310). MIT Press.

Moscovitch, M., Cabeza, R., Winocur, G., & Nadel, L. (2016). Episodic memory and beyond: The hippocampus and cortex in transformation. *Annual Review of Psychology, 67*, 105–134.

Moscovitch, M., Nadel, L., Winocur, G., Gilboa, A., & Rosenbaum, R. S. (2006). The cognitive neuroscience of remote episodic, semantic and spatial memory. *Current Opinion in Neurobiology, 16*, 179–190.

Moskowitz, D. (2013). Dunkin' brands versus Starbucks: Numbers don't lie. Retrieved from The Motley Fool website: https://www.fool.com/investing/general/2013/12/10/dunkin-brands-vs-starbucks-numbers-dont-lie.aspx

Moulton, E., Barton, M., Robins, D. L., Abrams, D. N., & Fein, D. (2016). Early characteristics of children with ASD who demonstrate optimal progress between age two and four. *Journal of Autism and Developmental Disorders, 46*, 2160–2173.

Moura, A. C. A. de, & Lee, P. C. (2004). Capuchin stone tool use in Caatinga dry forest. *Science, 306*, 1909.

Mroczek, D. K., & Spiro, A. (2005). Change in life satisfaction during adulthood: Findings from the Veterans Affairs Normative Aging Study. *Journal of Personality and Social Psychology, 88*, 189.

Muehlenkamp, J. J., Claes, L., Havertape, L., & Plener, P. L. (2012). International prevalence of adolescent non-suicidal self-injury and deliberate self-harm. *Child and Adolescent Psychiatry and Mental Health, 6*(10). https://doi.org/10.1156/1753-2000-6-10

Mueller, T. E., Gavin, L. E., & Kulkarni, A. (2008). The association between sex education and youth's engagement in sexual intercourse, age at first intercourse, and birth control use at first sex. *Journal of Adolescent Health, 42*(1), 89–96.

Mueller, T. I., Leon, A. C., Keller, M. B., Solomon, D. A., Endicott, J., Coryell, W., Warshaw, M., & Maser, J. D. (1999). Recurrence after recovery from major depressive disorder during 15 years of observational follow-up. *American Journal of Psychiatry, 156*, 1000–1006.

Muenter, M. D., & Tyce, G. M. (1971). L-dopa therapy of Parkinson's disease: Plasma L-dopa concentration, therapeutic response, and side effects. *Mayo Clinic Proceedings, 46*, 231–239.

Mullen, M. K. (1994). Earliest recollections of childhood: A demographic analysis. *Cognition, 52*, 55–79.

Müller, K., & Schwarz, C. (2018). Fanning the flames of hate: Social media and hate crimes. http://dx.doi.org/10.2139/ssrn.3082972

Murayama, K., Miyatsu, T., Buchli, D., & Storm, B. C. (2014). Forgetting as a consequence of retrieval: A meta-analytic review of retrieval-induced forgetting. *Psychological Bulletin, 140*, 1383–1409.

Murphy, S. L., Xu, J., Kochanek, K. D., & Arias, E. (2018). Mortality in the United States, 2017. *National Center for Health Statistics Data Brief, No. 328*. National Center for Health Statistics.

Murray, C. (2002). *IQ and income inequality in a sample of sibling pairs from advantaged family backgrounds*. Paper presented at the 114th Annual Meeting of the American Economic Association.

Murray, H. A. (1943). *Thematic Apperception Test manual*. Harvard University Press.

Murray, H. A., & Kluckhohn, C. (1953). Outline of a conception of personality. In C. Kluckhohn, H. A. Murray, & D. M. Schneider (Eds.), *Personality in nature, society, and culture* (2nd ed., pp. 3–52). Knopf.

Myers, D. G., & Lamm, H. (1975). The polarizing effect of group discussion. *American Scientist, 63*(3), 297–303.

Myles, P. S., Leslie, K., McNeil, J., Forbes, A., & Chan, M. T. V. (2004). Bispectral index monitoring to prevent awareness during anaesthesia: The B-Aware randomized controlled trial. *Lancet, 363*, 1757–1763.

Nadasdy, A. (1995). Phonetics, phonology, and applied linguistics. *Annual Review of Applied Linguistics, 15*, 68–77.

Nader, K., & Hardt, O. (2009). A single standard for memory: The case of reconsolidation. *Nature Reviews Neuroscience, 10*, 224–234.

Nader, K., Shafe, G., & LeDoux, J. E. (2000). Fear memories require protein synthesis in the amygdala for reconsolidation after retrieval. *Nature, 406*, 722–726.

Nagasako, E. M., Oaklander, A. L., & Dworkin, R. H. (2003). Congenital insensitivity to pain: An update. *Pain, 101*, 213–219.

Nagell, K., Olguin, R. S., & Tomasello, M. (1993). Processes of social learning in the tool use of chimpanzees (*Pan troglodytes*) and human children (*Homo sapiens*). *Journal of Comparative Psychology, 107,* 174–186.

Nairne, J. S., Thompson, S. R., & Pandeirada, J. N. S. (2007). Adaptive memory: Survival processing enhances retention. *Journal of Experimental Psychology: Learning, Memory, and Cognition, 33,* 263–273.

Nakazato, M., Murakami, N., Date, Y., Kojima, M., Matsuo, H., Kangawa, K., & Matsukura, S. (2001). A role for ghrelin in the central regulation of feeding. *Nature, 409,* 194–198.

Naqvi, N., Shiv, B., & Bechara, A. (2006). The role of emotion in decision making: A cognitive neuroscience perspective. *Current Directions in Psychological Science, 15,* 260–264.

Nassi, J. J., & Callaway, E. M. (2009). Parallel processing strategies of the primate visual system. *Nature Reviews Neuroscience, 10,* 360–372.

Nathan, P. E., & Gorman, J. M. (2007). *A guide to treatments that work* (3rd ed.). Oxford University Press.

National Academies of Science, Engineering, and Medicine. (2019). Reproducibility and replicability in science. National Academies Press. https://doi.org/10.17226/25303

National Center for Health Statistics. (2012). *Health, United States, 2011* (with special feature on socioeconomic status and health). Hyattsville, MD: Author.

National Center for Health Statistics. (2016). Health of Black or African American non-Hispanic population. Atlanta: Centers for Disease Control and Prevention. http://www.cdc.gov/nchs/fastats/black-health.htm

National Highway Traffic Safety Administration. (2018). Traffic safety facts: Alcohol-impaired driving. US Department of Transportation (DOT HS 812 630).

National Science Foundation, National Center for Science and Engineering Statistics. (2018). Doctorate recipients from U.S. universities: 2017. *Special Report NSF 19-301.* Available at https://ncses.nsf.gov/pubs/nsf19301/

Nave, G., Jung, W. H., Linnér, R. K., Kable, J. W., & Koellinger, P. D. (2019). Are bigger brains smarter? Evidence from a large-scale pre-registered study. *Psychological Science, 30,* 43–54.

Neimark, J. (2004, July/August). The power of coincidence. *Psychology Today,* pp. 47–52.

Neisser, U. (Ed.). (1998). *The rising curve: Long-term gains in IQ and related measures.* American Psychological Association.

Neisser, U., Boodoo, G., Bouchard, T. J., Jr., Boykin, A. W., Brody, N., Ceci, S. J., Halpern, D. F., Loehlin, J. C., Perloff, R., Sternberg, R. J., & Urbina, S. (1996). Intelligence: Knowns and unknowns. *American Psychologist, 51,* 77–101.

Neisser, U., & Harsch, N. (1992). Phantom flashbulbs: False recollections of hearing the news about Challenger. In E. Winograd & U. Neisser (Eds.), *Affect and accuracy in recall: Studies of "flashbulb memories"* (pp. 9–31). Cambridge University Press.

Nelson, A. B., & Kreitzer, A. C. (2015). Reassessing models of basal ganglia function and dysfunction. *Annual Review of Neuroscience, 37,* 117–135.

Nelson, C. A., Zeanah, C. H., Fox, N. A., Marshall, P. J., Smyke, A. T., & Guthrie, D. (2007). Cognitive recovery in socially deprived young children: The Bucharest early intervention project. *Science, 318,* 1937–1940.

Nemeth, C., & Chiles, C. (1988). Modelling courage: The role of dissent in fostering independence. *European Journal of Social Psychology, 18,* 275–280.

Nes, L. S., & Sergerstrom, S. C. (2006). Dispositional optimism and coping: A meta-analytic review. *Personality and Social Psychology Review, 10,* 235–251.

Neugebauer, R., Hoek, H. W., & Susser, E. (1999). Prenatal exposure to wartime famine and development of antisocial personality in early adulthood. *Journal of the American Medical Association, 282,* 455–462.

Newbold, R. R., Padilla-Banks, E., Snyder, R. J., & Jefferson, W. N. (2005). Developmental exposure to estrogenic compounds and obesity. *Birth Defects Research Part A: Clinical and Molecular Teratology, 73,* 478–480.

Newman, A. J., Bavelier, D., Corina, D., Jezzard, P., & Neville, H. J. (2002). A critical period for right hemisphere recruitment in American Sign Language processing. *Nature Neuroscience, 5,* 76–80.

Newman, J. P., Wolff, W. T., & Hearst, E. (1980). The feature-positive effect in adult human subjects. *Journal of Experimental Psychology: Human Learning and Memory, 6,* 630–650.

Newman, M. G., & Stone, A. A. (1996). Does humor moderate the effects of experimentally induced stress? *Annals of Behavioral Medicine, 18,* 101–109.

Newschaffer, C. J., Croen, L. A., Daniels, J., Giarelli, E., Grether, J. K., Levy, S. E., Mandell, D. S., Miller, L. A., Pinto-Martin, J., Reaven, J., Reynolds, A. M., Rice, C. E., Schendel, D., & Windham, G. C. (2007). The epidemiology of autism spectrum disorders. *Annual Review of Public Health, 28,* 235–258.

Newsome, W. T., & Paré, E. B. (1988). A selective impairment of motion perception following lesions of the middle temporal visual area (MT). *Journal of Neuroscience, 8,* 2201–2211.

Ng, M., Fleming, T., Robinson, M., Thomson, B., Graetz, N., Margono, C., Mullany, E. C., Biryukov, S., Abbafati, C., Abera, S. F., Abraham, J. P., Abu-Rmeileh, N. M. E., Achoki, T., AlBuhairan, F. S., Alemu, Z. A., Alfonso, R., Ali, M. K., Ali, R., Guzman, N. A., . . . Gakidou, E. (2014). Global, regional, and national prevalence of overweight and obesity in children and adults during 1980–2013: A systematic analysis for the Global Burden of Disease Study 2013. *Lancet, 384,* 766–781. https://doi.org/10.1016/S0140-6736(14)60460-8

Niaura, R., Todaro, J. F., Stroud, L., Spiro, A., III, Ward, K. D., & Weiss, S. (2002). Hostility, the metabolic syndrome, and incident coronary heart disease. *Health Psychology, 21,* 588–593.

Niedenthal, P. M., Barsalou, L. W., Winkielman, P., Krauth-Gruber, S., & Ric, F. (2005). Embodiment in attitudes, social perception, and emotion. *Personality and Social Psychology Review, 9*(3), 184–211.

Nikles, C. D., II, Brecht, D. L., Klinger, E., & Bursell, A. L. (1998). The effects of current concern- and nonconcern-related waking suggestions on nocturnal dream content. *Journal of Personality and Social Psychology, 75,* 242–255.

Nir, Y., & Tononi, G. (2010). Dreaming and the brain: From phenomenology to neurophysiology. *Trends in Cognitive Sciences, 14*(2), 88–100.

Nisbett, R. E. (2009). *Intelligence and how to get it.* Norton.

Nisbett, R. E., Aronson, J., Blair, C., Dickens, W., Flynn, J., Halpern, D. F., & Turkheimer, E. (2012). Intelligence: New findings and theoretical developments. *American Psychologist, 67*(2), 130–159. https://doi.org/10.1037/a0026699

Nisbett, R. E., Caputo, C., Legant, P., & Maracek, J. (1973). Behavior as seen by the actor and as seen by the observer. *Journal of Personality and Social Psychology, 27,* 154–164.

Nisbett, R. E., & Cohen, D. (1996). *Culture of honor: The psychology of violence in the South.* Westview Press.

Nissen, M. J., & Bullemer, P. (1987). Attentional requirements of learning: Evidence from performance measures. *Cognitive Psychology, 19,* 1–32.

Noah, T., Schul, Y., & Mayo, R. (2018). When both the original study and its failed replication are correct: Feeling observed eliminates the facial-feedback effect. *Journal of Personality and Social Psychology, 114*(5), 657–664. https://doi.org/10.1037/pspa0000121

Nobes, G., Panagiotaki, G., & Engelhardt, P. E. (2017). The development of intention-based morality: The influence of intention salience and recency, negligence, and outcome on children's and adults' judgments. *Developmental Psychology, 53*(10), 1895–1911. https://doi.org/10.1037/dev0000380

Nock, M. K. (2009). Why do people hurt themselves? New insights into the nature and functions of self-injury. *Current Directions in Psychological Science, 18,* 78–83. https://doi.org/10.1111/j.1467-8721.2009.01613.x

Nock, M. K. (2010). Self-injury. *Annual Review of Clinical Psychology, 6,* 339–363. https://doi.org/10.1146/annurev.clinpsy.121208.131258

Nock, M. K., Borges, G., Bromet, E. J., Alonso, J., Angermeyer, M., Beautrais, A., Bruffaerts, R., Chiu, W. T., de Girolamo, G., Gluzman, S., de Graaf, R., Gureje, O., Haro, J. M., Huang, Y., Karam, E., Kessler, R. C., Lepine, J. P., Levinson, D., Medina-Mora, M. E., . . . Williams, D. (2008). Cross-national prevalence and risk factors for suicidal ideation, plans, and attempts. *British Journal of Psychiatry, 192,* 98–105.

Nock, M. K., Borges, G., & Ono, Y. (Eds.). (2012). *Suicide: Global perspectives from the WHO World Mental Health Surveys.* Cambridge University Press.

Nock, M. K., Green, J. G., Hwang, I., McLaughlin, K. A., Sampson, N. A., Zaslavsky, A. M., & Kessler, R. C. (2013). Prevalence, correlates and treatment of lifetime suicidal behavior among adolescents: Results from the National Comorbidity Survey Replication–Adolescent Supplement (NCSA-A). *Journal of the American Medical Association Psychiatry, 70*(3), 300–310. https://doi.org/10.1001/2013.jamapsychiatry.55

Nock, M. K., Kazdin, A. E., Hiripi, E., & Kessler, R. C. (2006). Prevalence, subtypes, and correlates of *DSM-IV* conduct disorder in the National Comorbidity Survey Replication. *Psychological Medicine, 36,* 699–710.

Nolen-Hoeksema, S. (2012). Emotion regulation and psychopathology: The role of gender. *Annual Review of Clinical Psychology,* 161–187.

Norby, S. (2015). Why forget? On the adaptive value of memory loss. *Perspectives on Psychological Science, 10,* 551–578.

Norcross, J. C., & Rogan, J. D. (2013). Psychologists conducting psychotherapy in 2012: Current practices and historical trends among Division 29 members. *Psychotherapy, 50,* 490–495.

Nosanchuk, T. A., & Lightstone, J. (1974). Canned laughter and public and private conformity. *Journal of Personality and Social Psychology, 29,* 153–156.

Nosofsky, R. M., Sanders, C., & McDaniel, M. (2018). A formal psychological model of classification applied to natural-science category learning. *Current Directions in Psychological Science, 27,* 129–135.

Nowak, M. A. (2006). Five rules for the evolution of cooperation. *Science, 314,* 1560–1563.

Nyborg, H., & Jensen, A. R. (2001). Occupation and income related to psychometric *g. Intelligence, 29,* 45–55.

Ochsner, K. N., Bunge, S. A., Gross, J. J., & Gabrieli, J. D. E. (2002). Rethinking feelings: An fMRI study of the cognitive regulation of emotion. *Journal of Cognitive Neuroscience, 14,* 1215–1229.

O'Connor, T. G., & Rutter, M. (2000). Attachment disorder following early severe deprivation: Extension and longitudinal follow-up. *Journal of the American Academy of Child and Adolescent Psychiatry, 39,* 703–712.

Ofshe, R. J. (1992). Inadvertent hypnosis during interrogation: False confession due to dissociative state, misidentified multiple personality, and the satanic cult hypothesis. *International Journal of Clinical and Experimental Hypnosis, 40,* 125–126.

Ohayon, M. M. (2002). Epidemiology of insomnia: What we know and what we still need to learn. *Sleep Medicine, 6,* 97–111.

Ohayon, M. M., Guilleminault, C., & Priest, R. G. (1999). Night terrors, sleepwalking, and confusional arousals in the general population: Their frequency and relationship to other sleep and mental disorders. *Journal of Clinical Psychiatry, 60,* 268–276.

Okdie, B. M., Ewoldsen, D. R., Muscanell, N. L., Guadagno, R. E., Eno, C. A., Velez, J. A., Dunn, R. A., O'Mally, J., & Smith, L. R. (2014). Missed programs (you can't TiVo this one): Why psychologists should study media. *Perspectives on Psychological Science, 9*(2), 180–195. https://doi.org/10.1177/1745691614521243

Okuda, J., Fujii, T., Ohtake, H., Tsukiura, T., Tanji, K., Suzuki, K., Kawashima, R., Fukuda, H., Itoh, M., & Yamadori, A. (2003). Thinking of the future and the past: The roles of the frontal pole and the medial temporal lobes. *NeuroImage, 19,* 1369–1380.

Olausson, P. O., Haglund, B., Weitoft, G. R., & Cnattingius, S. (2001). Teenage child-bearing and long-term socioeconomic consequences: A case study in Sweden. *Family Planning Perspectives, 33,* 70–74.

Olds, J. (1956, October). Pleasure center in the brain. *Scientific American, 195,* 105–116.

Ollers, D. K., & Eilers, R. E. (1988). The role of audition in infant babbling. *Child Development, 59,* 441–449.

Olsson, A., Kopsida, E., Sorjonen, K., & Savic, I. (2016). Testosterone and estrogen impact social evaluations and vicarious emotions: A double-blind placebo-controlled study. *Emotion, 16,* 515–523.

Olsson, A., & Phelps, E. A. (2007). Social learning of fear. *Nature Neuroscience, 10,* 1095–1102.

Oltmanns, T. F., Neale, J. M., & Davison, G. C. (1991). *Case studies in abnormal psychology* (3rd ed.). Wiley.

Olton, D. S., & Samuelson, R. J. (1976). Remembrance of places passed: Spatial memory in rats. *Journal of Experimental Psychology: Animal Behavior Processes, 2,* 97–116.

Ono, K. (1987). Superstitious behavior in humans. *Journal of the Experimental Analysis of Behavior, 47,* 261–271.

Open Science Collaboration, Nosek, B. A., Aarts, A. A., Anderson, J. E., & Kappes, H. B. (2015). Estimating the reproducibility of psychological science. *Science, 349* (6251), aac4716. https://doi.org/10.1126/science.aac4716

Orban, P., Lungu, O., & Doyon, J. (2008). Motor sequence learning and developmental dyslexia. *Annals of the New York Academy of Sciences, 1145,* 151–172.

Otto, M. W., Henin, A., Hirshfeld-Becker, D. R., Pollack, M. H., Biederman, J., & Rosenbaum, J. F. (2007). Posttraumatic stress disorder symptoms following media exposure to tragic events: Impact of 9/11 on children at risk for anxiety disorders. *Journal of Anxiety Disorders, 21,* 888–902.

Oudiette, D. & Paller, K. A. (2013). Upgrading the sleeping brain with targeted memory reactivation. *Trends in Cognitive Sciences, 17,* 142–149.

Owens, W. A. (1966). Age and mental abilities: A second adult followup. *Journal of Educational Psychology, 57,* 311–325.

Oztekin, I., Curtis, C. E., & McElree, B. (2009). The medial temporal lobe and left inferior prefrontal cortex jointly support interference resolution in verbal working memory. *Journal of Cognitive Neuroscience, 21,* 1967–1979.

Pagnin, D., de Queiroz, V., Pini, S., & Cassano, G. B. (2008). Efficacy of ECT in depression: A meta-analytic review. *Focus, 6,* 155–162.

Paivio, A. (1971). *Imagery and verbal processes.* Holt, Rinehart and Winston.

Paivio, A. (1986). *Mental representations: A dual coding approach.* Oxford University Press.

Palombo, D. J., Alain, C., Soderlund, H., Khuu, W., & Levine, B. (2015). Severely deficient autobiographical memory (SDAM) in healthy adults: A new mnemonic syndrome. *Neuropsychologia, 72,* 105–118.

Palombo, D. J., Bacopulos, A., Amaral, R. S. C., Olsen, R. K., Todd, R. M., Anderson, A. K., & Levine, B. (2018). Episodic autobiographical memory is associated with variation in the size of hippocampal subregions. *Hippocampus, 28,* 69–75.

Paluck, B. L., & Green, D. P. (2009). Prejudice reduction: What works? A review and assessment of research and practice. *Annual Review of Psychology, 60,* 339–367.

Pan, S. C., & Rickard, T. C. (2018). Transfer of test-enhanced learning: Meta-analytic review and synthesis. *Psychological Bulletin, 144,* 710–756.

Pandit, J. J., Andrade, J., Bogod, D. G., Hitchman, J. M., Jonker, W. R., Lucas, N., Mackay, J. H., Nimmo, A. F., O'Connor, K., O'Sullivan, E. P., Paul, R. G., Palmer, J. H. M., Plaat, F., Radcliffe, J. J., Sury, M. R. J., Torevell, H. E.,Wang, M., Hainsworth, J., Cook, T. M., & Royal College of Anaesthetists and the Association of Anaesthetists of Great Britain and Ireland. (2014). The 5th National Audit Project (NAP5) on accidental awareness during general anaesthesia: Summary of main findings and risk factors. *Anaesthesia, 69,* 1089–1101.

Pang, W., Esping, A., & Plucker, J. A. (2017). Confucian conceptions of human intelligence. *Review of General Psychology, 21*(2), 161–169. https://doi-org.ezp-prod1.hul.harvard.edu/10.1037/gpr0000103

Park, B., & Hastie, R. (1987). Perception of variability in category development: Instance- versus abstraction-based stereotypes. *Journal of Personality and Social Psychology, 53*(4), 621–635. https://doi.org/10.1037/0022-3514.53.4.621

Park, D. C., & McDonough, I. M. (2013). The dynamic aging mind: Revelations from functional neuroimaging research. *Perspectives on Psychological Science, 8*(1), 62–67. https://doi.org/10.1177/1745691612469034

Parker, E. S., Cahill, L. S., & McGaugh, J. L. (2006). A case of unusual autobiographical remembering. *Neurocase, 12,* 35–49.

Parker, G., Gibson, N. A., Brotchie, H., Heruc, G., Rees, A. M., & Hadzi-Pavlovic, D. (2006). Omega-3 fatty acids and mood disorders. *American Journal of Psychiatry, 163,* 969–978.

Parker, H. A., & McNally, R. J. (2008). Repressive coping, emotional adjustment, and cognition in people who have lost loved ones to suicide. *Suicide and Life-Threatening Behavior, 38,* 676–687.

Parkinson, B., & Totterdell, P. (1999). Classifying affect-regulation strategies. *Cognition and Emotion, 13,* 277–303.

Parkinson, C., Walker, T. T., Memmi, S., & Wheatley, T. (2017). Emotions are understood from biological motion across remote cultures. *Emotion, 17*(3), 459–477. https://doi.org/10.1037/emo0000194

Parrott, A. C. (2001). Human psychopharmacology of Ecstasy (MDMA): A review of 15 years of empirical research. *Human Psychopharmacology, 16,* 557–577.

Parrott, A. C., Morinan, A., Moss, M., & Scholey, A. (2005). *Understanding drugs and behavior.* Chichester, UK: Wiley.

Parsons, T. (1975). The sick role and the role of the physician reconsidered. *Milbank Memorial Fund Quarterly, Health and Society, 53*(3), 257–278.

Pascual-Ferrá, P., Liu, Y., & Beatty, M. J. (2012). A meta-analytic comparison of the effects of text messaging to substance-induced impairment on driving performance. *Communication Research Reports, 29,* 229–238.

Pascual-Leone, A., Amedi, A., Fregni, F., & Merabet, L. B. (2005). The plastic human brain cortex. *Annual Review of Neuroscience, 28,* 377–401.

Pascual-Leone, A., Houser, C. M., Reese, K., Shotland, L. I., Grafman, J., Sato, S., Valls-Solé, J., Brasil-Neto, J. P., Wassermann, E. M., Cohen, L. G., & Hallett, M. (1993). Safety of rapid-rate transcranial magnetic stimulation in normal volunteers. *Electroencephalography and Clinical Neurophysiology, 89,* 120–130.

Patall, E. A., Cooper, H., & Robinson, J. C. (2008). The effects of choice on intrinsic motivation and related outcomes: A meta-analysis of research findings. *Psychological Bulletin, 134*(2), 270–300.

Patterson, C. J. (2013). Sexual orientation and family lives. In G. W. Peterson & K. R. Bush (Eds.), *The handbook of marriage and the family.* Springer.

Patton, G. C., & Viner, R. (2007). Pubertal transitions in health. *Lancet, 369,* 1130–1139.

Paulozzi, L. J., Mack, K. A., & Hockenberry, J. M. (2014). Vital signs: Variation among states in prescribing of opioid pain relievers and benzodiazepines—United States, 2012. *Morbidity and Mortality Weekly Report, 63,* 563–568.

Paulus, M. (2016). It's payback time: Preschoolers selectively request resources from someone they had benefitted. *Developmental Psychology, 52*(8), 1299–1306. https://doi.org/10.1037/dev0000150

Pavlidou, E. V., Williams, J. M., & Kelly, L. M. (2009). Artificial grammar learning in primary school children with and without developmental dyslexia. *Annals of Dyslexia, 59,* 55–77.

Payne, J. D., & Kensinger, E. A. (2018). Stress, sleep, and the selective consolidation of emotional memories. *Current Opinion in Behavioral Sciences, 19,* 36–43.

Payne, J. D., Kensinger, E. A., Wamsley, E., Spreng, R. N., Alger, S., Gibler, K., Schacter, D. L., & Stickgold, R. (2015). Napping and the selective consolidation of negative aspects of scenes. *Emotion, 15,* 176–186.

Payne, J. D., Schacter, D. L., Propper, R., Huang, L., Wamsley, E., Tucker, M. A., Walker, M. P., & Stickgold, R. (2009). The role of sleep in false memory formation. *Neurobiology of Learning and Memory, 92,* 327–334.

Payne, J. D., Stickgold, R., Swanberg, K., & Kensinger, E. A. (2008). Sleep preferentially enhances memory for emotional components of scenes. *Psychological Science, 19,* 781–788.

Pearce, J. M. (1987). A model of stimulus generalization for Pavlovian conditioning. *Psychological Review, 84,* 61–73.

Pearson, J., & Kosslyn, S. M. (2015). The heterogeneity of mental representation: Ending the imagery debate. *Proceedings of the National Academy of Sciences, USA, 112,* 10089–10092.

Penfield, W., & Rasmussen, T. (1950). *The cerebral cortex of man: A clinical study of localization of function.* Macmillan.

Pennebaker, J. W. (1989). Confession, inhibition, and disease. *Advances in Experimental Social Psychology, 22,* 211–244.

Pennebaker, J. W., & Chung, C. K. (2007). Expressive writing, emotional upheavals, and health. In H. Friedman & R. Silver (Eds.), *Handbook of health psychology* (pp. 263–284). Oxford University Press.

Pennebaker, J. W., Kiecolt-Glaser, J. K., & Glaser, R. (1988). Disclosure of traumas and immune function: Health implications for psychotherapy. *Journal of Consulting and Clinical Psychology, 56,* 239–245.

Pennebaker, J. W., & Sanders, D. Y. (1976). American graffiti: Effects of authority and reactance arousal. *Personality and Social Psychology Bulletin, 2,* 264–267.

Penner, L. A., Albrecht, T. L., Orom, H., Coleman, D. K., & Underwood, W. (2010). Health and health care disparities. In J. F. Dovidio, M. Hewstone, P. Glick, & V. M. Esses (Eds.), *The Sage handbook of prejudice, stereotyping and discrimination* (pp. 472–489). Sage.

Pepping, C. A., MacDonald, G., & Davis, P. J. (2018). Toward a psychology of singlehood: An attachment-theory perspective on long-term singlehood. *Current Directions in Psychological Science.* https://doi.org/10.1177/0963721417752106

Perenin, M.-T., & Vighetto, A. (1988). Optic ataxia: A specific disruption in visuomotor mechanisms. I. Different aspects of the deficit in reaching for objects. *Brain, 111,* 643–674.

Perera, S., Eisen, R., Bhatt, M., Bhatnagar, N., de Souza, R., & Thabane, L. (2018). Light therapy for non-seasonal depression: Systematic review and meta-analysis. *British Journal of Psychiatry, 2,* 116–126.

Perera, T., George, M. S., Grammer, G., Janicak, P. G., Pascual-Leone, A., & Wirecki, T. S. (2016). The Clinical TMS Society consensus review and treatment recommendations for TMS therapy for major depressive disorder. *Brain Stimulation, 9,* 336–346.

Perilloux, H. K., Webster, G. D., & Gaulin, S. J. C. (2010). Signals of genetic quality and maternal investment capacity: The dynamic effects of fluctuating asymmetry and waist-to-hip ratio on men's ratings of women's attractiveness. *Social Psychological and Personality Science, 1*(1), 34–42. https://doi.org/10.1177/1948550609349514

Perlmutter, J. S., & Mink, J. W. (2006). Deep brain stimulation. *Annual Review of Neuroscience, 29,* 229–257.

Perloff, L. S., & Fetzer, B. K. (1986). Self-other judgments and perceived vulnerability to victimization. *Journal of Personality and Social Psychology, 50,* 502–510.

Perrett, D. I., Burt, D. M., Penton-Voak, I. S., Lee, K. J., Rowland, D. A., & Edwards, R. (1999). Symmetry and human facial attractiveness. *Evolution and Human Behavior, 20,* 295–307.

Pessiglione, M., Seymour, B., Flandin, G., Dolan, R. J., & Frith, C. D. (2006). Dopamine-dependent prediction errors underpin reward-seeking behavior in humans. *Nature, 442,* 1042–1045.

Petersen, A. C., & Grockett, L. (1985). Pubertal timing and grade effects on adjustment. *Journal of Youth and Adolescence, 14,* 191–206.

Petersen, J. L., & Hyde, J. S. (2010). A meta-analytic review of research on gender differences in sexuality, 1993–2007. *Psychological Bulletin, 136*(1), 21–38. https://doi.org/10.1037/a0017504

Peterson, C., & Siegal, M. (1999). Representing inner worlds: Theory of mind in autistic, deaf and normal hearing children. *Psychological Science, 10,* 126–129.

Peterson, C., Slaughter, V., Moore, C., & Wellman, H. M. (2016). Peer social skills and theory of mind in children with autism, deafness, or typical development. *Developmental Psychology, 52*(1), 46–57. https://doi.org/10.1037/a0039833

Peterson, C., Wang, Q., & Hou, Y. (2009). "When I was little": Childhood recollections in Chinese and European Canadian grade school children. *Child Development, 80,* 506–518.

Peterson, L. R., & Peterson, M. J. (1959). Short-term retention of individual verbal items. *Journal of Experimental Psychology, 58,* 193–198.

Petitto, L. A., & Marentette, P. F. (1991). Babbling in the manual mode: Evidence for the ontogeny of language. *Science, 251,* 1493–1496.

Petrie, K. P., Booth, R. J., & Pennebaker, J. W. (1998). The immunological effects of thought suppression. *Journal of Personality and Social Psychology, 75,* 1264–1272.

Petry, N. M., Alessi, S. M., & Rash, C. J. (2013). Contingency management treatments decrease psychiatric symptoms. *Journal of Consulting and Clinical Psychology, 81*(5), 926–931. https://doi.org/10.1037/a0032499

Petty, R. E., & Cacioppo, J. T. (1986). The elaboration likelihood model of persuasion. In L. Berkowitz (Ed.), *Advances in experimental social psychology* (Vol. 19, pp. 123–205). Academic Press.

Petty, R. E., Cacioppo, J. T., & Goldman, R. (1981). Personal involvement as a determinant of argument-based persuasion. *Journal of Personality and Social Psychology, 41,* 847–855.

Petty, R. E., & Wegener, D. T. (1998). Attitude change: Multiple roles for persuasion variables. In D. T. Gilbert, S. T. Fiske, & G. Lindzey (Eds.), *The handbook of social psychology* (4th ed., Vol. 1, pp. 323–390). McGraw-Hill.

Phelan, J., Link, B., Stueve, A., & Pescosolido, B. (1997, August). *Public conceptions of mental illness in 1950 in 1996: Has sophistication increased? Has stigma declined?* Paper presented at the American Sociological Association, Toronto, Ontario.

Phelps, E. A. (2006). Emotion and cognition: Insights from studies of the human amygdala. *Annual Review of Psychology, 57*(1), 27–53. https://doi.org/10.1146/annurev.psych.56.091103.070234

Phelps, E. A., & LeDoux, J. E. (2005). Contributions of the amygdala to emotion processing: From animal models to human behavior. *Neuron, 48*(2), 175–187. https://doi.org/10.1016/j.neuron.2005.09.025

Phillips, F. (2002, January 24). Jump in cigarette sales tied to Sept. 11 attacks. *Boston Globe,* p. B1.

Phills, C. E., Kawakami, K., Tabi, E., Nadolny, D., & Inzlicht, M. (2011). Mind the gap: Increasing associations between the self and Blacks with approach behaviors. *Journal of Personality and Social Psychology, 100*(2), 197–210. https://doi.org/10.1037/a0022159

Piaget, J. (1954). *The child's conception of number.* Norton.

Piaget, J. (1965). *The moral judgment of the child.* Free Press. (Original work published 1932.)

Piaget, J., & Inhelder, B. (1974). *The child's construction of quantities.* Routledge and Kegan Paul Ltd.

Piazza, J. R., Charles, S. T., Sliwinski, M. J., Mogle, J., & Almeida, D. M. (2013). Affective reactivity to daily stressors and long-term risk of reporting a chronic physical health condition. *Annals of Behavioral Medicine, 45,* 110–120.

Pietschnig, J., Penke, L., Wicherts, J. M., Zeiler, M., & Voracek, M. (2015). Meta-analysis of associations between human brain volume and intelligence differences: How strong are they and what do they mean? *Neuroscience & Behavioral Reviews, 57,* 411–432.

Pietschnig, J., & Voracek, M. (2015). One century of global IQ gains: A formal meta-analysis of the Flynn effect (1909–2013). *Perspectives on Psychological Science, 10*(3), 282–306. https://doi.org/10.1177/1745691615577701

Piff, P. K., Kraus, M. W., Côté, S., Cheng, B. H., & Keltner, D. (2010). Having less, giving more: The influence of social class on prosocial behavior. *Journal of Personality and Social Psychology, 99*(5), 771–784. https://doi.org/10.1037/a0020092

Piff, P. K., Stancato, D. M., Côté, S., Mendoza-Denton, R., & Keltner, D. (2012). Higher social class predicts increased unethical behavior. *Proceedings of the National Academy of Sciences of the United States of America, USA, 109*(11), 4086–4091. https://doi.org/10.1073/pnas.1118373109

Pinel, J. P. J., Assanand, S., & Lehman, D. R. (2000). Hunger, eating, and ill health. *American Psychologist, 55,* 1105–1116.

Pines, A. M. (1993). Burnout: An existential perspective. In W. B. Schaufeli, C. Maslach, & T. Marek (Eds.), *Professional burnout: Recent developments in theory and research* (pp. 33–51). Taylor & Francis.

Pinker, S. (1994). *The language instinct.* Morrow.

Pinker, S., & Bloom, P. (1990). Natural language and natural selection. *Behavioral and Brain Sciences, 13,* 707–727.

Pitcher, D., Garrido, L., Walsh, V., & Duchaine, B. C. (2008). Transcranial magnetic stimulation disrupts the perception and embodiment of facial expressions. *Journal of Neuroscience, 28*(36), 8929–8933.

Plack, C. J. (2018a). Pitch and periodicity coding. In *The sense of hearing* (3rd ed., Chap. 7, pp. 128–148). Routledge.

Plack, C. J. (2018b). Spatial hearing. In *The sense of hearing* (3rd ed., Chap. 9, pp. 171–191). Routledge.

Plavén-Sigray, P., Hedman, E., Victorsson, P., Matheson, G. J., Forsberg, A., Djurfeldt, D. R., Rück, C., Halldin, C., Lindefors, N., & Cervenka, S. (2017). Extrastriatal dopamine D2-receptor availability in social anxiety disorder. *European Neuropsychopharmacology, 27,* 462–469.

Plomin, R., & Caspi, A. (1999). Behavioral genetics and personality. In L. A. Pervin & O. P. John (Eds.), *Handbook of personality: Theory and research* (Vol. 2, pp. 251–276). Guilford Press.

Plomin, R., DeFries, J. C., McClearn, G. E., & McGuffin, P. (2001). *Behavioral genetics* (4th ed.). W. H. Freeman.

Plotnik, J. M., de Waal, F. B. M., & Reiss, D. (2006). Self-recognition in an Asian elephant. *Proceedings of the National Academy of Sciences, USA, 103,* 17053–17057.

Polanczyk, G., de Lima, M. S., Horta, B. L., Biederman, J., & Rohde, L. A. (2007). The worldwide prevalence of ADHD: A systemic review and metaregression analysis. *American Journal of Psychiatry, 164,* 942–948.

Polderman, T. J. C., Benyamin, B., de Leeuw, C. A., Sullivan, P. F., van Bochoven, A., Visscher, P. M., & Posthuma, D. (2015). Meta-analysis of the heritability of human traits based on fifty years of twin studies. *Nature Genetics, 47*(7), 702–709. https://doi.org/10.1038/ng.3285

Poldrack, R. A. (2018). *The new mind readers: What neuroimaging can and cannot reveal about our thoughts.* Princeton University Press.

Poliak, S., & Peles, E. (2003). The local differentiation of myelinated axons at nodes of Ranvier. *Nature Reviews Neuroscience, 4,* 968–980.

Poole, D. A., Lindsay, S. D., Memon, A., & Bull, R. (1995). Psychotherapy and the recovery of memories of childhood sexual abuse: U.S. and British practitioners' opinions, practices, and experiences. *Journal of Consulting and Clinical Psychology, 63,* 426–487.

Poon, S. H., Sim, K., Sum, M. Y., Kuswanto, C. N., & Baldessarini, R. J. (2012). Evidence-based options for treatment-resistant adult bipolar disorder patients. *Bipolar Disorders, 14,* 573–584.

Pope, A. W., & Bierman, K. L. (1999). Predicting adolescent peer problems and antisocial activities: The relative roles of aggression and dysregulation. *Developmental Psychology, 35,* 335–346.

Posner, M. I., & Raichle, M. E. (1994). *Images of mind.* W. H. Freeman and Company.

Postman, L., & Underwood, B. J. (1973). Critical issues in interference theory. *Memory & Cognition, 1,* 19–40.

Postmes, T., & Spears, R. (1998). Deindividuation and anti-normative behavior: A meta-analysis. *Psychological Bulletin, 123,* 238–259.

Powell, R. A., Symbaluk, D. G., MacDonald, S. E., & Honey, P. L. (2009). *Introduction to learning and behavior* (3rd ed.). Wadsworth Cengage Learning.

Prakash, R. S., Voss, M. W., Erickson, K. I., & Kramer, A. F. (2015). Moving towards a healthier brain and mind. *Annual Review of Psychology, 66,* 769–797.

Prasada, S., & Pinker, S. (1993). Generalizations of regular and irregular morphology. *Language and Cognitive Processes, 8,* 1–56.

Pressman, S. D., Cohen, S., Miller, G. E., Barkin, A., Rabin, B. S., & Treanor, J. J. (2005). Loneliness, social network size, and immune response to influenza vaccination in college freshmen. *Health Psychology, 24,* 297–306.

Price, J. L., & Davis, B. (2008). *The woman who can't forget: The extraordinary story of living with the most remarkable memory known to science.* Free Press.

Prince, M., Wimo, A., Guerchet, M., Ali, G.-C., Wu, Y-T, Prina, A. M., & Alzheimer's Disease International. (2015). World Alzheimer Report 2015: The global impact of dementia: An analysis of prevalence, incidence, cost and trends. Alzheimer's Disease International.

Prince, M., Wimo, A., Guerchet, M., Ali, G.-C., Wu, Y-T, Prior, H., Schwartz, A., & Güntürkün, O. (2008). Mirror-induced behavior in the magpie (*Pica pica*): Evidence of self-recognition. *PLoS Biology, 6,* e202.

Prior, H., Schwartz, A., & Güntürkün, O. (2008). Mirror-induced behavior in the magpie (*Pica pica*): Evidence of self-recognition. *PLoS Biology, 6,* e202.

Prochaska, J. J., & Sallis, J. F. (2004). A randomized controlled trial of single versus multiple health behavior change: Promoting physical activity and nutrition among adolescents. *Health Psychology, 23,* 314–318.

Procopio, M., & Marriott, P. (2007). Intrauterine hormonal environment and risk of developing anorexia nervosa. *Archives of General Psychiatry, 64*(12), 1402–1407.

Protzko, J. (2015). The environment in raising early intelligence: A meta-analysis of the fadeout effect. *Intelligence, 53,* 202–210. https://doi .org/10.1016/j.intell.2015.10.006

Protzko, J. (2016). Does the raising IQ-raising *g* distinction explain the fadeout effect? *Intelligence, 56,* 65–71. https://doi.org/10.1016/j.intell .2016.02.008

Protzko, J. (2017). Raising IQ among school-aged children: Five meta-analyses and a review of randomized controlled trials. *Developmental Review, 46,* 81–101. https://doi.org/10.1016/j.dr.2017.05.001

Protzko, J., Aronson, J., & Blair, C. (2013). How to make a young child smarter: Evidence from the database of raising intelligence. *Perspectives on Psychological Science, 8*(1), 25–40. https://doi.org/10.1177/1745691612462585

Provencal, N., & Binder, E. B. (2015). The neurobiological effects of stress as contributors to psychiatric disorders: Focus on epigenetics. *Current Opinion in Neurobiology, 30,* 31–37.

Punjabi, N. M. (2008). The epidemiology of adult obstructive sleep apnea. *Proceedings of the American Thoracic Society, 5,* 136–143.

Puterman, E., Lin, J., Blackburn, E. H., O'Donovan, A., Adler, N., & Epel, E. (2010). The power of exercise: Buffering the effect of chronic stress on telomere length. *PLoS ONE, 5,* e10837.

Pyc, M. A., & Rawson, K. A. (2009). Testing the retrieval effort hypothesis: Does greater difficulty correctly recalling information lead to higher levels of memory? *Journal of Memory and Language, 60,* 437–447.

Pyers, J. E., & Senghas, A. (2009). Language promotes false-belief understanding: Evidence from learners of a new sign language. *Psychological Science, 20*(7), 805–812.

Pyers, J. E., Shusterman, A., Senghas, A., Spelke, E. S., & Emmorey, K. (2010). Evidence from an emerging sign language reveals that language supports spatial cognition. *Proceedings of the National Academy of Sciences, USA, 107,* 12116–12120.

Querleu, D., Lefebvre, C., Titran, M., Renard, X., Morillon, M., & Crepin, G. (1984). Réactivité de nouveau-né de moins de deux heures de vie à la voix maternelle [Reactivity of a newborn at less than two hours of life to the mother's voice]. *Journal de Gynécologie Obstétrique et de Biologie de la Reproduction, 13,* 125–134.

Qureshi, A., & Lee-Chiong, T. (2004). Medications and their effects on sleep. *Medical Clinics of North America, 88,* 751–766.

Rabin, L. A., Fogel, J., & Nutter-Upham, K. E. (2011). Academic procrastination in college students: The role of self-reported executive function. *Journal of Clinical and Experimental Neuropsychology, 33,* 344–357.

Race, E., Keane, M. M., & Verfaellie, M. (2011). Medial temporal lobe damage causes deficits in episodic memory and episodic future thinking not attributable to deficits in narrative construction. *Journal of Neuroscience, 31,* 10262–10269.

Radford, E., & Radford, M. A. (1949). *Encyclopedia of superstitions.* Philosophical Library.

Raichle, M. E., & Mintun, M. A. (2006). Brain work and brain imaging. *Annual Review of Neuroscience, 29,* 449–476.

Rajaram, S. (2011). Collaboration both hurts and helps memory: A cognitive perspective. *Current Directions in Psychological Science, 20,* 76–81.

Rajaram, S., & Pereira-Pasarin, L. P. (2010). Collaborative memory: Cognitive research and theory. *Perspectives on Psychological Science, 6,* 649–663.

Ramachandran, V. S., & Blakeslee, S. (1998). *Phantoms in the brain: Probing the mysteries of the human mind.* Morrow.

Ramachandran, V. S., & Brang, D. (2015). Phantom touch. In T. J. Prescott, E. Ahissar, & E. Izhikevich (Eds.), *Scholarpedia of Touch* (pp. 377–386). Amsterdam, Netherlands: Atlantis Press.

Ramachandran, V. S., Brang, D., & McGeoch, P. D. (2010). Dynamic reorganization of referred sensations by movements of phantom limbs. *NeuroReport, 21,* 727–730.

Ramachandran, V. S., Rodgers-Ramachandran, D., & Stewart, M. (1992). Perceptual correlates of massive cortical reorganization. *Science, 258,* 1159–1160.

Ramirez-Esparza, N., Gosling, S. D., Benet-Martinez, V., & Potter, J. P. (2004). Do bilinguals have two personalities? A special case of cultural frame-switching. *Journal of Research in Personality, 40,* 99–120.

Rand, D. G. (2016). Cooperation, fast and slow: Meta-analytic evidence for a theory of social heuristics and self-interested deliberation. *Psychological Science, 27*(9), 1192–1206. https://doi.org/10.1177/0956797616654455

Rand, D. G., & Nowak, M. A. (2016). Human cooperation. *Trends in Cognitive Sciences, 17*(8), 413–425. https://doi.org/10.1016/j.tics.2013.06.003

Rapaport, D. (1946). *Diagnostic psychological testing: The theory, statistical evaluation, and diagnostic application of a battery of tests.* Year Book Publishers.

Rapoport, J., Chavez, A., Greenstein, D., Addington, A., & Gogtay, N. (2009). Autism-spectrum disorders and childhood onset schizophrenia: Clinical and biological contributions to a relationship revisited. *Journal of the American Academy of Child and Adolescent Psychiatry, 48,* 10–18.

Rasmussen, A. S., & Berntsen, D. (2011). The unpredictable past: Spontaneous autobiographical memories outnumber autobiographical memories retrieved strategically. *Consciousness and Cognition, 20,* 1843–1846.

Raven, J., Raven, J. C., & Court, J. H. (2004). *Manual for Raven's Progressive Matrices and Vocabulary Scales.* San Antonio: Harcourt Assessment.

Raz, N. (2000). Aging of the brain and its impact on cognitive performance: Integration of structural and functional findings. In F. I. M. Craik & T. A. Salthouse (Eds.), *The handbook of aging and cognition* (pp. 1–90). Erlbaum.

Reber, A. S. (1967). Implicit learning of artificial grammars. *Journal of Verbal Learning and Verbal Behavior, 6,* 855–863.

Reber, A. S. (1996). *Implicit learning and tacit knowledge: An essay on the cognitive unconscious.* Oxford University Press.

Reber, P. J. (2013). The neural basis of implicit learning and memory: A review of neuropsychological and neuroimaging research. *Neuropsychologia, 51,* 2026–2042.

Reber, P. J., Gitelman, D. R., Parrish, T. B., & Mesulam, M. M. (2003). Dissociating explicit and implicit category knowledge with fMRI. *Journal of Cognitive Neuroscience, 15,* 574–583.

Recanzone, G. H., & Sutter, M. L. (2008). The biological basis of audition. *Annual Review of Psychology, 59,* 119–142.

Rechtschaffen, A., Gilliland, M. A., Bergmann, B. M., & Winter, J. B. (1983). Physiological correlates of prolonged sleep deprivation in rats. *Science, 221,* 182–184.

Redick, T. S. (2015). Working memory training and interpreting interactions in intelligence interventions. *Intelligence, 50,* 14–20.

Redick, T. S., Shipstead, Z., Harrison, T. L., Hicks, K. L., Fried, D. E., Hambrick, D. Z., Kane, M. J., & Engle, R. W. (2013). No evidence of intelligence improvement after working memory training: A randomized, placebo-controlled study. *Journal of Experimental Psychology: General, 142*(2), 359–379. https://doi.org/10.1037/a002908

Reed, D. R. (2008). Birth of a new breed of supertaster. *Chemical Senses, 33,* 489–491.

Reed, G. (1988). *The psychology of anomalous experience* (rev. ed.). Prometheus Books.

Reeve, C. L., Heggestad, E. D., & Lievens, F. (2009). Modeling the impact of test anxiety and test familiarity on the criterion-related validity of cognitive ability tests. *Intelligence, 37*(1), 34–41. https://doi.org/10.1016/j.intell.2008.05.003

Regan, P. C. (1998). What if you can't get what you want? Willingness to compromise ideal mate selection standards as a function of sex, mate value, and relationship context. *Personality and Social Psychology Bulletin, 24,* 1294–1303.

Reichbach, G. L. (2012, May 16). A judge's plea for pot [op-ed article]. *New York Times.* http://www.nytimes.com/2012/05/17/opinion/a-judges-plea-for-medical-marijuana.html

Reis, H. T., Maniaci, M. R., Caprariello, P. S., Eastwick, P. W., & Finkel, E. J. (2011). Familiarity does indeed promote attraction in live interaction. *Journal of Personality and Social Psychology, 101*(3), 557–570. https://doi.org/10.1037/a0022885

Reiss, D., & Marino, L. (2001). Mirror self-recognition in the bottlenose dolphin: A case of cognitive convergence. *Proceedings of the National Academy of Sciences, USA, 98,* 5937–5942.

Renner, K. E. (1964). Delay of reinforcement: A historical review. *Psychological Review, 61,* 341–361.

Renner, M. J., & Mackin, R. (1998). A life stress instrument for classroom use. *Teaching of Psychology, 25,* 46–48.

Rensink, R. A. (2002). Change detection. *Annual Review of Psychology, 53,* 245–277.

Rensink, R. A., O'Regan, J. K., & Clark, J. J. (1997). To see or not to see: The need for attention to perceive changes in scenes. *Psychological Science, 8,* 368–373.

Repacholi, B. M., & Gopnik, A. (1997). Early reasoning about desires: Evidence from 14- and 18-month-olds. *Developmental Psychology, 33,* 12–21.

Rescorla, R. A. (2006). Stimulus generalization of excitation and inhibition. *Quarterly Journal of Experimental Psychology, 59,* 53–67.

Rescorla, R. A., & Wagner, A. R. (1972). A theory of Pavlovian conditioning: Variations in the effectiveness of reinforcement and nonreinforcement. In A. H. Black & W. F. Prokasy (Eds.), *Classical conditioning II: Current research and theory* (pp. 64–99). Appleton-Century-Crofts.

Ressler, K. J., & Mayberg, H. S. (2007). Targeting abnormal neural circuits in mood and anxiety disorders: From the laboratory to the clinic. *Nature Neuroscience, 10,* 1116–1124.

Ressler, K. J., & Nemeroff, C. B. (1999). Role of norepinephrine in the pathophysiology and treatment of mood disorders. *Biological Psychiatry, 46,* 1219–1233.

Rice, K. G., Richardson, C. M. E., & Clark, D. (2012). Perfectionism, procrastination, and psychological distress. *Journal of Counseling Psychology, 39,* 288–302.

Richards, M., Black, S., Mishra, G., Gale, C. R., Deary, I. J., & Batty, D. G. (2009). IQ in childhood and the metabolic syndrome in middle age: Extended follow-up of the 1946 British birth cohort study. *Intelligence, 37*(6), 567–572.

Richards, M., Black, S., Mishra, G., Gale, C. R., Deary, I. J., & Richardson, D. S. (2014). Everyday aggression takes many forms. *Current Directions in Psychological Science, 23*(3), 220–224. https://doi.org/10.1177/0963721414530143

Richardson, D. S. (2014). Everyday aggression takes many forms. *Current Directions in Psychological Science, 23*(3), 220–224. https://doi.org/10.1177/0963721414530143

Riggs, J. E. (1993). Stone-age genes and modern lifestyle: Evolutionary mismatch or differential survival bias. *Journal of Clinical Epidemiology, 46*(11), 1289–1291. https://doi.org/10.1016/0895-4356(93)90093-g (via Elsevier Science Direct).

Rigoli, F., Rutledge, R. B., Chew, B., Ousdal, O. T., Dayan, P., & Dolan, R. J. (2016). Dopamine increases a value-independent gambling propensity. *Neuropsychopharmacology, 41,* 2658–2667.

Rimer, J., Dwan, K., Lawlor, D. A., Greig, C. A., McMurdo, M., Morley, W., & Mead, G. E. (2012). Exercise for depression. *Cochrane Database of Systematic Reviews, 7,* CD004366.

Rinderu, M. I., Bushman, B. J., & Van Lange, P. A. M. (2018). Climate, aggression, and violence (CLASH): A cultural-evolutionary approach. *Current Opinion in Psychology, 19,* 113–118.

Rippon, G. (2019). *The gendered brain: The new neuroscience that shatters the myth of the female brain.* Penguin Books.

Risko, E. F., Anderson, N., Sarwal, A., Engelhardt, M., & Kingstone, A. (2012). Every attention: Variation in mind wandering and memory in a lecture. *Applied Cognitive Psychology, 26,* 234–242.

Risko, E. F., & Gilbert, S. J. (2016). Cognitive offloading. *Trends in Cognitive Sciences, 20,* 676–688.

Risman, J. E., Coyle, J. T., Green, R. W., Javitt, D. C., Benes, F. M., Heckers, S., & Grace, A. A. (2008). Circuit-based framework for understanding neurotransmitter and risk gene interactions in schizophrenia. *Trends in Neurosciences, 31,* 234–242.

Ritchey, A. J., & Ruback, R. B. (2018). Predicting lynching atrocity: The situational norms of lynchings in Georgia. *Personality and Social Psychology Bulletin, 44*(5), 619–637.

Rivera, L. A. (2012). Hiring as cultural matching: The case of elite professional service firms. *American Sociological Review, 77,* 999–1022.

Rizzolatti, G., & Craighero, L. (2004). The mirror-neuron system. *Annual Review of Neuroscience, 27,* 169–192.

Rizzolatti, G., & Rozzi, S. (2018). The mirror mechanism in the parietal lobe. *Handbook of Clinical Neurology, 151,* 555–573.

Rizzolatti, G., & Sinigaglia, C. (2010). The functional role of the parieto-frontal mirror circuit. *Nature Reviews Neuroscience, 11,* 264–274.

Roberts, G. A. (1991). Delusional belief and meaning in life: A preferred reality? *British Journal of Psychiatry, 159,* 20–29.

Roberts, G. A., & McGrady, A. (1996). Racial and gender effects on the relaxation response: Implications for the development of hypertension. *Biofeedback and Self-Regulation, 21,* 51–62.

Robertson, L. C. (2003). Binding, spatial attention and perceptual awareness. *Nature Reviews Neuroscience, 4,* 93–102.

Robins, L. N., Helzer, J. E., Hesselbrock, M., & Wish, E. (1980). Vietnam veterans three years after Vietnam. In L. Brill & C. Winick (Eds.), *The yearbook of substance use and abuse* (Vol. 11). Human Sciences Press.

Robins, R. W., Fraley, R. C., & Krueger, R. F. (Eds.). (2007). *Handbook of research methods in personality psychology.* Guilford Press.

Rodieck, R. W. (1998). *The first steps in seeing.* Sinauer.

Rodman, A. M., Powers, K. E., & Somerville, L. H. (2017). Development of self-protective biases in response to social evaluative feedback. *Proceedings of the National Academy of Sciences, USA, 114*(50), 13158–13163.

Roediger, H. L., III. (2000). Why retrieval is the key process to understanding human memory. In E. Tulving (Ed.), *Memory, consciousness, and the brain: The Tallinn conference* (pp. 52–75). Psychology Press.

Roediger, H. L., III, & Karpicke, J. D. (2006). Test-enhanced learning: Taking memory tests improves long-term retention. *Psychological Science, 17,* 249–255.

Roediger, H. L., III, & Karpicke, J. D. (2018). Reflections on the resurgence of interest in the testing effect. *Perspectives on Psychological Science, 13,* 236–241.

Roediger, H. L., III, & McDermott, K. B. (1995). Creating false memories: Remembering words not presented in lists. *Journal of Experimental Psychology: Learning, Memory, and Cognition, 21,* 803–814.

Roediger, H. L., III, & McDermott, K. B. (2000). Tricks of memory. *Current Directions in Psychological Science, 9,* 123–127.

Roediger, H. L., III, Weldon, M. S., & Challis, B. H. (1989). Explaining dissociations between implicit and explicit measures of retention: A processing account. In H. L. Roediger & F. I. M. Craik (Eds.), *Varieties of memory and consciousness: Essays in honour of Endel Tulving* (pp. 3–39). Erlbaum.

Roelofs, K. (2017). Freeze for action: Neurobiological mechanisms in animal and human freezing. *Philosophical Transactions of the Royal Society of London. Series B, Biological Sciences, 372*(1718), 20160206.

Rogers, R., & Hammerstein, O., II. (1949). *Some enchanted evening.* Concord Music Publishing LLC.

Rohrer, D. (2015). Student instruction should be distributed over long time periods. *Educational Psychology Review, 27,* 635–643.

Rohrer, D., Dedrick, R. F., & Sterschic, S. (2015). Interleaved practice improves mathematics learning. *Journal of Educational Psychology, 107,* 900–908.

Roig, M., Skriver, K., Lundbye-Jensen, J., Kiens, B., & Nielsen, J. B. (2012). A single bout of exercise improves motor memory. *PLoS One, 7,* e44594. https://doi.org/10.1371/journal.pone.0044594

Roisman, G. I., Masten, A. S., Coatsworth, J. D., & Tellegen, A. (2004). Salient and emerging developmental tasks in the transition to adulthood. *Child Development, 75,* 123–133. https://doi.org/10.1111/j.1467-8624.2004.00658.x

Rolls, E. T. (2015). Taste, olfactory, and food reward value processing in the human brain. *Progress in Neurobiology, 127–128,* 64–90.

Ronay, R., & Galinsky, A. D. (2011). Lex talionis: Testosterone and the law of retaliation. *Journal of Experimental Social Psychology, 47*(3), 702–705. https://doi.org/10.1016/j.jesp.2010.11.009

Rosch, E. H. (1973). Natural categories. *Cognitive Psychology, 4,* 328–350.

Rosch, E. H. (1975). Cognitive representations of semantic categories. *Journal of Experimental Psychology: General, 104,* 192–233.

Rosch, E. H., & Mervis, C. B. (1975). Family resemblances: Studies in the internal structure of categories. *Cognitive Psychology, 7,* 573–605.

Rose, S. P. R. (2002). Smart drugs: Do they work? Are they ethical? Will they be legal? *Nature Reviews Neuroscience, 3,* 975–979.

Roseman, I. J. (1984). Cognitive determinants of emotion: A structural theory. *Review of Personality and Social Psychology, 5,* 11–36.

Roseman, I. J., & Smith, C. A. (2001). Appraisal theory: Overview, assumptions, varieties and controversies. In K. R. Scherer, A. Schorr, & T. Johnstone (Eds.), *Appraisal processes in emotion: Theory, methods, research* (pp. 3–19). Oxford University Press.

Rosenbaum, J. E. (2009). Patient teenagers? A comparison of the sexual behavior of virginity pledgers and matched nonpledgers. *Pediatrics, 123*(1), e110–e120.

Rosenbaum, S. (2016, June 9). Models keep getting skinnier and skinnier. *New York Post,* https://nypost.com/2016/06/09/models-keep-getting-skinnier-and-skinnier/

Rosenberg, M. (1965). *Society and the adolescent self-image.* Princeton University Press.

Rosenhan, D. (1973). On being sane in insane places. *Science, 179,* 250–258.

Rosenthal, R., & Fode, K. L. (1963). The effect of experimenter bias on the performance of the albino rat. *Behavioral Science, 8,* 183–189.

Roser, M. E., Aslin, R. N., McKenzie, R., Zahra, D., & Fiser, J. (2015). Enhanced visual statistical learning in adults with autism. *Neuropsychology, 29,* 163–172.

Ross, L. (1977). The intuitive psychologist and his shortcomings: Distortions in the attribution process. *Advances in Experimental Social Psychology, 10,* 173–220.

Ross, L., Amabile, T. M., & Steinmetz, J. L. (1977). Social roles, social control, and biases in social-perception processes. *Journal of Personality and Social Psychology, 35,* 485–494.

Ross, M., Blatz, C. W., & Schryer, E. (2008). Social memory processes. In H. L. Roediger III (Ed.), *Learning and memory: A comprehensive reference* (Vol. 2, pp. 911–926). Elsevier.

Rossano, F., Carpenter, M., & Tomasello, M. (2012). One-year-old infants follow others' voice direction. *Psychological Science, 23*(11), 1298–1302. https://doi.org/10.1177/0956797612450032

Roth, B., Becker, N., Romeyke, S., Schäfer, S., Domnick, F., & Spinath, F. M. (2015). Intelligence and school grades: A meta-analysis. *Intelligence, 53,* 118–137. https://doi.org/10.1016/j.intell.2015.09.002

Roth, H. P., & Caron, H. S. (1978). Accuracy of doctors' estimates and patients' statements on adherence to a drug regimen. *Clinical Pharmacology and Therapeutics, 23,* 361–370.

Rothbart, M. K., & Bates, J. E. (2006). Temperament. In W. Damon, R. Lerner, & N. Eisenberg (Eds.), *Handbook of child psychology: Vol. 3. Social, emotional, and personality development* (6th ed., pp. 99–166). Wiley.

Rothbaum, B. O., & Schwartz, A. C. (2002). Exposure therapy for posttraumatic stress disorder. *American Journal of Psychotherapy, 56,* 59–75.

Rotter, J. B. (1966). Generalized expectancies for internal versus external locus of control of reinforcement. *Psychological Monographs: General and Applied, 80,* 1–28.

Rozin, P. (1968). Are carbohydrate and protein intakes separately regulated? *Journal of Comparative and Physiological Psychology, 65,* 23–29.

Rozin, P., Dow, S., Moscovitch, M., & Rajaram, S. (1998). What causes humans to begin and end a meal? A role for memory for what has been eaten, as evidenced by a study of multiple meal eating in amnesic patients. *Psychological Science, 9,* 392–396.

Rozin, P., Kabnick, K., Pete, E., Fischler, C., & Shields, C. (2003). The ecology of eating: Smaller portion size in France than in the United States helps to explain the French paradox. *Psychological Science, 14,* 450–454.

Rozin, P., & Kalat, J. W. (1971). Specific hungers and poison avoidance as adaptive specializations of learning. *Psychological Review, 78,* 459–486.

Rozin, P., Scott, S., Dingley, M., Urbanek, J. K., Jiang, H., & Kaltenbach, M. (2011). Nudge to nobesity: I. Minor changes in accessibility decrease food intake. *Judgment and Decision Making, 6,* 323–332.

Rubin, M., & Badea, C. (2012). They're all the same! . . . but for several different reasons: A review of the multicausal nature of perceived group variability. *Current Directions in Psychological Science, 21*(6), 367–372. https://doi.org/10.1177/0963721412457363

Rubin, Z. (1973). *Liking and loving.* Holt, Rinehart & Winston.

Rudman, L. A., Ashmore, R. D., & Gary, M. L. (2001). "Unlearning" automatic biases: The malleability of implicit prejudice and stereotypes. *Journal of Personality and Social Psychology, 81,* 856–868.

Running, C. A., Craig, B. A., & Mattes, R. D. (2015). Oleogustus: The unique taste of fat. *Chemical Senses, 40,* 507–516.

Rusbult, C. E., & Van Lange, P. A. M. (2003). Interdependence, interaction and relationships. *Annual Review of Psychology, 54,* 351–375.

Ruscio, A. M., Stein, D. J., Chiu, W. T., & Kessler, R. C. (2010). The epidemiology of obsessive-compulsive disorder in the National Comorbidity Survey Replication. *Molecular Psychiatry, 15,* 53–63.

Rushton, J. P., & Templer, D. I. (2009). National differences in intelligence, crime, income, and skin color. *Intelligence, 37*(4), 341–346.

Russell, B. (1945). *A history of Western philosophy.* Simon & Schuster.

Russell, J., Gee, B., & Bullard, C. (2012). Why do young children hide by closing their eyes? Self-visibility and the developing concept of self. *Journal of Cognition and Development, 13*(4), 550–576. https://doi.org/10.1080/15248372.2011.594826

Russell, J. A. (1980). A circumplex model of affect. *Journal of Personality and Social Psychology, 39,* 1161–1178.

Rutter, M., O'Connor, T. G., & the English and Romanian Adoptees Study Team. (2004). Are there biological programming effects for psychological development? Findings from a study of Romanian adoptees. *Developmental Psychology, 40,* 81–94.

Rutter, M., & Silberg, J. (2002). Gene–environment interplay in relation to emotional and behavioral disturbance. *Annual Review of Psychology, 53,* 463–490.

Ryan, R. M., & Deci, E. L. (2000). Self-determination theory and the facilitation of intrinsic motivation, social development, and well-being. *American Psychologist, 55,* 68–78.

Ryle, G. (1949). *The concept of mind.* Barnes & Noble.

Sacks, O. (1995). *An anthropologist on Mars.* Knopf.

Sacks, O. (1996). *An anthropologist on Mars* (ppbk). Vintage.

Saffran, J. R., Aslin, R. N., & Newport, E. I. (1996). Statistical learning by 8-month-old infants. *Science, 274,* 1926–1928.

Sahakian, B., & Morein-Zamir, S. (2007). Professor's little helper. *Nature, 450*(7173), 1157–1159.

Sala, G., & Gobet, F. (2018, September 8). Elvis has left the building: Correlational but not causal relationship between music skill and cognitive ability. https://doi.org/10.31234/osf.io/auzry

Salmon, D. P., & Bondi, M. W. (2009). Neuropsychological assessment of dementia. *Annual Review of Psychology, 60,* 257–282.

Salovey, P., & Grewal, D. (2005). The science of emotional intelligence. *Current Directions in Psychological Science, 14*(6), 281–285.

Salthouse, T. A. (1984). Effects of age and skill in typing. *Journal of Experimental Psychology: General, 113,* 345–371.

Salthouse, T. A. (1987). Age, experience, and compensation. In C. Schooler & K. W. Schaie (Eds.), *Cognitive functioning and social structure over the life course* (pp. 142–150). Ablex.

Salthouse, T. A. (1996a). General and specific mediation of adult age differences in memory. *Journal of Gerontology: Series B: Psychological Sciences and Social Sciences, 51B,* P30–P42.

Salthouse, T. A. (1996b). The processing-speed theory of adult age differences in cognition. *Psychological Review, 103,* 403–428.

Salthouse, T. A. (2000). Pressing issues in cognitive aging. In D. Park & N. Schwartz (Eds.), *Cognitive aging: A primer* (pp. 43–54). Psychology Press.

Salthouse, T. A. (2006). Mental exercise and mental aging. *Perspectives on Psychological Science, 1*(1), 68–87.

Salthouse, T. A. (2015). Do cognitive interventions alter the rate of age-related cognitive change? *Intelligence, 53,* 86–91. https://doi .org/10.1016/j.intell.2015.09.004

Salvatore, J. E., Kuo, S. I.-C., Steele, R. D., Simpson, J. A., & Collins, W. A. (2011). Recovering from conflict in romantic relationships: A developmental perspective. *Psychological Science, 22*(3), 376–383. https://doi .org/10.1177/0956797610397055

Sampson, R. J., & Laub, J. H. (1995). Understanding variability in lives through time: Contributions of life-course criminology. *Studies of Crime Prevention, 4,* 143–158.

Santelli, J. S., Kantor, L. M., Grilo, S. A., Speizer, I. S., Lindberg, L. D., Heitel, J., Schalet, A. T., Lyon, M. E., Mason-Jones, A. J., McGovern, T., Heck, C. J., Rogers, J., & Ott, M. A. (2017). Abstinence-only-until-marriage: An updated review of U.S. policies and programs and their impact. *Journal of Adolescent Health, 61,* 273–280.

Sara, S. J. (2000). Retrieval and reconsolidation: Toward a neurobiology of remembering. *Learning & Memory, 7,* 73–84.

Sarris, V. (1989). Max Wertheimer on seen motion: Theory and evidence. *Psychological Research, 51,* 58–68.

Sarter, M. (2006). Preclinical research into cognition enhancers. *Trends in Pharmacological Sciences, 27,* 602–608.

Satcher, D. (2001). *The Surgeon General's call to action to promote sexual health and responsible sexual behavior.* U.S. Government Printing Office.

Satterwhite, C. L., Torrone, E., Meites, E., Dunne, E. F., Mahajan, R., Ocfernia, M. C., Su, J., Xu, F., & Weinstock, H. (2013). Sexually transmitted infections among U.S. women and men: Prevalence and incidence estimates, 2008. *Sexually Transmitted Diseases, 40*(3), 187–193.

Sauter, D. A., Eisner, F., Calder, A. J., & Scott, S. K. (2010). Perceptual cues in nonverbal vocal expressions of emotion. *Quarterly Journal of Experimental Psychology, 63*(11), 2251–2272. https://doi.org/10.1080 /17470211003721642

Savage, C. R., Deckersbach, T., Heckers, S., Wagner, A. D., Schacter, D. L., Alpert, N. M., Fischman, A. J., & Rauch, S. L. (2001). Prefrontal regions supporting spontaneous and directed application of verbal learning strategies: Evidence from PET. *Brain, 124,* 219–231.

Savic, I., & Lindstrom, P. (2008). PET and MRI show differences in cerebral asymmetry and functional connectivity between homo- and heterosexual subjects. *Proceedings of the National Academy of Sciences, USA, 105*(27), 9403–9408.

Sawa, A., & Snyder, S. H. (2002). Schizophrenia: Diverse approaches to a complex disease. *Science, 295,* 692–695.

Sawyer, S. M., Azzopardi, P. S., Wickremarathne, D., & Patton, G. C. (2018). The age of adolescence. *Lancet: Child and Adolescent Health, 2,* 223–228.

Scarr, S., Pakstis, A. J., Katz, S. H., & Barker, W. B. (1977). Absence of a relationship between degree of White ancestry and intellectual skills within a Black population. *Human Genetics, 39*(1), 69–86.

Schachter, S. (1982). Recidivism and self-cure of smoking and obesity. *American Psychologist, 37,* 436–444.

Schachter, S., & Singer, J. E. (1962). Cognitive, social, and psychological determinants of emotional state. *Physiological Review, 69,* 379–399.

Schacter, D. L. (1987). Implicit memory: History and current status. *Journal of Experimental Psychology: Learning, Memory, and Cognition, 13,* 501–518.

Schacter, D. L. (1996). *Searching for memory: The brain, the mind, and the past.* Basic Books.

Schacter, D. L. (1999). The seven sins of memory: Insights from psychology and cognitive neuroscience. *American Psychologist, 54*(3), 182–203.

Schacter, D. L. (2001a). *Forgotten ideas, neglected pioneers: Richard Semon and the story of memory.* Psychology Press.

Schacter, D. L. (2001b). *The seven sins of memory: How the mind forgets and remembers.* Houghton Mifflin.

Schacter, D. L. (2012). Adaptive constructive processes and the future of memory. *American Psychologist, 67,* 603–613.

Schacter, D. L., & Addis, D. R. (2007). The cognitive neuroscience of constructive memory: Remembering the past and imagining the future. *Philosophical Transactions of the Royal Society of London, B, 362,* 773–786.

Schacter, D. L., Addis, D. R., & Buckner, R. L. (2008). Episodic simulation of future events: Concepts, data, and applications. *Annals of the New York Academy of Sciences, 1124,* 39–60.

Schacter, D. L., Addis, D. R., Hassabis, D., Martin, V. C., Spreng, R. N., & Szpunar, K. K. (2012). The future of memory: Remembering, imagining, and the brain. *Neuron, 16,* 582–583.

Schacter, D. L., Alpert, N. M., Savage, C. R., Rauch, S. L., & Albert, M. S. (1996). Conscious recollection and the human hippocampal formation: Evidence from positron emission tomography. *Proceedings of the National Academy of Sciences, USA, 93,* 321–325.

Schacter, D. L., & Curran, T. (2000). Memory without remembering and remembering without memory: Implicit and false memories. In M. S. Gazzaniga (Ed.), *The new cognitive neurosciences* (2nd ed., pp. 829–840). MIT Press.

Schacter, D. L., Dobbins, I. G., & Schnyer, D. M. (2004). Specificity of priming: A cognitive neuroscience perspective. *Nature Reviews Neuroscience, 5,* 853–862.

Schacter, D. L., Guerin, S. A., & St. Jacques, P. L. (2011). Memory distortion: An adaptive perspective. *Trends in Cognitive Sciences, 15,* 467–474.

Schacter, D. L., Harbluk, J. L., & McLachlan, D. R. (1984). Retrieval without recollection: An experimental analysis of source amnesia. *Journal of Verbal Learning and Verbal Behavior, 23,* 593–611.

Schacter, D. L., Israel, L., & Racine, C. A. (1999). Suppressing false recognition in younger and older adults: The distinctiveness heuristic. *Journal of Memory and Language, 40,* 1–24.

Schacter, D. L., & Loftus, E. F. (2013). Memory and law: What can cognitive neuroscience contribute? *Nature Neuroscience, 16,* 119–123.

Schacter, D. L. & Szpunar, K. K. (2015). Enhancing attention and memory during video-recorded lectures. *Scholarship of Teaching and Learning in Psychology, 1,* 60–71.

Schacter, D. L., & Tulving, E. (1994). *Memory systems 1994.* MIT Press.

Schacter, D. L., Wagner, A. D., & Buckner, R. L. (2000). Memory systems of 1999. In E. Tulving & F. I. M. Craik (Eds.), *The Oxford handbook of memory* (pp. 627–643). Oxford University Press.

Schaie, K. W. (1996). *Intellectual development in adulthood: The Seattle Longitudinal Study.* Cambridge University Press.

Schaie, K. W. (2005). *Developmental influences on adult intelligence: The Seattle Longitudinal Study.* Oxford University Press.

Schapira, A. H. V., Emre, M., Jenner, P., & Poewe, W. (2009). Levodopa in the treatment of Parkinson's disease. *European Journal of Neurology, 16,* 982–989.

Scherer, K. R. (1999). Appraisal theory. In T. Dalgleish & M. Power (Eds.), *Handbook of cognition and emotion* (pp. 637–663). Wiley.

Scherer, K. R. (2001). The nature and study of appraisal: A review of the issues. In K. R. Scherer, A. Schorr, & T. Johnstone (Eds.), *Appraisal processes in emotion: Theory, methods, research* (pp. 369–391). Oxford University Press.

Schiff, M., Duyme, M., Stewart, J., Tomkiewicz, S., & Feingold, J. (1978). Intellectual status of working-class children adopted early in upper-middle-class families. *Science, 200,* 1503–1504.

Schildkraut, J. J. (1965). The catecholamine hypothesis of affective disorders: A review of supporting evidence. *American Journal of Psychiatry, 122,* 509–522.

Schiller, D., Monfils, M. H., Raio, C. M., Johnson, D. C., LeDoux, J. E., & Phelps, E. A. (2010). Preventing the return of fear in humans using reconsolidation update mechanisms. *Nature, 463,* 49–54.

Schilling, O. K., Wahl, H.-W., & Wiegering, S. (2013). Affective development in advanced old age: Analyses of terminal change in positive and negative affect. *Developmental Psychology, 49*(5), 1011–1020. https://doi.org/10.1037/a0028775

Schmader, T., Johns, M., & Forbes, C. (2008). An integrated process model of stereotype threat effects on performance. *Psychological Review, 115,* 336–356.

Schmitt, D. P., Jonason, P. K., Byerley, G. J., Flores, S. D., Illbeck, B. E., O'Leary, K. N., & Qudrat, A. (2012). A reexamination of sex differences in sexuality: New studies reveal old truths. *Current Directions in Psychological Science, 21*(2), 135–139. https://doi.org/10.1177/0963721412436808

Schmitt, D. P., Realo, A., Voracek, M., & Allik, J. (2008). Why can't a man be more like a woman? Sex differences in personality traits across 55 cultures. *Journal of Personality and Social Psychology, 94,* 168–182.

Schneider, B. H., Atkinson, L., & Tardif, C. (2001). Child–parent attachment and children's peer relations: A quantitative review. *Developmental Psychology, 37,* 86–100.

Schoenemann, P. T., Sheenan, M. J., & Glotzer, L. D. (2005). Prefrontal white matter volume is disproportionately larger in humans than in other primates. *Nature Neuroscience, 8,* 242–252.

Schonberg, T., O'Doherty, J. P., Joel, D., Inzelberg, R., Segev, Y., & Daw, N. D. (2009). Selective impairment of prediction error signaling in human dorsolateral but not ventral striatum in Parkinson's disease patients: Evidence from a model-based fMRI study. *NeuroImage, 49,* 772–781.

Schott, B. J., Henson, R. N., Richardson-Klavehn, A., Becker, C., Thoma, V., Heinze, H. J., & Duzel, E. (2005). Redefining implicit and explicit memory: The functional neuroanatomy of priming, remembering, and control of retrieval. *Proceedings of the National Academy of Sciences, USA, 102,* 1257–1262.

Schreiner, T., & Rasch, B. (2015). Boosting vocabulary learning by verbal cueing during sleep. *Cerebral Cortex, 25,* 4169–4179.

Schubert, T. W., & Koole, S. L. (2009). The embodied self: Making a fist enhances men's power-related self-conceptions. *Journal of Experimental Social Psychology, 45,* 828–834.

Schultz, D., Izard, C. E., & Bear, G. (2004). Children's emotion processing: Relations to emotionality and aggression. *Development and Psychopathology, 16*(2), 371–387.

Schultz, W. (2016). Dopamine reward prediction error coding. *Dialogues in Clinical Neuroscience, 18,* 23–32.

Schultz, W., Dayan, P., & Montague, P. R. (1997). A neural substrate of prediction and reward. *Science, 275,* 1593–1599.

Schwartz, B. L. (2002). *Tip-of-the-tongue states: Phenomenology, mechanisms, and lexical retrieval.* Erlbaum.

Schwartz, C. E., Wright, C. I., Shin, L. M., Kagan, J., & Rauch, S. L. (2003). Inhibited and uninhibited infants "grown up": Adult amygdalar response to novelty. *Science, 300,* 1952–1953.

Schwartz, H. A., Eichstaedt, J. C., Kern, M. L., Dziurzynski, L., Ramones, S. M., Agrawal, M., Shah, A., Kosinski, M., Stillwell, D., Seligman, M. E. P., & Ungar, L. H. (2013). Personality, gender, and age in the language of social media: The open-vocabulary approach. *PLoS ONE, 8,* e73791.

Schwartz, J. H., & Westbrook, G. L. (2000). The cytology of neurons. In E. R. Kandel, G. H. Schwartz, & T. M. Jessell (Eds.), *Principles of neural science* (pp. 67–104). McGraw-Hill.

Schwartz, L., & Yovel, G. (2016). The roles of perceptual and conceptual information in face recognition. *Journal of Experimental Psychology: General, 145*(11), 1493–1511. http://dx.doi.org/10.1037/xge0000220

Schwartz, S., & Maquet, P. (2002). Sleep imaging and the neuropsychological assessment of dreams. *Trends in Cognitive Sciences, 6,* 23–30.

Schwartzman, A. E., Gold, D., & Andres, D. (1987). Stability of intelligence: A 40-year follow-up. *Canadian Journal of Psychology, 41,* 244–256.

Schweizer, T. A., Ware, J., Fischer, C. E., Craik, F. I. M., & Bialystok, E. (2012). Bilingualism as a contributor to cognitive reserve: Evidence from brain atrophy in Alzheimer's disease. *Cortex, 48,* 991–996.

Scott, R. M., & Baillargeon, R. (2017). Early false-belief understanding. *Trends in Cognitive Sciences, 21,* 237–249.

Scoville, W. B., & Milner, B. (1957). Loss of recent memory after bilateral hippocampal lesions. *Journal of Neurology, Neurosurgery, and Psychiatry, 20,* 11–21.

Scribner, S. (1984). Studying working intelligence. In B. Rogoff & J. Lave (Eds.), *Everyday cognition: Its development in social context* (pp. 9–40). Harvard University Press.

Sedlmeier, P., Eberth, J., Schwarz, M., Zimmermann, D., Haarig, F., Jaeger, S., & Kunze, S. (2012). The psychological effects of meditation: A meta-analysis. *Psychological Bulletin, 138,* 1139–1171.

Seeman, T. E., Dubin, L. F., & Seeman, M. (2003). Religiosity/spirituality and health: A critical review of the evidence for biological pathways. *American Psychologist, 58,* 53–63.

Seligman, M. E. P. (1971). Phobias and preparedness. *Behavior Therapy, 2,* 307–320.

Seligman, M. E. P. (1995). The effectiveness of psychotherapy: The *Consumer Reports* study. *American Psychologist, 48,* 966–971.

Selye, H., & Fortier, C. (1950). Adaptive reaction to stress. *Psychosomatic Medicine, 12,* 149–157.

Semenza, C. (2009). The neuropsychology of proper names. *Mind & Language, 24,* 347–369.

Semenza, C., & Zettin, M. (1989). Evidence from aphasia for the role of proper names as pure referring expressions. *Nature, 342,* 678–679.

Senghas, A., Kita, S., & Ozyurek, A. (2004). Children create core properties of language: Evidence from an emerging sign language in Nicaragua. *Science, 305,* 1782.

Senju, A., Southgate, V., White, S., & Frith, U. (2009). Mindblind eyes: An absence of spontaneous theory of mind in Asperger syndrome. *Science, 325,* 883–885.

Serpell, R. (1974). Aspects of intelligence in a developing country. *African Social Research, 17,* 578–596.

Seybold, K. S., & Hill, P. C. (2001). The role of religion and spirituality in mental and physical health. *Current Directions in Psychological Science, 10,* 21–23.

Shah, A., Hayes, C. J., & Martin, B. C. (2017). Characteristics of initial prescription episodes and likelihood of long-term opioid use—United States, 2006–2015. *Morbidity and Mortality Weekly Report, 66,* 265–269.

Shahaeian, A., Peterson, C. C., Slaughter, V., & Wellman, H. M. (2011). Culture and the sequence of steps in theory of mind development. *Developmental Psychology, 47*(5), 1239–1247. https://doi.org/10.1037/a0023899

Shallice, T., Fletcher, P., Frith, C. D., Grasby, P., Frackowiak, R. S. J., & Dolan, R. J. (1994). Brain regions associated with acquisition and retrieval of verbal episodic memory. *Nature, 368,* 633–635.

Shariff, A. F., & Tracy, J. L. (2011). What are emotion expressions for? *Current Directions in Psychological Science, 20*(6), 395–399.

Sharot, T. (2011). *The optimism bias: A tour of the irrationally positive brain.* Pantheon Books.

Shaw, J., & Porter, S. (2015). Constructing rich false memories of committing crime. *Psychological Science, 26,* 291–301.

Shaw, J. S., Bjork, R. A., & Handal, A. (1995). Retrieval-induced forgetting in an eyewitness paradigm. *Psychonomic Bulletin & Review, 13,* 1023–1027.

Shedler, J. (2010). The efficacy of psychodynamic psychotherapy. *American Psychologist, 65,* 98–109.

Sheese, B. E., & Graziano, W. G. (2005). Deciding to defect: The effects of video-game violence on cooperative behavior. *Psychological Science, 16,* 354–357.

Shepherd, G. M. (1988). *Neurobiology*. Oxford University Press.

Shepperd, J., Malone, W., & Sweeny, K. (2008). Exploring the causes of the self-serving bias. *Social and Personality Psychology Compass, 2*(2), 895–908.

Sherry, S. B., & Hall, P. A. (2009). The perfectionism model of binge eating: Tests of an integrative model. *Journal of Personality and Social Psychology, 96*(3), 690–709.

Shichuan Du, Y.-T., & Martinez, A. M. (2014, April 15). Compound facial expressions of emotion. *Proceedings of the National Academy of Sciences, USA, 111*(15), e1454–e1462. https://doi.org/10.1073/pnas.1322355111

Shiffman, S., Gnys, M., Richards, T. J., Paty, J. A., & Hickcox, M. (1996). Temptations to smoke after quitting: A comparison of lapsers and maintainers. *Health Psychology, 15*, 455–461.

Shih, M., Pittinsky, T. L., & Ambady, N. (1999). Stereotype susceptibility: Identity salience and shifts in quantitative performance. *Psychological Science, 10*, 80–83.

Shimamura, A. P., & Squire, L. R. (1987). A neuropsychological study of fact memory and source amnesia. *Journal of Experimental Psychology: Learning, Memory, and Cognition, 13*, 464–473.

Shin, H., & Ryan, A. M. (2014). Early adolescent friendships and academic adjustment: Examining selection and influence processes with longitudinal social network analysis. *Developmental Psychology, 50*(11), 2462–2472. https://doi.org/10.1037/a0037922

Shin, L. M., Rauch, S. L., & Pitman, R. K. (2006). Amygdala, medial prefrontal cortex, and hippocampal function in PTSD. *Annals of the New York Academy of Science, 1071*, 67–79.

Shinskey, J. L., & Munakata, Y. (2005). Familiarity breeds searching. *Psychological Science, 16*(8), 596–600.

Shiota, M. N., Neufeld, S. L., Yeung, W. H., Moser, S. E., & Perea, E. F. (2011). Feeling good: Autonomic nervous system responding in five positive emotions. *Emotion, 11*(6), 1368–1378. https://doi.org/10.1037/a0024278

Shipstead, Z., Redick, T. S., & Engle, R. W. (2012). Is working memory training effective? *Psychological Bulletin, 138*, 628–654.

Shomstein, S., & Yantis, S. (2004). Control of attention shifts between vision and audition in human cortex. *Journal of Neuroscience, 24*, 10702–10706.

Shore, C. (1986). Combinatorial play: Conceptual development and early multiword speech. *Developmental Psychology, 22*, 184–190.

Shulman, L., D'Agostino, E., Lee, S., Valicenti-McDermott, M., Seijo, R., Tulloch, E., Meringolo, D., & Tarshis, N. (2019). When an early diagnosis of autism spectrum disorder resolves, what remains? *Journal of Child Neurology, 34*(7), 382–386.

Siegel, E. H., Sands, M. K., Van den Noortgate, W., Condon, P., Chang, Y., Dy, J., Quigley, K. S., & Barrett, L. F. (2018). Emotion fingerprints or emotion populations? A meta-analytic investigation of autonomic features of emotion categories. *Psychological Bulletin, 144*(4), 343–393.

Siegel, S. (1984). Pavlovian conditioning and heroin overdose: Reports by overdose victims. *Bulletin of the Psychonomic Society, 22*, 428–430.

Siegel, S. (2005). Drug tolerance, drug addiction, and drug anticipation. *Current Directions in Psychological Science, 14*, 296–300.

Siegel, S. (2016). The heroin overdose mystery. *Current Directions in Psychological Science, 25*, 375–379.

Siegel, S., Baptista, M. A. S., Kim, J. A., McDonald, R. V., & Weise-Kelly, L. (2000). Pavlovian psychopharmacology: The associative basis of tolerance. *Experimental and Clinical Psychopharmacology, 8*, 276–293.

Siegrist, M., & Cousin, M. E. (2009). Expectations influence sensory experience in a wine tasting. *Appetite, 52*(3), 762–765. https://doi.org/10.1016/j.appet.2009.02.002

Siemer, M., Mauss, I., & Gross, J. J. (2007). Same situation—Different emotions: How appraisals shape our emotions. *Emotion, 7*(3), 592–600. https://doi.org/10.1037/1528-3542.7.3.592

Sigman, M., Spence, S. J., & Wang, T. (2006). Autism from developmental and neuropsychological perspectives. *Annual Review of Clinical Psychology, 2*, 327–355.

Silverman, A. M., Gwinn, J. D., & Van Boven, L. (2014). Stumbling in their shoes: Disability simulations reduce judged capabilities of disabled people. *Social Psychological and Personality Science, 6*(4), 464–471. https://doi.org/10.1177/1948550614559650

Simeone, J. C., Ward, A. J., Rotella, P., Collins, J., & Windisch, R. (2015). An evaluation of variation in published estimates of schizophrenia prevalence from 1990–2013: A systematic literature review. *BMC Psychiatry, 15*, 193.

Simons, D., Lleras, A., Martinez-Conde, S., Slichter, D., Caddigan, E., & Nevarez, G. (2006). Induced visual fading of complex images. *Journal of Vision, 6*, 1093–1101. https://doi.org/10.1167/6.10.9

Simons, D. J., & Chabris, C. F. (1999). Gorillas in our midst: Sustained inattentional blindness for dynamic events. *Perception, 28*, 1059–1074.

Simons, D. J., & Levin, D. T. (1998). Failure to detect changes to people during a real-world interaction. *Psychonomic Bulletin & Review, 5*, 644–649.

Simons, D. J., & Rensink, R. A. (2005). Change blindness: Past, present, and future. *Trends in Cognitive Sciences, 9*, 16–20.

Simonton, D. K. (2006). Presidential IQ, openness, intellectual brilliance, and leadership: Estimates and correlations for 42 U.S. chief executives. *Political Psychology, 27*(4), 511–526. https://doi.org/10.1111/j.1467-9221.2006.00524.x

Simpson, J. A., Collins, W. A., & Salvatore, J. E. (2011). The impact of early interpersonal experience on adult romantic relationship functioning: Recent findings from the Minnesota Longitudinal Study of Risk and Adaptation. *Current Directions in Psychological Science, 20*(6), 355–359. https://doi.org/10.1177/0963721411418468

Simpson, S. J., & Raubenheimer, D. (2014). Perspective: Tricks of the trade. *Nature, 508*, S66. https://doi.org/10.1038/508S66a

Singer, P. (1975). *Animal liberation: A new ethics for our treatment of animals*. Random House.

Singh, D. (1993). Adaptive significance of female physical attractiveness: Role of waist-to-hip ratio. *Journal of Personality and Social Psychology, 65*, 293–307.

Sirois, F. M. (2015). Is procrastination a vulnerability factor for hypertension and cardiovascular disease? Testing an extension of the procrastination–health model. *Journal of Behavioral Medicine, 38*, 578–589.

Siu, A. L., & U.S. Preventive Services Task Force. (2016). Screening for Autism Spectrum Disorder in young children: U.S. Preventive Services Task Force recommendation statement. *Journal of the American Medical Association, 315*, 691–696.

Skiena, S., & Ward, C. B. (2013). *Who's bigger?: Where historical figures really rank*. Cambridge University Press.

Skinner, B. F. (1938). *The behavior of organisms: An experimental analysis*. Appleton-Century-Crofts.

Skinner, B. F. (1948). "Superstition" in the pigeon. *Journal of Experimental Psychology, 38*, 168–172.

Skinner, B. F. (1953). *Science and human behavior*. Macmillan.

Skinner, B. F. (1957). *Verbal behavior*. Appleton-Century-Crofts.

Skinner, B. F. (1977). Why I am not a cognitive psychologist. *Behaviorism, 5*, 1–10.

Skinner, B. F. (1979). *The shaping of a behaviorist: Part two of an autobiography*. Knopf.

Skotko, B. G., Levine, S. P., & Goldstein, R. (2011b). Self-perceptions from people with Down syndrome. *American Journal of Medical Genetics Part A, 155*(10), 2360–2369. https://doi.org/10.1002/ajmg.a.34235

Slater, A., Morison, V., & Somers, M. (1988). Orientation discrimination and cortical function in the human newborn. *Perception, 17*, 597–602.

Slotnick, S. D., & Schacter, D. L. (2004). A sensory signature that distinguished true from false memories. *Nature Neuroscience, 7*, 664–672.

Small, D. M., Gerber, J. C., Mak, Y. E., & Hummel, T. (2005). Differential neural responses evoked by orthonasal versus retronasal odorant perception in humans. *Neuron, 47*(4), 593–605.

Smart, E., Smart, L., & Morton, L. (2003). *Bringing Elizabeth home: A journey of faith and hope*. Doubleday.

Smetacek, V. (2002). Balance: Mind-grasping gravity. *Nature, 415*, 481.

Smith, A. R., Chein, J., & Steinberg, L. (2014). Peers increase adolescent risk taking even when the probabilities of negative outcomes are known. *Developmental Psychology, 50*(5), 1564–1568. https://doi.org/10.1037/a0035696

Smith, C. N., Frascino, J. C., Hopkins, R. O., & Squire, L. R. (2013). The nature of anterograde and retrograde impairment after damage to the medial temporal lobe. *Neuropsychologia, 51,* 2709–2714.

Smith, E. E., & Jonides, J. (1997). Working memory: A view from neuroimaging. *Cognitive Psychology, 33,* 5–42.

Smith, E. N., Romero, C., Donovan, B., Herter, R., Paunesku, D., Cohen, G. L., Dweck, C. S., & Gross, J. J. (2018). Emotion theories and adolescent well-being: Results of an online intervention. *Emotion, 18*(6), 781–788. https://doi.org/10.1037/emo0000379

Smith, M. L., Glass, G. V., & Miller, T. I. (1980). *The benefits of psychotherapy.* Johns Hopkins University Press.

Smith, N., & Tsimpli, I.-M. (1995). *The mind of a savant.* Oxford University Press.

Snedeker, J., Geren, J., & Shafto, C. (2007). Starting over: International adoption as a natural experiment in language development. *Psychological Science, 18,* 79–87.

Snedeker, J., Geren, J., & Shafto, C. (2012). Disentangling the effects of cognitive development and linguistic expertise: A longitudinal study of the acquisition of English in internationally adopted children. *Cognitive Psychology, 65,* 39–76.

Sniekers, S., Stringer, S., Watanabe, K., Jansen, P. R., Coleman, J. R. I., Krapohl, E., Taskesen, E., Hammerschlag, A. R., Okbay, A., Zabaneh, D., Amin, N., Breen, G., Cesarini, D., Chabris, C. F., Iacono, W. G., Ikram, M. A., Johannesson, M., Koellinger, P., Lee, J. J., & Posthuma, D. (2017). Genome-wide association meta-analysis of 78,308 individuals identifies new loci and genes influencing human intelligence. *Nature Genetics, 49,* 1107. http://dx.doi.org/10.1038/ng.3869

Snowdon, R., Thompson, P., & Troscianko, T. (2012). *Basic vision: An introduction to visual perception* (2nd ed.). Oxford University Press.

Solomon, S., Greenberg, J., & Pyszczynski, T. (1991). A terror management theory of social behavior: The psychological functions of self-esteem and cultural worldviews. In M. P. Zanna (Ed.), *Advances in experimental social psychology* (Vol. 24, pp. 93–159). Academic Press.

Solomon, S., Greenberg, J., & Pyszczynski, T. (2004). The cultural animal: Twenty years of terror management theory and research. In J. Greenberg, S. L. Koole, & T. Pyszczynski (Eds.), *Handbook of experimental existential psychology* (pp. 13–34). Guilford Press.

Son, L. K., & Metcalfe, J. (2000). Metacognitive and control strategies in study-time allocation. *Journal of Experimental Psychology: Learning, Memory, and Cognition, 26,* 204–221.

Song, H., Fang, F., Arnberg, F. K., Mataix-Cols, D., de la Cruz, L. F., Almqvist, C., Fall, K., Lichtenstein, P., Thorgeirsson, G., & Valdimarsdóttir, U. A. (2019). Stress-related disorders and risk of cardiovascular disease: Population based, sibling controlled cohort study. *British Medical Journal, 365,* 1255.

Song, Y., Ma, J., Wang, H. J., Wang, Z., Hu, P., Zhang, B., & Agardh, A. (2014). Trends of age at menarche and association with body mass index in Chinese school-aged girls, 1985–2010. *Journal of Pediatrics, 165,* 1172–1177.

Sonnby-Borgstrom, M., Jonsson, P., & Svensson, O. (2003). Emotional empathy as related to mimicry reactions at different levels of information processing. *Journal of Nonverbal Behavior, 27,* 3–23.

Sparrow, B., Liu, J., & Wegner, D. M. (2011). Google effects on memory: Cognitive consequence of having information at our fingertips. *Science, 333,* 776–778.

Spearman, C. (1904). "General intelligence," objectively determined and measured. *American Journal of Psychology, 15,* 201–293.

Spelke, E. S. (2005). Sex differences in intrinsic aptitude for mathematics and science: A critical review. *American Psychologist, 60*(9), 950–958. https://doi.org/10.1037/0003-066X.60.9.950

Spencer, S. J., Logel, C., & Davies, P. G. (2016). Stereotype threat. *Annual Review of Psychology, 67*(1), 415–437.

Sperling, G. (1960). The information available in brief visual presentations. *Psychological Monographs, 74*(11), 1–29.

Spiegel, A. (2011). How psychology solved a WWII shipwreck mystery. NPR. https://www.npr.org/templates/transcript/transcript.php?storyId=140816037

Sporns, O., & Betzel, R. F. (2016). Modular brain networks. *Annual Review of Psychology, 67,* 613–640.

Sprecher, S. (1999). "I love you more today than yesterday": Romantic partners' perceptions of changes in love and related affect over time. *Journal of Personality and Social Psychology, 76,* 46–53.

Squire, L. R. (1992). Memory and the hippocampus: A synthesis from findings with rats, monkeys, and humans. *Psychological Review, 99,* 195–231.

Squire, L. R. (2009). The legacy of patient HM for neuroscience. *Neuron, 61,* 6–9.

Squire, L. R., & Kandel, E. R. (1999). *Memory: From mind to molecules.* Scientific American Library.

Squire, L. R., & Wixted, J. T. (2011). The cognitive neuroscience of memory since HM. *Annual Review of Neuroscience, 34,* 259–288.

Srivistava, S., John, O. P., Gosling, S. D., & Potter, J. (2003). Development of personality in early and middle adulthood: Set like plaster or persistent change? *Journal of Personality and Social Psychology, 84,* 1041–1053.

Sroufe, L. A., Egeland, B., & Kruetzer, T. (1990). The fate of early experience following developmental change: Longitudinal approaches to individual adaptation in childhood. *Child Development, 61,* 1363–1373.

St. Jacques, P. L., & Schacter, D. L. (2013). Modifying memory: Selectively enhancing and updating personal memories for a museum tour by reactivating them. *Psychological Science, 24,* 537–543.

Staddon, J. E. R., & Simmelhag, V. L. (1971). The "superstition" experiment: A reexamination of its implications for the principles of adaptive behavior. *Psychological Review, 78,* 3–43.

Stahl, A. E., & Feigenson, L. (2015). Observing the unexpected enhances infants' learning and exploration. *Science, 348*(6230), 91–94. https://doi.org/10.1126/science.aaa3799

Stanca, L. (2016). The geography of parenthood and well-being: Do children make us happy, where and why? In J. Helliwell, R. Layard, & J. Sachs (Eds.), *World Happiness Report 2016, Special Rome Edition* (Vol. II) (pp. 89–103). Sustainable Development Solutions Network. http://worldhappiness.report/#happiness2016

Stanovich, K. E. (2009). *What intelligence tests miss: The psychology of rational thought.* Yale University Press.

Stanovich, K. E., & West, R. F. (2000). Individual differences in reasoning: Implications for the rationality debate? *Behavioral and Brain Sciences, 23,* 645–726.

Statton, M. A., Encarnacion, M., Celnik, P., & Bastian, A. J. (2015). A single bout of moderate aerobic exercise improves motor skill acquisition. *PLoS One.* https://doi.org/10.1371/journal.pone.0141393

Staw, B. M., & Hoang, H. (1995). Sunk costs in the NBA: Why draft order affects playing time and survival in professional basketball. *Administrative Science Quarterly, 40,* 474–494.

Steele, C. M., & Aronson, J. (1995). Stereotype threat and the intellectual test performance of African Americans. *Journal of Personality and Social Psychology, 69,* 797–811.

Steele, C. M., & Josephs, R. A. (1990). Alcohol myopia: Its prized and dangerous effects. *American Psychologist, 45,* 921–933.

Steele, H., Steele, M., Croft, C., & Fonagy, P. (1999). Infant–mother attachment at one year predicts children's understanding of mixed emotions at six years. *Social Development, 8,* 161–178.

Stein, D. J., Phillips, K. A., Bolton, D., Fulford, K. W. M., Sadler, J. Z., & Kendler, K. S. (2010). What is a mental/psychiatric disorder? From *DSM-IV* to *DSM-V. Psychological Medicine, 40*(11), 1759–1765. https://doi.org/10.1017/S0033291709992261

Stein, M., Federspiel, A., Koenig, T., Wirth, M., Lehmann, C., Wiest, R., Strik, W., Brandeis, D., & Dierks, T. (2009). Reduced frontal activation with increasing second language proficiency. *Neuropsychologia, 47,* 2712–2720.

Steinbaum, E. A., & Miller, N. E. (1965). Obesity from eating elicited by daily stimulation of hypothalamus. *American Journal of Physiology, 208,* 1–5.

Steinberg, L. (2007). Risk taking in adolescence: New perspectives from brain and behavioral science. *Current Directions in Psychological Science, 16*(2), 55–59. https://doi.org/10.1111/j.1467-8721.2007.00475x

Steinberg, L., & Monahan, K. C. (2007). Age differences in resistance to peer influence. *Developmental Psychology, 43,* 1531–1543.

Steinberg, L., & Morris, A. S. (2001). Adolescent development. *Annual Review of Psychology, 52,* 83–110.

Steiner, J. E. (1973). The gustofacial response: Observation on normal and anencephalic newborn infants. In J. F. Bosma (Ed.), *Fourth symposium on oral sensation and perception: Development in the fetus and infant* (DHEW 73-546; pp. 254–278). U.S. Department of Health, Education, and Welfare.

Steiner, J. E. (1979). Human facial expressions in response to taste and smell stimulation. *Advances in Child Development and Behavior, 13,* 257–295.

Stellar, J. R., & Stellar, E. (1985). *The neurobiology of motivation and reward.* Springer-Verlag.

Stelmack, R. M. (1990). Biological bases of extraversion: Psychophysiological evidence. *Journal of Personality, 58,* 293–311.

Stemmler, G., Aue, T., & Wacker, J. (2007). Anger and fear: Separable effects of emotion and motivational direction on somatovisceral responses. *International Journal of Psychophysiology, 66*(2), 141–153. https://doi.org/10.1016/j.ijpsycho.2007.03.019

Stephens, R. S. (1999). Cannabis and hallucinogens. In B. S. McCrady & E. E. Epstein (Eds.), *Addictions: A comprehensive guidebook* (pp. 121–140). Oxford University Press.

Stern, J. A., Brown, M., Ulett, A., & Sletten, I. (1977). A comparison of hypnosis, acupuncture, morphine, Valium, aspirin, and placebo in the management of experimentally induced pain. In W. E. Edmonston (Ed.), *Conceptual and investigative approaches to hypnosis and hypnotic phenomena* (Vol. 296, pp. 175–193). New York Academy of Sciences.

Sternberg, R. J. (1986). A triangular theory of love. *Psychological Review, 93,* 119–135.

Sternberg, R. J. (1999). The theory of successful intelligence. *Review of General Psychology, 3*(4), 292–316. https://doi.org/10.1037/1089-2680.3.4.292

Sternberg, R. J. (2006). The Rainbow Project: Enhancing the SAT through assessments of analytical, practical, and creative skills. *Intelligence, 34*(4), 321–350. https://doi.org/10.1016/j.intell.2006.01.002

Sternberg, R. J., & Grigorenko, E. L. (2004). Intelligence and culture: How culture shapes what intelligence means, and the implications for a science of well-being. *Philosophical Transaction of the Royal Society B,* 1427–1434. https://doi.org/10.1093/acprof:oso/9780198567523.003.0014

Stevens, J. (1988). An activity approach to practical memory. In M. M. Gruneberg, P. E. Morris, & R. N. Sykes (Eds.), *Practical aspects of memory: Current research and issues* (Vol. 1, pp. 335–341). Wiley.

Stevenson, R. J., & Francis, H. M. (2017). The hippocampus and the regulation of human food intake. *Psychological Bulletin, 143*(10), 1011–1032. https://doi.org/10.1037/bul0000109

Stice, E., & Yokum, S. (2016). Neural vulnerability factors that increase risk for future weight gain. *Psychological Bulletin, 142*(5), 447–471. https://doi.org/10.1037/bul0000044

Stickgold, R., Malia, A., Maguire, D., Roddenberry, D., & O'Connor, M. (2000). Replaying the game: Hypnagogic images in normals and amnesics. *Science, 290,* 350–353.

Stockman, A., & Sharpe, L. T. (2000). Spectral sensitivities of the middle- and long-wavelength sensitive cones derived from measurements in observers of known genotype. *Vision Research, 40,* 1711–1737. See "cone fundamentals" at http://www.cvrl.org/

Stoet, G., & Geary, D. C. (2018). The gender equality paradox in STEM education. *Psychological Science.* Advanced online http://journals.sagepub.com/doi/full/10.1177/0956797617741719

Stone, A. A. (2018). Ecological momentary assessment in survey research. In D. L. Vannette & J. A. Krosnick (Eds.), *The Palgrave Handbook of Survey Research* (pp. 221–226). Palgrave Macmillan.

Stone, A. A., Schwartz, J. E., Broderick, J. E., & Deaton, A. (2010). A snapshot of the age distribution of psychological well-being in the United States. *Proceedings of the National Academy of Sciences, USA, 107*(22), 9985–9990. https://doi.org/10.1073/pnas.1003744107

Stone, J., Perry, Z. W., & Darley, J. M. (1997). "White men can't jump": Evidence for the perceptual confirmation of racial stereotypes following a basketball game. *Basic and Applied Social Psychology, 19*(3), 291–306. https://doi.org/10.1207/s15324834basp1903_2

Stone, M. H. (1997). Introduction: The history of obsessive-compulsive disorder from the early period to the turn of the twentieth century. In D. J. Stein & M. H. Stone (Eds.), *Essential papers on obsessive-compulsive disorder* (pp. 19–33). New York University Press.

Stoodley, C. J., Ray, N., J., Jack, A., & Stein, J. F. (2008). Implicit learning in control, dyslexic, and garden-variety poor readers. *Annals of the New York Academy of Sciences, 1145,* 173–183.

Storms, M. D. (1973). Videotape and the attribution process: Reversing actors' and observers' points of view. *Journal of Personality and Social Psychology, 27,* 165–175.

Strack, F. (2016). Reflections on the smiling registered replication report. *Perspectives on Psychological Science, 11,* 929–930. https://dx.doi.org/10.1177/1745691616674460

Strack, F., Martin, L. L., & Stepper, S. (1988). Inhibiting and facilitating conditions of the human smile: A nonobtrusive test of the facial feedback hypothesis. *Journal of Personality and Social Psychology, 54,* 768–777.

Strayer, D. L., Drews, F. A., & Johnston, W. A. (2003). Cell phone–induced failures of visual attention during simulated driving. *Journal of Experimental Psychology: Applied, 9,* 23–32.

Streissguth, A. P., Barr, H. M., Bookstein, F. L., Sampson, P. D., & Carmichael Olson, H. (1999). The long-term neurocognitive consequences of prenatal alcohol exposure: A 14-year study. *Psychological Science, 10,* 186–190.

Striano, T., & Reid, V. M. (2006). Social cognition in the first year. *Trends in Cognitive Sciences, 10*(10), 471–476.

Strohmetz, D. B., Rind, B., Fisher, R., & Lynn, M. (2002). Sweetening the till: The use of candy to increase restaurant tipping. *Journal of Applied Social Psychology, 32,* 300–309.

Strueber, D., Lueck, M., & Roth, G. (2006). The violent brain. *Scientific American Mind, 17,* 20–27.

Stuss, D. T., & Benson, D. F. (1986). *The frontal lobes.* Raven Press.

Suchman, A. L., Markakis, K., Beckman, H. B., & Frankel, R. (1997). A model of empathic communication in the medical interview. *Journal of the American Medical Association, 277,* 678–682.

Suddendorf, T., & Corballis, M. C. (2007). The evolution of foresight: What is mental time travel and is it unique to humans? *Behavioral and Brain Sciences, 30,* 299–313.

Sullivan-Singh, S. J., Stanton, A. L., & Low, C. A. (2015). Living with limited time: Socioemotional selectivity theory in the context of health adversity. *Journal of Personality and Social Psychology, 108,* 900–916.

Susman, S., Dent, C., McAdams, L., Stacy, A., Burton, D., & Flay, B. (1994). Group self-identification and adolescent cigarette smoking: A 1-year prospective study. *Journal of Abnormal Psychology, 103,* 576–580.

Susser, E. B., Brown, A., & Matte, T. D. (1999). Prenatal factors and adult mental and physical health. *Canadian Journal of Psychiatry, 44*(4), 326–334.

Sutin, A. R., Stephan, Y., & Terracciano, A. (2015). Weight discrimination and risk of mortality. *Psychological Science, 26*(11), 1803–1811. http://doi.org/10.1177/0956797615601103

Suzuki, L. A., & Valencia, R. R. (1997). Race–ethnicity and measured intelligence: Educational implications. *American Psychologist, 52,* 1103–1114.

Swann, W. B., Jr. (1983). Self-verification: Bringing social reality into harmony with the self. In J. M. Suls & A. G. Greenwald (Eds.), *Psychological perspectives on the self* (Vol. 2, pp. 33–66). Erlbaum.

Swann, W. B., Jr. (2012). Self-verification theory. In P. Van Lang, A. Kruglanski, & E. T. Higgins (Eds.), *Handbook of theories of social psychology* (Vol. 2, pp. 23–42). Sage.

Swann, W. B., Jr., & Rentfrow, P. J. (2001). Blirtatiousness: Cognitive, behavioral, and physiological consequences of rapid responding. *Journal of Personality and Social Psychology, 81*(6), 1160–1175.

Swayze, V. W., II. (1995). Frontal leukotomy and related psychosurgical procedures before antipsychotics (1935–1954): *A historical overview. American Journal of Psychiatry, 152*, 505–515.

Sweatt, J. D. (2019). The epigenetic basis of individuality. *Current Opinion in Behavioral Sciences, 25*, 51–56.

Swencionis, J. K., & Fiske, S. T. (2016) Promote up, ingratiate down: Status comparisons drive warmth-competence tradeoffs in impression management. *Journal of Experimental Social Psychology, 64*, 27–34.

Szechtman, H., & Woody, E. Z. (2006). Obsessive-compulsive disorder as a disturbance of security motivation: Constraints on comorbidity. *Neurotoxicity Research, 10*, 103–112.

Szpunar, K. K. (2010). Episodic future thought: An emerging concept. *Perspectives on Psychological Science, 5*, 142–162.

Szpunar, K. K., Khan, N. Y., & Schacter, D. L. (2013). Interpolated memory tests reduce mind wandering and improve learning of online lectures. *Proceedings of the National Academy of Sciences, USA, 110*, 6313–6317.

Szpunar, K. K., Watson, J. M., & McDermott, K. B. (2007). Neural substrates of envisioning the future. *Proceedings of the National Academy of Sciences, USA, 104*, 642–647.

Tajfel, H., Billig, M. G., Bundy, R. P., & Flament, C. (1971). Social categorization and intergroup behaviour. *European Journal of Social Psychology, 1*, 149–178.

Tajfel, H., & Wilkes, A. L. (1963). Classification and quantitative judgement. *British Journal of Psychology, 54*, 101–114.

Talhelm, T., Oishi, S., & Zhang, X. (2018). Who smiles while alone? Rates of smiling lower in China than U.S. *Emotion.* https://doi.org/10.1037/emo0000459

Tamir, M., Bigman, Y. E., Rhodes, E., Salerno, J., & Schreier, J. (2015). An expectancy-value model of emotion regulation: Implications for motivation, emotional experience, and decision making. *Emotion, 15*(1), 90–103. http://doi.org/10.1037/emo0000021

Tamir, M., & Ford, B. Q. (2012). Should people pursue feelings that feel good or feelings that do good? Emotional preferences and well-being. *Emotion, 12*, 1061–1070.

Tamminga, C. A., Nemeroff, C. B., Blakely, R. D., Brady, L., Carter, C. S., Davis, K. L., Dingledine, R., Gorman, J. M., Grigoriadis, D. E., Henderson, D. C., Innis, R. B. B., Killen, J., Laughren, T., McDonald, W. M., Murphy, G. M. M., Paul, S. M., Rudorfer, M. V., Sausville, E., Schatzberg, A. F., . . . Suppes, T. (2002). Developing novel treatments for mood disorders: Accelerating discovery. *Biological Psychiatry, 52*, 589–609.

Tanaka, K. Z., He, H., Tomar, A., Niisato, K., Huang, A. J. Y., & McHugh, T. J. (2018). The hippocampal engram maps experience but not place. *Science, 361*, 392–397.

Tang, D. W., Fellows, L. K., & Dagher, A. (2014). Behavioral and neural valuation of foods is driven by implicit knowledge of caloric content. *Psychological Science, 25*(12), 2168–2176. https://doi.org/10.1177/0956797614552081

Tang, Y.-P., Shimizu, E., Dube, G. R., Rampon, C., Kerchner, G. A., Zhuo, M., Liu, G., & Tsien, J. Z. (1999). Genetic enhancement of learning and memory in mice. *Nature, 401*, 63–69.

Tarantino, N., Tully, E. C., Garcia, S. E., South, S., Iacono, W. G., & McGue, M. (2014). Genetic and environmental influences on affiliation with deviant peers during adolescence and early adulthood. *Developmental Psychology, 50*(3), 663–673. https://doi.org/10.1037/a0034345

Taylor, E. (2001). *William James on consciousness beyond the margin.* Princeton University Press.

Taylor, S. E. (1989). *Positive illusions.* Basic Books.

Taylor, S. E. (2002). *The tending instinct: How nurturing is essential to who we are and how we live.* Times Books.

Taylor, S. E., & Brown, J. D. (1988). Illusion and well-being: A social psychological perspective on mental health. *Psychological Bulletin, 103*, 193–210.

Taylor, S. E., & Fiske, S. T. (1975). Point-of-view and perceptions of causality. *Journal of Personality and Social Psychology, 32*, 439–445.

Teasdale, J. D., Segal, Z. V., & Williams, J. M. G. (2000). Prevention of relapse/recurrence in major depression by mindfulness-based cognitive therapy. *Journal of Consulting and Clinical Psychology, 68*, 615–623.

Telch, M. J., Lucas, J. A., & Nelson, P. (1989). Non-clinical panic in college students: An investigation of prevalence and symptomology. *Journal of Abnormal Psychology, 98*, 300–306.

Tellegen, A., Lykken, D. T., Bouchard, T. J., Wilcox, K., Segal, N., & Rich, A. (1988). Personality similarity in twins reared together and apart. *Journal of Personality and Social Psychology, 54*, 1031–1039.

ten Brinke, L., Vohs, K. D., & Carney, D. R. (2016). Can ordinary people detect deception after all? *Trends in Cognitive Sciences, 20*(8), 579–588. https://doi.org/10.1016/j.tics.2016.05.012

Tepper, T. (2018). Americans say this is their biggest financial regret. https://www.bankrate.com/banking/savings/financial-security-may-2018/

Terman, L. M. (1916). *The measurement of intelligence.* Houghton Mifflin.

Tews, M. J., Stafford, K., & Tracey, J. B. (2011) What matters most? The perceived importance of ability and personality for hiring decisions. *Cornell Hospitality Quarterly, 52*, 94–101.

Teyler, T. J., & DiScenna, P. (1986). The hippocampal memory indexing theory. *Behavioral Neuroscience, 100*, 147–154.

Thakral, P., Madore, K. P., & Schacter, D. L. (2017). A role for the left angular gyrus in episodic simulation and memory. *Journal of Neuroscience, 37*, 8142–8149.

Thaler, K., Delivuk, M., Chapman, A., Gaynes, B. N., Kaminski, A., & Gartlehner, G. (2011). Second-generation antidepressants for seasonal affective disorder. *Cochrane Database of Systematic Reviews*, CD008591.

Thaler, R. H., & Sunstein, C. R. (2008). *Nudge: Improving decisions about health, wealth, and happiness.* Penguin Books.

Thase, M. E., & Howland, R. H. (1995). Biological processes in depression: An updated review and integration. In E. E. Beckham & W. R. Leber (Eds.), *Handbook of depression* (2nd ed., pp. 213–279). Guilford Press.

Thibaut, J. W., & Kelley, H. H. (1959). *The social psychology of groups.* Wiley.

Thomaes, S., Bushman, B. J., Stegge, H., & Olthof, T. (2008). Trumping shame by blasts of noise: Narcissism, self-esteem, shame, and aggression in young adolescents. *Child Development, 79*(6), 1792–1801.

Thomas, A., & Chess, S. (1977). *Temperament and development.* Brunner/Mazel.

Thompson, P. M., Giedd, J. N., Woods, R. P., MacDonald, D., Evans, A. C., & Toga, A. W. (2000). Growth patterns in the developing brain detected by using continuum mechanical tensor maps. *Nature, 404*, 190–193.

Thompson, P. M., Vidal, C., Giedd, J. N., Gochman, P., Blumenthal, J., Nicolson, R., Toga, A. W., & Rapoport, J. L. (2001). Mapping adolescent brain change reveals dynamic wave of accelerated gray matter loss in very early-onset schizophrenia. *Proceedings of the National Academy of Sciences, USA, 98*, 11650–11655.

Thompson, R. F. (2005). In search of memory traces. *Annual Review of Psychology, 56*, 1–23.

Thorndike, E. L. (1898). Animal intelligence: An experimental study of associative processes in animals. *Psychological Review Monograph Supplements, 2*, i–109.

Thurber, J. (1956). *Further fables of our time.* Simon & Schuster.

Thurstone, L. L. (1938). *Primary mental abilities.* University of Chicago Press.

Tienari, P., Wynne, L. C., Sorri, A., Lahti, I., Läksy, K., Moring, J., Naarala, M., Nieminen, P., & Wahlberg, K. E. (2004). Genotype–environment interaction in schizophrenia-spectrum disorder: Long-term follow-up study of Finnish adoptees. *British Journal of Psychiatry, 184*, 216–222.

Timmerman, T. A. (2007). "It was a thought pitch": Personal, situational, and target influences on hit-by-pitch events across time. *Journal of Applied Psychology, 92,* 876–884.

Tobey, E. A., Thal, D., Niparko, J. K., Eisenberg, L. S., Quittner, A. L., Wang, N. Y., & CDaCI Investigative Team. (2013). Influence of implantation age on school-age language performance in pediatric cochlear implant users. *International Journal of Audiology, 52*(4), 219–229. https://doi.org/10.3109/14992027.2012.759666

Todd, A. R., Bodenhausen, G. V., Richeson, J. A., & Galinsky, A. D. (2011). Perspective taking combats automatic expressions of racial bias. *Journal of Personality and Social Psychology, 100*(6), 1027–1042. https://doi.org/10.1037/a0022308

Toga, A. W., Clark, K. A., Thompson, P. M., Shattuck, D. W., & Van Horn, J. D. (2012). Mapping the human connectome. *Neurosurgery, 71,* 1–5.

Tolin, D. F. (2010). Is cognitive-behavioral therapy more effective than other therapies? A meta-analytic review. *Clinical Psychology Review, 30,* 710–720.

Tolman, E. C., & Honzik, C. H. (1930). Introduction and removal of reward and maze performance in rats. *University of California Publications in Psychology, 4,* 257–275.

Tolman, E. C., Ritchie, B. F., & Kalish, D. (1946). Studies in spatial learning: I: Orientation and short cut. *Journal of Experimental Psychology, 36,* 13–24.

Tomasello, M., & Call, J. (2004). The role of humans in the cognitive development of apes revisited. *Animal Cognition, 7,* 213–215.

Tomasello, M., Savage-Rumbaugh, S., & Kruger, A. C. (1993). Imitative learning of actions on objects by children, chimpanzees, and enculturated chimpanzees. *Child Development, 64,* 1688–1705.

Tomkins, S. S. (1981). The role of facial response in the experience of emotion. *Journal of Personality and Social Psychology, 40,* 351–357.

Torre, J. B. & Lieberman, M. D. (2018). Putting feelings into words: Affect labeling as implicit emotion regulation. *Emotion Review, 10,* 116–124.

Tracy, J. L., Randles, D., & Steckler, C. M. (2015). The nonverbal communication of emotions. *Current Opinion in Behavioral Sciences, 3,* 25–30.

Tranter, L. J., & Koutstaal, W. (2007). Age and flexible thinking: An experimental demonstration of the beneficial effects of increased cognitively stimulating activity on fluid intelligence in healthy older adults. *Neuropsychology, Development, and Cognition. Section B, Aging, Neuropsychology and Cognition, 15,* 184–207.

Treede, R. D., Kenshalo, D. R., Gracely, R. H., & Jones, A. K. (1999). The cortical representation of pain. *Pain, 79,* 105–111.

Treisman, A. (1998). Feature binding, attention and object perception. *Philosophical Transactions of the Royal Society B, 353,* 1295–1306.

Treisman, A. (2006). How the deployment of attention determines what we see. *Visual Cognition, 14,* 411–443.

Treisman, A., & Schmidt, H. (1982). Illusory conjunctions in the perception of objects. *Cognitive Psychology, 14,* 107–141.

Trivers, R. L. (1972). Parental investment and sexual selection. In B. Campbell (Ed.), *Sexual selection and the descent of man, 1871–1971* (pp. 139–179). Aldine.

Troy, A. S., Saquib, S., Thal, J., & Ciuk, D. J. (2018). The regulation of negative and positive affect in response to daily stressors. *Emotion.* https://doi.org/10.1037/emo0000486

Trull, T. J., & Durrett, C. A. (2005). Categorical and dimensional models of personality disorder. *Annual Review of Clinical Psychology, 1,* 355–380.

Tucker-Drob, E. M., Briley, D. A., & Harden, K. P. (2013). Genetic and environmental influences on cognition across development and context. *Current Directions in Psychological Science, 22*(5), 349–355. https://doi.org/10.1177/0963721413485087

Tulving, E. (1985). Memory and consciousness. *Canadian Psychologist, 25,* 1–12.

Tulving, E., Kapur, S., Craik, F. I. M., Moscovitch, M., & Houle, S. (1994). Hemispheric encoding/retrieval asymmetry in episodic memory: Positron emission tomography findings. *Proceedings of the National Academy of Sciences, USA, 91,* 2016–2020.

Tulving, E., & Schacter, D. L. (1990). Priming and human memory systems. *Science, 247,* 301–306.

Tulving, E., Schacter, D. L., & Stark, H. (1982). Priming effects in word-fragment completion are independent of recognition memory. *Journal of Experimental Psychology: Learning, Memory, and Cognition, 8,* 336–342.

Tulving, E., & Thomson, D. M. (1973). Encoding specificity and retrieval processes in episodic memory. *Psychological Review, 80,* 352–373.

Turner, D. C., & Sahakian, B. J. (2006). Neuroethics of cognitive enhancement. *BioSocieties, 1,* 113–123.

Turner, M. E., & Pratkanis, A. R. (1998). Twenty-five years of groupthink theory and research: Lessons from the evaluation of a theory. *Organizational Behavior and Human Decision Processes, 73*(2–3), 105–115. https://doi.org/10.1006/obhd.1998.2756

Tversky, A., & Kahneman, D. (1973). Availability: A heuristic for judging frequency and probability. *Cognitive Psychology, 5,* 207–232.

Tversky, A., & Kahneman, D. (1974). Judgment under uncertainty: Heuristics and biases. *Science, 185,* 1124–1131.

Tversky, A., & Kahneman, D. (1981). The framing of decisions and the psychology of choice. *Science, 211,* 453–458.

Tversky, A., & Kahneman, D. (1983). Extensional versus intuitive reasoning: The conjunction fallacy in probability judgment. *Psychological Review, 90,* 293–315.

Tversky, A., & Kahneman, D. (1992). Advances in prospect theory: Cumulative representation of uncertainty. *Journal of Risk and Uncertainty, 5,* 297–323.

Tyler, T. R. (1990). *Why people obey the law.* Yale University Press.

Uchikawa, K., Morimoto, T., & Matsumoto, T. (2017). Understanding individual differences in color appearance of "#TheDress" based on the optimal color hypothesis. *Journal of Vision, 17*(8), 10. https://doi.org/10.1167/17.8.10

Umberson, D., Williams, K., Powers, D. A., Liu, H., & Needham, B. (2006). You make me sick: Marital quality and health over the life course. *Journal of Health and Social Behavior, 47,* 1–16.

Uncapher, M. R., & Rugg, M. D. (2008). Fractionation of the component processes underlying successful episodic encoding: A combined fMRI and divided-attention study. *Journal of Cognitive Neuroscience, 20,* 240–254.

Ungerleider, L. G., & Mishkin, M. (1982). Two cortical visual systems. In D. J. Ingle, M. A. Goodale, & R. J. W. Mansfield (Eds.), *Analysis of visual behavior* (pp. 549–586). MIT Press.

Urban, N. B. L., Girgis, R. R., Talbot, P. S., Kegeles, L. S., Xu, X., Frankie, W. G., Hart, C. L., Slifstein, M., Abi-Dargham, A., & Laruelle, M. (2012). Sustained recreational use of ecstasy is associated with altered pre- and postsynaptic markers of serotonin transmission in neocortical areas: A PET study with [11c] DASB and [11c] MDL 100907. *Neuropsychopharmacology, 37,* 1465–1473.

Ursano, R. J., & Silberman, E. K. (2003). Psychoanalysis, psychoanalytic psychotherapy, and supportive psychotherapy. In R. E. Hales & S. C. Yudofsky (Eds.), *The American Psychiatric Publishing textbook of clinical psychiatry* (4th ed., pp. 1177–1203). American Psychiatric Publishing.

Uskul, A. K., & Over, H. (2014). Responses to social exclusion in cultural context: Evidence from farming and herding communities. *Journal of Personality and Social Psychology, 106*(5), 752–771. https://doi.org/10.1037/a0035810

Vacha, E., & McBride, M. (1993). Cramming: A barrier to student success, a way to beat the system, or an effective strategy? *College Student Journal, 27,* 2–11.

Vafaei, A., Ahmed, T., Falcão Freire, A., Zunzunegui, M. V., & Guerra, R. O. (2016). Depression, sex and gender roles in older adult populations: The international mobility in aging studies (IMIAS). *PLoS ONE, 11,* e0146867.

Valentine, T., Brennen, T., & Brédart, S. (1996). *The cognitive psychology of proper names: On the importance of being Ernest.* Routledge.

Vallacher, R. R., & Wegner, D. M. (1985). *A theory of action identification.* Erlbaum.

Vallacher, R. R., & Wegner, D. M. (1987). What do people think they're doing? Action identification and human behavior. *Psychological Review, 94,* 3–15.

van den Boom, D. C. (1994). The influence of temperament and mothering on attachment and exploration: An experimental manipulation of sensitive responsiveness among lower-class mothers with irritable infants. *Child Development, 65,* 1457–1477.

van den Boom, D. C. (1995). Do first year intervention effects endure? Follow-up during toddlerhood of a sample of Dutch irritable infants. *Child Development, 66,* 1798–1816.

Van Dessel, P., Mertens, G., Smith, C. T., & De Houwer, J. (2019). Mere exposure effects on implicit stimulus evaluation: The moderating role of evaluation task, number of stimulus presentations, and memory for presentation frequency. *Personality and Social Psychology Bulletin, 45*(3), 447–460. https://doi.org/10.1177/0146167218789065

van Honk, J., & Schutter, D. J. L. G. (2007). Testosterone reduces conscious detection of signals serving social correction: Implications for antisocial behavior. *Psychological Science, 18,* 663–667.

van IJzendoorn, M. H., Juffer, F., & Klein Poelhuis, C. W. (2005). Adoption and cognitive development: A meta-analytic comparison of adopted and nonadopted children's IQ and school performance. *Psychological Bulletin, 131,* 301–316.

van IJzendoorn, M. H., & Sagi, A. (1999). Cross-cultural patterns of attachment: Universal and contextual dimensions. In J. Cassidy & P. R. Shaver (Eds.), *Handbook of attachment: Theory, research and clinical applications* (pp. 713–734). Guilford Press.

Van Laningham, J., Johnson, D. R., & Amato, P. (2001). Marital happiness, marital duration, and the U-shaped curve: Evidence from a five-wave panel study. *Social Forces, 79,* 1313–1341.

van Praag, H. (2009). Exercise and the brain: Something to chew on. *Trends in Neuroscience, 32,* 283–290.

van Stegeren, A. H., Everaerd, W., Cahill, L., McGaugh, J. L., & Gooren, L. J. G. (1998). Memory for emotional events: Differential effects of centrally versus peripherally acting blocking agents. *Psychopharmacology, 138,* 305–310.

van Vliet, I. M., van Well, E. P., Bruggeman, R., Campo, J. A., Hijman, R., van Megen, H. J., van Balkom, L. M., & van Rijen, P. C. (2013). An evaluation of irreversible psychosurgical treatment of patients with obsessive-compulsive disorder in the Netherlands, 2001–2008. *Journal of Nervous and Mental Disease, 201,* 226–228.

Vargha-Khadem, F., Gadian, D. G., Watkins, K. E., Connelly, A., Van Paesschen, W., & Mishkin, M. (1997). Differential effects of early hippocampal pathology on episodic and semantic memory. *Science, 277,* 376–380.

Vasilenko, S. A., Maas, M. K., & Lefkowitz, E. S. (2015). "It felt good but weird at the same time": Emerging adults' first experiences of six different sexual behaviors. *Journal of Adolescent Research, 30,* 586–606. http://dx.doi.org/10.1177/0743558414561298

Vinter, A., & Perruchet, P. (2002). Implicit motor learning through observational training in adults and children. *Memory & Cognition, 30,* 256–261.

Vitkus, J. (1999). *Casebook in abnormal psychology* (4th ed.). McGraw-Hill.

Volkow, N. D., & Boyle, M. (2018). Neuroscience of addiction: Relevance to prevention and treatment. *American Journal of Psychiatry, 175,* 729–740.

Volkow, N. D., Jones, E. B., Einstein, E. B., & Wargo, E. M. (2019). Prevention and treatment of opioid misuse and addiction: A review. *Journal of the American Medical Association Psychiatry* (epub online December 5).

Volkow, N. D., Koob, G. F., & McLellan, A. T. (2016). Neurobiologic advances from the brain disease model of addiction. *New England Journal of Medicine, 374,* 363–371.

von Bartheld, C. S., Bahney, J., & Herculano-Houzel, S. (2016) The search for true numbers of neurons and glial cells in the human brain: A review of 150 years of cell counting. *Journal of Comparative Neurology, 524,* 3865–3895.

Von Frisch, K. (1974). Decoding the language of the bee. *Science, 185,* 663–668.

Vondra, J. I., Shaw, D. S., Swearingen, L., Cohen, M., & Owens, E. B. (2001). Attachment stability and emotional and behavioral regulation from infancy to preschool age. *Development and Psychopathology, 13,* 13–33.

Vrij, A., Granhag, P. A., Mann, S., & Leal, S. (2011). Outsmarting the liars: Toward a cognitive lie detection approach. *Current Directions in Psychological Science, 20*(1), 28–32.

Vukasovíc, T., & Bratko, D. (2015) Heritability of personality: A meta-analysis of behavior genetic studies. *Psychological Bulletin, 141,* 769–785.

Wade, K. A., Garry, M., & Pezdek, K. (2018). Deconstructing rich false memories of committing crime: Commentary on Shaw and Porter (2015). *Psychological Science, 29,* 471–476.

Wade, S. E., Trathen, W., & Schraw, G. (1990). An analysis of spontaneous study strategies. *Reading Research Quarterly, 25,* 147–166.

Wadhwa, P. D., Sandman, C. A., & Garite, T. J. (2001). The neurobiology of stress in human pregnancy: Implications for prematurity and development of the fetal central nervous system. *Progress in Brain Research, 133,* 131–142.

Wager, T. D., Rilling, J., K., Smith, E. E., Sokolik, A., Casey, K. L., Davidson, R. J., Kosslyn, S. M., Rose, R. M., & Cohen, J. D. (2004). Placebo-induced changes in fMRI in the anticipation and experience of pain. *Science, 303,* 1162–1167.

Wagner, A. D., Schacter, D. L., Rotte, M., Koutstaal, W., Maril, A., Dale, A. M., Rosen, B. R., & Buckner, R. L. (1998). Remembering and forgetting of verbal experiences as predicted by brain activity. *Science, 281,* 1188–1190.

Wagner, G., & Morris, E. (1987). Superstitious behavior in children. *Psychological Record, 37,* 471–488.

Wai, J., Putallaz, M., & Makel, M. C. (2012). Studying intellectual outliers: Are there sex differences, and are the smart getting smarter? *Current Directions in Psychological Science, 21*(6), 382–390. https://doi.org/10.1177/0963721412455052

Wainer, H., & Zwerling, H. L. (2006). Evidence that smaller schools do not improve student achievement. *Phi Delta Kappan, 88*(4), 300–303. https://doi.org/10.1177/003172170608800411

Wakefield, J. C. (2007). The concept of mental disorder: Diagnostic implications of the harmful dysfunction analysis. *World Psychiatry, 6,* 149–156.

Walden, T. A., & Ogan, T. A. (1988). The development of social referencing. *Child Development, 59,* 1230–1240.

Waldfogel, S. (1948). The frequency and affective character of childhood memories. *Psychological Monographs, 62*(4), i–39. https://doi.org/10.1037/h0093581

Walker, N. P., McConville, P. M., Hunter, D., Deary, I. J., & Whalley, L. J. (2002). Childhood mental ability and lifetime psychiatric contact. *Intelligence, 30*(3), 233–245. https://doi.org/10.1016/S0160-2896(01)00098-8

Wallbott, H. G. (1998). Bodily expression of emotion. *European Journal of Social Psychology, 28,* 879–896.

Walton, G. M., & Spencer, S. J. (2009). Latent ability: Grades and test scores systematically underestimate the intellectual ability of negatively stereotyped students. *Psychological Science, 20,* 1132–1139.

Waltzman, S. B. (2006). Cochlear implants: Current status. *Expert Review of Medical Devices, 3,* 647–655.

Wammes, J. D., Seli, P., Cheyne, J. A., Boucher, P. O., & Smilek, D. (2016). Mind wandering during lectures II: Relation to academic performance. *Scholarship of Teaching and Learning in Psychology, 2,* 33–48.

Wang, P. S., Aguilar-Gaxiola, S., Alonso, J., Angermeyer, M. C., Borges, G., Bromet, E. J., Bruffaerts, R., de Girolamo, G., de Graaf, R., Gureje, O., Haro, J. M., Karam, E. G., Kessler, R. C., Kovess, V., Lane, M. C., Lee, S., Levinson, D., Ono, Y., Petukhova, M., . . . Wells, J. E. (2007). Use of mental health services for anxiety, mood, and substance disorders in 17 countries in the WHO World Mental Health Surveys. *Lancet, 370,* 841–850.

Wang, P. S., Berglund, P. A., Olfson, M., & Kessler, R. C. (2004). Delays in initial treatment contact after first onset of a mental disorder. *Health Services Research, 39,* 393–415.

Wang, P. S., Berglund, P., Olfson, M., Pincus, H. A., Wells, K. B., & Kessler, R. C. (2005). Failure and delay in initial treatment contact after first onset of mental disorders in the National Comorbidity Survey Replication. *Archives of General Psychiatry, 62*(6), 629–640.

Wang, S.-H., & Baillargeon, R. (2008). Detecting impossible changes in infancy: A three-system account. *Trends in Cognitive Sciences, 12*(1), 17–23.

Wang, W., & Parker, K. (2014). *Record share of Americans have never married as values, economics and gender patterns change.* Pew Research Center's Social & Demographic Trends project. http://www.pewsocialtrends.org /2014/09/24/record-share-of-americans-have-never-married/

Wansink, B., & Wansink, C. S. (2010). The largest last supper: Depictions of food portions and plate size increased over the millennium. *International Journal of Obesity, 34,* 943–944.

Ward, B. W., Dahlhamer, J. M., Galinsky, A. M., & Joestl, S. S. (2014). Sexual orientation and health among US adults: National Health Interview Survey, 2013. *National Health Statistics Reports, 15,* 1–10.

Ward, Z. J., Long, M. W., Resch, S. C., Giles, C. M., Cradock, A. L., & Gortmaker, S. L. (2017). Simulation of growth trajectories of childhood obesity into adulthood. *New England Journal of Medicine, 377*(22), 2145–2153. https://doi.org/10.1056/NEJMoa1703860

Warneken, F., & Tomasello, M. (2009). Varieties of altruism in children and chimpanzees. *Trends in Cognitive Sciences, 13,* 397–402.

Warner, L. A., Kessler, R. C., Hughes, M., Anthony, J. C., & Nelson, C. B. (1995). Prevalence and correlates of drug use and dependence in the United States: Results from the National Comorbidity Survey. *Archives of General Psychiatry, 52,* 219–229.

Warren, K. R., & Hewitt, B. G. (2009). Fetal alcohol spectrum disorders: When science, medicine, public policy, and laws collide. *Developmental Disabilities Research Reviews, 15,* 170–175.

Warrington, E. K., & McCarthy, R. A. (1983). Category specific access dysphasia. *Brain, 106,* 859–878.

Warrington, E. K., & Shallice, T. (1984). Category specific semantic impairments. *Brain, 107,* 829–854.

Watanabe, S., Sakamoto, J., & Wakita, M. (1995). Pigeons' discrimination of painting by Monet and Picasso. *Journal of the Experimental Analysis of Behavior, 63,* 165–174.

Waters, T. E. A., Fraley, R. C., Groh, A. M., Steele, R. D., Vaughn, B. E., Bost, K. K., Verissimo, M., Coppola, G., & Roisman, G. I. (2015). The latent structure of secure base script knowledge. *Developmental Psychology, 51*(6), 823–830. https://doi.org/10.1037/dev0000012

Watkins, L. R., & Maier, S. F. (2005). Immune regulation of central nervous system functions: From sickness responses to pathological pain. *Journal of Internal Medicine, 257,* 139–155.

Watson, D., & Pennebaker, J. W. (1989). Health complaints, stress, and distress: Exploring the central role of negative affectivity. *Psychological Review, 96,* 234–254.

Watson, D., & Tellegen, A. (1985). Toward a consensual structure of mood. *Psychological Bulletin, 98,* 219–235.

Watson, J. B. (1913). Psychology as the behaviorist views it. *Psychological Review, 20,* 158–177.

Watson, J. B. (1919). *Psychology from the standpoint of a behaviorist.* J. B. Lippincott.

Watson, J. B. (1924). *Behaviorism.* People's Institute Publishing Co.

Watson, J. B. (1930). *Behaviorism.* (rev. ed.). University of Chicago Press.

Watson, J. B., & Rayner, R. (1920). Conditioned emotional reactions. *Journal of Experimental Psychology, 3,* 1–14.

Watson, R. I. (1978). *The great psychologists.* Lippincott.

Watzke, B., Rüddel, H., Jürgensen, R., Koch, U., Kristen, L., Grothgar, B., & Schulz, H. (2012). Longer term outcome of cognitive-behavioural and psychodynamic psychotherapy in routine mental health care: Randomised controlled trial. *Behaviour Research and Therapy, 50,* 580–587.

Weaver, I. C. G., Cervoni, N., Champagne, F. A., D'Alessio, A. C., Sharma, S., Seckl, J. R., Dymov, S., Szyf, M., & Meaney, M. J. (2004). Epigenetic programming by maternal behavior. *Nature Neuroscience, 7,* 847–854.

Webb, T. L., Miles, E., & Sheeran, P. (2012). Dealing with feeling: A meta-analysis of the effectiveness of strategies derived from the process model of emotion regulation. *Psychological Bulletin, 138*(4), 775–808.

Webster Marketon, J. I., & Glaser, R. (2008). Stress hormones and immune function. *Cellular Immunology, 252,* 16–26.

Wechsler, H., & Nelson, T. F. (2001). Binge drinking and the American college student: What's five drinks? *Psychology of Addictive Behaviors, 15*(4), 287–291. https://doi.org/10.1037/0893-164X.15.4.287

Wegner, D. M. (1989). *White bears and other unwanted thoughts.* Viking.

Wegner, D. M. (1994a). Ironic processes of mental control. *Psychological Review, 101,* 34–52.

Wegner, D. M. (1994b). *White bears and other unwanted thoughts: Suppression, obsession, and the psychology of mental control.* Guilford Press.

Wegner, D. M. (2002). *The illusion of conscious will.* MIT Press.

Wegner, D. M. (2009). How to think, say, or do precisely the worst thing for any occasion. *Science, 325,* 48–51.

Wegner, D. M., Ansfield, M., & Pilloff, D. (1998). The putt and the pendulum: Ironic effects of the mental control of action. *Psychological Science, 9,* 196–199.

Wegner, D. M., Broome, A., & Blumberg, S. J. (1997). Ironic effects of trying to relax under stress. *Behavior Research and Therapy, 35,* 11–21.

Wegner, D. M., Erber, R. E., & Zanakos, S. (1993). Ironic processes in the mental control of mood and mood-related thought. *Journal of Personality and Social Psychology, 65,* 1093–1104.

Wegner, D. M., & Gilbert, D. T. (2000). Social psychology: The science of human experience. In H. Bless & J. Forgas (Eds.), *The message within: Subjective experience in social cognition and behavior* (pp. 1–9). Psychology Press.

Wegner, D. M., Schneider, D. J., Carter, S. R., & White, T. L. (1987). Paradoxical effects of thought suppression. *Journal of Personality and Social Psychology, 53,* 5–13.

Wegner, D. M., Vallacher, R. R., Macomber, G., Wood, R., & Arps, K. (1984). The emergence of action. *Journal of Personality and Social Psychology, 46,* 269–279.

Wegner, D. M., & Wenzlaff, R. M. (1996). Mental control. In E. T. Higgins & A. Kruglanski (Eds.), *Social psychology: Handbook of basic mechanisms and processes* (pp. 466–492). Guilford Press.

Wegner, D. M., Wenzlaff, R. M., & Kozak, M. (2004). Dream rebound: The return of suppressed thoughts in dreams. *Psychological Science, 15,* 232–236.

Wegner, D. M., & Zanakos, S. (1994). Chronic thought suppression. *Journal of Personality, 62,* 615–640.

Weinstein, N. D. (1980). Unrealistic optimism about future life events. *Journal of Personality and Social Psychology, 39,* 806–820.

Weintraub, D., Papay, K., & Siderowf, A. (2013). Screening for impulse control symptoms in patients with de novo Parkinson disease: A case-control study. *Neurology, 80,* 176–180.

Weiser, M., Zarka, S., Werbeloff, N., Kravitz, E., & Lubin, G. (2010). Cognitive test scores in male adolescent cigarette smokers compared to non-smokers: A population-based study. *Addiction, 105*(2), 358–363. https://doi.org/10.1111/j.1360-0443.2009.02740.x

Weisfeld, G. (1999). *Evolutionary principles of human adolescence.* Basic Books.

Weissman, M. M., Markowitz, J. C., & Klerman, G. L. (2000). *Comprehensive guide to interpersonal psychotherapy.* Basic Books.

Weldon, M. S. (2001). Remembering as a social process. In D. L. Medin (Ed.), *The psychology of learning and motivation: Advances in research and theory* (Vol. 40, pp. 67–120). Academic Press.

Wellman, H. M., Fang, F., Liu, D., Zhu, L., & Liu, L. (2006). Scaling theory-of-mind understandings in Chinese children. *Psychological Science, 17,* 1075–1081. https://doi.org/10.1111/j.1467-9280.2006.01830.x

Wenzlaff, R. M., & Wegner, D. M. (2000). Thought suppression. In S. T. Fiske (Ed.), *Annual review of psychology* (Vol. 51, pp. 51–91). Annual Reviews.

Wesch, N. N., Law, B., & Hall, C. R. (2007). The use of observational learning by athletes. *Journal of Sport Behavior, 30,* 219–231.

Westbrook, A., & Frank, M. (2018). Dopamine and proximity in motivation and cognitive control. *Current Opinion in Behavioral Science, 22,* 28–34.

Westrin, A., & Lam, R. W. (2007). Seasonal affective disorder: A clinical update. *Journal of Clinical Psychiatry, 19,* 239–246.

Wexler, K. (1999). Maturation and growth of grammar. In W. C. Ritchie & T. K. Bhatia (Eds.), *Handbook of child language acquisition* (pp. 55–110). Academic Press.

Wheeler, M. A., Petersen, S. E., & Buckner, R. L. (2000). Memory's echo: Vivid recollection activates modality-specific cortex. *Proceedings of the National Academy of Sciences, USA, 97,* 11125–11129.

White, G. M., & Kirkpatrick, J. (Eds.). (1985). *Person, self, and experience: Exploring pacific ethnopsychologies.* University of California Press.

Whiten, A. (2017). Social learning and culture in child and chimpanzee. *Annual Review of Psychology, 68,* 129–154.

Whybrow, P. C. (1997). *A mood apart.* Basic Books.

Wiebe, S. A., Fang, H., Johnson, C., James, K. E., & Espy, K. A. (2014). Determining the impact of prenatal tobacco exposure on self-regulation at 6 months. *Developmental Psychology, 50*(6), 1746–1756. https://doi.org/10.1037/a0035904

Wiegner, L., Hange, D., Björkelund, C., & Ahlbrg, G., Jr. (2015). Prevalence of perceived stress and associations to symptoms of exhaustion, depression, and anxiety in a working age population seeking primary care: An observational study. *BMC Family Practice, 16,* 38.

Wiggs, C. L., & Martin, A. (1998). Properties and mechanisms of perceptual priming. *Current Opinion in Neurobiology, 8,* 227–233.

Wilcoxon, H. C., Dragoin, W. B., & Kral, P. A. (1971). Illness-induced aversions in rats and quail: Relative salience of visual and gustatory cues. *Science, 171,* 826–828.

Wiley, J. L. (1999). Cannabis: Discrimination of "internal bliss"? *Pharmacology, Biochemistry, & Behavior, 64,* 257–260.

Williams, C. M., & Kirkham, T. C. (1999). Anandamide induces overeating: Mediation by central cannabinoid (CB1) receptors. *Psychopharmacology, 143,* 315–317.

Williams, K. D. (2007). Ostracism. *Annual Review of Psychology, 58,* 425–452. https://doi.org/10.1146/annurev.psych.58.110405.085641

Willingham, D. T. (2007). Critical thinking: Why is it so hard to teach? *American Educator, 31*(2), 8–19.

Wilson, K., & Korn, J. H. (2007). Attention during lectures: Beyond ten minutes. *Teaching of Psychology, 34,* 85–89.

Wilson, T. D. (2011). *Redirect: The surprising new science of psychological change.* Little, Brown.

Wilson, T. D., Meyers, J., & Gilbert, D. T. (2003). "How happy was I, anyway?" A retrospective impact bias. *Social Cognition, 21,* 421–446.

Wilt, J., & Revelle, W. (2019). The Big Five, everyday contexts and activities, and affective experience. *Personality and Individual Differences, 136,* 140–147.

Wimmer, H., & Perner, J. (1983). Beliefs about beliefs: Representations and constraining function of wrong beliefs in young children's understanding of deception. *Cognition, 13,* 103–128.

Winblad, B., Amouyel, P., Andrieu, S., Ballard, C., Brayne, C., Brodaty, H., Cedazo-Minguez, A., Dubois, B., Edvardsson, D., Feldman, H., Fratiglioni, L., Frisoni, G. B., Gauthier, S., Georges, J., Graff, C., Iqbal, K., Jessen, F., Johansson, G., Jönsson, L., . . . Zetterberg, H. (2016). Defeating Alzheimer's disease and other dementias: A priority for European science and society. *Lancet Neurology, 15,* 455–532.

Windham, G. C., Eaton, A., & Hopkins, B. (1999). Evidence for an association between environmental tobacco smoke exposure and birthweight: A meta-analysis and new data. *Pediatrics and Perinatal Epidemiology, 13,* 35–57.

Winkler, A. D., Spillmann, L., Werner, J. S., & Webster, M. A. (2015). Asymmetries in blue-yellow color perception and in the color of 'the dress.' *Current Biology, 25,* R547–R548.

Winocur, G., Moscovitch, M., & Bontempi, B. (2010). Memory formation and long-term retention in humans and animals: Convergence towards a transformation account of hippocampal–neocortical interactions. *Neuropsychologia, 48,* 2339–2356.

Winterer, G., & Weinberger, D. R. (2004). Genes, dopamine and cortical signal-to-noise ratio in schizophrenia. *Trends in Neuroscience, 27,* 683–690.

Wise, R. A. (1989). Brain dopamine and reward. *Annual Review of Psychology, 40,* 191–225.

Wise, R. A. (2005). Forebrain substrates of reward and motivation. *Journal of Comparative Neurology, 493,* 115–121.

Wisniewski, H., Liu, G., Henson, P., Vaidyam, A., Hajratalli, N. K., Onnela, J. P., & Torous, J. (2019). Understanding the quality, effectiveness, and attributes of top-rated smartphone health apps. *Evidence-Based Mental Health, 22,* 4–9.

Wixted, J. T., & Ebbensen, E. (1991). On the form of forgetting. *Psychological Science, 2,* 409–415.

Wood, A., Rychlowska, M., & Niedenthal, P. M. (2016). Heterogeneity of long-history migration predicts emotion recognition accuracy. *Emotion, 16*(4), 413–420. https://doi.org/1037/emo0000137

Wood, J. M., & Bootzin, R. R. (1990). Prevalence of nightmares and their independence from anxiety. *Journal of Abnormal Psychology, 99,* 64–68.

Woods, S. C., Seeley, R. J., Porte, D., Jr., & Schwartz, M. W. (1998). Signals that regulate food intake and energy homeostasis. *Science, 280,* 1378–1383.

Woumans, E., Santens, P., Sieben, A., Versijpt, J., Stevens, M., & Duyck, W. (2015). Bilingualism delays clinical manifestation of Alzheimer's disease. *Bilingualism: Language and Cognition, 18,* 568–574.

Wrangham, R. W. (2017). Two types of aggression in human evolution. *Proceedings of the National Academy of Sciences, USA, 115*(2), 245–253.

Wraw, C., Deary, I. J., Gale, C. R., & Der, G. (2015). Intelligence in youth and health at age 50. *Intelligence, 53* (2015), 23–32.

Wren, A. M., Seal, L. J., Cohen, M. A., Brynes, A. E., Frost, G. S., Murphy, K. G., Dhillo, W. S., Ghatei, M. A., & Bloom, S. R. (2001). Ghrelin enhances appetite and increases food intake in humans. *Journal of Clinical Endocrinology and Metabolism, 86,* 5992–5995.

Wrenn, C. C., Turchi, J. N., Schlosser, S., Dreiling, J. L., Stephenson, D. A., & Crawley, J. N. (2006). Performance of galanin transgenic mice in the 5-choice serial reaction time attentional task. *Pharmacology Biochemistry and Behavior, 83,* 428–440.

Wundt, W. (1900–1920). *Völkerpsychologie. Eine untersuchung der entwicklungsgesetze von sprache, mythos und sitte* [Völkerpsychologie: An examination of the developmental laws of language, myth, and custom]. Engelmann & Kroner.

Wundt, W. (1912/1973). *An introduction to psychology.* Arno Press.

Wyatt, T. D. (2015). The search for human pheromones: The lost decades and the necessity of returning to first principles. *Proceedings of the Royal Society B: Biological Sciences, 282*(1804), 20142994. https://doi.org/10.1098/rspb.2014.2994

Wynn, K., Bloom, P., Jordan, A., Marshall, J., & Sheskin, M. (2018). Not noble savages after all: Limits to early altruism. *Current Directions in Psychological Science, 27,* 3–8.

Yamaguchi, S. (1998). Basic properties of umami and its effects in humans. *Physiology and Behavior, 49,* 833–841.

Yamane, G. K. (2007, November 1). Obesity in civilian adults: Potential impact on eligibility for U.S. military enlistment, *Military Medicine, 172*(11), 1160–1165. https://doi.org/10.7205/MILMED.172.11.1160

Yang, S., & Sternberg, R. J. (1997). Conceptions of intelligence in ancient Chinese philosophy. *Journal of Theoretical and Philosophical Psychology, 17,* 101–119.

Yik, M., Russell, J. A., & Steiger, J. H. (2011). A 12-point circumplex structure of core affect. *Emotion, 11*(4), 705–731.

Young, J. J., Silber, T., Bruno, D., Galatzer-Levy, I. R., Pomara, N., & Marmar, C. R. (2016). Is there progress? An overview of selecting biomarker candidates for major depressive disorder. *Frontiers in Psychiatry, 7,* 72.

Yu, Y., & Kushnir, T. (2014). Social context effects in 2- and 4-year-olds' selective versus faithful imitation. *Developmental Psychology, 50*(3), 922–933. https://doi.org/10.1037/a0034242

Yzerbyt, V., & Demoulin, S. (2010). Intergroup relations. In S. T. Fiske, D. T. Gilbert, & G. Lindzey (Eds.), *The handbook of social psychology* (5th ed., Vol. 2, pp. 1024–1083). Wiley.

Zahn-Waxler, C., Radke-Yarrow, M., Wagner, E., & Chapman, M. (1992). Development of concern for others. *Developmental Psychology, 28,* 126–136.

Zajonc, R. B. (1968). Attitudinal effects of mere exposure. *Journal of Personality and Social Psychology, 9,* 1–27.

Zeki, S. (1993). *A vision of the brain.* Blackwell Scientific.

Zeki, S. (2001). Localization and globalization in conscious vision. *Annual Review of Neuroscience, 24,* 57–86.

Zentall, T. R., Sutton, J. E., & Sherburne, L. M. (1996). True imitative learning in pigeons. *Psychological Science, 7,* 343–346.

Zentner, M., & Mitura, K. (2012). Stepping out of the caveman's shadow: Nations' gender gap predicts degree of sex differentiation in mate preferences. *Psychological Science, 23*(10), 1176–1185. https://doi.org/10.1177/0956797612441004

Zerwas, S., & Bulik, C. M. (2011). Genetics and epigenetics of eating disorders. *Psychiatric Annals, 41*(11), 532–538. https://doi.org/10.3928/00485713-20111017-06

Zhang, T. Y., & Meaney, M. J. (2010). Epigenetics and the environmental regulation of the genome and its function. *Annual Review of Psychology, 61,* 439–466.

Zickfeld, J. H., Schubert, T. W., Seibt, B., Blomster, J. K., Arriaga, P., Basabe, N., Blaut, A., Caballero, A., Carrera, P., Dalgar, I., Ding, Y., Dumont, K., Gaulhofer, V., Gračanin, A., Gyenis, R., Hu, C.-P., Kardum, I., Lazarević, L. B., Mathew, L., . . . Fiske, A. P. (2019). Kama muta: Conceptualizing and measuring the experience often labelled being moved across 19 nations and 15 languages. *Emotion. 19*(3), 402–424. https://doi.org/10.1037/emo0000450

Zihl, J., von Cramon, D., & Mai, N. (1983). Selective disturbance of movement vision after bilateral brain damage. *Brain, 106,* 313–340.

Zimbardo, P. (2007). *The Lucifer effect: Understanding how good people turn evil.* Random House.

Zimprich, D., & Martin, M. (2002). Can longitudinal changes in processing speed explain longitudinal age changes in fluid intelligence? *Psychology and Aging, 17,* 690–695.

Name Index

A

Aarts, H., 251
Abdolmohammadi, B., 53
Abel, T., 169
Abelson, J., 468
Abraham, T., 39, 40f
Abrams, D., 359f
Abramson, L. Y., 429
Acevedo, B. P., 364
Acevedo-Garcia, D., 287
Achter, J. A., 285
Acikalin, M. Y., 379f
Ackerman, P. L., 275, 281
Ackermann, H., 200
Adams, R. B., Jr., 163
Adamson, L. B., 263
Addington, A., 432
Addis, D. R., 176, 177, 188
Adelmann, P. K., 239
Adelson, E. H., 107
Adler, N. E., 391
Adolphs, R., 239
Agarwal, P. K., 223
Aggleton, J., 68
Agin, D., 49
Agnew, C. R., 365
Agrawal, M., 308
Agren, T., 169
Aguilar-Gaxiola, S., 451
Agyes, Y., 314
Ahankari, A., 298
Ahlbirg, G., Jr., 403
Ahlskog, J. E., 213
Ahmed, T., 335
Ahs, F., 421
Aiello, A. E., 424
Ainsworth, M. D. S., 307, 308
Ainsworth, S., 358
Ainsworth, S. E., 356
Ajoku, A. C., 183
Aknin, L. B., 310
al-Haytham, I., 29f
Alaie, I., 421
Alain, C., 176
Alam, D., 467
Albarracín, D., 43, 147, 378
Alberini, C., 169
Albert, M. S., 172, 184
Albrecht, T. L., 387
Albucher, R., 468
Alcoholics Anonymous, 460
Aldao, A., 335
Aleman, A., 467
Alessi, S. M., 455
Alfaro-Almagro, F., 82
Alferi, S. M., 405
Alger, S., 168
Ali, G.-C., 69
Alink, L. R., 299
Alkire, M. T., 187
Allen, N. B., 140

Allen, R. J., 166
Allen, V. J., 121
Allison, D. B., 247
Alloy, L. B., 428
Allport, G. W., 331, 358, 366
Almeida, D. M., 387
Almqvist, C., 312, 392
Alonso, J., 416, 451
Alpert, N. M., 161, 162, 172, 184
Alstrup, A., 247
Altiteri, P., 319
Alvarez, L., 45, 426f
Alvarez, V. E., 53
Alzheimer's Disease Neuroimaging
    Initiative, 69
Amabile, T. M., 179, 371
Amaral, R. S. C., 176
Amato, P., 322
Ambady, N., 238, 287
Amedi, A., 73
American Psychiatric Association,
    416
American Psychological Association,
    314, 472
Ames, M. A., 241f, 314
Ametaj, A. A., 465, 471
Amouyel, P., 69
Anand, S., 83
Anderon, S. W., 272, 273
Anderson, A. K., 161, 176, 232
Anderson, C. A., 34, 354, 356
Anderson, E., 169
Anderson, K., 282, 400, 432
Anderson, M. C., 171
Anderson, N. D., 181, 223
Anderson, R. C., 170
Anderson, R. J., 188
Anderson, S. W., 272, 273
Anderson, T., 61
Andone, I., 333
Andrade, J., 127
Andreasen, N. C., 430
Andres, D., 281
Andrewes, D., 78
Andrieu, S., 69
Andrusyna, T. P., 471
Angelini, A., 155
Angelone, B., 108
Angermeyer, M., 152
Angermeyer, M. C., 451
Annis, D. B., 220
Annis, L. F., 220
Anthony, J. C., 147, 152
Antoine, P., 181
Antoni, M. H., 396, 404, 405
Antony, J. W., 168
Anzellotti, S., 268
Appelbaum, M., 356
Apter, A., 443
Aquilar-Valfae, M. E., 335
Archer, J., 355

Ardekani, B. A., 69
Arena, P. L., 405
Arias, E., 442
Ariel, R., 171
Armstrong, D. M., 131
Armstrong, J. M., 312
Arnberg, F. K., 312, 392
Arndt, J., 252
Arnold, M., 400
Arnold, M. B., 232
Aron, A., 364, 365
Aronson, E., 118, 364, 380
Aronson, J., 286, 287, 288, 368
Arps, K., 252
Arriaga, P., 230
Asch, S. E., 14–15, 15f, 375
Asensio, E. M., 121
Aserinsky, E., 137
Ash, M., 282
Ashburner, J., 265
Ashby, F. G., 267, 268
Asher, S. J., 45
Ashikaga, T., 419
Ashmore, R. D., 369
Aslin, R. N., 218
Assanand, S., 406
Astington, J. W., 304
Atkins, M., 467
Atkinson, J. W., 251, 330
Atkinson, L., 309
Atkinson, R. C., 165
Au, J., 166
Aue, W. R., 222
Autrey, W., 360f
Avalosse, H., 279
Avena-Koenigsberger, A., 65
Axelrod, R., 357
Axt, J., 369
Ayduk, O., 250
Aynaw, Y., 245f
Azari, R., 462f
Azucar, D., 333
Azuma, H., 279
Azzopardi, P. S., 311

B

Baars, B. J., 11, 15
Babcock, J. C., 336
Baca-Motes, K., 380
Bachman, A. H., 69
Back, K., 362
Backman, C. W., 364
Bäckman, L., 319
Bacopulos, A., 176
Baddeley, A. D., 165, 166,
    170, 176
Badea, C., 367
Baek, J., 299
Bagby, R. M., 334
Bagnell, M. E., 392

Bahney, J., 54
Bahník, S., 163
Bahrick, H. P., 179, 187
Bai, D. L., 118
Bailey, H. R., 162
Bailey, J. M., 314
Baillargeon, R., 301, 302
Baird, J., 304
Bakeman, R., 263
Baker, C. I., 100
Baker, D. P., 281
Baker, T. B., 150
Bakermans-Kranenburg, M. J.,
    299
Bakia, M., 221
Balague, G., 23f
Baldessarini, R. J., 467
Baldwin, V. N., 181
Baler, R. D., 61
Bales, V. S., 246
Balkin, T. J., 144
Baltes, P. B., 319
Balthazart, J., 314
Banaji, M. R., 368
Bandelow, B., 462
Bandoli, G., 424
Bandura, A., 215, 216, 341
Bangerter, N. K., 82
Banks, M. S., 299
Bannerjea, A., 288
Banse, R., 236
Baptista, M. A. S., 198
Bar-Hillel, M., 247
Barad, M., 77
Barbee, A. P., 363
Barber, J. P., 453
Barbey, A. K., 278
Bard, P., 234
Bargh, J. A., 239, 251,
    252, 372
Barker, A. T., 83
Barker, J. E., 406
Barker, S. B., 287
Barkin, A., 397
Barkow, J., 347
Barlett, C., 356
Barlow, D. H., 420, 465, 471
Barnes, C. D., 356
Barnett, S. M., 285
Barnier, A. J., 178
Baron, R., 266
Baron-Cohen, S., 304, 436
Baronchelli, A., 374
Barr, H. M., 298
Barragán, R., 121
Barrett, L. F., 234, 236
Barron, A., 243f
Barsade, S. G., 279
Barsalou, L. W., 239
Bartlett, F., 13, 13f, 14
Bartol, C. R., 336

Bartoshuk, L. M., 120, 121
Basabe, N., 230
Basden, B. H., 178
Basden, D. R., 178
Bashat, D. B., 105
Basile, K. C., 249
Bass, C., 403
Bastian, A. J., 73
Bates, E., 262
Bates, J. E., 308
Bates, T. C., 82
Batson, C. D., 360
Batterink, L. J., 168
Batty, G. D., 275, 276
Baudry, M., 169
Baumeister, R. F., 249, 250, 346, 347, 356, 358, 374, 406
Bavelier, D., 19, 43
Bayley, P. J., 167, 168
Beale, E. E., 459
Beames, K. R., 356
Bear, G., 279
Beatty, M. J., 93
Beaty, R. E., 177
Beauchamp, G. K., 120
Beauchamp, M. H., 309
Beaupré, M., 238
Beautrais, A., 443
Bechara, A., 182, 236, 272, 273
Becht, A. I., 316
Beck, A. T., 428–429, 456, 458
Becker, C., 174
Becker, J. B., 312
Becker, N., 276
Beckham, D., 379f
Beckman, H. B., 403
Bedny, M., 268
Beedle, D., 467
Beek, M. R., 108
Beer, J. S., 345
Beevers, C. G., 429
Bell, J. R., 288
Bell, R., 163
Bellotto, B., 131f
Belmonte, M. K., 436
Belsky, J., 312
Bem, S. L., 335
Ben-Porath, Y. S., 329
Benartzi, S., 271
Benavides, M., 281
Benbow, C. P., 30, 285, 286
Bender, P. K., 356
Benedek, M., 177
Benenson, J. F., 356
Benes, F. M., 433
Benet, L., 368f
Benet-Martinez, V., 342
Bengio, Y., 102
Bennett, D. A., 69
Bennett, I. J., 218
Benoit, D., 309
Benoit, R. G., 176
Benson, D. F., 71
Benson, H., 396, 398
Benson, J. M., 151
Benyamin, B., 281
Bergen, J. R., 107

Berger, J., 378
Berger, S. A., 187
Berglund, P., 416, 426, 450, 451
Berglund, P. A., 450
Bergmann, B. M., 139
Berkowitz, L., 34, 354
Berkowitz, O., 378
Berman, J. S., 471
Bernal, G., 472
Bernier, A., 309
Bernstein, E. E., 397
Bernstein, I. L., 201
Bernstein, M. J., 163
Berntsen, D., 170
Berridge, K. C., 212
Berscheid, E., 362
Bertenthal, B. I., 118
Berthoud, H.-R., 67
Bertolote, J., 443
Bertrand, J., 261
Bessi, A., 43f
Bethea, C. F., 398
Betzel, R. J., 65
Beunen, G., 438
Bhargava, S., 133, 141
Bhatnager, N., 464, 467
Bhatt, M., 464, 467
Bhattacharya, K., 321
Bialystock, E., 265
Bickerton, D., 260
Bickman, L., 378
Biddle, J. E., 363
Biederman, J., 389, 438
Bienvenu, O. J., 428
Bierman, K. L., 318
Bigman, Y. E., 242
Billig, M. G., 358
Binder, E. B., 77
Binswanger, I. A., 198
Bioleau, I., 150
Birbaumer, N., 200
Birch, L. L., 247
Biro, S., 299
Bisby, J. A., 167
Bjork, E. L., 171
Bjork, R. A., 171, 188, 222, 224
Björkelund, C., 403
Bjorklund, P., 193
Bjorkqvist, K., 356
Björkstrand, J., 169, 421
Black, M. C., 249
Black, S., 275
Blackburn, E., 391
Blackburn, E. H., 391
Blair, C., 279, 286, 287, 288
Blair, I. V., 369
Blair, J., 441
Blaise, S. L., 459
Blake, K. R., 356
Blake, M. J., 140
Blake, P. R., 310
Blake, Y., 31f
Blakely, R. D., 61
Blakeslee, S., 73
Blanchard-Fields, F., 320
Blane, D., 276

Blascovich, J., 232, 392
Blaszkiewicz, K., 333
Blatt, S. J., 428
Blehar, M. C., 307, 308
Blendon, R. J., 151
Blesch, A., 65
Bliss, T. V. P., 169
Bliss-Moreau, E., 236
Bloch, L., 243, 264
Bloj, M., 104
Blomster, J. K., 230
Bloom, C. M., 210
Bloom, F. E., 61
Bloom, P., 263, 310, 311
Bloom, S. R., 244
Blozis, S. A., 313
Blumberg, B., 247
Blumen, H. M., 179
Blumenthal, J., 433
Blunt, J. R., 223
Boden, J. M., 356
Bodenhausen, G. V., 369
Boecker, H., 61
Boehm, J. K., 404, 405
Boeninger, D. K., 313
Boergers, J., 442
Bogod, D. G., 127
Bohan Brown, M. M., 247
Boinski, S., 216
Boisvert, C. M., 472
Bollen, J., 243f
Bolt, U., 31f
Bolton, D., 414
Bonanno, G. A., 394
Bond, C. F., 241
Bondi, M. W., 60
Bonnici, H. M., 83
Bonnie, R. J., 236
Bontempi, B., 167
Boodoo, G., 282, 286
Bookheimer, S. Y., 172
Bookstein, F. L., 298
Boomsma, D., 76, 284
Booth, R. J., 395
Booth-LaForce, C., 309
Bootzin, R. R., 140, 142
Borbely, A. A., 139
Borden, R., 32
Bordone, V., 281
Borges, G., 442, 451
Borghans, L., 275
Boring, E. G., 2, 10
Born, J., 60
Born, R. T., 107
Bornstein, R. J., 362
Borok, E., 244
Boss, S. M., 108
Bost, K. K., 309
Botvinick, M., 130
Botwin, M. D., 364
Bouazizi, M., 250f
Bouchard, C., 311
Bouchard, S. M., 273
Bouchard, T. J., 281, 334
Bouchard, T. J., Jr., 282, 286
Boucher, P. O., 223
Bouras, C., 53

Bouton, M. E., 199
Boutwell, B. B., 288
Bowdle, B. F., 356
Bower, G. H., 186
Bowie, T., 31f
Bowlby, J., 307
Bowman, B. A., 246
Boyce, J. K., 282
Boyce, W. T., 312
Boyd, R., 84
Boyer, R., 387
Boyers, A. E., 405
Boykin, A. W., 282, 286
Boyko, E. J., 392
Boyle, L. L., 334
Boyle, M., 147
Bozarth, M. A., 145
Brackett, M. A., 279
Bradley, D. C., 107
Brady, L., 61
Brady, T., 363f
Braff, D. L., 432
Brakefield, T. A., 314
Bramlett, M. D., 365
Brandeis, D., 288
Brandon, T. H., 150
Brandt, K. R., 176
Brang, D., 72, 73
Branje, S. T., 316
Bransford, J. D., 171
Brant, A. M., 284
Brassard, J., 387
Bratko, D., 334
Bratman, G. N., 396
Bratsberg, B., 281
Bratslavsky, E., 406
Braun, A. R., 144
Brazil, I. A., 441
Brechan, I., 43, 147
Brecht, D. L., 142
Brédart, S., 181, 182
Bredy, T. W., 77
Breggin, P. R., 472
Breiner, K., 236
Breland, K., 213
Breland, M., 213
Brennan, B. P., 425
Brennan, P. A., 120
Brennen, T., 181
Brenninkmeijer, V., 393
Breslow, L., 223
Bretherton, I., 309
Brewer, M. B., 358
Brier, A., 419
Briggs, J., 356
Briley, D. A., 283
Brink, J., 441
Broberg, D. J., 201
Broca, P., 18
Broch, H., 45
Broderick, J. E., 320
Brody, N., 279, 282, 286
Bromet, E. J., 451
Brooks, D., 221
Brooks, G. W., 419
Brooks, R., 305
Brooks-Gunn, J., 132, 312

Brosch, T., 235
Brotchie, H., 159, 464
Brown, A., 298, 380
Brown, A. S., 183
Brown, A. W., 247
Brown, B. B., 317
Brown, F., 180
Brown, G. M., 160
Brown, J. D., 347, 387
Brown, L., 365
Brown, M., 155
Brown, P. C., 221
Brown, R., 181, 187, 264
Brown, R. P., 42, 356
Brown, S. A., 149
Brown, S. C., 160
Brown, S. E., 149
Brown, T. A., 420
Brown, T. G., 273
Bruce, K., 245
Bruggeman, R., 468
Bruner, J. A., 264
Brunet, A., 169
Brüning, J. C., 244
Brunner, D. P., 139
Bruno, D., 428
Bryck, R. L., 74
Bryner, S., 178
Brynes, A. E., 244
Buccino, G., 71
Buch, T., 244
Buchanan, C. M., 312, 313
Buchanan, D. R., 363
Buchanan, T., 408
Buchanan, T. W., 186
Buchli, D., 171
Buchner, A., 163
Buck Louis, G. M., 312
Buckley, 360f
Buckner, R. L., 68, 173, 174, 177
Bucy, P. C., 235
Budson, A. E., 53, 68
Bukasovic, T., 334
Bulik, C. M., 245
Bull, R., 186
Bullard, C., 303f
Bullemer, P., 218
Bullis, J. R., 465, 471
Bulten, B. H., 441
Bunce, D. M., 223
Bundchen, G., 363f
Bundy, R. P., 358
Bunge, S. A., 236, 243, 288
Burger, J. M., 360, 377, 380, 407
Burgess, N., 167
Burke, D., 182
Burke, M., 354
Burke, S. L., 69
Burkhart, J. M., 217
Burks, S. V., 276
Burns, D. J., 163
Burns, L., 407
Burns, S. A., 163
Burns, T. C., 298
Burnstein, E., 360
Bursell, A. L., 239
Burt, D. M., 363

Buschkuehl, M., 166, 288
Bush, D., 167
Bush, G. W., 41f, 186
Bushdid, C., 119
Bushman, B. J., 34, 347, 354, 356
Busjahn, A., 76
Buss, D. M., 249, 362, 363, 364
Butcher, J. N., 420, 432
Butera, F., 424
Butler, A. C., 458
Butler, M. A., 54
Buunk, B. P., 393
Buzza, C., 235, 236
Byerley, G. J., 334
Byers-Heinlein, K., 298
Byrne, D., 364

C
Cabeza, R., 184, 320
Cacioppo, J. T., 353, 359, 378, 379
Cadario, R., 248
Caddigan, E., 91
Caggiano, J. M., 108
Cahill, L., 187, 188, 235
Cahill, L. S., 159, 464
Caldarelli, G., 43f
Calder, A. J., 237
Caldji, C., 77
Calkins, M. W., 21, 21f
Call, J., 217
Callaghan, T., 303
Callaway, E., 288
Callaway, E. M., 101
Callens, M., 279
Calvert, S. L., 356
Calvin, C. M., 276
Cameron, C. D., 243
Campbell, A., 335
Campbell, J. D., 346
Campbell-Sills, L., 424
Campo, J. A., 468
Campos, B., 237
Cannon, W., 234
Cantanese, K. R., 249
Cantor, N., 343
Cantu, R. C., 53
Canuto, A., 53
Cappa, S. F., 182
Capps, L. M., 304
Capuozzo, A., 168
Caputi, P., 276
Caputo, C., 371
Caramazza, A., 268
Card, D., 287
Card, N. A., 356
Cardena, E., 154
Cardeña, E., 154
Cardi, D. P., 100
Carey, N., 77
Carey, S., 309
Carik, F. I. M., 171
Carlsmith, J. M., 380
Carlson, S. J., 186
Carlson, S. M., 309
Carmichael Olson, H., 298
Carmody, J., 395
Carney, D. R., 239, 241

Carolson, E. A., 309
Caron, H. S., 403
Carpenter, A. C., 188
Carpenter, J. P., 276
Carpenter, M., 305, 310
Carpenter, S. K., 222
Carpenter, W., 398
Carré, J. M., 355
Carroll, J. B., 278
Carroll, M. D., 405
Carruth, N. P., 406
Carson, K. L., 61
Carson, R. E., 144, 420
Carstensen, L. L., 235, 320, 321
Carter, C. S., 61
Caruso, D. R., 279
Carver, C. S., 232, 404, 405
Casazza, K., 247
Casey, B. J., 236
Casey, K. L., 401
Casey, R. J., 363
Caspi, A., 333, 334, 364
Cassano, G. B., 467
Castel, A. D., 224
Castellani, R. J., 53
Catellanos, F. X., 438
Cattell, R. B., 278, 331
Catts, S. V., 288
Cavedo, M., 69
Cawthorn, R. M., 391
Cayeux, I., 120
CDaCI Investigative Team, 114
Ceci, S. J., 30, 160, 282, 286
Cellini, N., 168
Celnik, P., 73
Cellini, N., 168
Centola, D., 374
Cepeda, N. J., 222
Cerda, M., 198
Cerf-Ducastel, B., 121
Cervenka, S., 421
Cervone, D., 250
Cervoni, N., 77
Cesario, J., 369
Chabris, C., 84
Chabris, C. F., 108, 161
Chadha, A. S., 69
Chaiken, S., 378
Champagne, F. A., 77
Champney-Smith, K., 467
Chan, A. Y., 276
Chan, M. T. V., 127
Chandon, P., 248
Chang, L., 217
Chang, Y., 234
Chant, D., 432
Chao, L. L., 268
Chaplin, T. M., 335
Chapman, A., 89, 464
Chapman, H. A., 232
Chapman, J. E., 458
Chapman, M., 310
Charcot, J.-M., 8
Charles, S. T., 320, 387
Charlson, F. J., 450
Charlton, K., 240, 241

Charness, N., 285, 319
Charpak, G., 45
Chartrand, T. L., 239, 252
Chassin, L., 150
Chattopadhyay, S. K., 316
Chavez, A., 432
Cheavens, J. S., 243
Cheke, L. G., 83
Chen, E., 53, 282
Chen, F. S., 309
Chen, J., 249
Chen, S., 432
Chen, Z., 371
Cheney, D. L., 258
Cheng, B. H., 20
Cheng, D. T., 200
Cherlin, A. J., 365
Chernikova, M., 380
Cheshire, C., 361
Chess, S., 308
Chew, B., 213
Cheyne, J. A., 223
Chiang, J. J., 53
Chiesa, P. A., 69
Chiles, C., 375
Chin, A., 133
Chin, H. B., 316
Chiu, W. T., 152, 450
Choi, I., 371
Chomsky, N., 15–16, 16f, 263
Chou, S. P., 441
Christakis, E., 306
Christakis, N. A., 314, 374f
Christensen, K., 433
Christiansen, B. A., 149
Christie, I. C., 235
Christophe, A., 298
Chui, H., 321
Chun, M. M., 102
Chung, C. K., 395
Cialdini, R. B., 372, 374, 376, 380
Ciarrochi, J., 276, 279
Cicchetti, D., 309
Cicchetti, P., 235
Cicero, T. J., 151
Circarelli, T., 93
Ciszewski, A., 426
Ciuk, D. J., 243
Claes, L., 443
Clark, A. E., 321
Clark, C. A., 213
Clark, D., 399
Clark, H., 275
Clark, I. A., 167
Clark, J. J., 108
Clark, K., 21, 21f
Clark, K. A., 81
Clark, M. P., 21, 21f
Clark, R. A., 251, 330
Clark, R. D., 362
Clark-Polner, E., 234
Clarke, A., 102
Clarke, R. J., 181
Clasen, L. S., 438
Claux, M. L., 303
Claxton, A. B., 183
Cleary, A. M., 183

Cleckley, H. M., 439
Clerc, G., 464
Clinton, H., 41f
Clore, G. L., 364
Cnattingius, S., 316
Coatsworth, J. D., 316
Coe, C. L., 298
Cogan, D., 399
Cogan, R., 399
Coghill, R. C., 400, 401f
Cohen, A. B., 371
Cohen, A. E., 236
Cohen, D., 356
Cohen, G., 181
Cohen, G. L., 243
Cohen, M., 309
Cohen, M. A., 244
Cohen, N. J., 173
Cohen, S., 282, 359, 397
Coifman, K. G., 394
Colcombe, S. J., 73
Coleman, D. K., 387
Coleman, J. R. I., 283
Coleman, T., 298
Collibee, C., 315
Collins, A., 282, 432
Collins, J., 432
Collins, W. A., 309
Coltell, O., 121
Coman, A., 178
Comer, J. S., 465, 471
Condon, J. W., 364
Condon, P., 234
Conger, R. D., 313
Congleton, C., 395
Conklin, Q., 395
Conley, T. D., 362
Connelly, A., 176
Convit, A., 69
Conway, B. R., 104
Cook, M., 421
Cook, T. M., 127
Cook-Deegan, R., 288
Cooke, J. E., 243
Coolidge, C., 277
Cooper, H., 240, 241, 251
Cooper, J., 380
Cooper, J. R., 61
Cooper, M. L., 149
Cooper, W. H., 341
Corballis, M. C., 71
Corboy, J. R., 54
Cordaro, D. T., 236, 238
Corella, D., 121
Coren, S., 139
Corina, D., 19, 43
Corkin, S., 167, 181
Corp, D. T., 53
Correll, C. U., 462
Correll, J., 368, 369
Corti, E., 148
Coryell, W., 430
Coryell, W. H., 235, 236
Costa, P. T., 334
Costa, P. T., Jr., 335
Costanza, A., 53
Costello, N., 336

Côté, S., 20
Court, J. H., 278
Courville, A., 102
Cousin, M. E., 33f
Coyle, J. T., 433
Coyne, S. M., 356
Cradock, A. L., 314
Craig, B. A., 120
Craighero, L., 71, 217
Craik, F. I. M., 160, 171, 172, 174, 180
Cramer, R. E., 363
Crandall, C., 360
Crane, C. A., 149
Crano, W. D., 364
Craske, M. G., 422
Crawley, J. N., 60
Creelman, C. D., 93
Creery, J. D., 168
Crego, C., 77
Crepin, G., 298
Crinion, J. R., 265
Cristello, J. V., 460
Crockett, M. J., 243
Crocq, M.-A., 145
Croen, L. A., 436
Croft, C., 309
Crombag, H. F. M., 184
Cross, E. S., 217
Cross, P., 347
Cross-Disorder Group of the
        Psychiatric Genomics
        Consortium, 430
Crowder, R. G., 164
Cruess, D. G., 396
Crum-Cianflone, N. F., 392
Csigó, K., 468
Csikszentmihalyi, M., 340
Cuc, A., 68, 171, 178
Cuddy. A. J. C., 239
Cuellar, A. K., 430, 431
Culham, J. C., 102
Culver, J. L., 405
Cunitz, A. R., 165
Cunningham, D. G., 464
Cunningham, M. R., 363
Cunningham, W. A., 235
Curran, J. P., 363
Curran, T., 174
Currier, D., 443
Curtis, C. E., 172
Curtis, G., 468
Curtiss, S., 264
Cushman, F., 309
Custers, R., 251

D

D'Agostino, E., 437
D'Agostino, P. R., 371
D'Alessio, A. C., 77
D'Alessio, A. D., 461
D'Antonio, L., 223
Dael, N., 237
Dagher, A., 213, 248
Dahdaleh, N. S., 235, 236
Dahlhamer, J. M., 246
Daily, G. C., 396

Dall, S. R. X., 217
Dallenbach, K. M., 168
Dalton, P., 119
Daly, M., 355
Damasio, A. R., 167, 182, 236, 268,
        272, 273, 334
Damasio, H., 182, 236, 268, 272, 273
Damerius, L. A., 217
Danesh, J., 440
Daneshvar, D. H., 53
Daniel, H. J., 364
Daniel, K., 185
Daniels, J., 436
Danner, U. N., 273
Darley, J. M., 43, 359, 367
Darwin, C., 6, 6f, 238
Darwin, C. J., 164
Date, Y., 244
Daubenmier, J., 391
Dauer, W., 68
Daum, I., 200
David-Barrett, T., 321
Davidson, R. J., 237, 243, 252
Davies, P. G., 368
Davis, B., 159
Davis, K. L., 61
Davis, P. J., 321
Davis, R. B., 464
Davison, G. C., 424
Daw, N. D., 213
Dawson, D. A., 441
Dawson, G., 437
Day, J. J., 77
Dayan, E., 247
Dayan, P., 61, 213
de Araujo, I. E., 120
De Bolle, M., 335
De Fryut, F., 335
De Houwer, J., 362
de la Cruz, L. F., 312, 392
de Leeus, C. A., 281
de Lima, M. S., 438
De Neve, J. E., 314
de Oliveria, M. G., 216
de Queiroz, V., 467
de Ridder, D. T., 273
De Simoni, C., 166
de Souza, R., 464, 467
de Waal, F. B. M., 132, 283
De Wolff, M., 308
Deacon, B. J., 463
Deady, D. K., 363
Deardorff, J., 312
Deary, I. J., 275, 276, 285
Deaton, A., 320
DeBoer, J., 223
Deci, E. L., 251, 340, 373
Deckersbach, T., 162
Dedrick, R. F., 222
Deese, J., 184
Defries, J. C., 284
Degenhardt, L., 152
Dekker, M. C., 285
Dekker, S., 84
Deković, M., 316
Del Vicario, M., 43f
Delivuk, M., 89, 464

Demb, J. B., 160
Dement, W. C., 141
Dement, W. D., 80, 138, 139
Demeter, G., 468
Demler, M. A., 416, 426, 450
Demoulin, S., 359
Dempster, E. L., 431
Denburg, N., 272, 273
Denissen, J. J., 332, 333
Dennett, D., 131
Denny, B. T., 243
Denson, T. F., 243, 356
DePaulo, B. M., 240, 241, 321
Der, G., 275, 276
Der Foo, M. D., 279
Derbyshire, S., 154
Dermer, M., 363f
Dernier, O., 450
Descartes, R., 2, 3f
DeSimone, M., 30, 160
Desjardins, S., 387
Desmond, J. E., 160, 200
DeVilliers, P., 304
Devine, P. G., 369
Devlin, B., 245
Dewey, T., 41f
Dewhurst, S. A., 188
DeYoung, C. G., 188
Dhabhar, F. S., 391
Di Giulio, G., 471
Di Santo, D., 380
Diaconis, P., 45
DiBiase, H. D., 320
Dichgans, J., 200
Dickens, W. T., 281, 286, 287, 382
Dickinson, A., 205
Didden, R., 285
Didi, R., 464
DiDonato, T. E., 358
Dieckmann, N. F., 281
Diederich, N. J., 401
Diener, E., 321
Dienes, Z., 154
Dierks, T., 265
Dietz, W. H., 246
Diguer, L., 471
Dijk, D. K., 139
Dimberg, U., 239
Dimech, A. S., 69
Dion, K. L., 321
Diorio, J., 77
DiScenna, P., 167
Dishman, R. K., 397
Dismukes, R. K., 181
Disner, S. G., 429
Disterhoft, J. F., 200
Dittrich, W. H., 237
Dixon, R. A., 319
Dixon, R. M., 247
DiZio, P., 118
Djurfeldt, D. R., 421
Dobbins, I. G., 177
Dodge, K. A., 356
Dolan, R. J., 162, 181, 213
Dolan, S., 272, 273
Dolinski, D., 377
Dollard, J., 354

Domnick, F., 276
Donaldson, D., 442
Dong, H., 69
Donnerstein, E., 34
Donovan, B., 243
Doob, L. W., 354
Doucet, S., 120
Dougherty, D. D., 425
Dovidio, J. F., 358, 369, 387
Dow, S., 247
Dowd, S. M., 467
Downey, G., 250
Dowshen, S. A., 312
Doyle, A. E., 438
Doyon, J., 218
Dragoin, W. B., 201
Dreiling, J. L., 60
Dresler, M., 160
Drews, F. A., 93
Drieschner, K., 285
Droesch, M., 313f
Druen, P. B., 363
Druss, B., 450
Dube, G. R., 288
Dubé, M., 387
Dubin, L. F., 398
Duchaine, B. C., 239
Dudai, G. J., 168
Dudycha, G. J., 180
Dudycha, M. M., 168, 180
Duenwald, M., 394
Duffy, V. B., 121
Duncan, G. J., 166
Dunlop, S. A., 65
Dunlosky, J., 220, 222, 224
Dunn, E. W., 310
Dunn, J., 14
Dunne, E. F., 405
Dunning, D. L., 166
Dunphy, D. C., 317
Durrett, C. A., 439
Dusek, J. A., 398
Duval, S., 132
Duyck, W., 265
Duyme, M., 282
Duzel, E., 174
Dweck, C. S., 309
Dworkin, R. H., 116
Dy, J., 234
Dymov, S., 461
Dyrenforth, P. S., 321
Dziurawiec, S., 299
Dziurzynski, L., 308

E

Eagly, A. H., 43, 147, 335, 362
Eastwick, P. W., 362, 364
Eaton, A., 298
Eaton, W. W., 428
Eaves, L. J., 334
Ebbensen, E., 179
Ebbinghaus, H., 4, 179, 180f
Ebersole, C. R., 369
Eberth, J., 396
Ebner, F., 177

Eccles, J. S., 312
Echterhoff, G., 171, 177, 178
Eckholm, E., 426f
Ecklund, E. H., 2
Eddy, D. M., 269
Edwards, R., 363
Edwards, W., 269
Egeland, B., 309
Ehrhardt, A. A., 314
Eich, J. E., 170, 186
Eichenbaum, H., 173
Eichstaedt, J. C., 308
Eilers, R. E., 261
Einstein, A., 44, 84
Einstein, E. B., 151
Einstein, G. O., 181
Eisen, R., 464, 467
Eisenberg, D. M., 464
Eisenberg, L. S., 114
Eisenberg, M. L., 162
Eisenberg, N., 279
Eisenberger, N. I., 359
Eisenegger, C., 355
Eisenkraemer, R. E., 171
Eisner, F., 237
Ekman, P., 235, 237, 238, 239
El Haj, M., 181
Elbogen, E. B., 419
Elder, G. H., 313
Elder, R., 316
Eldridge, L. L., 172
Elfenbein, H. A., 238, 240, 279
Ell, S. W., 268
Elliott, R., 288
Ellis, A., 456t
Ellis, B. J., 312
Ellis, D. A., 200
Ellis, H. D., 299
Ellis, L., 314
Ellis, M. S., 151
Ellman, S. J., 139
Ellsberg, M., 356
Ellsworth, P. C., 232
Elman, D., 32
Elsey, J. W. B., 169
Emerson, R. C., 107
Emmorey, K., 264
Emre, M., 61
Encarnacion, M., 73
Endicott, J., 430
Engel, S. A., 172
Engelhardt, M., 223
Engelhardt, P. E., 309
Engle, R. W., 166
English and Romanian Adoptees
   Study Team, 307
Engman, J., 169, 421
Epel, E. S., 391
Epictetus, 429f
Epley, N., 371
Epstein, D. R., 140
Epstein, R., 313
Epstein, R. M., 462f
Erickson, K. I., 73
Erickson, K. L., 73
Ericsson, K., 285
Erikson, E. H., 316

Eron, L. D., 34
Ervin, C. R., 364
Eslinger, P. J., 281
Esping, A., 279
Espy, K. A., 298
Essex, M. J., 312
Estes, A., 437
Ethier, K. A., 313, 314, 315
Etkin, A., 428
Euclid, 29f
Euling, S. Y., 312
Evans, A. C., 311
Evans, G. W., 282, 387, 388
Evans, S. W., 282
Everaerd, W., 235
Everling, S., 102
Exner, J. E., 329
Eysenck, H. J., 332, 336, 471

F

Fabes, R. A., 279
Fagerlund, B., 433
Falcão Freire, A., 335
Falk, R., 45
Fallon, J., 187
Familiari, P., 155
Fan, R., 243f
Fancher, R. E., 12
Fang, F., 304, 312, 392
Fang, H., 298
Farah, M. J., 243f, 282, 288
Faraone, S. V., 438
Farooqi, I. S., 244
Farrar, M. J., 264
Farrelly, D., 364
Faulkner, G., 397
Faust, D., 472
Fava, N. M., 69
Favagehi, M., 391
Favazza, A., 443
Fazel, M., 405
Fazel, S., 440
Fazio, R. H., 380
Feczer, D., 193
Federspiel, A., 265
Fedor, S., 459
Fehr, E., 355
Fein, S., 378
Feinberg, M. E., 317
Feinberg, T. E., 344
Feingold, A., 361
Feingold, J., 282
Feinstein, J. S., 235, 236
Feldman, D. E., 72
Feldman, M. D., 462f
Felleman, D. J., 98
Fellow, L. K., 248
Fenton, C., 276
Ferguson, C. J., 356
Fernandez Nievas, I. F., 393
Fernández, G., 160
Fernandez, J. R., 243
Ferrari, A. J., 450
Ferretti, M. T., 69
Ferster, C. B., 207, 208, 209f, 210
Festinger, L., 362, 380

Fetzer, B. K., 407
Feudtner, C., 403
Fields, H. L., 401
Filley, C. M., 54
Fincher-Kiefer, R., 371
Fink, A., 177
Finkel, E. J., 362, 364
Finkelstein, K. E., 180
Finn, B., 224
Fiore, A. T., 361
Fiorillo, C. D., 212
Fischer, H., 465
Fischer, P., 359
Fischler, C., 406
Fiser, J., 218
Fisher, D. W., 69
Fisher, H., 365
Fisher, P. A., 74
Fisher, R. P., 171, 374
Fiske, A. P., 230
Fiske, S. T., 342, 367, 372
Fitch, C. A., 312
FitzGerald, T. H. M. B., 83
Fitzsimmons, C., 319
Fitzsimons, G. J., 379f
Flament, C., 358
Flanagan, J. R., 102
Flandin, G., 213
Fleeson, W., 341
Flegal, K. M., 245
Fleming, T., 246
Flens, E. A., 223
Fletcher, G. J. O., 364
Fletcher, P., 181
Fletcher, P. C., 162, 432
Flint, K. H., 313, 314, 315
Flores, S., 162
Flores, S. D., 334
Florian, S., 242
Flynn, E., 214
Flynn, J., 286, 287
Flynn, J. R., 281, 283
Flynn, L. M., 236
Foa, E. B., 394
Fode, K. L., 33
Fogel, J., 399
Foldman, S., 391
Foley, K., 187
Folkman, S., 392
Follmer, R. L., 235, 236
Folwarczny, M., 377
Fonagy, P., 309
Fontaine, K. R., 247
Forbes, A., 127
Forbs, C., 286
Ford, B. Q., 242
Ford, E. S., 246
Ford, J. H., 320
Forman, E. M., 458
Foroni, F., 239
Forsberg, A., 421
Forscher, P. S., 369
Forss, S. I. F., 217
Forster, B. B., 441
Fortier, C., 68
Foster, C. L., 216
Foster, D. F., 464

Fowler, J. H., 314, 374f
Fox, K. R., 459
Fox, M. J., 61f
Fox, N. A., 282
Frackowiak, R. S., 181, 182, 265
Fragaszy, D. M., 216
Fraley, R. C., 309, 330
Francesconi, M., 363
Franchow, E. I., 243
Francis, D., 77
Francis, H. M., 247
Frank, M. G., 238
Frankel, R., 403
Frankie, W. G., 150
Franklin, C. R., 459
Franklin, J. C., 459
Franks, J. J., 171
Franks, P., 462f
Franz, C. E., 462f
Frascino, J. C., 167
Fraser, S. C., 380
Frati, A., 155
Fredman, T., 216
Fredrickson, B. L., 321
Fredrikson, M., 169, 465
Freedman, A., 77
Freedman, G., 450
Freedman, J. L., 380
Freeman, S., 32
Freeston, I. L., 83
Fregni, F., 73
Freud, S., 135, 136, 142, 150
Freund, A. M., 320
Frey, D., 359, 361
Frick, A., 169, 421
Frick, R. W., 236
Fried, P. A., 298
Fried, Reed, G., 166
Friederici, A. D., 298
Friedman, B. H., 235
Friedman, J. M., 246, 247
Friedman, M., 392
Friesen, W. V., 235, 237, 238, 239
Frijda, N., 232
Frith, C. D., 181, 213, 432
Frith, U., 304
Frnak, M., 213
Frost, G. S., 244
Fry, D. P., 356
Fryar, C. D., 245, 246, 405
Fujii, T., 176
Fujioka, K., 247
Fukui, H., 273
Fukuyama, H., 273
Fulford, K. W. M., 414
Funder, D. C., 341
Furman, D. J., 428
Furman, W., 315
Furmanski, C. S., 172
Furmark, T., 169, 421, 465
Furukawa, Y., 150
Fuseli, H., 142f
Fuster, J. M., 68

G

Gabrieli, J. D. E., 68, 160, 236, 243
Gadermann, A. M., 416

Gadian, D. G., 176
Gaertner, S. L., 358
Gaga, L., 327, 328
Gage, P., 78–79, 334
Gais, S., 60
Gakidou, E., 246
Galanter, E., 91
Galati, D., 238
Galatzer-Levy, I. R., 428
Gale, C. R., 275, 276
Galea, S., 198, 424
Galef, B., 203
Galilei, G., 28f
Galinsky, A. D., 355, 369
Galinsky, A. M., 246
Gall, M., 279
Gallese, V., 71
Galling, B., 462
Gallistel, C. R., 214
Gallivan, J. P., 102
Gallo, D. A., 184
Gallouj, K., 181
Gallup, 47, 246
Gallup, G. G., 132
Galton, F., 82
Galvan, V. V., 167, 168
Gandy, S., 53
Ganzel, B. L., 388
Gao, X., 402
Garb, H. N., 419
Garber, J., 312
Garcia, J., 17, 17f, 201
Garcia, S. E., 316
Garcia-Moreno, C., 356
Gard, T., 395
Gardiner, J. M., 176
Gardner, C. O., 424
Gardner, H., 288
Gardner, M., 313
Gardner, R., 139
Garite, T. J., 298
Garland, E. L., 149
Garrido, L., 239
Garry, M., 186
Gartlehner, G., 89, 464
Gary, M. L., 369
Gathercole, S. E., 166
Gatz, M., 320
Gaulin, S. J. C., 363
Gavett, B. E., 53
Gavin, L. E., 316, 428
Gaykema, R. P. A., 400
Gaynes, B. N., 89, 464
Gazzaniga, M. S., 80
Ge, X. J., 313
Geary, D. C., 30, 286
Gee, B., 303f
Geenen, R., 332, 333
Gegenfurtner, K. R., 104
Genet, J. J., 243
Gentile, D. A., 356
George, O., 146
Georgellis, Y., 321
Georgiades, A., 431
Geraerts, E., 186
Gerbasi, M. E., 360
Gerber, J. C., 121

Geren, J., 262
Germanotta, S. J. A., 327, 328
Germine, L. T., 318
Gernsbacher, M. A., 30, 286
Gershoff, E. T., 204
Gerstorf, D., 321
Gert, G. W., 242
Gest, S. D., 317
Ghaffar, O., 172
Ghirardi, M., 169
Ghosh, A., 321
Giannakopoulos, G., 53
Giarelli, E., 436
Gibb, B. B., 428
Gibbons, F. X., 132
Gibler, K., 168
Gibson, C. E., 287
Gibson, N. A., 159, 464
Giedd, J. N., 311, 433
Gifford, R. K., 366
Gigerenzer, G., 269
Gignac, G. E., 82
Gigone, D., 358
Gil-Olarte, P., 279
Gilbert, D. T., 42, 186, 241, 250, 341, 371
Gilbertson, M. W., 426
Gilboa, A., 167, 168
Giles, C. M., 314
Giles, L., 364
Giles, M., 467
Gillespie, C. F., 307
Gillespie, N. A., 334
Gillette, J., 262
Gilliland, K., 336
Gilliland, M. A., 139
Gilmore, A. W., 184
Gilovich, T., 32, 346
Gino, F., 20
Giordani, B., 468
Giovanello, K. S., 172
Girgis, R. R., 150
Gitelman, D. R., 219
Giuliano, L., 287
Gjernes, M., 295
Gladue, B. A., 314
Glanzer, M., 165
Glaser, R., 391
Glass, D. C., 388
Glass, G. V., 471
Gleitman, H., 262
Gleitman, L., 262
Glenthøj, B., 433
Glenwick, D. S., 32
Glick, S. M., 399
Glotzer, L. D., 71
Glover, G. H., 160, 388
Glynn, L. M., 298
Gneezy, A., 380
Gneezy, U., 251
Gnys, M., 407
Gochman, P., 433
Goddard, H., 274, 275
Godden, D. R., 170
Godleski, S. A., 149
Goehler, L. E., 400
Goethals, G. R., 378

Goette, L., 276
Goetz, C. G., 401
Goetz, E. T., 170
Goetz, J. L., 237
Gofen, C., 408
Goff, D. M., 462
Goff, L. M., 186
Gogtay, N., 432
Gold, D., 281
Gold, J. J., 167
Golden, R. L., 315
Goldenberg, A., 243
Goldin, C., 368f
Goldman, M. S., 149
Goldman, R., 379
Goldstein, D. G., 271
Goldstein, N. J., 372
Goldstein, R., 285
Goldstone, R. L., 374
Golinkoff, R. M., 263
Gollwitzer, P. M., 251, 252, 372
Golsteyn, B. H. H., 275
Gonzaga, G. C., 237, 365
Goodale, M. A., 100
Goodfellow, I., 102
Goodman, J. C., 262
Goodman, N. D., 374
Goodnick, P., 431
Gooren, L. J. G., 235
Gootman, E., 281f
Gopnik, A., 305
Goralnick, J. J., 438
Gorczynski, P., 397
Gore, A., 186
Gorman, J. M., 465, 471
Gorno-Tempini, M. L., 182
Gortmaker, S. L., 314
Gosling, S. D., 333, 342
Gosney, M. A., 121
Gotlib, I. H., 428, 429
Gottesman, I. I., 75, 433
Gottfredson, L. S., 279
Gottfried, J. A., 120
Gough, C., 366
Gouldner, A. W., 374
Govoni, R., 181
Graber, J. A., 312
Grabowski, T. J, 182, 236
Grace, A. A., 433
Grace, L., 188
Gracely, R. H., 117
Graetz, N., 246
Graf, P., 173
Grafman, J., 369
Grafton, S. T., 71, 133, 217
Graham, S., 356
Grajski, K. A., 73
Grande, L. R., 360
Grandin, T., 436–437, 436f
Granhag, P. A., 241
Grant, B. F., 441
Grasby, P., 181
Grassian, S., 353
Graupmann, V., 361
Gray, H. M., 128
Gray, J., 336

Gray, J. A., 252
Gray, J. R., 188
Gray, K., 128
Gray, L. E., 312
Graziano, W. G., 356
Green, D. A., 93
Green, D. A. E., 83
Green, D. P., 370
Green, M. F., 432
Green, R. W., 433
Green, S. K., 363
Greenaway, K. H., 243
Greenberg, A. S., 247
Greenberg, J., 252
Greene, D., 251, 373
Greenson, J., 437
Greenspan, L., 312
Greenstein, D., 432
Greenstein, D. K., 438
Greenwald, A. G., 368
Greicius, M. D., 160
Greinke, Z., 415f
Greitemeyer, T., 359
Grether, J. K., 436
Grewal, D., 279
Gribble, P. L., 216
Griffiths, J. H., 205
Grigorenko, E. L., 279
Grilo, S. A., 316
Griskevicius, V., 244
Grockett, L., 313
Groh, A. M., 309
Groom, R. W., 354
Gropp, E., 244
Gross, J. J., 232, 236, 243, 394, 396
Gross, P. H., 43
Gross, S. J., 243
Groth, G., 362
Grothgar, B., 453
Grover, S., 321
Groves, B., 127
Groves, C. L., 356
Gruen, R. S., 314
Grün, F., 247
Grzyb, T., 377
Grzybala, P., 377
Gu, Q., 245
Guadagnoli, E., 402
Gudsnuk, K., 77
Guerchet, M., 69
Guerin, S. A., 184
Guerra, R. O., 335
Guil, R., 279
Guilford, J. P., 177
Gulleminault, C., 141
Günther, L., 400
Güntürkün, O., 69, 132
Gup, T., 466
Gur, R. C., 30, 286
Gurwitz, J. H., 402
Gusnard, D. A., 133
Gustafsson, J.-E., 278
Gustavson, D. E., 406
Guthrie, D., 282
Guthrie, I. K., 279
Guthrie, R. V., 21
Gutting, G., 7

Gwadry, F., 144
Gwinn, J. D., 370

H
Haarig, F., 396
Haas, A., 443
Haase, C. M., 243, 320
Hackman, D. A., 282
Hackman, J. R., 358
Haddad, L., 387
Hadzi-Pavlovic, D., 159, 464
Haedt-Matt, A. A., 245
Hagen, L., 248
Haggard, P., 130
Hagi, K., 462
Haglund, B., 316
Hahn, K. S., 396
Haidt, J., 238
Haier, R. J., 187
Haigh, E. A., 429
Hajratalli, N. K., 459
Halaas, J. L., 247
Halasz, J., 354
Halbrooks, D., 186
Hales, C. M., 405
Hall, G. R., 461
Hall, L. K., 187
Hall, P. A., 245
Haller, J., 354
Haller, S., 264
Hallett, M., 83
Halliday, R., 288
Halligan, P., 403
Halperin, S., 139
Halpern, B., 120
Halpern, D. F., 30, 286, 287
Hamani, C., 468
Hamby, S., 356
Hamermesh, D. S., 363
Hamidi, A., 395
Hamilton, A. F. C., 71, 72, 217
Hamilton, D. L., 366
Hamilton, J. P., 396, 428
Hamilton, W. D., 360
Hamlin, J. K., 310
Hammerstein, O., II, 363
Hampel, H., 69
Hanakawa, T., 273
Handal, A., 171
Hanel, P. H. P., 379
Hange, D., 403
Hansen, M. K., 400
Hanson, D. R., 75
Happé, F. G. E., 304
Harbluk, J. L., 182, 183
Harden, K. P., 283
Harden, M., 210
Harding, C. M., 419
Hardt, O., 168
Hare, B., 439
Hare, R. D., 360, 441
Harlow, H., 307f
Harlow, H. F., 78
Harmon-Jones, C., 380
Harmon-Jones, E., 232, 380
Harrigan, M., 468
Harris, B., 199

Harris, C. B., 178
Harris, D., 312
Harris, S. D., 405
Harris, V. A., 371
Harris, W. A., 313, 314, 315
Harrison, T. L., 166
Harro, J., 433
Harsányi, A., 468
Harsch, N., 187
Hart, B., 263, 282
Hart, B. L., 400
Hart, C. L., 276
Hart, W., 43, 147
Hartshorne, H., 341
Hartshorne, J. K., 318
Hartwell, N., 150
Harvey, R. H., 405
Hashtroudi, S., 182
Hasin, D. S., 441
Haslam, C., 266
Haslam, S. A., 266
Haslet, A., 405
Hassabis, D., 130
Hasselmo, M. E., 60
Hassin, R. R., 251
Hassmen, P., 396
Hasson, U., 105
Hastie, R., 358, 367
Hatemi, P. K., 334
Hatfield, E., 362, 364
Hauptman, P. J., 402
Haushofer, J., 355
Häusser, M., 57
Havertape, L., 443
Hawkins, R. X. D., 374
Haworth, C., 93
Haworth, C. M. A., 284
Hay, L., 26, 26f, 38f
Hayakawa, K., 247
Hayashi, T., 273
Hayes, C. J., 151
Hayes, J. E., 121
Hayes, S. C., 394
Hayne, H., 180
He, H., 167
Heap, M., 154
Heath, A. C., 334
Heatherton, T. F., 246
Heaven, P. C. L., 279
Heavey, C. L., 230
Hebl, M. R., 246
Heckers, S., 162, 433
Heckhausen, J., 320
Heckman, J. J., 275
Hedges, L. V., 285, 356
Hedley-Whyte, E. T., 53
Hedman, E., 421
Heerey, E. A., 304
Heeringa, S. G., 424
Heggestad, E. D., 286
Heine, S. J., 41
Heinrichs, M., 355
Heinze, H. J., 174
Heiphetz, L., 368
Heise, L., 356
Heitel, J., 316
Heiy, J. E., 243

Helenius, D., 433
Helliwell, J., 321
Helmholtz, H. v., 5
Helzer, J. E., 147
Henderlong, J., 251
Hendin, H., 443
Hendler, T., 105
Henin, A., 389
Henrich, J., 41, 357
Henriksen, G., 61
Henson, P., 459
Henson, R. N., 174
Hepburn, C., 358
Herbener, E. S., 364
Herbstman, J. B., 77
Herculano-Houzel, S., 54
Herjavec, R., 371f
Herman, C. P., 247
Herman, M., 369
Herman-Giddens, M. E., 312
Hermann, L. I., 336
Hermsen, S., 369
Herring, M. P., 397
Hershfield, H. E., 271
Herskovitch, P., 144
Hertenstein, M. J., 237
Herter, R., 243
Hertig, M. M., 73
Heruc, G., 159, 464
Herz, D. M., 213
Herz, R. S., 120
Herzig, K., 288
Hess, U., 238
Hesselbrock, M., 147
Hettema, J. M., 424
Heuer, S. K., 363
Hewitt, B. G., 298
Hewitt, J. K., 284
Heyes, C., 305
Heyes, C. M., 216
Heyman, G. M., 147
Heymsfield, S. B., 247
Hibbeln, J. R., 464, 464f
Hibberd, P. L., 398
Hichwa, R. D., 268
Hickcox, M., 407
Hickok, G., 72, 217
Hicks, K. L., 166
Higgins, E. T., 346, 406
Hijman, R., 468
Hilbar, D. P., 69
Hilgard, E. R., 154
Hilker, R., 433
Hill, C. R., 216
Hill, P. C., 398
Hill, S. S., 288
Hillman, C. H., 73
Hilts, P., 167
Hindes, A., 272, 273
Hines, M., 247, 407
Hintzman, D. L., 45
Hirano, A., 346f
Hiripi, E., 244
Hirsch, C., 150
Hirsh, J. B., 337
Hirsh-Pasek, K., 263
Hirshfeld-Becker, D. R., 389

Hirst, W., 68, 171, 178, 187
Hitch, G. J., 165, 166
Hitchman, J. M., 127
Hitler, A., 295–296
Ho, A. D., 223
Hoang, H., 271
Hobbes, T., 2, 3f
Hobson, J. A., 142, 143
Hockenberry, J. M., 151
Hockley, W. E., 170
Hodgkin, A., 57
Hodson, G., 358
Hoek, H. W., 244, 298
Hoeppner, B., 460
Hof, P. R., 53
Hoffman, V., 309
Hoffrage, U., 269
Hofmann, W., 250
Hogan, M. J., 245
Hollins, M., 115
Holmbeck, G. N., 316
Holmes, J., 166
Holmes, R., 237
Holmgren, M. A., 438
Holt-Lunstad, J., 353
Hölzel, B. K., 395
Homann, E., 428
Homans, G. C., 365
Homonoff, T., 252, 253f
Homsveld, H., 273
Honey, P. L., 205
Honzik, C. H., 211
Hooley, J. M., 431
Hopkins, B., 298
Hopkins, R. O., 167
Hoppenbrouwers, S. S., 441
Hoppmann, C. A., 321
Horiuchi, Y., 356
Horn, J. L., 278
Horner, A. J., 167
Horrey, W. J., 93
Horta, B. L., 438
Horton, R. S., 364
Hosking, S. G., 93
Hotson, J., 83
Hou, Y., 180
Hougaard, E., 460
Houle, S., 160, 172, 174
Howard, D. V., 218
Howard, J. D., 213
Howard, J. H., 218
Howard, M. O., 149
Howard-Jones, P., 84
Howes, M., 180
Howland, R. H., 428
Hsiang, S. M., 354
Hu, T., 69
Hua, X., 69
Huang, A. J. Y., 167
Huang, Y.-Y., 169
Hubel, D. H., 80, 98
Huber, B. R., 53
Huddar, N., 238
Hudson, J. I., 244
Huedo-Medine, T. B., 463
Huesmann, L. R., 34, 354
Huffman, J. C., 459

Hughes, M., 147
Hull, C. L., 242
Hummel, T., 121
Humphries, J. E., 275
Hunsley, J., 471
Hunt, E. B., 282
Hunt, L. L., 364
Hunt, M., 1f
Hunt, T., 247
Hunter, D., 285
Hurlburt, R. T., 230
Hurlemann, R., 235, 236
Hurst, N., 89
Hussey, E., 239
Hussey, M., 312
Hutchinson, J. B., 241
Hutchison, R. M., 102
Huxley, A., 57, 145
Huys, Q. J. M., 61
Hwang, A. J., 163
Hwang, W. C., 472
Hyde, J. S., 30, 286, 334, 362
Hyman, I. E., Jr., 108, 186
Hypericum Depression Trial Study
       Group, 464
Hyun, D. Y., 464

I

Iacoboni, M., 71
Iacono, W. G., 316
Iasanzaniro, M., 155
Ihori, N., 356
Illbeck, B. E., 334
Illes, J., 288
Illingworth, A. J., 399
Imberi, J. E., 360
Inagaki, T. K., 243
Inciardi, J. A., 148
Ingram, P., 154
Inhelder, B., 13f
Inniss, D., 245
Inui, A., 244
Inzelberg, R., 213
Inzlicht, M., 369
Iqbal, M. I., 150
Irvine, J. T., 279
Isaacowitz, D. M., 320
Isenberg, D. J., 358
Itakura, S., 303
Ittelson, W. H., 107
Iulita, M. F., 69
Iverson, G. L., 53
Iwata, J., 235
Iyengar, S., 364
Izar, P., 216
Izard, C. E., 239, 279

J

Jack, A., 218, 219
Jack, C. R., Jr., 69
Jack, I., 45
Jack, R. E., 237
Jacob, V., 316
Jacobson, N. C., 420
Jacobson, T., 309

Jaeger, A., 171
Jaeger, S., 396
Jaeggi, S., 166
Jaeggi, S. M., 288
Jakobson, L. S., 100
Jallinous, R., 83
James, K. E., 298
James, S., 346f
James, W., 1–2, 1f, 5, 6, 6f, 8, 9, 20, 22,
       84, 131, 233, 241, 333, 346
Jamison, K. R., 430f
Janet, P., 8
Janicak, P. G., 467
Janis, I. L., 358
Janoschek, R., 244
Jansen, H. A. F. M., 356
Jansen, P. R., 283
Jaroszewski, A. C., 459
Jarrett, K., 73f
Jasko, K., 380
Jason, L. A., 32
Jauk, E., 177
Javitt, D. C., 433
Jaynes, J., 132
Jefferson, T., 4, 277
Jefferson, W. N., 247
Jeffries, N. O., 438
Jelic, M., 356
Jenkins, J. G., 168
Jenkins, W. M., 73
Jenner, P., 61
Jennum, P., 144
Jensen, A. R., 276
Jeter, C., 31f
Jetten, J., 369
Jezzard, P., 19, 43
Jin, R., 416, 426, 450
Jing, H. G., 223
Joel, D., 213
Joestl, S. S., 246
Joffe, R. T., 334
John, O. P., 332, 333
Johns, M., 286, 368
Johnson, B. T., 463
Johnson, C., 245, 298
Johnson, D. C., 169
Johnson, D. J., 369
Johnson, D. R., 321, 322
Johnson, J. D., 34
Johnson, J. E., 464
Johnson, J. S., 264
Johnson, K., 115
Johnson, K. A., 371
Johnson, M. H., 299
Johnson, M. K., 182
Johnson, R. F., 428
Johnson, S., 30
Johnson, S. C., 309, 419
Johnson, S. L., 430, 431
Johnson, T., 234
Johnston, W. A., 93
Jollant, F., 273
Jolles, J., 84
Jonas, E., 361
Jonason, P. K., 334
Jonasson, M., 421
Jones, A. K., 117

Jones, E. B., 151
Jones, E. E., 371
Jones, J. H., 46
Jones, K., 221
Jones, M. J., 77
Jones, S. S., 305
Jonides, J., 288, 319
Jonker, W. R., 127
Jonsson, H., 460
Jonsson, P., 239
Joormann, J., 429
Jordan, A., 311
Jordan, S. A., 464
Josephs, O., 182
Josephs, R. A., 149
Judd, C. M., 368, 369
Judd, L. L., 428
Juffer, F., 282
Jung, W. H., 82
Jung-Beeman, M., 265
Jürgensen, R., 453

K

Kaas, J. H., 72
Kable, J. W., 82
Kabnick, K., 406
Kadis, J., 279
Kagan, J., 308, 330
Kahler, C. W., 460
Kahn, R. S., 467
Kahneman, D., 136, 270, 271, 272,
       322
Kahnt, T., 213
Kainbacher, M., 359
Kaiser, A., 264
Kalat, J. W., 244
Kalb, J., 239f
Kallio, S., 154
Kalokerinos, E. K., 243
Kamble, S., 238
Kamin, L. J., 205
Kaminski, A., 89, 464
Kan, P. F., 261
Kandel, E., 288
Kandel, E. R., 56, 167, 169, 173
Kane, F., 431
Kang, S. H. K., 223
Kangawa, K., 244
Kann, L., 313, 314, 315
Kant, I., 3, 3f, 4
Kantor, L. M., 316
Kanwisher, N., 102
Kaplan, L. M., 247
Kaprio, J., 247
Kapur, N., 182
Kapur, S., 160, 172, 174
Karazsia, B. T., 245
Kardes, F. R., 43
Karlson, K., 36f
Karminer, Y., 460
Karnaze, M. M., 186
Karpicke, J. D., 171, 222, 223
Kasai, K., 426
Kashiwagi, K., 279
Kaski, K., 321
Kassam, K. S., 133

Kasser, T., 362
Kassin, S. M., 186
Kastenmüller, A., 359
Kattan, H., 372f
Katz, B., 288
Katz, N., 358
Katz, S. H., 287
Kaufman, A. S., 281
Kawakami, K., 369
Kay, A., 252
Kay, J., 266
Kaye, W. H., 245
Kayser, D. N., 361
Kazdin, A. E., 459
Keane, M. M., 176
Keane, T. M., 426
Keator, D., 187
Keefe, F. J., 61
Keefe, J. R., 453
Keel, P. K., 245
Keenan, E. A., 380
Keesee, T., 369
Kegeles, L. S., 150
Kell, H. J., 285
Keller, A., 119
Keller, M. C., 284, 430
Kelley, H. H., 365
Kelley, M. R., 165
Kelley, W. M., 217
Kelly, G., 341
Kelly, J. F., 460
Kelly, L. M., 218
Kelm, Z., 403
Keltner, D., 20, 236, 237, 238, 304, 365
Kendler, K. S., 414, 424
Kennedy, S. H., 334, 468
Kenrick, D. T., 244, 362
Kenshalo, D. R., 117
Kensinger, E. A., 68, 168, 181, 187, 320
Keo-Meier, C. L., 336
Kepler, J., 28f
Kerchner, G. A., 288
Kern, M. L., 308
Kern, R. S., 432
Kerns, K. A., 243
Kerr, N. L., 358
Kerry, J., 41f
Kertesz, J., 321
Kessinger, T., 182
Kessler, R. C., 147, 152, 244, 307, 416, 417, 419, 420, 422, 423, 424, 425, 426, 428, 438, 450, 451, 464
Ketchum, K., 154
Keyes, K. M., 424
Khalid, N., 467
Khoshaba, D. M., 405
Khuu, W., 176
Kidd, J. R., 121
Kidd, S., 432
Kiecolt-Glaser, J. K., 391
Kiehl, K. A., 441
Kiens, B., 73
Kiernan, P. T., 53
Kieser, M., 464

Kihlstrom, J. F., 345
Kihn, L., 472
Kim, D. A., 232
Kim, G., 120, 305
Kim, J. A., 198
Kim, J. S., 73
Kim, P., 282, 388
Kindt, M., 169
King, B., 395
King, M. L. Jr., 370
King, P., 288
Kingstone, A., 223
Kinney, D., 317
Kinney, D. A., 318
Kinzler, K. D., 366
Kirchgessner, A., 53
Kirchner, W. H., 258
Kirkham, T. C., 152
Kirkpatrick, J., 279
Kirov, G., 467
Kirsch, I., 154, 463
Kirsch, P., 387
Kirsner, K., 14
Kirwan, C. B., 167, 168
Kish, D., 89
Kish, S. J., 150
Kita, S., 264
Kitayama, S., 360
Klarer, M., 400
Klatzky, R. L., 116
Kleiman, E. M., 459
Klein, O., 368
Klein, R. A., 163
Klein, S. B., 345
Klein Poelhuis, C. W., 282
Kleitman, N., 137, 138
Klerman, G. L., 453
Klibourn, K. M., 405
Klinger, E., 239
Kluckhohn, C., 331
Klump, K. L., 245
Klüver, H., 235
Knieps, L. J., 120, 305
Knight, J., 363f
Knowles, E. D., 371
Knowlton, B. J., 172, 218
Kobasa, S., 405
Kober, H., 236
Kobor, M. S., 77
Koch, U., 453
Kochanek, K. D., 442
Kochendorfer, L. B., 243
Koehn, A. J., 243
Koelling, R. A., 201
Koellinger, P. D., 82
Koenen, K. C., 424
Koenig, T., 265
Koestner, R., 251
Kohlberg, L., 310
Kohler, P. K., 316
Kohnert, K., 261
Koivula, N., 396
Kojima, M., 244
Kolb, B., 78
Koller, D., 221
Kolotkin, R. L., 246
Komter, A., 360

Konitzer, T., 364
Konrad, B. N., 160
Koob, G. F., 146, 149
Koot, H. M., 285, 316
Koppel, J., 171, 178
Koppenhoefer, M., 61
Kopsida, E., 355
Korkeila, M., 247
Korn, J. H., 223
Kornbrot, D. E., 187
Kornell, N., 224
Koschutnig, K., 177
Koskenvuo, M., 247
Koslov, K., 243, 387, 422
Kosonen, Z. K., 217
Kosslyn, S. M., 161–162
Koutstaal, W., 160, 288
Kozak, M., 142
Kraemer, D. J. M., 217
Kraemer, H. C., 415
Krahé, B., 356
Kral, P. A., 201
Kramer, A. F., 73
Krapoli, E., 283
Krasuski, J., 467
Kraus, M. W., 20
Krause, E. D., 471
Krauth-Gruber, S., 239
Kravitz, D. J., 100
Kravitz, E., 276
Kravitz, R. L., 462f
Kreibig, S. D., 235
Kreider, T., 233
Kreitzer, A. C., 68
Krimgold, B. K., 287
Krishna, A., 248
Kristen, L., 453
Kroeze, W. K., 61
Kroll, J., 422
Krueger, A. B., 322
Krueger, R. F., 330
Krueger, J. I., 346, 358, 359
Kruetzer, T., 309
Kruger, A. C., 216
Kruglanski, A. W., 243, 380
Kruk, M. R., 354
Krzyszycha, K., 377
Kubzansky, L. D., 404, 405
Kuenzli, E., 264
Kuffler, D. P., 72
Kugler, M. B., 378
Kuhl, P. K., 260
Kuipers, P., 232
Kulik, J., 187
Kulkarni, A., 316
Kumar, M., 396
Kumaran, D., 130, 176
Kunda, Z., 43
Kundakovic, M., 77
Kung, K. F., 247, 407
Kunis, M., 29f
Kunz, P. R., 374
Kunze, S., 396
Kupers, R., 144
Kurtz, S. P., 151
Kushner, R., 247
Kushnir, T., 305

Kuswanto, C. N., 467
Kvavilashvili, L., 187
Kwon, M.-K., 299

L

Labella, M. H., 356
Laboneté, B., 461
Labrie, V., 431
Lachman, B., 333
Lackner, J. R., 118
Lafer-Souza, R., 104
Lafferty, E., 316
LaFramboise, T., 472
Lahti, I., 435
Lai, C. K., 369
Lai, M. C., 436
Lai, Y., 144
Laird, A., 69
Lake, J., 464
Lakhan, S. E., 53
Lakin, J. M., 285
Läksy, K., 435
Lalonde, G., 309
Lam, P., 398
Lam, R. W., 428
Lamberth, J., 364
Lamm, H., 358
Lan, P. H., 53
Lancioni, G. E., 285
Landis, C. A., 139
Landru, H. D., 439–440
Landry, M., 154
Lane, C., 7
Lang, R., 285
Lange, C., 233
Langhans, W., 400
Langlois, J. H., 363
Langström, B., 465
Laogel, C., 368
LaPierre, S., 387
Larsen, S. F., 187
Larson, C. L., 243, 252
Larson, R., 316
Larsson, E. M., 169
Laruelle, M., 150
Lashley, K., 18
Lasko, N. B., 426
Latané, B., 32, 359
Lattal, K. A., 205
Lau, A., 472
Laub, J. H., 313
Laurin, K., 309
Lavie, P., 137
Lavori, P., 430
Law, B., 216
Law Smith, M. J., 363
Lawlor, D. A., 275
Lawrence, N. S., 273
Lazar, S. W., 395
Lazarus, J., 364
Lazarus, R. S., 232, 392
Le, B., 365
Le, V., 53
Lea, S., 237
Leader, T., 359f
Leal, S., 241

Leary, M. R., 347, 359, 374
LeBar, K. S., 235
Leckenby, N., 276
Lecky, P., 345
Lecrubier, Y., 464
Lederbogen, F., 387
Lederer, A., 262
Lederman, S. J., 116
LeDoux, J. E., 68, 168, 169, 201, 236
Lee, A. Y., 406
Lee, B. H., 428
Lee, D. N., 118
Lee, K. J., 363
Lee, N. C., 84
Lee, P. C., 216
Lee, S., 69, 437
Lee-Chiong, T., 140
Lefcourt, H. M., 343
Lefebvre, C., 298
Lefforge, N. L., 230
Lefkowitz, B., 287
Lefkowitz. E. S., 315
Legant, P., 371
Lehéricy, S., 213
Lehman, D. R., 406
Lehman, J. M., 404, 405
Lehmann, C., 265
Leirer, V., 319
Lemay, E. P., 365
LeMoyne, T., 408
Lemus, M. G., 428
Lench, H. C., 186
Lenton, A. P., 363
Lentz, M. J., 139
Leon, A. C., 150
Leon, D. A., 275
Leon, J., 281
Lepage, M., 172
Lepper, M. R., 251, 373
Lerch, J., 150
Lerman, D. C., 205, 329
Lerner, N., 279
Leslie, A., 304
Leslie, K., 127
Levenson, J. M., 77
Levenson, R. W., 235, 243
Lévesque, M., 238
Levin, D. T., 108
Levin, R., 142
Levine, B., 176
Levine, C. S., 53
Levine, J. D., 401
Levine, L. J., 186
Levine, R. V., 32f
Levine, S. P., 285
Levitan, R. D., 334
Levitt, A. J., 334
Levitt, J. T., 471
Levy, N., 380
Levy, S. E., 436
Lewin, K., 14, 14f, 341
Lewis, M., 132
Lewis, M. B., 239
Lewis, M. D., 464
Lewis, S., 298
Li, G., 247, 407
Li, H., 365

Li, T., 69
Li, Y. J., 371
Liberman, Z., 366
Libet, B., 129
Lichterman, R., 16f
Liddle, P. F., 441
Lieberman, M. D., 243, 336, 359, 374
Lieras, A., 91
Lievens, F., 286
Lifshitz, M., 154
Lightstone, J., 378
Lilienfeld, S. O., 330, 472
Lillard, A., 303
Lin, J., 391, 395
Lin, W.-J., 167
Lin, Y. H., 464
Lincoln, A., 1
Lindberg, L. D., 316
Lindberg, M. J., 43, 147
Lindenberger, U., 319
Lindquist, K., 236
Lindquist, S. I., 223
Lindsay, D. S., 182
Lindsay, J. J., 241
Lindsay, S. D., 186
Lindström, P., 314
Link, B., 419
Linnér, R. K., 82
Linz, D., 34
Liou, A. P., 247
Lippmann, W., 366
Lippold, S., 363
Liszkowski, U., 310
Little, T. D., 356
Liu, D., 77, 303, 304
Liu, G., 459
Liu, H., 397
Liu, J., 178
Liu, L., 304
Liu, Y., 93
Livingstone, M., 80
Locke, J., 3, 4, 4f
Löckenhoff, C. E., 335
Locksley, A., 358
Loehlin, J. C., 282, 286, 287
Loewenstein, G., 133
Loewke, J. D., 464
Loftus, E. F., 83, 154, 176, 184, 185
Lohr, J. M., 330
Lømo, W. T., 169
Londahl, E. A., 365
Long, M. W., 314
Long, P., 183
Lopes, P. N., 279
Lorenz, K., 307
Lorrain, D., 387
Losee, J., 287
Low, C. A., 321
Lowell, E. L., 251, 330
Lozano, A., 468
Lozano, B. E., 431
Lubach, G. R., 298
Lubin, G., 276
Lubinski, D., 285
Luborsky, L., 471
Lucas, J. A., 422

Lucas, R. E., 321
Luck, D., 139
Luck, S. J., 299
Ludwig, A. M., 137
Lueck, M., 355
Luevano, J.-M., 247
Lumley, M., 61
Lundbye-Jensen, J., 73
Lungu, O., 218
Lurquin, J. H., 406
Luszcz, M. A., 321
Lutzenberger, W., 200
Lyden, J., 198
Lykken, D. T., 334
Lynch, G. S., 169
Lynch, T., 61
Lynn, M., 363, 374
Lynn, R., 281
Lynn, S. J., 330
Lythcott-Haims, J., 408
Lyubomirsky, S., 329

M
Ma, X., 242
Ma, Y.-Y., 180–181
Maas, M. K., 315
MacDonald, D., 311
MacDonald, G., 321
MacDonald, S., 180
MacDonald, S. E., 205
Machineni, S., 247
Macintyre, S., 275
Mack, K. A., 151
MacKay, D. G., 182
Mackey, A. P., 288
Mackin, R., 386–387
MacLeod, M. D., 171
Macmillan, M., 78
Macmillan, N. A., 93
Macomber, G., 252
Macrae, C. N., 133, 369
Madden, L., 23f
Maddi, S. R., 405
Madey, S. F., 32, 346
Madigan, S., 309
Madore, K. P., 83, 177, 223
Maes, M., 400
Magnasco, M. O., 119
Maguire, E. A., 73, 167
Mahajan, R., 405
Maher, B. S., 334
Mahon, B. Z., 268
Mai, N., 107
Maier, S. F., 400
Maio, G. R., 379
Major, B., 387
Mak, Y. E., 121
Makel, M. C., 285
Makin, J. E., 298
Makris, N., 438
Malach, R., 105
Malamuth, N. M., 34
Malina, R. M., 438
Malone, B. E., 240, 241
Malone, P. S., 371
Malone, W., 347

Malooly, A. M., 243
Mampe, B., 298
Mandel, H., 425f
Mandela, N., 353
Mandler, G., 162
Mandy, W., 436
Maner, J. K., 356
Manhart, L. E., 316
Manier, D., 178
Mankiw, N. G., 363f
Mann, J. J., 443
Mann, S., 241
Mannix, L. M., 246
Manstead, A. S. R., 379
Maquet, P., 143
Maracek, J., 371
Marangell, L. B., 462, 463
Marcus, G., 83
Marcus, M., 312
Marengo, D., 333
Marentette, P. F., 261
Margoni, F., 310
Margono, C., 246
Margot, C., 120
Marien, H., 251
Maril, A., 160
Marino, L., 132
Markakis, K., 403
Markel, H., 461
Marketon, J. I., 391
Markey, A., 133
Markovits, H., 356
Markowetz, A., 333
Markowitz, J. C., 453
Marks, J. S., 246
Markus, H., 345
Marlatt, G. A., 149
Marles, R. J., 464
Marmar, C. R., 428
Marriott, P., 245
Marsh, A. A., 239
Marsh, E. J., 220, 222
Marshall, A. D., 426
Marshall, J., 311
Marshall, P. J., 282
Marteinsdottir, I., 465
Martin, A., 70, 71, 174, 268
Martin, B. C., 151
Martin, D., 271
Martin, J., 237
Martin, L. L., 239
Martin, M., 281
Martin, M. J., 313
Martin, N. G., 334
Martinez-Conde, S., 91
Martins, D., 213
Martins, S. S., 198
Martis, B., 467, 468
Martynowski, K., 377
Marucha, P. T., 391
Marufu, T. C., 298
Marzuk, P. M., 150
Masarik, A. S., 313
Maser, J. D., 430
Mashek, D., 365
Maslach, C., 393
Maslow, A. H., 244, 339, 347

Mason, A., 399f
Mason, M. F., 133
Masten, A. S., 316, 356, 458
Masuda, T., 19
Mataix-Cols, D., 312, 392
Mather, M., 320
Matheson, G. J., 421
Matsick, J. L., 362
Matsukura, S., 244
Matsumoto, D., 238
Matsumoto, T., 104
Matsuo, H., 244
Mattar, A. A. G., 216
Matte, T. D., 298
Mattes, R. D., 120
Matthews, G., 336
Matthews, K., 288
Mattick, R. P., 288
Mauss, I., 232
Mauss, I. B., 230
May, M. A., 341
May, R., 340
Mayberg, H., 468
Mayberg, H. S., 468
Mayer, A., 184
Mayer, J. D., 279
Mayo, R., 239
Mayr, E., 247
Mayr, U., 320
Mazure, C. M., 69
Mazziotta, J. C., 71
McAdams, D., 345
McArdle, N., 287
McAuley, E., 73
McAuliffe, K., 310
McBride, M., 220
McCabe, D. P., 224
McCabe, R. B., 364
McCain, J., 353
McCarley, R. W., 143
McCarthy, K. S., 453
McCarthy, R. A., 268
McCartt, A. T., 93
McClelland, D. C., 251, 330
McCluskey, T., 150
McConville, P. M., 285
McCrae, R. R., 334, 335
McCue, M., 399
McCullough, M., 237
McDaniel, M., 267
McDaniel, M. A., 181, 221, 223
McDermott, J., 102
McDermott, K. B., 176, 184, 223
McDonald, R. V., 198
McDonough, I. M., 319
McElree, B., 172
McElwain, N. L., 309
McEvoy, S. P., 93
McFarlane, A. H., 387
McFerran, B., 248
McGarty, C., 367
McGaugh, J. L., 68, 159, 167, 187, 188, 235, 464
McGeoch, P. D., 73
McGhee, D. E., 368
McGill, K. L., 387
McGovern, P. E., 461

McGowan, P. O., 77, 461
McGrady, A., 396
McGrath, J., 432
McGregor, D., 45
McGue, M., 281, 316, 334
McHaffie, J. G., 400, 401f
McHugh, T. J., 167
McIntyre, S. H., 221
McKee, A. C., 53
McKenzie, K., 432
McKenzie, K. E., 108
McKenzie, R., 218
McKetin, R., 288
McKone, K. M. P., 313
McLachlan, D. R., 182
McLaughlin, K. A., 424
McLaughlin, T. J., 402
McLean, C. P., 394, 449
McLean, J. P., 223
McLean, K. C., 345
McManus, T., 313, 314, 315
McNab, F., 266
McNally, R. J., 186, 394, 397, 422, 472
McNeely, H., 468
McNeil, G., 238
McNeill, D., 181
McNell, J., 127
McVeigh, T., 182
Meade, M. L., 178
Meaidi, A., 144
Meaney, M. J., 75, 77, 461
Means, B., 221
Mechelli, A., 265
Meder, D., 213
Medin, D. L., 266
Mednick, S. C., 314
Medvec, V. H., 32, 346
Meelis, W., 354
Meeus, W., 316
Meeus, W. J., 316
Mehl, M. R., 330
Mehta, M. A., 213
Mehu, M., 237
Meites, E., 405
Meldrum, R. C., 288
Mellon, R. C., 210
Meltzer, H. Y., 462
Meltzoff, A. N., 305
Melzack, R., 117
Memmi, S., 237
Memon, A., 186
Mendelsohn, G. A., 361
Mendes, W. B., 232, 243, 387, 422
Mendle, J., 313
Mendoza-Denton, R., 20
Mendrek, A., 441
Merabet, L. B., 73
Mercer, S. L., 316
Merikangas, K. R., 416, 426, 450
Merrill, L., 43, 147
Mertens, G., 362
Mervis, C. B., 261, 266
Merzenich, M. M., 73
Mesoudi, A., 217
Meston, C. M., 249, 249t
Mestre, J. M., 279

Mesulam, M. M., 219
Metcalfe, J., 224
Meter, K., 246
Methven, L., 121
Meuret, A. E., 422
Meyer, D. E., 288
Meyer, U., 400
Meyer-Bahlberg, H. F. L., 314
Meyer-Lindenberg, A., 387
Meyers, J., 186
Mez, J., 53
Michaela, R., 242
Michaelis, S. S., 462
Michaelson, L. E., 406
Mierop, A., 279
Miezin, F. M., 174
Miguel, E., 354
Miklowitz, D. J., 431
Mikolajczak, M., 279
Milad, M. R., 425
Miles, E., 243
Milgram, S., 377, 378
Mill, J., 431
Miller, C., 430
Miller, D. T., 347, 360, 374
Miller, G., 15
Miller, G. A., 165
Miller, G. E., 282, 392, 397
Miller, I., 431
Miller, M. L., 82
Miller, N. E., 244, 354
Miller, T. I., 471
Miller, T. W., 386
Miller, W. R., 403
Milne, A. B., 369
Milne, E., 369
Milner, A. D., 100
Milner, B., 68, 166, 173
Milyavsky, M., 243, 380
Mineka, S., 420, 421
Mink, J. W., 468
Minsky, M., 129
Minson, J. A., 358
Mintun, M. A., 81
Mintz, J., 432
Miranda, J., 472
Mirani, J., 187
Mischel, W., 250, 341
Mishkin, M., 100, 176
Mishra, A., 247
Mishra, G., 275
Mishra, H., 247
Misic, B., 65
Mita, T. H., 363f
Mitchell, B. D., 385
Mitchell, D. R., 441
Mitchell, J. P., 133, 174
Mitchell, K. J., 182
Mitura, K., 362
Miyake, A., 406
Miyamoto, Y., 242
Miyatsu, T., 171
Mock, L. O., 23f
Mogle, J., 387
Moise-Titus, J., 34
Mojtabai, R., 450
Mokdad, A. H., 246

Molaison, H., 166–167
Molden, D., 406
Moll, J., 369
Molloy, L. E., 317
Molnar-Szakacs, I., 71
Monae, J., 174
Monahan, J. L., 362
Monahan, K. C., 318
Moncrieff, J., 433
Monfils, M. H., 169
Monsivais, D., 321
Montag, C., 333
Montague, C. T., 244
Montague, P. R., 213
Montenegro, P. H., 53
Montgomery, N., 408
Montoya, R. M., 364
Monuteaux, M. C., 438
Mook, D. G., 39
Moon, S. M., 399
Moore, A. J., 137f
Moore, C., 304
Moore, E. G. J., 288
Moore, S. R., 77
Moore, T. J., 463
Moors, A. C., 362
Morein-Zamir, S., 288
Morgan, D., 237
Morillon, M., 298
Morimoto, T., 104
Morin, A., 132
Morinan, A., 148
Moring, J., 435
Morison, V., 299
Morris, A. S., 312
Morris, C. D., 171
Morris, E., 210
Morris, R., 459
Morris, R. G., 169
Morris, W. L., 321
Morrison, C., 67
Morrow, D., 319
Morrow, J. D., 391
Mortillaro, M., 237
Morton, J., 299
Mory, M., 317
Moscovitch, M., 167, 168, 172, 174, 247
Mosher, W. D., 365
Moskowitz, D., 366
Moskowitz, J. T., 391
Moss, M., 148
Mosteller, F., 45
Moura, A. C. A. de, 216
Mowrer, O. H., 354
Mroczek, D. K., 320
Muehlenkamp, J. J., 443
Mueller, J. S., 358
Mueller, T., 430
Mueller, T. E., 316
Muenter, M. D., 61
Muhlenbruck, L., 240, 241
Mullen, A., 160–161
Mullen, B., 359f
Mullen, M. K., 180
Müller, K., 40
Müller, N. C. J., 160

Munakata, Y., 284, 302
Munholland, K. A., 309
Muñoz, R. F., 243
Munson, J., 437
Munson, J. M., 221
Murai, T., 273
Murakami, N., 244
Muran, J. C., 453
Muraven, M., 406
Murayama, K., 171
Murnen, S. K., 245
Murphy, C., 121
Murphy, K. G., 244
Murphy, R., 221
Murphy, S. L., 442
Murphy, S. T., 362
Murray, C., 275
Murray, C. J. L., 450
Murray, H. A., 331
Myers, D. G., 358
Myles, P. S., 127

N

Nadasdy, A., 258
Nadeau, L., 273
Nadel, L., 167, 168
Nader, K., 168, 169
Nadolny, D., 369
Naef, M., 355
Nagasako, E. M., 116
Nagayama Hall, G. C., 356
Nagel, B. J., 73
Nagell, K., 216
Nairne, J. S., 162
Nakazato, M., 244
Nandi, A., 424
Naqvi, N., 273
Nash, J., 432f
Nassi, J. J., 101
Nathan, M. J., 220, 222
Nathan, P. E., 471
National Academies of Sciences,
    Engineering, and Medicine, 42
National Center for Health Statistics,
    149, 287
National Highway Traffic Safety
    Administration, 149
National Institute on Aging, 69
National Science Foundation, 21, 22
Naumann, L. P., 332
Nave, G., 82
Naveh-Benjamin, M., 181
Naylor, H., 288
Neale, J. M., 424
Neale, M. C., 247, 314
Neath, I., 165
Needham, B., 397
Neiles, K. Y., 223
Neimark, J., 45
Neisser, U., 187, 281, 282, 286
Nelemans, S. A., 316
Nelson, A. B., 68
Nelson, C. A., 282
Nelson, C. B., 147
Nelson, L. D., 380
Nelson, P., 422

Nelson, T. F., 376
Nemeroff, C. B., 61, 307
Németh, A., 468
Nemeth, C., 375
Nes, L. S., 272
Nesselroade, J. R., 320
Nestadt, G., 428
Neubauer, A. C., 177
Neuberg, S. L., 244
Neugebauer, R., 298
Nevarez, G., 91
Neville, H. J., 19, 43
Newbold, R. R., 247
Newman, A. J., 19, 43
Newman, M. G., 399, 420
Newport, E. L., 218, 264
Newschaffer, C. J., 436
Newsom, J. T., 380
Newsome, W. T., 107, 212
Ng, M., 246
Nguyen, P., 169
Niaura, R., 392
Nicolson, R., 433
Niedenthal, P., 237
Niedenthal, P. M., 239, 240
Nielsen, J. B., 73
Nielsen, T., 142
Niisato, K., 167
Nikles, C. D., II, 239
Niparko, J. K., 114
Nir, Y., 143
Nisbett, R. E., 19, 251, 282, 283, 285,
    286, 357, 371, 373
Nissen, M. J., 218
Nitsch, C., 264
Noah, T., 239
Nobes, G., 309
Nock, F., 66f
Nock, M. K., 243, 387, 422, 424, 442,
    443, 459
Nolen-Hoeksema, S., 428
Nomi, J. S., 183
Noom, M. J., 316
Noppeney, U., 265
Norby, S., 188
Norcross, J. C., 452
Norenzayan, A., 32f, 41, 371
Norman, G. R., 387
Norman, R. E., 450
Norton, M. I., 133
Nosanchuk, T. A., 378
Nosek, B. A., 163, 368, 369
Nosofsky, R. M., 267
Nowak, M. A., 357
Nowell, A., 285
Nowinski, C. J., 53
Nutter-Upham, K. E., 399
Nyberg, L., 172
Nyborg, H., 276

O

O'Brien, J. B., 268
O'Brien, K. F., 364
O'Connor, P. J., 397
O'Connor, T. G., 307
O'Daly, O., 273

O'Dean, S. M., 356
O'Doherty, J., 265
O'Doherty, J. P., 213
O'Donnell, K., 316
O'Donovan, A., 391
O'Leary, K. N., 334
O'Rahilly, S., 244
O'Regan, J. K., 108
O'Reilly, M., 285
Oakes, L. M., 299
Oaklander, A. L., 116
Ocfernia, M. C., 405
Ochsner, K. N., 236, 243
Odbert, H. S., 331
Odden, H., 303
Oettingen, G., 251, 252, 372
Ofshe, R. J., 154
Ogan, T. A., 305
Ogden, C. L., 245, 405
Ohayon, M. M., 140, 141
Ohtake, H., 176
Oishi, S., 240
Ojeda, S. R., 312
Ojemann, J. G., 174
Okuda, J., 176
Olausson, P. O., 316
Olds, J., 211
Olfson, M., 450, 451
Olguin, R. S., 216
Ollers, D. K., 261
Olsen, R. K., 176
Olsson, A., 201, 355
Olthof, T., 347
Oltmanns, T. F., 424
Olton, D. S., 213
Omalu, B., 53
Onnela, J. P., 459
Ono, K., 210
Ono, Y., 442
Open Science Collaboration, 42
Orban, P., 218
Orom, H., 387
Orr, S. P., 169, 426
Orsillo, S. M., 399
Ortiz, V., 358
Osgood, D. W., 317
Osterman, L. L., 356
Osypuk, T. L., 287
Ott, M. A., 316
Otto, M. W., 389
Ottoni, E. B., 216
Oudiette, D., 168
Ousdal, O. T., 213
Ouwehand, C., 273
Over, H., 359, 374
Owen, M. T., 263
Owens, E. B., 309
Owens, S., 431
Owens, W. A., 281
Oztekin, I., 172
Ozyurek, A., 264

P

Pace, A., 263
Padilla-Banks, E., 247
Pagnin, D., 467

Pai, S., 431
Paikoff, R. L., 312
Paivio, A., 161
Pakstis, A. J., 287
Palamara, P., 93
Paller, K. A., 168
Palmieri, M., 155
Palombo, D. J., 176
Paluck, B. L., 370
Pan, S. C., 222
Panagiotaki, G., 309
Pandeirada, J. N. S., 162
Pandit, J. J., 127
Pang, W., 279
Papademitris, X., 188
Papay, K., 213
Pardo, S. T., 336
Paré, E. B., 107
Park, B., 67, 368, 369
Park, D. C., 319
Parker, E. S., 159, 464
Parker, G., 159, 464
Parker, H. A., 394
Parker, K., 364
Parker, R., 33f
Parkinson, B., 243
Parkinson, C., 237
Parrish, T. B., 219
Parrott, A. C., 148, 150
Parsons, T., 402
Parvisi, J., 182, 236
Pascual-Ferrá, P., 93
Pascual-Leone, A., 73, 83
Pashler, H., 222
Pasupathi, M., 320
Patall, E. A., 251
Patrick, B., 353
Patten, S. B., 450
Patterson, C. J., 314
Patti, P. L., 438
Patton, G. C., 311
Paty, J. A., 407
Paulos, J., 45
Paulozzi, L. J., 151
Paulus, M., 311
Paunesku, D., 243
Pavlidou, E. V., 218
Pavlov, I., 10, 10f, 11, 17, 193, 194,
    195, 197, 200
Payne, B. K., 243
Payne, J. D., 168
Pearce, J. M., 198
Pearson, J., 161–162
Peles, E., 58
Peltonen, L., 76
Penfield, W., 71
Penke, L., 82
Penn, S., 276–277
Pennebaker, J. W., 330, 373, 395, 400
Penner, L. A., 387
Pennsylvania, T., 2
Pentland, J., 186
Penton-Voak, I. S., 363
Pepping, C. A., 321
Pereira-Pasarin, L. P., 178
Perenin, M.-T., 101
Perera, F. P., 77

Perera, S., 464, 467
Perilloux, H. K., 363
Perlis, R. H., 438
Perlmutter, J. S., 468
Perloff, L. S., 407
Perner, J., 303
Perrett, D. I., 363
Perrig, W. J., 288
Perron, B. E., 149
Perruchet, P., 216
Perry, G., 53
Perry, Z. W., 367
Pesce, A., 155
Peschardt, K., 441
Pescosolido, B., 419
Pescovitz, O. H., 312
Pessiglione, M., 213
Pete, E., 406
Petermann, A. G., 242
Peters, E., 281
Petersen, A. C., 313
Petersen, J. L., 362
Petersen, S. E., 173, 174
Peterson, C., 180, 304
Peterson, C. C., 304
Peterson, L. R., 164, 165
Peterson, M. J., 164, 165
Peterson, C., 304
Petitto, L. A., 261
Petrescu, P., 356
Petrie, K. P., 395
Petroni, F., 43f
Petronis, A., 431
Petry, N. M., 455
Petty, R. E., 378, 379
Petukhova, M., 420, 428
Pezdek, K., 186
Phelan, J., 419
Phelps, E. A., 68, 169, 201, 235, 236, 243f
Phillips, F., 407
Phillips, K. A., 414
Phillips, M. L., 273
Phills, C. E., 369
Piaget, J., 13, 13f, 300–301, 302, 304–305, 309
Piazza, J. R., 387
Picard, R. W., 459
Picasso, P., 205–206
Pichert, J. W., 170
Pickrell, J. E., 185
Pidsley, R., 431
Pierce, L., 20
Pierro, A., 380
Pietschnig, J., 82, 282
Piff, P. K., 20
Pillard, R. C., 314
Pincus, H. A., 451
Pinel, E. C., 42
Pinel, P. J., 406
Pines, A. M., 393
Pini, S., 467
Pinker, S., 262, 263
Pissiota, A., 465
Pitcher, D., 239
Pitman, R. K., 169, 426
Pittinsky, T. L., 287

Plack, C. J., 112, 113
Plante, C., 356
Platt, M. L., 379f
Plavén-Sigray, P., 421
Plener, P. L., 443
Pleskac, T. J., 369
Plomin, R., 283, 334
Plotnik, J. M., 132
Plucker, J. A., 279
Podolski, C.-L., 34
Poewe, W., 61
Pokorny, J., 395
Polanczyk, G., 438
Polderman, T. J. C., 281
Poldrack, R. A., 83
Polgar, J., 280
Poliak, S., 58
Polivy, J., 247
Pollack, M. H., 389
Pomara, N., 428
Ponto, L. L. B., 182, 236
Poole, D. A., 186
Poon, S. H., 467
Pope, A. W., 318
Pope, H. G., 244
Porte, D., Jr., 244
Porter, S., 186
Portera, L., 150
Portolés, O., 121
Posner, M. I., 81
Posthuma, D., 281, 283
Postman, L., 180
Postmes T., 359
Potter, J., 333
Potter, J. P., 342
Powell, R. A., 205
Powell, T., 181
Power, J. M., 200
Powers, D. A., 397
Powers, K. E., 318
Prakash, R. S., 73
Prakesh, R., 73
Prasada, S., 262
Prata, D., 213
Pratkanis, A. R., 358
Prentice, D. A., 360, 374
Prescott, C. A., 424
Pressman, S. D., 397
Préville, M., 387
Price, A. A., 405
Price, C. J., 182, 265
Price, J., 159
Priest, R. G., 141
Prince, M., 69
Prior, H., 69, 132
Pritchard, D. E., 223
Prochaska, J. J., 406
Procopio, M., 245
Protzko, J., 283, 288
Provencal, N., 77
Przedborski, S., 68
Przybyla, S. M., 149
Ptito, M., 144
Ptolemy, 29
Puetz, T. W., 397
Punjabi, N. M., 141
Putallaz, M., 285

Puterman, E., 391
Putnam, K. M., 243, 252
Pyc, M. A., 222
Pyers, J. E., 264, 304
Pzaiuk, M., 247

Q

Quatrone, R. P., 216
Quattrociocchi, W., 43f
Qudrat, A., 334
Queen, B., 313, 314, 315
Querleu, D., 298
Quing, F., 356
Quinter, V. E., 364
Quittner, A. L., 114
Qureshi, A., 140

R

Rabi, T., 281f
Rabin, B. S., 397
Rabin, L. A., 399
Race, E., 176
Raco, A., 155
Racsmány, M., 468
Radke-Yarrow, M., 310
Raichle, M. E., 81, 133, 174
Raio, C. M., 169
Rajaram, S., 178, 179, 247
Rajeevan, N., 188
Rajkai, C., 468
Ramachandran, V. S., 72, 73
Ramirez-Esparza, N., 330, 342
Ramones, S. M., 308
Rampon, C., 288
Ramus, S. J., 218
Rand, D. G., 357
Randles, D., 238
Ranvier, L.-A., 58
Rao, S., 184
Rapaport, D., 329
Rapoport, J. L., 432, 433, 438
Rasch, B., 168
Rash, C. J., 455
Rasmussen, A. S., 170
Rasmussen, T., 71
Ratliff, K. A., 163
Ratner, R. K., 360
Rau, H., 244
Raubenheimer, D., 247
Rauch, S. L., 161, 162, 172, 184, 330, 425, 426
Raven, J. C., 278
Rawson, K. A., 220, 222
Ray, N. J., 218, 219
Ray, R. D., 394
Rayner, R., 199
Raz, A., 154
Raz, N., 318
Reber, A. S., 218, 219
Reber, P. J., 219
Recanzone, G. H., 70, 73
Rechtschaffen, A., 139
Redick, T. S., 166
Reed, D. R., 121
Reed, G., 183

Rees, A. M., 159, 464
Reeve, C. L., 286
Regan, M. A., 93
Regan, P. C., 363
Reichbach, G. L., 153
Reid, S., 305, 363
Reis, D. J., 235
Reis, H. T., 362
Reiser, M., 279
Reishofer, G., 177
Reisner, S. L., 336
Reiss, D., 132, 283
Reiter, E. O., 312
Renard, X., 298
Renner, K. E., 205
Renner, M. J., 386–387
Rensink, R. A., 108
Rentfrow, P. J., 329
Resch, S. C., 314
Rescorla, R. A., 198, 200
Respass, J., 298
Ressler, K. J., 61, 468
Resurreccion, N., 405
Revelle, W., 333
Reynolds, C. A., 320
Rhoads, S. A., 239
Rhodes, E., 242
Rhu, E., 320
Ribeiro, J. D., 459
Ric, F., 239
Ricci-Bitt, P. E., 238
Rice, K. G., 399
Rich, A., 334
Richards, M., 275
Richards, M. H., 316
Richards, T. J., 407
Richardson, C. M. E., 399
Richardson, D. S., 356
Richardson-Klavehn, A., 174
Richeson, J. A., 369
Rickard, T. C., 222
Rietschel, L., 462
Riggs, J. E., 247
Rigoli, F., 213
Rilling, J. K., 401
Rimm, E. B., 405
Rimmer, J., 288
Rind, B., 374
Rinderu, M. I., 354
Rippon, G., 335
Riskin, B., 127
Risko, E. F., 223
Risley, T. R., 263, 282
Risman, J. E., 433
Ritchey, A. J., 359f
Ritter, J. M., 363
Ritz, T. 422
Rivera, L. A., 342
Rivers, S. E., 279
Rizzolatti, G., 71, 72, 217
Robbins, C. A., 184
Robbins, T. W., 288
Roberts, A. R., 363
Roberts, B. A., 276
Roberts, B. W., 333

Roberts, G., 364
Roberts, G. A., 396, 432
Roberts, R. D., 279
Robertson, K., 169
Robins, L. N., 147
Robins, R. W., 330
Robinson, J. C., 251
Robinson, M., 246
Robinson, M. D., 230
Rochat, P., 303
Rock, C., 392f
Rodgers-Ramachandran, D., 73
Rodieck, R. W., 94
Rodman, A. M., 318
Rodriguez, M., 69, 250
Roediger, H. L., 170, 223
Roediger, H. L., III, 171, 184, 186,
    221, 222, 223, 224
Roelofs, K., 232
Roer, J. P., 163
Rogan, J. D., 452
Rogeberg, O., 281
Rogers, R., 363
Rogers, S. J., 437
Rohde, L. A., 438
Rohrer, D., 222
Rohsenow, D., 149
Roig, M., 73
Roisman, G. I., 309, 316
Roldan, A., 462
Rollnick, S., 403
Rolls, E. T., 120
Romano, J. C., 218
Romero, C., 243
Romeyke, S., 276
Ronay, R., 355
Rosch, E. H., 266
Rose, J. L., 118
Rose, S. P. R., 288
Rosedahl, L., 267
Roseman, I. J., 232
Rosen, L. R., 314
Rosenbaum, J. E., 316
Rosenbaum, J. F., 389
Rosenbaum, R. S., 167, 168
Rosenbaum, S., 245
Rosenberg, M., 346
Rosenberg, T., 376
Rosenhan, D., 419
Rosenman, R. H., 392
Rosenthal, R., 33,
    336, 471
Roser, M. E., 218
Ross, D., 215
Ross, L., 179, 371
Ross, M., 347
Ross, S., 215
Rossano, F., 305
Rotella, P., 432
Roth, B., 276
Roth, B. L., 61
Roth, D. A., 247
Roth, G., 355
Roth, H. P., 403
Roth, R. H., 61
Rothbart, M. K., 308
Rothbaum, B. O., 199

Rothermel, J., 139
Rothstein, H. R., 356
Rotkirch, A., 321
Rotte, M., 160
Rotter, J. B., 343
Rouse, C., 368f
Rowe, J. B., 213
Rowland, D. A., 363
Roy, R., 387
Rozin, P., 244, 247, 406
Rozzi, S., 72, 217
Ruan, W. J., 441
Ruback, R. B., 359f
Rubin, M., 367
Rubin, Z., 364
Rubio-Stipec, M., 415
Rüddel, H., 453
Rudman, L. A., 369
Rugg, M. D., 181
Ruggiero, C., 431
Ruggles, S., 312
Running, C. A., 120
Rusbult, C. E., 365
Rushton, J. P., 275
Russell, J. A., 232, 239, 303f
Russin, A., 369
Rustichini, A., 251, 276
Rutledge, R. B., 213
Rutter, M., 75, 307
Ruttle, P. L., 312
Ryals, A. J., 183
Ryan, A. M., 316
Ryan, R. M., 239, 251, 313, 340
Rychlowska, M., 237, 240
Ryff, C., 405
Ryle, G., 2

S

Sabbagh, M. A., 303
Sacks, O., 173, 437
Sadalla, E. K., 362
Sadler, J. Z., 414
Sadler, M. S., 369
Safford, A., 239
Saffran, J. R., 218
Sagher, O., 468
Sagi, A., 308
Sagot, P., 120
Saha, S., 432
Sahakian, B. J., 288
Sakamoto, A., 356
Sakamoto, J., 205
Saks, E. R., 434
Salapatek, P., 299
Saleem, K. S., 100
Saleem, M., 356
Salerno, J., 242
Sallis, J. F., 406
Salmon, D. P., 60
Salovey, P., 279
Salthouse, T. A., 281, 288, 318, 319
Saltzman, L. E., 249
Salvatore, J. E., 309
Sampson, L., 198
Sampson, N., 152, 420, 428
Sampson, N. A., 450

Sampson, P. D., 298
Sampson, R. J., 313
Samuelson, R. J., 213
Sanbonmatsu, D. M., 43
Sanchez, J., 360
Sanders, C., 267
Sanders, D. Y., 373
Sandler, B., 35f
Sandman, C. A., 298
Sands, M. K., 234
Santelli, J., 316
Santens, P., 265
Sanulis, J., 237
Sapiro, G., 437
Saquib, S., 243
Sara, S. J., 168
Sariyska, R., 333
Saron, C., 237, 395
Sarris, V., 12
Sarter, M., 61
Sarwal, A., 223
Sasaki, A., 461
Satcher, D., 316
Satterwhite, C. L., 405
Saunders, J., 171
Sauter, D. A., 237
Savage-Rumbaugh, S., 216
Savage, C. R., 162, 172, 184
Savic, I., 314, 355
Sawa, A., 433
Sawalani, G. M., 356
Sawin, D. B., 363
Sawyer, B. D., 183
Sawyer, S. M., 311
Saxe, R., 268
Scalåa, A., 43f
Scalf, P. E., 73
Scarr, S., 287
Schaal, B., 120
Schachter, D. L., 162, 177
Schachter, S., 362, 407
Schacter, D. L., 68, 83, 160, 163, 167,
    170, 172, 173, 174, 176, 177, 179,
    182, 184, 186, 187, 188, 223
Schacter, S., 234
Schaefer, J. T., 363
Schäfer, S., 276
Schaffer, M. M., 266
Schaie, K. W., 281
Schalkwyk, L. C., 431
Schaller, E., 392
Schaller, M., 244
Schallert, D. L., 170
Schapira, A. H. V., 61
Scheffer, M., 243f
Scheitle, C. P., 2
Scherbov, S., 281
Scherer, K. R., 232, 236, 237, 238
Schiff, M., 282
Schildkraut, J. J., 428
Schiller, D., 169
Schilling, O. K., 320
Schkade, D. A., 322
Schlagman, S., 187
Schlauch, R. C., 149
Schlosser, S., 60
Schmader, T., 286

Schmidt, H., 101, 102
Schmitt D. P., 334, 362, 363
Schneider, B. H., 309
Schneiderman, N., 396
Schnyer, D. M., 172, 177
Schoenemann, P. T., 71
Scholey, A., 148
Schön, J. H., 48–49
Schonberg, T., 213
Schoon, I., 276
Schott, B. J., 174
Schraw, G., 220
Schreier, J., 242
Schreiner, T., 168
Schubert, T. W., 230
Schugens, M. M., 200
Schul, Y., 239
Schuldiner, K. L., 69
Schultz, D., 279
Schultz, W., 212, 213
Schulz, H., 453
Schutter, D. J. L. G., 355
Schwartz, A., 69, 132
Schwartz, A. C., 199
Schwartz, B., 289
Schwartz, C. E., 330
Schwartz, H. A., 308
Schwartz, J. E., 320
Schwartz, J. L. K., 368
Schwartz, L., 102
Schwartz, M. W., 244
Schwartz, N., 356
Schwartz, S., 143, 182
Schwartzman, A. E., 281
Schwarz, C., 40
Schwarz, M., 396
Schwarz, N., 322
Schwarzbach, J., 268
Schyns, P. G., 237
Scoboria, A., 463
Scott, A., 281f
Scott, D. J., 387
Scott, E. S., 236
Scott, S. K., 237
Scoville, W. B., 68, 166
Scribner, S., 279
Scrugs, P., 370
Seal, L. J., 244
Sears, R. R., 354
Seaton, D. T., 223
Seau, J., 53
Seckl, J. R., 77
Secord, P. F., 364
Sedlmeier, P., 396
Seeley, R. J., 244
Seeman, M., 398
Seeman, T. E., 398
Seetharaman, S., 210
Segal, N., 334
Segal, Z. V., 458
Segev, Y., 213
Segge, H., 347
Seibt, B., 230
Seidman, L. J., 438
Seijo, R., 437
Seli, P., 223
Seligman, M. E. P., 250, 421, 429, 471

Selye, H., 68, 389–390
Semenza, C., 181, 182
Semin, G. R., 239
Seminowicz, D., 468
Senghas, A., 264, 304
Senju, A., 304
Sergerstrom, S. C., 272
Serpell, R., 279
Setoodehnia, M., 299
Settanni, M., 333
Seybold, K. S., 398
Seyfarth, R. M., 258
Seymour, B., 213
Shackelford, T. K., 364
Shafe, G., 168
Shafto, C., 262
Shah, A., 151
Shah, P., 288
Shahaeian, A., 304
Shallice, T., 162, 181, 268
Shanabrough, M., 244
Shane, M. S., 188
Shanklin, S. L., 313, 314, 315
Shao, H., 428
Shariff, A. F., 238
Sharma, S., 77
Sharma, Y. S., 362
Sharot, T., 272
Sharp, C., 336
Sharp, W., 438
Shattuck, C. W., 81
Shaver, J. L., 139
Shavitt, S., 378
Shaw, B. M., 271
Shaw, D. S., 309
Shaw, J., 186
Shaw, J. S., 171
Shear, M. K., 465, 471
Shedler, J., 453
Sheehan, E., 166
Sheenan, M. J., 71
Sheeran, P., 243
Sheese, B. E., 356
Sheketoff, R., 309
Shenton, M. E., 426
Shepherd, G. M., 74
Shepperd, J., 347
Sherburne, L. M., 216
Sherry, S. B., 245
Sherwood, J. B., 398
Sheskin, M., 311
Shibuya, A., 356
Shields, B., 428f
Shields, C., 406
Shiffman, S., 279, 407
Shiffrin, R. M., 165
Shih, M., 287
Shimamura, A. P., 183
Shimizu, E., 288
Shin, H., 316
Shin, L. M., 330, 426
Shiner, R. L., 333
Shinskey, J. L., 302
Shiota, M. N., 237
Shipstead, Z., 166, 288
Shirer, W. R., 160
Shiv, B., 273

Shoda, Y., 250, 341
Shomstein, S., 93
Shore, C., 262
Shrout, P. E., 415
Shu, S., 271
Shulman, L., 437
Shurgot, B. A., 363
Shusterman, A., 264
Si-Hyeon, R., 280f
Siderowf, A., 213
Sieben, A., 265
Siebner, H. R., 213
Siegal, J., 144
Siegal, M., 304
Siegel, E. H., 234
Siegel, M., 180
Siegel, S., 198
Siegrist, M., 33f
Siemer, M., 232, 243
Sigafoos, J., 285
Sigman, M., 436
Silber, T., 428
Silberg, J., 75
Silberman, E. K., 453
Silver, J. M., 462
Silverman, A. M., 370
Silvia, P. J., 177
Sim, K., 467
Simeone, J. C., 432
Simmelhag, V. L., 210
Simons, D., 84, 91
Simons, D. J., 108
Simons, J. S., 83
Simonton, D. K., 277
Simpson, J. A., 309, 364
Simpson, S. J., 247
Singer, J. E., 234, 388
Singer, P., 47
Singh, S., 303
Sinigaglia, C., 71
Sipe, T. A., 316
Sirois, F. M., 399
Siu, A. L., 437
Skiena, S., 9
Skinner, B. F., 10–12, 11f, 15, 203–204,
    206–207, 208, 209f, 210, 263
Skinner, T., 279
Sklar, P., 438
Skotko, B. G., 285
Skriver, K., 73
Skytthe, A., 433
Slatcher, R. B., 330
Slater, A., 299
Slaughter, V., 304
Sletten, I., 155
Slichter, D., 91
Sliwinski, M. J., 387
Slora, E., 312
Small, D. M., 121
Smart, E., 385, 390, 394
Smart, L., 356
Smetacek, V., 65
Smilek, D., 223
Smith, A. M., 441
Smith, B., 392
Smith, C. A., 232
Smith, C. N., 167

Smith, C. T., 362
Smith, E. E., 319
Smith, E. N., 243
Smith, G. D., 276
Smith, M., 437
Smith, M. D., 365
Smith, M. L., 471
Smith, N., 257
Smith, S. M. 83
Smith, T. C., 392
Smoller, J. W., 438
Smyke, A. T., 282
Snedeker, J., 262
Sniekers, S., 283
Snowdon, R., 94
Snozzi, R., 355
Snyder, M., 368
Snyder, R. J., 247
Snyder, S. H., 433
Soderlund, H., 176
Sokolik, A., 401
Solomon, S., 252, 347
Somers, M., 299
Somerville, L. H., 318
Sommer, I. E., 467
Son, L. K., 224
Song, H., 312, 392
Sonnby-Borgstrom, M., 239
Sonne, L., 304f
Sonne, T., 304f
Soos, M. A., 244
Sorjonen, K., 355
Sorlí, J. V., 121
Sorrentino, R. M., 358
Sorri, A., 435
Soto, C. J., 332, 333
Soukup, J., 464
Soumerai, S. B., 402
Soussignan, R., 120
South, S., 316
Southgate, V., 304
Sparrow, B., 178
Spearman, C., 277
Spears, R., 359
Speizer, I. S., 316
Spelke, E. S., 264, 285, 301, 302
Spence, S. J., 436
Spencer, S. J., 286, 368
Spencer, T., 438
Sperling, G., 163
Sperry, R. W., 79
Spiegel, A., 14
Spielman, A. J., 139
Spiers, H. J., 73
Spilka, M. E., 61
Spillmann, L., 104
Spinath, F. M., 276
Spirito, A., 442
Spiro, A., 320
Spiro, A., III, 392
Sporns, O., 65
Sprecher, S., 187
Spreng, R. N., 168
Sprenger, T., 61
Squire, L. R., 68, 167, 168, 169, 173,
    174, 183, 218
Srivastava, S., 332, 333

Sroufe, L. A., 309
St. Jacques, P. L., 172
Staddon, J. E. R., 210
Stafford, K., 342
Stanca, L., 321
Stancato, D. M., 20
Stanton, A. L., 321
Starr, J. M., 276
Statton, M. A., 73
Stecker, R., 388
Steckler, C. M., 238
Steele, C. M., 149, 286, 368
Steele, H., 309
Steele, M., 309
Steele, R. D., 309
Steffes, J., 312
Steiber, N., 281
Steiger, H., 245
Steiger, J. H., 232
Stein, D. J., 414
Stein, J. F., 218, 219
Stein, L. M., 171
Stein, M., 265
Stein, M. B., 424
Stein, T. D., 53
Steinbaum, E. A., 244
Steinberg, L., 236, 312, 313, 318
Steiner, J. E., 238
Steiner, S. S., 139
Steinmetz, J. L., 179, 371
Steketee, G. S., 422
Stellar, E., 244
Stellar, J. R., 244
Stelmack, R. M., 336
Stennet, J., 238
Stephan, Y., 246
Stephens, R. S., 152
Stephenson, D. A., 60
Stepper, S., 239
Stern, J. A., 155
Stern, L. D., 45
Stern, R. A., 53
Sternberg, R. J., 279, 364
Sterschic, S., 222
Stevens, J., 162
Stevens, K. V., 170
Stevens, M., 265
Stevenson, M. R., 93
Stevenson, R. J., 247
Stewart, J., 282
Stewart, M., 73
Stewart, S. E., 425
Stibbard, J., 397f
Stice, E., 247
Stickgold, R., 168
Stickney-Gibson, M., 187
Stinson, F. S., 441
Stoet, G., 30
Stone, A. A., 132, 320,
    322, 399
Stone, J., 367
Stone, M. H., 425
Stone, S. I., 288
Stoodley, C. J., 218, 219
Stopp, C., 298
Storm, B. C., 171
Storm, T., 363f

Storms, 372
Strack, F., 239
Strasburger, V. C., 245
Strauss, J. S., 419
Strayer, D. L., 93
Streiner, D. L., 387
Streissguth, A. P., 298
Streit, F., 387
Striano, T., 310
Stringer, S., 283
Strober, M., 245
Strohmetz, D. B., 374
Strong, G., 365
Strosahl, K., 394
Stroud, L., 392
Strueber, D., 355
Stuart-Parrigon, K. L., 243
Stucky, B. D., 356
Stueve, A., 419
Stump, G. S., 223
Stuss, D. T., 71, 236
Suchman, A. L., 403
Suchy, Y., 243
Suddendorf, T., 71, 163, 177
Sullenberger, C., 319f
Sullivan-Singh, S. J., 321
Sullivan, P. F., 281
Sum, M. Y., 467
Suma, K., 263
Summerfield, C., 130
Sumner, F. C., 21
Sun, R., 238
Sun, Y. E., 77
Sunstein, C. R., 48, 48f, 247
Suppes, T., 61
Suri, G., 243
Surian, L., 310
Surprenant, A. M., 165
Surratt, H. L., 151
Susser, E., 298
Susskind, J. M., 232
Sutin, A. R., 246
Sutter, M. L., 70
Sutton, J., 178
Sutton, J. E., 216
Suzuki, K., 176, 356
Suzuki, L. A., 286
Svensson, O., 239
Swann, W. B., Jr., 329, 345
Swartz, H., 216
Swayze, V. W., II, 467
Swearingen, L., 309
Sweatt, J. D., 77
Sweeny, K., 347
Swencionis, J. K., 342
Swendsen, J., 69
Swets, J. A., 93
Swing, E. L., 356
Symbaluk, D. G., 205
Szechtman, H., 425
Szpunar, K. K., 176, 177, 223
Szyf, M., 461

T

Tabi, E., 369
Tabibnia, G., 243

Taft, C. T., 426
Tajfel, H., 358, 367
Tajima, S., 356
Talbot, P. S., 150
Talhelm, T., 240
Tamir, M., 242
Tamminga, C. A., 61
Tan, H. H., 279
Tanaka, K. Z., 167
Tang, C., 187
Tang, D. L., 77
Tang, D. W., 248
Tang, J., 461
Tang, Y.-P., 288
Tanji, K., 176
Tannenbaum, B., 77
Tarantino, N., 316
Tardif, C., 309
Tardiff, K., 150
Tardiff, T., 303
Tarshis, N., 437
Taylor, L. S., 361
Taylor, S., 397–398, 468
Taylor, S. E., 147, 188, 372
Taylor-Thompson, K. A., 236
Teasdale, J. D., 429, 458
Tedin, K., 364
Telch, M. J., 422
Tellegen, A., 232, 316, 329, 334
Temple, E., 388
Templer, D. I., 275
ten Brinke, L., 241
Tepper, T., 271
ter Schure, E., 232
Terman, L., 285–286
Terracciano, A., 246, 334, 335
Testa, M., 149
Tews, M. J., 342
Teyler, T. J., 167
Thabane, L., 464, 467
Thakral, P. P., 83, 177
Thal, D., 114
Thal, J., 243
Thaler, K., 89, 464
Thaler, R. H., 247
Thase, M. E., 428
Thaver, D., 393
Thibaut, J. W., 365
Thiede, K., 298
Thiede, K. W., 224
Thoma, V., 174
Thomaes, S., 347
Thomas, A., 308
Thomas, D. L., 82
Thomas, G., 364
Thomas, R. C., 223
Thomas, R. L., 178
Thompson, M. E., 356
Thompson, P., 94, 252, 347
Thompson, P. M., 81, 311, 433
Thompson, S. R., 162
Thompson, W. L., 161
Thomson, B., 246
Thomson, D. M., 170
Thorndike, E. L., 202–203
Thornton, A., 217
Thornton, L., 245

Thurber, J., 252
Thurstone, L., 277
Tice, D. M., 406
Tienari, P., 435
Tierney, S., 428
Tillfors, M., 465
Timko, C., 460
Tindale, R. S., 358
Titran, M., 298
Tobey, E. A., 114
Tobler, I., 139
Todaro, J. F., 392
Todd, A. R., 369
Todd, R. M., 176
Toga, A. W., 69, 81, 311
Tolin, D. F., 453
Tolle, T. R., 61
Tolman, E. C., 210, 211
Toma, R., 356
Tomaka, J., 392
Tomar, A., 167
Tomasello, M., 216, 217, 305, 310, 360
Tomkiewicz, S., 282
Tomkins, S. S., 239
Tong, J., 150
Tononi, G., 143
Torous, J., 459
Torre, J. B., 243
Torrone, E., 405
Toscani, M., 104
Tost, H., 387
Toth, S. L., 309
Totterdell, P., 243
Towne, W. F., 258
Townshend, P., 321f
Toyama, Y., 221
Tracey, J. B., 342
Tracy, J. L., 238
Tranel, D., 239, 268, 273
Tranter, L. J., 288
Trathen, W., 220
Traut-Mattausch, E., 361
Treanor, J. J., 397
Tredget, J., 467
Treede, R. D., 117
Treisman, A., 101, 102
Tremblay, J., 169
Trendafilov, B., 333
Trinder, J. A., 140
Trivers, R. L., 360
Trojanowski, J., 377
Trollips, S. R., 170
Troscianko, T., 94, 237, 252, 347
Trost, M. R., 362, 380
Troy, A. S., 243
Trull, T. J., 439
Truman, H., 41f
Trump, D., 41f
Tsai, N., 166
Tsakiris, M., 130
Tshering, S., 236
Tsien, J. Z., 288
Tsimpli, I.-M., 257
Tsujii, N., 238f
Tsukiura, T., 176
Tucker-Drob, E. M., 283

Tulloch, E., 437
Tully, E. C., 316
Tulving, E., 160, 170, 172, 173, 174, 176
Turchi, J. N., 60
Turk-Charles, S., 320
Turkheimer, E., 286, 287
Turnbaugh, P. J., 247
Turner, B. J., 459
Turner, D. C., 288
Turner, J. C., 367
Turner, M. E., 358
Turvey, M. T., 164
Tuszynski, M. H., 65
Tversky, A., 270, 271
Tyce, G. M., 61
Tyler, L. K., 102
Tyler, T. R., 377
Tylka, T. L., 245

U

U.S. Department of Health, Education and Welfare, 46
U.S. Preventive Task Force, 437
Uchikawa, K., 104
Uddin, M., 424
Uesiliana, K., 180
Ulett, A., 155
Ullrich, J., 358
Ulman, L., 242
Umberson, D., 397
Uncapher, M. R., 181
Underwood, B. J., 180
Underwood, W., 387
Ungar, L. H., 308
Ungerleider, L. G., 100
Urban, N. B. L., 150
Ursano, R. J., 453
Uskul, A. K., 359
Uutela, A., 396

V

Vacha, E., 220
Vafaei, A., 335
Vaidya, C. J., 68, 160
Vaidyam, A., 459
Valdimarsdóttir, U. A., 312, 392
Valencia, R. R., 286
Valentine, B. A., 362
Valentine, T., 181, 182
Valicenti-McDermott, M., 437
Vallacher, R. R., 252, 343
van Aken, M. A. G., 332, 333
Van Ast, V. A., 169
Van Bergen, P., 178
van Bochoven, A., 281
Van Boven, L., 370
van Broeck, N., 279
van de Leemput, I. A., 243f
van den Boom, D. C., 308
Van den Noortgate, W., 234
Van Dessel, P., 362
van Esch, L., 188
van Essen D. C., 98
van Haastert, N. L., 273

van Hoeken, D., 244
van Honk, J., 355
Van Horn, J. D., 81, 133
van IJzendoorn, M. H., 282, 299, 308
Van Koppen, P. J., 184
Van Lange, P. A. M., 354, 365
Van Laningham, J., 322
Van Megan, H. J., 468
Van Paesschen, W., 176
van Praag, 73
Van Rijen, P. C., 468
Van Rompay, M. I., 464
van Schaik, C. P., 217
Van Stegeren, A. H., 235
Van Vliet, I. M., 468
van Well, E. P., 468
Vancorenland, S., 279
Vandenberghe, R., 182
Vangel, M., 395
Vanyperen, N. W., 393
Varamesh, A., 243f
Varga, M., 144
Vargha-Khadem, F., 176
Varley, J., 437
Varol, O., 243f
Vasilenko, S. A., 315
Vaughn, B. E., 309
Vaughn, M. G., 149
Vazire, S., 330
Velazco, M. I., 120
Venard, J., 210
Verfaellie, M., 172, 176
Verniest, R., 279
Versijpt, J., 265
Viana, M., 467
Vianello, M., 163
Victorsson, P., 421
Vidal, C., 433
Vighetto, A., 101
Vilagut, G., 416
Viner, R., 311
Vinicor, F., 246
Vinter, A., 216
Visalberghi, E., 216
Visscher, P. M., 281
Vitiello, C., 287
Vitkus, J., 430
Vogrincic, C., 359
Vohs, K., 358
Vohs, K. D., 241, 249, 250, 346, 406
Volkow, N. D., 61, 147, 149, 151
Vollebergh, W. M., 316
von Bartheld, C. S., 54
von Bastian, C. C., 166, 406
von Clef, J., 120
von Cramon, D., 107
Von Frisch, K., 258
Vondra, J. I., 309
Voon, V., 468
Voracek, M., 82, 282
Vorndran, C. M., 205
Voss, M. W., 73
Vosshall, L. B., 119
Vrij, A., 241
Vukasovic, T., 334
Vul, E., 222
Vygotsky, L., 305

W

Wade, E., 182
Wade, K. A., 186
Wade, S. E., 220
Wadhwa, P. D., 298
Wagenaar, W. A., 184
Wager, T., 236
Wager, T. D., 401
Wagner, A. D., 160, 162, 184, 243f
Wagner, A. R., 200
Wagner, E., 310
Wagner, G., 210
Wagner, I. C., 160
Wagner, K. J., 61
Wahl, H.-W., 320
Wahlberg, K. E., 435
Wai, J., 285
Wainer, H., 43
Wakefield, J. C., 414
Wakita, M., 205
Walden, T. A., 120, 305
Waldfogel, S., 180
Walker, M. R., 32
Walker, N. P., 285
Walker, R., 321
Walker, T. T., 237
Wall, P. D., 117
Wallace, A. R., 6f
Wallbott, H. G., 237
Walls, S., 307, 308
Walsh, V., 239
Walter, J. K., 403
Walters, E. E., 416, 450
Walton, G. M., 286
Waltz, W., 399
Waltzman, S. B., 113
Walyzada, F., 462
Wammes, J. D., 223
Wamsley, E., 168
Wang, N. Y., 114
Wang, P. S., 419, 450, 451
Wang, Q., 180
Wang, S.-H., 302
Wang, T., 436
Wang, W., 364
Wangchuk, D., 236
Wansink, B., 247f
Wansink, C. S., 247f
Warburton, W., 356
Ward, A. J., 432
Ward, B. W., 246
Ward, C. B., 9
Ward, K. D., 392
Ward, P. B., 288
Ward, Z., 314
Wareham, N. J., 244
Wargo, E. M., 151
Warneken, F., 310, 360
Warner, L. A., 147
Warren, E., 21f
Warren, K. R., 298
Warrington, E. K., 268
Wartella, E., 34
Washburn, M. F., 21f
Wasserman, S., 301, 302
Watanabe, K., 283

Watanabe, S., 205
Waters, E., 307, 308
Waters, T. E. A., 309
Watkins, K. E., 176
Watkins, L. R., 400
Watkinson, B., 298
Watson, D., 232, 400
Watson, J. B., 9–10, 10f, 11, 16–17, 194, 199, 422
Watson, J. M., 176, 223
Watson, K. K., 379f
Watt, A., 205
Watts, C. H., 356
Watzke, B., 453
Waytz, A., 371
Weaver, I. C. G., 77
Webb, B. T., 334
Webb, T. L., 243
Webber, D., 243, 380
Weber, K., 53
Webster Marketon, J. I., 391
Webster, G. D., 363
Webster, M. A., 104
Wechsler, D., 275
Wechsler, H., 376
Wedekind, D., 462
Wegener, D. T., 378
Wegner, D. M., 128, 130, 133, 134, 135, 154, 178, 252, 341, 394, 406, 424
Weinberger, D. R., 61
Weiner, M. W., 69
Weinstein, N. D., 272
Weinstock, H., 405
Weintraub, D., 213
Weinzierl, M., 363f
Weise-Kelly, L., 198
Weiser, M., 276
Weisfeld, G., 317
Weiss, S., 392
Weissman, M. M., 453
Weitoft, G. R., 316
Weldon, M. S., 178
Welham, J., 432
Wellman, H. M., 303, 304
Wells, J. E., 152, 451
Wells, K. B., 451
Wemmie, J. A., 235, 236
Wenzlaff, R. M., 142, 406, 424
Werbeloff, N., 276
Werge, T. M., 433
Werker, J. F., 298
Wermke, K., 298
Werner, J. S., 104
Wertheimer, M., 12–13, 12f
Wesch, N. N., 216
Wescoff, M., 16f
Wesensten, N. J., 144
Westbrook, A., 213
Westerberg, C. E., 168
Westrin, A., 428
Wexler, K., 262
Whalley, L. J., 285
Whalley, M., 154
Wharton, S., 309
Wheatley, T., 237
Wheeler, M. A., 173

Whishaw, I. Q., 78
White, G. M., 279
White, J., 279
White, R., 431
White, S., 304, 346f
Whiteford, H. A., 450
Whitehead, J. P., 244
Whiten, A., 214, 216, 305
Whybrow, 430
Wicherts, J. M., 82
Wickens, C. D., 93
Wicklund, R. A., 132
Wickremarathne, D., 311
Widge, A. S., 425
Wiebe, S. A., 298
Wiegering, S., 320
Wiegner, L., 403
Wiesel, T. N., 98
Wiest, R., 265
Wiggs, C. L., 174
Wilcox, K., 334
Wilcoxon, H. C., 201
Wilens, T. E., 438
Wilhelm, S., 425
Wilkes, A. L., 367
Wilkes, M. S., 462f
Wilkey, S. A., 464
Wilkins, D., 150
Willems, E. P., 217
Williams, C. M., 152
Williams, D. R., 405
Williams, G. R., 246
Williams, J. M., 218
Williams, J. M. G., 458
Williams, K., 397
Williams, K. D., 359, 374
Williams, M. J., 371
Williams, R., 413, 415
Williams, W. M., 282, 285
Willingham, B., 238
Willingham, D. T., 42, 220, 222
Willison, D. J., 402
Wills, A. J., 266
Wilson, A. A., 160
Wilson, H. W., 314
Wilson, K. G., 223, 394
Wilson, M., 355
Wilson, T. D., 7, 42, 186
Wilson, V., 276
Wilt, J., 333
Wimmer, H., 303
Wimo, A., 69
Winblad, B., 69
Windham, G. C., 298, 436
Windisch, R., 432
Winkielman, P., 239
Winkler, A. D., 104
Winnett-Perman, C., 431
Winocur, G., 167, 168
Winter, C., 400
Winter, J., 437
Winter, J. B., 139
Winterer, G., 61
Wirth, M., 265
Wise, B. M., 108
Wise, R. A., 145, 212
Wish, E., 147

Wisniewski, H., 459
Witchel, S. F., 312
Withers, G. A., 121
Withey, W. J., 341
Wittchen, H. U., 420, 428
Wittenbrink, B., 368, 369
Wixted, J. T., 167, 168, 169, 222
Wolfradt, U., 379
Wolpe, P. R., 288
Womer, J., 403
Wong, A. T., 176
Wood, A., 237, 240
Wood, J. M., 142
Wood, R., 252
Wood, W., 335, 362
Woods, R. P., 311
Woods, S. C., 244
Woods, S. W., 465, 471
Woodward, A. L., 366
Woodward, M., 93
Woody, E. Z., 425
Woolcott, M., 374
Woollett, K., 73
Worchel, P., 364
Worthley, J. S., 182
Woumans, E., 265
Wrangham, R. W., 354, 356
Wraw, C., 276

Wren, A. M., 244
Wrenn, C. C., 60
Wright, C. I., 330
Wright, S., 140
Wrosch, C., 320
Wu, C.-H., 363
Wu, H., 77
Wu, J., 321
Wu, X., 309
Wu, Y-T., 69
Wundt, W., 5, 5f
Wyatt, T. D., 120
Wynn, K., 310, 311
Wynne, L. C., 435

X

Xu, A. W., 244
Xu, J., 82, 442
Xu, X., 150

Y

Yacoub, E., 82
Yamadori, A., 176
Yamaguchi, S., 120
Yang, S., 279
Yano, L., 288
Yantis, S., 93

Yap, A. J., 239
Yen, Y., 400, 401f
Yerramsetti, S. M., 395
Yeterian, J., 460
Yik, M., 232
Yokum, S., 247
Young, J. J., 428
Young, J. T. N., 288
Young, K. L., 93
Yount, S. E., 405
Yovel, G., 102
Yu, Y., 305
Yudofsky, S. C., 462
Yzerbyt, V., 359

Z

Zacks, J. M., 162
Zahn-Waxler, C., 310
Zahra, D., 218
Zajonc, R. B., 239, 362
Zampini, M., 268
Zanakos, S., 394
Zandi, P., 428
Zanesco, A., 395
Zanna, M., 361
Zappatore, D., 264
Zarka, S., 276
Zaslavsky, A. M., 416, 420, 428

Zeanah, C. H., 282
Zeiler, M., 82
Zeki, S., 70, 80
Zelaya, F., 273
Zellhoefer, J., 77
Zentall, T. R., 216
Zentner, M., 362
Zerwas, S., 245
Zetterberg, H., 69
Zettin, M., 182
Zhang, J., 461
Zhang, T. Y., 75
Zhang, X., 240
Zhang, X.-M., 356
Zhong, X., 361
Zhu, L., 304
Zhuo, M., 288
Zickfeld, J. H., 230
Ziegler, A., 362
Zihl, J., 107
Zimbardo, P., 377
Zimerman, S., 251
Zimmermann, D., 396
Zimprich, D., 281
Zollo, F., 43f
Zufall, F., 120
Zunzunegui, M. V., 335
Zwerling, H. L., 43

Abnormal, defining, 414
Absentmindedness, 180–181
Absolute thresholds, 91–92, 91t, 92f
Abuse
    age of puberty and, 312
    false memories of, 186
    hypnosis and memories of, 154
    language development and, 264
    suicidal behavior and, 442
Acceptance, 394
Accommodation
    in cognitive development, 300–301
    visual, 95
Accountability, 48
Accuracy motive in social influence, 378–380
    consistency and, 379–380
    information influence and, 378
    persuasion and, 378–379
Acetylcholine (ACh), 60
Achievement, need for, 251–252
Acorns, 271
Acquisition, in classical conditioning, 196–197,
    197f
ACTH. See adrenocorticotropic hormone (ACTH)
Action potential, 57–59, 57f, 60f
Action tendencies, 232–233
Activation–synthesis model, 143
Actor–observer effect, 371–372
Adaptation
    evolution and, 6, 6f, 8
    sensory, 90–91
    smell, 119–120
Adderall, 288, 466
Addiction, 145–148
    dangers of, 146, 148t
    DSM-5 categorization of, 416t
    individual risk for, 146–147
    RDoC approach on, 419
    what's considered addictive and, 147–148
A-delta fibers, 116–117
ADHD. See attention-deficit/hyperactivity
    disorder (ADHD)
Adolescence, 311–318
    brain tissue loss in, 433–434, 435f
    cognitive development in, 301f
    definition of, 311
    focus on peers vs. parents in, 316–318
    mental disorders of, 436–439
    nonsuicidal self-injury in, 443
    overparenting and, 408
    protraction of, 311–313, 312f
    schizophrenia in, 433–434, 435f
    sexuality in, 313–316
Adrenal glands, 68, 69f
    stress reactions and, 389
Adrenocorticotropic hormone (ACTH), 68, 389
Adulthood, 318–322
    changing abilities in, 318–320, 319f
    changing goals in, 320–321, 321f
    changing roles in, 321–322
    definition of, 318

Advertising, 378
Aerobic exercise, 396–397
Affect labeling, 243, 243f
African Americans. See also minorities
    intelligence tests and, 7, 286
    segregation and, 21
    stereotype threat and, 7, 286–287
    Tuskegee syphilis experiment and, 46
Afterimages, 98–99, 164
Agency, capacity for, 129
Aggression, 354–356, 357f
    biological influences on, 355–356, 356f
    conduct disorder and, 438–439
    culture and, 356, 357f
    definition of, 354
    frustration and, 354
    hate posts, hate crimes, and, 40
    media violence and, 34–35, 35f, 36–38, 36f, 37f,
        39
    observational learning and, 215–216
    proactive, 354
    reactive, 354, 355f
    sleep deprivation and, 139
Aging
    changing abilities in, 318–320, 319f
    intelligence in, 281, 281f
    stress and, 390–391
    taste perception and, 121
Agonists, 61
Agoraphobia, 422–423
Agreeableness, 332–333, 332t, 337
AI. See artificial intelligence (AI)
Air cribs, 11f
Al-Anon, 460
Alarm phase, 390, 390f
Alcohol, 148–149
    binge drinking and, 376
    dangers of, 148t
    prohibition of, 147f
Alcoholics Anonymous (AA), 460
Alcohol myopia, 149
Alpha waves, 138, 138f
Alprazolam, 462
Altered states of consciousness, 136
Alternate Uses Task (AUT), 177
Alternative für Deutschland (AfD), 40
Altruism, 359–360
Alzheimer's disease, 60
    bilingualism and, 265
    hippocampus and, 69
    intelligence and, 279
    treatment effectiveness, 471t
Ambivalent attachment, 308–309, 308f
American Psychological Association (APA), 20–21,
    46, 451
American Sign Language (ASL), 18–19, 114
    infant babbling in, 261, 261f
Ames room, 106–107, 107f
Amnesia
    anterograde, 167
    childhood or infantile, 180

posthypnotic, 154
    retrograde, 167
Amphetamines, 61, 150
    dangers of, 148t
    schizophrenia and, 433
Amphibians, 74
Amplitude
    of light waves, 94–95
    of sound waves, 109, 110f
Amputations, phantom limb syndrome after,
    72–73, 73f
Amygdala, 67f, 68
    classical conditioning and, 200–201
    during dreaming, 143–144, 143f
    in emotions, 235–236, 235f
    memory persistence and, 187–188, 188f
    in pain perception, 117
    personality disorders and, 441
    phobic disorders and, 421
    in sense of smell, 118–119
    in social phobia, 465, 465f
Anal stage, 339t
Analytic intelligence, 279
Anandamide, 152
Androgynous people, 335
Anesthesia, consciousness with, 127
Animals. See also specific animals
    altruism in, 360
    communication among, 258
    drug addiction in, 145
    ethics of research on, 47
    observational learning in, 216–217
    self-consciousness in, 132
    sickness response in, 400
    sleep needs in, 140, 140f
Anorexia nervosa, 246. See also eating disorders
ANS. See autonomic nervous system (ANS)
Antagonists, 61
Anterior cingulate cortex, 401
Anterograde amnesia, 167
Antianxiety medications, 462
Antidepressant medications, 428, 463–464, 463f
Antipsychotic drugs, 461–462
Antisocial personality disorder (APD), 439–441,
    440t
Anxiety
    in children over gun violence, 306
    defense mechanisms and, 338, 338t
    sleep disorders and, 140
Anxiety disorders, 416t, 420–424
    antianxiety medications for, 462
    cognitive behavioral therapy for, 458
    definition of, 420
    generalized anxiety disorder, 423–424
    panic disorder and agoraphobia, 422–423
    phobic, 420–422
    prevalence of, 416t, 417f
Anxious/inhibited personality disorders, 439, 440t
APA. See American Psychological Association
    (APA)
APD. See antisocial personality disorder (APD)

Aphasia, 265
Aplysia californica
    habituation and sensitization in, 194
    memory in, 169
Apnea, sleep, 141
Apparent motion, 107–108
Appearance, attraction and, 362–363, 363f
Appraisal, 232–233
Approach motivation, 252–253
Approval motive, 372, 374–377
    accuracy motive and, 378–380
    conformity and, 375–376
    normative influence and, 374
    obedience and, 376–377
Apps
    financial investment, 271
    for psychotherapy, 459
Area V1, 97, 99, 100f, 112, 112f
Artificial grammars, 218
Artificial intelligence (AI), 130, 459
ASD. *See* autism spectrum disorder (ASD)
ASL. *See* American Sign Language (ASL)
Asperger's syndrome, 436
Assimilation, 300–301, 301t
Association areas, 71
Associations, learning, 17
Atherosclerosis, 392
Ativan, 462
Attachment, 307–309
    definition of, 307
    effects of styles in, 308–309
    styles of, 307–308, 308f
Attachment styles, 307–309
Attention
    absentmindedness and, 180–181
    alcohol myopia and, 149
    cocktail-party phenomenon and, 131
    definition of, 102
    joint, 305, 305f
    testing and, 223
    in visual perception, 108–109
Attention-deficit/hyperactivity disorder (ADHD), 415
    bipolar disorder and, 430
Attitudes, 378
Attraction, interpersonal, 361–365
    physical factors in, 362–363, 363f
    psychological factors in, 363–364
    selectivity and, 361–362
    situational factors in, 362
Attractiveness, attraction and, 362–363, 363f
Attributions, 370–372
Atypical antipsychotic drugs, 462
Auditory cortex, 70, 111f
Auditory perception
    absolute threshold of, 91t
    prenatal, 298
    temporal lobe in, 70
Autism spectrum disorder (ASD), 436–437
    bipolar disorder and, 430
    implicit learning and, 218
    intelligence and, 279
    optimal outcome for, 437
    theory of mind development and, 304
Autocracy, 14, 14f
Autonomic nervous system (ANS), 62–63, 63f
Autonomy *vs.* shame/doubt, 317t

Autoreceptors, 59, 60f
Availability bias, 270, 270f
Avoidance motivation, 252–253, 253f
Avoidant attachment, 308–309, 308f
Avoidant personality disorder, 440t
Axons, 54, 54f, 55f, 59

Babbling, 260–261, 261f
Balance, 117–118
Barbiturates, 149
Basal ganglia, 67f, 68
Basilar membrane, 111, 111f
Beauty, 362–363
Behavior
    attribution of, 370–372
    brain damage and, 78–80
    definition of, 2
    environment and, 14–15
    grossly disorganized, 432
    interpersonal, 354–361
    involuntary, demand characteristic reduction and, 32
    law of effect on, 202–203
    the mind-body problem and, 129–130, 129f
    nervous system organization and, 62–65
    neurons in originating, 54–62
    neuroscience and, 52–87
    operant, 203
    sexual, 315–316
    shaping, 209
    social class and, 20
    social psychology on, 14–15
Behavioral activation system (BAS), 336
Behavioral confirmation, 367–368
Behavioral inhibition system (BIS), 336
Behavioral Insights Team, 48
Behavioral neuroscience, 19
Behaviorism, 9–12, 16. *See also* operant conditioning
    evolutionary psychology and, 16–17
    on language development, 263
    resistance to, 12–15
    Skinner in, 10–12, 11f
Behavior therapy, 455–456, 458
    for autism, 437
Beliefs, 378
    about mental disorders and treatment, 451
    consistency with, 379–380
Belmont Report, 46
Belonging, 347
Bem Sex Role Inventory, 335
Beneficence, in research, 46
Benzodiazepines, 462
    dangers of, 148t
Beta waves, 138, 138f
Beyond Freedom and Dignity (Skinner), 11–12
Bias
    availability, 270, 270f
    behavioral confirmation, 367–368
    correspondence, 371
    implicit, 369–370
    in intelligence tests, 285–288
    in memories, 186–187, 188
    optimism, 272
    perceptual confirmation, 367
    self-serving, 347–348
Big Five traits, 332–333, 332t

Bilateral asymmetry, 319–320, 320f
Bilingualism, 264, 265, 265f
    personality and, 342
Binaural cues, 113
Binding problem, 101–102
Binge drinking, 149, 376
Binge eating disorder (BED), 244–245. *See also* eating disorders
Binocular depth cues, 106, 106f
Binocular disparity, 106, 106f
Biofeedback, 396
Biological preparedness, 201
Biological treatments, 461–468
    antianxiety medications, 462
    antidepressants and mood stabilizers, 463–464, 463f
    antipsychotic medications, 461–462
    combined medication and psychotherapy, 465–466, 465f
    herbal and natural, 464, 464f
    nonmedication based, 466–468
Biopsychosocial perspective, 418, 418f
Bipolar cells, 96
Bipolar disorder, 416t, 429–431
    electroconvulsive therapy for, 467
    mood stabilizers for, 463–464
Birds, 74
    self-consciousness in, 132
Birth control, 316, 407
Blank slate, 4, 16–17
Blindness, 89
    category-specific organization in, 268, 268f
    change and inattentional, 108–109, 108f
    perspective-taking and stereotypes about, 370
    vision in dreams and, 144
Blind spot, 97, 98f
Blocking, 181–182
BMI. *See* body mass index (BMI)
Bobo doll experiments, 215–216, 215f
Body dysmorphic disorder, 417
Body mass index (BMI), 245–246, 246f
Body shape, 363
Boot-camp programs, 472, 472t
Borderline personality disorder, 440t
Boredom, 133f
Botox, 239
Brain
    activation in implicit learning, 219, 219f
    in adolescence, 311–312, 312f
    bilateral asymmetry in, 319–320, 320f
    in central nervous system, 62, 63–65, 64f
    cerebral cortex in, 68, 70–72, 70f
    concepts and categories and, 268, 268f
    decision making and, 272–273, 273f
    de-differentiation in, 319–320
    during dreams, 143–144, 143f
    dual process theories on, 136
    electrical activity in, 80, 80f
    emotions and, 235–236, 235f
    endocrine system and, 68, 69f
    environmental sensitivity of, 284
    evolution of, 74–75, 74f
    forebrain in, 66–67, 66f
    hemispheres of, 70–71, 70f, 79–80
    hindbrain in, 65–66, 66f
    hunger center in, 244
    investigations of the, 78–83

language development and, 265, 265f
midbrain in, 66, 66f
the mind–body problem and, 129–130, 129f
motivational and emotional centers of, 117
myths about, 84
neuroscience on, 18–19
obesity and, 247
in pain perception, 116–117, 116f
plasticity of, 72–74
pleasure centers, 211–212, 212f
prenatal development of, 297–298
satiety center in, 244
schizophrenia and, 433–434, 435f
sexual orientation and, 314
sign language and, 18–19
size of and intelligence, 82
structure of the, 65–74
subcortical structures in, 67–68, 67f
vision and, 99–101
visual pathways to, 94–99
Brain damage
amnesia from, 167
category-specific deficits and, 268
imitating with TMS, 83
memory blocking and, 182
memory misattribution and, 183–184, 184t
motion perception and, 107
personality change and, 334
risky decision making and, 272–273, 273f
studying, 78–80
visual streams and, 100–101
Brain imaging, 81–83, 81f, 82f
of working memory, 166
Brave New World (Huxley), 145
Broca's area, 18, 265, 265f
Brown v. Board of Education, 21
Bulimia nervosa, 246. *See also* eating disorders
Bullying, 356
Bupropion, 463
Burnout, 392–393
Bystander intervention, 359

Calories, 247, 248
Cambridge Laboratory of Industrial Research, 14
Cancer
Hay on the mind's ability to cure, 26, 26f, 38f
marijuana and, 153
rural areas and kidney, 43–44, 44f
Cannabis. *See* marijuana
Cardiovascular health, 391, 392
Case method, 39–40
Catatonic behavior, 432, 433f
Catecholamines, 389
Categories and categorization, 266–268
the brain and, 268, 268f
of mental disorders, 415–417, 419
in organizational encoding, 161–162, 161f
psychological theories of, 266–267
in stereotyping, 365–370, 366f, 367f
Category-specific deficit, 268
Causation, 34–35
coincidence and, 45
internal validity and, 38–39
manipulation of variables and, 35–37
third-variable problem and, 35, 35f
CBT. *See* cognitive behavioral therapy (CBT)
Celexa, 463

Cell body, 54, 54f, 55f
Cell membranes, 56
Cell phones
driving accidents and, 93
inattentional blindness and, 108–109
Centers for Disease Control and Prevention, 62
Central executive, 166
Central nervous system (CNS), 62, 63–65, 63f
Cephalocaudal rule, 299
Cerebellum, 65, 66f
Cerebral cortex, 67, 67f, 68, 70–72, 70f
C fibers, 117
Change bias, 187
Change blindness, 108–109, 108f
Chat-bots, 459
Chemical senses, 118–122
Child abuse, language development and, 264. *See also* abuse
Childhood
amnesia, 180
cognitive development in, 301f, 302–306
definition of, 302
development in, 299–311
mental disorders of, 436–439
moral development in, 309–311
sleepwalking in, 141
social development in, 306–309
Childhood disintegrative disorder, 436
Children
overparenting and, 408
parental happiness and, 321–322
Chimpanzees
observational learning in, 216–217
self-consciousness in, 132
Chromosomes, 75, 76f
stress and, 391
Chronic stressors, 387–388
burnout and, 392–393
Chronic traumatic encephalopathy (CTE), 53
Chunking, 165
Circadian rhythm, 138
CISD. *See* critical-incident stress debriefing (CISD)
Cisgender, 315
Citalopram, 463, 465
Classical conditioning, 194–202
acquisition, extinction, and spontaneous recovery in, 196–197, 197f
basic principles of, 195–198, 196f
cognitive elements of, 200
definition of, 195
drug overdoses and, 198
of emotional responses, 199
evolutionary elements of, 201
generalization and discrimination in, 197–198
neural elements of, 200–201
in phobic disorders, 422
second-order, 196
Claustrophobia, 420
Client-centered therapy, 454
Clinical social workers, 451
Cliques, 317
Closure, 103, 104f
Clozaril, 462
CNS. *See* central nervous system (CNS)
Co-authors, crediting, 49
Cocaine, 145, 147, 150, 461
Cochlea, 111, 111f

Cochlear implants, 113–114
Cocktail-party phenomenon, 131
Coercion, freedom from in research, 46
Cognitive behavioral therapy (CBT), 458, 465, 465f
effectiveness of, 471t
Cognitive development
in adulthood, 318–320, 319f
discovering other minds and, 303–305
discovering our cultures and, 305
in infancy, 300–306
language development and, 262–263
Cognitive dissonance, 380
Cognitive enhancers, 288–289
Cognitive maps, 211
Cognitive model of depression, 428–429, 429f
Cognitive neuroscience, 19
Cognitive psychology, 16
Cognitive restructuring, 456–457
Cognitive symptoms, 432
Cognitive therapy, 456–458
Cognitive unconscious, 136
Coincidences, 45
Collaborative inhibition, 178–179
Collaborative memory, 177–179
Collective cultures, 19
favors in, 361
College Undergraduate Stress Scale (CUSS), 386–387, 386t
Color afterimage, 98, 99f
Color perception, 98–99, 104
Color vision deficiency, 98–99
Commisures, 70
Common fate, 103, 104f
Common knowledge effect, 358
Communication
of emotions, 236–241
language and, 257–274
Comorbidity, 416
Companionate love, 364–365, 365f
Complexity, empirical method and, 29
Compliance, 403–404, 403f
Computerized axial tomography (CT), 81, 81f
Computers. *See also* apps
ENIAC, 16, 16f
personality measurement with, 330
in psychological treatment, 459
Concepts
the brain and, 268, 268f
definition of, 266
psychological theories of, 266–267
Conceptual knowledge, in object recognition, 102
Concrete operational stage, 301f, 302
Concussion (movie), 53
Concussions, 53
Conditioned response (CR), 195–196, 196f
Conditioned stimulus (CS), 195–196, 196f
Conditions, manipulation of, 36–38
random assignment and, 37–38
Conduct disorders, 416t
personality disorders and, 441
Conductive hearing loss, 113
Cones, 95–97, 96f, 97f, 98–99, 99f
Confidentiality, 47
Confirmation bias, 43
Conformity, 375–376
Congruence, 454
Conjunction fallacy, 270

Conscientiousness, 332–333, 332t, 337
Conscious motivations, 251–252
Consciousness, 126–157
    altered states of, 136
    basic properties of, 130–131
    contents of, 132–135
    definition of, 127
    in dreams, 141–142
    drugs and, 145–153
    hypnosis and, 153–155
    James on, 8
    levels of, 131–132
    mental control in, 133–135
    mind–body problem and, 129–130
    mysteries of, 128–130
    nature of, 130–135
    problem of other minds and, 128–129
    sleep and dreaming and, 136–145
    the unconscious mind and, 135–136
Conservation of quantity, 302
Consistency, 379–380
Consolidation of memory, 167–168
Construct validity, 31
Consumer psychologists, 23
Content morphemes, 259
Context, in memory retrieval, 170
Continuity, 103, 104f
Control
    health and, 405
    stress and perception of, 388
Conventional antipsychotic drugs, 462
Conventional stage, 210
Cooperation, 356–359
    definition of, 357
    in groups, 358–359
    risks of, 357–358
Coping
    rational, 394
    repressive, 394
Core network of brain regions, 176
Cornea, 95, 96f
Coronary heart disease (CHD), 392
Corpus callosum, 67f, 70, 71
Correlation, 34, 34t
    natural, 34–35
    third-variable problem and, 35, 35f
Correspondence bias, 371
Cortico-striato-thalamo-cortical loop, 425
Cortisol, 389
Counselors, 451
Couple therapy, 458
Courage, 289
CR. See conditioned response (CR)
Cravings, 212
Creative intelligence, 279
Creativity
    bipolar disorder and, 430
    divergent creative thinking, 177
Criminal personality, 440
Critical-incident stress debriefing (CISD), 7, 472, 472t
Critical thinking, 42–44
Critical thinking skills, 84
Crowding, 388
Crystallized intelligence, 278–279
CS. See conditioned stimulus (CS)
CT. See computerized axial tomography (CT)

Cue exposure therapies, 198
Cultural explanations of mental disorders, 417
Cultural idioms of distress, 417
Cultural psychology, 19
Cultural syndromes, 417
Culture
    adolescence and, 311–312
    aggression and, 356, 357f
    cognitive development and, 305
    definition of, 19
    display rules and, 239–240
    favors and, 361
    flavor perception and, 121–122
    intelligence tests and, 279, 286–288
    language development and, 262–263
    mental disorders and, 416–417, 417f
    nonsuicidal self-injury and, 443
    psychotherapy and, 472
    sexual orientation and, 314
    sexual selectivity and, 362
    social class and, 20
    terror management theory and, 252–253
    theory of mind and, 304
CUSS. See College Undergraduate Stress Scale (CUSS)
Cutting, self-, 443
Cyber-bullying, 356
Cytokines, 400

D.A.R.E program. See Drug Abuse and Resistance Education (D.A.R.E.)
Data
    correlation and, 34, 34t
    ethical analysis and reporting of, 47–49
    sharing scientific, 49
Daydreams, 133, 133f
DBS. See deep brain stimulation (DBS)
Deafness, 113–114
    babbling in infants and, 261, 261f
    theory of mind development and, 304
Debriefing, 47
Deception
    in emotional expression, 239–241, 240f
    in research, 46
Decision criterion, 93
Decision making, 269–274
    in adolescence, 312, 313f
    availability bias in, 270, 270f
    the brain and, 272–273
    conjunction fallacy and, 270, 270f
    framing effects in, 271
    in groups, 358
    the irrational reality in, 269
    judging frequencies and probabilities for, 269
    optimism bias in, 272
    prospect theory on, 272
    rational choice theory on, 269
    representativeness heuristic in, 270–271
Declaration of Helsinki, 46
Declaration of Independence, U.S., 4
Deep brain stimulation (DBS), 468, 468f
Default network, 133, 133f
Defense mechanisms, 338, 338t
Definitions, operational, 31
Deindividuation, 359
Déjà vu, 183
Delayed gratification, 250

Delayed reinforcement and punishment, 205, 205f
Delta waves, 138, 138f
Delusions, 432
Demand characteristics, 31–33
Democracy, autocracy and, 14, 14f
Demyelinating diseases, 54
Dendrites, 54, 54f, 55f, 59
Dentate gyrus/CA$_{2/3}$, 176
Dependence, in addiction, 146, 148t
Dependent personality disorder, 440t
Dependent variables, 37, 37f
Depressants, 148–149, 148t
Depression
    cognitive behavioral therapy for, 458
    cognitive model of, 428–429
    costs of, 450
    electroconvulsive therapy for, 467
    epigenetics in, 77
    gender and, 335
    herbal and natural products for, 464
    negative thoughts in, 428–429, 429f
    puberty timing and, 313
    risk for and prevalence of, 428
    sickness response in, 400
    sleep disorders and, 140
    telomere length and, 391
    transcranial magnetic stimulation for, 467
    treatment effectiveness, 471t
Depressive disorders, 416t, 427–431
    major depressive disorder, 415, 427
Depth perception, 105–107
Desirable difficulties, 222
Detectors, 31
Development, 294–325
    adolescence, 311–318
    adulthood, 318–322
    environment and, 298
    infancy and childhood, 299–311
    of language, 259–265
    prenatal, 296–298, 297f
Developmental psychology, 13
    definition of, 296
Dhat, 417
Diagnosis, definition of, 415
Diagnostic and Statistical Manual of Mental Disorders (DSM)-5, 415–417
Diagnostic criteria, 415
Diathesis–stress model, 418, 418f, 424
Diazepam, 149, 155, 462
Diet. See nutrition
Diffusion, 59, 60f
Diffusion of responsibility, 359
Diffusion tensor imaging (DTI), 81, 81f
Digital footprints, 333
Digit memory test, 160, 160f
Dihydroepiandosterone (DHEA), 248
Disaster preparedness, 306
Discrimination
    in classical conditioning, 198
    in operant conditioning, 205–206
    stress from, 387
Disease, definition of, 415
Disorganized attachment, 308–309, 308f
Disorganized speech, 432
Displacement, 338t
Display rules, 239–240
Dispositional attributions, 371

Disruptive disorders, 416t
Dissociative disorders, 416t
Distributed practice, 220–221, 220t
Divergent creative thinking, 177
Diversity. *See also* culture; minorities
    perspective-taking and, 370
    psychotherapy and, 472
Dizygotic twins, 76, 76f, 281
DNA (deoxyribonucleic acid), 75–77, 76f
Dogmatism, 28
Dolphins, self-consciousness in, 132
The Doors of Perception (Huxley), 145
Dopamine, 60–61, 68
    antipsychotic drugs and, 461–462
    phobic disorders and, 421
    pleasure centers and, 212
    reward learning and, 213
    schizophrenia and, 433
Dopamine hypothesis of schizophrenia, 433
Dorsal visual stream, 100–101, 100f
Double-blind studies, 33, 470
Dramatic/erratic personality disorders, 439, 440t
Dreams, 141–145
    the brain during, 143–144, 143f
    consciousness in, 141–142
    Freudian theory of, 9, 9f
    REM sleep and, 138–140, 138f, 139f
    theories on, 142–143
Drive-reduction theory, 242
Drives, 242
Drug Abuse and Resistance Education (D.A.R.E.),
    7, 472, 472t
Drug addiction
    classical conditioning and, 198
    dopamine in, 61
    to opioids, 61–62
Drugs
    addiction and, 145–148
    consciousness and, 145–153
    dangers of, 148t
    neurotransmitters mimicked by, 61–62
Drug therapy
    antidepressants for (*See* antidepressant medi-
        cations)
    antipsychotics for, 461–462
    for attention-deficit/hyperactivity
        disorder, 438
    combined psychotherapy and, 465–466, 465f
    psychoactive drugs for, 148–153
Drug tolerance, 146
DSM. *See Diagnostic and Statistical Manual of
    Mental Disorders (DSM)-5*
DTI. *See* diffusion tensor imaging (DTI)
Dualism, 2–3
Dual process theories, 136
Dynamic unconscious, 135
Dyslexia, 218–219

EAR (electronically activated recorder), 330
Early bloomers, 313
Ears. *See also* hearing
    anatomy of, 111f
    sound waves funneled by, 110, 111f
Eating disorders, 244–245, 245f, 416t
Echoic memory, 164
Echolocation, 89
Eclectic psychotherapy, 452

Ecological momentary assessment (EMA),
    132–133
Ecstasy. *See* MDMA (Ecstasy)
ECT. *See* electroconvulsive therapy (ECT)
Education
    intelligence and, 282–283, 288–289
    of psychologists, 21–23
    on sex, 316, 407
EEG. *See* electroencephalograph (EEG)
Effexor, 463
Ego, 338
Egocentrism, 303
Ego integrity *vs.* despair, 317t
Elaborative interrogation, 220t
Electroconvulsive therapy (ECT), 467
Electroencephalograph (EEG), 80, 80f
    of brain patterns during sleep, 138
Electromagnetic spectrum, 94–95, 94f
Electronically activated recorder (EAR), 330
Elephants, self-consciousness in, 132
Elimination disorders, 416t
Embryonic stage, 297, 297f
Emotion, 228–255
    action tendencies and, 232–233
    in adulthood, 320
    appraisals and, 232–233
    attachment and, 307–309
    the brain in, 235–236, 235f
    classical conditioning and, 199
    communication of, 236–241
    definition of, 230
    display rules on, 239–240
    in dreams, 142
    experience of, 230–232, 231f
    exposure therapy and, 456, 456t
    gender differences in expressing, 334–335
    hedonic principle and, 242–243
    memory persistence and, 187–188
    mental disorders and, 414
    motivation and, 241–253
    nature of, 228–236
    physical aspects of, 233–235
    positive and negative, 233
    theories, 233–235
    universality hypothesis on, 238
Emotional expression, 236–237
Emotional intelligence, 279
Emotion regulation, 243
Empathy, 289
    autism and, 436
    in person-centered therapy, 454
    in therapy, 471
Empirical method, 29
Empiricism, 4, 28–29
    scientific method and, 28–29
Encoding, 159–163
    definition of, 159
    memory retrieval and, 170–171
    organizational, 161f, 162
    semantic, 160, 161f
    survival-related information, 162–163, 163f
    visual imagery, 160–162
Encoding specificity principle, 170
Endocrine system, 68, 69f
Endorphins, 61, 151, 401
ENIAC, 16, 16f
Environment

aggression and, 354, 355f
attachment styles and, 308–309
in bipolar disorder, 430–431
child development and, 84
chronic stressors in, 387–388
conduct disorder and, 439
epigenetics and, 77
intelligence and, 281–283, 281f, 282f,
    283, 284
intelligence testing and, 287–288
obesity and, 247
phobic disorders and, 421–422
posttraumatic stress disorder and, 426
prenatal, 298
schizophrenia and, 435
social psychology on, 14–15
Environmental psychology, 388
Environmental sensitivity, 284
Epigenetics, 77
    in bipolar disorder, 430–431
    intelligence and, 283
Epilepsy, 79
Episodic buffer, 166
Episodic memory, 175–177
    imaging the future and, 176–177
ERP. *See* exposure and response prevention (ERP)
ESP (extrasensory perception), 45
Essay on Human Understanding (Locke), 4
Estrogen, 248–249
*Ethical Principles of Psychologists and Code of
    Conduct* (APA), 46
Ethical standards, 472–473
Ethics
    experimentation and, 45–49, 46f
    Little Albert experiments and, 199
Ethnicities. *See* culture; minorities; *specific ethnic
    groups*
Evidence
    coincidence and, 45
    critical thinking about, 42–44
    empirical method for gathering, 29
    ethical analysis and reporting of, 47–49
    expectations and, 43
    skepticism in evaluating, 44
Evolution, 6, 6f, 8
    classical conditioning and, 201
    operant conditioning and, 212–214
Evolutionary mismatch, 247
Evolutionary psychology, 16–17
    obsessive–compulsive disorder and, 425
    on personality and gender, 335
Exemplar theory, 266–267, 267f
Exercise
    brain plasticity and, 73
    endorphins in, 151
    stress and aerobic, 396–397
Exhaustion phase, 390, 390f
Existential approach, 340
Existentialist psychology, on personality,
    339–340
Existential therapies, 454–455
Expectancy theory, 149, 342–343
Expectations
    classical conditioning and, 200
    evidence evaluation and, 43–44
    observer bias and, 33, 33f
    placebo effect and, 469

Experiences. *See also* environment
  bias in memories and, 186–187
  brain plasticity and, 73–74
  of emotion, 230–232, 231f
  in judging others' minds, 128–129
  language development and, 262–263
  reexperiencing, 176
Experience-sampling, 132–133
Experimentation, 35–38
  ethics in, 199
  random assignment in, 37–38, 38f
  steps in, 36–37, 37f
  using animals, 47
Experiments, 7, 35–38
  double-blind, 33
  drawing conclusions from, 38–42
  ethical analysis and reporting of, 47–49
  ethics in, 45–49, 46f
  generalizability restriction and, 39–41
  manipulation of conditions in, 36–38, 36f
  observer bias in, 33
  reliability restriction in, 41–42
  replication of, 41–42
  representativeness restriction and, 39
Explanation, methods of, 29
Explicit memory, 173, 174–179
  episodic, 175–177
  semantic, 175
Exposure, to stressors, 394
Exposure and response prevention (ERP), 449
Exposure therapy, 456, 456t
*The Expression of the Emotions in Man and
    Animals* (Darwin), 237
External validity, 39
Extinction
  in classical conditioning, 197, 197f
  in operant conditioning, 206
Extrasensory perception (ESP), 45
Extraversion, 332–333, 332t, 336, 337
Extrinsic motivation, 250–251, 251f
Eyeblink conditioning, 200
Eyes. *See also* visual perception
  light detection in, 95
Eyewitness testimony
  memory misattribution in, 183f, 184
  reliability of, 185
  suggestibility and, 186

Faces, perception of, 102, 299
Face-vase illusion, 105, 105f
Facial expressions
  cause and effect of, 239
  communicative, 238–239
  cultural differences in, 238, 238f, 239–240, 240f
  deceptive, 239–241
  reading emotions in, 236–241, 237f
  universality of, 238, 238f
Facial feedback hypothesis, 239
Factors or personality. *See* traits
Fair-mindedness, 289
False-belief task, 303
False recognition, 184, 184t
Falsifiability, 28–29
Family therapy, 458
Farsightedness, 95, 96f
Fast mapping, 261
Fat cells, 247

Favors, 361
Fear
  fast and slow pathways in, 235–236, 235f
  personality disorders and, 441
  terror management theory and, 252–253
Feature detectors, 80
Feeding and eating disorders, 416t
Fetal alcohol syndrome (FAS), 298
Fetal stage, 297, 297f
Fight-or-flight response, 389, 397–398
Figure and ground perception, 103, 105
First impressions, 15, 15f
Five-factor personality model, 332–333,
    332t
Fixed-interval (FI) schedules, 207
Fixed-ratio (FR) schedules, 207–208
Flashbulb memories, 187–188
Flash sonar, 89
Flatworms, 74, 74f
Flavor perception, 118, 121–122
Flow experiences, 340
Fluid intelligence, 82, 278–279
Fluoxetine, 463
Flynn effect, 281, 282f
FMRI. *See* functional magnetic resonance imaging
    (fMRI)
Food. *See* nutrition
Food aversions, 201
Foot-in-the-door technique, 380
Forebrain, 66–67, 66f, 67f, 74, 74f
  in sense of smell, 118–119
Forensic psychologists, 23
Forgetting
  absentmindedness, 180–181
  blocking, 181–182
  collaborative memory and, 178
  pros and cons of, 188
  retrieval-induced, 171
  transience and, 179–180, 180f
Formal operational stage, 301f, 302–303
Fovea, 95, 97f
Framing effects, 271
Fraternal twins, 76, 76f, 281
Fraud, scientific, 48–49
Free association, 9, 453
Free will, 12
Freezing response, 200–201
Frequencies, judging, 269
Frequency, sound wave, 109, 110f
Freudian slips, 135, 337
Frontal lobe, 71
  in pain perception, 117
  in sense of smell, 118–119
Frustration–aggression hypothesis, 354
Full consciousness, 132
Functional brain imaging, 81, 82–83, 82f
Functionalism, 6–8, 11, 17
Functional magnetic resonance imaging (fMRI),
    18–19, 18f, 82–83, 82f
  of multitasking, 93
Function morphemes, 259
Fundamental attribution error, 371

GABA (gamma-aminobutyric acid), 61,
    149, 462
GAD. *See* generalized anxiety disorder (GAD)
Gamblers Anonymous, 460

Gambling
  addiction to, 147
  dopamine and reward learning in, 213
  risky decision making and, 272–273, 273f
Gate-control theory of pain perception, 117
Gateway drugs, 152
Gender
  age at puberty and, 312, 313
  aggression and, 355–356, 356f
  attention-deficit/hyperactivity disorder and,
      438
  autism and, 436
  bipolar disorder and, 430
  conduct disorder and, 438
  definition of, 315
  depression and, 428
  generalized anxiety disorder and, 423
  IQ and, 285
  neuroticism and, 333
  nonsuicidal self-injury and, 443
  obsessive–compulsive disorder and, 425
  personality and, 334–336
  personality disorders and, 440, 441
  sciences and, 30
  sexual desire and, 248–249
  sexual selectivity and, 361–362
  social support and, 397–398
  suicidal behavior and, 442
  talkativeness and, 330
Gender dysphoria, 416t
Gene editing, 288
General adaptation syndrome (GAS), 389–390, 390f
General factor *(g)*, 278
Generalizability restriction, 39–41, 41f
Generalization
  in classical conditioning, 197–198
  in operant conditioning, 205–206
Generalized anxiety disorder (GAD), 423–424
  cognitive behavioral therapy for, 458
Generativity *vs.* stagnation, 317t
Genes, 75–77, 76f
Genetic dysphasia, 264
Genetics
  attention-deficit/hyperactivity disorder and,
      438
  in bipolar disorder, 430–431
  in intelligence, 280–281, 283
  intelligence testing and, 287–288
  personality and, 334
  in schizophrenia, 433, 433f
  in sexual orientation, 314
  in taste perception, 120–121
Genital stage, 339t
Germany, hate crimes in, 40, 40f
Germinal stage, 296–297
Gestalt perceptual grouping rules, 103, 113
Gestalt psychology, 12–13
  perceptual organization and, 103
Gestalt therapy, 454–455
Ghost in the machine, 2
Ghrelin, 244
Glial cells, 54
Glutamate, 61
Google, memory and, 178
Grammar, 218
  definition of, 258
  emergence of rules in, 262

learning, 259–260
universal, 263–264
Grandiosity, 430
Ground, 103, 105
Group factors, 278
Group polarization, 358
Groups
cooperation in, 358–359
definition of, 358
Group therapy
couple and family, 458
self-help and support groups, 460
Groupthink, 358
Group treatments, 458–460
Gun violence, 306
Gyri, 70, 70f

Habituation, 194, 299
Hallucinations
in bipolar disorder, 430
in schizophrenia, 431–432
Hallucines, 9
Hallucinogens, 151–152
dangers of, 148t
Happiness, 233
intelligence and, 289
marriage and, 321–322
measuring, 31
Haptic perception, 115
Hardiness, 405
Harm, freedom from in research, 46
Hashish, 152
Hate crimes, 40
"Head Turn" technique, 260, 260f
Health. See also treatment of psychological
disorders
behaviors promoting, 405–407
discrimination and, 387
immune system and, 391–392
intelligence and, 276
negative effects of stress on, 390–391
personality and, 404–405
prayer and, 398f
psychology of illness and, 399–404
puberty timing and, 312
religiosity and, 398
self-regulation and, 405–406
stress and, 384–411
Health psychology, 404–407
definition of, 385
illness and, 399–404
Hearing, 109–114
absolute threshold of, 91t
loss of, 113–114
sensing sound and, 109–112
sound source perception in, 112–113
Heat, aggression and, 354, 355f
Hedonic motive in social influence, 372, 373, 373f
Hedonic principle, 242–243
Helplessness theory, 429
Herbal therapies, 464, 464f
Heroin, 147
overdoses, 198
Heuristic persuasion, 378–379, 379f
Heuristics, representativeness, 270–271
Hierarchy of needs, 244, 244f, 339
Hindbrain, 65–66, 66f

Hippocampus, 67f, 68, 69
in long-term memory, 166–167
memory priming and, 174
obesity and, 247
personality disorders and, 441
posttraumatic stress disorder and, 426, 426f
in semantic memory, 176
in sense of smell, 118–119
in social phobia, 465, 465f
Hispanics, intelligence testing and, 287. See also
minorities
Histrionic personality disorder, 440t
Homosexual, 315
Homunculus, 71
Honesty, 289
Honor system, 47–49
Hormones. See also specific hormones
in adolescence, 311–312
aggression and, 355–356, 356f
personality and, 335–336
postpartum depression and, 428
stress and, 389
Hostility, heart disease and, 392
How to Raise an Adult (Lythcott-Haims), 408
HPA (hypothalamic-pituitary-adrenocortical) axis,
389, 389f
Human Connectome Project, 81
Humanistic–existential approach, 339–340
Humanistic psychology, on personality, 339–340
Humanistic therapies, 454–455
Humility, 289
Humor, 398–399
Hunger, 244, 245f
eating disorders and, 244–245, 245f
obesity and, 245–248
Hypnagogic state, 137
Hypnic jerk, 137
Hypnopompic state, 137
Hypnosis, 153–155
Hypnotic analgesia, 155, 155f
Hypothalamus, 67, 67f, 68, 69f
in hunger, 244, 245f
in pain perception, 117
pleasure center in, 212, 212f
stress reactions and, 389
Hypotheses, 28–29
Hysteria, 8

Iatrogenic illness, 472
Ice cream, polio and, 35f
Iconic memory, 164, 164f
Id, 337
Idealism, 3
Identical twins, 76, 76f
intelligence in, 281
Identification, 338t
Identifying the Culprit: Assessing Eyewitness
Identification (National Academy of
Sciences), 185
Identity, social psychology on, 15
Identity vs. role confusion, 317t
Illness, 399–404
being a patient and, 402–403
immune system and, 391–392
patient–practitioner interaction and, 403–404
psychological effects of, 400
recognizing and seeking treatment for, 400–402

somatic symptom disorders, 402
telomere length and, 391
Illusions
of depth and size, 106–107, 107f
treatment of psychological disorders and,
469–470
of unique invulnerability, 406–407
Illusory conjunction, 101–102, 102f
Illusory motion, 12–13
Imagination
brain evolution and, 75
memory and, 176–177
Imipramine, 465
Imitation, 305
Immediate reinforcement and punishment, 205,
205f
Immune system, 391–392
Implicit Association Test (IAT), 368f
Implicit bias, 369–370
Implicit learning, 217–220
definition of, 217–218
neural pathways in, 219, 219f
Implicit memory, 173–174
Impossible events, 301–302, 301f
Impulse-control disorders, 416t
prevalence of, 416, 417f
Inattentional blindness, 108–109, 108f
Independent variables, 36–37, 37f
Individualistic societies, 19
favors in, 361
Industrial psychologists, 22–23, 22f
Industry vs. inferiority, 317t
Infancy
cognitive development in, 300–306
definition of, 299
development in, 299–311
distinguishing speech sounds in, 260–261, 260f
moral development in, 309–311
motor development in, 299, 300f
perceptual development in, 299
self-consciousness in, 132
social development in, 306–309
Infantile amnesia, 180
Influence. See social influence
Informational influence, 378
Information processing, cognitive psychology on,
16
Informed consent, 46
Ingroup favoritism, 358
Initiative vs. guilt, 317t
Inner ear, 111f
vestibular system in, 118
Inner hair cells, 111, 111f
Inside Out (movie), 185
Insight, developing, 453
Insomnia, 140, 471t
Instincts, 241–242
Institutional review boards (IRBs), 47
Instrumental behaviors, 202–203
Insula, 401
Intellectual disabilities, 284–285
Intellectual giftedness, 284–285
Intellectual virtues, 289
Intelligence, 257, 274–290
brain size and, 82
crystallized, 278–279
definition of, 274

Intelligence (*continued*)
    education and, 282–283
    environmental influences on, 281–283, 281f,
        282f, 283, 284
    fluid, 82, 278–279
    genetic influences on, 280–281
    group differences in, 285–288
    improving, 288–289
    individual differences in, 284–285
    intellectual virtues and, 289
    measuring, 274–276
    tests, 275–276, 276t, 279, 285–288
    two-factor theory of, 277–278
    types of, 279
    what it is, 276–280
Intentionality, 130
Intention offloading, 181
Intentions, in moral reasoning, 209
Interactionist theories of language development,
    264
Interleaved practice, 220t, 222
Intermittent reinforcement, 208
Intermittent reinforcement effect, 208
Internal validity, 38–39
Internal working models, 209f, 308–309
Interneurons, 56
Interpersonal psychotherapy (IPT), 453
Interposition, 106, 106f
The Interpretation of Dreams (Freud), 9f
Interval schedules, 207
Intimacy *vs.* isolation, 317t
Intrinsic motivation, 250–251, 251f
Introspection, 6
Introversion, 336
Inuit, 356
Invertebrates, 74
Involuntary behaviors, demand characteristic
    reduction and, 32
Ion pumps, 59
Ions, 56–59
IPT. *See* interpersonal psychotherapy (IPT)
IQ tests, 279. *See also* intelligence
    average IQ and, 284–285
    environmental sensitivity and, 284
    the Fynn effect and, 281, 282f
IRBs. *See* institutional review boards (IRBs)
Iris, 96f
Ironic processes of mental control, 134–135

James–Lange theory, 233–234, 234f
Japan
    cultural syndromes in, 417
    display rules in, 239
    foreground *vs.* background perception in, 19
Jiffy Lube University, 221
Joint attention, 305, 305f
Judgments
    brain activity during, 161f
    of frequencies and probabilities, 269
    of learning, 224
    primacy effect in, 15, 15f
Justice, experiments and, 46
Just noticeable difference (JND), 92

Kama muta, 230
K complexes, 138, 138f
Ketamine, 151–152

Kidney cancer, rural areas and, 43–44, 44f
Kin selection, 360
Kormoran (warship), 14

Labeling, 419–420
Language, 257–274
    brain areas in, 265, 265f
    brain evolution and, 75
    cognitive development and, 262–263
    culture and, 279
    deafness and, 114
    decision making and, 269–274
    definition of, 258
    development of, 259–263, 261t
    distinguishing speech sounds in, 260–261
    grammatical rules in, 262
    how we think and, 266–268
    learning a second, 264, 265, 265f
    left hemisphere processing of, 79–80, 79f
    milestones in development of, 261–262, 261t
    prenatal perception of, 298
    sign language, 18–19
    structure of human, 258–259, 259f, 260f
    temporal lobe in, 70
    theories of development of, 263–264
    theory of mind and, 304
    units of, 259f
Language development
    behaviorist theories of, 15
    Broca's area and, 18
    cognitive psychology on, 15–16
Latency stage, 339t
Latent learning, 211, 211f
Lateral geniculate nucleus (LGN), 97, 97f
Law of effect, 202–203
L-dopa, 61
Learning, 192–227. *See also* operant conditioning
    associations in, 193
    biological preparedness in, 201
    classical conditioning and, 194–202
    in the classroom, 220–224
    control of, 223–224
    definition of, 194
    epigenetics in, 77
    implicit, 217–220
    latent, 211, 211f
    memory retrieval and, 171
    mental disorders and, 414
    observational, 214–217
    operant conditioning and, 202–214
    reward, 213
    in sea slugs, 169
    shaping, 209
    from stress, 408
    techniques for, 220–223, 220t
    testing and, 222–223
    trial and error, 7
    working memory training and, 166
Learning styles, 84
Leptin, 244, 247
The Letters of William James (James), 1f
Light, sensing, 94–97, 94f, 104
Light waves, 94–95, 94f
Linear perspective, 105, 106f
Listening, 289
Little Albert experiments, 199, 422
Lobes, cerebral cortex, 70–71, 70f

Lobotomy, 467
Locus of control, 343, 343t
Longevity, intelligence and, 276
Long-term memory, 164f, 166–169, 175f
    collaborative, 177–179
    explicit, 174–179
    forms of, 173–179
    implicit, 173–174
Long-term potentiation (LTP), 169
Lorazepam, 462
Loss aversion, 252, 253f
Loudness, 109, 112
Love, 364–365, 365f
LSD (lysergic acid deithylamide), 151–152
LTP. *See* long-term potentiation (LTP)
Lying, 240–241, 240f

Magnetic resonance imaging (MRI), 81, 81f, 82
    functional, 18–19, 18f, 82–83, 82f
Major depressive disorder, 415, 427
Make It Stick: The Science of Successful Learning
    (Brown, Roediger, and McDaniel), 221
Malingering, 403
Mammals, 74
    pheromones in, 120
Mania, 430. *See also* bipolar disorder
Manipulation of conditions, 35–37, 36f
    ethics of, 48
MAOIs. *See* monoamine oxidase inhibitors
    (MAOIs)
Marijuana, 152–153
    dangers of, 148t
    legalization of, 153
Marriage, 321–322
    costs and benefits of, 365
    couple therapy and, 458
    same-sex, 314, 314f
Maslow's hierarchy of needs, 244, 244f, 339
Massed practice, 221–222
Materialism, 2–3
MDMA (Ecstasy), 148t, 150
Measurement, in research, 30–31
    construct validity of, 31
    demand characteristics and, 31–33
    in experiments, 37, 37f
    operational definitions and, 31
Medial forebrain bundle, 212, 212f
Medical model, 414–415
Medication-induced movement disorders, 416t
Medications
    adverse effects of, 416t
    antianxiety, 462
    antipsychotic, 461–462
    cognitive enhancers, 288–289
    combining psychotherapy and, 465–466, 465f
    compliance in taking, 403–404, 403f
    effectiveness of, 472
    herbal and natural therapies, 464, 464f
    placebo effect and, 401
    sleeping pills, 140
Meditation, 395–396, 457–458
Medulla, 65, 66f
Memory, 158–191
    absentmindedness and, 180–181
    in adulthood and aging, 318–319, 319f
    Bartlett on construction of, 13, 14
    bias in, 186–187

blocking, 181–182
chunking, 165
collaborative, 177–179
consolidation of, 167–168
déjà vu, 183
of dreams, 142
in the dynamic unconscious, 135
echoic, 164
encoding, 159–163
epigenetics in, 77
episodic, 175–177
exercise and, 73
explicit, 174–179
failures of, 179–188
flashbulb, 187–188
functional brain imaging studies of, 83
Google's effects on, 178
hippocampus in, 67f, 68, 69, 166–167, 174, 176
hypnosis and, 154
iconic, 164, 164f
implicit, 173–174
long-term, 164f, 166–169, 173–179
mental disorders and, 414
misattribution, 182–183, 182f, 184t
myths about, 84
neurons and synapses in, 169
organizational, 161f, 162
persistence of, 187–188, 188f
priming, 174
procedural, 174
prospective, 181
reconsolidation of, 168–169
reconstructive, 470
rehearsal and "chunking" of, 165, 165f
retrieval, 159, 170–173
semantic, 160, 175
sensory, 163–164, 164f
short-term, 164–166, 165f
sleep and, 34, 34t
sleep deprivation and, 139
source, 182–183
storage, 159, 163–169
suggestibility in, 184–186
transience, 179–180, 180f
visual imagery, 161–162, 161f
working, 165–166, 165f
Mental control, 133–135, 417
Mental disorders, 412–447
    anxiety, 420–424
    causation of, 418
    of childhood and adolescence, 436–439
    classifying, 415–417
    conceptualizing, 414–415
    costs of, 450, 466
    culture and, 417
    definition of, 414
    depressive and bipolar, 427–431
    DSM-5 categories of, 416t
    labeling and, 419–420
    medical model of, 414–415
    obsessive-compulsive, 424–425
    personality, 439–441
    posttraumatic stress disorder, 425–426
    prevalence of, 450
    psychotic, 431–436
    RDoC system on, 419
    self-harm behaviors, 441–443

    treatment of (See biological treatments; drug
        therapy; psychotherapy; treatment of psy-
        chological disorders)
Mental health
    intelligence and, 285
    overparenting and, 408
Mere exposure effect, 362
Mescaline, 145, 151–152
Metabolism, 247
Methamphetamine, 147
Microvilli, 120, 121f
Midbrain, 66, 66f, 67f
Middle ear, 110, 111f
Milgram's obedience studies, 377, 377f
Military service, PTSD and, 425–426, 426f
Mind. See also consciousness
    behavioralist views of, 9–12
    definition of, 2
    functionalist view of, 6–8
    neuroscience and, 18–19
    psychoanalytic theory on, 8–9
    science of the, 4–8
    structuralist view of, 5–6
    unconscious, 8–9
Mind–body problem, 129–130
Mindfulness meditation, 457–458
Minimal consciousness, 131–132
Minnesota Multiphasic Personality Inventory
    (MMPI), 329
Minorities. See also stereotypes
    discrimination and stress in, 387
    intelligence tests and, 286–288
    psychotherapy and, 472
    stereotype threat and, 7
    suicidal behavior and, 442
Mirror neurons, 71–72, 217, 217f
Misattribution, memory, 182–183, 182f,
    184t, 188
MMPI. See Minnesota Multiphasic Personality
    Inventory (MMPI)
Mnemonics, 220t
Mobs, 359, 359f
Modular view of objects, 102
Money, saving, 271
Monoamine oxidase inhibitors (MAOIs), 463–464,
    463f
Monoaural cues, 113
Monocular depth cues, 105–106, 105f,
    106f
Monozygotic twins, 76, 76f, 281
Mood disorders, 427–431
    bipolar, 430–431
    definition of, 427
    depressive, 427–430
    neurotransmitters in, 61
    prevalence of, 416, 417f
Mood stabilizers, 463–464, 463f
Moral development, 309–311
Moral reasoning, 309–310
Morphological rules, 259
Mothers. See also parenting
    attachment styles and, 307–309
    pheromones of, 120
    postpartum depression in, 428
    schizophrenia and, 435
    stress responses and, 77
    teenage, 316

Motion perception, 12–13, 12f, 107–108
Motion sickness, 118
Motivation, 241–253
    accuracy, 378–380
    approach vs. avoidance, 252–253
    approval motive, 374–377
    approval seeking, 372, 374–377
    conscious vs. unconscious, 251–252
    definition of, 241
    drives and, 242
    hunger, 244
    instincts and, 241–242
    intrinsic vs. extrinsic, 250–251, 251f
    mental disorders and, 414
    the nature of, 241–243
    obesity and, 245–248
    personality traits and, 331
    physical, 244–249
    sexual desire, 248–249, 249t
    social influence and, 372–381
Motor cortex, 71, 72f
    in category-specific processing, 268, 268f
    during dreaming, 143–144, 143f
Motor development
    definition of, 299
    in infancy, 299, 300f
Motor neurons, 56
Motor reflexes, 299
Motor skills
    development of, 299, 300f
    exercise and, 73
Movement
    frontal lobe in, 71
    spinal cord damage and, 64–65
MRI. See magnetic resonance imaging (MRI)
Multitasking, 93
Murder rates, 356
Myelin, 58, 58f
Myelination, 297
Myelin sheath, 54, 55f

Narcissism, 347–348
Narcissistic personality disorder, 440t
Narcolepsy, 141
Narcotics, 150–151
    dangers of, 148t
National Basketball Association (NBA), 271
National Institutes of Health, 81
National Science Foundation, 7, 48
Nativism, 4
    on language development, 263–264
Nativist theory of language development,
    263–264
Natural correlations, 34–35
Natural improvement, treatment effectiveness
    and, 469
Naturalistic observation, 32
Natural selection, 6, 6f, 8
Natural therapies, 464, 464f
Nature and nurture, 75–77
Nature-vs.-nurture, 4
Nearsightedness, 95, 96f
Need for achievement, 251–252
Negative punishment, 204
Negative reinforcement, 204
    in drug addiction, 146, 146f
Negative symptoms, 432, 462

Nervous system, 62–65, 63f
  central, 62
  definition of, 62
  peripheral, 62–63
Neurocognitive disorders, 416t
Neurodevelopmental disorders, 416t
Neuromyths, 84
Neurons, 54–62
  action of, 56–62
  action potential of, 57–59, 57f
  axons of, 54, 54f, 55f
  cell body of, 54, 54f, 55f
  chemical signaling between, 59–62
  components of, 54–55, 54f, 55f
  definition of, 54
  dendrites of, 54, 54f, 55f
  electric signaling by, 56–59
  feature detectors, 80
  interneurons, 56
  memory formation and, 169
  mirror, 71–72, 217, 217f
  motor, 56
  myelination of, 297
  postsynaptic, 59
  presynaptic, 59
  resting potential of, 56–57, 57f
  sensory, 56
  synapses between, 54f, 55, 55f
  types of, 56
Neuroscience, 18–19
  behavioral, 19
  classical conditioning and, 200–201
  cognitive, 19
  on decision making, 272–273, 273f
Neuroscience and behavior, 52–87
  brain structure and, 65–74
  genes, epigenetics, and environment in, 75–77
  nervous system organization, 62–65
Neuroticism, 332–333, 332t, 337
Neurotransmitters, 59, 60f
  in depressive disorders, 428
  exercise and, 397
  generalized anxiety disorder and, 424
  marijuana and, 152
  phobic disorders and, 421
  schizophrenia and, 433
  types and functions of, 59–61
New York Times, 7
Nicotine, 150, 407
  dangers of, 148t
Nicotine replacement systems, 407
Nightmares, 142
Night shift work, 140
Night terrors, 141
9/11 terrorist attacks, 68, 187, 388–389, 418
Nodes of Ranvier, 58, 58f
Nonsuicidal self-injury (NSSI), 443
Nontasters, 120
Norepinephrine, 61
  in depressive disorders, 428
Normative influence, 374
Norm of reciprocity, 374
Norms, 374
  obedience and, 376–377, 377f
NSSI. See nonsuicidal self-injury (NSSI)
Nucleus, 55f
Nucleus accumbens, 212, 212f

Nuremberg Code of 1947, 46
Nutrition, 406
  intelligence and, 288
  puberty timing and, 312
  self-regulation and, 405–406

Obedience, 376–377
Obesity, 245–248, 246f, 374f
  causes of, 246–247
  conquering, 247–248
  definition of, 245
  eating wisely and, 406
Object permanence, 301–302, 301f
Observational learning, 214–217
Observations
  empiricism and, 28–29
  incompleteness of, 30
  inconsistency in, 30
  measurement and, 30–31
  methods for, 30–33
  naturalistic, 32
  observer bias in, 33
Observer bias, 33
Obsessive-compulsive disorder, 416t, 424–425
  psychosurgery for, 468
  treatment of, 449, 450
Obsessive-compulsive personality disorder, 440t
Occipital lobe, 70, 70f
  in vision, 97
OCD. See obsessive-compulsive disorder
Odd/eccentric personality disorders, 439, 440t
Odorants, 118–119
Oklahoma City terrorist attack, 182
Olanzapine, 462
Oleogustus, 120
Olfaction, 118–120, 119f
Olfactory bulb, 119, 119f
Olfactory receptor neurons (ORNs), 119, 119f
Omega-3 fatty acids, 464, 464f
On the Origin of Species by Means of Natural
    Selection (Darwin), 6, 6f
Openness
  to experience, personality trait of, 332–333, 332t
  intelligence and, 284
Operant behavior, 203
Operant conditioning, 202–214
  basic principles of, 205–210
  cognitive elements of, 210–211
  definition of, 202
  discrimination and generalization in, 205–206
  evolutionary elements of, 212–213
  extinction in, 206
  law of effect and, 202–203
  neural elements of, 211–212, 212f
  reinforcement and punishment in, 203–205,
    204t
  shaping in, 209
  superstitions and, 209–210
Operant conditioning chamber. See Skinner box
Operational definitions, 31
  representativeness restriction and, 39
Opiates. See narcotics
Opioid epidemic, 151
  overdoses in, 198
Opioids, 61–62, 150–151
Opium, 150–151, 461
Optic nerve, 96–97, 99

Optimism, 404–405
Optimism bias, 272
Oral stage, 339t
Orbicularis oculi, 237, 240, 240f
Orderliness, 331
Organizational encoding, 161f, 162
Organizational judgments, 161f
Organizational psychologists, 22–23, 22f
Ossicles, 110, 111f
Outcome expectancies, 343
Outcomes, in moral reasoning, 209
Outer ear, 110, 111f
Ovaries, 68, 69f
Overdoses, 148t, 466
  classical conditioning and, 198
  opioid, 151
Overjustification effect, 373
Overregularization of grammar, 262

Pace of life, measurement of, 32f
Pain perception, 116–117, 116f
  facial expressions and, 238, 238f
  hypnosis and, 155, 155f
  recognizing and reporting, 400–402, 401f
  sleep deprivation and, 139
Pain withdrawal reflex, 64, 64f
Pancreas, 68, 69f
Panic attacks, 422–423
Panic disorder, 422–423, 465, 465f
  treatment effectiveness, 471t
Papillae, 120
Paranoid personality disorder, 440t
Paraphilic disorders, 416t
Parasympathetic nervous system, 63, 63f
Parenting
  of adolescents, 316–318
  attachment styles and, 307–309
  happiness and, 321–322
  personality and, 334
  sexual orientation and, 314
Parietal lobe, 70–71, 70f
  in touch perception, 115–116
Parkinson's disease, 468
  basal ganglia damage in, 68
  dopamine in, 61, 213
Paroxetine, 463
Passionate love, 364–365, 365f
Patient–practitioner interactions, 403–404
Patients, sick role of, 402–403
Paxil, 463
PCP (phencyclidine), 151–152
Peer pressure, 376
People for the Ethical Treatment of Animals, 47
Perceived control, 388
Perception
  of body position, movement, and balance,
    117–118
  constancy and contrast in, 102–105
  definition of, 90
  of depth and size, 105–107
  distortion of in depression, 428–429, 429f
  encoding memories from, 160–163
  gestalt psychology on, 12–13
  hallucinogens and, 152
  of hearing, 109–114
  in infancy, 299
  interpersonal, 365–372

mental disorders and, 414
  of motion and change, 107–109
  of others' minds, 128–129, 128f
  of pain, 116–117, 116f
  prenatal, 298
  of smell, 118–120, 119f
  of taste, 120–122, 121f
  of touch, 115–116, 115f
  visual, 101–109
Perceptual confirmation, 367
Perceptual constancy, 102–105
Perceptual contrast, 103–105
Perceptual grouping, 103, 113
Perceptual organization, 103
Peripheral nervous system (PNS), 62–63, 63f
Perseverance, 289
Persistence, 187–188
Personal constructs, 341–342
Personality, 326–351
  change in, 333
  definition of, 327
  describing and explaining, 328
  as existence, 340
  gender and, 334–336
  goals, expectancies, and, 342–343
  health and, 404–405
  humanistic–existential approach on, 339–340
  inventories, 328–329
  measuring, 328–330
  perceiver's, 341–342
  projective techniques on, 329–330, 329f
  psychodynamic approach on, 337–339
  the self-concept and, 344–345
  social–cognitive approach on, 341–343
  technology in measuring, 330
  trait approach to, 331–337
Personality disorders, 416t, 439–441
  antisocial, 439–441
  types of, 439, 440t
Person-centered therapy, 454
Person-situation controversy, 341
Perspective-taking, 289, 370
Persuasion, 378–379
Pessimism, 404–405
PET. See positron emission tomography (PET)
Phallic stage, 339t
Phantom limb syndrome, 72–73, 73f
Phenomenology, 128
Pheromones, 120
Philosophical dualism, 2–3
Philosophical empiricism, 4
Philosophical idealism, 3
Philosophical materialism, 2–3
Philosophical nativism, 4
Philosophical realism, 3
Phobic disorders, 420–422
  biological and environmental factors in,
    421–422
  definition of, 420
  risk for, 421
  social phobia, 421
  specific phobia, 420–421
Phonemes, 259
Phonological loop, 166
Phonological rules, 259
Photoreceptor cells, 95–97, 96f, 97f
Phototherapy, 464

Physical dependence, 146, 148t
Piercings, 39f
Pineal gland, 68, 69f
Pinna, 110, 111f, 113
Pitch, 109, 112
Pituitary gland, 67f, 68, 69f
  stress reactions and, 389
Placebo effect, 401, 469
Placebos, 469
Place codes, 112
Placeholders, 162
Plasticity, 72–74
Pleasure centers, in the brain, 211–212, 212f
PNS. See peripheral nervous system (PNS)
Polio, 35f
Polygraphs, 241
Pons, 66, 66f
Populations
  definition of, 39
  random sampling and, 40–41
Positive punishment, 204
Positive reinforcement, 204
  in drug addiction, 146, 146f
Positive symptoms, 431–432, 462
Positron emission tomography (PET), 82, 82f, 83
  memory retrieval and, 172, 172f
Postconventional stage, 210
Posthypnotic amnesia, 154
Postpartum depression, 428
Postsynaptic neurons, 59, 60f
Posttraumatic stress disorder (PTSD), 394,
    425–426
  9/11 terrorist attacks and, 388–389
  cognitive behavioral therapy for, 458
  epigenetics in, 77
  treatment effectiveness, 471t
Poverty. See socioeconomic status
Power, of detectors, 31
Practical intelligence, 279
Practice
  brain plasticity and, 73–74
  distributed, 220–221, 220t
  interleaved, 220t, 222
  massed, 221–222
Practice testing, 220t, 222–223
Prayer, 398f
Precognition, 183
Preconventional stage, 210
Prefrontal cortex
  calorie-rich foods and, 248
  during dreaming, 143–144, 143f
Prejudice, definition of, 358. See also racism
Prenatal development, 296–298, 297f
Preoperational stage, 301f, 302
Preparedness theory of phobias, 421
Preschool, intelligence and, 288
Prescriptions, in moral reasoning, 209
Presynaptic neurons, 59
Primacy effect, 15, 15f, 165
Primary auditory cortex, 70, 111f, 112f
Primary caregivers, 307
Primary gustatory cortex, 121
Primary mental abilities, 277–278
Primary olfactory cortex, 121
Primary reinforcers, 204
Primary sex characteristics, 311
Priming, 174, 175f

Principle of reinforcement, 11
Principles, in moral reasoning, 209
Principles of Physiological Psychology (Wundt),
    5, 5f
The Principles of Psychology (James), 2
Prisoner's dilemma, 357–358, 357f
Privacy, demand characteristic reduction and, 32
Proactive aggression, 354
Proactive interference, 180
Probabilities, judging, 269
Problem of other minds, 128–129
Procedural memory, 174
Procrastination, 399
Prohibition era, 147f
Projection, 338t
Projective techniques, 329–330, 329f
Prolonged exposure technique, 394
Proprioception, 117–118
Prospective memory, 181
Prospect theory, 272
Prototype theory, 266, 267f
Proximity, 103, 104f, 113
Proximodistal rule, 299
Prozac, 463
Pruning, brain, 433f, 434
Psilocybin, 151–152
Psychiatric social workers, 451
Psychiatrists, 451
Psychoactive drugs, 148–153
  definition of, 145
  depressants, 148–149
  hallucinogens, 151–152
  marijuana, 152–153
  narcotics, 150–151
  stimulants, 150
Psychoanalysis, 8–9, 453, 471
Psychoanalytic theory, 8–9, 142
Psychodynamic approach, 337–339
Psychodynamic psychotherapies, 452–453
  effectiveness of, 470–473
Psychodynamic therapy, 453
Psychological dependence, 146, 148t
Psychological disorders. See mental disorders
Psychological treatments, 452–461
  combined medication and, 465–466, 465f
  psychodynamic therapy, 452–453
Psychologists, 451
  becoming, 20–23
  education of, 21–23
  employment settings for, 22–23, 22f
  ethics for, 45–49
Psychology
  cognitive, 16
  definition of, 2
  developmental, 13
  evolutionary, 16–17
  evolution of, 1–25
  Gestalt, 12–13
  methods in, 26–51
  philosophical roots of, 2–4
  as a science, 7
  as science of the mind, 4–8
  social, 14–15
  subfields of, 22–23, 22f
Psychology from the Standpoint of a Behaviorist
    (Watson), 10
Psychopaths, 439–440

Psychopharmacology, 461
Psychophysics, 91–92
Psychosexual stages, 338, 339t
Psychosocial development stages, 316, 317
Psychosomatic illness, 402
Psychosurgery, 467–468
Psychotherapists, types of, 451
Psychotherapy
    approaches to, 452, 452f
    definition of, 452
    eclectic, 452
    psychodynamic, 452–453
Psychotic disorders, 416t, 431–436
    antipsychotic drugs for, 461–462
    dopamine in, 61
    epigenetics in, 77
PTSD. See posttraumatic stress disorder (PTSD)
Puberty, 311–312. See also adolescence
Public policy, use of research in, 48
Punishers, 204
Punishment
    immediate vs. delayed, 205, 205f
    in operant conditioning, 203–205, 204t
    overjustification effect with, 373
    primary, 204
    secondary, 204–205
Pupil (of the eye), 95, 96f
Pure tones, 109
Puzzle boxes, 202–203, 202f, 203f

Queer, 315

Racism. See also stereotypes
    intelligence tests and, 286–287
    stress from, 387
Random assignment, 37–38, 38f
Random sampling, 40–41
Rational choice theory, 269
Rational coping, 394
Rationalization, 338t
Ratio schedules, 207–208
RDoC. See Research Domain Criteria Project
    (RDoC)
Reactance, 373
Reaction formation, 338t
Reaction times, 5
Reactive aggression, 354, 355f
Reactivity, empirical method and, 29
Reading, intelligence and, 288
Realism, 3
    in moral reasoning, 209
Reappraisal, 243
Reasoning
    brain evolution and, 75
    moral, 209–311
Rebound effect of thought suppression, 134
Recency effect, 165
Receptors, 59
Reciprocal altruism, 360
Reciprocity norms, 374
Reconsolidation of memory, 168–169
Reconstructive memory, 470
Reexperiencing the past, 176
Referred pain, 117
Reflexes
    motor, 299
    spinal, 64, 64f

Refractory period, 58–59
Reframing, 394–395
Refugees, hate crimes against, 40
Regression, 338t
Rehearsal, memory and, 165, 165f
Reinforcement
    in drug addiction, 146, 146f
    immediate vs. delayed, 205, 205f
    intermittent, 208
    negative, 204
    in operant conditioning, 203–205, 204t
    positive, 204
    primary, 204
    principle of, 11
    schedules of, 206–208, 207f
    secondary, 204–205
Reinforcers, 204
    primary, 204
    secondary, 204–205
Relationships
    in adulthood, 320–321, 321f
    attachment styles and, 307–309
    internal working models on, 308–309
    peer, 316–318
    romantic, 317, 364–365
Relative height, 106, 106f
Relative size, 105, 105f
Relativism in moral reasoning, 209
Relaxation response, 396
Relaxation therapy, 396
Reliability, of detectors, 31, 31f
Reliability restriction, 41–42
Religion, 398, 398f
    dualism in, 2–3
Religiosity, 398
REM sleep, 138–140, 138f, 139f
    brain activation and deactivation in, 143–144,
        143f
Replication, 41–42
Representativeness heuristic, 270–271
Representativeness restriction, 39
Repression, 135, 338t
Repressive coping, 394
Reptiles, 74
Research, 26–51
    causation in, 34–35
    coincidence and, 45
    correlation in, 34
    cost and affordability of, 48
    critical thinking about, 42–44
    demand characteristics in, 31–33
    drawing conclusions in, 38–42
    empirical method in, 29
    ethical analysis and reporting of, 47–49
    ethics in, 45–49, 46f
    explanation methods in, 34–42
    generalizability restriction and, 39–41
    honor system in, 47–49
    nonrandom sampling in, 40–41
    observation methods in, 30–33
    observer bias in, 33, 33f
    random assignment in, 37–38, 38f
    reliability restriction in, 41–42
    replication of, 41–42
    representativeness restriction and, 39
    sampling in, 39–41
    scientific method in, 28–29

    scientific rigor of social sciences and, 7
    skeptical stance for, 44
    using animals, 47
Research Domain Criteria Project (RDoC), 419
Resistance phase, 390, 390f
Respect for persons, 45–47
Responses
    in behaviorism, 10–12
    Pavlov on, 10
Resting potential, 56–57, 57f
Reticular formation, 65, 66f, 336
Retina, 95, 97f
    in motion perception, 107
Retinal ganglion cells (RGCs), 96–97
Retrieval cues, 170–171
Retrieval-induced forgetting, 171
Retrieval of memories, 170–173
    components of, 172–173
    consequences of, 171–173
    cues for, 170–171
    definition of, 159
    memories changed by, 172
    state-dependent, 170
Retroactive interference, 179–180
Retrograde amnesia, 167
Reuptake, 59, 60f
Reward prediction error, 213
Rewards
    hedonic motive in social influence and, 372,
        373, 373f
    overjustification effect with, 373
Risk–benefit analysis, 46
Risk taking. See also drug addiction
    in adolescence, 312, 313f
    in bipolar disorder, 430
    decision making and, 272–273, 273f
    sexual behavior and, 405, 406–407
Risperdal, 462
Risperidone, 462
Ritalin, 288
Rods, 95–97, 96f, 97f
Romantic relationships, 364–365
    in adolescence, 317
Rooting reflex, 299
Rorschach Inkblot Test, 329, 329f
Rubin vase, 105, 105f

SAD. See seasonal affective disorder (SAD)
Saltatory conduction, 58
Same-sex marriage, 314, 314f
Samples
    definition of, 39
    generalizability restriction and, 39–41
    random, 40–41
Satiety center, 244, 245f
Sawtooth waves, 137, 138f
Scared Straight programs, 7, 472, 472t
Schedules of reinforcement, 206–208, 207f
    interval, 207
    ratio, 207–208
Schemas, 300–301, 301t
Schizoid personality disorder, 440t
Schizophrenia, 416t, 431–436
    antipsychotic drugs for, 461–462
    biological factors in, 433–434
    bipolar disorder and, 430
    brain tissue loss in adolescent, 433–434, 435f

dangers of labeling, 419, 420
definition of, 431
dopamine in, 61
epigenetics in, 77
personality disorders and, 440t
risk for, 432–433, 433f
social/psychological factors in, 434–435
symptoms of, 431–432
in twins, 77
Schizotypal personality disorder, 440t
School psychologists, 22, 22f
Scientific method, 28–29
SDT. See signal detection theory (SDT)
Sea slugs, 169
habituation and sensitization in, 194
Seasonal affective disorder (SAD), 427–428, 464
Secondary reinforcers, 204–205
Secondary sex characteristics, 311
Second-order conditioning, 196
Secure attachment, 308–309, 308f
Security, 347
Selective serotonin reuptake inhibitors (SSRIs),
        463–464, 463f, 465
Selectivity
of consciousness, 131
sexual behavior and, 361–362
Self-actualization, 339–340
Self-actualizing tendency, 339–340
Self-awareness, brain evolution and, 75
Self-concept, 344–345
Self-consciousness, 132
Self-control, 405–406
Self-esteem, 346–348, 346t
aggression and, 355–356
labeling mental disorders and, 420
sexual behavior and, 315
Self-explanation, 220t
Self-fulfilling prophecy, 367–368
Self-harm behaviors, 441–443
nonsuicidal self-injury, 443
suicidal, 441–443, 442f
treatment for, 459
Self-help groups, 460
Selfishness, social class and, 20
Self-narrative, 345
Self-regulation, 405–406
Self-reports, 328–329, 415
Self-selection, 38
Self-serving bias, 347–348
Self-verification, 345
Semantic encoding, 160, 161f
Semantic judgments, 161f
Semantic memory, 175
Sensation
of body position, movement, and balance,
        117–118
definition of, 90
during dreams, 144
in dreams, 142
hearing and, 109–114
psychophysics of, 91–92
sensory transduction and adaptation in,
        90–91
signal detection and, 92–93
of smell, 118–120, 119f
spinal cord damage and, 64–65
of taste, 120–122, 121f

thresholds for, 91–92, 91t
of touch, 115–116, 115f
Sensitivity, 92
Sensitization, 194
Sensorimotor stage, 300–301, 301t
Sensorineural hearing loss, 113
Sensory adaptation, 90–91
Sensory memory, 163–164, 164f
Sensory neurons, 56
Serial position effect, 165
Serial reaction time, 218
Serotonin, 61
depression and, 463–464
in depressive disorders, 428
phobic disorders and, 421
Severely deficient autobiographical memory
        (SDAM), 176
Sex, definition of, 315
Sex addiction, 147
Sex differences
in Alzheimer's and the hippocampus, 69
science participation and, 30
Sex education, 316, 407
Sexual abuse
age of puberty and, 312
false memories of, 186
hypnosis and memories of, 154
Sexual arousal, in REM sleep, 138
Sexual behavior, 315–316
attraction and, 362–364
health-promoting, 405, 406–407
relationships and, 364–365
selectivity in, 361–362
Sexual desire, 248–249, 249t
Sexual development, 311
in adolescence, 311, 313–316
Sexual dysfunctions, 416t
Sexually transmitted infections (STIs), 405, 407
Sexual orientation, 314–315, 314f
definition of, 315
Shape perception, 99, 100f
Shaping, 209
Short-term memory, 164–166, 165f
Sickness response, 400
Sick role, 402–403
Signal detection theory (SDT), 92–93
Sign languages, 114, 261, 261f
Signs, of mental disorders, 415
Similarity, 103, 104f
in attraction, 364
Simplicity, 103, 104f
Situational attributions, 371
Size perception, 105–107
Skepticism, 44
Skinner box, 11, 11f, 203, 203f
Sleep, 136–145
in bipolar disorder, 430
brain electrical activity in, 80
cycle of, 138–139, 138f, 139f
deprivation, 139
disorders, 140–141
dreams and, 141–145
generalized anxiety disorder and, 423
learning and, 168
memory and, 34, 34t
memory consolidation in, 168
need for, 139–140, 140f

Sleep apnea, 141
Sleeping pills, 140
Sleep paralysis, 141
Sleep spindles, 138, 138f
Sleep terrors, 141
Sleep–wake disorders, 416t
Sleepwalking, 141
Smell sense, 118–120, 119f
absolute threshold of, 91t
in dreams, 144
Smiles
cultural differences in, 238f, 240
deceptive, 240–241, 240f
Social anxiety disorder, 415
Social class, 20
Social cognition, 365–570
attribution and, 370–372
definition of, 365
stereotypes and, 365–370
Social–cognitive perspective
on personality, 341–343
on personality and gender, 335
Social development, 306–309
Social influence, 372–381
approval motive and, 372, 374–377
collaborative memory and, 177–179
definition of, 372
hedonic motive and, 372, 373
Socialization, 225. See also culture
aggression and, 355
intelligence and, 285
Social media
affect labeling in, 243
Big Five personality traits and, 333
confirmation bias in, 43
hate posts, hate crimes, and, 40, 40f
labels and manipulation of conditions
        with, 36f
personality research using, 330, 333
Social phobia, 421
cognitive behavioral therapy for, 458
exposure hierarchy for, 456, 456t
medication and psychotherapy for, 465, 465f
Social psychology, 14–15, 352–383
on aggression, 354–356
on altruism, 359–360
on cooperation, 356–359
definition of, 353
on favors, 361
interpersonal attraction, 361–365
interpersonal behavior and, 354–361
interpersonal influence, 372–381
interpersonal perception, 365–372
Social referencing, 305
Social sciences, scientific rigor in, 7
Social status, 346–347
Social support, 397–398
Social workers, 451
Socioeconomic status
attraction and, 362–363, 363f
bilingualism and, 265
framing effects and, 271
intelligence and, 275–276, 276f, 282
intelligence testing and, 287–288
language development and, 263
Sociopaths, 439–440
Sodium lactate, panic attacks and, 423

Solitary confinement, 353
Somatic nervous system, 62, 63f
Somatic symptom disorders, 402, 416t
Somatosensory cortex, 70–71, 72f, 73, 115–116
    in flavor perception, 121
    in pain perception, 116–117, 116f
Somnambulism, 141
Sonar, 89
Sound waves, 109–110
Source memory, 182–183
Specific factors, 278
Specific phobia, 420–421
Speech sounds, 260–261
Spinal cord
    in central nervous system, 62, 63–65, 64f
    damage to the, 64–65
Spinal reflexes, 64, 64f
Spirituality, 398
Split-brain procedure, 79–80, 79f, 80f
Spontaneous recovery, 197, 197f
Sports psychologists, 23, 23f
SSRIs. See selective serotonin reuptake inhibitors
    (SSRIs)
Stanford–Binet Intelligence Scale, 285–286
State-dependent retrieval, 170
Status, aggression and, 355–356
Stereotypes, 365–370
    gender, personality and, 335
    inaccuracy in, 366
    overcoming, 369–370
    overuse of, 366–367
    perspective-taking and, 370
    self-perpetuating, 367–368
    social psychology on, 15, 15f
    techniques for reducing, 369f
    unconscious and automatic, 368–369
Stereotype threat, 7, 286–287, 367–368
Stereotyping, 366
Stigma, mental disorders and, 419–420
Stimulants, 150
Stimuli
    in behaviorism, 10–12
    Pavlov on, 10
STIs. See sexually transmitted infections (STIs)
St. John's wort, 464
Storage of memory, 163–169
    consolidation in, 167–168
    definition of, 159, 163
    long-term, 164f, 166–169
    reconsolidation in, 168–169
    sensory, 163–164, 164f
    short-term, 164–166
    working memory, 165–166, 165f
Stream of consciousness, 131
Stress, 384–411
    bipolar disorder and, 431
    body management and, 395–397
    chronic, 387–388, 392–393
    definition of, 385
    discrimination and, 387
    epigenetics and responses to, 77
    events causing, 386–387
    immune system and, 391–392
    interpreting, 392
    managing, 394–399
    overparenting and, 408
    perceived control and, 388

physical reactions to, 389–392
psychological reactions to, 392–393
reactions to, 388–393
situation management and, 397–399
smoking and, 407
sources of, 386–388
Stressor-related disorders, 416t. See also
    posttraumatic stress disorder (PTSD)
Stressors, 385
    chronic, 387–388
Structural brain imaging, 81, 81f
Structuralism, 5–6, 11
Study techniques, effectiveness of, 220t
Subcortical structures, 67–68, 67f
Sublimation, 338t
Substance-related and addictive disorders,
    416t
    prevalence of, 416–417, 417f
Successive approximations, 209
Sucking reflex, 299
Suggestibility, 184–186, 188
Suicidal behavior, 441–443, 442f, 459
    herbal and natural products for, 464
Suicide, 413, 441–442
Suicide attempts, 442
Sulci, 70–71, 70f
Summarization, 220t
Sunk-cost fallacy, 271
Superego, 337
Support groups, 460
Suppression
    emotional, 243
    thought, 133–134, 143
Survival-related information encoding, 162–163,
    163f
Survivor memories, 14
Susceptibility, to hypnosis, 154
Sydney (warship), 14, 14f
Symmetry, in beauty, 363
Sympathetic nervous system, 63, 63f
Symptoms, of mental disorders, 415
    cognitive, 432
    negative, 432
    positive, 431–432
Synapses, 54f, 55, 55f
    long-term potentiation of, 169
    memory formation and, 169
Synaptic transmission, 59–62, 60f
Syntactic rules, 259, 260f
Systematic persuasion, 378
Systematizing, 436

Tabula rasa, 4, 16–17
Tactile Dome, 115f
Taijin kyofusho, 417
Tantrums, 455
Targeted memory reactivation (TMR), 168
Tastants, 120, 121f
Taste buds, 120, 121f
Tasters, 120
Taste sense, 120–122, 121f
    absolute threshold of, 91t
    in dreams, 144
    food aversions and, 201
TAT. See Thematic Apperception Test (TAT)
TEC. See Therapeutic Evaluative Conditioning
    (TEC)

Technology
    personality measurement with, 330
    in psychological treatment, 459
Tectum, 66
Tegmentum, 66, 67f
Telegraphic speech, 261–262
Telomeres, 391, 395
Temperament, attachment styles and, 308
Temporal codes, 112
Temporal lobe, 70, 70f
    in category-specific processing, 268, 268f
    in face perception, 102
    in hearing, 112, 112f
    in motion perception, 107
Tend-and-befriend response, 397–398
Terminal buttons, 59
Terrorist attacks, 68, 182, 187, 388–389, 418
Terror management theory, 252–253
Testes, 68, 69f
Testing
    intelligence, 275–276, 276t
    practice, 220t, 222–223
    stereotype threat and, 7
Testosterone, 248–249
    aggression and, 355, 356f
    personality and, 335–336
Tetrahydrocannabinol (THC), 152. See also
    marijuana
Texting while driving, 93
Texture gradient, 106, 106f
Thalamus, 67, 67f
    in pain perception, 116–117, 116f
    placebo effect and, 401
THC. See tetrahydrocannabinol (THC)
Thematic Apperception Test (TAT), 329–330
Theories, scientific method and, 28–29
Theory of mind, 303–305
Therapeutic Evaluative Conditioning (TEC),
    459
Theriac, 461
Thermoreceptors, 115
Theta waves, 138, 138f
Thinking. See also intelligence
    cognitive therapy for distorted, 456–458
    decision making and, 269–274
    in dreams, 142
    language and, 266–268
    mental disorders and, 414
Thinking Fast and Slow (Kahneman), 136
Third-variable problem, 35
Thorndike's puzzle box, 202–203, 202f, 203f
Thought suppression, 133–134, 143, 424
Threats, motivation by, 251, 251f
Thresholds, 57
    absolute, 91–92
Thyroid gland, 68, 69f
Timbre, 109–110, 110f, 112
Time magazine, 12
Time management, 399
Time-outs, 455
T mazes, 212–213
TMS. See transcranial magnetic stimulation
    (TMS)
Tobacco use, 147–148, 150, 407
    dangers of, 148t
Token economies, 455–456
Torture, 353

Touch sense, 115–116, 115f
    absolute threshold of, 91t
    in dreams, 144
    parietal lobe in, 70–71
Toxic inhalants, 149
    dangers of, 148t
Training, working memory, 166
Traits, 331–337. *See also* personality
    Big Five, 332–333, 332t
    as biological building blocks, 334–337
    core, 331–333
    definition of, 331
    genetics and, 334
    hierarchical structure of, 332f
    neurophysiology of, 336–337
    personality disorders and, 439, 440t
Transcranial magnetic stimulation (TMS), 83, 467
Transduction, 90–91
    auditory, 111, 111f
Transfer-appropriate processing, 171
Transgender people, 315
    hormones and personality changes in, 335–336
Transience, 131, 179–180, 180f
Trauma-related disorders, 416t. *See also*
        posttraumatic stress disorder (PTSD)
Treatment of psychological disorders, 448–475
    approaches to, 451–452
    autism, 437
    behavior therapy, 455–456
    biological, 461–468
    cognitive behavioral therapy, 456–458
    cognitive therapy, 456–458
    effectiveness of, 469–473, 471t
    ethical standards in, 472–473
    failure to seek or receive, 450–451, 466
    group treatments, 458–460
    harm caused by, 472, 472t
    humanistic and existential therapies,
        454–455
    illusions in, 469–470
    nonsuicidal self-injury, 443
    outcome studies on, 470
    psychodynamic therapies, 452–453
    psychological, 452–461
    rates of, 450
    rebooting, 459
    types of psychotherapists for, 451
Treatment outcome studies, 470
Tricyclic antidepressants, 463–464, 463f
Trust *vs.* mistrust, 317t
Truth, love of, 289
Tumblr, 104
Tuskegee syphilis experiment, 46
TV Guide, 12
12-step programs, 460
Twins and twin studies
    bipolar disorder and, 430–431
    brain environmental sensitivity in, 284
    genetics in, 76–77, 76f
    intelligence and, 281
    posttraumatic stress disorder and, 426
    schizophrenia and, 430–431, 433, 433f
    sexual orientation and, 314
Two-factor theory of emotion, 234–235
Two-factor theory of intelligence, 277–278

Type A behavior pattern, 392
Type B behavior pattern, 392

UK Biobank, 82
Umami, 120
Unawareness, demand characteristic reduction
        and, 33
Unconditional positive regard, 454
Unconditioned response (UR), 195–196, 196f
Unconditioned stimulus (US), 195–196, 196f
Unconscious, 127
    cognitive, 136
    definition of, 127
    dynamic, 135
    Freudian theory on, 8–9, 135–136
    sleep and, 137–145
    stereotyping and, 368–369
    the unconscious mind and, 135–136
Unconscious motivations, 251–252
Uncritical acceptance, 142
Unipolar depression, 415, 427
United Kingdom Behavioral Insights Team, 48
Unity, of consciousness, 130–131
Universal grammar, 263–264
Universality hypothesis, 238
UR. *See* unconditioned response (UR)
US. *See* unconditioned stimulus (US)
U.S. Public Health Service, Tuskegee experiment
        and, 46

Validity
    construct, 31
    external, 39
    internal, 38–39
Validity scales, 329
Valium, 149, 155, 462
Values, intellectual virtues and, 289
Variability
    empirical method and, 29
    stereotypes and, 366–367, 367f
Variable-interval (VI) schedules, 207
Variable-ratio (FR) schedules, 208
Variables
    definition of, 34
    dependent, 37, 37f
    independent, 36–37, 37f
    manipulation of, 35–37
    operational definition of, 39
    representativeness restriction and, 39
    third-variable problem and, 35, 35f
Variation, correlation and, 34
Ventral visual stream, 99–101, 100f
Ventromedial hypothalamus, 244
Verbal Behavior (Skinner), 15
Vertebrates, 74
Vestibular system, 118
Video games, aggression and, 37–38
View of Dresden with the Fraunkirche (Bellotto), 131f
Violence. *See also* aggression
    children's fears about, 306
    gender and, 355–356, 356f
    hate posts, hate crimes, and, 40
    in the media, aggression and, 34–35, 35f, 36–38,
        36f, 37f, 39
    mental disorders and, 419

Visible spectrum, 98
Vision
    absolute threshold of, 91t
    balance and, 118
    classical theory of, 29f
    loss of, 89
    in newborns, 299
Visual cortex, 80, 97
    in category-specific processing, 268, 268f
    during dreaming, 143–144, 143f
Visual imagery encoding, 160–162, 161f
Visual judgments, 161f
Visual perception, 94–109
    brain electrical activity and, 80
    of color, 98–99
    of depth and size, 105–107
    in dreams, 143–144
    of figure and ground, 103, 105
    of light, 94–97, 94f
    of motion and change, 107–109
    object recognition in, 102
    occipital lobe in, 70
    perceptual constancy and contrast in,
        102–105
    recognizing what we see and, 101–109
    of shape, 99, 100f
Visual streams, 99–101, 100f
Visuo-spatial sketchpad, 166

Walden II (Skinner), 11–12
Washington Post, 7
Wavelengths, 94–95, 94f
Weber's law, 92
Wechsler Adult Intelligence Scale (WAIS), 275–
        276, 276t
Wechsler Intelligence Scale for Children (WISC),
        275, 276t
Wellbutrin, 463
Wernicke's area, 112f, 265, 265f
"What" pathway, 99–100, 116
What Would You Do? (TV show), 46f
"Where" pathway, 100–101, 100f, 116
White House's Social and Behavioral Sciences
        Team, 48
Will, timing of conscious, 129–130, 129f
Wisdom, 289
Women
    intelligence tests and, 286–287
    in psychology, 21, 21f
    in science, 30
    violence against, 356
Wong-Baker FACES Pain scale, 402f
Working memory, 165–166, 165f
World War II
    memory research in, 14
    Nazi experiments in, 45–46

X (drug). *See* MDMA (Ecstasy)
Xanax, 462

You Can Heal Your Life (Hay), 26

Zygomaticus major, 237, 240, 240f
Zygotes, 296–297
Zyprexa, 462